D1426285

THE COLLECTED SCIENTIFIC PAPERS OF
PAUL A. SAMUELSON

VOLUME IV

THE COLLECTED SCIENTIFIC PAPERS OF PAUL A. SAMUELSON

Edited by Hiroaki Nagatani and Kate Crowley

THE MIT PRESS
Cambridge, Massachusetts, and London, England

Second printing, 1979

See pages 959–965 for acknowledgments of previously published material.

Copyright © 1977

by

The Massachusetts Institute of Technology

Printed and bound in the United States of America

Library of Congress Cataloging in Publication Data (Revise)

Samuelson, Paul Anthony, 1915–
    The collected scientific papers of Paul A. Samuelson.

    Vol. 3 edited by R. C. Merton; v. 4 edited by H. Nagatani and K. Crowley.
        Includes bibliographies.
        1. Economics—Collected works.
HB33.S2   330'.08   65–28408
ISBN 0–262–19167–9 (v. 4)

AUTHOR'S PREFACE

Since the 1966 publication date of the first two volumes of my scientific papers and the 1972 date of the third volume publication, this new harvest of papers has accumulated. I am grateful to the editors, Hiroaki Nagatani and Kate Crowley, who have gathered these items for publication in this fourth volume.

Theirs was the choice of items to include and exclude. Wisely, I think, they decided to err on the side of inclusion wherever a paper had scientific relevance and to err on the side of exclusion when it came to my many fugitive items of contemporary journalism. Theirs too was the choice of classification and order-of-appearance of the various papers.

Photo offset reproduction of the original papers has proved to be by all odds the optimal mode of presentation. The reader can cite the original page numbers, a great scholarly benefit. Extraneous new errors and corruptions of the text are avoided. The cost is minimal, a crucial consideration these days where a difficult mathematical text is concerned.

More than the previous editors, the present editors have labored to correct errors in the original versions. Hiroaki Nagatani, blessed with unbelievably sharp eyes and a sophisticated mathematical pencil, has worked through all the derivations. For the most part unobtrusively, he and Kate Crowley have corrected errors; in a few places where several lines of argument have had to be recast, the reader will be alerted to the

1977 editorial alterations by small but obvious variations in typography or by parenthetical editorial indications. I used to remark that the only thing better than an economic classic is its Japanese translation; readers of this volume will benefit from Mr. Nagatani's labors, which make available to them versions that are better than the originals.

Much intelligence and work went into the editing of these many papers. The earlier acts of Joseph E. Stiglitz and Robert C. Merton were not easy ones to follow. But Crowley and Nagatani have earned in their own right distinction for a hard job beautifully done. I am grateful to them for their successful efforts and for their friendship.

Paul A. Samuelson

Cambridge, Massachusetts
June 1977

EDITORS' PREFACE

The fourth volume of *The Collected Scientific Papers* consists of eighty-six articles, all the scientific contributions of Paul A. Samuelson from mid-1971 through 1976. Most of the articles were collected from professional journals, books, and festschrifts. Some were selected from non-professional sources, such as magazines, newspapers, and lectures. Although the major purpose of *The Collected Scientific Papers* is to give easy reference to Professor Samuelson's scientific papers, we have included many papers of a biographical nature, which give his insight into the professional development of many of his eminent colleagues.

The papers are grouped into ten parts, each part representing a field of economics; the articles are then arranged by subject within each part. Although this volume is the continuation of the first three volumes edited by Professors Joseph E. Stiglitz and Robert C. Merton, we have changed the classification system from that established in 1966 suited to the earlier works. Despite these changes, nine parts of this volume correspond roughly to the divisions of the previous volumes. Part IV, "Mathematical Biology and Economics of Population," contains work in an area in which Professor Samuelson has recently begun investigation.

We have corrected obvious typographical and mechanical errors. A few substantive corrections were made by Professor Samuelson, each with a clear statement that it is of 1977 vintage.

In the year in which we worked on this volume, Professor Samuelson, as usual, wrote an enormous amount. We must confess that it was a difficult task to keep up with his rate of production.

HIROAKI NAGATANI
KATE CROWLEY

Cambridge, Massachusetts
June 1977

CONTENTS

Volume IV

Contents

Part III. On Marxian Economics

Part IV. Mathematical Biology and Economics of Population

Contents

Part VII. Welfare Economics

Part VIII. Theory of Money and Inflation

Part IX. Lectures and Essays on Current Economic Problems

Part X. Essays on the Evolution of Economics

Contents

PART I

Theory of Consumption and Production

208

COMPLEMENTARITY
An Essay on the 40th Anniversary of the Hicks–Allen Revolution in Demand Theory

By PAUL A. SAMUELSON

Massachusetts Institute of Technology

Offered in tribute to Sir John Hicks and Sir Roy Allen. My thanks go to the National Science Foundation for financial aid, and to Kate Crowley and Lynn Mary Karjala for editorial assistance. My intellectual debts to Nicholas Georgescu-Roegen are great and obvious.

THE TIME is ripe for a fresh, modern look at the concept of complementarity. Whatever the intrinsic merits of the concept, forty years ago it helped motivate Hicks and Allen to perform their classical "reconsideration" of ordinal demand theory. And, as I hope to show, the last word has not yet been said on this ancient preoccupation of literary and mathematical economists.

The simplest things are often the most complicated to understand fully. For this reason, I have redrafted the present paper along the following lines: The main discussion is primarily literary. Then comes a mathematical section. Finally, I give a brief survey of the history of the subject.

I. *What Every Schoolboy Knows*

As Ludwig Wittgenstein would say, we "know" that coffee and tea are "substitutes" because we can drink one or the other; in the same way, we know that tea and lemon are "complements," because tea with lemon makes up our desired brew. And probably we feel that tea and salt are somewhere between being substitutes and being complements: relatively speaking, tea and salt are in the nature of "independents."

Beyond these simple classifications the plain man may hesitate to go. Thus, sometimes I like tea and lemon; sometimes I like tea and cream. What would you say is the relation between lemon and cream for me? Probably substitutes. I also sometimes take cream with my coffee. Before you agree that cream is therefore a complement to both tea and coffee, I should mention that I take much less cream in my cup of coffee than I do in my cup of tea. Therefore, a reduction in the price of coffee may *reduce* my demand for cream, which is an odd thing to happen between so-called complements; at least this is in contrast to the case of the tea-and-lemon complements where we should expect a reduction in the price of either to increase the demand for both (as I am induced to consume more cups of lemoned tea).

Things are not so plain sailing after all. We and Wittgenstein are not so sure what it is that we know. Actually three different strands of argumentation have been running through our discussion.

1. First, there is the "either-or" re-

lation of tea and coffee: at 4 o'clock we want a cup of something, and if coffee will not serve, tea will—or vice versa. Related to this first polar-case notion of either-or is the contrasting "and-both" relation of tea and lemon.[1]

2. Vaguely related to the above is a second line of argumentation. If you ask me why coffee and tea are substitutes and why tea and lemon are complements, prior to my naive preconceptions having been tainted by exposure to advanced Slutsky-Pareto sophistications, I'll probably be tempted to reply along the following lines:

"Add a pinch of tea to my previous ration of goods and services. Alternatively add a squeeze of lemon. Each makes me better off. But now add the tea and lemon doses together (*i.e.*, make them both now available to me). Because the benefit of tea and lemon together is greater than the sum of their separate benefits, surely I have a right to regard tea and lemon as complements.

"Likewise, imagine adding each of coffee and tea as alternatives. Since the benefit from both together is surely less than the sum of each's separate benefit (in the same sense that 2 extra cups of tea is supposed to give me less than twice the benefit of 1, as my yearning for further stimulation and warmth satiates), I regard coffee and tea as substitutes.

"Similarly, extra salt and extra tea give combined benefits about equal to the sum of each, and so they are roughly independents."[2]

---

[1] This first way of defining complementarity by perfect polar cases is probably prehistoric. An early definitive formulation is in Irving Fisher [22, 1892].

[2] This second way of defining complementarity might be called the Pareto-Georgescu criterion after Pareto [52, 1909] and Georgescu-Roegen [29, 1952]. Fig. 2 comes from the latter, as does Fig. 2. As will be shown around Equation [26], it is what provides point to the better known criterion given by the sign of the cross derivative of an introspectively felt cardi-

3. Finally, there is a third test to decide that tea and lemon are complements: it involves the fact that a rise in tea's price will cause a reduction in my demand for lemon. By this test criterion, coffee and tea will be said to be substitutes if a rise in the price of one causes the demand for the other to go up. By such a test, in the case where a 1 percent rise in salt's price causes a 1 percent cut in quantity of salt bought, leaving me with the same money that I spend in the same way on tea and the rest, we can pronounce salt and tea to be independents.[3]

Figure 1 summarizes the three pre-1934 complementarity measures. In 1*a*, indifference contours like *ccc* represent "perfect" complementarity; contours like *ss* represent "perfect" substitutes. In 1*b*, either U''' or U'''' or U''''' is introspectively felt by the consumer to represent a utility increment over U'' just equal to the U'' utility increment over U': the alternatives lead respectively to neoclassical complements, independents, or substitutes. In 1*c*, demand for good 1 is reduced to *cc* when the price p_2 of its complement is raised; *dd* is raised to *ss* when the price of its substitute is raised.

II. *Doubts and Second Thoughts*

None of the above plain arguments has made any reference to what is taught today in the graduate classroom as a proper measure of complementarity. Since the classic

---

nal utility function, $\partial^2 U/\partial q_1 \partial q_2$, which is usually called Edgeworth-Pareto (or, here, E-P for short), because of F. Y. Edgeworth [20, 1897, 1925] and Vilfredo Pareto [52, 1909]. But George Stigler [76, 1965] points out that it was already in R. von Auspitz and R. Lieben [11, 1889]. As is well known, Pareto was inconsistent in espousing it *after* he had given up *cardinal* utility in favor of better-or-worse, *ordinal* utility.

[3] This third way of defining complementarity by the sign of *ceteris paribus* cross elasticities, of $\partial q_i/\partial p_j$ or (they need not be the same!) by

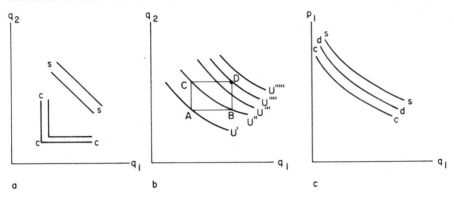

Figure 1

In 1*a*, contours like *ccc* are Fisher perfect complements; contours like *ss*, Fisher perfect substitutes. In 1*b*, if U'''', U'', and U' are equally-spaced in introspective utility, the goods are Edgeworth-Pareto independents (because U'''' passes right through the upper *D* corner of the *ABCD* box); if the equally-spaced contours are U''', U'', and U', the goods are complements (since the two changes together put you on U'''' lying above the U''' where the sum of each separately would put you); if U''''', U'', and U' constitute the equally-spaced contours, the two goods are substitutes, and the E-P cross-derivative of utility $\partial U^2/\partial q_1 \partial q_2$ is negative. In 1*c*, *dd* is the demand curve for q_1 in terms of its *own* price p_1. Then for third-definition complements, an increase in p_2 shifts *dd* downward to *cc*; for substitutes, higher p_2 shifts the *dd* curve upward to *ss*.

of Eugen E. Slutsky [73, 1915], and particularly since the independent early 1930's discovery and rediscovery of Slutsky's post-Paretian work by Allen and Hicks and by Henry Schultz, a fourth and rather different test has been suggested to determine how to classify pairs of tea, coffee, lemon, salt, ... If we were to describe this new procedure to the schoolchildren whom Wittgenstein taught in lower Austria, they would be astonished to learn that such post-Paretian concepts belong *to them*. The same astonishment might be registered by most in-laws of economic Ph.D.'s. "What?" they will ask, "to discover that tea and lemon are complements must I accompany any change in their prices or quantities by

a 'compensating' change in money income or in some other good or goods? Bless my soul, I'd never have suspected that. Pray, *why?*"

Actually, if you eavesdrop on the graduate classroom or peer into intermediate and advanced books on economic theory, you'll have some difficulty in learning the reason why. Indeed, Slutsky seems never to have proposed his compensated cross-price changes as an explicit measure of complementarity [73, 1915]. What you primarily find[4] in the 1930's discussions are various

---

$\partial q_j/\partial p_i$, is intuitive, and is at least implicitly in mind in most elementary discussions. Warning: All these and later measures are "local" or "point" measures.

[4] Of course, what you find in Slutsky [73, 1915] and Hicks-Allen [34, 1934] is something much more important than palaver about complementarity—namely recognition of the canonical simplicity demand analysis assumes when *ceteris paribus* terms ($\partial q_i/\partial p_i$, $\partial q_i/\partial p_j$, $\partial q_i/\partial income$) are used to form "compensated" compounds, $(\partial q_i/\partial p_j) + q_j(\partial q_i/\partial income)$ or $(\partial q_i/\partial p_j)_{\bar{u}}$.

5

desultory but cogent objections to the older complementarity definitions—demonstrations that not all of the three may agree with each other, that some may be ambiguous in terms of an observed demand situation that involves no introspection and no polar case, and that the third definition can be asymmetric in the sense that tea could be a substitute for salt while salt is independent of tea.

Before giving the post 1934 complementarity definition based on the work of Slutsky [73, 1915], Hicks [34, 1934; 35, 1939], Allen [4, 1934], and Henry Schultz [71, 1938], hereafter called the SHAS definition for short, let me examine some cases where the older definitions do seem to coexist peacefully. Suppose I always spend two-thirds of my income on warm beverage, and one-third on salt. Suppose also, by introspection under the interrogation of a Weber-Fechner[5] psychologist, I know that the marginal utility to me of each good halves when *its* consumption doubles, but is quite unaffected by a change in my consumption of the *other* good.

Then the first Fisher test does not apply: the beverage and salt are not *perfect* complements, nor are they *perfect* substitutes [22, 1892]. Because I have augmented observable price-quantity demand data by introspective information, the second Edgeworth-Pareto (E-P) definition can apply: by it salt and beverage are *independents,* since adding increments of salt and of beverage together does add to my cardinal utility exactly the sum of what each alone would add. The third test, based on $\partial beverage/$

∂p_{salt}, is easily seen to agree that the goods are *independents*: with higher p_s, I still have the same two-thirds of income to spend on beverage and its p_b has not changed; hence $\partial q_b/\partial p_s = 0$, and likewise $\partial q_s/\partial p_b = 0$.

So far so good. This was about the view of the world of Marshall [46, 1890, 1920]. He thought that broad categories of goods approximated to both these independences. But within each broad category, he recognized patterns of complementarity and substitutability. Let us construct a Santa Claus case where all this stays valid.

Suppose that my hot beverage could be either cups of coffee or double cups of tea-with-1-lemon-slice. All else in the problem remains the same. Now we have 4 quantities: q_c, q_t, q_l, q_s. Clearly the polar definitions also apply: (1) coffee and lemoned-tea are perfect substitutes; tea and lemon are perfect complements; beverage and salt are independents, and hence so must be each of the pairs: coffee-salt, tea-salt, lemon-salt —this both by the E-P cross-derivative-of-utility test and by the *ceteris paribus* price-elasticity test. What about tea and coffee, and lemon and coffee? They are clearly E-P substitutes and also $\partial q_i/\partial p_j$ substitutes.[6]

Our first signal of discord in Eden comes if I keep the previous example in every detail except to make one alteration: my marginal utility for salt never goes down; I am now a salt addict who fritters away all my extra income on salt. Tea, lemon, and coffee remain as before in their various interactions; and they still are E-P independents in comparison with salt. Also, changes

---

[5] See Stigler [76, 1965] for discussion of the psychological notions associated with the Weber-Fechner logarithmic law, and for related discussion of resolution of the St. Petersburg Paradox in Daniel Bernoulli [15, 1738] by positing a logarithmic utility function whose expected value is to be maximized in stochastic situations.

[6] Strictly speaking, Fisher's polar cases introduce discontinuities in the definition of partial derivatives $\partial^2 u/\partial q_i \partial q_j$ and $\partial q_i/\partial p_j$. But if we work with finite differences and interpret the qualitative results according to the spirit of the proposed tests, we verify that: any rise in p_t will, if anything, reduce q_c, and vice versa; any rise in p_c will, if anything, reduce q_t; adding tea and lemon together does add more than the sum of what each does separately, and adding lemoned-tea and coffee together adds less than

in the prices of tea, lemon, and coffee will have zero effects on q_s: so they are in that sense independent of salt. But is salt independent of them? No: raising p_s will lower the marginal utility of money income and *ceteris paribus* lower beverage, coffee, tea, and lemon consumption; so salt is a third-definition complement to the other goods, while each of them is an independent to salt. Not a very satisfactory outcome for a Wittgenstein who hopes for a clear-cut plain-man's conception of complementarity.[7]

No wonder that economists had been softened up for the SHAS fourth definition of complementarity, however little its intuitive content. Nature abhors a vacuum, and agnosticism over introspective utility left the economists of forty years ago without an E-P concept worth fighting for.

III. *Post-Slutsky Compensated Definitions*

Now for the fourth, SHAS definition.

---

what comes from adding the contributions of each separately.

[7] My examples have deviously selected for discussion two singular cases in which definitions 2 and 3 can be made to seem most equivalent: they are shown in Samuelson [61, 1942] to be first the singular logarithmic-utility case in which a p_j change does not affect Marshall's "marginal utility of money"; and second the case where one good has literally constant marginal utility. In the last case, when $n = 3$ and goods 2 and 3 are not the ones with constancy of marginal utility, the E-P $\partial^2 u/\partial q_2 \partial q_3$ and the $-\partial q_2/\partial p_3 = -\partial q_3/\partial p_2$ criteria will agree in sign, as is noted in Hicks (1939, p. 42); but this need *not* be the case for $n > 3$, and even for $n = 3$, we find that $\partial^2 u/\partial q_1 \partial q_2 = \partial^2 u/\partial q_1 \partial q_3 = 0$, at the same time that $\partial q_2/\partial p_1, \partial q_1/\partial p_2, \partial q_3/\partial p_1, \partial q_1/\partial p_3$ need not vanish and need not agree in sign; and hence it is not true, even for this singular case, that the different definitions agree when applied to *all* the goods. All remarks about this last case need qualifying when the p's are so high that none of q_1 is bought.

How to account for lingering hopes that $\partial\{\partial u/\partial q_1\}/\partial q_j$ and $\partial q_j/\partial p_i$ will "tend" to agree in

For Schultz [71, 1938] and the mathematical appendix of Hicks [35, 1939], this was definable by a slight modification to the cross-price-elasticity test of the third definition already discussed.

> *SHAS definition:* Instead of using the sign of the *ceteris paribus* cross-elasticity, $\partial q_i/\partial p_j$, we are to use a compensated price change. *In effect*, in increasing p_j, we are simultaneously to increase money income by an amount just sufficient to keep the consumer on the same indifference contour — to freeze $u = \bar{u}$ — and then ask for the sign of the change in q_i, namely of
> $$(\partial q_i/\partial p_j)_{\bar{u}} = (\partial q_i/\partial p_j) + q_j \partial q_i/\partial in\text{-}come = s_{ij} = s_{ji}$$
>
> $s_{ij} > 0$ implies substitutes
> $s_{ij} < 0$ implies complements
> $s_{ij} = 0$ implies SHAS
> independents

Hicks-Allen [34, 1934] and the main text of Hicks [35, 1939, p. 44] gave an equivalent definition for the case $n = 3$.[8] By it, goods 2 and 3 are respectively complements, substitutes, or independents,

---

sign? No doubt by the fact that when utility theory was first invented, for example by W. S. Jevons [42, 1871], it was invented with its common errors already in it — namely, with the belief that as $n \to \infty$, somehow the marginal utility of income, λ, becomes "approximately constant," with $\partial\lambda/\partial p_i = 0$, so that $\partial u[\ldots, q_i, \ldots, q_j, \ldots]/\partial q_i$ and observed partial-equilibrium demand functions, $p_i(\ldots, q_i, \ldots, q_j, \ldots)$ are proportional: then, provided every $\partial p_i/\partial q_j$ is "small" relative to every $\partial p_i/\partial q_i$, we deduce that $-\partial q_i/\partial p_j$ has the same sign as $\partial^2 u/\partial q_i \partial q_j$. The historical section cites Stigler's quotation from Jevons [76, 1965, p. 89 from 42, 1871, p. 147].

[8] See my mathematical section, around equations [18]–[22], for a discussion of how Hicks handles the more-than-three-good case by means of a third composite good made up of all other goods than the pair in question.

depending on whether as we stay on an indifference contour and increase q_3, lowering q_1 to keep us on the same $\bar{u}$, the marginal rate of substitution of q_2 for q_1 is raised, lowered, or stays the same.

This is some mouthful for Wittgenstein's plain man. Fortunately, Georgescu-Roegen can put the matter so that it more intuitively resembles the E-P test [29, 1952].

1. Increase q_2 alone to $q_2 + h_2$; and record the amount of q_1 you can sacrifice, $-h_1$, and stay at the same $\bar{u}$ level. 2. Increase q_3 above by just enough h_3 to permit the *same* compensating drop in q_1 of $-h_1$. 3. Now increase q_2 and q_3 *together* by those same amounts, h_2 and h_3, and record the resulting amount of q_1 that can be sacrificed. Is it just twice as large as h_1? more than $2h_1$? less than $2h_1$? In the first case, 2 and 3 are SHAS independents; in the second they are SHAS complements; in the third case SHAS substitutes. This way of perceiving the SHAS classification between q_2 and q_3 shows that it is not really a question solely of *their* interrelationship, but involves intimately each's relation to the third good. (All of·this is demonstrated in my mathematical section, around equation [23'].)

Figure 2[9] gives a test for SHAS complementarity that is thus seen to have a formal resemblance to Figure 1b's version of the E-P concept. Everywhere in Figure 2, we are in the same base level of utility: the contours in the q_2-q_3 plane represent iso-q_1 levels to keep utility at the base $\bar{u}$ level (an *ordinal* requirement). Every contour carries therefore a q_1 number—q_1', q_1'', q_1''', . . .— namely, the compensatory amount of q_1

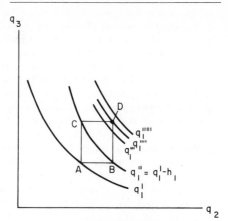

Figure 2

To determine Slutsky-Hicks, Allen-Schultz "compensated" complementarities, we plot iso-q_1 contours that keep me on the same base level of indifference, $\bar{u}$. (Higher contours therefore have *lower* q_1 levels.) As in 1b, now that we have our numbering metric, we can ask which one of the top three contours is equally-spaced in comparison with the bottom two contours. If q_1'''' going through D is it, the goods are SHAS independents; if q_1''' going below D is it, they are SHAS complements; if q_1''''' is it, we are in the more common case of SHAS substitutes.

needed, along with each point's q_2 and q_3, to keep me on the same level of indifference.

Now let me carefully identify a base contour, q_1', corresponding to some q_1'. And a second higher contour, q_1'' corresponding to (lower!) $q_1' - h_1$. Where in Figure 2 does

---

[9] F. A. Hayek [32, 1943] uses a similar diagram: but he'd use the q_2-q_3 diagram not as is done here to determine the SHAS complementarity of q_2 and q_3, but rather to determine the SHAS complementarity of q_1 and q_2 or of q_1 and q_3: if moving north from a point in my diagram makes the absolute slope become *less* steep, Hayek correctly infers that q_1 and q_2 are complements; a posteriori, then, if a move west

in my diagram makes the absolute slope more steep, goods q_1 and q_3 are complements (and only *one* of these can be complements at a given point if the contour is to be properly convex, which can be used to prove that only one pair of three goods can, for $n = 3$, be complements). See N. Georgescu-Roegen for geometry and discussion [29, 1952].

the still-higher equally-spaced contour occur that corresponds to $q_1^* = q_1' - 2h_1$, with $q_1^* - q_1'' = q_1'' - q_1'$? That question can be given an answer *without* asking me about my introspective cardinal utility! In Figure 2, if the contour q_1'''' that goes through the upper corner of the indicated box, D, represents the equally-spaced q_1 third contour $q_1^* = q_1' - 2h_1$, then q_2 and q_3 are *SHAS independents* (and s_{23} can be verified to vanish). If contour q_1''' *below* D represents q_1^*, the goods are *SHAS complements*. If the contour q_1''''' above D represents the critical q_1^*, q_2 and q_3 are *SHAS substitutes*.

What to think about the SHAS definitions? Despite their lack of immediate intuitive content for the plain man, they have the merit of being (a) observable from non-introspective (p,q) demand data; (b) of being symmetric, so that if tea is a substitute for salt, salt will be one for tea; (c) of being likely in the strong polar case of perfect substitutes to agree with the intuitive definition of Fisher [22, 1892]. However, (α) for $n = 2$, we can verify that $s_{12} > 0$ always, so SHAS complementarity becomes vacuous; (β) for $n > 2$, since we must stay on the same indifference contour, substitutability of goods for each other must clearly dominate over the small amounts of complementarity admissible.

Can we fulfill all the good requirements that the SHAS definitions do, and do no worse with respect to its drawbacks? I now propose a fifth definition of complementarity, based on observable money-metric utility, that goes some way to fulfilling this bill. Also, it easily adapts itself to a still better sixth concept that has even greater intuitive content, the use of von Neumann stochastic-metric utility.

IV. *Money's Worth as a Metric for Complementarity*

We have arrived at the finding that we human beings do not, on careful examination, turn out to possess any one clear-cut notion of complementarity and substitutability. So I shall have no quarrel with any agnostic who questions the importance of the whole subject of complementarity. But before he makes up his mind, I would propose a fifth test for complementarity and substitutability based on money-metric utility that he may find more appealing. This proposed method avoids most of the traditional objections. It is not entirely new since, I believe, people have had a glimpse of it long before political economy became a scholarly discipline and took up mathematical symbolisms, and since many economists have implicitly or explicitly employed it. Here it is.

Karl Marx commented on the fetishistic character of money and prices. Without pejorative or normative affect, let us build on this undoubted base. I inhabit an economic status. I am accustomed to facing a pattern of prices $(p_1, \ldots, p_n) = P$. Lord knows these are not strict and immutable constants: in recent years they tend to have been rising; but still I should be surprised if toothpaste became more expensive than caviar; and so, at least in my memory, I have a notion of "current prices," P^0. Also, depending on my current income, I consume a vector of goods $(q_1, \ldots, q_n) = Q$. Faced by my current expenditure or income, and prices, P^0, I customarily am demanding Q^0, or Q's in the neighborhood of Q^0. For simplicity, assume smooth differentiability of all (P,Q) demand relationships.

Now suppose I contemplate getting more of Q^0, going to $Q^0 + \Delta Q$: perhaps more tea; or more coffee; or both. It is natural for me to think: "I'd be as well off with Q^0 plus yonder pinch of tea, $\Delta Q^0 = $ (pinch of tea, no more coffee, . . .), as I would be with an extra .1 of 1 percent of money income e^0, Δe^0. Thus, if overtime is available, I'd work an extra minute a day to get it, etc." Naturally, no exactitude is needed or to be expected; and there is no need to assume that, for ΔQ so large as to take me out of my customary economic habitat, I would still be able even to guess at how my tastes and demand would run. All that is being assumed is this:

> *Axiom:* The indifference contours near one's customary living standard, Q^0, are to be given a cardinal numbering just equal to how much income, e, would be needed at prevailing prices, P^0, to (most cheaply!) attain that new contour of living standard as in ordinary index-number theory.

If wished, one can speak of "utility," $e(Q)$, that is objectively measurable by money spendable at prices P^0. Mathematically $e(Q)$ is given by $e[P^0;Q]$, where this last function[10] is defined behavioristically as

$$e[P^0;Q] = \underset{x_i}{\text{Minimum}} \sum_1^n p_j x_j \text{ subject to} \tag{1}$$
$$u[x_1, \ldots, x_n] = u[q_1, \ldots, q_n] = u[Q]$$

where $u[Q]$ is *any* indicator-numbering of the observable indifference contour (that for simplicity is assumed to exist and to have two or three continuous partial derivatives). Note that observing scientists have no need to use or rely on anyone's psychological introspection to measure this $e[P^0;Q]$ function. Such measurements could be inferred from the objective demand functions. Indeed, by revealed-preference data near $(P^0;Q^0)$, of the form $(P^1;Q^1)$, $(P^2;Q^2)$, . . . , one could hope to make all our qualitative and quantitative calculations. (If one wished for help from introspection, that introspection would not at all involve any mental "sensations," but

---

[10] It is more customary to write $e[P^0;Q]$ as defined here in a form involving utility indicators, namely as $e(P^0|u[Q])$, and that form is discussed in my mathematical section around equations [33]–[35]. However, the present innovation has the merit of eschewing all nonobservables, even in terms of representational symbols.

only estimates of how much one would buy at different prices and incomes!)

Now that we have a good solid utility metric to work with, those who hanker for a solid and simple measure of complementarity can feel back in the promised land from which Pareto and others of us modern ordinalists drove them out. And now they have no need to give up the bread they want and settle for the sophisticated stone preferred them by post-Slutsky writers.

Figure 3, which is reminiscent of Figure 1b, summarizes money-metric utility. At P^0 prices, I choose to be at Q^0. With higher or lower incomes, I would be higher or lower on the Engel income-consumption path EE'. For simplicity, EE' is shown to be a straight line near Q^0, an approximation that becomes exact as we contemplate limitingly small changes. Recall that we have resolved definitively, and in a nonintrospective way that can be read off the vertical intercepts, exactly what I mean by money-metric equally-spaced indifference contours. So now I do have a meaningful numbering of the indifference contours. And now you can apply the E-P-like cross-derivative test to see whether the two goods are complements or substitutes. (Actually, in Figure 3, the upper D corner of the $ABCD$ box lies *above* the top contour; so we know that the goods are money-metric complements rather than substitutes—a necessity in the two-superior-good convex-contour case, as prolonged study of the diagram can make clear.[11] But for $n > 2$, sub-

---

[11] Mathematics proves what geometry and common sense can confirm: no matter how numerous the goods, provided more is bought of each at higher incomes, money-metric complementarity must dominate over *substitutability* or independence. For weighting all *own* and *cross* terms by positive income elasticities requires them to cancel out to zero, since one new dollar of income raises money-metric utility by one dollar, with the marginal (money-metric) utility of income *never* diminishing. With each

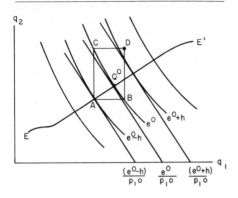

Figure 3

When money income, spendable at fixed prices, goes in equal steps, from e^0 to $e^0 + h$ or $e^0 - h$, the indifference contours depict money-metric utility. Note that every Q point then has an observable numerical value for money-metric utility. Note that always the upper corner of the box D comes *above* the third equally-spaced money-metric utility contour: so always in the two-superior-good case, the goods must be money-metric complements. (If you redraw the chart to make one good inferior, you'll find the goods are then money-metric substitutes.)

stitutability and independence are definite non-vacuous possibilities; and, as will be discussed,[12] if we "Weber-Fechnerize" money-metric utility or, better still, use observable risk-aversion behavior to con-

good being a "substitute for itself," the off-diagonal terms must average out to zero. Annoyingly, the shift in terminology between Hicks [33, 1932] and Hicks [34, 1934] causes the normal case for SHAS to be "substitution," while the same preference field regarded as a production function or money-metric utility has complementarity for its normal case. Hicks speaks of dual p-substitutes and q-substitutes in recognition of this vexing terminological snarl [36, 1956, Ch. 16].

[12] Cf. the mathematical section around equa-

vert it into my von Neumann risk-utility metric, we shall have a sixth complementarity concept that even-handedly permits all degrees of complementarity and of substitutability no matter how few or numerous the goods.)

By formal symmetry with the E-P cross-derivative, our point measure of money-metric complementarity is given by the cross-derivative of $e[P^0;Q]$ with respect to q_i and q_j; but evaluated at $Q = Q^0$: namely

$$e_{q_i q_j}[\cdot;Q^0] = \frac{\partial^2 e[P^0;Q^0]}{\partial q_i \partial q_j}$$

$$> 0, \text{ complements}$$
$$= 0, \text{ independents} \quad (2)$$
$$< 0, \text{ substitutes}$$

The mathematical section will give the relationship between money-metric utility and the SHAS or other complementarity definitions. Here we need only note that our new measure is free from many of the objections that were cogently raised against earlier concepts.

Money-metric utility:

(a) has an intuitive meaning,
(b) involves no introspection about unobservables,
(c) is symmetric for each of a pair of goods.

However, it has the drawback of elevating complementarity above substitutability in the normal-goods case. And it does not give people the Gossen-like law of diminishing marginal utility *of income*. Before showing how we can improve on money-metric utility to meet these objections, a word about its intuitiveness is in order.

Consider the recurring desire to calculate consumers-surplus measures from ob-

tions [34]–[35] and [53]–[54]. Warning: Figure 3 applies to $n = 2$ only. For $n > 2$, if we had other goods constant, what is here EE' will not be the true income-consumption path of Engel, and the equally-spaced money-metric contours will no longer be the same inches apart on the q_1 axis or on EE'.

served demand curves. In the cases where those calculations are most valid, what is being computed is precisely my money-metric utility or its logarithm! (an irony in view of my own long-standing lack of enthusiasm for consumer-surplus integrals). To see all this, consider the case where one good, call it q_1, has literally constant marginal utility by some numbering of the indifference contours. Then that numbering agrees with money-metric utility; and the area under an independent q_i good's demand curve, $\int q_i dp_i$ (or in the case of interdependent demands, the line integral of $\Sigma_2^n q_j dp_j$) will equal the changes in $e[P^0;Q]$, except for the dimensional scale factor $1/p_1^0$.

Or consider the economic theory of index numbers.[13] A properly constructed economic index of quantity will give precisely the present money-metric utility. Moreover, in the case where all people have the same homothetic tastes, adding their money-metric utilities (however illegitimate that is for any interpersonal welfare decisions) will definitely give us an exact measure of real social output that is free of the well-known index-number difficulties.

V. *Improving on Money-Metric Complementarity by Observed Risk Tolerance*

Actually, we are not yet quite back at the promised land of old-fashioned diminishing marginal utility. Our money-metric gives us, so to speak, diminishing returns to any subset of goods not on the Ernst Engel's income-consumption path; but when we adjust all goods optimally to extra income, it gives us, so to speak, constant returns to (income) scale! That is to say, the money-metric marginal utility *of income* is

---

[13] Cf. Samuelson and Swamy for a recent survey [69, 1974]. See there the Divisia-line-integral form of consumer's surplus in the homothetic case.

constant at unity. For how could it be otherwise? If you are measuring utility by money, it must remain constant with respect to money: a yardstick cannot change in terms of itself.

Wittgenstein's constituency may therefore wonder whether our new definitions do capture the intuitive notions of the plain man. Let us interrogate the fellow on the point.

Q. Do you have some utility notion which, unlike that of the money-metric, does exhibit diminishing-marginal utility of income in some intuitive, verifiable (*i.e.,* non-private) sense?

A. I might in the following sense. The dollar I stand to win in a fair gamble is worth less to me than the dollar I stand to lose. So you have to offer me better than even odds if I'm to agree to gamble and thereby maximize my expected value of (or first moment of) utility.

Q. For each x dollars you stand to lose below your present e^0 income, at 50–50 odds, how large must your gain, y, have to be for you to take the wager?

A. On reflection, I find that for each x lost, there is a definite amount of y gain you must give me at even odds to make me as well off as staying risklessly at e^0. Moreover, as x losses rise in equal steps, needed y gains rise at an increasing rate (so $y = g_e(x)$ is a strictly-convex increasing function for risk-averting me).

Q. Then on the basis of your observable $g_e(x)$ risk-tolerance function, I (Wittgenstein, or F. Ramsey, or John von Neumann) can stretch your money-metric utility $e[\,\cdot\,;Q]$ into a sixth concept of utility from which complementarity can be ideally computed.

Figures 4a and 4b show how this is done. The vv curve for observable von Neumann [51, 1944] diminishing marginal utility of income (*i.e.,* of money-metric utility obtainable at fixed P^0!) is determined by the condition that the y-gain-area on the right of $e^0 = e[P^0;Q^0]$ always just matches the

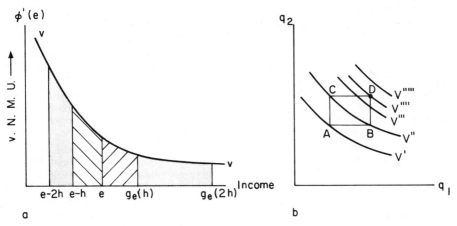

Figure 4

In 4a, to balance an even-odds loss from *e* of $h, the two inside areas must be equal; to balance the loss of a second $h, the outside shaded areas must be equal. Knowing the needed-gain function, $g_e(x)$, we can deduce the shape of the *vv* marginal utility function. In 4b, the von Neumann utility metric, derived from 4a, numbers our contours. If the same *V* change as between *V'* and *V'''* comes at, below, or above *D*, we have risk-utility-metric independence, complementarity, or substitutability.

x-loss-area on the left. This gives us our final von Neumann utility

$$V\lfloor Q\rfloor = b\phi\{e[\cdot;Q]\} \pm a, \qquad b > 0 \qquad (3)$$

where $\phi\{\ \}$ is no longer an *arbitrary* $f\{\ \}$ stretching, but has a definite $\phi''\{\ \}$ curvature, which will be negative for me if I am risk-averse. Figure 4b reproduces the same contours as Figure 3. But now, on the supposition that the *V'''* contour in Figure 4b is exactly the $e^0 + h$ contour in Figure 3, the fact of positive risk aversion says that the new von Neumann, third equally-spaced contour can be *anything* above *V'''*: hence it could fall above or below *D*, so that for all $n \geq 2$ all three categories of complementarity are now possible.

So we are at our journey's end, with an observable test for complementarity that has all the nice requirements ever felt to be needed, and which is subject to none of the numerous defects already alluded to.

Our test criterion is

$$\frac{\partial^2 V[q_1, \ldots, q_n]}{\partial q_i \partial q_j} \begin{array}{l} > 0, \text{ complements} \\ = 0, \text{ independents} \\ < 0, \text{ substitutes} \end{array} \qquad (4)$$

Here then are the possible distinct sign patterns of complementarity possible for a risk averter in the $n = 2$ and 3 cases, where the negative diagonal cross-terms and the 0 case of independents are not shown explicitly

$$\begin{bmatrix} \cdot & + \\ + & \cdot \end{bmatrix} \text{ or } \begin{bmatrix} \cdot & - \\ - & \cdot \end{bmatrix}$$

$$\begin{bmatrix} \cdot & + & + \\ + & \cdot & + \\ + & + & \cdot \end{bmatrix}, \begin{bmatrix} \cdot & - & + \\ - & \cdot & + \\ + & + & \cdot \end{bmatrix} \text{ or }$$

$$\begin{bmatrix} \cdot & - & - \\ - & \cdot & + \\ - & \cdot & + \end{bmatrix}, \begin{bmatrix} \cdot & - & - \\ - & \cdot & - \\ - & - & \cdot \end{bmatrix}$$

13

By contrast, for money-metric utility with no goods inferior and for SHAS, all the sign patterns after "or" are *not* possible.

Interpretation

Forty years is a long time to wait for a clarification of complementarity. Fortunately, and this tells us something about the empirical importance of complementarity classifications, few misleading implications stemmed from the SHAS digressions. Indeed there have been few econometric determinations of complementarity in all of this century, and fewer so refined that they could distinguish between the different esoteric definitions.

Therefore, the present analysis of complementarity in no way depreciates the intrinsic and lasting merits of the Hicks-Allen 1934 breakthrough. Though these two articles gave some emphasis to complementarity, their true contribution was to free nonstochastic demand analysis from all

cardinality of utility. As so often happens in the history of scientific thought, one gains attention and appreciation for one's innovations for reasons that prove to have been irrelevancies. If the authors had not given emphasis to the popular topic of complementarity (and had not brilliantly presented their innovations both in mathematics and in plain words!), their 1934 analysis could not have made the splash it did make and which, for more solid reasons, it deserved to make.[14]

Whatever the merits of the money-metric utility concept developed here, a warning must be given against its misuse. Since money can be added across people, those obsessed by Pareto-optimality in welfare economics as against interpersonal equity may feel tempted to add money-metric utilities across people[15] and think that there is ethical warrant for maximizing the resulting sum.[16] That would be an illogical perversion, and any such temptation should be resisted.

---

[14] Illustrating the same principle of the serendipity of irrelevant issues is the fact that stochastic utility, like that in Bernoulli [15, 1738], Ramsey [54, 1931], B. de Finetti [21, 1937], J. Marschak [45, 1950], or L. J. Savage [70, 1954], came back into prominence 30 years ago, not for the genuine reason that operations research, investment analysis, and Bayesian statistical decision making called for it, but because of the adventitious and accidental reason that a great mind like von Neumann needed metric-utility payoffs for his elegant, but not very useful, two-person zero-sum game theorem. Cf. von Neumann and O. Morgenstern [51, 1944]. However, cf. Wald [80, 1950] for a parallel

development of cardinal utility and loss functions in statistical decision making.

[15] Warning: A similar facile assumption crops up often in consumer's-surplus applications: "If we have no reason to regard one person's 'social marginal utility of money' to be higher or lower than another person's, we can go ahead and add them up—with the presumption that any policy decision that increases their (money-metric!) sum is 'probably a good thing.'" Let the reader beware!

[16] Different people's von Neumann utilities, not being measured in common money units, are less tempting to the perversion of simple addition. But, as argued in J. C. Harsanyi [31,

Mathematics of Complementarity

Here is a terse account of the highlights of the different complementarity concepts. The equations of this self-contained section are numbered in square brackets rather than parentheses. Any reader is free to skip to the final historical section.

Fisher 1893 polar definitions. For $n = 2$, (q_1, q_2), perfect complements are defined to occur when, for positive a_j,

$$u = f\{\mathrm{Min}[q_1/a_1, q_2/a_2]\}, \\ f'\{\ \} > 0, f''\{\ \} \gtrless 0 \qquad [1]$$

Or, more generally, when

$$u = f\{\mathrm{Min}[g_1(q_1), g_2(q_2)]\}, g_i'(\ ) > 0 \quad [2]$$

Perfect substitutes are defined to occur when

$$u = f\{b_1 q_1 + b_2 q_2\}, \ b_j > 0 \qquad [3]$$

Or, more generally, perfect substitutes occur when along an indifference contour $d^2 q_1/dq_2^2 = 0$. This is assured when the following relations prevail between *any* of u's first and second partial derivatives,

$$u_i = \partial u[Q]/\partial q_i, \\ u_{ij} = \partial^2 u[Q]/\partial q_i \partial q_j, \\ u_2[Q]/u_1[Q] = R(q_1, q_2), \ R_j = \partial R/\partial q_j:$$

$$0 \equiv R_2(q_1, q_2) - R(q_1, q_2)R_1(q_1, q_2) \quad [4]$$

$$0 \equiv u_2 u_{11} u_2 - 2u_1 u_{12} u_2 + u_1 u_{22} u_1 \quad [5]$$

This last expression, if recalculated for $U[Q] = f\{u[Q]\}$, will be found to have $f''\{\ \}$ cancel out; and it is therefore invariant to the particular utility numbering used.

Clearly [1] and [3] easily generalize to

1955], one of the few quantum-jump improvements on the classic A. Bergson clarification of welfare economics [13, 1938], it turns out that it *does* make sense to take ethically-weighted sums of individuals' von Neumann utilities: $\lambda^1 V^1[Q^1] + \lambda^2 V^2[Q^2] + \ldots, \lambda^i > 0$. On this see my 1965 afterthoughts, Samuelson [67, 1965, I, pp. 124–26].

$n \geqslant 2$: $(q_1, \ldots, q_n) = Q$. Note that a continuum between the polar cases of [1] and [3] is provided by a CES family of functions:

$$u = f\left\{\left[\sum a_j q_j^{\gamma}\right]^{1/\gamma}\right\}, 0 \neq \gamma < 1 \quad [6]$$

When $\gamma = 1$, we have [3]'s perfect substitutes (and infinite "elasticity of substitution" as measured by $1/[1 - \gamma]$). When $\gamma \to -\infty$, we have perfect complements (so-called "fixed proportions" or zero elasticity of substitution, $1/[1 - \gamma]$).

There is no natural point intermediate between Fisher's poles at which "independence" is definable. However, the limiting case where $\gamma \to 0$ can, by proper evaluation of certain indeterminate forms, be shown to achieve the Cobb-Douglas or Bernoulli case (with unitary elasticity of substitution, $1/[1 - \gamma]$):

$$u = f\{q_1^c q_2^{1-c}\} \quad \text{or} \qquad [7] \\ U = f\{c \log q_1 + (1 - c)\log q_2\}$$

Hicks [33, 1932] provided one possible point concept that fills in the continuum between Fisher's poles when $n = 2$ and the preferences are homothetic (*i.e.*, all income elasticities unity). In that case there exists a homogeneous-first-degree utility indicator

$$U[\lambda q_1, \lambda q_2] \equiv \lambda U[q_1, q_2], \lambda > 0 \quad [8]$$

This will be concave if the indifference curves are convex (*i.e.*, if $f\{U[Q]\}$ is quasi-concave). Then the 1932 elasticity of substitution is definable as

$$\sigma = \sigma_{12} = \sigma_{21} \qquad [9] \\ = U_1[Q] U_2[Q]/U_{12}[Q]U[Q]$$

When $\sigma \to 0$, we have Fisher's [1]. When $\sigma \to \infty$, we have his [3]. When $\sigma \equiv 1$, we have the Cobb-Douglas constant-relative-share function of [7]. For the CES family of [6], $\sigma = 1/[1 - \gamma]$.

For non-homothetic tastes and $n > 2$, the definitions become more complex. In the former case, [9] is better recast in terms of curvature of the indifference contour itself—as for example by some variant of [4], possibly in dimensionless form such as in

$$\sigma_{indif.} = \{d\log(q_2/q_1)/d\log(u_2[Q]/u_1[Q])\}_{\bar{u}} \quad [10]$$

There is a vast industry connected with partial elasticities of substitution for $n > 2$ which I omit.

Third definition by cross-elasticity. Fisher's definitions and their variants are observable from non-introspective, price-quantity data. Skipping for the moment the Edgeworth-Pareto second definition based on introspective feelings of utility, we note that when [1]'s perfect complementarity holds, a rise in p_i must reduce the q_j demand for its perfect complement (at the same time that q_i itself falls). For [3]'s perfect substitutes, a rise in p_i, if it has any effect at all on q_j, must increase it.

This suggests that we define complementarity, independence, or substitutability between goods i and j by either (or both, they need not be the same!) cross-elasticity sign

$$\partial q_i/\partial p_j < 0, \text{ complements}$$
$$> 0, \text{ substitutes} \quad [11]$$
$$= 0, \text{ independents}$$

However, when the two goods have unequal income elasticities, it can easily happen that $\partial q_1/\partial p_2$ and $\partial q_2/\partial p_1$ are of opposite signs. It seems a bit awkward to be able to say that tea is a complement to salt but salt is a substitute for tea. Or consider the special case

$$U = \log tea + (salt)^{1/2} \quad [12]$$

Faced with $(p_1, p_2, e = \Sigma p_j q_j)$, when p_1 alone rises you will spend the same $p_1 q_1$ on tea, and not change your salt q_2. Hence, by the $\partial q_2/\partial p_1$ test, salt is independent of tea. But now decrease p_2 alone. It can be shown that you will increase your $p_2 q_2$ on salt, having to cut down on your tea q_1. By the $\partial q_1/\partial p_2$ test, tea is a complement to salt—even

though we've seen salt to be an independent with respect to tea.

The SHAS fourth definition based on compensated elasticities. This ambiguity of sign of the cross derivative of *ceteris paribus* demand was undoubtedly one reason for Hicks and Allen to propose new definitions [34, 1934]. Very briefly, let's see why the ambiguity is possible.

Consider a regular case of convex indifference contours, with $f\{u[Q]\}$ strongly quasi-concave and smooth. Then

$$\underset{Q}{\text{Max}} \, u[Q] \text{ s.t. } \sum p_j q_j = e > 0$$
$$= u[D(P/e)] \quad [13]$$

where the observable demand functions are denoted by

$$Q = [q_1, \ldots, q_n]$$
$$= [d^1(p_1/e, \ldots, p_n/e), \ldots,$$
$$d^n(p_1/e, \ldots, p_n/e] \quad [14]$$
$$= [d^j(P/e)] = D(P/e)$$
$$= D(Y), y_j = p_j/e, \text{ normalized prices}$$

Slutsky [73, 1915] realized that the partial derivatives $e^{-1} d_i^j = \partial d^i(\ )/\partial p_i$ lack symmetry because they involve an asymmetric combination of cofactors of Pareto's bordered matrix.

$$\begin{bmatrix} 0 & u_j \\ u_i & u_{ij} \end{bmatrix} \text{ or } \begin{bmatrix} 0 & \lambda p_j \\ \lambda p_i & u_{ij} \end{bmatrix} \quad [15]$$

However, it was the key discovery by Slutsky, and later by Hicks and Allen independently, that the following compensated terms did display symmetry:

$$S = [s_{ij}] = [s_{ji}] = S^T$$
$$= [\partial q_i/\partial p_j + q_j \partial q_i/\partial e] \quad [16]$$
$$= [(\partial q_i/\partial p_j)_{\bar{u}}]$$
$$= e^{-1}[d_i^j[Y] + d^j[Y]d^i_{\log e}]$$
$$s_{ij} < 0, \text{ complements}; s_{ij} > 0, \text{ substitutes}$$

where $\partial d^i(p_1/e, \ldots, p_n/e)/\partial \log e = d^i_{\log e}$.

Because $(\partial q_i/\partial p_j)_{\bar{u}}$ obeyed symmetry, Hicks and Allen, and Henry Schultz, proposed use of these Slutsky coefficients (or dimensionless variants of them, such as $V = [v_{ij}] = [k_i E_{ij} + k_i k_j E_{ie}]$, where $k_i =$

$p_i q_i / e = y_i q_i$, $E_{ij} = \partial\log q_i / \partial\log p_j$, $E_{ie} = \partial\log q_i / \partial\log e$), as the SHAS (fourth) definition of complementarity.

For $n = 2$, always $s_{12} > 0$, so no SHAS complements are then possible. For $n = 3$, one at most of the pair of goods $(1,2)$, $(1,3)$, $(2,3)$ can be complements. Since the sums of rows or columns of the V matrix defined in the previous paragraphs must vanish, and since the diagonal terms V_{ii} must be negative, it is clear that every row must have complementarity coefficients that average out plus: in this sense, SHAS substitutability dominates complementarity.

Although s_{ij} and v_{ij} lack much intuitive content for a Wittgenstein, they do have the merit that in the alternative cases of 3 goods

$$u[\mathrm{Min}(q_1,q_2),q_3] \quad \text{or} \quad u[q_1 + q_2, q_3], \quad [17']$$

we do tend to find s_{12} respectively negative and positive, in agreement with out intuitions about Fisher's polar cases.

There remains one tedious task. Hicks and Allen [34, 1934], and Hicks [35, 1939], outside of his mathematical appendix, do not for the $n = 3$ case actually use s_{ij} as their SHAS measure. Instead of, say s_{23}, they use an equivalent, the sign of

$$h_{23}[Q] = h_{23}[q_1,q_2,q_3] = h_{32}[Q] \quad [17'']$$
$$= -(R_3^2[Q] - R^3[Q]R_1^2[Q]),$$
$$R^i[Q] = u_i[Q]/u_1[Q], \ (i=2,3)$$
$$R_j^i[Q] = \partial R^i[q_1,q_2,q_3]/\partial q_j, \ (j=1,2,3)$$

Finally, here is a brief proof of the equivalence of sign of the 1934 criterion $-(R_3^2 - R^3 R_1^2)$ and the 1915–1939 criterion $s_{23} = (\partial q_2/\partial p_3 + q_3 \partial q_2/\partial income)$. For $n = 3$, we have

$$e/p_1 = q_1 + (p_2/p_1)q_2 + (p_3/p_1)q_3$$
$$p_2/p_1 = R^2(q_1,q_2,q_3) \qquad [18']$$
$$p_3/p_1 = R^3(q_1,q_2,q_3)$$

To calculate s_{23}, make a compensated-change experiment, with $d(p_3/p_1)/dt = 1$, $d(e/p_1)/dt = q_3$. Then differentiating our above equations with respect to t, we can solve for all $dq_i/dt = \dot{q}_i$ including $\dot{q}_2 =$

s_{23}/p_1, by means of the following linear relations and Cramer's rule:

$$\begin{bmatrix} 1 & p_2/p_1 & p_3/p_1 \\ R_1^2 & R_2^2 & R_3^2 \\ R_1^3 & R_2^3 & R_3^3 \end{bmatrix} \begin{bmatrix} \dot{q}_1 \\ \dot{q}_2 \\ \dot{q}_3 \end{bmatrix} = \begin{bmatrix} q_3 - q_3 \\ 0 \\ 1 \end{bmatrix} [18'']$$

$$s_{23}/p_1 = \dot{q}_2 = \cfrac{\begin{vmatrix} 1 & 0 & R^3 \\ R_1^2 & 0 & R_3^2 \\ R_1^3 & 1 & R_3^3 \end{vmatrix}}{\begin{vmatrix} 1 & R^2 & R^3 \\ R_1^2 & R_2^2 & R_3^2 \\ R_1^3 & R_2^3 & R_3^3 \end{vmatrix}}$$

$$= \cfrac{-(R_3^2 - R^3 R_1^2)}{\begin{vmatrix} 1 & 0 & 0 \\ R_1^2 & R_2^2 - R^2 R_1^2 & R_3^2 - R^3 R_1^2 \\ R_1^3 & R_2^3 - R^2 R_1^3 & R_3^3 - R^3 R_1^3 \end{vmatrix}}$$

$$= -(R_3^2 - R^3 R_1^2) \div \text{positive determinant}$$

since the condition of convexity of the (sufficiently-many-times-differentiable) indifference contours implies that the $(n - 1)$ by $(n - 1)$ (symmetric!) matrix, $-(R_j^i - R^j R_1^i)$, must be almost-everywhere positive definite with positive principal minors. Q.E.D.

For more details and discussion of the $(n - 1)(n - 2)/2$ independent integrability conditions on the above matrix, see Samuelson [64,1950].

For $n > 3$, say $n = 4$, it is not the case that

$$-R_2^1[q_1,q_2,q_3,q_4] + R^2[q_1,q_2,q_3,q_4]R_3^1[q_1,q_2,q_3,q_4] \quad [19]$$

and s_{12} agree in sign. But as Hicks explains [35,1939], if we lump goods 3 and 4, or 3, ..., n in the general case, into a composite good whose components always have the same relative prices, we can show the equivalence of sign of s_{12} and

$$-R_2^1[q_1,q_2;q_{\mathrm{III}}] + R^2[q_1,q_2;q_{\mathrm{III}}]R_{\mathrm{III}}^1[q_1,q_2;q_{\mathrm{III}}] \quad [20]$$

where, by definition

$$\mathrm{Max}_{q_3,\dots,q_n} u[q_1,q_2,q_3,\dots,q_n] \quad [21]$$

s.t. $\sum_{3}^{n} p_j q_j = q_{III}$

$$= u[q_1, q_2; q_{III}; p_3, \ldots, p_n]$$
$$= u[q_1, q_2; q_{III}] \text{ for short}$$

$R^i[q_1, q_2; q_{III}] =$
$(\partial u[q_1, q_2; q_{III}]/\partial q_i)/(\partial u[q_1, q_2; q_{III}]/\partial q_{III})$

$R_j^i = \partial R^i/\partial q_i, \ R_{III}^i = \partial R^i/\partial q_{III}, \ (i, j = 1, 2)$

The neatness of the Hicks definition of the composite commodity q_{III} is that $u[q_1, q_2; q_{III}]$ has all the nice well-behaved properties of any $u[q_1, q_2, q_3]$, as for example convex indifference contours if those of $u[q_1, \ldots, q_n]$ were convex. Hence, we can derive well-behaved self-defining demand functions

$$q_i = d^i(p_1/e, p_2/e; p_{III}/e), \quad [22]$$
$$(i = 1, 2 \text{ and } III)$$

as the solution to

$$\underset{q_1, q_2, q_{III}}{\text{Max}} \ u[q_1, q_2; q_{III}]$$

s.t. $\sum_{1}^{2} p_i q_i + p_{III} q_{III} = e$ [23]

$$= u[d^1(\ ), d^2(\ ); d^{III}(\ )]$$

Finally, we can now motivate the procedure of Figure 2's test for SHAS complementarity. Along the $\bar{u}$ indifference contour, solve for q_1 as a convex function of q_2 and q_3:

$f\{\bar{u}\} = f\{u[q_1, q_2, q_3]\} \leftrightarrow$
$q_1 = \rho(q_2, q_3; \bar{u}) = \rho(q_2, q_3)$ for short

$\partial \rho(q_2, q_3)/\partial q_i = -R^i[\rho(q_2, q_3), q_2, q_3],$
                     $(i = 2, 3)$
$-\partial^2 \rho(q_2, q_3)/\partial q_i \partial q_j = (R_j^i - R^j R_1^i)$ [23']
$= h_{ij} = h_{ji}$, with sign of s_{ij}

Hence, Figure 2's contours of $\rho(q_2, q_3; \bar{u})$ can have the Georgescu-Pareto box-technique applied to them, with

$-\partial^2 \rho(q_2, q_3; \bar{u})/\partial q_2 \partial q_3$
> 0, SHAS complements
$= 0$, SHAS independents   [23'']
< 0, SHAS substitutes

The case of SHAS independence for 2 and 3 everywhere is given by

$q_1 = \rho(q_2, q_3; \bar{u}) \equiv \rho_2(q_2; \bar{u}) + \rho_3(q_3; \bar{u})$
$\partial^2 \rho/\partial q_2 \partial q_3 \equiv 0$ [23''']

A special case is where $\Sigma_2^3 \rho_j(q_j; \bar{u}) \equiv \bar{u} - \Sigma_2^3 U_j(q_j)$, which is the singular case where good 1 can be taken to have strictly constant marginal utility.

Edgeworth-Pareto complementarity based on introspective utility's cross-derivative. This presupposes that the consumer really does have in mind one privileged cardinal indicator of utility (*i.e.*, Vilfredo Pareto's *ophelimité*). If $u[Q]$ is not already it, we must apply the proper $f\{u\}$ stretching so that $U[Q] = f\{u[Q]\}$ is it.

Such a privileged, introspective utility scale has, of course, two arbitrary parameters: an origin constant, a, and a positive dimensional-unit constant, b. Then $a + bU[Q]$ is as admissible as $U[Q]$ itself and will yield the same E-P complementarity designation.

Examples of such an introspective $U[Q]$ could be the Bernoulli [7] logarithmic case, suggested also by psychologists' Weber-Fechner Law of stimulus and response. Thus, suppose that your perceived sensation of marginal utility of any good (a) halves when its q_i doubles, and (b) is unaffected when some other q_j changes. Then you must have

$U[Q] = k_1 \log q_1 + k_2 \log q_2 + \ldots, k_i > 0$
with $U[Q] \to -\infty$ as $q_i \to 0$.   [24]

In this case, adding tea and salt *together*, positive $\Delta q_1 = h_1$ and $\Delta q_2 = h_2$, brings me the same ΔU as the sum of the separate ΔU's that come from adding each positive Δq_i separately. Our test to verify this "E-P independence" is the vanishing of

$E[q_1, q_2, \ldots; h_1, h_2, \ldots] = E[Q; H]$
$= \{U[q_1 + h_1, q_2 + h_2, \ldots]$
$- U[q_1, q_2, \ldots]\}$ [25]
$- \{U[q_1 + h_1, q_2, \ldots] - U[q_1, q_2, \ldots]\}$
$- \{U[q_1, q_2 + h_2, \ldots] - U[q_1, q_2, \ldots]\}$

By Taylor's expansion, any thrice differentiable $U[Q]$ can lead to

$$E[Q;H] \equiv 0$$
$$+ 0h_1 + 0h_2 + \tfrac{1}{2}0h_1^2 + \tfrac{1}{2}0h_2^2$$
$$+ U_{12}[q_1,q_2,\ldots]h_1h_2 + R_3[Q;H] \quad [26]$$

where the $R_3[Q;H]$ remainder term will involve at least third-degree products, h_i^3 or $h_i^2h_j$, which will become ignorable relative to the sign of $U_{12}[Q]$.

Hence, the E-P criterion becomes

$$\frac{\partial^2 U[q_1,q_2,\ldots]}{\partial q_i \partial q_j} > 0, \text{ complements} \quad [27]$$
$$< 0, \text{ substitutes or rivals}$$
$$= 0, \text{ independents}$$

Remark: Although $U_{ij} \equiv 0$ with independence *everywhere* holds for [24]'s Bernoulli-Weber-Fechner case, and indeed for any case of additive functions $U_1[q_1] + U_2[q_2] + \ldots$, generally at two different Q points we *might* find opposite signs for $U_{12}[Q^a]$ and $U_{21}[Q^b]$. If $U_{12}[Q^a]$ is not zero, it will keep its same complementarity for *all* points in a finite neighborhood of Q^a, and for h_i, all sufficiently small, the [26] test for [25] will be valid. However, if $U_{12}[Q^a] = 0$, the R_3 remainder can no longer be ignored, and we shall have to test $U_{12}[Q]$ for all points in the neighborhood of Q^a to see whether it everywhere vanishes and $E[Q;H] \equiv 0$ as independence requires; actually, for $U_{12}[Q^a] = 0$, one could find that the sign of $E[Q^a;H]$ depends upon the exact composition of $H = (h_1,h_2,\ldots)$, possibly being plus for one choice, minus for another, and zero for still another. If $U[Q]$ is sufficiently "smooth," possessing continuous third-order partial derivatives would more than suffice, then we are assured of symmetry

$$U_{ij}[Q] \equiv U_{ji}[Q] \quad [28]$$

Hence, if tea is an E-P complement to cream, cream is also an E-P complement to tea.

We can now verify that our E-P criterion, *i.e.*, sign of $U_{ij}[\;]$, does depend on choice of $U[Q]$ as against $u[Q] = f\{U[Q]\}$

for arbitrary $f''\{\;\} \gtrless 0$. For $f\{U\} = a + bU[Q]$, the trivial linear-transformation case, we do find that $u_{ij}[Q] = bU_{ij}[Q]$ and that mere change in dimensional units cannot affect the algebraic sign upon which our E-P classification depends. But in general, we calculate

$$u_i[Q] = f'\{U[Q]\}U_i[Q], f'\{\;\} > 0$$
$$u_{ij}[Q] = f'\{U[Q]\}U_{ij}[Q] \quad [29]$$
$$+ f''\{U[Q]\}U_i[Q]U_j[Q]$$

Since $f''\{\;\}$ is unrestricted in sign or magnitude, obviously by making it large enough positive, we can always get u_{ij} to be positive at any one given point; or, by making $f''\{\;\}$ enough negative, we can make u_{ij} be negative. Thus, with any cardinal-utility stretching admissible as an indicator of ordinal utility, Pareto loses the definiteness of the E-P definition, and in his post 1900 writings he should have noticed that his ordinalist thinking has undermined the basis of his 1890's complementarity definitions. Thus, the Bernoulli $U = \Sigma k_j \log q_j$ gives E-P independence; but the *same* indifference contours and demand functions can come from the Cobb-Douglas formulation, $u = f\{U\} = \exp U = \Pi q_j^{k_j}$, and this gives positive $u_{ij}[Q]$ of E-P complementarity not $U_{ij}[Q] \equiv 0$.

Remark: True, we can *locally* make u_{ij} of any sign and magnitude. However, if along an indifference curve, $U_{12}[Q]$ is positive and somewhere is indefinitely large, we cannot find an $f''\{U^0\}$ sufficiently negative to make *all* u_{12} change sign. So, non-locally, there are limits to what we can do in changing E-P classifications: indeed near saturation boundaries, where some $U_i[Q]$ vanishes, the first term in [29] will dominate in sign. Despite Pareto's confusions, many of his non-local assumptions, such as $U[Q] = \Sigma U_j[q_j]$, do have non-introspective price-quantity implications for observable demand functions. Indeed it is this fact about "additive preferences," or weak and strong "tree properties," that Fisher, Ragnar Frisch, and other would-be measurers of "utility" use to perform their identifications. There is a vast modern literature on utility trees associated with the names of Leontief, Gorman, Strotz, F. Fisher, Houthakker, Samuelson, Pollak, Fishburn, and many others, for a survey of which see R. A. Pollak [53, 1972].

There is another way of seeing the non-invariance of the E-P measure. Equal utility steps for one $U[Q]$ will become unequal utility steps for a non-linear stretching $u[Q] = f\{U[Q]\}, f''\{\ \} \neq 0$. C and C' will *not* be the same when respectively defined by

$$U[B] - U[A] = U[C] - U[B] > 0 \quad [30]$$
$$f\{U[B]\} - f\{U[A]\} = f\{U[C']\} - f\{U[B]\}$$

C' will be preferred to C or not depending on whether $f''\{\ \}$ is negative or positive in this region of Q space. O. Lange [44, 1934] and other writers in the *Review of Economic Studies* in the mid-1930's noted that [30] implies $f\{U[C']\} \equiv f\{U[C]\}$ for all $A, B, C, C', \ldots$, if and only if $f''\{U\} \equiv 0$, a fact established in Frisch [27, 1926] and glimpsed by Pareto between intervals of forgetfulness.

Once Wittgenstein senses that much of our intuitive notion of complementarity involves three rather than two goods, something curious can be salvaged from old-fashioned E-P notions. Thus, I may be able to assert that "cream is *more* complementary to tea than coffee is." This means that cream-cum-tea does more for me *ordinally* (!) than coffee-cum-tea. Mathematically, define h_1, h_2, h_3 so that each alone gives the same gain in ordinal utility:

$$U[q_1 + h_1, q_2, q_3] = U[q_1, q_2 + h_2, q_3] \quad [31]$$
$$= U[q_1, q_2, q_3 + h_3]$$

Identifying (q_1, q_2, q_3) with (cream, tea, coffee), I now assert that

$$f\{U[q_1 + h_1, q_2 + h_2, q_3]\}$$
$$> f\{U[q_1, q_2 + h_2, q_3 + h_3]\}$$

and thus demonstrate the greater complementarity with tea of cream than of coffee!

This can be given an unambiguous, and observable, point definition. Thus, calculate at Q the algebraic sign of the invariant

$$\partial \log[(\partial f\{U\}/\partial q_1)/(\partial f\{U\}/\partial q_3)]/\partial q_2$$
$$= [(u_{12}/u_1) - (u_{32}/u_3)] \quad [32]$$
$$= [(U_{12}/U_1) - (U_{32}/U_3)] + (f''/f')[U_2 - U_2]$$

If this is positive, cream is verified to be "more complementary to tea" than coffee is. This more-than-two-good invariance of expressions like $(U_{ij}/U_i) - (U_{kj}/U_k)$ or of $(U_{ij}/U_iU_j) - (U_{kj}/U_kU_j)$ seems hitherto to have escaped notice, although W. E. Johnson came close to it [43, 1913].

Note that a preferred utility indicator cannot be inferred from non-stochastic, price-quantity data of demand. But, eschewing introspection, we may be able to define a privileged $U[Q]$ by revealed ordinal choices among stochastic or probability options. Bernoulli's $U = \log$ Wealth, Cramer's (Wealth)$^{1/2}$, as cited in D. Bernoulli [15, 1738] and G. Stigler [76, 1965, p. 113, n. 129], and von Neumann's [51, 1944] utility, whose expected value one acts to maximize, could thus give us an object to which the old-fashioned E-P definition could be applied, as will be seen when I discuss the sixth definition of complementarity. Note that the more risk-averse the person, the more concave his relevant $f\{u[Q]\}$ von Neumann utility, the more scope there is for negative cross-derivatives and substitutability. On the other hand, if the person is risk-neutral and Gossen's 1854 Law of Diminishing Marginal Utility does not apply to his von Neumann utility, then complementarity will "tend to rule the roost" — in the sense that for $n = 2$ and no goods inferior, the goods *must* be E-P-Neumann complements! Likewise for $n > 2$, complementarity must "dominate" (in a like sense that, by the quirk of the peculiar SHAS terminology, SHAS substitutability must always "dominate" over complementarity).

New money-metric complementarity. Here is a brief mathematical description of this paper's proposed measure of money-metric utility, to which E-P cross-derivative test-criteria are to be applied. Define the basic minimized-expenditure functions that L. W. McKenzie and modern duality theory show to be so useful [48, 1957]

$$e[P^0;Q] \equiv e(P^0|u[Q])$$

$$= \text{Min} \sum_1^n p_j^0 x_j \qquad [33]$$

s.t. $u[x_1, \ldots, x_n] = u[q_1, \ldots, q_n] = u[Q]$

Note that this defines the same $e[P^0;Q]$ function whether we use $u[Q]$ or $f\{U[Q]\}$; only the $e(P^0|u[Q])$ function depends on the choice of utility indicator, and in it the arbitrariness of $u[Q]$ is just offset by the arbitrariness of the dependence of $e(P^0|u[Q])$ on changes in its last argument. $e[P^0;Q]$ can be directly observed from demand data without any need for introspection.

For frozen P^0, $e[P^0;Q]$ or $e[\cdot;Q]$ becomes a perfectly good $U[Q]$ indicator. That is the essence of the proposed fifth, money-metric method for defining complementarity; once we live in a sea of money, Wittgenstein can ascertain that we do have an intuitive feeling for $e[\cdot;Q]$ and its cross-derivatives. $\partial^2 e[\cdot;Q]/\partial q_i \partial q_j = e_{q_i q_j} [\cdot;Q]$, particularly if we evaluate Q at (or very near) a point Q^0 corresponding to what we actually optimally buy at P^0, with $Q^0 = D(P^0/e^0)$. Thus, our local measure of money-metric complementarity is non-introspectively defined by

$$e_{q_i q_j} = \frac{\partial e[P^0;Q^0]}{\partial q_i \partial q_j} > 0, \text{ complements}$$
$$= 0, \text{ independents} \qquad [34]$$
$$< 0, \text{ substitutes}$$

There are the following shortcomings of this measure. First, it does depend upon P^0, one arbitrary set of recently ruling prices; for Q^1 far from Q^0, we might be at a loss to guess our own demand behavior, and for a P near to the prices at which it would be bought, P^1, we might arrive at a difference in sign for $e_{q_i q_j} [P^0;Q^1]$ and $e_{q_i q_j} [P^1;Q^1]$.

Second, by the very definition of money

as our utility metric, we lose Gossen's diminishing-marginal utility of extra income, e^0 or $e^0 + \Delta e^0$. Instead we find that a dollar's extra income always increases our money-metric utility by a dollar, and that the "marginal utility of money" is constant at all incomes at the defined level of unity. If we, so to speak, Weber-Fechnerize money-metric utility, by using log(money-metric U), we can recover our Gossen Law. But this does not seem the best way to improve our fifth concept. Instead, we get a better sixth concept of privileged von Neumann utility by applying to money-metric U that $f\{\text{money-metric } U\}$ stretching that the person's revealed preferences concerning risk show to be required (as discussed later).

Third, as already hinted at, if $n = 2$ and both goods are superior, goods 1 and 2 can never be money-metric substitutes or independents. Our classification then becomes vacuous. If this seems unbearable to anyone, he might avoid the dire fate by Weber-Fechnerizing money-metric utility, thereby getting back all three possibilities. (As remarked, this seems *ad hoc* and less preferable than going on to the sixth von Neumann concept.)

To illuminate the above remarks, consider how $e[\cdot; Q]$ differs in its cross-derivatives from some arbitrary $u[Q]$ in terms of which $e[\cdot;Q] = f\{u[Q]\}$. Let us concentrate on $e(P^0|u[Q])$ and calculate cross-derivatives:

$$e_{q_i}(P^0|u[Q]) = e_u(P^0|u[Q])u_i[Q]$$
$$e_{q_i q_j}(P^0|u[Q^0]) = e_u^0 u_{ij} + e_{uu}^0 u_i u_j \qquad [35]$$

Now suppose $u[Q]$ is the von Neumann utility metric and the person is risk averse; then, by this supposition, $e_{uu}^0 > 0$ and we realize that u_{ij} can be negative even though, in the two-superior-good case, $e_{q_i q_j}$ cannot be. Likewise, for $n > 2$ and all goods superior, even though the average cross-derivative of $e(|)$ or $e[\ \ ]$ must in some sense average out positive, this need not hold for the average u_{ij}, which can be even-handed in permitting substitutability and complementarity to occur.

For the homothetic case, the elegance of modern duality theory, cited in my historical appendix, applies. Then we have factorability

$$e[P;Q] \equiv p[P]q[Q]$$
$$= p[p_1, \ldots, p_n]q[q_1, \ldots, q_n]$$
$$\equiv \lambda^{-1}p[\lambda P]m^{-1}q[mQ], \lambda > 0, m > 0$$
$$= \sum_1^n p_j q_j \quad \text{if} \quad Q = D(P/e) \equiv eD(P)$$
$$< \sum_1^n p_j q_j \quad \text{if} \quad Q \neq eD(P)$$

[36]

The money-metric complementarity cross-derivatives, $e^{-1}e_{q_i q_j}$ or $q_{ij}[Q]/q[Q]$, have all the properties of factor-input complementarity in the neoclassical case of homogeneous production functions. Now we can show the contrast between money-metric complementarity and SHAS complementarity: the latter can be shown to be given by the partials $p_{ij}[Y]/p[Y]$, which are related to the money-metric partials in only an indirect (or complicated, dual) way.

Very briefly, here are the essential relations. Our basic demand function of [14], we know from modern duality theory relations like [36], now takes on the following simple forms

$$[q_i] = Q = D(P/e) = D(Y)$$
$$= eD(P), \text{ in the homothetic case}$$
$$= [\partial \log p(y_1, \ldots, y_n)/\partial y_i]$$
$$= \text{grad } p(Y)$$
$$= e \text{ grad } p(P)$$

[37]

$$[y_i] = Y = D^{-1}[Q]$$
$$= [\partial \log q(q_1, \ldots, q_n)/\partial q_i]$$
$$= \text{grad } q(Q)$$

Homotheticity means balanced income effects, since all income elasticities are unity. Therefore, all *ceteris paribus* cross-price effects are symmetric even in the absence of the Slutsky-Hicks compensated-income changes. Now we have

$$[\partial q_i/\partial y_j] = [\partial q_j/\partial y_i] = D'(Y) = D'(Y)^T$$
$$= \left(\frac{p_{ij}(Y)}{p(Y)} - \frac{p_i(Y)}{p(Y)} \frac{p_j(Y)}{p(Y)} \right) \quad [38]$$
$$= [\partial^2 \log p(Y)/\partial p_i \partial p_j]$$

$$[\partial y_i/\partial q_j] = [\partial y_j/\partial q_i]$$
$$= D^{-1'}(Q) = D^{-1'}(Q)^T$$
$$= \left(\frac{q_{ij}(Q)}{q(Q)} - \frac{q_i(Q)}{q(Q)} \frac{q_j(Q)}{q(Q)} \right) \quad [39]$$
$$= [\partial^2 \log q(Q)/\partial q_i \partial q_j]$$

Since $[\partial q_i/\partial y_j]$ and $[\partial y_i/\partial q_j]$ are inverse Jacobian matrices, we can express the exact relationship between the p_{ij} and q_{ij} coefficients. But first let us relate the former to the SHAS complementarity coefficients. We calculate for the homothetic case

$$[e^{-1}s_{ij}]$$
$$= \left(\frac{p_{ij}(Y)}{p(Y)} - \frac{p_i(Y)}{p(Y)} \frac{p_j(Y)}{p(Y)} + q_i q_j \right) \quad [40]$$
$$= [p_{ij}(Y)/p(Y)]$$

Hence, we relate the SHAS term s_{ij} to the money-metric-utility term $\partial^2 e/\partial q_i \partial q_j$ by the simple matrix relation, $D'(Y) = D^{-1'}(Y)^{-1}$. But we might as well apply this to the dimensionless elasticity expressions so beloved in literary economics. So we define dual complementary elasticities Σ_{ij}^* and Σ_{ij}

$$\Sigma_{ij}^* = e^{-1}s_{ij}/q_i q_j \equiv \Sigma_{ji}^*$$
$$= \frac{p_{ij}(Y)}{p(Y)} \div \frac{p_i(Y)}{p(Y)} \frac{p_j(Y)}{p(Y)}$$
$$= p(Y)p_{ij}(Y)/p_i(Y)p_j(Y)$$

$$\Sigma_{ij} = e_{q_i q_i}[Y;Q]/y_i y_j \equiv \Sigma_{ji} \quad [41]$$
$$= \frac{q_{ij}(Q)}{q(Q)} \div \frac{q_i(Q)}{q(Q)} \frac{q_j(Q)}{q(Q)}$$
$$= q(Q)q_{ij}(Q)/q_i(Q)q_j(Q)$$
$$= 1/\text{Hicks 1932 } \sigma_{ij}$$

Recall that $D'(Y)$ and $D^{-1'}(Q)$ are Jacobian matrices of inverse transformations, and are therefore inverses:

$I = D'(Y)D^{-1'}(Q)$ [42]

$= [\partial^2 \log p(Y)/\partial p_i \partial p_j] \ [\partial^2 \log q(Q)/\partial q_i \partial q_j]$

$= [q_i \delta_{ij}][\Sigma_{ij}^* - 1][k_i \delta_{ij}]$

$\cdot [\Sigma_{ij} - 1][y_i \delta_{ij}]$

where

$k_i = p_i q_i / e = y_i q_i, \qquad 0 \leqslant k_i \leqslant 1 = \sum_1^n k_j$ [43]

$\delta_{ij} = 0$ if $i \neq j$ and $\delta_{ii} = 1$ if $i = j$

Hence we have dual homothetic relations

$[\Sigma_{ij}^* - 1] = [k_i^{-1}\delta_{ij}][\Sigma_{ij} - 1]^{-1}[k_i^{-1}\delta_{ij}]$ [44]

$[\Sigma_{ij} - 1] = [k_i^{-1}\delta_{ij}][\Sigma_{ij}^* - 1]^{-1}[k_i^{-1}\delta_{ij}]$

For $n = 3$, we verify the elegant relations for the homothetic case of Hicks [37, 1970, equations [9] and [10]], once we replace his symbols δ_{ij} and s_{ij}^{-1} by our equivalent Σ_{ij}^* and Σ_{ij}:

$$\Sigma_{12}^* = \frac{\Sigma_{23}(k_2+k_3) + \Sigma_{13}(k_1+k_3) - \Sigma_{12}k_3}{\Sigma_{13}\Sigma_{21}k_1 + \Sigma_{23}\Sigma_{21}k_2 + \Sigma_{31}\Sigma_{32}k_3}$$ [45]

$$\Sigma_{12} = \frac{\Sigma_{23}(k_2+k_3) + \Sigma_{13}^*(k_1+k_3) - \Sigma_{12}^*k_3}{\Sigma_{13}^*\Sigma_{21}^*k_1 + \Sigma_{23}^*\Sigma_{21}^*k_2 + \Sigma_{31}^*\Sigma_{32}^*k_3}$$

From these dual relations, Hicks deduces a rule about the permitted departures from a positive sign of an Σ_{ij} or Σ_{ij}^* [37, 1970]. We can express the rule as follows: for homothetic three-good demand, either all three pairs of three goods are both money-metric complements and SHAS substitutes; or a pair of goods can depart from the normal in at most one of the definitions, a counterintuitive constraint. Thus, both SHAS and money-metric stand in need of some improvement to satisfy a deep Wittgenstein.

As a further illustration, consider a near-Fisher case where I spend half my income on whisky (*rather* indifferently between q_1 of bourbon or q_2 of rye) and half my income on martini cocktails (*rather* specifically requiring about one ounce of gin, q_3, to one drop of vermouth, q_4). Here we have $n = 4$, and by means of two well-known CES functions we can approach as close

as we like to Fisher's polar cases

$e[Y;Q] = p(Y)q(Q)$ [46]

$$q(Q) = \left[\sum_1^2 (n^{1/2}q_j)^\alpha\right]^{1/2\alpha}\left[\sum_3^4 (n^{1/2}q_j)^\beta\right]^{1/2\beta}$$

$$p(Y) = \left[\sum_1^2 (n^{1/2}y_j)^\gamma\right]^{1/2\gamma}\left[\sum_3^4 (n^{1/2}y_j)^\delta\right]^{1/2\delta}$$

$(1-\alpha)(1-\gamma) = 1, \quad \alpha \to 1, \quad \gamma \to -\infty$

$(1-\beta)(1-\delta) = 1, \quad \beta \to -\infty, \quad \delta \to 1$

All off-diagonal Σ_{ij} and Σ_{ij}^* are positive despite the fact that one pair of goods (bourbon and rye) are close to perfect Fisher substitutes and one pair (gin and vermouth) are close to perfect Fisher complements! So really it is the signs of $\Sigma_{12} - 1$ and $\Sigma_{34} - 1$, and not of Σ_{12} and Σ_{34} that correspond to intuitive Fisher notions; and, as will be seen, Weber-Fechnerizing our metric, or modifying it by Bernoulli-logarithmic or some other risk utility, will bring us closer to these $\Sigma_{ij} - 1$ coefficients.

On the other hand, when we encounter the same stubbornness of positive signs for SHAS Σ_{ij}^* coefficients, all that the most sophisticated Wittgenstein can do is to show that $\Sigma_{12}^* - \Sigma_{ji}^*$, where i is 1 or 2 and j is 3 or 4, is strongly positive; and show that $\Sigma_{34}^* - \Sigma_{ji}^*$ is then strongly negative; and, of course, that $\Sigma_{12}^* - \Sigma_{34}^*$ is strongly positive.

To test our formulas on an easy homothetic case, consider that of Mill-Marshall-Cobb-Bernoulli in which all income and own-price elasticities are unity, and all crude own-elasticities are zero.

$$e[Y;Q] = \left\{n^{1/2}\prod_1^n y_j^{k_j}\right\}\left\{n^{1/2}\prod_1^n q_j^{k_j}\right\}$$ [47]

$D(Y) = [k_i/y_i], \qquad D^{-1}(Q) = [k_i/q_i]$

$\Sigma_{ij} = \Sigma_{ij}^* = 1 \qquad$ if $i \neq j$

$\phantom{\Sigma_{ij} = \Sigma_{ij}^*} = 1 - k_i^{-1} \qquad$ if $i = j$

Money-metric complementarity in the general, non-homothetic case. First, we may state some general relations:

$$e[P^0;Q^0] = e^0 = \sum_1^n p_j^0 q_j^0, \ e[Y^0;Q^0] = 1$$ [48]

$$Q^0 = D(P^0/e^0), \ P^0/e^0 = Y^0 = D^{-1}(Q^0)$$

$$\partial e[P^0;Q^0]/\partial q_i = p_i^0, \ \partial e[P^0;Q^0]/\partial p_i = q_i^0$$

$$\partial e[Y^0;Q^0]/\partial q_i = y_i^0, \ \partial e[Y^0;Q^0]/\partial y_i = q_i^0$$

Next we may verify that e[P ;Q] is "locally concave in all Q that are near to Q^0. By definition

$$e[P^0;Q^0 + H] \leq \sum_1^n P^0(q_j^0 + h_j) \qquad [49]$$

for any H. Taking account of [48], [49] gives

$$e[P^0;Q^0 + H] - e[P^0;Q^0]$$
$$\leq \sum_1^n (\partial e[P^0;Q^0]/\partial q_j)h_j \qquad [50]$$

This assures us of our local concavity (only local because [50] is weaker than

$$e[P^0;Q + H] - e[P^0;Q]$$
$$\leq \sum_1^n (\partial e[P^0;Q]/\partial q_j)h_j$$

for **all** Q rather than only for [50]'s $Q = Q^0$).

[Note: Equations [49] and [50] have been rewritten by Samuelson in 1977.]

Given continuous higher derivatives of our functions, [50] guarantees that, for almost all Q^0, we have $\partial^2 e/\partial q_i \partial q_j$ a negative-semi-definite quadratic form

$$(h_1, \ldots, h_n) \left(\frac{\partial^2 e[P^0;Q^0]}{\partial q_i \partial q_j} \right) \begin{bmatrix} h_1 \\ \cdot \\ \cdot \\ \cdot \\ h_n \end{bmatrix} \leq 0 \qquad [51]$$

with the equality holding only if the (h_j) vector is proportional to the Engel income slopes $(\partial q_i/\partial e)$. It follows that, unless all other goods have zero income elasticities, a good must satisfy Gossen's Law of Diminishing Marginal [money-metric!] Utility. We are in this sense back in the Gossen (1854) old-fashioned promised land of diminishing marginal utility, but now on a rigorous and non-introspective basis.

We can now generalize the sign patterns of the homothetic case to the general case.

Theorem: Provided all goods have positive income elasticities, every good must be money-metric complementary with at least one good; and, between it and *any* other good, we must be able to find a path of complement pairs (*i.e.*, it must be a complement to a good that is a complement to a second good that is ... finally a complement to the specified other good, with the Mosenson-Dror combinatorials of SHAS sign patterns being valid here also [50, 1972]).

The two-good case illustrates how, when one good is an inferior good, both goods must be money-metric substitutes. Instead of the first normal pattern of the text's (5), we may now have its second pattern

$$\text{sign} \ \frac{\partial e(P^0;Q^0)}{\partial q_i \partial q_j} = \begin{pmatrix} - & - \\ - & - \end{pmatrix} \qquad [52]$$

Here a row cancels out to zero—as [51] tells us it must—when we apply to it opposite-signed income slopes as weights!

By formal manipulation, the general, non-homothetic relations between the money-metric elasticities and the SHAS elasticities could be derived: they will involve not only the k_i proportions but also the income elasticities $e(\partial q_i/\partial e)/q_i$.

Improved risk-utility metric. Confronted with various probabilities of different income, say with a probability density $m(e)de$, under a few plausible axioms of consistent choice, I can be shown to act to maximize the expected value of the $V\{e\}$ utility of income outcomes, namely to maximize $E\{V(e)\} = \int V(e)m(e)de$. Here $V\{e\}$ is determinate up to the usual linear transformation; its determinate $V''\{e\}/V'\{e\}$ determines its absolute risk tolerance, and eV''/V' its relative risk tolerance. As in

Samuelson, we can reverse the logic and, from revealed risk tolerance, infer the shape of $V\{e\}$, *i.e.*, infer the stretching of money-metric utility $e[\cdot;Q], f\{e[\cdot;Q]\} = V\{e[\cdot;Q]\} = V[Q]$, that we need to improve it [64, 1950].

As in my main text, a 50–50 coin experiment can be used, in which we solve the following for the unknown $V\{e\}$ function in terms of the observed gain-to-loss function $g_e(x)$, with $g_e(0) = 0, g_e'(0) = 1$,

$$V\{e\} \underset{x}{\equiv} \tfrac{1}{2}V\{e-x\} + \tfrac{1}{2}V\{e+g_e(x)\}$$

$$0 \equiv -\tfrac{1}{2}V'\{e-x\} + \tfrac{1}{2}g_e'(x)V'\{e+g_e(x)\}$$
$$0 = V''\{e\} + (1)V''\{e\} + g_e''(0)V'\{e\}$$
$$-\tfrac{1}{2}g_e''(0) = V''\{e\}/V'\{e\} \quad \text{for all } e \quad [53]$$

This g_e'' is related to the Pratt-Arrow measure of *absolute* risk aversion of K. J. Arrow [10, 1971]; a convenient measure of *relative* risk aversion is provided by $\tfrac{1}{2}eg_e''(0) = r\{e\} = r[Q]$.

Armed with these we can calculate *corrected money-metric* complementarities, in absolute or dimensionless form

$$\partial^2 V[Q]/\partial q_i \partial q_j \\ = V'\{e[\ ;\ ]\}[e_{q_iq_j} - \tfrac{1}{2}g_e'' e_{q_iq_j}] \quad [54]$$

$$C_{ij} = eV'\{\ \ \}(\partial^2 V/\partial q_i \partial q_j)/(\partial V/\partial q_i)(\partial V/\partial q_j)$$

$$= eV'\frac{V'e_{q_iq_j}}{V'e_{q_i}V'e_{q_j}} - r\{e\}$$

$$= \Sigma_{ij} - r[Q]$$

Thus, for risk averters, this $r\{e[\cdot;Q]\}$ correction pushes all complementarity coefficients toward substitutability — as we would expect when marginal utilities are made to diminish more rapidly.

We also see that the Pareto error, of continuing to talk about utility complementarity after he became an ordinalist, was not quite so bad an error after all [52, 1909]. True, when we change from one cardinal-utility-numbering to another by non-linear stretchings, we do lose the invariance of signs of the cardinal cross-derivatives and own-derivatives. But the absolute differences between the proper versions of them is, after 65 years, seen to be invariant (as W. E. Johnson tacitly glimpsed in 1913).

One could illustrate this by plotting *all* Σ_{ij} coefficients on the same line, locating them as beads depending on their algebraic values. Then if we stretch from money-metric utility to any other metric, in Pareto's ordinalist way, we merely displace the point at which the zero origin falls on the line: the order and spacing of the beads never changes! Thus, E-P are not so bad, and neither is Gossen: it makes good sense to say, lobster is more subject to diminishing marginal utility than bread, or lemon is more a complement to tea than coffee is.

As a final numerical example, recall our money-metric complementarities of unity in the Cobb-Douglas case. For $i \neq j, \Sigma_{ij} = 1$. Now if I show Bernoulli risk aversion according to $V\{e\} = \log e$, I calculate $r[\ ] = 1$, and I now have "independence," $C_{ij} = \Sigma_{ij} - r[\ ] = 1 - 1 = 0$ — as is intuitive. If I show Cramer risk aversion according to $V\{e\} = e^{1/2}, r[\ ] = \tfrac{1}{2}$, and $C_{ij} = 1 - \tfrac{1}{2} = \tfrac{1}{2}$. If like most investors, I show risk aversion greater than Bernoulli, say like $V\{e\} = -e^{-2}$, with $r[\ ] = 3$, we have all goods substitutes and $C_{ij} = 1 - 3 = -2$.

Historical Review

I. George Stigler, in his two 1950 *Journal of Political Economy* papers on "The Development of Utility," cited here in its only-slightly-amended Stigler [76, 1965, Ch. 5] pagination, has given so magisterial a survey of utility theory in the two centuries before Slutsky's 1915 classic, that I can here: (1) review some of the more technical issues, and (2) bring the story up to the last quarter century.[17]

[17] Occasionally, instead of referring to an author's original source, I shall refer to Stigler's citation of him: thus Bentham (1782, in Stigler, 76, 1965, p. 73) refers to the Bentham manuscript of that data cited in Stigler. Cf. P. N. Rosenstein-Rodan for further references to the continental literature [57, 1933].

II. Jeremy Bentham had stated: "The excess in happiness of the richer [of two men] will not be so great as the excess of his wealth" [12, 1802, in Stigler, p. 73], drawing from this vague assertion of $U''(e) < 0$ the now-standard corollaries that fair and less-than-fair gambling is bad, while insuring is good. His "minimum-sensible" jolts of just-recognizable increments of pleasure were supposed to provide him with his units of utility: thus, suppose that, after having e^0, I *just* notice that at e^1 I am better off; and after having e^1, *just* notice at e^2 that I am again better off. Then, for Bentham, and Edgeworth after him [19, 1881], $U(e^1) - U(e^0) = U(e^2) - U(e^1) = 1$, with subjective experience allegedly telling us that $e^2 - e^1 > e^1 - e^0$.

However, three-quarters of a century earlier, the St. Petersburg paradox had already alerted Daniel Bernoulli [15, 1738] and other mathematicians to the alleged observable fact: The ducat you stand to win is worth less to you than the one you stand to lose, implying negative $U''(e)$ and positive $g_e''(0)$ for any decision maker assumed to act to maximize the expected (or mean) value of $U(e)$ outcomes.[18] Bernoulli's own beautiful memoir (translated from the Latin in the 1954 *Econometrica*) suggested the special form where marginal utility halves when wealth doubles, and $U = \log e$. As discussed in Stigler [76, 1965, p. 114], by the mid-nineteenth century, the Weber-Fechner school of psychology professed to find this logarithmic function in diverse stimulus-response experiments. (Bentham, at one place, almost stumbles into it when he tacitly treats the transfer of a pound from a man with £10,000 to one

with £1,000 as a good thing *because* .0001 < .001.)

I skip Bentham's arcane taxonomies of pleasure and pain, his blithe interpersonal summing of utilities to form a social utility or welfare, and his cheerful equating of poetry and push-pin as equally legitimate pleasures. Mention though should be made of the fact that, foreshadowing most later hedonists, Bentham at one place admits that social utility can *not* be measured; but then, claiming (non-cogently) that we need to measure it, he goes on to treat it as if it were measurable, at least approximately.

III. The classical economists, and J. B. Say and Marx, could never succeed in relating vague utility notions to demand behavior and market price determination. A. A. Cournot elaborated demand with no utility underpinning [17, 1838]. John Stuart Mill did likewise [49, 1848], never dreaming that his international trade examples, in which constant proportions of income were spent on various goods, presupposed indifference contours that could have been generated by $U = \Sigma k_j \log q_j$. J. Dupuit discussed, so to speak, demand and marginal-utility curves in the same breath [18, 1844], foreshadowing the integrals of consumers-surplus and total utility of Fleeming Jenkin [41, 1870], Auspitz and Lieben [11, 1889], and Marshall [46, 1890, 1920]. Gossen (1854), knowing little mathematics, assumed linear marginal utility in his long lost classic. Jevons had independently conceived of additive concave utilities [42, 1871], $U = U_1(q_1) + U_2(q_2) + \ldots$ Like Bentham, Jevons at one place says utility can't be measured; but, recovering, goes on to do it anyway. His attempt, described by Stigler [76, 1965, p. 89], to perhaps measure marginal utility by the money demand curve on the basis of some unclear notion about the "approximate constancy" of the marginal utility of income, sounds like the present money-metric of utility but, in general, it is not. Only in the Santa Claus case where $U = mq_1 + f(q_2, q_3, \ldots)$, will this

---

[18] The St. Petersburg Paradox merely dramatized what should have been obvious without it: It suffices to prove $U''(e) < 0$ to know $\frac{1}{2}U(e+x) + \frac{1}{2}U(e-x) < U(e)$ for $x \neq 0$, without having to realize $U(e) < \sum_1^\infty 2^{-j}U(e - v + 2^{j+1}a)$ for every positive v and a.

Jevons-Marshall aspiration lead to the present general money-metric utility.

Walras, after a long struggle to extricate himself from his father's vague notion of *rareté* [81, 1874], finally resolved his difficulty by rediscovering Gossen's and Jevon's $U_i'(q_i)$ and attaching the name *rareté* to it. At one place, Walras explicitly recognized that observable p_j/p_1 depends only on relative marginal utilities, $U_i(q_i)/U_1(q_1)$ [76, in Stigler, 1965, p. 117, n. 148].

Edgeworth [19, 1881], and Irving Fisher [22, 1892] independently, generalized from additive-independent $U_1(q_1) + U_2(q_2)$ to $U(q_1,q_2)$, $\partial^2 U/\partial q_1 \partial q_2 \neq 0$, almost without comment. To be oversure that his indifference contours are convex, Edgeworth in effect adds to the arbitrary assumption that $\partial^2 U/\partial q_i^2 < 0$ the assumption of positive $\partial^2 U/\partial q_1 \partial q_2$ and necessary complementarity. But formal identification of complementarity definition with the sign of the cross derivative $\partial^2 U/\partial q_i \partial q_j$, the so-called Edgeworth-Pareto criterion, was first done by the Austrians Auspitz and Lieben [11, 1889]. Their work exploited the $mq_1 + f(q_2,q_3, \ldots)$ case graphically, agreeing with money-metric utility and foreshadowing Marshallian partial equilibrium and also the total revenue and cost diagrams of the 1930's, and of Cournot [17, 1838]. Not bad work for bankers.

What is now seen to be magnificent about Edgeworth's *Mathematical Psychics* is his 40 pages of discussion on indifference contours, exchange, recontracting, supply and demand, contract curves, and (deepest of all) the core [19, 1881]. None of it depends on one utility metric $U[Q]$ as against any other $u[Q] = f\{U(Q)\}$. But, of course, he makes much to do, in every language including the differential calculus, about measurable utility. At any delicate point we are fobbed off with a Tennyson quotation, an allusion to the equal difficulties of probabilistic inference, or to Lagrange-Hamilton maximum principles in physics. Here is a quite typical passage: "As electro-

magnetic force tends to a maximum energy, so also pleasure forces tend to a maximum energy. The energy generated by pleasure force is the physical concomitant and measure of the conscious feeling of delight [19, 1881, p. 13]." To dispel such Victorian smog, notice that physical concepts of the kinetic and potential energies of a frictionless pendulum are firmly anchored on prosaic *revealed observations* of pendulum position: we can define the potential energy of a frictionless pendulum at a given angle by the squared velocity (or "kinetic energy") at the plumb line after the pendulum was released from that angle; and it can then be checked by observation that in any undisturbed motion of the pendulum, at any point on its path, the sum of its observed squared velocity and the already-calculated potential energy is always the same.

That is all the law of conservation of (mechanical) energy amounts to; and Hamilton's least-action principle merely states the verifiable fact that, between two nearby points, the integral over time of the difference between the observed squared velocity and the calculable potential energy is less than for any other path between those two points that the pendulum might otherwise have taken in the same time. This is Hicks-Allen stuff, not Edgeworthian poetry.[19]

IV. Irving Fisher articulated the no-

---

[19] You might not realize from this account that Edgeworth is my most admired mathematical economist. He made it a point to know the literature in every language, and he went out of his way to give credit where credit was due. Before Pareto, he formulated Pareto-optimality; before von Neumann, he formulated the core; before Stackelberg, he provided the Stackelberg solution to duopoly (and the collusive solution, the Bertrand solution, . . .). As an analytical economist, he dwarfs Marshall; and besides, this self-taught barrister made genuine contributions to mathematical probability in an arid era of English mathematics.

tions of *perfect* complements, like Min [tea, lemon], and *perfect* substitutes, like U [coffee + .2 tea], drawing the L-shaped and parallel-straight-line indifference contours [22, 1892]. He repudiated the Bentham-Edgeworth attempt to found a psychological utility metric on the basis of "minimum-sensible" increments of sensation. Stigler describes Fisher's method of objectively measuring $U_2(q_2)$ by, in effect, integrating, for fixed q_1 and over variable q_2, the operationally observable $p_2/p_1 = R(q_1,q_2) = U'(q_2)/U'(q_1)$; in turn this logic can be followed for every good, yielding $U_1(q_1) + U_2(q_2) + \ldots$ that is unique up to an arbitrary scaling of $U_1'(\bar{q}_1)$ and arbitrary origin for $U_1(0) + U_2(0) + \ldots$ [76, 1965, p. 118]. Since Fisher was proud to have discovered, *before* reading Edgeworth [19, 1881], that $U(q_1,q_2,\ldots) \neq f\{U_1(q_1) + U_2(q_2) + \ldots\}$ in the general case, one wonders why he permitted himself in 1892, and 35 years later in the J. B. Clark *Festschrift*, to postulate the additive independence which alone gave him his utility metric [24, 1927]. A similar query is raised by the efforts after 1926 of Ragnar Frisch to determine a utility metric from budget data arbitrarily assumed to be compatible with a $U = f(q_1,q_3,q_4,\ldots) + g(q_2,q_3,q_4,\ldots)$ specification [27, 1926; 26, 1932]. Little empirical warrant for such tree-branch properties has been adduced in the 80 years since 1892, although the persistence of the belief in the trinity of food, clothing, and housing lends some plausibility to the hypothesis.

Fisher was about the first scholar to recognize the *redundancy* for demand analysis of a preferred utility metric. And yet he employed the $\partial^2 U/\partial q_i \partial q_j$ criterion for complementary and competing goods. Fisher also anticipated the 1913 Johnson analysis of demand by indifference curves [43, 1913], a tradition later exploited by Lerner, Leontief, Viner, and Meade in the field of international trade; also Fisher [22, 1892] and in his interest theories [23,

1907], enlarged on Walras' general equilibrium analysis. Briefly, Fisher, a student of Gibbs, anticipated the Pareto-Volterra integrability problem for the observable marginal rates of substitution in the case of more than two goods, just as the long-lost work of G. D. Antonelli [9, 1886] had anticipated Fisher. My review of the integrability problem [64, 1950], carries the story past Houthakker's strong Axiom of Revealed Preference, but the modern reader will have to supplement this by reading the works on integrability and transitivity by Georgescu-Roegen [28, 1936], M. Richter and J. Chipman [16, Chipman, *et al.*, 1971], H. Uzawa [77, 1960], and others.

V. Alfred Marshall has nothing interesting to add on these subjects, a fact recognized too rarely. Pareto is the real hero, but as is so often the case with him, his writings contain confusions. (A lone scholar, Pareto had no students or colleagues; like Diderot, God gave him every gift but the gift of dialogue.) Too often his disciples tried to make sense out of Pareto's slips, such as his belief that one can have a presumption about the algebraic sign of the *third* derivative of the indifference curve, when it would have served him better to correct such errors.

Pareto [52, 1909] agreed with Fisher that *any* index of utility, $u = f\{U(Q)\}$, is as good as any other for demand analysis. Yet Pareto continued to exposit a complementarity criterion based implicitly on the second cross derivative of his utility or *ophelimité*. (See the table on p. 269 of the 1909 French edition, p. 195 of the 1971 English translation.) It is puzzling to understand this inconsistency of using in his literary text the non-invariant cross derivative of a utility concept which he had already thrown away, both in his mathematical appendix and text. Undoubtedly, Pareto was confused. He does not realize that most of his complement examples—like those of such out and out hedonists as Bentham,

Edgeworth, and P. H. Wicksteed [82, 1933]—are for the most part *not* utility-metric at all: thus, Pareto speaks of shirts without buttons, lamps without oil, of wine *or* beer, or of martini-cocktail-like examples where more or less vermouth can go with a jigger of gin depending upon price ratios. No utility metric is needed for these, since it is obvious more money can in some sense be got from me for a blade to add to my knife handle than can be got from me for coffee to accompany my afternoon tea. Had the *Manuel's Appendix* explicitly calculated $f'\ U_{ij} + f''\ U_i U_j$, Pareto might have noticed his own cultural lag and confusion about non-invariants.

There is another possibility other than utter confusion to rationalize Pareto's seeming inconsistencies. He may have believed that: (1) any index of *ophelimité* is as good as any other for demand analysis; and (2) that we can even dispense with *all* indices of utility $u = f\{U\}$ and U, instead basing our analysis on behavioristically observable indifference contours; and yet he *also* believed (3) that, psychologically, people *do* have a preferred introspective utility metric, which he labels *ophelimité*, U, to distinguish it from mere indexes of *ophelimité* $f\ \{U(Q)\}$. Although one cannot accurately determine this existent *ophelimité*, one can do so, Pareto may have thought, conceptually to some degree of approximation. So the argument might go. Thus, at three brief places in the *Manuel* [52, 1909, pp. 169, 265, 556; 1971, pp. 118, 192, 395], Pareto suggests one might be able to assert that *ophelimité* in going from Q^0 to Q^1 equals that in going from Q^1 to Q^2. Lange [44, 1934], H. Bernardelli [14, 1935], F. Alt [8, 1936], Samuelson [60, 1938], and others in the mid-thirties *Review of Economic Studies* analyzed why invariances of the equalities $U(Q^1) - U(Q^0) = U(Q^2) - U(Q^1)$ and $f\{U(Q^1)\} - f\{U(Q^0)\} = f\{U(Q^2)\} - f\{U(Q^1)\}$ restrict $f\{U\}$ to linear form, $f\{U\} = \pm a + bU$, with $f''U_i U_j = 0$ and complementarity coeffi-

cients being unambiguously definable. Why refuse Pareto the license to contemplate two different axiom systems without being indicted for inconsistencies? Whatever license we do give him, we must recognize that he never made clear which of his expressions were invariant under non-zero f'' utility stretchings. And his discussion of the integrability problem is certainly confused and confusing.[20]

VI. W. E. Johnson [43, 1913] and Eugen E. Slutsky [73, 1915], particularly Slutsky, made many of the necessary clarifications, as did Allen and Hicks [34, 1934], Henry Schultz [71, 1938], Georgescu-Roegen [29, 1952; 29a, 1968], and others up until the present paper itself.

W. E. Johnson's paper is a remarkable one; even now not well understood except for its definitive two-good indifference-curve analysis of demand (a first in the literature?) [43, 1913]. And its last half has a complete marginal productivity theory of factor demand and of cost (including what would now be called Leontief-Gorman-Strotz-Pollak-Fisher tree-structures for sub-aggregates, additive or otherwise). Negative income elasticities are related to the way two adjacent indifference curves are located, in terms of how their indifference slopes change as one looks due east and due north. Though Johnson realizes that signs of $\partial^2 U/\partial q_i \partial q_j$ are *not* invariants

---

[20] Pareto was actually quite a creative mathematician, being an early writer on what would now be called the Laplace transform. But few better mathematicians could, in the early 1890's, have handled properly the matrices and quadratic forms of Weierstrass' constrained maxima subject to constraints. So Pareto got far, but he never got all the way. Even Slutsky, who does perfect the *ordinal*-utility analysis of demand, reads a bit awkwardly to the modern eye in his formulation of secondary sufficiency conditions [73, 1915]. However, a glance at post-Gibbs literature on thermodynamics will show that it rarely reached the technical proficiency of classical mathematical economics.

under utility stretchings, he cleverly (almost too cleverly) works with $\tau_{ij} = -U_{ij}/U_iU_j$ differences, which as we've seen and he tacitly noticed, are invariants. Thus, his equation (2) says that convexity of an indifference curve is equivalent to τ_{12} being less than the mean of τ_{11} and τ_{22}. His new definition, under which two goods are normally Johnson "complements," requires that τ_{12} be less than both τ_{11} and τ_{22}, and hence both income elasticities be positive; his rarer condition of two goods as "competing," comes when one income elasticity is negative. Johnson's new complementarity definitions, poorly motivated by his discussion, turn out to agree with our money-metric definition after all.

R. G. D. Allen [2, 1932; 3, 1933; 4, 1934], before his 1934 collaboration with Hicks, was taken with the Johnson complementarity definitions. Milton Friedman in a January 1934 unpublished paper (his maiden venture?) that is quoted copiously by Schultz [71, 1938, pp. 614–19], gives variants of Johnson's definition that apply on the borders where a good becomes satiated and where the U_{ij} signs become invariants because of the vanishing of a U_i or U_j in the expansion of $f'U_{ij} + f''U_iU_j$; Allen had also noted this phenomenon [2, 1932]. The concept has some intuitive appeal, but only at the uninteresting satiation border. Our money-metric measures of complementarity include the Friedman-Allen species of the Johnson genus at points where those are applicable.

VII. Eugen E. Slutsky, in a classic lost to notice from 1915 to 1934 [73, 1915], perfected what Pareto had begun: namely, the emancipation of analysis of observable $Q = D[P/e]$ demand behavior from any dependence upon non-invariant properties $f\{U(Q)\}, f'U_i$, or $f'U_{ij} + f''U_iU_j$, instead basing his analysis on bordered determinants (U_{ij} bordered by U_i and U_j) and their cofactors. He was the first to notice the simplicity imparted to the theory if, instead of working with *ceteris paribus* partial

derivatives $[\partial q_i/\partial p_j] = e^{-1}D'(P/e)$, one works with what he called "residual [compensated] variabilities," $s_{ij} = \partial q_i/\partial p_i + q_j\partial q_i/\partial e$: Slutsky [73, 1915, (52)] proves that $s_{ii} < 0$, and gives the empirically verifiable or refutable *integrability* conditions of symmetry, $s_{ij} \equiv s_{ji}$ [73, 1915, (55)]; also [73, 1915, (56)], that demand functions are homogeneous of degree zero in income and prices $D(e,P) \equiv D(P/e)$; his (57) and (58) establish generalized symmetry relations that have escaped further notice, such as $0 = \Sigma\Sigma(\partial q_i/\partial p_j)/q_iq_j$, where the summation is over all $i \neq j$ among any subset of goods $r \leq n$. He just stops short of noting the negative semi-definiteness of the $[s_{ij}]$ matrix, and that knowledge of this property of $D(P/e)$ *exhausts* the empirical content of utility maximization and indifference analysis, and is isomorphic with the assumptions of that theory—a fact, I believe, not adumbrated until my *Foundations of economic analysis* [62, 1947] and earlier revealed preference discussions.

On measurability of utility, Slutsky's (71) shows that $Q = D(P/e)$ can never determine a unique utility metric, U as against $f\{U\}$. After his (76), he presents verifiable empirical implications, for $n > 2$, of the assumption that $u \equiv f\{\Sigma U_j(q_j)\}$ for some existent $f\{\ \}$, from which I. Fisher [22, 1892; 24, 1927], Frisch [26, 1932], Houthakker [40, 1960], or later writers could have determined the $U_j(q_j)$ from $Q = D(P/e)$ observations. On complementarity, Slutsky clearly understands that the sign of any U_{ij} cannot be inferred from (P,Q) observations but only, at best, from psychological introspection or other means. He does not, in the Hicks-Allen [34, 1934] and Schultz [71, 1938] fashion, propose his compensated variations as measures of "complementarity," either for their own sake or as replacements for the Edgeworth-Pareto U_{ij} definition, an interesting abstinence. Had Slutsky's paper not appeared in a wartime Italian journal, its classic quality would have been recognized earlier and there would have been no need to rediscover its content in the 1930's.

VIII. Hicks and Allen realize that $f'U_{ij} + f''U_iU_j$ cannot be of any one definite sign if f'' is arbitrary [34, 1934]. Unlike Slutsky (whose work they didn't know) and Hicks' *Value and capital* [35, 1939], they resolutely eschew use of *any* $f\{U(Q)\}$, instead basing their analysis (more antiseptically even than Johnson) on observable marginal-rate-of-substitution functions, $p_i/p_1 = R^i(Q)$, knowing that these are equivalent in the integrable case to invariant relative marginal utilities $f'U_i/f'U_1 = u_i/u_1$. They rediscover, what surprisingly was known to G. B. Antonelli in his long-lost Italian classic [9, 1886], the verifiable integrability conditions $h_{ij} = (\partial R^i/\partial q_j) - R^i(\partial R^i/\partial q_1) = h_{ji}$, with $[h_{ij}]$ a negative-definite matrix if the indifference contours are convex and obey (what is now known as) the law of diminishing marginal rate of substitution. For $n = 3$, they in effect calculate $[\partial q_i/\partial p_j] = e^{-1}D'[P/e]$ coefficients in terms of the inverse of $[h_{ij}]$ and the income effects of $q_j\partial q_i/\partial e$: because of $h_{ii} < 0$, $s_{ii} = (\partial q_i/\partial p_i) + \bar{q}_i(\partial q_i/\partial e)$ is shown always to be negative, even though for inferior goods with $q_i(\partial q_i/\partial e) < 0$ the Giffen case of positive $\partial q_i/\partial p_i$ is seen to be possible. Except for Allen's non-integrable case, where $h_{ij} \neq h_{ji}$ and $s_{ij} \neq s_{ji}$, which I follow Hicks in ignoring here, the symmetry of h_{ij} and s_{ij} are capitalized on: a negative sign for s_{23} and h_{23} is defined to make goods 2 and 3 [SHAS] complements; a positive sign makes them substitutes; but, for $n = 3$, the latter category predominates, since if $s_{23} < 0$, it follows from homogeneity that $s_{12} > 0$ and $s_{13} > 0$. For $n = 2$, $s_{12} > 0$ is mandatory. The $n > 3$ case is not handled, but the remark in Hicks [34, 1934, p. 67], stating that other goods whose price ratios are constant can be treated as one composite good, is presumably to be applied to the $n > 3$ case in the manner so brilliantly employed later in *Value and capital* [35, 1939]. They notice that $\partial q_i/\partial p_j$ and $\partial q_j/\partial p_i$ can differ in sign when income effects are unbalanced, which presumably counts against those crude *ceteris paribus* cross-effects as possible measures of complementarity. From the undoubted fact that these $\partial q_i/\partial p_j$ terms can be (usefully!) split into $[s_{ij} - q_j(\partial q_i/\partial e)]$ components, Hicks and Allen properly call attention to the significance of $[s_{ij}]$ terms — but they rarely[21] stop to linger over the question of why complementarity in the intuitive sense should be connected with them. This summary, which runs in terms of dimensional derivatives rather than their elasticity expressions, too briefly conveys the content of this 1934 *tour de force*, which has revolutionized all subsequent economic theory.

IX. Henry Schultz provides a valuable transitional study [71, 1938]. There are more than a few confusions in it that could mislead a reader; because of the tragic auto crash in which he and his family perished, the corrections that the author might have made in later editions have never been made. Since only his penultimate chapter on general interrelations of demand has caught up with Slutsky (who it will be recalled was rediscovered by Schultz and by Hicks only in 1934), the earlier discussions, like an embryo, represent a case of ontogeny recapitulating phylogeny, which makes for some oddities of exposition.

---

[21] This is too strong. In Hicks' footnote a connection with "common sense" is essayed: "[In a certain sense it is] possible to say that [SHAS] competitive goods are easily substitutable; [SHAS] complementary goods not easily substitutable. This statement, so agreeable to common sense, turns out to be correct — so long as we speak in relative, not absolute, terms [34, 1934, p. 73]" My mathematical discussion shows, around equation [46]'s example of bourbon-rye and gin-vermouth, the sense in which this is plausible; but note that even E-P complementarity shares this desirable property, and that improved-money-metric complementarity gives absolute signs of the desired type.

Schultz [71, 1938, Ch. 1] reproduces Pareto's pre-Slutsky and pre-Hicks and Allen complementarity definitions, based inconsistently on the sign of U_{ij} in the face of the non-invariance of $f'U_{ij}+f''U_iU_j$—an inconsistency he came to recognize when he reproduced Slutsky's analysis of $eD'[P/e] = [\partial q_i/\partial p_j]$. The special case of $f\{\Sigma U_j(q_j)\}$ is analyzed, and the Jevons-Marshall hope is repeated, that as $n \to \infty$, the marginal utility of income will be "approximately constant" so that the (p_i,q_i) demand curve will provide the $\partial U/\partial q_i$ marginal utility except for a scale factor. Schultz returns [71, 1938, Ch. 18] to the U_{ij} complementarity: under his vague hope that λ in $U_i/p_i = \lambda$ is almost a constant, Schultz tries to measure the non-invariant U_{ij} empirically in (3.8)–(3.12) by $D^{-1\prime}(Q) = [\partial(p_i/e)/\partial q_j]$, thinking that this is consistent with the alternative inverse measures, $D'[P/e] = e[\partial q_i/\partial p_j]$. His empirical equations are not even specified to be homogeneous of degree zero! And the identification of symmetry-condition approximations is non-cogently related to the Hotelling correct integrability condition for firms' profit maximization subject to no budgetary constraint [38, 1932]. Incidentally, Hotelling correctly handles the budget-constrained demand problem [39, 1935].

Schultz [71, 1938, Ch. 19] finally arrives at Slutsky's correct and general $[s_{ij}]$ analysis, demonstrating its agreement for $n = 3$ to Hicks and Allen. Like Hicks [35, 1939, mathematical appendix], he explicitly proposes (pp. 622–23) the sign of s_{ij} as a test for complementarity between goods i and j, contrasting the new definition with the older U_{ij} definitions—*e.g.*, showing that $\Sigma U_j(q_j)$ with $U_j''(q_j) < 0$ involves independent goods by the $U_{ij} = 0$ test, but only substitutes by the new SHAS definition. Also, in this chapter, Schultz describes the Johnson-Allen-Friedman genus of complementarity, already described in my paragraphs on Johnson. Schultz also explores empirical testing of and determina-

tion of $[s_{ij}]$; but he does not get very far because his income data apply to *many* persons instead of one, his linear equations are inconsistently non-homogeneous, and his logarithmic equations are inconsistently specified.

The only argumentation given for the SHAS definition is in Schultz: "No definition has yet been suggested which corrects the basic limitation of the classical definition and which retains all its advantages. Of those which have been suggested, the Slutsky and Hicks-Allen definitions are the most promising" [71, 1938, p. 628].

X. Hicks [35, 1939, Ch. 3 and Appendix 9] adds no argument for the SHAS definitions beyond those of Hicks-Allen:[22] the unsatisfactoriness of the U_{ij} sign test of Pareto is properly stressed; also, it is shown that, when the marginal utility of money is constant in the $U = mq_1 + f(q_2,q_3, \ldots)$

---

[22] Hicks does clarify matters for the $n > 3$ case by elaboration of the notion of a composite commodity of goods purchasable at fixed prices [35, 1939, pp. 33–34, 44 and particularly 44, n. 1, and 311–12]. Cf. my mathematical discussion around equations [20]–[23]. Hicks points out that, for $n > 3$, h_{ij} and s_{ij} can differ in sign [36, 1956]; and it, in effect explores aspects of duality theory like the following:

generalize $e[P;Q^0]$ or $e(P|u[Q^0])$ to
$$e(p_1, \ldots, p_r; q_{r+1}, \ldots, q_n|u[Q^0])$$
$$= e(\ldots, p_r; \ldots), \ 1 \leqslant r \leqslant n$$
such that, for all r, there is equivalence between
$$\partial e(P|u[Q^0])/\partial p_i = q_i \quad (i = 1, \ldots, n)$$
and
$$\partial e(\ldots p_r; \ldots)/\partial p_i = q_i \quad (i = 1, \ldots, r),$$
$$1 \leqslant r \leqslant n$$
$$\partial e(\ldots p_r; \ldots)/\partial q_j = p_j \quad (j = r + 1, \ldots, n)$$
Then the elements of the Jacobians of $e(P\ |\ )$ and $e(\ldots, p_r; \ldots\ |\ldots)$ provide alternative definitions of SHAS-type q-complements and p-complements. Hicks contains remarks that seem puzzling: it seems to be said there that p-complements are somehow related to *ordinal* utility, q-complements somehow related to cardinal utility [36, 1956, pp. 83–84]. Actually, both are equally ordinal.

sense, the old E-P U_{ij} does agree with the new SHAS definition for $i > 1 < j$; and that the SHAS definitions do possess the desired symmetry properties. Finally, Hicks astutely formulates its concepts so that the inadmissible law of diminishing (absolute) utility is replaced by the law of diminishing (relative) marginal utilities or marginal rate of substitution, $h_{ii} < 0$, which says that a good is in this certain sense a substitute for itself; hence, he proposes that $h_{ij} > 0$ also be termed a test for substitutability, with a reversal of sign of h_{ij} then seeming, not unnaturally, to be a test of complementarity [35, 1939].

Even if one thinks that this analysis goes over the head of Wittgenstein's plain man, it has some appeal in its own right; and I think deserves better than the strictures in Stigler:

> It is difficult to see the purpose in Johnson's definition of complements, or, for that matter, in more recent versions such as that of Hicks and Allen. They cannot be applied introspectively to classify commodities (as the Auspitz-Lieben definition could be), so they offer no avenue to the utilization of introspection.... As a result, such criteria can be applied concretely only if one has full knowledge of the demand functions. If one has this knowledge, they offer [sic] no important advantage over simple criteria such as the crosselasticity of demand; if one does not have this knowledge, the simple criteria are still often applicable. The chief reason for presenting criteria in terms of utility, I suspect, is that, when familiar names are given to unknown possibilities, as illusion of definiteness of results is frequently conferred [76, 1965, pp. 134–35].

XI. This review covers[23] all but modern

[23] D. H. Robertson, on utility and all that [55, 1951; 56, 1954], received attention primarily from the already converted, and was received with condescending silence by the *avant garde* ordinalists with whom he hoped to debate; in view of the hard work he put into the matter, this is a pity. Comment here must be brief. If Sir Dennis really does feel introspectively a unique utility, that is his right, but nowhere does he give anything about its interesting implications. Certainly it is not the case

writings. A few guides to recent literature may be helpful. Samuelson and Swamy give a survey of the modern theory of index numbers [69, 1974]. Duality relations are

---

that a *privileged* cardinal indicator of ordinal non-stochastic utility *simplifies* the formulation of standard equilibrium; nor is it correct that cases of non-convex indifference contours are more optimally understood thereby; nor is it correct to fall in the old Knight error of thinking that: (1) the ordinalist fact of adding a new budget item at higher income, (2) presupposes that the law of diminishing cardinal utility applies to previous items, and (3) that this in turn demonstrates the necessary truth of an existent privileged cardinal indicator of utility. When an ordinalist essays consumer-surplus integrals to arrive at *one* non-privileged cardinal utility indicator, he in no sense backslides until he extends to it an illegitimate privilege; and ordinalism does *not* deprive itself of any valid quantitative results, such as how to compare direct and indirect taxes or decide how durable to make a road. In stochastic decision theory, a few consistent axioms of *ordinal* choice — such as, if A and B is "not preferred to" A and C at 50–50 odds, it will not be at any odds (including 0 or 1) — one will lead to a cardinal von Neumann metric of utility, $U[Q]$, unique up to a linear transformation, whose expected value is to be maximized; but it is *not* ordinalist backsliding to recognize this, and it is foolish to deny such a $2 + 2 = 4$ proposition. On complementarity, the only relevant passage is that in which Robertson [55, 1951, p. 24] quotes with approval a consumer-surplus calculation of Hicks [36, 1956] type, by which it appears that one loses more when deprived of tea and coffee *together* than the sum of their *separate* losses; had Robertson applied the same technique to lemon and tea, the example would have backfired; but, in any case, no measure applied to non-introspective (P,Q) data can throw light on the ultimate virtue of one $f\{u[Q]\}$ as against $u[Q]$. My main section's footnote 16 on Harsanyi [31, 1955] provides the only germ of truth in the notion that (ordinalist!) welfare economics benefits from or needs cardinal utilities.

discussed in Hotelling [38, 1932], R. Roy [58, 1942], J. Ville [79, 1946], Samuelson [62, 1947], R. W. Shephard [72, 1953], Samuelson [65, 1953], H. Uzawa [78, 1962], D. McFadden [47, 1963], H. S. Houthakker [40, 1960], Samuelson [67, 1965], S. N. Afriat [1, 1972], Samuelson [68, 1972], and many others, and indeed are already implied in R. G. D. Allen's *Mathematical analysis for economists* [7, 1938, Ch. 18].

Hicks analyzes factor demand for an industry and gives dual relations like those of [38] for $n = 3$ [33, 1932; 37, 1970]. Arrow [10, 1971] collects his earlier essays on risk bearing and gives references to the Pratt-Arrow risk-aversion measures akin to my $g_c''(x)$. The general invariance of $U_{ij}/U_iU_j - U_{ik}/U_iU_k$ differences seem to be new, although Johnson comes near to them [43, 1913].

Georgescu's Fig. 2 version of Pareto's criterion provided in [29, 1952] a topological condition necessary and sufficient for the existence of an "independent," additive utility function of the form, $U_1[q_1] + U_2[q_2]$ as follows: Let (a_1, a_2, b) be arbitrary positive numbers; then three positive, single-valued functions, $[\theta_0(x), \theta_1(x), \theta_2(x)]$ are defined by the respective identities: $f\{u[x, \theta_0(x)]\} \equiv f\{u[a_1, a_2]\}$, with $\theta_0[w - v]/[w - v] \leqslant 0; f\{u[x + \theta_1(x), \theta_0(x)]\} \equiv f\{u[a_1 + b, a_2]\} \equiv f\{u[x, \theta_0(x) + \theta_2(x)]\}$. Then global "independence" holds, if and only if, $f\{u[x + \theta_1(x), \theta_0(x) + \theta_2(x)]\} \equiv f\{u[a_1 + b, a_2 + \theta_2(a_1)]\}$. For $n > 2$, Debreu has given some elegant topological extensions of this 1952 relation in [17a, 1960].

I leave it to the reader to decide whether the skeptical remarks about complementarity in Samuelson [62, 1947, pp. 183–89] still stand in light of the present paper; but, in any case, my misleading criticism of Hicks [35, 1939] for its handling of the $n > 3$ case, is seen to need correction.

REFERENCES

1. AFRIAT, S. N. "The Theory of International Comparisons of Real Income and Prices." In DALY, J. D., ed. *International comparisons of prices and output*, Vol. 37. Studies in Income and Wealth. New York: National Bureau of Economic Research, 1972.

2. ALLEN, R. G. D. "Foundations of a Mathematical Theory of Exchange," *Economica*, May 1932, *12*, pp. 197–226.

3. ———, "On the Marginal Utility of Money and its Applications," *Economica*, May 1933, *13*, pp. 186–209.

4. ———, "A Comparison Between Different Definitions of Complementary and Competitive Goods," *Econometrica*, April 1934, *2*(2), pp. 168–75.

5. ———, "A Note on the Determinateness of the Utility Function," *Rev. Econ. Stud.*, Feb. 1935, *2*, pp. 155–58.

6. ———, "Professor Slutsky's Theory of Consumer's Choice," *Rev. Econ. Stud.*, Feb. 1936, *3*, pp. 120–29.

7. ———, *Mathematical analysis for economists*. London: Macmillan, 1938.

8. ALT, F. "Uber die Messbarkeit des Nutzens," *Z. nationalökon.*, 1936, *7*, pp. 161–69.

9. ANTONELLI, G. B., *Teoria mathematica della economica politica*. Pisa: 1886.

10. ARROW, K. J. *Essays in the theory of risk-bearing*. Chicago: Markham, 1971.

11. VON AUSPITZ, R. AND LIEBEN, R. *Untersuchungen über die theorie der preises*. Leipzig: Duncker & Humboldt, 1889.

12. BENTHAM, J. *Theory of legislation*. 1802.

13. BERGSON, A. "A Reformulation of Certain Aspects of Welfare Economics," *Quart. J. Econ.*, Feb. 1938, *52*, pp. 310–34.

14. BERNARDELLI, H. "Notes on the Determinateness of the Utility Function. Part II," *Rev. Econ. Stud.*, 1935-6, *2*, pp. 69-71.

15. BERNOULLI, D. *Specimen theoriae novae de mensura sortis*. 1738. English translation, "Exposition of a New Theory on the Measurement of Risk," *Econometrica*, Jan. 1954, *22*, pp. 23-26.

16. CHIPMAN, J.; HURWICZ, L.; RICHTER, M. AND SONNENSCHEIN, H. *Preferences, utility, and demand*. New York: Harcourt Brace Jovanovich, 1971.

17. COURNOT, A. A. *Researches into the mathematical principles of the theory of wealth*. 1838.

17a. DEBREU, G., "Topological Methods in Cardinal Utility Theory." In ARROW, K. J., et al., eds. *Mathematical Methods in Social Sciences*. Stanford: Stanford University Press, 1960, 16-26.

18. DUPUIT, J. "De la mesure de l'utilité des travaux publics," 1844. Reprinted in *De l'utilité et de sa mesure*. Torino: La Riforma Sociale, 1934.

19. EDGEWORTH, F. Y. *Mathematical psychics*. London: C. Kegan Paul, 1881.

20. ———, "The Pure Theory of Monopoly," 1897. Reprinted in EDGEWORTH, F. Y. *Papers relating to political economy*. London: Macmillan, 1925.

21. DE FINETTI, B. "La prévision: ses lois logiques, ses sources subjectives," *Annales de l'Institut Henri Poincaré*, 1937, *7*, pp. 1-68.

22. FISHER, I. *Mathematical investigations in the theory of value and prices*. New Haven: Yale University Press reproduction, 1925, of Yale Dissertation appearing in *Transactions of the Connecticut Academy of Arts and Sciences*, July 1892, *9*, pp. 1-124.

23. ———, *The rate of interest*. New York: 1907.

24. ———, "A Statistical Method for Measuring 'Marginal Utility' and Testing the Justice of a Progressive Income Tax." In HOLLANDER, J. H. ed. *Economic essays contributed in honor of John Bates Clark*. New York: Macmillan, 1927.

25. FRIEDMAN, M. "The Fitting of Indifference Curves as a Method of Deriving Statistical Demand Functions." Unpublished manuscript, January, 1934.

26. FRISCH, R. *New methods of measuring marginal utility*. Tübingen: J. C. B. Mohr, 1932.

27. ———, "Sur un problème d'économie pure," *Norsk Matematisk Skrifter*, 1926, Series I, No. 16, pp. 1-40.

28. GEORGESCU-ROEGEN, N. "The Pure Theory of Consumer's Behavior," *Quart. J. Econ.*, August 1936, *50*, pp. 545-93.

29. ———, "A Diagramatic Analysis of Complementarity," *Southern Econ. J.*, July 1952, *19*, pp. 1-20.

29a. ———, "Utility." In SILLS, D. H., ed. *The international encyclopedia of social sciences*. New York: Macmillan, The Free Press, 1968.

30. GOSSEN, H. *Entwicklung der gesetze des menschlichen verkehrs*. Berlin: [1854] 1927.

31. HARSANYI, J. C. "Cardinal Welfare, Individualistic Ethics, and Interpersonal Comparisons of Utility," *J. Polit. Econ.*, August 1955, *63*, pp. 309-21.

32. HAYEK, F. A. "The Geometrical Representation of Complementarity," *Rev. Econ. Stud.*, 1943, *10*(2), pp. 122-25.

33. HICKS, J. R. *Theory of wages*. London: Macmillan, 1932, 1963.

34. ——— AND ALLEN, R. G. D. "A Reconsideration of the Theory of Value," Parts I and II, *Economica, N. S.*, Feb. 1934, *1*(1), pp. 52-76; May 1934, *1*(2), pp. 196-219.

35. ———, *Value and capital*. Oxford: Clarendon Press, 1939.

36. ——, *A revision of demand theory.* Oxford: Clarendon Press, 1956.

37. ——, "Elasticity of Substitution Again: Substitutes and Complements," *Oxford Econ. Pap.*, 1970, *22*, pp. 289–96.

38. HOTELLING, H. "Edgeworth's Taxation Paradox and the Nature of Demand and Supply Functions," *J. Polit. Econ.*, Oct. 1932, *40*, pp. 577–616.

39. ——, "Demand Functions with Limited Budgets," *Econometrica*, Jan. 1935, *3*, pp. 66–78.

40. HOUTHAKKER, H. S. "Additive Preferences," *Econometrica*, April 1960, *28*(2), pp. 244–57.

41. JENKIN, F. "The Graphic Representation of the Laws of Supply and Demand, and Other Essays on Political Economy (1870)," *London School of Economics and Political Science, Reprints of Scarce Tracts*, 1931, No. 9.

42. JEVONS, W. S. *The theory of political economy.* London: Macmillan, 1871.

43. JOHNSON, W. E. "Pure Theory of Utility Curves," *Econ. J.*, Dec. 1913, *23*, pp. 483–513.

44. LANGE, O. "The Determinateness of the Utility Function," *Rev. Econ. Stud.*, June 1934, *1*, pp. 218–25.

45. MARSCHAK, J. "Rational Behavior, Uncertain Prospects, and Measurable Utility," *Econometrica*, April 1950, *18*, pp. 111–41.

46. MARSHALL, A. *Principles of economics.* London: Macmillan, 1890, 1920.

47. MCFADDEN, D. "Constant Elasticity of Substitution Production Function," *Rev. Econ. Stud.*, June 1963, *30*, pp. 73–83.

48. MCKENZIE, L. W. "Demand Theory Without a Utility Index," *Rev. Econ. Stud.*, June 1957, *24*, pp. 185–89.

49. MILL, J. S. *Principles of Political Economy.* London: 1848.

50. MOSENSON, R. AND DROR, E. "A Solution to the Qualitative Substitution Problem in Demand Theory," *Rev. Econ. Stud.*, 1972, *39*, pp. 433–41.

51. VON NEUMANN, J. AND MORGENSTERN, O. *Theory of games and economic behavior.* Princeton: Princeton University Press, 1944.

52. PARETO, V. *Manuel d'économie politique.* Paris: V. Giard & E. Brière, 1909.

53. POLLAK, R. A. "Generalized Separability," *Econometrica*, May 1972, *40*(3), pp. 431–53.

54. RAMSEY, F. *Foundations of mathematics.* London: Routledge, 1931.

55. ROBERTSON, D. H. *Utility and all that and other essays.* London: Allen & Unwin, 1951, 1954, pp. 13–41.

56. ——, "Utility and All What?" *Econ. J.*, Dec. 1954, *64*, pp. 665–78.

57. ROSENSTEIN-RODAN, P. N. "La complementarità, prima delle tre tappe della teoria economica," *La Riforma Sociale*, 1933, *44*, pp. 257–308.

58. ROY, R. *De l'utilité: Contribution à la théorie des choix.* Paris: 1942.

59. SAMUELSON, P. A. "A Note on the Pure Theory of Consumer's Behavior," "An Addendum," *Economica, N. S.*, Feb. 1938, *5*, pp. 61–71; August 1938, *5*, pp. 353–54. Reprinted in STIGLITZ, J. E. ed. *The collected scientific papers of Paul A. Samuelson.* Vol. I, Ch. 1, pp. 3–13; 13–14. Cambridge, Mass.: M.I.T. Press, 1966.

60. ——, "The Numerical Representation of Ordered Classifications and the Concept of Utility," *Rev. Econ. Stud.*, Oct. 1938, *6*, pp. 65–70, 344–56; *CSP*, I, Ch. 2, pp. 15–20.

61. ——, "Constancy of the Marginal Utility of Income." In LANGE, O. et al., ed. *Studies in mathematical economics and econometrics in memory of Henry Schultz.* Chicago: University of Chicago Press, 1942, pp. 75–91; *CSP*, I, Ch. 5, pp. 37–53.

62. ——, *Foundations of economic*

analysis. Cambridge, Mass.: Harvard University Press, 1947.

63. ———, "Probability and the Attempts to Measure Utility" (English and Japanese), *Econ. Rev.* (Keizai Kenkyu), July 1950, *1*(3), pp. 167–73; *CSP,* I, Ch. 12, pp. 117–23.

64. ———, "The Problem of Integrability in Utility Theory," *Economica, N. S.,* Nov. 1950, *17,* pp. 355–85; *CSP,* I, Ch. 10, pp. 75–105.

65. ———, "Prices of Factors and Goods in General Equilibrium," *Rev. Econ. Stud.,* 1953, *21*(1), pp. 1–20; *CSP,* II, Ch. 70, pp. 888–901.

66. ———, "Parable and Realism in Capital Theory: The Surrogate Production Function," *Rev. Econ. Stud.,* June 1962, *29,* pp. 193–206; *CSP,* I, Ch. 28, pp. 325–38.

67. ———, "Using Full Duality to Show that Simultaneously Additive Direct and Indirect Utilities Implies Unitary Price Elasticity of Demand," *Econometrica,* Oct. 1965, *33,* pp. 781–96. Reprinted in MERTON, R. C., ed. *The collected scientific papers of Paul A. Samuelson,* Vol. III, Ch. 134, pp. 71–86. Cambridge, Mass.: M.I.T. Press, 1972.

68. ———, "Unification Theorem for the Two Basic Dualities of Homothetic Demand Theory," *Proc. Nat. Acad. Sci.,* Sept. 1972, *69*(9), pp. 2673–74.

69. ——— AND SWAMY, S. "Invariant Economic Index Numbers and Canonical Duality: Survey and Synthesis," *Amer. Econ. Rev.,* Sept. 1974, pp. 566–94.

70. SAVAGE, L. J. *Foundations of statistics.* New York: Wiley, 1954.

71. SCHULTZ, H. *The theory and measurement of demand.* Chicago: University of Chicago Press, 1938.

72. SHEPHARD, R. W. *Cost and production functions.* Princeton: Princeton University Press, 1953.

73. SLUTSKY, E. "Sulla teoria del bilancio del consumatore," *Gior. degli econ.,* 1915, *51,* pp. 1–26. English translation "On the Theory of the Budget of Consumer." In STIGLER, G. J. AND BOULDING. K. E. eds. *Readings in price theory.* Chicago: Richard D. Irwin, 1952, pp. 27–56.

74. STIGLER, G. J. "The Development of Utility Theory. I," *J. Polit. Econ.,* August 1950, *58,* pp. 307–27.

75. ———, "The Development of Utility Theory. II," *J. Polit. Econ.,* Oct. 1950, *58,* pp. 373–96.

76. ———, *Essays in the history of economics.* Chicago and London: University of Chicago Press, 1965, Ch. 5.

77. UZAWA, H. "Preference and Rational Choice in the Theory of Consumption." In ARROW, K. J.; KARLIN, S. AND SUPPES, P. eds. *Mathematical methods in the social sciences.* Stanford: Stanford University Press, 1960.

78. ———, "Production Functions with Constant Elasticities of Substitution," *Rev. Econ. Stud.,* Oct. 1962, *29,* pp. 291–99.

79. VILLE, J. "The Existence Condition of a Total Utility Function and of an Index of Price," *Annales de l'Université de Lyon,* Section A, 1946, *9,* pp. 32–39. English translation in *Rev. Econ. Stud.,* 1951, *19,* pp. 123–28.

80. WALD, A., *Statistical decision functions.* New York: Wiley, 1950.

81. WALRAS, L. *Eléments d'économie politique pure.* (1874, 1926.) English translation by W. JAFFÉ, *Elements of pure economics, or the theory of social wealth.* Homewood, Ill.: Richard D. Irwin, 1954.

82. WICKSTEED, P. H. *Common sense of political economy,* Vols. I and II. London: Routledge, 1933.

83. WITTGENSTEIN, L. *The blue and brown books.* (Preliminary studies for the philosophical investigations.) New York: Harper & Row, 1965.

Invariant Economic Index Numbers and Canonical Duality: Survey and Synthesis

By P. A. SAMUELSON AND S. SWAMY[*]

Index numbers of prices and quantities, an invention of the last century, are important for macro-economic description and for sliding-scale wage and other contracts. Desirable properties for an index of many items have been postulated by Irving Fisher (1922) and others by analogy with the case of a single good's price or quantity. If a single good's price doubles, the index should double; the index between any two dates will not be changed if the base period of the index is changed from one date to another; a dimensional change in the good (as from grams to pounds) should not change the index, nor should a dimensional change in money (as from pennies to dollars or dollars to pounds); finally, for a single good, the product of the index number of price and the index number of quantity will equal the ratio of the values of total expenditure between any two compared dates.

Although Ragnar Frisch (1930) has proved that, when the number of goods exceeds unity, it is impossible to find well-behaved formulae that satisfy *all* of these Fisher criteria, we derive here canonical index numbers of price and quantity that do meet the spirit of all of Fisher's criteria in the only case in which a single index

number of the price of cost of living makes economic sense—namely, the ("homothetic") case of unitary income elasticities in which at all levels of living the calculated price change is the same. This seeming contradiction with Frisch is possible because the price and quantity variables are not here allowed to be arbitrary independent variables, but rather are constrained to satisfy the observable demand functions which optimize well-being.

The invariant quantity and price index numbers are shown to be "dual" in exactly the same sense that the production function and the minimum-unit cost function are dual; further, the price index function is shown to be the reciprocal of the indirect-utility dual function in its canonical, homogeneous first-degree form. By contrast, in the nonhomothetic demand case, the central role of the base quantity level of living in the price index is shown to have as a natural dual a central place for a base price level in an index of quantity expressed in terms of standardized dollars. Economic theory warns that no single index-number formula could correctly characterize alternative preference and indifference-contour patterns. Brief treatment is also given here to taste changes, to index-number approximation, to path-dependent and path-independent Divisia line integrals, and to index-number measures of changes in production possibilities; new ground is broken, and a fairly complete survey of the theory of index numbers is sketched. Some of our work

[*] Massachusetts Institute of Technology, and Indian Parliament, New Delhi, respectively. We owe gratitude to our common teacher Wassily Leontief. Samuelson acknowledges financial aid from the National Science Foundation that enabled Jill Pappas to give us valuable editorial assistance. We have benefitted from conversations or correspondence with Robert Pollak, Robert Summers, Dale Jorgenson, Hajime Hori, and Meir Kohn.

overlaps with the independent findings of Robert Pollak and Sydney Afriat, and of the now classic work of Ronald Shephard.

I. Economic Assumptions

One set of ordinal preferences is assumed to be observed involving n goods $(q_1, \ldots, q_n) = Q$. (Throughout we use capital letters for row vectors and lowercase or Greek letters for scalars.) Preferences can be summarized by any indicator of ordinal preference $u(Q)$ or $f\{u(Q)\}$ where $f'\{\ \} > 0$. The prices of the goods are $(p_1, \ldots, p_n) = P$. Expenditure on the goods is denoted by $e = p_1 q_1 + \ldots + p_n q_n = P \cdot Q = Q \cdot P$. Superscripts are used to denote the dates (or places) of the observations as in (Q^1, P^1), (Q^0, P^0), (q_j^1), (p_j^0), etc.

Historically,[1] one can discern three different approaches to index-number theory.

1) Jevons, Edgeworth, and other early writers tended to think of them as some kind of a mean or measure of central tendency of a universe of price changes over time. (Thus, if each price ratio could be regarded as a random item drawn independently from the same skew distribution, which is approximately lognormal, then the geometric mean would be the maximum likelihood statistic that most accurately estimates its parameter of location.)

2) Later, as with Irving Fisher, Walsh, Palgrave, Persons, Allyn Young, Frickey, and other writers of the World War I epoch, certain mechanical tests were applied to index-number formulas.[2] From the two-plus-two-equals-four tautology that the geometric mean of an array of positive numbers lies between the arithmetic and harmonic means, it was somehow thought that the arithmetic mean had "*upward*

bias." Exactly what zero bias meant was never thought through.

3) Finally, attention returned toward the economic theory of a price index[3] (associated with older names of Marshall, Lexis, Wicksell, . . . and more modern names of Könus, Pigou, Haberler, Keynes, Bortkiewicz, Gini, Bowley, H. Schultz, Staehle, Frisch, Leontief, Lerner, R. G. D. Allen, Wald, Ulmer, Wold, Samuelson, Theil, Afriat, Gilbert and Kravis, Beckerman, Pollak, Fisher and Shell, . . .). This paper confines itself to this economic approach, with its following definitions.

DEFINITION: *Economic Price Index: This must equal the ratio of the (minimum) costs of a given level of living in two price situations.*

Not quite so obvious as the price case is the corresponding definition for a quantity index.

DEFINITION: *Economic Quantity Index: This measures for two presented quantity situations Q^0 and Q^1, the ratio of the minimum expenditure needed, in the face of a reference price situation P^α, to buy their respective levels of well-being.*

Although most attention in the literature is devoted to price indexes, when you analyze the use to which price indexes are generally put, you realize that quantity indexes are actually most important. Once somehow estimated, price indexes are in fact used, if at all, primarily to "deflate" nominal or monetary totals in order to arrive at estimates of underlying "real

---

[1] The best general references are still the 1936 surveys of Frisch, Leontief, and Hans Staehle (1935). See also Samuelson (1947, ch. 6), which is in the spirit of Leontief. Note too our earlier citation of Pollak and Afriat. See also the useful survey by Richard Ruggles.

[2] See Fisher (1911, 1922) and Frisch (1930).

[3] See Melville Ulmer for the following quotation: "Writing in 1707, William Fleetwood, Bishop of Ely, set himself the task of determining the relative difference in money income which would provide for a student of the University of Oxford 'the same Ease and Favour' in his day and 260 years before" (p. 28). The fifteenth century B.C. Indian treatise *Arthastra* shows similar concerns.

magnitudes" (which is to say, *quantity* indexes!).

We begin by sketching the price case. Write the required index in the equivalent forms

$$(1.1) \quad p[P^1, P^0 \mid u(Q^a)] \equiv p(P^1, P^0; Q^a)$$

By its definition, the price index can be written as

$$(1.2) \quad p(P^1, P^0; Q^a)$$
$$= e(P^1; Q^a)/e(P^0; Q^a)$$
$$= e[P^1 \mid u(Q^a)]/e[P^0 \mid u(Q^a)]$$

where by definition

$$(1.3) \quad e(P; Q^a) \equiv e[P \mid u(Q^a)]$$
$$= \underset{Q}{\text{Min}} \, P \cdot Q$$

such that $\quad u(Q) = u(Q^a)$

It follows from their definition that these e functions are homogeneous of degree one and concave in the prices; and for regular, reversible demand curves where the indifference contours are strongly convex from below, e will also be a quasi-concave function of Q.

We now describe mathematically the economic quantity index.[4] By its definition, we can write this in the following notation:

$$(1.4) \quad q(Q^1, Q^0; P^a) = e(P^a; Q^1)/e(P^a, Q^0)$$

Here P^a is the arbitrarily chosen price standard for which the quantity comparison is to be made.

The fundamental point about an economic quantity index, which is too little stressed by writers, Leontief and Afriat

[4] For a somewhat different definition of the quantity index in the general nonhomothetic case, see Pollak, pp. 60–61. In terms of later sections' dual "indirect utility function," $u^*(P/e)$, our general price and quantity indexes can be described thus: solve $u^*(P^a/e) = u(Q^0)$ and $u^*(P^a/eq) = u(Q^1)$ for $q = q(Q^1, Q^0; P^a)$, the quantity index; and solve $u(Q^a) = u^*(P^0/e) = u^*(P^1/ep)$ for $p = p(P^1, P^0; Q^a)$, the price index.

being exceptions, is that it must itself be a cardinal indicator of ordinal utility. That is, $q(Q, Q^0; P^a)$ must, for Q^0 and P^a fixed, be itself of the form $f\{u(Q)\}$. Likewise $q(Q^1, Q; P^a)$ must, for Q^1 and P^a fixed, be another version of $-f\{u(Q)\}$. These facts are guaranteed by our economic definition. But the point is worth stressing because it shows at the beginning that we cannot hope for one ideal formula for the index number: if it works for the tastes of Jack Spratt, it won't work for his wife's tastes; if, say, a Cobb-Douglas function can be found that works for him with one set of parameters and for her with another set, their daughter will in general require a non-Cobb-Douglas formula! Just as there is an uncountable infinity of different indifference contours—there is no counting tastes—there is an uncountable infinity of different index-number formulas, which dooms Fisher's search for *the* ideal one. It does not exist even in Plato's heaven.[5]

The fundamental and well-known theorem for the existence of a price index that is invariant under change in level of living Q^a, is that each dollar of income be spent in the same way by rich or poor, with all income elasticities exactly unity (the homothetic case). Otherwise, a price change in luxuries could affect only the price index of the rich while leaving that of the poor relatively unchanged. This basic theorem was well known already in the 1930's, but is often forgotten and is repeatedly being rediscovered.

HOMOGENEITY PRICE THEOREM: *If, and only if, preferences are homothetic, with all income elasticities unitary, and with one $f\{u(Q)\}$ being of the canonical form $q(Q) \equiv \lambda^{-1} q(\lambda Q)$, a homogeneous first-degree function, will there exist an invariant index,*

[5] This point, forcefully made in Samuelson (1947, p. 154) has served to intimidate many (but, alas, not all) searchers for the nonexistent. See for example Doris Iklé, on which we comment later.

(1.5) $p(P^1, P^0; Q^a)$

$$\equiv p(P^1, P^0; Q^b) \equiv p(P^1, P^0)$$
$$= p(P^1)/p(P^0)$$

for all (Q^a, Q^b)

Proof for this will be reserved for the next section.

On reflection, it will also be clear that in the homothetic case, and only then, will the quantity index be the same for *any* chosen price standard P^α.

HOMOGENEITY QUANTITY THEOREM: *If, and only if, preferences are homothetic with all income elasticities unitary with $q(Q) = \lambda^{-1}q(\lambda Q)$ being an admissible cardinal indicator of utility, will for all P,*

(1.6) $q(Q^1, Q^0; P^\alpha)$

$$\equiv q(Q^1, Q^0; P) \equiv q(Q^1, Q^0)$$
$$= q(Q^1)/q(Q^0)$$

Proof of this theorem will be reserved for the next sections, which will also relate the invariant indexes of price and quantity to 1) the duality theory of production and cost, elaborated by R. W. Shephard, Samuelson (1953), Hirofumi Uzawa, and Daniel McFadden; 2) the duality theory of direct and indirect utility, associated with Harold Hotelling, René Roy, Hendrik Houthakker (1960), Samuelson (1965), and Pollak; 3) the interrelations between the two dualities, as in Samuelson (1972); and 4) certain new aspects of duality.

II. Duality of Prices and Quantity Indexes

The following theorem establishes the exact canonical form of the invariant $p(P^1, P^0)$ index.

FIRST DUALITY THEOREM: *Ratios of the homogeneous first-degree function $p(P) \equiv \lambda^{-1}p(\lambda P)$ and $q(Q) \equiv \lambda^{-1}q(\lambda Q)$, provide respectively, the invariant canonical price and quantity indexes, namely*

(2.1) $p(P^1, P^0) = p(P^1)/p(P^0)$

$$q(Q^1, Q^0) = q(Q^1)/q(Q^0)$$

where $q(Q)$ has been defined as a homogeneous first-degree numerical indicator of homothetic preferences, unique up to an arbitrary scale or dimensionality constant, and where $p(P)$ is its dual defined by

(2.2) $p(P) = \underset{Q}{\text{Min}}\ P \cdot Q/q(Q)$

$$p(P/e)q(Q) \le 1$$

with equality holding only for optimal $(Q, P/e)$ demand pairing $Q = D(P/e)$, $P/e = D^{-1}(Q)$, and where $p(P/e)$ is concave, homogeneous first-degree in its arguments. In the regular case when $u(Q)$ is strongly quasiconcave, the $q(Q)$ function will have these same properties as its dual $p(P/e)$, and the dual to the dual of $q(Q)$ will be $q(Q)$ itself. The reader may verify the dual counterpart to (2.2)

$(2.2')$ $q(Q) = \underset{P}{\text{Min}}\ Q \cdot P/p(P)$

and, also, that the contour, $p(p_1/p_q, \dots)$ $= 1$, defines the useful "factor-price frontier," p_q being the price of the q output. We take these duality relations as established by cited works of Shephard, Samuelson, Afriat, and others.

We now proceed to prove the two homogeneity theorems. We begin with sufficiency of homothetic tastes for the independence of the price index from the chosen level of living. Provided $q(Q)$ $= \lambda^{-1}q(\lambda Q)$, the homothetic case, $P \cdot Q/q(Q)$ $\equiv P \cdot \lambda Q/q(\lambda Q)$ and takes on for fixed P and $q(Q) = q(Q^a)$ all the values that it takes on for the same fixed P and no restrictions on the Q. Hence, by its definition in (1.3) and setting $\lambda = q(Q^i)^{-1}$,

(2.3) $e(P; Q^i) = \underset{Q}{\text{Min}}\ P \cdot Q$

such that $q(Q) = q(Q^i)$

$$= q(Q^i) \underset{Q}{\text{Min}}\ P \cdot Q/q(Q) =$$

$$= q(Q^i)p(P),$$

from the definition of (2.2)

Therefore

$$(2.4) \quad p(P^1, P^0; Q^i) = e(P^1; Q^i)/e(P^0; Q^i)$$
$$= q(Q^i)p(P^1)/q(Q^i)p(P^0)$$
$$= p(P^1)/p(P^0)$$
$$q(Q^1, Q^0; P^\alpha) = q(Q^1)p(P^\alpha)/q(Q^0)p(P^\alpha)$$
$$= q(Q^1)/q(Q^0)$$

which proves sufficiency of homotheticity.

To prove necessity of homotheticity, note that the functional equation

$$(2.5) \quad \frac{e(P^1; Q^i)}{e(P^0; Q^i)} \equiv \frac{e(P^1; Q^j)}{e(P^0; Q^j)}$$

implies for the monotone $e(;)$ function that it be factorable into

$$(2.6) \quad e(P; Q) = a(P)b(Q)$$

where we know that $a(P) = \lambda^{-1}a(\lambda P)$ because e always is homogeneous first-degree in its P arguments. Shephard and Afriat have noted (2.6)'s factorization theorem for the homothetic case, and valid for it only.

The invariance of the price index is seen to imply and to be implied by the invariance of the quantity index from its reference price base

$$(2.7) \quad q(Q^1, Q^0; P^\alpha) = \frac{e(P^\alpha; Q^1)}{e(P^\alpha; Q^0)} \equiv \frac{e(P^\beta; Q^1)}{e(P^\beta; Q^0)}$$
$$= \frac{a(P^\alpha)}{a(P^\alpha)} \frac{b(Q^1)}{b(Q^0)}$$

To keep our necessity argument brief, we revert to a calculus proof. From the classical formulation of Lionel McKenzie or the standard envelope theorem of maximization subject to a parameter, we know

$$(2.8) \quad \partial e(P; Q)/\partial p_i = q_i \quad (i = 1, \ldots, n)$$

$$(2.9) \quad \frac{\partial e/\partial p_i}{\partial e/\partial p_j}$$

$$= \frac{\partial\{a(P)b(Q)\}/\partial p_i}{\partial\{a(P)b(Q)\}/\partial p_j}, \quad \text{from (2.6)}$$
$$= q_i/q_j = \{\partial a(P)/\partial p_i\}/\{\partial a(P)/\partial p_i\}$$
$$= \text{function of } (p_2/p_1, \ldots, p_n/p_1) \text{ alone}$$

But this last relation is evidently the case only when homotheticity prevails. Hence, necessity of homotheticity as well as sufficiency is proved.

III. Indirect Utility Duality and Dual Dualities

In this compressed survey, we note briefly the relationship between the $[p(P), q(Q)]$ duality and the indirect-direct utility duality $[u(Q), u^*(P/e)]$ where

$$(3.1) \quad u^*(P/e) = \underset{Q}{\text{Max}}\, u(Q)$$

such that $Q \cdot P/e = 1$

Note that $u^*(P/e)$ differs in sign from the full duality of Samuelson (1965). When $u(Q) \equiv q(Q) \equiv \lambda^{-1}q(\lambda Q)$ and $P/e = D^{-1}(Q)$, it is easily shown as in (2.3) and Samuelson (1972), that

$$(3.2) \quad u^*(P/e) = eu^*(P) = u(Q)$$
$$u(Q)p(P) = u(Q)[u^*(P)]^{-1} = e,$$

from (2.2) and (3.2)

$$p(P) = 1/u^*(P)$$

Hence

$$(3.3) \quad p(P^1, P^0) = u^*(P^0)/u^*(P^1)$$

This leads to the unification theorem of the last-cited paper.

DOUBLE DUALITY THEOREM: *For $u(Q) \equiv q(Q)$, the "production dual" $p(P/e)$ equals the reciprocal of the "indirect-utility" dual, $u^*(P/e)$.*

Some further aspects of duality may be mentioned. Swamy has found it convenient to utilize a related duality that treats a numeraire good asymmetrically. Solve for

q_1, the expression

(3.4) $u(q_1, \ldots, q_n) = u(Q^a)$

to define a new $m(q_2, \ldots, q_n; Q^a)$ primal function.

(3.5) $-q_1 = m(q_2, \ldots, q_n; Q^a)$

$= m[q_2, \ldots, q_n \mid u(Q^a)]$

(3.6) $\partial m(q_2, \ldots; Q^a)/\partial q_i = p_i/p_1$

$(i = 2, \ldots, n)$

Then it is seen that $e(P; Q^a)/p_1$ is dual to $m(q_2, \ldots; Q^a)$ in the sense that

(3.7) $e(P; Q^a)/p_1$

$= m^*(p_2/p_1, \ldots, p_n/p_1; Q^a)$

$= \underset{Q}{\text{Min}} \sum_1^n p_j q_j/p_1$

such that $q_1 + m(q_2, \ldots; Q^a) = 0$

$e(P; Q^a)/p_1 = \underset{q_{i+1}}{\text{Min}} [-m(q_2, \ldots, q_n; Q^a)$

$+ \sum_2^n (p_j/p_1)q_j]$

(3.8) $\partial m^*(p_2/p_1, \ldots, p_n/p_1; Q^a)/\partial(p_i/p_1) = q_i$

$(i = 2, \ldots, n)$

This Hicks-Allen marginal rate of substitution parent function $m(\ )$ and its dual $m^*(\ )$ hold for the general nonhomothetic case. However, in the special homothetic case where some $u(Q) = q(Q) \equiv \lambda^{-1} q(\lambda Q)$

(3.9) $q_1 + m(q_2, \ldots; Q^a)$

$\equiv \frac{1}{\lambda} \lambda q_1 + m(\lambda q_2, \ldots; \lambda Q^a)$

$m[q_2, \ldots, q_n \mid q(Q)]$

$\equiv \lambda^{-1} m[\lambda q_2, \ldots, \lambda q_n \mid \lambda q(Q)]$

$q_1/q^* = -m[q_2/q^*, \ldots, q_n/q^* \mid 1]$

where q^* is a parameter taking on any scale we wish and the function on the right is the solution for q_1/q^* of the implicit-function equation

(3.10) $1 = q(q_1/q^*, q_2/q^*, \ldots, q_n/q^*)$

IV. Passing Fisher's Tests: The Homothetic Case

We can now show that *all* of the traditional test criteria of Fisher (1911) for an index number are satisfied by the canonical pair $[p(P^1, P^0), q(Q^1, Q^0)]$ in the homothetic case.

COMPLETENESS THEOREM: *These canonical index numbers satisfy, for any number of goods $n \geq 1$, the Fisher test criteria appropriate to the primitive $n = 1$ case.*

(4.1)   (i) If $P^1 = \lambda P^0$, $p(P^1, P^0) = p(\lambda P^0, P^0)$

$\equiv \lambda$,

"general mean of price relatives"

(4.2)   (ii) $p(P^1, P^0)p(P^0, P^1) \equiv 1$,

"time-reversal test"

(4.3)   (iii) $p(P^2, P^1)p(P^1, P^0) \equiv p(P^2, P^0)$,

"circular-reversal test"

Properties (i)-(iii) are seen to be *also* exactly satisfied for $q(Q^1, Q^0)$, where q and p, and Q^i and P^i, are interchanged respectively.

(iv) Dimensional change from q_j to $q_j\dagger$

$= d_j q_j$, $q\dagger = d_{n+1}q$, $e\dagger = d_{n+2}e$,

$d_j > 0$, leave indexes invariant[6]

---

[6] The literature, from Fisher on, including Samuelson (1967, p. 25) and Swamy (1965, p. 620), is inadequate on the dimensional invariance test. Properly speaking, once one has introduced the appropriate dimensional constants, we impose thereby no restrictions on the functional form of the index number. Thus, write in our notation the Frisch-Fisher index functions of $4n$ rather than $2n$ variables, namely $f(P^1, Q^1; P^0, Q^0)$. Now subject all q's to arbitrary dimensional changes $q_j\dagger = d_j q_j$, $d_j > 0$. We must now have $f\dagger(P^1\dagger, Q^1\dagger; P^0\dagger, Q^0\dagger)$ give identical results as $f(P^1, Q^1; P^0, Q^0)$. But note that $f\dagger(\ )$ is a *new and different function* from $f(\ )$. As an example, consider $f = p(P^1)/(p(P^0) = (p_1^1 + p_2^1)/(p_1^0 + p_2^0)$, which seems to fail the (ill-conceived) test. Actually, as we can see from the case $(d_1, d_2) = (2, 1)$, it leads to the proper $f\dagger = (p_1^1\dagger d_1^{-1} + p_2^1\dagger d_2^{-1})/(p_1^0\dagger d_1^{-1} + _2 p_2^0\dagger d_2^{-1}) = (\frac{1}{2}p_1^1\dagger + p_2^1\dagger)/(\frac{1}{2}p_1^0\dagger + p_2^0\dagger) \equiv f$. See Percy W. Bridgman for proper treatment of dimensional analysis in the natural sciences and logic. (Samuelson, it should be said, no longer regards his brief discussion in (1967, pp. 24–25) as fully optimal; it is superseded by the present paper.) Further

(4.4) $p\dagger(P\dagger^1, P\dagger^0) \equiv p(P^1, P^0)$

$q\dagger(Q\dagger^1, Q\dagger^0) \equiv q(Q^1, Q^0)$

"dimensional test"

(4.5)   (v) $p(P^1, P^0)q(Q^1, Q^0) \equiv e^1/e^0$

"factor-reversal[7] test"

Property (i) follows immediately from the first-degree homogeneity property of $p(P)$ as defined in (1.6). Property (iii) follows immediately from the ratio form of $p(P^1, P^0)$ as $p(P^1)/p(P^0)$ and it implies (ii) as a special binary case, as well as implying the general case

(4.6) $p(P^n, P^{n-1})p(P^{n-1}, P^{n-2}) \ldots p(P^1, P^0)$

$\equiv p(P^n, P^0)$

Property (iv) follows from

$q(Q) = q(q_1, \ldots, q_n)$

$= q(q_1\dagger d_1^{-1}, \ldots, q_n\dagger d_n^{-1})$

$= d_{n+1}^{-1}q\dagger(q_1\dagger, \ldots, q_n\dagger)$

$= d_{n+1}^{-1}q\dagger(Q\dagger)$

---

discussion of the Frisch-Fisher axioms is provided in Samuelson (1974a).

[7] Since we do not impose the strong requirement that the *same* formula apply to p as to q, for reasons to be discussed later, our condition (v) might well be called the "weak factor-reversal test," in contrast to the more common "strong" case where $p(X, Y) \equiv f(X, Y) \equiv q(X, Y)$. Nonetheless, as indicated in Samuelson (1965) and Swamy (1970), the Cobb-Douglas does provide one singular case where $p(P)$ and $q(Q)$ are "strongly self-dual," namely the Cobb-Douglas case where each has the form $f(X) = n^{\frac{1}{2}}\prod_1^n x_j^{k^j}$, $\sum_1^n k_j = 1$. Samuelson has recently discovered an infinity of other self-dual cases; and Wahidul Haque of Toronto seems to have made similar, as yet unpublished, discoveries. The unwary may be tempted by a fallacious way of getting non-Cobb-Douglas invariant indexes that will satisfy the strong rather than weak factor-reversal tests. Let $q(Q)$ and $p(P/e) = p(Y)$ be dual functions of different form. Why not mate them to get a new pair of the form $\{[q(Q)p(Q)]^{1/2}, [q(Y)p(Y)]^{1/2}\}$? Alas, these last are not dual to each other. Even though

$q(Q)p(Y) \leq 1, q(Y)p(Q) \leq 1$

$[q(Q)p(Y)]^{1/2}[q(Y)p(Y)]^{1/2} \leq 1$

the equality signs will *not* hold simultaneously for the optimal-demand pairings $Q = D(Y)$, $Y = D^{-1}(Q)$, unless $D(X) \equiv D^{-1}(X)$, the strongly self-dual case that holds from the beginning, with no need for mating!

$P \cdot Q/q(Q) = \sum_1^n p_j q_j [q(Q)]^{-1}$

$= d_{n+2}^{-1}\sum_1^n p_j\dagger d_j d_j^{-1} q_j\dagger d_{n+1}$

$\cdot [q\dagger(Q\dagger)]^{-1}$

$= d_{n+2}^{-1}d_{n+1}P\dagger \cdot Q\dagger/q\dagger(Q\dagger)$

$p(P) = d_{n+2}^{-1}d_{n+1}p\dagger(P\dagger)$

(4.7) $p\dagger(P\dagger^1, P\dagger^0) = \dfrac{d_{n+1}^{-1}p(P^1)}{d_{n+1}^{-1}p(P^0)} = p(P^1, P^0)$

(4.8) $q\dagger(Q\dagger^1, Q\dagger^0) = \dfrac{d_{n+1}q(Q^1)}{d_{n+1}q(Q^0)} = q(Q^1, Q^0)$

Property (v)'s factor-reversal test is seen to be satisfied from the original definition of the quantity index, combined with (2.3)'s definition of $p(P)$ and the identities

(4.9) $p(P^1, P^0)q(Q^1, Q^0) =$

$p(P^1)q(Q^1)/p(P^0)q(Q^0) = e^1/e^0$

This completes the proof. It remains only to note that, for $n=1$, $p(P^1, P^0) = p_1^1/p_1^0$, $q(Q^1, Q^0) = q^1/q^0$ and all of Fisher's properties (i)–(v) follow trivially.

How have we shown to be possible what Frisch (1930) proved to be impossible? Of course, that is not quite what we have done.

First, and least essential, Frisch followed the old practice of adding a regularity condition that we have not postulated. It is the so-called "determinateness test," which requires that, as some $p_j \to 0$ or ∞, the index should not go to 0 or infinity. This condition, it seems to us, is an odd one and not at all a desirable one. Thus, this Frisch regularity condition is *necessarily* violated in the trivial one-good case where $n=1$, and it rules out the non-satiation assumptions often made in standard economic theory.[8]

[8] For critical discussions on Frisch's 1930 treatment

Second, writing in 1930 before the economic theory of index numbers had, thanks to Frisch's own work and that of others, displaced the mechanical earlier formulations, Frisch had no need to insist upon the demand-dependence holding between $Q = (q_1, \ldots, q_n)$ and $P/e = (p_1/e, \ldots, p_n/e)$. His index formulas are postulated from the beginning to be functions of the arbitrary [!] $4n$ variables (P^1, Q^1, P^0, Q^0), rather than of the $2n$ variables (Q^1, Q^0) *or* the $2n$ variables $(P^1/e^1, P^0/e^0)$.

In any case, it is easy for us to specify instances of existent well-behaved and admissible price and quantity index numbers that satisfy *all* the tests (i)–(v), including the strong form of (v)'s factor-reversal test in which $p(\,,\,)$ and $q(\,,\,)$ are identical functions.

Thus, let the expenditures on each good be constant positive fractions of total expenditure $(k_1 = 1 - \sum_2^n k_j, k_2, \ldots, k_n)$, the Cobb-Douglas case.[9] Then

---

of this determinateness point, see the references in Swamy (1965) to Subramanian, Mizutani, and Wald. Fisher made little of this requirement in his 1922 book, merely carrying it over from his 1911 classic. As mentioned, to insist on this test requirement would be to rule out the nonsatiation assumptions often made in economic theory. Thus, if $q = (2q_1q_2)^{1/2}$, lowering any one price enough should yield bliss beyond that of any preassigned finite increment of income; and why rule this out? For both $q(Q)$ and $p(P)$ to satisfy this strict criterion would by itself and without reference to other test criteria entail a self-contradiction. We do not deny sympathy with Frisch's practical point that " ... the withdrawal or entry of any [new] commodity will often have to be performed as a limiting case when either the quantity ... or the money value ... decreases toward zero, respectively increases from zero" (1930, p. 405). Thus, $q = \sum a_j q_j$, $p = \mathrm{Min}[\ldots, p_j/a_j, \ldots]$ would handle this kind of case where one new gadget adds only a bit to well-being. But we do not wish to impose *our* wishes on the economic agents who can have any tastes they wish—including cases where some good (potassium, say) is vitally necessary in minimum ratios, or alternative cases of nonsatiation. Therefore, with good conscience we do not impose the self-contradictory determinateness test.

[9] Actually, for the homothetic quadratic-utility function the Ideal index is exact, which is the Buscheguennce-Alexander case mentioned in Samuelson (1947) and in Afriat. In view of the discussion of (4.18), this suggests that, along the $Q = D(Y)$ function of the quadratic-

---

$$(4.10) \qquad q(Q) = n^{\frac{1}{2}} \prod_1^n q_j^{k_j}$$

$$p(P) = n^{\frac{1}{2}} \prod_1^n p_j^{k_j}$$

$$q(Q^1, Q^0) = \prod_1^n (q_j^1/q_j^0)^{k_j}$$

$$= \prod_1^n (q_j^1 \dagger / q_j^0 \dagger)^{k_j}$$

$$p(P^1, P^0) = \prod_1^n (p_j^1/p_j^0)^{k_j}$$

$$= \prod_1^n (p_j^1 \dagger / p_j^0 \dagger)^{k_j}$$

$$p(P^1, P^0)q(Q^1, Q^0) = \prod_1^n (k_j e^1/k_j e^0)^{k_j} = e^1/e^0$$

$$= \prod_1^n [(p_j^1/p_j^0)(q_j^1/q_j^0)]^{k_j}$$

The difference between our procedure, in which either of the $2n$ variables (q_j^1, q_j^0) or $(p_j^1/e^1, p_j^0/e^0)$ determines the other set, is brought out by examining the last two lines in (4.10).

Obviously,

$$(4.11) \qquad \prod_1^n \left(\frac{p_j^1 q_j^1}{p^0 q^0}\right)^{k_j} = \frac{\sum_1^n p_j^1 q_j^1}{\sum_1^n p_j^0 q_j^0}$$

is *not* an identity in the $4n$ indicated variables *all* regarded as *arbitrary*. But it *is* an identity satisfied by all values of the $4n$ variables that also satisfy (4.10)'s optimality demand relations

$$(4.12) \quad p_j^i q_j^i = k_j e^i \quad (j = 1, \ldots, n; i = 0, 1)$$

We can now answer this question: What is the widest class of admissible invariant index numbers $[q(Q^1, Q^0), p(P^1, P^0)]$? Ob-

---

homogeneous case, the Ideal index does satisfy the circular test after all. Of course, the Ideal index satisfies only the weak form of (v).

(4.13a) $\qquad q = \left[\sum_1^n a_j q_j^\gamma \right]^{1/\gamma}, \quad 0 \neq \gamma < 1, \quad \text{``CES''}$

$\qquad\qquad p = \left[\sum_1^n p_j^\delta / a_j \right]^{1/\delta}, \quad (1-\gamma)(1-\delta) = 1$

(4.13b) $\qquad q = \sum_1^n a_j q_j, \quad \text{``Laspeyres-Paasche quantity index''}$

$\qquad\qquad p = \text{Min} \left[p_1/a_2, \ldots, p_n/a_n \right]$

(4.13c) $\qquad q = \text{Min} \left[q_1/a_1, \ldots, q_n/a_n \right], \quad \text{``fixed proportion case''}$

$\qquad\qquad p = \sum_1^n a_j p_j, \quad \text{``Laspeyres-Paasche price index''}$

$\qquad\qquad \lim \gamma \to 1 \text{ of } (4.13a) \text{ } CES \text{ case}$

(4.13d) $\qquad q = n^{1/2}(a_1 q_1)^{k_1}(a_2 q_2)^{k_2} \ldots (a_n q_n)^{k_n}$

$\qquad\qquad 1 - \sum_1^n k_j = 0, \, k_j > 0, \, \lim \gamma \to 0 \text{ of } (4.13a), \text{ the Cobb-Douglas case}$

$\qquad\qquad p = n^{1/2}(p_1/a_1)^{k_1}(p_2/a_2)^{k_2} \ldots (p_n/a_n)^{k_n}$

(4.13e) $\quad q(Q) = q_1 \sum_1^n \left[\log(a_j q_j/q_1) - \exp(b_j q_j/q_1) \right]$

---

viously, there are as many as there are arbitrary homogeneous first-degree functions $q(Q) \equiv \lambda^{-1} q(\lambda Q)$ or $p(P) \equiv \lambda^{-1} p(\lambda P)$. Thus, we can generate new homothetic preference functions and invariant indexes *ad lib*. The examples (4.13a)–(4.13e) illustrate that there are uncountably many more "exact" index-number formulas than those few previously recognized: the Cobb-Douglas geometric-mean case; the so-called Ideal index; etc.

We must give a brief but unavoidably technical digression to explain why there does not exist, for *any* old-fashioned index-number formula arbitrarily preassigned, some indifference contours for which the formula is exact. Fisher (1922) gives literally thousands of different formulas of the general form

(4.14) $\quad f(Q^1, P^1; Q^0, P^0) \equiv g(Q^1, Y^1; Q^0, Y^0),$

$\qquad\qquad Y \equiv P/e$

$\qquad g(Q^0, Y^0; Q^1, Y^1) g(Q^1, Y^1; Q^0, Y^0) \equiv 1$

Since (4.14) follows the usual presupposition that the price and quantity $g(\ )$ function are to be "of the same form," the next section's discussion of test (i^*) will show that only in the homothetic case will the generalized mean property hold for $q(\lambda Q^0, Q^0; P^\alpha) \equiv \lambda$ as well as for $p(\lambda P^0, P^0; Q^\alpha) \equiv \lambda$. So we may examine (4.14)'s possibilities under the simplifying assumption of homotheticity. It is well known for this case that the relations hold that appear as (6.3) and (6.3') below, and which we now borrow for use here

(6.3) $\quad p_i/e = \partial \log q(q_1, \ldots, q_n)/\partial q_i$

$\qquad\qquad\qquad\qquad (i = 1, \ldots, n)$

$\qquad Y = grad \log q(Q)$

Hence, you might at first think that setting

(4.15) $\quad q(Q) \equiv g(Q, grad \log q(Q); Q^0, Y^0) q(Q^0)$

would, in the homothetic case, yield a first-order partial differential equation that, given the form of $g(\ )$, could be solved for a corresponding $q(Q)$, in terms of whose indifference contours the $g(\ )$ formula would be exact. However, for this to yield a consistent result, it is necessary that $g(\ )$ have certain special properties. Thus

(4.16) $q(Q) \equiv \lambda^{-1} q(\lambda Q)$ implies

$$g(\lambda Q, \lambda^{-1}Y; Q^0, Y^0) \equiv \lambda g(Q, Y; Q^0, Y^0)$$

Also, consider *all* Q^0 on a base indifference curve passing through an arbitrarily selected point Q^*, with $q(Q^0) = q(Q^*) = 1$. In terms of (3.5), $[(Q^0, Y^0)]$ can then be written as

(4.17) $\overset{0}{q_1} = - \ m(\overset{0}{q_2}, \dots, \overset{0}{q_n}; \overset{*}{Q})$

(4.17′) $\overset{0}{y_1} = \Big[-m(\overset{0}{q_2}, \dots, \overset{0}{q_n}; \overset{*}{Q})$

$$+ \sum_2^n \overset{0}{q_j} \partial m / \partial \overset{0}{q_j} \Big]^{-1}$$

(4.17″) $\overset{0}{y_i} = \overset{0}{y_1} \partial m / \partial \overset{0}{q_i}$ $(i = 2, \dots, n)$

Hence, we can replace the $2n$ parameters (Q^0, Y^0) in $g(\ )$ by $n-1$ arbitrary $\overset{0}{q_2}, \dots, \overset{0}{q_n}$ parameters along the base indifference contour. Now (4.15) becomes (after we substitute (4.17), (4.17′), (4.17″) into it):

(4.18) $q(Q) = h[Q, grad \ log \ q(Q); \overset{0}{q_2}, \dots, \overset{0}{q_n}]$

$\equiv \lambda^{-1} h[\lambda Q, \lambda^{-1} grad \ log \ q(Q); \overset{0}{q_2}, \dots, \overset{0}{q_n}]$

$q(Q^*) \equiv h[Q^*, grad \ log \ q(Q^*); \overset{0}{q_2}, \dots, \overset{0}{q_n}]$

If an arbitrary Fisher or new formula of type given in (4.14) is to be exact for some preference field, the solution to (4.18) must be independent of $\overset{0}{q_2}, \dots \overset{0}{q_n}$! And why, in general, should general $f(\ )$, $g(\ )$, $h(\ )$ formulas have this needed property? As an example, we should be surprised if the Iklé proposed formula has this property; we do not even know whether its quantity index is unity on all Q^1 points for which $u(Q^1) = u(Q^0)$.

The last part of this section is basic to

deep insight into the meaning of the five Fisher-Frisch tests in the general non-homothetic case to which we now turn. For the pathologies considered in (4.18)'s solution are as nothing compared to the pathologies to be expected in the general nonhomothetic case.

V. Commentary on Fisher-Frisch Tests in the General Nonhomothetic Case

We have already spoken on the gratuitousness of the determinateness test that requires an index not to go to zero or infinity as a subset of its variables go to these limits; and also of the erroneous interpretation of the requirement of dimensional invariance. We must stress again that the factor reversal test offers no stumbling block for our definitions of $p(P^1, P^0; Q^a)$ and $q(Q^1, Q^0; P^a)$ if, as we should do logically, we drop the *strong* requirement that the *same* formula should apply to $q(Q)$ as to $p(P)$. A man and wife should be properly matched; but that does not mean I should marry my identical twin!

Where most of the older writers balk, however, is at the circular test that frees us from one base year. Indeed, so enamoured did Fisher become with his so-called Ideal index

(5.1) $p(P^1, P^0)$

$= [(P^1 \cdot Q^0 / P^0 \cdot Q^0)(P^1 \cdot Q^1 / P^0 \cdot Q^1)]^{1/2}$

$=$ square root of (Laspeyres $\times$ Paasche)

$= (\lambda_p \pi_p)^{1/2}$

that, when he discovered it failed the circular test, he had the hubris to declare " . . . , therefore, a *perfect* fulfillment of this so-called circular test should really be taken as proof that the formula which fulfills it is erroneous" (1922, p. 271). Alas, Homer has nodded; or, more accurately, a great scholar has been detoured on a trip whose purpose was obscure from the beginning.

If all the other tests were satisfied, but the circular test were violated and if $q(Q, Q^0; P^\alpha)$ is to be one cardinal indicator of utility, we would be facing a contradiction. Thus, suppose we are given the data

(5.2) $q(Q^2, Q^0; P^\alpha) = q(Q^1, Q^0; P^\alpha)$

From the circular test we could infer

(5.3) $q(Q^2, Q^1; P^\alpha) = 1$

and from it

(5.3') $u(Q^2) = u(Q^1)$

The last is a proper inference. Yet if (5.2) did not imply (5.3) it could not imply (5.3')! Also the following contradictions would be possible if the circular test could be violated.

(5.4) $q(Q^2, Q^0; P^\alpha) = q(Q^1, Q^0; P^\alpha) = 1$

$q(Q^3, Q^0; P^\alpha) = q(Q^1, Q^0; P^\alpha) = 1$

$q(Q^3, Q^2; P^\alpha) > 1$

This leads to the absurd intransitivity

(5.5) $u(Q^2) = u(Q^1)$

and $u(Q^3) = u(Q^1)$,

but $u(Q^3) > u(Q^2)$

Conclusion: So long as we stick to the economic theory of index numbers, the circular test is as required as is the property of transitivity itself. And this regardless of homotheticity or nonhomotheticity.

Furthermore, as will be shown in our next section on approximation, Fisher missed the point made in Samuelson (1947, p. 151) that knowledge of a third situation can add information relevant to the comparison of two given situations. Thus Fisher contemplates Georgia, Egypt, and Norway, in which the last two each have the same price index relative to Georgia:

> We might conclude, since "two things equal to the same thing are equal to each other," that, therefore, the price levels of Egypt and Norway must be equal, and this would be the case if we

compare Egypt and Norway *via* Georgia. But, evidently, if we are intent on getting the very best comparison between Norway, we shall not go to Georgia for our weights . . . [which are], so to speak, none of Georgia's business. [1922, p. 272]

This simply throws away the transitivity of indifference and has been led astray by Fisher's unwarranted belief that only fixed-weights lead to the circular test's being satisfied (an assertion contradicted by our $p(P^1)/p(P^0)$ and $q(Q^1)/q(Q^0)$ forms).

We may now ask the question, "In the nonhomothetic case, how do the index numbers fare relative to the Fisher test criteria?" That his five tests cannot then be successfully passed is seen by verifying the following:

(5.6)   (i*) $p(\lambda P^0, P^0; Q^\alpha) \equiv \lambda$

$q(\lambda Q^0, Q^0; P^\alpha) \not\equiv \lambda$

Thus, as our quantity index is defined, even the first of Fisher's tests fails in the nonhomothetic case, as any example will reveal. A simple instance is where

(5.7) $u(Q) = \text{Min} [q_1 + 1, q_2]$

$Q^0 = (2, 3), \quad Q^1 = \lambda Q^0, \quad \lambda > 1$

$q(\lambda Q^0, Q^0; P^\alpha) = \dfrac{(3\lambda - 1)p_1^\alpha + 3\lambda p_2^\alpha}{2p_1^\alpha + 3p_2^\alpha}$

$= \lambda - \dfrac{(\lambda - 1)p_1^\alpha}{2p_1^\alpha + 3p_2^\alpha} < \lambda$

If, like Pollak, one employs a quantity definition that satisfies Fisher's (i*), then one of the other tests, such as (v*), will fail in the nonhomothetic case—and this even though the $(Q^1, P^1; Q^0, P^0)$ are not treated as $4n$ arbitrary independent variables, but rather do respect the equilibrium demand relations

(5.8) $Q^i = D(P^i/P^i \cdot Q^i)$ $(i = 0, 1)$

It is easy to show that our defined pairs $p(P^1, P^0; Q^0)$ and $q(Q^1, Q^0; P^1)$, or $p(P^1, P^0; Q^1)$ and $q(Q^1, Q^0; P^0)$, satisfy *all* the other Fisher tests (ii–v), (v) being understood as the "weak" factor-reversal test of footnote 7. But before showing this, it is well to elucidate that, in the nonhomothetic case, there is no real symmetry or full-duality between the definitions of price and of quantity indexes. One sees this from the original definitions, from examining footnote 4's mathematical asymmetric formulations of the definitions in terms of the genuinely dual variables $(P/e, Q) \equiv (P/P \cdot Q, Q) \equiv (Y, Q)$. A formulation in terms of the nondual variables $(P, Q) \equiv (Ye, Q)$, as in $p(P^1, P^0; Q^a)$ and $q(Q^1, Q^0; P^a)$, could not be expected to be completely dual. Put differently, we can match (5.6)'s asymmetric property in which $q(, ;)$ fails a test in the non-homothetic case by the following asymmetric formulation in which $p(, ;)$ fails a test—or, more fairly, lacks a property the $g(, ;)$ enjoys. Thus, by basic demand theory with its lack of money illusion, it never matters for the quantity index if we multiply all reference prices P^a by a common factor λ, and use λP^a. Thus, by contrast with (5.6), we have

$$(5.9) \quad q(Q^1, Q^0; \lambda P^a) \equiv q(Q^1, Q^0; P^a)$$

$$p(P^1, P^0; \lambda Q^a) \not\equiv p(P^1, P^0; Q^a)$$

If Fisher had adjoined to (i*) the requirement that the quantity index is never to be affected by scale changes in P^1 or P^0 (which leave their "weightings" unchanged), we'd learn in the nonhomothetic case that both indexes must fail this widened (i*) test. It is only from the fact that in the homothetic case, the references used, P^a or Q^a, never matter (cancelling out, so to speak), that (5.6) and (5.9) get satisfied in the homothetic case.

We now speedily show the sense in which the tests (ii*)–(v*) can all be satisfied even in the nonhomothetic case.

$$(5.10) \quad (ii^*) \quad p(P^1, P^0; Q^a)p(P^0, P^1, Q^a) \equiv 1$$

$$= \frac{e(P^1; Q^a)e(P^0; Q^a)}{e(P^0; Q^a)e(P^1; Q^a)}$$

$$q(Q^1, Q^0; P^a)q(Q^0; Q^1; P^a) \equiv 1$$

$$= \frac{e(Q^1; P^a)}{e(Q^0; P^a)} \frac{e(Q^0; P^a)}{e(Q^1; P^a)}$$

$$(5.11) \quad (iii^*) \quad p(P^2, P^1; Q^a)p(P^1, P^0; Q^a)$$

$$\cdot p(P^0, P^2; Q^a) \equiv 1$$

$$q(Q^2, Q^1; P^a)q(Q^1, Q^0; P^a)$$

$$\cdot q(Q^0, Q^2; P^a) \equiv 1,$$

by similar proofs;

$$(5.12) \quad (iv^*) \quad p\dagger(P\dagger^1, P\dagger^0, Q\dagger^a)$$

$$\equiv p(P^1, P^0; Q^a)$$

$$q\dagger(Q\dagger^1, Q\dagger^0; P\dagger^a)$$

$$\equiv q(Q^1, Q^0; P^a),$$

by the same earlier dimensional analysis.

When it comes to the factor-reversal test, we easily verify the "crossed" condition

$$(5.13) \quad (v^*) \quad p(P^1, P^0; Q^1)q(Q^1, Q^0; P^0)$$

$$\equiv e^1/e^0$$

$$\equiv p(P^1, P^0; Q^0)q(Q^1, Q^0; P^1)$$

But, in general,

$$(5.14) \quad p(P^1, P^0; Q^i)q(Q^1, Q^0; P^i) \not\equiv e^i/e^0$$

$$(i = 0, 1)$$

$$p(P^1, P^0, Q^a)q(Q^1, Q^0; P^a) \not\equiv e^1/e^0$$

for arbitrary (Q^a, P^a)

From this review of the general case, it will be appreciated how much more simple is the homothetic case. If only it were as realistic[10] as it is elegant! This is said not

[10] Fortunately, in the case of production theory, because of the degree of interest that attaches to constant returns to scale, homotheticity is not always so unrealistic. See Ulmer, ch. 4, for an attempt to estimate limits even in the nonhomothetic case. More promising is the quadratic interpolation method of Abraham Wald that Ulmer discusses in his appendix A along with the ambitious attempt of Frisch (1932). Afriat favors the linear Engel-curve approximation: $e(P; Q) = \theta(P)\phi(Q) + \mu(P)$.

in regret, but as a reminder that more is asked of index numbers than can be delivered, as for example when union contracts and government sliding-scale agreements are all made to depend on the consumers price index appropriate at best to one real-income stratum.

VI. Divisia Indexes

Before leaving the general survey, a word about the little understood Divisia line integrals is in order. The typical argument for Divisia indexes is inadequate in its treatment of the invariance of the line integrals under change of path between endpoints. Too often it goes something like this Schumpeter version

$$(6.1) \qquad d \sum_1^n p_j q_j = \sum_1^n p_j dq_j + \sum_1^n q_j dp_j$$

or in vector notation

$$d(P \cdot Q) = P \cdot dQ + Q \cdot dP$$

$$P^1 \cdot Q^1 - P^0 \cdot Q^0 = \int_c P \cdot dQ + \int_c Q \cdot dP$$

$$= I_q + I_p$$

where c indicates the contour taken by $[p_j(t), q_j(t)]$ between the endpoints, t^1 and t^0. However, for each different path going from the end points t^0 to t^1, the invariant left-hand difference gets broken down on the right-hand side into noninvariant partition between the I_q and I_p line integrals.

More sophisticatedly, beg the case of existence and suppose there somehow exist composite scalar measures of quantity and price, $\bar{q}$ and $\bar{p}$, such that

$$(6.2) \quad \bar{q}\bar{p} = Q \cdot P, \quad log\ \bar{q} + log\ \bar{p} = log \sum_1^n p_j q_j$$

$$log\ Q^1 \cdot P^1 - log\ Q^0 \cdot P^0$$

$$= \int_c \left[\sum_1^n p_j q_j \right]^{-1} \sum_1^n p_j dq_j$$

$$+ \int_c \left[\sum p_j q_j \right]^{-1} \sum q_j dp_j = J_q + J_p$$

$$\bar{q}^1 = \bar{q}^0 \exp J_q, \qquad \bar{p}^1 = \bar{p}^0 \exp J_p$$

But, again, this begs the case as to whether the invariant total $J_q + J_p$ is composed of separate line integrals that are invariant under arbitrary change of the $[Q(t), P(t)]$ path, c, between the fixed endpoints. In general, from the theory of Pfaffians and inexact differential expressions, the integrability conditions needed to ensure invariant line integrals are *not* realized.

However, as seen in Samuelson (1965, equation (5)), for Y defined as P/e,

$$(6.3) \quad Q = grad\ log\ p(Y)$$

$$= [\partial\ log\ p(y_1, \ldots, y_n)/\partial y_i]$$

$$(6.3') \quad Y = grad\ log\ q(Q)$$

$$= [\partial\ log\ q(q_1, \ldots, q_n)/\partial q_i]$$

Hence, independently of path

$$(6.4) \quad log\ [q(Q^1)/q(Q^0)]$$

$$= \int_c grad\ log\ q(Q) \cdot dQ = \int_c Y \cdot dQ$$

$$= \int_{t^0}^{t^1} \sum_1^n y_j(t) q'_j(t) dt$$

$$= \int_{t^0}^{t^1} \sum_1^n [y_j(t) q_j(t)]$$

$$\cdot [d\ log\ q_j(t)/dt] dt \equiv J_q$$

$$(6.4') \quad log\ [p(P^1)/p(P^0)]$$

$$= log\ [p(Y^1)/p(Y^0)] + log\ [e^1/e^0]$$

$$= \int_c grad\ log\ p(Y) \cdot dY + log\ [e^1/e^0]$$

$$= \int_c Q \cdot dY + log\ [e^1/e^0]$$

$$= \int_{t^0}^{t^1} \sum_1^n [q_j(t) y'_j(t)] dt + log\ [e^1/e^0]$$

$$= \int_{t^0}^{t^1} \sum_1^n [y_j(t)y_j(t)][d \log q_j(t)/dt]dt$$

$$+ \log [e^1/e^0]$$

$$= \int_{t^0}^{t^1} \sum_1^n [y_j(t)q_j(t)]$$

$$\cdot [d \log p_j(t)/dt]dt + 0$$

$$= J_p$$

This provides a proper proof that if and only if homotheticity prevails, we can define canonical index numbers by Divisia line integrals that will be invariant under arbitrary path change

$$(6.5) \quad q(Q^1)/q(Q^0) = \exp \int_{t^0}^{t^1} \left[\sum_1^n y_j(t)q_j(t) \right]$$

$$\cdot [d \log q_j(t)/dt]dt$$

$$(6.5') \quad p(P^1)/p(P^0) = \exp \int_{t^0}^{t^1} \left[\sum_1^n y_j(t)q_j(t) \right]$$

$$\cdot [d \log p_j(t)/dt]dt$$

If one's data happen to come along a continuous arc $[p_i(t), q_i(t)]$ and if homotheticity is a legitimate assumption (as it often may be in production theory), one may fit the surfaces $p(Y)$ and $q(Q)$ to the data by the above normalized Divisia-index expressions. This is not a better method of surface fitting than an arbitrary variety of other methods of the type to be discussed in later sections, but for the data given on a continuous arc, it is a convenient method and one that must be as good as any other.

When, as is invariably the case, our data are at discrete intervals, then even if they happen to come in a determinate time sequence, it is no longer necessarily the case that the best way of utilizing the data is to attempt to approximate the normalized Divisia integrals by one or another method of numerical integration (for example, Simpson's rule, Euler-Maclaurin formulas, etc.).[11]

Our investigation of the history of Divisia indexes is worth reporting. Schumpeter, chapter 8, gives the typical cavalier exposition that ignores the problem of lack of path invariance of the line integrals. But already in Divisia's original work in the 1920's, as in Divisia (1928) and in other references given in Dale Jorgenson and Zvi Griliches on the subject, the problem is ignored—as it is in the Frisch 1936 "Survey" and in the works by Dresch and most others in the G. C. Evans Berkeley camp (Shephard being a notable exception). The remarkable 1946 paper of Ville gives the first proof we could find that, only with homotheticity, do we get the vital path invariance. (Incidentally, our duality relations, (6.3) and (6.3') above

---

[11] Actually, if the data are "close together," or the rate of change of events is very "slow," it will normally be better to use *all* the data points *simultaneously* in the fitting process as in equations (7.14) and (7.16) below. Thus, let $n=2$ and suppose you have N observations of vector pairs listed consecutively in time: $[y(t_1), q(t_1); y(t_2), q(t_2); \ldots ; y(t_N), q(t_N)]$. Then, without regard to t_i positioning, we can calculate N pairs of $[y_2/y_1, q_2/q_1]$ and from them fit the best functional relationship $y_2/y_1 = R(q_2/q_1)$ as in (7.13) below.

On an NSF grant, Meir Kohn of the M.I.T. Graduate School has kindly applied our ϵ-power series technique of Section VII to see whether the familiar device of "chaining" index numbers is an optimal mode of calculation. As suspected, calculating the Divisia integrals interval by interval by chaining does do better than merely using the pair of remote endpoints: as we show in (7.14) and later, the latter procedure gives an error-remainder term proportional to $T^3\epsilon^3$ whereas Kohn's Divisia-index chaining gives an error-remainder term proportional only to $T\epsilon^3$, where T is the number of equally spaced time intervals. Using *all* the (T+1) vectors of data *simultaneously* should be able, certainly in the $n=2$ case of our discussion around equation (7.14), to annihilate error terms in ϵ^3, $\epsilon^4, \ldots$, and in favorable cases even in ϵ^T. In unpublished work, Spencer Star and Robert E. Hall have shown that one gets a better discrete-data approximation to the Divisia line integrals when one assumes that, within each subinterval $\Delta t = t_{i+1} - t_i$, $y_j q_j$ is assumed constant (at the mean of its t_{i+1} and t_i values) than if one merely calculates $\int Y \cdot dQ$ for the interval by the approximation $Y(t_i) \cdot [Q(t_{i+1}) - Q(t_i)]$. Star and Hall give exact error calculations in terms of (not necessarily observable) covariance integrals; and, actually, in some realistic cases, the $T^3\epsilon^3$ coefficient may be small (even if not smaller than the $T\epsilon^3$ term).

51

are already in Ville, but the Houthakker Strong Axiom seems *not* to be *quite* there.) Wold, Richter, Gorman, Samuelson, Jorgenson and Griliches, Hulten, and other modern writers are aware of homotheticity's key role. In production theory, unlike consumer's demand analysis, this is not so bizarre a hypothesis: however, where the homothetic isoquants do not correspond to constant-returns output function, exp J_q gives at best canonical $q(Q^1)/q(Q^0)$ not *Output*^{1}/*Output*^{0}; moreover, one cannot then blithely identify p_i/e expressions with percentage marginal productivities $\partial \log Output/\partial q_i$.

VII. Approximations

In this paper we have thus far been concerned primarily with exact formulations and not with the problem of approximation. However, the two have become confused and so we do make some needed observations upon the problem of approximation and empirical estimation based upon incomplete information, particularly since the theory of revealed preference and maximization does provide some correct limits on exact functions.

Thus, from the definition of $e(P^1; Q^0)$ as minimized expenditure to achieve the $u(Q^0)$ level of satisfaction, we derive *alternative* one-sided bounds

$$(7.1) \quad p(P^1, P^0; Q^0) = \frac{e(P^1; Q^0)}{e(P^0; Q^0)} \leq \frac{P^1 \cdot Q^0}{P^0 \cdot Q^0}$$
$$= \lambda_p$$

$$(7.1') \quad p(P^1, P^0; Q^1) = \frac{e(P^1; Q^1)}{e(P^0; Q^1)} \geq \frac{P^1 \cdot Q^1}{P^0 \cdot Q^1}$$
$$= \pi_p$$

Here λ_p and π_p stand for the familiar Laspeyres and Paasche price indexes. Likewise we denote by λ_q and π_q the corresponding base-period weighted and given-period weighted quantity indexes with $\lambda_p \pi_q = e^1/e^0 = \lambda_q \pi_p$. Then, by symmetry,

similar alternative one-sided limits hold for quantity indexes, namely

$$(7.2) \quad q(Q^1, Q^0; P^0) \leq \frac{P^0 \cdot Q^1}{P^0 \cdot Q^0} = \lambda_q$$

$$(7.2') \quad q(Q^1, Q^0; P^1) \leq \frac{P^1 \cdot Q^1}{P^1 \cdot Q^0} = \pi_q$$

As became clarified in the 1930's it is in general invalid to combine the above alternative single-limit expressions into the frequently met assertion

$$(7.3) \quad \pi_p \leq p(P^1, P^0; Q^i) \leq \lambda_p$$

Only in the special homothetic case in which

$$p(P^1, P^0; Q^1) \equiv p(P^1, P^0; Q^0) = p(P^1)/p(P^0)$$

can we validly[12] derive the following double limit

$$(7.4) \quad \pi_p \leq p(P^1, P^0) = p(P^1)/p(P^0) \leq \lambda_p$$

$$(7.4') \quad \pi_q \leq q(Q^1, Q^0) = q(Q^1)/q(Q^0) \leq \lambda_q$$

It is true that for the general case one can almost trivially assert a double limit of the following form

$$(7.5) \quad \text{Min} [\ldots, p_j^1/p_j^0, \ldots]$$
$$\leq p(P^1, P^0; Q^0) \leq \lambda_p$$
$$\leq \text{Max} [\ldots, p_j^1/p_j^0, \ldots]$$

and likewise for $p(P^1, P^0; Q^i)$ with λ_p

---

[12] Franklin Fisher and Karl Shell for the most part invoke the nonvalid double-limit (7.4), acknowledging in their fn. to p. 6, fn. 7 on p. 38, that it is not generally valid. But the reader must be warned against their reason for why the double-bound is not generally valid. Instead of attributing its invalidity to nonhomotheticity, they say: "In fact this [double-bound] proposition is not true [even with unchanged tastes] if price and income changes are large." It is incorrect that *largeness* of $(P^1 - P^0, Q^1 - Q^0)$ has anything to do with the failure of the double-bound. Even if these changes were indefinitely small, it would not be true that $\lambda_q \leq q(Q^1, Q^0; p_i) \leq \Pi_q$, as the failure of (iv*) in our earlier discussion of (5.7) reveals and as (7.25) will discuss further for the example $Q^1 = Q^0(1+\epsilon)$, $|\epsilon|$ arbitrarily small.

omitted. These follow from the easily demonstrated fact that a price index number is a *generalized internal mean* of its price ratios $[\ldots, p_j^1/p_j^0, \ldots]$. But these double limits are often so wide as to be practically not worth very much. Thus, in the homothetic case, (7.4) generally gives a sharper bound on the left than (7.5). And, as was pointed out in connection with (5.6) and (i*) interchanging all q_j for p_j in (7.5) will *not* in the nonhomothetic case give a valid (7.5') that provides similar bounds on $q(Q^1, Q^0; P^\alpha)$.

Another odd confusion crops up repeatedly in the literature. *If* we know that $u(Q^1) = u(Q^0)$, then it is valid to write the two-sided bounds

$$(7.6) \qquad \pi_p \leq p(P^1, P^0; Q^a) \leq \lambda_p,$$
$$u(Q^1) = u(Q^0) = u(Q^a)$$
$$\pi_q \leq q(Q^1, Q^0; P^\alpha) = 1 \leq \lambda_q \quad \text{for all } P^\alpha$$

But since we know $q = 1$ by hypothesis, no bounds on q are needed! Nor do the bounds on p add any information since, in this case, we *already* know the *exact* value of p as e^1/e^0!

Let us return to the homothetic case in which (7.4) and (7.4') are valid double-bounds. Is it not tempting to take some symmetric mean of the upper and lower bounds of Paasche and Laspeyres in the hope of getting a "more accurate approximation" and avoiding "upward or downward bias"? Fisher's Ideal index already mentioned in footnote 9, which in our notation is $(\lambda_p \pi_p)^{1/2}$, is precisely such an attempt. And, even though it fails the general circular test, we would welcome it as an approximation if in some sense it tended to produce "more accurate, less biased" results.

At long last, after half a century, we can a little bit vindicate Fisher in his choice of the "Ideal" index number, $(\lambda_p \pi_p)^{1/2}$ or $(\lambda_q \pi_q)^{1/2}$, not as an exact formula for $p(P^1)/p(P^0)$ or $q(Q^1)/q(Q^0)$—for there can

be no one formula to cover two different sets of tastes—but as one "locally sufficient" function of homothetic (P, Q) observations that will approximate to the true magnitude up to terms of the *second* degree in the deviations between the two situations. To interpret what this means, we now proceed to develop a new power-series technique that enables one to make rigorous sense about degrees of goodness of approximations.

Specifically, for $Y = P/e$ and the two situations close together in *ratios*, so that $Q^1 - \alpha Q^0$ and $Y^1 - \alpha^{-1} Y^0$ are "small numbers," write

$$(7.7) \qquad \alpha Y^1 = Y^0 + \epsilon \dot{Y}^0 + \tfrac{1}{2}\epsilon^2 \ddot{Y}^0 + \cdots$$
$$\alpha^{-1} Q^1 = Q^0 + \epsilon \dot{Q}^0 + \tfrac{1}{2}\epsilon^2 \ddot{Q}^0 + \cdots$$
$$Y^1 \cdot Q^1 = 1 + 0 = Y^0 \cdot Q^0$$
$$= 1 + \epsilon(Y^0 \cdot \dot{Q}^0 + \dot{Y}^0 \cdot Q^0)$$
$$+ \tfrac{1}{2}\epsilon^2(Y^0 \cdot \ddot{Q}^0 + 2\dot{Y}^0 \cdot \dot{Q}^0$$
$$+ \ddot{Y}^0 \cdot Q^0) + \cdots$$
$$Y^0 \cdot \dot{Q}^0 = - \dot{Y}^0 \cdot Q^0,$$
$$- \ddot{Y}^0 \cdot Q^0 = Y^0 \cdot \ddot{Q}^0 + 2\dot{Y}^0 \cdot \dot{Q}^0, \text{ etc.}$$

From (6.3'), we know that

$$(7.8) \qquad \partial q(Q)/\partial q_i = q(Q)y_i \quad (i = 1, \ldots, n)$$

Substituting (7.7) and (7.8) into $q(Q^1)$ gives

$$(7.9) \qquad \alpha^{-1} q(Q^1)/q(Q^0)$$
$$= 1 + \epsilon Y^0 \cdot \dot{Q}^0 + \tfrac{1}{2}\epsilon^2 [Y^0 \cdot \ddot{Q}^0 + 2 Y^0 \cdot Q^0$$
$$+ (\dot{Y}^0 \cdot Q^0)^2] + \cdots$$

By (6.3') and the definitions of λ_q and π_q

$$(7.10) \qquad \alpha^{-1} \lambda_q = \alpha^{-1} Y^0 \cdot Q^1 = 1 + \epsilon Y^0 \cdot \dot{Q}^0$$
$$+ \tfrac{1}{2}\epsilon^2 Y^0 \cdot \ddot{Q}^0 + \cdots$$
$$\alpha^{-1} \pi_q = \alpha^{-1}(Y^1 \cdot Q^0)^{-1} = \{1 + \epsilon \dot{Y}^0 \cdot Q^0$$
$$+ \tfrac{1}{2}\epsilon^2 \ddot{Y}^0 \cdot Q^0 + \cdots\}^{-1}$$
$$= 1 - \epsilon \dot{Y}^0 \cdot Q^0 + \tfrac{1}{2}\epsilon^2 [2(Y^0 \cdot \dot{Q}^0)^2$$
$$- \ddot{Y}^0 \cdot Q^0] + \cdots$$
$$= 1 + \epsilon Y^0 \cdot \dot{Q}^0 + \tfrac{1}{2}\epsilon^2 [2(Y^0 \cdot Q^0)^2$$
$$+ 2\dot{Y}^0 \cdot \dot{Q}^0 + Y^0 \cdot \ddot{Q}^0] + \cdots$$

(7.10') $\quad \alpha^{-1}(\pi_q\lambda_q)^{1/2}$

$$= 1 + \epsilon Y^0 \cdot \dot{Q}^0 + \tfrac{1}{2}\epsilon^2[Y^0 \cdot \ddot{Q}^0$$
$$+ \dot{Y}^0 \cdot \dot{Q}^0 + (\dot{Y}^0 \cdot Q^0)^2] + \cdots$$

But this last expression, whose first three coefficients are simple linear unweighted means of the λ_q and π_q expressions' coefficients, is seen to be identical up to ϵ^2 terms with the true index of (7.9). Hence, we have established the following:

ACCURACY THEOREM: *In the homothetic case, any symmetric mean of the Laspeyres and Paasche index numbers (including the Ideal index's geometric mean) will approximate the true index number up to the third order in accuracy.*

(7.11) $\quad q(Q^1)/q(Q^0) - (\lambda_q\pi_q)^{1/2}$
$$= 0 + \epsilon 0 + 0\epsilon^2 + \epsilon^3 r(\epsilon)$$

where the remainder $r(\epsilon)$ is finite at $\epsilon = 0$.

The truth of this finding, that the Ideal index gives a second-order or osculating approximation to the true homothetic index, could have been vaguely suspected from the finding in Samuelson (1953a, p. 8, n. 1) that the symmetric mean of overcompensated and undercompensated demand functions provides a high-order, osculating approximation to the Slutsky-Hicks just-compensated demand along the indifference contours.

The Ideal index is of course not alone in this accuracy. *Any* symmetric internal mean of the locally sufficient Laspeyres and Paasche indexes will provide as high accuracy. For example, $p(P^1)/p(P^0)$ is well-approximated by any generalized symmetric mean function $m(\lambda_p, \pi_p)$, where

(7.12) $\quad \text{Min } (x, y) \leq m(x, y)$
$$\equiv m(y, x) \leq \text{Max } (x, y)$$

One would have to go to ϵ^3 terms to decide whether one symmetric mean can be said to be better than another, as for example

whether $\tfrac{1}{2}(\lambda_q + \pi_q)$ gives a better approximation than $(\lambda_q\pi_q)^{1/2}$ to a particular given $q(Q)$.

Of course, all this applies only to the homothetic case, as we shall see.

The fact that the Ideal index, for Q and P/e treated as independently varying vectors, flunks the circular test does not vitiate it as a local approximation. Approximations often violate transitivity. For example, 1.01 and .99 are each within 1 percent approximations to 1.0, but *that* does not make them have this property with respect to each other!

*The Homothetic Case with
Only Two Goods*

Given *only* two observations $[P^\beta, Q^\beta]$, $(\beta = 0, 1)$, no more information can be squeezed out about the unknown $q(Q)$ or $p(P)$ functions than from these $m(\lambda, \pi)$ functions. But if we have more than two observations, $(\beta = 0, 1, 2, \ldots)$, say k in all, we can of course do better. It appears that the independent inner-products $P^\beta \cdot Q^\alpha$ are no longer "locally sufficient" information parameters for highest-order accuracy. Let us sketch briefly for the $n = 2$ case how k observations might give us approximations to $q(Q)$ accurate up to ϵ^k terms. Write

(7.13) $\quad q(q_1, q_2) = q_1 q(1, q_2/q_1) = q_1 g(q_2/q_1)$
$$p_1/p_2 = \frac{g(q_2/q_1) - (q_2/q_1)g'(q_2/q_1)}{g'(q_2/q_1)}$$
$$= \exp{-h[\log (q_2/q_1)]}$$

Now from k nearby paired values of $[\log q_2^k/q_1^k, \log (p_2/p_1)^k]$, fit a polynomial approximation to $h[\;]$, namely

(7.14) $\quad h[z] = h + h_1 z + \ldots + h_{k-1} z_{k-1}$

Knowing $h[z]$, we use the differential equation for $g(\;)$ in (7.13) to get its corresponding form, and then we have $q(q_1, q_2) = q_1 g(q_2/q_1)$ and can calculate our index numbers of high-order accuracy, by $q(Q^\beta)/q(Q^0)$.

As mentioned in footnote 11 on Divisia index chaining, even when our data come in consecutive time or space sequence, one does not get an optimal estimate of an existent $q(Q)$ function by using binary chaining, in which one estimates $q(Q^T)/q(Q^0)$ by chained separate products $[q(Q^1)/q(Q^0)][q(Q^2)/q(Q^1)] \ldots [q(Q^T)/q(Q^{T-1})]$. Instead, when the data are sufficiently close and each $Q^t = Q^0 + \epsilon \dot{Q}^0 + \ldots$, one gets a lower coefficient of the ϵ^3 and higher-order error terms by using all data simultaneously to make closest estimates of the coefficients in

$$(7.15) \quad q[\epsilon] = q(Q[\epsilon]) = q[0] + q'[0]\epsilon$$
$$+ q''[0]\epsilon^2/2 + \ldots$$

The Homothetic Case with More Goods

For $n > 2$, the problem is of course more complicated, even in this homothetic case. Only a sketch can be given here. For the homothetic case we are fortunate in that the Antonelli-Slutsky-Hotelling-Hicks integrability conditions take a very simple form and enable us to reduce the problem to that of determining one function of n variables: $\phi(Q) = \log q(Q)$ being the most convenient one. It was seen in (6.3') and (7.8) that $Y = \text{grad } \phi(Q) = (\partial \phi(Q)/\partial q_j)$. Because $q(Q)$ is first-degree homogeneous, we can reduce the problem to that of determining a surface in the $n-1$ variables $(q_j/q_1) = (z_2, \ldots, z_n) = Z$, namely $\phi(1, Z) = \psi(Z)$ whose gradient equals the modified prices $W = (w_2, \ldots, w_n) = (q_1 y_2, \ldots, q_1 y_n)$.

Now suppose we are given for $t = 0$, $1, \ldots, T$ data situations the observed vector pairs $[Z^t, W^t] = [z_2^t, \ldots, z_n^t; w_2^t, \ldots, w_n^t]$. Then we can fit a polynomial surface to $\psi(Z)$ of the form

$$(7.16) \quad h(z_2, \ldots, z_n) = a_0 + \sum_{j=1}^{n} a_{1j}(z_j - z_j^0)$$
$$+ \frac{1}{2} \sum_{i=1}^{n} \sum_{j=1}^{n} a_{2,ij}(z_i - z_i^0)(z_j - z_j^0) + R_3$$

$$(7.17) \quad \text{grad } h(Z^0) = W^0 = [w_j^0] = [a_{1j}]$$

Thus, to determine only $n-1$ coefficients a_{1j} to $h(Z)$, we need only one (Z^0, W^0) observation. But for a quadratic approximation to $h(Z)$, we must determine the $n-1$ coefficients a_{1j} plus $n(n-1)/2$ independent $a_{2,ij}$ coefficients: this requires $(n-1) \cdot [1 + \frac{1}{2}n]$ equations in all; but since, for each t in (7.17), we get $n-1$ equations, we need at least $T = 1 + \frac{1}{2}n$ situations to be able to derive a quadratic approximation. Thus, for $n-1 = 1$, and T situations we can, as in (7.14) determine $\psi(Z)$ as a T degree polynomial. For $n-1 = 2$, we would need to determine 5 coefficients for a quadratic approximation; hence $T = 3$ known values for $[(q_2/q_1)^t, (q_2/q_1)'^t; (q_1 y_2)^t, (q_1 y_3)^t]$ would give us 6 equations, which is 1 more than the minimum number needed. For general $n-1$, we need approximately $n/2$ equations to get a quadratic approximation. Note, however, that for data close together so that the (7.12) power series applies, we can with a large enough number of situations T, in principle, determine the $q(Q)$ surface to as great accuracy as we desire. Of course, the T situations must not be collinear, as when all (q_i/q_1) proportions never change at all. And, as is known from the theory of interpolation of noisy data, one might want to use redundant observations to filter out error noise and make best estimates of true message, utilizing least squares and other techniques for providing data. If the $q(Q)$ and $\psi[Z]$ functions are not indefinitely differentiable, or if their higher derivatives oscillate wildly, one will prefer low-degree polynomial fitting to high.

Before leaving this little explored domain, we should mention that when $q(Q)$ is actually changing through time—as in our Section VIII dealing with changing tastes —chaining makes some sense, even though it may be hard to state what then makes good sense.

The Nonhomothetic Two-Good Case

The nonhomothetic case also presents, even for $n=2$, more intrinsic difficulties. With only 2 observations, we do not perceive that there is *any* way of getting $q(Q^1, Q^0; P^\alpha)$ to an accuracy of ϵ^2. However, given 3 nearby and noncollinear observations on (q_1, q_2, y_1, y_2), we should be able to do so. Thus, let

$$(7.18) \qquad Q^t = Q^0 + \epsilon A^t, \qquad (t = 1, 2)$$
$$det\, [A^1, A^2] \neq 0$$

and suppose we also have observations on (Y^2, Y^1, Y^0). Then in

$$(7.19) \quad y_2/y_1 = [\partial u(Q)/\partial q_2]/[\partial u(Q)/\partial q_1]$$
$$= r(q_1, q_2)$$

we can use our three paired observations $[q_1^t, q_2^t, (y_2/y_1)^t]$, $(t=0, 1, 2)$, to provide some approximation to the marginal rate of substitution function, $r(\ ,\ )$, that is linear in terms of some functions of the variables.

Often, it is alternatively assumed, as for example in Wald, that we have knowledge of two or more Engel's paths from budget studies in different price situations. Then we know two empirical functions, $f[q_2; (p_2/p_1)^t]$ in the following

$$(7.20) \quad r(q_1, q_2) = (p_2/p_1)^t \qquad (t = 0, 1)$$
$$q_1 = f[q_2; (p_2/p_1)^t]$$

and can use linear interpolation, either on the q's, their logarithms, or any other stretchings, to get the $f[\ ;\ ]$ and $r(\ ,)$ functions up to accuracy of terms $\{(p_2/p_1)^1 - (p_2/p_1)^0\}^2$.

Given the $r(\ ,)$ function or a close approximation to it, we then, as in Samuelson (1948, p. 245), solve the differential equation

$$(7.21) \qquad -dq_2/dq_1 = r(q_1, q_2)$$

to get

$$(7.22) \qquad q_2 = u(q_1; \overset{\#}{q_2}), \qquad \overset{\#}{q_2} \equiv v(q_1; \overset{0}{}; \overset{\#}{q_2})$$
$$\overset{\#}{q_2} = v^{-1}(q_1; q_2) = f\{u(Q)\}$$

Having derived one indicator of utility, our index number problems are solved.

The Nonhomothetic Many-Good Case

Here we shall be brief and avoid duplicating the exposition of Wald, and shall not be assuming knowledge of any full Engel's paths. Write

$$(7.23) \quad u(Q) = (Q - Q^0) \begin{pmatrix} 1 \\ b_2 \\ \vdots \\ \vdots \\ b_n \end{pmatrix} + \frac{1}{2}(Q - Q^0)$$
$$\cdot [a_{ij}](Q - Q^0)^T + R_3$$

Although we shall here neglect R_3 remainders and speak only of quadratic approximations, our method generalizes to cubic and higher-degree approximations. Note that we have chosen to employ the convention of setting $u(Q^0) = 0 = 1 - \partial u(Q^0)/\partial q_1$. By the familiar tangency of price ratios and indifference contours, we know

$$(7.24) \quad \frac{\partial u(Q^t)/\partial q_i}{\partial u(Q^t)/\partial q_1} = (p_i/p_1)^t,$$
$$(t = 0, 1, \dots, T; i = 2, \dots, n)$$
$$0 = \partial u(Q^t)/\partial q_i - (p_i/p_1)^t \partial u(Q^t)/\partial q_1$$
$$0 = b_i - (p_i/p_1)^0$$
$$0 = \left[(p_i/p_1)^0 - \sum_1^n a_{ij} q_j^t \right]$$
$$- (p_i/p_1)^t \left(1 - \sum_1^n a_{1j} q_j^t \right)$$

These last are $(n-1)T$ relations linear in the unknown a_{ij} coefficients, of which, because of the symmetry of the a_{ij} coefficients, there are only $n(n+1)/2$ unknown a_{ij} coefficients. This means that for $T > \frac{1}{2}(n-1)+1.5$ and no degeneracy or

(7.25)

$$u(Q) = q_2(1 + q_1), \qquad Q^0 = (1, 1), \qquad Q^1 = (1 + \epsilon, 1 + \epsilon)$$

$$(p_2/p_1)^0 = (1 + 1)/1 = 2, \qquad (p_2/p_1)^1 = (2 + \epsilon)/(1 + \epsilon)$$

$$e(P^\alpha; Q^1) = \underset{Q}{\text{Min}} \{q_1 + (p_2/p_1)^\alpha q_2\} \text{ such that } q_2(1 + q_1) = (1 + \epsilon)(2 + \epsilon)$$

$$e(p^\alpha; Q^1) = \underset{q_1}{\text{Min}} \left\{ q_1 + \frac{(p_2/p_1)(1 + \epsilon)(2 + \epsilon)}{1 + q_1} \right\}$$

$$= 2[(p_2/p_1)^\alpha (1 + \epsilon)(2 + \epsilon)]^{1/2} - 1$$

$$= 2[2(p_2/p_1)^\alpha]^{1/2} \left[1 + \frac{3}{2}\epsilon + \frac{\epsilon^2}{2} \right]^{1/2} - 1$$

$$= 2[2(p_2/p_1)^\alpha]^{1/2} \left[1 + \frac{3}{4}\epsilon - \frac{1}{32}\epsilon^2 + \dots \right] - 1$$

$$q(Q^1, Q^0; P^\alpha) = \frac{2[2(p_2/p_1)^\alpha]^{1/2} \left[1 + \dfrac{3}{4}\epsilon - \dfrac{1}{32}\epsilon^2 + \dots \right] - 1}{2[2(p_2/p_1)^\alpha]^{1/2} - 1}$$

collinearity, we can in principle calculate all our desired functions: $u(Q)$, $q(Q, Q^0; P^\alpha)$, $p(P, P^0; Q^\alpha)$. If the T observations obey the power-series form of (7.12) generalized to nonhomotheticity, then for $\epsilon \to 0$ but $\epsilon \neq 0$, we can calculate the $q(, ;)$ and $p(, ;)$ index numbers that will be accurate up to powers of ϵ as high as we like—if only we are given T sufficiently large.

Nonoptimality of Ideal Index for Nonhomothetic Case

We have already noted that, in the nonhomothetic case, the quantity index can fail Fisher's first test of being a generalized mean of the ratios (q_j^1/q_j^0), and can differ from them even when they all have a common value. Since $(\lambda_q \pi_q)^{1/2}$ will equal that common ratio, it is evident that the Ideal index cannot give high-powered approximation to the true index in the general, nonhomothetic case. A simple example will illustrate the degree of this failure as shown in (7.25). Specifically, for $(p_2/p_1)^\alpha = (p_2/p_1)^0$,

(7.26)
$$q(Q^1, Q^0; P^0)$$

$$= \frac{2[2] \left[1 + \frac{3}{4}\epsilon - \frac{1}{32}\epsilon^2 + \dots \right] - 1}{2[2] - 1}$$

$$= 1 + \epsilon - \frac{1}{24}\epsilon^2 + \dots$$

$$< \lambda_q = 1 + \epsilon = \pi_q = (\lambda_q \pi_q)^{1/2}$$

for $\epsilon \neq 0$ but sufficiently small.

It is thus seen that there is *not* agreement to the second-order of ϵ^2 terms. This example also warns against the common fallacy mentioned in footnote 12: even if (P^1, P^0, P^α) and (Q^1, Q^0) are "sufficiently close together," it is not true that the Laspeyres and Paasche indexes provide two-sided bounds for the true index. In this example, the true index lies *outside* the $[\lambda_q, \pi_q]$ interval!

VIII. Taste Changes

As in Samuelson[13] and Fisher-Shell, we

[13] Samuelson in present notation, says: "We can validly state: $p > 1$ [*i.e.*, $\pi_q > 1$] implies that the first batch of goods is higher than the batch II on the indifference curves that prevailed in period I [*i.e.*, the

show what can be said about index numbers when tastes change, being generated in situations 0 and 1 not by uniform $u(Q)$ but respectively by $u^0(Q)$ and $u^1(Q)$. We now generalize the $e(\ ,\ ;\ )$, $p(\ ,\ ;\ )$, and $q(\ ,\ ;\ )$ functions for $(i=0,\ 1)$ to

$$(8.1) \quad e^i(P;\ Q) = \underset{X}{\text{Min}}\ P\cdot X$$

such that $u^i(X) = u^i(Q)$, $(i=0,\ 1)$

$$p^i(P^1,\ P^0;\ Q^a) = e^i(P^1;\ Q^a)/e^i(P^0;\ Q^a)$$

$$q^i(Q^1,\ Q^0;\ P^a) = e^i(P^a;\ Q^1)/e^i(P^a;\ Q^0)$$

$$e^i(P^j;\ Q^j) = P^j\cdot Q^{ji}$$

$$\neq e^j = P^j\cdot Q^j,\ (j \neq i)$$

Note that $p^i(P^1,\ P^0;\ Q^i)$ never involves Q^j at all, and neither do ratios involving $P^i\cdot Q^i$ and $P^i\cdot Q^j$. So the valid one-sided price bounds of (7.1) remain valid.

$$(8.2) \quad p^1(P^1,\ P^0;\ Q^1) \geq \pi_p$$

$$(8.2') \quad p^0(P^1,\ P^0;\ Q^0) \leq \lambda_p$$

Likewise, since neither $q^i(Q^1,\ Q^0;\ P^i)$ nor ratios involving such terms as $P^i\cdot Q^i$ and $P^i\cdot Q^j$ ever involve P^j at all (or the new and unobserved P^{ji} that would have to prevail *if* Q^j were to be the best buy at $u^i(Q)$ tastes), the one-sided quantity bounds of (7.2) remain valid:

$$(8.3) \quad q^1(Q^1,\ Q^0;\ P^1) \geq \pi_q$$

$$(8.3') \quad q^0(Q^1,\ Q^0;\ P^0) \leq \lambda_q$$

However, even in the homothetic case where $e^i(P;\ Q) = p^i(P)q^i(Q)$, the two-sided limits of (7.1) can never validly apply, being replaced only by

---

period of P^0, Q^0]" (1950, p. 24). Since $q(Q^1,\ Q^0;\ P)$ has just been shown to be approximated by λ_q up to terms of linear order in ϵ, if we are interested in the tastes of the period of $(P^1,\ Q^1)$, we are well advised to follow the (8.3) suggestion above and give primacy to the Paasche π_q index. If, as is unlikely, we knew that tastes shift slowly—like ϵ^3 rather than ϵ—we would do better in the homothetic case to use a symmetric mean of λ_q and π_q, achieving ϵ^2 rather than ϵ accuracy.

$$(8.4) \quad \lambda_p \leq p^0(P^1)/p^0(P^0)$$

$$\leq \frac{P^1\cdot Q^{10}}{P^0\cdot Q^0} \gtreqless \frac{P^1 Q^1}{P^0 Q^0} = \pi_p$$

$$\lambda_p = \frac{P^1\cdot Q^0}{P^0\cdot Q^0} \gtreqless \frac{P^0\cdot Q^1}{P^0\cdot Q^{01}}$$

$$\leq p^1(P^1)/p^1(P^0) \leq \pi_p$$

Here Q^{01} are what would have been bought at P^0 if tastes of 1 had prevailed, etc.

Even the weak factor-reversal fails to be satisfied under changing tastes, since

$$(8.5) \quad p^i(P^1,\ P^0;\ Q^1)q^i(Q^1,\ Q^0;\ P^0) \gtreqless e^1/e^0$$

$$(i = 0,\ 1)$$

$$p^i(P^1,\ P^0;\ Q^0)q^i(Q^1,\ Q^0;\ P^1) \gtreqless e^1/e^0$$

This failure greatly reduces the significance of the valid (8.2) price bounds since they can never be of any use in providing deflators of money expenditures that will produce estimates of real quantity magnitudes.[14] So it is fortunate that we have the valid direct quantity bounds of (8.3).

One use for (8.2) is in estimating cost of living allowances or adjustments for, say, foreign employees who face P^1 and need to be given enough (unknown) income, e^1_x, to be able to enjoy, at 0 situation tastes, a level of living just as good as Q^0. Then (8.3) provides the valid bound on e^1_x,

$$(8.6) \quad e_x \overset{\text{def.}}{=} e^0 p^0(P^1,\ P^0;\ Q^0)$$

$$\leq e^0 \pi_p = P^0\cdot Q^0 \frac{P^1\cdot Q^0}{P^0\cdot Q^0}$$

$$\leq P^1\cdot Q^0$$

This solution is so simple as to be almost anticlimactic. It merely restates the commonsense observation that, if you give someone abroad enough money to buy

---

[14] Fisher-Shell, at the end of their preface's first page, seem to suggest that the price index bounds they reach, such as (8.2)'s Paasche, can be used as deflators—which may be in some contradiction to (8.5), unless the deflation process is restricted to be of (8.6) type.

exactly the Q^0 goods he consumes at home, then he'll be at least as well off as he was at home, a so-called "over-compensated" change.

For two-country real-income comparisons, both tastes provide relevant $q^i(\ ,\ ;\ )$ indexes. Often estimates of quantity changes are desired over more than two periods (so that one can spot acceleration, takeoffs, revolutions, or mundane cycles). If tastes are changing cumulatively (with or without acceleration, takeoffs, or cycles), it would not seem sensible to give primacy to the last-available year's tastes. This would involve recomputing every year against the new year; and such a procedure would ignore the useful information contained in the presumption that, between each two close-by periods, tastes have presumably not changed much. So a chaining procedure seems sensible. Thus, disregarding the primacy established here of relations like (8.2), one might well compute between successive periods the Ideal quantity indexes, chaining them together by appropriation multiplications; or one could use Divisia-like indexes if nonhomotheticity is not too great;[15] or one could use one or another of the improved approximations developed for unchanging tastes in our earlier sections.

Suppose the purpose is *to calculate average price changes* so that money wage rates and other contracts can be periodically "escalated." The vague and implicit purpose underlying such contracts is presumably that the worker is to be "as well off in Period 1 (or the period just following it) as he was in the base Period 0." This sounds almost as if Period 0's tastes are to provide the appropriate criterion, so that

(8.3')'s Laspeyres bound is appropriate rather than (8.3)'s Paasche bound.

Probably, though, one should not try to read anything so definite into people's vague notions of equity. When a General Motors cost-of-living contract continues in effect for year after year, it seems doubtful that primacy should be given to the bygone tastes of its first year of life. More likely, we shall want to concentrate on the tastes of its year or 3-year renewal. But, in so concentrating, there seems no reason why either the end-of-the-year or beginning-of-the-year tastes should be particularly favored. This again suggests chaining, perhaps in the even-handed form of multiplying together successively computed Ideal price indexes of adjacent periods.

In concluding this section, we note that quality changes in the vectors of goods Q^0 and Q^1 provide some further complications to make the allowances for taste changes even more difficult. As an example, suppose the later period adds a good q_{n+1} that was not available at any price in the earlier period. We must set its price then at infinity: $p_{n+1}^0 = \infty$.

This makes our only valid bound on the price index calculated under the later period's taste, (8.2) involving the Paasche index, so wide as to be useless:

$$(8.7) \quad p^1(P^1, P^0; Q^1) \geq P^1 \cdot Q^1 / P^0 \cdot Q^0 = 0$$

since infinite p_j^0 makes the last denominator infinite. Fortunately, our valid Paasche-quantity bound still does apply: it makes sense to ask, "How much could my later-period's income drop to leave me as well off as I would be with my present tastes if I had to consume today the Q^0 I used to consume?" Now we apply (8.2') and give the answer: "If my income fell so that I could still buy Q^0 today, I'd assuredly still be as well off as then."

If, as following 400 A.D., goods both get lost and discovered, then no generally valid and useful bounds apply to prices or

[15] If one knows something about Engel-law deviations from homotheticity and something about Gerschenkron-Clark-Kuznets laws of changing comparative advantages with development, one should be able to improve upon the Ideal or Divisia indexes with their homotheticity dependence for high-order accuracy. This analysis is developed in Samuelson (1974b).

to quantities under any pattern of tastes (uniform or changing). That's the way things are.

IX. Index Numbers of Production Possibilities

Writers such as Hicks, Kuznets, and Little are cited in Samuelson (1950) where the focus is shifted away from cost-of-living consumption index numbers based on indifference contours to the attempt to infer uniform improvements in production-possibility frontiers. See also Abram Bergson, Richard Moorsteen, and Fisher-Shell, Essay II, for other more recent discussions.

Thus, let $X = (x_1, \ldots, x_n)$ now stand for amounts of goods produced. Let the frontier of what is producible be, for fixed totals of factor inputs and technology in the background, written as the implicit transformation function

$$(9.1) \quad 0 = f(X; x) = f(x_1, \ldots, x_n; x),$$
$$\partial f / \partial x_j > 0 \qquad (j = 1, \ldots, n)$$

where x is a scalar parameter of aggregate size that plays a role much like that played in demand theory by q in the $q(Q)$ function. Assume first that $\partial f / \partial x$ is known to be negative; an increase in x can then be seen to shift the p-p frontier outward, making more of all goods producible.

If $f(\ )$ is convex (from below) in all its X arguments (so that its contours in the $(x_1, x_2, \ldots)$ space for fixed x are concave!) and if $\partial f / \partial x$ is one-signed, an increase in x must increase the maximum national income attainable for any fixed set of positive prices. That is,

$$(9.2) \qquad y(Y; x) = \operatorname*{Max}_{x} Y \cdot X$$

subject to $f(X; x) = 0$

This is exactly parallel to the fact in consumption theory that minimized $P \cdot Q$ subject to fixed level of u is a monotone function of the utility indicator u. Therefore,

to compare the production possibilities of two situations, for which we have observations (X^1, Y^1) and (X^0, Y^0), we should be able to define index numbers involving $Y \cdot X$ ratios that run exactly parallel to the consumption index numbers. Specifically, define for the index of quantity change

$$(9.3) \quad x(X^1, X^0; Y^\alpha) = y(Y^\alpha; X^1)/(Y^\alpha; X^0)$$

Just as the cost-of-living case is enormously simpler in the homothetic case, so can we get richer analytic results in the special "neutral-technical-change or homothetic case" where (8.1) can be specialized to the form

$$(9.4) \qquad x = x(x_1, \ldots, x_n) = x(X)$$
$$= \lambda^{-1} x(\lambda X)$$

but where, because of the law of diminishing returns, $x(X)$ is convex, homogeneous first-degree and not concave (as in the consumer's diminishing marginal rate of substitution case). Reminder: The convexity of the $x(X)$ function should not be confused with the concavity of its contours in the $(x_1, x_2, \ldots)$ space.

It will come as no surprise to anyone who has followed our analysis thus far that running parallel to the homothetic consumption theory of price and quantity index numbers and their duality relations is a homothetic production-theory version of price and quantity index numbers. (The only difference is that convexity leads to maximization where concavity led to minimization and all bounds are reversed as in Samuelson (1950).)

Tersely, we define the dual to $x(X)$ as

$$(9.5) \qquad y(Y) = \operatorname*{Max}_{x} Y \cdot X / x(X)$$

$$y(Y)x(X) \geq Y \cdot X$$

with the equality sign holding if, and only if, the (X, Y) satisfy optimizing demand (or, better, "supply") pairings. As quantity and price index numbers, we define

$$x(X^1, X^0) = x(X^1)/x(X^0) \equiv x(X^1, X^0; Y^\alpha)$$

$$y(Y^1, Y^0) = y(Y^1)/y(Y^0) \equiv y(Y^1, Y^0; P^\alpha)$$

for *any* Y^α and x.

These satisfy all Fisher's suitably-generalized tests, having the properties

(9.6)

    (i) $y(\lambda Y^0, Y^0) \equiv \lambda$

    (ii) $y(Y^1, Y^0)y(Y^0, Y^1) = 1$

    (iii) $y(Y^2, Y^1)y(Y^1, Y^0)y(Y^0, Y^2) = 1$

    (iv) $y\dagger(Y\dagger^1/Y\dagger^0) \equiv y(Y^1, Y^0)$

            for $y_j\dagger = y_j d_j^{-1}, \quad d_j > 0$

Similarly, $x(X^1, X^0)$ satisfies the time reversal, circular reversal, and dimensional invariance tests and provides a generalized internal mean of the x_j^1/x_j^0 ratios; hence the (9.6) tests are passed by quantity as well as price indexes.

The (weak) factor-reversal test is also, by duality of (8.4), satisfied.

(9.7) $y(Y^1, Y^0)x(X^1, X^0) = Y^1 \cdot X^1/Y^0 \cdot X^0$

Except that convexity on the supply functions makes us reverse the double Laspeyres-Paasche inequalities, we have just as in (7.4) and (7.4′)

$$\lambda_y = Y^1 \cdot X^0/Y^0 \cdot X^0 \leq y(Y^1, Y^0)$$
$$\leq Y^1 \cdot X^1/Y^0 \cdot X^1 = \pi_y$$
$$\lambda_q = Y^0 \cdot X^1/Y^0 \cdot X^0 \leq x(X^1, X^0)$$
$$\leq Y^1 \cdot X^1/Y^1 \cdot X^0 = \pi_q$$

Of course, in the nonhomothetic case we lose one of the bounds and must be content with the following counterparts to (8.4), involving inequality reversals

(9.8) $y(Y^1, Y^0; Y^1) \leq \pi_y$

(9.8′) $y(Y^1, Y^0; Y^0) \geq \lambda_y$

As before, various approximate interpolations to unknown $y(Y)$ or $x(X)$ functions can be made on the basis of observed (Y^i, X^i) pairs, which are subject to the duality partial derivative relations like

those of (6.3)

(9.9) $(\partial x/\partial x_i)/(\partial x/\partial x_1) = y_i/y_1$

                      $(i = 2, \ldots, n)$

    $(\partial y/\partial y_i)/(\partial y/\partial y_1) = x_i/x_1$

Suppose the data we observe were *simultaneously* (q_i) amounts consumed and (x_i) amounts produced in a closed economy, with producers' competitive prices (y_i) identical to those facing consumers (p_i): i.e., suppose $X \equiv Q$, $Y \equiv P$. Then (9.7)'s reversal of our Paasche-Laspeyres inequalities of (7.4) would at first glance seem to threaten us with contradictions of the following type

$$a \leq z \leq b \quad \text{and} \quad b \leq z \leq a$$

Actually, such simultaneous inequalities imply no contradiction but only the equality

$$a = z = b$$

As applied to $q(Q)$, $x(X)$, $p(P)$, and $y(Y)$, this implies that the only admissible changes under our straightjacket of assumptions would be balanced changes in the $(Q = X$ and $P = Y)$ variables. This is balanced growth with a vengeance—not surprising when homothetic tastes encounter homothetic or neutral technical change. With $(Q^1 = \alpha Q^0$ and $P^1 = \beta P^0)$, neither the $x(\ )$ nor the $q(\ )$ functions can be identified, because there is no scatter. However,

(9.10) $x(\alpha X^0)/x(X^0) \equiv \alpha \equiv q(\alpha Q^0)/q(Q^0)$,

          $y(\beta Y^0)/y(Y^0) \equiv \beta \equiv p(\beta P^0)/p(P^0)$,

a wholly natural consistency.

In many cases, as in a comparison of the production potentialities of two regions, we do not know that the x parameter uniformly shifts the frontier *outward*. This is what the investigator wants to infer. Hence, he cannot assume that $\partial f/\partial x$ is one-signed in (9.1). But, on the supposition that we deal with stable competitive[16] prices, with the frontiers always being concave, we can infer an outward or inward shift of X^1's frontier near the point X^0 from the index number comparison

(9.11) $x(X^1, X^0; Y^0) \lessgtr 1$

One-sided inequalities, like those of (7.4′), will be valid in the nonhomothetic case, but of course with signs reversed:

(9.12) $x(X^1, X^0; Y^0) \geq \lambda_q$

(9.12′) $x(X^1, X^0; Y^1) \leq \pi_q$

If $\lambda_q > 1$, (9.12) tells us that $x(X^1, X^0; Y^0) > 1$ and X^1's frontier lies outside X^0. Alternatively, if $\pi_q < 1$, then $x(X^1, X^0; Y^1) < 1$ and we can infer that X^0's frontier lies outside X^1. But, if we are given only (X^i, Y^i) data and $\lambda_q < 1$ and $\pi_q > 1$, no qualitative inference is possible about any shiftings. Since frontiers, unlike indifference contours, can twist in the general nonhomothetic case so as to intersect, we cannot infer anything about π_q from $\lambda_q > 1$, or anything about λ_q from $\pi_q < 1$.

It could happen that *both* situations are simultaneously better than each other in this sense, that there has been a *twist* of the frontiers, as revealed by

(9.13) $x(X^1, X^0; Y^0) \geq \lambda_q \geq 1 > \pi_q$
$\geq x(X^1, X^0; Y^1)$

This implication of inequality of $x(X^1, X^0; Y^0)$ and $x(X^1, X^0; Y^1)$, the former exceed-

ing unity and the latter falling short of unity, would be impossible in the homothetic case (where twists of the frontiers are in any case ruled out); but, as mentioned, it is not surprising in the nonhomothetic case where frontiers may cross, in contrast to the case of noncrossing indifference contours.

We must warn that it is never possible, on the basis of $[Y^1, X^1; Y^0, X^0]$ observations alone, to infer that the one frontier lies *inside* the other in the neighborhood of the latter's observed point. This is because the one-sided inequality of (9.12) then becomes

(9.14) $1 > \lambda_q < x(X^1, X^0; Y^0) \lessgtr 1$

We leave this brief survey with the remark that Moorsteen and Bergson often work, not with our $x(X^1, X^0; Y^\alpha)$ index numbers, but rather with the following variant concept:[17]

---

[16] If technology cannot be "lost" or "forgotten," and if X^0 precedes X^1 in time, then the fact that the earlier options are still available means that the frontier cannot shift inward: at worst one can take convex combinations of points on both frontiers, so that the new concave frontier, if anything, always shifts outward. This, however, assumes that the X vector includes (possibly as negative items) the stock of inputs; if any of the latter are omitted, then reduction of their stock in the background could shift the observed frontier inward. Also, in interregional cross-sectional comparison, as between *U.S.* and *USSR* production potentialities, we cannot assume the same effective laws of technology at both X^0 and X^1; so X^1 need not dominate X^0, and twists of the frontier are admissible.

[17] As mentioned in fn. 4, the Pollak quantity index of demand resembles this Moorsteen-Bergson variant to our $x(X^1, X^0; Y^\alpha)$. Pollak defines his q index by solving $u(\lambda^1 Q^\alpha) = u(Q^1)$, $u(\lambda^0 Q^\alpha) = u(Q^0)$ for the ratio λ^1/λ^0 as a function of $(Q^1, Q^0; Q^\alpha)$. This fails (v^*)'s factor-reversal test but passes the quantity version of (i^*). In the homothetic case, Pollak's $q(\ )$ agrees with our $q(Q^1, Q^0, P^\alpha) = q(Q^1)/q(Q^0)$. It might be pointed out that a price index, different from our $p(P^1, P^0; Q^\alpha)$, could be defined by a logic dual to that of Pollak's here: Define $p\{P^1, P^0; P^2\}$ or λ^1/λ^0 where $u^*(P^2\lambda^1) = u^*(P^1)$, $u^*(P^2\lambda^0) = u^*(P^0)$. For homothetic demand *only* will $p\{P^1, P^0; P^2\} \equiv \rho(P^1, P^0; Q^\alpha)$ and will $p\{, ;\}$ satisfy Fisher's original (i^*) requiring $p\{\lambda P^0, P^0; P^2\} \equiv \lambda$. [Added in proof: Hicks, ch. 19, noting that $\lambda_q > \lambda_p$ in the homothetic case and the case where Q^0 and Q^1 are indifferent, and attributing this to a "substitution effect," writes $\lambda_q - \pi_q$ in the nonhomothetic case where Q^1 and Q^0 are not indifferent, as the sum of such a substitute effect and a so-called "income effect." However, even if no good is inferior, when demand is nonhomothetic, there will always be somewhere southwest of any Q^0 point, an infinity of Q^1 points for which $\pi_q > L_q$. Our attention has been called belatedly to the useful analysis of Nissan Liviatan and Don Patinkin, which among many other points notices the importance of nonhomotheticity. Also to Richard Geary, who attempts to organize the (Q^k, P^k) for N countries where prices are in local currencies by defining 1) certain average world prices, $\bar{p}_i$ in our notation and 2) standardized exchange rate parities for the α country in terms of the hypo-

"What *multiple* of X^1 could have been produced on X^0's frontier? Call it $m(X^1, X^0)^{-1}$. Likewise define $n(X^0, X^1)$ as the *multiple* of X^0 producible on X^1's frontier."

These two last measures, m and n, can be shown necessarily to equal each other only in the homothetic case, and then they will equal our $x(X^1)/x(X^0) = x(X^1, X^0; P)$; but $m(,)$, $n(,)$, and $x(, ;)$ need not agree in the general, nonhomothetic case. Of course, depending upon whether or not $m(X^1, X^0) \lesseqgtr 1$, X^0 lies outside, on, or inside X^1's frontier. In general, it is not possible to say that the $x(X^1, X^0; Y^\alpha)$ concept is more or less useful than the $m(X^1, X^0)$ and $n(X^0, X^1)$ concept; exactly the same one-sided bounds applies, in the nonhomothetic case, to $m(X^1, X^0)$ as $x(X^1, X^0; Y^0)$ but their magnitudes relative to each other are ambiguous.

$$(9.15) \quad \lambda_q \leq x(X^1, X^0; Y^0) \gtreqless m(X^1, X^0) \geq \lambda_q$$

$$\pi_q \geq x(X^0, X^1; Y^1) \gtreqless n(X, X^1) \geq \pi_q^{-1}$$

Only in the homothetic frontier case do we get the two-sided identities

$$(9.16) \quad \pi_q \geq n(X^0, X^1) = x(X^1)/x(X^0)$$
$$= m(X^1, X^0) \geq \lambda_q$$

---

thetical world currency, E^α, so that

$$\overline{P} = [\overline{p}_j] = \left[\sum_{\alpha=1}^{N} E^\alpha p_j^\alpha q_j^\alpha \Big/ \sum_{\alpha=1}^{n} q_i^\alpha \right] \quad (j = 1, \ldots, n)$$

$$E^\alpha = \sum_{j=1}^{n} \overline{p}_j q_j^\alpha \Big/ \sum_{j=1}^{n} p_j^\alpha q_j^\alpha \quad (\alpha = 1, \ldots, N)$$

Then E^α is applied as a deflator to $P^\alpha \cdot Q^\alpha$ to get a measure of real income $E^\alpha P^\alpha \cdot Q^\alpha = \overline{P} \cdot Q^\alpha$. In the easiest cases where we know the exact answer, as in the homothetic case, $n = 2$ and α takes on a continuum with $p_2^\alpha/p_1^\alpha = \pi(\alpha)$, $q_2^\alpha/q_1^\alpha = \theta(\alpha)$, π and θ being observable functions, the Geary measure does *not* give the correct $p(P^\alpha)/p(P^\beta)$ and $q(Q^\alpha)/q(Q^\beta)$ even though these correct functions are uniquely inferrable. So Geary's method seems to be a throwback to the Fisher-Pearson-Frickey mechanical methods. Like them, it may turn out to have some heuristic merits for approximating useful results.

To the extent that the production possibility frontier is almost linear with high elasticity of substitution, λ_q approximates $m(X^1, X^0)$ better than it does $x(X^0, X^1; Y^0)$; to the extent that the frontier has low elasticity of substitution, λ_q approximates $x(X^0, X^1; Y^0)$ better than it does $m(X^1, X^0)$.

Finally, we mention the "Gerschenkron effect," namely that when a society's frontier is augmented more in terms of one good (say, machines) than another (say, bread), the quantity mix of demand allegedly moves to favor the most-augmented good whereas its price ratio moves against that good. This common sense empirical likelihood would be a deductive necessity if tastes for the two goods were homothetic and with normal curvature. For then, from the double-limit theorem of homothetic tastes in (7.3), we can infer

$$(9.17) \quad \pi_q \leq q(X^1)/q(X^0) \leq \lambda_q$$

Hence, we have deduced the well-known phenomenon, noted by Kravis-Gilbert and numerous writers such as Samuelson (1974b).

SERENDIPITY THEOREM: *Each region tends empirically to fare better in terms of a comparison involving its own prices and mix, provided*

$$(9.18) \quad \{(x_2/x_1)^1 - (x_2/x_1)^0\}$$
$$\{(p_2/p_1)^1 - (p_2/p_1)^0\} < 0$$
$$(9.19) \quad x(X^1, X^0; P^1)$$
$$< \pi_q < \lambda_q < x(X^1, X^0; P^0)$$
$$(9.20) \quad n(X^0, X^1)^{-1} < \pi_q < \lambda_q < m(X^1, X^0)$$

Again, there is no advantage or disadvantage in the Moorsteen-Bergson variant of (9.20) over (9.19)'s conventional production index numbers. The proof of $\pi_q < \lambda_q$ in the Gerschenkron case follows immediately by arithmetic from the assumed fact that the $[(p_2/p_1), (x_2/x_1)]$ have a negative Pearsonian correlation coefficient between the two situations (reminding one of the old-fashioned discussions of "weight-bias").

X. Concluding Warning

Empirical experience is abundant that the Santa Claus hypothesis of homotheticity in tastes and in technical change is quite unrealistic. Therefore, we must not be bemused by the undoubted elegances and richness of the homothetic theory. Nor should we shoot the honest theorist who points out to us the unavoidable truth that in nonhomothetic cases of realistic life, one must not expect to be able to make the naive measurements that untutored common sense always longs for; we must accept the sad facts of life, and be grateful for the more complicated procedures economic theory devises.

REFERENCES

S. N. Afriat, "The Theory of International Comparisons of Real Incomes and Prices," in J. D. Daly, ed., *International Comparisons of Prices and Output*, Nat. Bur. Econ. Res. Stud. in Income and Wealth, Vol. 37, New York 1972, 15–94.

A. Bergson, *National Income of the Soviet Union since 1928*, Cambridge 1961.

P. W. Bridgman, *Dimensional Analysis*, rev. ed., New Haven 1931.

F. Divisia, *Économie Rationnelle*, Paris 1928.

F. Fisher and K. Shell, *The Economic Theory of Price Indices*, New York 1972.

I. Fisher, *Purchasing Power of Money*, New York 1911.

———, *The Making of Index Numbers*, Cambridge 1922.

R. Frisch, "Necessary and Sufficient Conditions Regarding the Form of an Index Number Which Shall Meet Certain of Fisher's Tests," *J. Amer. Statist. Assn.*, Dec. 1930, *25*, 297–406.

———, *New Methods of Measuring Marginal Utility*, Tübingen 1932.

———, "Annual Survey of General Economic Theory: The Problem of Index Numbers," *Econometrica*, Jan. 1936, *4*, 1–38.

R. C. Geary, "A Note on the Comparison of Exchange Rates and Purchasing Power Between Countries," *J. Royal Statist. Soc.*, Part I, 1958, *121*, 97–99.

A. Gerschenkron, *A Dollar Index of Soviet Machinery Output*, Santa Monica 1951.

J. R. Hicks, *A Revision of Demand Theory*, Oxford 1956.

H. Hotelling, "Edgeworth's Taxation Paradox and the Nature of Demand and Supply Functions," *J. Polit. Econ.*, Oct. 1932, *40*, 577–616.

H. Houthakker, "Additive Preferences," *Econometrica*, Apr. 1960, *28*, 244–57; "Errata," *Econometrica*, July 1962, *30*, 633.

———, "Some Problems in the International Comparison of Consumption Patterns," in *L'Evaluation et le Rôle des Besoins de Consommation dans les Divers Régimes Economiques*, Paris 1963.

D. M. Iklé, "A New Approach to Index Numbers," *Quart. J. Econ.*, May 1972, *86*, 188–211.

D. Jorgenson and Z. Griliches, "The Explanation of Productivity Change," *Rev. Econ. Stud.*, July 1964, *34*, 249–82.

W. W. Leontief, "Composite Commodities and the Problem of Index Numbers," *Econometrica*, Jan. 1936, *4*, 39–59.

N. Liviatan and D. Patinkin, "On the Economic Theory of Price Indexes," *J. Econ. Develop. Cult. Exchange*, Apr. 1961, *9*, 502–36.

D. McFadden, "Constant Elasticity of Substitution Production Function," *Rev. Econ. Stud.*, June 1963, *30*, 73–83.

L. W. McKenzie, "Demand Theory Without a Utility Index," *Rev. Econ. Stud.*, June 1957, *24*, 185–89.

R. H. Moorsteen, "On Measuring Productive Potential and Relative Efficiency," *Quart. J. Econ.*, Aug. 1961, *75*, 451–67.

R. A. Pollak, "The Theory of the Cost of Living Index," unpublished paper, Univ. Pennsylvania, June 1971.

R. Roy, *De l'Utilité; Contribution à la Théorie des Choix*, Paris 1942.

R. Ruggles, "Price Indexes and International

Price Comparisons," in *Ten Economic Studies in the Tradition of Irving Fisher*, New York 1967.

P. A. Samuelson, *Foundations of Economic Analysis*, Cambridge 1947.

——, "Consumption Theory in Terms of Revealed Preference," *Economica*, Nov. 1948, *15*, 243–58; reprinted in J. E. Stiglitz, ed., *The Collected Scientific Papers of Paul A. Samuelson*, Vol. I, Cambridge 1966, 64–74.

——, "Evaluation of Real National Income," *Oxford Econ. Pap.*, Jan. 1950, *2*, 1–29; reprinted in J. E. Stiglitz, ed., *The Collected Scientific Papers of Paul A. Samuelson*, Vol. II, Cambridge 1966, 1044–72.

——, "Consumption Theorems in Terms of Overcompensation Rather Than Indifference Comparisons," *Economica*, Feb. 1953, *20*, 1–9.

——, "Parable and Realism in Capital Theory: The Surrogate Production Function," *Rev. Econ. Stud.*, June 1962, *29*, 193–206; reprinted in J. E. Stiglitz, ed., *The Collected Scientific Papers of Paul A. Samuelson*, Vol. I, Cambridge 1966, 325–38.

——, "Using Full Duality to Show that Simultaneously Additive Direct and Indirect Utilities Implies Unitary Price Elasticity of Demand," *Econometrica*, Oct. 1965, *33*, 781–96; reprinted in R. C. Merton, ed., *The Collected Scientific Papers of Paul A. Samuelson*, Vol. III, Cambridge 1972, 71–86.

——, "Unification Theorem for the Two Basic Dualities of Homothetic Demand Theory," *Proc. Nat. Acad. Sci., U.S.*, Sept.

1972, *69*, 2673–74.

——, (1974a) "Remembrances of Frisch," *European Econ. Rev.*, 1974 forthcoming.

——, (1974b) "Analytical Notes on Real Income Measures," *Econ. J.*, 1974 forthcoming.

J. A. Schumpeter, *Business Cycles*, Vol. II, New York 1939, 452–58.

R. W. Shephard, *Cost and Production Functions*, Princeton 1953.

H. Staehle, "A Development of the Economic Theory of Price Index Numbers," *Rev. Econ. Stud.*, Feb. 1935, *3*, 163–88.

S. Star and R. E. Hall, "An Approximate Divisia Index of Total Factor Productivity," Univ. British Columbia department of economics disc. pap. 73–19, Oct. 1973.

S. Swamy, "Consistency of Fisher's Tests," *Econometrica*, July 1965, *33*, 619–23.

——, "On Samuelson's Conjecture," *Indian Econ. Rev.*, Oct. 1970, *5*, 169–75.

H. Theil, *Economics and Information Theory*, Chicago 1967.

M. J. Ulmer, *The Economic Theory of Cost of Living Index Numbers*, New York 1949.

H. Uzawa, "Production Functions with Constant Elasticities of Substitution," *Rev. Econ. Stud.*, Oct. 1962, *29*, 291–99.

J. Ville, "The Existence Condition of a Total Utility Function and of an Index of Price," *Rev. Econ. Stud.*, 1951, *19*, 128–32, a translation of a 1946 paper from the *Annales de l'Université de Lyon*.

A. Wald, "A New Formula for the Index of Cost of Living," *Econometrica*, Oct. 1939, *7*, 319–31.

H. Wold, *Demand Analysis*, New York 1953.

210

ANALYTICAL NOTES ON INTERNATIONAL
REAL-INCOME MEASURES[1]

I. *Quantity Index Numbers*

THEORETICAL diagrams can throw light on international index-number approximations to real income comparisons of a rich country (like the United States) and a poorer country (like Italy or India). Waiving discussion of distributional issues, Fig. 1, p. 599, shows a representative man of the rich country sitting on his high indifference curve at A; and a representative man of the poor country sitting on his low indifference curve at B. Man A's expansion of the luxury item X is relatively greater than his expansion of the necessity item Y. Less theoretically inevitable, but (I am told) empirically usual, is the presumption that in the richer countries the prices of luxuries are lower relative to the prices of necessities.[2] I suppose this presumes the poor country has a comparative advantage in necessities, and that there are irreducible transport costs in international trade.

The Engel's path through A is shown as $A'A$ (a straight line only for diagrammatic simplicity, although Afriat (1972) has proposed such an approximation for empirical econometric estimating). The Engel's curve through B is shown as BB'; by Engel's laws that define luxuries, BB' must lie above $A'A$ if the same tastes characterise rich men and poor men and luxuries are posited to be cheaper in the rich country. This assumption of uniform tastes is fairly[3] crucial, since without it the purpose of most quantitative real-income comparisons is obscure. In this brief discussion I operate on the assumption of uniform tastes: a rich fool is merely a poor fool with more real income.

B's real income falls short of A's. By how much? Since B's luxuries are one-sixth of A's, and B's necessities are two-thirds of A's, presumably B's income is somewhere between one-sixth and two-thirds of A's. An index number of B real income, based on A at $1 \cdot 00$ (not 100), presumably lies between $0 \cdot 167 = 1/6$ and $0 \cdot 667 = 2/3$.

The usual economic theory of quantity index numbers, as summarised for example in Samuelson and Swamy (1974), provides more precise real-income definitions. At A's prices, with only three-eighths of A's actual money

[1] I owe thanks to the National Science Foundation for financial aid. I have benefited from conversations and correspondence with Professors Houthakker, Balassa, and David; but none of them is to blame for my shortcomings.

, [2] This presumption, we shall see later, is reversed in the case of personal services. Hair-cuts, domestic servants and other services that have shown no productivity improvements tend to be dear in high-wage countries, as is discussed in the 1964 papers of Balassa and Samuelson cited in my bibliography. Note: throughout, by "luxuries" I mean only goods whose income elasticities exceed unity.

[3] Some progress in analysis can be made even if tastes are assumed to be different, as is shown in Samuelson (1950), Fisher and Shell (1972), and Samuelson and Swamy (1974). Note: the q's of this paper are quantities consumed, not produced. Samuelson (1950) and Samuelson and Swamy (1974) contrast the index number problem involved in production theory.

income, he could be just as well off as he would be at B. (The diagram, we shall see in a moment, tells us this.) So the rich-country quantity index, A_q, is defined as *exactly* $3/8 = 0.375$, which does lie between our broad bounds. But B has only two-sevenths of the income he would need at B's prices to be just as well off as he would be at A. So the (poor country) quantity index, B_q, is defined as exactly two-sevenths $2/7 = 0.286$, which also lies between the broad bounds.

We now have two different exact quantity indexes, which do not agree with each other. Actually, the rich-country index gives a lower estimate of its superiority than does the poor country index; and, even-handedly, the poor country index gives a lower estimate of *its* relative position than does the rich-country index. Evidently, it always looks better to ride the other fellow's horse! This is no accident, being a theorem from our basic axiom that luxuries are relatively cheap in the richer country where they are abundant.

> *Theorem.* If (p_i/p_j) and (q_i/q_j) are (by technology and tastes!) nega-tively correlated and Engel's laws make one set of goods have income elasticities greater than unity and the rest have income elasticities less than unity, then a country's real income position is always less when its own price structure is used to define its real income index number. (I might call this the Engel–Gerschenkron effect.)[1]

Which is *the correct* quantity index, the rich-country index A_q or the poor-country index B_q? There is no sensible way of answering the question, except to say: "On the assumption of the same tastes, both exact indexes will always agree in their qualitative ranking of the two (or more) countries." Perhaps to Americans the more conservative rich-country index will have more

---

[1] Engel's laws refer to the empirical fact that food expenditures are less than unity in income elasticity. The "Gerschenkron effect" refers to his finding that, as a country grows, comparing it with its own past or with a poorer country involves greater estimates of growth if you use poorer-state price weights than if you use richer-state price weights. The reason for this is the negative correlation between relative price changes and relative quantity changes, as discussed in Gerschen-kron (1951). The combination of Engel and Gerschenkron gives the effect here analysed. It is useful to note when it would not and when it would occur. If tastes followed Engel's laws, resource endow-ments were everywhere similar, and technical change between the positions of the poor and rich countries were Hicks-neutral, so that every resource increases proportionally in productivity, then luxuries would be relatively *dear* in the rich country rather than relatively cheap. If necessities are relatively land-intensive and luxuries labour-intensive and if a country is poor only because of high population density, luxuries would again be relatively dear in the rich country rather than cheap. If population densities are fairly uniform but rich countries differ from poor countries only by "Harrod-neutral technical change", where labour alone becomes more productive, then provided Engel's laws do not cause income elasticities to deviate too much from unity, the Rybczynski–Samuelson theorems about incidence on relative prices of changes in supply of factors most inten-sively needed by various goods can give us the relative cheapness of labour-intensive luxuries that accords with the conventional wisdom and the Gerschenkron effect—and with Fig. 1 and Table I. By departing from static competitive assumptions, we can directly explain the cheapness of the goods most important for rich-country consumption along Adam Smith and Allyn Young lines of in-creasing returns: assuming increasing returns and learning by doing, we can deduce along Ohlin and Linder lines the relative cheapness of the goods whose production has expanded most in the advanced countries. Of course, we know from the doctrines of imperfect competition that market price ratios observed in a regime of decreasing costs no longer measure the technological slopes of the economy's production-possibility frontier.

intuitive appeal. Perhaps to Indians the more conservative poor-country index will have more intuitive appeal.[1] Perhaps some analysts will regard it as more even handed and symmetric to split the difference or to take a geometric mean—in the Irving Fisher Ideal Index fashion—of the two exact indexes A_q and B_q, $(A_q B_q)^{\frac{1}{2}}$.

Note: in terms of their own definitions, A_q and B_q—which Samuelson and Swamy write as $q(Q^B, Q^A; P^A)$ and $q(Q^B, Q^A; P^B)$—are each an *exact* index and not an approximation to something else. And some mean of them will be an exact measure of $C_q = q(Q^B, Q^A; P^C)$ for some (alas unknown) P^C somewhere intermediate between P^A and P^B. Because Engel's laws show that goods differ systematically in their income elasticities, the search for a single real-income index number is the search for a chimera. Fortunately, the economic historian looking for "takeoffs", accelerations, industrial revolutions, or only prosaic business-cycle fluctuations, is likely to be told the same conclusive or inconclusive story by the one index as by the other.[2]

Fig. 1 depicts the A_q quantity index as Oa'/Oa, and the B_q index by the necessarily smaller Ob/Ob'. Explanation: a is the intersection of A's tangential budget line with the arbitrary reference ray OC; b is the intersection of B's

---

[1] In his maiden analytical publication, ECONOMIC JOURNAL, September 1908, pp. 472–3, the young Keynes noted that the official 1905–7 real wage comparison of Ireland or the Midlands to London, being based on a fixed-weight arithmetic mean of price relatives based on London, understated London's real wage as compared to shifting the base to Ireland and thereby using in effect the harmonic mean, which is known to be less than the arithmetic. (I have provided the missing explanation; incidentally if the 4 : 1 value weights for non-rent items and rents had been appropriate for all places, the weighted geometric mean would have been optimal—not because it is "between" the two other means but because the economic theory of index numbers tells us that "Cobb–Douglas" indifference contours lead canonically to the weighted geometric mean.) I do not know Keynes's 1909 Adam Smith Prize Essay on index numbers, but by 1911 Keynes, in his comments on Hooker's 1890–1910 study of price movements (*Journal of Royal Statistical Society*, 75, December 1911, pp. 45–7) somehow took for granted that the most recent period base, or Paasche price index, was to be preferred to the original period base of Laspeyres (which Hooker had used). Against the authority of Edgeworth and other savants who thought that weights do not matter much (they would not if *random* weights were used on a great number of price relatives drawn from the *same* skewed universe), Keynes pointed out that L_p/P_p is great when the periods are apart by decades, a valid generalisation beyond Hooker's sample of the negative correlation of price and quantity relatives to be expected empirically. The alchemy from talent to genius had not yet begun.

[2] Suppose, as with the fourteenth line of footnote 1, p. 596, that the only difference between India at B and America at A is Harrod-neutral technical change that increased the productivity of U.S. labour, but if you can imagine it, leaves America and India with the same population/land density. Then imagine America, the tortoise, standing still at A while India the hare rapidly undergoes Harrod-neutral invention until it catches up to A. Let this technical change proceed at a steady absolute or percentage rate. Then plotting the arc of rising A_q and rising B_q will show the latter beginning below the former but both converging to unity. Clearly there is a certain *bias* which makes A_q average out to a higher growth rate than B_q, even though, by hypothesis, both are generated by the same steady pace of Harrod-neutral innovation. There is thus some case to be made for measuring real growth rates by some more even-handed mean, such as the Fisher Ideal Index $(L_q P_q)^{\frac{1}{2}}$. Alternatively, one might argue: "The A_q path is the genuine one, in that its price reference never changes. The slowdown on the B_q path, which will be greatest at first and least as the measures converge near to each other and 1, is not so much a slowdown in technical progress (by hypothesis this is steady in the Harrod-neutral sense); rather it is the case that along B_q, the decline in the terms of trade of the luxury good (which is dictated by the Engel–Gerschenkron-effect hypothesis) means that the price weight is declining of the faster-growing luxury good and thereby genuinely lowering the B_q average rate of growth."

tangential budget line with OC. B' is where B *would* be if, at his own prices, he were on the same indifference contour $B'A$ as A; A' is where A *would* be if, at his prices, he were on the same indifference contour BA' as B. And a' is the intersection of the A' tangent line with OC; b' the intersection of the B' tangent line with OC. Clearly since the BB' and $A'A$ Engel's paths cut the OC ray from above and b and b' lie outside a' and a, we have the inequality

$$B_q = Ob/Ob' < Oa'/Oa = A_q . \qquad . \qquad . \qquad (1)$$

I am assuming that the reader, from Samuelson and Swamy or elsewhere, knows that Ob/Ob' measures $\Sigma P^B Q^B/\Sigma P^B Q^{B'}$ and $Oa'/Oa = \Sigma P^A Q^{A'}/\Sigma P^A Q^A$, and realises that country B could have been put in the denominators if it had been chosen as the base-reference point.

TABLE I

International Quantity and Price Comparisons

	Country A			Country B		
	P^A	Q^A	$Q^{A'}$	P^B	Q^B	$Q^{B'}$
Y necessity	$10	3	$1\frac{1}{2}$	#1,000	2	$3\frac{3}{5}$
X luxury	$5	6	$1\frac{1}{2}$	#2,000	1	$5\frac{1}{5}$

Official Exchange Rate 150 #/$* = R^{BA}

$$\Sigma P^A Q^A = \$60 \qquad\qquad \Sigma P^B Q^B = \#4,000 \qquad\qquad \Sigma P^A Q^B = \$25$$

$$\Sigma P^A Q^{A'} = \$22.50 \qquad\qquad \Sigma P^B Q^{B'} = \#14,000 \qquad\qquad \Sigma P^B Q^A = \#15,000$$

$$A_q = \frac{\Sigma P^A Q^{A'}}{\Sigma P^A Q^A} = \tfrac{3}{8} = 0.375 \qquad B_q = \frac{\Sigma P^B Q^B}{\Sigma P^B Q^{B'}} = \tfrac{2}{7} = 0.286$$

$$L_q = \frac{\Sigma P^A Q^B}{\Sigma P^A Q^A} = \tfrac{5}{12} = 0.417 \qquad P_q = \frac{\Sigma P^B Q^B}{\Sigma P^B Q^A} = \tfrac{4}{15} = 0.267$$

$$P_q \leqslant B_q < (A_q B_q)^{\frac{1}{2}} < A_q \leqslant L_q$$

$$0.267 \leqslant 0.286 < 0.327 < 0.375 \leqslant 0.417$$

$$\Sigma P^B Q^B/\Sigma P^A Q^A = \frac{4,000}{60} = 66.7\#/\$, \quad A_p = \frac{66.7\#/\$}{0.375} = 166\#/\$$$

$$B_p = \frac{66.7\#/\$}{0.286} = 233\#/\$, \quad \sqrt{(B_p A_p)} = 196\#/\$$$

$$L_p = \frac{\Sigma P^B Q^A}{\Sigma P^A Q^A} = \frac{\#15,000}{\$60} = 250\#/\$, \quad P_p = \frac{\Sigma P^B Q^B}{\Sigma P^A Q^B} = \frac{\#4000}{\$25} = 160\#/\$$$

$$P_p \leqslant A_p < (A_p B_p)^{\frac{1}{2}} < B_p \leqslant L_p$$

$$160\#/\$ < 166\#/\$ < 196\#/\$ < 233\#/\$ < 250\#/\$$$

Table I provides an independent description of the problem, supplementing Fig. 1's data by information on absolute domestic-currency prices, P^A and P^B.

Unfortunately the statistician—Kravis, Gilbert, C. Clark, David, Balassa, ...—cannot calculate these exact quantity index numbers until he knows the exact shape of the indifference curves. Generally, he knows at best, from one set of statistical quantity data and local-currency price data, the points A and B and the tangent slopes running through those respective points. He does not know A' and B' even approximately. All he can know is that B' lies above the tangent line through A and that its needed intersection b' lies below the b'' intersection of the ray and a line through A parallel to B's budget line. Likewise, all he can know about A' is that it lies below the a'' intersection of the

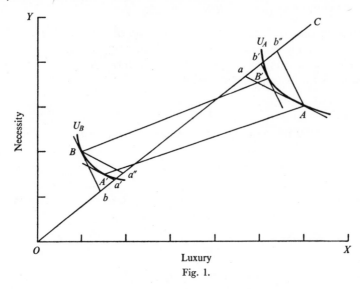

Fig. 1.

ray and a line through B parallel to A's budget line. So, at best, by use of the well-known Laspeyres and Paasche index numbers, L_q and P_q, the statistician can get single bounds on these respective exact quantity index numbers A_q and B_q. That is, Laspeyres

$$L_q = \Sigma P^A Q^B / \Sigma P^A Q^A = Oa''/Oa$$

gives an upper bound to the true rich-country index A_q; and Paasche $P_q = \Sigma P^B Q^B / \Sigma P^B Q^A = Ob/Ob''$ gives a lower bound to the true poor-country index B_q, because b'' must lie above b'.

Always, we have for smooth strongly convex tastes the well-known bounds:

$$P_q = Ob/Ob'' < Ob/Ob' = B_q \qquad . \qquad . \qquad (2a)$$
$$L_q = Oa''/Oa > Oa'/Oa = A_q \qquad . \qquad . \qquad (2b)$$

In general, we cannot combine these into valid double bounds. Only under special taste assumptions—such as all income elasticities the same, at unity— can different real incomes be given valid double bounds.

However, under our special Engel–Gerschenkron-effect assumption about technology and tastes, inequality (1) holds and we can combine it with (2a) and (2b), to get the valid double bounds:

$$P_q \leqslant B_q < A_q \leqslant L_q \cdot \qquad . \qquad . \qquad . \qquad (3)$$

For L-shaped non-smooth indifference contours that admit of no substitutability at all, the outside equalities will actually prevail.

This completes the basic theoretical exposition.[1] From it, I find it hard to support the enthusiasm in David (1972, 1973) for preferring the Laspeyres L_q index over the Paasche P_q index. The contention in Balassa (1973, 1974) that some splice of L_q and P_q is in order, such as Fisher's Ideal Index $(L_q P_q)^{\frac{1}{2}}$, does seem a bit more even-handed[2] in terms of pure theory.

II. *Price Index Numbers*

What does all this mean for price indexes, which up until now I have not considered at all? I assume that the typical researches into international prices, such as those of Professor Kravis, are designed to provide price indexes that can be used as deflators of relative money expenditures to give best estimates of true quantity indexes. I shall here confine myself to single observations on Q^A and Q^B and their concomitant domestic-currency price vectors P^A and P^B. Then—as in Samuelson and Swamy—it is well known that the two exact price indexes, A_p and B_p, are given by the factor reversal identities

$$A_p A_q = B_p B_q = \Sigma P^A Q^A / \Sigma P^B Q^B = \text{money-expenditure index} \quad (4)$$

However, it is also well known from index number theory that these factor reversal identities hold for Laspeyres and Paasche indexes only when we *cross* them with each other

$$L_p P_q = P_p L_q = \Sigma P^A Q^A / \Sigma P^B Q^B \quad . \quad . \quad (5)$$

In terms of these identities, the price index dual to (1) becomes

$$A_p < B_p . \quad . \quad . \quad . \quad . \quad (1^*)$$

The price index dual to (2) gives for smooth strongly convex tastes the following valid single bounds:

$$B_p < L_p . \quad . \quad . \quad . \quad . \quad (2a^*)$$

$$A_p > P_p . \quad . \quad . \quad . \quad . \quad (2b^*)$$

And (3)'s valid quantity double bound gives rise to the following dual double bound on price indexes:

$$P_p \leqslant A_p < B_p \leqslant L_p . \quad . \quad . \quad . \quad (3^*)$$

Again, it does seem even-handed to use an Ideal index approximation $(P_p L_p)^{\frac{1}{2}}$ as a deflator. Also, even if Professor David does for some reason wish to give

[1] Reference may be made to the Samuelson–Swamy demonstration of how to make exact statements about (local) degree of accuracy of index numbers and of how optimally to utilise (P, Q) observations of many situations to estimate the indifference contours.

[2] Samuelson–Swamy prove that, if income elasticities are unity, and $A_q \equiv B_q$, then the Ideal index (and any symmetric mean of L_q and P_q) are locally most-accurate estimates of A_q and B_q. However, with the deviation from unitary income elasticities dictated by Engel's laws a better compromise between L_q and P_q may be computable from Kravis-type data on *many* countries by the approximation methods sketched in Samuelson–Swamy.

primacy to the United States (or rich country) quantity index, A_q, he would seem safer with the (2b*) P_p Paasche single bound[1] on the A_p price index, and he would presumably be more accurate since he would be nearer to his desideratum in the double bound (3*).

III. *Purchasing Power Parity Doctrines and Calculations*

One February day in 1973 the United States moved from being decidedly the most affluent nation to being definitely below Sweden. Does anybody believe in such violent 24-hour changes in relative real incomes? You must if you rely on official or market exchange rates for your purchasing power parity deflators. To avoid such nonsense, which becomes apparent nonsense only on the occasions when exchange rates happen to make great moves in short periods of time, we need the tools discussed here and estimated statistically by scholars like Professor Kravis. Anyone who studies Table I's discrepancy between (*a*) the official exchange rate of 150 of B's # for each 1 of A's \$ and (*b*) actual A_p, B_p, L_p, P_p price index numbers, will realise the basic reality: If Swedish real incomes *per capita* exceeded those in the United

---

[1] Professor David raises the interesting question as to whether it is not preferable to stay with a biased one-sided bound, since at least you then know where you stand with respect to the true measures as against some splicing of two-sided bounds. Thus, let one of the true quantity measures defined for some definite price structure—be $T_q(t)$ at time t. Suppose you wish to make statements about $T_q(1)$, $T_q(2)$, $T_q(3)$, ..., such as whether there is an acceleration:

$$T_q(3) - T_q(2) \gtreqless T_q(2) - T_q(1).$$

Then, are you safer to work with what you know to be always an upper-bound, $L_q(1)$, $L_q(2)$, $L_q(3)$ rather than with what may average out to be more accurate, namely $[L_q(t) \, P_q(t)]^{\frac{1}{2}}$ but whose bias you cannot know? Or safer always to work with what you know to be a lower bound, such as $P_q(t)$? As far as guessing at the signs of accelerations, one-sided bounds *cannot* give you safe judgments. While the difference between 7 and 6 is assuredly equal to that between 6 and 5, the difference between a number less than 7 and a number less than 6 cannot be known to agree in sign with the difference between that number less than 6 and a number less than 5. Inequalities are preserved only when one forms positive sums from them, not when one forms differences as in growth-rate measurements.

Professor David also puts stress on the apparent empirical fact that price ratios are less variable for the United States than for other countries; presumably this has something to do with its continental size or statistical coverage, since there is no law that presumes greater price stability from mere affluence itself. Does this differential price stability militate in favour of the rich-country price and quantity indexes (and the P_p or L_q bounds)? I am not sure. If the price variation is genuine and not statistically spurious, variability around B would enable us to get a more accurate guess of B's indifference contours near B than of A's indifference contours near A. This knowledge would be most useful for approximating to A_q. On the other hand, even if the variable price and quantity data were both genuine, it would be B's *short-run* contours that are traced out; and there is good reason to doubt that such short-run contours tell us much about our needed long-run contours of taste. If the price data around B simply reflect errors of observation and noise, there is something to be said for concentrating on L_q rather than P_q. But where does that leave us with respect to L_p and P_p? Do we assume that the Q^B data are also noisy? If so, what reliance can we place on the $\Sigma P^A Q^B$ and $\Sigma P^B Q^B$ terms that consumers of Kravis–David index numbers will need in their deflating operations? If, as can easily be imagined, the Q^B data are better than the P^B data, what assumption can you make about the $\Sigma P^B Q^B$ data used when deflating by a price index? Surely, it would then be better to estimate L_q directly if you can. But in years after a Kravis study you may only have $\Sigma P^A Q^A$, $\Sigma P^B Q^B$, L_p, and P_p data. Perhaps, for David reasons, the last may be least reliable of all; then you might be best advised to use $[\Sigma P^A Q^A / \Sigma P^B Q^B]/L_p$ as a lower-bound estimate of the poor-country's quantity index, B_q!

States in post-devaluation March, they did so *already* in pre-devaluation January; any instantaneous cheapening of certain Swedish imports in February relative to her exports does bring a real improvement in her real income, but careful calculation of the resulting change in $q(Q^B, Q^A; P)$ will show that such effects are not quantitatively as large in the short as in the long run—and they cannot validly be extrapolated to provide reliable quantitative estimates of the ultimate long-run benefits from appreciation-induced movements in the terms of trade.

A price index between countries whose goods are denominated in different currencies is, by definition, a measure of "purchasing power parity". Thus, in Table I, A_p and B_p are of the dimensionality "$\#/\$$", or "number of units of B's currency per unit of A's currency". There is no reason, though, for the official exchange-rate parity to agree precisely with purchasing power parity: thus, in Table I, the official rate is 150 $\#/\$$ at the same time that the A_p and B_p rates are respectively 166 $\#/\$$ and 233 $\#/\$$. Of course, under perfect competition, free trade without tariffs, quotas, or exchange controls, relative prices of one good could not deviate regionally if transport costs were zero. In that case only, *each* competitive good's international price ratio—*e.g.* p_x^B/p_x^A—would have to equal the official free exchange rate *exactly*, as a result of quick acting competitive arbitrage; and what is true for each and every good, must be true for the average index number of price, A_p and its then precise equivalents B_p, P_p, L_p, $\sqrt{(P_p L_p)}$. Fig. 1 would have to be redrawn under costless free trade, to have A and B lie on the same Engel's path with $A_q \equiv B_q \equiv L_q \equiv P_q$.

What Gustav Cassel, and Ricardo before him, had in mind in connection with the doctrine of purchasing power parity was something more than the above trivial doctrine of arbitrage among near-transport-free staple commodities. In any case, what they should have[1] had primarily in mind was the homogeneity fact lying at the root of the classical Quantity Theory of Money: namely that a scale change in all nominal prices of P^A would ultimately have no substantive effects on any of the *real* magnitudes, Q^A, Q^B, p_x^B/p_y^B, p_x^A/p_y^A, in a classical determinate system. Thus, if Cassel could imagine a balanced World War I inflation that raised *all* P^A prices 100 % more than all P^B prices —and if [if!] nothing else substantive changed—then Cassel could predict that *in the long run* the exchange rate of A would halve relative to that of B.

Such dogmas, useful or misleading, are no concern of the statistician tackling an actual Fig. 1 or Table I. To the knowing eye these tell their own story. Thus, the fact that p_x^B/p_y^B is not equal to p_x^A/p_y^A, being rather four times as large, tells us something about transport costs, tariffs, or competitive imperfections between the two regions. In terms of transport costs as the sole impediment to free trade, it is evident that both goods could *not* be transportable at *less* than 100 % markup on their F.O.B. prices. If m_y is the percentage

---

[1] As Balassa reminds me, Cassel is so prolific and careless a writer that it is rather a thankless task to defend him against vulgar errors.

markup of the delivered price of necessities exported from B to A calculated at the free official rate, and m_x is the corresponding percentage markup of luxuries exported from A to B, competitive arbitrage imposes the inequality

$$\frac{p_x^B/p_y^B}{p_x^A/p_y^A} \leqslant (1+m_x)(1+m_y) \qquad . \qquad . \qquad . \qquad (6)$$

Only if the equality holds in (6) can the goods be moving both ways in international trade. Because the direction of trade could be reversed if the price conditions were right, an opposite-signed inequality holds in (6) in terms of $(1+M_x)^{-1}(1+M_y)^{-1}$, where M_x and M_y are percentage markups for exports in the opposite direction. Indeed (6) is the relative price version of the absolute price arbitrage inequalities

$$(1+M_x)^{-1}p_x^A R^{BA} \leqslant p_x^B \leqslant (1+m_x)p_x^A R^{BA} \qquad . \qquad . \qquad (7)$$

$$(1+M_x)^{-1} \leqslant \frac{p_x^B/p_x^A}{R^{BA}} \leqslant 1+m_x$$

where R_{AB} is the free exchange rate of number of B's # unit per A's \$, p_x is any good's competitive price, and m_x and M_x are respective transport-cost or tariff markups of x when exported from B to A and A to B.

Since a valid exact price index—like A_p, B_p, or $p(P^B, P^A; Q)$ in Samuelson and Swamy—must be a general mean of the individual-goods price ratios, p_x^B/p_x^A, the second form of (7), gives us the wide bounds on permissible deviations of free exchange rates from exact purchasing power parities:

$$(1+\max\{M\})^{-1} \leqslant \frac{p(P^B, P^A; Q)}{R^{BA}} \leqslant 1+\max\{m\} \qquad . \qquad (8)$$

where $\max\{M\}$ and $\max\{m\}$ are the largest of the percentage markups.

These bounds are too wide to be of any usefulness—since some so-called "domestic goods" involve m's and M's that are practically infinite.

Years ago Houthakker (1962) and I (1964)[1] discussed whether narrower bounds could be found on purchasing power parity. If there were a tremendous number of footloose *rentiers* (as there are not), who would move between

---

[1] In my (1964) footnote 2, I quote a 1962 passage of Houthakker: "...recent figures indicate that an average basket of commodities bought for \$1 in the U.S. would cost only 3.11 marks in Germany, while the official exchange rate is four marks to the dollar. We may say, therefore, that the dollar was overvalued with respect to the mark by 22 per cent." That his underlying argument is of greater analytical complexity is shown by the following quotation I reproduced two pages later from Houthakker's 1962 Joint Economic Committee congressional testimony: "...For foreign trade to be in long-run balance (still abstracting from capital movements) it is necessary roughly speaking that unit labor costs, converted at official exchange rates, be the same everywhere... Information about unit labor costs in different countries is hard to obtain directly but there is an indirect and much simpler way of making the comparisons. In the long run wages are equal to the marginal product of labor in terms of commodities sold locally and for export. Domestic production competes with imports, which means that prices are equalized and that marginal product can also be measured in terms of commodities consumed rather than commodities produced. The competitive position of different countries can therefore be evaluated from the relative price levels of consumption goods...not only [of] commodities that enter into international trade, but also...all

A and *B* whenever *their* cost of living was not equalised and would do so in such numbers as to force by their own shifts in demands enough changes in the regional price levels to bring about equality in their cost of living, we would have

$$R^{BA} = p(P^B, P^A; Q^{\text{rentier}}) \qquad . \qquad . \qquad . \qquad (9)$$

This is a caricature of the Cassel position, although in the text of a dogmatic writer like Cassel one can find plenty of such unconscious self-parodies.

Actually, Balassa (1964) and I appealed in the 1964 discussions to some systematic forces that might be expected to invalidate any purchasing-power parity approximation like (9). We, independently, pointed out that in advanced countries personal services are relatively dear compared to goods— hair-cuts versus autos, maids versus washing machines. Hence, poor countries are good places to retire to or to vacation in; but not enough retirees do relocate to keep an advanced country from seeming to have an "overvalued" currency in terms of Houthakker-like calculations of $p(P^A, P^A;)$.

Our analysis permits us now to appraise the likely direction of bias that results from the often-met estimates of real income based on official currency parities. Thus, suppose the *per capita* income of an American is reckoned in dollars as $\Sigma P^A Q^A = \$5,000$; the *per capita* income of a Japanese is reckoned in yen at $\Sigma P^B Q^B = 900,000$ yen; and the actual official exchange rate is at $R^{BA} = 300$ yen to the dollar. Then as an alleged approximation to the true A_q, B_q, or some blend of them, we are often presented with the currency-parity estimate

$$O_q = [\Sigma P^B Q^B / \Sigma P^A Q^A]/R^{BA} = [900,000/5,000]/300 = 0·6 \quad (10)$$

What are the presumed inequalities relating true A_q or B_q and O_q? No one answer can be universally true as a matter of pure logic alone. However, if one had for a sample of places and times, observations on A_q and B_q, or at least on L_q and P_q, one might regress the crude O_q measures for that sample on one of these actual measures or on some blend of them such as $(L_q P_q)^{\frac12}$. And then one might form, in the David or Balassa or some other manner, an empirical rule of thumb of the four-ninths, five-ninths, or such-and-such fashion.

Why might one expect that O_q has a downward bias compared to a poor country's true position relative to a rich? In 1964 I argued that this is a reasonable expectation on the basis of the following hypotheses or axioms (and I believe this is consonant with Balassa's arguments):

(1) Some domestic goods exist in both countries, with heavy transport costs that inhibit their easy movement in international trade and that permit

---

other commodities." In terms of Samuelson (1971) and the present, we can agree that the ratio of wage rates, $(W^B/W^A)/R^{BA}$ has an equilibrium level, r^*; and that therefore $R^{BA} > (W^B/W^A)/r^*$ makes A have an overvalued currency. But Professor Houthakker and I agree that this is a far cry from identifying $(W^B/W^A)/r^*$ itself with *any* price index of the form $p(P^B, P^A)$, once transport costs are not negligible. Events since 1962 validated Houthakker's surmise about an overvalued dollar, a surmise I then shared despite my quibbles of logic.

of price divergences from crude purchasing-power-parity arbitrage relations. Examples are hair-cuts, basic house construction, etc.

(2) For whatever reason, the technical advances as between rich and poor countries and as between later and earlier times tend to be concentrated in non-domestic goods. Thus, haircuts everywhere take 20 minutes of a man's time; but manufactures and commercial agricultural products fall in real-resource costs through time, and tend to involve higher productivity in rich countries almost as a condition of their being rich countries.

Then it follows, regardless of whether domestic goods tend to have high or low income elasticities, that domestic goods will be relatively cheap in poor countries in comparison with crude p-p-p arbitrage calculations. (When I travel abroad and find hair-cuts cheap relative to converted United States prices, I know I am in a low-wage country with adverse double-factoral terms-of-trade relative to the United States.) But note that *non*-domestic-goods relative price levels, $p(P^B, P^A;)$ are truly approximated well by R^{BA} p-p-p calculations.

So, combining the non-bias of non-domestic goods with the systematic bias of domestic goods, we derive the inequality we seek as

$$R^{BA} > p(P^B, P^A;) \qquad . \qquad . \qquad . \qquad . \qquad (11)$$

$$O_q = [\Sigma P^B Q^B / \Sigma P^A Q^A]/R^{BA} < [\Sigma P^B Q^B / \Sigma P^A Q^A]/p(P^B, P^A)$$
$$= \text{true real-income measure} \quad (12)$$

This substantiates the Balassa–Samuelson contention that free-trade exchange rates, even in the absence of exchange controls and disequilibrium, tend to look "over-valued" for the rich countries in crude equal-cost-of-living comparisons when domestic goods are relatively dear in the high-income countries. (In Fig. 1, based upon the opposing assumption of cheap luxuries in the rich country, the parity of the dollar "looked" undervalued at $150 \,\#/\$$, even though Fig. 1 might have been describing a long-run equilibrium situation. In Table I,

$$O_q = [\Sigma P^B Q^B / \Sigma P^A Q^A]/R^{BA} = [4{,}000/60]/150 = \tfrac{4}{9}, \qquad (13)$$

which exceeds all the true measures for the poor country relative to the rich country and makes the latter look worse than it truly is.)

IV. *General Analysis*

We have just noted that those domestic goods loosely called "services" are one item of luxury goods. Thus, A. G. B. Fisher and Colin Clark proposed three stages for a developing economy: first agricultural, then manufacturing, then services. Clearly, if *all* luxuries were in the form of such services, and if such domestic goods were deemed to be relatively dear in rich countries, we should have a reversal of the Engel–Gerschenkron axiom upon which Fig. 1 and the inequalities of (1)–(5) are based. For, it will be recalled, our earlier analysis assumed that luxuries are relatively cheap in the rich country, so that $B_q < A_q$.

Let us see what results from reversing the basic empirical axiom. The reader can now alter Fig. 1 in the following way: interchange B and A', and A and B'; then the upper Engel line will have to be labelled $A'A$ rather than BB', and the rich country's line will now be above the poor country's instead of below. With this reversal of roles, we see that the inequalities of (1) and (1*) must now be exactly reversed, becoming

$$A_q < B_q, \quad B_p < A_p \qquad . \qquad . \qquad . \qquad (14)$$

And now the double bounds of (3) and (3*) become disappointingly ambiguous, taking the form

$$L_q \gtreqless A_q < B_q \gtreqless P_q, \quad L_p \gtreqless B_p < A_p \gtreqless P_p \qquad . \qquad . \qquad (15)$$

No longer do the observable Laspeyres and Paasche indexes bracket with certainty any true measures, which is not to deny that a symmetric mean like $(L_p P_p)^{\frac{1}{2}}$ may still have some appeal as being more "even-handed".[1]

It would be desirable to get empirical information on whether the Engel–Gerschenkron case dominates or its opposite. At first, I fell into the common trap of thinking that the strong empirical evidence that P_q is almost always found to be less than L_q settled the issue. But deeper analysis of the general case shows that the sign of $(L_q - P_q)$ does not unconditionally govern the sign of $(A_q - B_q)$, or vice versa, i.e., only $L_q - P_q < 0 > B_q - A_q$ is ruled out; hence, $L_q - P_q > 0$ permits $B_q - A_q \gtreqless 0$. Fig. 2 shows the general case. Only the regions above the indifference contour matter; and any point like A must fall into one of these three regions α, β and γ, which are formed by the intersection of the ray through B, OBB'', and the Engel's curve through B, BB'.

It will be seen that all points in α obey the Engel–Gerschenkron axiom and satisfy $B_q < A_q$ as in (1). But in β and γ that axiom is reversed; and we have $A_q < B_q$, as in (14). However, it is only in β that we have a reversal of the usual Kravis–Könus relation $P_q < L_q$. When all income elasticities are unity, P_q can never lie above L_q. But it is wrong to fall into the common error of thinking that two points, B and A that are "close together" must satisfy $P_q < L_q$. All the points in β satisfy $L_q < P_q$, and clearly there are an infinity of points in β that are as near as we wish to B. The germ of truth in the belief that $L_q < P_q$ is less to be expected than its opposite rests, perhaps, in the vague realisation of β as being only one region in comparison with α and γ as being two regions; and, more cogently, in the realisation that, to the degree that income elasticities fail to diverge much from unity, BB'' and BB' differ not too much in angle and form a β region of limited area.[1]

[1] In α, P_q and L_p bracket both B_q and A_q. In β, A_q and B_q bracket both L_q and P_q; so the latter necessarily bracket some weighted average of the former. In γ, P_q and L_q may bracket both A_q and B_q, or one only of them, or may be bracketed by both of them; what is impossible is that the maximum of one pair be less than the minimum of the other.

Once we have two good Santa Claus examples, it is a hard empirical task to determine which axioms apply. Price elasticities and income elasticities often get confounded in reality. Thus, as Professor Balassa has reminded me, a rich country may spend relatively more on services than a poor even though its physical q_2/q_1 is less than the poor country's, provided its p_2/p_1 is

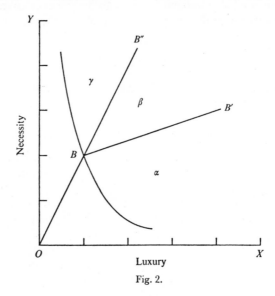

Fig. 2.

sufficiently greater: in 1950, Gilbert–Kravis find that the United States spends relatively less on services than Italy. This does not deny that services are luxuries. Rather it tells us that supplying services is an inferior good: in an affluent society that is at all egalitarian, few will be willing to undergo the subordination and obsequiousness associated with personal services. Processed food, T.V. dinners, and household gadgets are the ersatz services of the rich nations.

V. *Summary*

The complex arguments can be briefly reviewed.

1. If domestic goods are relatively dear (cheap) in the rich countries, those countries will have their real income overstated (understated) if we use exchange rates to calculate O_q, as in (10). This will be the case whether the domestic goods tend to be luxuries or to be necessities. Crude purchasing-power-parity calculation of the type $p(p^B, p^A;)/R^{BA}$ will make the rich country's currency look "undervalued" ("overvalued") even if true balance of payment equilibrium prevails.

2. If luxuries tend to be relatively cheap in the rich countries, the usual Paasche–Laspeyres index numbers will bracket the true real-income measures. The exact true measure calculated in a country's own prices will

give it a lower exact real-income measure than if calculated in the other country's prices. To use a blend of the Paasche and Laspeyres indexes, such as Fisher's "Ideal" geometric mean, does seem more even-handed than to use either alone.

3. If luxuries (like services) tend to be relatively dear in the richer countries, the true measure using a country's own prices will give a more favourable comparison for it than if using the other country's prices.

4. Only empirical research can establish whether relative p's and q's are negatively correlated, and whether luxuries are relatively cheap or dear on balance.

PAUL A. SAMUELSON

Massachusetts Institute of Technology.

Date of receipt of typescript: December 1973.

ANNOTATED REFERENCES

Afriat, S. N. (1972), "The Theory of International Comparisons of Prices and Outputs," in D. J. Daly (ed.), *International Comparisons of Prices and Incomes*, Vol. 37 in National Bureau of Economic Research's Conference on Research in Income and Wealth (Columbia University Press, New York). Contains bibliography of earlier works. His linear approximation, or "marginal price indexes", appear in his section 4.

David, P. A. (1972), "Just How Misleading Are Official Exchange Rate Conversions?" ECONOMIC JOURNAL, 82 (September), pp. 979–90; Balassa, B. (1973), "Just How Misleading Are Official Exchange Rate Conversions?: A Comment," *ibid.* 83 (December); David, P. A. (1973), "The Rule of Four-Ninths Upheld: A Rejoinder to Professor Balassa," *ibid.* 83 (December); Balassa, B. (1974), "The Rule of Four-Ninths: A Further Comment," *ibid.* (June). This debate raises dozens of interesting issues: some are resolved by the present theoretical analysis; others could benefit from appropriate extensions of it.

Fisher, F. M. and Shell, K. (1972), *Economic Theory of Price Indices* (Academic Press, New York).

Gilbert, M. and Kravis, I. B. (1954). *An International Comparison of National Products and the Purchasing Power of Currencies* (Paris, OECD). This has long been the standard empirical reference, along with its more elaborate 1958 sequel; the forthcoming multi-country researches under Kravis's general direction will provide a similar basic benchmark. Gerschenkron, A. (1951), *A Dollar Index of Soviet Machinery Output*, 1927–8 to 1937 (Santa Monica, California, Rand Corp.).

Houthakker, H. (1972), "Exchange Rate Adjustment," *Factors Affecting the U.S. Balance of Payments: Joint Economic Committee Compilation of Studies* (Government Printing Office, Washington D.C.), pp. 289–304; Samuelson, P. A. (1964), "Theoretical Notes on Trade Problems," *Review of Economic Statistics*, 46 (May), pp. 145–54, reproduced as ch. 65 in Samuelson (1965), *Collected Scientific Papers*, II (MIT Press, Cambridge, Mass.); Balassa, B. (1964), "The Purchasing Power Parity Doctrine: A Reappraisal," *Journal of Political Economy*, 72 (December), pp. 584–96; Samuelson, P. A. (1971), "An Exact Hume–Ricardo–Marshall Model of International Trade," *Journal of International Economics*, 1 (February), pp. 1–18, ch. 163 in *Collected Scientific Papers*, III (1972).

Samuelson, P. A. and Swamy, S. (1974), "Invariant Economic Index Numbers and Canonical Duality: Survey and Synthesis," *American Economic Review* (December). This gives a fairly complete survey of the existing theory of economic index numbers, bibliography, and various extensions to the theory and to the goodness of approximating techniques.

REMEMBRANCES OF FRISCH

P. A. SAMUELSON*

M.I.T., Cambridge, Mass. 02139, U.S.A.

The paper reviews Frisch's enormous contribution in the progress of economics over the last decades. Special attention is paid to Frisch's work on 'macrodynamic modelling', utility measurement from demand data index number theory and axiomatics in economics.

1. Introduction

Ragnar Frisch dominated analytical economics from the early 1930's founding of the Econometric Society to his wartime internment in a Nazi concentration camp. He combined fertility and versatility with depth. Although this was the golden decade in which the world came to realize his genius, both in the years before, and the years after, Frisch made numerous important contributions to (a) economic theory, (b) economic measurement, (c) economic policy, and (d) scientific methods in statistics, mathematics, and economics. Arrow's 1960 Frisch *Festschrift* review and Johansen's 1970 Nobel survey of Ragnar Frisch's scientific achievements tell the story so well that I can here be more impressionistic and personal.

2. Macrodynamic modelling

The number one problem between the great wars was macroeconomic: boom and bust. Frisch, who was a great coiner of names (e.g. 'econometrics' itself), almost invented the word 'macroeconomic'. In fact, when Alvin Hansen replied to an inquiry from Edwin Nourse as to who did originate it, Hansen said: 'I don't know. Probably Samuelson'. When this was put to me, I in turn replied: 'No. I popularized the term and embalmed it in a textbook. But it was not in my first, 1948 edition; I find this to my surprise, since it was already popular then. Surely, it was Ragnar Frisch in his classic 1933 Cassel *Festschrift* piece on models that dynamically resonate to exogenous shocks'. To verify this, I examined the cumulative index to *Econometrica*. Sure enough, this index designated articles of the 1930's as macroeconomic, microeconomic, etc. But on going to those back issues, I could not find the term there. The indexer had used hindsight in

*I owe thanks to the National Science Foundation for financial aid and to Norma Wasser for editorial assistance.

his classifications. What I did find there was the Frischian adjective 'macro-dynamic', a coinage embraced by Tinbergen, Kalecki, and other pioneers. [Incidentally, macroeconomic models – and I believe the word 'model' itself may have been introduced by Frisch in its present economic sense – have two distinguishable meanings: the first and most common has a connotation of Keynesian effective demand among economy totals, as with the simplified Keynesian system $Y = I + c(Y)$; the second which really belongs to micro-economics as applied to simplified global models or aggregates, is of the J. B. Clark distribution type as where aggregate output is produced by aggregate land and aggregate labor and becomes distributed by marginal productivity equations such as $w = \partial Q(L, T)/\partial L$ and $r = \partial Q(L, T)/\partial T$. Cursory research on the origin of macroeconomics, to my surprise, turned up the word's first use in the second sense, in the Lawrence Klein 1946 *Econometrica* debates about aggregation in (essentially micro) models. It is a small step from 'macrodynamics' as applied to, say, $\varepsilon \, dY/dt = I - [Y - c(Y)]$ to 'macroeconomics' that includes the latter as well as the statical $0 = I - [Y - c(Y)]$. Since macroscopic versus microscopic are terms long familiar in the thermodynamic contrast between regarding a balloon of gas as (a) an elastic substance whose pressure and volume are reciprocals at constant temperature or as (b) the resultant of a large number of unobserved particles whose mean number and intensity of collisions with the balloon's walls can be deduced by kinetic theory – it was virtually inevitable that economics would evolve toward the convenient macro–micro terminology.]

Frisch's 1933 Cassel paper employed the Wicksellian imagery of the economy as a rocking horse set into characteristic periodicity by the impact of enough random shocks to offset its frictional dampening. Simplest representations of these, which depart from his literal 1933 text, would be linear:

$$\ddot{y} + \varepsilon \dot{y} + a^2 y = s(t), \qquad\qquad 0 < \varepsilon \doteq 0, \tag{1}$$

$$\Delta^2 Y + a^2 \Delta Y + (a^2 - \varepsilon)Y = S(t), \qquad 0 < \varepsilon \doteq 0, \quad a^2 < 4,$$

where $s(t)$ and $S(t)$ are exogenous forces that could be stochastic, and $\Delta Y(t) = Y(t+1) - Y(t)$. The impact of a dramatically written exposition that comes at the right time is hard to exaggerate. I remember how my old teacher Schumpeter, perhaps Frisch's most fervent admirer, marveled at the miracle that imaginary numbers, $1 = \sqrt{-1}$ in e^{it}, could drive 'real' alternating current and 'actual' business cycles. I don't think he ever really understood that the complex number system is merely a convenient way of handling the algebra[1] of the real sinusoidal

---

[1] All complex roots of characteristic polynomials associated with the constant-coefficient differential and difference equations must, since they arise from real coefficients, come in conjugate complex pairs. When one fits real boundary conditions for the functional equations, the complex constants of the exponential components also come in conjugate pairs, so that *all* imaginaries drop out when we employ real trigonometric functions in the solutions. Since complex numbers are looked upon by sophisticated mathematicians as paired real numbers subject to certain rules, one could demystify them completely by working only with such 2-element

solutions associated with (1)

$$k(t) = c_1 e^{-\alpha t} \sin (\beta t + c_2), \qquad \alpha < 0, \tag{2}$$

$$K_t = C_1 \gamma^t \sin (\delta t + C_2), \qquad |\gamma| < 1,$$

that served as decaying weights in the solutions to (1) of the form

$$y(t) = \int_{-\infty}^{t} k(t-\tau)s(\tau)d\tau, \tag{3}$$

$$Y(t) = \sum_{-\infty}^{t} K_{t-\tau}S_\tau.$$

Even prior to 1933, Frisch had worked out the 'echo' fluctuations of replacement or renewal theory. Tinbergen had studied the dynamic functional equations of the shipbuilding cycle. And at the end of the 1920's, Henry Schultz, Ricci, Tinbergen and Rosenstein–Rodan had independently worked out the cob-web dynamics of H. L. Moore's lagged-supply, contemporaneous-demand identified econometric model.

As a young student, what I found mystifying was the meaning of the infinite number of sinusoidal components of Frisch's more transcendental mixed difference-differential equation of the following type:

$$\dot{y}(t) + ay(t-1) = s(t), \qquad 0 < a < -e^{-1}, \tag{4}$$

and its Hertz–Herglotz–Lotka solution in the infinite Dirichlet series form

$$y(t) = \sum_{-\infty}^{\infty} a_j e^{\lambda_j t} = \sum c_j e^{\alpha j} \sin (\beta_j t + dj), \tag{5}$$

where $(\lambda_1, \lambda_2, \ldots)$ are the infinite complex roots of (2)'s associated transcendental equation

$$\psi(\lambda) = \lambda + ae^{-\lambda} = 0. \tag{6}$$

It is easy to verify that two roots, λ_1, λ, will be negative real numbers; and Frisch showed that the rest must be conjugate complex numbers with real parts more negative than either real root. Since World War II, such 'retarded' equations have been much studied by electrical engineers here and in Russia, as can be seen in Bellman–Finney; but after 1911, similar methods were often used on the

vectors and recasting even the Fundamental Theorem of Algebra in terms of 2-dimensional vector additions, substraction, rotations, etc.

Again and again, methods of pioneers could be usefully employed after they are gone. When I read Tobin's devastating 1970 QJE critique of the power of observed leads and lags between money and income to bear out Friedman's monetaristic causality, it occurred to me that the Kennelly complex impedance algebra could have been used to portray the leads and lags between sinusoidal $M, \dot{M}, Y, \dot{Y}$, etc.

Lotka–Feller equations of renewal and reproduction.[2] I satisfied myself that, for $y(t)$ prescribed on the interval $-1 \leq t \leq 0$ as $\bar{y}(t)$, one could recursively calculate (2)'s solution by quadratures

$$y(t) = -a \int_{k-1}^{t-1} y(\tau)d\tau + y(k), \qquad k \leq t \leq k+1. \tag{7}$$

And knowing that an arbitrary function, the profile of Helen of Troy in Schumpeter's example taken from the *Encyclopedia Brittanica*, can be expanded in terms of a Fourier-like expansion of infinite sinusoidals, my uneasiness concerning the meaninglessness of the separate harmonic components was put to rest. (I ought, though, to have realized that these components had this much reality: if exogenous sinusoidal forces were put on the system with about the periodicity of say the third root, λ_3, namely $s(t) \doteq a \sin (\beta_3 t + b)$, then there might be some detectable response in the form of an amplified $y(t) = c(\sin \beta_3 t + d)$ component. Since, however, $\alpha_3 > 1$, it is doubtful that this resonance could in fact be observed amidst the noise of the lower and higher harmonics.

In leaving Frisch's work of the 1930's on stochastic difference, differential, and other functional equations, let me point out that a great man's work can, in its impact on lesser men, have bad as well as good effects. Thus, by 1940, Metzler and I as graduate students at Harvard fell into the dogma – I use the word 'dogma' in the non-pejorative sense of Crick's dogma on DNA and RNA, as a leading hypothesis – that all economic business-cycle models should have *damped* roots. We accepted Frisch's criticism of the Kalecki procedure of imposing constraints on his parameter-estimating equations so that roots would be neither damped nor undamped; to explain Kalecki's supposed constancy-of-amplitude-of-capitalism's-fluctuations, Frisch's mechanism of exogenous shocks seemed preferable, in that it led to stationary time series rather than random-walk build up of variance incompatible with Kalecki's trendless amplitudes; besides we thought that, empirically, the U.S. economy of the 1933–1940 period behaved like a system incapable of self-fulfilling bootstrap returns to prosperity.

Since simulation experiments on present-day macromodels of Tinbergen–Klein type seem to confirm this dampedness feature, what was so bad about the dogma? Well, it slowed down our recognition of the importance of non-linear autorelaxation models of van der Pol–Rayleigh type, with their characteristic amplitude features lacked by linear systems. And, in my case, it led to suppressing development of the Harrod–Domar exponential growth aspects that kept thrusting themselves on anyone who worked with accelerator–multiplier systems.

[2] A feature of *Econometric* meetings around the onset of World War II was somewhat comical polemics between A.J. Lotka and Gabriel Preinrich, the latter criticizing the use of such series expansion in solving $B(t) = \int_0^n \alpha(a)\beta(a)B(t-a)\,da$, where $\alpha(a)$ and $\beta(a)$ are the age-specific survival and female-fertility functions. Lotka's claim to scientific fame needs no mention; but Preinrich, also a lone-wolf scholar, was one of the first to anticipate the Bellman dynamic programming technique of working backwards from the terminus iteratively, this in connection with the optimal-time-to-replace-equipment problem.

3. Microeconomic theory and measurement

Much of Frisch's energy from 1925 to 1935 was devoted to utility measurement from demand data. In this, as in his early index-number interests, he was much affected by Irving Fisher's 1892 (and 1927) efforts. Frisch's visit in the early 1930's to Yale and the University of Minnesota did much to spread his fame.[3] He, Fisher and Schumpeter were the leaders in founding the *Econometric Society* and Frisch was for many years the strong editor of *Econometrica*.

Since observed demand behavior on an individual's (P, Q) choices is invariant under a monotone stretching, $f\{u(Q)\}$, of any arbitrary cardinal indicator of utility, how could Frisch or Fisher hope to measure $u(Q)$ from $Q = D[e; P]$ data, where $Q = (q_1, \ldots q_n)$, $P = (p_1, \ldots, p_n)$, and $e = \Sigma PQ = \Sigma p_j q_j$? The trick, of course, is to postulate that for some reason there exists an additive form, $u = f_1(q_1) + f_2(q_2, \ldots, q_n)$. In that case, only for $f\{u\} = a^2 u \pm b$ would the 'independence' of q_1 and q_n be maintained in the sense of $\partial^2 f\{u\}/\partial q_1 \partial q_2 \equiv 0$. Rarely has anyone found much empirical warrant for the assumption that $\partial(p_n/p_2)/\partial q_1 = 0$ vanishes or is in some sense small. So why were Frisch, Fisher, and their many readers so interested in such statistical measurements? The answer, I suppose, lay in their strong interest in making policy welfare pronouncements about how to frame redistributive taxation that would maximize total social utility.

After Bergson's 1938 *Quarterly Journal of Economics* clarification of the ordinal nature of social welfare functions, there was perhaps less reason for attaching importance to such cardinal measurements. Harsanyi's 1955 work on welfare economics and stochastic rationality, however, resurrected additive cardinality of utility relevant by reference to Bernoulli–Ramsey–Savage stochastic decision making. However, this need not involve the same $f\{u\}$ stretching as the one that yields the additive-tree form $f_1(\ ) + f_2(\ )$.

Criticisms of a $f_1(q_1) + f_2(q_2, \ldots, q_n)$ specification, like those above, have very properly themselves been subjected to criticism. Arrow's 1960 appreciation of Frisch suggests that my own earlier criticisms have been too strong. He may well be right. The matter is worth objective reexamination.

First, one must agree with Arrow that there is more interest today in the axiomatics and the possibilities of additive-preference structures than there was in the 1940's. This is primarily due to von Neumann and Morgenstern's successful resurrection of the criterion of maximizing under uncertainty the expected value of a cardinal utility function of outcomes that is unique up to a linear transformation. The fact that psychologists have been using and testing additive structures is also part of the intellectual atmosphere. However, as is well known,

---

[3]On one of Frisch's periodic visits to Cambridge, he distressed Schumpeter by insisting on taking the subway – which was actually the rational way of going from Harvard Square to the rail station for everyone but Schumpeter.

the plausible additivity characterizing probabilities as applied to *mutually-exclusive* outcomes or states of the world tells us little or nothing about the plausibility of *non*-stochastic demand relations like $\partial(p_n/p_2)/\partial q_1 \equiv 0$.

Second, Arrow is quite correct in his Popperian view that finding out what valid *restrictions* can be put on the empirical facts is what science is all about. If one could learn from data, or be able to propose from plausible analysis of experience (and later verify the plausibility of the hypothesis), that $\partial(p_n/p_2)/\partial q_1 \equiv 0$ or $\partial \log (p_n/p_2)/\partial \log q_1 \equiv 7 \times 10^{-8}$, this would be a scientific triumph – much like learning that all apples released from rest fall four times as far in 2 short ensuing periods as they do in 1 (and, because of discernible friction, come to err a bit from this on the underside). But the goal of sharpening down one's hypotheses, of limiting generality, Arrow properly reminds us must be put to the test of evidence. 'The moon is made of green cheese' is a methodologically flawless hypothesis: a color photographer in a cheese shop can even provide some empirical warrant for it; and it had never been refuted by (naive!) evidence before the last decade of rockets; nevertheless, ridding science of such *false* limitations on generality, is also what science is about. (Drilling to find where oil isn't differs not all that much from drilling to find where it is.)

Third, turning to the testimony of evidence, I believe Arrow is quite right to correct any overstatement to the effect that Fisher, Frisch and other analyzers of demand data had performed *no* testing of their hypotheses to see whether the data testified against them. For $n = 2$ and $p_2/p_1 = R(q_1, q_2)$, an observed surface, there are plenty of ways of testing whether there exists any $f_i(q_i)$ such that $R(q_1, q_2) = f_2'(q_2)/f_1'(q_1)$. Of course, this testing can't be done with 3 points like (1, 1) (1, 2), (2, 1); but it can be done by addition of (2, 2), although there would remain the problem of stochastic variation, errors in observation, and the issue of when an hypothesis that is not borne out *exactly* is borne out 'tolerably'. Popper would say it should not be left to the critics of cardinal-utility measuring to work out these empirical testability requirements and to carry them out on the data: we should all be our own critics, imperialistically reserving the fun for ourselves. It is not my impression that prior to the 1940's much stringent testing had been done by friends or foes of additivity, or that there was much available data worth doing it on. I am not sure that the situation has changed much in this respect; and my amateurish sampling years ago of psychologists' experimentings did not put to rest my concern in this matter.

Fourth, in the absence of definitive experimental or other observations, one relies on looser experience: on judgment itself based on historical and cross-sectional observations. Is it plausible that a substance like sugar has the needed property of independence, $\partial(p_i/\partial p_j)/\partial$ sugar $\equiv 0$? Surely lemon demand is affected? And other calorie demand? And insulin demand? I know a Nobel organic chemist who seriously thinks that sucrose may be the villain in modern degenerative diseases. So $\partial\{p_{\text{wheel chairs}}/p_{\text{cadillacs}}\}/\partial$ sugar may be appreciable. Are these fanciful speculations? Then replace them by your own honest reflections on the matter. I am not so much interested here in persuading anyone, or myself, on the issue as in asking the following hard question: 'As against any such doubts based on loose experience, how much weight should a fair man give to a demonstration that on some sample of budget data, $\log(p_2/p_1)$ is (if it is) approximately the same shaped function of x_2 at one level of x_1 as at another?' My own temptation would be to say: 'If $p_2/p_1 = R(x_1, x_2)$ data can be conveniently graduated by $\log(p_2/p_1) = \log f_2'(x_2) - \log f_1'(x_1) = g_2(x_2) + g_1(x_1)$, I'd not pass up the opportunity just because of casual folk-wisdom. But if different ethical programs were to hang on the correctness of the specification, I'd insist upon a much more rigorous testing of whether $\partial^2 \log(p_2/p_1)\partial \log x_1 \partial \log x_2$ was zero or virtually so.'

Finally, turning to what use can be made of the utility measurements by welfare economics, let's stipulate that my demand is generated by $f\{q_1^{0.4} + q_2^{0.4}\}$. Suppose yours is too. Or suppose yours is generated by $f\{-q_1^{-2} - q_2^{-2}\}$ or $f\{q_1^{0.39} + q_2^{0.39}\}$. What difference ought this to make for progressive taxation, or for a vote on a redistributional rationing proposal that is not Pareto-optimal? Reread the Fisher-type literature on this with an open mind and you may be left with my impression that the most important step of all has received relatively little attention.[4] To add to the difficulty of the problem, suppose all women gamble to maximize expected value of $-\{(q_1^{0.4} + q_2^{0.4})^{2.5}\}^{-6}$ and all men gamble to maximize expected value of $-(q_1^{-2} + q_2^{-2})^{+3}$. If I've managed my arithmetic right, their bets and portfolio decisions will be the same; but their demand behavior will be different, the women so to speak being shrewder substituters of one good for another when relative prices change. Would Fisher tax men and women differently? Would you want to?

I am trying to make several points. Ramsey–Neumann–Savage–Marschak cardinal utility is not at all the same as Fisher–Frisch cardinal utility. Along the lines argued in my 1965 piece commemorating Abba Lerner's 60th birthday (and argued in Rawl's book on justice), I could make a case for some relevance for F–F utility. Here are examples:

[4] Fisher's beautifully exposited 1927 Clark paper, after realizing (p. 779) that people will ask whether we can 'properly compare her [one 1900 woman's] want [utility or marginal utility] for eggs or dollars with that of another woman', answers 'Yes – approximately at least . . . [because] in actual practical human life, we do proceed on just such an assumption. . . . Philosophic doubt is right and proper, but the problems of life cannot, and do not wait . . . By common sense we cut our gordion knots.' Etc. etc. Even if you can swallow this, why work with $f_1(q_1) + f_2(q_2)$ rather than $f\{f_1(q_1) + f_2(q_2)\}$, which leads to entirely different conclusions about progressive taxation? And why, in discussing the bearing of cardinal utility measurements for tax policy, put all the weight of the argument on the one laconic sentence (p. 185): 'This is all on the assumption that the tax is to be laid according to the principle of equal [utility] sacrifices to people of different incomes.' Equal-sacrifice indeed: is there a more gratuitous precept of justice? Frisch's 1932 discussion is more eclectic: he considers a variety [of what many will consider equally gratuitous traditional precepts], and correctly states what the flexibility or elasticity of marginal utility of income implies for taxing according to each alternative criterion; but he never chooses among them, and never discusses the crucial question: 'Why work with $f_1(q_1) + f_2(q_2, \ldots) = u$ rather than with $f\{u\} = e^u$ or any other stretching?'

1. All people gamble to maximize expected value of $q_1^{0.9} + q_2^{0.9}$. If each thinks he is as likely to have high incomes as low, all will unanimously vote for a completely egalitarian tax system (incentive effects assumed ignorable). The same will be true if all people gamble to maximize expected value of $q_1^{0.4} + q_2^{0.4}$ or of any strictly-concave $u(q_1, q_2)$. But suppose there are some disincentive effects that all people are somehow symmetrically exposed to and that the dead-weight loss from these increases with the degree of egalitarian-progressiveness of the tax system. Then a society made up solely of the former group – being less risk averse and less appreciative of mutual-insurance social programs – will *unanimously* vote for *less* progression of the tax system than a society made up solely of the latter more-risk-averse group.

The above arguments are highly abstract and unlikely to be applicable in real world situations where those who can rationally know that they are likelier to end up with silver spoons will never agree on unanimous introduction of egali-tarian measures. But the above arguments, invoking R–N–S–M utility, are logically valid. Can anything like them be found for Fisher–Frisch utility's possible relevance? Let me try with the following, even more esoteric, argument.

2. Men spend and act to maximize expected value of $q_1 + q_2$. Women spend and act to maximize $(q_1^{0.4} + q_2^{0.4})^{2.5}$. Both are indifferent to the risks of fair gambling. Neither would attach importance to redistributive taxes if each believes that every person has an equally-likely shot at both high and low incomes. Assume also that the two goods are producible at constant labor costs. How would each person vote on the following proposal: 'Society will allocate its fixed total labor at random among Σq_1 and Σq_2. Those totals will be allocated at random among the individuals. How much of society's labor would you be prepared to sacrifice permanently for the privilege of being able to swap your rations with others who by chance get different (q_2/q_1) allocations from your own?' In a society of men only, the unanimous vote would be: 'Pay nothing for the swapping privilege.' In a society of women only, a definite positive pay-ment could be deducted beyond which there would be no unanimous vote forthcoming. Notice, and this is the point of the exercise, Frisch's measurement from demand data of what he calls flexibility of marginal utility, 0.6 for women and 0 for men, does have some relevance for the welfare voting. [But it does so, not for the light it throws on how marginal utility falls *with income* – as risk tolerators, neither men nor women have any falling off of marginal (R–N–S–M) utility! – but rather for the light it throws on the elasticity of substitution *between* goods along an indifference curve and what this implies for people's tolerance for *distortion of proportions* of their consumption goods.] Note, though, the existence of a F–F additive cardinal utility was not really involved. To see this, consider $p_2/p_1 = R(q_1, q_2) \equiv R(q_2/q_1)$, $(q_2/q_1)R/R' = \sigma > 0$, but $\partial^2 \log R/\partial q_1 \partial q_2 \neq 0$ and $R(q_2/q_1)$ not equal to $(q_2/q_1)^\gamma$ for any γ. Then Frisch could never measure cardinal utility his way. Yet if both men and women are risk tolerant and women have a lower (no longer constant) σ at every (q_2/q_1)

than men do, then the same argument about a female society unanimously voting to pay more for Pareto-optimal swapping privileges might still be made.

3.1. Index number theory

Even if measurement of cardinal utility is deemed unimportant for its own sake, we can be grateful for the advances in demand analysis that were spin offs from Frisch's interest in utility. Index number theory in particular was noteably added to by Frisch. His masterly 1936 survey and other writings on this subject would be valuable, even if one had limited interest in the utility-measurement model

$$u = f_1(q_1) + f_2(q_{\text{II}}[q_2, \ldots, q_n]), \qquad f_i'' < 0, \tag{8}$$

$$q_{\text{II}}[\lambda Q] \equiv \lambda q_{\text{II}}[Q],$$

where u is to be maximized subject to the budget constraint

$$p_1 q_1 + p_{\text{II}} q_{\text{II}}[Q] = e, \tag{9}$$

$$p_{\text{II}} = p_{\text{II}}[p_2, \ldots, p_n] = \min_{q_{i+1}} \sum_{2}^{n} p_i q_i / q_{\text{II}}[q_2, \ldots, q_n].$$

Here I have used modern duality theory, in the 1974 Samuelson–Swamy fashion, to analyze the quantity index $q_{\text{II}}[Q]$ and its conjugate price index $p_{\text{II}}[P]$.

One innovation proposed by Frisch, which is related to earlier work done by Bowley and Könus, is his Double-Expenditure method. Confronted with two price situations P^0 and P^1, and given knowledge of two Engel's consumption-income-path data for a rational person, $Q = D[P^0/e]$ and $Q = D[P^1/e]$, how shall we guess what point $Q^1 = D[P^1/e^{1*}]$ is 'almost' on the same level of indifference as a given point $Q^0 = D[P^0/e^{0*}]$? Frisch's solution is to pick e^{1*} such that

$$\Sigma P^1 Q^1 \cdot \Sigma P^0 Q^1 = \Sigma P^1 Q^0 \cdot \Sigma P^0 Q^0. \tag{10}$$

For homothetic or unitary-income elasticity demand, this is equivalent to use of Fisher's Ideal index number; namely, pick e^{1*} so that

$$[\Sigma P^1 Q^1 / \Sigma P^1 Q^0]^{\ddagger} [\Sigma P^0 Q^1 / \Sigma P^0 Q^0]^{\ddagger} = 1. \tag{11}$$

Könus–Buscheguennce and S.S. Alexander have proved that the Ideal index will be exact for a homogeneous quadratic, as for example $u = q_1 q_2$, $\log u = \log q_1 + \log q_2$; here that Double-Expenditure method would also be exact for such a Cobb–Douglas Bernoulli case. Samuelson–Swamy have proved that the Ideal index has high degree local accuracy for the general homothetic case; so the Double-Expenditure method must share in this local accuracy, independently of Bowley–Frisch–Wald quadratic specification. Frisch's 1938 numerical examples suggest that, in some non-homothetic cases at least, the Double-Expenditure method will be more accurate than the Ideal index (which is not surprising in that Samuelson–Swamy found that the Ideal index loses its local-accuracy property when homotheticity is denied); and in his 1939 editorial footnote on Wald's quadratic method, he reports that numerical experiments show the Double-Expenditure method to be more accurate than Wald's formula as often as Wald's is more accurate than it. Using the Samuelson–Swamy power-series methods, someone should be able to answer the unresolved question :'Knowing two near-by Engel's curves, generated by $P^1 = P^0 + \varepsilon \Delta P^0$, around some base point Q^0 the true quantity index number $q(Q^1, Q^0; P^0)$ will be expressible by a power series in ε. So will the Ideal index number formula. So will Frisch's double-expenditure formula. So will Wald's general quadratic formula. Query 1: How many terms vanish in the difference between the true formula and each of the proposed formulas in the non-homothetic case? Which has the most vanishing coefficients? Among the best formulas from this point of view, is there any smallness of absolute value of the last non-vanishing coefficient that would make one good formula better than another?'

These seem to me answerable questions. My guess is that Wald's formula cannot be beat, and that it always has its 2nd degree coefficient in ε^2 vanish; whereas the Ideal index, in general, will have a non-vanishing 2nd degree coefficient. I suspect that the Double-Expenditure formula may share the Wald ε^2 local-accuracy problem: if it does, its simplicity recommends it a best method when observations are in hand on 2 Engel's paths; if my guess is bad and the Double-Expenditure formula does not have as many vanishing coefficients in ε as Wald's formula, this would go a long way toward offsetting the testimony of Frisch's arithmetical examples.

Just as one brings a wreath to the shrine of a fallen warrior, one brings as tribute to a great scholar a scientific finding in his own tradition. As a different species in the same genus as Frisch's Double-Expenditure method, let me suggest a plausible variant, which may be called 'The mean of the under-compensated and overcompensated states'. Like Frisch and Wald, I assume we know 2 nearby Engel's paths: the function $Q = D[e; P^0]$ and $Q = D[e; P^1]$. How shall we find, corresponding to a point $Q^0 = D[e^0; P^0]$ a new point $Q^{10} = D[e^{10}; P^1]$ such that approximately $u[Q^{10}] \doteq u[Q^0]$?

To do so, I propose we solve the easy equation for the *under*compensated p^1 income e^{1L}, and the *over*compensated P^1 income, e^{1U}, as roots of the respective Laspeyres and Paache equations:

$$\frac{\Sigma P^0 D[e^{1L}; P^1]}{\Sigma P^0 Q^0} = 1 = \frac{\Sigma P^1 D[e^{1U}; P^1]}{\Sigma P^1 Q^0}. \tag{12}$$

Then let the desired e^{10} be *any* symmetric mean of the calculated lower e^{1L} and upper e^{1U}. Since it was proved in my 1953 paper on over- and under-compensated demands that their mean has an osculating higher-order approximation to the just-compensated Slutsky–Hicks demand, it is reasonable to hope that this proposed method has the highest order local accuracy obtainable, better perhaps than the Ideal index for the posed problem, as good as Wald's more complicated formula and no worse than the Double-Expenditure method of Frisch. If I had Frisch's buoyant energy and drive, I would apply this method to his 1938 numerical examples to provide light on the method's practical accuracy.

3.2. Axiomatics and index numbers

Particularly in his early years, Frisch made two interesting contributions to the fascinating, sometimes overrated, field of axiomatics. As Arrow reminds us, in Frisch's first 1926 venture into economics, he began with an excellent axiomatization of utility and of utility differences. This both resolved some of the well-known ambiguities in Pareto's work and anticipated the similar ideas of the mid-1930's associated with such names as Lange, Bernardelli, Phelps Brown, Allen, Samuelson, Alt and many others. Then there was his interesting 1930 analysis of the mechanical tests which Irving Fisher had proposed that a good price and quantity index number should satisfy. What is interesting about this is his proof of an Impossibility Theorem, which in logic is of the same form as Arrow's more important 1949–1953 Impossibility Theorem on Non-Existence of a 'Well-Behaved' Constitutional Welfare Function.

In effect, Frisch proves that no formula exists for a price and quantity index which (i) will be a generalized mean of price or quantity ratios, (ii) will have the transitivity (or 'independence of irrelevant alternative') property of satisfying the 'circular reversal' test of invariance under transformation of the base situation, and (iii) will satisfy the so-called 'factor-reversal' test, so that the product of the price and quantity index numbers will equal the index number of expenditure on the goods.

Samuelson–Swamy show that, when one leaves the swamp of mechanical index number construction for the firm terrain of the economic theory of index numbers, there do after all exist solutions that meet all reasonable requirements. This is not a conclusion that Frisch would have found repugnant or surprising, since his 1936 article on the economic indexes mentions (p. 10) that prices and quantities *cannot* be regarded as independently variable if we are dealing with utility-maximizing demand data. A brief sketch of this discussion will be useful, particularly since it can now resolve in the negative the open question of whether the Cobb–Douglas geometric-mean case is the *only* one that generated completely 'self-dual' demand functions and satisfies the spirit of the Fisher–Frisch test axioms in their strong form.

To explain all this, I write down the price index on a 4-n variable function,

$$f(p_1^1, \ldots, p_n^1, q_1^1, \ldots, q_n^1; p_1^0, \ldots, p_n^0, q_1^0, \ldots, q_n^0) \qquad (13)$$
$$= f(P^1, Q^1; P^0, Q^0),$$

a formulation which, so to speak, provides the important zeroth-axiom of the model. In its weak form, the system would write down the quantity index as a possibly different function of 4-n variables with the positions of the P's and Q's interchanged. In its strong (gratuitously strong, in my opinion) form, the *same* $f(\ )$ formula is to apply to quantities, but of course with the transposition of variables $f(Q^1, P^1; Q^0, P^0)$. As we'll see, only in the singular case of self-dual demand, where $Q = D[P/e]$ and $P/e = D^{-1}[Q] = D[Q]$, will the strong axiom be of any economic relevance.

Ignoring demand dependences between variables, Frisch and Fisher impose certain 'desirable' tests as axioms on the $f(\ )$ function. These are usually six in number. However, Samuelson–Swamy and other commentators have shown that two of these are misconceived: the requirement for dimensional invariance is not optimally framed; and the regularity condition, that no partial derivative of $f(\ )$ shall go to zero or infinity, is not only seen to be undesirable on reflection but can also be shown to involve a self-contradiction within the economic analysis of dual demand – so that *any* axiom system possessing it as an axiom will spawn a trivial Impossibility Theorem.[5] Even if someone hesitates to jettison these two axioms, he will find that the basic Impossibility Theorem is proved from the subset of 4 axioms that I do retain.

Here then are the strong test-axioms:

(i) $f(\lambda P^0, Q^1; P^0, Q^0) \equiv \lambda$,   'generalized mean',

(ii') $f(P^1, Q^1; P^0, Q^0)f(P^0, Q^0; P^1, Q^1) \equiv 1$,   'time-reversal',

(ii) $f(P^2, Q^2; P^1, Q^1)f(P^1, Q^1; P^0, Q^0)f(P^0, Q^0; P^2, Q^2) \equiv 1$,

'circular reversal',

(iii) $f(P^1, Q^1; P^0, Q^0)f(Q^1, P^1; Q^0, P^0) \equiv \Sigma P^1 Q^1 / \Sigma P^0 Q^0$,

'factor-reversal'.

Remark: In the more-general 'weak' form, we'd replace $f(Q^1, P^1; Q^0, P^0)$ by a separate function $g(Q^1, P^1; Q^0, P^0)$, requiring it also to satisfy (i), (ii'), and (ii). Then it is easy to show that when demand is not homothetic, the general case with $D[P/e] \neq eD[P]$, no pair of index numbers can satisfy (ii) and both (i) and (iii): the usual economic definition makes the quantity-index violate (i) in the general case; but Pollak and others, operating in the same tradition as the

[5]Fisher and Frisch are right in pointing out that inventing one new product, whose price previously was to effectively infinity, often confers only a limited, finite benefit on the consumer. But that does not justify their 'determinateness axiom' in the crude form they give it. Also, why deny there might be subsets of goods that are indispensable in the sense that no increments in other goods could compensate fully for their becoming unavailable? Why rule out oxygen in advance? Also, one can agree that changing units from single eggs to dozens of eggs should not matter, any more than changing dollars to cents should matter. But proper use of dimensional analysis merely requires that any $f(\ )$ formula adjusted to one set of units be *readjusted* to another set; it does *not* require that $f(\ldots, \alpha p_i^1, \ldots, \alpha^{-1} q_i^1 \ldots; \ldots \alpha p_i^0, \ldots \alpha^{-1} q_i^0, \ldots) \equiv f(\ldots, p_i^1, \ldots, q_i^1, \ldots; \ldots p_i^0, \ldots q_i^0, \ldots)$. Thus $f = \Sigma P_j^1 / \Sigma P_j^0$ is not ruled out on dimensional grounds; for if this formula were valid in one set of units, it would be transformable at a different set of units into a new formula $f = \Sigma \alpha_j p_j^1 / \Sigma \alpha_j p_j^0$.

Moorsteen production analysis, defines the quantity index to satisfy (i) and violate (iii). In the unitary-income-elasticity homothetic case, as we'll see, all of (i), (ii), (iii) – and a foriori (ii') – are simultaneously satisfied.

From (ii) alone, we easily deduce an infinity of solutions all of the form

$$f(P^1, Q^1; P^0, Q^0) \equiv cf(P^1, Q^1)/f(P^0, Q^0), \tag{14}$$

where the constant c equals $f(P^2, Q^2; P^2, Q^2)$ for arbitrary (P^2, Q^2). If we adjoin to (ii) either (i) or (iii), we easily deduce that $c = 1$ as (ii') requires. Hence, (ii') can be eliminated as an axiom and proved as a theorem in any model that involves (ii) and one of the other axioms.

An infinity of solutions of (ii) and (i) exist, all of the form

$$\frac{f(P^1, Q^1)}{f(P^0, Q^0)} \equiv f(P^1)/f(P^0) \equiv \frac{\lambda^{-1} f(\lambda P^1)}{f(P^0)}. \tag{15}$$

Thus, $f(P)$ must be homogeneous of the first degree, and independent of the Q's! To prove this verify the homogeneity from

$$\frac{f(\lambda P^0, Q^0)}{f(P^0, Q^0)} \equiv \lambda. \tag{16}$$

And verify the independence of the Q's from

$$\frac{f(\lambda P^0, Q^1)}{f(P^0, Q^0)} \equiv \lambda, \tag{17}$$

regardless of differences between Q^1 and Q^0.

What solutions, if any, are there to (ii) and (iii)? One obvious, if trivial, solution is

$$f(P^1, Q^1; P^0, Q^0) \equiv \Sigma P^1 Q^1 / \Sigma P^0 Q^0$$

itself! But, as can be easily verified, it does not satisfy (i) as well as satisfying (ii) and (iii). Any other solution would have to be of the following form

$$\frac{cf(P^1, Q^1)f(Q^1, P^1)}{f(P^0 Q^0)f(Q^0, P^0)} \equiv \frac{\Sigma P^1 Q^1}{\Sigma P^0 Q^0}. \tag{18}$$

Evaluating the constant c for $(P^1, Q^1) \equiv (P^0, Q^0)$ shows that $c = 1$. Hence, any solution to (ii) and (iii) implies for $f(P, Q)$ the functional equation

$$f(P, Q)f(Q, P) \equiv \Sigma PQ, \tag{19}$$

of which $f(P, Q) = (\Sigma PQ)^{\frac{1}{2}}$ is one particular solution.[6]

Whether, for P and Q *independently* variable, there exists any other solution than this trivial one, I do not know. But the answer is not crucial, since adjoining

---

[6]In the weak form of the axiom system, when the quantity index is not constrained to be the same function as the price index, (19) would be replaced by $f(P, Q)q(Q, P) \equiv \Sigma PQ$.

(i) to (ii) and (iii) leads directly to the relation

$$f(P, Q)f(Q, P) \equiv f(P)f(Q) \equiv \Sigma PQ. \tag{20}$$

Certainly, for P and Q independently variable and $n > 1$, there exists no $f(\ )$ function with the required property – and the same can be said of the weak version where $f(Q)$ is replaced by $g(Q)$. Hence, we see the truth of what is essentially Frisch's 1930 Impossibility Theorem.

Impossibility Theorem: No index number formulas exist that can, for arbitrarily independent prices and quantities, satisfy the Fisher tests of being a generalized mean of price and quantity ratios, the circular-reversal test, and the factor-reversal test.

An infinity of formulas satisfy (i), (iii) and the binary time-reversal test (ii'). The so-called Ideal index, $f = (P^1Q^0)^{\frac{1}{2}}(P^1Q^1)^{-\frac{1}{2}}(P^0Q^1)^{\frac{1}{2}}(P^0Q^0)^{-\frac{1}{2}}$, is one example. So enamoured was Fisher of this that he tried to make a virtue of its failing the circular-reversal test. However, economically, if equality of $f(Q^2, P^2; Q^0, P^0)$ and $f(Q^1, P^1; Q^0, P^0)$ does *not* mean that Q^1 and Q^2 are indifferently good, what is left of the economic theory of index numbers?

Let us now turn away from the mechanical theory to the economic theory of index numbers associated with Frisch, Konus, Bowley, Staehle, Leontief, Allen, Pigou, Keynes, Kuznets, Hicks, Haberler, Samuelson, Ulmer, Afriat, Pollak, Samuelson–Swamy, Fisher–Shell and many others. So long as we stick to the unitary-income-elasticity, homothetic case ('expenditure proportionality' in Frisch's terminology), canonically duel quantity and price index numbers exist. The 1930 Impossibility Theorem no longer applies once we go from 4-n variable space to 2-n variable space, ceasing to treat P and Q as arbitrarily and independently variable but rather constraining them by the satisfaction-maximizing demand functions, $Q = D[P/e]$, equal $eD[P]$ in the homothetic case. Actually, for the homothetic case, Samuelson–Swamy show that

$$\min_{X} \Sigma PX \text{ subject to } u(X) = u(Q) \tag{21}$$

$$= q(Q)p(P) \equiv \alpha^{-1}q(\alpha Q)\beta^{-1}p(\beta P),$$

where $q(Q) = f\{u(Q)\}$ is a first-degree homogeneous cardinal indicator of utility and $p(P)$ is its Shepard–Samuelson–Afriat dual

$$p(P) \equiv \min_{X} \Sigma PX/q(X) \le \Sigma PQ/q(Q), \tag{22}$$

$$p(P)q(Q) \le \Sigma PQ.$$

For $q(Q)$ concave, or $u(q)$ quasi-concave with convex indifference contours, the equality in (22) will hold if, and only if, $Q = D[P/e]$.

With P and Q so constrained by demand, we find (i), (ii), and (iii) lead, in (20), to

$$g(Q^1, P^1; Q^0, P^0) = q(Q^1)/q(Q^0), \tag{23}$$

$$\frac{p(P^2)q(Q^1)}{p(P^0)q(Q^0)} = \frac{\Sigma P^1 Q^1}{\Sigma P^0 Q^0}, \qquad p(P)q(Q) = \Sigma PQ. \tag{24}$$

This last can now be satisfied by

$$q(D[P/e])p(P) \equiv e. \tag{25}$$

If, as a stunt, we insist on the strong version's identity of price-index and quantity-index formula, $g(Z) \equiv f(Z)$ or $p(Z) \equiv q(Z)$, then (20) becomes

$$q(P)q(Q) = \Sigma PQ. \tag{26}$$

Possibility Theorem: With P and Q constrained by homothetic demand, (i), (ii), and (iii) can all be satisfied, in strong or weak form, in an infinity of ways, of which one strong form is the Cobb–Douglas case

$$q(Q) = n^{\frac{1}{2}}q_1^{k_1} \ldots q_n^{k_n}, \quad \sum_1^n k_j = 1, \quad k_j \geqq 0,$$

$$p(P) = n^{\frac{1}{2}}p_1^{k_1} \ldots p_n^{k_n},$$

$$Q = D[P/e] = (k_j e/p_j).$$

For $n = 2$, let $Q = D[P/e]$ be generated by the self-symmetric homogeneous marginal-rate-of-substitution and budget functions

$$s[p_2/p_1, q_2/q_1] = 0, \qquad \Sigma PQ = e,$$

$$s[x, y] \equiv s[y, x],$$

$$\{\partial s/\partial x\}\{\partial s/\partial y\} > 0.$$

Then for each of the infinite number of admissible symmetric $s[\ ,\ ]$ functions, there exists a derived $q(Q)$ and $q(P)$ function that satisfies axioms (i), (ii), and (iii) under the $Q = D[P/e]P/e = D[Q]$ constraint.

Similar self-dual solutions, other than Cobb–Douglas, have been independently found, I have learned, by Professors Wahidul Haque of Toronto, Giora Hanoch of Jerusalem, Ryuzo Sato of Brown University.

In a sense, Frisch's pre-1936 and classical works on index numbers have been satisfactorily integrated.

4. Finale

In writing about a scholar like Ragnar Frisch, your pen runs away with you. I have left myself no space to speak of Frisch's clear-sighted clarification of the need to go beyond reduced forms to structural specification, a necessary formulation for proper identification, prediction, and policy[7] judgments and a correction of crude crypto-positivism. This led to the great methodological advances of Haavelmo, Wold, Koopmans, and other Cowles pioneers, and its impetus is not yet spent. Nor have I left myself opportunity to *skoal* his elucidation, along with Jan Tinbergen's, of the number of independent controls needed to achieve multiple targets.

Only those who lived before the Age of Frisch can appreciate his incremental-product contribution to political economy and the human cause. He splashed us with surplus.

---

[7]On specific policy matters, I cannot forbear mentioning that his 1932 'circulation planning model' was an independent discovery, like that of Kalecki and J.M. Clark, of the crucial income analysis of John Maynard Keynes and Richard Kahn.

References

Arrow, K.J., 1960, The work of Ragnar Frisch, in: Frisch Festschrift, Econometrica 28, 175–192.

Bergson, A., (Burk), 1938, A reformulation of certain aspects of welfare economics, Quarterly Journal of Economics 52, 310–334.

Fisher, I., 1892, Mathematical investigations into the theory of value and price.

Fisher, I., 1927, A statistical method for measuring 'marginal utility' and testing the justice of a progressive income tax, Economic essays in honor of John Bates Clark (MacMillan, New York).

Frisch, R., 1926, Sur une problème d'économie pure, Norsk Matematisk Forenings Skrifter I, no. 16, 299–335.

Frisch, R., 1930, Necessary and sufficient conditions regarding the form of an index number which shall meet certain of Fisher's tests, Journal of the American Statistical Association 25, 397–406.

Frisch, R., 1932, New methods of measuring marginal utility (Tübingen) 142 pp.

Frisch, R., 1933, Propagation problems and impulse problems in dynamic economics, Economic essays in honor of Gustav Cassel (London) 171–205.

Frisch, R., 1936, Price index comparisons between structurally different markets, Congrès International des Mathématiciens (Oslo) 220–222.

Frisch, R., 1939, The double-expenditure method, Econometrica 6, 85–90.

Frisch, R., 1959, A complete scheme for computing all direct and cross demand elasticities in a model with many sectors, Econometrica 27, 177–196.

Harsanyi, J.C., 1955, Cardinal welfare, individualistic ethics, and interpersonal comparisons of utility, Journal of Political Economy 63, 309–321.

Johansen, L., 1969, Ragnar Frisch's scientific contributions to economics, Swedish Journal of Economics LXXI, 302–324.

Samuelson, P.A., 1953, Consumption theorems in terms of overcompensation rather than indifference comparisons, Economica (New series) 20, no. 77, 1–9. (Also reproduced in: The collected scientific papers of Paul A. Samuelson, vol. 1.)

Samuelson, P.A., 1964, A.P. Lerner at sixty, Review of Economic Studies 31, no. 87, 169–178. (Also reproduced in: The collected scientific papers of Paul A. Samuelson, vol. 3.)

Samuelson, P.A. and S. Swamy, 1974, Invariant economic index numbers and canonical duality: Survey and synthesis, American Economic Review (forthcoming). (This gives references in its bibliography to relevant work by Afriat, Shephard, Pollak, Swamy, Fisher and others.)

Savage, L.J., 1954, Foundations of statistics (John Wiley, New York).

Strotz, R.H. and E. Malinvaud, eds., 1960, Festschrift on Ragnar Frisch's 65th birthday, Econometrica 28, 171–494. (This is also referred to as Frisch Testschrift.)

Wald, A., 1939, A new formula for the index of cost of living, Econometrica 7, 313–331.

212

Unification Theorem for the Two Basic Dualities of Homothetic Demand Theory

PAUL A. SAMUELSON

Department of Economics, Massachusetts Institute of Technology, Cambridge, Mass. 02139

Contributed by Paul A. Samuelson, July 17, 1972

ABSTRACT　　When income elasticities of demand are all unity, every dollar being spent in the same proportions at all levels of income, a homogeneous-first-degree, concave utility function exists to serve as an unequivocal measure of real output. Dual to it, and with identical concavity and homogeneity properties, is the minimized-cost-per-unit-of-output, a function of prices. Distinct from this production dual is the indirect-utility dual, representing, except for algebraic sign, the maximized level of utility attainable as a function of prices relative to income. These basic alternative dualities are shown to be related by a unifying theorem: The logarithm of either of the pair of production-dual functions has for its indirect-utility dual the logarithm of the other function. What is shown to be the same thing, the indirect-utility dual of the output function is, except for sign, the reciprocal of the output's production-dual.

Optimality Demand Relations

If income elasticities are unity, the case of *homothetic* preferences, it is known that one cardinal indicator of utility can be written as a homogeneous-first-degree function, unique except for scale, namely

$$f[u(Q)] = q(Q) \equiv m^{-1}q(mQ), f'[\ ] > 0 < m \qquad (1)$$

where throughout lower-case symbols stand for scalars and capital letters stand for row vectors, as with quantities of goods $Q = (q_1,\ldots,q_n) = (q_j)$, prices $P = (p_j)$, normalized prices $Y = P/e$, where $e = p_1q_1 + \ldots + p_nq_n = P \cdot Q = Q \cdot P$.

In the regular cases considered here any cardinal indicator of utility, $u(Q)$, will be quasi-concave with positive partial derivatives and no satiation. This requires that the homogeneous-first-degree function $q(Q)$ be concave with positive partial derivatives.

The observed demand functions, $Q = D[P/e] = D[Y]$, $Y = D^{-1}[Q]$, are generated as the utility maximizing solution subject to the budget constraint

$$\text{Max}_{Q} \, q(Q) \text{ subject to } Y \cdot Q = 1 \qquad (2)$$

$$= q(D[Y]) = -q^*(Y)$$

where $q^*(Y)$ will be soon defined as the indirect-utility dual to $q(Q)$. This constrained maximum implies

$$\frac{\partial q(Q)/\partial q_1}{p_1/e} = \cdots = \frac{\partial q(Q)/\partial q_n}{p_n/e}$$

$$= \left[\sum_1^n q_j \partial q(Q)/\partial q_j \right] \bigg/ \sum_1^n q_j p_j/e = q(Q)/1 \quad (3)$$

Hence, as in Samuelson [1],

$$Y = \text{gradient} \log q(Q) = [y_j]$$

$$= [\partial \log q(Q)/\partial q_j] = D^{-1}[Q] \quad (4)$$

$$[\partial y_i/\partial q_j] = [\partial^2 \log q(Q)/\partial q_i \partial q_j] = [\partial^2 \log q(Q)/\partial q_j \partial q_i]$$

$$= [\partial y_j/\partial q_i]$$

Since $q(Q)$ is concave, and $\log q$ is concave, so will be $\log q(Q)$, and indeed strongly concave in the regular case, with its Hessian matrix of second partial derivatives negative definite rather than semi-negative-definite as with homogeneous $q(Q)$. This Hessian matrix of $\log q(Q)$ serves as the Jacobian matrix of the demand functions of $D^{-1}[Q]$; being symmetric negative definite, it will have an inverse matrix with the same properties. Hence by a global theorem of Gale and Nikaido [2] on on uniqueness of inversion, we can derive from $D^{-1}[Q]$ our desired demand functions $Q = D[Y]$. Actually, as is well known and easily shown, just as $D^{-1}[Q]$ can be written as the gradient of an existent function $\log q(Q)$, so this implies that $D[Y]$ can be written as the gradient of a defined existent function of prices. The next sections will relate this existent function to the indirect-utility dual of $\log q(Q)$ and to $\log p(P)$, and where $p(P)$ will be defined as the production dual to $q(Q)$ itself.

PRODUCTION DUALITY

As in Shephard [3] and Samuelson [4], we define $q(Q)$'s production dual $p(P)$ by

$$p(P) = \underset{Q}{\text{Min}} \; P \cdot Q / q(Q) \leq P \cdot Q / q(Q) \qquad (5)$$

with the equality holding only for (Q,P) and (Q,Y) pairings that can be shown by explicit differentiation of (5) to satisfy the optimality equations of (3). From (5) directly, we verify that $p(P)$ is homogeneous-first-degree, $p(P) \equiv m^{-1}p(mP)$ because $q(Q)$ has this property. It is not hard to verify that concavity of $q(Q)$ implies concavity of $p(P)$, and that the contour, $p(p_1/p_q, \; p_2/p_q, \dots) = 1$, provides the important "factor-price frontier." From the symmetry relations

$$p(P)q(Q) \leq P \cdot Q = Q \cdot P = e \qquad (6)$$

$$p(Y)q(Q) \leq 1 = p(Y)q(D[Y]) = p(D^{-1}[Q])q(Q)$$

we see that just as $p(\;)$ is dual to $q(\;)$, so is $q(\;)$ dual to $p(\;)$. Thus, the dual of the dual to a function is reflexively itself.

It follows by dual symmetry that we can write parallel to (3)

$$\frac{\partial p(Y)/\partial y_1}{q_1} = \dots = \frac{\partial p(Y)/\partial y_n}{q_n} = \frac{Y \cdot \text{grad} p(P)}{Y \cdot Q} = p(P) \quad (7)$$

the necessary conditions for

$$q(Q) = \underset{P}{\text{Min}} \; Q \cdot P / p(P) \qquad (8)$$

Likewise we use dual symmetry to derive the parallel to (4)

$$Q = D[Y] = \text{grad} \log p(Y) \qquad (9)$$

$$[\partial q_i / \partial y_j] = [\partial q_j / \partial y_i] = [\partial y_i / \partial q_j]^{-1}$$

In a forthcoming paper, Swamy and Samuelson [5] show that $p(P^1)/p(P^0)$ and $q(Q^1)/q(Q^0)$ provide exact index numbers of price change and quantity change between two situations (P^0,Q^0) and (P^1,Q^1), thus resolving for the homothetic case the century-old search for ideal index numbers.

INDIRECT-UTILITY DUAL

On the basis of pioneering work by Hotelling, Roy, Houthakker, Gorman, and others, the full indirect-utility dual is introduced in Samuelson [1]. This must not be confused with the production dual of the last section.

By definition, the full indirect-utility dual to $u(Q)$ (with its proper reversal of algebraic sign) is given by

$$\underset{Q}{\text{Max}} \; u(Q) \text{ subject to } Y \cdot Q = 1 \qquad (10)$$

$$= u(D[Y]) = -u^*(Y)$$

It should be noted that the full dual as defined here is of opposite sign to the classical indirect utility function, a convention with simplifying advantage.

Hence,

$$u(Q) + u^*(Y) \leq 0 \text{ for } Y \cdot Q = Q \cdot Y = 1 \qquad (11)$$

and where the equality sign holds only for optimal pairings $Q = D[Y]$ and $Y = D^{-1}[Y]$. From the symmetry of (11) we see that the demand problem can be formulated as maximizing the left-hand side of (11) with respect to either set of variables Q or Y with the other set held constant. Hence, it is clear that both the direct and the indirect demand functions must have the same properties, and so must $u(\ )$ and $u^*(\ )$. Just as $u^*(\ )$ is dual to $u(\ )$, so is $u(\ )$ dual to $u^*(\ )$, with the result that the dual to the dual of any function is itself reflexively, $u(Q) \equiv u^{**}(Q)$. (In the above statement, the word indirect has been omitted for brevity.) In the general case where $u(Q)$ is quasi-concave in its arguments, with its indifference contours being convex from below, $u^*(Y)$ will thereby be quasi-concave in its arguments too. Indeed the form of the functions is indistinguishable.

UNIFYING THE TWO DUALITIES

We can now specialize $u(Q)$ to $\log q(Q)$ and relate the two alternative definitions of duality. For observed pairings, $Q = D[Y]$, $Y = D^{-1}[Y]$, we know

$$p(Y)q(Q) = 1 \qquad (12)$$

$$\log p(Y) + \log q(Q) = 0$$

$$u^*(Y) + u(Q) = 0$$

By identifying the respective functions of P and of Q, we see that if we choose in the beginning for our $u(Q)$ the particular utility indicator $\log q(Q)$, then we shall get for its full indirect-utility dual $u^*(Y) = \log p(Y)$. This suggests our unifying theorem.

THEOREM. *For homothetic demand, the cardinal utility indicator, $q(Q) \equiv m^{-1}q(mQ)$, that is homogeneous-first-degree and concave has a production dual $p(Y)$ or $p(P) \equiv m^{-1}p(mP)$ with similar properties. Then (a) the full indirect-utility dual to $\log q(Q)$, which except for sign represents the maximum of this function attainable with the given budget of normalized prices Y, will be found to be $\log p(Y)$; (b) the full indirect-utility dual to $q(Q)$ itself will be, with its sign reversed, the reciprocal of the production dual, $-q^*(Y) \equiv p(Y)^{-1}$*

Since the proof of (a) has already been sketched, it remains only to prove (b). We note that, if $u(\ )$ and $u^*(\ )$ are indirect-utility duals, so are $f[u(\ )]$ and $-f[u^*(\ )]$ from the definition in (10). Hence, pair up

$$f[u(Q)] = \exp u(Q) = \exp \log q(Q) = q(Q) \qquad \textbf{(13)}$$

$$-f[u^*(Y)] = -\exp [-u^*(Y)] = -\exp [-\log p(Y)]$$
$$= -p(Y)^{-1} = q^*(Y)$$

$$-q^*(Y) \equiv p(Y)^{-1} \qquad \text{Q.E.D.}$$

It is worth emphasizing that being able to summarize the information contained in n different demand functions of n variables in terms of the gradient of a single function of n variables represents a tremendous economy of description, a fact well known to students of Gibbsian thermodynamics.

The author thanks the National Science Foundation for financial assistance to this preliminary report of more extensive duality, complementarity, and elasticity relations. Over the years, he has benefited from conversations with Robert Pollak of the University of Pennsylvania.

1. Samuelson, P. A. (1965) "Using full duality to show that simultaneously additive and indirect utilities implies unitary price elasticity of demand," *Econometrica* **33**, 781–796; reproduced (1972) as chap. 134 of *The Collected Scientific Papers of Paul A. Samuelson, III*, ed. Merton, R. C. (M.I.T. Press, Cambridge, Mass.), pp. 71–86.
2. Gale, D. & Nikaido, H. (1965) "The Jacobian matrix and global equivalence of mappings," *Mathematische Annalen* **159**, 81–93.
3. Shephard, R. (1953) *Cost and Production Functions* (Princeton University Press, Princeton, N.J.).
4. Samuelson, P. A. (1962) "Parable and realism in capital theory: the surrogate production function," *Review of Economic Studies,* **29**, 193–206; reproduced (1966) as chap. 28 of *The Collected Scientific Papers of Paul A. Samuelson, I*, ed. Stiglitz, J. E. (M.I.T. Press, Cambridge, Mass.), 325–338.
5. Samuelson, P. A. & Swamy, S., "Invariant economic index numbers and canonical duality: Survey and synthesis," in press.
6. Pollak, R. A., "The theory of the cost of living index," pre-publication study of June, 1971 from the Bureau of Labor Statistics, the National Science Foundation and the University of Pennsylvania. (Available from the University of Pennsylvania.)

Relative Shares and Elasticities Simplified: Comment

By Paul A. Samuelson*

The taxonomy of changing factor shares in a competitive industry's output, as factor supplies (or prices) shift, has, again, been ably discussed.[1] These results can be included under the following terse exposition.

I

Denote the neoclassical (homogeneous-first-degree, concave) production function as $q = f(x_1, \ldots, x_n)$. Then write $X_i = log_e x_i = ln\ x_i$ and

(1) $\quad ln\ f(x_1, \ldots, x_n) = ln\ f(e^{X_1}, \ldots, e^{X_n})$

$$= \alpha(X_1, \ldots X_n)$$

The relative share of the ith factor,

$$p_i x_i \Big/ \sum_1^n p_j x_j = \alpha_i$$

is then given by

(2) $\quad \alpha_i = \partial \alpha(X_1, \ldots, X_n)/\partial X_i$

$$= \alpha_i(X_1, \ldots, X_n)$$

where subscripts on a function denote partial differentiation, as in $\partial \alpha / \partial X_i = \alpha_i, \partial^2 \alpha / \partial X_i \partial X_j = \alpha_{ij}$, etc.

By definition, total relative shares sum to unity; hence

(3) $\quad \partial \left(\sum_1^n \alpha_i \right) \Big/ \partial X_j = 0$

$$= \sum_1^n \alpha_{ij}(X_1, \ldots, X_n)$$

Effects on α_i, from a relative change in factor i alone are given simply by the sign of α_{ii}, or equivalently of $\alpha_{ii}/\alpha_i \alpha_i$, and $\alpha_{ii}/\alpha_i(1-\alpha_i)$ (the latter being $1-\sigma_i^{-1} = 1 + [x_i f_{ii}/(1-\alpha_i)f_i]$, the "Samuelson" criterion). Effects on α_i from a sole change in

factor j are given by α_{ij} or $\alpha_{ij}/\alpha_i \alpha_j$ (which are closely related to the "partial elasticities" concepts, $ff_{ij}/f_i f_j$, of Hicks, Allen, McFadden, Sato-Koizumi, and many others).

To determine how the share of some subset of factors, say $\alpha_1 + \ldots + \alpha_r$, $r < n$, changes relative to some other subset's, $\alpha_{r+1} + \ldots + \alpha_m$, $m < n$, when some factor x_j alone changes, we need only calculate the sign of

(4) $\quad \partial \left(ln \sum_1^r \alpha_i - ln \sum_{r+1}^m \alpha_i \right) \Big/ \partial X_j$

$$= \left(\sum_1^r \alpha_i \right)^{-1} \left(\sum_1^r \alpha_{ij} \right)$$

$$- \left(\sum_{r+1}^m \alpha_i \right)^{-1} \left(\sum_{r+1}^m \alpha_{ij} \right)$$

Thus, if $r = 2$, $m = 3 = j$, as in Sato-Koizumi's example of a change in brown labor's supply and the effects of this upon its share relative to that of white and black laborers' combined, (4) becomes $(\alpha_1 + \alpha_2)^{-1}(\alpha_{13} + \alpha_{23}) - \alpha_3^{-1}\alpha_{33}$. If $m = n = 3$, (4) becomes $-\alpha_{33}[(1-\alpha_3)^{-1} + (\alpha_3)^{-1}]$.

II

This completes all there is to say.[2]

Mention, however, should be made of the obvious duality relations that hold for the minimum-unit cost function in terms of factor prices, $c(p_1, \ldots, p_n)$, which is dual to the production function and has all its qualitative properties. Now we work with

(5) $\quad \alpha[Y_1, \ldots, Y_n] = ln\ c(e^{Y_1}, \ldots, e^{Y_n})$

$$\alpha^i[Y_1, \ldots, Y_n] = \partial \alpha[Y_1, \ldots, Y_n]/\partial Y_i$$

where now brackets (rather than parentheses) differentiate between factor prices and factor quantities, and superscripts (rather than subscripts) indicate differentiation with

* Institute professor, Massachusetts Institute of Technology. I owe thanks to the National Science Foundation.

[1] See Ryuzo Sato and Tetsunori Koizumi. This gives references to Hicks, Robinson, McFadden, Samuelson, Sato-Koizumi, and others.

[2] I have skipped the Sato-Koizumi discussion of "direct and shadow elasticities," dealing with a change in "x_i/x_j," since, when $n > 2$, such Robinsonian changes are ill-defined.

respect to factor prices (rather than factor quantities).

Now, if we ask the effects on factor shares of changes in one of many factor prices (instead of factor quantities), all our previous formulas can immediately have their duals written, merely by changing subscripts to superscripts! Thus, instead of α_{ii} we write α^{ii}, etc.[3]

[3] The informed reader can verify the following symmetric relations between the "dual" functions:

(6) $\alpha[Y_1, \ldots, Y_n] + \alpha(X_1, \ldots, X_n) \geq 0$

for $Y_i = ln(p_i/\sum p_j x_j)$ and with (6)'s equality sign holding if, and only if,

(7) $Y_i = -X_i + ln\,\alpha_i(X_1, \ldots, X_n)$

    $X_i = -Y_i + ln\,\alpha_i[Y_1, \ldots, Y_n]$

In conclusion, and with no implication of criticizing earlier writers (including myself), this terse exposition may usefully point up the fact that most elasticity discussions are empty of substance: for the most part, whether they are partial elasticities or total elasticities, they merely give names to effects that need to be measured—except for their occasional function of relating some of the different needed measurements to each other.

REFERENCES

R. Sato and T. Koizumi, "The Production Function and the Theory of Relative Shares," *Amer. Econ. Rev.*, June 1973, *63*, 484–89.

214

A Quantum-Theory Model of Economics: Is the Co-ordinating Entrepreneur Just Worth His Profit?[1]

P. A. SAMUELSON

I INTRODUCTION

If an industry consists of symmetric firms with rising marginal costs, its total output is produced at minimum total costs when industry output is divided evenly among the firms. The optimal number of such firms will grow in jumps as industry output increases smoothly; but asymptotically, as industry output Q becomes large relative to the scale of each firm's U-shaped cost curve, the optimal number of firms, n^*, will be proportional to Q and the curve of industry's average cost will become asymptotically horizontal, no longer rising and falling perceptibly as each new firm is added.

All this has been well known for a third of a century.[2] But it pays no explicit attention to the need to pay the co-ordinating entrepreneur, if only for reason of his opportunity cost. Why does the firm's marginal cost curve ever rise if it can have *all* the inputs at fixed prices and can replicate processes in scale and also sub-divide them in scale? Why should it then not have a horizontal long-run marginal and average cost curve? Often, tacitly or explicitly, economists assume that the 'firm' needs a co-ordinating manager (or management), whose time and attention devoted to it involves some indivisible, minimum quantum of time and energy. Moreover, as more and more inputs are directed by him, his effective command

[1] Financial aid from the National Science Foundation and editorial assistance from Mrs Jillian M. Pappas are gratefully acknowledged.
[2] See M. F. W. Joseph, 'A Discontinuous Cost Curve and the Tendency to Increasing Returns', *Economic Journal*, vol. 43 (1933), pp. 390–8; P. A. Samuelson, 'The Monopolistic Competition Revolution', in R. E. Kuenne (ed.), *Monopolistic Competition Theory: Studies in Impact — Essays in Honour of Edward H. Chamberlin*, (New York, Wiley, 1967), pp. 105–38, particularly pp. 129–35.

or span of attention gets stretched, so that the marginal cost of output from those inputs rises in much the same fashion that MC rises when any continuously-divisible fixed factor is held constant.

The essence of the present case of a co-ordinating entrepreneur is that it involves a granular factor that, by hypothesis, can change only in integral steps: you can contemplate $1, 2, 3 \ldots n, n+1$ of such agents; but not $1/2, \sqrt{2}$, or π.

To be sure, our case does not cover all models of co-ordinating management. In compensation, its results will apply to any integrally-lumpy factor – as when homogeneous land, for some reason, can be re-allocated only by the acre or by the square inch rather than completely continuously. Also, this analysis throws light on the valuation of taxi-cab medallions or other variants of artificial permits needed for a new business or new plant.

II PREVIEW

Suppose any 'manager' will leave the industry if his residual profits from production, after paying the hired factors, systematically fall below π. How high π is above zero depends on a general equilibrium analysis not here discussed; however, the present partial-equilibrium analysis is an important strand in that general equilibrium story. Suppose new managers will be attracted into the industry when there is a reasoned expectation that managers will earn in it residual profit of π or more.

Then, pretty clearly, as industry demand grows large enough to support numerous competitive firms, its healthy long-run equilibrium will involve price marked up above non-management unit cost by the π amount of needed-manager profit. What is the 'function' that any one representative manager is providing, to his firm or the industry or the consumer or society, that can 'justify' his profits being levied against the consumer?

Thanks to the writings of such Cambridge economists as Joan Robinson,[3] students of competitive price have realized that the lumpy entrepreneur usually gets his lumpy marginal productivity just as a divisible factor gets its smooth marginal productivity. But this has never been properly demonstrated.

Specifically, entrepreneur's profit becomes ('virtually') π in long-

[3] J. V. Robinson, 'Euler's Theorem and the Problem of Distribution', *Economic Journal*, vol. 44 (1934), pp. 398–414, particularly p. 409.

run equilibrium and π is the loss to society of having industry's output produced by one less (or, one more) firm out of many firms. What society loses when the entrepreneur is removed is his competitively determined profit. Charging that profit is needed to get production in each firm the optimal amount *beyond* the lowest point on the curve of hired-factor unit cost!

This lumpy, or quantum theory of marginal product is a remarkable case. Mathematically, we know that the production function which is smoothly differentiable in real variables

$$Y = F(X_1, X_2, \ldots)$$

and which is concave and homogeneous to the first degree, leads simply to marginal-productivity, imputation relations

$$\begin{cases} W_i = \partial F(X_1, X_2, \ldots)/\partial X_i & (i = 1, 2, \ldots) \\ Y = \sum_i W_i X_i. \end{cases}$$

All this holds by virtue of Euler's theorem.

But $\partial F/\partial X_1$ is not the same as

$$(\Delta F/\Delta X_1)_{x_2} = F(X_1 + 1, X_2) - F(X_1, X_2),$$

and Euler has no theorem to compel

$$X_1(\Delta F/\Delta X_1)_{x_2} + X_2(\Delta F/\Delta X_2)_{x_1} \equiv F.$$

Yet, as we shall see, for large enough X_i, $\partial F/\partial X_i$ and $\Delta F/\Delta X_i$ become identical. Indeed, it can be easily shown that even for $F(X_1, X_2, \ldots)$ 'almost homogeneous', satisfying

$$F(\lambda X_1, \lambda X_2, \ldots) = \lambda F(X_1, X_2, \ldots)$$

only for λ integral, this same asymptotic equivalance will hold.

III STATEMENT OF THE BASIC ASYMPTOTIC THEOREM

Although it is evident that Joan Robinson in her heuristic discussion of Euler's theorem has a clear understanding of the relationships involved, I cannot recall a rigorous statement or demonstration of the following basic quantum theory result

$$(1)\ \lim_{Q \to \infty} \left\{ \{n^{**}(Q) - 1\}C[Q/\{n^{**}(Q) - 1\}] - n^{**}(Q)C[Q/n^{**}(Q)] \right\}$$
$$= \pi = C'(q^{**})q^{**} - C(q^{**})$$

where the total cost paid out optimally by the industry to the hired factors is denoted by $n^{**}(Q)C[Q/n^{**}(Q)]$ and $n^{**}(Q)$ is defined by

(2) $$\underset{n}{\text{Min}}\left\{nC[Q/n]+\pi n\right\} \overset{def}{\equiv} n^{**}(Q)\left\{C[Q/n^{**}(Q)]+\pi\right\}$$

and where $C[q]$ is each manager's total cost curve of hired factors (exclusive, of course, of any entrepreneurial profit, whether of the opportunity-cost, the short-run quasi-rent, or the long-run competitively-determined type).

What the fundamental relation (1) asserts is that, if a firm is selling at a competitive price equal to its marginal cost and that marginal cost is competitively above the average cost outlay to hired factors, then the profit doled out to it as a residual rent is equal to its opportunity cost and, more interestingly, is asymptotically for large enough scale precisely equal to its marginal product, even though that marginal product is of *finite* quantum type rather than of smooth-partial-derivative type.

IV PROOF

Here I shall briefly sketch the salient relations. The heavy curves in Figure 18.1 merely reproduce my textbook diagram (*Economics* (1970), p. 457) of the cost curves when entrepreneur's opportunity cost or profit is ignored; marginal cost curves have been added here. The upper curve superimposes the profit magnitude π, so that the curve represents cost-cum-profits that must at least prevail if each Q were to hold for ever and each firm in the industry were content to stay in it and, at the same time, no larger numbers of firms would be able to cover in profits their needed opportunity costs, π.

To anyone who understands the lower curve diagram and its logic, this new diagram should be self-explanatory. Let me comment on its features.

1. Because of need to pay profit to hold managers, every firm produces *beyond* the bottom of the lower hired factor U-shaped curve. This 'overproduction' in each firm is optimal and approximates to the amount $q^{**}-q^*$, where q^{**} is the point at which the excess of MC over hired-factor AC just equals the needed profit-per-unit, π/q^{**}.

2. The competitive industry acts *as if* the upper curve of cost-plus-needed-profit were its actual cost curve. Residual profits are,

par excellence, short-run rents or (in Marshall's terminology) quasi-rents; but they are truly long-run costs.

3. What the unit-cost diagram cannot show clearly is that the profit π equals the saving in industry cost from not losing the last

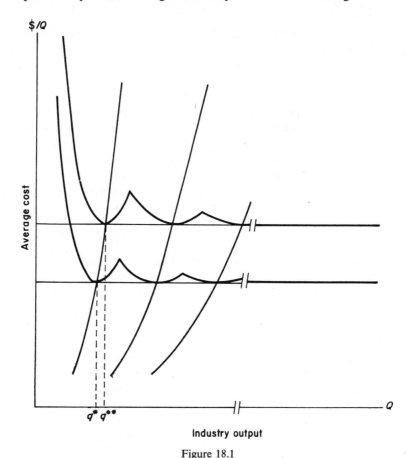

Figure 18.1

entrepreneur. Figure 18.2 sketches the total-cost aspect of this. Now the scale is tremendously reduced so that the initial less-than-100 firm stage is only a speck near the origin. The straight lines show that we are at a scale involving a really large number of firms, and it is only then that we get our asymptotic results with strictly parallel lines. Also, the vertical distance depicting π has been grossly exaggerated so that the diagram can be understood; naturally, the profit of one firm is very small compared to the total cost of the whole industry.

The ray marked n^{**} represents fixed-factor outlays (exclusive of π!), growing in proportion to industry output with number of firms

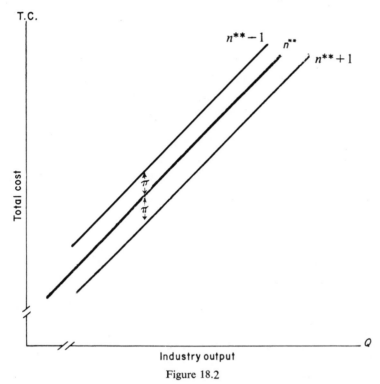

Figure 18.2

[Note: This figure was altered by Samuelson in 1977.]

n^{**} rising in optimum proportion to Q, namely as Q/q^{**}. Not shown is the still lower ray that would result if π were zero, and the bottom-of-the-lower-U output, q^* rather than q^{**}, was achieved by each firm.

The rays marked $n^{**}-1$ and $n^{**}+1$ are parallel to the n^{**} ray and are equally-spaced above it. The essence of the present demonstration is that the space between the $n^{**}\pm1$ ray and the n^{**} ray must be precisely π as $Q\to\infty$ and all curves become strictly straight lines.

Writing $n^{**}(Q)$ as n for short, we have

$$(n-1)C[Q/(n-1)] - nC[Q/n]$$

$$= n\frac{C[Q/(n-1)] - C(Q/n)}{[Q/(n-1) - Q/n]}Q\frac{1}{n(n-1)} - C[Q/(n-1)]$$

$$= [\triangle C/\triangle Q][Q/(n-1)] - C[Q/(n-1)]$$

$$(3) \qquad \to C'(q^{**})q^{**} - C(q^{**}) = \pi$$

as

$$Q/n^{**}(Q) \to q^{**} \text{ for } Q \to \infty.$$

This proves that asymptotic finite marginal product of a lumpy factor does converge to its remuneration. QED

Strictly speaking, I should append to this demonstration that entrepreneur's residual profit equals the cost saving to the industry his presence provides, a related demonstration on marginal product itself. Since the mathematical proof[4] would be straightforward, I shall leave to the reader the demonstration that

$$(4) \qquad \lim_{\lambda \to \infty}\left\{Q[\lambda x_1 + 1, \lambda x_2, \ldots] - Q[\lambda x_1, \lambda x_2, \ldots]\right\}$$
$$= \partial Q[x_1, x_2, \ldots]/\partial(x_1)$$

if Q is any smooth homogeneous-first-degree function. That is,

$$\lim_{\lambda \to \infty}(\Delta Q/\Delta x_i) = \partial Q/\partial x_i$$

even though Δx_i is kept at a large positive number rather than going to zero. This property causes jigsaw-puzzle versions of the economic world to approach hydraulic versions of the world – provided that sufficient *replication* in scale is possible.

Moral: *Large numbers smooth!*

[4] Allyn Young, Frank Knight and Joan Robinson assume in their heuristic proofs that the factors hired by the withdrawn firm or acre of land go to work at sensibly *unchanged* marginal productivity for other firms or at the external margin: hence society loses the infra-marginal product of the withdrawn factor, which is its residual rent. I have merely made this rigorous by careful lim $n \to \infty$ argumentation. See Robinson, op. cit., p. 409; F. H. Knight, 'The Ricardian Theory of Production and Distribution', *Canadian Journal of Economics and Political Science*, vol. 1 (1935), pp. 3–25, 171–96, particularly p. 181 where Knight attributes the argument to Allyn Young's section of R. T. Ely, *Outlines of Economics*, 4th edn (New York, Macmillan, 1923), p. 410.
Hint: rewrite (4) as

$$\{Q[\lambda x_1 + \lambda\lambda^{-1}, \lambda x_2 \ldots] - Q[\lambda x_1, \lambda x_2, \ldots]\}\lambda\lambda^{-1} = \{Q[x_1 + \lambda^{-1}, x_2, \ldots] - Q[x_1, x_2, \ldots]\}\lambda^{-1}$$

which clearly goes to $\partial Q/\partial x_1$ as $\lambda^{-1} \to 0$.

PART II

Theory of Capital and Growth

215

INTEREST RATE DETERMINATIONS AND OVERSIMPLIFYING PARABLES: A SUMMING UP*

Paul A. Samuelson

1. Prologue

Economists properly attach considerable importance to correct descriptions and understandings of the distribution of income and of wealth, and also to any discernible trends over time in these phenomena. Behind an esoteric dispute over 'reswitching' or heterogeneity of capital there often lurk contrasting views about fruitful ways of understanding distributional analysis and affecting its content by alternative policy measures.

It may therefore be useful by way of introduction to review some stages of thought. Like Nabokov, I say 'Speak memory'. Rather than contaminate the Freudian filter by doing research to document my theses, it may be of greater interest to let the subconscious tell its own story. Then the discrepancies between actual fact and recall may themselves tell an interesting story.

1.1. Before the General Theory

Prior to 1936 most economists thought that pricing of the factors of production determined income distribution once one ascertained the ownership pattern of the different factors of production and worked out the evolving implied changes in that ownership pattern. Thus, people who chanced upon mountains of silver in the Rockies became rich. Those with high genetic cunning and good educational opportunity became affluent. Those with no ownership of land, machinery, bonds, shares or learned skills stayed poor. The result is

*I owe thanks to Norma Wasser for editorial assistance and to the National Science Foundation for financial support.

the familiarly skewed income distribution, described by Lorentz curves and/or truncated Pareto distributions.

Prior to 1936 the fact of the business cycle had not escaped notice. Periods of increased unemployment tended to increase inequality as measured by a Gini–Lorentz coefficient for the whole distribution or at least for the lower part of the distribution. Risk-takers with heavy overhead cost commitments tended to have volatile profits, the declines being especially sharp during unanticipated declines in business activity. Most economists would, I think, have agreed with Adam Smith that if the Dutch for decades or a century thriftily undertook much capital formation and the English did not, then, other things equal, steady-state per capita consumption levels would be high in Holland and interest rates would tend to be low there. Also, most economists would have agreed with Fisher, Schumpeter, Wicksell, Cannan, and (by 1932) Hicks that inventions could shift relative incomes in favor of or against particular factor owners – the unskilled, the landowners, those in the mousetrap industry, and even the possessors of a diversified business portfolio.

1.2. First Keynesian models

When Keynes' (1936) *General Theory* came along, his followers could simplify their expositions by assuming that each level of short-term employment and output would, relative to the stocks of diverse capital goods inherited from the past, be accompanied by a determinate income distribution. The overall saving ratio at each income level would in consequence be a determinate weighted-average of the saving propensities of the poor and rich, the skilled and unskilled, the wage–salary earner, *rentier*, and residual profit claimant.

An extreme form of this simplifying hypothesis was the strong 1938 view of Kalecki on constancy of relative shares: alleged horizontal variable unit costs constituting wages meet alleged stable average elasticities of perceived oligopolists' demand; result, fairly constant ratio of quasi-rent property earnings to wage earnings. Whatever limited plausibility this model had in 1938 and has not lost by 1974, it was simple[1]. More complicated were the attempts by

---

[1]Since depreciation charges do not shrink fully in proportion to contraction of underemployment income levels, this is not so much a theory of the constancy of wage–property income shares as a theory of cyclical variability of the net profit

Harrod (1936) in his *Trade Cycle* to postulate the direction in which the average perceived elasticity of demand moved at high and low unemployment levels.

To sum up, the Keynesian writings of the late 1930s were not inconsistent in their distribution theory with the pre-1936 mainstream analysis of perfect- and imperfect-competition pricing as applied to factors as well as goods.

Kalecki's second model of income distribution (Kalecki, 1942) determined *absolute* factor shares as a function of exogenous investment (or, possibly, saving) decisions. This wartime effort escaped general notice. It also escaped inconsistency with his earlier relative shares model by its premise that the level of underemployment equilibrium was defined as being determined at that income level where both models could be satisfied. This second, so-called Widow's–Cruse Kalecki model, which has given stimulus to some later macroeconomic distribution models, has sometimes been thought to have paradoxical features. Actually, the second Kalecki model of profits is quite consistent with the crudest neoclassical Cobb–Douglas theory of marginal productivity, as applied to a *General-Theory* 'multiplier' model of variable underemployment income under fluctuating autonomous investment. All that is peculiar about the Kalecki model is its empirical assumption that only profit receivers save. Its seeming paradoxes become acute only when we add to the fable the bizarre assumption that profit receivers

---

share, with the wage share rising somewhat in recession and falling in booms. Bowley's law (of alleged invariance of the wage share) would emerge in the long run only if, along with the postulated constant elasticity of perceived oligopolists' demands, there is also a postulated long-run constancy of average degree of excess capacity over the business cycle. Not much of a satisfactory 'explanation' is provided, in my view, by reposing the question, 'Why constant shares?', replacing it by 'Why these convenient postulated constancies? (and *are* they constant? and are there no alternative ways of fruitfully posing the questions?).' Perfect competition would require: (a) unitary elasticity-of-substitution short-run production functions to explain constancy of factor shares in boom and depression, and (b) less-than-unity elasticity-of-substitution functions to explain a fall in residual-profit share in recession. The minimal elements I would consider relevant to an adequate analysis of such non-constancies and constancies as are empirically displayed by different income shares include: (1) less-than-infinite-elasticity of firm demand, (2) increasing returns to scale, (3) the existence of contractual obligations that benefit some factors and hurt others, (4) some limitation on short-run factor substitutability, (5) inability to foresee perfectly the undulations of the trade cycle that the future will bring, and (6) differential stickiness in adjustment of wage rates and administered prices.

save *all* their income. As is well known in any Keynesian multisector analysis, any money spent in a sector which saves nothing comes
back fully to the rest of the world. There is no real paradox in this.
Thus, in a Cobb–Douglas competitive technology where only profits
are saved and only wages are consumed, the relative profit share
never varies; but, as the multiplicand of investment falls, the
absolute level of income to which the relative shares are applied
drops just enough to make the resultant implied absolute profit share
equal to the lowered level of investment. If, in the interest of less
unrealism, we assume that the elasticity of substitution is less than
unity, Kalecki's new equilibrium will not have to fall as much. A rise
in relative wage share induced by the recession, under his saving-
out-of-profit assumption (and under the less extreme assumption
that workers are less thrifty than property owners), will lower the
average community saving ratio and thus lower the multiplied
decline in employment and income.

For some years after 1940 the focus of attention in the literature
shifted away from distributive shares to the movement of the whole
of the national product. Although Keynes did not include the
accelerator explicitly in his *General Theory*, in his *Eugenics Review*
lecture (Keynes, 1937) he recognized that there would be forces
tending to induce investment and capital formation in a growing
economy. Hansen's theory of secular stagnation, as induced by what
would today be called a reduction in the *natural rate of growth* in
consequence of demographic and natural resource trends, involved
a similar preoccupation. Also, Harrod, Hansen, I, and many others
worked out cyclical interrelations between the accelerator and
multiplier. As soon as such a system ceased to have all of its
exponential roots damped – and such a phenomenon became
inevitable once investigators shortened the lag periods of the model
or worked with instantaneous-lag differential-equation versions –
self-fulfilling exponential growth paths emerged.

Harrod's (1939) article on dynamic growth was appreciated by
only a few connoisseurs, but by the time of his (Harrod, 1947) essay
on dynamic growth, a wider audience had become receptive.
However, the usual Harrod and Domar analyses – they are not quite
the same thing, of course – had no particular connection with the
distribution of income. In part this is a consequence of their crude
assumption that there is a constant average propensity to save for

the sum of all factor sharers taken together[2]. But even if there were systematic patterns of relative sharing to be associated with each fractional degree of unutilization of potential full employment income, along an exponential path of natural growth there would be no need to postulate any shifts in income distribution: as the system widens in balanced growth, all intensive relations and proportions can remain invariant.

Although there is nothing in the basic logic of the Harrod–Domar model that is inconsistent with neoclassical marginal productivity (as Ramsey's (1928) saving model might have made clear, and as Solow's (1956) analysis showed), Harrod in fact seemed to think of the capital–output ratio as a hard technical parameter. Indeed, we make the best sense of his distinctions between the warranted and natural rates of growth if we postulate for an exposition of his theory a fixed proportions aggregate production function, of the form $C + dK/dt = \min(L/a, K/b) - dK$, where b is the accelerator regarded as a fixed parameter in the Leontief fashion, d is the exponential rate of depreciation, $1/d$ being the average length of life of capital equipment. Either it is assumed that L grows at some *natural* exponential rate or equivalently, under the assumption of 'Harrod-neutral' or 'labor-augmenting' technical change, that L/a grows in proportion to e^{gt}, where $g = (dL/dt)/L + |(da/dt)/a|$ is the relevant natural rate of growth. In such a fixed-coefficient model, one would indeed have reason to be preoccupied with the Keynesian

---

[2]Actually, by the time of Kuznets' (1940) lectures on long-term trends, it was realized that this crude assumption was not so crude after all. (There is no merit to the notion, entertained at one time by George Stigler as I recall, that a constant saving/income propensity is incompatible with Keynes' *General Theory*. Keynes never had need to postulate a convex saving function, $S(Y)$ with $S''(Y) > 0$.) Denison's law of constant average propensity to save at successive full employment levels, my own analysis of the long-run forces making for higher desired consumption standards (in a race with the enhanced per capita full-employment supply of goods), the parallel researches of Duesenberry and Modigliani on rising habitual trends of autonomous and emulative consumption, Friedman's permanent income hypothesis and, most importantly of all, Modigliani's life-cycle hypothesis, all testify to the coarseness of any simple identification of saving with non-wage income. Kuznets has estimated that about 80% of net product is wage and salary income, or implicit wage earnings of farmers, professionals, and unincorporated enterprises. But the modern revival of interest in 'human capital' makes us recognize that much capital formation escapes the yardstick of the national income statisticians and only an unknown fraction of the 80% earnings of personal services represents the quasi-rents of raw, *genetic*, uneducated labor.

issue of whether there will be enough investment opportunities to sweep any oversaving under the rug without causing unemployment. So long as Harrod operates with a saving ratio s that is constant despite any mention of the distribution of income between wages and property, his warranted rate of growth is definable as s/b, a hard parameter or hard constant. There is no *a priori* reason why this warranted rate should not exceed or fall short of the natural rate g.

Moreover, as soon as an economist tries to break up the average s into a properly weighted average of separate propensities to save (out of profits s_K, and out of wages s_L, with the weights being respectively the relative profit share α_K or α, and relative wages share α_L or $(1 - \alpha)$) he does need a theory of distribution. However, it is precisely in the fixed-coefficient-model interpretation of the Harrod dynamic system that the neoclassical relations of marginal productivity fail to apply to supply such a distribution theory.

Nature abhors a vacuum. And even where there is no vacuum, creative scholars rush in to supply alternative theories of distribution. By 1950 a rash of macroeconomic distribution theories had begun to sprout. An example would be Boulding (1950) or Frank Hahn's macrodistribution theory. (Frank Hahn, like the late German banker, Albert Hahn, the early discoverer of underconsumption models of the Keynes type, who later turned orthodox, is in a position to claim: 'The theory is not much good, but I was the first to discover it.') Rather than try to enumerate various versions of macroeconomic distribution models, it will suffice here to mention the many works of the 1950s by Joan Robinson and Nicholas Kaldor. Although both of these authors have been critical of neoclassical models, their writings do not seem to express identical views. In particular, one must distinguish between short-run theories of distribution, and long-run theories (meaning by long run, the theories that are postulated to hold in steady states of exponential or 'golden-age' growth).

Not everybody has an elaborated short-run distribution theory. But in Kaldor (1955) there is hypothesized a meaningful, conceptually refutable, macroeconomic theory. It is based on a *General Theory* version of exogenous fluctuating investment, $I = dK/dt$. But this is grafted onto a full-employment model that Kaldor likens to Keynes' *Treatise*, with its paradoxes of Widow's Cruses. On the basis of the empirical hypothesis that s_K is definitely greater than s_L

(indeed, in extreme cases the latter can be zero and the former unity, as in certain Kalecki models), and on the basis of an unelaborated empirical hypothesis about the differential stickiness in the presence of threatening unemployment and overcapacity of money wages as compared to money prices, Kaldor assumes that any decline in autonomous investment has zero or negligible intermediate-run effects on unemployment or total output. Instead, wage rates and wage bills rise relative to flexibly falling prices and declining residual profits by just enough to reduce the profit share by just enough to make full-employment saving shrink down to the postulated fall in investment.

That is one way of filling the vacuum created by a fixed-coefficient assumption that negates marginal productivities. It is not, I have to confess, one which commends itself to my own readings of contemporary and historical experience in the US or other developed economies. But this is not the place to evaluate such inferences.

When it comes to the long run, however, there seems to be more common ground for the different macroeconomic distribution theorists. Perhaps this agreement is more apparent than real, constituting agreement about a bizarre case not deemed to be of any true relevance in the realistic world of capitalistic or mixed economies of the twentieth century. Thus, one must not take it for granted that, just because Joan Robinson has done valuable deductive analysis on the properties and tautologies appropriate to golden-age exponential states, she regards such states as being approximated to the tolerable degree that would be necessary to make their tautologies actually useful to the observer and policy-maker in modern mixed economies. Kaldor's stylized version of capitalist development, which is not all that different from those of Cassel, Pigou or for that matter, Say, may not be deemed sufficiently realistic by other Cambridge economists concerned with epochs of capitalist unemployment and underemployment.

In any case, Kaldor assumes in effect that the missing equation to determine factor shares comes from the condition that, whatever the natural rate of growth that the system has imposed on it, there will be full-employment growth at the permissible rate, with the share of profits α having adjusted by the amount needed to make the system's warranted rate of growth equal to the imposed natural rate of growth. Given (s_K, s_L, g), there is a unique root for α^*, determined by equating the warranted and natural growth rates: $g = \{\alpha s_K + (1 - \alpha)s_L\}/b$. This will have a non-negative solution for factor shares[3], provided g is within the range of $\min(s_L, s_K)/b$ and $\max(s_L, s_K)/b$. The razor-edge case of Harrod, where $s_L \equiv s_K \equiv s$, is fatal for this view since: (1) it presupposes a miraculous coincidence of g and s/b, and then (2) leaves distributive shares, α and $1 - \alpha = \alpha_L$, quite indeterminate. As far as the statics of α^* are concerned, we could as well have s_L greater than s_K as less than it. But since Kaldor implicitly assumes that prices are more flexible downward than wage rates, such a reversal of inequalities would lead to the statical equilibrium's being unstable and irrelevant in a world where perturbations to equilibrium have to occur.

The basic tautology of exponential growth states tells us nothing about the merits of macroeconomic versus alternative theories. Thus, the crudest neoclassical model – involving, say an aggregate Cobb–Douglas function in 'leets' (homogeneous capital) and propensities to save out of wages as high or higher than out of profits – is quite compatible with the stated tautology in every and any run, long or short, golden age or otherwise. It is merely that the capital–output ratio b is regarded by it as the variable that (along with $(dK/dt)/K$) adjusts to the Cobb–Douglas-given α^*. Even Kalecki's quite different theory of α^* is compatible with it, provided the degree of excess capacity of his oligopolists adjusts b to the level needed by the tautology if all growth is to remain in balance. The tautology is valid if: (1) Pasinetti's relation, profit rate $= g/s_K$, is valid. But the tautology is valid even if: (2) we are in what has been infelicitously called an 'anti-Pasinetti' equilibrium with $s_L > \alpha^* s_K$. The tautology is valid in a multisector model of general dynamic equilibrium, in which there are many heterogeneous capital goods and many alternative blueprint activities for producing the various outputs and in which the perfection of competition is not assumed to be perfect in every market.

As soon as one wishes to analyze a system that is not necessarily in steady-state exponential balanced-growth equilibrium, the main logical difficulty that arises is the absence of perfect foresight and/or

[3] If $1 - \alpha^*$ is so small as to force real wage rates below the 'subsistence' level, g will no doubt be adversely affected. If α^* is so small as to make the profit rate fall below some needed minimum, liquidity traps and 1936 Keynesian stagnation–unemployment may ensue.

the absence of a full complement of futures markets out to infinity. Among other things, we are plunged into the so-called 'Hahn problem' with a vengeance: how do the real-world markets and the participators in those markets avoid moving off into finite-time-self-fulfilling tulip manias and South Sea bubbles? This logical problem is not less acute for a non-neoclassical activities model than for a multisector smooth heterogeneous-capital model (with or without joint products).

Dobb's (1973) recent book seems to be typical of critics of mainstream economics who have read the works of Sraffa and his Cambridge colleagues. He is left with no purely Marxian theory of distribution. He certainly cannot accept a Clark or even a Walrasian–Malinvaud paradigm. Golden-age tautologies seem of dubious relevance.

It is better to be left with an empty mind than with one filled with nonsense – with deductive inconsistencies and fanciful empirical hypotheses. But, speaking for myself, the weight of evidence suggests to me that there are deep-seated causes for the Lorentz–Pareto distributions of actual income. They can be changed (for good and evil) by governmental policies and by trade-union and other collusions. But they do stubbornly resist such changes in their *real* magnitudes, and their laws of motion over time seem to me to be best understood and forecasted in terms of hypotheses about relative factor supplies, the nature of technological invention and innovation, and (to a lesser degree) in terms of changes in the degree of imperfection of competition in commodity and factor markets.

This prologue has attempted to provide the background against which the various models of time-phased production (my term for what used to be loosely called capital theory) have to be analyzed.

2. Interest theory with and without homogeneous capital

In May 1952, on returning from a Paris econometric conference on risk (the one where Arrow first presented his fundamental break-through on optimal contingent contracts), I visited Cambridge. It must have been a Monday, for I was taken to a seminar in Kahn's rooms at King's where Robinson was presenting her doubts about quantifying the notions of roundaboutness of production and deepening of capital. Youth, like old and middle age, is inclined to be impatient and I was a bit surprised to encounter discussion of such basics at so late a date. But it was a memorable occasion since, so to speak, the act of conception of Robinson's important (1956) *Accumulation of Capital* must already have taken place.

At the time I stated that, along Fisher lines (1907, 1930), there is a basic tradeoff between vectors of consumption goods at one time and such vectors at earlier and later time periods, this transformation frontier being defined as of some still earlier date's vector of heterogeneous capital goods being specified, along with some later date's vector of heterogeneous capital goods also being specified. (This mode of thought was familiar to me because I had been working since 1949 on the Rand monograph, *Linear Programming and Economic Analysis*, on which Dorfman and Solow subsequently became co-researchers (Dorfman *et al.*, 1958). In my widely circulated Rand memorandum (Samuelson, 1949) I had developed intertemporal efficiency conditions for such a model and had conjectured the truth of the production turnpike theorem that lacked adequate proof until Radner's (1961) paper.)

The intertemporal transformation frontier would be concave (weakly or strongly) if increasing returns to scale were ruled out and if summability of the fruits of independent activities were feasible. With concavity, the second dose of chocolates I sacrifice today can be expected to give me a smaller additional dose of chocolates tomorrow than would the first of today's dose sacrificed. The real own rate of interest, regarded as some measure of the tradeoff between chocolates today and next period, could be expected to decline the greater today's abstention from consumption. (This aspect of 'diminishing returns' survives through all reswitching, backward switching, Wicksell effects, denial of marginal productivity smoothness, and rejection of homogeneous capital in favor of vectors of heterogeneous capitals of the putty or clay varieties. Although I had worked out for my paper on factor price equalization (Samuelson, 1953) the concept of the factor–price frontier that is *always* negatively inclined in the absence of joint products, it was not until my paper on Marx (Samuelson, 1957) that I stated this universal truth that stands up despite the reswitching and other phenomena mentioned above (Robinson, 1973).)

What I have said thus far is not so much wrong as vague and oversimplified. Without smoothness in the underlying technology, so that partial derivatives can be everywhere defined, we would lack exact relations for the profit rate i_t of the form

$$1 + i_t = - \partial C_{t+1}/\partial C_t, \tag{1}$$

where C stands for one element of the consumption vector (say chocolates), and where the partial derivative signs indicate that such other variables as initial and terminal capital vectors and other consumptions are being held constant. Instead, in the absence of smoothness, $1 + i_t$ would lie within the range set by 'left- and right-hand' $-\Delta C_{t+1}/\Delta C_t$ expressions. Those of us who had been analyzing the Harrod–Domar accelerator growth model[4] on the lines of the inflexible accelerator

$$C_{t+1} + K_{t+1} - K_t = \min (K_t/\beta, L_t/a_0) - dK_t,$$
$$C_t \geq 0, \qquad K_{t+1} - K_t \geq dK_t \tag{2}$$

recognized that the step-like range of indeterminacy of the interest-profit rate could, in this fixed capital–output model, be so wide as to make the wage share anything from 0 to 100% of national income. So I should not have been so smug in my own mind.

Moreover, reflecting during the plane trip going home, I fell into a definite trap, a trap that an example of reswitching could have kept me out of. Suppose society begins at a given *plateau* of consumption (chocolates only or a market basket of consumption goods) with all vectors of capital goods being constant in time. Now suppose, for an interval, the society does some 'abstaining' or 'waiting' (let it be by decree of the planning board in a socialist state if Baron Rothschild's saving and investing seems repugnant). Then, subsequently society can almost always have a *higher* plateau of consumption goods (unless, improbably, we are already at the golden-rule satiation level of maximum consumption). What makes this possible is the new vector of maintained capital goods in the background, which in *some* of its elements must now be numerically greater. A second spell of equal chocolates abstinence prolonged for the same length of time, as we have already seen, cannot lead to a greater new increment of plateau of consumption. But I went

---

[4]Where possible, I give discrete-time versions of models to reduce extraneous complications. Exponential depreciation holds in (2), with $1/d$ the average life expectancy of equipment.

beyond this to assert: suppose you observe an interest or profit rate (they are the same thing in the absence of uncertainty) at the original level and at the new level. (In a Pontryagin–Kantorovich optimal control society the observed interest rate would be dual-variable shadow prices in the planning board's computers; in Victoria's England, these could be on loan contracts of low risk type.) Then I rashly held: Samuelson's false theorem – the rate of interest will be (if anything) lower at the higher plateau of consumption. I am unable to cite a paper where I wrote this down explicitly. But if I were to examine a variorum edition of my elementary *Economics*, some-where around the sixth edition, traces of this view could be found in the appendix on interest theory; and in one or another of my letters to Robinson one might find this false theorem.

The theorem is false even in a domain where reswitching cannot occur[5]. It is false even in a model where marginal productivity determinants of the profit rate *could* be true (as in a two-capital good model that is smooth). It is false even in a model with one homogeneous capital good and in which marginal productivity smoothnesses exist to validate marginal productivity relations (but where the no-joint product postulate is denied as in the multiple turnpike case of Liviatan and Samuelson). It is false even in a model where we assume perfect futures markets exist for all times and all goods and in which warranted dynamic paths can be rigorously defined and are actually followed.

Although the possibility of reswitching is *not necessary* for there

---

[5] Even if that other false theorem, which for my sins I planted in the mind of Levhari, had not been false (what an if!), Samuelson's false theorem would be false, since indecomposability of the Leontief–Sraffa matrix (which Levhari wrongly thought could rule out reswitching) cannot rule out the innumerable contradictions to Samuelson's false theorem. Why the false theorem is false, which is to say why I should have discerned this fact from the beginning, is indicated briefly in footnotes 6 and 9 of Samuelson (1966, pp. 577, 579) and Samuelson (1965, vol. III, pp. 239, 241). This can be seen even more clearly in a simple joint-product model with one capital good like that of Liviatan–Samuelson: if $C_{t+1} = F[L_t, K_t; K_{t+1} - K_t]$ is concave in its arguments, then $\partial^2(K_{t+1} - K_t)/\partial K_t^2 \leq 0$ and $\partial^2 C_{t+1}/\partial C_t^2 \leq 0$; but that is no reason why the relation between $\partial(K_{t+1} - K_t)/\partial K_t = r_t$ and C_t cannot, for $K_{t+1} - K_t = 0$ and r_t away from zero, be a positive one, for this depends upon complicated complemen-tarity cross derivatives of F and not on the definiteness of its Hessian matrix. Credit must go to Pasinetti, Garegagni, Morishima and Bruno–Burmeister–Sheshinski for demonstrating the possibility of reswitching even in an indecomposable model; see 'Paradoxes in capital theory: a symposium', *Quarterly Journal of Economics*, 80 (1966), 503–583 for their papers, the Levhari and Samuelson recantation, and my 'A summing up'.

to be a positive rather than negative relation between the producible level of steady-state consumption and the steady-state profit rate, reswitching is dramatically *sufficient* to reveal this and show the falsity of Samuelson's false theorem: to use the example of my paper (Samuelson, 1966) on reswitching, if above a 100% interest rate the economy returns to the golden-rule factor proportions appropriate to below 50%, clearly the plateau of consumption at 51% is lower than at 101%. Without disagreeing in substance with Robinson's 1973 view of reswitching as unimportant, we see that it can play a useful role in alerting economists to more important possibilities in the background.

3. The too-special paradigm

All of the above can be summarized by saying that the most general neo-neoclassical case of a concave, homogeneous, Fisher–Solow intertemporal frontier

$$0 = T(K_t^1, \ldots, K_t^n; L_t, L_{t+1}, \ldots, L_{t+T-1}; C_{t+1}^1, \ldots, C_{t+1}^m, \ldots,$$
$$C_{t+T}^1, \ldots, C_{t+T}^m; K_{t+T}^1, \ldots, K_{t+T}^n)$$
$$= T(K_t; L_t, \ldots, L_{t+T-1}; C_{t+1}, \ldots, C_{t+T}; K_{t+T}), \quad \text{for short,} \quad (3)$$

does not, repeat not, have *all* the familiar properties of the simpler Clark–Ramsey–Solow–Swan–Meade parable

$$C_{t+1} + K_{t+1} - K_t = L_t f(K_t/L_t) - dK_t, \quad \text{NNP,}$$
$$r_t = f'(K_t/L_t) - d = R_t - d, \quad \text{profit rate or } i_t, \qquad (4)$$
$$w_t = f(K_t/L_t) - (K_t/L_t)f'(K_t/L_t), \quad \text{wage rate,}$$

where $f''(\ \ )$ is well defined and negative, $C_t \geq 0$, $K_{t+1} - K_t \geq -dK_t$; d is the rate of exponential depreciation of K, and $1/d$ the average length of life of K.

This is the simplest neoclassical case, with one homogeneous malleable physical capital, one sector, no joint production, smooth substitutability and all successful saving–investment being able to go into the one capital stuff without need for extensive planning foresight. For it, the Harrod–Domar growth model of eq. (2) takes on simple, over-simple, form: *any* path is a warranted path; if labor grows exponentially and net saving and consumption are *any* monotone functions of output (or of separate factor shares), asymptotically the actual path will approach the natural rate of growth, as Solow (1956) showed in detail and as Tobin (1955) discussed in monetary terms. For such an over-simple case, Clarkian marginal productivity gives the distribution between labor and property at every instant in terms of K/L proportions, and forms part of the general-equilibrium equation system that determines all the variables. (However, only for the Cobb–Douglas case of unit elasticity of substitution σ will Bowley's constant relative shares invariably hold. For σ much below unity, increasingly close to zero, eq. (4) will approach the fixed capital–output case of eq. (2) with relative shares swinging from 0 to 100% at the slightest change in K/L.)

Robinson's insistence on the desirability of going beyond this over-simple case deserves praise. In particular, it has been an important advance for economists of all schools to discover just which of the steady-state properties of eq. (4) do *not* necessarily hold for the most general case of eq. (3).

It is worth listing some dozen steady-state properties of eq. (4) that may or may not apply in general:

$$- \partial C_{t+1}/\partial C_t = 1 + r_t$$

or

$$\lim_{h \to 0} \{-\Delta C_{t+1}/(C_t + h - C_t)\} \le 1 + r_t$$

$$\le \lim_{h \to 0} \{-\Delta C_{t+1}/(C_t - h - C_t)\} \quad (5a)$$

$$\partial^2 C_{t+1}/\partial C_t^2 \le 0$$

or

$$\Delta^2 C_{t+1}/\Delta C_t^2 \le 0, \tag{5b}$$

$$W/P_i = f_i(r) = f(r), \quad \text{factor–price frontier } \textit{tradeoff}, \tag{5c}$$

$$r = f'(K/L), \quad \text{marginal productivity}, \qquad f'' < 0, \tag{5d}$$

$$C/L = \gamma(r), \quad \text{monotone decreasing}, \qquad \gamma'(\ ) < 0, \tag{5e}$$

$$C/L = \theta(K/L), \quad \text{monotone increasing}, \qquad \theta'(\ ) > 0, \tag{5f}$$

K/Q or capital–output ratio declining with profit rate, $\qquad$ (5g)

K/L declining with profit rate, $\qquad\qquad$ (5g')

no reswitching possible, (5h)

no 'backward switching' possible, (5i)

elasticity of (r, w) frontier=wage share/profit share, (5j)

no foresight needed to determine composition of investment,
(5k)

no putty–clay versus putty–putty distinction needed. (5l)

Some interpretations of these too-terse properties are needed. In all forms of (5a) and (5b), 'other' variables are understood 'to be held constant': initial and terminal (*vectors* of) *capitals*; consumptions of other time periods; other elements in the market-basket vectors of consumption goods; etc. In (5c), if there are many capital goods and/or sectors of non-joint production, the real wage in terms of *every* good's price will form a factor–price frontier with the negative slope of a tradeoff. In (5e) and (5f), if there are many consumption goods, then others are to be held constant; and if, instead of having a steady state with zero population growth, we have one with positive natural rate of growth g, then the monotone relations are to hold only for r's greater than g and K/L less than the golden rule $(K/L)^*$ corresponding to $r^* = g$. In (5g) and (5g'), if there are many capital goods, the capital–output ratio will have to be expressed in some *numéraire's* value units, $\Sigma P_i K_i / \Sigma P_i Q_i$ and $\Sigma P_i K_i / WL$. In (5i), backward switching is defined in the Robinson manner as a case where, at interest rates below the switch rate, the technique used is less labor intensive in the sense that net available final output (or C in the steady state with $g = 0$) is higher rather than lower there. As thus defined, backward switching of (5i) is identical with denying (5a) and my false theorem.

3.1. Relations universally valid and not

Those who have followed the literature of the past 20 years know that these many properties of the Clarkian paradigm do *not* all hold generally. In every Cambridge, and wherever informed economic theory is taught, there is no 1976 disagreement on this. Thus, any reswitching example shows that although (5h) is implied by eq. (4), (5h) does not have to hold in general and thus so much the worse for

(4). The same reswitching example negates the false theorem of (5e) and (5i).

Suitably interpreted, (5a), (5b), and (5c) do stand up in the most general case of eq. (3). When there is only one activity technique available, the second form of (5a) alone becomes relevant and its limits may be so wide as not to be useful; as the number of activity-technique options increases in the von Neumann fashion, and providing the options are varied, the second forms of (5a) and (5b) may approach arbitrarily close to the first derivative forms. So long as we rule out intrinsic joint production, the negatively sloped factor–price frontier of (5c) remains valid, a fact that makes it impossible for both Marxian laws of declining rate of profit and of immizerizing declining real wage to hold. (No matter what the character of viable technical change, if intrinsic joint production holds, like that of wool–mutton and going beyond mere putty-durable machines subject to exponential decay, Burmeister and Kuga have shown that a factor–price tradeoff can still be defined and that it is dual to the consumption-growth rate frontier in the usual Weizsäcker–Bruno duality fashion.)

All the other relations, (5d)–(5l), are in some sense special to the simplest neoclassical parable. Since one can affirm or deny $13 - 3 = 10$ propositions in $2^{10} = 1024$ different ways, it is a necessary deductive task to delineate alternative models in which subsets of (5d)–(5l) hold or do not hold. I shall only mention a sample of these non-controversial relationships.

Thus, as Garegnani properly pointed out to me prior to completion of my 1962 paper (Samuelson, 1962), and as I might have realized from the consideration that *one* arbitrary function cannot determine *two* arbitrary functions, it is only when the same production function can be written for the consumption good and the capital good sector, so that they in effect collapse into one sector, that the elasticity of the steady-state (r, w) factor–price frontier provides a measure of wage–profit shares in the national income[6]. The relation (5g) was established in my surrogate capital parable (Samuelson, 1962), for (4) and for one-sector heterogeneous capital extensions that include some cases of Robinson's (1956) blueprints of alterna-

---

[6]von Weizsäcker showed, a decade ago, that the elasticity of the $(W/P_c, r)$ frontier does measure, even when the two sectors differ in their L_i/K_i ratios, the relative shares in the golden-rule configuration where $r = g$, the natural rate of growth of all elements of the system.

tive techniques. Burmeister has emphasized repeatedly that it is (5g′) rather than (5g) which is crucial for the truth of (5e), i.e. the only way steady-state consumption can be high at interest rates in greater excess of the golden-rule rate is for $\Sigma \, P_i \, dK_i/dr$ to fail to be negative, not for $d \, \Sigma \, (P_iK_i/P_qQ)/dr$ to fail to be negative. The relation (5k) shows that for (4)'s parable there are no intertemporal-efficiency conditions of my 1949 type needed, so that 'mistakes' in planning or in market behavior are of no great concern. The (5k) and (5l) conditions are also related to Robinson's (1973) discussion of 'pseudo production functions', namely steady-state relations that cannot correctly be used to describe time-phased input–output relations that hold in *unbalanced* dynamic paths. The distinction between putty–putty and putty–clay in (5l) is related to the realistic possibility that, once a capital good is produced, then *ex post* its qualitative properties are frozen in conformity to its original planned use in a particular sector and particular technique. It may then be non-transferable or only transferable at a great penalty. However, *ex ante*, there may be a great variety of alternative forms that it might take, with the result that the *short-run* family of production functions may have members that each are close to fixed proportions or to low elasticity of substitution, even though the *long-run* envelope of these functions may show great substitutability and even smoothness!

3.2. *Legitimate and illegimate use of pseudo production function*

The putty–clay version of a simple model provides an interesting demonstration. We may as well consider a Uzawa two-sector model as a Solow one-sector model, thereby eliminating some arguments about special simplicities of the latter. In the most naive, malleable, neoclassical form, the Uzawa model becomes for sectors zero and one:

$$C_{t+1} = F^0(L^0_t, K^{10}_t) \geq 0,$$
$$G_{t+1} = F^1(L^1_t, K^{11}_t) = K^1_{t+1} - (1 - d_1)K^1_t \geq 0, \qquad (6)$$
$$0 \leq K^1_t \leq K^{10}_t + K^{11}_t, \qquad K^{1i}_t \geq 0 \qquad (i = 0, 1).$$

But now let us go from putty–putty to putty–clay, so that once the K^1 destined for the consumption good sector gets frozen into its K^{10}

form it cannot be used as K^{11}, and likewise for K^1 frozen into K^{11} that cannot be shifted to K^{10} use. Now the model becomes

$$C_{t+1} = F^0(L_t^0, K_t^{10}) \geq 0,$$

$$G_{t+1}^0 + G_{t+1}^1 = F^1(L_t^1, K_t^{11}), \qquad G_t^i \geq 0, \tag{7}$$

$$K_{t+1}^i = K_t^{1i} + G_t^i - d_i K_t^{1i} \geq 0 \qquad (i = 1, 2).$$

Suppose that $F^i(\ ,\ )$ are smooth with existent partial derivatives. Then it is routine to prove that the steady-state profit rate $r_t \equiv r$ is equal to the net marginal own-productivity of physical capital, which will necessarily be a declining function of the $K^1/L = (K^{10} + K^{11})/L$ ratio. (If instead of a zero population growth rate we postulate a steady-state exponential golden age with $L_{t+1}/L_t = 1 + g$, then for each g a similar statement can be made. But whether r will be higher or lower for higher K^1/L will now depend on whether the consumption good sector is relatively more or relatively less labor intensive than the capital good sector.)

With (7)'s putty–clay, we cannot add more L_t^0 to given K_t^{10} and get any extra product. It would seem that marginal productivity fails. But, it can be verified rigorously, the steady-state profit rate $r \equiv r_t$ can be correctly deduced from the marginal-productivity partial derivatives of $F^i(\ ,\ )$ in (7) or (6). These production functions, one may agree, are 'pseudo' in the sense that (6) cannot legitimately describe the time-phased transient unbalanced paths of (7). But they are legitimate in predicting the observable relations between (7)'s steady state r and $(K^{10} + K^{11})/L$. So perhaps the expression 'steady-state surrogate production functions' would be a better name than 'pseudo production function' for the legitimate use of (6) to summarize (7)'s steady-state properties.

This is no mere trick. Suppose (7) is in a steady state and a bomb destroys some of K_t^{10} and K_t^{11}. Then own-rate of profit will not be equal to each other and to the previous profit rate. One (or both) own-rates of profit will rise because of 'capital scarcity'. Only a reduction of consumption by somebody's doing without can restore the old capital plenty and the old steady-state profit rate: if capitalists consume nothing, that drop in consumption must come from a decline in the real wage because (so to speak!) workers have less equipment or 'leets' to work with in the post-bombing transition[7].

References

Arrow, K. J. (1963–1964), The role of securities in the optimal allocation of risk-bearing, *Review of Economic Studies*, 31, 91–96; a translation of: Le role des valeurs boursières pour la repartition la meilleur des risques, *Econometrie*, Colloques Internationaux du Centre National de la Recherche Scientifique, XI (1953) 41–47; reproduced as Arrow (1971, ch. 4).

Arrow, K. J. (1971), *Essays in the Theory of Risk Bearing*, Markham: Chicago.

Boulding, K. (1950), *Reconstruction of Economics*, Wiley: New York.

Burmeister, E. and Dobell, A. R. (1970), *Mathematical Theories of Economic Growth*, Macmillan: New York.

Dobb, M. H. (1973), *Theories of Value and Distribution since Adam Smith*, Cambridge University Press: London.

Domar, E. D. (1946), Capital expansion, rate of growth, and employment, *Econometrica*, 14, 137–147; reproduced as Domar (1957, ch. 3) which also contains his (1947), (1948), and (1952) *American Economic Review* essays.

Domar, E. D. (1957) *Essays in the Theory of Economic Growth*, Oxford University Press: New York.

Dorfman, R., Samuelson, P. and Solow, R. (1958), *Linear Programming and Economic Analysis*, McGraw-Hill: New York.

Fisher, I. (1907), *The Rate of Interest: Its Nature and Determination and Relation to Economic Phenomena*, Macmillan: New York.

Fisher, I. (1930), *The Theory of Interest: As Determined by Impatience to Spend Income and Opportunity to Invest It*, Macmillan: New York; A. M. Kelley: New York (1965).

Hahn, F. (1950), *The Share of Wages in National Income*, Weidenfeld & Nicolson: London.

Harcourt, G. C. (1972), *Some Cambridge Controversies in the Theory of Capital*, Cambridge University Press: Cambridge.

Harrod, R. F. (1936), *The Trade Cycle*, Clarendon Press: Oxford.

Harrod, R. F. (1939), An essay in dynamic theory, *Economic Journal*, 49 (Apr.).

Harrod, R. F. (1947), *Economic Journal*, 57.

Harrod, R. F. (1948), *Toward a Dynamic Economics*, Macmillan: London, which gives references to Harrod's important earlier (1936) *The Trade Cycle* and his (1939) *Economic Journal* essay in dynamic economics.

Kaldor, N. (1955), Alternative theories of distribution, *Review of Economic Studies*, 23, 83–100.

[7]Dropping Uzawa–Robinson 'leets' (equals 'steel' spelled backwards), can we doubt that something like this must happen no matter how heterogeneous the capital goods sector. Thus, with capitalists saving all their profits, bombing every element of the capital sector will take us out of the golden-rule state: all own-profit rates can sink back into that golden-rule state at best only asymptotically in time (as in the one-sector Solow–Phelps case, but with the Hahn complication that the system must properly allocate available capital formation among the different capital goods).

Kaldor, N. (1956), A model of economic growth, *Economic Journal*, 67 (Dec.).

Kalecki, M. (1938), *Essays in the Theory of Economic Fluctuations*, Farrar & Rinehart: New York (1939).

Kalecki, M. (1942), A theory of profits, *Economic Journal*, 52.

Keynes, J. M. (1936), *The General Theory of Employment, Interest and Money*, Macmillan: London.

Keynes, J. M. (1937), Some economic consequences of a declining population, *Eugenics Review Lecture*, vol. 29, No. 1 (Apr.) London.

Liviatan, N. and Samuelson, P. (1969), Notes on turnpikes: stable and unstable, *Journal of Economic Theory*. 454–475; reproduced as Samuelson (1965, vol. III, ch. 141).

Pontryagin, L. S., Boltyanski, V. G., Gamrelidze, R. V. and Mishchenko, E. F. (1962), *The Mathematical Theory of Optimal Processes*, Interscience Publishers: New York. Kantorovich, from 1939 onward, independently developed aspects of what we call linear programming – as did Hitchcock, Koopmans and von Neumann prior to Danzig's (1947) development of the simplex method.

Radner, R. (1961), Prices and the turnpike, III: paths of economic growth that are optimal with regard only to final states: a turnpike theorem, *Review of Economic Studies*, 28, 98–104; related turnpike contributions are in the same issue by Hicks and Morishima, and subsequent work was done by Furuya and Inada, McKenzie, Koopmans, Samuelson, Drandakis and many others.

Ramsey, F. P. (1928), A mathematical theory of saving, *Economic Journal*, 38.

Robinson, J. V. (1956), *The Accumulation of Capital*, Macmillan: London.

Robinson, J. V. (1973), On the unimportance of reswitching, *Quarterly Journal of Economics*, 89 (Feb.).

Samuelson, P. (1949), Market mechanisms and maximization, III, Rand Corporation research memorandum, 29 June; reproduced as Samuelson (1965, vol. I, ch. 33, pp. 471–492).

Samuelson, P. (1953), Prices of factors and goods in general equilibrium, *Review of Economic Studies*, 21, 1–20; reproduced as Samuelson (1965, vol. II, ch. 70, pp. 888–907); the first section of the appendix defines the minimum-unit-cost function dual to the production function whose contours are the factor-price frontier: both Shephard and Champernowne at about the same time, independently, arrived at similar concepts.

Samuelson, P. (1957), Wages and interest: a modern dissection of Marxian economic models, *American Economic Review*, 47, 884–912, particularly p. 894; reproduced as Samuelson (1965, vol. I, ch. 29, pp. 341–369, particularly p. 351). The factor–price frontier's negative slope guarantees the incompatibility of falling profit rate *and* falling real wage; at most one of these Marxian laws can hold.

Samuelson, P. A. (1962), Parable and realism in capital theory: the surrogate production function, *Review of Economic Studies*, 21, 193–206.

Samuelson, P. A. (1964), *Economics*, McGraw-Hill: New York, 6th edn.; pp. 595–597 and fig. 5 are wrong in seeming to deny that a sacrifice of present consumption to get to a higher plateau of income could be accompanied by a rise in the interest rate. Ultimately, sufficiently near to the zero golden-rule rate, the alleged 'diminishing-returns' relation must hold, but earlier there can be reversals. [Consider a smooth heterogeneous-capital model, $C^t = F[L, K^t, K^{t+1}]$, where $K^t = (K^t_1, \ldots, K^t_n)$ and $(F_i, F_{n+j}) = (\partial F/\partial K^t_j, \partial F/\partial K^{t+1}_j)$ and L is constant and hereafter omitted from F. Let $F_i/F_{n+i} = 1 + r$ define a steady-state relation $C = \gamma(r)$, with $\gamma'(r)$ not necessarily negative as in the one-sector (5e). Now suppose $K^t \equiv K^0$, $t < t^0$ with $F[K^0, K^0] = \gamma(r^0) = C^0$. For $t^0 < t < t^1$ impose $F[K^t, K^{t+1}] = C^0 - H$, and for $t > t^1$, $F[K^t, K^{t+1}] \equiv C^0 + G$, where G is to be maximal. Then fig. 5 (1964) is correct in suggesting that $G/(t^1 - t^0)$ is a concave function of H, $g(H)$, with $g'(0)$

proportional to r^0 as $(t^1 - t^0) \to 0$. But it would be wrong to claim that $g'(H)$ is proportional to the r^1 that will be reached in the post-t_2 steady state, when H is finite (since, among other things, when $\gamma'(r^0) > 0$, $r^1 \nless r^0$ for small finite H). Moreover, it would be wrong to claim that $G_2 < G$ when we impose: $K^t \equiv K^0$, $F[K^0, K^0] = C^0 = \gamma(r^0)$, $t < t^0$; $F[K^t, K^{t+1}] = C^0 - H$, $t^0 < t < t^1$; $F[K^t, K^{t+1}] \equiv C^0 + G - H$, $t^2 < t < t^2 + (t^1 - t^0)$; and $F[K^t, K^{t+1}] = C^0 + G + G_2$, with G_2 to be maximal. I omit the subtle proofs, but affirm the following kernel of universal truth: from any $C = F[L, K^t, K^{t+1}]$ which is not already in a golden-rule state (so that $r^t > 0$ if $L = L^0$ or $r^t > g$ if $L = L^0 e^{gt}$), by *sacrificing current* attainable steady-state per capita consumption, the system may attain *higher ultimate* steady-state per capita consumption on a perpetual basis, *and in doing so it will lower the interest or profit rate*. Some myths are valid.]

Samuelson, P. (1965), *Collected Scientific Papers*, MIT Press: Cambridge, Mass.

Samuelson, P. A. (1966), A summing up, *Quarterly Journal of Economics*, 80, 444–448; reproduced as Samuelson (1965, vol. III, ch. 148).

Samuelson, P. (1973), *Economics*, 9th edn., McGraw-Hill: New York.

Solow, R. M. (1956), A contribution to the theory of economic growth, *Quarterly Journal of Economics*, 70 (Feb.).

Solow, R. M. (1958), *Linear Programming and Economic Analysis*, McGraw-Hill: New York, Dorfman and Samuelson co-authors.

Tobin, J. (1955), A dynamic aggregative model, *Journal of Political Economy*, 63 (Apr.).

von Weizsäcker, C. C. (1963), Bemerkungen zu Einem 'Symposium' Über Wachstums-theorie und Produnktionfunktionen, *Kyklos*, 16, 438–457. For references to Bruno, Hicks and Burmeister–Kuga dualities and generalizations, see Burmeister and Dobell (1970) which contains numerous references; another good source for references is Harcourt (1972).

216

STEADY-STATE AND TRANSIENT RELATIONS:
A REPLY ON RESWITCHING *

PAUL A. SAMUELSON

Nature of a pitfall, 41. — Substantive vindication– 43. — Deeper issue of nonsteady-state analysis, 45.

Economics owes much to Joan Robinson for her many contributions across the whole spectrum of the subject: imperfect competition, Keynesian macroeconomics, international trade, Marxian-analysis contributions and critiques, growth theory, economic philosophy, and much more. Her 1975 paper [1] will be of interest to those who have not followed closely the complex discussions of modern capital theory and, as well, to those who have. But beyond this, it represents a valuable addition to our meagre store of autobiographical accounts of the actual process by which scientific ideas get formed, modified, and motivated.

Autobiography has a tendency to evoke autobiography, and Professor Robinson's account revives some of my own memories. This, however, is not the occasion for such an exercise. What is appropriate is that I review my own contribution to this *Journal's* Symposium on Reswitching in the light of her remarks, to discover whether and where my pen may have slipped, and as gracefully as possible acknowledge in the interest of scientific truth any errors turned up. For, as Professor Robinson says, the purely *logical* parts of economic arguments should not remain subject to irresolution or dispute.

When the sixteen pages of my "A Summing Up" [2] are subjected to a merciless audit, both in the light of Professor Robinson's present remarks and of the voluminous literature on the subject since, what does the trial balance show? I must report that my 1966 discussion seems to stand up very well, and it would be hypocritical of me to give it other than a clean bill of health as a representation

* I owe thanks to the National Science Foundation for financial aid, and to Kate Crowley for editorial help.

1. J. Robinson, "The Unimportance of Reswitching," this *Journal*, LXXXIX (Feb. 1975), 32–39.
2. P. Samuelson, "A Summing Up," this *Journal*, LXXX (Nov. 1966), 568–83. This appeared in the symposium in which L. Pasinetti, P. Garegnani, M. Morishima, and Bruno-Burmeister-Sheshinski had all provided valid counterexamples to the false assertion that, in an indecomposable Leontief-Sraffa system, reswitching is allegedly impossible — as was admitted explicitly and unreservedly in D. Levhari and P. Samuelson, "The Reswitching Theorem is False," this *Journal*, LXXX (Nov. 1966), 518–19.

of my 1975 views. Indeed, readers who need help in digesting Professor Robinson's text at its more terse places might be aided in understanding by simultaneously consulting this 1966 summary on reswitching.

Since my purpose here is not to win an argument, but to avoid an unnecessary one and to narrow down the recognized area of disagreement, let me briefly examine what it is that could possibly lead a critic to think that in "A Summing Up" the author did illegitimately utilize for analysis of *transient* passages (between or out of steady states) the functions and technical relations that are valid only *across different steady states*. For, it is that charge that Professor Robinson seems to be making.[3]

NATURE OF A PITFALL

First, begin with a general truth untouched by reswitching or by difference of opinion about the existence of capital aggregates and about the usefulness of production functions with smooth-substitutability properties.

FACTOR-PRICE FRONTIER THEOREM: *If all goods can be produced over time, at constant returns to scale, with no joint production, out of themselves and out of one or more primary factors, then there exists a quasi-concave monotonic factor-price trade-off frontier relating (i) the rate of interest or profit and (ii) the real wages (or rents or prices) of those primary factors in terms of any one of the good's price. I.e.,*

$$(1) \qquad 1+r = h_i(W_1/P_i, W_2/P_i, \ldots) \qquad (i=1, \ldots, n),$$

where an increase in all or any subset of $(W_1/P_i, W_2/P_i, \ldots)$ *will lower* r *and where for fixed* r *the trade-off between* $(W_1/P_i, W_2/P_i, \ldots)$ *is a convex function.*

This factor-price frontier, whose existence was sensed by Smith, Ricardo, v. Thünen, and other classical economists, somehow did not get enunciated and named in the economic literature until a late date. For the one-primary-factor case of labor only, if Piero

---

3. Cf. Robinson, *op. cit.*: "At the end of it all, Professor Samuelson still thought that he could use a pseudoproduction function in describing a process of accumulation through time. . . ." A related criticism will be found in G. C. Harcourt, *Some Cambridge Controversies in the Theory of Capital,* (Cambridge: Cambridge University Press, 1972), around p. 123 and perhaps elsewhere. Professor Harcourt very kindly called to my attention recently a dozen passages in the 1966 text that might lay themselves open to misinterpretation, and I have noted a score more that should be unambiguously clarified by the discussion to follow. Note 7, p. 44, returns to this point.

Sraffa had published in 1930 his 1960 book, the factor-price frontier would not have had to be independently discussed after 1949 by R. Shephard, D. Champernowne, J. R. Hicks, myself, and many others.[4]

It is important to realize that this theorem applies outside the Santa Claus world of oversimplified neoclassical analysis. It holds for Parts I and III of Sraffa's book, and for general von Neumann systems that involve no joint productions (or only joint productions of the type that still admit of nonsubstitution theorems).

But note this. For it *steady-state analysis is implied* in which

$$r^t = r^{t \pm 1}, \ (W_j/P_i)^t \equiv (W_j/P_i)^{t \pm 1}, \ \ldots, \ \text{etc.}$$

It is false to think that, as a system moves *out of a steady state,* its prices and quantities will be found *along* the same trade-off loci. Even a neoclassical case will illustrate this. Consider a one-sector "leets" model of Ramsey-Solow-Swan-Meade type, where

(2) $C + \dfrac{dK}{dt} = F(L, K) = L \, F(1, K/L) = L \, f[K/L]$

$f'[\ \ ] > 0, f''[\ \ ] < 0.$

Then, independently of the time trend of $K/L = k(t)$, the profit or interest rate, $r = f'[k(t)]$, and the wage, $w = f[k(t)] - k(t)f'[k(t)]$, *do* always lie on the steady-state factor-price frontier definable from $f[\ \ ]$ in the form

(3) $r = h(w), \ h'(w) < 0.$

This, however, is special to oversimplified neoclassical fables.

But consider any *general* non-one-sector model. A simplest case would be a two-sector model in which the capital-goods-jelly stuff (leets), K, were producible by labor alone; and consumption (corn) is produced out of K, and labor by a neoclassical function. Even in this oversimplified case where capital-deepening is unambiguously possible, when $k(t)$ is changing, there is no universally valid relation of the $r = h(w)$ type. Indeed, since the relative price

4. R. Shephard, *Cost and Production Functions* (Princeton: Princeton University Press, 1953); D. Champernowne, "The Production Function and the Theory of Capital," *Review of Economic Studies,* XXI, No. 2 (1953), 112–35; P. Samuelson, "Prices of Factors and Goods in General Equilibrium," *Review of Economic Studies,* XXI, No. 1 (1953), 1–20; P. Samuelson, "Wages and Interest," *American Economic Review,* XLVII (Dec. 1957), 884–912; P. Sraffa, *Production of Commodities by Means of Commodities* (Cambridge: Cambridge University Press, 1960); J. Hicks, *Capital and Growth* (Oxford: Oxford University Press, 1965); P. Samuelson, "A Modern Treatment of the Ricardian Economy, I and II," this *Journal,* LXXIII (Feb., May 1959), 1–35, 217–31; P. Samuelson, "Parable and Realism in Capital Theory," *Review of Economic Studies,* XXIX (June 1962), 193–206. The duality theory related to this frontier goes back forty years to the work of Harold Hotelling and thirty years to that of René Roy.

of corn and leets is declining when $k'(t) > 0$, the own rate of interest or profit *is different in terms of each good*, being less for corn than for leets as capital is accumulating. By uninteresting coincidence this example does happen to involve the leets-own-profit rate and the corn real wage as falling along the steady-state $r = h(w)$ relation even in transient growth. Professor Robinson would be quite right to convict a writer of error who asserted that the observed relation between the own-*corn*-profit rate and the real-wage-in-corn also fell along the $r = h(w)$ function (the "pseudofunction" in her elliptic reference).[5]

For me to have said this in 1966, or thought it, would indeed have required a 1967 correction or a 1975 recantation. But I sinned neither in thought nor word. Indeed, even in 1962,[6] I did not perpetrate such an error in my surrogate production function discussion; and in 1966 I went out of the way to avoid all such pitfalls.

SUBSTANTIVE VINDICATION?

Where then does the possibility of misinterpretation arise? It arises from the ambiguity of English speech and grammar. Thus, in my first paragraph, I speak of "switching back at a low interest rate . . ." and of ". . . as the interest rate falls in consequence of abstention from present consumption. . . ." Suppose that here, and in a score of other innocent passages, I had rewritten these as ". . . a switch back had *permanently* occurred at a *permanent* low interest rate to the techniques *permanently* viable at a *permanent*

5. If deepening is "slowed down," so that lim $k'(\ ) \to 0$, the error in using the $h(W/P_c)$ relation for the own-corn-profit rate would $\to 0$, an observation that I could not have repeatedly made over the years if I were not alertly conscious of the pitfall. If we modify the example so that both sectors use some of K and make putty-clay rather than putty-putty assumptions, Professor Robinson's warning will be all the more in order, and I second it.

6. "Parable and Realism in Capital Theory," *op. cit.*, reproduced as Chapter 28 in *CSP*, I, 325–338. I have acknowledged my deep debt to Professor Garegnani for keeping me from the error of thinking that the equal-intensity assumption of the argument was not crucial to some of its simplifications. From neoclassical considerations alone I should not have been in even momentary doubt on the matter, since how can *one* function, $r = h(w)$, contain the content of *independent* two-sector functions,

$$\frac{dK}{dt} + \delta K = G = F_1[L_1, K_1], \quad C = F_2[L_2, K_2]?$$

My 1975 audit of this 1962 paper would omit or qualify the word "exactly" in its sixth paragraph; would explicitly include L_{t-1}, L_t, L_{t+1} in the final $T(\ ) = 0$ relation; and would replace the simple $\partial C_{t+1}/\partial C_t$ and $\partial C_t/\partial L_t$ derivatives by their generalized values as "left-hand and right-hand limiting derivatives," or what is the same thing, by the dual variables of the problem, which serve as slopes of supporting hyperplanes and satisfy *inequalities* at corners where fixity of coefficients prevails. I am glad now to reinforce Professor Robinson's warning that, in transient states, the 1962 schedules will *not* be observed.

high interest rate *subsequent* to successful saving-investment abstaining in the past from then-current consumption [as envisaged by the neoclassical writers being quoted]." If I had done this, even a hostile critic could not have managed to fall into a misunderstanding; and a critic of neoclassical views, sensitized to past propensities of some writers to err on related matters, would have had no reason to quarrel with my revised text.

So, to narrow down misunderstanding, I authorize any reader to make such purely verbal alterations at a score of places.

This done, how much of my substantive argument evaporates, or is vitiated, or needs amendation and elucidation? None that I can see. No diagram needs redrawing. No substantive contention need be withdrawn or qualified.

Since it is only too easy to be blind to one's own shortcomings, I have gone to some pains to check this complacent conclusion by reference to a detailed criticism on the same point by Professor Geoffrey Harcourt.[7] The conclusion stands.

7. Harcourt, *op. cit.*, pp. 122–23, compliments my 1966 discussion for "handsomely admit[ting] the logic of the neo-Keynesian criticisms," but quotes a passage, as a sample of still others, that is supposed (as an aside) to violate "Joan Robinson's strictures that it is most important not to apply theorems obtained from the analysis of differences to situations of change (or, at least, to be aware of the act of faith in doing this). . . ." Because of length I do not reproduce the supposedly offending quotation, which consists of the complete sentences of the first paragraph on p. 577 of my 1966 paper. What it plainly says is correct, and I would write it again, namely the following: if above 100 percent interest rate and below 50, technique A is viable over technique B, society can go from 101 percent equilibrium to 49 percent equilibrium without any physical movements at all. And so it can, as in my Table I between, say, time 7 and time 23 with all the intermediate times shown there skipped; or, as between time 4 and 5 (!) with the only changes between the equilibrium being the change in price tags that are *not* shown in the table. The point of the passage quoted was *not* to claim that the described move in time does go along the steady-state curve of my Figure Vb but to point out that it does not. Let me, however, not stick to the quoted passage but try rather to be responsive to the spirit rather than the letter of Professor Harcourt's unease. Suppose he had found a passage to quote that went like this: "In going from the 51 percent profit point on the curve to the 49 percent profit point, the system goes through old-fashioned abstinence of present consumption for higher future consumption; but in going from the 101 percent point to the 99 percent point, it reverses the neoclassical parable and is splashed with current consumption and does negative abstinence." If my pen had written that, would I be caught out in mortal or venial sin? Not at all. Not only does such a passage not say that the movement takes place *along* the steady-state locus, but to anyone who understands it and my Table I, it clearly indicates the contrary! The slopes between the 1.01 and 0.99 points and the 0.51 and 0.49 points in the relevant steady-state diagrams are the *reverse* of the described transient algebraic abstinences and splashings, and no "act of faith" would permit of other than this even in the simplest neoclassical model. I believe that Professor Harcourt and I do not remain in any essential disagreement on substantive matters, but he does have the right to ask of me why a system might move along the warranted paths I so skillfully built into my discussion. Here we leave the realm of

DEEPER ISSUE OF NONSTEADY-STATE ANALYSIS

I do not think that the real stumbling block has been the failure of a literary writer to understand that when a mathematician says, "y rises as x falls," he is implying nothing about temporal sequences or anything different from "when x is low, y is high." More important, I think there may well remain differences of opinion between some in Cambridge, England, and some in Cambridge, Massachusetts, over *whether nonsteady-state analysis can be meaningfully formulated and handled.* Thus, my 1966 Table I, p. 581, presents a warranted dynamic path, in which a system goes from one steady state to another. No reader who contemplates my exposition has reason to think that the technological relations of the transition are falsely derived there from relations valid only for the steady state. They clearly are not. But, what is a different and not a "logical" point, a skeptic may legitimately doubt that (i) a planned economy would have the wit to follow such an "intertemporally-efficient" warrantable path; or, withdrawing doubt about planned systems, a skeptic might legitimately doubt that (ii) a competitive market system will have the "foresight" or the perfect-futures markets to *approximate* in real life such warranted paths that have the property that, if everyone knew in advance they would occur, each will be motivated to do just that which gives rise to them.

Another deeper issue has to do with hard-to-prove differences in empirical presumption. Thus, Sir John Hicks, in his 1972 Nobel

---

logic, but, too briefly, I would reply: Consider that a war breaks out between time 4 and 5 in my Table I (not amended as in this footnote). Perspicacious planners, or avaricious speculators in forward markets, act to produce the expansion of final output needed in the temporary war years. Etc., etc.

Countless other less dramatic scenarios could be written: change in optimal-control planners' Ramseyan time preference, a slow trend toward later retirements, tolerably well discerned by market participants, etc., etc. The warranted paths of my Table I are simply two of an infinity of alternatives. They were selected as the *fastest* transient paths, not for realism but to illuminate the nice Solow theorem on transition states of the 1967 Dobbs *Festschrift*, a theorem that Professor Robinson dismisses by the characterization that it merely says ". . . the definition of a switch point does define a switch point." (The one point where my 1966 exposition does seem ungenerous is in my terming this theorem as "merely" a "bookkeeping" or "general accounting relationship, as applied to a constant-returns-to-technology." An adversary in a debate would not merit the sneering "merely" much less an admired colleague.) To conclude the reply to Professor Harcourt's query, the vast literature on the "Hahn problem" should be consulted to form a reasoned opinion on how tolerably inefficient or efficient are market and planned systems in the real world in transient and steady-state analysis; I am not aware that my own part in this discussion contains *invalid* "habits of thought so ingrained as for him [me] to be unconscious of their presence," but I shall be happy to recant if such logical errors can be found.

Lecture,[8] comes full circle to his 1932 view that a successful raising of real wage rates (perhaps by real-wage sliding-scale contracts) is likely in the short and long run to result in a reduction of employment. By contrast, one who believes technology to be more like my 1966 reswitching example than like its orthodox contrast, will have a more sanguine view about how successful militant power by organized labor can be in causing egalitarian shifts in the distribution of income away from property even in the long run. Indeed under such a reswitching technology, anyone who believes in the tautologies of the exponential paths of textbook-land might vote Social Credit to promote an easy euthanasia of the capitalist class merely by having the state (perhaps out of across-the-board taxation) finance larger shares of capital formation: when it relieves the profit savers of half the task, the tautological profit rate will halve, etc., according to the tautology,

$$r = (\text{growth rate/fraction-of-profits-saved}) \times (1-f),$$

where f is the fraction of capital formation done by the government's fiscal system.

So even after logical issues have been put in their proper uncontroversial place, the arguments can go on as to whether the distribution of income does or does not depend significantly in real life on the *relative supplies of labor and of diverse capital goods*.[9]

8. J. R. Hicks, "The Mainstream of Economic Growth," Nobel Prize Lecture, April 27, 1973, Stockholm, in *Les Prix Nobel en 1972*, The Nobel Foundation, Stockholm, 1972, 235–46, particularly p. 244ff. Professor Hicks is well aware of reswitching and other possibilities and therefore punctuates his text with the word "*usually*." A perfectionist might want him to insert that qualification at a few other places, but I think that on a sensible interpretation of his text this can be taken as understood. No doubt too, except for the limitation of space, he would have spelled out in greater detail the time sequence of incidence of the postulated increase in real wages, but enough is given to register his empirical judgment about the importance of reswitching and related phenomena. For purposes of an anthology of readings, I had not been able to identify in Professor Robinson's voluminous writings a clear statement of exactly what, outside steady states, her theory of income distribution is. (In this respect Professor Kaldor is different, and one is splashed almost with an embarrassment of riches). But it is clear that her theory is not neoclassical. And, from an aside (thrown off in her lecture before the 1970 World Econometric Congress in Cambridge) concerning the putative ability of Philippine workers to affect the distribution of income by militancy, I would infer that her empirical insights would not coincide with this of Sir John.

9. One who believes that class power can wrest great gains in absolute and relative income shares within a market system need not necessarily reject neoclassical constructs involving smooth marginal productivities and simple capital aggregates. For, as pointed out in P. Samuelson and F. Modigliani, "The Pasinetti Paradox in Neoclassical and More General Models," *Review of Economic Studies*, XXXIII (Oct. 1966), 269–301, particularly around p. 213 and Figure 4, a one-sector model with $dK/dt + C = [(aL)^{-100} + (bK)^{-100}]^{-.01}$ and almost-zero elasticity of substitution would act much like a Pasinetti-Kaldor model with a fixed capital-output coefficient; on the other hand, a finite-

In concluding this conciliatory note dealing solely with the logical points raised about my own works, I should say that failure to deal with other aspects of Professor Robinson's account does not mean that I would consider hers an optimal formulation of the issues agreed upon or in controversy.[10] It is valuable as *her* account: from *Rashomon*, we know how different the single reality will appear to different actors in the same drama. There may even be a viewpoint from which Professor Robinson's final Nonexistence Theorem belongs in the realm of deductive logic — like the Nonsubstitution or the Pythagorean Theorems, or the Impossibility Theorems of Frisch and of Arrow — but on this matter I must still reserve judgment.

Massachusetts Institute of Technology

---

activities model can be found, which at the same time that it lacks marginal productivities that "determine" real wages and interest rates, has comparative-static and dynamic-path properties that come as near as we like to Cobb-Douglas Clarkian models.

10. We all owe Professor Robinson so much that there is not the usual sting in such words as ". . . just a bluff," or "The professors at M.I.T. took over my book of blueprints and tried to. . . ." Any reader of my three volumes of collected papers can verify that, whatever Walras did or did not do, I have on several occasions developed *logically correct*, nonsimple models of not-necessarily-steady-state economic development that eschewed use of *any* capital aggregate, and the same is true of many other writers. But it has been my sad experience that when a challenge in the realm of logic has been successfully met, that tends to move the objection into the realm of realism and relevance. Only into the logical realm does the present note enter. Also, politeness should not be confused with imitation: the activity analysis of von Neumann and programming theory was used by scholars all over the world before Professor Robinson used the terminology of blueprints, and yet it was appropriate that those who conducted discussions with the author of the *Accumulation of Capital* should have paid her the compliment of using her terminology. It is understandable that strong convictions should lead to strong language, as any reader of the "capital controversies" can document in quantitative detail, author by author.

PARADOXES OF SCHUMPETER'S ZERO INTEREST RATE

Paul A. Samuelson

Today, a quarter of a century after I rejected Lord Robbins' contention that at Schumpeter's zero interest rate people would dissave, I must agree that Professor Whitaker makes a good point against me. Specifically, I agree with his proposition [1] that in a zero-population-growth, zero-interest-rate, golden-rule state, there is a hitch connected with decentralized decision-making by hedonistic consumers each of whom assumes that he can trade freely without ever affecting prices at all. This admission, given without reservation, does not mean that my critique of Robbins and defense of Schumpeter did not have some valid points. Let me, therefore, put into the record the following observations.

1) Suppose we first deal with Robinson Crusoe. He lives forever and has no time discount. He faces a Ramsey-Solow technology: $C + dK/dt = F(K,L) = f(K)$ for L constant, and $f'(K) = 0$ has a golden rule root at the Schumpeter point K^*.

Maximizing the integral $\int_0^\infty u[c]dt$, where $u[f(K^*)] = 0$, implies that for initial $K(0)$ equal to K^*, Crusoe will most definitely not dissave even though he knows the interest yield of capital will

---

[1] Dr. Duncan McCrae, in a forthcoming paper seems independently to have arrived at a similar conclusion: cf., D. McCrae, "Production and Investment in an Equilibrium Economy," Working Paper, No. 18, M.I.T., March 1968. I have not had the opportunity to read a recent Harvard Working Paper by David Starrett dealing with these matters but I benefited from talking with him.

always be zero. (Rereading of Robbins does not tell me whether he failed to see this, as I once thought he did.)

2) Suppose we add a second Crusoe, exactly alike, and a third, and an Nth. Endow them with initial capital stocks K^*/N. Then, the only symmetric Pareto-optimal solution is, for all N, that in which no one ever dissaves. They live on their wages, or what is the same thing, on per capita product which their capital and labor make possible.

Dispensing with any idealized constructs of "perfect competition," we can conclude that no departure from this zero-marginal-productivity-of-capital state would ever take place.

Hence, the root of the difficulty is in the economist's notion of decentralized decision-making under ideally perfect competition. For a philosopher who regards idealized poles as asymptotic states that can be approached but never quite reached (like Kelvin $0°$ in thermodynamics), the Whitaker-McCrae phenomenon cannot be used to controvert Schumpeter's vision of the circular flow.

3) In simple exchange systems, we can define the "point of perfect competition" as that point to which the core shrinks as we replicate the number of symmetric competitors. Here, define the core for $n = 0, 1, \ldots, N$ Robinson Crusoes. Then let N become large. For N large enough we should be able to rule out any outcome which differs by as much as ε from $K_i(t) \equiv K^*/N$. By this definition of competition — which I hasten to admit was not that of Robbins, Schumpeter, or your humble servant in 1943 — the Schumpeter zero-interest rate state *is* the competitive equilibrium and the only one.

4) When mathematicians, like Debreu, speak of a competitive equilibrium, they do not insist that it is to be the only one but merely that it be *self-warranting* in the sense of satisfying all the conditions of the problem. Certainly for the Schumpeter problem, if zero interest is not *the* solution, there is no other solution (despite Robbins' final paragraph which suggests to me that he, at least momentarily, thought otherwise).

Observe, a system from $t = 0$ to $T = 1$ billion years, a permanent system. Let us observe its competitive prices and its actual behavior. What are the admissible observations that we could not fault?

They are *exactly* those of Schumpeter which Robbins criticized — namely $K(t) \equiv K^*$ and interest rate identically zero.

Suppose we keep T finite and let it be longer or shorter than one billion years. No matter what *its* finite length, the Schumpeter solution is the only one that satisfies the competitive equilibrium so that an external observer cannot fault it.

So, without disagreeing with the spirit of Whitaker and McCrae, one can make this defense of Schumpeter even under decentralized perfect competition. As I have insisted elsewhere [2] in discussing the Phelps-Koopman concept of "permanent insufficiency," what Whitaker can validly object to is *a strategy by the consumer of never eating his lollipop.* No court can ever convict him of the crime of not having eaten his lollipop. For, with time preference zero, the decision to eat it "later" can never be shown to involve loss. The opportunity keeps.

5) Before concluding, let me mention that a common criticism of Schumpeter's zero interest rate is the fact that it involves infinite capitalized value of permanent land (or for that matter of permanent labor power). In my obituary article [3] on Schumpeter, I touched on an aspect of this problem that could cause difficulty even for such a critic of Schumpeter as Knight or Robbins. Let me resurrect that paradox from its footnote.

Suppose our production function involves only capital, K, and permanent land, L, with no labor. With land fixed at unit level, the production function is $f(K)$ as before. But let the full function be Cobb-Douglas, $Q = L^a K^{1-a}$. Now assume a

---

[2] P. A. Samuelson, "A Turnpike Refutation of the Golden Rule in a Welfare Maximizing Many-Year Model," in K. Shell (ed.), *Essays in the Theory of Optimal Economic Growth* (Cambridge, Mass.: M.I.T. Press, 1967).

[3] P. A. Samuelson, "Schumpeter as a Teacher and Economic Theorist," reproduced as chapter 116 in J. E. Stiglitz (ed.), *Corrected Scientific Papers of Paul A. Samuelson* (Cambridge, Mass.: M.I.T. Press, 1966), but originally appearing in May 1951 issue of the *Review of Economics and Statistics.*

standard Solow model with output the sum of consumption and capital formation and with the amount saved and invested a constant positive fraction of income, s. Then

$C + dK/dt = L^a K^{1-a}$ GNP identity

$dK/dt = sL^a K^{1-a}$ saving assumption

$R = \partial Q/\partial L = a(K/L)^{1-a}$ marginal-productivity rent

$r = \partial Q/\partial K = (1-a)(L/K)^a$ marginal-productivity interest

From the second of these relations we can calculate the time-shape of output, then proceed to calculate the time-shape of land rent and of interest.

Having determined the path of development of the current variables, we can next proceed to calculate the present discounted value of land, knowing that the interest rate will be positive at all finite times. When we evaluate the integral of present discounted value, we shall find that unless the fraction of income saved is less than the fractional share of capital, i.e., $s < a$, land is *already* infinite in value, prior to the Schumpeter point's being actually reached!

Does this mean that, empirically, a Solow process with Cobb-Douglas function is unrealistic because it would make people feel so rich that they would surely not wish to save a fixed positive fraction of their factor incomes over their lifetimes? I leave this puzzle to the reader, but not before thanking Professor Whitaker for his cogent criticism of my arguments.

218

ECONOMICS OF FORESTRY IN AN EVOLVING SOCIETY*

PAUL A. SAMUELSON
Massachusetts Institute of Technology

A debate that has raged for centuries is unlikely to be resolved by me in one lecture. However, I shall do my best to set forth the issues and indicate what ought to be the crucial factors that a jury should consider in rendering its verdict on the matter. The issue is one between forestry experts and the general public on the one side and professional economists and profit-conscious businessmen on the other. At first blush this would seem to suggest that economists are on the side of the interests and are not themselves members of the human race. But, as I hope to show, sound economic analysis is needed to do justice to the cases put forward by either of the adversary parties.

SUSTAIN OR NOT SUSTAIN?

To vulgarize and oversimplify, *there has been a tradition in forestry management which claims that the goal of good policy is to have sustained forest yield, or even "maximum sustained yield" somehow defined.* And, typically, economists have questioned this dogma.

If laissez-faire enterprisers tended to be led by that invisible hand Adam Smith talked about to achieve in fact sustained forest yields, and even maximum sustained forest yields, no doubt there would be a school of economists called into existence to give their blessings to the doctrine of maximum sustained yield. In that case there would be no great debate. The economists in the liberal arts division of the university, on those rare occasions when they deign to think about the practical problems of forest management, would come out with the same conclusions and dicta as would the professional foresters in the school of forestry. Moreover, the professors in the biological departments, and the lay public generally, would heartily approve of the actual solution in this best of all possible worlds.

Life is not like that and it hasn't been for a long time. The medieval forests of Britain, and of Europe, tended to be chopped down as society moved into the Industrial Revolution. The virgin forests that graced the New World when Columbus arrived here have increasingly been cut

*This paper was presented initially as a lecture at a symposium on "The Economics of Sustained Yield Forestry," at the University of Washington, Seattle, Washington, November 23, 1974. I owe thanks to the National Science Foundation for financial aid, and to Kate Crowley for editorial assistance. Also to Vicki Elms for help with the bibliography, and to Barbara Feldstein for composition. It was Professor Barney Dowdle of the University of Washington who, knowing of my innocence of forestry economics, inveigled me into making these preliminary researches.

down once the calculus of dollar advantage began to apply. When I informed a graduate student that I was preparing this lecture, he mentioned to me the rumor that a nearby consulting firm had applied dynamical programming analysis to the problem of how old — or rather how young — a tree should be when it is to be optimally cut in the steady state. Allegedly, its computer spun out of control and generated a negative, or for all I know, imaginary, root for the equation: apparently at realistic profit rates, it doesn't pay to keep a forest in existence at all. This is probably only a tall story, but it does well illustrate the fact that standard managerial economics, and actual commercial practice, both tend to lead to an optimal cutting age of a forest that is much shorter than the 80 or even 100 years one often encounters in the forestry literature.

EXTERNALITIES AND INTERVENTION

This apparent clash between economists and foresters is not an isolated one. Biological experts in the field of fisheries are sometimes stunned when they meet economists who question their tacit axiom that the stock of fish in each bank of the ocean ought to be kept as a goal at some maximum sustained level. Similarly, hard-boiled economists are greeted with incredulity if and when they opine that it may be optimal to grow crops in the arid plain states only until the time when the top soil there has blown away to its final resting place in the ears and teeth of Chicago pedestrians.

Everybody loves a tree and hates a businessman. Perhaps this is as it should be, and perhaps after the profession of economics is 1,000 rather than 200 years old, the human race will be as conditioned to abhor economists as it has become to abhor snakes. But really, these matters need arguing in court so the informed jury, and I do mean the informed jury of human beings, can make up its mind.

Let me say in advance of the argument, there is no ironclad presumption that profit seeking laissez-faire will lead to the social optimum. Thus, suppose that a living redwood tree helps purify the air of smoggy Los Angeles. Suppose sowing the land to short-lived pine trees prevents floods 500 miles downstream. Then we may well have here a case of what modern economists recognize as "externalities." We economists these days spend much of our time analyzing the *defects* of competitive free entry and push-shove equilibrium when important externalities are involved. If therefore in the great historic debate on sustained yields, foresters and conservationists had brought into court an elaboration of the respects in which forestry is an activity beset with important externalities, carefully and objectively described, Ph.D.'s in economics would be found on both sides of the case under trial. Indeed, if the externalities involved could be shown to be sufficiently important, I am naive enough to believe that all economists would be found on the side of the angels, sitting thigh next to thigh with the foresters. (*All* economists agree? Well, almost all.)

"PRIVATE" VERSUS "COMMON" PROPERTY

Earlier I mentioned fisheries. Even those economists who ostrich-like tend always to play down externalities if they can, have long recognized that there is a "common property" element in hunting and fishing: even though I were to have to pay rent to someone who owns a particular acre of the ocean in order to put down my net there, my act of fishing there can hope to draw on fish with might migrate from nearby acres. So we have in the case of fisheries a special kind of externality that makes it nonoptimal to have *decentralized rent-charging owners* of subdivisions of a common fishing bank. Government regulation and centralized decision making for the whole fishing pool, if it can be arranged in this age of nationalism, is obviously preferable to free competition as Gordon (1954), Scott (1955), and Crutchfield (1962) have analyzed.

From a cursory glance at the literature of forestry, both technical and economic, I do not perceive foresters to be making as a case for timber what is true for fisheries, or for oil drilling. It is true that forest fires are a hazard that adjacent timber lands may face in common. And if the units of land owned by each forester-owner were very, very small, the externalities between adjacent plots would render decentralized competitive decision-making nonoptimal. However, for the most part, timber ownership will not under laissez-faire tend to stay so pulverized, since it is quite feasible to have the span of ownership widened to the optimal degree without creating monopoly or vitiating the assumptions of workable competition.

At the beginning, therefore, even before entering into the serious argument, let us make a deposition that the following would be a false issue in the debate:

Abolishing private ownership in land or abandoning public regulation of forest land owned by the government is not an alternative to maximum sustained yield that is advocated by anybody. This would certainly result in unnecessary decimation of the forest. Indeed, as Vernon Smith (1968) has shown in one of his models, it could result in extinction of *all* forests; but even if a realistic model of complete push-shove free-free entry led to a maintainable sustained-yield steady state, the average age of the forest stands in such a Hobbesian jungle might well involve rotation periods so short as to be absurd, which is why in medieval Germany severe limits were properly placed on the use by the public of crown and public forest lands.

COMPETITIVE LAND RENTS

The economists who oppose maximum sustained-yield do not advocate any such absurd push-shove procedure. They assume that the cultivator who plants a tree on one acre of land owns or rents the right to exclusive garnering of the fruits of that which he has planted. Similarly, if I own yonder acre or have leased it from a public or private owner, and if I desist in chopping down a tree that is not yet ripe, I expect to find it still there when I do come to chop it down. In return for this exclusive use of my own area of cultivation, I expect to pay a land rent. If I own the land outright, I pay it *to myself* at an opportunity cost rate that is perfectly well determined in a freely competitive market. Or I pay the rent to a private owner, who knows he can rent that land to somebody else like me if not to me. Or I pay a rent to a government that owns the land.

This rate of land rental can be high or low. If the total amount of land available for growing the timber that society needs, and which is close enough to the market to be able to avoid heavy transportation charges, is severely limited in amount, then the appropriate competitive land rent will be high. If on the other hand land is extremely plentiful, its scarcity rent will be very low. It will not even matter for the purpose of our analysis if well-located land is so plentiful as to be redundant. In that case, its competitive land rent will be zero, but even though land rent is zero I shall still need to have *exclusive* rights to the fruits of my earlier labor and other investment inputs, independently of whether in other acres of the redundant territory push-shove free-free entry is permitted.

ASSUMPTIONS FOR THE ANALYSIS

Let me first review the correct economic principles that would be applicable if forestry can be regarded simply as sources of wood saleable in competitive markets. This initially assumes away externalities such as flood control, pollution abatement, species preservation, vacationers' enjoyments, etc.

Although I am not a specialist in the field of forest economics, I have been reading a couple of dozen different analyses ranging over the last two centuries that grapple with optimal steady-state rotation periods. The economic analysis in most of them is wrong. In some it is very wrong. In others it is not quite right. In at least one case, the remarkable 1849 German article by Martin Faustmann, the analysis does come close to an essentially correct solution.

These remarks are not intended to give a harsh indictment of foresters or of economists who have worked in the field of forestry. The mistakes made in the forestry literature can be duplicated aplenty in the intermediate textbooks of pure economics.

Thus, Irving Fisher was the greatest single economic writer on interest and capital, and his 1930 *Theory of Interest* summarized his life work in that field. Yet at MIT we ask graduate students on quizzes to identify and correct Fisher's false solution as to when a tree should be cut (a false solution that he seems to share with the great von Thunen (1826) and the brilliant Hotelling (1925) as well as with some excellent economists who have written on forestry in recent decades). Again, Kenneth Boulding is one of our leading economists; but his rule of maximizing the so-called "internal rate of return" has led many a forestry economist down the garden path (Boulding 1935). A 1960 review of the literature by G. K. Goundrey comes out with the wrong Boulding solution, and yet his analysis purports to lean on such excellent authorities as Wicksell, Scitovsky, Kaldor, Metzler, and Scott; alas, it did not lean more heavily on Faustmann (1849), Preinrich (1938), Alchian (1952), Bellman (1957), Gaffney (1957), Hirshleifer (1958), and perhaps Samuelson (1937).

If an unambiguous solution to the problem is to be definable, of course certain definite assumptions must be made. If the solution is to be simple, the assumptions must be heroic. These include: (1) knowledge of future lumber prices at which all outputs can be freely sold, and future wages of all inputs; (2) knowledge of future interest rates at which the enterprise can both borrow and lend in indefinite amounts; and (3) knowledge of technical lumber yields that emerge at future dates once certain expenditure inputs are made (plantings, sprayings, thinnings, fellings, etc.). Finally, it is assumed (4) that each kind of land suitable for forests can be bought and sold and rented in arm's length transactions between numerous competitiors; or, if the government owns public lands, it rents them out at auction to the highest of numerous alternative bidders and conducts any of its own forestry operations so as to *earn the same maximum rent* obtainable at the postulated market rate of interest. For the special steady-state model, the future prices and interest rates must be assumed to be known constants. Moreover, our problem is not one merely of managerial economics; rather we must deduce the competitive prices that clear the industry's market.

Assumptions would not be heroic if they could be easily taken for granted as being exactly applicable. Stochastic factors of climate, lightning, forest fires, and disease must in real life qualify the technical assumptions made in (3) above. At the least, therefore, as a second approximation, one must introduce probabilities and expected values into the decision calculus.

Similarly, tomorrow's lumber price is not knowable exactly, much less the price of lumber a score of years from now when today's seedling will mature. So, in other than a first approximation, the assumptions under (1) need to be complicated.

Finally, future interest rates are not knowable today. Moreover, the inherent uncertainties involved in interest and profit yields also serve to falsify the assumption in (2) that the enterprise is able at each date both to borrow and to lend in indefinite amounts at one interest rate (even one knowable at *that* date if not now). Once we recognize that the enterprise is in an imperfect capital market, we will not be able to deduce its optimal forestry decisions independently of knowledge about its owners' personal preferences concerning consumption outlays of different dates (and concerning their "liquidities" at different dates).

CORRECT CAPITAL ANALYSIS

Our problem is now well posed. What principles provide its solution? What is the exact nature of the solution?

(i) Does it yield a steady-state rotation period as long as that which achieves the foresters' traditional "maximum sustained yield"?

(ii) Is the optimal rotation that *shorter* period which maximizes the present discounted value over the first planting cycle of the cash receipts that come from the sale of cut lumber minus the cash expenses of planting and cutting inputs (excluding from the net cash receipts stream any adjustments for implicit and explicit land rent)?

(iii) Is the optimal rotation period that still shorter period which maximizes Boulding's "Internal Rate of Return," computed as that largest rate of interest which when applied to the net dollar cash receipts over one complete cycle reduces the resulting present discounted value to zero (and, be it noted, ignores land rent in setting up the net algebraic cash receipts!)?

(iv) Alternatively, is the optimum the rotation period that results from maximizing (a) the present discounted value of all net cash receipts excluding explicit or implicit land rents, but calculated over the *infinite chain* of cycles of planting on the given acre of land from now until Kingdom Come; or (b) what may sound like a different criterion, the rotation period that results from maximizing the present discounted value of net algebraic receipts over the first cycle, but with the market land rental included in those receipts, it being understood that the land rental that each small enterprise will be confronted with will be the *maximum* rental that ruthless Darwinian competition can contrive?

If you have been testing yourself by trying to answer the objective-type quiz that I have just propounded, you will receive a perfect A+ if you gave the following answers:

(i) No, the rotation period that maximizes sustained yield is so long that, at the postulated positive interest rate and inevitable market rent for land, it will bankrupt any enterprise that endeavors to realize it.

(ii) No, maximizing the present discounted value, over *one* planting cycle, of cash receipts from cut timber sold minus cash receipts for inputs that do planting, thinning, and cutting will give you a somewhat too long rotation period and will not enable you to cover the land rent that will be set by your more perspicacious competitors. However, your error will not be so very great in the case the length of each cycle is very great and/or the rate of interest per annum is very large, so that the discounted value today of a dollar payable at the end of the cycle is negligible. Still, employing this method that is so frequently advocated by sophisticated economists will lead you to the following absurdity: an increase in initial planting cost will have *no effect at all* on your optimal rotation period, up to the point that it makes it unprofitable to put the land you own into lumber, even when you are philanthropic enough to forego obtainable positive land rent. It is a solution that pretends that the Archimedean forest lever never needs the land fulcrum to work with.

(iii) No, ignoring land rent and maximizing the internal rate of return will give you so short a rotation period that, at the postulated interest rate, you will not be able to pay yourself the positive land rental set by competition. Moreover, maximizing the interal rate of return will give you the nonsensical result that you should select the same rotation period when the interest rate, the price of time, is high or low; and, when initial planting costs are zero, it will give a meaningless infinite return.

(iv) Finally, yes, (a) and (b), which really are exactly the same method, constitute the only correct method. The first formulation, in terms of an infinite chain of repeated cycles, was already proposed in the brilliant 1849 German article by Martin Faustmann. A glance at its recent English translation convinces me of his remarkable merit, even though at first glance one does not find in it the exact explicit conditions for optimal cutting age of the forest stand. I do not know that the economics literature caught up with this degree of sophistication prior to the 1938 *Econometrica* survey article on depreciation by Gabriel Preinrich, which was itself a notable anticipation of the dynamic programming that Richard Bellman made routine in the postwar period. The second approach, which I cannot recall seeing explicitly in print, will perhaps be more intuitively understandable at a first approach to the subject; and, in any case, land rent has tended not to be given the proper analysis it needs.

In a moment I shall illustrate all this by means of a specific model, which though not very realistic will be familiar to economists since the time of Stanley Jevons. From it, you will infer the presumption that commercial exploitation of forestry will lead to a departure from the goal of maximum sustained yield even greater than may have been realized by adherents and critics of forestry dogmas. The higher the effective rate of interest, the greater will be the shortfall of the optimal rotation age compared to the age that maximizes steady-state yield. As the interest rate goes to zero, the economists' correct optimum will reach the limit of the foresters' target of maximum sustained yield. Only if an explicit land rent charge is introduced into the cash stream will Boulding's maximized internal rate of return avoid incorrect results; but in that case, Ockham's razor can cut it down as redundant (worse than that, as involving incomplete, implicit theorizing.) Actually, as we have seen in (b) above, including in competitive land-rent can save from error the popular method of maximizing present discounted value calculated over only the first cycle; however, to know *how much* rent so to include, one must impose the condition that it be just large enough to reduce to zero that maximized discounted value over one cycle, and this rent so calculated will turn out to be after capitalization exactly what the Faustmann-Preinrich-Bellman-Hirshleifer solution deduced. It should be noted that, in the special case where the land for timber growth is redundant and therefore free, maximizing over a single cycle will singularly give the correct answer, and maximizing the internal rate of return will with equal singularity also give the same answer. Since at least one writer, Goundrey (1960), has alleged that timber land in Canada is so plentiful as to be free, it is worth emphasizing that even in this case the three methods nominated by economists will deduce a rotation period significantly shorter than the foresters' maximum because of the positive interest rate. The foresters, without realizing it, are correct only when the true interest rate is literally zero.

THE BOGEY OF COMPOUND INTEREST

I cannot conclude this general survey of wrong and right ways of analyzing the actual equilibrium that will emerge in the competitive steady-state without expressing my amazement at the low interest rates which abound in the forestry literature. Faustmann, writing in the middle of the nineteenth century, uses a four percent rate. Thunen, writing at the same time, uses a five percent interest rate. The 1960 Goundrey survey also uses a five percent rate. These will seem to an ordinary economist and businessman as remarkably low. The notion that for such gilt-edge rates I would tie up my own capital in a 50-year (much less a 100-year) timber investment, with all the uncertainties and risks that the lumber industry is subject to, at first strikes one as slightly daft. I can only guess that such low numbers have been used either as a form of wishful thinking so foresters or forest economists can avoid rotation ages so short they show up the forester's "maximum sustained yield"; or because the writers have not had the heart to face up to the discounting almost out of existence of receipts payable half a century from now.

Let us make no mistake about it. The positive interest rate is the enemy of long-lived investment projects. At six percent interest, money doubles in 12 years, quadruples in 24, grows 16-fold in 48 years, and 256-fold in 96 years. Hence, the present discounted value today of $1 of timber harvest 96 years from now is, at six percent, only 0.4 of one cent!

Foresters know this and fight against compound interest. Thus, an economist cannot help but be amused at the 1925 gem by the Assistant Chief, Board of Research, U.S. Forest Service, Ward Shepard. Entitled "The Bogey of Compound Interest," this argues that if you have a forest stand in the steady state, no interest need be involved: your cutting receipts exceed your planting expenses! This is so absurd as to be almost believable to the layman — up to the moment when the economist breaks the news to the farmer, lumber-company president, or government official that he can mine the forest by cutting it down without replanting and sell the land, thereafter putting the proceeds into the bank or into retiring the public debt and subsequently earn interest forever.

"Bogey" has two meanings. The first, which is Shepard's naive meaning, is that compound interest is a fictitious entity which, like the Bogey Man, is wrongfully used to frighten little children. The second and here more legitimate meaning of bogey is that defined in Webster's Dictionary as "a numerical standard of performance set up as a mark to be aimed at in competition." Compound interest is indeed the legitimate bogey that competitors must earn in forestry if they are not to employ their land, labor, and disposable funds in other more lucrative uses.

Competitive theory can be reassuring as well as frustrating to the forester. There is a popular notion that interest calculations may be applied to decisions for next year as against the immediately following years. "But," it is not infrequently argued, "when what is at issue is a tree or dam whose full fruits may not accrue until a century from now, the brute fact that our years are numbered as three score and ten prevents people from planting the trees that will not bear shade until after they are dead — altruism, of course, aside."

To argue in this way is to fail to understand the logic of competitive pricing. Even if my doctor assures me that I will die the year after next, I can confidently plant a long-lived olive tree, knowing that I can sell at a competitive profit the one-year-old sapling. Each person's longevity and degree of impatience to spend becomes immaterial in a competitive market place with a borrowing, lending, and capitalizing interest rate that encapsulates all which is relevant about society's effective time preferences.

INFLATION AND INCOME TAXES

What interest rate is appropriate for forestry? I hesitate to pronounce on such a complex matter. A dozen years ago I might incautiously have said 12 percent or more. And, just recently you could have got 12 percent per annum on $100,000 left with safety in the bank for three months. But this of course represented in part the 1974 10+ percent annual inflation rate, a rate which the price rise in lumber could also presumably share. Indeed timber lands are often recommended as an inflation hedge: if the interest rate is 12 percent and the price of lumber rises at 12 percent per annum, it is a standoff and in effect there is a zero real interest rate.

Fortunately, I was able to show back in 1937, correcting a misleading interpretation in Keynes' 1936 *General Theory*, that so long as price changes are anticipatable, it does not matter in what "own-rates-of-interest" you calculate to make decisions (such as at what optimal age to cut a tree), the optimal physical decision will always be invariant. This means that essentially all we need in order to discuss forest economics correctly is to concentrate on (1) the *real* rate of interest (i.e., the actual interest rate on money minus the presumed known rate of overall price inflation), and (2) the real price of lumber outputs and inputs (i.e., the percentage real rate of rise for $P_{lumber}/P_{general}$).

There is another complication. If marginal tax rates are (say) 50 percent, a 12 percent yield before tax is a 6 percent yield after tax. It would seem to make quite a difference for optimal rotation decisions whether we must use a 12 or a 6 percent discount rate. Actually, and this may seem discouraging to the foresters' dream of maximum sustained yield, one can correctly use the higher pre-tax rate in making optimal decisions provided the income tax authorities really do properly tax true money income at uniform prices. More specifically, I showed in Samuelson (1964) that, if foreseeable depreciation and appreciation are taxed when they occur, a person always in the 50 percent (or 99 percent) bracket will make the same optimal decisions as a person always in the zero percent bracket.

But are actual U.S. or Canadian tax systems "fair" in their income taxation? Of course not. As a forest grows in size and value, instead of taxing this certain accretion of true income in the Henry Simons fashion, the tax is deferrable until the wood is cut. So forestry may provide a "tax loophole," which can distort decisions toward the longer rotation period of the foresters' maximum sustained yield, particularly if capital-gains tax-treatment is available at lower rates.

To sum up, I might mention that William Nordhaus (1974) recently showed at Brookings that *real* profit yields have been falling in recent years. Thus, his Table 5 suggests that real before-tax yields on corporate capital have tended to average only about 10 percent in the early 1970's as against over 15 percent 20 years earlier. This seems better for forest economics than in earlier decades, but still bad enough. Tax loopholes may further improve the viability of longer rotation periods. Also, I remember Frank Knight's being quoted as saying that, in effect, *real* lumber prices have risen historically about enough to motivate holding on to forest inventories — a dubious generalization, but one that reminds us that lumber price cannot be taken as a hard constant in realistic analysis. Before a nation, or regions it trades with, completely depletes a needed item, the price of that item can be expected to rise.

DEFINING MAXIMUM SUSTAINED YIELD IN A CLASSIC CASE

You might think that the practical man's notion of sustained yield, or of maximum sustained yield, would be clear-cut. But if you do, you haven't had much experience with analyzing so-called common sense notions. Certainly maximum sustained yield in forestry does not suggest all land wasted on soybeans and other goodies should be plowed and planted with trees. Nor does it mean that land devoted to forests should be manicured and fertilized by all the labor in society, labor not needed for subsistence calories and vitamins, in order to produce the most lumber that land is capable of in the steady state.

The amount of lumber a virgin forest is capable of producing in a wild state approaches closer to the notion's content. But biologists have long realized that Darwinian evolution leads to an ecological equilibrium in which many trees grow to be too old in terms of their wood-product efficiency; and, in any case, a virgin forest left unmolested by man is like a librarian's perverted dream of a library where no books are ever permitted to be taken out so that the inventory on the shelves can be as complete as possible.

One presumes that "maximum sustained yield" is shorthand for a reasonable notion like the following:

Cut trees down to make way for new trees when they are past their best growth rates. Follow a planting, thinning, and cutting cycle so the resulting (net?) lumber output, averaged over repeated cycles or, what is the same thing, averaged over a forest in a synchronized age class distribution, will be as large as possible.

Jevons, Wicksell, and other economists have for a century analyzed a simple "point-input point-output, time-phased" model that can serve as the paradigm of an idealized forest. Labor input of L_t does planting on an acre of forest land at time t. Then at time $t + T$, I can cut lumber of Q_{t+T}, freeing the land for another input of L_{t+T} and output $Q_{t+2T}, \ldots,$ and so forth in an infinite number of cycles. Biology and technology give me the production function relating inputs and output, namely

(1)
$$Q_{t+T} = f(T)$$
$$f'(T) > 0, \quad a < T < b; \quad f'(b) = 0$$

Actually, as we'll see, $f(T)$ is short for $f(s, L; T)$, where L is labor input at the beginning of one planting cycle and s is the land used throughout that complete cycle (which can be set at $s = 1$).

In the steady state, a new part of each forest is being planted at every instant of time, an old part is being cut down at age T, and forest stands of all ages below T are represented in equal degree. If we wish to calculate the average product per unit of land of the synchronized forest, we can follow one cycle on one part of the forest, and divide the Q it produces in T periods by T to get average product per year. So one measure of gross sustained yield would be $f(T)/T$. However, this neglects the fact that workers must be paid wages. These are payable in dollars at rate W; and the lumber is sold in dollars at the competitive price P. But we could think of the workers who do the initial planting as being paid off in kind, in lumber they can sell at price P. So their wage in lumber, $(W/P)L$, must be subtracted from gross output $f(T)$ in order to form "average sustainable net lumber yield" of $[f(T) - (W/P)L]/T$.

Figure 1 shows the story. The point of maximum $f(T)$ is shown at B, where $f'(b) = 0 > f''(b)$. The point of maximum sustained gross yield T_q, is shown where a ray through the origin, OG, is tangent to the $f(T)$ curve. The point of maximum sustained net yield, is given by tangency at T_r of a similar ray, EN, from the expense point, E, to the net curve $f(T) - (W/P)L$.

Maximum sustained gross yield, as here defined, is at a maximum, not when $T = b$. To wait until each tree slowly achieves its top lumber content is to fail to realize that cutting the tree to make the land available for a faster-growing young tree is truly optimal. Ignoring all wage subtractions, sustained yield of gross lumber is maximized at the lower rotation age, T_g, defined by

(2)
$$Max_T \ [f(T)/T] = f(T_g)/T_g \ ,$$

where

$$f'(T_g) = f(T_g)/T_g, \quad T_g < b \ .$$

FIGURE 1

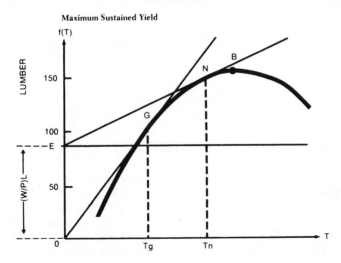

Maximum Sustained Yield

T_g is rotation period for maximum *gross* sustained yield irrespective of initial planting costs. T_n is rotation period for maximum *net* sustained yield.

Since a short rotation period makes us pay the same wages more often, once we introduce wage subtractions, we arrive at a forester's true "maximum sustained (net) yield" at a rotation age somewhat greater than T_g, namely at T_n defined as

$$(3) \qquad \underset{T}{Max} \; [f(T) - (W/P)L]/T = [f(T_n) - (W/P)L]/T_n \,,$$

where [1]

$$f'(T_n) - f(T_n)/T_n = -(W/P)L/T_n, \quad T_g < T_n < b.$$

This provides us with an unambiguous and useful definition of "maximum sustained net yield." And it is this definition of sustained yield that I shall compare with what will actually emerge as steady-state competitive equilibrium, and with the various optima that one or another economist has proposed when poaching on the territory of forest economics.

THE TRUE COMPETITIVE SOLUTION

The above Jevons model will illustrate the false economic solutions and the correct solution.

First, consider the most popular method which maximizes present discounted value or PDV, calculated over one planting cycle only and involving cash receipts other than land rent. This gives T_1, defined by the equations below as

$$(4) \qquad f(T_1)e^{-rT_1} - (W/P)L \geqslant 0 = \underset{T}{Max} \, [f(T)e^{-rT} - (W/P)L],$$

where

$$f'(T_1)/f(T_1) = r$$

and

$$T_1 < b \quad \text{when} \quad r > 0,$$

where r is the market-given competitive interest rate at which everyone can borrow and lend in unlimited amounts. This is the famous Jevons relation, which had already been glimpsed by Thunen and which Fisher was later mistakenly to apply to a forest growing on limited land. (Only if land is so abundant as to be redundant and rent-free, so that P/W falls to equal $f(T_1)L^{-1}$, will T_1 give the correct competitive rotation period

---

1. Note that, as $(W/P) \to f(T)/L$, so that land rent is zero even at $r = 0$, $T_n \to b$.

of the forest. As we'll see, the correct rotation period, call it T_∞, will be shorter than T_1; but unlike T_1 it must always fall short of T_n.)

A defect in many good economic discussions is to present alternative maximum criteria, as if it were a matter of choice which to adopt. One such is to maximize the so-called internal rate of return, defined by

$$(5) \qquad \underset{T}{Max}\ \varrho\ =\ \underset{T}{Max}\ \{T^{-1} \log [f(T)\ (P/WL)]\}\ =\ r_i\ =\ f'(T_i)/f(T_i),$$

$$=\ T_i^{-1} \log [f(T_i)\ (P/WL)]\ =\ r_i$$

where

$$f'(T_i)/f(T_i)\ =\ T_i^{-1} \log [f(T_i)\ (P/WL)]$$

$$T_i < T_1 \quad \text{when} \quad r_i > r.$$

Anyone who misguidedly adopts this foolish T_i rotation period will find that he either goes broke or is permanently sacrificing return on original capital that could be his. (To prove that $T_i < T_1$, note that increasing r can be shown to lower T_1; also note that for $r = r_i$, T_1 and T_i would coincide. Hence, the T_1 for smaller r would be greater than T_i. Q.E.D.)

Finally, as Faustmann showed in 1849, the correct description of what will emerge in competitive forest-land-labor-investment equilibrium is an optimal rotation period shorter than the forester's T_n and Thunen-Fisher's T_1, but longer than Boulding's T_i, namely T_∞ as defined by either of the following equivalent formulations.

$$R_\infty\ \underset{T}{Max}\ Rs\ =\ \underset{T}{Max}\ R \quad \text{for } s = 1, \text{subject to}$$

$$(6a)$$

$$0\ =\ \underset{T}{Max}\ \{Pf(T)e^{-rT} - WL - R \int_0^T e^{-rT} dt\}\ =$$

$$Pf(T_\infty)e^{-rT_\infty} - WL - R_\infty [1 - e^{-rT_\infty}]r^{-1}$$

or,

$$(6b) \qquad \underset{T}{Max}\ [Pf(T)e^{-rT} - WL][1 + e^{-rT} + (e^{-rT})^2 + \ldots]$$

$$=\ \underset{T}{Max}\ [Pf(T)e^{-rT} - WL]/[1 - e^{-rT}]\ =$$

$$=\ \underset{T}{Max}\ (R/r)\ =\ [Pf(T_\infty)\ e^{-rT_\infty} - WL]/[1 - e^{-rT_\infty}]\ =\ R_\infty/r,$$

land's value, where

(6c) $\qquad f'(T_\infty) - r\dot{f}(T_\infty) = +r[Pf(T_\infty)e^{-rT_\infty} - WL]/[1 - e^{-rT_\infty}]$

$$= r(R_\infty/r) = r \ \ land \ \ value = R_\infty$$

$$T_i < T_\infty < T_1 \ and \ T_\infty < T_n \ for \ R_\infty > 0.$$

The first line of (6b) is the correct Faustmann-Gaffney-Hirshleifer formulation. Its equivalence with the maximum-land-rent formulation of (6a) is seen from solving the last relation of (6a) for R and noting its equivalence with the second relation of (6b) except for the extraneous constant r.

Figure 2 shows the familiar relation among the different rotation periods. Note that a reduction in P/W would lower the curve in the figure until at the zero-land-rent state the line through E with slope r would just touch the new curve at the new *coinciding* points T_i and T_1 and T_∞. It can be shown that, as $r \to 0$.[2]

DIGRESSION: LABOR AND LAND VARIABLE

The general problem recognizes that Q_{t+T} output can, for each T, be affected by how much labor, L_t, one uses initially and how much land, $s_{t:t+T}$, one uses throughout the time interval t to $t+T$. Hence, we replace $f(T)$ in the steady state by

(1') $\qquad\qquad Q = f(s, L; T) \equiv \lambda^{-1}f(\lambda s, \lambda L; T)$

and $f(\ )$ concave in (s, L) jointly; $f(\ )$ can be smoothly differentiable in the neoclassical fashion, or it can take the fixed-coefficients form $f(Min[s/\alpha, L/\beta]; T)$ where (α, β) are positive constants that can be set equal to unity by proper choice of input units. For brevity, I analyze the neoclassical case.

---

2. This is better brought out by my maximum rent formulation of (6a) than by Faustmann's infinite number of cycles as in (6b) here. Thus for $r = 0$ (6a) becomes equivalent to

$$subject \ to \ 0 = \underset{T}{Max} \ \{f(T) - (W/P)L - R \int_O^T dt\}$$

Maximize R, namely

$$\underset{T}{Max} \ \{[f(T) - (W/P)L]/T\} = [f(T_n) - (W/P)L]/T_n$$

where T_n is defined by my earlier equation (3). B. Ohlin, I now learn, worked out much of this as a graduate student: cf. Ohlin (1921).

FIGURE 2

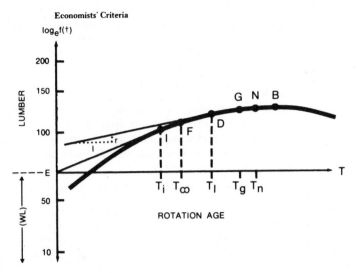

Economists' Criteria

Using the rate of interest (r) as a discount factor, economists like von Thünen and Irving Fisher favored cutting trees when percentage growth of gross lumber just equals the interest rate, giving T_i as optimal age where D's slope just equals r on ratio chart. Boulding and those who say, maximize internal rate of return, select lower T_i where slope of ray through E is at its steepest because of tangency at I. Correct competitive solution is that of Martin Faustmann (1849), which maximizes *present discounted* value over infinity of cycles (not just one cycle as with Fisher): correct T_∞ is between T_i and T_1 and maximizes land rent of steady-state forest. If $r \to 0$, $T_\infty \to T_n$, the point at which the net sustained yield is maximized.

Competitive equilibrium requires, for given $(r, W/P)$,

$$(7) \quad 0 = \operatorname*{Max}_{T, s, L} \{f(s, L; T)e^{-rT} - (W/P)L - (R/P)s \int_O^T e^{-rt} dt\}$$

$$= f(s_\infty, L_\infty; T_\infty) e^{-rT_\infty} - (W/P)L_\infty - (R/P)_\infty s[1 - e^{-rT_\infty}]r^{-1}$$

where $[L_\infty/s_\infty, T_\infty, (R/P)_\infty]$ are roots of

$$(8a) \quad e^{-rT} \partial f(1, L/s; T)/\partial L = W/P$$

$$(8b) \quad e^{-rT} \partial f(1, L/s; T)/\partial s = (R/P)[1 - e^{-rT}]r^{-1}$$

$$(8c) \quad \partial f(1, L/s; T)/\partial T - rf(1, L/s; T) = (R/P)$$

These equations are not all independent; and, of course, even if total land available for forestry, $\bar{s}$, is knowable in advance because such land has no other viable use, we need to know the consumer's demand for labor, and the workers' supply of labor to forestry as against alternative uses, before the extensive scale of (Q_∞, L_∞) are determined. It is worth noting that, in the steady state, there is a fundamental three-variable factor-price frontier of the form

(9) $$r = \psi(W/P, R/P)$$

where ψ is a monotone-decreasing function that has contours that are convex. Figure 3 shows such contours for equi-spaced values of r: the fact they are alternately bunched and spread out indicates that, in the Sraffa fashion, the relation between r and any one variable can be wavy, with variable curvature.

SIMPLE GENERAL EQUILIBRIUM: STATIC AND DYNAMIC

An oversimplified case can illustrate the general equilibrium of lumber and other prices, and can show that some efficiency properties are produced by that equilibrium. Suppose the total supply of land is fixed at $s = \bar{s}$, and that it is suitable only for forestry. Suppose the total

FIGURE 3

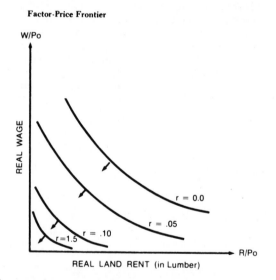

Factor-Price Frontier

REAL LAND RENT (in Lumber)

The higher the rate of interest, the lower will be the land rent that can be earned in forestry for each real wage given in terms of lumber price. The tradeoff between such real wage rates and land rents will be the convex contours of frontiers shown here; however, equal increments of profit rate may have quite unequal shift effects upon contours.

steady-state supply of labor is fixed at $\bar{L}$, to be divided between L for forestry and $\bar{L}$-L for the other (composite) good. Let Q be the steady-state output of wood, as produced by the production function in (1'); and let C be the output of the other good, which is producible instantaneously from $\bar{L}$-L alone, by $C = (\bar{L}\text{-}L)/c$. Finally, suppose everyone spends his income on lumber and the other good in the same way whether rich or poor, and in the same way as does any other person. Therefore, demand curves can be regarded as generated by the "homothetic" collective utility function, $U[C, Q] \equiv \lambda^{-1} U[\lambda C, \lambda Q]$, where U is a concave first-degree-homogeneous function with standard regularity properties. With the interest rate at which society neither saves nor dissaves given by time preference rate ϱ, so that $r = \varrho > 0$, the full equilibrium is defined by

(10a)
$$C = (\bar{L} - L)/c$$
$$Q = f(\bar{s}, L; T)$$

(10b)
$$W/P_C = c^{-1}$$
$$W/P_Q = e^{-\rho T} \partial f(\bar{s}, L; T)/\partial L$$
$$P_Q/P_C = c^{-1} e^{\rho T} [\partial f(\bar{s}, L; T)/\partial L]^{-1}$$

(10c)
$$\partial f(1, L/\bar{s}; T)/\partial T - \varrho f(1, L/\bar{s}; T) = (R/P_Q)$$

(10d)
$$P_Q/P_C = \frac{\partial U(C, Q)/\partial Q}{\partial U(C, Q)/\partial C}$$

Here (10a) gives the steady-state production functions. (10b) gives the labor and land marginal productivity relations, discounted when necessary, and with the implied steady-state price ratios. (10c) gives the Faustmann optimal-rotation relation to determine T_∞. (10d) gives the needed demand relations. Note that, with T determined, we can use (10a) to express the right-hand side of (10d) in terms of L as the only unknown; substituting the right-hand side of (10b)'s last relation into the left-hand side of (10d), (10d) become one implicit equation for the one unknown, namely L. So an equilibrium does exist (and, under strong sufficiency conditions, it may well be unique). However, is there anything at all socially optimal about this positivistic competitive solution? Is there ever any "intertemporal efficiency" to this market equilibrium? The answer can be shown to be yes in a certain definable sense.

Specifically, imagine a Ramsey planner who maximizes an integral of discounted social utility, with discounting at an exponential rate of time preference, $r = \varrho$, in $\exp(-\varrho t)$. His steady-state optimality relations will be of the exact same form as the steady-state competitive relations.

The following simple example can help to illustrate the general principles involved.

OPTIMAL PROGRAMMING AND FORESTRY ROTATION

Thus, restrict T to only integral values — say to either $T = 1$ or $T = 2$; and replace the equality in (10c) that determines T_∞ by a corresponding inequality condition. And suppose a planner for this society acts to solve a Ramsey (1928) optimal-control problem, namely for t restricted to integral values,

(11)
$$Max \sum_{t=0}^{\infty} U[C(t), Q(t)]e^{-\rho t} \text{ subject to}$$

$$C(t) \leqslant c^{-1}[L - L_1(t) - L_2(t)]$$

$$\overline{S} \geqslant S_1(t) + S_2(t) + S_3(t)$$

$$L_i(t) \geqslant 0, S_i(t) \geqslant 0$$

$$Q(t) = f[S_1(t-1), L_1(t-1); 1] + f[Min[S_2(t-2), S_3(t-1)], L_2(t-2)],$$

with specified initial conditions

$$L_1(-1), S_1(-1), S_2(-2), S_2(-1), S_3(-1).$$

Such a problem is known to have a determinate solution, with implied optimal T_∞ rotation periods that can prevail at each time. And normally it will have the property that as $t \to \infty$, the optimal solution approaches the "turnpike" defined by the steady-state equations (10) above, once they are modified for discrete time periods. Of course, for still lower ϱ, a different solution will be optimal, and presumably the optimal T_∞, call it $T_\rho = 1$, becomes optimal in the steady state. See Samuelson (1973) for indicative analysis concerning the dynamic aspects of profit-including prices.

NON-STEADY-STATE CONSIDERATIONS

The forester's notion of sustained yield is a steady-state notion. The economist's shorter rotation period for the forest, due essentially to a positive interest rate, is also a steady-state notion. But life is not now in a steady-state. It never was. It never will be. Incessant change is the law of life. You might correctly infer from this that economists' simple notion of stationary equilibrium needs to be generalized and replaced by the notion of a perpetual Brownian motion, as dramatized by the perpetual dance of the colloidal particles one sees in the microscope as they are buffeted to and fro around an average position of equilibrium by ever-present molecules, numerous and random, but unseen. A beginning has been made at the frontier of modern economics toward replacing equilibrium by an *ergodic probability distribution*. Since my time here is limited, I shall only refer to the works of Mirrlees (1965), Brock and Mirman (1972), R. C. Merton (1973), Samuelson (1971). But it is not the purely probabilistic perturbation of equilibrium that is important for the great debate on sustained yield. What is important is the realistic presence of *systematic trends* or *transients*, which move away from one steady-state equilibrium and which need not settle down to a newer one. It is no paradox that steady-state analysis is useful in the understanding of realistic trend analysis.

Foresters are concerned with sustained yield precisely because they have lived in a world where virgin stands have been decimated. It is only too easy to understand why, with new technologies and consumer tastes and with the cheapening of transport of exports to affluent North America and Western Europe, much land that was once devoted here to trees is transferred to other uses.

We have seen that the rotation age in the virgin forest is greater than what competitive enterprise will countenance. Indeed, were it not that, so to speak by accident, historical governments own much timber land, there would be even fewer trees in North America today. Our analysis warns that applying what is sound commercial practice to government's own utilization of public forests, or what is the same thing, renting out public land to private lumbering interests at the maximum auction rent competition will establish — this is a sure prescription for future chopping down of trees.

NO TREES LEFT?

Is this prospect a good or bad thing? That cannot be decided in advance of lengthy discussion. Surely, from the vantage point of the final third of the twentieth century, few will agree with the beginning-of-the-century claim of Dean Fernow (1913) that wood is our most important necessity, second only to food in societal importance. Wood is only wood, just as coal is only coal, plastics are only plastics, and, some would say, as bubblegum is only bubblegum. Proper transient analysis does not justify the implied fear that, once forests cease to be cultivated at maximum sustained yield, the descent is inevitable to the hell of zero timber anywhere in the world where we engage in trade. As wood becomes scarce, it will become more expensive. As it becomes expensive, people will economize on its use. But so long as there remain important needs for wood that people will want to satisfy, the price of wood will rise to the level necessary to keep a viable supply of it forthcoming. This in a sense is a "doctrine of sustained yield," but of course not the traditional forester's doctrine of maximum sustained yield. Indeed, by contrast with deposits of oil, coal peat, and high-concentration ores, all of which are constantly being irreversibly mined, trees bottle up sunshine into cellulose in a reversible cycle.

Nothing said so far should rule out that, in a world where preparation for war is only prudent, governments may have some interest in subsidizing activities that will lower the probability that in emergency times the nation will find itself bereft of steel, uranium, food, energy, and certain kinds of wood. This is not ruled out by sound economics; but it is only fair to mention that economists have a good deal to say by way of criticism of the efficiency with which governments program their subsidies for national defense purposes.

CONSERVATION AND FLOOD CONTROL

When people in a poor society are given a choice between staying alive in lessened misery or increasing the probability that certain species of flora and fauna will not go extinct, it is understandable that they may reveal a preference for the former choice. Once a society achieves certain average levels of well-being and affluence, it is reasonable to suppose that citizens will democratically decide to forego some calories and marginal private consumption enjoyments in favor of helping to preserve certain forms of life threatened by extinction. It is well-known that clearcutting forests is one way of altering the Darwinian environment. Therefore, pursuit of simple commercial advantage in forest management may have as a joint product reversible or irreversible effects upon the environment. When information of these tradeoffs is made available to the electorate, by that same pluralistic process which determines how much shall be spent on defense and other social goods, and how much shall be taxed for interpersonal redistributions of income, the electorate will decide to interfere with laissez-faire in forest management. This might show itself, for example, in forest sanctuaries of some size located in some density around the nation: the optimal cutting age there and indeed the whole mode of timber culture will have little to do with Faustmann copybook algorithm. Or, putting the matter more accurately, I would have to say the future vector of real costs and real benefits of each alternative will have to be scrutinized in terms of a generalization of the spirit and letter of the Faustmann-Fisher calculus.

Everything said about species conservation can, with appropriate and obvious modifications, be said about the programming of a nation's geographical resources to provide benefits for vacationers, campers, sportsmen, and tourists. Even the unspeakable fox hunter is an endangered species, and it is part of the political decision-making process to decide at what sustained level he is to be permitted to flourish.

Beyond pointing out these simple truisms, I need only mention in the present connection that, when a sophisticated cost-benefit calculus is applied to each of these areas, it is unlikely the optimal solution will include many virgin forests located in inaccessible places. Land use is shot through with externalities. Zoning, public regulations, and various use taxes will presumably be the rational way recommended by economists who study these matters. The organization of land use activities is likely, in the good society, to fall heavily inside the walls of government and regulatory authorities; but there seems reason to believe part of the problem can be effectively franchised out to enterprisers motivated by the hope of financial return. So far, in awarding television licenses or gasoline and restaurant franchises on public highways, governments have been disappointing in the efficiency with which they have worked out such arrangements. But this does not necessarily mean that turning over our landscape to the untender mercies of push-shove laissez-faire is better, or more feasible, than improving the efficiency with which the public sector organizes these activities.

Earlier I accepted the denial that externality problems which crop up in fisheries are equally applicable to forest economics. But that was in connection with the forest merely as a producer of cellulose. Ecologists know that soil erosion and atmospheric quality at one spot on the globe may be importantly affected by whether or not trees are being grown at places some distance away. To the degree this is so, the simple Faustmann calculus and the bouncings of the futures contracts for plywood on the organized exchanges need to be altered in the interests of the public (i.e., the interests of both Pareto-optimality and interpersonal-equity). Again, when the implied optimal sustained yield pattern comes to be estimated, it might well involve numerous clusters of trees planted hexagonally over much of the nation's terrain, rather than huge isolated forest reserves.

THE CLAIMS OF POSTERITY

My time is almost up. Yet I've only been able to scratch the surface of what needs to be explored in depth by catholic men of good will. At the least I must conclude by touching on an issue that goes to the heart of the controversy. Suppose that the competitive interest rates which will guide commercial forestry practices turn out to be very far from zero — say, 10 percent or even more. Must one necessarily accept this penalty on the use of time as the untouchable correct rate of discount a good society will want to recognize in its capital and intergenerational decision-making? This is not an easy question to answer. My earlier equation systems (7) and (8) show there are indeed theoretical models from which market solutions emerge which *also agree* with a technocrat's computation of a society's welfare optimum. So perhaps there is some presumption in favor of the market solution, at least in the sense that a vague burden of proof can be put against those who argue for interferences. At least many of today's mainstream economists would so argue.

I personally think the issue is more open. But I do not wish to pronounce on a matter that time does not permit us to do full justice to. Let me simply conclude therefore with some overly brief comments.

1. Economists like Cambridge's Pigou and Ramsey, or such Rawlsian writers as Phelps and Riley (1974), have asserted that we ordinary citizens in our day-to-day and lifetime decision-making about spending, consuming, and saving actually act in *too myopic* a way. If we display time-preference rate of 6 or 10 percent per annum, those rates are not the law of Moses and the Prophets. When we gather together periodically to form social compacts, set down constitutions, and elect representative legislators, a democracy may well decide that government coercion (involving taxing, fiscal changes in the public debt, and control by the central bank of the money supply) ought to alter the trends of capital formation and the amounts of capital bequeathed by each generation to subsequent generations. This is an argument for having lower interest rates at some future date when the policies described have become effective. It is not necessarily an argument for programming the use of publicly-owned forests now with a hypothetical interest rate much lower than interest rates that prevail elsewhere. The latter rates may very well be needed to ration optimally the supply of capital in its actual limited state.

2. There is still some debate among economists as to whether the interest rates appropriate for a government to use should be at all lower than those of private enterprise, and in particular, of the smaller private enterprises and corporations. Marglin (1963) has argued in this fashion, and so in a sense Arrow and Lind (1970) seem to have argued. Hirshleifer (1966) has given arguments against such a dichotomy; Diamond and Mirrlees (1971) have applied the powerful techniques of Ramseyian second-best analysis to analyze the problem. Pending the ultimate verdict of the informed jury in this matter, it seems safe to guess that no simple historical notion of "maximum sustained yield" will be likely to be recommended as optimal.

Whatever else my analysis today may have accomplished, I daresay it will provide corroboration to the old theorem that, when economists and forecasters meet to reason together, economists are likely stubbornly to act like economists. This is an indictment to which I would have to plead guilty, and throw myself on the mercy of your indulgent sentence. Let the penalty fit the crime!

BIBLIOGRAPHICAL NOTES

Rather than burden my text with footnotes, I include here some sketchy comments on previous writings. The notion is ancient that wood is so important and the time periods of forestry are so long that the state cannot leave the matter to commercial laissez-faire. See, for example, the

Roman and German background as discussed in Fernow (1902, 1913);
Fernow takes for granted that the ideas of Adam Smith are pernicious
when applied to long-lived forests.

The foresters' notion of "sustained yield," with allowable cut to be
regulated by how much the average tree age is above or below
the optimal age that maximizes steady-state lumber yield per acre is
already present in the 1788 "Austrian Cameral Valuation Method."
With a little charity, we might interpret this as an attempt to reduce cut
of trees below the age T_g at which $f'(T_g) = f(T_g)/T_g$ (as in my Equation
(2)), and to encourage cut at older ages.

In the early nineteenth century discounting future receipts at compound interest had reared its head. A momentary 1820 flash of insight by
Pfeil, which he later regretted, called for "a rotation based on maximum
soil rent" (Fernow 1913, p. 139), as in my Equation (6). Von Thunen
(1826, 1966, Hall English edition, p. 121) seems to anticipate the
(incorrect!) Jevons-Fisher relation $f'(T_1)/f(T_1) = r$ (of my Equation (4))
in his statement: "When the right methods are adopted, only trees of the
same age will stand together; and they will be felled (just?) before the
relative increment in their value sinks to (r =) 5 percent — the rate of
interest I have assumed to prevail throughout the Isolated State."

The highwater mark comes in 1849 when Martin Faustmann corrects
an attempt by E. F. von Gehren to use present discounted values to put
a fair price on (1) forest land taken by eminent domain for alternative
agricultural uses, and (2) existing forest stands on that land. Because
von Gehren uses too long a rotation age for his postulated interest rate,
applies bad approximations to true compound interest, and mistakenly
values unripe trees at their then-current wood value rather than at their
best future value properly discounted, he arrives at wrong and inconsistent results. He concluded, for example, that land value is negative when
he subtracted too high a stand value from total land-cum-stand value.

Faustmann corrects all this, applying the infinite cycle formula —
maximum $[Pf(T)e^{-rT} - WL][1 + e^{-rT} + \ldots]$ for our idealized case —
as in my Equation (6b). He shows that evaluating each tree or
age-cohort, or evaluating a synchronized forest, must always lead to the
same result, a truth denied as late as 1951 by Lutz and Lutz (1951, p.33).
I rely on the excellent translation of Faustmann and von Gehren given
in Gane (1968). In my quick reading, I judge Faustmann to know how to
calculate the correct optimal rotation age; but I cannot recall exactly
where he has done so, if he has indeed done so.

By this century, Irving Fisher (1906, 1907, 1930) has made present
discounted value calculations standard in the economics literature.
However, Fisher (1930, p. 161-165) still incorrectly calculates over one
cycle rather than over an infinity of repeated cycles, deducing in effect
as mentioned the relation for T_1 of my Equation (2), rather than the
right Faustmann-Ohlin-Preinrich-Bellman-Samuelson relation for T_∞ of

Equation (6c). Hotelling (1925) also concentrates on one cycle of a machine; and Goundrey (1960) claims the economist writers on forestry like Scott (1955) are still concentrating on one cycle. Lutz and Lutz (1951) give numerous alternatives including the correct infinite-cycle, but they fail to deduce just *when* this correct method is mandatory (and, as noted, they become confused on the synchronized-forest case). Preinrich (1938), Alchian (1952), Bellman (1957) provide more accurate discussion of the infinite-cycle case: but until this present paper, I have not seen an adequate elaboration of the maximum-land-rent aspect of the forestry problem. Hirshleifer (1970, p. 88-90) has the correct Faustmann solution and refers in his work to Gaffney (1957). I have to agree with Gaffney that Fisher is wrong, even though Hirshleifer is right in thinking that his principle of maximizing a *proper* PDV is not wrong. Ohlin (1921), I belatedly discover, gives an exactly correct analysis.

The "internal rate of return," r_i, today quite properly associated with Boulding (1935, 1941 and 3 later editions), was already explicitly or implicitly in Bohm-Bawerk (1889), Fisher (1907), Keynes (1936). Samuelson (1937) and Hirshleifer (1958) have debunked "maximizing" this r_i as a proper goal for decision-making by either a perfect or an imperfect competitor, but the corpse will not stay buried. Under free-entry and perfect competition, maximizing proper PDV *happens when PDV is zero also* to make r_i by tautology at a maximum. The only other possible defense for maximum-r_i is farfetched in any application, but has to my knowledge independently been glimpsed or proved by Boulding, Samuelson, Solow, Gale, and Chipman. If there is available to you a time-phased vector of net algebraic cash receipts, which you can initiate at *any* intensity *with no diminishing returns* (as you force down lumber prices, force up wage rates, run out of free forest lands, and bid up the land rent you must pay!), then any dollars that you initially have can ultimately be made, by investment and reinvestment into the postulated golden goose, to grow proportionally to $e^{r_i t}$; hence, having a higher r_i will ultimately come to dominate any lower r_i. However, under these unrealistic assumptions, r_i will come to form r, the market interest rate, itself; for if one could borrow at $r < r_i$, infinite scale would be optimal for this activity, a "meaningless" situation in a finite world; or, in the present application, the fact that trees grow on finite land will require positive rent payments that undermine any excess of r_i over r.

I found Goundrey (1960) a valuable survey, even if in the end he mistakenly comes out in favor of maximum internal rate of return. For the forestry literature on sustained yield, see items like Shepard (1925) and Waggener (1969).

On the proper discount rate to be used for governmental welfare decisions, see Ramsey (1928), Marglin (1963), Arrow and Lind (1970), Hirshleifer (1966), and Diamond and Mirlees (1971).

REFERENCES

Alchian, A. A., 1952, *Economic Replacement Policy*. The Rand Corporation, Santa Monica, Calif.

Arrow, K. J. and Lind, R. C., 1970, "Uncertainty and the evaluation of public investments," *American Economic Review*, 60, 354-378.

Austrian Government, 1965, "The Austrian Cameral Valuation Method." *The Forestry Chronicle*, 41, 84-92. English translation of the 1896 republication.

Bellman, R., 1957, *Dynamic Programming*. Princeton University Press, Princeton.

Boulding, K. E., 1935, "The theory of a single investment," *Quarterly Journal of Economics*, 49, 475-494.

_____ , 1941, 1948, 1955, 1966. *Economic Analysis*. Harper & Bros., New York.

Brock, W. and L. Mirman, 1972. "The stochastic modified golden rule in a one sector model of economic growth with uncertain technology," *Journal of Economic Theory* (June).

Chipman, J. A., 1972, "A renewal model of economic growth," *SIAM* (January). Also p. 43-83 in Day, R. H. and Robinson, S. M., eds., *Mathematical Topics in Economic Theory and Computation*, Society for Industrial and Applied Mathematics, Philadelphia, 1972.

Crutchfield, J. A. and Zellner, A., 1962, "Economic aspects of the Pacific halibut fishery," *Fishery Industrial Research I.*, U.S. Dept. of the Interior, Washington, D.C.

Diamond, P. A. and Mirrlees, J., 1971, "Optimal taxation and public production I-II," *American Economic Review*, 61, 8-27, 261-278.

Faustmann, M., 1849, "On the Determination of the Value Which Forest Land and Immature Stands Possess for Forestry," English edition edited by M. Gane, *Oxford Institute Paper 42*, 1968, entitled "Martin Faustmann and the Evolution of Discounted Cash Flow," which also contains the prior 1849 paper by E. F. von Gehren.

Fernow, B. E., 1902, *Economics of Forestry*, Thomas Y. Crowell & Co., New York.

_____ , 1913, *A Brief History of Forestry*, 3rd Edition, University Press Toronto, Toronto.

Fisher, I., 1906, *The Nature of Capital and Income*, Macmillan, New York.

_____ , 1907. *The Rate of Interest*, Macmillan, New York.

_____ , 1930, *The Theory of Interest*, Macmillan, New York, particularly p. 161-165.

Gaffney, M., 1957, "Concepts of financial maturity of timber and other assets," *Agricultural Economics Information Series 62*, North Carolina State College, Raleigh, N.C., September.

Gordon, H. S., 1954, "The economic theory of a common-property resource: The fishery," *Journal of Political Economy*, 62, 124-142.

Goundrey, G. K., 1960, "Forest management and the theory of capital," *Canadian Journal of Economics*, 26, 439-451.

Hirshleifer, J., 1958, "On the theory of optimal investment decision," *Journal of Political Economy*, 66, 198-209.

_____ , 1966, "Investment decision under uncertainty: Applications of the state-preference approach," *Quarterly Journal of Economics*, 80.

_____ , 1970, *Investment, Interest and Capital*, Prentice-Hall, Inc., Englewood Cliffs.

Hotelling, H., 1925, "A general mathematical theory of depreciation," *Journal of the American Statistical Association,* 20, 340-353.

Koopmans, T. C., 1967, "Intertemporal distribution and optimal aggregate economic growth," pp. 95-126 in *Ten Economic Studies in the Tradition of Irving Fisher*, John Wiley & Sons, New York.

Lutz, F. and Lutz, V., 1951, *The Theory of Investment of the Firm* (particularly Chs. 2 & 8). Princeton University Press, Princeton.

Marglin, S. A., 1963, "The social rate of discount and the optimal rate of investment," *Quarterly Journal of Economics*, 77, 95-111.

Merton, R. C., 1975, "An asymptotic theory of growth under uncertainty," *Review of Economic Studies*, 42, 375-394.

Mirrlees, J. A., "Optimum accumulation under uncertainty," Unpublished MS, December 1965.

Nordhaus, W. D., 1974, "The falling share of profits," *Brookings Papers on Economic Activity*, Okun, A. M. and Perry, G. L., eds., pp. 167-217. The Brookings Institution, Washington, D.C.

Ohlin, B., 1921, "Till fragen om skogarnas omloppstid," *Ekonomisk* Tidskrift, "Festschrift to Knut Wicksell."

Phelps, E. S., and Riley, J. G., "Rawlsian growth: Dynamic programming of capital and wealth for intergenerational maxi-min justice," Columbia University and UCLA. (Paper for private circulation, early 1974).

Preinrich, G. A. D., 1938, "Annual survey of economic theory: The theory of depreciation," *Econometrica*, 6, 219-241.

Ramsey, F. P., 1928, "A mathematical theory of saving," *Economic Journal*, 38, 543-559.

Samuelson, P. A., 1937, "Some aspects of the pure theory of capital," *Quarterly Journal of Economics*, 51, 469-496. Also reproduced in Stiglitz, J. E., ed., *Collected Scientific Papers of Paul A. Samuelson*, 1, pp. 161-188, M.I.T. Press, Cambridge, Mass. 1966.

—————— , 1964, "Tax deductibility of economic depreciation to insure invariant valuations," *Journal of Political Economy* (December) 604-606. Also pp. 571-573 in Merton, R. C., ed., *Collected Scientific Papers of Paul A. Samuelson*, 3, M.I.T. Press, Cambridge, Mass.

—————— , 1971, "Stochastic speculative price," *Proceedings of the National Academy of Sciences*, U.S.A., 68, 335-337. Also pp. 894-896 in Merton, R. C., ed., *Collected Scientific Papers of Paul A. Samuelson*, M.I.T. Press, Cambridge, Mass. 1972.

—————— , 1973, "Reply on Marxian matters," *Journal of Economic Theory*, 11, 64-67.

—————— , 1973, "Optimality of Profit-Including Prices Under Ideal Planning," *Proc. Nat. Acad. Sci. USA*, 70, 2109-2111.

Scott, A., 1955, "The fishery: The objectives of sole ownership," *Journal of Political Economy*, 63, 116-124.

—————— , 1955, *Natural Resources: The Economics of Conservation*, University of Toronto Press, Toronto.

Shepard, W., 1925, "The bogey of compound interest," *Journal of Forestry*, 23.

Smith, V. L., 1968, "Economics of production from natural resources," *American Economic Review*, 58, 409-431.

Thunen, J. H. von, 1826, *Isolated State*, English edition edited by Peter Hall, 1966. Pergamon Press, London.

Waggener, T. R., 1969, "Some economic implications of sustained yield as a forest regulation model," University of Washington, Contemporary Forestry Paper 6.

CAPITAL SHORTAGE, OR GLUT?

"To teach is to affirm." The late Crane Brinton of Harvard, who was himself a great teacher of intellectual history, could not wholeheartedly agree, reminding us that "To teach is also to raise doubt."

So I must raise some important questions. Is it true that capital is now particularly scarce? True that we need less consumer spending and more saving? (After all, it was just one President back who was urging the American people to save an extra 1½ per cent of their incomes.)

Is it true that the environmentalist lobby is lowering the yield on corporate capital, thereby depleting the funds out of which new capital formation is financed and killing off the incentive for savers to invest in new productive plant and equipment? Are profits minuscule after being corrected to take account of inflationary windfall capital gains on inventories and true replacement costs of plant and equipment being used up? And if so, how does this square with an alleged *scarcity* rather than plethora of capital?

These all are important questions. And we know from the last summit meeting of business economists and businessmen held in the White House by President Nixon that nine out of ten men of the business establishment would answer all these questions with a confident yes.

They may well turn out to be right. But a panel of assistant professors of economics cannot be sure.

CLAIMS

First, we can make a deposition that it would always be nice to have more productive capital. But that is not to say much. 'Twould be nice to have better consumption standards, nice to have (costlessly) more useful public goods and humane government income transfers.

Second, there is this much truth in the capital-scarcity thesis: a number of our basic-materials industries—paper, steel, chemicals, plastics, domestic oil refining—have been on round-the-clock operations even in the current recession. Perhaps this apparent lack of excess capacity would have come as less of a surprise to analysts if the Federal Reserve had revised its inadequate index of capacity earlier.

Third, environmental concern is a legitimate concern. To the degree that it acts like any other useful activity—air-conditioning demand, travel demand, indoor-tennis-court demand—environmental concern will add to capital demand. Far from being merely a net drag on industry, it is also a creator of profit opportunities, as the producers of pumps, catalysts and filter systems know.

So much can be granted to the thesis of capital scarcity.

COUNTERCLAIMS

Here are points on the other side.

1. If capital is scarce, its yield both before and after taxes *should be up, not down*. The yield is in fact down all over the world, way down. William Nordhaus of Yale has computed the decline in the 1974 Brookings Papers on Economic Activity. After carefully correcting for fictitious inflation gains, he finds that "genuine" after-tax rates of return on capital have fallen to between 5 and 6 per cent in the 1970s. By contrast, they averaged above 8 per cent in the late 1940s,

and again in the mid-1960s. Lest you think that it is merely the tax collector at work here, Nordhaus reports a comparable *before*-tax decline in corporate capital yield.

The story is more dramatic in Italy and the U.K. Nor are Germany and Japan immune from this worldwide competing of capital against capital.

2. It is definitely not the case that U.S. families are saving less of their disposable incomes than in recent decades. On the contrary, we are now saving in the 1970s a significantly *larger fraction* of our incomes. Also, corporations seem to plow back savings, in the form of earnings not paid in dividends, much as before. What comes hard these days is new equity capital.

3. In view of the fact that existing assets of U.S. enterprise can be bought at bargain terms, can one wonder that new issues are hard to float? James Tobin, also of Yale, calculates in the July Morgan Guaranty Survey that the ratio of what U.S. assets sell for in Wall Street and what they actually cost to reproduce is only two-thirds of what it was a decade ago.

Capital scarce? Then why does it sell at such a discount in the free market?

OPTIMUM SOCIAL SECURITY IN A LIFE-CYCLE GROWTH MODEL*

By Paul A. Samuelson[1]

INTRODUCTION

An exact model of steady-state, exponential-growth social security, characterized by two parameters of benefit levels and real-capital owned, is introduced into the life-cycle model of Modigliani, Diamond, Cass and Yaari, and Samuelson. Its incidence is shown to be such that, by an infinite number of different combinations of its parameters, the optimal social security program can be found to convert laissez faire equilibrium into golden-rule equilibrium that maximizes lifetime wellbeing of every subsequent generation. The infinity of optimal patterns results from the fact that greater public thrift will rationally lower the need for private thrift and, uncertainty aside, the precise allocation between the two is a matter of indifference. Indeed, "fully-funded social security," in this model always drives out an equivalent amount of "private saving," only the total mattering. However, once elements of private myopia are introduced into the model, it can be shown that a social security program that is second-best in its induced real capital formation can still add much to true citizenry wellbeing.

SANS SOCIAL SECURITY

Let the wellbeing of the representative person who works for a period when young and retires for a period when old be $u[c^1, c^2]$ as in Samuelson [7, 8, 9]. Let labor grow forever like $(1 + g)^t$, and output be given neoclassically by $L_t f[K_t/L_t]$, as in Solow [6]. Then the two-part golden rule to achieve, at growth rate g, maximum steady-state lifetime wellbeing is given by

$$(1) \qquad c_g^1 + \frac{c_g^2}{(1 + g)} = f(k_g) - gk_g$$

$$(2) \qquad f'[k_g] = g$$

$$(3) \qquad \frac{\partial u[c_g^1, c_g^2]/\partial c^1}{\partial u[c^1, c^2]/\partial c^2} = 1 + g.$$

However, unless g happens to equal the optimum population growth rate g^*, that maximizes $u[c_g^1, c_g^2]$ with respect to g and ensures the goldenest golden rule of Samuelson [8], the laissez faire life-cycle saving model of Modigliani [4, 5], Diamond [2], Tobin [10], Cass and Yaari [1], and von Weizsäcker [11] will not

* Manuscript received April 17, 1975.

[1] I owe thanks to the National Science Foundation and to the National Institute of Health for financial aid, and to Lynn Mary Karjala for editorial assistance.

asymptotically evolve into $u[c_g^1, c_g^2]$, but rather into $(k_{\ddagger}, c_{\ddagger}^1, c_{\ddagger}^2, r_{\ddagger} \gtreqless g)$, the roots of

$$(4) \qquad c^1 + \frac{c^2}{(1 + r)} = f[k] - rk$$

$$(5) \qquad f'[k] = r$$

$$(6) \qquad \frac{\partial u[c^1, c^2]/\partial c^1}{\partial u[c^1, c^2]/\partial c^2} = 1 + r$$

$$(7) \qquad (f[k] - rk) - c^1 \equiv \frac{c^2}{(1 + r)} = k(1 + g).$$

This last equation states the equality of saving when young with the system's productive capital (and out of which, interest and principal, the retired consume).

If $r_{\ddagger}$ of (4)–(7) happens to equal g, we are in the golden-rule state satisfying (1)–(3) and, as shown by the Samuelson [8] Serendipity Theorem, we are then at the goldenest g^*.

WITH SOCIAL SECURITY

We can now add a social security program to the system and endeavor to convert laissez faire's $u[c_{\ddagger}^1, c_{\ddagger}^2]$ into the higher $u[c_g^1, c_g^2]$.

A steady-state social security system taxes each worker τ and pays benefits to each retired person of β, while owning k^s of real capital per laborer. Private owned capital per capita is then $k - k^s$. The budget identity of the steady-state social security program is given as

$$\beta L_{t-1} \equiv \tau L_t + r_t k_t^s L_t - (k_{t+1}^s L_{t+1} - k_t^s L_t)$$

or, when L_t grows like $(1 + g)^t$ and we are in the steady state

$$(8) \qquad \frac{\beta}{(1 + g)} \equiv \tau + (1 + r)k^s - (1 + g)k^s.$$

We may use this identity to eliminate β as an unknown, thereby characterizing each steady-state social security program by its two independent parameters, τ and k^s. (Note: the transient burden of building up to k^s involves straightforward dynamic analysis that casts no new light on the comparative statics of steady states; it is reserved for explicit analysis elsewhere.)

Now we generalize (4)–(7) to the following four equations to determine the four unknowns, $k(\tau, k^s)$, $c^1(\tau, k^s)$, $c^2(\tau, k^s)$, $r(\tau, k^s)$:

$$(9) \qquad c^1 + \frac{c^2}{(1 + r)} = f[k] - rk - \tau + \frac{\beta}{(1 + r)}$$

$$= f[k] - rk - \tau + (1 + r)^{-1}(1 + g)[\tau + (r - g)k^s]$$

$$(10) \qquad f'[k] = r$$

$$(11) \qquad \frac{\partial u[c^1, c^2]/\partial c^1}{\partial u[c^1, c^2]/\partial c^2} = 1 + r$$

$$(12) \qquad \frac{c^2}{(1+r)} - (1+r)^{-1}(1+g)[\tau + (r-g)k^s] = (1+g)(k-k^s).$$

The incidence of a change in either τ or k^s can be worked out by straightforward total differentiation of (9)–(12) with respect to either of those parameters, giving linear relations to solve for $\partial c^i(\tau, k^s)/\partial \tau$, $\partial c^i(\tau, k^s)/\partial k^s$, etc.

OPTIMUM SOCIAL SECURITY

But to solve the problem of achieving the golden-rule state, we need not go through that analysis. Instead, we can force $r = g$ in (9), (10), (11), and note what values of (τ, k^s) are then needed to satisfy (12), namely (τ_g, k_g^s) in the following

$$(13) \qquad \frac{c_g^2}{(1+g)} = \tau_g + (1+g)(k_g - k^s).$$

THEOREM 1. *By an appropriate steady-state, life-cycle social security system, we can support a golden-rule state instead of bearing with a laissez faire equilibrium that is not in that state. And that golden-rule steady state can be supported by an infinity of different social security programs (some involving more rather than less social capital, k^s, and less rather than more current taxing, τ_g). It is really indifferent in the steady state whether we are doing much or little of lifetime saving in our purely private capacities or via our democratic social security system.*

Obviously in applying an abstract theorem like this, the severe idealizations of the model will have to be qualified. (Thus, private savings may be channeled under uncertainty in a qualitatively more efficient way; or, in a system of depression rigidities, when private thrift becomes abortive, public thrift may be more effective.) Also, when private myopia is deemed to require merit-want intensification of social security, the fuller analysis will need to take into account that private $k - k^s$ will be displaced in some degree by an increase in β and τ, and this quite aside from induced longer retirement analyzed in Feldstein [3].

It should also be obvious that "ever-fully-funded" social security, so beloved by actuaries and so necessary in a voluntary system, can accomplish nothing in this model.

THEOREM 2. *Any increase in "fully-funded" social security merely displaces exactly as much private capital as the public capital it brings into being.*

Thus, by definition of full funding,

$$\beta L_{t-1} = \tau L_{t-1}(1+r)$$
$$= k^s L_t(1+r)$$

or

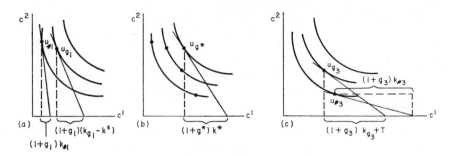

FIGURE 1

IN 1(b) WHERE THE GROWTH RATE IS JUST AT THE OPTIMUM POPULATION GROWTH RATE, HIGH-
EST WELLBEING IS AT u_{g^*}; PRIVATE SAVING WITH ZERO SOCIAL SECURITY OR WITH "FULLY-
FUNDED SOCIAL SECURITY" CAN SUPPORT THIS GOLDENEST STATE.

IN 1(a) WHERE THE GROWTH RATE g_1 EXCEEDS THE OPTIMUM RATE g^*, LAISSEZ FAIRE WILL
LEAD TO $u_{\sharp_1}$ WHERE LIFETIME SAVINGS JUST MATCH THE $k_{\sharp_1}$ LEVEL OF PER CAPITA CAPITAL AND
WHERE $r_{\sharp_1}$ FALLS SHORT OF g_1. AN OPTIMAL SOCIAL SECURITY PROGRAM THAT IS "OVER-FUNDED"
CAN GENERATE ONE OF THE SET OF k^s SOCIALLY-OWNED REAL CAPITAL WHICH CAN SUPPORT
PERMANENTLY THE GOLDEN-RULE LIFETIME WELLBEING OF u_{g_1}.

IN 1(c) WHERE THE SOCIAL RATE IS BELOW THE OPTIMUM RATE g^*, LAISSEZ FAIRE WILL LEAD
TO THE PERMANENTLY INEFFICIENT POINT $u_{\sharp_3}$, WITH $r_{\sharp_3}$ BELOW g_3. A PAY-AS-YOU-GO PONZI-LIKE
PROGRAM CAN RAISE THE PERMANENT LEVEL OF THE SYSTEM TO THE GOLDEN-RULE POINT u_{g_3}.
ALWAYS AN INFINITE NUMBER OF DIFFERENT BLENDS OF PAY-AS-YOU-GO AND OVER-FUNDING
CAN ACHIEVE ANY DESIRED STATE.

$$(14) \qquad\qquad \tau = k^s(1 + g) = \frac{\beta}{(1 + r)}.$$

If we put (14) into (9)–(12), that system degenerates into the laissez faire equilibrium of (4)–(7): then large τ merely lowers private $k - k^s$ as much as k^s rises,
a trivially obvious result once we realize that the representative man is no different off if much or little of his "spontaneous" thrift is embalmed in private
or public capital.

If $k_{\sharp} < k_g$ and $c_g^2/(1 + g) < k_g(1 + g)$, it is obvious that $gk^s - \tau_g$ in (13)
must be positive—which can happen only if $k^s > 0$ and social security is *more*
than fully funded (as that term is defined in (14)). If, as in Cass and Yaari [1],
$k_{\sharp} > k_g$, as when growth rates become very low or very negative, $c_g^2/(1 + g) >
k_g(1 + g)$ and $\tau_g - gk^s$ must be positive, which can be salubriously realized
under pay-as-you-go social security with

$$k^s = 0$$

and

$$\tau_g = \frac{c^2}{(1 + g)} - (1 + g)k_g.$$

Increases in g so long as $k_{\sharp}$ remains above k_g will improve lifetime wellbeing
and reduce the τ_g of pay-as-you-go social security, until at the Samuelson [8]
optimum growth rate g^*, *no* social security program is needed (and the only

optimal ones have to be fully-funded).

A concluding warning is in order. Reserved for later treatment is the analysis needed for transient analysis out of steady states. Thus, begin with laissez faire equilibrium at too high an interest rate. If we now aim to attain golden-rule steady state with positive social capital, it is clear that (with β and τ non-negative!) ever-pay-as-you-go social security cannot be utilized to accomplish this; but this truth does not deny that, *after* enough k^s has been built up and can be maintained out of its own earnings, the requisite steady-state social security program could forever after be a purely pay-as-you-go one with $\beta_g = (1 + g)\tau_g$.

Figure 1 illustrates how optimal social security programs can convert private life-cycle saving into golden-rule states.

FINAL REMARKS

1. Just because a system is observed in a permanent steady-state equilibrium, $u[c^1, c^2]$, which is lower than the golden-rule $u[c_g^1, c_g^2]$ by virtue of the fact that the interest rate exceeds the growth rate, $r > g$, this does not mean that it will necessarily wish to move toward the higher u_g level; for to do so, must necessarily imply transient sacrifice of utility by some generations, and society's systematic rate of time preference might reckon this to be a bad bargain. In short, the hypothesized non-golden-rule steady state is not (repeat, not) *intertemporally* inefficient.

2. Many social security systems, like the New Deal U.S. system, may be deemed most valuable precisely because the myopia ignored by the present models does in fact prevail. People live miserably in old age because they do not realize when young what are the consequences of their private saving habits. So by democratic fiat, they paternalistically impose on themselves a within-life pattern of consumption that favors old age at the expense of young. Precisely because of the myopia that makes paternalism optimal, once citizens are subject to social security taxation and benefits they do not see clearly how they can undo by private-saving offsets what the mandatory system is doing to them. So, both because of themselves and yet despite themselves, they contrive social security that makes them better off.

This can be formalized by a model in which the $u[c^1, c^2]$ function "upon which people act" is different from the "true" $v[c^1, c^2]$ in terms of which they definitely wish to be guiding their decisions. Subject to (9)–(12), we pick (τ, k^s) to maximize $v[c^1(\tau, k^s), c^2(\tau, k^s)]$.

Massachusetts Institute of Technology, U.S.A.

REFERENCES

[1] CASS, D. AND YAARI, M., "Individual Savings, Aggregate Capital Accumulation, and Efficient Growth," in K. Shell, ed., *Essays on the Theory of Optimal Economic Growth* (Cambridge, Mass: MIT Press, 1967), 233–268.

[2] DIAMOND, P., "National Debt in a Neoclassical Growth Model," *American Economic Review*, LV (December, 1965), 1126–1150.

[3] FELDSTEIN, M., "Social Security and Private Savings: International Evidence in an Extended Life Cycle Model," unpublished Discussion Paper Number 361, Harvard Institute of Economic Research, Harvard University, (May, 1974).

[4] MODIGLIANI, F., "The Life-Cycle Hypotheses of Saving Twenty Years Later," in M. Parkin, ed., *Contemporary Issues in Economics* (Manchester: Manchester University Press, 1974).

[5] ———— AND R. BRUMBERG, "Utility Analysis and the Consumption Function: An Interpretation of Cross-Section Data," in K. K. Kurihara, ed., *Post Keynesian Economics* (New Brunswick, N. J.: Rutgers University Press, 1954).

[6] SOLOW, R. M., "A Contribution to the Theory of Economic Growth," *Quarterly Journal of Economics*, LXX (February, 1956), 65–94.

[7] SAMUELSON, P. A., "An Exact Consumption-Loan Model of Interest with or without the Social Contrivance of Money," *Journal of Political Economy*, LXVI (December, 1958), 467–482. Reprinted in Joseph E. Stiglitz, ed., *The Collected Scientific Papers of Paul A. Samuelson*, Volume I (Cambridge, Mass: MIT Press, 1966), Chapter 21.

[8] ————, "The Optimum Growth Rate for Population," *International Economic Review*, XVI (October, 1975), 531–538.

[9] ————, "The Two-Part Golden Rule Deduced as the Asymptotic Turnpike of Catenary Motions," *Western Economic Journal*, VI (March, 1968), 85–89. Reprinted in Robert C. Merton, ed., *The Collected Scientific Papers of Paul A. Samuelson*, Volume III (Cambridge, Mass.: MIT Press, 1972), Chapter 138.

[10] TOBIN, J., "Life Cycle Saving and Balanced Growth," in W. Fellner *et al.*, eds., *Ten Economic Studies in the Tradition of Irving Fisher* (New York: John Wiley and Sons, Inc., 1967), 231–256.

[11] VON WEIZSÄCKER, C. C., *Steady State Capital Theory* (Berlin: Springer Verlag, 1971).

THE OPTIMUM GROWTH RATE FOR POPULATION*

By Paul A. Samuelson[1]

INTRODUCTION

THE WELL-KNOWN THEORY of optimum population was concerned with that stationary *plateau* of population which, taking into account limitations of un-augmentable land and economies of scale, maximizes per capita output and consumption. In conventional post-Keynesian models of capital growth, by Harrod, Robinson, and Solow, natural resources are not assumed to be limiting and constant returns to scale is maintained, with the result that the *level* of population is indifferent. In the usual version of that growth model, the slower the rate of exponential growth the higher can be the level of steady-state consumption; on the other hand, in a life-cycle pure-consumption model of the 1958 Samuelson type, which permits no trades with nature, the faster the population growth the better, since more children means better support for retired parents. By contrast, the present analysis, which takes into account differentiated periods of life, work and retirement, and also investment in capital goods, derives the conditions for an optimum intermediate population *growth rate* and proves, as a serendipity theorem, that under laissez faire private savings would *just* suffice to support this growth-rate state if biological and cultural factors happened to mandate it.

STANDARD STATICAL THEORY

Labor and land inputs, L and T, produce output Q by a production function

$$(1) \qquad Q = F(L, T) .$$

For fixed T, the optimum of per capita output is given where

$$(2) \qquad \partial\left\{\frac{F(L, T)}{L}\right\}\Big/\partial L = 0 .$$

If $F(L, T)$ is concave and homogeneous-first-degree, the lower the population the better. If scale economies exist to make $F(L, T)$ strongly convex in initial T

* Manuscript received April 17, 1975.

[1] Financial aid from NIH Grant 1 R01 HD-09081-01 is gratefully acknowledged. Thanks go to Lynn Mary Karjala for editorial assistance.

and the law of diminishing returns makes it ultimately strongly concave, an optimum L^* will come at a finite positive level.

This result is not essentially changed if we add a vector of capital goods, $K = (K_1, \ldots, K_n)$, each producible out of L, T, and K. Specifically, for $n = 1$ and K scalar, we generalize (1) and (2) to

(3)
$$Q_t = C_t + K_{t+1} - K_t = F(L_t, K_t, T_t)$$

$$\operatorname*{Max}_{L,K} \left\{ \frac{F(L, K, T)}{L} \right\} = \frac{F(L^*, K^*, T)}{L^*}$$

$$\frac{\partial F(L^*, K^*, T)}{\partial K} = 0$$

$$L^* \frac{\partial F(L^*, K^*, T)}{\partial L} - F(L^*, K^*, T) = 0 .$$

Meade [4] gives standard analysis of the static case.

STANDARD DYNAMICAL THEORY

Solow [12] defines the conventional capital growth model, in which (3) holds but with land ignorable:

(4)
$$Q_t = C_t + K_{t+1} - K_t = F(L_t, K_t) , \qquad\qquad C_t \geq 0$$

$$= L_t f\left(\frac{K_t}{L_t}\right), \qquad\qquad f'(\ ) > 0, \quad f''(\ ) < 0 .$$

In this version $F(\ ,\ )$ is concave and first-degree-homogeneous; also it is understood that gross capital formation is non-negative, so that $K_{t+1} - K_t \geq -\delta K_t$, where δ is some non-negative fractional rate of exponential depreciation. Also

(5)
$$\frac{C_t}{L_t} + \left[\frac{K_{t+1} - K_t}{K_t} \right]\left(\frac{K_t}{L_t}\right) = f\left(\frac{K_t}{L_t}\right)$$

$$c_t = f(k_t) - \frac{K_{t+1} - K_t}{K_t} k_t$$

where the lower-case per capita symbols are defined by (5).

If labor is assumed to grow exponentially, like $(1 + g)^t$, and the system is in balanced-growth or steady-state configuration, with capital also growing at that same exponential rate, we have for steady-state per capita magnitudes

(6)
$$c = f(k) - gk , \qquad\qquad g \geq -\delta .$$

As shown by Swan [13], Phelps [6], von Weizsäcker [16], and others, the golden-rule state for maximum c at each prescribed g rate is that in which the interest rate and growth rate are equal, and where the profit and investment shares of income are equal

$$(7) \qquad \text{Max}_{k} \{f(k) - gk\} = f(k_g) - gk_g = c_g$$

$$(8) \qquad f'(k_g) = g$$

where k_g and c_g are the optimal or golden-rule values of k and c for each given g.

It follows directly that the less algebraic is the growth rate g, the greater in that model will be c_g. Actually,

$$(9) \qquad \frac{dc_g}{dg} = -k_g < 0.$$

Thus, by this model a declining population would yield higher per capita income as people can live off "narrowing" of capital, and the fastest feasible decline would be the best, in which $g = -\delta$.

OPTIMUM LIFETIME WELLBEING

The important researches of Modigliani [5] stress the importance for understanding saving of the fact that people's earning years are followed by years of retirement. For such a life-cycle model, but where K can be ignored in (4), Samuelson [8] showed that the greater the growth rate g, the greater would be income available to the retired, whether from optimal social security or private intergenerational loans. The same Ponzi or chain-letter analysis leads to results opposite that of the previous section: The faster the permanent growth rate in a pure-consumption-loan model, the greater is lifetime wellbeing of the representative person!

Diamond [2] and Samuelson [11] combined the Solow model of (4) and (6), with its pivotal role for capital, with the 1958 Samuelson model of overlapping generations. What can now be shown here is that there will exist an optimum rate of growth, g^*, *the goldenest golden-rule state* that maximizes lifetime wellbeing of the representative man or generation.

For simplicity, assume one period of work when young, followed by one period of retirement when old. Let $u[c^1, c^2]$ be a quasi-concave indicator (ex ante or ex post) of ordinal wellbeing, where c^1 and c^2 are per capita real consumptions when young and old respectively. At time t, there are L_t of young workers, who consume in total $L_t c_t^1$; the rest of consumption is by the old and, deaths at a young age being ignored, is given by $L_{t-1} c_t^2$. Now (4) generalizes to

$$(10) \qquad L_t c_t^1 + L_{t-1} c_t^2 + K_{t+1} - K_t = L_t f\left(\frac{K_t}{L_t}\right)$$

$$u_t = u[c_t^1, c_{t+1}^2].$$

Warning: c^2 never refers to c-squared; but rather to c in the second period of life.

On the supposition of balanced exponential growth, with

$$g = \frac{L_{t+1} - L_t}{L_t} = \frac{K_{t+1} - K_t}{K_t},$$

(10) gives rise to the following expression for steady-state u,

(11)
$$u[c^1, c^2] = u\left[f(k) - gk - \frac{c^2}{1 + g}, c^2 \right]$$

$$u_g = \max_{k, c^2} u\left[f(k) - gk - \frac{c^2}{1 + g}, c^2 \right]$$

$$= u\left[f(k_g) - gk_g - \frac{c_g^2}{1 + g}, c_g^2 \right]$$

where optimal k_g, c_g^2 and

$$c_g^1 = f(k_g) - gk_g - \frac{c_g^2}{1 + g}$$

satisfy

(12a)
$$f'(k_g) = g$$

(12b)
$$\frac{u_1[c_g^1, c_g^2]}{u_2[c_g^1, c_g^2]} = 1 + g.$$

The first of these is the familiar Swan-Phelps golden-rule production relation of (8). The second, in (12b), is the "biological interest rate" relation of Samuelson [8]. Together they constitute the two-part golden rule.

We can now vary g to find the optimum growth rate, g^*, at which we are in the goldenest golden-rule state of all, at which u_g is maximized

(13)
$$u^* = \max_g u_g = \max_g u\left[f(k_g) - gk_g - \frac{c_g^2}{1 + g}, c_g^2 \right]$$

$$= u\left[f(k^*) - g^*k^* - \frac{c^{2*}}{1 + g^*}, c^{2*} \right]$$

where g^* is the root of

(14)
$$0 = -k_g + \frac{c_g^2}{(1 + g)^2},$$

$$1 + g^* = \left(\frac{c_g^2}{k_g} \right)^{1/2}.$$

Since k_g and c_g^2 are themselves functions of g from (12), (14) is an implicit, not an explicit equation for g^*. Though u in (11) is a concave function of (k, c^2) and of g, it is not concave in all three variables together. Therefore, the necessary conditions of (12a), (12b), and (14) must be supplemented by secondary conditions in order to be sufficient for a true maximum; and multiple solutions to these equations might occur. The truly optimizing g^* might be greater or less than zero depending upon $u[\ ]$, $f(\ )$, and other econometric aspects of the problem.[2]

---

[2] Since g is constrained to be not less than $-\delta$, the maximum rate at which capital can be milked, the equalities in (14) have to be modified in the Kuhn-Tucker manner to invoke "$\geq$" rather than "$=$", with the latter having to hold when $g > -\delta$. I owe thanks to Professor Guillermo Calvo of Columbia for reminding me of the inequality possibilities.

The longer the relative period of retirement becomes, as from improvements in old-age mortality, the more likely g^* will represent positive growth.

SERENDIPITY OF PRIVATE SAVING AT OPTIMUM GROWTH

Given an arbitrary population growth rate, g, private saving will *not* generally lead to the golden-age state k_g or u_g. If population growth is very great, life-cycle saving will not generate at the interest rate g enough saving to match the capital formation needed to "widen" capital in pace with the rapid labor growth. So, as in Diamond [2], for such large g, the laissez faire equilibrium will be at $k(\infty; g) < k_g$. Similarly at very low g, negative g for example, laissez faire equilibrium will be at $k(\infty; g) > k_g$, which has been shown by Phelps [7] and Koopmans [3] to be permanently inefficient.

Therefore, if g is a given and society insists upon achieving the golden rule optimum of (k_g, u_g), society must resort to a public debt or to some form of compulsory social security. Thus, at g so low that private saving becomes excessive, pay-as-you-go social security that taxes the young to provide for the old will serve to displace enough capital formation from the private saving that would otherwise occur just to achieve the desirable reduction in overall thrift! Contrariwise, when population growth is above the optimum growth rate g^*, compulsory social security invested in real capital at an "excessive" scale, judged by private standards, raises c_g. Such extensive social security must be actually invested in new capital formation, and cannot be merely pay-as-you-go as will be shown in Samuelson [9].

A remarkable theorem can now be discerned.

SERENDIPITY THEOREM. *At the optimum growth rate g^*, private lifetime saving will just support the most-golden golden-rule lifetime state.*

To prove this, note that the Modigliani-Diamond condition for private-saving steady-state equilibrium is that what workers choose to "save" must just match what the system needs for extensive growth. That is, $k(\infty; g)$ is determined in the model of (10) by the life-cycle saving and investment condition

$$(15) \qquad (1 + g)k(\infty; g) = \frac{c^2(\infty; g)}{1 + r}.$$

Here $k(\infty; g)$ and $c^2(\infty; g)$ are the long-run lifecycle equilibrium asymptotic values.

Hence, for $g = g^*$, $k(\infty; g^*)$ satisfies the optimality condition for k^*. So our theorem is proved that, if g is somehow changed to g^*, laissez faire private saving will just support the equilibrium. (Since there might be multiple Modigliani equilibria, the horrible thought arises that the goldenest golden-rule state might fall on one of them that is unstable, a matter that needs further investigation.)

All this applies to the case where g represents the rate of population growth and where there is no labor-augmenting technical change. If both are present, say at rates g and g', we must replace $(1+g)$ in all our formulas by $(1+g)(1+g')$. Provided $u[c^1, c^2]$ is homothetic, we can still have steady-state equilibrium, with both c^{2*} and k^* growing proportionally to $(1+g')^t$. Then for $1+g'$ given, the optimum $1+g^*$ can be determined as in (14), but with $(c^{2*}/k^*)^{1/2}/(1+g')$ there.

Note that the present theory of the optimum ignores the pleasures of parent-hood analyzed at the end of Phelps [7], but can easily adjust to them. Note also that, like the statical optimum population, the present optimum growth point has one-sided stability, being stable from above but unstable from below: if people were educated to insisting upon having the u^* level of living before producing the number of children needed for g^*, any tendency to have too many children would result in lowered wellbeing and a corrective cutback in fertility; however, any shortfall of fertility would result in lowered living standards and further shortfalls, causing a self-aggravating drop in g below g^*.

Figure 1 summarizes graphically the optimal rate of population growth.

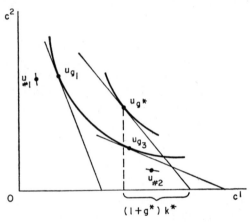

FIGURE 1

THE GOLDENEST GOLDEN AGE OF ALL IS REACHED AT u_{g^*}, WHERE THERE IS TANGENCY BETWEEN THE LIFETIME $u[c^1,c^2]$ CONTOURS AND THE LINE WITH SLOPE $-(1+g^*)$ AND HORIZONTAL INTERCEPT $f[k^*] - g^*k^*$. AT HIGHER GROWTH RATE, g_1, THE GOLDEN RULE STATE COMES AT u_{g_1}; AT LOWER GROWTH RATE, g_3, THE GOLDEN RULE STATE COMES AT u_{g_3}. UNDER LAISSEZ FAIRE PRIVATE SAVING, WHEN GROWTH IS AT g_1 OR g_3, EQUILIBRIUM COMES AT INTEREST RATES THAT DEPART EVEN MORE FROM g^*, WITH LIFETIME WELLBEINGS AT $u_{\#1}$ AND $u_{\#3}$.

CONCLUSIONS

The assumptions of the present argument have been heroically oversimplified. Most of these simplifications can be remedied, as for example, when we replace a scalar K by a vector heterogeneous capital goods and specify more periods of work than of retirement, as in Tobin [14], and make the age of retirement an endogenous variable.[3] Ultimately, positive exponential population growth will presumably bring back into importance the scarcity of natural resources ignored by the model. (However, the possibility of land-augmenting invention, in which $F(K_t, L_t, \theta_t T)$ with θ_t growing at as rapid an exponential rate as K_t and L_t, cannot be dismissed out of hand.)

But even if we do not care to take literally the findings of this model of optimal growth, it still can provide pregnant insights.

The sense in which social security can be eased by a Ponzi-like bonus from exponential growth is one such insight, as in Samuelson [10] or Cass and Yaari [1]. But more ominous for the future of planned parenthood is the following possibility thrown up by the analysis.

For several generations people may benefit on a lifetime basis by having numerous children to support them well in their old ages, out of filial piety or by means of social security. And yet until the end of time their increases in population will cause the law of diminishing returns to be brought into play to leave all subsequent generations in a worsened situation. To the degree that childhood dependency is intrinsically less costly relative to old-age dependency, this dyshygienic temptation becomes all the more dangerous.

Massachusetts Institute of Technology, U.S.A.

REFERENCES

[1] CASS, D. AND YAARI, M., "Individual Saving, Aggregate Capital Accumulation, and Efficient Growth," in K. Shell, ed., *Essays on the Theory of Optimal Growth* (Cambridge, Mass.: MIT Press, 1967), 233–268.

[2] DIAMOND, P., "National Debt in a Neoclassical Growth Model," *American Economic Review*, LV (December, 1965), 1126–1150.

[3] KOOPMANS, T. C., "On the Concept of Optimal Economic Gtowth," *Scripta Varia* (Vatican City: Pontificia Academia Scientarium, 1965), 225–287.

[4] MEADE, J. E., *Economic Analysis and Policy* (Oxford: Clarendon Press, 1936), Part IV.

[5] MODIGLIANI, F., "The Life Cycle Hypothesis of Saving Twenty Years Later," in M. Parkin, ed., *Contemporary Issues in Economics* (Manchester: Manchester University Press, 1974).

[6] PHELPS, E. S., "The Golden-Rule of Accumulation: A Fable for Growthmen," *American Economic Review*, LI (September, 1961), 638–643.

[7] ————, *Golden Rules of Economic Growth: Studies of Efficient and Optimal Investment* (New York: W. W. Norton and Co., 1966), Essays 5 and 12.

[8] SAMUELSON, P. A., "An Exact Consumption-Loan Model of Interest with or without the Social Contrivance of Money," *Journal of Political Economy*, LXVI (December, 1958), 467–482. Reprinted in Joseph E. Stiglitz, ed., *The Collected Scientific Papers of Paul A. Samuelson*, Volume I (Cambridge, Mass.: MIT Press, 1966), Chapter 21.

[9] ————, "Optimum Social Security in a Life-Cycle Growth Model," *International Economic Review*, XVI (October, 1975), 539–544.

[10] ————, "Social Security," *Newsweek* (February 3, 1967), 88.

[3] Since completing this paper, I have been able to prove the Serendipity Theorem for a general n-period-of-life model. However, J. Mirrlees has given me reasons to wonder whether it holds when bequests occur. In private correspondence on the present manuscript, C.C. von Weizsäcker informs me that he hopes to include the present theorems in the forthcoming second edition of his [15], giving neat proofs by combining his theorems [15, (86–87 and 80)] on the equality of "waiting period" and the definable "period of production" and golden-rule relations.

[11] ————, "The Two-Part Golden Rule Deduced as the Asymptotic Turnpike of Catenary Motions," *Western Economic Journal*, VI (March, 1968), 85–89. Reprinted in Robert C. Merton, ed., *The Collected Scientific Papers of Paul A. Samuelson*, Volume III (Cambridge, Mass.: MIT Press, 1972), Chapter 138.

[12] SOLOW, R. M., "A Contribution to the Theory of Economic Growth," *Quarterly Journal of Economics*, LXX (February, 1956), 65–94.

[13] SWAN, T. W., "Of Golden Ages and Production Functions," Gamorgi IEA paper, 1960. Reprinted in K. Berrill, ed., *Economic Development for Asia* (London: Macmillan and IEA, 1964).

[14] TOBIN, JAMES, "Life Cycle Saving and Balanced Growth," in W. Fellner *et al.*, eds., *Ten Economic Studies in the Tradition of Irving Fisher* (New York: John Wiley and Sons, Inc., 1967), 231–256.

[15] VON WEIZSÄCKER, C. C., *Steady State Capital Theory* (Berlin: Springer Verlag, 1971).

[16] ————, *Wachstum, Zins und Optimale Investitsionsquote* (Basel: Kyklos Verlag, 1962).

THE OPTIMUM GROWTH RATE FOR POPULATION:
AGREEMENT AND EVALUATIONS*

By Paul A. Samuelson[1]

Mea culpe. SAMUELSON [4] POINTED OUT that increased rate of population growth has the well-known disadvantage of reducing consumption goods per capita because of the need to "widen" capital in proportion to the population growth; but that increased population growth has the advantage, analyzed in Samuelson [3] and elsewhere, of giving retired persons more working individuals to support them. It was therefore suggested that there might be an intermediate rate of population growth—positive, zero, or negative—depending upon the parameters of the problem—at which the disadvantages of further growth were just cancelled by the advantages. At such a point we would have the optimal rate of population growth, the one which maximizes per capita lifetime utility of consumptions. The necessary conditions for this optimum rate were given (and, incidentally, a "serendipity theorem" was discovered according to which, if that optimal rate were mandated by actual propensities to procreate, it would turn out to be the case that voluntary life-cycle personal savings would just suffice to support the equilibrium without recourse to social security alterations of life-cycle consumption patterns).

Professor Deardorff [1] has provided a valuable corrective to the over-simple view that was implicit in my earlier paper. It is true I had warned that (1) the optimal population rate might occur at the lowest rate admissible in the standard Solow-Harrod-Robinson one-sector capital model (at the limiting rate of decline equal to the maximum depreciation rate of capital, for which gross capital formation is zero). Also, (2) I had mentioned the possibility of multiple solutions to the first-order necessary conditions since my maximand was noted *not* to be concave in all its variables. Still, the reader would be correct in inferring that the author believed it to be the usual and normal case that the crucial equation for the optimum corresponded to a *maximum* of welfare, not a *minimum*, and that there was some presumption that one unique local and global maximum rate of population growth exists.

By a class of counter-examples and by useful general analysis, Professor Deardorff has shown that it can well be the case that the only root to my extremum condition corresponds to a *minimum* rather than a maximum of well-being. My necessary first-order condition then defines the model's globally *worst* rate of population growth: far better, then, to have population decline at the fastest rate that the milking of capital can match; and, paradoxically, equally blissful in the Deardorff specification of the model is the fastest possible exponential rate of population growth.

* Manuscript received March 1, 1976; revised April 14, 1976.
[1] My thanks go to the National Health Institutes Grant 1 RO1 HD-09081-01 for financial aid.

My hat is off to Professor Deardorff. I have learned from his analysis; no less important, I have "unlearned" some implicit fallacies. It is well that readers forthwith be provided with his important correctives.

Within the limits of my present leisure and the patience of the editors, the optimal thing for me to do is to add some relevant reactions and provide answers to a subset of the open questions posed by the Deardorff analysis.

1. GRAPHICAL EXPOSITION

Figure 1 shows what was implicitly in my mind prior to the Deardorff correctives. In 1(a) we have the standard one-period-of-life Solow model involving one sector that produces with a single malleable capital good either consumption or new capital goods. The lower the rate of population growth, g, the less the need to "waste" resources on the "widening" of capital: hence, steady-state per capita consumption is at its maximum when population declines as fast as capital depreciates, at rate $-\delta$, so that gross investment is zero and consumption maximal.

In 1(b), people consume at different ages of life, including an age of retirement. Production comes from labor in preretirement years. The 1958 pure-consumption-loan model rules out investing in "nature" or "technology," since

SOLOW MODEL   LIFE-CYCLE "LOAN" CASE   COMBINED MODEL

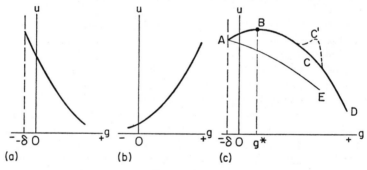

FIGURE 1

IN (a) IS SHOWN THE STANDARD ONE-SECTOR CAPITAL MODEL IN WHICH ANY IN-CREASE IN POPULATION GROWTH RATE OCCASIONS GREATER NEED TO "WIDEN" GOLDEN-RULE CAPITAL STOCK, THEREBY LESSENING AVAILABLE PER CAPITA STEADY-STATE CONSUMPTION. IN (b) IS SHOWN THE LIFE-CYCLE MODEL IN WHICH HIGHER POPULATION GROWTH MEANS MORE ACTIVE WORKERS PER RETIRED PER-SON, THEREBY ENABLING REPRESENTATIVE PERSONS TO HAVE HIGHER LIFETIME UTILITY. IN (c) THE TWO MODELS ARE COMBINED. ABCD, WITH OPTIMUM POPULA-TION GROWTH AT g^* CORRESPONDING TO MAXIMUM POINT B ILLUSTRATES THE SAMUELSON [4] IMPLICIT PRESUMPTION. ALTERNATIVE CASE OF AE HAD NOTED POSSIBILITY OF A BOUNDARY MAXIMUM WITH DECLINING POPULATION. ALTERNA-TIVE CASE OF ABC'D HAD RECOGNIZED THE POSSIBILITY OF MULTIPLE MAXIMA BE-CAUSE OF LACK OF CONCAVITY OF MAXIMAND.

there are no capital goods. Paradoxically, high population growth gives retired people many workers to rely on: the optimal steady-state level of lifetime for the representative person in every generation is *highest* when g is highest. The rising curve in 2(a) shows this. (For simplicity, let the measure of lifetime utility, *u*, be represented by some homogeneous-first-degree, concave function of per capita consumptions at all ages: thus, with the proper tastes, a two-period-of-life model could involve $u = \text{Min}\,[c^1, c^2/\omega], \omega > 0$.)

Figure 1(c) shows the result of combining the models of 1(a) and 1(b), as in the classical article on public debt of Diamond [2]. The result was thought to be like ABCD, with B the best state of well-being when population growth was at its optimum, g^*. However, caution had suggested the possibility that tastes and technology would produce the *alternative* pattern AE; or, possibly, the alternative pattern ABC'D.

The Deardorff example shows that we must reckon with the possibility sketched crudely in Figure 2(a). If the ABC pattern prevails, then Equation (14), Samuelson [4, (534)], has for its root, $g^\dagger$, the *worst* population growth rate and not g^*, the optimal growth rate. Another possibility, arising for certain admissible parameter values in Deardorff's Cobb-Douglas functions for gross output and for utility, would be given by an indefinite extention of the falling AB branch, so that any algebraic population growth greater than $-\delta$ reduces lifetime well-being from the infinite bliss level obtainable at $g^* = -\delta$.

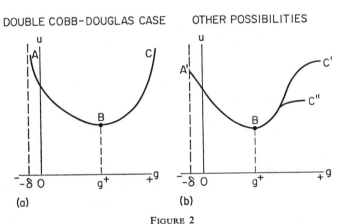

DOUBLE COBB-DOUGLAS CASE   OTHER POSSIBILITIES

(a)   (b)

FIGURE 2

(a) SHOWS DEARDORFF CASE OF COBB-DOUGLAS ISOQUANTS AND UTILITY CON-
TOURS FOR DIFFERENT PERIODS OF LIFE. IN ABC THE POINT B REPRESENTS A
MINIMUM $g^\dagger$, RATHER THAN A MAXIMUM g^*. INFINITELY BETTER "BLISS"
LEVELS ARE ACHIEVABLE AT VERY HIGH POPULATION GROWTH RATES OR AT
POPULATION DECLINE EQUAL TO RATE OF CAPITAL DEPRECIATION. IN (b) ARE
SHOWN VARIANT CASES IN WHICH NO INTERMEDIATE MAXIMUM g^* EXISTS.
BETTER THAN C'' AND MINIMUM POINT B IS A' ON ABC''; BETTER THAN A' AND
B ON ABC' IS C' POINT. WARNING IS GIVEN THAT HIGH-g OPTIMA WILL EVEN-
TUALLY RUN AFOUL OF SCARCITIES OF LAND AND NATURAL RESOURCES, ELE-
MENTS NEGLECTED IN THE OVERSIMPLE MODEL.

In 2(b) I have sketched some alternative patterns that are in the spirit of the Deardorff example, even though they are not compatible with exact Cobb-Douglas functions. A'BC'' admits only of feasible states of *limited* lifetime well-being. Since the right-hand upper bound, C'', is below A', society is permanently better off in population decline at A' than in any pattern of population growth (or of *very* slow decline). When A'BC' prevails, strong population growth is better than any rate of population decline. In both cases, the point B represents a pessimorum state, the worst of all possible worlds.

2. REALISMS?

Recourse to realism is the last refuge employed by theoretical scoundrels caught out in muddled deductions. To save face by appealing to facts or idealized facts is not my purpose here. However, the original purpose of the 1975 exercises was to shed possible light on the vital public policy questions involved in social security, Modigliani lifecycle saving-investing patterns, apparent declining patterns of demographic fertility, and normative discussions of family planning.

In sympathetic agreement with the spirit and letter of the Deardorff analysis, I should like to explore some implications for policy and real-life description of the amended analysis.

2.1. An important purpose of the original analysis was not so much to enable society to identify g^* and normatively to move to it, as to learn what is implied for society's net welfare potentialities by the post–1957 drop in birth rates. Samuelson [5] on optimal social security was designed as a companion piece for [4], and accordingly they were published together back-to-back.

Paradoxically, Deardorff's minimizing $g^\dagger$ is as encouraging as Samuelson's maximizing g^* to reduce the fears that declining population growth makes old-age security more difficult. In the neighborood of an extremum, *whether* it is a minimum or a maximum, a function does not change much.

2.2. Now that population seems on the wane, there is some comfort in the final Deardorff conclusion, that under his stipulated conditions "..the old result of neo-classical growth theory, that economies benefit from low or negative population growth, still stands."

Thus, economists like Professor Martin Feldstein may be right in their concern that the present mode of financing social security undermines fruitful capital formation. And others may be right in worrying that the survivors of the 1940's baby boom will have too-few working descendants to support them tolerably in retirement. Still these concerns are *not* fully additive: to the degree that slower population growth calls for less widening of capital, one trend somewhat cancels out the other. Also, to ease the transition problem there is the third trend toward having more women work and pay social security taxes. With lower burdens of dependent children, and with our retirement benefit formulas biased toward giving small incremental rewards to spouses who choose to work in taxed occupations as against spouses who work in the home without pay, the hump of retired persons in the early decades of the next century becomes more "manageable."

2.3. Strictly speaking, within the literal confines of Deardorff's Cobb-Douglas-like models, or in my $A'BC'$ variant of Figure 2b, very high population growth is not demonstrably worse than population decline; it is only moderate population growth that is demonstrably inferior.

Does the conclusion that society can benefit permanently from very high population growth really make sense? Almost surely not. But it is not Deardorff who can be blamed for this odd conclusion: his deductions are valid deductions from my postulated technology in which land and natural resources never become scarce enough to set limits on production.

The land of exponential growth of all things in balance with self-generating labor, à la Harrod, Joan Robinson, Solow, Meade, Pasinetti, et al., is indeed a never-never land undreamed of in the philosophy of the Club of Rome or realistic thinkers. At best, we must replace the Samuelson [4 (Equation (4))] relations like $F(L_t, K_t)$ by relations like (3) there, $F(L_t, K_t, T_t)$, where T_t is non-producible land and natural resources. Even if we postulate that "necessity is the mother of invention," and allow for something like land-augmenting technical change in our production functions, does it make sense to believe that populations which triple per generation can induce the needed inventions to put off forever the bogey of diminishing returns from scarce land, mineral deposits, and energy deposits?

Surely, this does not make good sense. We must face the danger of relying on alleged high-well-being states stemming from super-rapid population growth. The final warning in Samuelson [4] was directed against this danger.[2]

3. BOUNDEDNESS OF LIFETIME WELL-BEING?

Here I want to stay within the strict confines of the Harrod-Robinson-Solow model of all things reproducible out of primary labor alone. *Within it*, does Deardorff's case of *infinite* well-being at a *finite* rate of population decline make plausible sense? Also, does an *indefinitely augmentable* level of well-being at higher and higher rates of population growth make sense?

My queries are in no sense criticisms of Professor Deardorff. He has taken my

---

[2] To illustrate, let $F[L_t, K_t, T_t] = (\tau_t T_t)G[L_t/T_t, K_t/T_t]$. Then one might for a long time maintain high g and $(K_{t+1} - K_t)/K_t = (L_{t+1} - L_t)/L_t = g$, and at the same time have the technical improvement parameter τ_t grow fast enough to lead to results like those of $F[L_t, K_t]$ as analyzed in Samuelson [4, 5] and Deardorff [1]. Yet, in the end, society might find that maintained high population growth leads to impoverishment in the form of low and declining per capita $u[c^1, c^2]$ or Min$[c^1, c^2/\omega]$. What helps in the short run may insidiously hurt in the long run. See the final section of my Mathematical Appendix for an optimal-control treatment of how these considerations lead to a transient approach to the optimal stationary population level, and how that transient path is biased (other things being equal) toward greater population growth by the favorable intralife cycle effects.

postulates and validly deduced what they lead to in the double-Cobb-Douglas case. What I am querying is whether it makes good sense for one to admit as *feasible* technology and tastes the kinds of elasticities of substitution *holding over all the space of* $(K/L, c^2/c^1)$ *ratios* that are implied by Cobb-Douglas and related functions. Any thought experiment is permissible. But when the purpose of a simplified model is to throw light on the putative workings of a complicated model, some thought experiments seem less interesting than other ones.

Nice neat "Inada conditions," in which $F[1, k]/k$ and $\partial F[1, k]/\partial k$ run the gamut from ∞ to 0 as k runs from 0 to ∞, simplify the theorist's daily tasks, assuring him of interior solutions and so forth. However, God or Darwin did not create the universe to give lazy theorists an easy life. When the chips are down, one feels forced to admit that unitary elasticity of substitution, σ, would at most prevail over some intermediate range of k: at all K/L ratios, even the highest ones, one expects per capita output, $F[1, k]$, to be only finite; at all K/L ratios, even the lowest ones, one expects capital's gross yield, $\partial F[1, k]/\partial k$, to be only finite. These conditions rule out Cobb-Douglas and any CES function with $\sigma > 1$. Indeed, it may be most realistic to suppose that only a maximum K/L ratio can be technically useful, so that σ must fall rapidly to zero at a finite k, thus ruling out all CES functions with positive σ. (My Appendix analyzes the case of $\sigma = 0$.)

On reflection, one also feels impelled to put "realistic" restrictions on the global behavior of $u[c^1, c^2]$. To see this, consider how Deardorff [1, (Equation (27))] contrives infinite $u[\ ]$ bliss for $g \to \infty$. It does so by virtue of the following story being true in the background:

> At very high g, every retired person stands on the shoulders of innumerable workers. From their *finite* (and modest!) total per capita productions, he is splashed with luxurious old-age c^2. But this is only "just recompense" for the fact that in his own working years he enjoyed *infinitesimal* consumption levels.

Could one really believe that any almost infinite old-age c^2 could compensate one for an almost-infinitesimal standard of living in the first sixty-five years of life? As Dr. Samuel Johnson would say, all reason, all experience is against it. Mathematically, along any $\bar{u}$ contour, no increase in c^2 can compensate for cuts in c^1 below some critical level.

The Deardorff infinity of bliss above A in Figure 2(a) does not come about as the result of some pathology of the specified function for $u[c^1, c^2]$. Rather, as indicated above, it requires us to believe in the following scenario in the background:

"As $g \to -\delta$ from above, capital endowment per laborer approaches infinity; even with zero further technical change, the real wage is capable of being made to be infinite (or *indefinitely* large just by maintaining a minute rate of *gross* capital formation and waiting until the number of workers shrinks indefinitely relative to the more slowly declining stock of K)."

Once we accept that realism requires σ to fall indefinitely toward zero at high finite K/L ratios, the fairy-tale-implied infinite real wage and per capita output becomes incredible and has to be ruled out.

At very low K/L ratios, the razor of realism requires us to lop off infinitely high yields on capital. Indeed in this 200th year of Smith's *Wealth of Nations*, we realize that there *must* be a realistic realm of increasing returns to scale when K and L rise together from zero or when K rises from zero and L holds at a finite level; thus, our assumption that $F[L, K]$ is homogeneous-first-degree cannot possibly be strictly true for either or both of $[L, K]$ extremely small!

4. NOLO CONTENDERE?

What is the moral? It seems to me that we find ourselves either back again at my original qualitative patterns of Figure 1(c), namely ABC, ABC', or AE³; or, we are in one of the patterns I've suggested for Figure 2(b), A'BC', A'BC'', or A'B extended ever downward. Even if A'BC' prevailed, for Club of Rome reasons already mentioned as being non-ignorable, I believe that the A' of declining population growth would have to be preferred to the illusory attraction of C' and its basic impermanence and eventually perhaps to any allegedly positive g^*.

Needless to say, none of these last tentative conclusions is in any sense critical of Professor Deardorff's analysis. It is that analysis which has flushed out the false from the true. And it is he who has explicitly warned that it is Cobb-Douglas technology's assumption of an indefinitely augmentible capital-output ratio that converts a declining population rate of $-\delta$ into a state of ineffable bliss.

Economists are in Professor Deardorff's debt, none more than I.

Massachusetts Institute of Technology, U.S.A.

BRIEF MATHEMATICAL APPENDIX

1.

The reader may replace Cobb-Douglas and similar specifications by fixed-coefficient specifications à la Cambridge, East Anglia:

$$(1) \qquad u[c^1, c^2] = \text{Min}\left[c^1, \frac{c^2}{\omega}\right], \qquad \omega > 0$$

$$(2) \qquad f(k) = \text{Min}\left[\lambda, \frac{k}{\bar{k}}\right], \qquad \bar{k}^{-1} > \delta > 0$$

where $\bar{k}$ is the Leontief-Kaldor-Pasinetti gross capital-output ratio, and λ^{-1} is the technical labor-output ratio. Here I am following the Deardorff [1] alteration of my 1975 notation in which the new $f(\ )$ function refers to *gross* output

---

³ If σ remains bounded above zero as $k \to \infty$, for most reasonable forms of $u[\ ]$, we find $g^* = -\delta$ must be a local boundary maximum with finite u^*, as Professor Mirrlees reminds me.

inclusive of depreciation, δk, rather than to my original net output function.

Now my old relations (10)–(14), and Deardorff's relations (1)–(15), boil down when the capital-labor ratio is technically determined to

$$(3) \quad u[c_g^1, c_g^2] = c_g^1 = [f(k_g) - \delta k_g - g k_g][1 + \omega(1 + g)^{-1}]^{-1}$$
$$= \Gamma(g) = \lambda(1 - \delta \bar{k} - g\bar{k})(1 + g)(1 + g + \omega)^{-1}, \; g < \bar{k}^{-1} - \delta$$
$$\equiv 0, \qquad\qquad\qquad\qquad\qquad\qquad g \geq \bar{k}^{-1} - \delta.$$

Clearly, it never pays to let population grow at a faster rate than that in which the system is able to keep its capital formation up, even with zero consumption.

The maximum of $\Gamma(g)$ on the g interval $[-\delta, \bar{k}^{-1} - \delta]$ depends on the respective strengths of the $(\omega, \lambda, \delta, \bar{k})$ parameters.

Low values for ω, which means people attach scant importance to consumption in retirement, tend to make $g^* = -\delta$, with optimal population declining. High enough values for ω must lift g^* above $-\delta$ if $\bar{k} < 1$. Studies of Kuznets and others usually find that the capital-output ratio equals 2 to 4 calendar years. But this does not mean that $\bar{k}$ is empirically between 2 and 4. The reason for this is that the length of time involved in one of our present periods is measured in decades, not in calendar years. So $\bar{k}$ might be put at a small fraction. The reader can experiment with selections of $(\omega, \delta, \bar{k})$ to find alternative cases in which optimal g^* falls either at $-\delta$, or in between $-\delta$ and $\bar{k}^{-1} - \delta$.

As we've seen, small enough ω does make $g^* = -\delta$. And large enough ω with small $\bar{k}$ does give rise to a *single* intermediate maximal g^*. Thus, for $\delta = .05$, $\bar{k} = 4/21$, $\omega = .8$, we find that $g^* = .57 < (21/4) - .05$ does represent such an intermediate maximum, much like B in my Figure 1(c).

2.

Since there are compelling reasons to be concerned about eventual limits of land and natural resources, optimal growth rates based on production functions $F(L, K)$, rather than on $F(L, K, T)$, become academic.[1] It is worth devoting a few words to the case where land scarcity defines an optimal steady-state level for (L, K), defined by

$$(4) \quad \underset{L, K}{\text{Max}} \left\{ \frac{F(L, K, T)}{L} \right\} = \frac{F(L^*, K^*, T)}{L^*}$$

where (L^*, K^*) are unique roots of

$$(5) \quad \frac{\partial F(L^*, K^*, T)}{\partial L} = \frac{F(L^*, K^*, T)}{L^*}$$
$$\frac{\partial F(L^*, K^*, T)}{\partial K} = 0 .$$

---

[1] There is a printer's error at the end of the first page Samuelson. [4, (531)], where "convex in initial L" should replace "convex in initial T."

What are the effects of adding to lifetime wellbeing integrand expressions of the form

(6)
$$U\left[\frac{C(t)}{L(t)}\right] = U\left[\frac{\{F(L, K, T) - \dot{K}\}}{L}\right], \qquad \dot{K} = \frac{dK}{dt}$$

a term to reflect the advantage to retired people of having many in the working ages to support them, of the general form

(7)
$$V\left[\frac{\dot{L}(t)}{L(t)}\right], \quad V' > 0, \quad V'' < 0, \quad \dot{L} = \frac{dL}{dt}.$$

We see that the optimal transient path, in going from a postulated excess world population today to the desired optimal steady state with smaller population, will be slowed down a little in getting there.

The optimal transient path is given by the solution to the following control problem:

(8)
$$\underset{L(t), K(t)}{\text{Max}} \int_0^\infty \left(U\left[\frac{\{F(L, K, T) - \dot{K}\}}{L}\right] + V\left[\frac{\dot{L}}{L}\right] \right) dt \qquad \text{s.t.}$$

$$K(0) = K_0 \gtreqless K^*, \quad L(0) = L_0 > L^*.$$

We may by convention set the arbitrary origin constant in $U[\ ]$ so that

(9)
$$U\left[\frac{F(L^*, K^*, T)}{L^*}\right] = 0, \quad U'[\ ] > 0, \quad U''[\ ] < 0.$$

Then with $-U''$ and $-V''$ uniformly large enough, and $L(0) - L^*$ small enough, the optimal infinite-time program will be that unique solution to the following Euler-Pontryagin extremal conditions that has $[L(t), K(t)] \to [L^*, K^*]$:

(10)
$$\frac{d}{dt}\{-U'[F(L, K, T)L^{-1} - \dot{K}L^{-1}]\}$$

$$= U'[F(L, K, T)L^{-1} - \dot{K}L^{-1}]F_K(L, K, T),$$

$$\frac{d}{dt}\left\{V'\left[\frac{\dot{L}}{L}\right]L^{-1}\right\}$$

$$= -L^{-1}\left(\frac{\dot{L}}{L}\right)V'\left[\frac{\dot{L}}{L}\right] + U'[F(L, K, T)L^{-1} - \dot{K}L^{-1}]L^{-1}$$

$$\times [F_L(L, K, T) - L^{-1}F(L, K, T)]$$

$$K(0) = K_0, \quad L(0) = L_0$$

$$\lim_{t \to \infty} \begin{cases} K(t) = K^* \\ L(t) = L^*. \end{cases}$$

It can be shown that the descent of $L(t)$ to L^* is slowed down by the $V[\ ]$ term with its emphasis on population growth as a good thing in itself. (The pleasure of having children has precisely the same $V[\ ]$ effect on the optimal program.) Should L^* be greater than present $L(0)$, the $V[\ ]$ effect should speed up slightly the optimal growth to L^*. This shows that, even for those interested only in ultimate steady population states, the tradeoff between the intralife benefit from larger $\dot{L}/L$ and the capital-widening debit from larger $\dot{L}/L$ has to be reckoned with.

REFERENCES

[1] DEARDORFF, A. V., "The Growth Rate for Population: Comment," *International Economic Review*, XVII (June, 1976), 510–515.

[2] DIAMOND, P., "National Debt in a Neoclassical Growth Model," *American Economic Review*, LV (December, 1965), 1126–1150.

[3] SAMUELSON, P.A., "An Exact Consumption-Loan Model of Interest with or without the Social Contrivance of Money," *Journal of Political Economy*, LXVI (December, 1958), 467–482. Reprinted in Joseph E. stiglitz, ed., *The Collected Scientific Papers of Paul A. Samuelson*, volume I (Cambridge, Mass.: MIT Press, 1966), Chapter 21.

[4] ————, "The Optimum Growth Rate for Population," *International Economic Review*, XVI (October, 1975), 531–538.

[5] ————, "Optimum Social Security in a Life-Cycle Growth Model." *International Economic Review*, XVI (October, 1975), 539–544.

[6] SOLOW, R. M., "A Contribution to the Theory of Economic Growth," *Quarterly Journal of Economics*, LXX (February, 1956), 65–94.

223

The General Saddlepoint Property
of Optimal-Control Motions*

PAUL A. SAMUELSON

*Department of Economics, Massachusetts Institute of Technology,
Cambridge, Massachusetts, 02139*

Received October 19, 1971

1. In classical mechanics, the variational condition [1]

$$\delta \int_0^T L(\dot{x}, x)\, dt = 0, \tag{1}$$

where x stands for $(x_1, ..., x_n)$, implies the Euler extremal conditions

$$(d/dt)\, \partial L/\partial \dot{x}_i - \partial L/\partial x_i = 0, \qquad (i = 1,..., n) \tag{2}$$

or the equivalent canonical relations of Hamilton

$$\begin{aligned} dp_i/dt &= -\partial H(p, x)/\partial x_i \\ dx_i/dt &= +\partial H(p, x)/\partial p_i \end{aligned} \qquad (i = 1,..., n), \tag{3}$$

where the conjugate momenta $p = (p_1, ..., p_n)$ and the Hamiltonian energy function H are defined in terms of the Lagrangian function $L(\dot{x}, x)$ by the standard Legendre transformation

$$L(\dot{x}, x) + H(p, x) = \sum_{i=1}^{n} p_i \dot{x}_i,$$

$$p_i = \partial L(\dot{x}, x)/\partial \dot{x}_i, \qquad \dot{x}_i = \partial H(p, x)/\partial p_i, \tag{4}$$

$$\partial L(\dot{x}, x)/\partial x_i + \partial H(p, x)/\partial x_i = 0.$$

At a stationary point of motions,

$$\begin{aligned} \dot{x}_i &= 0, \qquad x_i(t) = x_i^* \\ p_i &= p_i^* = \partial L(0, x_i^*)/\partial \dot{x}_i. \end{aligned} \qquad (i = 1,..., n), \tag{5}$$

* My thanks go to the National Science Foundation for financial assistance and to the Rand Corporation for a visit there twenty years ago. Jill Pappas provided appreciated editorial aid.

Levhari and Liviatan show in a companion paper [2] that, if $L(\dot{x}, x)$ is strongly concave near $(0, x^*)$ with a Hessian matrix of second partial derivatives that is negative definite, then the characteristic exponents associated with the motions around the stationary point cannot be pure imaginaries.

Contours of H, which are constant along the extremal motions, are therefore excluded from forming closed contours around the $(0, x^*)$ point. Thus, the periodic sinusoidal motions of classical harmonic motion are ruled out.

2. Unanswered is the question whether, if $L(\dot{x}, x)$ is concave around $(0, x^*)$ but with vanishing Hessian matrix there—so that its Taylor's expansion were of higher-order form

$$L(\dot{x}, x) = 0 + 0 \sum_1^n \dot{x}_i + 0 \sum_1^n (x_i - x_i^*) + 0 \sum_1^n \sum_1^n (x_i - x_i^*)(x_j - x_j^*)$$

$$+ 0 \sum_1^n \sum_1^n \dot{x}_i \dot{x}_j + 0 \sum_1^n \sum_1^n \dot{x}_i(x_j - x_j^*) + \cdots \tag{6}$$

the contours of constant H along which the motions take place can or cannot form closed contours.

3. The following general theorem rules out such a possibility.

THEOREM. *If one of the L and H has an extremum at* $(0, x^*; p^*, x^*)$, *the other must have a saddlepoint there.*

To prove this, let $L(\dot{x}, x)$ be cancave in $(\dot{x}, x)$ with

$$L(0, x^*) \geqslant L(\dot{x}, x). \tag{7}$$

Then

$$\max_{\dot{x}_i} L(\dot{x}, x) - \sum_1^n p_i \dot{x}_i = -H(p, x) \tag{8}$$

For fixed (x_i), it is a familiar property [3] of dual Legendre transformations that

$$0 \geqslant \sum_1^n \varDelta p_i \, \varDelta \dot{x}_i = \sum_1^n \varDelta(\partial L/\partial \dot{x}) \, \varDelta \dot{x}_i = \sum_1^n \varDelta p_i \, \varDelta(\partial H/\partial p_i). \tag{9}$$

Hence H is concave in (p_i) wherever L is concave in $\dot{x}_i$.

More generally,

$$0 \geqslant \sum_1^n \Delta(\partial L/\partial \dot{x}_i)\, \Delta \dot{x}_i + \sum_1^n \Delta(\partial L/\partial x_i)\, \Delta x_i$$

$$= \sum_1^n \Delta p_i \Delta(\partial H/\partial p_i) + \sum_1^n \Delta(-\partial H/\partial x_i)\, \Delta x_i. \qquad (10)$$

Hence, H must be a convex function in (x_i) when L is a concave function in $(\dot{x}_i, x_i)$.

Conclusion. When $L(\dot{x}, x)$ is concave in its arguments, $H(p, x)$ will be concave in p and convex in x. Hence,

$$H(p, x^*) \leqslant H(p^*, x^*) \leqslant H(p^*, x), \qquad (11)$$

so that H does enjoy a saddlepoint at the stationary turnpike $(0, x)$ and the neighboring contours of efficient motions cannot be closed contours or periodic motions [4].   Q.E.D.

It would be erroneous to try to state the converse of the present theorem. If one of L and H has a saddlepoint, that need not imply that the other has an extremum. Thus, suppose $L = \frac{1}{2}\dot{x}^2 - \frac{1}{2}x^2 + \alpha \dot{x}x$, possessing a saddlepoint: then it can be shown that H, for α sufficiently large, is an indefinite quadratic form in (p, x), enjoying no extremum at $(0, 0)$. Only special kinds of saddlepoints are Legendre transforms of extrema.

4. Note that our analysis has not only ruled out extremals of the form

$$\ddot{x} = -x \qquad (12)$$

in the fashion of Levhari and Liviatan when dealing with $L = -\frac{1}{2}\dot{x}^2 - \frac{1}{2}x^2$. It also rules out periodic extremals of the singular form

$$\ddot{x} = -x^3. \qquad (13)$$

Thus, if $L = \frac{1}{2}\dot{x}^2 + \frac{1}{4}x^4$, $H = \frac{1}{2}p^2 - \frac{1}{4}x^4$ with a saddlepoint at $(0, 0)$.

5. We can even dispense with the requirement that $L(0, x^*)$ represents a unique interior maximum defined by $\partial L(0, x^*)/\partial x_i = 0$. It should still be possible to prove that

$$\max_{x(t)} \int_0^\infty \{L(\dot{x}, x) - L(0, x^*)\}\, dt \qquad \text{for} \quad x(0) = x^0 \qquad (14)$$

has a solution, near $(0, x^*)$ where $L(0, x^*) \geqslant L(0, x)$, with the property

$$\lim_{t \to \infty} x(t) \equiv x^*, \tag{15}$$

no matter what the initial value of x^0.

Thus, consider

$$L = -\tfrac{1}{2}(\dot{x}_1{}^2 + \dot{x}_2{}^2) - \tfrac{1}{2}(x_1{}^2 + x_2{}^2) \tag{16}$$

with extremals having to satisfy

$$(\ddot{x}_1 + \ddot{x}_2) = (x_1 + x_2) \tag{17}$$

and the solution to (14)'s infinite-time program satisfying the indeterminate relations

$$(x_1 + x_2) = (x_1{}^0 + x_2{}^0)\, e^{-t}. \tag{18}$$

Every solution of (18) does clearly satisfy

$$\lim_{t \to \infty} (x_1 + x_2) = (x_1{}^* + x_2{}^*) = 0. \tag{19}$$

6. We may even prove the saddlepoint property when L has corners. Thus, let

$$L = -\tfrac{1}{2}\dot{x}^2 - \tfrac{1}{2}\,|\,x\,|. \tag{20}$$

Now $H = -\tfrac{1}{2}p^2 + \tfrac{1}{2}\,|\,x\,|$ which does have a saddlepoint at $(0, 0)$. The solution to (14) will here become

$$\begin{aligned} x &= (-\tfrac{1}{2}t + |\,x_0\,|^{1/2})^2 & 0 \leqslant t < 2\,|\,x_0\,|^{1/2} \\ &\equiv 0 & 2\,|\,x^0\,|^{1/2} \leqslant t \end{aligned} \tag{21}$$

if $x_0 > 0$; and the negative of this if $x_0 < 0$. Hence,

$$\lim_{t \to \infty} x(t) = x^* = 0. \tag{22}$$

7. Bang-bang solutions of the Pontryagin type arise when $L = 2x^{1/2} - x - \dot{x}$ and we have the restrictions, $L \geqslant 0$ and $\dot{x} \geqslant -|\,a\,|$. Then $(0, 1)$ is a stationary equilibrium of saddlepoint type. For $x(0) < 1$, $\dot{x}$ goes to the maximum possible and stays there for a finite time until $x(t)$ reaches $x^* = 1$. For $x(0) > 1$, $\dot{x}$ stays at $-|\,a\,|$ for $[x(0) - 1]/|\,a\,|$ periods until $x(t)$ descends to $x^* = 1$, where it remains ever afterward.

It is not hard to fabricate examples in which $(0, x^*) = (0, \infty)$ or $(0, -\infty)$, and yet the general saddlepoint property is preserved.

Finally, consider $L \equiv -\frac{1}{2}\dot{x}^2$ everywhere, or at least in some finite neighborhood of $(0, 0)$. Then (14)'s solution becomes, for any $x(0)$ in this neighborhood, $x(t) \equiv x(0) \equiv x^*$, where the set of optimal long-term x^* is *any* value of x in that neighborhood.

8. Note that all the pathological examples of the last three sections involve concave L but without a nonsingular Hessian at $(0, 0)$, and they do rule out pure imaginary characteristic exponents. Equally important, they rule out closed contours and periodic oscillations of extremal motions; and they rule out lack of an infinite-time motion that approaches a stationary turnpike in the limit.

9. Suppose now L depends explicitly on t and must be written as $L(\dot{x}, x, t)$. H is still defined by a Legendre transformation; but now $H(p, x, t)$ is not constant along an extremal motion, since $dH/dt = \partial H/\partial t$.

In the case of exponential time discount, $L = e^{-\delta t}F(\dot{x}, x)$, the Euler Eq. (2) can have time eliminated from them, which is not possible for the canonical Eq. (3)—unless the p's are transformed into new variables that are not of the standard canonical type.

For $\delta = 0$, the Euler equations have a stationary point $[0, x^*(\delta)]$, $\delta = 0$, shown to be of saddlepoint type. Levhari and Liviatan have shown that the characteristic exponents are continuous functions of δ and come in even–odd pairs that satisfy

$$\lambda_{2i-1}(\delta) + \lambda_{2i}(\delta) = \delta. \tag{23}$$

For F concave in its arguments, whether weakly or strongly, the general saddlepoint property can rule out

$$\lambda_i(0) = \pm |b| \sqrt{-1}, \qquad |b| > 0. \tag{24}$$

For $n = 1$, it is known [5] that no λ can be complex. Hence, for $\lambda_i(0) \neq 0$, continuity argument can rule out complex $\lambda_i(\delta)$ for δ sufficiently small: for this rules out a double root at $\delta = 0$, and if the quadratic's discriminant is not zero there, it will remain positive for δ in some neighborhood of zero. Hence for δ small and $n = 1$,

$$\lambda_1 = a(\delta) + 0\sqrt{-1}, \qquad \lambda_2 = \delta - a(\delta) - 0\sqrt{-1} \qquad \text{if } a(0) \neq 0.$$

For $n > 1$, we can have

$$\lambda_{2i-1}(0) = a + b\sqrt{-1}, \qquad \lambda_{2i}(0) = -a - b\sqrt{-1},$$
$$\lambda_{2i+1}(0) = a - b\sqrt{-1}, \qquad \lambda_{2i+2}(0) = -a + b\sqrt{-1},$$

so long as a is not the only coefficient to vanish. For $a \neq 0$, and δ suffi-ciently small, continuity implies that the saddlepoint property is preserved in the sense that,

$$\lambda_{2i-1}(\delta) \text{ has real part of opposite sign to } \lambda_{2i}(\delta). \qquad (25)$$

Section 18, after the canonical equations have been analyzed, will return to the case of large positive δ and loss of the saddlepoint property.

10. The case where $F = -\frac{1}{2}\dot{x}^2 - \frac{1}{4}x^4$ is instructive in showing that, even when the Hessian is singular, for δ sufficiently small, the saddlepoint property of the stationary point $(0, 0)$ is still ensured. Now the Euler equation becomes

$$\ddot{x} - \delta\dot{x} - x^3 = 0. \qquad (26)$$

With $\lambda_1 = \delta$ and $\lambda_2 = 0$, we must go beyond linearized approximation to determine stability.

Graphical analysis of the trajectories in the phase space $(x, \dot{x}) = (x, y)$ will show that two of them pass through the $(0, 0)$ equilibrium point. The first, which enters the origin with positive slope δ corresponding to λ_1, approaches asymptotically the linear approximation

$$\ddot{x} - \dot{x} = 0, \qquad x(t) = ce^{\delta t} = \dot{x}(t)/\delta, \qquad c \neq 0. \qquad (27)$$

This motion is unstable, and is approached by all motions except those on the other trajectory through the origin, which resembles $y = -x^3$ in general shape: all points on this razor's edge give rise to "stable" motions that approach the equilibrium asymptotically with singular speed of convergence.

Using the method followed by Liviatan and Samuelson [6], we can quickly prove these properties analytically. Let $y' = dy/dx$ represent the slope of a trajectory through any (x, y) point. Then

$$\dot{x}y' = \ddot{x} = \delta\dot{x} + x^3. \qquad (28)$$

Substitution and repeated differentiation with respect to x gives

$0 = yy' - \delta y - x^3 = 0,$

$0 = yy'' + y'^2 - \delta y' - 3x^2 = 0;$ at $(x, y) = (0, 0)$, $y' = \delta$ or 0,

$$\qquad (29)$$

$0 = yy''' + 3y'y'' - \delta y'' - 6x = 0;$ for any $y' = 0$ at $(0, 0)$, $y'' = 0$,

$0 = yy'''' + 4y'y''' + 3y''^2 - \delta y''' - 6;$ for $y' = 0$ at $(0, 0)$, $y''' = -6/\delta$.

Hence, for $\delta > 0$, there is a singular trajectory through the origin with a stationary inflection point. Since it passes through the second and fourth quadrants, it does correspond to stable motion. Clearly, it provides the optimizing solution to (14)'s infinite-time program, with asymptotic convergence like

$$\dot{Z} = -aZ^3, \qquad dZ/Z^3 = -adt,$$
$$Z = \pm\alpha(t + |\beta|)^{-1/2}. \tag{30}$$

11. This completes the analysis relevant to the usual economic or optimal-control problem. Because L and H are dual Legendre transforms, we can use the present theorem—that an extremum of one implies a saddlepoint for the other—to characterize the usual conservative oscillations of pendulum physics. Thus, if the H energy contours are closed as at a center, the Lagrangian kinetic potential $L = T(\dot{x}, x) - V(x)$, must have a saddlepoint property

$$L(0, x) \leqslant L(0, x^*) \leqslant L(\dot{x}, x^*), \tag{31}$$

where x^* corresponds to a minimum of potential energy, $V(x^*) \leqslant V(x)$. Here x^* represents the pendulum hanging down, pointing at 6 o'clock. With L convex in $(\dot{x})$ to provide a minimizing solution to Hamilton's action integral $\int L\, dt$, it follows that H must be convex in p. Together with the fact that (p^*, x^*) is a center, and thus an extremum point for H, this implies that H is convex in (p, x) near there. The present theorem thus confirms that L is convex in $\dot{x}$ and concave in x, as asserted.

Pendulum vibrations of simple harmonic motion illustrate this.

$$L = T - V = \tfrac{1}{2}\dot{x}^2 - \tfrac{1}{2}x^2, \qquad H = T + V = \tfrac{1}{2}p^2 + \tfrac{1}{2}x^2 \tag{32}$$

are seen to be respectively a saddlepoint and a minimum. The H^* minimum is equal to the minimum of potential energy $V^* = V(0) = 0$.

12. To point up the contrast between these vibrations typical of physics and the catenary motions typical of economics and optimal control, let the hand of a clock rotate frictionlessly under the pull of gravity. Six o'clock represents an equilibrium point like that just described, with conservative oscillations around it for small enough displacements.

A second point of, physically unstable, balance is the vertical upright position of 12 o'clock. The potential energy is clearly at a maximum there, as will be H with respect to x for $\dot{x} = 0$. On the other hand, at this x^* point, H will be a minimum for $\dot{x} = 0$ since any motion at all can only add to the kinetic and total energy. The possible motions fall into four classes: the two main classes are those which approach 12 o'clock with enough or not enough initial velocity to pass through it. Between these are the watershed cases. The stable axis of the saddlepoint is that in which the velocity is just enough to keep the hand moving upward, but just weak enough to prevent an overshoot: hence the frictionless hand approaches 12 o'clock asymptotically, but never quite gets there. The time-reversal of this case provides the other, unstable watershed, corresponding to the unstable axis of the saddlepoint.

13. A warning is perhaps in order [7] that there are at least three different kinds of saddlepoints to be met in connection with standard variational problems. That of the present paper should not be confused with the other two.

As is well known from the cited standard references, the Euler necessary conditions for the primal problem of the form (1)

$$\delta \int_0^T L(\dot{x}, x, t) \, dt = 0$$

can also be derived from the variational condition

$$\delta \int_0^T \left[\sum_1^n p_j \dot{x}_j - H(p, x, t) \right] dt = 0, \tag{33}$$

where H and L are connected by the usual Legendre transformations. This suggests that this last integral assumes a stationary value in function space with respect to simultaneous variation in the functions $[x_i(t), p_i(t)]$. Actually, it is straightforward to verify the equivalence of the following:

$$\max_{x_i(t)} \int_0^T L(\dot{x}, x, t) \, dt \qquad \text{s.t. } x(0) = x^0, \qquad x(T) = x^T \tag{34}$$

and

$$\min_{p_i(t)} \max_{x_i(t)} \int_0^T \left[\sum_1^n p_j \dot{x}_j - H(p, x, t) \right] dt \tag{35}$$

s.t. no boundary conditions on the p's and the above boundary conditions on the x's. The Euler conditions for this new problem become the canonical equations (3), namely,

$$dp_i/dt + \partial H/\partial x_i = 0,$$
$$-\dot{x}_i + \partial H/\partial p_i = 0. \tag{36}$$

Since L is concave in $(\dot{x}_i, x_i)$, H is concave in (p_i) and convex in (x_i), which suffices for the asserted min-max saddlepoint. If the original problem (34) had involved a minimum instead of a maximum that would merely involve a sign change in all the expressions and simply reverse the min-max interpretation to max–min.

14. Inasmuch as the last saddlepoint is in function space, there is less danger of its being confused with the H's saddlepoint at the stationary point. However, *everywhere* on an extremal motion we can define also a third saddlepoint as follows.

Rewrite (34) in the form closer to that used by Pontryagin [8] and other writers on control theory

$$\max_{u_i(t)} \int_0^T L(u, x, t)\, dt \qquad \text{s.t. } x(0) = x^0, \qquad x(T) = x^T, \qquad (37)$$

and

$$\dot{x}_i = u_i, \qquad (i = 1,..., n)$$

Eschewing for simplicity the inequality versions of the theory, we use the classical Lagrangian-multiplier technique to require

$$\delta \int G\, dt = \delta \int_0^T \left\{ L(u, x, t) + \sum_1^n \lambda_j(t)(\dot{x}_j - u_j) \right\} dt = 0, \qquad (38)$$

$$\partial L/\partial u_i - \lambda_i = 0 \qquad (i = 1,..., n),$$

$$d\lambda_i/dt - \partial L/\partial x_i = 0,$$

$$\dot{x}_i = u_i.$$

When L is strongly concave in the u's, an optimal (u^*, x^*, λ^*) will at *every* point on the trajectory yield a saddlepoint for the bracketed Lagrangian expression $G(u, \lambda; x, \dot{x}, t)$,

$$G(u, \lambda^*; x^*, \dot{x}^*, t) \leqslant \min_{\lambda_i} \max_{u_i} G(u, \lambda; x^*, \dot{x}^*, t)$$

$$= G(u^*, \lambda^*; x^*, \dot{x}^*, t) = G(u^*, \lambda; x^*, \dot{x}^*, t). \qquad (39)$$

Here $\dot{x}^*$ is required to be the optimal $\dot{x}$ for the extremal motion's (λ^*, x^*, t).

15. As a final digression, I must warn that the literature on variational mechanics is very cavalier in its treatment of maximum and minimum conditions. So long as the physicist can set the first variation of something equal to zero, he couldn't care less about extrema,

EXAMPLE. In simple harmonic motion, where $L = \frac{1}{2}\dot{x}^2 - \frac{1}{2}x^2$, the extremal motion $x = x^0 \sin t$ does not minimize Hamilton's integral,

$$\int_0^T L \, dt, \quad \text{for} \quad T > \pi.$$

Similar violations of the Principle of Least Action occur when an actual motion passes through a Jacobi conjugate point, as in the case where a shell sinks a ship by indirect rather than direct surface fire.

EXAMPLE. In simple harmonic motion, where L is not convex in *both* variables $(\dot{x}, x)$, although the primal problem (34) does have a well-defined minimum for $T < \pi$, instead of getting a maximum in (35) we get another minimum. Indeed, for the extremum problem of (35), because $\dot{x}$ enters linearly and therefore degenerately, it is the curvature with respect to x that is decisive for max or min; by contrast, for the primal problem, it is the curvature with respect to $\dot{x}$ that is alone decisive.

EXAMPLE. As an alternative to (35)'s derivation of the extremal equations, consider the variant attributed to Helmholtz

$$\delta \int_0^T \psi \, dt = \delta \int_0^T \{L(u, x, t) + [(\partial L/\partial u)(\dot{x} - u)]\} \, dt = 0. \quad (40)$$

This does lead directly to the canonical equations.

However, the point $(u^*, \dot{x}, x)$, where $u^* = \dot{x}$ does *not* provide a minimum of ψ with respect to u when the primal problem has a maximum, but rather *also* a maximum.

EXAMPLE. In continuum mechanics, the vibrations of a continuous string may be regarded as the limit of a series of beads, as their number per meter grows and the size of each diminishes. In the limit, a double integral is to have its first variation vanish just as a single Hamiltonian integral has its first variation vanish before the limit is reached and while we still deal with a finite number of particles. Despite the fact that Hamilton's integral *is* minimized for n beads no matter how large is n, when $n \to \infty$ and we contemplate the limiting double integral, we find that the variationally defined functions that describe the string's motions are incapable of providing a true minimum to the double integral [9]. Thus Mother Nature is not even a myopic minimizer, a fact that the physicist is scarcely aware of,

16. There remains the task of demonstrating that the min–max definition of a saddlepoint does coincide with the stability–instability properties.

Whether or not the Hessian matrix of $H(p, x) = H(p_1, ..., p_n, x_1, ..., x_n)$

$$\begin{bmatrix} H_{pp} H_{px} \\ H_{xp} H_{xx} \end{bmatrix}$$

has H_{pp} negative definite and H_{xx} positive definite, the mere fact that H is strictly concave in p and strictly convex in x suffices to rule out closed contours around a center or oscillatory motions around an unstable or stable focus.

Thus, in the canonical equations

$$\dot{p} = -\partial H/\partial x$$

$$\dot{x} = +\partial H/\partial p,$$

multiply both sides by the row vector $[x - x^*, p - p^*]$ and utilize the fact that at $[p^*, x^*]$ the gradient of $H(p, x)$ vanishes. This yields

$$d\phi/dt = d\left[\sum_1^n (x_i - x_i^*)(p_i - p_i^*)\right]\Big/dt$$

$$= -\sum_1^n (x_i - x_i^*)(\partial H/\partial x_i - 0)$$

$$+ \sum_1^n (p_i - p_i^*)(\partial H/\partial p_i - 0) < 0, \qquad (41)$$

provided that $(p_i, x_i) \neq (p_i^*, x_i^*)$, by virtue of the posited curvature properties.

Suppose there were a solution, $[p_i(t), x_i(t)]$, periodic with period T. Then the left-hand expression in (41), ϕ, would not have decreased after the elapse of T—which is a contradiction to the right-hand side's inequality. For $n > 1$, we can similarly rule out a motion on a closed contour that is a finite distance away from equilibrium, since ϕ would be bounded on that contour, which again contradicts (41)'s requirement that ϕ always be decreasing at a rate bounded above zero.

For $n = 1$, a stable or unstable focus would require that ϕ become alternately positive and negative, which also contradicts (41)'s inequality. Thus, the usual two dimensional characterization of a saddlepoint as ruling out a center or focus is confirmed. For $n > 1$, we can rule out a stable focus by making each $(p_i - p_i^*)$ initially of the opposite sign to each $(x_i - x_i^*)$: hence, ϕ begins negative and cannot, by (41)'s inequality, ever go to its zero value at equilibrium. Reversing time, we can similarly rule out an unstable focus by making each $(p_i - p_i^*)$ initially of the same sign as $(x_i - x_i^*)$.

17. When $L(\dot{x}, x, t)$ involves t explicitly in the form $e^{-\delta t}F(\dot{x}, x)$, $H(p, x, t)$ takes the form beautifully analyzed by Kurz [10]:

$$H(p, x, t) = e^{-\delta t}h[pe^{\delta t}, x], \tag{42}$$

where $h(\Pi, x)$ is the Legendre transform of $F(\dot{x}, x)$, namely,

$$F(\dot{x}, x) + h(\Pi, x) = \sum_{1}^{n} \Pi_j \dot{x}_j, \tag{43}$$

$$\Pi_i = \partial F(\dot{x}, x)/\partial \dot{x}_i \qquad (i = 1,..., n).$$

Now the canonical equations become

$$\dot{p}_i = -e^{-\delta t} \partial h[pe^{\delta t}, x]/\partial x_i = -e^{-\delta t}h_{n+i}[pe^{\delta t}, x],$$
$$\dot{x}_i = \partial h[pe^{\delta t}, x]/\partial(p_i e^{\delta t}) = h_i[pe^{\delta t}, x]. \tag{44}$$

Corresponding to the equilibrium point $(0, x^*)$, we now have

$$[p^*(t), x^*] = [\Pi^*(\delta) e^{\delta t}, x^*(\delta)],$$

where $[\Pi^*(\delta), x^*(\delta)]$ is the stationary point of the time-free system derived from (44) by the Kurz transformation of variables, $\Pi_i(t) = e^{\delta t}p_i(t)$, namely,

$$\dot{\Pi}_i = -h_{n+i}[\Pi, x] + \delta \Pi_i$$
$$\dot{x}_i = h_i[\Pi, x]. \qquad (i = 1,..., n), \tag{45}$$

If the Hessian matrix of $F[\dot{x}, x]$ is negative-definite near $[0, x^*(0)]$, then, for δ sufficiently small, continuity arguments can establish that the characteristic exponents for (45)'s stationary point have real parts that come in opposite-signed pairs.

18. It will be instructive to consider the general quadratic case both in Euler and Hamiltonian form. Let

$$L = -e^{-\delta t}[\tfrac{1}{2}\dot{x}^2 + ax\dot{x} + \tfrac{1}{2}x^2], \qquad -1 \leqslant a \leqslant 1. \tag{46}$$

The Euler equations can be reduced to

$$\ddot{x} - \delta\dot{x} - (1 + \delta a)x = 0. \tag{47}$$

The canonical equations can be derived from

$$H = e^{-\delta t}[-\tfrac{1}{2}(pe^{\delta t})^2 - ape^{\delta t}x + \tfrac{1}{2}(1 - a^2)\,x^2], \tag{48}$$

namely,

$$\dot{p} = e^{-\delta t}[ape^{\delta t} + (a^2 - 1)\,x],$$
$$\dot{x} = -pe^{\delta t} - ax. \tag{49}$$

These lead to the time-free relations in $(x, \Pi) = (x, pe^{\delta t})$

$$\dot{\Pi} = (a + \delta)\,\Pi + (a^2 - 1)\,x,$$
$$\dot{x} = -\Pi - ax. \tag{50}$$

with characteristic exponents around the stationary point $(\dot{x}, x; \Pi, x) = (0, 0; 0, 0)$ defined by

$$0 = \begin{vmatrix} a + \delta - \lambda & a^2 - 1 \\ -1 & -a - \lambda \end{vmatrix} = \lambda^2 - \delta\lambda - (1 + \delta a). \tag{51}$$

For $\delta > 0$ and small, the characteristic roots are of opposite signs. For $-\delta < a^{-1} < 0$, all roots have real parts that are positive: hence, the equilibrium point $(0, x^*; 0, x^*)$ is absolutely unstable. It would thus appear that the problem (14) has no solution satisfying well-behaved transversality conditions at $T = \infty$.

The Arrow–Kurz pathological example of the cited 1968 Kurz paper is essentially the present case with $a = -1$: thus, let the (constant) own rate of interest be set equal to one by proper choice of time periods, and interpret x as $K - \bar{c}$. Then (46) is equivalent to

$$I = \int_0^T e^{-\delta t}U(c)\,dt = \int_0^T -e^{-\delta t}\tfrac{1}{2}(c - \bar{c})^2$$

$$= \int_0^T -e^{-\delta t}\,\tfrac{1}{2}(K - \bar{c} - \dot{K})^2\,dt. \tag{52}$$

If we do not, for any finite T or for $T = \infty$, specify any terminal condition K_T or terminal transversality condition, we can obviously set

$$\dot{K} = K - \bar{c}, \qquad K(t) = \bar{c} + (K^0 - \bar{c})\,e^t \tag{53}$$

and maximize (52)'s integrand and the integral I at zero. Out of all the solutions of the Euler equation, the optimum one is the particular solution

$$0 = d^2[\bar{c} + (K^0 - \bar{c})\,e^t]/dt^2 - \delta d[\bar{c} + (K^0 - \bar{c})\,e^t]/dt$$
$$+ (\delta - 1)[(K^0 - \bar{c})\,e^t]$$
$$= (K^0 - \bar{c})\,e^t[1 - \delta + (\delta - 1)]. \tag{54}$$

In maximizing (52), the assumption is made that $\dot{K}(t)$ is under no inequalities: thus, if $K^0 < \bar{c}$, we are to disinvest at whatever rate is needed to keep consumption at the satiation level. Suppose, however, that the capital stock depreciates at most at the rate $bK(t)$, and that gross investment cannot be negative. Then

$$\dot{K} + bK \geqslant 0, \tag{55}$$

and the solution of (53) is not feasible for all T. For $\bar{c} > K^0 > \bar{c}(1 + b)^{-1}$, (53)'s solution holds up to

$$t^\dagger = \log[b\bar{c}/(1 + b)(\bar{c} - K^0)]. \tag{56}$$

For $t > t^\dagger$, (55)'s equality of maximum disinvestment takes over and the solution is of the form

$$K(t) = \bar{c}(1 + b)^{-1} \exp - b(t - t^\dagger), \qquad t > t^\dagger. \tag{57}$$

For $\bar{c} > K^0 < \bar{c}(1 + b)^{-1}$, $t^\dagger$ can be taken as zero and (57) always holds. For $K > \bar{c}$, the solution of (53) holds forever. As Kurz remarks, the unstable turnpike $k = \bar{c}$ can be thought of as being bracketed by stable turnpikes at $K = 0$ and $K = \infty$.

19. The singular case where the Hessian of L, or some of its diagonal blocks, vanish, can be illustrated by our earlier example of (26):

$$L = -e^{-\delta t}(\tfrac{1}{2}\dot{x}^2 + \tfrac{1}{4}x^4),$$

$$H = e^{-\delta t}[-\tfrac{1}{2}(pe^{\delta t})^2 + \tfrac{1}{4}x^4].$$

The canonical equations become

$$\dot{p} = -e^{-\delta t}x^3,$$
$$\dot{x} = -pe^{\delta t}. \tag{58}$$

The time-free equations become

$$\dot{\Pi} = \delta\Pi - x^3,$$
$$\dot{x} = -\Pi, \tag{59}$$

which are seen to reduce directly down to (26). The linearized version of (58) becomes

$$\dot{P} = 0 \qquad \bigg\} \quad P = P^0,$$
$$\dot{X} = -Pe^{\delta t} \bigg\} \quad X = (X^0 + P^0\delta^{-1}) - P^0\delta^{-1}e^{\delta t}. \tag{60}$$

Because of degeneracy of the matrix we must go beyond linear analysis to demonstrate that the saddlepoint property holds. Similarly, we must go beyond the linearized version of (59)

$$\dot{\Pi} = \delta\Pi \quad \bigg\} \quad \Pi = \Pi^0e^{\delta t},$$
$$\dot{X} = -\Pi \bigg\} \quad X = (X^0 + \Pi^0\delta^{-1}) - \Pi^0\delta^{-1}e^{\delta t}, \tag{61}$$

to demonstrate the saddlepoint property, namely, back to (59) and (26).

20. Quadratic examples hide the fact that the characteristic exponents are generally to be defined by polynomials of the form

$$0 = a_0(\delta)\,\lambda^2 + a_1(\delta)\lambda + a_2(\delta)\lambda + \delta[a_3(\delta) + a_4(\delta)], \tag{62}$$

where the a_i are functions of δ rather than constants. This means that the final dependence of the λ roots on δ can be very complicated. Thus even though large δ tends to add a positive component to the real parts of the λ_i, it need not follow that all real parts become positive.

Thus, consider the standard one-sector Ramsey case

$$\max \int_0^\infty e^{-\delta t}U[f(K) - \dot{K}]\,dt,$$

where U and f are strictly concave and $U'[c] > 0$ for all c.

The Euler equation and its associated linearized form become

$$0 = -d/dt\, U'[f(K) - \dot{K}] + U'[f(K) - \dot{K}][f'(K) - \delta], \tag{63}$$

$$0 = \ddot{Y} - \delta\dot{Y} - a_2Y,$$

$$f'(K^*) = \delta, \qquad U' > 0, \qquad U'' < 0, \tag{64}$$

$$a_2 = \{f''(K^*)\,U'[f(K^*) - 0]/U''[f(K^*) - 0]\} > 0.$$

No matter how positive δ becomes, and therefore no matter how positive becomes the mean of the two characteristic roots, there still always remains a negative and a positive root. Thus, increasing time preference cannot ultimately lead to absolute instability in a Ramsey problem where $f(k)$ satisfies the Inada conditions with $f'(K) = \delta$ having a K^* solution for all positive δ that is monotone decreasing.

The above assumes that $U' > 0$, with no satiation. In the alternative case, where

$$U'[f(K^{**})] = 0, \qquad K^{**} < K^*,$$

(64) becomes

$$0 = \ddot{Y} - \delta\dot{Y} - [f'(K^{**})]^2\, Y + \delta f'(K^{**})Y = 0. \tag{65}$$

This generalizes the Arrow–Kurz pathology of instability to all cases in which $\delta > f'(K^{**})$, implying two characteristic exponents with positive real parts.

21. For many purposes of analysis, it is not enough that the vector point (x^*, y^*) yield a strong saddlepoint

$$f(x^*, y) < f(x^*, y^*) < f(x, y^*) \quad \text{for all } y \neq y^* \quad \text{and} \quad x \neq x^*. \tag{66}$$

For this, it would suffice that, at (x^*, y^*), f be strictly concave in x alone and strictly convex in y alone, with nothing stipulated about curvature when x and y are varied together.

EXAMPLE.

$$f = -y^{2n} + x^{2m} + xyg(x, y), \tag{67}$$

where g is an arbitrary function with a finite value at $(0, 0)$ and n and m are arbitrary integers.

A stronger property is that f be strictly convex in x and strictly concave in y at *any* nearby point to (x^*, y^*).

To illustrate these considerations, consider the gradient algorithm for reaching the maximum of any concave function, or the minimum of any convex function, namely,

or
$$\dot{y}_i = +\partial\psi(y_1,\ldots, y_n)/\partial y_i$$
$$(i = 1,\ldots, n), \tag{68}$$
$$\dot{x}_i = -\partial\phi(x_1,\ldots, x_n)/\partial x_i.$$

These will approach the interior extrema points (y_i^0) and (x_i^0), since

$$d\left[\tfrac{1}{2}\sum_1^n (y_i - y_i^0)^2\right]\bigg/ dt = \sum_1^n (\partial\psi/\partial y_i - 0)(y_i - y_i^0) < 0, \qquad (69)$$

$$d\left[\tfrac{1}{2}\sum_1^n (x_i - x_i^0)^2\right]\bigg/ dt = -\sum_1^n (\partial\phi/\partial x_i - 0)(x_i - x_i^0) < 0. \qquad (70)$$

To find a strong saddlepoint, this suggests a mixed-gradient method applied seperately to the r maximizing and s minimizing variables, namely,

$$\begin{aligned}
\dot{y}_i &= +\partial f(x, y)/\partial y_i \qquad (i = 1,...,r), \\
\dot{x}_j &= -\partial f(x, y)/\partial x_j \qquad (j = 1,...,s).
\end{aligned} \qquad (71)$$

In a 1949 Rand memorandum [11], I utilized such methods and later, in a notable series of papers, Arrow and Hurwicz [12] generalized such methods to handling the saddlepoints of constrained programming problems.

The mixed-gradient Eq. (71) have some superficial resemblence to the canonical equations. More than 20 years ago I proved local convergence of (71) provided the saddlepoint was "regular," in the sense that the Hessian diagonals $[\partial^2 f(x^*, y^*)/\partial x_i\, \partial x_j]$ and $[\partial^2 f(x^*, y^*)/\partial y_i\, \partial y_j]$ were, respectively, positive definite and negative definite. Thus

$$d\left[\tfrac{1}{2}\sum_1^r (y_i - y_i^*)^2 + \tfrac{1}{2}\sum_1^s (x_j - x_j^*)^2\right]\bigg/dt$$

$$= \sum_1^r (y_i - y_i^*)[\partial f(x, y)/\partial y_i] - \sum_1^s (x_i - x_i^*)[\partial f(x, y)/\partial x_i]$$

$$= \theta(x, y). \qquad (72)$$

Since $\theta(x, y)$ is necessarily negative at all points surrounding (x^*, y^*), local convergence of the mixed-gradient motions is assured.

For years I tried to prove similar local convergence when regularity is not assumed but only that the saddlepoint inequalities be strong. That effort was, however, doomed to be abortive, as examples like the following show:

$$\begin{aligned}
f(x, y) &= -(1/80)\, y^{80} + (1/80)\, x^{80} - x^{16}y^4, \\
\dot{y} &= -y^{79} - 4x^{16}y^3, \qquad (73) \\
\dot{x} &= -x^{79} + 16x^{15}y^4, \\
d[\tfrac{1}{2}(y^2 + x^2)]/dt &= -(y^{80} + x^{80}) + 12(x^8)^2(y^2)^2. \qquad (74)
\end{aligned}$$

Along either axis, where $x^0 = 0$ or $y^0 = 0$, the process is clearly convergent. But away from there, the second positive term on the right-hand side of (74) dominates the first negative term, and the process pretty clearly diverges.

This pathology is possible since f in (73) ceases to be convex in x away from $x = 0$. If $f(x, y)$ is convex in x and concave in y everywhere in the neighborhood of (x^*, y^*), we are assured that the mixed-gradient process converges, by virtue of

$$d\left[\tfrac{1}{2} \sum_{1}^{r} (y_i - y_i^*)^2 + \tfrac{1}{2} \sum_{1}^{s} (x_i - x_i^*)^2 \right] \Big/ dt$$

$$= \sum_{1}^{r} (y_i - y_i^*)(\partial f/\partial y_i - 0) + \sum_{1}^{s} (x_i - x_i^*)(-\partial f/\partial x_i + 0) < 0 \quad (75)$$

for $(x, y) \neq (x^*, y^*)$.

REFERENCES

1. Standard references are E. T. WHITAKER, "Analytical Dynamics," 4th ed., Cambridge University Press, Cambridge, 1936; C. LANCZOS, "The Variational Principles of Mechanics," University of Toronto Press, Toronto, 1949; R. COURANT AND D. HILBERT, "Methods of Mathematical Physics, I," Interscience Publishers, New York, 1953 (translated from the 1923 and 1930 German versions).
2. DAVID LEVHARI AND NISSAN LIVIATAN, On stability in the saddlepoint sense, J. Econ. Theory, 4 (1972), 88–93.
3. Compare P. A. SAMUELSON, Structure of minimum equilibrium systems, in "Essays in Economics and Econometrics: A Volume in Honor of Harold Hotelling," (R. W. Pfouts, Ed.), University of North Carolina Press, 1960; reproduced in "The Collected Scientific Papers of Paul A. Samuelson, I" Chap. 44, (J. E. Stiglitz, Ed.), M.I.T. Press, Cambridge, MA, 1966, where numerous uses are made of Legendre transformations and duality.
4. Standard works classifying the stability of stationary points distinguished between centers, nodes, foci, and saddlepoints. But the descriptive label "saddlepoint" as so used is usually not connected up in any extended discussion with the min–max definition of saddlepoint. Compare R. BELLMAN, "Stability Theory of Differential Equations," McGraw–Hill, New York, 1953; E. A. CODDINGTON AND N. LEVINSON, "Theory of Ordinary Differential Equations," McGraw–Hill, New York, 1955; W. HURWICZ, "Lectures on Ordinary Differential Equations," M.I.T. Press, Cambridge, MA, 1958. See my final section for light on this.
5. P. A. SAMUELSON, Efficient paths of capital accumulation in terms of the calculus of variations, in "Mathematical Methods in the Social Sciences, 1959" (K. J. Arrow, S. Karlin, and P. Suppes, Eds.), Stanford University Press, Palo Alto, CA, 1960. An erratum slip with the book pointed out an omitted term in Eq. (35), which unfortunately was also omitted from its reproduction in "The Collected Scientific Papers of Paul A. Samuelson, I," (J. E. Stiglitz, ed.), Chap. 26 (see Ref. [3]).

6. N. Liviatan and P. A. Samuelson, Notes on Turnpikes: Stable and Unstable, *J. Econ. Theory* **1** (1969), 454–475, especially pp. 468–9.

7. See Courant and Hilbert, *J. Econ. Theory*, **1** (1969), 234, for a related involutary extremum formulation by Fredrichs.

8. L. Pontryagin, V. Toltyanskii, R. Gamreudze, and E. Mishchenko, "The Mathematical Theory of Optimal Processes," Interscience Publishers, New York, 1962.

9. I believe the key to the paradox is the fact that as *n* grows large, the time until a first Jacobi conjugate point gets small, shrinking to zero in the limit, and thereby precluding minimization for any time, however small. Along with Gauss, Hertz, and Appel, I have tried to replace minimizing over a distance with selecting instantaneous accelerations that minimize an action expression. Compare P. A. Samuelson, Some Notions on Causality and Teleology in Economics, *in* "Cause and Effect" (D. Lerner, Ed.), pp. 99–143, particularly pp. 130–2, The Free Press, New York, 1965. This paper is to be reproduced in the forthcoming Volume III of my "Collected Scientific Papers" (R. C. Merton, Ed.,) M.I.T. Press, Cambridge, MA.

10. M. Kurz, The general instability of a class of competitive growth processes, *Rev. Econ. Studies*, **35** (1968), 155–174. Some ambiguities in the relation between the time-dependent characteristic exponents of the Jacobian of the time-dependent Hamiltonian function and the stability of the system appear on pages 161 and 165. Fortunately the author's examination of the stability of the time-free associated system resolves all difficulties.

11. P. A. Samuelson, "Market Mechanisms and Maximization," Parts I and II, March 28, 1949, Part III June 29, 1949, RAND Corporation; reproduced *in* "The Collected Scientific Papers of Paul A. Samuelson, I," (J. E. Stiglitz, Ed.) *op. cit.*, Chapter 44.

12. K. J. Arrow, L. Hurwicz, and H. Uzawa, "Studies in Linear and Non-Linear Programming," Stanford University Press, Stanford, CA, 1958.

THE PERIODIC TURNPIKE THEOREM[1]

P. A. SAMUELSON

Massachusetts Institute of Technology, Department of Economics, Cambridge 02139, U.S.A.

(*Received* 19 *January* 1976)

Key words: Optimal control, economic turnpike, periodic extremal

IN DEMONSTRATING that the familiar corn-hog cycle, rather than being a speculative aberration, may be deduced as a rational and optimal way of storing harvest gluts of grain in the form of hog meat, Samuelson (1976) chanced upon a generalization of the usual *turnpike theorem*. If the integrand in an optimal control problem is a strictly periodic function of time instead of being time-free,[2] then what used to be defined as a turnpike plateau can now be defined as a turnpike that is a periodic function of time. And it will again be the case that, for fixed initial and terminal conditions, but with the time interval of the maximization being made limitingly *large*, the true optimal program will spend *most* of its time arbitrarily *close* to the new, periodic turnpike.

Here, very briefly I shall summarize with minimal proofs the new extension. There do remain some uncompleted tasks concerned with investigation of the necessity and sufficiency of various sets of regularity assumptions. Although I confine my exposition to the consumption version of turnpike theory, the analogous application to production theory will be evident.

REVIEW

Consider a typical optimal growth problem in economics

$$J\{y^0, y^1, \theta\} = \underset{y(t)}{\text{Max}} \int_{t^0}^{t^0+\theta} L[y'(t), y(t)] \, \mathrm{d}t \qquad \text{s.t.} \, y(t^0) = y^0, \qquad (1)$$
$$y(t^0 + \theta) = y^1$$

---

[1] The last quarter of a century has spawned a vast economic literature on the triple-limit property called the turnpike theorem, a phenomenon not studied in physics or biology. For the production variant of the turnpike theorem, see Samuelson, 1949, 1960, 1967a, 1969, 1971a; Dorfman, Solow & Samuelson, 1958; Radner, 1961; Morishima, 1961, 1964; Hicks, 1961, 1965; Furuya & Inada, 1962; McKenzie, 1963a, 1963b, 1968; Nikaido, 1964; Koopmans, 1964, 1965; Kuhn, 1963; Drandakis, 1966; Gale, 1967; Vanek, 1968; Burmeister & Dobell (and Turnovsky), 1970. The early paper of von Neumann (1931) dealt with stationary states of balanced growth; Solow & Samuelson (1953) dealt with a special one-joint-process economy; a complete bibliography would include many further important names. For the consumption turnpike theorem, which in a degree was implicit in the early work, Ramsey (1928), and in Samuelson & Solow (1956), see Cass, 1965, 1966; Samuelson, 1965, 1967b, 1968a, 1968b, 1970a, 1971a, 1972, 1973; Kurz, 1968, 1968b; Shell, 1966, 1967; Shell & Stiglitz, 1967; Caton & Shell, 1971; Liviatan & Samuelson, 1969; Levhari & Liviatan, 1972; Brock, 1973; Brock & Scheinkman, 1974; Tinbergen, Chakravarty, von Weizsäcker, Uzawa, Phelps, Bruno, Ryder and many others have written on these and related matters. For stochastic generalizations, see Mirrlees, 1965; Samuelson, 1971b; Brock & Mirman, 1972; Stigum, 1971; Merton, 1975.

[2] When systematic time preference is invoked to generalize the standard Ramsey case, the conventional integrand will depend on time through appearance in the integrand of the factor, $\exp(\delta t)$. The same generalization will apply to the periodic case, as in Eqns (36) and (40). When labor grows at the exponential rate $\exp(gt)$ in a Solow–Ramsey model, provided *per capita* consumption enters into the integrand as $u[C/L] = u[c]$, the Ramsey case easily generalizes to have Golden–Rule turnpikes.

$$= \int_{t^0}^{t^0 + \theta} L[Y'(t),\ Y(t)]\ dt$$

where $[Y(t),\ Y'(t)]$ are short for $[Y(t;\ y^0,\ y^1,\ \theta),\ \partial Y(t;\ y^0,\ y^1,\ \theta)/\partial t]$; $L[y',\ y]$ is strictly concave in its arguments, with existent continuous partial derivatives up to the second order, written for short as

$$L_y[y',\ y] = \partial L[y',\ y]/\partial y,\ L_y'[y',\ y] = \partial L[y',\ y]/\partial y'$$

$$L_{yy}[y',\ y] = \partial^2 L[y',\ y]/\partial y^2,\ L_{y'y'}[\ ] = \partial^2 L[\ ]/\partial y'^2$$

$$L_{y'y}[\ ] = \partial^2 L[\ ]/\partial y' \partial y,\ L_{yy'}[\ ] = \partial^2 L[\ ]/\partial y \partial y'$$

and where the optimal, $Y(t)$, does satisfy the Euler and boundary conditions

$$\frac{d}{dt} \{L_{y'}[Y'(t),\ Y(t)]\} - L_y[Y'(t),\ Y(t)] = 0 \tag{2}$$

$$Y(t^0) = y^0,\ Y(t^0 + \theta) = y^1$$

In Ramsey (1928), y is a capital stock and $L \equiv u[f(y) - y']$, where $u[\ ]$ is a concave utility and $f(y)$ a concave production function.

In (1) and (2), $y(t)$ may be interpreted as a scalar, or as a row vector of n functions $[y_j(t)]$. When $n > 1$, $L_y[\ ]$ and $L_{y'}[\ ]$ are interpreted as column vectors of partial derivatives, $(\partial L[y',\ y]/\partial y_j)$ and $(\partial L[y',\ y]/\partial y_j')$; $L_{yy}[\ ]$ and the other second derivatives are then square matrices, $(\partial^2 L[\ ]/\partial y_i \partial y_j)$, and so forth; $y^0 = (y_j^0),\ y^1 = (y_j^1)$; $y' L_{y'}[\ ]$ is an inner product; etc.

The catenary turnpike theorem, among its formulations, can be expressed as follows.

Consumption Turnpike Theorem

For the system defined in (1) and (2),

$$\lim_{\theta \to \infty} Y(t^0 + \omega\theta;\ y^0,\ y^1,\ \theta) = y^* \text{ or } \bar{y},\ 0 < \omega < 1 \tag{3}$$

where y^* is the turnpike defined by

$$\underset{y}{\text{Max}}\ L[0,\ y] = L[0,\ y^*] = 0 \tag{4}$$

$$L_y[0,\ y^*] = 0, \tag{5}$$

$$\underset{y(t)}{\text{Max}} \int_0^\theta L[y',\ y]\ dt \qquad \text{s.t. } y(t^0) = y(t^0 + \theta) \tag{6}$$

$$= \int_0^\theta L[0,\ y^*]\ dt$$

$$\frac{d}{dt} \{L_y'[0,\ y^*] - L_y[0,\ y^*]\} \equiv 0,\ y^* \equiv Y(t;\ y^*,\ y^*,\ \theta) \tag{7}$$

Figures 1a and 1b give reminders of the meaning of this turnpike theorem. In Fig. 1a, as θ grows from θ' to θ'' and to θ''', the optimal path is seen to approach ever closer to the y^* turnpike for most of the time. In Fig. 1b, as θ grows, the horizontal scale is correspondingly compressed so that the whole time interval is portrayed as constant at unity. On this diagram, as $\theta \to \infty$, the members of the sequence of corresponding paths approach for each abscissa the turnpike. Figure 1c shows

219

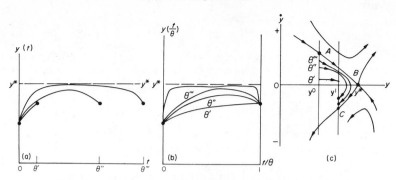

Fig. 1. All extremals hug close to the y^* turnpike most of the time as $\theta \to \infty$.

$(y^*, 0)$ to be a saddlepoint in phase space: as θ grows, the appropriate extremal path joining the two fixed meridians of y^0 and y^1, approaches limitingly close to the locus ABC.

Remark: If $\theta = \infty$ in (1) and y^1 is not imposed, the optimal permanent path deduced by Ramsey (1928) does in Fig. 1a approach the turnpike asymptotically, $Y(t; y^0, y^*, \infty) = \overline{Y}(t; y^0)$, where for all y^0, $\overline{Y}(t; y^0) \to y^*$ as $t \to \infty$. The motion is shown in 1c by the "stable" axis of the saddlepoint, AB. If $n = 1$, $\overline{Y}(t; y^0)$ is definable by the "natural-energy integral":

$$L[\overline{Y}'(t; y^0), \overline{Y}(t; y^0)] - L[0, y^*] - Y'(t; y^0) L_{y'}[\overline{Y}'(t; y^0), \overline{Y}(t; y^0)] = 0 \tag{8}$$

If $n > 1$, (8) must be supplemented by $n - 1$ of the Euler conditions of (2).

A "local proof" of the theorem can rely on the demonstration that, for (y^0, y^1) sufficiently near to (y^*, y^*), the behavior of the extremals defined by the non-linear Euler relation of (2) will have the same qualitative topological properties (actually "saddlepoint" properties) as that of the *associated linear system* in $z(t) \approx y(t) - y^*$

$$0 = L^*_{y'y'} z''(t) + (L^*_{y'y} - L^*_{yy'}) z'(t) - L^*_{yy} z(t) \tag{9}$$

where $L^*_{y'y'}$ is short for $L_{y'y'}[0, y^*]$, etc.

For $n = 1$, the middle term will vanish; and the strict concavity of $L[y', y]$ implies that, almost always, the first and last of these coefficients will be of opposite signs.[3] Thus, the solution to (9) must have the catenary or hyperbolic form

$$z(t) = a_1 \exp(+\lambda t) + a_2 \exp(-\lambda t), \lambda = +(L^*_{yy}/L^*_{y'y'})^{1/2} \tag{10}$$

As the time horizon becomes large, while the boundary conditions remain the same, $(a_1 \exp(+\lambda\omega\theta)$, $a_2 \exp(-\lambda\omega\theta)) \to (0,0)$, so that intermediate values $z(t_0 + \omega\theta) \to 0$ as $\theta \to \infty$. This entails that $|Y(t^0 + \omega\theta; y^0, y^1, \theta) - y^*|$ can be made as small as we like by letting $\theta \to \infty$ while fixing ω at a fractional value.

PERIODIC ECONOMICS

Suppose there is a 24-h, 29-day, 365-day, or 40-month fluctuation in tastes and technology.

---

[3] For $n > 2$, as is discussed later just before Eqn (36), the coefficients in (9) are square matrices that come from the Hessian of $L[y', y]$. Now opposite-signed complex roots can occur: $(+\lambda_1, -\lambda_1; +\lambda_2, -\lambda_2; \ldots, +\lambda_r, -\lambda_r, \leqslant n)$. In that case the generalized catenaries can be locally oscillatory, being a superposition of terms like $\Sigma_1^r [c_j \exp(t \operatorname{Re} \lambda_j) + d_j \exp(-t \operatorname{Re} \lambda_j)] \sin(v_j t + \gamma_j)$, where the c_j and d_j are worst polynomials in t, and where $\lambda_j = \operatorname{Re} \lambda_j + iv_j$.

That should not materially affect the optimal program over long periods of time. That it will not can now be demonstrated.

Consider a natural generalization of (1)

$$J\{y^0, y^1, t^0, t^1\} = \underset{y(t)}{\text{Max}} \int_{t^0}^{t^1} L[y'(t), y(t), t]\, dt \qquad \text{s.t. } y(t^0) = y^0, \qquad (11)$$
$$y(t^1) = y^1$$

$$= \int_{t^0}^{t^1} L[Y'(t), Y(t), t]\, dt$$

where $L[y', y, t]$ is strictly periodic in t as well as continuing to be strictly concave in (y', y) and twice differentiable

$$L[y', y, t] \equiv L[y', y, t + \tau], 0 < \tau < \infty \qquad (12)$$

$$L_{y'}[\ ], L_y[\ ], L_t[\ ], L_{yy}[\ ], L_{yt}[\ ], \dots \text{ well-defined}$$

$$L[y', y, t] \text{ strictly concave in } (y', y)$$

and where $Y(t)$, now short for $Y(t; y^0, y^1, t^0, t^1)$, satisfies

$$0 = \frac{d}{dt}\{L_{y'}[Y'(t), Y(t), t] - L_y[Y'(t), Y(t), t] \qquad (13)$$

$$Y(t^0) = y^0, Y(t^1) = y^1.$$

By analogy with the definition of the constant turnpike given by (7), we can hope to define a periodic turnpike, $\bar{y}(t)$, if it exists, by the following properties:

$$\bar{y}(t) \equiv \bar{y}(t + \tau) \qquad (14)$$

$$0 = \frac{d}{dt}\{L_{y'}[\bar{y}'(t), \bar{y}(t), t]\} - L_y[\bar{y}'(t), \bar{y}(t), t]. \qquad (15)$$

EXISTENCE OF PERIODIC TURNPIKES

Sufficient conditions for the existence of such a periodic turnpike can be stated in a variety of ways. One set is that

$$\underset{y^0}{\text{Max}}\, J\{y^0, y^0, 0, 2\tau\} = 2 \underset{y^0}{\text{Max}}\, J\{y^0, y^0, 0, \tau\} = J\{\bar{y}(0), \bar{y}(0), 0, 2\tau\} = 2J\{\bar{y}(0), \bar{y}(0), 0, \tau\}. \qquad (16)$$

Another sufficient condition is that $L[y', y, t]$ be quadratic with periodic coefficients like those in

$$L[y', y, t] = \tfrac{1}{2}a_{00}(t)\, y'(t)^2 + a_{01}(t)\, y'(t)\, y(t) + \tfrac{1}{2}a_{11}(t)\, y(t)^2$$

$$+ a_0(t)\, y'(t) + a_1(t)\, y(t), a_i(t) \equiv a_i(t + \tau), a_{ij}(t) \equiv a_{ij}(t + \tau), (i, j = 0, 1) \qquad (17)$$

and where

$$a_{00}(t) < 0, a_{11}(t) < 0, a_{00}(t)\, a_{11}(t) - a_{01}(t)^2 > 0.$$

Then (13) becomes a linear second-order differential equation with constant coefficients, shown in Coddington & Levinson (1955, Ch. 3) and other standard works, necessarily to have a periodic solution, $\bar{y}(t) = \bar{y}(t + \tau)$.

Even in the time-free case of $L[y', y]$, there need not be a finite y^* turnpike. Thus, in the Bernoulli–Solow model, $L = \log[ay^\alpha - y']$, $0 < \alpha < 1$, $L_y[ay^\alpha - 0] = \alpha/y = 0$ has no finite root for y^*. One wonders whether, in the periodic case, it would suffice to ensure existence of a periodic turnpike that

$$L_y[x, y, t] = 0 \quad \text{for} \quad 0 < y = f(x, t) < M < \infty, \; -m \leqslant x \leqslant +m < \infty. \tag{18}$$

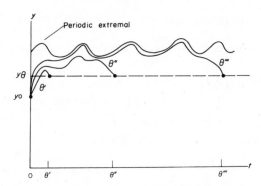

Fig. 2. Schematic diagram of the presumed asymptotic approach to the periodic turnpike as the time horizon widens.

One suspects this because, as noted in Carathéodory (1967, Ch. 17), it is sufficient for the existence of a periodic solution that there exist a finite y^{0*} such that

$$\text{Max } J\{y^0, y^0, 0, \tau\} = J\{y^{0*}, y^{0*}, 0, \tau\} \tag{18.1}$$

$$0 = J_{y^0}\{y^{0*}, y^{0*}, 0, \tau\} + J_{y^1}\{y^{0*}, y^{0*}, 0, \tau\}$$
$$= -L_{y'}[y'^*, y^{0*}, 0] + L_{y'}[y'^*, y^{0*}, \tau] \tag{18.2}$$

for some y'^* and y^{0*} satisfying

$$0 = \frac{\mathrm{d}}{\mathrm{d}t} L_{y'}[y'(t), y(t) \; t], - L_y[y'(t), y(t), t] \tag{18.3}$$

$$y(0) = y(\tau) = y^{0*}, \; y'(0) = y'(\tau) = y'^*$$

Another conjecture needing to be investigated is that a periodic turnpike exists for ε small enough, and

$$L(y', y, t; \varepsilon) \equiv L(y', y, t + \tau; \varepsilon), \; \varepsilon > 0$$

$$L(y', y, t; 0) \equiv L(y', y, 0; 0) \tag{19}$$

$$\lim_{\varepsilon \to 0} |L_\varepsilon(y', y, t; 0)| < M > \infty.$$

Even in the easy case of a Solow one-sector model with an annual weather cycle, the problem of existence of a periodic turnpike involves mathematics not to be found in the standard advanced textbooks of differential equations. Consider the specific case

$$\text{Max}_{y(t)} \int_0^\theta \log \left[3(1 - \varepsilon \sin t)^{1/3} y(t)^{1/3} - gy(t) - y'(t)\right] dt \tag{20}$$

$$y(0) = y^0, \, y(\theta) = y^1$$

$$d \log \left[3(1 - \varepsilon \sin t)^{1/3} y(t)^{1/3} - gy(t) - y'(t)\right]/dt - (1 - \varepsilon \sin t)^{1/3} y(t)^{-2/3} + g = 0 \tag{21}$$

This last Euler condition is of the periodic form

$$0 = F[y''(t), y'(t), y(t), t] \equiv F[y''(t), y'(t), y(t), t + 2\pi]. \tag{22}$$

But whether the conjecture is true that a periodic solution exists to it, $\bar{y}(t) = \bar{y}(t + 2\pi)$, even for $|\varepsilon|$ small, requires delicate investigation.

An example with an existent periodic turnpike, and which satisfies many of the different sufficiency conditions, is the following:

$$\text{Max}_{y(t)} \int_{t^0}^{t^1} \log \left[\{y(t) + \varepsilon \sin t\}^{1/3} - gy(t) - g\varepsilon \sin t\} - \{y'(t) + \varepsilon \cos t\}\right] dt. \tag{23}$$

An obvious transformation of variable reduces this to a standard turnpike problem:

$$x(t) = y(t) + \varepsilon \sin t$$

$$\text{Max} \int_{t^0}^{t^1} \log \left[x(t)^{1/3} - gx(t) - x'(t)\right] dt \tag{24}$$

$$x(t^0) = y^0 + \varepsilon \sin t^0, \, x(t^1) = y^1 + \varepsilon \sin t^1$$

The fact that the terminal conditions oscillate as t^1 grows does not alter the applicability of the standard theorem, since that theorem implies increasing insensitivity of the path with respect to the same finite variation of x^1 as $t^1 - t^0 \to \infty$. Simple as the example is, it shows that the present discussion is not without content.

From now on, attention is confined to those cases in which a periodic extremal does exist, $\bar{y}(t)$ and for which

$$Y(t; \bar{y}(0), \bar{y}(0), 0, \tau) \equiv \bar{y}(t) = \bar{y}(t + \tau) \tag{25.1}$$

$$J\{\bar{y}(0), \bar{y}(0), 0, k\tau\} = \int_0^{k\tau} L[\bar{y}'(t), \bar{y}(t), t] \, dt, \quad (k = 1, 2, \ldots)$$

$$= k \, \text{Max}_{y(t), \, y^0} \int_0^\tau L[y'(t), y(t), t] \, dt \quad \text{s.t. } y(0) = y(\tau) = y^0 \tag{25.2}$$

$$= k \, \text{Max}_{y(t)} \int_0^\tau L[y'(t), y(t), t] \, dt \quad \text{s.t. } y(0) = y(\tau) = \bar{y}(0)$$

$$0 = J_{y_0}\{\bar{y}(0), \bar{y}(0), 0, \tau\} + J_{y_1}(\bar{y}(0), \bar{y}(0), 0, \tau) = -L_{y'}[\bar{y}'(0), y'(0), 0, 0] + L_{y'}[\bar{y}'(0), \bar{y}(0), 0, \tau]. \tag{25.3}$$

THE GENERALIZED TURNPIKE THEOREM

As before, we hold terminal conditions constant, y^0 and y^1, and let $t^1 - t^0$ grow indefinitely. The sequence of resulting optimal programs can be made to spend an arbitrary fraction of the total time within an epsilon distance of the periodic turnpike.

Periodic Consumption Turnpike Theorem

For $\bar{y}(t)$ a unique periodic solution of the Euler equation

$$0 = \frac{d}{dt} L_{y'}[\bar{y}'(t), \bar{y}(t), t] - L_y[\bar{y}'(t), \bar{y}(t), t], \tag{26}$$

$$\bar{y}(t) = \bar{y}(t + \tau), \tag{27}$$

necessarily

$$\lim_{t^1 - t^0 \to \infty} Y(\omega t^0 + (1 - \omega) t^1; y^0, y^1, t^1, t^0) = \bar{y}(\omega t^0 + (1 - \omega)t^1), 0 < \omega < 1. \tag{28}$$

A heuristic "local proof" proceeds much as before, making use of the celebrated theorem of Poincaré that the characteristic exponents associated with a periodic solution of variational system must come in opposite signed pairs.

Write $y(t) = \bar{y}(t) + az(t)$, so that the Euler relation becomes

$$L_{y'y'}[y', y, t][\bar{y}'' + az''] + L_{y'y}[y', y, t][\bar{y}' + az'] + L_{y't}[y', y, t] - L_y[y', y, t] = 0. \tag{29}$$

Now differentiate (29) with respect to a, use (26) and set a equal to zero to derive the *linear* so-called variational equations

$$\bar{L}_{y'y'}z + \{\bar{L}_{y'y} - \bar{L}_{yy}\}z' - \bar{L}_{yy}a = 0 \tag{30}$$

where $\bar{L}_{y'y'}$ is short for $L_{y'y'}[\bar{y}', \bar{y}, t]$, and where all such coefficients have periodicity τ. For $n = 1$, the middle coefficients will vanish and, almost always the first and third coefficients will be respectively negative and positive.

It follows from Poincaré's theorem that the most general solution of (30) can be put in the form

$$z(t) = c_1(t) \exp(+\lambda_1 t) + c_2(t) \exp(-\lambda_1 t), \lambda_1 > 0 \tag{31}$$

where the $c_j(t)$ coefficients have the same periodicity τ as the coefficients in (30). With $z(t^0)$ and $z(t^1)$ held constant

$$[c_1(t)\exp(+\lambda\omega(t_1-t_0)), c_2(t)\exp(-\lambda_1\omega(t_1-t_0))] \tag{32}$$

With $\lambda_1 > 0$, the qualitative behavior of the linear system's $z(t)$, determines locally the exact qualitative behavior of $y(t) - \bar{y}(t)$, it being understood that $|y(t^0) - \bar{y}(t^0)| + |y(t^1) - \bar{y}(t^1)|$ is sufficiently small. The qualitative behavior might with some poetic license be called that of an "oscillatory saddlepoint."

Also, if $t^1 \to \infty$ and y^1 is not restricted, we have the following permanently-optimal program which asymptotically converges to the periodic turnpike in the same way that Ramsey's optimal permanent paths approach asymptotically to his "bliss turnpike."

$$J\{y^0, t^0\} \equiv J\{y^0, t^0 + \tau\} \tag{33}$$

$$= \max_{y(t)} \int_{t^0}^{\infty} L[y', y, t] \, dt \qquad \text{s.t. } y(t^0) = y^0$$

$$= \int_{t^0}^{\infty} L[\bar{y}'(t; y^0, t^0), \bar{y}(t; y^0, t^0), t] \, dt$$

$$= \text{Max} \left[\lim_{k \to \infty} J\{y^0, y^1, t^0, t^0 + k\tau\} \right]$$
$$\quad \underset{y^1}{}$$

$$= J\{y^0, \bar{y}(t^0), t^0, \lim_{k \to \infty} k\tau\}$$

where

$$\bar{y}(t; y^0, t^0) \underset{t}{\equiv} Y(t; y^0, \bar{y}^0, \lim_{k \to \infty} k\tau) \tag{34}$$

$$\lim_{t \to \infty} \left[\bar{y}(t; y^0, t^0) - \bar{y}(t)\right] \exp\left(+ \lambda_1 t\right) = \text{constant.} \tag{35}$$

As we go from $n = 1$ to higher n, how are these results modified? As indicated in footnote 3, the coefficients of the linear system (30) are now $n \times n$ matrices, submatrices of the $2n \times 2n$ Hessian matrix of $L[y', y, t]$ with respect to $[y', y]$. Since the Hessian is symmetric, the middle coefficient is a skew-symmetric matrix. Since the Hessian, almost always, is negative definite, the opposite-signed characteristic exponents $(\pm \lambda_1, \pm \lambda_2, \ldots, \pm \lambda_n)$ will have real parts that do not vanish. Now complex roots can occur to produce sinusoidal catenaries. Also, roots may be repeated so that the periodic coefficients, $c_j(t)$, which are now each column vectors, may be polynomials involving powers of t with periodic coefficients. Nothing essential is altered in our general conclusions.

So far there has been no systematic time preference or discounting in our integrands. For $L[\ ]$ periodic and strictly concave, we can introduce some small amount of discounting without affecting our qualitative results—just as in the standard turnpike case. Thus, consider

$$J\{y^0, y^1, t^1, t^0; \delta\} = \int_{t^0}^{t^1} \exp \delta(t^0 - t) L[y', y, t] \, dt \tag{36}$$

where

$$L[y', y, t] \equiv L[y', y, t + \tau], 0 < \delta < \varepsilon \tag{37}$$

$$H = \begin{bmatrix} L_{y'y'} & L_{y'y} \\ L_{yy'} & L_{yy} \end{bmatrix} \text{ negative definite} \tag{38}$$

$$\bar{y}(t; \delta) = \bar{y}(t + \tau; \delta) \text{ a periodic turnpike satisfying} \tag{39}$$

$$\frac{d}{dt} L_{y'}[\bar{y}', \bar{y}, t] - L_y[\bar{y}', \bar{y}, t] - \delta L_{y'}[\bar{y}', \bar{y}, t] = 0. \tag{40}$$

Periodic Turnpike Theorem with Discounting

Then any optimal path, satisfying the Euler condition and frozen boundary conditions, $y(t^0)$, $y(t^1)$, will have the following "turnpike" property, provided δ is sufficiently near to zero,

$$\lim_{t^1 - t^0 \to \infty} Y(\omega t^0 + [1 - \omega] t^1; y^0, y^1, t^1, t^0; \delta) = \bar{y}(\omega t^0 + [1 - \omega] t^1; \delta). \tag{41}$$

$$0 < \omega < 1$$

If $|\delta|$ becomes "large", Kurz (1968), Liviatan & Samuelson (1969), and others have shown that "multiple" turnpikes may exist. One still will have asymptotic close approximations to such turnpikes, but to which one will depend on boundary conditions imposed. Also, with $\delta > 0$, one can encounter the fascinating Sutherland (1970) phenomenon of a periodic extremal in a discrete-time optimal-control problem whose technology and tastes possess no periodic components. This phenomenon has little intrinsic relation to the present discussion: in any case, for any $L[y', y]$ exp $(-\delta t)$ with a negative definite Hessian matrix at $L[0, y^*]$, the Sutherland phenomenon cannot occur for δ in the neighborhood of zero.

Utilizing the formulation in Samuelson (1960), one can adapt all this to the production-turnpike case. Now one faces a constrained maximum problem, and converts $L[\ ]$ into a saddlepoint problem:

$$\underset{\lambda(t)}{\text{Max}} \ \underset{y_j(t)}{\text{Max}} \int_{t^0}^{t^1} L[y_1', y_2', y_1, y_2, \lambda(t), t] \, dt \tag{42}$$

$$= \underset{\lambda(t)}{\text{Min}} \ \underset{y_j(t)}{\text{Max}} \int_{t^0}^{t^1} \{f(y_1, y_2, y_2', t) + \lambda[y_1' - f(y_1, y_2, y_2', t)]\} \, dt$$

$$\text{s.t. } y_1(t^0) = y_1^0, y_2(t^0) = y_2^0, y_2(t^1) = y_2^1.$$

With $f(\ )$ concave and of periodicity τ, as $t^1 - t^0 \to \infty$, the optimal program between (y_1^0, y_2^0) and (y_2^0) remains almost all the time indefinitely close to a periodic von Neumann extremal of maximal "balanced" growth.

It is a matter of taste whether one works, as I have done, with primal variables and their velocities. Alternatively, one can work with canonical equations and phase variables that depict dual prices along with primal quantities. Also, one can utilize the inequality approach of Pontryagin, Valentine, and Kuhn and Tucker. More important, problems of *global* behavior need to be handled by methods more sophisticated than the classical tools here employed.[4]

Acknowledgement—Dedicated to Tjalling Koopmans of Yale University on the occasion of the 1975 Nobel Award in Economics. I owe thanks to the National Science Foundation for financial aid, and to Kate Crowley for editorial assistance.

REFERENCES

1. BROCK W. A. & SCHEINKMAN J. A., Global asymptotic stability of bounded trajectories generated by modified Hamiltonian dynamical systems: A study in the theory of optimal growth, *J. Econ. Lit.* To be published.
2. BURMEISTER E. & DOBELL A. R., *Mathematical Theories of Economic Growth*, Macmillan, New York (1970).
3. CARATHÉODARY C., *Calculus of Variation and Partial Differential Equations of the First Order, Part II: Calculus of Variations*, Holden-Day, San Francisco (1967). (translation of 1935 German original).
4. CASS D., Optimum growth in an aggregative model of capital accumulation, *Rev. Econ. Stud.* 32, (1965), 233–240.
5. CASS D. & SHELL K., The structure and stability of competitive dynamical systems, Technical Report No. 169, Institute for Mathematical Studies in the Social Sciences, (1974); *J. Econ. Lit.* To be published.

[4]Some further conjectures will occur to the reader. Suppose $L = L[y', y, a_1(t), a_2(t)]$, where $a_1(t) = a_1(t + \tau_1)$ and $a_2(t) = a_2(t + \tau_2)$. If τ_2/τ_1 is rational, equal to p/q, we are back in our periodic case, with some single minimum period. Thus if τ_1 and τ_2 are integers, the common period can be taken as $\tau_1\tau_2$ or their least common multiple. However, suppose $\tau_1 = 999$ and $\tau_2 = 1,000$. Then for long subperiods of the 999,000-year cycle, the clocks move close together and the system acts much like a system with a 9995-period cycle. Therefore, for a wide class of frozen terminal states, when $t^1 - t^0$ is large (but finite, and perhaps much less than 999,000 periods), optimal programs may be "almost almost-periodic," in a definable sense.

Suppose, however, that τ_1 and τ_2 are incommensurable, as when $a_1(t) = \sin t, a_2(t) = \sin \pi t, \tau_1/\tau_2 = \pi$. Then, one guesses, that almost-periodic turnpikes can be defined, and that, for $t^1 - t^0 \to \infty$ and (y^0, y^1) frozen, optimal programs do hug close to them for most of the time.

6. CASS D., Optimum growth in an aggregation model of capital accumulation: A Turnpike Theorem, *Econometrica* **34**, 833–850, (1966).
7. CASS D., Optimum growth in an aggregative model of capital accumulation, *Rev. Econ. Stud.* **32**, 233–240, (1965).
8. CODDINGTON E. A. & LEVINSON N., *Theory of Ordinary Differential Equations*, McGraw-Hill, New York (1955).
9. DORFMAN R., SAMUELSON P. & SOLOW R., *Linear Programming and Economic Analysis*, McGraw-Hill, New York (1958).
10. DRANDAKIS E., On efficient accumulation paths in the closed production model, *Econometrica* **34**, 331–346, (1966).
11. FURUYA H. & INADA K., Balanced growth and intertemporal efficiency in capital accumulation, *Int. Econ. Rev.* **3**, 94–107, (1962).
12. GALE D., On optimal development in a multi-sector economy, *Rev. Econ. Stud.* **34**, 1–18, (1967).
13. HICKS J. R., Prices and the Turnpike I: The story of a Mare's next, *Rev. Econ. Stud.* **28**, 77–88, (1961).
14. HICKS J. R., *Capital and Growth*, Clarendon Press, Oxford (1965).
15. KOOPMANS T. C., Economic growth at a maximal rate, *Quart. J. Econ.* **78**, 355–394, (1964).
16. KOOPMANS T. C., *On the Concept of Optimal Economic Growth*, pp. 225–287. Pontifical Academy of Sciences (1965).
17. KUHN H., Paris lecture (1961).
18. KURZ M., The general stability of a class of competitive growth processes, *Rev. Econ. Studies* **35**, 155–174, (1968a).
19. KURZ M., Optimal economic growth and wealth effects, *Int. Econ. Rev.* **9**, 348–357, (1968b).
20. LEVHARI D. & LIVIATAN N., On stability in the saddlepoint sense, *J. Econ. Theory* **4**, 88–93, (1972).
21. LIVIATAN N. & SAMUELSON P. A., Notes on Turnpikes: Stable and Unstable, *J. Econ. Theory* **1**, 454–475, (1969); reproduced as Ch. 141 in *Collected Scientific Papers of Paul A. Samuelson*, Vol. III.
22. MCKENZIE L. W., The Dorfman–Samuelson–Solow Turnpike Theorem, *Rev. Econ. Rev.* **4**, 29–43, (1963a).
23. MCKENZIE L. W., Turnpike theorem for a generalized Leontief model, *Econometrica* **31**, 29–43, (1963b).
24. MCKENZIE L. W., Accumulation programs of maximum utility and the von Neumann facet, in *Value, Capital and Growth*, J. N. Wolfe (ed.). Edinburgh University Press, Edinburgh (1968).
25. MERTON R. C., An asymptotic theory of growth under uncertainty, *Rev. Econ. Stud.* **42** (3), 375–393, (1975).
26. MIRRLEES J. A., Optimum accumulation under uncertainty, unpublished Oxford memo, December 1965.
27. MORISHIMA M., Proof of a Turnpike Theorem: The 'No Joint Production Case', *Rev. Econ. Stud.* **28**, 89–97, (1961).
28. MORISHIMA M.,*Equilibrium, Stability, and Growth*. Clarendon Press, Oxford (1964).
29. NIKAIDO H., Persistence of continued growth near the von Neumann Ray: A strong version of the Radner Turnpike Theorem *Econometrica* **32**, 151–162, (1964).
30. RADNER R., Paths of economic growth that are optimal only with respect to final states, *Rev. Econ. Stud.* **28**, 98–104, (1961).
31. RAMSEY F. P., A mathematical theory of saving, *Econ. J.* **38**, 543–559,
32. SAMUELSON P. A., *Market Mechanisms and Maximization, Part III: Dynamics and Linear Programming*, Rand Corporation, Santa Monica, Cal. (1949); reproduced as Chapter 33 in *Collected Scientific Papers of Paul A. Samuelson*, Vol. I, MIT Press, Cambridge, Mass. (1962), ed. J. E. Stiglitz; hereafter referred to as *CSP*.
33. SAMUELSON P. A., Efficient paths of accumulation in terms of the calculus of variations, in K. Arrow *et al.* (eds.), *Mathematical Methods in the Social Sciences*, Standard University Press (1959), 77–88; appears as Chapter 26 in *CSP*, I.
34. SAMUELSON P. A., A catenary Turnpike Theorem involving consumption and the golden rule, *Amer. Econ. Rev.* **55**, 486–496, (1965); reproduced as Chapter 136 in *CSP*, III.
35. SAMUELSON P. A., Indeterminancy of development in a heterogeneous-capital model with constant saving propensity, in K. Shell (ed.), *Essays on the Theory of Optical Economic Growth*, MIT Press, Cambridge, Mass. (1967a), 219–231; reproduced as Chapter 150 in *CSP*, III MIT Press, Cambridge, Mass., (1972), R. C. Merton (ed.).
36. SAMUELSON P. A., A turnpike refutation of the golden rule in a welfare maximizing many-year plan, in Shell (ed.), *op. cit*, 1967b, 269–288; reproduced as Chapter 137 in *CSP*, III.
37. SAMUELSON P. A., The two-part golden rule reduced as the asymptotic turnpike of catenary motions, *West. Econ. J.* **6**, 85–89, (1968a); reproduced as Chapter 138 in *CSP*,·III.
38. SAMUELSON P. A., Local proof of the turnpike theorem, *West. Econ. J.*[now *J. Econ. Inquiry*] **7**, 1–8, (1969); reproduced Chapter 139 in *CSP*, III.
39. SAMUELSON P. A., Classical orbital stability deduced for discrete-time maximum systems, *West. Econ. J.* **8**, 110–119, (1970a); reproduced as Chapter 158 in *CSP*, III.
40. SAMUELSON P. A., Law of Conservation of the Capital Output Ratio, *Proc. Natn. Acad. Sci., U.S.A.* **67**, 1477–1479, (1970b); reproduced as Chapter 142 in *CSP*, III.
41. SAMUELSON P. A., Turnpike theorem even though tastes are intertemporally dependent, *West. Econ. J.* **9**, 21–26, (1971a); reproduced as Chapter 140 in *CSP*, III.
42. SAMUELSON P. A., Stochastic Speculative Price, *Proc. Natn. Acad. Sci., U.S.A.* **68**, 335–337, (1971b); reproduced as Chapter 206 in *CSP*, III.
43. SAMUELSON P. A., The general saddlepoint property of optimal-control motions, *J. Econ. Theory* **5**, 102–120, (1972).
44. SAMUELSON P. A., Optimality of profit-including prices under ideal planning, *Proc. Natn. Acad. Sci.* **70**, 2109–2111, (1973).

45. SAMUELSON P. A. & SOLOW R. M., A complete capital model involving heterogeneous capital goods, *Quart. J. Econ.* **70**, 537–562, (1956); reproduced as Chapter 25 in *CSP*, I.

46. SHELL K., Toward a theory of inventive activity and capital accumulation, *Amer. Econ. Rev.* **56**, 62–68, (1966).

47. SHELL K., Optimal programs of capital accumulation for an economy in which there is exogenous technical change, in K. Shell (ed.), *Essays on the Theory of Optimal Economic Growth*, MIT Press, Cambridge, Mass. (1967).

48. SHELL K. & STIGLITZ J. E., The allocation of investment in a dynamic economy, *Quart. J. Econ.* **81**, 592–609, (1967).

49. SOLOW R. M. & SAMUELSON P. A., Balanced growth under constant returns to scale, *Econometrica* **21**, 412–424, (1953); reproduced as Chapter 24 in *Collected Scientific Papers of Paul A. Samuelson, Vol. I*.

50. UZAWA H., Optimal growth in a two-sector model of capital accumulation, *Rev. Econ. Stud.* **31**,   (1964).

51. VANEK J., *Maximal Economic Growth: A Geometric Approach to von Neumann's Growth Theory and the Turnpike Theorem*, Cornell University Press, Ithaca, New York (1968).

52. VON NEUMANN J., A model of general economic equilibrium, *Rev. Econ. Stud.* **13**, 1–9, (1945), *translated* from the German given ealier at Princeton in 1931 and Vienna, 1936.

PART III

On Marxian Economics

225

MARX AS MATHEMATICAL ECONOMIST

Steady-State and Exponential Growth Equilibrium

Paul A. Samuelson

Massachusetts Institute of Technology

Introduction

What do Marx and Metzler and Markov have in common? The German radical in London exile, the small-town Kansas boy, and the Petersburg aristocrat all worked with matrices of nonnegative elements.

So important are these in varied branches of science that we could speak of Marx–Leontief–Sraffa input–output matrices; of Metzler–Keynes–Chipman–Goodwin–Machlup–Johnson many-country multiplier matrices; of Metzler–Hicks–Mosak–Arrow–Hurwicz gross-substitutes matrices; of Markov–Frechet–Feller–Champernowne–Solow transition-probability matrices; and in pure mathematics itself, of Perron–Frobenius–Minkowski matrices a, with nonnegative elements, and the related $(I - a)^{-1}$ matrices with either positive or nonnegative elements. Or, divorcing them from any one application, we could call them Morishima–Solow–Dosso–McKenzie–Kemp matrices, after writers who explicated their general properties and applications. I am sure that I have omitted some important names and some important fields of application.[1]

---

[1] I vaguely recall that these matrices arose a century ago in connection with electric network theory.

Just when the New Left seems beginning to lose interest in the mature Marxism of *Das Kapital*—in favor of the *Grundrisse* and early philosophical writings of the Young Marx (alienation and all that)—the Leontief–Sraffa analytical literature is beginning to pay deserved homage to Marx's seminal contribution to the study of "simple reproduction" and "extended reproduction."

Tongue somewhat in cheek, I once referred to Karl Marx as "...from the viewpoint of pure economic theory...a minor Post-Ricardian...a not uninteresting precursor of Leontief's input–output of circular independence..." [1]. This is a bit less fulsome than Professor Morishima's recent evaluation: "...economists are in the wrong...in undervaluing Marx, who should in my opinion be ranked as high as Walras in the history of mathematical economics."[2] I do not know where Professor Morishima's tongue was when his quill penned these lines, but one can hope that the truth will eventually be found within these valid bounds!

Ignoring the fact that Marx is an important ideological figure, I propose in this essay to explore the nature of Marx's key analytical contribution to economic theory—one that links him directly with Leontief and modern Harrod–Robinson–Solow growth theory, and links him indirectly with Keynes, Metzler, Hicks, and the rest.

I. Two Claims to Fame

I agree with Morishima (and I think, with Joan Robinson and Nicholas Kaldor) that Marx's Volume II models of simple and extended reproduction have in them the important germ of general equilibrium, static and dynamic. If Schumpeter reckoned Quesnay, by virtue of his *Tableau Économique*, among the four greatest economists of all time,[3] Marx's advance on Quesnay's *Tableau* should win him a place inside the Pantheon.

One's respect for Friedrich Engels as an editor goes up when one wades through Marx's Volume II, made up as it was of incomplete, overlapping, and tedious manuscripts and notes written at different times. However, by going three-quarters of the way through the book and singling out the tableau of simple reproduction found there (Tableau 1), one can claim immortal fame for Marx. This was presumably arrived at by Marx in the 1860's.

Before reviewing the meaning of the symbols, we may consolidate Marx's right to fame by adding his tableau of extended reproduction (Tableau 2),

[2] Morishima [2]. I salute this valuable work, and respect its differences of conclusions from my own. The quotation is from p. 1.

[3] After Walras, and along with Cournot and either Smith or Marshall (from his 1935–1936 Harvard lectures; I cannot remember which one of the last two).

TABLEAU 1

SIMPLE REPRODUCTION

Department I,
    Capital goods: 4000 of c_1 + **1000** of v_1 + **1000** of s_1 = 6000 total
Department II,
    Consumption goods: **2000** of c_2 +   500 of v_2 +   500 of s_2 = 3000 total

---

TABLEAU 2

EXPANDING REPRODUCTION
(at 10% Rate per Period)

Present period

I: 4400 of c_1 + 1100 of v_1 + 1100 of s_1 = 6600

II: 1600 of c_2 + 800 of v_2 + 800 of s_2 = 3200

Next period

I: 4840 of c_1 + 1210 of v_1 + 1210 of s_1 = 7260 = $(1 + \frac{1}{10})6600$

II: 1760 of c_2 + 880 of v_2 + 880 of s_2 = 3520 = $(1 + \frac{1}{10})3200$

---

taken almost from the book's end. This seems to come from the 1870's; and from the internal evidence of Marx's expositions, one senses that he had not mastered the intricacies of the extended reproduction case in quite the way he had that of simple reproduction.[4]

[4] These tableaux are taken, in trivially modified notations, from Volume II, Part III, Chapter XX, Section 11 (p. 459 of the 1909 Kerr edition), Chapter XXI, Section III (pp. 598 and 599). We might have been able to avoid some sterile disputes over Marx's "transformation" of his notions of "values" into his Volume III discussion of bourgeois prices if Marx had carried through a straightforward conversion of his p. 459 simple reproduction example, with its equal-organic composition or direct-labor intensity property, into the following alternative to his quoted p. 598 examples, recorded here for future reference.

TABLEAU 1*

I: 4400 of c_1 + 1100 of v_1 + 1100 of s_1 = 6600
II: 1600 of c_2 + 400 of v_2 + 400 of s_2 = 2400

This preserves the technology and initial labor supply of his simple reproduction example, but displays balanced growth of 10% per period. Thus in the following period 4400 would be replaced by 4400(1 + 0.1), and all entries would be amplified by the same (1 + 0.1) factor.

II. Simple Reproduction

We may quickly explain Marx's terminology. Society is split into two industries or departments:

Department I, which produces a capital good—to keep notions simple, suppose it to be a raw material such as coal.

Department II, which produces a consumption good—corn for simplicity, to be consumed by workers for their needed sustenance and reproduction and by capitalists for their luxurious spending of surplus value or profit.

It will simplify exposition *not* to regard each department as the consolidation of several different capital-goods and consumption-goods industries. Though it would not be hard to replace coal by a durable machine, we avoid all problems of depreciation and periods of turnover by sticking with a raw material (such as coal) consumed completely in each production use.

Technically, corn is produced by labor and by coal. There is no great novelty here. But coal is produced by labor and by *itself*—a great leap out of what came to be known as the Ricardo–Austrian world (with "triangular hierarchy" of earlier and later stages of production) and into the Leontief–Sraffa world of circularly interdependent input–output.

A. Explanation of Symbols

The v_1 and v_2 in Tableau 1 represent the 1000 and 500 of direct wage costs—"variable capitals" in standard Marx terminology. The c_1 and c_2 represent the 4000 and 2000 of raw material costs for coal—"constant capitals."

Marx assumes that "surplus" or capitalists' profit happens to be equal to the wage cost in each industry. As we would say, half of *all* values added goes to property and half to labor, with Net National Product happening to be distributed in equal shares.[5]

---

[5] Incidentally, Marx's long quibble with Adam Smith over Smith's assertion that "...the price of every commodity finally dissolves into one or another of these...parts (wages, profit, ...)" which "...are the final...sources of all income as well as exchange value" is refuted after all by Marx's own analysis! When Smith resolves price into $\sum (s + v)$, he obviously is referring to summed value added, even being quoted by Marx on p. 427 to say: "The value which laborers add to the material resolves itself...," Marx nodded, and failed to point out that Net National Product = 3000 of Department II's final corn; and *not* the gross total 6000 + 3000 of I and II together, since Smith would have agreed with Marx that it would involve double counting to count in the labor needed to produce corn's needed net coal *along* with that of coal itself. (I return to this dispute in footnote 12.)

Modern economists, Smith, and Marx would today agree that Net National Product equals both the sum of values added and the flow of *final* products:

$$\text{NNP} = \sum_1^2 (v_j + s_j) = \sum_1^2 \{(c_j + v_j + s_j) - c_j\}.$$

B. Equal Rates of Surplus Value and of Profit

Because of the happy accident that this first example of Marx chances to involve equal "organic compositions of capital" in all departments (i.e., equal fractions of total cost in the form of direct wages, or equal v_i/c_i), we can luckily have equality in all industries of *both* the rates of surplus value s_i/v_i and the usual bourgeois rates of profit or interest $s_i/(c_i + v_i)$—at 100% and 20%, respectively. That is, in Tableau 1,

$$1000/1000 = s_1/v_1 = 1.00 = \text{uniform } s/v = s_2/v_2 = 500/500 \quad \text{(1a)}$$

$$1000/(4000 + 1000) = s_1/(c_1 + v_1)$$

$$= 0.20 = \text{uniform } s/(c + v)$$

$$= s_2/(c_2 + v_2) = 500/(2000 + 500). \quad \text{(1b)}$$

C. Zero Saving

The wage half of NNP, $\sum v_i$, goes to buy half of Department II's corn output for needed real-wage subsistence. Since there is no accumulation in simple reproduction, capitalists spend all their incomes, $\sum s_i$, on the other half of the corn, performing zero net saving. Hence,

$$\sum_1^2 (v_i + s_i) = c_2 + v_2 + s_2. \quad \text{(2)}$$

It follows then, by arithmetic tautology, that the total of coal used up in all industries, $\sum c_i$, must just equal all of Department I's coal production. Or (2) implies

$$\sum_1^2 c_i = c_1 + v_1 + s_1, \quad \text{(3)}$$

since by definition

$$\sum_1^2 (v_i + s_i) + \sum_1^2 c_i \equiv \sum_1^2 (c_i + v_i + s_i). \quad \text{(4)}$$

Ricardo, the Physiocrats, and other classical economists would, in certain moods, regard subsistence wages as a cost not unlike that involved for coal; hence, they would subtract from NNP labor-subsistence costs, $\sum v_i$, to get Neat Product, *Produit Net*, or Net–Net National Product:

$$\text{NNNP} = \sum_1^2 s_j = \sum (\{(c_j + v_j + s_j) - c_j\} - \sum v_j).$$

Fortunately, Marx's vendetta with Smith and his predecessors led him, in this case, to the pure gold of simple and extended reproduction.

Marx clearly sees, and somewhat belabors, a further implication of either (2) or (3): namely, simple reproduction requires

$$c_2 = v_1 + s_1. \tag{5}$$

That is why in Tableau 1 I wrote these numbers in boldface, so that the reader could see their equivalence. Since the sum of the first column equals the sum of the first row's terms, striking out the upper-left-hand element shared in common by the row and column, $4000 = c_1$, gives us this equivalence.

D. CHANGING THE RATE OF "EXPLOITATION"

Suppose that, by some mechanism (not well explained by Marx), workers are now to get a lower subsistence wage. Then there must result a higher rate of surplus value and of profit—even if technology remains unchanged.

Thus, suppose the same laborers can now be made to work for wages low enough to give them only 1200 rather than 1500 of the producible corn. Then we must now have a rate of surplus value of 150% rather than 100%. Similarly, with *fully* as much insight, we can say that the rate of profit must now be 25% rather than 20%. To see this, calculate

$$(3000 - 1200)/1200 = 1.50 > 1.00 = 1500/1500$$
$$(3000 - 1200)/(6000 + 1200) = 0.25 > 0.20 = 1500/(6000 + 1500).$$

In this special case of equal organic compositions of capital, the price ratio of a ton of coal relative to a bushel of corn will be unaffected by a change in the profit rate. If, instead, corn were more labor intensive than coal (as in Marx's Tableau 2, where $v_2/c_2 > v_1/c_1$), a rise in the rate of profit would raise the market price of coal relative to that of corn. But in no case could a change in the real wage and a rise in (the equalized-across-industries) rate of surplus value alter in any way the ratio of corn's Volume I "value" to coal's "value." This ratio will still remain equal to the ratio of embodied total labor contents ("direct" and "indirect") of the two goods.

I recall no evidence that Marx ever knew how to calculate the infinite-term matrix series that decomposes each good into its total labor content—namely, the matrix series

$$a_0 + a_0 a + a_0 a^2 + \cdots$$

where a_0 is the row vector of direct labor requirements and a is the square matrix of input–output coefficients. (See footnote 12 that comments further on his quarrel with Adam Smith.)

However, he could in principle have calculated the total labor requirement of the simple reproduction 3000 corn by replacing *all* $(v_i + s_i)$ by a new equivalent $(v_i^* + 0)$. Then $\sum (v_i^* + 0)$ is the total labor cost of the corn. And to get the total labor cost of each unit of *net* coal, or of the $6000 - 4000 = 2000$ *net* coal, he had only to reckon the $v_1^* + 0$ total.

E. The Three-Sector Model

I leave mathematical analysis of simple reproduction until after extended reproduction is discussed. But, in concluding the zero-growth case, we may notice that Marx could treat capitalists' consumption of luxury corn as a separate luxury Department III. Now Tableau 1 takes the form given in Tableau 3.

TABLEAU 3

I:	4000 of c_1 + 1000 of v_1 + 1000 of s_1 = 6000	Capital goods
II:	1000 of c_2 + 250 of v_2 + 250 of s_2 = 1500	Subsistence goods
III:	1000 of c_3 + 250 of v_3 + 250 of s_3 = 1500	Luxury goods

This is a familiar three-sector model in the Marxian literature. And for it we have obvious equalities between respective rows and columns:

$$c_1 + c_2 + c_3 = c_1 + v_1 + s_1$$
$$v_1 + v_2 + v_3 = c_2 + v_2 + s_2 \qquad (6)$$
$$s_1 + s_2 + s_3 = c_3 + v_3 + s_3 .$$

And, corresponding to (5), we have the equivalent three-sector relation

$$c_2 + c_3 = v_1 + s_1 \qquad (5')$$

with numerous similar implications of (6). Note that any two of (6)'s three relations implies the remaining third one, as well as implying (5').

F. Changed Pattern of Luxury Consumptions

What if capitalists chose to spend two fifths of their incomes on coal, and three fifths rather than five fifths on corn? At least in this simple case, Marx could probably arrive at the correct new form of the two-sector model of simple reproduction (Tableau 4). No longer is $c_2 = v_1 + s_1$, now that Department I is providing *more* coal than the system *uses up as intermediate* $\sum c_j$.

Note that Tableau 4 is in fact identical to footnote 4's extended reproduction variant of Marx's first simple reproduction tableau (Tableau 1), namely, the footnote's Tableau 1*. That is why I decided to pick this numerical amount of luxury coal consumption—to prepare the way for exponential-growth equilibrium.

TABLEAU 4

SIMPLE REPRODUCTION
$\frac{2}{5}$ Luxury Spending on Coal, $\frac{3}{5}$ on Corn, Zero Saving

I: 4400 of c_1 + 1100 of v_1 + 1100 of s_1 = 6600

II: 1600 of c_2 + 400 of v_2 + 400 of s_2 = 2400

III. Balanced Expanding Reproduction

A gap of years separated Marx's writing on simple and extended reproduction. Perhaps this explains why he did not proceed directly from his original simple reproduction example of Tableau 1 to Tableau 1*, its new equilibrium configuration when capitalists accumulate part of their incomes to finance golden-age exponential growth of all parts of the system, including the labor supply.

Thus, let capitalists save half their $\sum s_j$ incomes. With a uniform profit rate assumed to remain at 20%, we know from modern Kalecki–Robinson–Kaldor tautologies that a balanced growth rate of 10% per period is then implied.[6] If coal production is, like everything else, to rise at this rate, our new tableau must have coal output available for next period, $c_1 + v_1 + s_1$, equal to $\frac{11}{10}$ of the total used up, $\sum c_j$, of this period. With the same initial labor supply of Tableau 1, we have our new Tableau 1* (which is not in *Das Kapital*).

To explain the interrelations of Tableau 1*, note that the half of 1500 of $\sum s_j$ saved comes to 750; this total of net saving is exactly enough to match the increment of capital between the two periods. Thus, we have the saving-investment identity

$$0.5 \sum s_j = 750 = S = I = \{6600 \text{ of coal produced} -6000 \text{ of coal used up}\}$$
$$+ \{1650 \text{ of new corn-wage outlay}$$
$$- 1500 \text{ of old corn-wage outlay}\}$$
$$= \{600\} + \{150\} = 750. \quad \text{Q.E.D.}$$

A three-sector rearrangement of Tableau 1* can illuminate how $\sum v_j$, $\sum s_j$, and $\sum c_j$ get "spent" (see Tableau 1**).

---

[6] In Marx's own extended reproduction case (Table 2), this tautology would not be available—since, with unequal organic compositions of capital and insistence on uniform rates of surplus value, we encounter unequal rates of profit and inapplicability of the tautology. See Morishima [2, Chapter 12] on the "dynamic" transformation problem, for demonstration of the greater complexity of the relationship between the rates of growth, saving, and uniform surplus value, in comparison with the first two and the rate of uniform profit.

TABLEAU 1*

EXTENDED REPRODUCTION
(10% Growth Rate; 0.5 Saving Rate Out of Profits)

First period

I: 4400 of c_1 + 1100 of v_1 + 1100 of s_1 = 6600

II: 1600 of c_2 + 400 of v_2 + 400 of s_2 = 2400

    6000   1500   1500   9000

Next period

I: 4800 of c_1 + 1210 of v_1 + 1210 of s_1 = 7260 = 6600(1 + 0.1)

II: 1760 of c_2 + 440 of v_2 + 440 of s_2 = 2640 = 2400(1 + 0.1)

    6600   1650   1650   9900   9000(1 + 0.1)

Etc.

TABLEAU 1**

EXTENDED REPRODUCTION
(10% Growth Rate; 0.5 Saving Rate of Profits)

I**:   4000 of c_1 + 1000 of v_1 + 1000s_i = 6000 of "nonfinal" coal

II**:   1000 of c_2 + 250 of v_2 + 250s_2 = 1500 of "subsistence" corn wages

III**: $\begin{matrix} a \\ b \\ c \end{matrix}$: $\left.\begin{matrix} 500 \\ 400 \text{ of } c_3 + \\ 100 \end{matrix}\right.$ $\left.\begin{matrix} 125 \\ 100 \\ 25 \end{matrix}\right\}$ of v_3 + $\left.\begin{matrix} 125 \\ 100 \\ 25 \end{matrix}\right\}$ of s_3 = 1500 = $\left\{\begin{matrix} 750 \text{ of luxury corn} \\ \text{consumption} \\ 600 \text{ of new coal} \\ \text{inventory} \\ 150 \text{ of new corn} \\ \text{inventory for} \\ \text{wage "advances"} \end{matrix}\right.$

Note that in this rearrangement[7] the sum of the columns do match the sum of the respective rows. Again verify that the two final columns of "values added" and the final two rows of "flow of *final* products (consumption + net capital formation)" do each equal Net National Product or National Income. I see no reason to doubt that both Adam Smith and Marx could agree on this.

[7] If corn and coal have unequal organic composition, in any model with uniform profit rates, the aggregation in Department III** of diverse (c_i, v_i, s_i) magnitudes would make the resulting totals sensitive to the weightings of the various subaggregates. By contrast, using Volume I's regime of equalized rates of surplus value would leave the breakdown between aggregate v_3 and s_3 invariant; moreover, a mere change in the rate of surplus value would not affect the relative size of c_3 to $v_3 + s_3$. This simplification of analysis is not matched by real-world simplification.

A. COMPARATIVE EXPONENTIAL-GROWTH STATES

When we " go " from the simple reproduction of Tableau 1 to the extended reproduction of Tableau 1**, we are not describing an actual transition process that takes place in the real world. All we are doing is comparing (a) an equilibrium system that has always been, and will always be, in no-growth balance with (b) an equilibrium system that has always been, and will always be, in 10%-growth balance. Marx seems to understand this, as suggested by his shrewd observation (p. 572):† "It is further assumed that production on an enlarged scale has actually been in process previously."

Yet in some of Marx's attempts to compute a valid extended reproduction Tableau, he begins with a no-growth configuration and goes through an algorithm designed to end him with a balanced-growth equilibrium. Morishima [2, pp. 117–122] nicely clears up the steps in Marx's algorithm. As Morishima observes (p. 118):

> Marx then introduced his very peculiar investment [saving] function, such that (i) capitalists of Department I devoted a constant proportion of their surplus value to accumulation. . .[whereas] (iii) capitalists of Department II adjusted their investment [behavior] so as to maintain the balance between the supply and demand for capital goods.

Morishima shows that Marx's algorithm, whatever you or I may think of its illogical split in capitalists' behavior, does converge in two periods to an admissible configuration of true balanced growth. And (on p. 120) Morishima contrasts this exact two-period convergence of Marx with the disappointingly slow rate of convergence to balanced-growth golden-age states of neoclassical growth models.

Such a pejorative comparison seems odd. Marx presumably is not purporting to describe a real-life transition. The algorithm does not take place in the capitalist marketplace, but rather at Marx's desk in the British Museum. There are an infinite number of alternative unrealistic algorithms that could also be conjured up. For that matter, once we permit ourselves unrealistic saving behavior, why not pick on one of the infinite number of alternative models each with the property of converging in *one* step from simple reproduction.[8]

---

† All page references to Marx's *Capital* are to the 1909 Kerr edition.

[8] Thus, start with Tableau 1. Let the 6000 of coal be diverted, not 4000 to Department I and 2000 to Department II, but 4400 to I and 600 to II. And let all capitalists still save nothing for this initial period. Then Tableau 1 goes in one step to the first state of Tableau 1*; and forever after all capitalists can save half their incomes and have the system grow at 10% per period bringing 10% more labor into the system in each period. When organic compositions are unequal, one of course cannot keep, in the one-stage transition to the expanding model, both the labor total and the coal-input total the same as in the steady state. "Putty–clay" models, as against "putty–putty" models, become even more complicated.

This would be an arbitrary scenario, but neither more nor less arbitrary than Marx's suggested algorithm.

IV. A Digression on Morishima's Alternative to Marx

Morishima [2, pp. 122–126] proposes to replace Marx's admittedly "unnatural" behavior equations by what he hopes will be more reasonable assumptions about saving behavior. He ends with the matrix difference equations for the two departments' values, $y(t)$, of the form $y(t) = My(t + 1)$, where M is a positive matrix with characteristic roots less than unity in absolute value. [The coefficients of M depend on the (a_0, a) technical coefficients, and on the consumption propensities of the classes: if the technology satisfies Hawkins–Simon conditions for productivity of a net surplus above subsistence requirements, and if the percent saved from profits cannot exceed unity, M should be well behaved.] As is well known from the work of Jorgenson [3] Solow [4], Morishima [5], Dorfman–Samuelson–Solow [6], and others, such a "backward-defined" difference equation must be damped moving *backward* in time, and antidamped or explosive as we follow it forward in time. One wonders then why Professor Morishima wishes to propose it as the "fundamental equation of the theory of reproduction."

Actually, it is expecting too much of a pioneer like Marx that he should solve adequately the non-steady state behavior of a system. This problem taxes modern ingenuity. Indeed, we have here the indeterminacy of the famous Hahn problem, on which Hahn [7], Stiglitz [8], Shell [8, 9], Samuelson [10], Burmeister [11], and many others have written much in the last decade. Whatever the ultimate solution of the Hahn problem—i.e., the problem of how a *heterogeneous*-capital *many*-sector model can be expected to develop under competition when *overall* saving propensities are *alone* given—the Morishima proposal seems not to constitute a "self-warranting" permanent time solution. His variant of what Dorfman–Samuelson–Solow [6] called a "Leontief trajectory" (defined as a path that *insists on the equalities*, and rules out the feasible inequalities, of the dynamic relations) will necessarily become self-contradictory, generating negative physical quantities and ultimately in effect recognizing bankruptcy.

To see that static equalities cannot hold on a consistent self-warranting solution, consider the easier case of a Ramsey-planned Marxian system that acts to maximize, say, $\sum_0^\infty (1 + \rho)^{-t} \log x_t y_t$, where x_t and y_t are per capita corn and coal consumptions, ρ is a planner rate of time preference equal to $(1 + \text{profit rate of } 20\%)/(1 + \text{growth rate of } 10\%)$, available labor supply grows at 10% per period, Marx's implicit technology prevails, and we begin with prescribed initial stocks of corn and coal appropriate to an outmoded simple reproduction state. Then it can be shown that the system will

asymptotically change itself optimally into the extended reproduction configuration proportional to Tableaux like my earlier Tableaux 2 or 4. In the
transition, the dual variables of price will *not* have the steady state values that
the system both begins and ends with and which Marx and Morishima seem
implicitly to use. One sees heuristically (the Furuya–Inada theorem generalized)
that, if there is a self-warranting (perfect-futures market!) path consistent with
strictly constant fractions of profit saved, it must asymptotically approach
the golden-age state and not explode away from it in the Morishima manner.
[For certain special utility functions, such as $U = \log x_t y_t$ or $(x_t y_t)^\gamma / \gamma$, constant average saving propensities may hold.]

I dare not state arguments as heuristic as these except with the greatest
diffidence and absence of self-confidence.

V. Marx as Advancer of Mainstream-Economics Analytical Technique

First, let us observe that there is nothing "radical" or "leftish" about
these tableaux—even for the mid-nineteenth century. On the contrary, they
could be used to convey a 1931 Hayek message[9] that the Douglas Social
Credit cranks are wrong in believing that there is a necessary flaw in the
circulation system that must lead to underconsumption and unemployment.
Indeed, in some moods, Engels and Marx wrote with scorn of Rodbertus's
naive underconsumptionist views. And, after the turn of the century, Tugan–
Baronowsky or a Domar could use these compound-interest models of Marx
to refute a crude Luxemburg–Hobson thesis of *necessary*-and-*inevitable*
eventual underconsumption in a closed capitalistic system.[10]

Second, careful examination of Marx's analysis will show that, despite his
frequently reiterated belief that he is correcting this or that contemporary
vulgar economist or earlier bourgeois writer, there is no sense in which these
tableaux, properly understood, *refute* earlier mainstream writers. Merely one
case in point is the one already mentioned, in which Marx thought he was correcting Smith's erroneous belief[10a] that wages and profit (rent being ignored)

---

[9] See, for example, Hayek [12], where the easier Austrian case is shown to have identity
between total value added and flow of final product.

[10] Not too much should be read into this last sentence. We must remember that the
Harrod–Domar "warranted rate of growth" that Marx is anticipating need not be equal
to the "natural rate of growth of the labor supply" in a realistic not-necessarily-Marxist
model of actual population and labor-price growth. We must remember too the "instability" or knife-edge property of the warranted rate in a fixed-coefficient technology. And,
finally, we must remember the possible indeterminacy of the Hahn problem of heterogeneous-capital's dynamic behavior when only *aggregate* saving propensities are hypothesized.

[10a] In private correspondence, Professor William Baumol has expressed the view that
Marx's only, or main, difference with Smith's view of price as equal to wages plus profits

form the "components" of price; but, as seen, once the straightforward differentiation between gross and net totals is respected, Marx's own analysis serves to confirm Smith's formulation. Indeed Marx deserves high praise for demonstrating this formulation in the important and novel "non-Austrian" case of circular interdependence. In summary, Marx's tableaux of simple and extended reproduction constitute an important extension and generalization—to the case of circular interdependence—of the orthodox techniques of equilibrium analysis employed by Smith, Ricardo, or Mill.

VI. Living in Marx's Skin: Numerical Examples Generalized

It is a somewhat odd feeling to immerse one's self in the numerical-example world of an earlier writer like Marx. Perhaps only by doing so can one infer how he arrived at his insights, and recognize the limitations of his perceptions. Nor will it do, when you are reading the gropings, backslidings, and discoverings of a Kepler, to become irritated and wish to clap him on the shoulder and say—from the vantage point of post-Newtonian celestial mechanics—"Why can't you see this and that?"

A. POSSIBLE CLASS OF NUMERICAL TABLES OF SIMPLE REPRODUCTION

One expects pioneering work to be somewhat rough. Elegance can come later after genius encounters diminishing returns in new insights. Having no students, no colleagues, and no readers, Marx understandably wanders a bit in his derivations. Let us stand back and see the general rules that one can follow to generate *any* tableau of simple reproduction and of extended reproduction.

It simplifies things to begin by combining all value-added terms: work with two $(v_i + s_i)$ terms rather than four such terms; call them $d_i = v_i + s_i$ for short. So long as we stick with Marx's value formulation, where d_i is always broken up into the same proportional fraction, only the (c_i, d_i) totals need be considered.

Not any four positive numbers $\begin{bmatrix} c_1 & d_1 \\ c_2 & d_2 \end{bmatrix}$ can provide a tableau of simple reproduction. Only those with column sums equal to respective row sums can serve. This makes the off-diagonal elements equal, $c_2 = d_1$, and leaves us with only three arbitrary degrees of freedom. Since mere scale does not matter, we are free to set column 2's total value added or NNP equal to unity, leaving us with only two degrees of freedom. We may select the two elements of the

---

was that this was only a superficial surface relation (as indeed it is). Baumol may be right; but the reader should review the thousands of words on Smith in Volume II and decide whether that is *all* Marx finds wrong with Smith's view.

main diagonal arbitrarily: thus every admissible tableau comes from picking for d_2 an arbitrary fraction, and for c_1 an arbitrary positive number.

Suppose we consider the narrower case of equal organic compositions of capital, not for its realism but because the simplicities of algebra that Marx employed turn out to be legitimate for it. Then we have only one degree of freedom left, since the rows (or columns) must be proportional. Instead of the general simple reproduction case

$$\begin{bmatrix} c_1 & 1 - d_2 \\ 1 - d_2 & d_2 \end{bmatrix},$$

we have

$$\begin{bmatrix} (1 - d_2)^2/d_2 & 1 - d_2 \\ 1 - d_2 & d_2 \end{bmatrix},$$

as for example, $\begin{vmatrix} 4/3 & 2/3 \\ 2/3 & 1/3 \end{vmatrix}$, that corresponds to Marx's Tableau 1 (p. 271).

As we will see, for fixed technology, it will not be the case that the (c_i, d_i) preserve the same magnitudes when the real subsistence wage changes, changing the uniform rate of profit with it. Only in the equal-organic-composition case will this be true—for the reason that only in such a case will equalized-profit-rates be compatible with the alternative of equalized-rate-of-surplus-value model (in which it must be always true that the c_i and d_i breakdowns are invariant to changes in the real wage).

B. POSSIBLE TABLEAUX OF EXTENDED REPRODUCTION

Actually, a square array of *any* four positive numbers is admissible to define such a growth tableau, since no longer do respective column and row sums have to correspond. The ratio $(c_1 + d_1)/(c_1 + c_2)$ defines a growth rate, $1 + g$, whether it be greater or less than unity. However, since scale does not matter, we have only three degrees of freedom once we fix column 2's NNP or total value added at unity. Two arbitrary elements of the first column plus an arbitary fraction for one element of the second column define an admissible extended reproduction tableau. For example,

$$\begin{bmatrix} c_1 & 1 - d_2 \\ c_2 & d_2 \end{bmatrix} \quad \text{or} \quad \begin{bmatrix} c_1 & 1 - d_2 \\ (1 - d_2 - c_1 g)/(1 + g) & d_2 \end{bmatrix},$$

as in Table 2's $\begin{bmatrix} 22/19 & 11/19 \\ 8/19 & 8/19 \end{bmatrix}$.

Turn now to the singular case of equal organic compositions of capital, where a change in the profit rate within fixed technology leaves invariant the expanded reproduction (c_i, d_i) tableau for a given balanced-growth rate (it being understood that the saving ratio changes appropriately and scale is immaterial). Since now the columns and rows must be proportional, we lose one of our three degrees of freedom. Now instead of the general case of three arbitrary elements, such as (g, c_1, d_2) only (g, d_2) are assignable: e.g.,

$$\begin{bmatrix} (1 - d_2)^2/(g + d_2) & 1 - d_2 \\ (1 - d_2)d_2/(g + d_2) & d_2 \end{bmatrix},$$

as in $\begin{bmatrix} 44/30 & 22/30 \\ 16/30 & 8/30 \end{bmatrix}$ of Tableau 1*, that corresponds to Marx's Tableau 1 modified to grow at 10% per period.

VII. Handling Marx's Underlying Technology

As far as I have been able to discover, Marx apparently never pierced below the veil of his pound, franc, or labor-hour tableaux to their underlying technology. This was not so much fetishism on his part, as that the implied problem may not have occurred to him or may have seemed to him to be too hard algebraically. That it was probably not the latter reason is suggested by the fact that it apparently never occurred to him to master even that one case where the algebra would have been easy to handle—namely, the Ricardo–Austrian case where the coal that labor needs to produce corn is itself producible by labor *alone*. Let us shift to this simple case for expository clarity.

A. THE "TRIANGULAR" RICARDO–AUSTRIAN HIERARCHY

Let us suppose 1 labor in Department I produces 1 coal. And, in Department II, $\frac{1}{2}$ labor plus $\frac{1}{2}$ coal produces 1 corn. Then coal and corn each have total labor requirements (direct plus indirect) of 1.

B. BOURGEOIS PRICING REGIME

Using capital letters (C_i, V_i, S_i) for equalized-profit-rate regimes, the correct simple reproduction tableaux at zero profit, 100%, and 200% profit rates are given in Tableau 5. Note that the D_i/C_i or $(V_i + S_i)/C_i$ ratios are quite different depending on the real corn wage and corresponding profit rate: e.g., for the 100 and 200$\%$ profit rates of Tableau 5, we find $(0.5 + 1.5)/1 \neq (0.5 + 4.0)/1.5$.

A word of explanation of these tableaux may help. For simple reproduction, one-half of society's labor—the total of which can be taken as unity—must go to produce coal, all of which is used with the other half of labor to produce consumed corn. Nothing is saved out of profits (whose share of NNP depends on the posited rate of profit). This is the technocratic bedrock at the base of all examples.

At 100% profit rate, the 0.5 of labor used to produce 0.5 of coal gets marked up by 100%. So 0.5 coal costs 1.0 in all. Hence, the cost of corn is the sum of this 1.0 of coal plus 0.5 of labor, all marked up by 100%, until

TABLEAU 5

Profit Rate	
0%	0 of C_1 + 0.5 of V_1 + 0 of S_1 = 0.5
	0.5 of C_2 + 0.5 of V_2 + 0 of S_2 = 1
100%	0 of C_1 + 0.5 of V_1 + (1.0)(0 + 0.5) = 1.0
	1 of C_2 + 0.5 of V_2 + (1.0)(1 + 0.5) = 3
200%	0 of C_1 + 0.5 of V_1 + (2.0)(0.5 + 0) = 1.5
	1.5 of C_2 + 0.5 of V_2 + (2.0)(1.5 + 0.5) = 6

corn ends costing 3.0 in all. Likewise a 200% profit markup on all $(C_i + V_i)$ outlays at every stage would lead to Department II's corn receipts of 6.0 in all.

To distinguish actual capitalistic pricing at uniform profit rates in all departments from Marx's Volume I regime of values reckoned at uniform rates of surplus value in all departments (i.e., uniform markups on direct labor alone), I have used capital letters, $C_i + V_i + S_i = C_i + V_i + R(C_i + V_i)$ against Marxian lower case letters, $c_i + v_i + s_i = c_i + v_i + r(v_i)$. A uniform rate of profit is written as R; a uniform rate of surplus value is written as r.

C. "VALUES" REGIME

The "values" regimes alternative to the above "prices" regimes produce the corresponding three tableaux (given in Tableau 6) which at $r = 0$, 2.0, and 5.0, respectively, provide the comparable subsistence real wage in corn terms that was provided by $R = 0$, 1.0, and 2.0, respectively. If you calculate the three $(c_i, d_i = v_i + s_i)$ numbers for these three quite different distributions of incomes between laborers and capitalists, you find them all exactly the same

TABLEAU 6

Rate of surplus value	
0%	0 of c_1 + 0.5 of v_1 + 0 of s_1 = 0.5
	0.5 of c_2 + 0.5 of v_2 + 0 of $0.s_2$ = 1
200%	0 of c_1 + 0.5 of v_1 + (2.0)0.5 of s_1 = 1.5
	1.5 of c_2 + 0.5 of v_2 + (2.0)0.5 of s_2 = 3
500%	0 of c_1 + 0.5 of v_1 + (5.0)0.5 of s_1 = 3
	3.0 of c_2 + 0.5 of v_2 + (5.0)0.5 of s_2 = 6

except for inessential scale, each being proportional to $\begin{bmatrix} 0 & 1/2 \\ 1/2 & 1/2 \end{bmatrix}$. That is definitely not at all the case for the (C_i, D_i) numbers of realistic competitive pricings, which are respectively proportional to

$$\begin{bmatrix} 0 & \frac{1}{2} \\ \frac{1}{2} & \frac{1}{2} \end{bmatrix}, \quad \begin{bmatrix} 0 & \frac{1}{3} \\ \frac{1}{3} & \frac{2}{3} \end{bmatrix}, \quad \begin{bmatrix} 0 & \frac{1}{4} \\ \frac{1}{4} & \frac{3}{4} \end{bmatrix}.$$

D. Extended Reproduction Alternatives

Now, in parallel, I show the way the tableaux must look at the same balanced growth rate of 100% per period in the alternative prices and values regimes. All have to be generated by the same technology, in which $\frac{2}{3}$ of society's labor goes to Department I to produce twice as much coal as was produced in the previous period for use in this period's Department II corn production.

To these same physical labor-coal-corn magnitudes, I apply the respective "prices" and "values" appropriate to the stipulated (R or r) rates, (0% or 0%), (100% or 200%), and (200% or 500%). This gives the first-period tableaux (Tableau 7) each with $1 + g = 1 + 1.0$, so that in the subsequent period each tableau will have all of its elements *double*.

TABLEAU 7

R	
0%	0 of $C_1 + \frac{2}{3}$ of $V_1 + 0$ of $S_1 = \frac{2}{3}$
	$\frac{1}{3}$ of $C_2 + \frac{1}{3}$ of $V_2 + 0$ of $S_2 = \frac{2}{3}$
100%	0 of $C_1 + \frac{2}{3}$ of $V_1 + (1.0)\frac{2}{3}$ of $S_1 = \frac{4}{3}$
	$\frac{2}{3}$ of $C_2 + \frac{1}{3}$ of $V_2 + 1.0(\frac{2}{3} + \frac{1}{3})$ of $S_2 = \frac{6}{3}$
200%	0 of $C_1 + \frac{2}{3}$ of $V_1 + 2.0(0 + \frac{2}{3})$ of $S_1 = \frac{6}{3}$
	$\frac{3}{3}$ of $C_2 + \frac{1}{3}$ of $V_2 + 2.0(\frac{3}{3} + \frac{1}{3})$ of $S_2 = \frac{12}{3}$

r	
0%	0 of $c_1 + \frac{2}{3}$ of $v_1 + 0$ of $s_1 = \frac{2}{3}$
	$\frac{1}{3}$ of $c_2 + \frac{1}{3}$ of $v_2 + 0$ of $s_2 = \frac{2}{3}$
200%	0 of $c_1 + \frac{2}{3}$ of $v_1 + (2.0)\frac{2}{3}$ of $s_1 = \frac{6}{3}$
	$\frac{3}{3}$ of $c_2 + \frac{1}{3}$ of $v_2 + (2.0)\frac{1}{3}$ of $s_2 = \frac{6}{3}$
500%	0 of $c_1 + \frac{2}{3}$ of $v_1 + (5.0)\frac{2}{3}$ of $s_1 = \frac{12}{3}$
	$\frac{6}{3}$ of $c_2 + \frac{1}{3}$ of $v_2 + (5.0)(\frac{1}{3})$ of $s_2 = \frac{12}{3}$

The substantial differences between the Tableau 5 price regimes and the Tableau 6 value regimes are obvious. The greater algebraic simplicity of the market-unrealistic right-hand-side tableaux is also apparent. All three of the right-hand value tableaux are, except for scale,[11] identical in everything but the three uniform fractional allocations of the d_i of value added between wages and surplus, v_i and s_i.

VIII. Indeterminacy of Wage and Distributive Shares?

Suppose any of the preceding elementary relationships not fully understood by Marx were explained to him. What difference would it make to his *Weltanschauung* and fundamental vision about capitalist development? Quite possibly none of importance.

A. ROOTS OF THE POLEMIC AGAINST SMITH'S VIEW OF PRICE OR WAGES-PLUS-PROFITS

Marx might concede that some of his strictures against Smith's formulation of price as composed of wage-plus-profit components would have to be withdrawn or reworded.[12] But I think his animus against Smith's "explanation" of price as wage-cost-plus-profit goes deeper. Putting things this way, he

[11] These scale changes arise from my choice of normalizing the elements of the tableaux by conveniently stating the V_i and v_i elements in terms of actual labor-hour allocations.

[12] In Volume II, Part III, Chapter XIX, Section II, 3, fourth paragraph of the section, pp. 431–432, Marx comes close to admitting that Smith is correct in decomposing price into all the values added, $v + s$, of all the earlier stages—provided we stay in a Ricardo–Austrian triangular hierarchy of production (where everything can be "ultimately" produced out of labor above). But he denies that this will work in the case of circular interdependence, where without initial raw materials production can never get off the ground: so, in effect, he is missing the fact that the multiplier chain already referred to, $a_0(I + a + \cdots + a^t + \cdots)$, is a *convergent* infinite series. Had he constructed the tableaux of Section VII and compared them with his general case, he would still have avoided all error and realized that *final* product, or NNP, can be taxonomically split up into its $V_i + S_i$ or $v_i + s_i$ components (*pace* Sraffa [30]). The cited passage where Marx comes near to clearing up his own confusion bears quoting:

> Smith...admits...that the price of corn does not only consist of v plus s, but contains also the price of the means of production consumed in the production of corn.... But, says he, the prices of all these means of production likewise resolve themselves into v plus s.... He forgets, however, ...that they also contain the prices of the means of production consumed in their production. He refers us from one line of production to another, and from that to a third. The contention that the entire price of commodities resolves itself "immediately" or "ultimately" into v plus s would not be a specious subterfuge in the sole [!] case that the product...[depends ultimately on] products ...which are themselves produced by the investment of mere variable capital, by a mere investment in labor-power [i.e., what I here dub the Ricardo–Austrian hierarchy of non-circularly-dependent production] [Volume II, p. 431].

might legitimately have felt, tends to *justify* the state of affairs in which capitalists get much of what might otherwise go to labor.

Marx is here revealing more than a value judgment against unearned property incomes. He seems also to be stressing that there is nothing inevitable, nothing determined by lasting economic principle, in an existing share of profit in price formation. There is an implicit prediction by Marx that, by power or otherwise, labor could *alter* the status quo of high profits and low wages.

But there is also more here than a value judgment, and a hortatory call to action on the part of the proletariat. There is, I think, a perception by Marx that NNP $= \sum v + \sum s$ (or price equals the sum of wages and surplus) is, by itself, an indeterminate system. The economic system of his predecessors, he feels, lacks the conditions needed to determine whether 4 is $2 + 2$, or $1 + 3$, or $4 + 0$.

B. Marx's Anticipation of Robinsonian Critique?

This perception strikes a resonant response in our own age. Joan Robinson, building on Sraffa's work and her own earlier writings, says as much: Microeconomists lack an equation to determine the profit rate and profit share.[13] Their's is an *indeterminate system*—once microeconomists' fanciful marginal-productivity conditions are denied by virtue of (a) heterogeneity of capital goods, and (b) fixity of input proportions in nonsmooth production functions.[14]

---

[13] Of course, one might supply the missing link from a Kalecki–Kaldor–Robinson–Pasinetti long-run tautology of macroeconomic theory. But that is another story, and not one easily found in Smith, Ricardo, Marshall, or Walras—or, for that matter, in Marx.

[14] In order to achieve clarity on exact differences of opinion between different modern schools, it would be well to ignore smooth neoclassical production functions in any Department. But one might still stipulate, as being realistic or interesting, that in Tableaux 1 or 2, there are many alternative ways of producing coal and corn out of labor and raw materials. Thus, in Department I, along with (a_{01}, a_{11}) coefficients of $\frac{2}{3}$ coal needed to produce 1 of coal, along with say $\frac{1}{3}$ labor, we might have the alternative technical options $(\frac{1}{3}, \frac{2}{3})$, $(\sqrt{2}/3, \sqrt{2}/3)$, $(\frac{1}{30}, \frac{20}{3})$ and $(\frac{20}{3}$ and $\frac{1}{30})$. And, at the same time, we might have in Department II, a half-dozen equally varied technical options: i.e., varied "pages" in Joan Robinson's book of technical blueprints.

As a matter of logical clarity, it would be useful to know whether those who dislike Cobb–Douglas and other simplified Clarkian production functions would agree or disagree with the proposition that this sheaf-of-varied-option cases produces pretty much the same results as would two Clarkian functions of coal and labor inputs for Departments I and II. Thus, a Ramsey planner with low time preference in $\sum (1 + \lambda)^{-t} V[c_t]$ would give up corn consumption in the present in order to build up coal stocks for greater future efficiency in producing corn, etc., etc.—much as in the Clarkian case. If this is not a bone of contention, its conclusion perhaps need not be—namely, that in the Marxian system, the inherited stock of coal per capita (or the amount accumulated at the expense of current consuming) will be an important factor bearing on whether it is likely to involve a high or low trend for the profit rate.

From the side of Böhm–Fisher time preference, the missing equation for the steady state profit rate might be sought; but to do so would not be to incur the pleasure and approval of the Cambridge–Italian school, or of Karl Marx.

I do not wish to pronounce any opinion at this time on whether Marx was insightful or obtuse in regarding the profit component of price and NNP as being undetermined by mainstream bourgeois political economy. I merely wish to advance the hypothesis that we understand much of Marx's *Weltanschauung* if we employ this interpretive hypothesis. And we understand better why he was attracted to a subsistence-wage hypothesis (however far-fetched, empirically and analytically, such an hypothesis appeared to his critics).

IX. The Number One Issue in Appraising Karl Marx's Theoretical Innovations

I leave to the Appendix the Leontief–Sraffa–Metzler elucidation of Marx's models of simple and extended reproduction. But we must not let a preoccupation with Marx as a *mathematical* economist divert us from trying to form a just opinion of how novel and fundamental was what he and Engels and Lenin regarded as his most innovative and insightful contribution to political economy—namely, Marx's way of handling "surplus value."

What Marx claimed as most originally his is also precisely that which mainstream economists have been most unanimous in rejecting. It is precisely Marx's models in Volume I and Volume II of equalized-rates-of-positive-surplus-value-markups-on-direct-wages-alone that have seemed bizarre to most non-Marxian economists. "Reactionaries" like Pareto or "liberals" like Wicksteed, as well as pedants like Böhm–Bawerk, are only the most dramatic examples of the near-universal rejection by non-Marxian political economists of these Volume I and Volume II paradigms as (a) gratuitously unrealistic, (b) an unnecessary *detour* from which Marx in Volume III had to beat a return, even though a return he was too stubborn or too unperceptive or too unscientific to admit.

This, I think, has been the Number One issue in the debates about Marxian economics throughout the years of my professional life as an economist and indeed both before and after the 1894 posthumous appearance of *Capital's* Volume III.

Failure to recognize and focus on this clearly defined question seems to me to account for a good deal of the confusion and cross-talk in pro-Marxian and anti-Marxian economics debate. What is less important, some of the misinterpretation of my own Marxian analyses (commented on in footnote 24 in the Appendix) seem to me to stem from a failure to realize that it was this issue that has motivated my own exploration in understanding, appraising, and developing Marxian analyses. And it is on this key issue that two such different people as Joan Robinson and I have been so singularly in agreement.

The issue, to repeat, is this:

What are the merits or disadvantages of hypothesizing models of (a) uniform s_i/v_i mark-ups, alongside of, or as against, models of (b) uniform $S_i/(C_i + V_i)$ markups? What, if any, are the advantages of equalized-rates-of-surplus-value regimes, in comparison with the regimes of Marx's predecessors, contemporaries, and successors, which stipulate that competitive arbitrage enforces equalized-rates-of-profit by industries? What valid insights come from a macroeconomic ratio, $\sum s_j/\sum v_j$ or $\sum S_j/\sum V_j$, that are not already (better?) contained in a $\sum S_j/\sum (C_j + V_j)$ ratio?

To guide the reader in more rapid understanding of my argument, let me state at once that I have arrived at a definite view as to how this Number One question should be answered. On the basis of much reflection and analysis of the problem, and after a valiant attempt to read every Marxian and non-Marxian argument that bears on the issue, here is my own opinion.

Save as only an admitted first approximation, justifiable for dramatic emphasis and hortatory persuasiveness or defended because of its obvious greater simplicity of algebraic structure, the paradigm of equalized-rates-of-surplus-values is an unnecessary detour from the alternative paradigm of equalized-rate-of-profit that Marx and mainstream economists inherited from Ricardo and earlier writers. This digressing Marxian alternative paradigm not only lacks empirical realism as applied to competitive arbitrage governing capital flows among industries and competitive price relations of different goods and services, but also it is a detour and a digression to the would-be student of monopolistic and imperfect competition, to the would-be student of socialism, to the would-be student of the modern mixed economy and its laws of motion, to the would-be student of the historic laws of motion of historic capitalism (including, be it stressed, of earlier golden or nongolden ages of precommodity exchanges among artisans and farmers).

Specifically, logical analysis—like that here, and enumerated at greater length in my 1971 discussion [13][15] of the Marxian "transformation problem"—will *refute* the more sophisticated notion[16] that, although the equal-rates-of-profit behavior equations are indeed

---

[15] See also refs. [14] and [15], and my two replies [16, 17]. See also Samuelson [18] which carries further the Weizsäcker–Samuelson demonstration that, even in a planned socialist society, uniform $R^* = S_j/(C_j + V_j)$, rather than $r^* = s_j/v_j$, would be needed for efficient dynamic asymptotes. My earlier articles on Marx and Ricardo are also relevant [19–22]. The elements of Marxian analysis are given in my *Economics* [23].

[16] This point, which I argue is not valid, is perhaps most clearly made by Meek [24]. In ref. [13], p. 417], my parody tries to make the point that the macroeconomic total of profit does not (repeat not) require or benefit from any s/v analysis. The present chapter spells out my arguments for this thesis. I have tried to appraise impartially Meek's thesis [24, p. 95]: "For, according to him [Marx], the profit which the capitalists receive in each branch of industry must be conceived of as accruing to them by virtue of a sort of a redivision of the aggregate surplus value produced over the economy as a whole." And my findings are as adverse to this as they are to Marx's contention (Volume I, Chapter IX, Section 1, p. 239, n. 2): "We shall see, in Book III, that the rate of profit is no mystery, so soon as we know the laws of surplus-value. If we reverse the process, we cannot comprehend either the one or the other." A careful search of Marx's earlier and later writings does not produce any evidence that he was able to make good on this claim in the eyes of a competent analyst who understands all the issues—pro-Marxian and anti-Marxian. A referee has also made this point. Baumol [25] has made a similiar claim for Marx, and in [31] I have assayed to refute the cogency of the line of argument Baumol attributes to Marx.

more valid *micro*economically (to parcel out the *macro*economic *total* of surplus among the different subaggregate departments), nonetheless the insights of the s/v or $\sum s/\sum v$ Marxian paradigm are crucial (or at least "useful") in "explaining" and "understanding" how the total of social product gets divided into paid labor and the exploiter's surplus in the years of developing capitalism. To repeat, there is no validity to this doctrine of surplus-value-paradigm-needed-macroeconomically-to-determine-the-rate-of-profit-that-microeconomically-partitions-out-the-surplus.

This is not the place to provide a comprehensive analysis of the pros and cons of these issues, as discussed by Marx, Hilferding, Dobb, Sweezy, Mandel, Meek, and many others. What is appropriate in this discussion of Marx as mathematical economist is to take notice of writings of Bortkiewicz, Sraffa, Robinson, Okishio,[17] Bródy,[18] Johansen,[19] and, most of all, Morishima.

From the standpoint of this Number One question I have scrutinized each page of Morishima's *Marx's Economics: A Dual Theory of Growth* [2], and each equation and footnote. My resulting judgment is that there is no reason given there that leads me to want to weaken the above view on the Number One question.[20]

---

[17] Okishio [26]. If I had known of the article earlier, I would have referred to it in the bibliography of my 1971 paper. Its views essentially coincide with my own (although I do not think its attempt to resolve differences in labor qualities into differences in producible education does justice to the empirical complexity of realistic "primary" factors).

[18] Bródy [27] provides a valuable and original analysis of Marx along general Leontief lines.

[19] To my 1971 bibliography should now be added the article by Johansen [28].

[20] Volume I's discussion can make this clear. Since in that volume, Marx talks repeatedly of successive stages of production, such as the spinning of yarn and the weaving of it into cloth, he is evidently already in what Leontief, Sraffa, and Böhm would dub a more-than-one-department world. But, even without the mathematics given in the Appendix, we can easily jot down a truly one-department-model—to see whether I am right in denying that S/V reveals some insight that conventional $S/(C + V)$ analysis deceptively conceals.

Suppose to produce 1 corn at the end of a period, it takes at the beginning of the period, $a_0 = \frac{1}{2}$ of labor along with $\frac{1}{2}$ of corn as raw material or seed. Then if labor can be reproduced instantly for less than 1 corn, an exploitative positive rate of profit is deducible. Thus, if subsistence corn per unit of L is $m = \frac{1}{3}$ corn, the competent reader can verify that R^* is 50%. He can verify that half the gross product goes for raw materials. Of the remaining half of Net National Product, one-third goes to labor and two-thirds goes to profit receivers (to consume now in simple reproduction cases; or, in extended reproduction cases, to consume a fixed fraction and plow back into extensive growth of the system the remaining fraction saved).

We have full insight into the problem, by mainstream economic concepts that are Ricardian (i.e., pre-Marxian), Millian (i.e., contemporaneous with Marx), Wicksellian, or Sraffian (i.e., post-Marxian). We know: At any profit rate R higher than R^*, workers will get too low a real wage to reproduce themselves; at any profit rate lower than R^*, there would be opportunity for infinite-sure-thing arbitrage—in which I borrow to buy corn, pay workers with it, and use it as raw material, then sell the product at a return greater than what I have to pay as interest, and without risk, make as much as I like. So we see, from capitalist pricing and accounting and avaricious arbitrage exactly how and why exploitation takes place.

If we want to write down a $C + V + S = C + V + R^*(C + V)$ tableau, here is how it would read for each unit of steady state labor:

> 1 of corn as raw material $+ \frac{1}{3}$ of corn as subsistence wage $+ 0.5(1 + \frac{1}{3})$ of corn profit
>
> $= 2$ of corn produced gross (of which the 1 of NNP is seen to be divided up into $\frac{1}{3}$ for labor and $\frac{2}{3}$ for exploiter).

Thus, we know all there is to know both in pecuniary and physical terms.

Now, is there any *new insight* possible from concentrating on the ratio of surplus to wages alone, S/V? Since with only one department there cannot be differing organic compositions of capital, we know from the beginning that the surplus-value innovations of Volume I must give us exactly the same answer as mainstream economics. So, was that trip really necessary? Or somehow desirable? Surely, on reflection, one will see that in this case, where it does no harm and requires no transformation algorithm, it also does not one iota of extra good. One might as usefully squander one's time in considering still a third regime in which we concentrate on S/C ratios.

To be sure, one can describe the same degenerate 1-department tableau by saying that the rate of surplus value is 200%: i.e., $r^* = 2.00$. Admittedly, a 200% rate *sounds* more exploitative than a 50% rate. But that is only for illiterates, since (as Marx clearly points out) the 200% of S/V is the same absolute loot for the exploiter merely expressed as a fraction of the smaller base V, rather than the base $(C + V)$.

But have we not added the vital fact that "living labor" is the true source of all product and *a fortiori* exploitative profits? No; conventional analysis tells us that without labor, there is no product at all. And it tells us that, without beginning-of-the-period raw material, there is also no product. That is not an apologetic for profit; it is a technical fact: mainstream economics fully recognizes that, if the m minimum of subsistence goes up, R^* will fall; and if the workers—by power or education—insist on an m up to 1, they can get all the NNP and bring R^* to zero. But, you may say, there may be strong political reasons why workers will not succeed in doing this or will be prevented from organizing to raise m and their real wage. You may be right. But you will be equally right or wrong or insightful in terms of R^* analysis as in parallel r^* analysis. And further, you will be able with R^* to understand the Sraffa dated-labor resolution, à la Adam Smith, of price into wages and profit in all the (infinite but converging) earlier stages of production—namely

$$P = a_0(1 + R^*) + a_0 a(1 + R^*)^2 + \cdots + a_0 a^{t-1}(1 + R^*)^t + \cdots$$
$$= a_0(1 + R^*)/[1 - a(1 + R^*)]$$

which Marx, throughout all his jousting with Adam Smith, was never able to get straight when $R > 0$. [Indeed, this makes one wonder whether he actually ever was able to rigorously perceive that, for $R^* = 0$, price does indeed equal total embodied labor content (direct plus indirect).] Now try to make that same correct resolution in the surplus-value r^* regime, with its gratuitous neglect of compound interest, and its quite unmerited belief that only the last-stage's direct labor contributes to profit. Tell that to a capitalist who hires a worker to plant a 10-year rather than a 5-year tree. On these workers' "live labor," will the exploiters' profit end up the same? Of course not.

I have discussed elsewhere the views of others of these writers. Specifically, I wish to iterate that my view on these matters is quite divorced from the disputes over the inadequacies of neoclassicism. I would be quite content to call my position on this Number One question Sraffian, or Robinsonian, or Ricardian, or Passinettian, or Leontiefian. (For example, in a regime of values, with uniform rates of surplus value, the realistic possibility of reswitching could not logically occur: The technique that minimizes "values" at $r = 0$ will minimize them for all r's—a shortcoming of the "values" model.)

X. Final Summing Up

The preceding analysis does demonstrate that Karl Marx deserves an honored place among economic pioneers of steady state and balanced growth equilibrium. What is valid in this seminal contribution is in no sense contrary to mainstream economics of Marx's predecessors, contemporaries, or successors. Even if we end with the view that Marx was not so much a mathematical economist as "merely" a great economist, this recognition of his analytical abilities in no sense diminishes our appreciation of him as an original and creative shaper of the science of political economy. In science, your ultimate grade depends on the best performance you achieve, and not on your worst or even average performance.

I leave to the Appendix the more rigorous summarizing of these models, and discussion of Morishima's criticism of my Marxian writings.

Appendix

1. TECHNICAL COEFFICIENTS OF PRODUCTION

Let X_{ij} be the amount of the ith good used as input for the industry producing the jth nonnegative output, X_j; let L_j be the direct labor used by the jth industry. All these are nonnegative. Then $a = [a_{ij}] = [X_{ij}/X_j]$ represents the nonnegative Marx–Markov–Metzler–Leontief matrix, and $a_0 = [L_j/X_j]$ represents the row vector of direct labor requirements.

2. EXAMPLES

Some possible cases are the following.

$$\begin{bmatrix} a_0 \\ \hline a \end{bmatrix} = \begin{bmatrix} 1 & 1 \\ \hline 0 & 0 \\ 0 & 0 \end{bmatrix}, \quad \text{Smith's deer–beaver case;} \tag{2.1}$$

$$\begin{bmatrix} a_0 \\ \cdots \\ a \end{bmatrix} = \begin{bmatrix} 1 & \frac{1}{2} \\ \hline 0 & \frac{1}{2} \\ 0 & 0 \end{bmatrix}, \qquad \text{the Ricardo–Austrian coal–corn case of} \atop \text{my six tableaux;} \qquad (2.2)$$

$$\begin{bmatrix} a_0 \\ \cdots \\ a \end{bmatrix} = \begin{bmatrix} \alpha & \beta \\ \hline 1-\alpha & 1-\beta \\ 0 & 0 \end{bmatrix}, \qquad \begin{array}{l} \text{Marx's tableaux of corn–coal:} \\ \alpha = \beta \text{ as in Tableau 1,} \\ \alpha < \beta \text{ as in Tableau 2;} \end{array} \qquad (2.3)$$

$$\begin{bmatrix} a_0 \\ \cdots \\ a \end{bmatrix} = \begin{bmatrix} 1-\alpha_1-\beta_1 & 1-\alpha_2-\beta_2 \\ \hline \alpha_1 & \alpha_2 \\ \beta_1 & \beta_2 \end{bmatrix}, \qquad \text{the general two-department case.} \qquad (2.4)$$

In every case, I have followed the convention of selecting units so that "total" labor requirements ("direct" plus "indirect") are unity.

3. ADMISSIBLE CASES

In case (2.4) we could have $1 - \alpha_2 - \beta_2 = 0$; but in order that every good require, directly or indirectly, some labor input, we could *not* then also have either α_2 or $1 - \alpha_1 - \beta_1$ zero. Sraffa chooses to require that there exist at least one good (a basic) that is directly or indirectly required by all goods (including itself). But there seems no reason to rule out cases (2.1) and (2.2).

The simplest case to talk about is where a_0 and a have strictly positive elements: $a_0 > 0$, $a > 0$. But it is almost as simple if nonnegative a is "indecomposable" and at least one element of a_0 is positive. (Indecomposability is verified when $(I + a + \cdots + a^{n-1})$ is strictly positive.) Ricardo and Marx often adjoined to "necessary" goods a set of "luxury" goods, i.e., goods which are not themselves needed as inputs for the necessary goods. This gives

$$\begin{bmatrix} a_0 \\ \cdots \\ a \end{bmatrix} = \begin{bmatrix} a_{0,I} & a_{0,II} \\ \hline a_{I,I} & a_{I,II} \\ 0 & a_{II,II} \end{bmatrix}.$$

Here $a_{I,I}$ must be nonnegative and indecomposable and at least one element of $a_{0,I}$ must be positive. Columns of $a_{I,II}$ must have a positive element. The subscript I refers to necessary goods; the subscript II, to "luxury" goods (which must be understood to be able to include a wage-subsistence good such as corn).

4. GENERAL TIME-PHASED SYSTEM

These input–output relations are the steady state plateaux of the actual time-phased technology and allocation relations.

$$X_j(t+1) = F_j[L_j(t), X_{1j}(t), \ldots, X_{nj}(t)] \qquad (j = 1, \ldots, n) \qquad (4.1)$$

$$= \text{Min}[L_j(t)/a_{0j}, X_{1j}^{(t)}/a_{1j}, \ldots, X_{nj}^{(t)}/a_{nj}] \qquad (4.1')$$

$$X_j(t) = X_{j1}(t) + \cdots + X_{jn}(t) + B_j(t) \qquad (4.2)$$

where $B_j(t)$ is the nonnegative "final consumption" in the tth period of the jth good. (Whenever an a_{ij} is zero rather than positive, we can follow the convention of disregarding its X_{ij}/a_{ij} term.)

In (4.1) we can have *any* continuous production function (not necessarily possessing well-defined partial derivatives of marginal productivity). Only joint production and externalities are ruled out.

However, much of the Marx and Leontief literature chooses to concentrate on the single-fixed-technology case shown in (4.1'). It is well to notice that in (4.1') any pattern of nonnegative a's and a_0's are permitted, provided only that every good requires directly or indirectly some positive labor. In short, the so-called Hawkins–Simon conditions—that are necessary and sufficient if something of every good is to be producible for *steady* net consumption— need *not* be stipulated to hold in general. (It is worth pointing out that the belated discovery of the H–S conditions came out of Hawkins' study of a dynamic *Marxian* system!)

5. STEADY STATE PLATEAUX

For steady states, we equate variables at all times:

$$
\begin{aligned}
X_j(t) &= X_j(t+1) = \cdots = X_j \\
X_{ij}(t) &= X_{ij}(t+1) = \cdots = X_{ij} \\
L_j(t) &= L_j(t+1) = \cdots = L_j \\
B_j(t) &= B_j(t+1) = \cdots = B_j.
\end{aligned}
\qquad (5.1)
$$

If the consumption $[B_j]$ are to be capable of taking on all-positive values, we must be able to satisfy the steady state form of (4.1') and (4.2).

$$
\begin{aligned}
L_1 + \cdots + L_n &= L > 0, \qquad X_{ij} \geq 0 \\
X_i - (X_{i1} + \cdots + X_{in}) &= B_i > 0 \qquad (i = 1, \ldots, n)
\end{aligned}
\qquad (5.2)
$$

$$
\begin{aligned}
a_{01} X_1 + \cdots + a_{0n} X_n &= L > 0 \\
X_i - (a_{i1} X_1 + \cdots + a_{in} X_n) &= B_i > 0 \qquad (i = 1, \ldots, n)
\end{aligned}
\qquad (5.2')
$$

or, in matrix terms,

$$\left[\begin{array}{c} a_0 \\ \hline I - a \end{array}\right] X = \left[\begin{array}{c} L \\ \hline B \end{array}\right] > 0. \tag{5.3'}$$

6. Hawkins–Simon Conditions for Positive Steady State Consumptions

Suppose nonnegative a can be rearranged by renumbering of corresponding rows and columns into the partitioned form

$$\left[\begin{array}{cccc} A_{0,I} & A_{0,II} & \cdots & A_{0,N} \\ \hline A_{I,I} & A_{I,II} & \cdots & A_{I,N} \\ 0 & A_{II,II} & \cdots & A_{II,N} \\ \vdots & \vdots & & \vdots \\ 0 & 0 & \cdots & A_{N,N} \end{array}\right] \tag{6.1}$$

where each diagonal $A_{I,I}, \ldots, A_{N,N}$ matrix is indecomposable, except possibly the last, but where elements above this diagonal can be zero (provided, of course, that every indecomposable set is tied directly or indirectly to a positive A_0 element). [Examples would be (2.4) with (β_1, α_2) the only vanishing elements; or with β_1 and $1 - \alpha_2 - \beta_2$ the only vanishing elements.]

Then the Hawkins–Simon conditions say: "It is necessary and sufficient for producible steady state production of any one consumption good (and of all such) that every principal-minor subsystem of $I - a$ (and of $I - A_{J,J}$) have a positive determinant."

Our examples (2.1)–(2.4), because of their normalized-to-unity form automatically satisfy the H–S conditions for a "steady state surplus economy." This is so because the condition

$$\sum_{j=1}^{n} a_{ij} < 1 \qquad (i = 1, \ldots, n) \tag{6.2}$$

is a sufficient condition for H–S. It is of course not necessary, since changing units of goods can always destroy it; but H–S holds, if and only if, for *some* choice of units, *every* diagonal matrix in (6.1) can be made to have its row sums satisfy

$$a_{0i} = 1 - \sum_{j} a_{ij} \geqq 0 \tag{6.3}$$

with the strong inequality holding for at least one of its columns. Clearly, (6.2) is an overly strong case of (6.3).

7. Subsistence-Wage Theory of Labor's Cost of Reproduction

We must now introduce the Marx-like notion that labor itself has a cost of production and reproduction. If $L(t + 1)$ satisfied equations like those satisfied by $X_j(t + 1)$ in (4.1), we would have a von Neumann system in which labor could be treated like any other "nonprimary" input. But Marx never quite articulated that case.

Marx failed to develop in detail his subsistence-wage process. Perhaps the simplest version is to assume that, from the reserve army of unemployed or the countryside, the system can always get the $L(t) = \sum_{j=1}^{n} L_j(t)$ it needs *now* at the beginning of the period's production process. It gets each such unit of $L(t)$ by providing it with the column vector of subsistence-goods requirements $[m_i]$, where one or more of these nonnegative elements is strictly positive. (In the typical Marxian model, when workers consume different goods from those used as inputs, the only positive m_i elements belong to rows of A_{NN} in (6.1) that consist exclusively of zeros. If capitalists' luxury consumption items are different from those of workers' subsistence consumption, there may be still other rows of A_{NN} in which the elements are zero.[21] But the results would be essentially similar if m_i were positive for *all* i).

8. TECHNOCRATIC SUBSISTENCE-WAGE MODEL

Without using Marx's "value" concepts or (as yet) those of bourgeois prices, I review the familiar Leontief–Sraffa technocratic formulation of a steady state, where workers get subsistence wage consumption mL, or M for short, and capitalists get the rest, $B - M$. We have, from (5.3'):

$$X = aX + B = (I - a)^{-1}B$$
$$a_0 X = a_0(I - a)^{-1}B = L > 0 \qquad (8.1)$$
$$a_0(I - a)^{-1}(B - M) = L - a_0(I - a)^{-1}mL.$$

Here the row vector $a_0(I - a)^{-1}$ represents the total technocratic labor requirements (direct plus indirect) required in the steady state to produce unit amounts of the respective goods. If $B - M = 0$, so that the system is just producing needed wage subsistence, and "exploitation" were zero, goods

---

[21] By Seton's 1957 device of "feeding coefficients," we could handle subsistence wages by adding to each original a_{ij} the new requirement $a_{0j}m_i$. Or, in the case where a unit of work in each jth industry requires a different amount of subsistence to be paid at the beginning of the period, namely, m_{ij}, we add to a_{ij} the term $a_{0j}m_{ij} = k_{ij}$. Here I shall not make m_i depend on j, and shall not employ the feeding-coefficient notation even though it has its advantages. Thus, let $[a_{ij} + k_{ij}]$ be indecomposable. Then positive principal minors of $[I - a_{ij} - k_{ij}]$ is the *strengthened* Hawkins–Simon condition that guarantees not merely the producibility of positive B, but also that enough be producible to leave something over for employers' positive profit. In our notation, this is equivalent to $a_0[I - a]^{-1}m < 1$, so that $a_0(1 + R)[I - a(1 + R)]^{-1}m = 1$ have a positive R root for the profit rate. The reader of Morishima will note that there is no need to *duplicate* this condition by an *equivalent* requirement that $a_0(1 + r)[I - a]^{-1}m = 1$ have a positive r root for the "rate of surplus value." This last adds (and subtracts) nothing to the analysis of realistic competitive equilibrium. (For simplicity, I posit length of working day constant.)

might actually be priced (relative to the wage) at these undiluted-labor-theory-of-value $a_0(I - a)^{-1}$ levels.

9. COEFFICIENT OF "EXPLOITATION"

We could for any system calculate as a measure of exploiters' "share" in social production:

$$\rho \overset{\text{def}}{=} a_0(I - a)^{-1}(B - M)/a_0(I - a)^{-1}M \geqq 0. \tag{9.1}$$

(This is sometimes given the Marxian name, ratio of "unpaid" to "paid" labor.) Under the rude undiluted labor theory of value, we would have ρ and $B - M$ zero rather than positive. This ρ coefficient has the pleasant property that changes in capitalists' tastes among different $B - M$ consumption will not affect the magnitude of ρ. However, as we should expect, changes in the consumption of subsistence m or M requirements, like changes in any a_{0j} or a_{ij}, will change ρ. For example, reducing any one m_i, or any one a_{0j} needed for some m's production, will necessarily raise ρ.

10. EXPLOITATION PRICING

To verify that there is never an advantage, save to those of limited algebraic ability, in *ever* considering Marx's regime of equalized-positive-rates-of-surplus value, I proceed on conventional bourgeois Ricardo–Sraffa–Leontief lines. For each uniform profit rate R, the row vector of prices (relative to the wage numéraire), written as $P[1 + R]$, will consist of monotone-increasing functions of R, $P_j[1 + R]$, satisfying competitive-arbitrage steady state pricing

$$P_j[1 + R] = \left\{a_{0j} + \sum_{i=1}^{n} P_i[1 + R]a_{ij}\right\}(1 + R) \qquad (j = 1, \ldots, n). \tag{10.1}$$

In matrix terms

$$P[1 + R] = a_0(1 + R) + P[1 + R]a(1 + R)$$
$$= a_0(1 + R)[I - a(1 + R)]^{-1} > 0. \tag{10.1'}$$

11. EFFECT OF VARYING LEVEL FOR EXPLOITATIVE PROFIT RATE ON RELATIVE PRICES.

Generally, as R increases from 0 to its maximum value at which $[I - a (1 + R)]^{-1}$ remains finite, $R = R_{\max} \leqq \infty$, the $P_j[1 + R]$ prices will grow at *unequal* percentage rates. Hence, the ratio $P_{1+j}[1 + R]/P_1[1 + R]$ can rise, or can fall, or in general can both rise and then later fall. However, Marx realized that in the case he called "equal organic composition of capital," such price ratios could never change. We may express this in the following propositions.

Marx–Sraffa Theorem If, and only if,

$$a_{0j}(1 + R)/P_j[1 + R] \equiv a_{01}(1 + R)/P_1[1 + R] \qquad (j = 2, \ldots n) \quad (11.1)$$

for *some* nonnegative R, will this identity be true for *all* admissible R. And, in that case, for an observed equilibrium profit rate, $R = R^*$:

$$P_j[1 + R^*] \equiv P_j[1](1 + \rho) \tag{11.2}$$

where ρ is the exploitation coefficient of Section 9, which can be defined, as we will see in the next section, once the subsistence-requirement vector is known, as a unique function of the $R = R^*$ profit rate that is implied by the condition of a real wage rate at the subsistence level.

12. Defining the Subsistence-Theory's Equilibrium Profit Rate

The equilibrium profit rate is defined as the unique $R = R^*$ level at which

$$P[1 + R]m = 1 \tag{12.1}$$

where

$$1/P[1 + R]m = W[R] \tag{12.2}$$

defines the "factor-price tradeoff frontier" linking the real wage and the profit rate. Because $P_j'[1 + R] > 0$, necessarily $W'[R] < 0$.

13. "Exploitative Rate" Greater than Profit Rate

An easy Marx-like tautology is that, for equilibrium R positive

$$\rho > R \tag{13.1}$$

provided only that some one positive intermediate input a_{ij} is needed to produce the subsistence-wage basket.[22]

14. The Equal-Organic Case of Constant Relative Prices

When all $a_{0j}(1 + R)/P_j[1 + R]$ have uniform values $\alpha[R]$, as in (11.1), each price takes on the special simple form of (11.2):

$$P_j[1 + R] = (1 + \rho[R])P_j[1] \tag{14.1}$$

---

[22] To see this, define the monotone-increasing function

$$g[R_2] = a_0[I - a(1 + R_2)]^{-1}m = P[1 + R_2]m/(1 + R_2).$$

By definition of R^* and ρ^*,

$$1 = P[1 + R^*]m = g[R^*](1 + R^*) = P[1](1 + \rho^*)m = g[0](1 + \rho^*).$$

For $R^* > 0$, $g[R^*] > g[0]$ and hence $r^* > R^*$, the final proof that the defined exploitation rate ρ exceeds the profit rate numerically. This tautology has no empirical content (and no empirical relevance or insight).

where the monotone function $\rho[R]$ is defined in terms of $\alpha[0] = \alpha$ by

$$\rho[R] = R/[1 - (1 - \alpha)(1 + R)] > R, \qquad 0 < R \leq R_{\max} = \alpha/(1 - \alpha). \quad (14.2)$$

This follows from easy substitution into (10.1). As a convenient check, we note that the exploitation rate ρ corresponding to the positive subsistence-equilibrium profit rate R^* is given as

$$\rho = \rho[R^*] = (L - P[1]M)/P[1]M = (P[1]m)^{-1} - 1. \quad (14.3)$$

15. SIMPLE REPRODUCTION TABLEAU

L is given. It produces steady state gross outputs (X_i), which, at the equilibrium profit rate R^* sell at $P_j[1 + R^*]$. The revenues of each jth industry $P_j[1 + R^*]X_j$ are equal to costs of production defined by

$$P_j[1 + R^*]X_j = \{a_{0j}X_j\} + \left\{\sum_{i=1}^{n} P_i[1 + R^*]a_{ij}X_j\right\}$$
$$+ R^*\left\{a_{0j}X_j + \sum_{i=1}^{n} P_i[1 + R^*]a_{ij}X_j\right\} \qquad (j = 1, \ldots, n).$$
$$(15.1)$$

This can be rearranged into my text's $C + V + S$ arrangement:

$$\left\{\sum_{i=1}^{n} P_i[1 + R^*]a_{ij}X_j\right\} + \{a_{0j}X_j\} + R^*\left\{\sum_{i=1}^{n} P_i[1 + R^*]a_{ij}X_j + a_{0j}X_j\right\}$$
$$\equiv \{C_j\} + \{V_j\} + R^*\{C_j + V_j\} = C_j + V_j + S_j \qquad (j = 1, \ldots, n). \quad (15.1')$$

The prime cause of stumbling (and sterility) in the usual $C + V + S$ analysis is the failure to relate these magnitudes to the underlying technology, and the related failure to break down C_j into its price and quantity factors. These capital letters, note, represent the bourgeois pricing regime in which

$$S_1/(C_1 + V_1) = S_2/(C_2 + V_2) = \cdots = R^* \quad (15.2)$$

where R^* is the equilibrium profit rate.

In matrix terms, by the usual transposition of the row vectors of (15.1'), we get the simple reproduction tableau,

$$P[1 + R^*]aX + a_0 X + R^*\{P[1 + R^*]aX + a_0 X\} = P[1 + R^*]X \quad (15.1'')$$

where the composition of X is determined by the $B - M$ selected by the capitalists subject to the simple reproduction no-saving condition

$$P[1 + R^*](B - M) = \sum_{j=1}^{n} S_j. \quad (15.3)$$

Except for the usual transposition of row and column, we then have the well-defined tableau of simple reproduction[23]

$$P[1 + R^*]a(I - a)^{-1}B + a_0(I - a)^{-1}B$$
$$+ R^*\{(P[1 + R^*]a + a_0)(I - a)^{-1}B\} = P[1 + R^*]X. \quad (15.4)$$

16. EXTENDED REPRODUCTION

Now, what about the case of extended reproduction, with growth rate $g =$ (saving rate out of profits)$/R^*$? Then we must have dynamically

$$aX(t + 1) \leq X(t) - B(t), \qquad a_0 X(t + 1) \leq L(t). \quad (16.1)$$

For $L(t) \equiv L_0(1 + g)^t$ and *all* variables growing in proportion

$$X(t) = (1 + g)^t X, \qquad B(t) - (1 + g)^t B, \qquad M(t) = (1 + g)^t mL_0. \quad (16.2)$$

Then (16.1) becomes

$$a(1 + g)X = X - B, \qquad a_0(1 + g)X = L_0. \quad (16.3)$$

Evidently (16.3) relating the coefficients of the $(1 + g)^t$ expression is just like (5.3), but with all (a_0, a) coefficients blown up by $(1 + g)$ to allow for "widening" of capital goods.

As before, $B(t)$ gets split up into $M(t)$ and capitalists' expenditures for consumption, an amount determined by that part of their profit income which they do not invest. But as final product, we now have added to consumption B the vector of net capital formation gX.

---

[23] I have qualms about calling ρ by the commonly met Marxian expression "the ratio of 'unpaid labor' [which workers perform for the exploiting employers' ultimate benefit] to 'paid labor' [which workers do for themselves]." This expression tempts one to think that ρ is an indicator of "profit share in NNP $\div$ labor share in NNP." But, in a general competitive regime, such an identification is not valid. Actually, a shift in employer's tastes toward consumption goods with low $a_{0j}/P_j[1]$ will raise profit's NNP share to its upper limit; conversely, a shift to high $a_{0j}/P_j[1]$ will depress it to its lower limit; yet ρ itself remains constant between these limits independently of how, at the fixed profit rate R^*, capitalists select their luxury consumption. Although

$$\text{Min}[S_j/V_j] \leq \rho \leq \text{Max}[S_j/V_j],$$

it will generally *not* be the case that, "in the aggregate,"

$$\rho = \sum_j S_j / \sum_j V_j.$$

Only for the uninteresting lowercase "values" definition of s_j/v_j will each of these equal ρ. But my defined ρ *never* has need for any $s_1/v_1 = s_2/v_2$ concepts.

Applying prices $P[1 + R^*]$ to (16.3), we get the extended reproduction tableau for the system at time $t = 0$, namely,

$$\left\{ \sum_{i=1}^{n} P_i[1 + R^*]a_{ij}X_j \right\} + \{a_{0j}X_j\} + R^* \left\{ \sum_{i=1}^{n} P_i[1 + R^*]a_{ij}X_j + a_{0j}X_j \right\}$$

$$= P_j[1 + R^*]X_j + \sum_{i=1}^{n} P_i[1 + R^*]a_{ij}gX_j \qquad (j = 1, \ldots, n). \qquad (16.4)$$

The last term on the right, involving gX_j, represents net capital formation needed for widening of capital.

The left-hand side of (16.4) can be rewritten in the familiar form

$$C_j + V_j + R^*\{C_j + V_j\} \qquad (i = 1, \ldots, n)$$

of the extended reproduction tableaux—as in my text's equal-profit-rate tableaux.

17. THE ALTERNATIVE "VALUES" REGIME OF MARX

Now we must jettison Sections 10–16. ("Erase and replace." Or "Consider a dual accounting system.") I have argued that there is no good reason for a person well versed in algebra and logic to waste a moment on this alternative regime. (It is not a "dual" regime in the usual sense of dual—as for example Peter's game strategy as compared to Paul's dual strategy; or the primal linear programming maximum problem and its *dual* minimum problem; or the conjugate variables of coordinates and *dual* momenta in mechanics; or the point–line dualities of projective geometries; or the production function and its *dual* minimum unit cost of production; or optimal-control variables and their Pontryagin *dual* shadow prices; or of the duality theorem relating $P[1]X$ from (10.1) to $a_0(I - a)^{-1}X$ of (8.1) and also discussed in Morishima's first chapter.

Still, this final section may be useful to those of us who wish, if only for antiquarian reasons, to be clear on the logical differences between the concepts involved in Marx's detour and those involved in a regime of ruthless competition.

The same subsistence wage defines, in the "values" regime, not "prices" written in capital letters, P, but "values," written as $(p_1, \ldots, p_n) = p$. It is understood that, as a useful convention, these prices are expressed in wage-numéraire units. They are defined in terms of a parameter r, the rate of equalized markups on direct wages alone and are written as $p_j[1 + r]$. Alternatively to the behavior equation of arbitrage in (10.1), we now *arbitrarily* postulate with Marx

$$p_j[1 + r] = a_{0j} + \sum_{i=1}^{n} p_i[1 + r]a_{ij} + ra_{0j} \qquad (j = 1, \ldots, n). \qquad (17.1)$$

In matrix terms this gives

$$p[1 + r] = a_0 + p[1 + r]a + ra_0 = a_0(I - a)^{-1}(1 + r)$$
$$= p[1](1 + r) = P[1](1 + r). \tag{17.2}$$

Note that, for $r = 0$ and no exploitation, we do not get something *better* than our bourgeois $P[1]$ of embodied labors. Actually, we get the *identical* technocratic total labor requirements (direct plus indirect) of the undiluted labor theory of value, namely, $p[1] \equiv P[1]$. However, once workers do not get all the product, it is false in logic and in history (century by century) that there was ever a time when (17.2) could have been expected to prevail under the unequal organic composition of capital.

The equilibrium rate of surplus value, $r = r^*$, set by the minimum subsistence postulate of each laborer's consumption being m, is determined as the unique root of

$$p[1 + r]m = 1 = p[1]m(1 + r), \qquad r^* = (p[1]m)^{-1} - 1. \tag{17.3}$$

It is an easy exercise, along the lines of footnote 22, to prove that the technocratically defined exploitative coefficient, ρ of (4.1), must equal r^*:

$$r^* = \rho = P[1](B - mL)/P[1]mL = p[1](B - mL)/p[1]mL. \tag{17.4}$$

When we apply the X terms of (5.3') or (16.3) to (17.2), we get the simple reproduction or extended reproduction tableaux of Marx's "values" regimes (as in Volume II of *Capital*). Thus, in matrix terms

$$\{c\} + \{v\} + \{s\} = \{c\} + \{v\} + r\{v\} = \{p[1 + r^*]aX\} + \{a_0 X\} + r\{a_0 X\} \tag{17.5}$$

as in my text's simple and extended reproduction "values" tableaux.

Of course, by the stated Marx–Sraffa theorem, if $a_{0j}/P_j[1]$ are the same α for all industries, the two alternative regimes coincide, with

$$p_j[1 + \rho[R]] \equiv P_j[1 + R] \qquad (j = 1, \ldots, n)$$

and where $\rho[R]$ is defined as in (14.2).

In general, the "transformation problem" consists of the procedure that relates r^* to R^* taking into account the common subsistence-wage basket imposed on the alternative regimes. (Morishima uses the name "dynamic transformation problem" for discussion that relates "the saving rate out of profit" to "the saving rate out of surplus values," at a common growth rate imposed on the alternative regimes.)

How can one describe the greater algebraic simplicity of the values regime in comparison with the prices regime? Chiefly in three aspects:

$$\frac{p_j[1 + r]}{p_1[1 + r]} \equiv \frac{p_j[1](1 + r)}{p_1[1](1 + r)} = \frac{p_j[1]}{p_1[1]} \qquad \text{for all } r. \tag{17.6}$$

No similar relation holds for general $P_j[1 + R]/P_1[1 + r]$.

Instead of having to solve an nth degree polynomial for the subsistence-wage profit rate R^*, as in (12.1), in (17.3) we need solve only a *linear* equation

$$1 = (p[1]m)(1 + r) \qquad (17.7')$$

for r^*!

Finally, suppose we have a reproduction tableau

$$c + v + s$$

for one real wage and r^*. Suppose there is now a change in r^*, but (for some odd reason) the capitalists spend on consumption goods in the same proportion that the workers spend. (Neither Marxians nor non-Marxians vouch for realism in this.) Then, by dropping our no-longer-useful convention of measuring always in wage-numéraire units, we can immediately write down the new reproduction tableau as equal to, or proportional to,

$$\{c'\} + \{v'\} + \{s'\} = \{c\} + \{\beta(v + s)\} + \{(1 - \beta)(v + s)\}.$$

That is, we simply repartition the total $v + s$ of each industry into new proportionate parts as between wages and surplus, leaving their c and $v + s$ unchanged. This simplicity explains how Marx could consider a variety of cases without having to know how to handle his tableaux in detail.

Have I omitted an advantage for "values" when it comes to aggregating into more manageable subaggregates? Yes, deliberately. For I perceive no such advantages in the $p[1 + r]$ or $p[1]$ weights over the $P[1 + R^*]$ or $P[1 + R]$ weights. Since R, empirically, is poorly approximated by the biased value of $R = 0$, the $p[\cdot]$ values weights are unnecessarily biased. Apparently, Professor Morishima and I have not reached agreement on this point, since his case for values seems in significant part to hinge on this dubious aggregation question. (I like his generalization of the Marx–Sraffa theorem, but I think it is *better* stated in $P_j[1 + R]$ terms.)

Have I omitted an advantage for the $s_1/v_1 = s_2/v_2$ values regime when it comes to computing "employment multipliers" in the $L = \sum A_{0j} B_j = a_0(I - a)^{-1} B$ relation for societies' net-production-possibility frontier?[24] Yes, deliberately. For, *all* we need is $P[1] = a_0(I - a)^{-1}$ concepts of the *bourgeois* analysis for the $R^* = 0$ case.

---

[24] I owe to an unpublished review by von Weizsäcker [29] a similar point. Also for the point that $P_j[1], p_j[1]$, or $p_j[1 + r]$ weights are worse than $P_j[1 + R]$ weights would be for some positive R provides a more realistic approximation than $R = 0$. Arguing that $P_j[1]$ weights are more fixed than $P_j[1 + R]$ weights when R is changing is like arguing that a frozen weather vane is less capricious than one which is changed by the wind!

18. CONCLUSION

I append in a terse footnote my elucidation of positions that Morishima has taken explicit exception to.[25] But I believe that this Appendix could be expanded to show that there is never macroeconomic or microeconomic advantage in rate-of-surplus-value analysis.

[25] The Morishima index has 16 references to me by name. Some, like those referring to pp. 29, 56, 140, 181, and 185 contain citations that represent no disagreements. Those on pp. 70 and 78 point out that the equal-internal-organic-composition of capitals case of Section VII of my 1971 *JEL* paper [13] is, for more-than-two department systems, a sufficient but not necessary condition—to which I gladly agree and authorize the reader to go through an "erase-and-replace" algorithm: *erase* the section's first word "The" and *replace* it by "A." And I agree that this singular case is not empirically realistic or even admissible for those Marx models in which wage goods are not used for production and other goods are: I never thought otherwise. All that I wished to do was show that Marx's algorithm need not always be wrong; but that *even* where it is not, his claim that we need "value" systems to reveal active exploitation processes is completely unfounded, *logically* and *empirically*, *macro*economically and microeconomically. [Although Morishima thinks that the issue of these two pages are relevant to his criticisms on other pages, I believe that once misunderstandings of my arguments are cleared away, such issues as whether $C_j + V_j = c_j + v_j$ (or, for Morishima's notation, $C_j^p + V_j^p = C_j + V_j$) are quite irrelevant and uninteresting.]

On p. 129 Morishima argues that Marx would have rejected the Neumann–Malthus model of Section IV of my *JEL* paper. That is no point against me (even *if* one argues that the logic of the passages Morishima quotes are relevant and cogent to the issue). I tried to fill the lacunae in Marx's models with possible realistic demographic and migration patterns. And, as a special limiting case of that model, I was able to generate exactly his exploitation conditions and to do it without departing from bourgeois competitive conditions.

On p. 115, Morishima somehow thinks that Dorfman–Samuelson–Solow (1958) [6] fall into the error of believing that competition requires profit to be zero. On pp. 224, 227, and 229 of Chapter 9 of ref. [6] where $P[1] = a_0 + P[1]a$, the authors are obviously dealing with the statical, instantaneous, or time-satiated Leontief system—as the chapter's beginning warns in its early statement: "Subsequent chapters will deal with dynamic models involving time and stock of capital, and also more general models...of Leon Walras and J. B. Clark," I, for one, regret that we did not explicitly deal with the special steady state case $P[1 + R] = \{a_0 + P[1 + R]\}(1 + R)$ in the book, but the very fact that all three of us in those same years were writing papers with $R > 0$ should have prevented any such odd interpretation of our view of the real competitive world. (In the same 1958 year, my *QJE* papers on Ricardo appeared [21, 22] with pre-Sraffa models of exactly this type, with or without joint production.) Making a Marx versus no-Marx issue on this is straining.

Most of the rest of the references—as for example, on pp. 39, 46–47, 59–61, 72, 74, and 85—involve the same set of misunderstandings, in which I (either alone, or in the good company of Marx, or of Paul Sweezy or Joan Robinson) am supposed to have made misleading assertions. Here is a typical sentence of mine, quoted no less than three times (pp. 47, 59, 74): "Volume I's first approximation of equal positive rates of surplus value, S_j/V_j, is not a simplifying assumption but rather—to the extent it contradicts equal profit rates $S_i/(V_i + C_i)$—a complicating detour." That sentence, the reader can confirm in context, purports to say precisely this:

ACKNOWLEDGMENTS

I owe thanks to the National Science Foundation for financial ·aid, and to Norma Wasser for editorial assistance. I have also benefited from helpful comments by Professor Edward Ames of Stony Brook.

REFERENCES

1. Samuelson, P. A., "Economists and the History of Ideas (Presidential Address)," *American Economic Review* **52** (March 1962), 1–18, reproduced as Chapter 113 in my *Collected Scientific Papers*, Volume II. Cambridge, Massachusetts: MIT Press, 1966. The quotation appears on p. 12 of the former, or p. 1510 of the latter.
2. Morishima, M., *Marx's Economics; A Dual Theory of Growth*. London and New York: Cambridge Univ. Press, 1973.
3. Jorgenson, D. W., "Stability of a Dynamic Input-Output System," *Review of Economic Studies* **28** (February 1961), 105–116.
4. Solow, R. M., "Competitive Valuation in a Dynamic Input-Output System," *Econometrica* **27** (January 1959), 30–53.

If, as generally holds, $C_i/(C_i + V_i) \neq C_j/(C_j + V_j)$, where these refer to an actual competitive system, then the $S_i/(C_i + V_i) = S_j/(C_j + V_j)$ real-world arbitrage equivalences imply $S_i/V_i \neq S_j/V_j$, except as an unuseful first approximation; and any alternative model or accounting regime, where by definition uniform s_i/v_i rates are postulated and equal $s_i/(v_i + c_i)$ rates denied, represents an unuseful detour.

Now that is what is said. It could be right or wrong; the reader must weigh my many arguments, here and elsewhere, on this; and he may read the Morishima book line for line for light it throws on this Number One question.

But now see what interpretations are put on the quotation. It is supposed to overlook that $C_i + V_i \equiv c_i + v_i$ equivalences may not hold [and why should they?]. It is supposed to fail to see that $s_i/v_i = s_j/v_j$ is no logical contradiction to $S_i/V_i \neq S_j/V_j$. Perhaps when different writers use different letters for similar things, such misinterpretations are unavoidable. But no one who reads this paper and Morishima's book need be left with the view that we disagree on all the things his text thought we did.

Morishima's transformation algorithm is isomorphic to that of Seton [32] (and for that matter 1907 Bortkiewicz). So is mine. So *if* mine is [and it is] an "erase and replace algorithm," so must be his. To speak of a "dual accounting system" is to be isomorphic with what my *JEL* paper [13] said. If one reads the remaining dissents with quoted positions of mine, they are generally of the type, "Samuelson doesn't recognize that Marx is trying to reveal the deceptiveness of capitalist accounting in terms of price," to explain and uncover the divergences between what is written here as $P_j[1 + R]$'s and $p_j[1 + r]$'s or $p_j[1]$'s, or $(P_j[1 + R]m)^{-1}$ and $(P_j[1]m)^{-1}$, to illuminate exploitation, to show how profit has its source in living labor, etc. Of course I recognize that Marx was trying to do that (he said so repeatedly), and thought he had. But why should Morishima and I believe that he had *succeeded* in such a useful program? That is the Number One question, and I could not find a single theorem in the Morishima book that predisposes one toward a favorable verdict on the question. (This includes the more-than-one proposition awarded the adjective "fundamental.")

Space does not here permit the more detailed evaluation of Morishima's criticisms that one could make, nor the explicit singling out for praise of his many novel contributions.

5. Morishima, M., "Prices, Interest and Profits in a Dynamic Leontief System," *Econometrica* **26** (July 1958), 358–380; *Equilibrium, Stability and Growth*. London and New York: Oxford Univ. Press, 1964.

6. Dorfman, R., Samuelson, P., and Solow, R., *Linear Programming and Economic Analysis*, Chapter 11, pp. 283–300. New York: McGraw-Hill, 1959.

7. Hahn, F. H., "Equilibrium Dynamics with Heterogeneous Capital Goods," *Quarterly Journal of Economics* **80** (November 1966), 633–646.

8. Shell, K., and Stiglitz, J. E., "The Allocation of Investment in a Dynamic Economy," *Quarterly Journal of Economics* **8** (1967), 592–609.

9. Caton, C., and Shell, K., "An Exercise in the Theory of Heterogeneous Capital Accumulation," *Review of Economic Studies* **38** (January 1971), 13–22.

10. Samuelson, P. A., "Indeterminacy of Development in a Heterogeneous-Capital Model with Constant Saving Propensity," in *Essays in the Theory of Optimal Growth* (K. Shell, ed.). Cambridge, Massachusetts: MIT Press, 1967.

11. Burmeister, E., Caton, C., Dobell, A. R., and Ross, S., "The 'Saddlepoint Property' and the Structure of Dynamic Heterogeneous Capital Good Models," *Econometrica* **39** (January 1973).

12. Hayek, F. A., "The 'Paradox' of Saving," *Economica* **11** (May 1931), 125–169.

13. Samuelson, P. A., "Understanding the Marxian Notion of Exploitation: A Summary of the So-Called Transformation Problem between Marxian Values and Competitive Prices," *Journal of Economic Literature* **9** (June 1971), 399–431. Reproduced as Chapter 153, pp. 276–308, of my *Collected Scientific Papers* (hereafter *CSP*), Volume III. Cambridge, Massachusetts: MIT Press, 1972).

14. Samuelson, P. A., "The 'Transformation' from Marxian 'Value' to 'Competitive' Prices: A Process of Replacement and Rejection," *Proceedings of the National Academy of Sciences* **67** (September 1970), 423–425 (*CSP*, Volume III, Chapter 152, pp. 268–275).

15. Samuelson, P. A., and von Weizsäcker, C. C., "A New Labor Theory of Value for Rational Planning through Use of the Bourgeois Profit Rate," *Proceedings of the National Academy of Sciences* **68** (June 1971), 1192–1194 (*CSP*, Volume III, Chapter 155, pp. 312–136).

16. Samuelson, P. A., "The Economics of Marx: An Ecumenical Reply," *Journal of Economic Theory* **10** (March 1972), 51–56.

17. Samuelson, P. A., "Samuelson's 'Reply on Marxian Matters '," *Journal of Economic Theory* **11** (March 1973), 64–67.

18. Samuelson, P. A., "The Optimality of Profit-Inducing Prices under Ideal Planning," *Proceedings of the National Academy of Sciences* **70**, No. 7 (July 1973), 2109–2111.

19. Samuelson, P. A., "Wages and Interest: A Modern Dissection of Marxian Economic Models," *American Economic Review* **47** (December 1957), 884–912 (*CSP*, Volume I, Chapter 29, pp. 341–369).

20. Samuelson, P. A., "Reply," *American Economic Review* **50** (September 1960), 719–721 (*CSP*, Volume I, Chapter 30, pp. 370–372).

21. Samuelson, P. A., "A Modern Treatment of the Ricardian Economy: I. The Pricing of Goods and of Labor and Land Services," *Quarterly Journal of Economics* **73** (February 1959), 1–35 (*CSP*, Volume I, Chapter 31, pp. 373–407).

22. Samuelson, P. A., "A Modern Treatment of the Ricardian Economy: II. Capital and Interest Aspects of the Pricing Process," *Quarterly Journal of Economics* **73** (May 1959), pp. 217–231 (*CSP*, Volume 1, Chapter 32, pp. 408–422).

23. Samuelson, P. A., *Economics*, 9th ed., Chapter 42 Appendix. New York: McGraw-Hill, 1973.

24. Meek, R., "Some Notes on the Transformation Problem," *Economic Journal* **66** (March 1956), 94–107 (reprinted in Meek, R., *Economics and Ideology and Other Essays*, pp. 143–157. London: Chapman and Hall, 1967.

25. Baumol, W., "Values versus Prices, What Marx 'Really' Meant," *Journal of Economic Literature* **11** (December 1973).

26. Okishio, N., "A Mathematical Note on Marxian Theorems," *Weltwirtschaftliches Archiv* **2** (1963), 297–298.

27. Bródy, A., *Proportion, Prices and Planning: A Mathematical Restatement of the Labor Theory of Value*. Budapest: Akadémie Kiadó, and Amsterdam: North-Holland *Publ.*, 1970.

28. Johansen, L., "Labour Theory of Value and Marginal Utilities," *Economics of Planning* **3** No. 2 (September 1963).

29. von Weizsäcker, C. C., "Morishima on Marx" (Working Paper No. 7, Institute of Mathematical Economics, University of Bielefeld), 1972.

30. Sraffa, P., *Production of Commodities by Means of Commodities*, Appendix D, 3, 94. London and New York: Cambridge Univ. Press, 1960.

31. Samuelson, P. A., "Insight and Detour in the Theory of Exploitation: A Reply to Baumol," *Journal of Economic Literature* **11** (March 1974).

32. Seton, F., "The 'Transformation Problem'," *Review of Economic Studies* **25** (June 1957), 149–160.

Optimality of Profit-Including Prices Under Ideal Planning

(Marx's model)

PAUL A. SAMUELSON

Department of Economics, Massachusetts Institute of Technology, Cambridge, Mass. 02139

Contributed by Paul A. Samuelson, May 7, 1973

ABSTRACT   **Although prices calculated by a constant percentage markup on all costs (nonlabor as well as direct-labor) are usually admitted to be more realistic for a competitive capitalistic model, the view is often expressed that, for optimal planning purposes, the "values" model of Marx's *Capital*, Volume I, is to be preferred. It is shown here that an optimal-control model that maximizes discounted social utility of consumption per capita and that ultimately approaches a steady state must ultimately have optimal pricing that involves equal rates of steady-state profit in all industries; and such optimal pricing will necessarily deviate from Marx's model of equal rates of surplus value (markups on direct-labor only) in all industries.**

PRODUCTION RELATIONS

A fixed-coefficients model of Leontief–Sraffa type can illustrate the difference between Marxian values and bourgeois prices, as discussed in Samuelson (1) and Weizsäcker–Samuelson (2). Let total labor at time t, $x^t = (1 + g)^t$, grow exponentially at rate g per period, and let (x_j^t) be its amount allocated to the jth of n industries. Then per capita outputs satisfy

$$q_j^{t+1} = \text{Min}[x_j^t/a_{0j}(1 + g),\ q_{1j}^t/a_{1j}(1 + g),$$
$$\ldots,\ q_{nj}^t/a_{nj}(1 + g)] \quad [1]$$

$$= c_j^{t+1} + \sum_{i=1}^{n} q_{ji}^{t+1}, \qquad (j = 1,\ldots,n)$$

where (c_j) represents per capita amounts consumed of the jth good and (q_{ji}) the amount of the jth good used as input for the ith industry.

The relations **1** are equivalent to the matrix relations

$$1 \geq a_0(1 + g)q^{t+1}, \qquad q^{t+1} \geq 0, \qquad (t = 0,1,\ldots) \quad [2a]$$

$$c^t \leq -a(1 + g)q^{t+1} + q^t, \qquad c^t \geq 0 \qquad [2b]$$

where

$$\begin{bmatrix} \dfrac{a_0}{a} \end{bmatrix} = \begin{bmatrix} a_{01} & \cdots & a_{0n} \\ a_{11} & \cdots & a_{1n} \\ \cdot & & \cdot \\ \cdot & & \cdot \\ \cdot & & \cdot \\ a_{n1} & \cdots & a_{nn} \end{bmatrix} \geq 0.$$

$$[3]$$

Bourgeois competitive prices, relative to the wage of labor, are defined as the row vector of functions.

$$a_0(1 + R)[I - a(1 + R)]^{-1} = A_0[1 + R]$$
$$= (A_{01}[1 + R],\ldots,A_{0n}[1 + R]) \quad [4]$$

where R is the interest or profit rate.

Marxian values are defined in present notation as

$$a_0[I - a]^{-1}(1 + r) = A_0[1](1 + r)$$
$$= (A_{01}[1],\ldots,A_{0n}[1])(1 + r) \quad [5]$$

where r is the rate of surplus value (markup on direct-labor outlay only) equalized in all industries.

OPTIMAL CONTROL PROBLEM

Suppose an omniscient planner acts to maximize social welfare for the rest of time. Specifically, he seeks

$$\text{Max} \sum_{t=0}^{\infty} u(c_1{}',\ldots,c_n{}')/(1 + \rho)^t$$

$$\text{subject to } \mathbf{2} \text{ and initial } (q_j{}^0). \quad [6]$$

Here $u[c_1,\ldots,c_n] = u[c]$ is a concave function with positive partial derivatives $\partial u/\partial c_i = u_i[c]$, and the property that as any c_i goes to zero, $u_i[c] \to \infty$. The rate of time preference, ρ, is taken as nonnegative.

Since all $u_i[c]$ are positive, the equalities in **2b** will surely hold at every t. For, why throw away valuable consumable goods? However, if q^0 is sufficiently skimpy, the inequality can initially prevail in **2a**. On the other hand, provided $g < \rho$, it can be shown to be optimal to abstain from enough current consumption to build up the per capita stock of q's enough to make the equality in **2a** hold for all t beyond some finite time. We can assume, therefore, that we begin with q^0 large enough so that the **2a** equalities always prevail.

Substituting **2b** into **6** and appending the price-weighted **2a** constraints as Lagrangian–Pontryagin appendages, we convert **6** into the saddlepoint problem

$$\underset{q^t}{\text{Max}}\ \underset{\lambda^t}{\text{Min}}\ L = \underset{q^t}{\text{Max}}\ \underset{\lambda^t}{\text{Min}}\ \sum_{t=0}^{\infty} \{u[q^t - a(1 + g)q^{t+1}]$$
$$+ \lambda^{t+1}[1 - a_0(1 + g)q^{t+1}]\}(1 + \rho)^{-t}. \quad [7]$$

The Euler extremal conditions of form

$$\partial L/\partial q_j{}^t = 0, \qquad \partial L/\partial \lambda^t = 0, \qquad (j = 1,\ldots,n; t = 1,2,\ldots)$$
$$[8]$$

reduce, after cancellation of $(1 + \rho)^{-t+1}$, to the equalities of **2a** and

$$u_j[q^t - a(1 + g)q^{t+1}] - \sum_{i=1}^{n} u_i[q^{t-1}$$
$$- a(1 + g)q^t]a_{ij}(1 + g)(1 + \rho) - \lambda^t a_{0j}(1 + g)(1 + \rho) = 0,$$
$$(j = 1,\ldots,n; t = 1,2,\ldots). \quad [9]$$

A well-established property of such systems, first discussed by Ramsey (3), is that there exists a stationary solution to the optimal-control problem (a so-called "turnpike" or "modified-bliss" or "golden-age" configuration). Less universally true, but typically expected to be present in the conventional cases studied by economists, is the property that the stationary solution is "stable" in the sense that for initial conditions $(q_j{}^0)$ sufficiently near to the stationary state $(q_j{}^*)$, the permanent-time optimal path will asymptotically approach the turnpike. This is certainly true in the standard one-sector model. Thanks to Sutherland (4), we know of singular exceptions to this heuristic expectation. Later I discuss such an example to show that it only strengthens the case against Marxian values.

Such cases aside, adjoining to **2a** and **9** the proper transversality condition at infinity, we find our solution satisfies

$$\lim_{t \to \infty} (q_j, \lambda) = (q_j^*, \lambda^*) \qquad [10]$$

$$1 - a_0(1 + g)q^* = 0$$

$$u_j[q^* - a(1 + g)q^*]$$
$$- \sum_{i=1}^{n} u_i[q^* - a(1 + g)q^*]a_{ij}(1 + g)(1 + \rho)$$
$$= \lambda^* a_{0j}(1 + g)(1 + \rho) \qquad (j = 1,\ldots,n).$$

The last of these can be solved for

$$u_j[q^* - a(1 + g)q^*] = \lambda^* A_{0j}[(1 + g)(1 + \rho)],$$

$$(j = 1,\ldots,n) \quad [11]$$

from the definition of $A_{0j}[\ ]$ in **4**.

Hence, the relative marginal social utilities, to which any steady-state welfare prices must be equated, do satisfy

$$u_j[c^*]/u_1[c^*] = A_{0j}[1 + R]/A_{01}[1 + R],$$

$$(j = 2,\ldots,n) \quad [12]$$

which are the bourgeois competitive prices of **4** with $1 + R = (1 + g)(1 + \rho)$ QED.

This establishes the fundamental result.

THEOREM. *Optimal steady-state valuation for maximum per capita welfare as defined in **6** must satisfy equal rates of profit per industry (and hence, generally, unequal rates of surplus value or of markups on direct-labor alone).*

DYNAMIC PRICING

In an obvious way, the present theorem generalizes to any optimal balanced growth the golden-rule optimality condition deduced in the cited Weizsäcker–Samuelson paper, which assumed $\rho = 0$. The present demonstration worked with fixed coefficients a_0 and a. If these coefficients are at all variable, the case against Marxian values of **5** and in favor of Walras–Ricardo pricing of (now-minimized) elements of **4** is all the stronger.

Even where the system satisfies regularity conditions that deduce the asymptotic relevance of steady-state pricing in accordance with **4**, there will be long periods of time when an optimal program calls for changing prices, as defined in **9**. The correct steady-state relations of **4** readily generalize to these correct dynamic pricing relations in a way that the Marxian relations of **5** cannot.

OSCILLATORY PATHOLOGY

It is instructive to consider the singular, but possible case, first pointed out by Sutherland (4), in which the system fails to approach the steady-state turnpike but instead oscillates periodically along its optimal path. I am indebted to Prof. Martin Weitzman of MIT for an ingenious modified variant of Sutherland's example that nicely illustrates the need for periodic dynamic cum-profit pricing.

Weitzman assumes

$$\begin{bmatrix} a_0 \\ \hline a \end{bmatrix} = \begin{bmatrix} 1 & 1 & 0 \\ 0 & 0 & 0 \\ 0 & 0 & 1 \\ 0 & 0 & 0 \end{bmatrix}, u[c_1^t, c_2^t, c_3^t] = (c_1^t c_3^t)^{1/2}, \quad [13]$$

i.e., direct labor alone can in one period produce bread or grapejuice; grapejuice alone ripens in one more period into wine. Consumers then always spend half their incomes on bread, half on wine, having no interest in grapejuice except as it contributes to availability of wine.

A planner maximizes, for $g = 0$, $1 + \rho = D$, after substitutions,

$$\underset{c_1{}^t}{\text{Max}} \sum_1^\infty (1 - c_1{}^{t-1})^{1/2}(c_1{}^t)^{1/2}D^{-t} \quad \text{s.t.} \quad c_1{}^0 \text{ given.} \quad [14]$$

The Euler condition implies

$$c_1{}^{t+1}/(1 - c_1{}^t) = D^2/[c_1{}^t/(1 - c_1{}^{t-1})] \quad [15]$$

$$= y = D^2/y^{t-1} . \quad [16]$$

Note that **15** and **16** define the meaning of y^t. Also that, from now on, for brevity, I skip the subscript in $c_1{}^t$.

A turnpike is obviously at

$$y^{t+1} = y^t = y^* = D = c^*/(1 - c^*) \quad [17]$$

$$c^* = D/(1 + D).$$

But an optimal motion of period 2 is defined by

$$y^{2t} \equiv y^0 \equiv c^1/(1 - c^0) \quad [18]$$

$$y^{2t+1} = D^2/y^{2t} = D^2(1 - c^0)/c^1$$

$$c^1 = \{D^2(1 - c^0)/c^0\}/\{1 + D^2(1 - c^0)/c^0\}$$

with

$$(\dots c^{2t}, c^{2t+1}, c^{2t+2}, c^{2t+3}, \dots) = (\dots, c^0, c^1, c^0, c^1, \dots).$$

Actually, such a periodic notion is the only permanent-time optimal motion satisfying the transversality condition at infinity.

A numerical example, in which $D = 2$, $c^0 = 1/6$, gives $c^* = 2/3$, $c^1 = 20/21$.

What about prices? Their steadiest state is to oscillate in an every-other period fashion. The relative price ratio is given by

$$(P_3/P_1)^{2t} = c^0/(1 - c^1) = 7/2 \quad [19]$$

$$(P_3/P_1)^{2t+1} = c^1/(1 - c^0) = 8/7$$

Suppose we, by convention, set the money wage to be a constant, $W^t \equiv W$. Then the profit rate must fluctuate periodically, with D_e for even years and D_o for odd years. Also

$$D^2 = D_o E_e \quad [21]$$

$$P_j{}^{2t} = WD_o, \qquad P_j{}^{2t+1} = WD_e \qquad (j = 1,2) \quad [22]$$

$$P_3{}^{2t} = P_2{}^{2t-1}D_o, \qquad P_3{}^{2t+1} = P_2{}^{2t}D_e$$

$$= WD_eD_o \qquad\qquad = WD_oD_e$$

$$= WD^2 \qquad\qquad\qquad = WD^2$$

$$P_3{}^{2t}/P_1{}^{2t} = WD^2/WD_0 \;, \qquad P_3{}^{2t+1}/P_1{}^{2t+1} = WD^2/WD_e$$

$$= D_e \qquad\qquad\qquad\qquad = D_0$$

$$= 7/2 \qquad\qquad\qquad\qquad = 8/7$$

As a check $D_eD_0 = 4 = D^2$, as in 21. [Note: The preceding paragraph, with Equations [19]-[22], was altered by Samuelson in 1977.]

Note: Not even periodic "values" pricing, with uniform Marxian markup on direct-labor alone (*none* on grapejuice ripening into wine!), can sustain the planner's ideal optimal path.

Remark: Weitzman's example has the remarkable property, lacked by Sutherland's original cited example, that for R in $D = 1 + R$ sufficiently near to zero, we still have oscillations. (Actually, at $R = 0 = D - 1$, we encounter some problems for convergence of the infinite sum.)

Weitzman, by his example, and by one that is isomorphic with Sutherland's technology, refuted my suspicions that (*1*) Sutherland's pathological, permanent oscillations depend on *jointness* of production; or that (*2*) the pathology depends on bang-bang boundary inequalities of Pontryagin–Kuhn–Tucker type rather than nice Euler–Weierstrass equalities of an interior maximum. However, the fact that, subtracting ever so small positive ϵ from Weitzman's exponent of $1/2$ will kill permanent oscillations, confirms the view that, if in Max $\Sigma_1{}^\infty U[Z^t, Z^{t+1}]D^{-t}$, where Z^t is a scalar, U is so strongly concave in terms of its arguments as to have at the $Z^t = Z^*$ golden-rule state a negative definite Hessian matrix of second-cross derivatives:

$$U_{ii}{}^* < 0, \; U_{11}{}^*U_{22}{}^* - U_{12}{}^{*2} > 0 \qquad (i = 1,2) \qquad [23]$$

then permanent undamped oscillations are *impossible* in an optimal infinite-time solution. The stability of the Euler solutions to

$$0 = DU_2(Z^{t-1}, Z^t) + U_1(Z^t, Z^{t+1}) \qquad [24]$$

around the turnpike level

$$0 = DU_2(Z^*, Z^*) + U_1[Z^*, Z^*] \qquad [25]$$

depends on the stability of the associated linear system for deviation from equilibrium $z^t \sim Z^t - Z^*$,

$$0 = DU_{21}{}^*z^{t-1} + (U_{11}{}^* + DU_{22}{}^*)z^t + U_{12}{}^*z^{t+1}. \qquad [26]$$

This in turn, for $D = 1$ and all values of D sufficiently near to 1, depends on the characteristic roots of the associated polynomial

$$0 = DU_{21}{}^* + (U_{11}{}^* + DU_{22}{}^*)\lambda + U_{12}{}^*\lambda^2. \qquad [27]$$

But, because of 23, the discriminant here is positive and none of the reciprocal real roots can be 1 or -1. Hence, a damped root is assured, which guarantees topologically a permanent-path asymptote to the Z^* turnpike. To supplement this all-too-heuristic preliminary discussion, the reader will wish to consult earlier work by Kurz (5), Liviatan and Samuelson (6), Levhari and Liviatan (7), and Samuelson (8).

I thank the National Science Foundation for financial aid and Norma Wasser for editorial assistance. My debt to Prof. Martin Weitzman is great and obvious. The present application draws upon the post-Ramsey contributions of many writers—as for example, Uzawa, Koopmans, Cass, Samuelson, Morishima, Gale, and many others.

1. Samuelson, P. A. (1970) "The 'transformation' from Marxian 'values' to competitive 'prices'," *Proc. Nat. Acad. Sci. USA* **67**, 423–425.
2. Von Weizsäcker, C. C. & Samuelson, P. A. (1971) "A new labor theory of value for rational planning through use of the bourgeois profit rate," *Proc. Nat. Acad. Sci. USA* **68**, 1192–1194.
3. Ramsey, F. P. (1928) "A mathematical theory of saving," *Econ. J.* **38**, 543–59.
4. Sutherland, W. R. S. (1970) "On optimal development in a multi-sectoral economy: The discounted case," *Rev. Econ. Stud.* **37**, 585–90.
5. Kurz, M. (1968) "The general instability of a class of competitive growth processes," *Rev. Econ. Stud.* **35**, 155–174.
6. Liviatan, N. & Samuelson, P. (1969) "Notes on turnpikes: Stable and unstable," *J. Econ. Theory* 454–475.
7. Levhari, D. & Liviatan, N. (1972), "On stability in the saddle-point sense," *Journal of Economic Theor.* **4**, 88–93.
8. Samuelson, P. (1972) "The general saddlepoint property of optimal-control motions," *J. Econ. Theor.* **5**, 102–20.

227

The Economics of Marx: An Ecumenical Reply[*]

I am sorry to have incurred the displeasure of my old friend Abba Lerner [2, 1972] by my conciliatory statement that, *if* there is insight into the laws of motion of capitalism from Marx's hypothesis that real wages get set at a susbsistence cost-of-reproduction-of-man level, then that same insight can be expressed (and better expressed if we want to avoid contradiction with the arbitrage laws of ruthless competition) in terms of a model of "prices" (in which rates of profit on all cost outlays are uniform throughout all industries) rather than in terms of a *Capital* (Volume I) model of surplus-value (in which the rates of surplus in ratio to direct wage cost alone are assumed uniform for all industries). Perhaps I should have called stronger attention to the italicized "if," but I did explicitly warn all readers that I was meticulously refraining from pronouncing any judgments on empirical fruitfulness in order to concentrate on the purely-deductive logic of the Marxian and related models.

It would be sophomoric not to realize that, when there are other bottlenecks to production than labor, in the form of land and other primary natural resources and in terms of the time-phasing of production which requires us

to face up to the use of raw materials and to non-instantaneous production processes, then the undiluted labor theory of value will not hold. But I ask any jury to read my paper and decide whether I am to be scolded for having overlooked these qualifications; or, rather, commended for having pointed them all out—as well as the often-neglected consideration that heterogeneous labor cannot be reduced to a common denominator of socially-necessary labor independently of demand conditions unless any two such kinds of labor happen, singularly, to be infinitely substitutable for each other in *every* use. My section on the shortcomings of the labor theory of value deals with these issues; the whole rest of my paper deals with the complication that the passage of time makes in causing price ratios to deviate from embodied-labor-contents ratios.

I do plead guilty to having dealt with matters that are of interest for the history of economic thought; but I hope the judge's sentence will not be a harsh one in view of the extenuating circumstance that my paper did appear in a journal devoted to historical subjects. I also wonder whether the charge by the prosecuting attorney is not overly strong: only a Rip van Winkle who has snoozed through the economic discussions these last twenty years among such modern economists as Joan Robinson, Solow, von Neumann, Sraffa, Dorfman-Solow-Samu-

[*] My thanks go to the National Science Foundation for financial aid and to Ms. Jillian Pappas for editorial assistance.

elson, Pasinetti, von Weizsäcker, Kaldor, Swan, Meade, Uzawa, and others too numerous to list could claim that models in which labor is the only nonproducible factor "have no place in today's economic analysis." To whatever the degree that my formulations and emphasis "impinge on the honor of scientific inquiry," I do not think I would add to that honor by refusing to Marxian scholars the indulgences that we so freely grant each other.

In this connection I must confess that I did lean over backwards, in comparing formulations that are peculiarly Marxian (as in the case of Volume I's values) with more traditional bourgeois concepts, to try to make the best sense out of them that I could, explicitly passing up a few opportunities to expose confusions and logical contradictions. If such be lapses from impartiality, I hope the sin will be considered a venial one, particularly since a Machiavellian reader might suspect me of the opposite tactic in the form of giving the Marxian theory all the rope it could use.

Actually, there is much in Lerner's writings on these subjects with which I am in essential agreement. How could it be otherwise when, man and boy, I have received so much consumers' surplus from the socially-necessary labor time and forgone embodied-sunshine that I have invested in reading his works? Therefore, most of this note can be devoted to the constructive task of elucidating some of the properties of these Marxian constructs, a task that seems to have been much neglected both by the system's partisans and its opponents.

First, though, let me say a word on a problem that does concern Lerner and many others. Suppose you think that the best way to express the concept of "exploitation" is in a formulation that states, both as an ethical axiom and a feasible program for rectification of the distribution of income, that whenever a non-laborer receives part of the social product there should be a presumption that this "unearned increment" be transferred from him to the propertyless laborers; and that the historic labor theory of value only muddies up the issues. Are you given no pause by the fact that eloquent expositions of this view over a third of a century, many of the best being by Lerner himself, have not succeeded in exorcizing or putting to rout

the Marxian formulations based upon deviations of capitalistic or mixed-economy pricing from labor-theory-of-value norms? I ask this as a question. Whatever its answer, it would indeed be a cause for self-reproach *if*, in my attempt to be "objective," my formulations make life more difficult for "sophisticated Marxists" to arrive at a better understanding of truth. Rereading my paper as a whole, I cannot honestly report that it strikes me as undermining those who seek to make Marxism a living science rather than an embalmed ideology; but it may be that I underestimate the degree to which papers like mine serve as ammunition for nonsophisticated traditionalists in their polemics against new thinking.

It may be that we live in an age where "science as usual" is no longer a tenable position. I've quoted elsewhere the answer by the great antifascist scholar, Gaetano Salvemini, to a question by one of his history students, who asked whether one should publish a truth that might give comfort to the enemies of mankind. Salvemini instantly replied: "Publish, though the heavens fall!" Perhaps in a simpler age no one really expected the heavens to fall. Yet, what one loses in the short run by foresaking guile, one picks up in the long run by earning a reputation for being without guile. So let me reiterate what some may deem an admission.

Even if we regard Marx's value analysis of Volume I as only an *approximation*, for the understanding of a subsistence wage model it *is* a simplifying description. (As I argued, it was simple enough for Karl Marx, who possessed mathematical ability but lacked mathematical training, to understand at a time when he could not manage the algebra of the more consistent model being approximated.) To illustrate this, let me propose to Professor Lerner a little game, one which he is to solve working against the clock as if he were a student in an hour exam rather than a scholar in the library with all the time in the world to think through every aspect of a problem.

For the next edition of my textbook I have worked out a little coal-corn example to illustrate stationary equilibrium and balanced growth. Two hours of direct labor produces one unit of coal. To produce one unit of corn takes two hours of direct labor and in addition one unit of coal as intermediate product. One does not have to be a student of Leontief to realize that, if workers are to be provided daily with one unit of corn as subsistence, each must work four hours a day: two hours of live labor, so to speak, in corn plus the two hours of dead labor in the needed coal. If, in contrast, the market real wage gets set so low that workers have to work 12 hours a day for their one corn of subsistence, Marx would say, "Since workers work eight hours of the day for employers and only four hours for themselves, there is a mark-up over wages of 200 percent as the 'rate of surplus value'."

Now all this is truly a *simple* way of putting things—even if it is not quite exact in the way that it implicitly treats what would be the correct market costing of the coal. You do not have to be a Lerner to understand this terse exposition. But let us now state the *same* facts in the correct bourgeois or Ricardian way. If, in five minutes time, you can work out what will be the correct uniform rate of profit and the corresponding relative prices, then you are indeed a wizard at logic and calculation. (This is because you are guessing the correct solution of a quadratic equation; if I was not addressing a beginner audience, you might have to solve a 15th degree polynomial for a 15-sector model.)

It will be noted that this trivial example departs from the timeless labor-only technology of the undiluted labor theory of value *both* in the Volume I approximation case of "values" *and* in the exact Volume III case of "price of production." Hence the example provides a nice refutation of the preconception that Professor Lerner begins with in his opening paragraph. "Transforming values into prices of production," which is what I surveyed, is not—either to sophisticated Marxists or careful readers of my paper—a process of going from an unrealistic labor-only timeless model to a more realistic model that admits the heterogeneity of labor and the presence of scarce primary factors such as land. Before and after the transformation we stay with the assumption of no land, no heterogeneity of labor, and a significant problem of the time-phasing of production. And we stay with the assumption that Lerner considers "ridiculous" or tautologically "meaningless"—namely that the real wage gets fixed at

the minimum of subsistence or cost of reproduction of labor power. This assumption is so central that I find it odd to find it described by the adjective "silent."

Before moving on to points of analytical substance, it would be churlish of me not to agree that it was probably unfortunate to use the adjective "exploitative" as a synonym for "minimum-of-subsistence" as applied to the wage rate. At the least, I should have stressed the pejorative nature of the word.

Finally, any reader who agrees that I was too "conciliatory" in the section Professor Lerner quotes should feel free to exclude that section. After the censor has deleted my p. 422, the article will be as much of value as before.[1]

Laws of Motion of Values and Prices

Imagine a "values" or a "prices" system that runs for a century or for decades after its start in 1867. What hypotheses or prophecies does the logic of the model imply?

Marx himself enunciated a Law of the falling rate of profit—and also, more ambiguously, a Law of immiseration of the working class, which with some straining is often interpreted as the hypothesis that the real wage will fall. What has been glimpsed in the literature, but not I think sufficiently emphasized, is the logical incompatibility of these two laws as stated.

---

[1] In my original paper I tried to take notice of every alternative treatment of the transformation problem that I could locate in the literature. Inevitably, I missed a few, as for example one by my friend Nicholas Georgescu-Roegen in the 1960 Frisch *Festschrift*, and reprinted from *Econometrica* in *Analytical economics: Issues and problems* [1, 1966, Ch. 12]. As new solutions accumulate I hope, at another time, to comment on them. Since my article appeared, C. C. von Weizsäcker's valuable monograph has become available [6, 1971].

I might also mention that while Lerner finds me too soft on Marx, some other correspondents have written to say that I do not do justice to Marx's views about the central importance of labor when I characterize his "values" as merely marked-up labor. For the transformation problem all that is necessary to say is that the actual numbers in Marx's own tables are in fact *proportional* to embodied labor contents—but that is not to assert that all there is to Marx is a set of arithmetical tables.

The following theorems provide an important correction:

LAW OF INCREASING RATE OF PROFIT

(*a*) Every viable new invention must, if the competitive real wage should stay the same (whether at the subsistence or any other level), necessarily lead to a higher competitive rate of profit.

(*b*) In a regime where Volume I's values prevail, every viable new invention must, if that regime's real wage should stay the same (whether at the subsistence or any other level), necessarily lead to a higher rate of surplus-value.

For a proof of this law, the reader need only look at my Figures 2(c) and 2(f). These depict the now-familiar factor-price tradeoff between real wages and the rates of return, a relation already perceived by Ricardo and von Thünen but rediscovered in the modern literature only a dozen years ago. A viable invention, whether "labor-saving" or "capital-saving," will in either regime shift its frontier *outward:* moving outward from one negatively-sloped curve to another can obviously rule out any southwest movement as Marx's simultaneously-held two laws would require. Q.E.D.

The same thing can be put in another way, one more appropriate in view of the known fact that profit rates wandered rather trendlessly in the century after *Das Kapital:*

LAW OF INCREASING REAL WAGES

(*a*) Whenever viable inventions or successful thrift cause the competitive profit rate to stay the same or to fall, the real wage (whatever its commodity composition) must necessarily rise.

(*b*) Within a regime of values, the effect of viable inventions and/or accumulation of superior capital goods must, if the rate of surplus-value falls or stays the same, necessarily cause the real wage to be higher.

No separate proof of this law is needed since it is merely a variant of the law of rising profit. What does need observing is this:

In 1894 an acute reader, with the more than a million words of text of *Das Kapital* before him, should have been led *on the basis of it* to extrapolate for the next decades or centuries in the advanced countries a steady growth in real wage rates and/or in profit rates, pretty much as actually happened. Preoccupation with non-labor bottlenecks, such as future land scarcity, as in the case of the neoclassical economist Knut Wicksell, would have led to more dire forebodings than turned out to be actually warranted for the advanced societies and preoccupation with qualifications introduced by joint production would have been picayunish.

How neglected a field for analytical research Marxian models have been that this truism should have largely escaped notice![2] So rosy a conclusion, if noticed, would no doubt have been resisted by those hopeful of a near-term collapse of capitalism and an imminent socialist revolution. My point is that a correct understanding of the Marxian tableaux would itself offer little comfort for such radical critics. No doubt an erudite scholar could quote copious references recognizing these simple deductive truths. I must rest content with citing Joan Robinson's 1942 essay [4] on Marx.[3]

Let us see what is misleading about the usual Marxian derivation of the necessary fall in the profit rate,[4] *R*, of the following type:

[2] My brief quotation in footnote 34, p. 422, of Engel's 1891 words shows that he momentarily glimpsed this truth but apparently did not appreciate its vital significance: ". . . with every new invention . . . this surplus of its [labor's] product over its daily cost increases" [3, 1968; this is the 1891 introduction by Engels to a reissue of Marx's 1849, *Wage labour and capital*].

[3] "Marx can only demonstrate a falling tendency in profits by abandoning his argument that real wages tend to be constant. This drastic inconsistency he seems to have overlooked, for when he is discussing the falling tendency of profits he makes no reference to the rising tendency of real wages which it entails" [4, pp. 42–43]. One blemish must be noted: there is a suggestion on p. 44 that the ingenious reader could contrive an exception, *i.e.*, provide a numerical example in which the rate of profit falls while the real wage is constant (by having output in her example rise to below 105, say to 104). Written before the ideas of Leontief and Sraffa became widespread, this is an understandable slip of the pen, one which unfortunately is repeated in the 1966 second edition through oversight.

[4] In my main paper I used lower-case letters for value-regime magnitudes and capital letters for their price-regime counterparts, namely (c_j, v_j, s_j) versus (C_j, V_j, S_j). To be logical I should have used R rather than r for $(\Sigma S_j)/(\Sigma C_j + \Sigma V_j)$. Hence, here I shall distinguish R so defined from

$$R = \frac{\Sigma S}{\Sigma C + \Sigma V}$$

$$= \frac{\Sigma S}{\Sigma V} \frac{\Sigma V}{\Sigma C + \Sigma V} \quad .$$

= Rate of surplus value

$\times$ (1 − organic composition of capital)

(1) $R = SV (1 - K)$

Obviously, if SV stays constant and K rises, it is an inescapable tautology that R must fall. As Marx and Engels looked around Manchester and London and observed the advancement of technology and the elaboration of capital equipment, how natural it was to postulate "steady growth in $\Sigma C/\Sigma V$ or K." Couple this with the conviction that exploitation of labor continued unabated, and identify this insight with the postulate "constancy of SV, the rate of surplus value." The rest of the demonstration then becomes pure arithmetic. Let us see why these postulates represent misinterpretations of the processes Marx had in mind.

There are several different confusions involved here. The primary one is this: in those cases where unchanged rate of surplus-value can be loosely identified with unchanged real wage, the only reason why profit-maximizing managers incur the additional expense of a high organic composition of capital is because such new techniques do provide them with *extra* rather than unchanged surplus-value. In other words, Marx is often holding constant what cannot be held constant except by contradiction to ruthless exploitative competition.

Indeed the Marx-like reasoning is precisely what might go on in the mind of an entrepreneur as he *rejects* a new roundabout technique that does *not* pay: "What, shall I let this highly-capital-intensive innovation that produces no extra surplus-value for me rob me of my profit? No, I shall reject it." To this an acute logician might be tempted to object:

$r = (\Sigma s_j)/(\Sigma c_j + \Sigma v_j)$. Likewise I might better have used for the rate of surplus-value not the lower-case letter s, but should have distinguished $(\Sigma s_j)/(\Sigma v_j)$ from $(\Sigma S_j)/(\Sigma V_j)$. I shall now call these respectively sv and SV, with industry counterparts being sv_j and SV_j. The organic composition of capital also requires two symbols, K and k for $(\Sigma C_j)/(\Sigma C_j + \Sigma V_j)$ and $(\Sigma c_j)/(\Sigma c_j + \Sigma v_j)$; industry K_j and k_j are defined by omitting the "Σ" symbols.

"Maybe one single entrepreneur doesn't want to adopt the new technique, but competition may force *all* of the entrepreneurs to do so, even against their will—in the sense that they would curse the day the new technique got invented." But on second thought, our logician will realize that in those situations where inventions do force a reduction in the rate of profit, it is precisely because the cheapening of goods' prices is greater than the subsequent increase in money wage rates—or in short, as students of Leontief and Sraffa know, the forcing down of the profit rate is the concomitant of the forcing up of the real wage rate.

I say this is the primary confusion involved in the conventional Marxist tautologous derivation of a lower profit rate. But there are others. Consider for example the case where production gets elaborated into more numerous stages of production. Naturally then the average ratio of labor costs in any one stage must fall relative to other costs, and must fall relative to the fraction of total value-added represented by interest. In such cases it is unnatural to couple an increase in the organic composition of capital with an unchanged rather than an increased rate of surplus-value. Incidentally, the increase in SV or sv need involve little cause for self-congratulation on the part of the capitalists, for the real wage they have to pay may be little reduced and the profit they earn little increased; nor need such an outcome be a matter of great concern to the workers, since the posited increase in the rate of surplus-value is not associated with a cut in wages: this shows once again that giving the title of "rate of exploitation" to the technical ratio which is the "rate of surplus-value" can be a very misleading procedure. (I mean misleading to Marxian critics themselves.)

Three related cases can help to drive home the fact that viable improvements in technology cannot, despite the formula (1), drive down the rate of profit without increasing the real wage.

First, consider a one-good case. Corn is produced by nine units of labor and .1 unit of corn. Along comes a new invention with a higher organic composition of capital, say requiring .2 of corn. Now it is easy enough to specify such cases in which the rate of profit will fall: thus, if the direct labor requirements stay at nine, the higher organic composition will mean less profit left over than before at every rate of unchanged surplus-value. But who in his right mind would adopt a process that costs more of one input and no less of any other? Certainly no viable competitor. For the invention to be a viable one, it would have to bring some advantage along with the disadvantage of a higher organic composition of capital. Thus, suppose that .2 of corn goes along with a reduction of required direct labor to 8½. The invention still will not be viable *at any positive profit rate*. Only if the .2 of corn is accompanied by direct labor requirement of less than eight will the new invention be capable of displacing the old technique—and even then it will be able to do so only at low-enough profit rates, since at profit rates above 400 percent, no economy on direct labor can ever make the invention pay. Summary: in a one-good world every viable increase in organic composition automatically raises the rate of surplus-value.

All this supposes that when a new invention is chosen, it must be selected over the old technique which remains feasible. Thus, one may lose the wheel to lightning or a thief; but one cannot lose the notion of roundness. To be meticulously pedantic, there have been cultures which have lost technological knowledge—but that is not the bourgeois capitalism that Marx and Engels so eloquently described in *The communist manifesto*.

The second case to illustrate the confusion is that in which the organic compositions of capital are equal in all industries but are greater after the invention than before. Again it can be shown that a viable invention means that, at the same or lower profit rates, the new regime has a higher rate of surplus-value and real wage than before. A reader well-versed in Marx should be able to replicate the formal proof.

The third case easy to analyze is the singular one I introduced, in which the internal-organic compositions of capital are equal for all industries. In this case, let us concentrate on the factor sharing implied in producing the batch of consumption-wage-goods, again under the simplifying Santa Claus assumption that the iron ration of subsistence involves the same propor-

tions of goods as do the constant-capitals needed for production. Concentrating only on a society producing goods in these singular proportions, we will find that there is no need to distinguish between R and r, SV and sv, or K and k. Actually, in this singular case, it is as if we had one composite good, with its specified direct labor requirements and its specified amount of itself needed as raw materials. Hence we are back in the one-good world of my first case. After some manipulation, Marx's formula (1) can now be thrown into the form

$$R = \frac{w_{max} - w}{w} (1 - K)$$

Now an invention will be viable only if it raises the maximum real wage that could be paid workers if profits were zero, which I have written as w_{max}. If now we keep the rate of surplus-value the same, we are giving labor a higher real wage proportional to the increase in technical product. If capital's share stays the same fraction, and an increase in the capital-output ratio takes place (for that is what the organic composition of capital can be correlated with in this singular case), it is no wonder that the profit rate falls. Once again the well-known fact that the capital-output ratio has not steadily risen in the last century should deter one from facilely assuming a grand law of the rising organic composition of capital.

I have not taken the time to work through every possible permutation and combination of assumptions. But any reader should be convinced that the truth of my two upside-down Marxian laws are valid derivations of the Marxian systems and that they do not contradict the familiar Marx tautology of (1).[5]

[5] One should not try to prove too much. It is easy for me to write down valid cases in which a viable invention will raise K, leave SV the same, and lower R. The point is that every such case involves a real wage that rises even though the Marxian "rate of exploitation" remains the same. The actual facts of American and European history for the last century involve a good approximation to Bowley's Law of constancy of the share of wages in rising national income, along with a fairly stable capital-output ratio. This pattern of rapidly rising real wages is quite compatible with constancy of

In conclusion, let me say that the propositions that I have enunciated should be carefully audited by economists of all descriptions. For I have found that it is a solitary existence when writing about Marx, and one misses the constructive give-and-take from other economists that serves so effectively to correct the mistakes of the lone-wolf scholar. Karl Marx

---

the rate of surplus value, although it is only in singular cases that factor shares and SV can be tightly correlated.

By the way, here is the answer to the puzzle presented to Lerner: in the regime of prices, instead of having uniform rates of surplus-value (or mark-ups on labor alone) of 200 percent, we must have a uniform profit rate of exactly 100 percent per period; coal then will cost twice 2 labor hours, and corn will cost 12 labor hours—$\{2(2 \text{ hrs.}) + 2 \text{ hrs.}\}$ $(1 + 1)$. Price ratio of corn-to-coal will be $12/4 = 3$ as against values ratio of $2 = 12/6 = 4$ of embodied labor / 2 of embodied labor. Profit rate of $R = 1$ is the relevant root of the quadratic $2(1 + R)^2 + 2(1 + R) = 12$. Note that in the correct version workers are still, so to speak, working 8 hours of the day for the other fellow.

would be the first to understand this remark.

PAUL A. SAMUELSON
Massachusetts Institute of Technology

REFERENCES

1. GEORGESCU-ROEGEN, N. *Analytical economics: Issues and problems.* Cambridge, Mass.: Harvard University Press, 1966.
2. LERNER, A. P. "A Note on 'Understanding the Marxian Notion of Exploitation'," *J. Econ. Lit.*, March 1972, *10*(1), pp. 50–51.
3. MARX, K. and ENGELS, F. *Selected works.* New York: International Publishers, 1968.
4. ROBINSON, J. An *essay on Marxian economics.* London: MacMillan, 1942 and 1966.
5. SAMUELSON, P. "Understanding the Marxian Notion of Exploitation: A Summary of the So-Called Transformation Problem Between Marxian Values and Competitive Prices," *J. Econ. Lit.*, June 1971, *9*(2), pp. 399–431.
6. VON WEIZSÄCKER, C. C. *Steady state capital theory.* Berlin: Sprinter-Verlag, 1971.

228

Samuelson's "Reply on Marxian Matters"

Martin Bronfenbrenner [1, 1973] has generously tried to clarify issues raised by my two JEL papers on Marxian analysis and various replies that have come into the *Journal*. All interested in the overdue task of secularizing Marxian economics will be grateful to him. To further the process of convergence toward understanding, I offer the following brief commentary on the most important points raised.

1. *Values model as an "approximation" to competitive price model?* This is an issue of some interest. But it was not at all dealt with by my two papers. All that needs to be said here is this:

i Since "values" and "prices" agree when organic compositions of capital are equal, their results must perforce be strongly positively correlated when labor intensities are not too different.

ii An invention that, for the same profit rate, lowers the ratio of prices to the wage, will also lower the ratio of values to the wage when the rate of surplus value is held constant in a Volume I regime of values.

iii On the other hand, for many purposes the values approximation to prices is a shockingly poor one. Thus, in choosing among different technologies, anyone who works completely in the realm of values will find that, at *every* rate of surplus value, the technology chosen to minimize values is precisely that appropriate to a system with stocks of raw material as plentiful as in an undiluted labor-theory-of-value state. The prices regime has the advantage that it selects at each profit rate only that technology optimal for it (including, be it noted, the possibility of reswitching); also, as will be seen shortly, such minimized prices can properly signal the terms on which choice of the consumption-goods mix should be made for maximum welfare in planned optimal-control steady state.

2. *The "algorithmic transformation" from the "values" model to the "prices" model (or vice versa), is it truly a process of rejection of the former and replacement by the latter?* Here is my true crime. I pointed out the blunt truth. And this has been construed as an attack on Marx, covert or explicit.

Why is this truth thought to be an attack on Marx? And why is the simple truth to be regarded as the blunt truth? Non-Marxians and Marxians can profitably ponder over the questions. While they are doing so, let me develop two related points.

i My vantage point in the discussion was *not* neoclassical. It was Sraffian! Or alternatively stated, it was pre-Marxian: it was not what Cobb-Douglas or J. B. Clark (or, heaven forbid, what Böhm-Bawerk) would have said; it is what Ricardo and Smith would have said, once the ground rules were explained to them about (a) stationary states, (b) profit-seeking competition, (c) etc. What I said is exactly what Joan Robinson, no neoclassicist, has been saying all along—only I said it at such tedious length and in such pedantical detail that, one would have thought, no reader could find anything to quarrel with except its boringness.

ii Wassily Leontief (whom the besieged editor of this *Journal* asked to serve as a referee of one or another submission) has suggested to me that the valid "erase-and-replace" point could not help being recognized as valid if I would show how to transform from some third fantastic model to either of the "values" or "prices" models. I fear Leontief is an optimist, but let me put the matter to the test.

Contrast a "values model" (with its equal percentage markup on labor outlays) with a bizarre "gibberish model" (defined to involve equal percentage markup on raw-materials outlays only). I banish to an extended footnote[1]

---

[1] Assume technically that 1 labor and 1 coal produces 1 corn; and 1 labor produces 1 coal. Let the minimum-subsistence wage be 1/6 corn per 1 labor. The "values" regime is then implied to be: rate of surplus value = 200 percent, (value of coal)/wage = 3, (value of corn)/wage = (1)3 + 3 = 6. In short, $(X_1, X_2) = (3,6)$. Now for the gibberish regime, where Y_1 stands for the "gibberish equilibrium value" in each of the two departments relative to the wage: $Y_1 = 0 + 1 + g0 = 1$; $Y_2 = (1)(1) + 1 + g(1)(1)$; and $Y_2 = 6$, if and only if the equalized rate of gibberish, g, is 500 percent or $g = 5.0$ Now, do we need a Bortkiewicz or an aficionado of matrix algebra to tell us how we get from $(X_1, X_2) = (3,6)$ to $(Y_1, Y_2) = (1,6)$? Of course not. We drop (thud!) the X_1 equations and replace them by the gibberish-de-

the arithmetic of the "*algorithm* of transformation," which, despite Bronfenbrenner's tentative wording (". . . such an algorithm, if [!] it exists . . ."), cannot help but exist. Here, I merely summarize the algorithm's exact logical nature: "To go from the regime of 'gibberish equilibrium' to that of 'values equilibrium,' (a)

---

fined Y_1 equations. Or, if we use Bortkiewicz's route, we write $Y_1 = X_1(Y_1/X_1)$. Q.E.D. [Incidentally, Bronfenbrenner's own suggestion for the transformation process, as given in his footnote 4, is *identical* to the Bortkiewicz-Seton-Samuelson algorithm once he completes it by solving his two relations for his unknown p_1/p_2 conversion ratio, leading to Bortkiewicz's quadratic equation for the 2-department case.]

A different point: When Bronfenbrenner writes, "Marx tried nobly with inadequate mathematical background—as had David Ricardo a generation before him—to work out the transformation algorithm for his system," he incorrectly diagnoses where the difficulty of the problem is. Thus, Ricardo's tergiversations in connection with the labor theory of value [I love thee. I love thee not. I love . . .] had little to do with his inability to grapple with the correct algebra of equalized-profit rates. It had to do with the first point that I have termed a non-issue for this *JEL* discussion: Ricardo debated with himself as to whether it was or wasn't a good enough *expository approximation* to make total costs proportional to labor costs alone. As far as I can recall, Ricardo never wrote down an incorrect cost-cum-profit relation in those cases where he chose to grapple with the non-simplified case. The issue is not one of esoteric matrix operations, but only of clear thinking.

Lest the present exchange set back the cause of mutual understanding, let me comment on Bronfenbrenner's two ambiguities in Marx "most relevant to our present discussion." First, in every tableau of prices that Marx derived *after* his transformation from values to prices, Marx writes down (as he should and must!) *unequal* rates of surplus value. Therefore, why muddy the clear waters with this query? Second, it is of no significance what scale units are used so long as any analyst is free to equate between the two regimes any one (but only one!) of the following alternatives: (*i*) sum of surpluses, (*ii*) sum of industries' gross outputs evaluated in each regime's relative evaluation, or (*iii*) a chosen numeraire good's unity reference point. Where Marx went unambiguously wrong was in equating *both* (*i*) and (*ii*), which is impossible save in my Santa Claus case of equal-internal-organic compositions. The validity of my contention on this point, be it noted, stands even if we drop a minimum-subsistence wage as unrealistic.

ignore the behavior equations of gibberish, and (b) write down the behavior equations postulated for values."

Could anything be more plain? Or less controversial?

3. "I *find my paradigm easier to understand, you find your paradigm easier to understand, and there is no commensurability between them?*" Here is a point that must be handled with delicacy. Perhaps one can specify cases where such argumentation can be validly made. Without pronouncing on that issue, I have to state that nine out of ten times when such arguments are used, they are misused.

One Indo-European language may be as good as another for many purposes, but it is not the case that Anglo-Saxon units of measure are as good as the metric system. A map maker who uses Euclidean geometry for areas of the globe cannot claim that his geometry is as good as that of an opponent who happens to have been brought up on spherical geometry. When Thomas Kuhn published his *Structure of scientific revolutions* in 1962, I formed the impression that his treatment of the incommensurability of different paradigms did not do justice to the degree to which one paradigm in the physical sciences often unambiguously "dominates" another. (Dr. Kuhn has since made clear that he is of a similar opinion.) But, all such surmises aside, I knew that in the social sciences the Kuhn paradigm about paradigms would be rampantly misused. This prediction has, alas, been abundantly fulfilled.

With specific application to the present subject, there is really no room for subjective judgment as to whether two *different* "transformations" can *both* be correct. This is not a matter on which, depending upon which side of the Berlin Wall you happen to have been educated, you are entitled to choose your preferred algorithm.

And what is quite a different point, if one is trying to describe correctly the arbitrage conditions that will prevail under competitive capitalism, where capitalists are free to move their funds from one department or industry to another, no one can validly assert "given my training and background and mathematical adequacies, I find it more convenient to stick with a values model than with a prices model

—however *you* may feel." (Marx, himself, did not make such a defense for a values Tableau. Successfully or unsuccessfully, he was *pursuing* the correct procedure.)

Bronfenbrenner's comparing the number of apostates from one tradition to another is germane to some issues but not, I think, to a logical procedure that leads to self-contradiction.

4. *Exception to profit-wage tradeoff?* To narrow the area of dispute, let me agree with Bronfenbrenner that it is only in a competitive closed economy with labor the only non-producible factor that simultaneous worsening of the real wage and the profit are impossible. Without diagrams, we realize that an open economy, which faces an adverse turn in its terms of trade, can experience both lower profit rate and lower real wage; and if we add further primary factors to labor—land, etc.—the correct theorem becomes "The profit rate cannot fall in a closed competitive economy at the same time that all real remunerations are also falling." To derive important results like these requires Sraffian-Leontief methods and not those of Volume I.

5. *Semantics of word "exploitation."* On the issue of the terminology of "exploitation" under bourgeois pricing, I agree with Bronfenbrenner (and Lerner and Lange earlier) that an ethical observer could chose to deplore as "exploitation" any distribution of GNP that fails to give labor 100 percent of the product.

Normative Versus Descriptive Evaluatings

Any discussion designed to clarify misunderstanding should also, if it can, advance the state of the subject. Before turning to Bronfenbrenner's six writers, I shall go into some welfare-economics issues.

Sometimes one hears it said, "Granted that the Volume III bourgeois prices model is a more correct realization of the logic of the competitive capitalist system, still the Volume I values model [even if it should be deemed redundant in providing the macroeconomic underpinning of the prices' microeconomics] is more applicable in the rational planned society that will supersede capitalism."

Von Weizsäcker and I [3, 1971] have demonstrated this to be false. Let me describe here, using the corn-coal example, a new and different theorem asserting the optimality in the omniscient good society of the "prices" pricing and the non-optimality of the "values" pricing.

Marx often spoke scathingly of Robinson Crusoe economics, a view one can sometimes sympathize with. In the writings of von Wieser, Pareto, Barone (and later denied by von Mises), there is an alternative to Crusoe—the ideal communist state. Let me stick with Sraffian-Marx coal-corn technology, but consider a Ramsey optimal-control Planner who maximizes social utility from now and forever. Thus, he omnisciently maximizes

$$u[c_1{}^0, c_2{}^0] + \frac{1}{1+\rho} u[c_1{}^1, c_2{}^1]$$
$$+ \frac{1}{(1+\rho)^2} u[c_1{}^2, c_2{}^2] + \cdots \qquad (1)$$

out to infinity, where $(c_1{}^t, c_2{}^t)$ are the coal and corn consumed per capita in the tth period. (The form of $u[,]$ is almost immaterial: it could be $\log c_1 + \log c_2$, or $-c_1{}^{-1} - c_2{}^{-1}$, or $c_1{}^{.3} c_2{}^{.4}$, etc.)

Now how shall the Planner "evaluate" coal and corn? At the (3,6; or 6/3) of the values regime, or at the (2, 6; or 6/2) of the prices regime? The following theorem is valid:

Theorem of rational evaluation. An optimal planned state will (generally) come ultimately into a stationary state. In such a steady state, its rational evaluation of corn-to-coal must be at a P_2/P_1 of the Vol. III prices regime and not at any $Value_2/Value_1$ of the Vol. I values regime.

To be specific, assume $\rho = 0$ so that there is no time preference. Assume for expositional exaggeration that available labor doubles every period. Then every technocrat, whether he be Marxian or anti-Marxian, knows the golden-rule theorem of wider-than-neoclassical applicability: the profit rate must be uniformly equal to the growth rate in every department, 100 percent, (and, hence, the rates of surplus value must be unequal for efficiency).

Lest anyone think this to be a special truth associated with the golden rule, let me point out that if $\rho = 50$ percent systematic time preference, and labor grows at $g = 33\frac{1}{3}$ percent per period—so that $(1+\rho)(1+g) = (1.50) (1.33\frac{1}{3}) = 1 + 1.0$—the same bourgeois pricing of 2 corn-for-each-6 coal is optimal for so-

ciety's consumption decisions. And using the 3
corn-for-each-6 coal of the Vol. I regime
would result in perpetual loss of social welfare!

I omit proofs of this Ramseyan "turnpike"
theorem. Note that it holds for an anti-margin-
alist fixed-coefficient technology.[2]

Reactions to Quoted Writers

It is a bit odd to be commenting on abortive
articles that have not been accepted for publication. But here are some paragraphs on each
of Bronfenbrenner's six writers, numbered in
his ordering.

1. Yes, monetary analysis is important. But
there seems no need to bring that issue into the
present discussion.

2. In a fixed-coefficient technology, no sup-
ply-of-capital-goods-cum-marginal-productivity
relations are available to determine a unique
profit rate and set of real wages. I fail to see
why *that* realization should make a modern

---

[2] See my forthcoming paper entitled "Optimality
of Profit-including Prices Under Ideal Planning."
Mention is made there of some singular cases, discussed by Sutherland, where oscillations around
the turnpike may prevail. Also, note that if consumption involves completely fixed coefficients, as
when $u \equiv \min[c_1/b_1, c_2/b_2]$, these optimality conditions become vacuous.

The optimality of equal-profit-rate pricing is all
the greater if, as in the third section of P. Sraffa's
*Production of commodities by means of commodi-
ties* [2, 1960] there is more than one technology
blue print available. Suppose, above 200 percent
profit rate and below 50 percent, method A gives
lowest bourgeois prices. Between 50 percent and
200 percent let method B do so. Now, if $\rho = 2.5$ in
equation (1), method A will ultimately be optimally used. But, if suddenly ρ changes to .45 in
an unforseen but permanent way, method A will
still be used (but presumably with more coal and
less corn consumed in the new steady state).
Alternatively, suppose we change from $\rho = 2.5$ to
$\rho = .75$, known to hold "for a long time" and
then known to be followed by a permanent change
in ρ down to $\rho = .45$. What should ideally happen
is an omniscient Planner's optimal program? He
will shift from A asymptotically to B, hold to B
for a long time, and then optimally shift back to
A. Why, when he is in B, does he put up with
the lower plateau of consumption and instantaneous utilities? Because he lacks enough raw
materials for the A regime (and, actually, if he
had them, he'd want at $\rho = .75$, to dip into them
or decumulate them). Not only are steady state
price ratios optimal, but as well their dynamic
version (inclusive of forseeable capital-gains
terms) would be optimal for the Socialist Planner.

Marxist prefer the Vol. I equal-rates-of-sur-
plus-value model to the Sraffian Vol. III prices
regime with equal profit rates. If class power is
to supply the missing equation for distribution, it
can do so for pre- and post-Marxian equation
systems with not the slightest loss of efficiency.

3. I agree that it is needful to distinguish
between (i) the undiluted-labor-theory-of-
value case, where the rates of profit and of surplus value agree in both being zero, and in
which all exchange evaluations (whether of
"values" or prices, of Vol. I or Vol. III) are
equal to total necessary labor hours (direct-
plus-indirect, live-plus-dead), and between
(ii) the case of Vol. I tableaux in which there
is a positive rate of surplus values and in which
proportionality to labor contents (rather than
equality) prevails. However, terminologically I
did refer to case (ii) as well as to case (i) by
the term "values" for the reason that it is case
(ii) with which Marx begins in his Vol. III, Ch.
IX tables of transformation.

4. My own analysis stipulated that Marx's
technical transformation slip was unimportant
(and could be non-existent in my preferred
case of equal-internal-organic compositions—
unimportant in comparison with the miscon-
ception that macroeconomic profit rates *have
to be based* on macroeconomic rates of surplus
value, and *not* vice versa). But I ask the informed reader to decide—once this point has
been granted, and all the mysteries of matrix
mumbo jumbo are understood—in what sense
the matrix expression $a_0[I-a]^{-1}(1 + s.v.)$ is truly
better at "establishing economic categories as
social categories expressive of social relations
and structure" than is the matrix expression
$a_0(1 + P_r) [I-a(1 + P_r)]^{-1}$. On reflection, is
there not seen to be involved in such a false perception an almost-comical fetishism and word
play?

5. The quoted assertion ". . . from a Marxian point of view, there is no way of understanding price formation except by way of the
value concept" is left with only religious content once Marxians perceive for themselves
that they can as well go from prices to values
as vice versa.

6. Sraffa (and Marx[3] before him) proved

---

[3] See the discussion in my footnote 1 of Bronfenbrenner text's first alleged ambiguity in Marx.

that, when organic compositions differ [whether measured by $c_i/v_i \neq c_j/v_j$ or $c_i/(c_i + v_i) \neq c_j/(c_j + v_j)$], equal rates of profit imply necessarily unequal rates of surplus value, which can be shown to be as true of a proper durable-capital model as of a raw-materials model. Also, the point has already been made that any workers' society which makes its allocation and consuming decisions on the basis of positive equal-rates-of-surplus-values will be inefficiently and unnecessarily embracing deadweight loss of welfare. Even if the case contemplated is that of a decision-making workers' cooperative, which is a small island in the vast sea of competitive capitalism, then it is still true that the cooperative will lower its members' welfare by picking a_{ij} coefficients different from those of the bourgeois Sraffa analysis.

In conclusion, let me applaud the movement toward secularizing Marx, the economist. As Joan Robinson has said, he deserves the compliment of being taken seriously as a scholar.

PAUL A. SAMUELSON
Massachusetts Institute of Technology

REFERENCES

1. BRONFENBRENNER, M. "Samuelson, Marx, and their Latest Critics," *J. Econ. Lit.*, March 1973, *11*(1), pp. 58–63.
2. SRAFFA, P. *Production of commodities by means of commodities*. London and New York: Cambridge University Press, 1960.
3. VON WEIZSÄCKER, C. C. and SAMUELSON, P. A. "A New Labor Theory of Value for Rational Planning Through Use of the Bourgeois Profit Rate," *Proceedings of the National Academy of Science*, 1971, *68*, pp. 1192–94.

Insight and Detour in the Theory of Exploitation: A Reply to Baumol

By Paul A. Samuelson

Massachusetts Institute of Technology

I am grateful for editorial assistance of Norma Wasser, and financial aid from the National Science Foundation. Despite our friendly differences, I've benefitted from correspondence with Professors Baumol and Morishima.

Thesis

THE THESIS Professor Baumol advances about the proper interpretation of Marx deserves careful analysis because it duplicates a point that many think important [1, Baumol, 1974]. Essentially, it can be put in 38 words, 38 of Marx's actual words:

"We shall see, in Book III, that the rate of profit is no mystery, so soon as we know the laws of surplus-value. If we reverse the process, we cannot comprehend the one or the other" [5, 1906, p. 239, n. 2].

The valuable Meek paper that I cited in my 1971 survey of the transformation problem[1] put the essential point this way:

[1] See also my September 1970 *Proceedings of the National Academy of Sciences* (*PNAS*), [17, 1970] reproduced in my *Collected scientific papers*, [10, 1972], as Ch. 154, pp. 309–311; my May 1967 AER centennial paper [13, 1967], reproduced there as Ch. 152, pp. 268–275; my June 1971 paper with C. C. von Weizsäcker in the *PNAS*, [20, 1971], reproduced as Ch. 155, pp. 312–316. Also two replies by me in the *JEL* 10 and 11 [15, 1972; 14, 1973]. My paper in the July 1973 *PNAS*, "The Optimality of Profit-Inducing Prices Under Ideal Planning," [16, 1973] carries further the Weizsäcker-Samuelson demonstration that, even in a planned socialist society, uniform $R^* = S_j/(C_j + V_j)$, rather than $r^* = s_j/v_j$, would be needed for efficient dynamic asymptotes. In the George Halm *Festschrift* [4, 1973] and Alice Bourneuf *Festschrift* [2, forthcoming], I present analysis relevant to A. Emmanuel's neo-Marxian analysis in *Unequal exchange: A study of the imperialism of trade* [3, 1972]. My earlier 1957 AER and 1959 *QJE* articles on Marx and on Ricardo are also relevant [19, 1957; 9, 1959]; they are reproduced in the 1965 *Collected scientific papers*, [10, 1965] Chapters 339–408. The ninth edition of my *Economics* (McGraw-Hill, New York, 1973), Ch. 42 Appendix gives the elements of Marxian analysis [11, 1973].

". . . according to him [Marx], the profit which the capitalists receive in each industry must be conceived of as accruing to them by virtue of a sort of redivision of the aggregate surplus value produced by the economy as a whole" [6, 1956, p. 95].

Baumol's own words are these:

". . . the primary transformation was not from values into prices but, as Marx and Engels repeatedly emphasize, from *surplus* values into the non-labor income categories that are recognized by 'vulgar economists,' *i.e.*, profits, interest, and rent." [1, 1974, p. 52].

Baumol believes in homeopathic remedies. To offset my mathematical-economic misconceptions, he invokes the high authority of Professor Morishima's mathematical analysis of Marx in his new book [8, 1973]. Baumol's citations are from Chapter 7, pp. 72–86, and most particularly to pp. 80–84. The following Morishima passages seem germane.

Marx thought he had successfully removed the mask of capitalism . . . [writing in Volume III] 'the rate of profit is from the very outset distinct from the rate of surplus value . . . this serves . . . to obscure and mystify the actual origin of surplus value . . . The individual capitalist . . . rightly believes that his profit is not derived solely from the labour employed by him . . . This is quite true as far as his average profit is concerned. To what extent this profit is due to aggregate exploitation of labour on the part of the total social capital . . . this interrelation is a complete mystery to the individual capitalist; all the more so, since no bourgeois theorists, the political economists, have so far revealed it.'

"Thus it is clear that the transformation problem has the aim of showing how 'the aggregate exploitation of labour on the part of the total social capital' is, in a capitalist economy, obscured by the distortion of prices from values; the other aim is to show how living labour can be the sole source of profit . . . Marx . . . was very successful in [his conclusion about] the necessity of aggregate exploitation of labour by capitalists for the existence of positive profit. (Morishima, pp. 85–6.)

On p. 52, Morishima examines "Marx's proposition that surplus value is the source of profit . . . This result may be claimed as the Fundamental Marxian Theorem."

One could list another score of similar quotations.[2]

[2] The reader must judge whether Baumol's citing of the "famous challenge in the Engels 1885 preface to Volume II" has relevance [1, 1974, p. 56].

Antithesis

I deny that "surplus value is the source of profit" in any useful sense. I deny that Marx (or Morishima or Baumol) have anywhere cogently given us reason to believe that one can get to profits *only after* we know the laws of surplus value. And I accept Baumol's challenge to show that my "erase and replace" demonstration of the transformation problem applies, not merely to the transition from industry microeconomic "values" to industry "prices," but *equally* to the (unnecessary-detour) transition from "*surplus* values into profits." It will be seen to be logically untenable to agree with my "erase and replace" analysis of the values-prices transformation, and withhold agreement from my "erase and replace" analysis of the surplus-value-profit transformation. For these are identical.

I shall show that a useful Morishima theorem,[3]

Actually, Ricardo never had reason to expect industries with *different* direct-labor intensities to have equal rates of surplus value (*i.e.*, to have equal ratios of profits to direct-wage outlays). So there is nothing to be reconciled. And of course when Volume III came in 1894, and after its proposals were audited by Veblen, Böhm-Bawerk, Bortkiewicz, Sweezy, Dobb, Meek, Winternitz, Seton, Morishima (including his 1973 book), it was never shown (and was never possible to show) that one can reconcile equal positive $S_j/V_j = S_i/V_i$ with unequal $V_j/C_j \neq V_i/C_i$ and equal $S_j/(V_j + C_j) = S_i/(V_i + C_i)$ — in either the "prices" (accounting) regime or in the 1867–1885 "values" (accounting) regime so long as we stay in *any one* regime. Only by going, with or without the use of an eraser, from one to the other of the mutually-incompatible regimes, can one go from one of the equality sets to the other. (By mutually-incompatible accounting regimes, one signifies the fact that competitive capitalism can *empirically* conform in its exact configuration to *at most one* of the two alternative regimes.)

Baumol's quotations from the Engels-Marx correspondence of the 1860's shows that Engels was aware of difficulties in the case which, after Marx's 1883 death, he was forced to argue for. Engels' challenge was not one of his happier performances as my later quotation from Veblen suggests.

[3] As in my 1971 paper [18, 1971], I write a_0 for the direct labor requirements row vector, a for the square matrix of input-output raw material coefficients, m for the column vector of each worker's subsistence requirements. But to keep all "prices" variables distinct from "values" variables, I use capital letters for prices-variables and lower-case letters for values-variables, writing the profit rate as R and the rate of surplus value as r. Likewise $c_j + v_j + s_j = c_j + v_j + rv_j$ is the values counterpart of the prices relation $C_j + V_j + S_j = C_j + V_j + R(C_j + V_j)$. Morishima writes my a_0 as (l_j), my a as $\begin{bmatrix} A_I & A_{II} \\ 0 & 0 \end{bmatrix}$, my $c_j + v_j + s_j$ as

to any non-antiquarian, can dispense completely with all the $s_j/v_j = s_i/v_i$ innovations of Volume I (innovations which I claim to be uninsightful diversions and detours). And, for those who like me have an antiquarian's interest in relating Marx's detour to the geodesic turnpikes of competitive analysis, I shall show that there is complete reversible symmetry between the two alternative accounting regimes: "profit is the source of surplus value" is as formally valid as vice versa; "only if the profit rate R^* can be positive [in the matrix sense, $R^* > 0$ in $a_0(1 + R^*) [I-a (1+R^*)]^{-1} m = 1$], can the rate of surplus value r^* be positive [in the sense, $r^* > 0$ in $a_0 [I-a]^{-1} (1+r^*)m = 1$]"—this is as valid as vice versa; and preferable to either is the strengthened Hawkins-Simon condition $a_0 [I-a]^{-1}m < 1$ if and only if $R^* > 0$].

Since I have recently covered some of this ground elsewhere, I shall here be brief [12, 1974].

★　★　★

Let me clear the decks of some extraneous details to concentrate on Marx's thesis, which if valid, would be of considerable interest.

First, although Baumol apparently believes that a writer is allowed only one thesis—or one primary thesis—one may deem it safer to assume that there may be more than one. And certainly Marx and the school of Marxism have been concerned with many different facets other than that which Baumol concentrates on. Therefore, the many writers—non-Marxist or Marxist—whom Baumol chides for not seeing *his* simple truth I think need not plead guilty to any mortal sins.

Second, and related, may we put down to the account of conscious or unconscious humor any writer's belief that there is plainly to be read by any intelligent reader some simple resolution of the am-

$C_j + V_j + S_j$, my $C_j + V_j + S_j$ as $Cf + Vf + Sf$, my R as π, my r as e, my $P[1 + 0] = a_0[I-a]^{-1}$ as $(\lambda_1, \ldots,)$, my n as $n + m$, my $P[1 + R] = a_0(1 + R)[I - a(1 + R)]^{-1}$ as $(p_{j,w})$. In the "values" tableaux, $(c_j + v_j + rv_j)$, I use $p[1 + r] = a_0[I - a]^{-1} (1 + r) = p[i](1 + r)$, to signify $p[1 + r]aX + a_0X + ra_0X = p[1 + r]X;$ what I express as $p[1 + r]$ or $p[1 + e]$ would for Morishima become $(\lambda_j(1 + e))$. My $(m_1, \ldots, m_j, \ldots)$ Morishima writes as $(0, \ldots, 0, b_{n+1}, \ldots, b_m)$. Some of the discrepancies between us vanish when one realizes the differences in notations. For brevity only, I shall assume the length of the working day, T in Morishima's notation, to be fixed at unity; to assume it variable, as Marx often did, would only strengthen my argument.

biguities discerned in an early writer like David Ricardo or Karl Marx? There is Wittgenstein humor in a sentence like this gem of Baumol's: "Only a very few [!] commentators, notably R. Marshall and J. Viner and P. Sraffa, saw Ricardo's analysis for what it so plainly [!] was . . ." Years ago the world's greatest living authority laughed at the naiveté of my question: "Did Ricardo 'believe' in a labour theory of value?" And, as a student of Viner and a reader of Marshall, I can testify that both those teachers recognized that Ricardo's mode of exposition laid him intrinsically open to misunderstandings. (When one highway corner claims 50 times the number of lives of another, we are obtuse to explain its accidents by the propensity of *its* drivers to drink or to nap. Why don't people argue about the "meanings" of Wicksell the way they do about those of Ricardo and Marx?)

Third, the diligent reader can judge whether I am right in thinking that the present Baumol thesis was *not* overlooked in my earlier writings on the transformation problem—which is not to suggest that the present reincarnation of the issue is a waste of time.

How does one go about "proving" assertions like these above? I see no way other than to isolate the final insights agreed to by all parties, and examine how one arrives at them. How, via the analysis of rates of surplus value, do we arrive at the goal of explained distribution of actual incomes? What other paths can lead to that distribution? Which paths cannot? What are the arguments advanced by the various protagonists, and what is their cogency?

★　★　★

Baumol's testimony. Most of Baumol's paper is concerned with what Marx's purpose was. On the question of whether that purpose was successful in some sense or another, I can find only a few relevant paragraphs in Baumol's text.

First, there is his simple parable, describing how "*non* wage incomes are *produced* and then how this aggregate is *redistributed.*" [Baumol's italics.] Upon exegesis, the jury will conclude that there is no cogency in this contention. There exists in actuality no *prior* determination of the total non-wage surplus, after which its aggregate can be redistributed. I do not say this as a bourgeois economist writing within a non-Marxian paradigm. I say this within the Volume I-II-III paradigm, and as a matter of logic.[4] It involves the fallacy of *petitio principii* to assert, as Baumol does, to explain Marx's *intention,* "each [industry] . . . contributes to a storehouse containing total surplus value . . . [which] contribution is proportionate to the quantity of labor it uses . . . the transformation process . . . takes from each according to its work force, and returns to each according to its total investment" [1, 1974, p. 53]. Let's see what is actually involved in competitive income distribution.

(i) If there were zero profit or surplus, the value-added in each industry would be wages only: this is the pre-Marx classical labor theory of value. The simultaneous determination by long-run competitive supply and demand would determine goods' prices at their embodied labor contents, direct-plus-indirect labor. All the Net National Products would go to wages, and the consumption expenditure of such incomes would go for the flow of final NNP product. No quarrels here.

(ii) Suppose the profit rate is positive for whatever reason (*e.g.,* because labor can be reproduced at the cost of its subsistence bundle, *m,* which is less than what the labor can produce in the steady state net after reproducing its used up cooperating raw materials). Then the NNP flow of final product is composed of labor's consumption plus that of the capitalist property owners; within each industry, the prosaic accounting of value-added (a concept already glimpsed in Adam Smith) records its wage payments and its profit payments; summed, these industry value-addeds define the NNP, which has no logical existence other than as the macroeconomic sum of the microeconomic items, all simultaneously defined. To digress, in a corrected Baumol parable, each industry "puts into" the pot in value-added what it takes out.

Only simpletons think that accounting labels cause the world to move. The apple falls the same whether Newton watches or enunciates its constant acceleration. Profit or surplus is no less ugly or reprehensible or correctable when it is proportional to each industry's *total* investment outlay on raw materials and on direct-labor wage payments; and,

if we want to understand real-world competitive exploitation, and to predict how distribution will change when invention, consumption-demand, or subsistence-requirements change, we preserve insight by concentrating on the reality of avaricious competitive arbitrage rather than on irrelevant Platonic abstractions or dual accounting systems.

None of this soft pedals for a moment the basic fact that, if you take away all living labor, you take away *all* product. Nor does it distract attention from Marx's basic reality: The worker does not own the raw materials and machinery that is needed if his labor is to produce product (use values). That is why the worker must sell or rent out his labor power rather than be sole producer and appropriator of *all* the product he sets his hand and brain to.

Living labor, yes. But it is a bad pun to confuse this with "live labor" in the sense of *direct* labor, to the neglect of labor "previously" performed and embodied in raw materials and in equipment—*i.e.,* "dead" or indirect labor.

That there is no cogent sense in which at each stage surplus or profit springs out of the direct labor alone and not out of the needed raw materials can be shown by any simple example.[5] Let 1 coal now be producible by 1 mine-labor a short period ago. And let 1 coal now with 1 farm-labor now produce 1 corn a period from now. Suppose corn is the "end-all" of economic activity. Then, eschewing any neoclassical variability of production methods, we have in terms of production causation:

$$\text{Corn}_t = \text{Min}[\text{mine-labor}_{t-2}, \text{farm-labor}_{t-1}]$$

[4] This does not assert that a "macroeconomic" theory of profits, like Kalecki's widow's cruse model, is self-contradictory or illogical. It does point out that there is no semblance of such a theory in any of the three Volumes of Marx. Incidentally, a Kalecki-Kaldor-Pasinetti macro theory finds the uniform rate of profit more useful than a detour through a uniform rate of surplus value.

[5] A more complicated example can do better justice to Marx's non-Austrian circular-flow models. Let $\frac{1}{2}$ coal and $\frac{1}{2}$ mine labor now produce 1 coal a brief period from now. And let $\frac{1}{2}$ coal and $\frac{1}{2}$ farm labor produce 1 corn a period from now. Then

$$\text{Corn}_t = \text{Min}\ [\frac{1}{2}\text{ farm-labor}_{t-1}, \frac{1}{4}\text{ coal-labor}_{t-2},$$
$$\frac{1}{8}\text{ coal-labor}_{t-3}, \ldots, + \frac{1}{2^k}\text{ coal-labor}_{t-k}, \ldots]$$

an infinite-sequence that converges to steady-state corn production producible out of steady-state total labor $L_t = \bar{L}$ to

$$\overline{\text{Corn}} = 1\ \bar{L} = (\frac{1}{2} + \frac{1}{4} + \frac{1}{8} + \ldots + \frac{1}{2^k} + \ldots)\ \bar{L}$$

with half society's steady state labor on the farm and half in the mines. This NNP of producible corn will go to wage earners in a share of a anywhere from 1 to 0 depending upon where the profit rate per period, R, falls in the range $0 \leqslant R \leqslant 1$, where $a = 2(1 + R)^{-1} - 1$.

and in the steady state with a given labor supply of $L_t \equiv \bar{L}$, we have

$$\overline{\text{Corn}} = \text{Min}\left[\frac{\bar{L}}{2}, \frac{\bar{L}}{2}\right] = \tfrac{1}{2}\,\bar{L}$$

In terms of physical causation, and any ethical consequences inferrable from that, no more can be said.

Nothing in these technocratic facts or in the brute facts of competitive arbitrage is illuminated by the 1867–85 innovations that postulate dual accounting identities $s_1/v_1 = s_2/v_2$. As Veblen said, not unsympathetically, Marx never even deigns to prove his contention. As I say, neither Baumol nor Morishima nor anyone else has provided a shred of the lacking proof needed to show why $s_i/v_i = s_j/v_j$ is a useful concept to anyone who understands the self-standing $C_j + V_j + R(C_j + V_j)$ conventional tableau.

Beyond Baumol's parable and aside from his evidence bearing on Marx's *intention,* there is only one other part of his paper that addresses itself to whether or not Marx's intention misfired. In the first paragraph of his section on transformed profits as a mere surface manifestation, Baumol criticizes himself and other bourgeois economists like me for "treating Volume I as an unnecessary detour." He does so by turning from the issue of relative shares (which both sides deem *non*-trivial) to the issue of relative industry prices only. He says, "What is all that important, . . . from the point of view of the objectives of Marx's analysis . . . about an explanation of the determination of competitive prices."

But Baumol has not reckoned with my contention that, all microeconomic price details aside, when we properly transform from rate-of-surplus-value accounting regime to actual rate-of-competitive-profit regime, we take an eraser and replace the $a_0[I-a]^{-1}(1+r^*)m = 1$ relation that defines "the rate of surplus value, r^*" by the *alternative* relation $a_0(1+R^*)\,[I-a(1+R^*)]^{-1}m = 1$ that defines the "competitive rate of profit, R^*;" and literally nothing in the way of understanding of the latter's actual distribution relation is "revealed," is "uncovered" or is "laid bare" by the pre-eraser detouring. All that Baumol need do to end disagreement between us is to admit that what he calls Marx's intention actually misfires—in that, *from Marx's own standpoint of explaining actual wage-profits distribution,* the Volume I analysis is indeed a detour. Or Baumol should provide cogent argument for the first

time that demonstrates why such a conclusion is wrong.

★   ★   ★

Morishima's testimony. This book is of great interest for its own sake [8, 1973]. What light does it throw on the contention that analysis of

$$c_j + v_j + s_j = c_j + v_j + rv_j$$

where r is the uniform rate of surplus value, is an uninteresting and redundant detour for the economist interested in the statics and dynamics of the distribution of income?

After careful reading of the book, I find no cogent argumentation that compels, predisposes, or even tempts one to withdraw the view that the pre-Volume III model with $s_j/v_j = s_i/v_i = r$ (= e in Morishima's notation) is essentially only a diversionary detour. To appraise this thesis of mine, I divided the book's many interesting theorems into three classes:

A. Those theorems that are stated, or can be restated, to apply to the model of mainstream economics in which $S_j/(C_j + V_j) = S_i/(C_i + V_i) = R$ [π in Morishima's notation] including the case where $R = 0 = \pi$, the "classical labor theory of value."

B. Those theorems that relate the $s_j/v_j = s_i/v_i$ *dual* accounting system to the pre-Marxian *primal* accounting system of $S_j/(C_j + V_j) = S_i/(C_i + V_i)$ much in the way that a bi-lingual dictionary relates, say, my children's private nursery language to standard English.[6]

[6] "Duality" is an O.K. word these days, because of its insights into linear programming and game theory, direct-and-indirect utility analysis of demand, price-quantity symmetries in planning and growth models, Legendre transformations in Hamilton-Pontryagin control theory, classical thermodynamics, and in analysis of rationing, point-line symmetries of projective geometry and convex set theory, "and-or-not" symmetries of Schröder-Peirce symbolic logic; node-branch symmetries of network theory, etc. It represents at best a poor pun in English, at worst a source of confusion, to employ the Morishima usage of "*dual* accounting regimes" to denote competitive pricing and Marxian Volume I regimes. In this sense, obsolete phlogiston-caloric and living Cornot-Clausius-Gibbs energy-entropy thermodynamics are "dual accounting regimes," related by eraser transformation algorithms! If only Marxian surplus values added the insights to competitive profits that Maxwell-Boltzmann-Gibbs kinetic theories of statistical mechanics added to phenomenological thermodynamics—but, alas, not even the great skills of a Morishima can accomplish this.

C. Those theorems that apply exclusively to the dual system of values, and which yet do have an independent interest to an economist who has no penchant for antiquarian study in the history of doctrines and ideas.

My finding: Class C was a null set. The few interesting theorems in the book framed exclusively for the dual "values" regime could, upon straightforward reformulation, be expressed *solely* in terms of empirically-observable regimes of competitive-arbitrage pricing, and hence could be put into Class A. Class C's emptiness recognized, Class B dwindles in its interest.

Let me give some illustrations:

1. There is a beautiful modern theorem about non-negative matrices, a, a_0, $(I-a)^{-1}$, $a_0(I-a)^{-1}$, and the same matrices when all (a_0, a) coefficients are multiplied by $(1 + R)$ and R is not so large as to make $det[I - a(1 + R)]$ change its positive sign. In Hicks, *Value and capital*, the theorem states that the percentage change in an own good's price is, under certain assumptions about gross substitutes and defined changes in tastes, greater than for any cross-good's price change. In Leontief input-output analysis, the theorem states that a unit increase in hats will cause a greater percentage change in gross hat production than in gross shoe or belt production. In Keynes-Metzler n-country multiplier analysis, the theorem says that an increase in United States net investment will raise American income more than it will raise the United Kingdom's income. Connoisseurs know how neatly Morishima has enunciated and generalized this nice result in his non-Marxian writings.

Now, in his book on Marx, Morishima points out a version of the same theorem: an increase in an input requirement in industry j, say an increase in a_{ij} or a_{0j} (*i.e.*, of raw material or labor requirements), will increase the pure-labor cost of good j by a greater percentage than it will increase the pure-labor cost of another good k. It is a nice result. But what power, in the Neyman-Pearson sense, does such a result have for interesting any economist in rate-of-surplus versus rate-of-profit analysis? None! The theorem holds as well for "prices" as for "values"; as well for the primal bourgeois accounting regime as for the dual Volume I regime; it holds at every admissible positive profit rate.

I could give many other examples of Class A theorems.

2. Let's look at a typical Class B theorem of antiquarian interest only. The rate of surplus value, e or r^*, will be numerically greater than the rate of profit, R^* or π, in any system where some subsistence-good requires directly or indirectly some non-labor input. It can be specified for such a system that $I \neq [I - a]^{-1} \geq 0$, $a_0[I - a]^{-1} > 0$, and $a_0[I - a]^{-1}m < 1$, for m the non-negative, non-zero column vector of subsistence for worker. Then we see from the algebra that $f(R_1, R_2) = a_0 (1 + R_1)$ $[I - a(1 + R_2)]^{-1}m$ is positive for admissible positive R's and is strongly monotone in each and both of its arguments. Consequently Morishima neatly demonstrates that the respective roots, R^* and r^*, of

$$f(R, R) = 1 \text{ and } f(r, 0) = 1$$

must satisfy $0 < R^* < r^*$ since $f(r^* + k^2, r^* + k^2) > f(r^*, 0)$. But if my contention is correct that the $f(r, 0) = 1$ dual regime of Volume I is an uninsightful detour, who but an antiquarian will be interested in this simple algebraic result?

As C. C. von Weizsäcker discussed in "Morishima on Marx," [21, 1973], the harmless algebra theorem that $a_0(1 + R^*)[I - a(1 + R^*)^{-1} m = 1$ has a positive root iff $a_0[I - a]^{-1} (1 + e^*) m = 1$ has a positive e^* root, should *not* be construed to mean that a positive interest rate is solely possible under "exploitation" of poor laborers by rich capitalists. We can have a positive profit rate when all people are alike. Algebra should never *obscure* sociology and power relations! All that is valuable is conveyed by the Volume III non-Marxian theorem: *If and only if* $a_0[I - a]m < 1$ *will there be possible a positive profit rate and feasible positive non-subsistence consumption.* No $s_j/v_j = e > 0$ relations are involved.

3. Under Class C is a Marx-Sraffa theorem such as (a) the ratio of values in the dual accounting regime are never affected by the increase in the rate of surplus value, even though (b) the ratio of prices will be generally affected by changes in the rate of profit, in any system where the ratios of direct-wage to other costs are not uniform between industries. What is interesting about this theorem is the part which already belongs in Class A—namely the alegebra of how any price$_j$/price$_k$ is affected by a change in R from zero to larger values. Morishima's beautiful generalization of this Marx-Sraffa theorem, which can be stated as giving sufficient conditions for a subset of the goods to keep invariant relative *prices* [!] as the profit rate changes, belongs

to my Class A rather than to Class B or Class C.

4. Again, for antiquarians (I include myself in this harmless avocation), Morishima provides as a Class B theorem his useful generalization of my equal-internal-composition sufficiency condition to a wider "linear dependence" sufficiency condition. I applaud this. Morishima's e coefficient is computable from technocratic data alone, without our ever detouring to a dual accounting regime of $s_j/v_j = s_i/v_i = e$, and without ever going beyond the *pre*-Marx classical labor theory of value. But, of course, the ratio "surplus labour"/"necessary labor" $= e$ does not equal the observable Profit Share/Wage Share; nor will e equal observable aggregate *competitive* $\Sigma S_j/\Sigma V_j$, or any one industry competitive S_j/V_j, even though it is bounded by the maximum and minimum of observable $[S_j/V_j]$. A change in capitalists' tastes toward goods of greater wage intensity will, even at unchanged profit and real wage, result in a lowering of observable a even though e has the defect of being invariant under such taste changes.

5. One could go on listing how Morishima's findings could be, from the present viewpoint, more usefully reformulated. Even his rare mistakes can be made to be independent of any detours. Thus, on p. 142, he says "the following treatment based on the [Morishima] true formula (12) may be claimed as the first rigorous proof of the law [of the Marxian falling rate of profit]" [8, 1973]. What Morishima purports to show is this: Consider a "neutral" invention that enables us to replace an industry's labor and raw material requirements $[a_{0j}$ and a_{ij}, for fixed $j]$ by a new set of requirements in which total labor costs $[A_{0j}$ in $a_0(I-a)^{-1}$ remains the same but which the direct labor requirements $[a_{0j}]$ are reduced at the expense of an increase in raw material requirements [one or more a_{ij}]. Such an alleged increase in the organic composition of capital will, at the same real wage and r^* level, necessarily depress the rate of profit. So goes the assertion.

Heaven defend Marx from his defenders! The trap I warned against in my 1972 JEL ecumenical reply to Lerner [15, 1972, p. 56] has sprung here. The invention Morishima prescribes, which he calls by the harmless word "neutral," is a "*dis*improvement" at every positive profit rate, not an "improvement." It will be *avoided* in ruthless competition like the plague. It will never come into effect under the new equilibrium. His rigorous proof is no proof

at all, and no proof of a false proposition is ever possible. Indeed, once the system has a choice of technique—pre- and post-invention—concentrating on zero-profit embodied-labor magnitudes becomes highly dangerous (and irrelevant!) for aggregation or any other purpose. Volume I's dual regime gives outsights, not insights.

7. Morishima's claim, even if it were true, as it is not—that zero-profit embodied-labor contents give better weights for aggregation purposes than do prices calculated at positive interest rates that are in a nearer neighborhood of actual observed systems—is better formulated and criticized by avoiding any detour to $s_j/v_j = s_i/v_i = e > 0$ analysis. No need to belabor these points further.[7]

I conclude that Baumol's writing a check on Morishima to reinforce his thesis leaves him overdrawn at the bank.

Synthesis

Let me state for dogmatic clarity what I believe to be the position to which, at some future date, Marxian and non-Marxian economists will both agree. (My pen also has a sense of humor.)

1. *No* new analytical insight is given, statically or dynamically, by Marx's own novelties of theoretical analysis that involve—*macro*economically or microeconomically—the concept of the "rate of surplus-value," either in the form of s_j/v_j or of S_j/V_j, $\Sigma s_j/\Sigma v_j$ or $\Sigma S_j/\Sigma V_j$,

    (a) into the explanation of the distribution of income between labor wages and property capital return, or

    (b) into the determination of society's general profit rate (or total of profit return), or

---

[7] A reader who has mastered the present considerations will be in a position to judge whether, in his occasional stricture against my writings on Marx, Morishima has scored valid points that should cause me to recast my wordings. There is no point in discussing Morishima's p. 6 mention that his "discussion of the transformation problem . . . is very different from his [Samuelson's] in its conclusions, in spite of the surprising similarity in the mathematics used . . . I [Morishima] am very much more sympathetic than he [Samuelson] is" [8, 1973]. If you overhear two persons, saying respectively, "2 + 2 = 4 and Marx was a genius" and "2 + 2 = 4 and Marx fathered an illegitimate son," you must not think that they are necessarily disagreeing or that you can cogently infer which one is more sympathetic to Karl Marx! In the cited Metzler *Festschrift*, I have replied more specifically, albeit briefly, to points raised by Morishima about my Marxian writings [7, 1974].

(c) into the microeconomic empirical configuration of goods and prices in a system of perfect or imperfect competition (or of imperfect knowledge, or of stochastic exogenous disturbance) or

(d) into the realities of the class struggle or the understanding of power relations between groups and governments, internationally or nationally, or

(e) into the ethical nature of "exploitation" and inequality of income.

2. More concretely, I assert:

There is no cogent argument, in Baumol, or, for that matter in Morishima's 200 pages of mathematics, or in the vast literature already surveyed on the transformation problem, that would

(a) make one want to qualify the verdict that the Volumes I and II excursion into the realms of $s_j/v_j = s_i/v_i$ was anything but a detour, anything but at best a wasteful redundancy and at worst a digression that fails to "penetrate" and "lay bare," and "reveal" the "deceptive character" of "capitalist accounting."

All this is claimed *within* the paradigm of Marxian rejection of the legitimacy of positive property income at the expense of labor wages gettng 100 per cent of the Net National Product.

3. What I am arguing is this. If Baumol wishes to regard the transformation problem as, not a transition from "values" to "prices," but as a transition "from surplus values into . . . profits," then to understand competitive distribution of income I claim it to be equally true that what is involved *is use of the eraser to rub out the irrelevant detour's uninsightful accounting system, and then the replacing of that system by the empirically-relevant equalized-rate-of-profit behavior equations* that the economists use who preceded Marx, who were contemporary with him, and who have succeeded him. Marx's own investigation into the trends of distribution, the cycles of activity, and the modes of steady reproduction and exponential growth, I am arguing here, were hampered, not helped, by his novel rate-of-surplus-value analysis.

★ ★ ★

Qualifications: Are there no qualifications to this rather sweeping indictment? Yes, the following:

1. The algebra of the surplus-value regime is easier to handle. So, for purposes of elementary exposition and layman persuasion, there is merit in the Volume I models. Just as one does not criticize

Walras for not using in 1874 the topological methods von Neumann was to use in 1931 to prove existence of a general equilibrium system, I do not fault Marx—but rather praise him—for coming so close in the 1860's to a correct tableau of steady-state and exponential-growth-equilibrium. But no one would dream today of maintaining that Walras' 1874 counting of equations and unknowns is as good or is better than use of fixed-point theorems; likewise, I argue it is absurd, after praising Marx for his early efforts, to extoll his surplus-value model over the model that dominates it in every virtue.

2. To the degree that differences in direct-labor intensities are deemed minor or that their effects are macroeconomically ignorable, the "values" or surplus-value regime may be a useful first-approximation to the "prices" or profit regime.

3. In the history of thought, we realize that detours may serve useful purposes. An error of Newton is rightly dismissed as such by a modern student of live physics. But to the antiquarian of dead physics, to the historian interested in the psychology of discovery and innovation, errors are often as interesting as truths. Many seminal contributions have grown out of misunderstandings. I doubt that many important contributions of Marx, such as circular-flow balanced growth models, would have been developed by him if he had not, for extraneous reasons, been preoccupied with his detour paradigms. But just as we do not burn down our houses to broil our daily chops, there is no reason why the admirer of Marx should go through his historic circuitous detours and redundancies.

Summary. Karl Marx did pioneering work that foreshadowed a number of modern analytical models of economics. He also has an important position in the history of ideas and in non-analytical aspects of political economy, the social sciences, and philosophy.

Nonetheless, a careful rereading of his claims and those made on his behalf does not disclose cogent arguments that should impel a Marxian or non-Marxian to agree that his novel analytical innovations concerning positive equalized rates of surplus value are other than a detour to one who would understand 19th-century or earlier-century distribution of income and to one who would understand the laws of motion of any economic system.

If I am wrong in my answer to this question—which has been *the* number one question among pro- and anti-Marx analysts from 1867 to the present day—presentation of some new and cogent argumentation controverting my contention can dispose of it.

REFERENCES

1. BAUMOL, W. "The Transformation of Values: What Marx 'Really' Meant (An Interpretation)" *J. Econ. Lit.*, March 1974, *12*(1), pp. 51–62.

2. [BOURNEUF, A.] *Pathways to macroeconomics. Festschrift.* Edited by D. A. BELSLEY; E. J. KANE; P. A. SAMUELSON AND R. M. SOLOW. Columbus: Ohio State University Press, forthcoming.

3. EMMANUEL, A. *Unequal exchange: A study of the imperialism of trade.* With additional comments by Charles Bettelheim. Translated from the French by BRIAN PEARCE. New York and London: Montly Review Press, [1969] 1972.

4. [HALM, GEORGE N.] *Festschrift. Leading issues in international economic policy. Essays in honor of George N. Halm.* Edited by C. FRED BERGSTEN and WILLIAM G. TYLER. Lexington, Mass., Toronto and London: D. C. Heath, 1973.

5. MARX, K. *Capital. A critique of political economy.* Chicago: Charles H. Kerr and Co., Volume I (1906); Volumes II and III (1909).

6. MEEK, R. L. "Some Notes on the Transformation Problem," *Econ J.*, March 1956, *66*, pp. 94–107; reprinted in R. L. MEEK. *Economics and ideology and other essays; Studies in the development of economic thought.* London: Chapman and Hall, 1967, pp. 143–157.

7. [METZLER, LLOYD] *Festschrift. Trade, stability and macroeconomics.* Edited by G. HORWICH and P. A. SAMUELSON. New York: Academic Press, 1974.

8. MORISHIMA, M. *Marx's economics: a dual theory of value and growth.* New York: Cambridge University Press, 1973.

9. SAMUELSON, P. "A Modern Treatment of the Ricardian Economy," in two articles, *Quart. J. Econ.*, Feb. 1959, *73*(1), pp. 1–35; May 1959, *73*(2), pp. 217–231; reprinted in *Collected scientific papers* [See no. 10].

10. ——, *Collected scientific papers.* Edited by J. Stiglitz. 3 vols. Cambridge, Mass.: M.I.T. Press, [1965] 1972.

11. ——, *Economics.* 9th edition. New York: McGraw-Hill, 1973.

12. ——, "Karl Marx as a Mathematical Economist," In G. HORWICH and P. A. SAMUELSON, eds. [METZLER, LLOYD] *Festschrift. Trade, stability and macroeconomics.* New York: Academic Press, 1974.

13. ——, "Marxian Economics as Economics," *Amer. Econ. Rev.*, May 1967, *57*(2), pp. 616–623.

14. ——, "Samuelson's Reply on Marxian Matters'," *J. Econ. Lit.*, March 1973, *11*(1), pp. 64–68.

15. ——, "The Economics of Marx: An Ecumenical Reply," *J. Econ. Lit.*, March 1972, *10*(1), pp. 51–57.

16. ——, "The Optimality of Profit-Inducing Prices Under Ideal Planning," *Proceedings of the National Academy of Sciences,* July 1973, *70*(7), pp. 2109–2111.

17. ——, "The 'Transformation' from Marxian 'Values' to Competitive 'Prices': A Process of Rejection and Replacement," *Proceedings of the National Academy of Sciences,* Sept. 1970, *67*(1), pp. 423–425.

18. ——, "Understanding the Marxian Notion of Exploitation: A Summary of the So-called Transformation Problem Between Marxian Values and Competitive Prices," *J. Econ. Lit.*, June 1971, *9*(2), pp. 399–431.

19. ——, "Wages and Interest: A Modern Dissection of Marxian Economic Models," *Amer. Econ. Rev.*, Dec. 1957, *47*, pp. 884-912; reprinted in *Collected scientific papers* [See no. 10].

20. ——, AND VON WEIZSÄCKER, C. C. "A New Labor Theory of Value for Rational Planning Through Use of the Bourgeois Profit Rate," *Proceedings of the National Academy of Sciences,* June 1971, *68*, pp. 1192–1194.

21. VON WEIZSÄCKER, C. C. "Morishima on Marx." *Econ. J.*, Dec. 1973, *83*, pp. 1245–1254.

230

Rejoinder: Merlin Unclothed, A Final Word

Happily our dialectic registers didactic progress. Like the truth-seeking child in Hans Christian Andersen's tale of the Emperor's Clothes, I ventured a riskily strong statement in the hope of provoking from two formidable scholars a cogent defense of Marx as having *succeeded* in his avowed purpose of revealing the secrets of profit and income determination from his Volume I paradigm, in which the rate of surplus value is equalized industry by industry.

The issue is a momentous one. For, proper as it is to cast Karl Marx in the role of Prometheus, so too did he aspire to the role of a Merlin, who reveals the mysteries below the surface of things that cannot yield to conventional political economy.

There is a school in the history of science whose practitioners are concerned primarily with how earlier scientists perceived their own problems. In caricature, we can say it is all one to them whether Newton wrote on gravitation, alchemy, or the Secret of the Number of the Beast in Deuteronomy. They would never dream of grading earlier writers for error or fruitfulness. To look back so on earlier writers is, I believe, to *look down* on them as hopelessly handicapped Neanderthals who lacked our advantages.

I begrudge no one his pastime. But, in the realm of cumulative knowledge, I believe there is a place for what might be called Whig History of Science. In it we pay past scholars the compliment of judging how their works contributed (algebraic) value-added to the collective house of knowledge. Economics, I know, is not a hard natural science. Still I have thought it valuable to treat Marx not as an historic deity or oddity, but rather to appraise his arguments on the transformation problem in the way a journal referee would treat any serious contributor. If it had been the case that Professors Baumol and Morishima had been able to supply the demonstration I puzzled over—that the *prices tab-*

leau of the observed world can be understood only (or, even better) *after* the novel *values tableau* of Marx has been mastered—I would have regarded that as an important finding for modern-day political economy. But, alas, apparently the challenge must still stand.[1]

★   ★   ★

Political biases of the economist can contaminate the search for truth in this imperfect world. Hence, as a check on the degree to which my biases may

---

[1] Reading recent works by two other authors worthy of respect and just evaluation, I must record no reason to modify my thesis. Cf. M. Dobb, *Theories of value and distribution since Adam Smith,* Ch. 6 on Marx [1, 1973]. To illustrate for Dobb's readers the crucial analytic point, suppose (as is possible) that equal organic composition of capital does happen to obtain in the real world. Then the transformation problem is agreed by all to be trivially simple, and indeed hardly necessary. In that case my need to object to a values tableau as a digression from understanding of the actual prices plateau evaporates. But one is still left, even in this case, with no new insights, statically or dynamically, in the distribution of income or the share of wages by Marx's innovations concerning rates of surplus value, commodity fetishism, modes of production involving productive labor in a collective or social division of labor. A Sraffian, Clarkian, neo-Walrasian, would merely be *reposing* the problem of how inventions, thrift, composition of demand, and relative factor supplies alter (1) the R^* profit rate, by asking how these factors alter (2) the now-trivially-related rate of surplus value r^*.

Cf. also the excellent E. Wolfstetter "Surplus Labour, Synchronized Labour Costs and Marx's Labour Theory of Value" [3, 1973]. This affirms the truth that, for normative purposes under socialist planning or Pareto-optimal market exchanges, it is prices tableaux not values tableaux that are relevant when they differ. On p. 799 this also makes the point of Morishima's (10) in his *Reply* that, within the values tableau there is a common s_j/v_j that can be interpreted as the fraction of labor not worked for the subsistence wage itself. But one is left with no interest in this once he has grasped the "neutral" technocratic theorem: $a_0 [I - a]^{-1} m < 1$ implies and is implied by R^* positive in $a_0 (1 + R^*) [I - a (1 + R^*)]^{-1} m = 1$. Similarly, with von Weizsäcker, let labor grow like $L_0 (1 + g)^t$, workers' consumptions like $L_0 m (1 + g)^t$. Then this will be feasible only if the following "neutral" theorem applies: $a_0 (1 + g) [I - a (1 + g)]^{-1} m < 1$, if and only if $R^* > g$ provides a root for $a_0 (1 + R^*) [I - a (1 + R^*)]^{-1} m = 1$.

I accept Morishima's correction that in his book he did say that actual price weights might serve for aggregation as well as value weights. I reproach myself for not having made this clear. But of course this only reinforces my point about the dispensability of $c_j + v_j + r^* v_j$ tableaux in comparison with $C_j + V_j + R^* (C_j + V_j)$ tableaux.

have infected and contaminated my analysis's objectivity, I think it will be of interest that, just as Baumol by serendipity found fascinating letters of Marx and Engels in a lower-Manhattan ashcan, by similar happy chance I came upon the following answer to what I have called the Number One Problem by America's leading Leftist, Thorstein Veblen. Joseph Dorfman recently unearthed this 1895 item,[2] written, it is interesting to note, before Böhm-Bawerk's critique and while Thorstein Veblen was serving as the underpaid sub-editor of the *Journal of Political Economy:*

> Among the surprises of economic literature is the fate that has overtaken Karl Marx's theory of surplus-value in the third volume of his *Kapital,* lately published. Advocates, expositors and critics of the Marxian economics have exercised their ingenuity in futile attempts to reconcile that theory with obvious facts, while its author has put them off with the assurance that the whole mystery would be explained and made right in the Third Book of his work. In the mean time the Marxian dogma of surplus-value has served the present generation of "scientific" socialists as their fundamental "scientific" principle and the keynote of their criticism of existing industrial relations, and its acceptance (on faith) by the body of socialists, avowed and unavowed, has contributed not a little to the viciousness of their attack on the existing order of things. And now, after the theory, accepted literally and with full naiveté, has done service for a generation as the most redoubted engine of socialist propaganda, the "Third Book" comes along and explains with great elaboration, in the course of some 200 pages, that the whole of that jaunty structure is to be understood in a Pickwickian sense. It appears now that the need which has been felt for some reconciliation of this theory of the rate of surplus-value with the everyday facts of the rate of profits is due simply to a crude and gratuitous misapplication of the Marxian doctrine of surplus-value to a question with which it has nothing to do. That theory has none but the most remote and intangible relation to any concrete facts.

[2] That this was not a momentary aberration from Veblen's view will appear from a close reading of his famous 1906 essays in the *Quart. J. Econ.,* "The Socialist Economics of Karl Marx, I, II." Cf. relevant Veblen passages of 1893, 1895, 1897, and 1922 in Dorfman's *Thorstein Veblen: Essays, reviews and reports—Previously uncollected writings* at pp. 419, 263–4 and 444–5, 462, 241 [2, 1973].

The full extent of the relation between "surplus-value" and "profits" is this (and even this suffers material qualification in the course of the discussion), that the aggregate profits in any industrial community at any given time may also be styled "aggregate surplus-value." The rate of surplus-value bears no tangible relation to the rate of profits. The two vary quite independently of one another. Nor does the aggregate profits in any concrete case, in any given industry or enterprise, depend on or coincide in magnitude with the aggregate surplus-value produced in that industry or enterprise. For all useful purposes the entire surplus-value theory is virtually avowed to be meaningless lumber [2, Dorfman, 1973, pp. 263–264].

PAUL A. SAMUELSON

REFERENCES

1. DOBB, M. *Theories of value and distribution since Adam Smith: Ideology and economic theory.* New York and London: Cambridge University Press, 1973.
2. DORFMAN, J., ed. *Thorstein Veblen: Essays, reviews and reports—Previously uncollected writings.* Clifton, N.J.: Augustus M. Kelley, 1973.
3. WOLFSTETTER, E. "Surplus Labour, Synchronised Labour Costs and Marx's Labour Theory of Value," *Econ. J.,* Sept. 1973, *83* (331), pp. 787–809.

Economic essays on value, competition, and utility. By V. K. DMITRIEV. Edited with an introduction by D. M. NUTI. Translated by D. FRY. New York and London: Cambridge University Press, 1974. Pp. 231. $18.50.

Dmitriev is a romantic and shadowy figure, who founded Russian mathematical economics around the turn of the century, and whom most of us would never have heard of if L. von Bortkiewicz, in one of his two important 1907 papers of Marx's transformation problem, had not written: "The above algebraic of the solution of the [Ricardo-Marx] price-problem has been taken, in its essentials, from a work by W. K. Dmitrieff . . . . this remarkable work, which appeared in Russian, (apparently a first work!) . . . bears evidence of an exceptional theoretical talent and presents something really new . . ." [2, Bortkiewicz, 1907, p. 22]. Now that Mr. Nuti has given us this beautifully edited translation of the rare 1904 book of three essays, we can see that Bortkiewicz's (uncharacteristic!) enthusiasm for Dmitriev is well founded; we can be grateful for the resurrection of his reputation by Russian experts of the west, such as A. Nove, A. Zauberman, and M. Kaser; and we can well understand why V. Nemchinov and other Soviet experts should since 1959 have pointed with pride to the early contributions of their own countryman, contributions that also served to provide an indigenous rather than imported legitimacy to the use of mathematics in analyzing the post-Stalin Soviet economy.

From the useful biographical note, one learns that Dmitriev (1868–1913) was a figure rather like Chekhov: he died young of tuberculosis; he wished to study medicine but, deprived of opportunity for that, he studied political economy. Never apparently having had the opportunity to sit in the university chair his talents so clearly qualified him for, he eked out an inadequate living as a minor tax official in the provinces, during which few years he wrote the important first essay of 1898 that guarantees him imperishable fame. By virtue of his need and health, he seems never to have had the opportunity to carry out his plan to go beyond these three essays to write subsequent essays on rent, industrial crises, and on the theory of monetary circulation. One hopes that a Sraffa will some day arise to find some preliminary manuscripts on these appetizing subjects.

All three essays are interesting. At an initial reading, I judge that the first 57-page essay will seem most impressive to the modern economist, dealing as it does with the dependence of competitive prices on wage rates and the interest or profit rate. Here Dmitriev provides important clarification of issues that seized Ricardo and Marx: as Mr. Nuti properly stresses, Dmitriev in 1898 anticipated much of the Leontief and Sraffa systems; and, one may add, something of the von Neumann system as well. Next to such caviar, the meat and potatoes of the essays on Cournot's theory of monopoly and on the pre-twentieth-century developments of marginal utility must suffer by comparison—until we reflect how original a lone Russian of the 1890's would have had to be to improve on the esoteric delicacies of the 1838 Cournot.

On the basis of his first half dozen pages, Dmitriev deserves undying fame. He shows there, perhaps for the first time ever, just how to reckon *total socially-necessary (steady-state) labor requirements or cost* of competitive goods. If 1 deer can be hunted by 1 day's direct labor alone, Smith knew how to reckon its labor cost. If 1 coat can be made out of 2 day's direct labor of sewing plus the 1 day's hunting in producing the deerskin raw materials, Ricardo (and his predecessors) and his Austrian and Walrasian successors) knew how to reckon its *total* labor cost at 3, equals 2 direct (or "live") labor plus 1 indirect (or "dead" labor embodied in the deer carcass). We do not need a Dmitriev, or a Leontief or Sraffa, to handle these Santa Claus Ricardian-Austrian examples, whose so-called supra-diagonal input-output matrix, or hierarchical structure as between unambiguously *earlier* and *later* stages of production, do permit us to decompose all labor costs backward in a finite number of steps into their historic components. Indeed as Smith glimpsed in his reckoning of the prices of national product in terms of the value-added components of wages and interest (land rent being ignored by me for the moment), market competitive price can be decomposed into wages plus profit-interest mark-ups, namely for our coat example as

$$P/W = 2(1 + r) + 1(1 + r)^2 > 3 \text{ if } r > 0 \quad [1]$$

if r, the interest or profit rate is positive.

Suppose, however, it takes corn-seed to make corn. Or that it takes labor and coal to make corn, at the same time that it takes labor and corn to make coal. Then we lack that Austrian supra-diagonal structure which renders the historic decomposition process *finite in its number of steps*. This difficulty Marx perceived in his repeated Volume II joustings with Smith's decomposition of price into wages plus profit [5, Marx, 1885]. Yet in his brilliant "steady-reproduction tableaux" of that volume, Marx in effect solved the problem by deriving synchronized steady-state labor requirements needed to produce steady-state flow of coats. Dmitriev, perhaps knowing only the 1867 Volume I of *Das Kapital*, leaves nothing *implicit* in his resolution of the matter, saying (p. 43):

> It is asked how it is possible to calculate the amount of labour expended for the production of a given economic good from the very beginning of history . . . [when] there is no doubt that at present capital is invariably produced by capital . . . [so] that it is an impossible task to calculate the amount of labour expended in a given product from the time of the creation of the first capital by labour alone. However, there is no need for such a calculation: the sum of the labour expended on the production of a given product may be determined without such historical digressions.

Instead he proceeds by making the (heroic!) assumption that each good, 1,2, . . . , does have a *finite* total labor requirement (heroic because without a Ricardian-Austrian hierarchy, we know that special so-called Hawkins-Simon conditions must be assumable, so that less than

1 corn-seed is needed to produce 1 corn output and so that no good require directly or *indirectly* more than 1 unit of itself for its own production). Then, in his Equations (6), Dmitriev boldly cuts the Gordian knot of circular interdependence by writing down the *simultaneous-equation* system for steady-state total labor requirements (or, for what on p. 71 he shows to be the same thing, for zero-profit competitive prices).

That Dmitriev's equations are identical with those of Leontief and Sraffa can be seen by writing them in modern conventional matrix notation.[1] Or, suppose that corn is the sole good, requiring $a_{11} = \frac{1}{2}$ of corn-seed as input to produce 1 of corn and requiring $a_{01} = 2$ units of direct labor. Dmitriev's (6) then takes the simple form

$$
\begin{aligned}
N_1 &= a_{01} + N_1 a_{11} = a_{01}[1 - a_{11}]^{-1} \quad [2] \\
&= 2 + \tfrac{1}{2} N_1 = 2[1 - \tfrac{1}{2}]^{-1} = 2[2] \\
&= 4 \text{ labor units} \quad Q.E.D.
\end{aligned}
$$

Dmitriev, like Marx in Marx's criticisms of Adam Smith, apparently did not realize that although one is correct in believing that total labor requirements, N_j, can be computed *without* a full "historical digression" into labor requirements of *all* earlier stages, nevertheless one *can* rigorously make that full "historical decomposition." Thus, in the corn-seed and corn case, we find

$$
\begin{aligned}
N_1 &= 4 = a_{01}(1 - a_{11})^{-1} \quad [3] \\
&= a_{01}(1 + a_{11} + (a_{11})^2 + \ldots) \\
&= a_{01} + [a_{01}(a_{11}) + a_{01}(a_{11})^2 + \ldots] \\
&= 2 + [2(\tfrac{1}{2}) + \{2(\tfrac{1}{2})\}\tfrac{1}{2} + \ldots] \\
&= 2 + 2[(\tfrac{1}{2}) + (\tfrac{1}{2})^2 + \ldots + (\tfrac{1}{2})^k + \ldots] \\
&= 2 + 2[1], \ 0 < a_{11} = \tfrac{1}{2} < 1
\end{aligned}
$$

[1] The usual matrix notation, as in Dorfman, *et al.* [3, 1958] writes the row vector of direct labor requirements as $[a_{0j}] = \mathbf{a_0}$; the square n-by-n matrix of inputs required per unit of outputs as $[a_{ij}] = \mathbf{a}$; I as the n-by-n identity matrix consisting of zeros everywhere except for ones in the main diagonal. Often what is here written as **a** is written as **A**; but there is some convenience in reserving the latter symbol for the inverse matrix $[I - a]^{-1} = [A_{ij}] = \mathbf{A}$; then total labor requirements, Dmitriev's $[N_j]$, is written as the row vector $[A_{0j}] = \mathbf{A_0} = a_0[I - a]^{-1}$. When the interest rate r is not zero, the final equation of competitive prices (relative to the money wage set at one as numeraire) becomes $P = a_0(1 + r)[I - a(1 + r)]^{-1} = A_0\{r\}$, where the curly brackets indicate the functional dependence on the profit rate r (so that $A_0\{0\}$ is identically the same as A_0 above).

where the expression in square brackets is assured to be an infinite *but convergent* series for *all* earlier indirect labor requirements.

One could not expect economists of 1776, 1817, 1867 or 1898 to realize that, as applied to a viable many-good system of commodities used to produce commodities, a similar matrix infinite series will assuredly validly converge, namely

$$P = a_0[I - a]^{-1}$$
$$= a_0[I + a + a^2 + \ldots + a^k + \ldots]$$
$$= a_0 + [a_0 a + a_0 a^2 + \ldots + a_0 a^k + \ldots] < \infty$$

Thus, Smith was, in principle, correct in his breakdown of price into the value-added components of wages plus profits (or of wage-and-rents plus profits when land is not ignorable as superabundant).

Dmitriev's remarkable anticipation of Leontief must now be apparent. Secondly, his next dozen equations anticipate the way the interest rate enters into a Sraffian or Ricardian or Walrasian system. It is interesting that he ignores completely the Marxian practice of *Capital*'s Volume I, of trying to relate the capitalist's *surplus* to the *direct* wage outlay alone. Dmitriev, like Sraffa, [10, 1960], eschews any mention of equalized industry rates of surplus value on wages alone. Thus, Dmitriev gives equations like my [1] above; or, as with Böhm-Bawerk, he considers cases where a uniform application of labor is repeated for several different periods, and shows that changes in the profit rate will have systematic effects on relative prices, even if the same total labor is required, unless it happens that the time profile of application of the labor is the same between the two goods.

All of Dmitriev's examples seem to be of the supra-diagonal, hierarchical type that permit of a historical decomposition into wages and interest in a finite number of steps. So, in a sense, he retreats from his brilliant beginning, never quite reattaining the full Sraffa generality of my last footnote. But he is aware that, given the money wage rate, the rate of profit, and the absence of joint products or land-rent complications, all competitive prices of goods produced are determinable *independently of how much of each good demand conditions dictate*. In this sense, Dmitriev employs the zero- and positive-profit nonsubstitution theo-

rems of Georgescu-Roegen, Samuelson, Morishima, Mirrlees, and many others.

Thirdly, Bortkiewicz could clearly have learned from Dmitriev what Sraffa, Kaldor, and other modern commentators on the Ricardian and Marxian systems, have called the corn-own-rate equilibrium level of profit, or what was called the subsistence-exploitation rate of profit in my review of the Marxian transformation problem [9, Samuelson, 1971].

Dmitriev, like D. Champernowne, Samuelson, Sraffa, and others, clearly defines a factor-price tradeoff frontier, relating a rising real wage rate to a falling profit rate. But how to get the missing equation to pick out one equilibrium profit rate and real wage? Dmitriev claims that Ricardo, correctly in Dmitriev's view, got the missing equation from stipulating a minimum-subsistence real wage rate, in terms of corn or a more general array of subsistence goods. How that subsistence level is determined, by physiology, custom, and the class struggle, Dmitriev believes falls outside the "scope" and "competence" of "political economy"; but he harbors no doubts on the relevance for his times of the subsistence wage. He says: "Hardly anyone will dispute that the *only* process determining the level of profit at the *present time* is the process of production of the means of subsistence of the workers" (p. 73). My own reading of the economic history of demographic, wage, and profit trends in Europe and North America at the turn of the century makes this seem a most dubious conclusion, even coming from a writer in Tsarist Russia—which perhaps only goes to demonstrate the power of analytical superstructure on economists' perception of reality. It is a pleasure, however, to agree with Dmitriev's demolishing (pp. 75–76) of J. Thünen's odd compromise between subsistence wage and the total-of-product wage, the formula for the geometric mean of them that he had put on his tombstone and which he purported to derive by the maximization of a certain gratuitous ratio.

My one sector corn-seed and corn example of Equation [2] can illustrate the equilibrium profit theory Dmitriev attributes to Ricardo. Although each labor unit can produce in the steady-state ¼ a unit of corn, suppose that the minimum of subsistence of corn required to produce and reproduce one labor unit is less than ¼, say ¹/₁₀. Then only at a unique positive profit rate, will the competitive real wage advanced to the workers be equal to the stipulated subsistence. Plotting the factor-price frontier with the real corn wage rate on the vertical axis and the profit rate on the horizontal axis, we move horizontally on the ¹/₁₀ level to encounter the unique profit rate of .429 or 42 6/7 percent.

This theory attributed by Dmitriev to Ricardo, I would think can be more persuasively attributed to various versions of the Marxian system. For, in Ricardian long-run, land is not really ignorable. So even in the simplest case of homogeneous, but limited land, we have instead of a 2-variable factor price tradeoff, a 3-variable factor-price tradeoff frontier: this relates the profit rate, r, to the corn real wage, W/P_1, and the corn real rent rate, R/P_1: $r = f(W/P_1, R/P_1)$, not $f(W/P_1)$. Ricardo, much in the manner that Dmitriev criticizes as superficial in Adam Smith, determines from accumulation proclivities or supply-of-capital considerations how large will be ultimate population and labor-land density, and only at that level is the Ricardian ultimate profit rate determinable. For agreement on this interpretation see N. Kaldor [4, 1955], P. A. Samuelson [8, 1959], L. Pasinetti [6, 1959], M. Blaug [1, 1962], or the introduction to Sraffa's edition of Ricardo's *Principles* [7, 1817—1953]. On the other hand, Marx-like systems often do regard land as ignorable, so that my review of the Marxian transformation problem [9, Samuelson, 1971] dealt with precisely what Dmitriev is discussing.

Dmitriev, however, like so many Marxian and non-Marxian writers, falls into the trap of ignoring the intertemporal technological tradeoffs that characterize transient paths from one steady state to another; and he ignores the possibility that a model in which labor supply is producible out of subsistence can grow or decay rather than have to stay in the steady state. Therefore, the exploitation rate of profit defined by Marx or Dmitriev is in no necessary sense inconsistent with a Fisher-Senior general equilibrium model of the long-run interest rate as determined both by subjective time preference decisions about saving and consuming and by alternative opportunities to make intertemporal investments—or inconsistent with a

Modigliani life-cycle saving model—with or without the copious alternative technical blue prints that characterize so-called "neoclassical" branches of mainstream economics.

Dmitriev's last two essays are of interest in their own right. He realizes that the second, and longest, deals with imperfection of competition. Dmitriev is less sanguine than Cournot that, as sellers become more numerous than one, perfect competition will be rapidly approached in the limit. He is concerned that even with several sellers there may be a tendency to collude on a common price, particularly when each seller is known to have spare capacity and the ability to put some of his productivity into storage. There is also an interesting argument that Chamberlin would like concerning wastes of competition when we are neither in perfect monopoly nor in perfect competition. One can join the editor in commending Dmitriev's suggestive discussions of business-cycle aspects of oligopoly.

The final essay deals with the marginal utility background of demand. Once Dmitriev faces up to imperfect, rather than perfect, competition, demand becomes important. More than that, once he faces up to Ricardo's scarcity of land, he realizes the error in thinking that distribution of income can be divorced from the full conditions of demand. Ricardians simply erred in thinking that they could avoid the complication of land rent by going out to the "external no-rent margin." This can be seen from the fact that a shift in utility from land-intensive corn to labor-intensive cloth will, even at the same profit rate, lower the rent/wage factor shares and total profit share as well. Little new ground concerning marginal utility emerges from the third essay. Thus, Dmitriev shows no Paretian awareness that utility need not be cardinally measurable. Still, a 1904 discovery of such pre-Gossen theorists as Galiani, Rossi, Bernoulli, DeMolinari, Senior, Dupuit, and Weber-Fechner, deserves praise.

Reading Dmitriev's book helps give one an impression of just which authors were well known in turn-of-the-century Russia. English writers, to say nothing of American, play a much smaller role in Dmitriev's thinking than do, say, Italian writers. German, Austrian, and French economists bulk large, even though Dmitriev tends to be a bit hard on the Austrians. Readers of Dmitriev will also be left with the sad impression that his influence, except possibly through Bortkiewicz, was almost nil both on mainstream economists and on their critics, which is a pity. I think the editor's sharp nose is correct in sniffing out the aroma of a *bourgeois*, or even general-equilibrium, economist coiled inside Dmitriev.

Economists are much in Mario Nuti's debt. Only one who has edited a work like this can appreciate the intelligent effort that has gone into this edition. I tried the experiment of writing this review prior to reading the editor's introductory essay. I found it reassuring that we seem to be in agreement on most essentials, and am grateful that I could improve my first draft by benefitting from Mr. Nuti's analysis.

PAUL A. SAMUELSON
Massachusetts Institute of Technology

REFERENCES

1. BLAUG, M. *Economic theory in retrospect.* Homewood, Ill.: Irwin, 1962.
2. VON BORTKIEWICZ, L. "Value and Price in the Marxian System," *Archiv für Sozialwissenschaft und Sozialpolitik,* 1906, *23* (1), pp. 1–50; 1907, *25*(1), pp. 10–51; 1907, *25*(2), pp. 445–88; reprinted in English in *Int. Econ. Pap.,* 1952, *2,* pp. 5–60.
3. DORFMAN, R.; SAMUELSON, P. A. AND SOLOW, R. M. *Linear programming and economic analysis.* New York: McGraw-Hill, 1958.
4. KALDOR, N. "Alternative Theories of Distribution," *Rev. Econ. Stud.,* 1955–1956, *23* (2), pp. 83–100.
5. MARX, K. *Capital,* Vol. I (1867); Vol. II (1885); Vol. III (1894).
6. PASINETTI, L. "A Mathematical Formulation of the Ricardian System," *Rev. Econ. Stud.,* Feb. 1960, *27,* pp. 78–98.
7. RICARDO, D. *The works and correspondence of David Ricardo.* Edited by P. SRAFFA. Cambridge, England: Cambridge University Press, 1953.
8. SAMUELSON, P. A. "A Modern Treatment of the Ricardian Economy" in two articles, *Quart. J. Econ.,* Feb. 1959, *73,* pp. 1–35; May 1959, *73*(2), pp. 217–31; reprinted in P. SAMUELSON, *Collected scientific papers.* Edited by J. STIGLITZ. Cambridge, Mass.: MIT Press, 1965, Chs. 31, 32, pp. 373–442.
9. ———. "Understanding the Marxian Notion of Exploitation: A Summary of the So-Called Transformation Problem Between Marxian Values and Competitive Prices," *J. Econ. Lit.,* June 1971, *9*(2), pp. 399–431.
10. SRAFFA, P. *Production of commodities by means of commodities.* Cambridge, England: Cambridge University Press, 1960.

PART IV

Mathematical Biology and Economics of Population

A Biological Least-Action Principle for the Ecological Model of Volterra-Lotka

(predator–prey/ecology/least-action)

PAUL A. SAMUELSON

Department of Economics, Massachusetts Institute of Technology,
Cambridge, Mass. 02139

Contributed by Paul A. Samuelson, April 21, 1974

ABSTRACT   The conservative model of Volterra for more-than-two predator-prey species is shown to be generated as extremals that minimize a definable Lagrange-Hamilton integral involving half the species and their rates of change. This least-action formulation differs from that derived two generations ago by Volterra, since his involves twice the number of phase variables and it employs as variables the cumulative integrals of the numbers of each species that have ever lived. The present result extends the variational, teleological formulations found a decade ago by the author to the more-than-two species case. The present result is anything but surprising, in view of the works by Kerner, Montroll, and others which apply Gibbs' statistical mechanics to the all-but-canonical equations of the standard Volterra model. By a globally linear transformation of coordinates, the Volterra equations are here converted into a *completely* canonical system isomorphic with the classical mechanics models of Newton, Lagrange, Hamilton, Jacobi, Boltzmann, Gibbs, Poincaré, and G. D. Birkhoff. The conservative nature of the Lotka-Volterra model, whatever its realism, is a crucially necessary condition for the applicability of the variational formalisms, microscopically and macroscopically.

REVIEW

Volterra (ref. 1) postulates the skew-symmetric ecological system of predator-prey

$$dN_i/dt = N_i\{\epsilon_i + \beta_i^{-1}\sum_{j=1}^{n} a_{ij}N_j\}, \qquad (i = 1,\ldots,n = 2m)$$

$$= N_i \beta_i^{-1} \sum_{j=1}^{n} a_{ij}(N_j - N_j^*), \qquad \beta_i > 0 \qquad [1]$$

$$N_j^* > 0, \qquad a_{ij} + a_{ji} = 0, \qquad \det[a_{ij}] \neq 0 \qquad [2]$$

where $N_i(t)$ represents the number at time t of the i-th species, and there is skew-symmetry of the nonsingular matrix, $a = (a_{ij}) = (-a_{ji}) = -a^T$. This is an essential feature of this model of perpetual conservative fluctuation around a positive equilibrium point, (N_i^*). For $n = 2$, Eq. 1 is the classic predator–prey model of Lotka (ref. 2) and Volterra.

By the nonsingular transformation of variables,

$$y_i = \ln \beta_i N_i, \qquad \exp y_i = \beta_i N_i \qquad [3]$$

$$\exp y_i^* = \beta_i N_i^* = x_i^*, \qquad (i = 1, \ldots, n)$$

Eq. 2 becomes

$$dy_i/dt = \sum_{1}^{n} A_{ij}(\exp y_i - x_i^*), \qquad (i = 1, \ldots, n) \qquad [4]$$

$$A_{ij} + A_{ji} = \beta_i^{-1}(a_{ij} + a_{ji})\beta_j^{-1} = 0, \qquad \det[A_{ij}] \neq 0$$

This can be written in equivalent form

$$dy_i/dt = \sum_{j=1}^{n} A_{ij} \, \partial H[y_1, \ldots, y_n]/\partial y_j \qquad (i = 1, \ldots, n) \qquad [5]$$

where H is a Hamiltonian function defined as

$$H[y_1, \ldots, y_n] = H[y] \text{ for short}$$

$$= \sum_{1}^{n} H_i[y_i] = \sum_{1}^{n} \int_{y_i^*}^{y_i} [\exp v_i - x_i^*]dv_i \qquad [6]$$

$$= \sum_{1}^{n} [\exp y_i - (1 + y_i - y_i^*)x_i^*]$$

$$> H[y_i^*, \ldots, y_n^*] = 0, \qquad \text{for } (y_1, \ldots, y_n) \neq (y_1^*, \ldots, y_n^*)$$

$$\partial H[y]/\partial y_i = H_i'[y_i] = \exp y_i - x_i^*, \qquad (i = 1, \ldots, n)$$

Since $H_i''[y_i] = \exp y_i > 0$, $H[y]$ is a convex function in the Volterra system.

That H is constant along any motion is seen from

$$dH/dt = \sum_{1}^{n} (\partial H[y]/\partial y_i)(dy_i/dt) \qquad [7]$$

$$= \sum_{1}^{n} \sum_{1}^{n} (\partial H[y]/\partial y_i)A_{ij}(\partial H[y]/\partial y_j)$$

$$= \frac{1}{2} \sum_{1}^{n} \sum_{1}^{n} (\partial H[y]/\partial y_i)(A_{ij} + A_{ji})(\partial H[y]/\partial y_j)$$

$$\equiv 0 \text{ from Eq. } 4$$

Equations **5** are in the all-but-canonical form of Kerner (ref. 3). For the 2-species prey–predator case of Lotka-Volterra, an original dimensional transformation of variables can assure that $A_{12} = -1$, $A_{21} = 1$ in Eq. **5**. And then Eq. **5** is *completely* in Hamilton's canonical form, namely

$$\begin{aligned} dy_1/dt &= -\partial H[y_1,y_2]/\partial y_2 \\ dy_2/dt &= +\partial H[y_1,y_2]/\partial y_1 \end{aligned} \qquad A = \begin{bmatrix} 0 & -1 \\ +1 & 0 \end{bmatrix} \qquad [8]$$

where (y_1,y_2) are interpretable as a generalized momentum and its conjugate space coordinate (p,q), and $H[\ ]$ is akin to the sum of kinetic and potential energies. Essentially on this basis, the present least-action principle was derived for the $n = 2$ case in Samuelson (refs. 4 and 5).

I now provide the same least-action formulation, or more exactly, the same Hamilton's-Principle minimizing formulation, for the multi-species case of $n = 2m \geq 2$; new coordinates $(z_1,\ldots,z_n)$ are defined by globally linear transformations of $(y_1,\ldots,y_n)$, nonsingular but not orthogonal rotations, namely by

$$z_i = \sum_{1}^{n} b_{ij} y_j, \qquad (i = 1, \ldots, n) \text{ or } z = By \qquad [9]$$

$$y_i = \sum_{1}^{n} b^{ij} z_j, \qquad \det B \neq 0, \qquad \text{or } y = B^{-1}z$$

This defines a new transformed Hamiltonian function

$$\tilde{H}[z_1, \ldots, z_n] = \tilde{H}[z] \qquad [10]$$

$$= \sum_{j=1}^{n} H_j[\sum_{k=1}^{n} b^{jk} z_k]$$

$$\partial \tilde{H}[z]/\partial z_i = \sum_{j=1}^{n} b^{ji} H_j'[y_k] = \sum_{j=1}^{n} b^{ji} \partial H[y]/\partial y_j$$

Because $H[y]$ is convex, so must be $\tilde{H}[z]$.

In matrix notation, the system can be written in terms of $y = (y_i)$ and $H_y = (\partial H[y]/\partial y_i)$ as in Eq. **5**, or in terms of the new variables $z = (z_i)$ and $\tilde{H}_z[z] = (\partial \tilde{H}[z]/\partial y_i)$, namely as

$$dy/dt = AH_y[y] \qquad [5]$$

$$dz/dt = \tilde{A}\tilde{H}_z[z], \qquad \tilde{A} + \tilde{A}^T = 0, \qquad \tilde{A} = BAB^T$$

$$= BAB^T \tilde{H}_z[z] \qquad [11]$$

In conventional vector notation Eq. **5** is equivalent to $dy/dt = A\nabla H[y]$. Equations **11** are seen to be still in all-but-canonical form, even though $H[z]$ has lost its simplistic form of being a sum of n functions of a single variable.

However, since every nonsingular skew-symmetric matrix A is known to be congruent to a "canonical" skew-symmetric matrix, we are assured, as in textbooks like Perlis (ref. 6), that there exists a nonsingular B which makes $\bar{A}$ of the desired exact-canonical form, namely

$$
\begin{bmatrix}
0 & \cdots & 0 & -1 & \cdots & 0 \\
\cdot & & \cdot & & & \cdot \\
\cdot & & \cdot & & & \cdot \\
0 & \cdots & 0 & 0 & \cdots & -1 \\
1 & \cdots & 0 & 0 & \cdots & 0 \\
\cdot & & \cdot & & & \cdot \\
\cdot & & \cdot & & & \cdot \\
0 & \cdots & 1 & 0 & \cdots & 0
\end{bmatrix}
=
\begin{bmatrix}
0 & -I_m \\
I_m & 0
\end{bmatrix}
\qquad [12]
$$

For such a B and A, and there are $(2m)!/(m!)^2$ ways of picking m variables out of $2m$ variables to be our m new Lagrangian space variables in the above partitioning of Eq. 12, we have arrived at *exact* canonical equations:

$$
dz_i/dt = -\partial\tilde{H}[z_1,\ldots,z_{2m}]/\partial z_{m+i}
$$

$$
dz_{m+i}/dt = +\partial\tilde{H}[z_1,\ldots,z_{2m}]/\partial z_i \ (i = 1,\ldots,m = n/2) \quad [13]
$$

If we identify $(z_1,\ldots,z_m)$ with $(p_1,\ldots,p_m) = p$ and link $(z_{m+1}, \ldots,z_{2m})$ with $(q_1,\ldots,q_m) = q$, Eq. 14 takes on the more familiar canonical appearance

$$
dp/dt = -\partial H[p,q]/\partial q, \qquad dq/dt = +\partial H[p,q]/\partial p \quad [14]
$$

Now it is routine to work back from Eq. 14's exact canonical form to the Hamilton–Lagrange action integral that is being minimized. Shortening (dq_i/dt) to (q_i') or q', we use the following Legendre transformation to define as a conjugate function to the Hamiltonian function $H[p,q]$ a new Lagrangian integrand function $L[q',q]$, namely

$$
L[q_1',\ldots,q_m',q_1,\ldots,q_m] + \tilde{H}[p_1,\ldots,p_m,q_1,\ldots,q_m] \qquad [15.1]
$$

$$
= \sum_1^m p_j q_j'
$$

$$
q_i' = \partial\tilde{H}[p,q]/\partial p_i \qquad (i = 1,\ldots,m) \qquad [15.2]
$$

$$
p_i' = \partial L[q',q]/\partial q_i' \qquad [15.3]
$$

$$
\partial H[p,q]/\partial q_i + \partial L[q',q]/\partial q_i = 0 \qquad [15.4]
$$

Numerically solving Eq. 15.2 for unique p's in terms of (q',q) is always possible because of the convexity of $\tilde{H}[p,q]$; substituting the resulting p's in Eq. 15.1 does define $L[q',q]$ uniquely; from the convexity of $\tilde{H}[p,q]$ on all of its variables, it can be shown as in Samuelson (ref. 7) that $L[q',q]$ must be convex in $(q_1',\ldots,q_m')$ and concave in $(q_1,\ldots,q_m)$, having a minimax saddlepoint at $(q',q) = (0,\ldots,0, q_1{}^*,\ldots,q_m{}^*)$.

Applying Eq. **15** to Eq. **14**'s canonical equations, we arrive, as in Bliss (ref. 8) at the Euler extremal conditions

$$d/dt\ \partial L[q',q]/\partial q_i' - \partial L[q',q]/\partial q_i = 0 \qquad [16]$$

$$(i = 1,\ldots,m = n/2)$$

These are equivalent to the variational conditions reminiscent of Newton-Lagrange classical mechanics

$$\delta \int_{t^0}^{t^1} L[q_1',\ldots,q_m', q_1,\ldots,q_m]dt = 0 \qquad [17]$$

Because $L[q',q]$ is strictly convex in q', the Euler necessary conditions of Eq. **16** can be shown to be also sufficient for a *strong* minimum to the Lagrange-Hamilton integral of Eq. **17** provided $t^1 - t^0$ is not too large. Hence, the motions defined by Eq. **16**, and by our original system Eqs. **1** do provide a true minimum for the following biological "action" integral

$$I = \underset{q_i(t)}{\mathrm{Min}} \int_{t^0}^{t^1} L[q_1'(t),\ldots,q_m'(t),q_1(t),\ldots,q_m(t)]dt \qquad [18]$$

$$q_i(t^0) = q_i{}^0, \qquad q_i(t^1) = q_i{}^1 \qquad (i = 1,\ldots,m)$$

so long as $t^1 - t^0$ is a positive number sufficiently small to exclude Jacobi conjugate points.

Perhaps there is irony that the bitter struggle for Darwinian survival is here describable by a minimizing teleological ("best-of-all-possible-worlds") formulation. In any case, all the powerful theorems of the variational case now are seen to be applicable to the Volterra model, e.g., Poincaré's theorem on pairs of opposite-signed characteristic exponents at fixed points and for periodic motions, Liouville's theorem on conservation of volume in phase space, and related Poincaré's integral invariants. The works of Kerner had prepared one to believe in all these things but it should be useful to have an exact canonical formulation.

GENERALIZATIONS

As argued in Samuelson (ref. 9), there is no particular empirical or analytical warrant for the linearity of Eq. **1**'s right-hand bracketed expressions with the implied additivity properties of $H[y_1,\ldots,y_n]$. Cheap generalizations of Eqs. **1** and **3** are provided by

$$dy_i/dt = \sum_{j=1}^{n} A_{ij}\partial H[y_1,\ldots,y_n]/\partial y_j \qquad [19]$$

$$A_{ij} + A_{ji} = 0, \qquad \det[A_{ij}] \neq 0, \qquad (i,j = 1,\ldots,n = 2m)$$

where $H[y_1,\ldots,y_n]$ is *any* convex function not necessarily of Eq. **6**'s additive form $H_i[y_i]$. As Kerner has observed, there is no necessity that the A_{ij} elements of A in Eq. **19** be independent of the y's rather than $A_{ij}[y_1,\ldots,y_n]$. Also, we can lighten a bit the strong integrability condition $\partial(\partial H/\partial y_i)\partial y_j \rightleftharpoons \partial(\partial H/\partial y_j)/\partial y_i$. Thus, generalize Eq. **19** to

$$dy_i/dt = \sum_{j=1}^{n} A_{ij}[y_1,\ldots,y_n]f_j[y_1,\ldots,y_n] \qquad [20]$$

$$A_{ij}[y] \equiv -A_{ji}[y], \quad f_j[y_1{}^*,\ldots,y_n{}^*] = 0, \qquad \det(A_{ij}[y]) \neq 0$$

$$f_k[y](\partial f_i[y]/\partial y_j - \partial f_j[y]/\partial y_i) + f_i[y](\partial f_j[y]/\partial y_k$$
$$- \partial f_k[y]/\partial y_j) + f_j[y](\partial f_k[y]/\partial y_i - \partial f_i[y]/\partial y_k) \equiv 0,$$
$$(i,j,k = 1,\ldots,2m = n)$$

These last "integrability" conditions suffice to ensure existence of an integrability factor, $\gamma[y_1,\ldots,y_n] = \gamma[y]$, such that along any motion

$$\gamma[y]\sum_1^{n} f_i[y]dy_i/dt$$

$$= \frac{1}{2}\sum_1^{n}\sum_1^{n} f_i[y](A_{ij}[y] + A_{ji}[y])f_j[y] \qquad [21]$$

$$= 0 = dJ[y_1,\ldots,y_n]/dt$$

where J is an existent function that represents a generalization of Hamilton's H, and which can be assumed to have a minimum at $(y_i{}^*)$ provided the $f_i[y]/f_1[y]$ functions satisfy straightforward curvature conditions that suffice to make J quasiconvex, so that $J[y] \leq J[y^0]$ forms a convex set. Since J is a constant along any motion, wherever some $y_i{}^0 \neq y_i{}^*$ so that $H[y^0] > H[y^*]$, the motions never settle down and y_i must fluctuate forever.

CONTRASTING VOLTERRA EXTREMALS

Volterra's own variational formulation (ref. 10) is something different from Eq. **18**. It is in terms of $2n = 4m$ phase variables $(N_1,\ldots,N_{2m},V_1,\ldots,V_{2m})$, where

$$N_i(t) = V_i'(t), \qquad (i = 1,\ldots,n = 2m) \qquad [22.1]$$

$$V_i(t) = \int_\tau^t N_i(s)ds$$

$$L[V_1',\ldots,V_n',V_1,\ldots,V_n] \qquad [22.2]$$

$$= \sum_1^{n} \beta_j V_j'\ln V_j' + \frac{1}{2}\sum_1^{n}\sum_1^{n} a_{ji}V_i'V_j + \sum_1^{n} \beta_j\epsilon_j V_j$$

$$\delta \int_{t^0}^{t^1} L[V_1',\ldots,V_{2m}',V_1,\ldots,V_{2m}]dt = 0 \qquad [22.3]$$

One easily verifies that the Euler equations implied by Eq. **22.3** are precisely equivalent to Eq. **1** when Eq. **1** is expressed in the symbols defined by Eq. **22.1**. The Legendre transformation applied to Volterra's L gives its conjugate $4m$-variable

Hamiltonian function, in terms of which he can write canonical equations in $4m$ phase variables.

Volterra's original stationary point corresponds in the $4m$ space of $(V_1', \ldots, V_n', V_1, \ldots, V_n)$, where $V_i'(t) \equiv N_i(t) \equiv N_i^*$, to linearly growing cumulative variables, $V_1, \ldots, V_m$, so that the Poincaré characterizations of fixed points of a variational problem become inapplicable. However, Volterra's formulation has the convenient property that his integrand, $L[V', V]$, can be written down immediately without need to transform variables or solve the implicit equations of the Legendre transformation; and his second-order Euler equations to Eq. **22** turn out not to involve (V_j), but only (V_j', V_j'').

Kerner gives a more natural variational formulation alternative to Volterra's Eq. **22.3**. It also involves a phase space of $2n = 4m$ variables. Kerner's, however, is not a least-action principle but a stationary-action-principle.

In present notation, avoiding any Legendre-transformation, Kerner sets

$$\delta \int_{t^0}^{t^1} \left(\frac{1}{2} \sum_1^n \sum_1^n A^{ij} y_i y_j' - \sum_1^n H_i[y_i] \right) dt = 0 \quad [\mathbf{23.1}]$$

$$[A^{ij}] = [A_{ij}]^{-1} = -[A^{ji}]$$

with implied Euler equations, for $(i = 1, \ldots, n = 2m)$

$$\sum_1^n A^{ij} y_j' = H_i'[y_i] \quad [\mathbf{23.2}]$$

$$y_i' = \sum_1^n A_{ij} H_j'[y_j]$$

Since, however, the integrand in Eq. **23.1** is linear in the velocities (y_j'), the actual motions that take place between two points in time do not give a minimum to the integral but only a stationary value. As Kerner observes (ref. 3, p. 98 of the cited 1972 reprint of his 1959 discussion), the canonical equations to Eq. **23** are degenerate, which is fortunate since we wish to end up with n first-order differential equations and not $2n$. By contrast with Eq. **23**, Eq. **18** has only $n/2$ y's in its integrand, and its $2(n/2)$ canonical equations are precisely the number needed; the stronger convexity of its integrand in the velocities does ensure a true *least*-action.

NUMERICAL EXAMPLE

Here is a case where lettuce, N_1, is eaten by the other three species. Rabbits, N_2, eat lettuce and are eaten by the other two species. Foxes and dogs, N_3 and N_4, eat rabbits and lettuce but not each other. Now Eq. **1** becomes

$$N_1/N_1 = 4 + 1^{-1}(-2N_2 - 6N_3 - 4N_4)$$

$$\dot{N}_2/N_2 = 1 + 2^{-1}(2N_1 - 6N_3 - 8N_4)$$

$$\dot{N}_3/N_3 = -3 + 3^{-1}(6N_1 + 6N_2)$$

$$\dot{N}_4/N_4 = -2 + 4^{-1}(4N_1 + 8N_2)$$

$$(N_j{}^*) = \left(1, \frac{1}{2}, \frac{1}{3}, \frac{1}{4},\right)$$

Defining $y_i = \ln\beta_i N_i$, with $x_i^* = 1$, $y_i^* = 0$, we write our system as

$$dy_i/dt = \sum_1^4 A_{ij}[\exp y_j - 1] \qquad (i = 1,\ldots,n)$$

$$= \sum_1^4 A_{ij}\,\partial H[y]/\partial y_j, \text{ where } H = \sum_1^4 [e^y - 1 - y_i]$$

Or, in matrix form,

$$dy/dt = AH_y[y]$$

$$A = \begin{bmatrix} 0 & -1 & -2 & -1 \\ 1 & 0 & -1 & -1 \\ 2 & 1 & 0 & 0 \\ 1 & 1 & 0 & 0 \end{bmatrix} = -A^T$$

This almost canonical form can be transformed into exact canonical form

$$dz/dt = \tilde{A}\tilde{H}_z[z]$$

$$dz/dt = \begin{bmatrix} dp/dt \\ dq/dt \end{bmatrix} = \begin{bmatrix} -\tilde{H}_q[p,q] \\ +\tilde{H}_p[p,q] \end{bmatrix}$$

where

$$\tilde{A} = BAB^T$$

$$= \begin{bmatrix} 1 & -1 & 1 & -1 \\ 0 & 1 & -1 & 1 \\ 0 & 0 & 1 & -1 \\ 0 & 0 & 0 & 1 \end{bmatrix} \begin{bmatrix} 0 & -1 & -2 & -1 \\ 1 & 0 & -1 & -1 \\ 2 & 1 & 0 & 0 \\ 1 & 1 & 0 & 0 \end{bmatrix}$$

$$\begin{bmatrix} 1 & 0 & 0 & 0 \\ -1 & 1 & 0 & 0 \\ 1 & -1 & 1 & 0 \\ -1 & 1 & -1 & 1 \end{bmatrix}$$

$$= \begin{bmatrix} 0 & 0 & -1 & 0 \\ 0 & 0 & 0 & -1 \\ 1 & 0 & 0 & 0 \\ 0 & 1 & 0 & 0 \end{bmatrix}; B^{-1} = \begin{bmatrix} 1 & 1 & 0 & 0 \\ 0 & 1 & 1 & 0 \\ 0 & 0 & 1 & 1 \\ 0 & 0 & 0 & 1 \end{bmatrix}$$

$$\tilde{H}[p_1, p_2, q_1, q_2] = H_1[p_1] + H_2[p_1 + p_2] + H_3[p_2 + q_1]$$
$$+ H_4[q_1 + q_2] = [\exp{(p_1)} - p_1 - 1] + [\exp{(p_1 + p_2)}$$
$$- p_1 - p_2 - 1] + [\exp{(p_2 + q_1)} - p_2 - q_1 - 1]$$
$$+ [\exp{(q_1 + q_2)} - q_1 - q_2 - 1]$$

The Legendre transformation can be attained to any degree of accuracy by numerically inverting Eq. **15.2**'s set of implicit equations, but cannot be expressed in terms of standard, tabulated functions—the usual case in Hamilton-Lagrange systems outside of textbook examples.

A final warning is in order. The conservative nature of the Volterra system Eq. **1** is so strong and special as, perhaps, to constitute a prima-facie case *against* rather than for it as a useful description of ecological reality.

I owe thanks to Professors H. A. Freeman and Joel Yellin of M.I.T. for helpful discussions, to Kate Crowley for editorial assistance, and to the National Science Foundation for financial aid. My indebtedness to the works of Volterra, Kerner, and Montroll *et al.* (ref. 11) will be obvious.

1. Volterra, V. (1931) *Leçons sur la théorie mathématique de la lutte pour la vie* (Gauthier-Villars, Paris).
2. Lotka, A. J. (1925) *Elements of Physical Biology* (Williams & Wilkins, Baltimore).
3. Kerner, E. H. (1972) *Gibbs Ensemble; Biological Ensemble* (Gordon & Breach, New York), containing reprints of his 1957, 1959, 1961, and 1964 articles from the *Bulletin of Mathematical Biophysics* and a new introduction.
4. Samuelson, P. A. (1965) "Some notions on causality and teleology in economics," in *Cause and Effect*, ed. Lerner, D. (The Free Press, New York), pp. 99–143; this is reproduced in *Collected Scientific Papers of P. A. Samuelson*, Vol. III, MIT Press, Cambridge, Mass., 1972, as chap. 169; see particularly p. 126 of the original or p. 455 of the reproduction.
5. Samuelson, P. A. (1967) "A universal cycle?" in *Methods of Operations Research*, ed. Henn, R. (Verlag Anton Hain, Muhlgasse), Vol. III, pp. 307–320, reproduced in *Collected Scientific Papers*, Vol. III, as chap. 170.
6. Perlis, S. (1952) *Theory of Matrices* (Addison-Wesley Press, Reading, Mass.), chap. 5.
7. Samuelson, P. A. (1972) "The general saddlepoint property of optimal-control motions," *J. Econ. Theory* **5,** 102–120.
8. Bliss, G. A. (1946) *Lectures on the Calculus of Variations* (Univ. of Chicago Press, Chicago).
9. Samuelson, P. A. (1971) "Generalized predator-prey oscillations in ecological and economic equilibrium," *Proc. Nat. Acad. Sci. USA* **68,** 980–983; reproduced as chap. 171 in *Collected Scientific Papers*, Vol. III.
10. Volterra, V. (1937) "Applications de mathématiques à la biologie," *L'Enseignement Mathématique*, **37,** 297–330; reproduced as Chap. XXIV in Volterra, V., *Opera Matematica*, Vol. V, where most of his ecological papers appear.
11. Goel, N. S., Maitra, N. C. & Montroll, E. W. (1971) *Rev. Mod. Phys.* **43,** 241–276.

233

Speeding Up of Time with Age in Recognition of Life as Fleeting

Paul A. Samuelson

A child claims that summer drags forever. His grandfather regrets how fast the summer flew by. To a Watsonian behaviorist in psychology or a Paretian behaviorist in economics, this may be deemed a matter of talking at cross purposes, of comparing cheese with incommensurable chalk.

However, it is a testable matter of fact whether people do, autobiographically, report that "time seems to pass more quickly as I grow older." Many have so reported. And, independently, various writers have hit upon a Weber-Fechner type of purportive logarithmic "explanation." Commonly, the argument goes much as follows.[1]

Posit that one begins life with a clean slate. (Ethologists will hardly agree.) Let each passing day, or month, or year of objective calendar time, t, bring with it a more or less constant average rate of new "sensations," "experiences," or bits of stimulus somehow measured. By any age, t, one has accumulated the lifelong integral of such "experience."

Then, by hypothesis, the sense of the speed at which, subjectively, actual time passes may be posited to be determined by the *percentage of incremental experience received, in comparison with total recorded inventory of past experience.*

This sounds vague, but it can be reduced to operationally meaningful, refutable form. Write $\dot{X}(t)$ for the instantaneous rate at age t of new current sense perceptions, somehow measured (as for example by how many photons are falling on the retina of the eye or the camera of the brain). Then the integral of sense perceptions ever received by age t is

$$X(t) = \int_0^t \dot{X}(u)du \tag{7.1}$$

$$= kt, \quad if \ \dot{X}(u) \approx k, \text{ a constant} \tag{7.2}$$

By appropriate choice of time units, we could make k equal to unity.

Now consider a special "subjective or internal time," θ, with the posited property that two calendar intervals will seem subjectively of the

---

I owe thanks to the National Science Foundation for financial aid, and I have an intellectual debt to Nicholas Georgescu-Roegen of Vanderbilt University for his subtle appreciation of the deep issues underlying my final section and his helpful criticisms throughout.

154

same duration if and only if in each such interval there has been the same percentage (or logarithmic) increment of accumulated experience:

$$\theta_3 - \theta_2 = \theta_2 - \theta_1 \quad \text{if and only if}$$
$$\ln X(t_3) - \ln X(t_2) = \ln X(t_2) - \ln X(t_1) \tag{7.3}$$

Taking Newtonian limits, we thus hypothesize the following rate relations between θ, X, and t:

$$\frac{d\theta}{dt} = c^{-1} \frac{d[\ln X(t)]}{dt}$$

$$= c^{-1} \frac{d[\ln(kt)]}{dt}$$

$$= c^{-1}t^{-1}$$

$$\frac{dt}{d\theta} = ct \tag{7.4}$$

$$t = t_0 e^{c\theta} \tag{7.5}$$

$$\theta = c^{-1}\ln(t/t_0) \tag{7.6}$$

By convention, we may set $\theta = 0$ at age of first recalled memory, say at age 4 with $t_0 = 4$; the scaling constant c depends on the arbitrary dimensional units we choose to measure subjective time in—so that we can set $c = 1$ if we agree on the proper (inessential) rate correspondence at age t_0 between the two time magnitudes. However, any positive scaling will do as well as any other.

All the ambiguous talk about "photons, sensations, experiences, and bits of stimulus" can be dispensed with once we realize that the objective testable assertion of (7.5) about reporting of subjective judgments can be summed up as follows:

People do (or don't) report that between ages four and eight the passage of subjective time is about equal to that between eight and sixteen, and that between sixteen and thirty-two, . . . , and that between arbitrary age t^* and age $2t^*$: similarly, time elapsed from t^* to bt^* must seem the same as from t^{**} to bt^{**}, for all (b, t^*, t^{**}).

Since it is a common observation that the very old, particularly when health is failing, begin to complain about the slowness of time, the logarithmic hypothesis at best might apply only up to late middle age.

Square Root and Power Rules

All the above is by way of review. Suppose, however, persons alternatively report:

Between four and nine there seems to be the same duration of subjective time as between nine and sixteen—*not* as between nine and twenty and one quarter as the Weber-Fechner rule required. Moreover, between four and twenty-five, time flew by just as it did between nine and thirty-six, or between sixteen and forty-nine, . . . , or between ages $(t^*)^2$ and $(t^* + 1)^2$.

Evidently my θ is then following a square-root rather than logarithmic rule. In place of (7.3), (7.4), and (7.5), I seem to have the square-root-rule relations:

$$\theta_3 - \theta_2 = \theta_2 - \theta_1 \leftrightarrow t_3^{\frac{1}{2}} - t_2^{\frac{1}{2}} = t_2^{\frac{1}{2}} - t_1^{\frac{1}{2}} \qquad (7.7)$$

$$d\theta/dt = \frac{1}{2} c^{-1} t^{-\frac{1}{2}} \qquad (7.8)$$

Inessential dimensional constants aside, we can summarize such regularities in the square-root rule that is the alternative counterpart to (7.6)'s logarithmic rule:

$$\theta = t^{\frac{1}{2}} \qquad (7.9)$$

More generally, people could be tested to see whether they follow $t^{\frac{1}{2}}$ or t^α for α any positive position, or t^α/α for any nonzero α less than or equal to one:

$$\theta = t^\alpha/\alpha \quad 0 \neq \alpha \leqslant 1 \qquad (7.10)$$

For $\alpha \to 0$, this can be made to approach $ln\ t$.

For time to seem to slow down rather than speed up with age, we would have to posit $\alpha > 1$. If calendar and subjective time seem always to agree, $\alpha = 1$.

We can test, and not prejudge, whether time speeds up, by examining the curvature of reported

$$\theta = f(t) \qquad (7.11)$$

where $f(t)$ is a concave (from below) function if time does seem to pass faster with age, or is a convex function if it seems to slow down with age. If the decade of the thirties drags in comparison with early and subsequent decades, $f(t)$ would have to go through an inflection point of changing curvature then.

The Forward Look

My main purpose here is not to rederive the logarithmic rule, nor even to generalize it to a square-root or unspecified-power rule. Rather it is to analyze a quite different mechanism that might help explain the subjective speeding up of time that people report after forty.

A historical incident will illustrate what is involved. Eric Bell[2] writes the following account about the great algebraist, Evariste Galois (1811–1832), who was killed in a duel at the age of 21. All night before his hopeless duel, Galois

> . . . had spent the fleeting hours feverishly dashing off his scientific last will and testament, writing against time to glean a few of the great things in his teeming mind before the death which he foresaw would overtake him. Time after time he broke off to scribble in the margin, ''I have not the time; I have not the time,'' and passed on to the next frantically scrawled outline. What he wrote in those desperate last hours before dawn will keep generations of mathematicians busy for hundreds of years.

Weill's *Knickerbocker Holiday* reports the same message in the love song

It's a long, long time from May to December
But the days grow short when you reach September.

What is emphasized here is not the backward-looking duration from birth to each age but rather the perceived elapsing time interval from that age to life's end.

If humans, like the one-hoss shays of Oliver Wendell Holmes's poem, were destined to live to one certain age—say, the Biblical three score and ten—each passing year would reduce life expectancy by just that much. The subjective sense that this next year you will have lost 1/20 of remaining life, then 1/19, . . . , and then 1/2 might be expected to be perceived as a speeding up of the passing of calendar time with age.

It is usually not given to us to know exactly when we shall die. However, one does not have to be a trained actuary to know that the force of mortality greatly increases with age (at least after one passes through the shoals of infancy). Life expectancy decreases with age:

$$de^0(t)/dt < 0 \qquad (7.12)$$

for most values of t, where $e^0(t)$ represents the average number of years a person of age t may expect to live before dying.

One simple approximation for the subjective speeding up of time would be to postulate

$$d\theta/dt = be^0(t), b > 0 \qquad (7.13)$$

$$\theta = f(t) = b\int_0^t e^0(u)da, f'(t) < 0$$

$$t = f^{-1}[\theta] = g(\theta), g''(\theta) > 0 \qquad (7.14)$$

In the unrealistic one-hoss shay case of sudden death:

$$\theta(t) = b\int_0^t (70 - u)du = b(70t - 1/2t^2), 0 < t < 70 \qquad (7.15)$$

Early in life, calendar time and subjective time would agree in this case rather closely (as if, in (7.10), α were near to unity). Later in life, time would seem to flit by ever faster; until, at 69-plus, it could reach a Galois-like intensity.

The early writers on probability recognized that chance elements in mortality caused one to lose less than a year of expectancy with each passing year. Realistic actuarial tables today keep $e^0(t)$ positive at all ages, albeit shrinking rapidly for centenarians. A crude example, simpler than the formulas of Gompertz and other actuaries, would be the case where

$$\theta(t) = \int_0^t e^{-u}du = 1 - e^{-t} \qquad (7.16)$$

$$t = -\ln(1 - \theta) \qquad (7.17)$$

This would entail at all ages a positive acceleration term, $d^2\theta/dt^2$, as is required if time is to seem to speed up as one grows older.

To show that it would not be possible to distinguish from report data between the backward- and the forward-looking hypotheses, note the similarity of implications of (7.13) and (7.11):

$$d\theta/dt = be^0(t), be^{0'}(t) < 0 \qquad (7.18a)$$

$$d\theta/dt = f'(t), f''(t) < 0 \qquad (7.18b)$$

Also, one can replace $be^0(t)$ by some monotone-increasing function of $e^0(t)$, such as $\theta[e^0(t)]$, or use some other parameter of shrinking life left.

Qualifications

Young people, it is said, believe they will live forever. So, perhaps, the hypothesis of subjective speeding up of time from the perception of years-of-remaining-life flitting by should be reserved for the older ages only. How old?

D'Alembert, in his rather absurd attempt to resolve the famous St. Petersburg Paradox, proposed that people (do? or ought to?) treat sufficiently small positive probabilities as literally zero. When challenged to specify how small they would have to be for this, Buffon suggested that a man of fifty-six in good health does not wake up and think he will die that day. So any probability below the force of mortality at fifty-six for one day, reported by Stigler (1950, n. 126) to have been $p = 0.0001$ in the eighteenth century and $p = 0.00005$ in 1950, can be taken to be zero.[3] (Since men do not cancel their term insurance each morning, this is indeed absurd.) However, the fact that Buffon has not met with more scornful readers may suggest that only after age sixty is the presence of the grim reaper most consciously felt.

Similarly, at extreme old ages, the release of death may be increasingly welcomed. And time may again seem to drag as observable alertness diminishes and vital signs decelerate. No simple hypothesis should be expected to be able to fit the full diversity of life-cycle experience.

Problem of Existence of Subjective Time

Thus far I have been taking for granted that there may really exist for some of us a coherent notion of subjective time, $\theta = f(t)$. My present effort would not be worthy of him whom it seeks to honor, Nicholas Georgescu-Roegen, if I left this deep issue at the implicit and unresolved stage.

Therefore, I now propose to explore the testable conditions that are necessary and sufficient for the very existence of such a (θ, t) structure.

Begin with the testable hypothesis that a given individual reports that, when given any two arbitrary ages of life, t_1 and t_3, the individual is always able to report to you an intermediate age, t_2, which he feels does "subjectively split" the interval into two subintervals of equal seeming duration:

Axiom A: $t_2 = M(t_1,t_3)$ is an observable function with the following properties:

A_1: $M(t_1,t_3)$ is to be continuous (and perhaps "smooth")

A_2: $M(t_1,t_3) \equiv M(t_3,t_1)$, a harmless symmetry condition

A_3: $M(t_1,t_3'') > M(t_1,t'_3)$ if $t_3'' > t_3'$

A_4: $M(t,t) \equiv t$, a "mean," with $Min(t_1,t_3) \leqslant M(t_1,t_3) \leqslant Max(t_1,t_3)$

Axiom A does not suffice to ensure that a subjective time function, $\theta = f(t)$, does exist. We must stipulate more about the $M(\ ,\ )$ function if $t_2 = M(t_1, t_3)$ is always to agree with

$$\theta_3 - \theta_2 = \theta_2 - \theta_1 \leftrightarrow f(t_3) - f(t_2) = f(t_2) - f(t_1) \qquad (7.19)$$

Equation (7.19) says, in effect, that the $M(t_1, t_2)$ mean must be a so-called associative mean. Thus, the percentage-increment-of-experience paradigm could be summed up in the language of the geometric mean: namely, time between 4 and 8 seems to pass on quickly as between 8 and 16 because 8 is the geometric mean of 4 and 16: $8 = \sqrt{(4 \times 16)}$, $\log 8 = \frac{1}{2}(\log 4 + \log 16)$; and likewise for times between a and $\sqrt{(ab)}$ in comparison with those between $\sqrt{(ab)}$ and b.

For $\theta = f(t) = -t^{-1}$ in (7.10) or (7.11) or (7.19), the autobiographer replaces the geometric mean by the "harmonic mean" in splitting any time interval into two seemingly long subintervals. Then the time between 4 and 6.4 seems of the same duration as between 6.4 and 16, because $6.4 = (\frac{1}{2}2^{-1} + \frac{1}{2}16^{-1})^{-1}$, the harmonic mean—or more generally, $(a, c > a)$ are split by b, the harmonic mean, $(\frac{1}{2}a^{-1} + \frac{1}{2}b^{-1})^{-1} = b$.

If there is neither speeding up nor slowing down of subjective time, we have the ordinary arithmetic mean

$$b = M(a, c) = \frac{1}{2}a + \frac{1}{2}c \qquad (7.20)$$

Time would seem to slow down with age if $f(t)$ were a convex rather than concave function, like the "quadratic mean" of Pythagoras, $b = (\frac{1}{2}a^2 + \frac{1}{2}c^2)^{\frac{1}{2}}$.

The most general case of a so-called associative mean has been discussed by mathematicians, as in Hardy-Littlewood-Polya (1934, Theorem 215). In the present context, equations (7.11) and (7.19) say that b "subjectively splits" a and c, $a \leqslant c$, into two equal subintervals (a,b) and $(b\,c\cdot)$, if and only if

$f(b) = \tfrac{1}{2}f(a) + f(c), f(x)$
    strictly increasing and continuous, implying $a \leqslant b \leqslant c$ (7.21)

Abel's Identity

But really, Axiom A does not require that a relation like (7.21) correspond to one's reported $M(t_1, t_2)$ function. There may not be a coherent subjective time sense, $\theta = f(t)$. Why should my autobiographical reportings, even if made after calm and careful reflection, satisfy all the straitjackets of the paradigm that posits the true existence of a definite sense of subjective time?

The task of deductive analysis is to point out what are the testable restrictions on empirically observable data of the subjective-time paradigm. The task of empirical observers is to test, and possibly refute or fail to refute, these testable relations. Therefore, to Axiom A must be added the following form of the Abel (1826) Identity.

> Axiom B: If t_1 and t_5 are "subjectively split" by $t_3 = M(t_1, t_5)$, t_1 and t_3 are "split" by $t_2 = M(t_1, t_3)$, and t_3 and t_5 are "split" by $t_4 = M(t_3, t_5)$ then it must be the case (a testable, refutable condition) that t_2 and t_4 are just split by $t_3 = M(t_2, t_4)$. Mathematically, this implies that the functional identity of Abel (1802–1829) holds on $M(t_1, t_2)$ in the form
> $$M(M(t_1, M(t_1, t_5)), M(M(t_1, t_5), t_5)) \equiv M(t_1, t_5)$$

If this holds, given any finite interval of calendar time, we can divide the continuum into as many fine equal-subjective-time intervals as we desire: thus, select any two nearby ages on the interval; call them t_0 and t_{0+h}. By solving the following relations for $[t_{0+2h}, t_{0+3h}, \ldots, t_{0+nh}, \ldots]$, and for $[t_{0-h}, t_{0-2h}, \ldots, t_{0-nh}, \ldots]$, we have our desired equal θ intervals: $[\theta_0 - nH, \theta_0 - (n-1)H, \ldots, \theta_0 - H, \theta_0, \theta_0 + H, \theta_0 + 2H, \ldots, \theta_0 + nH]$:

$$t_{0+h} = M(t_0, t_{0+2h}), \; t_{0+2h} = M(t_{0+h}, t_{0+3h}), \; \ldots$$
$$t_{0+(n-1)h} = M(t_{0+(n-2)h}, t_{0+nh}) \; t_0 = M(t_{0-h}, t_{0+h}),$$
$$t_{0-h} = M(t_{0-2h}, t_0), \; \ldots, \; t_{0-(n-1)h} = M(t_{0-(n-2)h}, t_{0-nh}) \quad (7.22)$$

Graphical Construction

Figure 7–1 depicts contour lines of the $M(t_1, t_2)$ function, free of any unobservable solipsistic magnitudes. If only Axiom A applied to a person who reported a "speeding up of time," the smooth contours could be any curves that are convex near the 45-degree line. These contours are shown in Figure 7–1a, for which there exists no coherent sense of subjective time, $\theta = f(t)$. This is because the mean, $M(t_1, t_2)$, is not capable of there being written as an "associative mean."

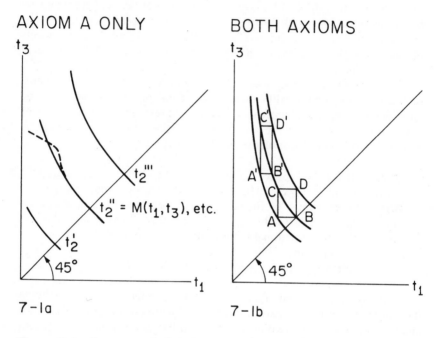

AXIOM A ONLY

t_3

t_2'''

$t_2'' = M(t_1, t_3)$, etc.

t_2'

45°

t_1

7–1a

BOTH AXIOMS

t_3

C' D'

A' B'

C'

D

A

B

45°

t_1

7–1b

Figure 7–1. Contours of the $M(t_1, t_3)$ Function. The contours shown connect all pairs of points (t_1 and t_3) that are split by equal $t_2 = M(t_1, t_3)$. In 7–1a arbitrary contours that satisfy Axiom A are shown as convex near the 45° line of symmetry. (Note the broken non-convex segment shown as a possibility for the middle contour away from the 45° line.) In 7–1b, along with Axiom A there is added the important Abelian Axiom B, so that there exists a coherent notion of subjective time, $\theta(t)$, and so that the $M(t_1, t_3)$ function is an "associative mean." From the two lower contours, by completing the Georgescu box ABC-and-D, we can derive the equally-spaced contours of "subjective time." (By selecting two initial contours close enough together, we can make our grid of measurement as fine as we like.)

Figure 7–1b imposes Axiom B as well as Axiom A. The resulting contours are compatible with the existence of a surface that generates those contours, and is capable of being written in the Gossen-Jevons additive form

$$M(t_1, t_2) = f^{-1}[\tfrac{1}{2}f(t_1) + \tfrac{1}{2}f(t_2)] \tag{7.23}$$

We may then avail ourselves of the Georgescu device, discussed in Georgescu-Roegen (1952) and Samuelson (1974), of constructing from any two close-together contours the implied equal-spacing contours by repeated "completing of the Georgescu box."[4] Without Abel's testable identity being satisfied, the whole construction would fail to apply.

Cardinal-Utility Increments

There is another way of looking at the problem of the operational implications for observable behavior of the existence of a subjective time scale. It has the merit of tying up the discussion with now-classical economic discussions of the possible cardinality of utility.

Pareto, three-quarters of a century ago, realized that consumer demand could be understood in terms of a person's merely having to decide whether one batch of goods is (ordinally) worse or better than another batch of goods, without having to be able to decide whether the increment in something called "utility" was greater or less in going from batch A to B than the increment in "utility" in going from C to D. Pareto (1909), Bowley (1923), Frisch (1926), Lange (1934–35), Phelps Brown (1934), Bernardelli (1934–35), R. G. D. Allen (1935), Samuelson (1938), Alt (1936), and many others realized the following:

If (U_1, U_2, U_3, U_4) are indicators of four levels of "utility," $U_1 < U_2 < U_3 < U_4$, then any monotone stretching of this U scale, call it $u = f(U)$, $f'(\ ) > 0$, would give new consistent indicators of "utility," $u_1 = f(U_1) < u_2 = f(U_2) < u_3 = f(U_3) < u_4 = f(U_4)$. However, the algebraic signs of increments of indicators of utility would agree if and only if $f(\ )$ is restricted to being a *linear* stretching: $f(U) \equiv a + bU, b > 0; |b| > 0;$ i.e.,

sign of $\dfrac{\{[f(U_2) - f(U_1)] - [f(U_3) - f(U_4)]\}}{\{[U_2 - U_1] - [U_3 - U_4]\}}$ always agrees with

if and only if $f''\{U\} \equiv 0.$ (7.24)

Samuelson (1938) pointed out, however, that it already begs the case to talk of ΔU and Δu increments. Going from batch of goods

$(q_1{}^a, \ldots, q_n{}^a) = Q^a$ to $(q_1{}^b, \ldots, q_n{}^b) = Q^b$, or alternatively from $(q_1{}^c, \ldots, q_n{}^c) = Q^c$ to $(q_1{}^d, \ldots, q_n{}^d) = Q^d$, a person might be able to make comparisons without those comparisons referring to the *difference* of some scalar magnitude, $U(Q^b) - U(Q^a)$ or $U(Q^d) - U(Q^c)$. Under certain regularity conditions, the person has a function of the $2n$ variables, $(q_1{}^b, \ldots, q_n{}^b; q_1{}^a, \ldots, q_n{}^a)$ that relates these "steps' in his mind or preference: call this

$$V(X; Y) = V(x_1, \ldots, x_n; y_1, \ldots, y_n), \text{ or}$$
$$v = \phi\{V(x; y)\} = v(X; Y), \phi'\{\ \} > 0, \phi''\{\ \} \gtreqless 0 \quad (7.25)$$

This is postulated to have the property:[5]

$\phi\{V(Q^a; Q^b)\} > \phi\{V(Q^c; Q^d)\}$ when $(Q^a$ to $Q^b)$ is deemed "more significant" than $(Q^c$ to $Q^d)$.

Likewise for $\phi\{V(Q^c; Q^d)\} > \phi\{V(Q^a; Q^b)\}$ or $\phi\{V(Q^a; Q^b)\} = \phi\{V(Q^c; Q^d)\}$.

What I showed almost forty years ago is the following: There will exist some $\phi\{\ \}$ and $f\{\ \}$ that make $\phi\{V(X; Y)\} \equiv f\{U(Y)\} - f\{U(X)\}$ if and only if the following variant of Abel's identity is verifiably true:

Abel-Samuelson: Whenever Q^a-to-Q^b is deemed equally significant to Q^c-to-Q^d, it must be the case that Q^a-to-Q^c is deemed equally significant to Q^b-to-Q^d.

Alternative Axioms for Subjective Time

Figure 7–2 applies this same logic to the question of the existence of a coherent subjective time scale, and *all* that this implies for observable behavior. It plots in the space of (t_1, t_2) contours of all the points of "seemingly equal subjective time" intervals. Thus, the 45° line represents the passage from any initial time to itself, the shortest possible subjective time interval. With the convention $t_1 \leqslant t_2$, we need only fill in the upper half of the positive quadrant.

The contours are positively sloped, in contrast to the usually negatively sloped indifference contours of the economist: this is because an increase in initial t_1 can only be compensated for by an increase in terminal t_2 if we are to be on the contour of equal-seeming time duration. The seeming speeding up of subjective time with age imposes no simple curvature condition on these contours.

Figure 7–2a obeys only the first axiom of the new formulation.

Axiom I: Reportable contours of equal time duration are indicated by the function

$$\tau = \tau(t_1, t_2), t_1 \leq t_2$$

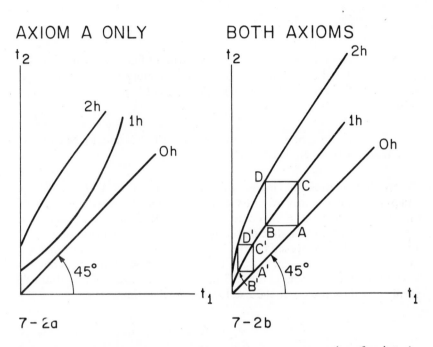

AXIOM A ONLY

t_2

2h

1h

0h

45°

7–2a

BOTH AXIOMS

t_2

2h

1h

0h

D C

D' B A

C'

A' 45°

B'

7–2b

Figure 7–2. Contours of $\tau(t_1, t_2)$**.** The contours connect pairs of points (t_1 and t_2) that have the same subjective-seeming duration of time between them. Thus, the points on the 45° line each correspond to zero subjective-seeming duration of time, since on that line t_1 and t_2 correspond to the same instant of time. In 7–2a, the contours only satisfy Axiom I and actually correspond to no coherent sense of subjective time. In 7–2b, however, the contours also satisfy the Abelian Axiom II: now with a coherent sense of subjective time, the Georgescu boxes, like ABC-and-D, can be used to construct, from the 45° line of 0h and the contour for 1h, the new contour for 2h. Likewise, from nh and $(n-1)h$, one can complete the box to construct the $(n+1)h$ contour. By selecting the 1h contour near enough to the 45° line, we can make the grid as fine as we like.

where

I.1 $\tau(t_1, t_2)$ is continuous in its arguments

I.2 $\tau(t_1, y)$ is monotone strictly increasing in y and $\tau(x, t_2)$ is monotone strictly decreasing in x

I.3 $\tau(x, x) \equiv \tau(y, y)$

Nevertheless, from Axiom I alone we cannot find a stretching of $\tau(t_1, t_2)$ that puts it in the form needed for a coherent subjective time structure. We must add a second refutable axiom to rule out Figure 7–2a and rule in Figure 7–2b.

Axiom II: If $\tau(a, b) = \tau(c, d)$, then necessarily $\tau(\text{Min}[a, c], \text{Max}[a, c]) = \tau(\text{Min}[b, d], \text{Max}[b, d])$

By "completing the Georgescu box," formed as at A on the 45° line and B and C on a nearby arbitrary contour, labeled $\theta = h$ we can calculate the D point on the $\theta = 2h$ contour. The whole of that new contour is constructed by letting A slide on the 45° line from the origin out to infinity. Then, apply the Georgescu box technique to points generated from $\theta = h$ to $\theta = 2h$, to get points on $\theta = 3h$. Clearly, by prescribing our initial $\theta = h$ contour arbitrarily near to the 45° line, we can in effect make h arbitrarily small, and thus trace out the existent subjective time scale,

$$\theta = f(t) = \psi\{\tau(t_1, t_2)\}, \ \psi'(\tau) > 0, \tag{7.26}$$

to as great accuracy as can be desired. (Experimentally, as Georgescu-Roegen reminds me, it is realistic to expect "threshold" effects so that few of us would be able to gauge minute equivalent subjective-time intervals. But this is to say that, at the fine scale level, we do do not verify the existence of a coherent set of autobiographical reports about seeming durations: our axioms, by their violation, reveal the absence of subjective-time structures when they do not exist!)

Mathematically, Axioms I and II are equivalent to putting the following (testable!) restrictions on continuous, monotone $\tau(t_1, t_2)$:

$$\begin{cases} \tau(y,y) = \tau(x,x) \leqslant \tau(x,y), \ y \geqslant x > 0 \\ \tau(a,b) = \tau(c,d), \ d \geqslant b \geqslant a \leqslant c \\ \text{if and only if} \\ \tau(a,c) = \tau(b,d) \end{cases} \tag{7.27}$$

This strong Abelian condition can be satisfied for a $\tau(t_1, t_2)$ function if and only if

$$\tau(t_1, t_2) = f^{-1}[\tfrac{1}{2}f(t_1) + \tfrac{1}{2}f(t_2)] \tag{7.28}$$

where $f(t)$ is a uniquely determined function, up to the linear transformation $a + bf(t)\, b > 0$, and where $f^{-1}[x]$ is the inverse function defined by $x = f(t)$.[6] Axioms A and B on $M(t_1, t_2)$ are essentially equivalent to Axioms I and II on $\tau(t_1, t_2)$.

Conclusion

The discussion here has been artfully arranged so that no phenomena of introspection, which are in principle unobservable, are ever involved. Even a radical behaviorist will, on reflection, find no cause for legitimate complaint.

Whether actual human beings do or do not satisfy the various axiomatic hypotheses to a tolerable degree of approximation is not a task for the logician to decide. The matter must be put to the test of experience, once the analyst has clarified how that can be done.

Notes

1. For the Weber-Fechner law, see any psychology text; or, in economics, G. J. Stigler (1950), which discusses the views of d'Alembert that I later comment on and also discusses the St. Petersburg Paradox. On the plane from Boston to Nashville for the Georgescu Festschrift, I discovered in Georgescu (1971) the words: "There is some evidence that the hours seem shorter as we grow older because—as has been suggested [by K. Pearson (1899)]—the content of our consciousness increases at a decreasing [percentage?] rate."

2. The quotation comes from Eric Bell (1937, Chapter 20 on Galois, p. 375).

3. G. J. Stigler (1950).

4. See N. Georgescu-Roegen (1952). Debreu (1960) later also gave some conditions for strong separability of variables, but in contrast to those of Georgescu-Roegen (1952) they are only applicable to a function of more than two variables. See also P. A. Samuelson (1974).

5. Georgescu-Roegen (1954) points out in his n. 66 that "lexicographic" orderings can exist, which cannot be described by a single-scale

cardinal indicator function or by any of its monotonic stretchings. I agree that the present formulation, therefore, still needs to be qualified to avoid what Georgescu calls the "ordinalist error." Debreu (1954) has also given valuable analysis of Eilenberg conditions necessary or sufficient if a transitive preference ordering is to be representable by one numerical function (and hence, after stretchings, by an infinity of such numerical functions).

6. See Samuelson (1947), Chapter 5, Equation [15]) for an alternative test for independence. If $M(t_1, t_3)$ has continuous partial derivatives of requisite order, the Abel identity can be shown to have for its full empirical implications the condition $\partial^2 \log M(t_1, t_3)/\partial t_1 \partial t_3 \equiv 0$. The similar condition on $\tau(t_1, t_2)$ is that $\partial^2 \log \tau(t_1, t_2)/\partial t_1 \partial t_2 \equiv 0$.

Bibliography

Abel, Niels Henrik. 1826. "Recherche des fonctions de deux quantités variables indépendantes x et y, telles que $f(x,y)$, qui ont la propriété que $f(z,f(x,y))$ est une fonction symetrique de z, x et y." *Journel fur die reine und angewandte Mathematik,* herausgegeben von Crelle, Bd. I, Berlin. Reproduced as Chapter VI in *Oeuvres Complètes de Niels Henrik Abel* (ed. L. Sylow & S. Lie) (Christiania: Grondahl & Son, 1881).

Allen, R. G. D. "A Note on the Determinateness of the Utility Function." *Review of Economic Studies* 2 (1936): 155–58.

Alt, F. "Über die Messbarkeit des Nutzens." *Zeitschrift für Nationalökonomie* 7 (1936): 161–69.

Bell, E. *Men of Mathematics.* New York: Simon & Schuster, 1937.

Bernardelli, H. "Notes on the Determinateness of the Utility Function." *Review of Economic Studies* 2 (1934–35).

Bowley, A. L. *Mathematical Groundwork of Economics.* Oxford: Clarendon Press, 1924.

Brown, E. H. Phelps. "Demand Functions and Utility Functions: A Critical Examination of Their Meaning." *Econometrica* 2, no. 1 (1934): 51–58.

Debreu, G. "Representation of a Preference Ordering by a Numerical Function." In R. M. Thrall et al. (eds.), *Decision Processes.* New York: Wiley, 1954.

——— "Topological Methods in Cardinal Utility Theory." In Arrow, K. J., Karlin, S., and Suppes, P. (eds.). *Mathematical Methods in the Social Sciences, 1959 (Proceedings of the First Stanford Symposium).* Stanford, California: Stanford University Press, 1960.

168

Frisch, R. "Sur un problème d'économie pure." *Norsk Matematish Foreignings Skrifter* 1, no. 16 (1926): 1–40.

Georgescu-Roegen, N. "A Diagrammatic Analysis of Complementarity." *Southern Economic Journal* (1952): 1–20.

——— "Choice, Expectations and Measurability." *Quarterly Journal of Economics* 68 (1954): 503–34.

——— "Threshold in Choice and the Theory of Demand." *Econometrica* 26 (1958): 157–68; reproduced as Chapter 5 in *Analytical Economics: Issues and Problems.*

——— *Analytical Economics: Issues and Problems.* Cambridge, Mass.: Harvard University Press, 1966.

——— *The Entropy Law and the Economic Process.* Cambridge, Mass.: Harvard University Press, 1971.

Hardy, G. H., Littlewood, J. E., and Polya, G. *Inequalities.* Cambridge: The University Press, 1934.

Lange, O. "The Determinateness of the Utility Function." *Review of Economic Studies* 1 (1934): 218–28; 2–3 (1934–35): 76–77.

Pareto, V. *Manuel d'economie politique.* Paris: V. Giard & E. Briere, 1909.

Pearson, K. *The Grammar of Science.* London: Scott, 1892.

Samuelson, P. A. "Complementarity: An Essay on the Fortieth Anniversary of the Hicks-Allen Revolution in Demand Theory." *Journal of Economic Literature* (1974): 1255–89.

——— *Foundations of Economic Analysis.* Cambridge, Mass.: Harvard University Press, 1947.

——— "The Numerical Representations of Ordered Classifications and the Concept of Utility." *Review of Economic Studies* 6 (1938): 65–70, 344–56; reproduced in *The Collected Scientific Papers of P. A. Samuelson* I, Chapter 2, 15–20.

Stigler, G. J. "The Development of Utility Theory." *Journal of Political Economy* 58 (1950): 307–27, 373–96; reproduced as Chapter 5 in Stigler, G. J. *Essays in History of Economics.* Chicago: University of Chicago Press, 1965.

A Dynamical Model for Human Population

(sex ratio/monogamy/birth rates/death rates/fertility)

JOEL YELLIN* AND P. A. SAMUELSON†

* Department of Political Science and Center for Policy Alternatives and
† Department of Economics, Massachusetts Institute of
Technology, Cambridge, Mass. 02139

Contributed by P. A. Samuelson, April 21, 1974

ABSTRACT   We analyze a simple, deterministic model
of the dynamics of population changes in a bisexual,
reproductive system based on marriage. Our model is one
of a general class, special cases of which have been previously discussed within the framework of population
biology by D. G. Kendall, L. A. Goodman, J. H. Pollard,
and others. Here, we extend and complete previous
analyses of systems characterized by first-degree homogeneous, unbounded marriage functions, allowing for
arbitrary birth and death rates.

The dynamics of the model is determined by three
coupled first-order, nonlinear differential equations,
similar to those used in the description of chemical reactions and of radioactive decay chains. Solutions of the
differential equation system are classified according to the
associated patterns of birth and death rates of the two
sexes, and growth and stability properties are discussed.

This preliminary report gives conditions sufficient to
insure the existence of a unique, exponential mode of
population growth or decay, with a finite ratio of the
sexes. We also exhibit other conditions which, in contrast
to the standard, linear demographic analysis of Lotka,
guarantee that the sex ratio asymptotically becomes
infinite.

The model manifests a delicate balance between the
vital parameters that alerts one to the possibility of self-
aggravating distortions of the sex ratio, once a monog-
amous society's fertility falls below the replacement
value.

This is a preliminary report of the results of an investigation
into the stability properties of reproductive systems whose
dynamics are independent of overall scale, and in which age-
specific fertility and mortality rates are (provisionally) assumed to be non-age-specific, and constant through time.
Special cases of this general class have previously been partially analyzed by D. G. Kendall (1), L. A. Goodman (2), J. H.
Pollard (3), and others.

Scale-independent model

Our population model is defined by the following assumptions:

1. There are two sexes with total numbers $T_1(t)$ and $T_2(t)$.
2. Monogamy prevails, with $T_3(t)$ marriages existing at time t. The number of single individuals of each sex is therefore

$$N_1(t) = T_1(t) - T_3(t); \quad N_2(t) = T_2(t) - T_3(t). \quad [1]$$

3. The population is replenished only through births to married couples. The fertility rates, per marriage, for female and male births are f_1 and f_2 respectively, and are independent of parental ages.
4. The (instantaneous) rate at which marriages occur depends nonlinearly on the then-existing stocks of single individuals $N_1(t)$ and $N_2(t)$, vanishing when either N_i vanishes, and increasing without limit as either N_i increases. We will write this (nonnegative) rate as $M[N_1(t), N_2(t)]$.
5. The mortality rates (λ_1, λ_2) of single individuals are constants, independent of age, as is the mortality rate of couples, λ_3, due to death (or divorce, or permanent sterilization, etc.).
6. The dynamics of the system is independent of its overall scale, and of the common scale of its components.

Dynamical equations

Given the assumptions above, the behavior of the system is determined by the following set of differential equations:

$$dN_1/dt = -\lambda_1 N_1 + f_1 T_3 - M[N_1, N_2] \quad [2a]$$

$$dN_2/dt = -\lambda_2 N_2 + f_2 T_3 - M[N_1, N_2] \quad [2b]$$

$$dT_3/dt = -\lambda_3 T_3 + M[N_1, N_2]. \quad [2c]$$

The interpretation of [2] is straightforward. For example, in [2a] the rate of change of the number of single women is negatively proportional to the fraction of single women dying at time t, $-\lambda_1 N_1(t)$, and to the marriage rate $-M$. The rate of female births is proportional to the number of existing marriages, and makes a positive contribution of $f_1 T_3(t)$ to $dN_1(t)/dt$. Similarly, for the growth conditions on the number of single men $N_2(t)$.

Though we take mortality and fertility rates to be fixed quantities independent of population growth, a more realistic model would include, for example, the nonlinearity which arises from the relations between agricultural production, the supply of arable land, and population density.

It is often convenient to work with the totals (T_1, T_2), in which case the set [2] translates as:

$$dT_1/dt = -\lambda_1 T_1 + (f_1 - \lambda_3 + \lambda_1) T_3 \equiv -\lambda_1 T_1 + \beta_1 T_3 \quad \text{[3a]}$$

$$dT_2/dt = -\lambda_2 T_2 + (f_2 - \lambda_3 + \lambda_2) T_3 \equiv -\lambda_2 T_2 + \beta_2 T_3 \quad \text{[3b]}$$

$$dT_3/dt = -\lambda_3 T_3 + M[T_1 - T_3, T_2 - T_3] \quad \text{[3c]}$$

which defines the quantities β_i. Note that for population growth, both the β's must be positive. However, as we shall see below, positivity of the β's, while necessary, is not sufficient to insure a growing population.

In [2] and [3], λ_3 is to be interpreted as a disappearance rate of marriages, due to the death of either partner, or to divorce. In this simple treatment, divorce or the death of one marriage partner can be considered to result in an accretion to the stocks of single individuals available for later fecund marriages; such an accretion is tacitly included in our fertility rates f_i.

In the discusssion to follow, we allow the fundamental parameters (f_i, λ_i) to range over all positive values, and we then qualitatively analyze the associated dynamical behavior of the system. Our procedure differs from that of previous writers, who imposed certain further restrictions on the parameters in order to explicitly take the accretions mentioned above into account. An example of such additional restrictions may be found in refs (1) and (3), where it is assumed that $\lambda_3 = \lambda_1 + \lambda_2, f_1 > \lambda_2, f_2 > \lambda_1$, and therefore that the resulting values of the β_i—i.e., $\beta_1 = f_1 - \lambda_2; \beta_2 = f_2 - \lambda_1$—are positive.

Our analysis is not restricted to these special cases, since in the age-specific models needed for more realistic description there will often be a higher average age for married persons, and for surviving partners of terminating marriages, than for single persons of the same sex—with implied effects on average (f_i, λ_i) parameters not consistent with any such simple restrictions. We do, however, note the special implications of any such postulated restrictions on the parameters.

Restrictions on the marriage function $M[N_1, N_2]$

To insure scale-independence, we ask that the (positive) marriage function M be first-degree homogeneous in its arguments, so that

$$M[qN_1, qN_2] = qM[N_1, N_2] \quad \text{[4]}$$

for all positive q. We do not insist that $M[x, y]$ be a symmetric function of x and y.

We further suppose that no marriages take place if either stock of single individuals vanishes, so that for positive N_i

$$M[0, N_2] = 0 = M[N_1, 0]. \quad \text{[5]}$$

Furthermore, we require that the marriage rate increase

when the number of single individuals of either sex rises, so that

$$\partial M[N_1,N_2]/\partial N_i > 0 \qquad [i = 1,2], \qquad [6]$$

again for positive (N_1,N_2).

The general class of models we consider is characterized by the set [3]— or [2]— and by Eqs. [4]–[6]. Particular cases within this class are distinguished by further detailed assumptions on the behavior of the function M. In this preliminary note, we consider the class of M functions for which

$$\lim_{N_i/N_j \to \infty} M[N_1,N_2]/N_i = 0 \qquad (i,j = 1,2; \ i \neq j) \quad [7a]$$

and

$$\lim_{N_i/N_j \to \infty} M[N_1,N_2]/N_j = \infty \qquad (i,j = 1,2; \ i \neq j). \quad [7b]$$

Equation [7a], which places restrictions on the behavior of $M[1,x]/x$ and $M[x,1]/x$ for large x, can be interpreted as expressing the assumption that the more single individuals there are of one sex alone, the lower is the ultimate marriage rate, per unit of that sex.

Equation [7b], which translates as unbounded behavior of $M[1,x]$ and $M[x,1]$, can be interpreted as the assumption that single females can, for a fixed positive supply of single males, achieve any preset rate of marriages per unit time. (That does not imply, however, that there are ever more weddings than bachelors available to be grooms!)

We note parenthetically that there exists an alternative possibility of bounded M, with

$$\lim_{N_i/N_j \to \infty} M[N_1,N_2]/N_j = C_j < \infty, \qquad (i, j = 1,2; i \neq j)$$
$$[8]$$

in contrast to [7b]. This asymptotic requirement is favored by many demographers, and is manifested by the harmonic mean $M[x,y] = xy/(x + y)$, and also by $M[x,y] = \mathrm{Min}(x,y)$. [See e.g., Pollard (3), Chap. 7].

It turns out that the bounded behavior [8] increases the chances of pathological sex-ratio distortion. In this preliminary report we therefore concentrate primarily on the *a priori* more favorable case [7b], and show that unstable, infinitely unbalanced, sex-ratios can still occur.

Two-dimensional intensive system

Since our marriage functions are first-order homogeneous, we can choose to write the system in terms of the ratios

$$x_1 = N_1/T_3, \qquad x_2 = N_2/T_3 \qquad [9]$$

of single individuals to married couples. This reduces [2] and [3] to the two-dimensional system

$$dx_i/dt = (\lambda_3 - \lambda_i)x_i + f_i$$
$$- (1 + x_i)M[x_1,x_2], \qquad (i = 1,2). \quad [10]$$

The question of stability of the sex ratio reduces to a discussion of the possible existence of stable nodes in the (finite) positive quadrant of the (x_1,x_2) plane. As we shall see below, the number and distribution of critical points depend on the detailed behavior of the marriage function, $M[N_1,N_2]$.

Qualitative dynamics

For any particular marriage function, our system is defined in a five-dimensional space of positive parameters $(\lambda_1,\lambda_2,\lambda_3,f_1,f_2)$. Our basic question then is: given a particular pattern of relative sizes of these parameters, is there positive population growth, immediately or ultimately, and does the sex ratio

$$R(t) = T_2(t)/T_1(t) \quad [11]$$

approach a constant, positive, finite value which is stable under perturbation of the initial conditions?

In particular, we are interested in determining whether there exist trajectories $T_i(t)$ which represent "interior rays" of balanced-growth, exponential change, in which

$$\mathbf{T}(t) = \mathbf{k}\,e^{rt} \quad [12]$$

where the constant vector $\mathbf{k}$ has components $k_i > 0$, and where $k_1/k_3 > 1$, $k_2/k_3 > 1$, and r is real. (The exponential rate r is positive for population growth, negative for decay, and zero for stationary replacement.) Furthermore, if such an interior ray (or rays) does exist, we would like to know if it is stable under small and/or arbitrary perturbations of the initial conditions, and whether its stability and growth properties are altered under small changes in the fundamental parameters (f_i,λ_i).

We know that there always do exist two modes of one-sex exponential decay, which we call "exterior rays." For example, if the system begins with females only, they die out at an exponential rate λ_1, and the whole system moves along a trajectory

$$\mathbf{T}(t) = [T_1(0),0,0]\exp(-\lambda_1 t). \quad [13]$$

Likewise there is also a T_2 exterior ray $[0,T_2(0),0]\exp(-\lambda_2 t)$. Note that there is no T_3 exterior ray, since any initial stock of married couples $T_3(0)$ immediately produces births at a rate

$$dN_i(0)/dt = f_i T_3(0), \qquad (i = 1,2). \quad [14]$$

A major part of our problem is to distinguish between situations in which there exist interior rays that asymptotically determine the behavior of the system, and those in which $R(t)$ tends to 0 or ∞, so that the system eventually reaches an exterior ray on the T_1 or T_2 axis.

We can easily derive necessary conditions for the existence of interior rays by substituting [12] into [3]. This leads to the three conditions

$$k_i/k_3 = (f_i + \lambda_1 - \lambda_3)/(r + \lambda_i) > 0, \qquad (i = 1,2) \quad [15a]$$

$$r + \lambda_3 = M[k_1/k_3, k_2/k_3] > 0. \qquad [15b]$$

Any generalized "eigenvalue," or exponential rate r, must satisfy, along with the associated "eigenvector" $\mathbf{k}$, the basic nonlinear relations [15], in order that there can exist an internal ray. Equations [15] lead to a rather complicated classification of trajectories of [3] with respect to the general topology of our parameter space, and we therefore first discuss the simple, symmetric situation in which the birth and death rates of the two sexes are equal.

Symmetric case

Let us suppose that the birth and death rates of the two sexes satisfy the symmetry conditions

$$\lambda_1 = \lambda_2 = \lambda; \quad f_1 = f_2 = f. \qquad [16]$$

Then for symmetric initial values $N_1(t) = N_2(t) = N(t)$, [1] reduces to a *linear* system in $[N(t), N_3(t)]$ and [15] to a *linear* system in $[k, k_3]$. This case has been previously discussed in part by other writers, who suggested that it is always associated with one interior ray along which there is balanced exponential change. However, complete analysis reveals that: (a) for symmetric growth rates $r^* \leq -\lambda$—a range of values resulting from negative β's in [3]—such an internal ray need not be asymptotically reattained if the initial sex ratio $R(0)$ is perturbed; (b) even the slightest perturbation of $\lambda_1 - \lambda_2$ and/or $f_1 - f_2$ away from zero can quite possibly lead to the nonexistence of any interior ray whatsoever; (c) in the particular symmetric case with $f + \lambda = \lambda_3$, a degeneracy occurs in which there are an infinity of critical points in the (x_1, x_2) plane, and a corresponding infinity of interior rays in $[T_i]$ space.

The degenerate case is a key indicator of the topology of our parameter space, and we briefly discuss its properties. To achieve degeneracy, it is necessary to impose, in place of the symmetry conditions [16], the stronger conditions

$$\lambda_3 - \lambda = \lambda_3 - \lambda_i = f_i = f; \quad \beta_i = 0. \qquad [17]$$

The relations [17] eliminate the T_3 terms from [3a] and [3b], so that the male and female populations decay at the common exponential rate λ, and the sex ratio $R = T_2(0)/T_1(0)$ is permanently fixed.

Equation [17] implies there are an infinity of critical points of [10] in the finite (x_1, x_2) plane, and an associated infinity of interior rays in the $[T_i]$ space. To derive that result, substitute [17] in [10], and note that dx_1/dt and dx_2/dt then vanish simultaneously everywhere on the curve

$$f = M[x_1,x_2]. \qquad [18]$$

Clearly, if we break the degeneracy [17], even by an infinitesmal amount, the curves $dx_i/dt = 0$ will no longer be coincident, and, generally, there will be, at most, only a finite number of critical points in the (x_1,x_2) plane.

For illustrative purposes, let us examine a particular simple perturbation from degeneracy. We will still treat both sexes symmetrically, choosing

$$f - \lambda_3 + \lambda = f_i - \lambda_3 + \lambda_i \equiv \beta, \qquad [19]$$

but keeping $f_1 = f_2$ and $\lambda_1 = \lambda_2$.

It is easily verified that negative β in [19] corresponds to a declining population, while positive β may be associated with either growth or decline. Explicitly, from the now-linear case of [15], the general symmetric growth rate is found to be

$$r^* = -\lambda + \frac{-f - m + \beta + \sqrt{(f - \beta - m)^2 + 4fm}}{2}, \qquad [20]$$

where $r^* \gtreqless -\lambda$ depending on whether $\beta \gtreqless 0$, and where $m = M[1,1]$. The replacement criterion for the watershed between growth and decay is $r^* \gtreqless 0$ depending on whether $mf \gtreqless \lambda_3(\lambda + m)$. For $\beta < 0$, the symmetric critical point is a saddle; for $\beta > 0$ it is a stable node.

We will see in the following section that the incompatibility of unbalanced sex-ratio pathology with population increase, found in this special symmetric case, carries over to more general considerations in which there is an arbitrary pattern of birth and death rates (λ_i,f_i).

Our summary of the general case will further show that infinitesmal variations of (λ_i,f_i) around the degeneracy point [17] or around the symmetry axes of [16] can cause the system to lose all its finite critical points, so that its asymptotic behavior in the extensive space $[T_i]$ takes it to an exterior ray with a sex ratio of zero or infinity.

Summary of results

To display our general results, it is helpful to subdivide the parameter space (λ_i,f_i) into regions defined by certain inequality relations. For that purpose, we introduce the quantities

$$\Delta_i = \lambda_3 - \lambda_i. \qquad (i = 1,2) \qquad [21]$$

which incapsulate the relevant roles of the λ's in [10]. Each distinct sector of parameter space will then be categorized, for example as

$$\Delta_1 < f_1 < f_2 < \Delta_2, \qquad [22]$$

340

there being essentially 4! such distinct cases to analyze. The detailed behavior of trajectories $\mathbf{T}(t)$ associated with each such sector is summarized in Table 1, where we have avoided redundancy by listing only the $4!/2$ sectors with $f_2 > f_1$.

As shown in table 1, there turn out to be five topologically distinct possibilities:

(A) *One stable critical point in the finite* (x_1,x_2) *plane.* This occurs for sectors 1 and 2 in Table 1. Here, as in Lotka's linear analysis, all trajectories asymptotically result in a balanced sex ratio; overall, the population may grow or shrink. Case (A) is the only one which can be compatible with the growth of all components.

(A') $K+1$ *stable nodes,* K *saddle points in the finite* x_i *plane.*

This applies to sector 3 in Table 1. In this case, and also for (B) and (C) below, it can be shown that in general a chain of critical points exists, with saddle points and stable nodes distributed roughly along a hyperbolic curve whose asymptotes lie along the axes $x_1 = 0$ and $x_2 = 0$. Saddle points and stable nodes alternate along this hyperbola. For case (A'), the two nodes at the ends of the chain are stable; all trajectories therefore result in balanced sex ratios, just as in case (A). For case (A'), the population shrinks.

Remark: In cases (A'), (B) and (C) certain singular values of the parameters result in points of tangency between the two curves $dx_i/dt = 0$ of [10], and there can even be an uncountable infinity of points in common. Furthermore, it can be shown that for particularly simple choices of $M[x_1,x_2]$, e.g. $M = x_1^\alpha x_2^{1-\alpha}$, $0 < \alpha < 1$, there is at most a pair of critical points in the finite plane. We note also that all our critical points are associated with real exponents. There are no complex foci, and there is no limit cycle behavior in the x_i plane.

(B) $K+1$ *saddle points,* K *stable nodes in the finite* x_i *plane.*

This occurs for sectors 4–6 in Table 1, in which at least one of the β_i is negative. In general, we again have a chain of critical points, but here, unlike (A'), the two ends of the chain are saddle points. Therefore, trajectories lying beyond the two separatrices dividing the saddle points at the ends of the chain from their stable-node neighbors will always result in unbalanced sex ratios. In case (B) the population shrinks.

Cases (A) and (B) occur when

$$U = (f_1 - \Delta_2)(f_2 - \Delta_1) = (f_1 - \lambda_3 + \lambda_2)(f_2 - \lambda_3 + \lambda_1) > 0$$

[23]

It can be shown from [10] that the relation [23] insures that the curves $dx_1/dt = 0$ and $dx_2/dt = 0$ cross at least once in the positive quadrant of the (x_1,x_2) plane. Cases (C) and (D), to be discussed below, are associated with negative U.

(C) K *stable nodes,* K *saddle points in* x_i *plane.*

341

This occurs for sectors 7 and 8 in Table 1. The chain of critical points now has a saddle point on one end, and a stable node on the other. There is now a watershed defined by the separatrix dividing the last saddle point from its neighboring stable node. Trajectories on the saddle point side of this separatrix always result in unbalanced sex ratios.

Cases (A'), (B), and (C) have the property that K can be reduced to zero, independently of the shape of $M[x_1,x_2]$, by changing the relative scale of the marriage function. In particular, if we write $M[N_1,N_2] = M[1,1] \{M[N_1,N_2]/M[1,1]\}$ and permanently fix the expression in curly brackets, then $M[1,1]$ becomes a parameter characterizing the "strength"— or scale—of the marriage function, and this strength plays a role in determining K in sectors 3 through 8.

In case (C)—as in Cases (A') and (B)—the population shrinks.

(D) *No critical points in the finite* (x_1,x_2) *plane.* In these cases, sectors 9–12 in Table 1, one sex has both a higher birth rate and a lower death rate than the other, with the result that the sex ratio asymptotically approaches 0 or ∞. Specifically, a sufficient condition for the nonexistence of a balanced-growth path is

$$(\Delta_1 - \Delta_2)(f_1 - f_2)(f_2 - \Delta_1)(f_1 - \Delta_2) < 0. \qquad [24]$$

The Kendall-Pollard restriction to positive β's rules out the saddles of sections 4–6, and also the exterior ray sectors 10–12, while permitting sector 9. Sector 9's disastrous blowup of the sex ratio may seem intuitively obvious from the fact that one of the sexes there has a higher birth rate and a lower death rate than the other. But such intuitive explanations are dangerous for at least two reasons: (1) $\lambda_1 > \lambda_2$ and $f_1 < f_2$ causes *no* infinite distortion of the asymptotic sex ratio in sector 2. In sector 2 birth rates will be sufficiently high, and the sex ratio N_2/N_1 asymptotically approaches a positive limit, greater than unity but finite. (2) The following brief discussion of a non-marriage, bisexual deterministic model shows one can always avoid infinite sex ratios, even with $\lambda_1 \gg \lambda_2$ and $f_1 \ll f_2$, if monogamy does not prevail.

A bisexual, non-marriage model

Consider, along with the earlier cited writers, a system with no marriage institution, and write, instead of [2] and [3]:

$$dN_1(t)/dt = -\lambda_1 N_1(t) + f_1 H[N_1(t),N_2(t)] \qquad [25a]$$

$$dN_2(t)/dt = -\lambda_2 N_2(t) + f_2 H[N_1(t),N_2(t)] \qquad [25b]$$

where $H(x,y)$ is again an unbounded, positive function, homogeneous of order 1, vanishing on the boundaries of the positive quadrant, and possessing a positive gradient, just as did M.

The system [25] always moves asymptotically to a finite

sex-ratio, as one easily sees by transforming to a one-dimensional system in $Z = N_2/N_1$,

$$dZ/dt = (\lambda_1 - \lambda_2)Z + H(1,Z)(f_2 - f_1 Z) \qquad [26]$$

and using the properties of H to show that dZ/dt changes sign from positive to negative once along the positive Z axis, independent of the signs or magnitudes of $\lambda_2 - \lambda_1$, f_2 and f_1.

Population decline and sex-ratio pathology

Finally, we note that a striking feature of the results of Table 1 is the absence of pathological behavior of the sex ratio in the presence of overall population growth. Growth is always associated with a unique, stable interior ray. There is a simple geometric explanation of why this is so. Visualize $[T_i]$ space, with a vertical T_3 axis. Then note, from [3], that above (below) their respective planes

$$-\lambda_i T_i + (\lambda_i + f_i - \lambda_3) T_3 = 0 \qquad (i = 1,2), \qquad [27]$$

dT_1/dt and dT_2/dt are positive (negative). Similarly, below (above) the hyperbolic surface

$$-\lambda_3 T_3 + M[T_1, T_2] = 0, \qquad [28]$$

dT_3/dt is positive (negative). For sufficiently large f_1 and f_2, the planes [27] intersect the surface [28] in such a way as to create an irregularly shaped cone, with its apex at $T_i = 0$, within which all three dT_i/dt are positive. With the exception of the apex, the surface of this cone lies completely within the positive octant, and all trajectories entering it can never escape, but instead go off to infinity. Again, the cone is bounded above by the surface [28], and below by the planes [27].

This trapping phenomenon for growing population is a feature of systems with marriage functions even more general than those we consider here. The essential properties of M which insure trapping are that it vanish for vanishing stocks of single individuals, and that it grow at least linearly as its arguments increase together.

Conclusion

In conclusion, it is important to emphasize that models such as ours lack two features which play crucial roles in the population dynamics of real societies: (1) the effects of biomedical and cultural change on mortality and fertility; (2) the feedback caused by resource limitations on output. Such effects might be admitted by allowing our fundamental parameters to be explicit functions of time, and of population density itself.

We thank Professors J. M. Deutch and R. M. Solow of M.I.T. for a number of helpful discussions; Professors J. E. Cohen of Harvard University and A. J. Coale of Princeton alerted us to the

343

Table 1. *Dynamics of scale- and age-independent reproductive systems, with unbounded, homogeneous marriage functions of order one*

Sector	Condition	Behavior in (x_1, x_2) plane — Critical points[a] — Stable	Saddle	Case[d]	Behavior in $[T_i]$ space — Range of growth rates r, for interior rays[e]	Population growth or decay
1	$\Delta_2 < \Delta_1 < f_1 < f_2$	1	0	A[f]	$[-\lambda_1, f_1 - \lambda_3]$	Either
2	$\Delta_1 < \Delta_2 < f_1 < f_2$	1	0	A[f]	$[-\lambda_2, f_1 - \lambda_3]$	Either
3	$\Delta_2 < f_1 < \Delta_1 < f_2$	$1 + K$	K	A′	$[f_1 - \lambda_3, -\lambda_1]$	Decay
4	$f_1 < f_2 < \Delta_2 < \Delta_1$	K	$1 + K$	B	$[f_2 - \lambda_3, -\lambda_2]$	Decay
5	$f_1 < f_2 < \Delta_1 < \Delta_2$	K	$1 + K$	B	$[f_2 - \lambda_3, -\lambda_1]$	Decay
6	$f_1 < \Delta_2 < f_2 < \Delta_1$	K	$1 + K$	B	$[-\lambda_2, f_2 - \lambda_3]$	Decay
7	$\Delta_2 < f_1 < f_2 < \Delta_1$	K[b]	K[b]	C	$[f_1 - \lambda_3, f_2 - \lambda_3]$	Decay
8	$f_1 < \Delta_2 < \Delta_1 < f_2$	K[e]	K[e]	C	$[-\lambda_2, -\lambda_1]$.	Decay
9	$\Delta_1 < f_1 < \Delta_2 < f_2$	No critical points	No critical points	D[f]	Decaying exterior ray	
10	$\Delta_1 < f_1 < f_2 < \Delta_2$	No critical points	No critical points	D	Decaying exterior ray	
11	$f_1 < \Delta_1 < f_2 < \Delta_2$	No critical points	No critical points	D	Decaying exterior ray	
12	$f_1 < \Delta_1 < \Delta_2 < f_2$	No critical points	No critical points	D	Decaying exterior ray	
—	$f = f_1 = \Delta_1 = f_2 = \Delta_2$	∞	0	Degenerate[d]	$-\lambda$	Decay
—	$\Delta_1 = \Delta_2 < f_1 = f_2$	1	0	Symmetric[d]	$[-\lambda, f - \lambda_3]$	Either
—	$f_1 = f_2 < \Delta_1 = \Delta_2$	K	$1 + K$	Symmetric[d]	$[f - \lambda_3, -\lambda]$	Decay

Shown here is the qualitative behavior of trajectories of the differential equation system [3], and of the associated two-dimensional system [10].

The parameter space $(\Delta_1 = \lambda_3 - \lambda_1; \Delta_2 = \lambda_3 - \lambda_2; f_1; f_2)$ has been divided into four sectors defined by the inequality relations listed in column two. Behavior in the twelve regions with $f_2 > f_1$ is shown; behavior in the remaining twelve regions is easily abstracted from the table by consistently interchanging subscripts 1 and 2. Also shown is trajectory behavior for two symmetric cases discussed in the *text*.

[a] Our listing of critical points assumes, as is almost always the case, no points of tangency between the curves $dx_i/dt = 0$ of equation [10]. Note also that by suitably choosing the marriage rate scale $M[1,1]$, the integer K characterizing the number of critical points in sectors 3 through 8 can be made to vanish.

[b] These critical points exist only for sufficiently large $M[1,1]$.

[c] These critical points exist only for sufficiently small $M[1,1]$.

[d] See discussion in *text*.

[e] Range of possible exponential rates r, in parameter space, for interior ray solutions of the form $k e^{rt}$, with least values listed first. As the marriage rate scale $M[1,1]$ runs from 0 to ∞, r takes all values in the given range. Note that the range of r in each case corresponds to the central interval in column two. When there are multiple possible r's, as in sectors 3–8, all fall in the specified range.

[f] Sectors 1, 2, and 9 have two positive β's, as required by the Kendall-Pollard reasoning discussed in the *text*.

fact that the cited works of Kendall, Goodman, Pollard, and others had anticipated some of our results. We would like to express our appreciation to the National Science Foundation for its financial support of this research.

1. Kendall, D. G. (1949) "Stochastic processes and population growth," *J. Roy. Stat. Soc.* **B11,** 230–264, in particular pp. 248–249.
2. Goodman, L. A. (1953) "Population growth of the sexes," *Biometrics* **9,** 212–225, in particular pp. 216–218.
3. Pollard, J. H. (1973) *Mathematical Models for the Growth of Human Population* (Cambridge Univ. Press, Cambridge).

235

Time Symmetry and Asymmetry in Population and Deterministic Dynamic Systems*

Paul A. Samuelson

Massachusetts Institute of Technology, Cambridge, Mass.

Received September 10, 1975

Greville and Keyfitz [1974] have discussed ambiguities in backward, rather than forward, projections of population growing according to the familiar Lotka-Leslie linear model. This is a species of a general genus analyzed here. A sequel will deal with stochastic, non-deterministic models.

1. *Reversible Conservative Newtonian Systems*

Laplace's grandiose world equation purported to predict the future of the universe from its initial phase conditions (positions and velocities). It could as well be used to predict (or postdict) the history of the system *forever* in the past.

More specifically, so long as one stays with the frictionless approximations of conservative Newtonian mechanics, the future and past trajectories have identical and indistinguishable properties. A simplest illustration is that of a pendulum stipulated to obey simple harmonic motion:

$$d^2y/dt^2 = -a^2y \tag{1.1}$$

That its solution is the same backward, for $-t$ as well as t, is seen from writing (1.1) in equivalent form:

$$d^2y/d(-t)^2 = -a^2y. \tag{1.2}$$

By contrast, if the pendulum is subject to simple viscous friction, (1.1) becomes

$$d^2y/dt^2 = -a^2y - b[dy/dt], \qquad b > 0. \tag{1.3}$$

The new backward version becomes

$$d^2y/d(-t)^2 = -a^2y + b[dy/d(-t)], \qquad b > 0. \tag{1.4}$$

That the forward and backward "projections are qualitatively different can

* I owe thanks for financial aid to NIH Grant #1 R01 HD-09081-01, to Kate Crowley for editorial assistance, and to Hiroaki Nagatani for research assistance that eliminated many errors.

be seen from the different behavior of total energy (kinetic energy plus potential energy); respectively, (1.3) and (1.4) lead to

$$\lim_{t \to \infty}[\tfrac{1}{2}(dy/dt)^2 + \tfrac{1}{2}a^2y^2] = 0 = \lim_{t \to \infty} y(t; y_0, y_0') \qquad (1.3')$$

$$\lim_{(-t) \to \infty} [\tfrac{1}{2}\{dy/d(-t)\}^2 + \tfrac{1}{2}a^2y^2] = +\infty. \qquad (1.4')$$

It is bizarre to consider a damped oscillator as having followed its indicated law of motion *forever in the past*, since it would have to have had velocities and positions indefinitely vast! Still, up to *any specified past date*, there is no *logical* difficulty in projecting backward where it would have to have been according to the stipulated model of its motion. The existence theorems for defining and extending the solutions of well-behaved differential equations encounter no Greville–Keyfitz problem of an ambiguous generalized inverse; but there is a meta-mathematical problem of feasibility.

Remark 1. By the nineteenth century thermodynamic models were framed, according to which the loss of *mechanical* energy of the macroscopic pendulum through friction was accompanied by an increase in the microscopic internal kinetic energy of molecules that constitutes their heating up due to friction. The combined system, in *all* its microscopic variables, is hypothesized to keep the time-reversible and conservative properties of (1.1) and (1.2), and to differ from the basic properties of (1.3) and (1.4). How to reconcile this assumed microscopic time reversibility with apparent macroscopic time-irreversibility of growth of "entropy" has spawned a vast literature in statistical mechanics and probability, involving such names as Boltzmann, Zermelo, Löschmidt, Poincaré, Gibbs, P. T. Ehrenfest, and many others into the present day.

Remark 2. The superficial mathematical sign of Newtonian time-reversibility is the presence of *even* derivatives only in the laws of motion: (1.1) and (1.2) involve accelerations and positions but no velocities; and $t^{2k} = (-t)^{2k} = (-1)^2 t^{2k}$. However, "gyroscopic *velocity* terms that do no work" frequently appear in fractionless rotating systems. A deeper explanation of Newton–Laplace time-symmetry comes from Poincaré's beautiful theorem that the "characteristic exponents" of a *variational* system, defined for a stationary point or for a periodic solution, must come in *opposite-signed pairs*, as in Whittaker [1937] and Samuelson [1967]. Thus, (1.1) could also be described as follows:

$$\operatorname*{Min}_{y(t)} \int_a^b \tfrac{1}{2}[(dy/dt)^2 - a^2y^2]\, dt, \qquad y(a) = y_a, \qquad y(b) = y_b,$$
$$b - a \text{ not too large}$$
$$\delta \int_a^b \tfrac{1}{2}[(dy/dt)^2 - a^2y^2]\, dt = 0, \qquad (1.5)$$
$$(d/dt)(dy/dt) = -a^2y, \qquad y(t) = c_1 e^{ait} + c_2 e^{-ait} = c_3 \sin(at + c_4)$$

where c_3 and c_4 are real numbers that depend on the boundary y_a and y_b, and where $\pm ai$ are roots defined by the characteristic polynomial associated with the differential equation

$$x^2 + a^2 = (x - ai)(x + ai) = 0$$

2. Conservative Lotka–Volterra Ecological Systems

The time reversibility of Newton-Laplace happens to be shared by the over-esteemed predator-prey model of Volterra, as discussed in Lotka [1925], Volterra [1927, 1937], Kerner [1972], and Goel, Maitra, and Montroll [1971]. Its simplest form gives

$$
\begin{aligned}
dN_1/dt &= r_1(1 - N_2/N_2{}^*)\,N_1\,, & r_1 &> 0,\quad N_2{}^* > 0 \\
dN_2/dt &= -r_2(1 - N_1/N_1{}^*)\,N_2\,, & r_2 &> 0,\quad N_1{}^* > 0.
\end{aligned}
\tag{2.1}
$$

For any positive initial numbers for prey and predators, $(N_1{}^0, N_2{}^0)$, the subsequent motions oscillate periodically around the equilibrium configuration, $(N_1{}^*, N_2{}^*)$, with an amplitude that depends on the initial displacement from equilibrium. Each such motion is characterized by the constancy of a definable Hamilton "energy" expression of the form

$$H[N_1(t; N_1{}^0, N_2{}^0), N_2(t; N_1{}^0, N_2{}^0)] \underset{t}{\equiv} H[N_1{}^0, N_2{}^0] \geqslant H[N_1{}^*, N_2{}^*] = 0. \tag{2.2}$$

Now let us run the motion-picture camera backwards. So to speak, instead of seeing tigers figuratively pursuing rabbits clockwise around closed contours in phase space, we seem to see rabbits preying on tigers along counterclockwise closed orbits. This is because the backward projections in history satisfy

$$
\begin{aligned}
dN_2/d(-t) &= +r_2(1 - N_1/N_1{}^*)\,N_2\,, \\
dN_1/d(-t) &= -r_1(1 - N_2/N_2{}^*)\,N_1\,.
\end{aligned}
\tag{2.3}
$$

There is seen to be perfect isomorphism between the structure of (2.3) and (2.1) once we interchange N_2 and N_1.

By contrast, once we leave the infinitely-improbable razor's edge in which

$$\partial(N_i^{-1}dN_i/dt)/\partial N_i \equiv 0, \qquad (i = 1, 2), \tag{2.4}$$

we lose the conservation property of (2.3) and time symmetry, as for example with the case of Kolmogorov [1936], Samuelson [1967], May [1972], in which a locally-unstable stationary point is surrounded by a stable limit cycle. Projected backward, such a system shows the opposing qualitative behavior of an apparently stable equilibrium surrounded by an unstable limit cycle.

On reflection, one realizes that the case of the stable limit cycle may meet some infinity asymptotes when projected backward. But, for *finite* past times, there need not be insuperable problems. Quite different is the case of the logistic model, which must be subject to backward "explosion."

3. *Verhulst–Pearl Explosiveness*

Let the numbers of a single species obey the model

$$dN/dt = r(1 - N/N^*)N, \qquad r > 0, \ N^* > 0, \ 0 \leqslant N(0) = N^0 \gtrless N^* \quad (3.1)$$

as in Verhulst [1844] or Pearl [1922], or in the chemist's Law of Mass Action. Then

$$\lim_{t \to \infty} N(t; N^0) = N^*, \qquad N^0 > 0. \quad (3.2)$$

The case where $N^0 = 0$ leads of course to no interesting future or past. The case where N^0 is negative would seem to have no feasibility relevance.

The history of the system obeys quite different relations:

$$dN/d(-t) = -r(1 - N/N^*)N, \qquad 0 \leqslant N^0 \gtrless N^*, \quad (3.3)$$

with

$$\lim_{(-t) \to \infty} N(t; N^0) = 0, \qquad 0 \leqslant N^0 < N^*. \quad (3.4)$$

However, a new wrinkle appears if we set initial N^0 above N^*, so that the species has always been historically shrinking in numbers. Now (3.3) can be projected backward only for a *limited*, finite time! Thus, there is a finite positive m such that

$$\lim_{(-t) \to m} N(t; N^0) = \infty, \qquad N^0 > N^*, \qquad m = (1/r) \log_e[N^0/(N^0 - N^*)]. \quad (3.5)$$

It is *empirically* absurd that species number should have been indefinitely large a *finite* time ago; it is *logically* impossible that the logistic law should have held in the regions above equilibrium for any *long* finite time in the past!

Amateur population projectors, either to raise the consciousness of the public or their own, have been known to create a similar difficulty for *permanent* forward projection population. Thus extrapolations based on laws like

$$N^{-1}dN/dt = \text{polynomial in } N, \quad (3.6)$$

can seem to begin realistically, and yet may lead to the absurdity of a big-bang blowup to infinity of numbers at 11 AM, July 4, 1984. An example is provided by $N^0 = 200$ million and

$$dN/dt = N^2 - cN,$$

where c is just a mite below N^0 and where $N(t; N^0) \to \infty$ as $t \to M < \infty$.

Remark. It is not hard to give strong sufficiency conditions on $f(t, y)$ so that the differential equation $dy/dt = f(t, y)$ can be extended indefinitely far into either the past or into the future. If a blowup at finite time is to occur, $f(\ )$ cannot be a bounded function.

And if f is bounded, a solution can be projected from $y(0)$ over the interval of time $(-\infty, \infty)$. The less easy problem is to give *weak sufficiency* conditions that guarantee this, and to give *strong necessary* conditions whose violation means that indefinite-time projection is impossible: thus, $f(t, y) = y$ is not bounded, but still its solution, e^t, is definable for all t; however, when $f(t, y) = f(y)$ stands for a vector of n functions of $(y_1, ..., y_n)$, the problem becomes a much broader one than merely calculating the convergence of $\int_a^b dy/f(y)$ as a and b approach roots of $0 = f(y)$ or $\pm\infty$.

4. *Forgetting What is Never (Completely) Forgotten*

Greville and Keyfitz [1974, p. 136] present the following initial diagnosis of the "awkwardness" of backward projection of a stable population algorithm:

[1] ... continued forward projection by the Leslie matrix can be shown to lead to the stable age distribution provided only there are two fertile ages prime to one another. Like any ergodic process, this one may be described as forgetting its past: irrespective of the original age distribution, the same stable age distribution will be reached.

That the identical stable condition is reachable through different paths is what makes impossible the retrieval of the path once the stable condition has been reached.

[2] If a plane is covered with lines, defined for example by a differential equation, one can in general proceed in either direction from a point, following the unique line through that point. But where a number of paths converge in a focus or other singularity, the trail is lost; a path cannot be followed through a singularity in a space that has one dimension for each age category, and the problem is to trace a path back from the singularity or from a point near it.

[3] It seems a paradox of the pure theory of population dynamics that the past is less easily accessible than the future. The difficulty arises because the Leslie matrix is singular.

I have numbered these three lines of argument separately in order to distinguish between their logics. Actually, it seems to me that statement [3] contains all that need to be said or that can be validly asserted: if one faces two populations, each subject to the same age-specific fertility and mortality assumptions and each agreeing in age-frequencies below the oldest, they will give rise to *exactly* the same age-frequencies forever in the future, *even* if they differ in frequency at the oldest age itself; this is by virtue of the singularity of the Leslie matrix, and makes it obvious that one cannot from knowledge of tomorrow's complete frequencies ever hope to "recover" today's.

But this has nothing at all to do with the ergodic or global stability property of the Leslie matrix. This assertion will be verified when we later come to consider as our *complete* system, the vector of age-frequencies of the child-bearing time of life and the pre-puberty years. Its Leslie matrix is stable: it is constantly forgetting its past, as it approaches its rendezvous with its ergodic or stable-age distribution destiny. Yet, *formal* backward projection is uniquely possible forever. (We shall show, however, that a new logical difficulty must eventually arise, one that in no way depends upon absence of a unique inverse but rather on the fact that the inverse of a primitive non-negative matrix must have negative elements—and in enough time back they must lead to a non-sensical population state.)

The essential point is this: a stable state may be forever forgetting its past, and yet will never have completely forgotten it. The trace elements left in the memory reservoir suffice to determine the past of a nonsingular algorithm, even when it is strongly damped.

The proposition that I have labeled [2] has to be reinterpreted from this point of view. Consider our damped harmonic oscillator of (1.3). It approaches the fixed point $(0, 0)$ from any point in the $(y, dy/dt)$ plane. Yet, from any point, even those "near" the singularity, the exact backward projection is unique. The same is true of the singularity itself: if at any t, we are literally at $(0, 0)$ we shall *always* be there; *and we must always have been there* if the postulated law of behavior is assumed valid! What must be realized is this: in the (y, y') space, $(0, 0)$ is a singularity with $dy'/dy = [d(y')/dt]/[dy/dt] = 0/0$, an indeterminate expression. But in the (y, y', t) space, there is a unique event-line going through $(0, 0, 1975)$ or *any* other point (y_0, y_0', t_0).

Warning: All along I have been talking about exact computations, not numerical computations rounded off to some finite number of decimal places of accuracy. Greville and Keyfitz have a valid point, as we shall see later, when the relations become "numerically ill-conditioned" as one converges on a stable equilibrium point.

Remark 1.   A reader of proposition [2] might first think of a differential equation $dy/dt = f(t, y)$ which is continuous but fails to satisfy a Lipschitz or other condition for uniqueness. Thus, $f(t, y) = y^{1/3}$ is mentioned in Coddington and Levinson [1955, p. 7] as having an infinity of solutions on the t interval $[0, 1]$ (or for that matter on $[-1, 0]$). But the Volterra or Leslie–Lotka differential equations that are damped are not of this type: and it is to be noted that *both* forward and backward projections from $(0, 0)$ are impossible uniquely under the pathology of this remark.

Do there exist *applied* mathematical systems with similar ambiguities? Yes.

In optimal control of Pontryagin type, $f(t, y)$ may not even be single-valued at certain boundary points. See Shell [1967] for many examples of the following type:

$$\text{Max} \int_0^{\infty} e^{-0.5t} C(t) \, dt \text{ s.t. } C = K^{1/2} - \dot{K} \geqslant 0 \leqslant \dot{K}, \qquad K(0) < 100.$$

The Euler–Pontryagin solution consists of

$$K(t) = [\tfrac{1}{2}t + K(0)^{1/2}]^2, \qquad 0 < t < 20 - 2K(0)^{1/2}$$
$$\equiv 100, \qquad t > 20 - 2K(0)^{1/2}$$

The differential equations-inequations that define this solution can be projected forward uniquely on the positive t interval; but many different initial conditions at time $t = 0$ could give rise to the same solution, namely $K(t) \equiv 100$, at far-distant dates. One would have to generalize the notion of an "inverse" and of a "generalized inverse" to treat this type of problem by such language.

6. Existent Inverses for Differential-Equation Systems

In any case, a general differential-equation system that satisfies Lipschitz or continuous differentiability conditions sufficient to define a unique solution through an initial point will always have a well-defined inverse and inverse-to-inverse. Thus, let

$$y_i' = f_i(y_1, ..., y_n), \qquad (i = 1, ..., n) \tag{6.1}$$

with $\partial f_i / \partial y_j$ well defined everywhere. Then we are guaranteed the solution $[Y_i(t; y_1^0, ..., y_n^0)]$ on an interval $-\eta \leqslant t \leqslant \eta$. For $0 < h < \eta$, consider the transformation:

$$y_i^h = Y_i(h; y_1^0, ..., y_n^0) \qquad (i = 1, ..., n), \tag{6.2}$$

with Jacobian matrix

$$J_h = [\partial Y_i(h; y_1^0, ..., y_n^0)/\partial y_j^0] = [\partial y_i^h / \partial y_j^0]. \tag{6.3}$$

Since .

$$\lim_{h \to 0} J_h = I, \qquad \text{the identity matrix}, \tag{6.4}$$

J_h must be nonsingular for h small enough. Its inverse is the Jacobian of the transformation

$$y_i^0 = Y_i(-h; y_1^h, ..., y_n^h) \tag{6.5}$$
$$J_{-h} = J_h^{-1}.$$

For a conservative variational system, the determinant $| J_t |$ is identically one for all positive and negative real t, by virtue of Liouiville's theorem on conservation of volume in phase space. For a damped system $| J_t | \to 0$ as $t \to \infty$. This means that the inverse J_t^{-1}, even though it exists and permits backward projection, is increasingly sensitive to minute errors in inputs and calculation roundoffs. As $t \to -\infty$, $| J_t | \to \infty$ for damped systems.

Section 11 will return to some global pathologies that can arise in demographic differential equations. However, as far as local projectability backward and forward is concerned, there can arise no problem for differential-equation systems that possess the smoothness and continuity of the well-known existence theorems.

7. Utter Irreversibility for Hardy's Genetic Relation

Consider a general difference equation system, defining for integral t,

$$y_i(t + 1) = f_i[y_1(t),..., y_n(t)], \qquad (i = 1,..., n), \tag{7.1}$$

where the $f_i[\ ]$ functions are single valued.

For $[y_i(0)] = y^0$ given, we can recursively define a forward solution $[Y_i(t; y^0)]$, $t > 0$.

Suppose further that the Jacobian matrix $J(y_1,..., y_n) = [\partial f_i[y_1,..., y_n]/\partial y_i] = J(y)$ is everywhere well-defined and y^* is an equilibrium solution

$$y_i^* = f_i[y_1^*,..., y_n^*] \qquad (i = 1,..., n).$$

Provided $J(y^*)$ is nonsingular, for all y^0 "not too far from y^*", the Implicit Function Theorem guarantees us that we can define a unique nearby $[y_i(-1)]$. And provided that all the characteristic or latent roots of the nonsingular $J(y^*)$ are less than one in absolute value, we know that the forward solutions are stable in the sense that

$$\lim_{t \to \infty} Y_i(t; y^0) = y_i^*, \quad (i = 1,..., n), \quad \sum_i | y_i^0 - y_i^* | < \eta. \tag{7.2}$$

However, there is no T such that, for $y^0 \neq y^*$, in an open small neighborhood of y^*,

$$Y_i(t; y^0) \equiv y_i^*, \qquad t > T, \quad (i = 1,..., n). \tag{7.3}$$

Also, provided η in (7.2) is made small enough, the number of backward projections, $t = -1, -2,..., -T$, can be made as large as we wish. (If the system is linear, and all real numbers in E^n are admissible for $(Y_i(-k; y^0))$, T is always infinite). Again, note that matrices near $J(y^*)^{-T}$ become ill-conditioned for large T if $J(y^*)$ has latent roots all less than 1 in absolute value.

G. H. Hardy [1908], although its author was a mathematical snob un-interested in applied mathematics (but one who, in Norbert Wiener's words, had earned the right to be a snob), considered the following nonlinear iteration for large-sample fractional frequencies of (AA) and (aa) genotypes in a popula-tion:

$$
\begin{aligned}
x_1(t+1) &= [x_1(t) + \tfrac{1}{2}\{1 - x_1(t) - x_2(t)\}]^2, \qquad x_i(0) \geqslant 0 \\
&= \tfrac{1}{4}[1 + \{x_1(t) - x_2(t)\}]^2 \\
x_2(t+1) &= [x_2(t) + \tfrac{1}{2}\{1 - x_1(t) - x_2(t)\}]^2 \\
&= \tfrac{1}{4}[1 + \{x_2(t) - x_1(t)\}]^2.
\end{aligned}
\tag{7.4}
$$

Hardy point out the remarkable feature of this random-mating process, namely

$$
x_1(t+1) - x_2(t+1) = x_1(t) - x_2(t), \tag{7.5}
$$

$$
\begin{aligned}
x_i(1) = x_i(2) &= \cdots = x_i(t), \qquad\qquad t > 0 \\
&= [x_i(0) + \tfrac{1}{2}\{1 - x_1(0) - x_2(0)\}]^2, \qquad (i = 1, 2)
\end{aligned}
\tag{7.6}
$$

$$
x_1(t) + x_2(t) = \tfrac{1}{2} + \tfrac{1}{2}[x_1(t) - x_2(t)]^2, \qquad (t = 1, 2, \ldots). \tag{7.6'}
$$

It is so damped it converges in 1 step.

Suppose, therefore, that we observe an arbitrary $[x_1(0), x_2(0)]$. It can never be projected back to a unique $[x_1(-1), x_2(-1)]$. Unless it satisfies (7.6'), there will be *no* $[x_j(-1)]$ that could have given rise to it; if it does satisfy (7.6'), there are an infinity of $[x_j(-1)]$ that could have generated it, namely $[x_1(0) + z, x_2(0) + z]$ for all algebraic z such that $[x_j(-1)] \geqslant 0$, which implies

$$
-\mathrm{Min}[x_1(0), x_2(0)] \leqslant z \leqslant \tfrac{1}{2}(1 - x_1(0) - x_2(0)).
$$

Clearly the Jacobian of (7.4), $J[x_1, x_2]$ must be singular. Indeed it is.

$$
\begin{aligned}
\det J &= \begin{vmatrix} + \tfrac{1}{2}[1 + (x_1 - x_2)] & - \tfrac{1}{2}[1 + (x_1 - x_1)] \\ - \tfrac{1}{2}[1 + (x_2 - x_1)] & + \tfrac{1}{2}[1 + (x_2 - x_1)] \end{vmatrix} \\
&= \tfrac{1}{4}[1 - (x_1 - x_2)^2] \begin{vmatrix} 1 & -1 \\ -1 & 1 \end{vmatrix}_{x_1, x_2} \equiv 0.
\end{aligned}
\tag{7.7}
$$

The nature of this beautiful pathology, which presumably has a Darwinian survival value, is best seen by tranforming variables

$$
\begin{aligned}
y_1(t) &= x_1(t) - x_2(t), \\
y_2(t) &= x_1(t) + x_2(t).
\end{aligned}
\tag{7.8}
$$

Then (7.4) becomes

$$y_1(t + 1) = y_1(t),$$
$$y_2(t + 1) = \tfrac{1}{2} + \tfrac{1}{2} y_1(t)^2, \tag{7.9}$$

with Jacobian

$$J\{y_1, y_2\} = \begin{bmatrix} 1 & 0 \\ y_1 & 0 \end{bmatrix}, \qquad |J| \underset{y}{\equiv} 0. \tag{7.10}$$

Clearly (7.9) does not permit us, from knowledge of $y_1(t + 1)$ and $y_2(t + 1)$, to determine $y_1(t)$ *and* $y_2(t)$. The last of these is simply not defined.

Moreover, we learn something more from the example. If the *H–W* process has been going on in the past, we cannot let $[y_i(0)]$ be an arbitrary vector. As soon as we know $y_1(0)$, then $y_2(0)$ is not free to be anything other than $\tfrac{1}{2} + \tfrac{1}{2} y_1(0)^2$. The same point holds for the observable (AA) and (aa) fractional frequencies if they are to be the result of *previous* large-sample random matings: such $[x_1(t), x_2(t)]$ or $[x_1(0), x_2(0)]$ must be constrained to satisfy the equilibrium locus already contained in (7.6′)

$$x_1^* + x_2^* = \tfrac{1}{2} + \tfrac{1}{2}[x_1^* - x_2^*]^2. \tag{7.11}$$

8. A Digression on the Hardy-Who? Law

Hardy wrote his 1908 note to correct a view attributed to G. U. Yule, namely that (AA) and (aa) frequencies had to settle at $(\tfrac{1}{4}, \tfrac{1}{4})$ rather than any of the infinity of other solutions of (7.11) if Mendel's hypotheses were true. Independently of Hardy, early in the same year, Dr. W. Weinberg [1908] is credited with essentially Hardy's law, as C. Stern [1943] has pointed out. Relying on the passage of Weinberg translated by Stern [1943, pp. 137–138], we seem to find Weinberg beginning his sequences with zero (Aa) and (aA) frequencies, so that initially $x_1(0) + x_2(0) = 1$; Weinberg correctly deduces permanent equilibrium in one step as given in (7.6) here. Hardy appears to be a bit more general in that he would permit $x_1(0) + x_2(0)$ to be anything, *including zero*, and still he is able to deduce permanent equilibrium in one step.

Sewall Wright [1968, p. 374], no mean authority, in effect seems to suggest that the Hardy–Weinberg Law might be dubbed the Yule–Castle Law:

> As early as 1902, however, the biometrician, Yule,... showed there would be no decline in variability in an indefinitely large population derived from a cross, since each pair of alleles would continue indefinitely under random mating to be represented in the three genotypes in the ratio 1:1, and zygotes would continue to be present according to the square of this ratio. Castle (1903) generalized these conclusions for any gene ratio. These principles attracted no attention until pointed out by both Hardy and Weinberg in 1908. This persistence of genetic variability under Mendelian heredity removes Fleeming Jenkin's criticism of Darwin's theory.

With some charity, and charity is needed, Yule may be deemed to have found that singular instance of Weinberg's specialization of Hardy in which $x_1(0) = x_2(0) = 0$ leads to (AA, Aa and aA, aa) of $(\frac{1}{4}, \frac{1}{2}, \frac{1}{4})$ forever after, or $[x_1(1), x_2(1)] = [\frac{1}{4}, \frac{1}{4}]$. In the paper cited by Wright, Castle [1903], gives merited criticism of various mistatements of Yule, and Castle demonstrates that he probably would have been able to deduce the Hardy–Weinberg Law if he had ever addressed himself to the problem in its full generality. C. C. Li [1967, p. 74] claims for Castle [1903] anticipation of the Hardy–Weinberg relation in these words:

> Castle (1903) has shown that all of the populations (4, 4, 1), (9, 6, 1), (16, 8, 1), (25, 10, 1), etc. ... [which Castle had deduced would prevail after certain *selection* procedures had prevailed, and which in our terminology would involve $[x_i(0)]$ respectively at (4/9, 1/9), (9/16, 1/16), (16/25, 1/25), (25/36, 1/36), or in general at $[(k-1)^2/k^2, 1/k^2]$, for integral k and which do provide $[x_i{}^*]$ solutions to the equilibrium relation (7.11)] ... will continue to be the same under random mating in the absence of selection. This is only slightly short of the algebraic expression $(m^2, 2mn, n^2)$ given explicitly by Weinberg in 1908. ... Castle's general conclusion: "as soon as selection is arrested, the race remains stable at the degree of purity then attained," is in substance the same as what has later been known as the Hardy–Weinberg law.

Bruce Wallace [1968] cites Karl Pearson [1904], as does Stern [1943]. It would be ironical if Pearson, the intemperate critic of the intemperate defenders of particulate inheritance, should have validly antedated Hardy and Weinberg. Pursuing the reference in Hardy [1908, p. 138] to Pearson [1904, p. 60], one verifies that Pearson there does give the special result close to that Yule had arrived at, namely that $[x_1(0), x_2(0)] = [\frac{1}{4}, \frac{1}{4}]$ does correspond to $[x_1{}^*, x_2{}^*]$ equilibrium forever.

My tentative conclusion: Hardy is most general. If the slightly less generality of Weinberg's initial conditions, $x_1(0) + x_2(0) = 1$, is deemed a triviality or a misleading inference from a fragmentary translation, the Hardy–Weinberg Law can be judged to be well named. The Castle–Weinberg–Hardy law is also a possibility, the progression of names corresponding to a progression of generality.

Professor Joel E. Cohen, now of Rockefeller University, when he read the above lines as a member of the Harvard Society of Fellows, put to me in 1971 the following question: Could any iteration other than that of Hardy–Weinberg, have the biologically important property of converging in one step? My answer is this: Yes, there are an infinity of such. Consider any not-necessarily linear iteration

$$x_i(t+1) = f_i[x_1(t),..., x_n(t)], \qquad (i = 1,..., n). \tag{8.1}$$

Let there exist a globally 1-to-1 transformation of variables

$$z_j = Z_j\{y_1,\ldots,y_n\}, \qquad (j = 1,\ldots,n)$$

$$y_j = Z_j^{-1}\{z_1,\ldots,z_n\} = Y_j\{z_1,\ldots,z_n\},$$

(8.2)

such that the substitution of (8.2) into (8.1) leads to the following iteration

$$z_i(t+1) = z_i(t), \qquad (i = 1,\ldots,r), \quad 1 \leqslant r < n$$

$$z_{r+j}(t+1) = F_{r+j}[z_1(t),\ldots,z_n(t)], \qquad (j = 1,\ldots,n-r).$$

(8.3)

Hardy–Weinberg's (7.4), (7.8) and (7.9) provide but one special species of the general genus (8.1), (8.2), and (8.3). What may be the survival value of this property, and how it manages to originate and evolve genetically, are interesting open questions.

Incidently, when the number of mating units is small enough to make the statistical variation around the mean relations of interest, almost certainly either (A) or (a) will become extinct in a long period of time. Yule's special case, where (AA) and (aa) have the equal proportions, $(\frac{1}{4}, \frac{1}{4})$, is the configuration with the *largest expected time* before extinction of all (aA) combinations under random mating and survival. Such a state may itself thus have survival value or "fitness," and perhaps tend to be achieved.

The full Markov transitional matrix to describe the sampling variations through time is itself *reducible*, so that the probability of having (Aa) combinations goes down with time: when all such combinations are no longer possible, one can never recover the past history of the stochastic process that led to extinction of such mixed combinations. In a sequel investigation I consider time-reversibility problems of Markov and other stochastic processes.

9. Backward Projection of the Lotka–Leslie Population Model

With invariant age-specific mortality and female fertility, a population is self-propelled from any initial state that involves positive numbers of females in the pre-puberty and childbearing ages asymptotically into a stable relative age distribution and exponential growth proportional to $(\lambda^*)^t$. The parameters of the system are the fractions of females surviving from age j to $j+1$, (p_j) or $(p_1, p_2, \ldots, p_{n-1}, 0)$, and the rates at which mothers of age j, bear female offspring, $(f_j) = (0,\ldots, 0, f_q,\ldots, f_m, 0,\ldots, 0)$. Here we count new-born babies as of age 1; q is the age of puberty, and m is the oldest fertile age; the f's are assumed to be nonzero for two ages prime to each other, as with two adjacent post-puberty years. Then the numbers of females of age i at time t are determined by the autonomous model

$$
\begin{bmatrix} N_1(t+1) \\ N_2(t+1) \\ \cdots \\ N_m(t+1) \\ \hline N_{m+1}(t+1) \\ \cdots \\ N_n(t+1) \end{bmatrix}
=
\left[\begin{array}{ccccccc|cccc}
0 & \cdots & 0 & f_q & \cdots & f_m & 0 & \cdots & 0 & 0 \\
p_1 & \cdots & 0 & 0 & \cdots & 0 & 0 & \cdots & 0 & 0 \\
\cdot & \cdots & \cdot & \cdot & \cdots & \cdot & \cdot & \cdots & \cdot & \\
0 & \cdots & 0 & p_q & \cdots & 0 & 0 & \cdots & 0 & 0 \\
\cdot & \cdots & \cdot & \cdot & \cdots & \cdot & \cdot & \cdots & \cdot & \\
\hline
0 & \cdots & 0 & 0 & \cdots & 0 & \cdot & \cdots & 0 & 0 \\
\cdot & \cdots & \cdot & \cdot & \cdots & \cdot & & & & \\
0 & \cdots & 0 & 0 & \cdots & p_m & 0 & \cdots & 0 & 0 \\
\cdot & \cdots & \cdot & \cdot & \cdots & \cdot & \cdot & \cdots & \cdot & \\
\cdot & \cdots & & & & \cdot & \cdot & \cdots & \cdot & \\
0 & & 0 & 0 & & 0 & 0 & \cdots & p_{n-1} & 0
\end{array} \right]
\begin{bmatrix} N_1(t) \\ N_2(t) \\ \cdots \\ N_m(t) \\ \hline N_{m+1}(t) \\ \cdots \\ N_n(t) \end{bmatrix}
$$

$$(9.1)$$

or in self-defining matrix notation

$$N(t+1) = AN(t), \qquad \det A = (-1)^{n-1} f_n p_{n-1} \cdots p_2 p_1 = 0. \qquad (9.2)$$

Neville–Keyfitz [1974] set $m = n - 1$ for simplicity: the qualitative complexity of the general case can be achieved with $n = 4$, $q = 2$. Bernardelli [1941] first gave (9.1); Leslie [1945] elaborated on the analysis.

Since A has a final column of zeros, it is obviously singular and possesses no inverse. In common sense terms, we realize that two populations identical initially in all but the oldest age frequency will give rise to the same $N(1)$ vector. Hence, knowledge of $N(1)$ can never lead to knowledge of a unique $N(0)$; likewise, $N(0)$ cannot be projected backward to an $N(-1)$ unique in *all* its elements.

However, consider the subset of frequencies prior to old and infertile ages: $Y(t) = [y_j(t)] = [y_1(t),...,y_m(t)] = [N_1(t),...,N_m(t)]$. Because A is seen to be a reducible matrix, with a $(n - m)^2$ block of zeros in its upper-righthand corner, $Y(t)$ satisfies an autonomous system that is invertible backward uniquely, namely

$$Y(t+1) = aY(t), \qquad \det a = (-1)^{m-1} f_m p_1 p_2 \cdots p_{m-1} > 0, \qquad (9.3)$$

where a is defined as the first m rows and columns of A.

From (9.1) or (9.3) one immediately solves for

$$N_1(t) = N_2(t+1)/p_1,..., N_{m-1}(t) = N_m(t+1)/p_{m-1}$$
$$N_m(t) = [N_1(t+1) - 0 - \cdots - f_q\{N_{q+1}(t+1)/p_q\} \qquad (9.4)$$
$$- \cdots - f_{m-1}\{N_m(t+1)/p_{m-1}\}]/f_m .$$

Therefore, a is easily inverted to give

$$Y(t-1) = a^{-1}Y(t)$$

$$= \begin{bmatrix} 0 & p_1^{-1} & \cdots & 0 & \cdots & 0 \\ \vdots & \vdots & & \vdots & & \vdots \\ 0 & 0 & \cdots & 0 & \cdots & p_{m-1}^{-1} \\ f_m^{-1} & 0 & \cdots & -f_q(p_q f_m)^{-1} & \cdots & -f_{m-1}(p_{m-1}f_m)^{-1} \end{bmatrix} Y(t)$$

$$= \begin{bmatrix} 0 & D_m^{-1} \\ f_m^{-1} & -f_j(p_j f_m)^{-1} \end{bmatrix} Y(t) \tag{9.5}$$

where D_m is a $(m-1) \times (m-1)$ diagonal matrix with $(p_1,\ldots,p_{m-1})$ in its main diagonal.

Clearly, our reduced system is determinate forever forward and backward from knowledge of an arbitrary vector $Y(0)$, namely as $a^t Y(0)$, $(t = 0, \pm 1, \pm 2,\ldots)$.

THEOREM 1.   *For arbitrary initial vector* $[N_1(0),\ldots, N_m(0)] = Y(0)$, *the system can be projected uniquely backward and forward to the only pattern consistent with the postulated algebraic invariances having held and holding forever.*

Remark. So long as f_m is known exactly as a positive number, the exact backward projection is algebraically possible. But, as Professor Keyfitz has properly reminded me, the fertility in the oldest fertile category is by its nature low; hence f_m is a small number, knowable only to a limited accuracy and sensitive to the grouping categories used. Hence, the practical backward projection necessarily involves inverting a matrix that is ill-conditioned with an almost zero determinant. In economics we call this a case of "pushing on a string," not an exercise tempting to engage in.

COROLLARY TO THEOREM 1.   *The initial old-age frequencies* $[N_{m+1}(0),\ldots, N_n(0)]$ *cannot be specified arbitrarily in a system that has always been subject to invariant p's and f's for n past periods, since from knowledge of* $Y(0)$, *we can compute*

$$[N_1(-m),\ldots, N_1(-n+1)] = [(p_1 p_2 \cdots p_m)^{-1}N_{m+1}(0),\ldots, (p_1 p_2 \cdots p_{n-1})^{-1}N_n(0)]$$

The algebraic possibility of backward projection forever by (9.5) is, however, somewhat illusory when it comes to the empirical significance of the result, as the following shows.

Theorem 2.   *Unless the initial non-zero, non-negative* $Y(0)/N_1(0)$ *is already in the steady-state age distribution* $Y^*/y_1{}^*$

$$aY^* = \lambda^* Y^*, \qquad 0 < Y^*, \qquad Y^* \text{ proportional to } \begin{bmatrix} 1 \\ p_1(\lambda^*)^{-1} \\ (p_1 p_2)(\lambda^*)^{-2} \\ (p_1 p_2 \cdots p_{m-1})(\lambda^*)^{1-m} \end{bmatrix}$$

the system cannot have always been subject to the Lotka–Leslie invariances, and it cannot be meaningfully projected backward for more than a finite number of periods since it must inevitably generate negative age frequencies, an empirical and logical monstrosity. It can be projected forward indefinitely with the asymptotic approach to steady-state exponential growth in the sense that

$$Y(t) \approx \alpha Y^*(\lambda^*)^t \qquad \text{or} \qquad \lim_{t \to \infty} Y(t)(\lambda^*)^{-t} = \alpha Y^* \tag{9.6}$$

where α is a positive scalar that depends on the initial $Y(0)$ vector, and where $\lambda^* = \lambda_1$ is the Perron–Frobenius dominant characteristic root of the primitive nonnegative a matrix, so that

$$\det[a - \lambda I] = (\lambda^* - \lambda)(\lambda_2 - \lambda) \cdots (\lambda_m - \lambda), \qquad \lambda^* = \lambda_1 = |\lambda_1| > |\lambda_{1+i}| > 0, \tag{9.7}$$

$$\lambda^* \gtreqless 1 \qquad \textit{if and only if} \qquad \sum_{j=q}^{m} f_j(p_{j-1} p_{j-2} \cdots p_2 p_1) \gtreqless 1. \tag{9.8}$$

As $Y(0)$ becomes closer and closer to the stable age distribution, the number of periods of meaningful backward projection, T, becomes indefinitely large, reaching infinity only when $Y(0)$ is proportional to the characteristic column vector Y^*.

Corollary to Theorem 2.   *Suppose $N(t)$ is known to have satisfied the Lotka–Leslie invariances since $t = -T < -n$, and we observe*

$$N(0) = [Y(0), N_{m+1}(0),..., N_n(0)].$$

Then we can recover by meaningful backward projection all of $[Y(-1), Y(-2),..., Y(-T)]$, and hence from the mortality parameters, p_j, we can recover:

$[Y(-T + 1), N_{m+1}(-T + 1)]$

$[Y(-T + 2), N_{m+1}(-T + 2), N_{m+2}(-T + 2)]$

. . . .

$[Y(-T + n - m), N_{m+1}(-T + n - m),..., N_n(-T + n - m)] = N(-T + n - m)$

$N(-T + n - m + 1)$

. . . .

$N(-1).$

We can never recover, for positive i, any of $N_{m+1}(-T)$, $N_{m+1+i}(-T+1)$,..., $N_n(-T+n-m-1)$; *since, however, these were* not *generated ab ovo from the postulated behavior laws, it is just as well that the system does not pretend to be able to predict them!*

The proof of Theorem 2 is immediate from the classical fact that every characteristic vector, Y_{1+i}, corresponding to λ_{i+1} rather than to the Perron–Frobenius λ^* root, must have some elements that are not positive or zero numbers. The forward and backward solutions consist of superpositions of polynomials in t times $\lambda_i^t Y_i$ components: since $|\lambda_{i+1}|^{-1} > \lambda_1^{-1} = (\lambda^*)^{-1}$, any divergence of $Y(0)$ from a scalar times Y^* will generate non-zero coefficients of such components with negative numbers and one or more of them will have to come to outweigh the positive numbers of the Y^* component.

That Theorem 2 is significant is shown by an easy example that cannot be *meaningfully* projected backward for even a single period. Let $N_{q+1}(0)$ be the only non-zero component of $Y(0)$: this implies $N_m(-1) < 0$—to keep $N_1(0)$ zero in the presence of positive fertile $N_q(-1)$ and all other components of $Y(-1)$ known to be zero.

For there to be absence of meaningful backward projection, m need not be finite. Consider the case most suitable for errorless aggregation: $0 < p_j \equiv p < 1$, $0 < f_j = f$, for *all j*. Then

$$S(t+1) = \sum_{j=1}^{\infty} N_j(t+1) = (f+p)\, S(t), \qquad (9.9)$$

$$S(t) = (f+p)^t\, S(0), \qquad (t = 0, \pm 1, \pm 2,...),$$

$$\lambda^* = f+p, \qquad Y^*/y_1^* = [\{p/\lambda^*\}^{i-1}] \qquad (i = 1, 2,...).$$

(9.10)

It would appear from (9.10) that (9.9) can be projected backward and forward forever. But this is not true of the infinite disaggregated vector, $Y(t+1) = aY(t)$; for unless $Y(0)$ already obeys $Y(0)/y_1(0) = Y^*/y_1^*$, $a^{-k}Y(0)$ will have negative elements for some finite k.

To prove Theorem 2, note the spectral representation of the solution to (9.1):

$$Y(t; Y^0) = c_1(\lambda^*)^t\, Y^* + \sum_{k=2}^{r} c_k \lambda_k^t Y_k,$$

$$\lambda^* = \lambda_1 = |\lambda_1| > |\lambda_{1+k}| > 0.$$

(9.11)

where the c_i are scalar polynomials in t whose coefficients depend on Y^0 (and on the multiplicity of the distinct $r - 1$ λ_{1+k} roots). Unless Y^0 is such that $(c_2,..., c_r)$ vanish, then as $t \to -\infty$, the λ_k^t terms present with the least absolute value for λ will dominate $Y(-t; Y^0)$ and will necessarily generate negative elements for the solution vector in view of the fact that Y_{1+k} can never be a positive vector.

Remark 1. The "nearer" to a stable age distribution is the initial $Y(0)$ vector (as measured by "smallness" of c_{1+k} coefficients), the greater will be the number of meaningful backward projections possible. Hence, no bound on that number, T, can be specified in advance. Greville–Keyfitz (1974, p. 137) attach importance to the (root or) roots of highest absolute value among λ_{1+k}, usually for human populations a pair of conjugate-complex roots, $(\lambda_2, \lambda_3) = (a + ib, a - ib)$. Our easy example raises the question of why one would want to project backward by having births satisfy $c_1 y_{11}^*(\lambda^*)^t + \{c_2 y_{12}\lambda_2{}^t + c_3 y_{13}\lambda_3{}^t\}$. If the system has been obeying (9.1) for a "long time," from "almost all" initial conditions prevailing back then, the neglected remainder $\sum_4^r c_k y_{1k}\lambda_k{}^t$ will now be small relative to $\sum_1^3 c_k y_{1k}\lambda_k{}^t$ and will stay small for a *few* backward iterations: this provides some rationale for interest in the subdominant harmonics of the total spectral chord.

Remark 2. As Coale conjectured in 1957 and Lopez [1961] proved, even when the (p_j, f_j) coefficients are not constant through time, if the current state of the system can be regarded as the product of a great number of Leslie a_t matrices operating on an ancient initial population distribution, that product matrix will have rank "almost of" 1. Hence, the observed age distribution will be pretty much independent, according to the Coale–Lopez theorem on quasi-ergodicity, of the ancient initial age distribution. One might at first think that this rules out as unlikely pathological age distributions like my horrible examples that are not projectable backward for even a few periods before generating negative people. But such is not a cogent inference. If a recent war were to kill off most young women, the Coale–Lopez theorem does not assert that the age distribution cannot then be distorted; rather it merely says that it will be distorted in about the same way as it would have been if the Civil War had not happened a century back.

A later section will show that sometimes it is the falsity of linear approximation that permits projections to go negative. But, in a one-sex model, linearity may be biologically permissible and the impossibility of permanent backward projection may be intrinsic.

A brief word may be in order relating the present discussion to the Greville and Keyfitz [1974] analysis. They propose projecting backward *linearly*, using a matrix X:

$$N(t) = XN(t + 1), \quad \text{backward projection,} \qquad (9.12a)$$

$$N(t + 1) = AN(t), \quad \text{forward projection.} \qquad (9.12b)$$

These forward and bacward projections can be consistent, for $N(0)$ arbitrary, only if

$$N(0) = AN(-1) = AXN(0). \tag{9.13}$$

For $N(0)$ *arbitrary*, this implies

$$AX = I, \tag{9.14}$$

an impossible condition to meet when $\det(A) = 0$, so that A^{-1} does not exist. Clearly something has to give. They cut the Gordian corner by suggesting that X at least be a "generalized inverse" to A, satisfying the requirements

$$A \equiv AXA, \tag{9.15a}$$

$$X \equiv XAX. \tag{9.15b}$$

The first of these ensures that, if we project forward once, then backward once, and then again forward once, we end with the correct result from projecting forward once. Aesthetic enough: but why would one ever want to get forward one step by other than a direct single iteration?

An alternative approach to realize the consistency condition of (9.13) will be to concentrate not on *arbitrary* $N(0)$ data, but rather on those $N(0)$ which could in fact have been generated by an invariant Lotka–Leslie process from actual historical conditions. For such cases, it makes sense to project backward to where the system *must* have been if the Lotka–Leslie invariances had been operative over the periods for which we can project backwards.

Thus, we now ask that (9.13) hold, not for *arbitrary* $N(0)$, but rather for *all* $N(0)$ compatible with the Lotka–Leslie invariances having held throughout the lifetimes of the oldest observed cohorts. Now (9.13) takes on the specialized form

$$N(0) = AN(-1) = AXN(0), \quad \text{for } N(0) = \alpha_1\lambda_1 N^1 + \alpha_2\lambda_2 N^2 + \cdots + \alpha_m\lambda_m N^m$$
$$m > n. \tag{9.13'}$$

where (α_j) are scalars, (λ_j) are the m nonzero latent roots of A (which we may "almost always" take to be distinct, in order to sidestep uninteresting complexities), and where (N^j) are suitable-normalized right-hand eigenvectors of A corresponding to the respective λ_j roots.

It can be shown, but not here, that X must then take the form implied in my Theorem 2. In particular, the first m rows and columns of X must be a^{-1} of (9.5). Greville and Keyfitz [1974, Eq. (3.2)] shows that my X does not satisfy the (9.14) identities, not being of the proper form for that. However, it can be verified that the spirit of those identities is satisfied where it makes most demographic sense for them to be satisfied: i.e., where (9.13′) holds

$$[A - AXA]\, N(0) \equiv 0 \equiv [X - XAX]\, N(0),$$
(9.15′)

$$N(0) = \sum_1^m \alpha_j \lambda_j N^j, \qquad m < n.$$

My X is unique, and it does embody all the knowledge of the fertility coefficients (f_j) and of *all* the implied (λ_j) spectral roots.

The discussion thus far does not do justice to the Greville and Keyfitz endeavor. Even if the method proposed here were exact in a universe where (f_j, p_j) coefficients never changed and could be observed and calculated exactly, and where one could ignore complications that come from ill-conditioning by making exact calculations with rational numbers subject to no-roundoff error, the real world that we face is certainly not such an ideal universe. In practise, it might be the case that the (p_j) coefficients are more invariant through time than the (f_j) coefficients. Furthermore, each is only a sample aspect of reality, subject to error and sensitive to classification intervals. Given approximate knowledge of the $(f_j p_1 \cdots p_{j-1})$ coefficients, one can in principle make an estimate of the first few characteristic roots $(\lambda_1, \lambda_2, \lambda_3, \ldots)$. If age specific fertility and mortality have not been changing much for some time, it is reasonable to suppose that births and *any* (!) age category, such as $N_{n-3}(t)$, satisfy the approximate recursion relation

$$N_{n-3}(t) = c_1 N_{n-3}(t - 1) + c_2 N_{n-3}(t - 2) + c_3 N_{n-3}(t - 3)$$
$$+ \text{ignorable remainder},$$
(9.15″)

$$c_1 = \lambda_1 + \lambda_2 + \lambda_3, \qquad c_2 = -\lambda_1\lambda_2 - \lambda_2\lambda_3 - \lambda_1\lambda_3, \qquad c_3 = \lambda_1\lambda_2\lambda_3.$$

This approximation can be tested on $N_{n-3}(0)$ and

$$[N_{n-3}(-1), N_{n-3}(-2), N_{n-3}(-3)]$$
$$= [N_{n-2}(0)/p_{n-3},\, N_{n-1}(0)/p_{n-2}p_{n-3},\, N_n(0)/p_{n-1}p_{n-2}p_{n-3}].$$

If it passes this test reasonable well, (9.15″) can be extrapolated backward one period to estimate $N_{n-3}(-4)$, from which we derive our desired estimate of $N_n(-1)$, namely

$$N_n(-1) = N_{n-3}(-4)\, p_{n-3}p_{n-2}p_{n-1}.$$

If (9.15″) does not prove to be a good approximation, one might estimate the (c_1, c_2, c_3) coefficients directly from data on $[N_{n-3}(-j), N_{n-4}(-j), N_{n-5}(-j)]$;

or one might use (f_j) coefficients that were in vogue when today's elderly were in *their* fertile years.

In principle, this seems to me akin to the Greville–Keyfitz procedure, and it does avoid the compounded errors from projecting births backward for a century. However, if a war or immigration has vitiated (p_j) coefficients in the past, or a change in family style has made today's (f_j) coefficient inapplicable in the past, all can agree that it is pointless to use (f_j, p_j) coefficients and A to recover past data. Wittengenstein concluded portentuously: "What we cannot speak about we must pass over in silence." On the present problem, he might have said: "Where backward inference cannot be properly made, we should not pretend to make it."

There is a point of view from which the whole problem might seem to disappear. A distinguished Scandinavian actuary has somewhere said that it is not good practice to assume a *finite* bound on the length of life, that it is better actuarial practice to stipulate *very low* probabilities that anyone live to the age beyond Methusalah rather than assert that this is impossible, an assertion that could always become embarrassing. Were this logic acceptable, my n might strictly speaking be infinite as p_j becomes a very small but positive number for all j. However, at a second glance we see that the problem is now all the more complicated. First, if people might always live another day, why couldn't (with sufficiently low, positive probability) there be a positive chance that a 100-year-old woman would bear a daughter? The logic that keeps all p_j positive might keep all f_j positive. In that case, the Feller [1939] worry over whether the spectral representation is complete reasserts itself as the Lopez [1961] result on this matter becomes inapplicable. Second, and much worse, if the infinite vector $N(0) \equiv Y(0)$ is not already in the stable age distribution, how could one constructively make sure that the $N(-1)$ implied by projecting the mortality table backward was consistent with the observed births $N_1(0)$? namely, $N_1(0) = \sum_1^\infty f_j p_j^{-1} N_{j+1}(0)$? and likewise for nonnegative $N_1(-k)$?

In concluding the discussion of the singularity of the Leslie matrix, we may sum up by considering the autonomous, nth order difference equation that births satisfy:

$$N_1(t) = 0 N_1(t-1) + \cdots + F_q N_1(t-q) + \cdots + F_m N_1(t-m)$$
$$+ 0 N_1(t-m-1) + \cdots + 0 N_1(t-n), \qquad m < n \qquad (9.16)$$

where $F_i = f_i(p_1 p_2 \cdots p_{i-1})$.

Applying the time-reversal transformation, this cannot be written as an nth order relation, because $f_n = 0$. Since $f_m > 0$, it can be written only as an mth order relation,

$$N_1(t) = -F_m^{-1} F_{m-1} N_1(t+1) - \cdots - F_m^{-1} F_q N_1(t+m-q) - 0$$
$$- \cdots - 0 + F_m^{-1} N_1(t+m). \qquad (9.17)$$

The solution of this, for *all* signed integers of t, can be given its spectral representation in terms of the roots of the mth degree characteristic polynomial or their reciprocals. And such a finite series of exponentials can be exactly tailored to fit births preassigned to be non-negative numbers over any specified initial m periods; but the same cannot be done for $n > m$ periods.

10. *Lotka's Continuous-Time Case*

This last discussion provides a convenient way to handle the demographic integral equations of Lotka, as in Sharpe and Lotka [1911], Lotka [1928, 1939], Feller [1939], and Lopez [1961]. Now instead of $N_j(t)$, we have $N(a, t)$, the frequency of females of age a at time t; instead of $p_1 p_2 \cdots p_{j-1}$ we have the survival fraction of female babies who are alive at age a, $p(a)$; instead of f_j, we have the age-specific female fertility function $m(a)$. Writing births at time t as $B(t) = N(0, t)$, we have

$$N(a, t) = p(a) B(t - a) = p(a) N(0, t - a), \qquad a \geqslant 0,$$

$$N(a, t) = \frac{p(a)}{p(a - b)} N(a - b, t - b), \qquad a \geqslant b \geqslant 0. \tag{10.1}$$

$$B(t) = \int_0^\infty m(a) N(a, t)\, da$$

$$= \int_0^m m(a) N(a, t)\, da, \qquad m(a) \equiv 0, \quad 0 < a < q \quad \text{or} \quad m < a$$

$$= \int_0^\infty K(a) B(t - a)\, da$$

$$= \int_q^m K(a) B(t - a)\, da, \qquad \text{for } K(a) \stackrel{\text{def}}{\equiv} m(a) p(a)$$

$$= \int_{t-\infty}^t K(t - x) B(x)\, dx$$

$$= \int_{t-m}^{t-q} K(t - x) B(x)\, dx. \tag{10.2}$$

$$p(0) = 1, \qquad p(n) = 0, \qquad p'(a) \leqslant 0, \qquad 0 \leqslant a < n > m > q, \tag{10.3}$$

$$K(a) \text{ and } m(a) > 0 \qquad \text{for } q < a < m$$

$$\equiv 0 \qquad \text{for } 0 < a < q \quad \text{or} \quad m < a$$

$$N(a, t) \equiv 0, \qquad a > n.$$

Suppose that $N(a, 0)$ is initially arbitarily prescribed in the fertile ages or earlier as an integrable function:

$$N(a, 0) \geqslant 0, \qquad 0 \leqslant a \leqslant m$$

$$\int_0^m N(a, 0)\, da > 0.$$

The a unique nonnegative forward projection of pre-old-age $N(a, t)$ is defined by

$$B(t) = \int_0^t K(t - x)\, B(x)\, dx + G(t), \qquad t > 0, \qquad (10.4)$$

$$G(t) = \int_0^{t-m} K(t - x)\, [N(x, 0)/p(x)]\, dx, \qquad 0 < t < m$$

$$\equiv 0, \qquad\qquad\qquad m < t. \qquad (10.5)$$

$$N(a, t) = p(a)\, B(t - a), \qquad t > a \geqslant m$$

$$= \frac{p(a)}{p(a - t)}\, N(a - t, 0), \qquad t \leqslant a \leqslant m. \qquad (10.6)$$

Equation (10.4) is a Volterra integral equation of the second kind, known to have a unique solution for $B(t)$, for $t > 0$. One representation of the solution is in terms of the resolvent kernel to $K(t - x)$, $k(t - x)$, namely

$$B(t) = G(t) + \int_0^t k(t - x)\, G(x)\, dx, \qquad t > 0, \qquad (10.7)$$

$$k(t) = K(t) + \int_0^t k(t - x)\, K(x)\, dx \geqslant 0, \qquad k(t) \equiv 0, \quad 0 < t < q$$

$$= K + K \cdot K + K \cdot K \cdot K + \cdots, \qquad (10.8)$$

where, symbolically

$$f \cdot g = \int_0^t f(t - x)\, g(x)\, dx = \int_0^t g(t - x)\, f(x)\, dx = g \cdot f. \qquad (10.9)$$

With $q > 0$, there will actually be for any t only a finite number of nonzero terms in the infinite series' sum of (10.8): with m also finite, the exact number of non-zero terms will be $[t/q] - [t/m]$, where here the bracket symbol $[x]$ means the greatest integer not greater than x, namely $[x] = k$ where $k \leqslant x < k + 1$. The "generations present" at any t range from generation $[t/m] + 1$ to generation $[t/q]$. For large t, the number of terms will be close to $(q^{-1} - m^{-1})t$. Thus, for $q = 15$ and $m = 50$, at $t < 15$, we have 0 terms; at $15 < t < 30$, 1 term of first-generation births; at $30 < t < 45$, 2 terms; between 45 and 50, 3 terms; between 50 and 60, we lose the first-generation births and again have only 2 terms; ...; at 511 we have $[511/15] - [511/50] = (510/15) - (500/50) = 24$ terms, representing generations 11 to 34. [By contrast, in the renewal equation to come in (10.25), where $q = 0$, we have an infinite number of terms:replacements of replacements of ... of those dying in the first "instant of life." Nonetheless, the infinite series converges very rapidly, being dominated by $M \exp Mt$, where M is an upper bound of $K(t)$, namely $0 \leqslant K(t) < M$.].

A natural interpretation can be given to $k(t)$ as the $B(t)$ that would be generated by a unit pulse of new female babies, i.e., by initial $N(a, 0)$ set equal to Dirac's Delta function, $\delta(a - 0)$, as in Lotka [1928].

The integral equation (10.4) can also be written in the form

$$B(t) = \int_{t-m}^{t-q} K(t - x) B(x) \, dx, \qquad t > 0. \tag{10.10}$$

On the right-hand side, $B(x)$ must be defined so that for negative values it satisfies

$$B(t) = \bar{B}(t) = N(-t, 0)/p(-t), \qquad -m < t < 0. \tag{10.11}$$

Both $k(t)$ and [hence] $B(t)$ are known to approach asymptotically an exponential growth rate, whose magnitude will be defined in (10.16):

$$k(t) \approx k_1 e^{rt}, \qquad B(t) \approx B_1 e^{rt}, \qquad r \gtreqless 0$$

$$\lim_{t \to \infty} k(t) \, e^{-rt} = k_1 > 0 < B_1 = \lim_{t \to \infty} B(t) \, e^{-rt}. \tag{10.12}$$

$$k_1 = 1 \bigg/ \int_0^m aK(a) \, e^{-ra} \, da, \qquad B_1 = k_1 \int_0^m G(a) \, e^{-ra} \, da. \tag{10.13}$$

Provided $0 < q < m < \infty$, formal Dirichlet exponential series, of the Hertz–Herglotz type, can be given for the solutions

$$k(t) = k_1 e^{rt} + \sum_{j=2}^{\infty} k_j e^{u_j t}(\cos v_j t + \alpha_j), \qquad t > 0, \tag{10.14}$$

$$B(t) = B_1 e^{rt} + \sum_{j=2}^{\infty} B_j e^{u_j t}(\cos v_j t + \beta_t), \qquad t > -m, \tag{10.15}$$

where $(r, u_2 \pm iv_2, u_3 \pm iv_3, ...)$ are the infinite R roots of the transcendental equation

$$T(R) = \int_q^m K(a) \, e^{-Ra} \, da - 1 = 0, \qquad 0 \gtreqless r > u_2 \geqslant u_3 \geqslant \cdots. \tag{10.16}$$

The k_{1+j} and B_{1+j} are almost always constants, save in the singular case where for some $j > 1$, $u_j + iv_j$ is a repeated root, for which case k_j and E_j become polynomials in t. Their coefficients can be calculated by straighforward generalizations of expressions like those in (10.13). Lopez [1961] has shown that $\bar{B}(t)$, arbitrarily given as an integrable function on the initial t interval $(-m, 0)$, is representable by the infinite series of (10.15) when $m < \infty$.

Projecting t backward indefinitely must make some higher harmonic, $B_j e^{u_j t} \cos(v_j t + \beta_t)$, come to dominate $B_1 e^{rt}$, and thereby inevitably produce nonsensical negative numbers, except in the singular case where to begin with the age distribution is in its equilibrium state

$$N(a, 0)/N(0, 0) \equiv p(a)\, e^{-ra}. \tag{10.17}$$

Remark. Lotka and Lopez have provided good reasons to believe that all of the above formal arguments can be demonstrated to be rigorous, without troublesome forward-convergence problems. However, as $-t$ becomes large, a problem of convergence for (10.15) does need to be investigated.

Now that $B(t)$ is projectable backward and forward, for as long as the postulated invariances are supposed to hold, we see that the old-age frequencies $N(m + x, 0)$ and $N(m + x, t)$ *cannot* be arbitrarily prescribed but rather must be solved for. The details of Theorems 1 and 2 apply, once obvious modifications are made.

Also, from (10.4)–(10.8), we easily deduce a Fredholm integral equation

$$N(a, t) = \int_0^m K_{t/m}(a, x)\, N(x, 0)\, dx, \qquad 0 \leqslant a \leqslant m, \quad t \geqslant m. \tag{10.18}$$

$$K_{t/m}(a, x) \geqslant 0, \qquad K_{t/m}(a, x) > 0 \qquad \text{for } t \text{ large enough}$$

$$N(a, m) = \int_0^m K_1(a, x)\, N(x, 0)\, dx$$

$$N(a, 2m) = \int_0^m K_2(a, x)\, N(x, 0)\, dx$$

$$\cdots \tag{10.19}$$

$$N(a, [i + 1]\, m) = \int_0^m \left\{ \int_0^m K_1(a, x)\, K_i(x, z)\, dx \right\} N(z, 0)\, dz$$

$$= \int_0^m K_{i+1}(a, z)\, N(z, 0)\, dz.$$

Can we define heuristically some kind of an "inverse" to $K_1(a, x)$, $K_1^{-1}(a, x)$? It would seem that we could by means of formal extrapolation backward of the Dirichlet series (10.15). Without assaying rigor, any such inverse cannot be nonnegative when $K_1(a, x)$ must be nonnegative. By formal definition, I suppose something like the following must hold, where to be safe I have replaced Riemann integrals by Stieltjes integrals (with the notational understanding $\int_0^m f(x)\,dg(x) = \int_0^m f(x)\,g(dx)$, equal if $g'(x)$ everywhere exists, $\int_0^\infty f(x)\,g'(x)\,dx$):

$$N(a, 0) = \int_0^m K_1^{-1}(a, dz)\,N(z, m)$$

$$= \int_0^m K_1^{-1}(a, dz)\left\{\int_0^m K_1(z, x)\,N(x, 0)\,dx\right\}$$

(10.20)

$$\int_0^m K_1^{-1}(a, dz)\,K_1(z, x) \equiv \delta(a - x),$$

(10.21)

where $\delta(\;)$ is the Dirac Delta function such that

$$f(x) \equiv \int_0^1 \delta(u - x)\,f(u)\,du, \qquad 0 \leqslant x \leqslant 1.$$

An example to illustrate the possibility of nonsensical historical projection backward for even an instant would be the case where

$$N(a, 0) \equiv 0, \qquad 0 < a < q$$

$$N(a, 0) \equiv 1, \qquad q < a < m.$$

(10.22)

Since $N(a, 0-)$ was just recently positive in the fertile years, how could births have been zero for some time?

In conclusion, one must be wary of nonsensical negative numbers in other standard Lotka problems. Thus, in Lotka [1931] there is posed an arbitrary growth for total population, $N(t) = \int_0^n N(a, t)\,da = \bar{N}(t)$; and then, on the basis of a given invariant life table, $p(a)$, the necessary pattern of births is sought. I.e., we want the solution for $B(t)$ of the integral equations

$$\bar{N}(t) = \int_0^n p(a)\,B(t - a)\,da, \qquad -\infty < t < \infty.$$

(10.23)

$$\bar{N}'(t) = B(t) + \int_0^n p'(a)\,B(t - a)\,da$$

$$= B(t) + \int_{t-n}^t p'(t - a)\,B(a)\,da.$$

(10.24)

Suppose for simplicity $p(a) = e^{-a}$. Then (10.23) becomes equivalent to

$$\bar{N}'(t) = B(t) - \bar{N}(t).$$

(10.24')

Unless restrictions are put on growth of $\bar{N}(t)$, as for example that $\bar{N}'(t) \geqslant -\bar{N}(t)$, a nonsensical result for $B(t)$ will emerge.

More generally, let $\Pi(t)$ be the "renewal function," which is the reciprocal kernel to $-p'(t)$, satisfying for $t > 0$

$$\Pi(t) = -p'(t) + \int_0^t [-p'(t-x)\,\Pi(x)\,dx > 0,$$

$$-p'(t) = \Pi(t) - \int_0^t \Pi(t-x)\,[-p'(x)]\,dx > 0. \qquad (10.25)$$

Then, if behavior of the system as $t \to \infty$ is suitable,

$$B(t) = \bar{N}'(t) + \int_0^t \Pi(t-x)\,\bar{N}'(x)\,dx, \qquad t > 0$$

and $\bar{N}'(t)$ must not be so negative over any interval as to make $B(t)$ ever be negative. It is curious that Lotka seems never to have used the renewal function of Lotka [1939a] and Feller [1939] to solve the problem posed in Lotka [1937a, 1937b].

Thus, by means of $\Pi(t)$, he could have verified the good sense of a proof that (a) a population will asymptotically acquire a stable age distribution if it starts from an arbitrary $N(a, 0)$ and has its $B(t)$ determined to keep $\int_0^n N(a, t)\,da$ growing like e^{ut}. His [1937a] strictures against R. R. Kuczynski, merited though they be in many respects, seem almost to deny that (a) is a well-posed problem and is in no contradiction to a misunderstanding of his [1937b] theorem (b) that any $N(a, 0)$ which gives rise to $\int_0^n \int_0^n K_t(x, a)\,N(a, 0)\,da\,dx$ that is growing exponentially over *any* time interval, $-\infty < t < \infty$, must *already* be in the stable age distribution, $cp(a)\,e^{-ra}$, of (10.17). Samuelson [1976] clarifies this.

11. *Erroneous Linearity the Culprit in Producing Nonsensical Negative Projections?*

Since the Lotka–Leslie linear model would make biological sense in a one-sex world, the answer to this heading's query must, in general, be in the negative. However, it will be of interest to discuss some 2-sex models of D.G. Kendall [1949], which have been generalized by L. A. Goodman [1953], Keyfitz [1971], J. H. Pollard [1973], Yellin and Samuelson [1974], and many others.

Writing male and female numbers as $[M, F] \equiv [x_1, x_2]$, the simplest case is the symmetric one in which

$$dx_1/dt = \Lambda(x_1, x_2) - \mu x_1, \qquad \Lambda(1, 1) = \lambda > 0, \quad \mu > 0$$
$$dx_2/dt = \Lambda(x_1, x_2) - \mu x_2$$
$$0 \leqslant \Lambda(x_1, x_2) \equiv \Lambda(x_2, x_1), \qquad \Lambda(0, x_2) \equiv 0 \equiv \Lambda(x_1, 0) \qquad (11.1)$$
$$\Lambda(\alpha x_1, \alpha x_2) \equiv \alpha\Lambda(x_1, x_2),$$
$$[\partial\Lambda/\partial x_j] > 0 \text{ well defined on } (x_1, x_2) > 0.$$

This system can be easily shown to be projectable forward from positive initial $[x_1(0), x_2(0)] = [x_1^0, x_2^0]$ forever in a positive solution $[X_j(t; x_1^0, x_2^0)]$ such that

$$\lim_{t\to\infty}[X_2(t; x_1^0, x_2^0)/X_1(t; x_1^0, x_2^0)] = 1,$$

$$\lim_{t\to\infty}\{X_j(t; x_1^0, x_2^0)\exp[-(\lambda-\mu)t]\} = c(x_1^0, x_2^0) > 0, \qquad (j = 1, 2),$$

(11.2)

for all positive initial conditions, as follows from the extreme symmetry conditions.

However, let us replace $\Lambda(x_1, x_2)$ by a linear expression, $\frac{1}{2}\lambda(x_1 + x_2)$, acknowledging the biological oddness of having births when one sex is zero in number. Then our system becomes

$$dx_j/dt = \tfrac{1}{2}\lambda(x_1 + x_2) - \mu x_j, \qquad (j = 1, 2). \tag{11.3}$$

From positive initial (x_1^0, x_2^0), we have

$$\lim_{(+t)\to\infty}[X_2(t; x_1^0, x_2^0)/X_1(t; x_1^0, x_2^0)] = 1. \tag{11.4}$$

And, except in the singular case of equilibrium forever, where $x_2^0/x_1^0 = 1$,

$$\lim_{(-t)\to\infty}[X_2(t; x_1^0, x_2^0)/X_1(t; x_1^0, x_2^0)] = -1. \tag{11.5}$$

Thus, almost all *backward* projections of the linear case must eventually give nonsensical negative numbers, the only exception being when the system is already in its equilibrium configuration, growing proportional to $\exp(\lambda - \mu)t$.

Suppose that instead of replacing (x_1, x_2) by a linear expression, we had respected the biological requirement that

$$\Lambda(0, x_2) \equiv 0 \equiv \Lambda(x_1, 0). \tag{11.6}$$

Then could we be assured that $[X_j(t; x_1^0, x_2^0)]$ stays positive and finite for all backward projections in time?

The case where $\Lambda(x_1, x_2) = \lambda(x_1 x_2)^{1/2}$ satisfies (11.6), but still runs into the difficulty of having a big-bang infinite blowup for the sex ratio in its recent history. I.e., if initially $x_2^0/x_1^0 > 1$, as we move back in history x_2/x_1 must have been bigger and bigger. But at a finite date in the past, $t = -T^*$, this female/male ratio went to infinity:

$$\lim_{t\to-T^*}\frac{X_2(t; x_1^0, x_1^0[1 + \epsilon^2])}{X_1(t; x_1^0, x_1^0[1 + \epsilon^2])} = \infty, \tag{11.7}$$

where t drops from 0 to the critical $-T^*$ that depends on the initial sex disparity

$|x_1^0 - x_2^0| > 0$. This infinite blowup reminds one of the logistic discussion around Eq. (3.5).

To demonstrate this, consider the following relations:

$$dx_j/dt = \lambda(x_1 x_2)^{1/2} - \mu x_j, \qquad (j = 1, 2), \qquad (11.8)$$

$$y_j = +(x_j)^{1/2}, \qquad x_j = y_j^2, \qquad (11.9)$$

$$dy_1/dt = \tfrac{1}{2}\lambda y_2 - \tfrac{1}{2}\mu y_1,$$
$$dy_2/dt = \tfrac{1}{2}\lambda y_1 - \tfrac{1}{2}\mu y_2, \qquad (y_1^0, y_2^0) > 0. \qquad (11.10)$$

This last is a linear system. Its solutions can be written down on sight because of the symmetry:

$$y_1(t) = \tfrac{1}{2}(y_1^0 + y_2^0)\, e^{\frac{1}{2}(\lambda - \mu)t} + \tfrac{1}{2}(y_1^0 - y_2^0)\, e^{-\frac{1}{2}(\lambda + \mu)t}$$
$$y_2(t) = \tfrac{1}{2}(y_1^0 + y_2^0)\, e^{\frac{1}{2}(\lambda - \mu)t} + \tfrac{1}{2}(y_2^0 - y_1^0)\, e^{-\frac{1}{2}(\lambda + \mu)t}. \qquad (11.11)$$

For positive t, it stays positive with $y_2/y_1 \to 1$ as $t \to \infty$.

For negative t the solution to (11.10) is also given by (11.11). But if $y_2^0 > y_1^0$, $y_1(t)$ must cease to be positive for $t = -T < 0$, where

$$T = -\frac{1}{\lambda} \log_e \frac{y_2^0 - y_1^0}{y_1^0 + y_2^0}. \qquad (11.12)$$

It follows that the solution to our original non-linear system (11.8) can be projected backward when $x_2^0 > x_1^0$ only to this same T,

$$T = -\frac{1}{\lambda} \log_e \frac{(x_2^0)^{\frac{1}{2}} - (x_1^0)^{\frac{1}{2}}}{(x_1^0)^{\frac{1}{2}} + (x_2^0)^{\frac{1}{2}}}. \qquad (11.13)$$

As $t \to -T$ from above, the motion approaches tangency with the vertical x_2-axis, and is not analytically continuable beyond that time. Our differential equations (11.8) fail to satisfy at $t = -T$ Lipschitz or other conditions that guarantee a solution, since $\partial(x_1 x_2)^{1/2}/\partial x_1 \to \infty$ as $x_1 \to 0$.

Selecting $\Lambda(x_1, x_2)$ to be the harmonic mean, as in Keyfitz [1971] removes the backward difficulty. Generally, suppose it is biologically reasonable to put a limit on $\Lambda(x_1, 1)$, namely

$$\lim_{x_1 \to \infty} \Lambda(x_1, 1) = \Lambda(\infty, 1) < \infty. \qquad (11.14)$$

This will remove the difficulty, as experimenting with the economists' *CES* family

$$\lambda(x_1^\gamma + x_2^\gamma)^{1/\gamma}, \qquad \gamma < 0 \qquad (11.15)$$

will verify; but (11.14)'s bounds create a new difficulty for a stable sex ratio.

In general, consider as in Yellin-Samuelson [1974, Eqs. (25-25)], but with bound relations like (11.4) now imposed

$$dx_j/dt = f_j \Lambda(x_1, x_2) - \mu_j x_j, \qquad (j = 1, 2)$$
$$0 < \Lambda(x_1, x_2) \not\equiv \Lambda(x_2, x_1), \qquad \mu_j > 0, \quad f_j > 0$$
$$\Lambda(0, x_1) = \Lambda(x_2, 0) = 0, \qquad \Lambda(\alpha x_1, \alpha x_2) \equiv \alpha \Lambda(x_1, x_2) \qquad (11.16)$$
$$\partial \Lambda(x_1, x_2)/\partial x_j > 0 \qquad \text{for} \quad (x_1, x_2) > 0$$
$$\Lambda(1, \infty) < \infty, \qquad \Lambda(\infty, 1) < \infty.$$

If $|\mu_1 - \mu_2|$ is large enough, the sex ratio can be more and more unbalanced as t grows, a situation not possible in the Lotka–Leslie linear case and one therefore that has tended to be overlooked in the population literature. However, it can be shown here what for quite general form of the two-sex fertility function are necessary and sufficient conditions for asymptotic convergence to a stable sex ratio and exponential growth.

THEOREM. *If and only if $-f_2\Lambda(\infty, 1) < \mu_1 - \mu_2 < f_1\Lambda(1, \infty)$, the nonlinear two-sex system of* (11.16) *will approach a positive stable sex ratio and exponential growth, as can be verified from the following relations:*

$$f_1\Lambda(1, Z) - f_2\Lambda(Z^{-1}, 1) + \mu_2 - \mu_1 = 0, \text{ has one positive}$$
$$\text{root for } Z^* = (x_2/x_1)^* \text{ if } -f_2\Lambda(\infty, 1) < \mu_1 - \mu_2 < f_1\Lambda(1, \infty) \qquad (11.17)$$
$$dZ/dt = d(x_2/x_1)/dt$$
$$\qquad = (\mu_1 - \mu_2)Z + \Lambda(1, Z)(f_2 - f_1 Z) = \psi(Z)$$
$$\psi(Z^*) = 0, \qquad \psi'(Z^*) < 0, \qquad Z^* > 0$$
$$\lim_{t \to \infty} Z(t; Z^0) = Z^*, \qquad 0 < Z^0 < \infty$$
$$\{\partial Z(t; Z^0)/\partial t\}(Z^0 - Z^*) < 0, \qquad Z^0 \neq Z^*.$$

In Keyfitz [1971, p. 92], Eq. (4.4) was trying to give warning that, for large discrepancies in the sex death rates, the formula for the sex ratio implied by a harmonic-mean fertility function would go negative—a meaningless result that merely warms of an asymptotic approach of (x_1/x_2) or (x_2/x_1) to zero as in the above theorem.

To find out whether, as $-t$ becomes large, the solution remains positive forever, consider as in the logistic blow up discussion around Eq. (3.5), the divergence of the following integral

$$-t = \int_0^{-t} d\theta = - \int_{z^0}^{z} dz/\psi(z), \qquad (11.18)$$

as $Z \to \infty$. For large Z we can replace $\psi(z)$ by $[\mu_1 - \mu_2 - \Lambda(1, \infty)f_1]z$, and $\int dz/z$ certainly does diverge as $Z \to \infty$.

This does prove that a backward solution can be extended indefinitely for (11.16). If $\Lambda(x_1, x_2) = [c_1 x_1^\gamma + c_2 x_2^\gamma]^{1/\gamma}$, $\gamma > 0$, one could then demonstrate an historical big-bang blowup of the x_2/x_1 ratio at a finite calendar date.

Is an actual population model capable of a big-bang blowup of its x_2/x_1 at a finite date *forward* in time? Pollard [1973, Fig. 7.4.1] gives a linear case of a 2-sex marriage model with this property.

As with Kendall [1949], Goodman [1953], Pollard [1973], Yellin–Samuelson [1974], consider the model for growth of (single males, single females, married couples) $= (N_1, N_2, N_3)$:

$$dN_j/dt = f_j N_3 - \mu_j N_j - M[N_1, N_2], \qquad (j = 1, 2),$$
$$dN_3/dt = M[N_1, N] - \mu_3 N_3, \qquad M[\alpha N_1, \alpha N_2] \equiv \alpha M[N_1, N_2],$$
$$\partial M[N_1, N_2]/\partial N_j > 0, \qquad (j = 1, 2) \quad \text{for } (N_1, N_2) > 0. \qquad (11.19)$$
$$M[0, N_2) \equiv 0 \equiv M[N_1, 0]. \qquad (11.20)$$

When Pollard makes $M[\ ]$ linear, disregarding (11.20), his $M = \frac{1}{2}\nu(N_1 + N_2)$ can lead to negative N_1 when $Z^0 = N_2^0/N_1^0$ begins large enough. (Later, $N_1(t)$ will again become positive on its way to a rendezvous with positive $N_2^*/N_1^* = Z^*$, as in the symmetric case where $f_1 = f_2$, $\mu_1 = \mu_2$ and $Z^* = 1$.)

Although the linear "approximation develops a bigbang for $Z(t)$ at $t = T > 0$, it is doubtful that any actual system could generate positive marriages when one sex is absent.

12. *Teleology and Time Reversibility*

Near the ends of both Section 1 and 4, I referred to the relationship between the deterministic, *causal* differential equations of dynamics and the purposeful solving of an extremum problem; and Samuelson [1965] discusses some further relations between teleology and causality. Here brief mention can be made of time-reversibility aspects of the problem. The discussion will not be systematic in order to be brief.

Much of classical mechanics consists of second-order differential equations of Lagrange–Hamilton type

$$d\{\partial L[q', q] \, \partial q_i'\}/dt - \partial L[q', q]/\partial q_i = 0 \qquad (i = 1, ..., n), \qquad (12.1)$$

where q_j' and $L[q', q]$ are short for dq_j/dt and $L[q_1', ..., q_n', q_1, ..., q_n]$. Provided $L[\ ]$ is strictly convex in $(q_1', ..., q_n')$, these solutions provide, for $t^1 - t^0$ sufficiently small, a strong minimum for the following Hamilton integral

$$\operatorname*{Min}_{q(t)} \int_{t^0}^{t^1} L[q', q] \, dt, \qquad q(t^0) = q^0, \qquad q(t^1) = q^1. \qquad (12.2)$$

If $L[\ ]$ is not also convex in (q', q), making t^1 large may cause the motion to go through a Jacobi conjugate point and, as is discussed in Bliss [1946], this may destroy the extremum property of the motion. Still, over every local finite interval of t on an extended interval (t^0, t^1), we shall have a strong minimum for $\int_{t-\eta}^{t+\eta} L\, dt$, η positive and sufficiently small. Indeed, when the Hessian matrix

$$H[q', q] = [\partial^2 L/\partial q_i'\, \partial q_j'],$$

is everywhere positive definite, we can always project a solution forward and backward: now (12.1) can be written in matrix terms as

$$q'' = H[q', q]^{-1}\, \partial L[q', q]/\partial q - H[q', q]^{-1}\, G[q', q]\, q'$$
$$\partial^2 L[q', q]/\partial q'\partial q = [\partial^2 L/\partial q_i'\partial q_j] = G[q', q]. \tag{12.3}$$

With H and H^{-1} positive definite, (12.3) satisfies the existence-theorem conditions that suffice to give a unique solution through any observed point

$$[y_1'(t^0),..., y_n'(t^0), y_1(t^0), y_1(t^0),..., y_n(t^0), t^0],$$

point on the t interval $(t^0 - \eta, t^0 + \eta)$.

Oddly, the same cannot be said about projectability forward and backward of a discrete-time minimum problem of the form

$$\operatorname*{Min}_{q(t)} \sum_{t^0}^{t^1-1} f[q(t), q(t+1)], \qquad q(t^0) = q^0, \qquad q(t^1) = q^1, \tag{12.2'}$$

where $q(t)$ is again a vector of q's.

The counterpart of Euler's extremal conditions (12.1) now becomes

$$f_{\mathrm{II}}[q(t), q(t+1)] + f_{\mathrm{I}}[q(t+1), q(t+2)] = 0, \qquad (t = t^0,..., t^1 - 2)$$
$$q(t^0) \text{ and } q(t^1) \text{ given.} \tag{12.1'}$$

The short-hand matrix notation in (12.1') is defined by

$$_{\mathrm{II}}[x_1,..., x_{2n}] = (\partial f[x_1,..., x_{2n}]/\partial x_{n+j}) \qquad (j = 1,..., n)$$
$$f_{\mathrm{I}}[x_1,..., x_{2n}] = (\partial f[x_1,..., x_{2n}]/\partial x_j)$$
$$f_{\mathrm{I,I}}[\ ] = (\partial^2 f[\ ]/\partial x_i\partial x_j) \qquad (i, j = 1,..., n) \tag{12.4}$$
$$f_{\mathrm{I,II}}[\ ] = (\partial^2 f[\ ]/\partial x_i\partial x_{n+j})$$
$$f_{\mathrm{II,II}}[\ ] = (\partial^2 f[\ ]/\partial x_{n+i}\partial x_{n+j})$$
$$f_{\mathrm{I,I}}[\ ]^T = f_{\mathrm{I,I}}[\ ], \qquad f_{\mathrm{II,II}}[\ ]^T = f_{\mathrm{II,II}}[\ ], \qquad f_{\mathrm{I,II}}[\ ]^T = f_{\mathrm{II,I}}[\ ].$$

The counterpart of H being positive definite in (12.3) is that

$$f_{\text{II,II}}[q(t), q(t+1)] + f_{\text{I,I}}[q(t+1), q(t+2)] \text{ be pos. def.} \qquad (12.5)$$

This does *not*, however, assure us that the implicit difference equations of (12.1′) can be put into either of the explicit forms comparable to (12.3), namely

$$q(t+2) = \psi[q(t+1), q(t)], \qquad (12.3')$$

$$q(t) = \phi[q(t+1), q(t+2)]. \qquad (12.3'')$$

These solutions are locally possible, if at all, only if $\det(f_{\text{I,II}}[q(t), q(t+1)])$ is one signed. Actually, if (12.3′) is valid, so will be (12.3″).

The following trivial example shows that neither may be valid.

$$f[x_1, x_2] = U[x_1] + V[x_2], \qquad n = 1 \qquad (12.6)$$
$$0 = f_{\text{II}}[q_1(t), q_1(t+1)] + f_{\text{I}}[q_1(t+1), q_1(t+2)]$$
$$= V'[q_1(t+1)] + U'[q_1(t+1)], \qquad (t = t^0, t^0+1, ..., t^1-2).$$

Hence, regardless of assigned $q_1(t^0)$ and $q_1(t^1)$,

$$q_1(t) \equiv q_1{}^* \qquad t^0 < t < t^1. \qquad (12.7)$$

Thus, if we observe $[q_1(1984), q_1(1985)] = (q_1{}^*, q_1{}^*)$, we cannot be sure what $q_1(1983)$ or $q_1(1986)$ had to be in the optimal-control problem. Forward and backward projectibility are not assured by the curvature of the minimization.

The minimum problems in (12.2) and (12.2′) involved integrands and summands not involving t explicitly. Often, however, in engineering and economic programming problems, exponential time-discount factors of the form e^{-rt} or R^{-t} are involved, for reasons having to do with positive interest rates or the natural way people have perspective in their regard for the near and distant future. Hence, (12.2) and (12.2′) become respectively,

$$\underset{q(t)}{\text{Min}} \int_{t^0}^{t^1} L[q', q]\, e^{-rt}\, dt, \quad r > 0, \qquad q(t^0), q(t^1) \text{ given}, \qquad (12.8)$$

$$\underset{q(t)}{\text{Min}} \sum_{t^1}^{t^1-1} f[q(t), q(t+1)]\, R^{-t}, \quad R > 1, \qquad q(t^0), q(t^1) \text{ given}. \quad (12.8')$$

Positive r and $R-1$ does introduce some interesting time-asymmetry. Now (12.1) and (12.1′) become

$$d\{\partial L[q', q]/\partial q'\}/dt - \partial L[q', q]/\partial q - r\partial L[q', q]\, \partial q' = 0, \qquad (12.9)$$

$$Rf_{\text{II}}[q(t), q(t+1)] + f_{\text{I}}[q(t+1), q(t+2)] = 0. \qquad (12.9')$$

With L strictly convex in $[q', q]$ and f strictly convex in $[q(t), q(t + 1)]$, we can be sure that (12.9) and (12.9′) have unique stationary solutions $q(t) \equiv q^*$ for $r = 0$ or $R = 1$. But for $r > 0 < R - 1$, the following equations may have more than one q^* solution, as shown in Liviatan and Samuelson [1969]:

$$0 = -\partial L[0, q^*]/\partial q - r\partial L[0, q^*]/\partial q', \tag{12.10}$$

$$0 = Rf_{II}[q^*, q^*] + f_I[q^*, q^*]. \tag{12.10'}$$

For "small deviations" near equilibrium, the motions depend on the roots of

$$0 = \det[L_{I,I}^* \lambda^2 + (L_{I,II}^* - L_{II,I}^*)\lambda - L_{II,II}^* - r(L_{I,I}^*\lambda + L_{I,II}^*)]$$

$$= (\lambda_1 - \lambda)(\lambda_2 - \lambda) \cdots (\lambda_{2n-1} - \lambda)(\lambda_{2n} - \lambda)\det(+L_{I,I}^*) \tag{12.11}$$

$$r = \lambda_1 + \lambda_2 = \lambda_3 + \lambda_4 = \cdots = \lambda_{2n+1} + \lambda_{2n} > 0,$$

$$0 = \det[f_{II,I}^* + (f_{II,II}^* + f_{I,I}^*)\gamma + f_{I,II}^*\gamma^2 + (R - 1)(f_{II\,I}^* + \gamma f_{II,II}^*)]$$

$$= (\gamma_1 - \gamma)(\gamma_2 - \gamma) \cdots (\gamma_{2n-1} - \gamma)(\gamma_{2n} - \gamma)\det(+f_{I,II}^*) \tag{12.11'}$$

$$R = \gamma_1\gamma_2 = \gamma_3\gamma_4 = \cdots = \gamma_{2n-1}\gamma_{2n}.$$

Equations (12.11) and (12.11′), due respectively to Kurz [1968] and to Levhari and Liviatan [1972], generalize the Poincaré theorem about opposite-signed pairs of roots and reciprocal component solutions, $e^{\lambda_1 t}$ and $e^{\lambda_2 t} = e^{-\lambda_1 t}$ or γ_1^t and $\gamma_2^t = 1/\gamma_1^t$. But note that the asymmetric e^{-rt} and R^{-t} factors that appear to be damped in time lead to solutions that are biased to be anti-damped in time. Thus, the pendulum of (1.1) has a motion, when we introduce e^{-rt} into the integrand of (1.5), of the form

$$y''(t) - ry'(t) + ay(t) = 0, \tag{12.12}$$

$$y(t) = c_1 e^{(1/2)rt} \cos[\tfrac{1}{2}(4a^2 - r^2)^{\tfrac{1}{2}}t + c_2], \qquad 0 < r < 2a,$$

$$\lim_{\theta \to \infty} \frac{\int_0^\theta |y(t)|\,dt}{\int_0^\theta |y(-t)|\,d(-t)} = \infty.$$

In the case met in economics where $L[\ ]$ is convex in (q', q), we have the generalized catenary motions

$$\operatorname*{Min}_{y(t)} \int_0^T \tfrac{1}{2}[(y')^2 + a^2 y^2]\,e^{-rt}\,dt, \qquad r > 0 \tag{12.13}$$

$$y''(t) - ry'(t) - a^2 y(t) = 0,$$

$$y(t) = c_1 e^{((1/2)r+\alpha)t} + c_2 e^{((1/2)r-\alpha)t}, \qquad 0 < \alpha = \tfrac{1}{2}(r^2 + 4a^2)^{1/2}$$

$$\lim_{\theta \to \infty} \frac{\int_0^\theta |y(t)|\,dt}{\int_0^\theta |y(-t)|\,d(-t)} = \infty \qquad \text{for almost all } [y(0), y(T)].$$

In the discrete-time analogue to (12.13), one encounters relations like

$$y(t) = c_1 \gamma_1{}^t + c_2 \gamma_2{}^t$$
$$= c_1[R(1+\beta)]^t + c_2(1+\beta)^{-t}, \qquad \beta > 0 \quad \text{when} \quad R > 1$$

$$\lim_{N \to \infty} \frac{\sum_0^N |y(t)|}{\sum_0^N |y(-t)|} = \infty, \qquad \text{for almost all } [y(t^0), y(t^1)]. \tag{12.14}$$

Another time-asymmetry in causal and teological optimizing systems may be mentioned briefly. Let $a = [a_{ij}]$ be a matrix of positive elements with *column sums less than unity*. Then Keynes [1936] and Metzler [1973, Chaps. 2, 10] multi-sector-multiplier models of international spending obey matrix relations

$$y(t+1) = ay(t) + f(t), \tag{12.15}$$

where $[f_1(t), ..., f_n(t)]$ are autonomous multiplicands of investments. Because $a^k \to 0$ as $k \to \infty$, when $[f_j(t)] \equiv [f_j]$ the system dampens down

$$\lim_{t \to \infty} y(t) \to y^* = [I - a]^{-1} [f_i], \tag{12.16}$$

Almost always $\det[a] \neq 0$, and a^{-1} and a^{-k} exist. The system can then be projected backward forever, but usually with nonsensical and explosive elements for $k \geqslant 1$; in the spectral representation of a^{-t}, the subdominant roots come to outweigh the Perron–Frobenius dominant root, for the reason that

$$1 > \lambda_1 > |\lambda_2| \geqslant |\lambda_3| \geqslant \cdots \geqslant |\lambda_n| > 0$$
$$\lambda_1^{-t} < |1/\lambda_2|^t \leqslant |1/\lambda_3|^t \leqslant \cdots \leqslant |1/\lambda_n|^t, \qquad t > 0. \tag{12.17}$$

For Leontief planning programs, an exactly similar $[a_{ij}]$ input-output matrix is involved, where a_{ij} gives the amounts of input i needed at t to produce 1 output of j at $t+1$. But now the planning dynamics runs backward! Instead of (12.15), we have

$$x(t) = ax(t+1) + c(t), \tag{12.18}$$

where $c(t)$ represents the specified amount of military consumption goods needed. To have guns for a war in 1984, $c_1(1984)$, we need iron in 1983, $a_2 c_1(1984)$; but for iron then, we need coal in 1982, $a_{32} a_{21} c_1(1984)$; etc.

Moving backward in time, and only then, is (12.18) nicely damped and positive for $x(t^0) = x(1984) > 0$. Thus, for $x(1984)$ given and $c(t) \equiv 0$,

$$\lim_{t \to -\infty} x(1984 + t) = \lim_{t \to -\infty} a^{-t} x(1984) = a^\infty x(1984) = 0. \tag{12.19}$$

Finally, the famous "turnpike theorem" of growth economics, as in Ramsey [1928], von Neumann [1946], Dorfman, Samuelson, and Solow [1958], Radner

[1961] or Morishima [1964], can at first seem to create an illusion of time-asymmetry. Thus, in the optimal saving version of (12.13), let the horizon, T, go to infinity. Then the transversality condition at infinity requires that c_1 in (12.13) equal zero and the solution, the Ramsey locus to modified bliss, becomes damped forward in time:

$$y^*(t) = y(t^0)\, e^{(\frac{1}{2}r-\alpha)(t-t^0)}$$

$$\lim_{t\to\infty} y^*(t) = 0 = y^*.$$

(12.20)

The time-asymmetry is, however, spurious. Supose we pose the problem as follows:

$$\operatorname*{Min}_{y(t)} \int_{-\infty}^{0} \tfrac{1}{2}[(y')^2 + a^2 y^2]\, e^{-rt}\, dt \qquad y(0) \text{ given.} \qquad (12.21)$$

Its solution, which is the only permanently backward-projectable extremal motion, requires the suppression of c_2 not c_1 . This gives

$$y(t) = u(t^0)\, e^{(\frac{1}{2}r+\alpha)(t-t^0)}, \qquad t < t^0$$

$$\lim_{t\to-\infty} y(t) = 0.$$

(12.22)

Although the motions seem to fan out like a cornucopia, this fanning out occurs in both directions of time. The present, so to speak, is at the apex of two cones joined at now.

13. World Equation

The rockbottom case of deterministic dynamics is one in which there is a finite number of states of the world. Number the states $(1, 2,..., S)$. A world system is "causal-forward," if "given that the system is in state j at time t, we can be sure that at time $t + 1$ it will be at state $i = f(j)$, where

$$[f(1),...,f(S)], \qquad 1 \leqslant f(j) \leqslant S, \quad (j = 1,..., s), \qquad (13.1)$$

is a well-defined sequence of integers."

Only if $f(j) \neq f(k)$ for $j \neq k$, will a causal-forward system also necessarily be "causal-backward," in the sense that "if we know the system is at $t + 1$ in state i, we can be sure that at time t, equal $(t + 1) - 1$, it was in state $f^{-1}(i)$, where we have the well-defined sequence

$$[f^{-1}(1),...,f^{-1}(S)] \qquad 1 \leqslant f^{-1}(i) \leqslant S, \quad (i = 1,..., S). \qquad (13.2)$$

Clearly, when $f^{-1}(\ )$ is well-defined,

$$f^{-1}(f(j)) \equiv j, \qquad (j = 1,..., S)$$

$$f(f^{-1}(i)) \equiv i, \qquad (i = 1,..., S).$$

(13.3)

The example where for $S = 2$,

$$f(1) = f(2) = 1,$$

shows that no $f^{-1}(\ )$ inverse need exist. In that case, beginning at t in state 1, the subsequent position of the system is given forever as being in 1. I.e.,

$$1 = f(1) = f(f(1)) = \cdots$$

Similarly, beginning at t in state 2, the subsequent orbit is Laplacianly certain, happening also to be in state 1 forever

$$1 = f(2) = f(f(2)) = \cdots.$$

With S finite, and $[f(j)]$ well defined, it is clear that, from any initial condition j_0, the orbit must ultimately become *strictly* periodic. Thus, define $f_t(j)$ recursively,

$$f_1(j) \equiv f(j), f_2(j) = f(f_1(j)),..., f_t(j) = f(f_{t-1}(j)). \tag{13.4}$$

Then

$$f_{t+T}(j) \equiv f_t(j) \text{ for some } T \text{ and } t > t^*. \tag{13.5}$$

Here, T and t^* will depend on S and the nature of $f(\ )$.

There are always S^S different forward-causal dynamic laws (and, alternatively, the same number of possible backward-causal dynamic laws). On the other hand, there are only $S!$ forward-backward-causal dynamic laws. Thus, consider $S = 2$. The forward-causal cases for $[f(1), f(2)]$ are

$$[1 \quad 1] \quad [1 \quad 2]$$
$$[2 \quad 1] \quad [2 \quad 2].$$

Alternatively, there are 4 similar patterns that could be specified for backward-causal laws.

However, one cannot *independently* impose both a backward- and a forward-causal law. Only in the forward-causal cases [1 2] or [2 1] could there *also* be a backward-causal law holding: the pairs that go together for $[f(\ ); f^{-1}(\ )]$ would be [1 2; 1 2] or [2, 1; 2 1]. Every forward-causal path has an ultimate period of 2; some, such as [1 2], [1 1], [2 2] also have period 1.

The reader can verify the following periodicities for $f(\ )$

[2 3 1], period 3 forward and backward

[1 3 2], period 2 forward and backward

[2 3 2], ultimate period 2 forward.

Degenerate Markov transition probability matrices can be used to describe these dynamic relations. Let the system be in state k at t if the following S-row vector of $S - 1$ zeros and one 1 has a 1 in its kth element:

$$x(t) = [\delta_{kj}], \tag{13.6}$$

where δ_{ij} is the Kronecker delta, $\delta_{ii} = 1$, $\delta_{ij} = 0$ if $i \neq j$.

$$x(t + 1) = x(t) A$$
$$[x_j(t + 1)] = [x_j(t)] [a_{ij}] \tag{13.7}$$
$$= [x_j(t)] [\delta_{f(i),j}].$$

A has row sums all equal to unity.

For $x(t) = [\delta_{kj}]$, so that the system is in state k at t, (13.7) says that at $t + 1$ it will be in state $f(k)$, namely

$$x(t) A = [\delta_{kj}] [\delta_{f(i),j}]$$

$$= \left[\sum_{i=1}^{s} \delta_{ki} \delta_{f(i),j} \right] = [\delta_{kk} \delta_{f(k),j}]$$

$$= [\delta_{f(k),j}] = x(t + 1). \qquad \text{Q.E.D.}$$

Thus, let $[f(1), f(2), f(3)] = [3\ 1\ 2]$. Then

$$A = [\delta_{f(i),j}] = \begin{bmatrix} 0 & 0 & 1 \\ 1 & 0 & 0 \\ 0 & 1 & 0 \end{bmatrix},$$

$$\begin{bmatrix} 1 & 0 & 0 \\ 0 & 1 & 0 \\ 0 & 0 & 1 \end{bmatrix} A = \begin{bmatrix} 0 & 0 & 1 \\ 1 & 0 & 0 \\ 0 & 1 & 0 \end{bmatrix} \text{ as required.}$$

In order that a system be backward-causal as well as forward-causal, there must also be a matrix, call it A^*, such that

$$x(t) = x(t + 1)A^*, \tag{13.8}$$

where A^* has the same form as A, namely $S - 1$ zeros in each of its rows and one 1. If A^* exists, it must algebraically be A's inverse, A^{-1}. It will exist, if and only if, $f(j) \neq f(k)$ for $j \neq k$. And, in this case,

$$A^{-1} = A^* = A^T. \tag{13.9}$$

Hence, for every 2-way causal system, the matrix $A = [\delta_{f(i),j}]$ is an orthogonal or unitary matrix. This requires that the nonnegative permutation matrix be cyclic. Actually, for some integer q,

$$A^q \equiv I, \tag{13.10}$$

from which the periodicity of orbits follows.

A quick test for reversibility of the forward system is whether

$$\det[a_{ij}] \neq 0. \tag{13.11}$$

However, the requirement $f(j) \neq f(k)$, $k \neq j$, or that the sums of the columns as well as of the rows be unity, is even quicker to test.

There is no reason to keep S finite. For a countable infinity of states of the world, forward-causality can be defined by an infinite A matrix with zeros in every row everywhere except for one 1; a 2-way causal system is one in which A also has a single 1 in each column. That we can no longer expect necessary periodicity when S is infinite can be seen from the systematic climb

$$f(j) = j + 1, \qquad (j = 1, 2,...) \quad j = 0, \pm 1, \pm 2,...$$

In the stochastic sequel to this paper, we shall encounter generalizations of these degenerate Markov matrices, in which the a_{ij} are fractional but with row sums still unity.

The case of an uncountable number of states of the world, indexed by the real numbers on the x interval $[0, 1]$ leads to

$$x(t + 1) = f[x(t)]. \tag{13.13}$$

If a continuous $f[x]$ is to be causal-forward and causal-backward, $f[x]$ must be strictly monotone, and either $(f[0], f[1]) = (1, 0)$ or $(0, 1)$. Then f^{-1} will exist and have the same properties. Also

$$f^{-1}[f(x)] \equiv x, \qquad f[f^{-1}(y)] \equiv y. \tag{13.12}$$

14. *Conclusion*

This completes a survey of time symmetry and asymmetry in the deterministic case. The parallel and new problems that arise in probabilistic models will be sampled in a forthcoming sequel.

Underlying the distinction between systems projectable forward and backward is the fundamental difference between the ability of the laboratory scientist to "control" his experiments, and the ability of the astronomer, meteorologist, and econometrician merely to observe the sequence of reality that happens to stagger into his camera sights.

Before Galileo released the ball on his inclined plane, before he began to hum the tune that served as his metronome and clock, the curtain had not gone up. Likewise with Isaac's scenario of the falling apple before he cut its stem. To the laboratory scientist, this property of the system to have only a future is a source of no discomfiture. (Nor does he mourn when the apple hits the mud and the symphony ends; no more does the optimizing archer mourn when his arrow's flight comes to an end in the bull's eye.)

By contrast, the moon was falling toward the earth before the fatherless babe was born in Lincolnshire; and continued so to fall after the Master of the Mint was interred in Westminster Abbey. It was Newton the theologian who stipulated a Watchmaker to wind up the planets and then set them free, an hypothesis he need not have feigned.

To the observer of a world he never made, time must have a more symmetric, two-sided structure. He has the faith that the thunder rumbled and the lightning flashed even when he was not there in the forest to witness. And, in a universe where laws of motality and fertility are subject to evolutionary change, a model based on particular behavior laws has, strictly speaking, only a *present*; the past was not *its* past; the future will not be *its* future; and, again strictly speaking, its present has only a Platonic existence as a convenient fiction not unambiguously identifiable. The art of science is to infer the invariant aspects of that which is ever changing.

REFERENCES

BERNARDELLI, H. 1941. Population waves. *J. Burma Res. Soc.* **XXXI**, Part I, 1–18.

BLISS, G. A. 1946. "Lectures on the Calculus of Variations," University of Chicago Press, Chicago, Ill.

CASTLE, W. E. 1903. The laws of heredity of Galton and Mendel, and some laws governing race improvement by selection, *Proc. Amer. Acad. Arts Sci.* **39**, 223–242.

COALE, A. J. 1972. "The Growth and Structure of Human Populations: A Mathematical Investigation," Princeton University Press, Princeton, N.J.

CODDINGTON, E. A. AND LEVINSON, N. 1955. "Theory of Ordinary Differential Equations," McGraw-Hill, New York.

DORFMAN, R., SAMUELSON, P. A. AND SOLOW, R. M. 1958. "Linear Programming and Economic Analysis," McGraw-Hill, New York.

FELLER, W. 1941. On the integral equation of renewal theory, *Ann. Math. Stat.* **12**, 243–267.

GOEL, N. S., MARTRA, N. C. AND MONTROLL, E. W. 1971. On the Volterra and other nonlinear models of interacting populations, *Rev. Mod. Phys.* **43**, 231–276.

GOODMAN, L. A. 1953. Population growth of the sexes, *Biometrics* **9**, 212–225.

GREVILLE, T. N. E. AND KEYFITZ, N. 1974. Backward population projection by a generalized inverse, *Theor. Pop. Biol.* **6**, 135–142.

HARDY, G. H. 1908. Mendelian proportions in a mixed population, *Science* (July 10, 1908), 49–50.

KENDALL, D. G. 1949. Stochastic processes and population growth, *J. Roy. Stat. Soc.* **B11**, 230–264.

KERNER, E. H. 1972. "Gibbs Ensemble; Biological Ensemble," Gordon and Breach, New York.

KEYFITZ, N. 1971. The mathematics of sex and marriage, In "Proceedings of the Sixth Berkeley Symposium on Mathematical Statistics and Probability Vol. IV, Biology and Health," University of California Press, Berkeley, Calif.

KOLOMOGOROV, A. N. 1936. Sulla teoria di Volterra della lotta per l'esistenza, Giorn. Instituto Ital. Attnan 7, 74–80.

KURZ, M. 1968. The general instability of a class of competitive growth processes, Rev. Econ. Studies 35, 155–174.

LESLIE, P. H. 1945. On the use of matrices in certain population mathematics, Biometrika 33, 183–212.

LEVHARI, D. AND LIVIATAN, N. 1972. On stability in the saddlepoint sense, J. Econ. Theory 4, 88–93.

LI, C. C. 1967. Castle's early work on selection and equilibrium, Amer. J. of Human Genet. 19, 70–74.

LIVIATAN, N. AND SAMUELSON, P. A. 1969. Notes on turnpikes: Stable and unstable, J. Econ. Theory 1, 454–475.

LOPEZ, A. Problems in stable population theory, Office of Population Research, Princeton, N.J.

LOTKA, A. J. 1925. "Elements of Physical Biology," Williams and Wilkins, Baltimore Md.

LOTKA, A. J. 1928. The progeny of a population element, Amer. J. Hygiene VIII, 875–901.

LOTKA, A. J. 1931. The structure of a growing population, Human Biol. 3, 459–493.

LOTKA, A. J. 1939a. A contribution to the theory of self-renewing aggregates, with special reference to industrial replacement, Ann. Math. Stat. 10, 1–25.

LOTKA, A. J. 1939b. On an integral equation in population analysis, Ann. Math. Stat. 10, 144–161.

MAY, R. M. 1973. "Model Ecosystems," Princeton University Press, Princeton, N.J.

METZLER, L. 1973. "Collected Papers," Harvard University Press, Cambridge, Mass.

MORISHIMA, M. 1964. "Equilibrium Stability and Growth," Clarendon Press, Oxford.

PEARL, R. 1922. "The Biology of Death," Lipincott, Philadelphia.

PEARSON, K. 1904. Mathematical contributions to the theory of evolution. On a generalised theory of alternative inheritance, with special reference to Mendel's laws. Philos. Trans. Roy. Soc. London 203, 53–86.

POLLARD, J. H. 1973. "Mathematical Models for the Growth of Human Population, Cambridge University Press, Cambridge, Mass.

PONTRYAGIN, L. S., BOLTYANSKII, V. G., GAMKRELIDZE, R. V. AND MISHCHENKO, E. F. 1962. "The Mathematical Theory of Optimal Processes," New York.

RAMSEY, F. P. 1928. A mathematical theory of saving, Econ. J. 38, 543–559.

SAMUELSON, P. A. 1967. A universal cycle?, In "Methods of Operations Research," (Henn, R., Ed.) Verlag Anton Hain, Muhlgasse, Vol. III, 307–320. Reproduced In "Collected Scientific Papers," Vol. III, Chapter 170.

SAMUELSON, P. A. 1968. Reciprocal characteristic root property of discrete-time maxima, Western Econ. J. Reproduced in Samuelson, P. A. 1967. "Collected Scientific Papers," Chapter 157, pp. 324–327.

SAMUELSON, P. A. 1970. Classical orbital stability deduced for discrete-time maximum systems, Western Econ. J. 110–119. Reproduced in Samuelson, P. A. "Collected Scientific Papers," Chapter 158, pp. 328–338.

SAMUELSON, P. A. 1971. The general saddlepoint property of optimal-control motions, J. Econ. Theory 5, 102–120.

SAMUELSON, P. A. 1976. Resolving a historical confusion in population analysis, *Human Biology*, forthcoming September issue.

SHARPE, F. R. AND LOTKA, A. J. 1911. A problem in age distribution, *Philosophical Magazine*, Series 6, No. 1, **21**, 435–438.

SHELL, K. 1967. "Essays on the Theory of Optimal Economic Growth," MIT Press, Cambridge, Mass.

STERN, C. 1943. The Hardy–Weinberg law, *Science* **97**, 137–138.

VERHULST, P. F. 1844. *Mem. Acad. Roy. Bruxelles* **18**, 1.

VOLTERRA, V. 1927. Una Teoria Matematica Sulla Lotta Per L'Esistenza, *Scientia* **XLI**, 85–102.

VOLTERRA, V. 1931. "Leçon sur la Théorie Mathématique de la Lutte Pour la Vie," Gauthier-Villars, Paris.

VOLTERRA, V. 1937. Acta biotheoretica, III, Reproduced in Volterra, V. "Opera Matemicha" **V**, 414.

WALLACE, B. 1968. "Topics in Population Genetics," W.W. Norton, New York.

WEINBERG, W. 1908. Uber den Nachweis der Vererbung beim Menschen, *Jahreshefte Verein fur vaterlandische Naturkunde in Wuttemberg* **64**, 368–382.

WHITTAKER, E. T. 1937. "A Treatise on Analytical Dynamics of Particles and Rigid Bodies," Cambridge University Press, London.

YELLIN, J. AND SAMUELSON, P. A. 1974. A dynamical model for human population, *Proc. Nat. Acad. Sci.* **71**, 2813–2817.

YULE, G. W. 1902. Mendel's laws and their probable relations to intra-racial heredity, *The New Phytologist* **1**, 193–237.

236

Resolving a Historical Confusion in Population Analysis[1]

Paul A. Samuelson[2]

ABSTRACT

That "a population subject to invariant age-specific mortality and fertility will asymptotically approach an exponential rate of balanced growth or decay with a stable relative age distribution" was first established in 1911 by Lotka and Sharpe. (Euler had clearly glimpsed this truth in a private communication of around 1760.) Bortkiewicz proved in 1911 the quite different and more obvious proposition: "Any population subject to invariant age-specific mortality, must be growing exponentially in all its parts." Kuczynski, an eminent demographer in his own right, understandably irritated Lotka by his repeated attributions of the Lotka result to Bortkiewicz, thus leading Lotka to deny incorrectly the truth of valid third theorems like the following: "A population with invariant age-specific mortality and with exponential growth in its *total* numbers will *asymptotically* approach a stable age distribution." The present analysis surveys the misunderstandings, sorts out the issues and errors in the debates, and supplies overdue generalizations and extensions.

As Robert K. Merton (1973) has so well discussed, creative scientists are not immune to preoccupation with priorities: *their* priorities. Alfred J. Lotka (1880-1949), the father of self-renewal models in linear population analysis, was least of all an exception in this regard. A lone pioneer throughout much of his career,[3] with no cadre of graduate students and colleagues, he could naturally be expected to be a bit prickly over failures to recognize and acknowledge his important contributions to demography.

[1]I owe thanks to the National Institutes of Health for financial aid on demographic research, NIH Grant #1-R01 HD-09081-01, and to Vicki Elms for help in preparing the manuscript. Wilma Winters, librarian at the Harvard Center for Population Studies, provided me with appreciated help in locating rare items. And I owe gratitude to Professor Ansley Coale for providing me with a Princeton library English translation of Bortkiewicz (1911), and with xerox pages from Kuczynski (1932), which might be Lotka's own copy bequeathed with his other demographic collection to the Princeton Office of Population Research. More than a third of a century ago, I benefitted from some correspondence with Dr. A. J. Lotka on aspects of these questions; however, from so cursory a dialogue, I was not able to sort out then the present formulation of the issues. Professor Nathan Keyfitz's invitation to include this material in the Smith and Keyfitz (1976) collection of historical items provided the final stimulus for the present effort, and I owe thanks to David P. Smith for translation of the Süssmilch (1761) account of Euler's important private communication. All interpretations must, of course, be on my own responsibility.

[2]Massachusetts Institute of Technology, Cambridge, Massachusetts.

[3]See Spengler (1968) on Lotka; also, the obituary notices by Dublin (1950) and Notestein (1950).

The present brief note attempts to sort out a controversy that arose some 40 years ago between Lotka and another able self-made demographer, R. R. Kuczynski (1876-1947). The matter has an interest at two levels. Substantively, a reader of their polemics has still been left in ignorance of the true merits of the points being argued—whether Bortkiewicz (1911) and other writers had already established the asymptotic approach to a stable exponential equilibrium of a population subject to invariant (one-sex) age-specific mortality *and fertility,* an accomplishment properly attributed today primarily to Lotka. Psychologically, as an exercise in how new science gets itself done, the matter is also of secondary interest. Once emotions entered in, Lotka ceased to be his own best advocate and came gratuitously to denigrate legitimate theorems in demography that are of interest for their own sake. I shall briefly sort out the truths and misunderstandings of the discussion.

ACT I

The story begins with Lotka (1929), a review of Kuczynski (1928), a book with an honorable role in the history of demography for its forceful pointing out an impending decline in European population levels, a decline shown to be concealed by the swollen numbers of people of fertile age inherited from earlier generations of higher fertility. Kuczynski could have benefitted from the fundamental findings of Sharpe and Lotka (1911) and Lotka (1913, 1922). Perhaps he did not then know of the 1911 integral-equation finding; and perhaps he had neither the mathematical equipment nor the inclination to master it even were it called to his attention. For the purpose of discerning a shift from a growing to an ultimately declining population, Kuczynski could rely on a common-sense criterion,[4] the *net reproduction rate* (i.e., the expected number of female babies that will be born to a representative female baby who throughout her life will be subject to current age-specific mortality and fertility rates).

Lotka's review is favorable on Kuczynski's substantive thesis, but accuses him of not acknowledging that his analysis is taken from Dublin and Lotka (1925), a work said to receive only cursory acknowledgment by Kuczynski.

Kuczynski (1930) replies sturdily that the finding about swollen fertile-age numbers is in fact an ancient staple in the literature, even having been

---

[4]Edwin Cannan, a no-new-fangled-nonsense economist if there ever was one, showed by arithmetic projections of the absolute number of English births that ultimate U.K. population decline was likely. See Cannan (1895).

dealt with by Kuczynski in an 1897 book [when Lotka was only 17 and Kuczynski only 23]; moreover, the concept of the net reproduction rate that Kuczynski relied on, Kuczynski points out, was put forth by his mentor, Richard Böckh, as far back as 1886.[5]

In his rebuttal to Kuczynski, Lotka (1930) had to scale down his accusations. But he does assert the incompleteness of the early work Kuczynski cited. And he makes the valid point that, although the net reproductive rate is an accurate indicator of whether the intrinsic rate of population growth is positive or negative, it only gives the rate of growth per ambiguous "generation," and *not* per *year*, so that it falls short of the full analysis of Sharpe and Lotka and of Dublin and Lotka. He concludes with the barb that, if he had known that the discussion of Dublin and Lotka (1925) on the net reproduction rate had been anticipated earlier, *he*, Lotka, would have felt obliged to acknowledge it—whatever Kuczynski's scholarly code might be.

This ends Act I of the drama. The antagonists are now sensitized to each other. In the years between 1930 and 1937, Lotka apparently became increasingly of the opinion that Kuczynski's publications were spreading misleading accounts of the true priorities. This finally culminated in two publications, Lotka (1937a, 1937b), which attempt to set the record straight and clarify the truth. To understand them, I first review some now familiar fundamentals. And then I formulate a number of distinguishable propositions or theorems that are needed to judge the various allegations.

REVIEW OF FUNDAMENTALS: MORTALITY RELATIONS

Let $N(a,t)$ be the number of people (females presumably) of age a at time t, with total population number at t give by

$$N(t) = \int_0^\infty N(a,t)da = \int_0^n N(a,t)da, \quad a < n < \infty \tag{1}$$

where n is the maximum length of life. Let $p(a)$ be the fraction of new-born females surviving to age a. Then with births at t given as a prescribed function of time, $N(0,t) = B(t)$,

$$N(a,t) = p(a)B(t-a) \tag{2}$$

$$= \frac{p(a)}{p(a-\theta)} N(a-\theta, t-\theta), \quad 0 < \theta < a$$

$$p(0) = 1, \ p(n) = 0, \ p'(a) \leq 0$$

[5]Cf. Kuczynski (1935, p. 207, n. 2) and his citation of Böckh (1886).

$$\partial N(a,t)/\partial a + \partial N(a,t)/\partial t = [p'(a)/p(a)]N(a,t) \tag{3}$$

$$N(t) = \int_0^n p(a)B(t-a)da \tag{4}$$

$$N'(t) = B(t) + \int_0^n p'(a)B(t-a)da \tag{5}$$

A solution to (5), and under suitable specifications to (4), can be given by the "renewal function" so useful in industrial-equipment as well as actuarial analysis, $\Pi(t)$, as discussed in Feller (1941) and Lotka (1933, 1939a) namely by

$$B(t) = N'(t) + \int_{-\infty}^t \Pi(t-a)N'(a)da \tag{6}$$

where $\Pi(t-a)$ is the Volterra resolvent kernel to $p'(t-a)$, defined as the solution to

$$\Pi(t) = -p'(t) - \int_0^t p'(t-a)\Pi(a)da \tag{7}$$

$$= -p'(t) - \int_0^t \Pi(t-a)p'(a)da$$

One way of solving for $\Pi(t)$ is via its Laplace transform

$$\bar{\Pi}(\omega) = \int_0^\infty \Pi(t)e^{-\omega t}dt \tag{8}$$

$$-\bar{p}'(\omega) = \int_0^\infty - p'(t)e^{-\omega t}dt$$

$$\bar{\Pi}(\omega) = -\bar{p}'(\omega) - \bar{p}'(\omega)\,\bar{\pi}(\omega)$$

$$= \frac{-\bar{p}'(\omega)}{1+\bar{p}'(\omega)}$$

Alternatively, writing symbolically,

$$f(t) = -p'(t), \ f(t)\cdot g(t) = \int_0^t f(t-a)g(a)da$$

$$= g(t)\cdot f(t)$$

$$\Pi(t) = f(t) + f(t)\cdot f(t) + f(t)\cdot f(t)\cdot f(t) + \ldots \tag{9}$$

which is a rapidly converging explicit solution, known to have the property

$$\lim_{t\to\infty} \Pi(t) = c_0 = 1/\int_0^n - ap'(a)da = 1/\int_0^n p(a)da > 0 \tag{10}$$

Also, with n finite, $\Pi(t)$ can be written as an infinite series of exponentials, of Hertz-Herglotz-Lotka type:

$$\Pi(t) = c_0 + \sum_{-\infty}^\infty e^{m_j t}c_j \tag{11}$$

where m_j are the infinite number of complex roots of the transcendental equation

$$\int_0^n - p'(a)e^{-ma}da = 1 \tag{12}$$

The sole real root is $m_0 = 0$, and the real parts of all the conjugate complex roots are demonstrably negative

$$m_j = \mu_j + iv_j, \; m_{-j} = \mu_j - iv_j$$

$$0 = m_0 > \mu_j \; (j=1,2,\ldots) \tag{13}$$

If any m_j root is multiple, the coefficients c_j and c_{-j} will be polynomials in t rather than constants.

It is worth noting that the non-real roots of (12) are also the roots of

$$\int_0^n p(a)e^{-ma}da = 0 \tag{12'}$$

as an integration by parts will verify.

REVIEW: FERTILITY AND MORTALITY RELATIONS

So far nothing has been said about fertility rates. Writing the number of female births at time t to mothers of age a as $B(a,t)$, we define an invariant age-specific fertility function, $m(a)$, by

$$m(a) \underset{t}{\equiv} B(a,t)/N(a,t) \geqslant 0 \tag{14}$$

$$m(a) \equiv 0, \; 0 < a < \alpha$$

$$m(a) > 0, \; \alpha \leqslant a \leqslant \beta < n$$

$$m(a) \equiv 0, \; \beta < a$$

A population self-propelled by invariant age-specific mortality and fertility functions, $p(a)$ and $m(a)$, and starting out from an initial non-negative age distribution, $N(0,a)$, will have births and numbers that forever after satisfy

$$B(t) = \int_\alpha^\beta m(a)p(a)B(t-a)da, \; t > n > \beta > \alpha > 0 \tag{15}$$

$$= \int_0^t m(t-a)p(t-a)B(a)da + \int_t^n m(a)\frac{p(a)}{p(a-t)} N(a-t,0)da, \; 0 < t < n$$

$$= \int_0^t \phi(t-a)B(a)da + G(t), \; t>0$$

where

$$\phi(a) \equiv m(a)p(a) \tag{17}$$

$$G(t) = \int_t^n m(a)\frac{p(a)}{p(a-t)}N(a-t,0)da \geqslant 0, \; 0 < t < n$$

$$\equiv 0, \; n < t$$

Just as $\Pi(t-a)$ was the resolvent kernel of $-p'(t-a)$ in (6) $-$ (9), so is there a useful resolvent kernel to $\phi(t-a)$, which I write as $\phi^*(t-a)$, and which provides a solution to $B(t)$ in (16) and has the other listed verifiable properties:

$$B(t) = G(t) + \int_0^1 \phi^*(t-a)\, G(a)\, da$$

$$\phi^*(t) = \phi(t) + \int_0^1 \phi(t-a)\, \phi^*(a)\, da$$

$$= \phi(t) + \int_0^t \phi^*(t-a)\, \phi(a)\, da$$

$$= \phi(t) + \phi(t)\cdot\phi(t) + \ldots$$

$$= Q_0 e^{r_0 t} + \sum_{-\infty}^{\infty} Q_j e^{r_j t}, \quad Q_0 > 0$$

where r_0 is the sole real root and r_j are the complex roots, necessarily infinite in number when β is a finite positive number, of the transcendental equation

$$\psi(r) = \int_0^\infty \phi(a) e^{-ra}\, da - 1 \tag{20}$$

$$r_0 > \text{real coefficients of } r_{\pm j}, \ (j=1,2,\ldots) \tag{21}$$

The $(Q_{\pm j})$ are constants or polynomials in t, and like Q_0 can be determined from the initial condition $N(a,0)$.

To determine whether $r_0 \gtreqless 0$, we can employ the useful Böckh (1886) net reproduction rate as a criterion, namely

$$r_0 \gtreqless 0 \leftrightarrow \int_0^n m(a)p(a)da = \int_0^n \phi(a)da \gtreqless 1 \tag{22}$$

As was done in (8), the Laplace transform may be used to solve for $\phi^*(t)$ in terms of known $\phi(t)$. Lotka (1928) gave the interpretation of $\phi^*(t)$ as the progeny of a Dirac pulse of new births at initial time zero:

$$N(a,0) = \delta(a-0) \tag{23}$$

$$\int_0^n N(a,0)da = \int_0^n \delta(a-0)da = 1$$

From (19) and (20), or from more general analysis of Feller, one can prove

$$\lim_{t\to\infty} \phi^*(t)e^{-r_0 t} = Q_0 = -1/\psi'(r_0) > 0 \tag{24}$$

$$\lim_{t\to\infty} B(t)e^{-r_0 t} = b_0 > 0 \tag{25}$$

$$\lim_{t\to\infty} N(a,t)e^{-r_0 t} = b_0 p(a)e^{-r_0 a} \tag{26}$$

$$\lim_{t \to \infty} \frac{N(a,t)}{N(0,t)} = p(a)e^{-r_0 a} \qquad (27)$$

These two-dozen-odd equations are now standard in the demographic literature, as discussed in Lopez (1961), Keyfitz (1968), Coale (1972), Pollard (1973), and elsewhere. All of these relations owe much to Lotka; in particular there can be no doubt that equations (15)-(20), (25)-(27) are primarily due to him, so that any account which failed to indicate this fact is open to criticism by an impersonal jury, to say nothing of criticism by the injured scientist himself.

A Bouqet of Theorems

To illuminate the disputed issues, let me write down a number of relevant theorems. The list could be amplified, abbreviated, or arranged differently.

The first three theorems involve essentially nothing more than the actuarial assumption of age-specific mortality.

Theorem 1A. Suppose that, for a finite time interval,

$t_0 - \delta < t < t_0 + \delta$

(i) p(a) applies, so that from (3)

$\partial[\ln N(a,t)]\partial a + \partial[\ln N(a,t)]/\partial t \equiv d[\ln p(a)]/da$

(ii) the age distribution is stable, in the sense that

$N(a,t)/N(0,t) \equiv c(a)$:

Then $N(0,t) = B(t) \equiv B(0)e^{ut}$, $t_0 - \delta < t < t_0 + \delta$, $u \gtreqless 0$

$N(a,t)/N(0,t) \equiv p(a)e^{-ua}$

$b \equiv B(t)/N(t) = 1/\int_0^\infty p(a)e^{-ua}da$

$d \equiv D(t)/N(t) = -[\int_0^\infty p'(a)e^{-ua}da]/\int_0^\infty p(a)e^{-ua}da$

$u \equiv b - d$

Bortkiewicz (1911) essentially states and proves Theorem 1A; however, it would be surprising if a thorough search did not turn it up in the earlier actuarial literature. With charity, and some charity is needed, Lotka (1907a, 1907b), his maiden demographic papers, can be construed to have glimpsed the truth of 1A.

To prove 1A, using my notation rather than that of Bortkiewicz (1911), combine (i) and (ii) to derive

$$0 \equiv \partial \ln[N(a,t)/N(0,t)]/\partial t \tag{28}$$

$$\equiv (d \ln [p(a)]/da - \partial \ln[N(a,t)]/\partial a) - B'(t)/B(t)$$

$$c(a) = p(a)e^{-ua}, \tag{29}$$

$u = B'(t)/B(t)$, a constant of any sign.

No doubt Bortkiewicz (1911) and Lotka (1907a, 1907b) thought of δ as ∞ or as a large number; however, so long as $\delta > 0$, the theorem holds.

Theorem 1 B. Suppose for all positive time, $t \geqslant 0$,

    (i) $p(a)$ applies, and
    (ii) $B(t) = B(0)e^{ut}$, $u \gtrless 0$, $t \geqslant 0$

Then

$$N(a,t) \equiv p(a)B(t-a),$$
$$\equiv B(0)[p(a)e^{-ua}]e^{ut}, \ t \geqslant n$$
$$N(t) = B(0)b^{-1}e^{ut}, \ b^{-1} = \int_0^\infty p(a)e^{-ua}da$$

This almost trivial theorem, whose proof is direct from substitution, is in Euler (1760), paragraph 17; in perusing this celebrated early paper, I was surprised to find that Euler (1760) seems to have not gone beyond 1B in its fertility analysis, despite his earlier promising remarks that, the multiplication of a population "depends, of course, on the number of marriages and upon fertility. . . ." However, in Euler's private communication to Süssmilch, reported in Süssmilch (1761) and discussed in my footnote 6, Euler did anticipate a case of the Sharpe-Lotka Theorem 2A about to be discussed.

Theorem 1C. Suppose, for *all* $t \geqslant 0$,

    (i) $p(a)$ applies, and
    (ii) $N(t)$ is of exponential growth

$$N(t) = N(0)e^{ut}, \ t \geqslant 0, \ u \gtrless 0 \quad :$$

Then

$$\lim_{t \to \infty} \frac{N(a,t)}{N(0,t)} = p(a)e^{-ua}$$

$$\lim_{t \to \infty} B(t)e^{-ut} = bN(0), \; b^{-1} = \int_0^n p(a)e^{-ua}da > 0$$

If u were zero, and $N(a,0)$ were Dirac's $\delta(a-0)$, this would be the renewal equation for $\Pi(t) \equiv B(t)$. However, the theorem is true whatever the admissible specifications of $N(a,0)$, and it is far from absurd or trivial.

To prove the theorem, utilize (5) and (6). Thus, for $N(t) = e^{ut}$, $u > \mu_{\pm j}$,

$$N'(t) \equiv ue^{ut} \tag{30}$$

$$\equiv B(t) + \int_0^t p'(t)B(t-a)da - H(t),$$

$$H(t) \equiv \int_t^n - \frac{p'(a)}{p(a)} \; N(a,t)da \geq 0, \; 0 < t < n$$

$$\equiv \int_t^n \frac{p'(a)}{p(a)} \; N(a-t,0)da$$

$$H(t) \equiv 0, \; n < t$$

Any general solution to (30) is known from the principle of superposition to be the sum of the special exponential solution proportional to e^{ut} plus $Y(t)$, the general solution to the following homogeneous integral equation:

$$Y(t) = \int_0^n p(a)Y(t-a)da \tag{31}$$

$$= \sum_{-\infty}^{\infty} h_j e^{m_j t}, \text{ where } m_j \text{ is as in } (12').$$

When the h's are tailored to admissible initial $H(t)$, the fact that all μ_j are negative guarantees that as t grows large, the non-exponential $Y(t)$ is damped down to zero. Q.E.D.

Remark: The fact that numbers in any age group can never be negative puts a restriction on how fast total $N(t)$ can fall exponentially: thus, if u in e^{ut} were more negative than the real part of some m_j in (13), μ_j, that would not be an admissible observed situation unless $B(t)$ was *already* exactly proportional to e^{ut}.

This serves as a reminder that one could strengthen the hypothesis in all three theorems to require their postulated conditions to hold for *all* time, $-\infty < t < \infty$. In that case, Theorems 1A and 1B have conclusions that hold for *all* time. And the conclusion of Theorem 1C *holds not merely asymptotically but for all t*, as in the following:

Theorem 1C': Suppose, for $-\infty < t < \infty$,

(i) $p(a)$ applies,
(ii) $N(t) \equiv N(0)e^{ut}$, $-\infty < t < \infty$
(iii) $N(a,t)$ must, of course, *always* be non-negative

Then

$$N(a,t)/N(0,t) \equiv p(a)e^{-ut}$$

$$B(t) \underset{t}{\equiv} N(0)e^{ut}/\int_0^n p(a)e^{-ua}da$$

$$N(a,0) \equiv [N(0)/\int_0^n p(a)e^{-ua}da]p(a)e^{-ua}$$

For proof, recall that any *initial* deviation from the stable distribution would, when projected backward in the fashion of Samuelson (1976), generate negative numbers from the backward-anti-damped (!) oscillatory components implied to be present. This shows that there can be no such initial deviation.

The condition of non-negativity, (iii), is important, even if usually left implicit. Thus, Lotka (1931, 1939b) seems a bit casual in assuming that a particular formal solution for $B(t)$ is unique in $\int_0^\infty p(a)B(t-a)da = $ a prescribed $N(t)$ function. We can add to such a special solution terms like $\Sigma k_{\pm j}e^{m_j t}$ and have new *formal* solutions: however, with μ_j all negative in (12')'s $m_{\pm j} = \mu_j \pm \nu_j$, these "appendages" would make $B(t)$ negative as $t \to -\infty$; and it is this property that Lotka should utilize in a cogent treatment.

All theorems up to now, 1A, 1B, 1C, or 1C', have involved only age-specific mortality data as contained in the $p(a)$ survival function. They have not involved age-specific fertility data from an $m(a)$ function, all e^{ut} growth functions having been postulated or deduced from postulates *not* involving $m(a)$. They all belong to the pre-Sharpe-and-Lotka era of Euler, Bortkiewicz, and Lotka (1907a, 1907b). The next set of theorems depend on both $m(a)$ and $p(a)$ belonging to the post-1911 age of Lotka.

The first theorem is the basic one of Sharpe and Lotka (1911), with Bernardelli (1941) and Leslie (1945) equivalences holding for discrete-time, discrete-age models.

Theorem 2A: Suppose, for $t \geq 0$,

(i) $p(a)$ applies,

(ii)   age-specific fertility, $m(a)$, applies

$$B(t) = \int_\alpha^\beta m(a)N(a,t)da, \ t \geq 0$$

(iii) initial $N(a,0)$ is an arbitrarily given, non-negative, integrable function with some females not yet beyond the fertile ages

$$\int_0^\beta N(a,0)da > 0 \quad :$$

Then

$$\lim_{t \to \infty} B(t)e^{-r_0 t} = c_0 > 0$$

397

$$\lim_{t \to \infty} N(t)e^{-r_0 t} = c_0 \int_0^n p(a)e^{-r_0 a} da$$

$$\lim_{t \to \infty} \frac{N(a,t)}{N(0,t)} = p(a)e^{-r_0 a}$$

$$\lim_{t \to \infty} N(a,t)e^{-r_0 t} = p(a)e^{-r_0 a} c_0$$

$$\psi(r_0) = \int_\alpha^\beta m(a)p(a)e^{-r_0 a} \, da - 1, \ r_0 \text{ real}$$

$$c_0 = \frac{\int_0^\beta e^{-r_0 a} G(a)da}{\int_\alpha^\beta a\phi(a)e^{-ra}da}; \ G(t) \text{ as defined in (17)}$$

Warning: My $\psi(r)$ is often written in the demographic literature as $\psi(r) - 1$.

Two corollaries may be stated.

> Corollary 2A. Depending upon whether the net reproduction rate, $\int_\alpha^\beta m(a)p(a)da$, is greater than, less than, or equal to unity, the population will ultimately grow, decay, or approach a constant level.

> Corollary 2AA. The algebraic sign of r_0, the asymptotic or intrinsic rate of natural self-propelled increase, is determined by the algebraic sign of $\int_\alpha^\beta m(a)p(a)da - 1 = \psi(0)$, which represents the rate of growth per (ambiguous) "generation."

For $|r_0|$ not too large, good approximations are given to r_0 by r_0', r_0'', r_0''':

$$r_0' = -\psi(0)/\psi'(0) = (R_0 - 1)/R_1 = (R_0 - 1)/\mu R_0$$

$$R_j = \int_\alpha^\beta a^j \phi(a)da, \ \mu = R_1/R_0, \ \text{average age of becoming a mother}$$

$$\sigma^2 = (R_2/R_0) - \mu^2 = \text{variance of net fertility}$$

$$r_0'' = \frac{\mu - \sqrt{\mu^2 - 2\sigma^2 \ln R_0}}{\sigma^2}$$

$$r_0''' = r_0' - \psi(r_0')\psi'(r_0')$$

Corollary 2A is essentially due to Böckh (1886) who intuitively inferred it, and from whom Kuczynski (1928, 1932, 1935) derived his understanding.

Corollary 2AA was popularized by Dublin and Lotka (1925), but its essentials had already been stated in Lotka (1913). The first approximation given above can be derived from various series expansions of $\psi(r)$ and related functions, or as a Newton-Raphson approximation using an initial $r_0 = 0$; the final approximation given above involves a second Newton-Raphson whirl; the intermediate approximation has alternative derivations—from certain ratios of power expansions involving cumulants, or from fitting a Gaussian function to m(a)p(a) (with its bizarre implication of some mothers who are not themselves conceived!). S. D. Wicksell, and others, have given alternative non-Gaussian graduations.

Lotka's formal proofs of 2A were made rigorous by Feller (1941); however, Lopez (1961) showed that the finiteness postulated for β guaranteed that the roots of $\psi(r) = 0$ were infinite in number and sufficed to provide an arbitrary B(t) on the interval $(-\beta, 0)$ with its Fourier-like expansion, $\sum_{-\infty}^{\infty} c_j e^{\eta_j t}$.

A different theorem from 2A is provided by the following:

> Theorem 2B: Suppose that, for *all* time, $-\infty < t < +\infty$,
> (i)   p(a) applies,
> (ii) m(a) applies,
> (iii) $N'(t)/N(t) \equiv$ a constant, $-\infty < t < \infty$

Then, the asymptotic stable state of 2A holds already, and holds all the time

$$N(a,0)/N(0,0) \equiv p(a)e^{-r_0 a}$$

$$\underset{t}{\equiv} N(a,t)/N(0,t), \quad -\infty < t < \infty$$

$$B(t) \equiv B(0)e^{r_0 t}, \quad N(t) \equiv [B(0) \int_0^n p(a)e^{-r_0 a} da]e^{r_0 t}$$

$$N(a,t) \equiv [B(0)p(a)e^{-r_0 a}]e^{r_0 t}$$

$$\psi(r_0) = \int_\alpha^\beta m(a)p(a)e^{-r_0 a} da - 1 = 0$$

Theorem 2B was stated very loosely in Lotka (1937a), and a purported proof of its more careful restatement was offered in Lotka (1937b).

A final theorem may be distinguished from 2A and 2B.

> Theorem 2C: Suppose that, for a time period as long as the length of life, namely for $0 < t < \gamma \geqslant n$,
>
> (i)   p(a) applies,
> (ii) m(a) applies,
> (iii) $N'(t)/N(t) \equiv$ a constant
>
> Then
>
> $$N(a,0) = B(0)p(a)e^{-r_0 a}, \quad \psi(r_0) = 0$$

$$N(a,t) \equiv [B(0)p(a)e^{-r_0 a}]e^{r_0 t}, \ t \geqslant 0$$

$$N(a,t)/N(0,t) \equiv p(a)e^{-r_0 a}, \ t \geqslant 0$$

$$B(t) \equiv B(0)e^{r_0 t}, \ N(t) \equiv [B(0) \int_0^n p(a)e^{-r_0 a}da]e^{r_0 t}, \ t \geqslant 0$$

Remark: If the time interval in the hypothesis of 2C, λ, were permitted to be less than n, the conclusion that a stable age distribution already holds from the beginning could be shown by numerous counter-examples to be definitely false, contrary to what some of the remarks in Lotka (1937a) seem to me to suggest and thereby undermining his contention.

A proof of 2C would show that $N'(t)/N(t)$ would undergo a transient oscillation if any complex-root harmonic $e^{r_j t}$ were present: since this is ruled out by hypothesis, the only admissible initial $N(a,0)$ is *already* in the stable configuration $p(a)e^{-r_0 a} B(0)$.

ARBITRATING THE QUARRELS

We are now armed to judge the litigants. Lotka (1937a) begins by alleging that Kuczynski's writings "probably" caused a recent monograph, German Statistical Office (1935), to credit to Bortkiewicz (1911)[6] the first formulation of the Sharpe-Lotka results of my Theorem 2A and my Equa-

[6]On the attainment of stability Bortkiewicz says only (1911, pp. 63, 69-70. This translation, located at Princeton, is of unknown authorship):

Three qualifying hypotheses underlie the following statements. It is assumed: 1) that in the population an unchanging order of deaths prevails; 2) that the current age distribution likewise is invariable, and 3) that no immigration or emigration takes place.

Accordingly the "stationary" and the "stable" population appear in a sense, as the terms will be used here, almost as ideal types, to which reality never exactly corresponds, but to which it comes all the closer, the less significant the actual changes of the death order and the age distribution, and, relatively speaking, the smaller the immigration and emigration.

The above hypotheses can be considered as the three characteristics which are held in common with the two concepts of the stationary and stable population. In addition, there comes a fourth characteristic: with the stationary population there is a continual constancy, whereas with the stable population a continual accretion in the total number of persons living.

... [T]he geometric progression as a standard norm for the growth of the population was established by L. Euler. He proceeded from one human couple, and let it as well as its offspring propagate from generation to generation according to certain invariable conditions. These conditions referred to age of marriage, the number of children begotten by each couple, and the number dying. Hence it resulted that the

tion (20). The jury must agree that what Bortkiewicz did accomplish, namely Theorem 1A, cannot possibly be identified with Theorem 2A. So Lotka's complaint, if accurate, is a serious one.

In support of his charge against Kuczynski, Lotka (1937a, p. 104) quotes the following passage from Kuczynski (1935, p. 226):

> Bortkiewicz had come to the conclusion that a population constantly subject to the same mortality and with a constant rate of increase must ultimately become stable, that is to say has a stable age composition, a stable birth rate and a stable death rate.

The reader will find this a bit odd, since Kuczynski's quoted words can be construed as attributing to Bortkiewicz not Theorem 2A, but rather my Theorem 1C, which seems to be a perfectly valid theorem, albeit as far as I know not appearing explicitly in the pre-1976 literature.

Lotka goes on to remark that there is no m(a) fertility function in Bort-kiewicz, saying in Lotka (1937a, p. 104, n. 2) that even "Kuczynski [1932, p. 43] admits this in his otherwise misleading history of the 'stable'

---

number of living at the end of every calendar year forms a line which, in its further course, approaches more and more a geometric progression.

The key second paragraph reads in the original German: "Demnach erscheinen die "stationäre" und die "progressive" Bevölkerung in dem Sinne, wie diese Termini hier gebraucht werden, gleichsam als Idealtypen, denen die Wirklichkeit niemals genau entspricht, denen sie aber um so näher kommt, je unerheblicher die thatsächlich vor sich gehenden Wandlungen der Absterbeordnung und der Altersverteilung und je geringer, relativ genommen, die Zahlen der Ein- und Auswandernden sind."

The statement suggests that real populations may *resemble* the stable ideal type, and not that they *approach* stability. Kuczynski may have given it the second meaning, taking the comment that the geometric is a standard norm as supportive evidence. (The illustration by Euler is from a personal communication to J. P. Süssmilch [1761, Vol. 1, pp. 291-299]. It is summarized in the introduction to paper 10 in the Smith and Keyfitz [1976] volume.) Euler's example treats 1 female and 1 male as a "couple", and in effect postulates B(t) = B(t−22) + B(t−24) + B(t−26), D(t) = B(t−40), a Bernadelli-Leslie case that is "cyclic" because of an unfortunate choice of even numbers only: along with dominant $(\lambda^*)^t$ terms go also dominant $(-\lambda^*)^t$ terms and no strict approach to a stable age distribution at both odd and even ages.

[7]I am unable to discern the cogency of Lotka's (1937b) purported proof that if N(t) is observed to be in exponential growth (over *some* consecutive time periods? over all time periods?—which is another thing), N(a,t) is *already* in the stable configuration. The following discrete-time example meets the only hypotheses he purports to use in his demonstration—yet it is not "already in the stable distribution," and *after* (t=0,1,2) its N(t) ceases to grow like N(0)(2)^t! The example is based on [p(0), p(1), p(2), p(3)] = [1,2^{-1},2^{-2},2^{-3}], B(0) = 1,032, [m(0), m(1), m(2), m(3)] = [2,0,0,0], with initial (and asymptotic!) increase of N(t) like $(1+1)^t$, but lacking such exact exponential growth in the near future.

population." Lotka goes on to argue that (1) Kuczynski has not correctly stated what Bortkiewicz (1911) did do—which Lotka correctly states was to *begin* with a stable age distribution and *to deduce from it* a balanced exponential growth rate proportional to my e^{ut} [not to be confused with my e^{rot} since u is *not* deduced from an m(a)p(a) integral], and then to find a numerical estimate for u that made the $p(a)e^{-ua}$ theoretical distribution fit tolerably well the turn-of-the-century German data.

The jury must agree with Lotka's contention under (1), which is that Bortkiewicz (1911) proves my Theorem 1A. Kuczynski, like Homer, nodded. Lotka (1937a, p. 106) however goes a bit far in writing: "All this was old in the literature (which Kuczynski fails to point out)... ," having already been done in Lotka (1907a, 1907b) with English and Welsh data. First, we might deem 1907 not to be long before 1911. Second, Lotka's 1907 utterances of Theorem 1A was, as noted already, loose at best and no semblance of an adequate proof was provided. Third, Bortkiewicz's work is thorough to the point of being tedious, much of it going back to the 1890's, while Lotka's maiden publications are brief and suggestive notes.

(2) Lotka (1937a, pp. 106-107) goes on seemingly to argue that what Kuczynski wrongly attributes to Bortkiewicz is in any case not worth doing, being "inherently absurd" in the light of Lotka's claim that, exponential growth in total self-propelled population *already* implies realization of the

Period, t	Births, N(0,t)	N(1,t)	N(2,t)	N(3,t)	Total N(t)
0	1,032	88	192	48	1,360
1	2,064	516	44	96	$2 \times 1{,}360$
2	4,128	1,032	258	22	$2^2 \times 1{,}360$
3	8,256	2,064	516	129	$85 + (2^3 \times 1{,}360)$

The example was fabricated by perturbing an exact exponential solution to the self-propelled Sharpe-Lotka system through adding to a stable initial state, [N(j,t)] = [1,024, 256, 64, 32], a non-exponential solution, [8, −168, 128, 16], of higher harmonics *fitted* to the initial conditions that total N(t) of the add-on *initially* vanish as for t=(0,1,2). Only if Lotka postulates initial exponential growth of N(t) over a long enough initial interval—the whole length of life, $n > \beta$—will it become impossible for me to find such a perturbing add-on. No hint of this appears in his purported proof. The demonstration goes off the tracks because he seems to confuse a functional-equation requirement of the type

$$f(a,t)/g(a,t) \text{ independent of t for all a}$$

with his actual type

$$[f_1(t) + f_2(t)]/[g_1(t) + g_2(t)] \text{independent of t.}$$

I must make clear that these last interpretations of mine have to be regarded as only tentative.

stable age distribution—as in Theorem 2B here. It escapes me why the truth of 2B should make it absurd for Bortkiewicz [if only he had done it!] to have formulated Theorem 2A. [or, Kuczynski aside, for Bortkiewicz to have formulated Theorem 1C]. Indeed, taken literally, Lotka seems to be cutting his own throat and that of Sharpe! Obscurely, Lotka (1937a, p. 106) argues that if Bortkiewicz had done what he is credited with doing, there would have been no need "for Kuczynski to go through the agonizing labor of testing the approach . . . to the stable distribution in 15 pages of closely printed figures" of Kuczynski (1932, c. p. 65).

This Lotka point seems dubious. The 1911 Sharpe-Lotka proof, or the 1941 proof of Feller of Theorem 2A is admittedly better than Kuczynski's numerical exercise, which (a) starts from an m(a)p(a) such that $\int_0^n m(a)p(a)da = 1$ and the population is in *stationary*, stable equilibrium, (b) suddenly lowers m(a) by 10%, and then (c) by laborious numerical projection depicts the 70 years of transient approach to a new exponential equilibrium with negative r_0. Still numerical exercises are frequently performed, and for a non-mathematician like Kuczynski this was a particularly valuable and insightful thing to do.

Lotka (1937a) concludes with his imperfect statement of the truth of Theorem 2B—perhaps not being clear in his own mind that, for the age distribution of a self-propelled system to necessarily *already* be in its stable form, the posited exponential growth for N(t) would have had to have held forever or at least as in my 2C for n $\approx$ 100 years. Lotka (1937b), when it comes to provide a more careful statement of 2B and a proof, evidently assumes that his hypotheses hold *for all* time, $-\infty < t < \infty$; and even then I cannot follow the cogency of his proof.[7]

From my literal account of Lotka's 1937 papers, one can perhaps conclude that the plaintiff has not optimally pressed his case. But the jury cannot conclude from this that the defendant, Kuczynski, is without fault in Kuczynski (1935) or Kuczynski (1932). This requires special investigation, the results of which do not clear Kuczynski of fault in the matter.

Let me audit Kuczynski (1935), a much better-known work than Kuczynski (1932), and which purports to be a basic exposition. Around pp. 6-7, the author concentrates on the qualitative problem of intrinsic growth of population, or decay, properly pointing out that Böckh's net reproduction rate provides an appropriate answer. Fair enough. He goes on to document at length, p. 207. n. 2, how Böckh, Kuczynski, Kirschberg, Rahts had computed in the 1884-1912 period dozens of fertility tables for Germany, Sweden, Denmark, and France—so that Dublin and Lotka (1925) was something of a Johnny-come-lately. Fair enough as documentation of the Kuczynski (1930) reply to the Lotka (1929) review.

But it was quite misleading for Kuczynski to gloss over the difference between the rate of growth per annum, r_0, and the rate of growth per generation: Kuczynski (1935, p. 207) misleadingly says that, from his 1884 calculation of a Berlin fertility table, Böckh ". . . concluded that the real rate of increase of the Berlin population in 1879 was $\frac{2,172}{2,053} - 1 = 6$ per cent." The growth rate per year or decade is of course not .06, and Böckh could not give the correct number.

To conserve time and reduce tedium, I shall reproduce some further misleading passages from Kuczynski (1935, p. 224) with my bracketed editorial comments.

> Will a population constantly subject to the same fertility and the same mortality ultimately become stable?
> The mathematical elements of this problem have for a long time [how long? and when before Sharpe and Lotka of 1911?] attracted the attention of both European [name one!] and American mathematicians. They [Lotka and who else?] have come to the conclusion that a population with a constant fertility and mortality will in fact ultimately become stable [yes, Lotka, Feller, Leslie, Lopez]. A comparatively easy approach to the computations necessary for ascertaining the age composition and the birth and death rates of the stable populations is to be found in the report represented by Bortkiewicz to the 1911 congress of the International Statistical Institute [literally correct as written, but Kuczynski (1932, p. 41, n.1.) had already noted that Lotka (1907b) had already done this; and, in any case, this literally true assertion is a non sequitur in its seeming implication that Theorem 1A or 1C is Theorem 2A].

There soon follows the p. 226 passage on Bortkiewicz that Lotka quoted in protest, and which I showed to be ambiguous. Kuzcynski (1935, p. 226) goes on to say:

> . . . But one of his [Bortkiewicz's] assumptions, the stable rate of increase, was not and could not be based on the actual conditions presented by some specific statistical example [being *not* based on any m(a) data, as Lotka pointed out was devastating to Kuczynski's apparent link up of Bortkiewicz with Theorem 2A], his findings, interesting as they were from a theoretical standpoint [misleading in that "theoretical" verus "statistical" is being confused with the Theorem 1A versus Theorem 2A issue], did not attract the attention of demographers.
> The attentions of demographers [Kuczynski at least] was indeed only aroused when 14 years later the American mathematician, Lotka, who for a long time had studied the theoretical properties of the stable population [which one? the 1A case? or the 2A case?] published with Dublin. . . . Their approach is highly mathematical and we shall confine ourselves here to showing how through Lotka's formulae the stable yearly rate of increase (r) may be derived from the net reproduction rate [and the first and second moments of m(a)].

A cross that mathematical pioneers in a subject must always bear is to have their pearls dismissed as theoretical and vaguely impractical; later, after capitulation, they receive their revenge.

It is true that in the rarer item, Kuczynski (1932), the author deals at greater length with Lotka's contributions, quoting from him copiously and correcting his numerical errors [but still writing the same misleading sentence about Bortkiewicz!]. At one point, Kuczynski (1932, Appendix, pp. 62-63) makes this explicit acknowledgment:

> It goes without saying that we would not have devoted so much space [more than 17 pages!] to the presentation of the trend of Dublin and Lotka's argument and to the translation of their mathematical operations into simple arithmetic if we were not convinced that some of the methods which they apply are of great scientific value and if we did not feel the strong desire that those methods be applied in the future also by such statisticians as are unfamiliar with higher mathematics. We wish even to state expressly that the computation of the exact rate of increase in the stable population, as presented in this study of Dublin and Lotka, in our opinion, marks the only great progress that has been made in the methodology of measuring net reproduction since Boecke in 1886 published his first table of fertility. But just because we so emphatically recommend the application of those methods we feel obliged to show that the manner in which they themselves applied them to statistical data is inadequate.

This is merited if qualified praise, and all the greater the pity that a reader like myself can find it only in the Appendix of a work so rare that, in the end, I had to rely on a xerox from a copy in the Princeton Office of Population library, a copy which I judge from some marginal caligraphy, in comparison with some samples of Lotka's handwriting in my own possession, to have come from Lotka's own copy and which must have been among his books bequeathed to Princeton.

Before concluding, I ought to venture an opinion as to whether Kuczynski was being deliberately ungenerous to Lotka. At the conscious level, I think not. Kuczinski was always a plain spoken scholar, and such people never hesitate to point out the motes that they see in the eyes of others. In this regard he was not extreme: certainly, Bortkiewicz customarily meted out more trenchant criticisms than did Kuczynski, and R. A. Fisher's quill was dipped in stronger acid than Kuczynski's. Moreover, as I read and reread Kuczynski, both a third of a century ago when I developed a mild interest in the matter and recently in the preparation of this article, I sensed that he may really never have fully understood the magic of Lotka's Theorem 2A. He sensed that, if you knew r_0 you could derive the stable age distribution, and then from that you could compute from p(a) alone the death rate; he may also have sensed the element of simultaneity involved, because only if you had happened to guess the right r_0 would your resulting death rate, when subtracted from the birth rate computable from m(a), be consistent with the originally assumed r_0. But he shows signs of being unclear on the essential logic involved.[8] Nevertheless, I ought to point out explicitly that there is a way of reading his train of thought which makes his individual sentences about Bortkiewicz *literally true*, even though misleading in their context. Thus, Kuczynski, in the end seems to have considered the following procedure as optimal: First compute r_0 from the first few moments of the fertility table m(a)p(a) (a result he ought to have clearly excluded Bortkiewicz from in favor of Lotka); second, use Bortkiewicz (or pre-Sharpe Lotka) to get the actuary's stable age distribution and the implied death rate (and, as a residual, the birth rate). This will be faster and digitally more accurate, Kuczynski decided, than computing out a Monte Carlo version of Lotka's Theorem 2A. But why did he not make this clear?

Perhaps at the unconscious level, Kuczynski was a bit grudging in his treatment of Lotka, writing passages, (1932, p. 65), like

> A good mathematician may be a poor statistician; a good statistician may be a poor mathematician. And since the author of this book, if anything, is a poor mathematician. . . .

A Gestalt psychologist trained in Vienna would expect the reader to complete the *chiasmus* by regarding Lotka as the poor statistician.

---

[8]This surmise is corroborated by Kuczynski (1931, pp. 20, 32, 166): writing apparently simultaneously with his *Fertility and Reproduction*, the author eschews relations like those in (22) and Corollary 2AA, even though he already knows them, in favor of stable-state relations like

$$r \equiv N'(t)/N(t) \equiv B(t)/N(t) - D(t)/N(t)$$

$$r = \frac{\int_\alpha^\beta m(a)p(a)e^{-ra}da}{\int_0^n p(a)e^{-ra}da} - \frac{\int_0^n - p'(a)e^{-ra}da}{\int_0^n p(a)e^{-ra}da}$$

$$= \theta(r) = \frac{\psi(r) + 1}{\bar{p}(r)} + \frac{r\bar{p}(r) - 1}{\bar{p}(r)}$$

$$= \frac{\psi(r)}{\bar{p}(r)} + r$$

where real r is put in the indicated Laplace Transforms and where we solve for the unique r_0 root. Keyfitz (1968, p. 176) calculates r_0 iteratively from

$$r_0'' = \theta(r_0'), \quad r_0''' = \theta(r_0''), \dots$$

Even more rapid convergence would occur for the Newton-Raphson variant

$$r_0'' = r_0' - \theta(r_0')/\theta'(r_0')$$

A sociologist of science like Merton would not be surprised to observe that controversy sours both contestants. Lotka (1925, p. 112, n.7) praised Euler's early anticipations, writing, "An exceedingly interesting effort of early date to demonstrate the ultimate approach to geometric increase of the birth rate, independently of the initial conditions (e.g., starting with a single pair of parents) is to be found in L. Euler [1760]." This is generous praise—as I have argued even over-generous, if Lotka did not in 1925 know Euler's private communication to Süssmilch (1761), and seemingly involving an error like that of Kuczynski's mistake in attributing to Bortkiewicz Theorem 2A rather than 1A—but understandable praise of a great scholar. However, once he has become alarmed for his own property rights, Lotka (1937a, p. 107) takes a shriller tone in defending his own originality, now writing: ". . . This must be abundantly clear to anyone who takes the trouble to examine the pertinent publications, from the first crude approach by Euler (based on highly unrealistic assumptions, and quite inapplicable to actual statistical data), . . ."

As a final word, I ought to emphasize that the reason for now discussing this historical *contretemps* in detail has to do primarily with the need *to clarify the substance of the matter*. By no means was this controversy of unprecedented virulence: neither scholar ever stood in an extreme position with respect to temperament or emotion; both always conducted themselves with honor and dignity.

Moreover, in a sense Lotka has been the ultimate victor. It is he who is accorded full scholarly homage today. The danger is that, if anything, it is Kuczynski's commendable role in the development of the subject that will be lost. Thus, Lotka appears with a full page of references in the excellent Keyfitz (1968, pp. 424-5) bibliography; the works of Kuczynski escape notice. The one notice taken of Kuczynski in J. H. Pollard (1973, p. 82) is only in connection with his 1932 computation of a male NRR for France after World War I that exceeds unity whereas the female NNR falls short of it, a dramatic consequence of war casualties that ironically, Lotka had adverted to in his original cited review of Kuczynski. Richard Böckh receives no citations in either text. Again, a Merton would understand how the brighter light drowns out the earlier light. And I would venture to assert that the ultimate triumph of mathematics follows a Law, not perhaps the one named for Sir Thomas Gresham, but not the less operative for all of that.

Received: 8 October 1975.

LITERATURE CITED

BERNARDELLI, H. 1941 Population waves. Journal of Burma Research Society 31, Part I: 1-18.

BÖCKH, R. 1886 Statistik des Jahres 1884. Statistisches Jahrbuch der Stadt Berlin, Volume 12 (Berlin).

BORTKIEWICZ, L. V. 1911 Die Sterbeziffer und der Frauenüberschuss in der stationären und in der progressiven Bevölkerung. Bulletin de l'Institut International de Statistique 19: 63-183; English translation (translator unknown), Princeton University Library.

CANNAN, E. 1895 The probability of a cessation of the growth of population in England and Wales during the next century. Economic Journal 5: 505-515; abridged reproduction in Smith and Keyfitz (1976) Paper 22.

COALE, A. J. 1972 The growth and structure of human populations: A mathematical investigation. Princeton University Press, Princeton, N. J.

DUBLIN, L. I. 1950 Alfred James Lotka, 1880-1949. J. Amer. Statistical Assoc. 45: 138-139.

DUBLIN, L.I. AND A. J. LOTKA 1925 On the true rate of natural increase of a population. J. Amer. Statistical Assoc. 20: 305-339.

EULER, L. 1760 Recherches générales sur la mortalité et la multiplication. Mémoires de l'Académie Royale des Sciences et Belles Lettres 16: 144-164; abridged reproduction in Smith and Keyfitz (1976) Paper 11.

EULER, L. 1761 See Süssmilch.

FELLER, W. 1941 On the integral equation of renewal theory. The Annals of Mathematical Statistics 12: 243-267; abridged reproduction in Smith and Keyfitz (1976) Paper 16.

GERMAN STATISTICAL OFFICE 1935 Neue Beiträge zum deutschen Bevölkerungsproblem, Berlin.

KEYFITZ, N. 1968 Introduction to the mathematics of population. Addison-Wesley Publishing Co., Reading, Mass.

KUCZYNSKI, R. R. 1928 The balance of births and deaths, Volume I. Western and Northern Europe. Macmillan Co. for The Brookings Institution, New York.

―――― 1930 A Reply to Dr. Lotka's Review of 'The Balance of Births and Deaths,' J. Amer. Statistical Assoc. 25: 84-85.

―――― 1931 The balance of births and deaths. Volume II, Eastern and Southern Europe. The Brookings Institution, Washington, D. C.

―――― 1931/32 Fertility and reproduction. Falcon Press, New York.

―――― 1935 The measurement of population growth. Sedgewick & Jackson, Ltd., London; reproduced by Gordon and Breach Science Publishers, New York, 1969.

LESLIE, P. H. 1945 On the use of matrices in certain population mathematics, Biometrika 33: 183-212.

LOPEZ, A. 1961 Problems in stable population theory. Office of Population Research, Princeton, N. J.

LOTKA, A. J. 1907a Relation between birth rates and death rates. Science, N.W. 26: 21-22; unabridged reproduction in Smith and Keyfitz (1976) Paper 12.

―――― 1907b Studies on the mode of growth of material aggregates. Amer. J. Science, 24: 199-216.

―――― 1913 A natural population norm. J. Washington Acad. Sciences, 3: 241-248, 289-293.

———— 1922 The stability of the normal age distribution. Proc Nat'l Acad. Sciences, **7**: 339-345; unabridged reproduction in Smith and Keyfitz (1976) Paper 14.

———— 1925 Elements of physical biology. Williams & Wilkins, Baltimore; reproduced in posthumous edition with bibliography as: Elements of mathematical biology. Dover Publications, Inc., New York. 1956.

———— 1928 The progeny of a population element. Amer. J. Hygiene, **8**: 875-901.

———— 1929 Review of "The Balance of Births and Deaths, Vol. I, Western and Northern Europe" by R. Kuczynski (New York: Macmillan, 1928). J. Amer. Statistical Assoc. **24**: 332-333.

———— 1930 Rejoinder to "A Reply to Dr. Lotka's Review of The Balance of Births and Deaths by R. Kuczynski," J. Amer. Statistical Assoc. **25**: 85-86.

———— 1931 The structure of a growing population. Human Biology, **3**: 459-493.

———— 1937a Notes A historical error corrected. Human Biology, **9**: 104-107.

———— 1937b Population analysis: A theorem regarding the stable age distribution. J. Washington Acad. Sciences, **27**: 299-303.

———— 1939a A contribution to the theory of self-renewing aggregates, with special reference to industrial replacement. Annals of Mathematical Statistics, **10**: 1-25.

MERTON, R. K. 1973 The sociology of science theoretical and empirical investigations. The University of Chicago Press, Chicago.

NOTESTEIN, F. W. 1950 Alfred James Lotka: 1880-1949. Population Index, **16**: 22-29, containing a Lotka bibliography of 114 items.

POLLARD, J. H. 1973 Mathematical models for the growth of human populations. Cambridge University Press, Cambridge.

SAMUELSON, P. A. 1976 Time symmetry and asymmetry in population and general dynamic systems. J. Theoretical Population Biology, **8**: (forthcoming in February, 1976).

SHARPE, F. R. AND A. J. LOTKA 1911 A problem in age-distribution. Philosophical Magazine, **21**: 435-438; unabridged reproduction in Smith and Keyfitz (1976) Paper 13.

SMITH, D. AND N. KEYFITZ, eds. 1976 Contributions to mathematical demography. Springer-Verlag, Berlin, Heidelberg, New York. (forthcoming).

SPENGLER, J. J. 1968 Alfred J. Lotka. International Encyclopedia of the Social Sciences. Crowell Collier Macmillan, New York. **9**: 475-476.

SÜSSMILCH, J. P. 1761 Die göttliche Ordnung **1**: 291-299; abridged translation in Smith and Keyfitz (1976), Paper 10.

237

An Economist's Non-Linear Model of Self-Generated Fertility Waves

PAUL A. SAMUELSON*

Although the classical economists, such as Adam Smith, Robert Malthus, David Ricardo, and John Stuart Mill, had considered population analysis part of economics, by the early twentieth century economists had decided that demographic movements were largely exogenous to the economic system and were to be turned over to sociologists and other non-economists for scientific discussion. Richard Easterlin[1] was an exception to this trend, who endeavoured to explain by economic analysis the post-World-War II baby boom and, what is more notable, to explain the decline in fertility since 1957. The Easterlin theory, moreover, has possible interesting implications for prediction of a revival of fertility at some future date.

The Easterlin theory is therefore worthy of careful analysis for its own sake. It is also an interesting model in non-linear population analysis and one well calculated to illustrate how far wrong demographers can be if they insist on extrapolating to the non-linear domain the nice stable age distribution asymptotes of the linear Lotka–Bernardelli model.[2]

The purpose of this paper is to give an oversimplified version of the Easterlin theory, and subject it to rigorous analysis, both in the large and in the neighbourhood of equilibrium. Since the degree of oversimplification is excessive, readers will understand that the formulation is illustrative only, designed to bring out the logic of more complicated hypotheses.

* I owe thanks for financial aid to NIH Grant #1 R01 HD-09081-01 and Hiroaki Nagatani and Joel Yellin for research assistance that eliminated many errors.

[1] For classical economists' population dynamics, see an exposition such as that of W. J. Baumol, *Economic Dynamics* (New York: Macmillan, 1951). The original paper by Easterlin is R. A. Easterlin, 'The American Baby Boom in Historical Perspective', *American Economic Review*, **60** (1961) pp. 869–911, reproduced under the same title as *Occasional Paper No. 79* of the National Bureau of Economic Research (1962). But see also the same author's 'Towards a Socioeconomic Theory of Fertility: A Survey of Recent Research on Economic Factors in American Fertility', in S. J. Behrman *et al.* (eds), *Fertility and Family Planning: A World View* (Ann Arbor: University of Michigan Press, 1969); 'On the Relation of Economic Factors to Recent and Projected Fertility Changes', *Demography*, **3** (1966), pp. 131–153; 'Relative Economic Status and the American Fertility Swing' (unpublished paper, 1975); and R. A. Easterlin and G. Condran, 'A Note on the Recent Fertility Swing in Australia, Canada, England and Wales and the United States', in *Migration, Foreign Capital and Economic Development: Essays in Honor of Brinley Thomas* (forthcoming). I am indebted to Nathan Keyfitz for the reference to N. Keyfitz, 'Population Waves', in T. N. E. Greville (ed.), *Population Dynamics* (New York: Academic Press, 1972), pp. 1–38, and to Ansley Coale for the valuable reference to R. D. Lee, 'Natural Fertility, Population Cycles and the Spectral Analysis of Series of Births and Marriages', *Journal of the American Statistical Association*, **70** (1975), pp. 295–304, which also cites as relevant T. R. Malthus, *An Essay on the Principle of Population, 1798*, Anthony Flew (ed.) (Baltimore: Penguin Books, 1970); G. U. Yule, 'Changes in the Marriage and Birth Rates in England and Wales during the Past Half Century', *Journal of the Royal Statistical Society*, **69** (1906), pp. 18–132; J. Grauman, 'Comment' in Universities–National Bureau of Economic Research, *Demographic and Economic Change in Developed Countries* (Princeton: Princeton University Press, 1960); R. D. Lee, 'The Formal Dynamics of Controlled Populations and the Echo, the Boom and the Bust', *Demography*, **11** (1974), pp. 563–585.

[2] The classical post-1911 work of A. J. Lotka, H. Bernardelli and P. H. Leslie is surveyed in N. Keyfitz, *Introduction to the Mathematics of Population* (Reading, Mass.: Addison–Wesley, 1968); A. J. Coale, *The Growth and Structure of Human Populations: A Mathematical Investigation* (Princeton: Princeton University Press, 1972); and J. H. Pollard, *Mathematical Models for the Growth of Human Populations* (Cambridge: Cambridge University Press, 1973). See J. Yellin and P. A. Samuelson, 'A Dynamical Model for Human Population', *Proceedings of the National Academy of Sciences*, **7** (1974), pp. 2813–2817, for a development of the Kendall marriage model that illustrates the pitfall of expecting a non-linear model *necessarily* to approach an exponential balanced growth. D. G. Kendall, 'Stochastic Processes and Population Growth', *Journal of the Royal Statistical Society*, **B11** (1949), pp. 230–264. See P. Das Gupta, 'On Two-Sex Models Leading to Stable Populations', *Theoretical Population Biology*, **3** (1972), pp. 358–375, for invalid conjectures concerning the representation of non-linear solutions by infinite series of Lotka-type exponentials.

In a nutshell, Easterlin suggests that families in the childbearing age groups will have more children if they are enjoying a standard of living and of economic security greater than their parents enjoyed when they were conceived and reared. Thus, those of parental age in the early 1950s were born in the 1930s when the Great Depression led to small numbers of births and when economic life was risky. Being so few in numbers in the 1950s, the usual laws of economic demand predispose their adult earnings to be high and relatively secure. They then in turn have many children. By contrast, those of parental age in the late 1960s and early 1970s were products of the war baby boom. They are relatively numerous, and the remorseless laws of the market place yield them relatively low and relatively insecure incomes.

Thus, the Easterlin hypothesis can explain fertility waves not unlike those actually experienced in the United States during the last 40 years.[3] The Easterlin theory is all the more valuable for its scarcity among economic theories, standing out in welcome relief from the rather sterile verbalizations by which economists have tended to describe fertility decisions in terms of the jargon of indifference curves, thereby tending to intimidate non-economists who have not mis-spent their youth in mastering the intricacies of modern utility theory.[4]

SIMPLIFIED EASTERLIN MODEL

Let there be two age groups: $N_1(t)$, the number of persons (or females) in the prime child-bearing stage of life; $N_2(t)$ the number of those some 20 years older who are not yet quite past childbearing age but are nearing it. Let female births at t be written interchangeably as $B(t)$ or B_t, of whom $p_1 B_t$ survive to constitute $N_1(t+1)$ and $p_1 p_2 B_t$ survive to constitute $N_2(t+2)$. The p's of mortality can be assumed to be constants. Let (f_1, f_2) be the age-specific female fertility rates, as in the Lotka–Bernardelli–Leslie standard analysis. But, unlike the standard case, f_1 here will depend upon the ratio of numbers in the two adult age groups, namely on $N_1(t)/N_2(t)$. When this ratio is high, the relative incomes of those of prime child-bearing ages may be expected to be low and insecure, so that f_1 is assumed by Easterlin to be a declining function of N_1/N_2, $f_1[N_1/N_2]$ with $f_1'[N_1/N_2] < 0$.

Now our autonomous dynamic system can be reduced to:

$$B(t) = f_1 N_1(t) + f_2 N_2(t) = f_1 p_1 B(t-1) + f_2 p_1 p_2 B(t-2) \tag{1}$$
$$= p_1 f_1 [p_1 B(t-1)/p_1 p_2 B(t-2)] B(t-1) + f_2 p_1 p_2 B(t-2)$$
$$= a_1 [B(t-1)/B(t-2)] B(t-1) + a_2 B(t-2)$$
$$a_1 [B(t-1)/B(t-2)] \equiv p_1 f_1 [B(t-1)/p_2 B(t-2)]$$
$$a_1'[N_1/N_2] < 0; \quad a_2 \equiv f_2 p_1 p_2 \quad a \text{ constant.}$$

---

[3] The flavour of Easterlin's analysis is indicated by quoting some samples of his 1961 paper: '... the favorable impact ... of a swing in the rate of growth of demand – itself much larger than heretofore – was felt with much greater force [after 1939]... As a result, the rate of change of fertility reproduced the swing in labor demand in significant measure for the first time' (p. 894). 'As for prediction of the shorter-term future, the decade of the sixties, ... a relative weakening in the exceptional labor market engaged by young persons in the recent past is implied, and a consequent adverse response in the fertility rate (though not necessarily in the *number* of births)' (p. 899). 'The implications of the present analysis for the longer-term future of fertility change are in contrast with those likely to be suggested by the typical demographic discussion of our fertility history ... [namely] a resumption of the primary trend [of a long-term secular decline in fertility]. ... One might imagine a more-or-less self-generating mechanism, by which in one period a decline in the rate of labor market entry causes a concurrent rise in the rate of change of fertility, and this in turn leads with a lag of around two decades, to a rise in the rate of labor-market entry and a consequent decline in the rate of change of fertility' (p. 900). Obviously, I have not done justice to Dr Easterlin's careful qualifications.

[4] See H. Leibenstein, 'An Interpretation of the Economic Theory of Fertility', *Journal of Economic Literature*, 12 (1974), pp. 457–479, for a survey of economists' theories of fertility, including that of the Chicago School theorists, Gary Becker and T. W. Schultz, and others in the *Journal of Political Economy* (March/April 1973) supplement entitled *New Economic Approaches to Fertility*.

For prescribed initial $[N_1(0), N_2(0)] = [N_1^0, N_2^0]$ or $[B_{-1}, B_{-2}]$, the system forever after determines its own development,

$$B(t) = \beta(t; N_1^0, N_2^0) = b(t; B_{-1}, B_{-2}), \ t \geq 0. \tag{2}$$

Those accustomed to the standard Lotka model will surmise that there exists an asymptotic exponential rate of increase with stable age distribution:

$$\underset{t \to \infty}{\text{Lim}} \ B(t) (1+r)^{-t} = \text{constant dependent on } (B_{-1}, B_{-2}) \tag{3}$$

$$\underset{t \to \infty}{\text{Lim}} \ [N_1(t)/B(t)] = p_1(1+r)^{-1}$$

$$\underset{t \to \infty}{\text{Lim}} \ [N_2(t)/B(t)] = p_1 p_2 (1+r)^{-2}$$

where $1+r = \lambda^*$ is the root of

$$\lambda^2 = a_1[\lambda]\lambda + a_2 \tag{4}$$

This is not a quadratic equation. However, if $|a_1'[\ ]|$ is small enough, there will certainly be such a real root, with $r < 0$ as $a_1[1+r] + a_2 < 1$ to a good approximation. (If a_1 were a constant as in the linear Lotka model, the quadratic equation would have a second negative root, λ_2, $|\lambda_2| < |\lambda_1 = \lambda^* = 1+r$, which provides transient oscillations in births.)

Readers of Easterlin will expect oscillations around the stable age distribution of an every-other generation type, oscillations which are *additional* to those incurred as a Lotka model irons out abnormalities in its initial age distribution. And they will not be disappointed. Indeed, if $a_1'[\lambda]$ is sufficiently negative near $\lambda^* = 1+r$, the exponential mode of growth will be unstable with respect to the slightest perturbation, which will send it into a 'limit-cycle' motion reminiscent of the famous cobweb model of the pig cycle.[5]

To see all this, solve the problem for $B(t)/B(t-1) = Y(t)$. Then (1) reduces to the non-linear first-order difference equation

$$Y(t+1) = a_1[Y(t)] + a_2 Y(t)^{-1} \tag{4}$$
$$= F[Y(t)], \ Y(t) > 0$$

With $a_1[Y]$ a positive function that is non-increasing in its argument, there will be exactly one positive root,[6] $Y^* = \lambda^* = 1+r$, to

$$Y = F[Y] = a_1[Y] + a_2 Y^{-1}, \ Y > 0 \tag{5}$$

If $a_1[Y]$ were a constant,[7] Lotka and Leslie could easily prove that

[5] See M. Ezekiel, 'The Cob-Web Theorem', *Quarterly Journal of Economics*, **52** (1938), pp. 255–280, for a survey of the famous cobweb model, or the mathematical analysis and references in P. A. Samuelson, 'Dynamic Process Analysis', in H. S. Ellis (ed.), *A Survey of Contemporary Economics* (Homewood, Ill.: Richard D. Irwin for the American Economic Association, 1948–1952), Ch. 10, pp. 352–387, and 'Mathematics of Speculative Price', in R. H. Day and S. M. Robinson (eds), *Mathematical Topics in Economic Theory and Computation* (Philadelphia: Society for Industrial and Applied Mathematics, 1972). This 1971 John von Neumann Lecture is reprinted in *SIAM Review*, **15** (1973), pp. 1–42.

[6] There is no meaningful definition possible for any further root. However, there is a definable limit, for $B_{-1}/B_{-2} \neq Y^*$ and $|a_1'[\ ]|$ small, to

$$\underset{t \to \infty}{\text{Lim}} \ \frac{b(t+1; B_{-1}, B_{-2})(Y^*)^{-t-1} - b(t; B_{-1}, B_{-2})(Y^*)^{-t}}{b(t; B_{-1}, B_{-2})(Y^*)^{-t} - b(t-1; B_{-1}, B_{-2})(Y^*)^{-t+1}} = \lambda_2 = +Y^* F'[Y^*] < 0,$$

When $a_1[\ ]$ is a constant this is the second Lotka root. When $a_1'[\ ]$ is a small negative number, the non-linear λ_2 contains an Easterlin amplification of the Lotka transient component. When $|a_1'[\ ]|$ is large and Y^* unstable, the limit must be taken backward as $t \to -\infty$ and initial B_{-1}/B_{-2} is near Y^*.

[7] Keyfitz, *loc. cit* in footnote 1, gives a *linear* model that somewhat resembles my (1). In the absence of economic effects on fertility, he postulates (in my notation), $B(t) = R_0 B(t-1)$, $0 < R_0 < 1$. Easterlin effects lead him to modify this to $B(t) = R_0 B(t-1) + \gamma[R_0 B(t-1) - B(t-2)]$, $r > 0$, so that $B(t) = c_1 R_0^t + c_2 (-\gamma)^t$. Such a linear system is everywhere damped, or anti-damped, or conservative; it can never approach a limit cycle of definite

$$-1 < F'[Y^*] = -a_2/(Y^*)^2 = \lambda_2/\lambda_1 < 0 \qquad (6)$$

and that Y^* is a globally stable root, approached asymptotically by every solution $y[t; Y_0]$ that begins with initial positive Y_0 – namely

$$\lim_{t \to \infty} y[t; Y_0] = Y^*, \; Y_0 > 0 \qquad (7)$$

However, with $a_1'[Y^*]$ a large enough negative number, we now have

$$F'[Y^*] = a_1'[Y^*] - a_2(Y^*)^{-2} < -1 \qquad (8)$$

Hence, Y^* is locally unstable, and any initial growth at a uniform exponential rate proportional to $(Y^*)^t$ will, when perturbed ever so little, diverge from that steady path.

Indeed, if we keep $a_1[Y]$ bounded between m and $m+h = M$, but let $a_1'[Y^*]$ vary with a parameter $1/\varepsilon$, then for ε near enough to zero we can be sure that an every-other-generation limit cycle will be asymptotically approached. An example is provided by:

$$
\begin{aligned}
a_1[Y,\varepsilon] &\equiv M > m \qquad \text{for } Y < 1 - \varepsilon^{-1} \\
a_1[Y,\varepsilon] &\equiv m > 0 \qquad \text{for } Y > 1 + \varepsilon^{-1}
\end{aligned}
\qquad (9)
$$

$$a_1[Y,\varepsilon] = \frac{1}{2}(M+m) + \frac{1}{2}\frac{(M-m)}{2\varepsilon}(Y-1), \; 1 - \varepsilon^{-1} < Y < 1 + \varepsilon^{-1}$$

$$a_2 = 1 - \frac{1}{2}(M+m)$$

Here a_2 is adjusted to make $r = 0 = Y^* - 1$, so that the population happens to have a steady state with no growth. If we begin with $B_{-1} = B_{-2}$, the system will stay forever until disturbed, at $B(t) \equiv B_{-1}$, $Y(t) \equiv Y^* \equiv 1$. However, the slightest initial disturbance, $Y_0 > Y^*$ will, when ε is small enough, lead to oscillations of $B(t)/B(t-1)$ every other generation, approaching a stable periodic motion of the type

$$
\begin{aligned}
B(2t)/B(2t-1) &= A^* > Y^* \\
B(2t+1)/B(2t) &= B^* < Y^*
\end{aligned}
\qquad (10)
$$

To solve for the exact (A^*, B^*) values we find the (A, B) roots of

$$B = F[A], \; Y^* < A = F[B], \; A = F[F[A]], \; B = F[F[B]] \qquad (11)$$

eschewing the trivial root $(A, B) = (Y^*, Y^*)$. The example in (9) is designed so that, for ε small enough, there will be exactly one such pair of stationary roots to the iteration

$$Y_{t+2} = F[F[Y_t]] \equiv F_2[Y_t] \qquad (12)$$

amplitude. Lee (1975), *loc. cit* in footnote 1, gives a non-linear system, similar to my (1) but involving so great a number of phase variables that its exact qualitative properties cannot be determined. However, in the neighbourhood of its exponential-growth mode, he does provide linear small-vibration approximations and even tests the implied spectrum against the historical 1900–1972 spectral periodogram: the observed 40-year cycle is reported not to be captured by the model. Belatedly, I have learned that Lee [1974, Figure 3] clearly anticipated this 'limit-cycle' finding, saying (p. 567): '... the equilibrium point [of a two-age non-linear model] may be unstable, in which case violent oscillations may lead to extinction ... or a stable "limit cycle" may occur, with perpetual oscillation'. Also, I applaud Lee's recognition that, quite aside from cohorts' relative-security effects, environmental constraints and the law of diminishing returns cause Lotka–Leslie coefficients to be variable functions not constants, so that the long-run intrinsic rate of increase, $1 + r^*$, must be unity in such models rather than *any* positive number as in the conventional linear models. Like reasoning led to my view: 'No economist could have devised the [standard, *conservative*] Lotka–Volterra [predator–prey] model, which ignores diminishing returns and the ratios of the species to fixed land.' See P. A. Samuelson, 'A Universal Cycle?', in R. Henn (ed.), *Methods of Operations Research* (Meisenheim: Verlag Anton Hain, 1967), pp. 307–320.

For ε very large, we will have

$$-1 < \partial F[Y^*;\varepsilon]/\partial Y < 0 \qquad (13)$$

Therefore, as is probably realistic, *the population does settle down to its Lotka stable-growth state, but with a detectable extra tendency to resonate in doing so, with a damped every-other-generation Easterlin component.* However, when the Easterlin effect is very strong, we do have a stable limit cycle, as in (10).

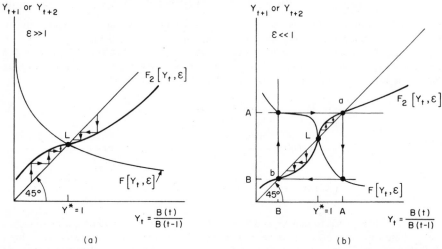

FIGURE 1. In (a) where the Easterlin fertility response to relative labour demand is weak, equilibrium at Y^* is locally and globally stable in the Lotka linear fashion – but with amplified every-other-generation transient component. In (b), where ε is small and the Easterlin effect large, the Lotka equilibrium at L is locally unstable – the slightest perturbation near L sends the system into asymptotic fertility oscillations that approach the limit cycle, $B(2t)/B(2t-1) \to A$, and $B(2t+1)/B(2t) \to B$, as $t \to \infty$.

Figure 1 illustrates the topology of the $F_2[Y_t]$ iteration. In 1(a), there is shown a damped system that returns to its Lotka exponential growth mode. In 1(b) is shown a stable limit cycle of the economic 'cobweb' type encountered in the corn-hog literature.

238

Scale Economies and Non-labor Returns at the Optimum Population*

What the landlord can collect in rent was proved to be more than the extra product society achieves by the improved allocation of labor to land that results from a shift from push-shove squatterism to a regime of private property in land.[1] Once you understand it, this proposition will hardly cause surprise: for, as Frank Ramsey liked to quote from William Blake, "Truth cannot be expressed so as to be understood without being believed."

My earlier case of a labor-land model can clarify some issues in the theory of optimum population.

Constant Return to Scale

If we adhere to the dogma that production functions on all lands are everywhere homogeneous of the first degree, the highest per capita real income is achieved when there has been enough euthanasia of laborers, foetuses, or conceptions to reduce the labor supply to the point of total euthanasia of the land-owner's rent. In examples where labor's marginal productivity curve falls from the beginning, and where some labor is essential if there is to be any product, the optimal labor supply is infinitesimal, with each infinitesimal of labor getting all the (maximized per capita) product and with land rent zero. No doubt an infinitesimal labor supply will seem absurd: Adam without Eve; or Adam's grin without even his rib. But that only points out the absurdity of assuming first-degree homogeneity at very small, even quantum-physics scales.

First-degree homogeneity will seem a bit less absurd in cases where initial small, but finite, amounts of labor, L, do not find it optimal to spread over all the (best) land available. In this case, the marginal-product-of-labor curve begins with an initial horizontal branch. Any point on this represents optimum population size, and all involve zero land rent. Squatterism would involve no pushing and shoving; and even if private property in land were permitted, land ownership would not be worth assuming (much like the modern cases where slumlords abdicate their no longer worthwhile status).

All these simple properties of the constant-returns case would hardly need restating were it not for a Knightian error that still permeates the literature. In *Risk, Uncertainty, and Profit*, Knight asserted three stages for a two-input first-degree-homogeneous neoclassical pro-

*M.I.T., Cambridge, Mass. August, 1974
*Aid from the National Science Foundation is gratefully acknowledged.
[1] P.A. Samuelson, "Is the Rent-Collector Worthy of His Full Hire?", Eastern Economic Journal, Vol. 1, No. 1 (January 1974), 7-10; essentially the same theorem was individually enunciated by Martin Weitzman. See J.S. Cohen and M.L. Weitzman, "A Marxian Model of Enclosures," Journal of Development Economics I, 1975, 287-336, particularly section 5, pp. 304-316.

duction function. As we vary L, holding land (denoted by T) constant, Knight assumed that the normal *second* stage was that in which output, Q, rose, but in which labor's average product, Q/L, and marginal product, $\partial Q/\partial L$, declined as L/T increased. But he thought that this stage was followed by a third stage in which output fell as more L became available to work with fixed T. And he deduced, correctly, that if a third stage of negative $\partial Q/\partial T$ existed, then a first stage had to exist in which, as we increase a variable factor, average output rises. On the assumption that there are no "disposability costs," having more of an input *available* cannot hurt you: there is no need for you to spread your labor over all the continent of land available if you could do better by cultivating only a subset, leaving the rest fallow. Once we replace the possibility of $\partial Q/\partial T < 0$ by the restriction $\partial Q/\partial T \geq 0$, we rule out Knight's first and third stages, replacing them by the case just analyzed: an initial horizontal MP stage, and a terminal horizontal total-Q stage (for the *other* factor, of course).

What needs to be mentioned is that this correction to Knight's analysis rules out, for the constant-returns case, those versions of the optimal population as occurring at the point where an arch of rising and falling average product is at its maximum and is being intersected by a falling marginal product curve. There is no such admissible upward branch of the arch. The curve is at its maximum from the beginning, and at most possesses a horizontal stretch of optimal-population points.

Empirical Realism

In the actual world, however, there do exist rising branches of average product. That is because, on reflection, we realize that constant returns to scale at indefinitely small scales is an absurdity. Once the logical legiti-

macy of first-degree homogeneity is rejected, the field is open for observational determination of the scale (if it exists!) at which some semblance of approximation to constant returns happens to assert itself.

Now, as Meade's 1936 elementary textbook[2] discussed (Pt. 4, Ch. 2) an optimum level of population can be meaningfully defined. If we envisaged a socialist state with no time-phasing or "capital" problems, per capita total product might be what is to be maximized. Identifying population with L, a point of maximum Q/L can be found at the top of the arch, with falling $\partial Q/\partial L$ intersecting it there. Hence, if labor is "paid" "its" marginal physical product, it will get all the total optimized product, leaving no product to be given to non-laborers.

However, it must *not* be inferred from this that the marginal product of land is zero and that adding additional good land could do nothing for total product. For, now we have abandoned constant returns to scale; and thereby lost Euler's Theorem which identifies one factor's marginal product as what is left over when another factor is given its marginal product.

But now we face a problem for a market economy that wants to be at its optimum population level. For it perfect competition is (by continuity and smoothness) almost certain to be *not* perfectly workable or viable. For it, long-run marginal cost will fall short of price in some important sectors of the economy. I say this is "almost certain" and not "certain," because one can conjure up special asymptotic cases in which one can be "near" the optimum population and hope to have all or most marginal costs "near" to competitive prices. Competition may then be tolerably workable.

[2] J. E. Meade, *An Introduction to Economic Analysis and Policy* (Oxford, 1936).

Inside the Boxes

The concept of an optimum population is hard to give empirical content to. Repeatedly it is rejected as one of those "empty boxes" of economic theory that the historian and statistician cannot fill with meaningful measurements. But repeatedly it keeps rearing its head. A can full of worms is not empty of those worms just because you and I can't measure them.

Edward Denison, the most careful measurer of sources of economic growth, has always estimated a component of growth due to increasing returns to scale. Thus, in his 1974 Brookings monograph, *Accounting for United States Economic Growth, 1929–1969*, Denison on p. 127 attributes more than 10 percent of our average $3\frac{1}{3}$ annual growth rate for 1929–1969 to Economies of Scale: 0.36 out of 3.33 total of per year growth.

In terms of a simple-minded Cobb-Douglas production function of the form

$$Q = T(t)L^a T^b$$

presumably a and b add up to more than unity and $T(t)$ is a trend factor. Then

$$(dQ/dt)/Q = T'(t)/T(t) + a(dL/dt)/L$$

One way I could indicate the strength of increasing returns to scale would be to say that $[a - (1 - b)](dL/dt)/L$ as a fraction of $(dQ/dt)/Q$ is roughly .36/3.33; but of course neglecting "capital" inputs cannot do justice to Denison's measurements.

If Denison is at all near to the mark in his estimate of the degree to which there prevails increasing rather than constant returns to scale—as measured for non-Cobb-Douglas functions locally by the excess over unity of $(\partial Q/\partial L)(L/Q) + (\partial Q/\partial T)(T/Q)$, call it I for

increasing returns—should one be worried about the viability of competition? This is difficult to say since the real world involves a vector of many commodities $(Q_1, \ldots, Q_n)$, not just Q, and a vector of many kinds of labors and land $(L_1, \ldots, L_m, T_1, \ldots, T_r)$ and not just L and T, and it also involves time-phasing problems of all kinds of capital goods. Dodging that question, we can emphasize how increasing returns, $I > 0$, enables non-labor marginal productivities to be positive at the point of optimum population, by stating the following:

Proposition: Where $Q/L = F(L,T)/L$ is at its maximum for fixed T, we must have

Non-labor-marginal-productivity Imputation

= Degree of Increasing Returns[3]

Or, $I = (T\partial Q/\partial T)/Q$

With constant returns and $I = 0$, we verify that land rent or $\partial Q/\partial T$ must be zero.

Conclusion

Adam Smith insisted that the division of labor is limited by the extent of the market. Those disciples of his who revere perfect competition have not sufficiently emphasized that, to the degree that unexhausted scale efficiencies prevail, Smith's invisible hand of perfect competition is handicapped. And, alas, it is peculiarly at a point of optimum population that these handicaps are likely to be significantly present.

---

[3]If there are non-primary non-labor inputs, like a vector of heterogeneous capitals $(K_1, K_2, K_3, \ldots)$, and if their steady-state totals are assumed to be proportional to L. Non-labor-marginal-productivity Imputation in this formula will not be $\Sigma K_j(\partial Q/\partial K_j)/Q + \Sigma T_i(\partial Q/\partial T_i)/Q$, but only the last terms involving primary factors that cannot be enhanced by changes in population.

239

Social Darwinism

By Paul A. Samuelson

American business ideology at the turn of the century embraced a crude notion that might makes right. The fittest survive, and *should* survive. For every survivor, there must be a dozen perishers. But they also serve who only perish, just as they also serve who are the anvil against which the hardest metal is formed.

Fruits of this vulgar Social Darwinism (or, more accurately, Social Spencerism) were such dicta as:

■ "The public be damned" (attributed to William Vanderbilt).

■ "The poverty of the incapable . . . starvation of the idle and those shoulderings aside of the weak by the strong . . . are the decrees of a large, far-seeing benevolence" (Herbert Spencer).

■ The "formula of most schemes of humanitarianism is this: A and B put their heads together to decide what C shall be made to do for D. I call C the Forgotten Man" (William Graham Sumner, decidedly not FDR).

■ ". . . the laboring man will be protected and cared for not by the labor agitators, but by the Christian men to whom God in his infinite wisdom has given the control of the property interests of the country . . ." (George F. Baer).

This ideology did not meet its own first test—survival. How could it be sold to the majority of the electorate, since it was they who were billed as patsies in its scenario?

SOCIOBIOLOGY

A new and, I think, more interesting version of Social Darwinism is now being floated. I refer to the attempt to understand the changing behavior and structure of various groups from the standpoint of *selection*. A subject called sociobiology exists by virtue of the Cartesian syllogism, "I have a textbook written about me, therefore I am a discipline." The textbook is the handsome new work of Edward O. Wilson, Harvard's authority on insects. I predict it will earn esteem.

The old Social Darwinism had regarded altruism as dysgenic: thus, Josephine Shaw Lowell advised charity givers never to give a basket of food that would last *more than one day* lest they encourage poverty. Not so with the new Social Darwinism, which has rediscovered Prince Kropotkin's *survival value of reciprocal altruism*. According to this, an ant colony could do worse than follow the precepts of Jesus. The sterile ant soldiers, who mobilize to protect the fecund queen, are really acting to perpetuate the genes of their corporation! And so with a mother who starves herself that her child may live and reproduce her genes. Or with a hero who dies in Flanders or Vietnam so that the American stock can multiply.

SURVIVAL

As an economist I've long found heuristic worth in Darwin's concept of survival value. I bet on the corporation with quixotic pricing to go to the wall. And if a new energy source is likely to prove viable, e.g., solar or wind, I seek signs that it is making its way in the competitive market.

But economics is a rather safe area.

I foresee greater problems for the sociobiologists when they try to tackle problems of race and sex. How do you keep distinct a Shockley from a Wilson? A Hitler from a Huxley?

Consider woman's role. What will happen to a sociobiologist who speculates that women have been bred by the struggle for existence to be immobile in order to better take care of the young?

Or examine the following argument that wishes to be taken seriously. (A) Homosexuality may be *genetically* inheritable in some degree. (B) Homosexuals tend to have fewer offspring. (C) To explain why genes for homosexuality persist, the ingenious sociobiologist may venture the following hypothesis: (D) Homosexuals are well suited to perform certain social roles, and (E) they perhaps are thereby enabled to favor their own nephews, nieces and siblings. Ergo, (F) reciprocal altruism and natural selection solve the puzzle.

Re-examine the above paragraph. Is it not calculated to maximize social controversy? Every link in the syllogism's chain is problematic and provocative. Do the data on twins establish heritability of homosexuality? Do gay people favor kin? Etc., etc. All that we have, or can have, is a mass of speculation, a collection of inconclusive anecdotes designed to touch off social resentments and controversy.

To survive in the jungle of intellectuals, the sociobiologist had best tread softly in the zones of race and sex.

PART V

Stochastic Theory of Economics

240

MATHEMATICS OF SPECULATIVE PRICE*

PAUL A. SAMUELSON†

This paper is dedicated to a great mind, L. J. Savage of Yale.

Abstract. A variety of mathematical methods are applied to economists' analyses of speculative pricing: general-equilibrium implicit equations akin to solutions for constrained-programming problems; difference equations perturbed by stochastic disturbances; the *absolute* Brownian motion of Bachelier of 1900, which anticipated and went beyond Einstein's famous 1905 paper in deducing and analyzing the Fourier partial-differential equations of probability diffusion; the economic *relative* or geometric Brownian motion, in which the logarithms of ratios of successive prices are independently additive in the Wiener–Gauss manner, adduced to avoid the anomalies of Bachelier's unlimited liability, and whose log-normal asymptotes lead to rational pricing functions for warrants and options which satisfy complicated boundary conditions; elucidation of the senses in which speculators' anticipations cause price movements to be fair-game martingales; the theory of portfolio optimization in terms of maximizing expected total utility of all outcomes, in contrast to mean-variance approximations, and utilizing dynamic stochastic programming of Bellman–Pontryagin type; a molecular model of independent profit centers that rationalizes spontaneous buy-and-hold for the securities that exist to be held; a model of commodity pricing over time when harvests are a random variable, which does reproduce many observed patterns in futures markets and which leads to an ergodic probability distribution. Robert C. Merton provides a mathematical appendix on generalized Wiener processes in continuous time, making use of Itô formalisms and deducing Black–Scholes warrant-pricing functions dependent only on the certain interest rate and the common stock's relative variance.

1. Introduction. Great mathematicians have often been important contributors to applied science. One has only to think of the names of Newton, Gauss, Euler and Poincaré. Now that the social and managerial sciences have emerged as professional disciplines, spinoffs from pure mathematics play an increasing role in their development. John von Neumann made two immortal contributions to economics. Best known to the outside world is his theory of games; no less seminal for modern economic analysis was his 1931 input–output model of dynamic general equilibrium.

The subjects that I shall survey today were not, as far as I can remember, within the direct range of von Neumann's research interests. But the methods and techniques he stressed infiltrate every branch of modern economics.

2. Shadow prices. Is there any other kind of price than "speculative" price? Uncertainty pervades real life and future prices are never knowable with precision. An investor is a speculator who has been successful; a speculator is merely an investor who has lost his money.

* Received by the editors March 9, 1972. The twelfth John von Neumann Lecture delivered at the Symposium on Mathematical Analysis of Economic Systems sponsored in part by a grant from the Office of Naval Research at the 1971 Fall Meeting of the Society for Industrial and Applied Mathematics, held at the University of Wisconsin, Madison, Wisconsin, October 11–13, 1971.

Reprinted from *Mathematical Topics in Economic Theory and Computation*, R. H. Day and S. M. Robinson, eds., Society for Industrial and Applied Mathematics, Philadelphia, 1972, pp. 1–42.

† Massachusetts Institute of Technology, Cambridge, Massachusetts 02139. The writing of this paper was supported in part by a grant from the National Science Foundation.

In the Santa Claus examples of textbooks, however, there are theoretical prices that play a role in organizing the resource allocation of a competitive society. The simplest example I can give that still has some richness of texture is the following ideal case of "homothetic general equilibrium," as sketched in Samuelson [93].

There are n goods and services, $q_1, \cdots, q_n$, each producible out of r factors of production $V_1, \cdots, V_r$ by concave, homogeneous-first-degree production functions. The sum of the amounts of each factor used in the respective n industries is an assigned positive constant. Finally, the owners of the incomes from the factors all spend their incomes in the same common proportions at all income levels, so as to maximize an ordinal utility function: one admissible cardinal indicator of the utility to be maximized is seen to be concave, homogeneous-first-degree in its consumption arguments.

Certain regularity conditions being assumed—such as existence of repeated partial derivative, nonsatiability, strong concavity, and others familiar in the economics literature—the system is defined by

$$q_j = Q^j(V_{1j}, \cdots, V_{rj}), \qquad\qquad j = 1, \cdots, n,$$

$$\sum_{j=1}^{n} V_{ij} = V_i, \qquad\qquad i = 1, \cdots, r,$$

(2.1)
$$p_j \partial Q^j / \partial V_{ij} = w_i, \quad j = 1, \cdots, n, \quad i = 1, \cdots, r,$$

$$u = u[q_1, \cdots, q_n],$$

$$p_j = \partial u / \partial q_j, \qquad\qquad j = 1, \cdots, n.$$

Here (p_j) is the vector of prices of the goods (q_j), expressed in "real GNP" units; (w_i) is the vector of real prices of the factors (V_i); V_{ij} is the nonnegative amount of the ith factor allocated to the jth industry; u is the real GNP, invariant to redistributions of incomes among individuals because of our strong assumption of uniform, homothetic tastes.

The $n + r + nr + 1 + n$ "independent" relations of (2.1) do suffice to determine the $n + nr + n + r + 1$ unknown variables: $(q_j), (V_{ij}), (p_j, w_i), u$, as can be proved by the nonalgebraic consideration that (2.1) can be shown to be equivalent to an interior maximum solution to

(2.2) $$U(V_1, \cdots, V_r) = \max_{V_{ij}} u[Q^1(V_{11}, \cdots, V_{r1}), \cdots, Q^n(V_{1n}, \cdots, V_{rn})]$$

subject to

$$\sum_{j=1}^{n} V_{ij} = V_i.$$

Even if we weaken the assumed regularity conditions, the equality–inequality version of (2.1) can be shown to have a solution by the Kuhn–Tucker version of (2.2).

Now the (p_j, w_i) prices are prices never seen on land or sea outside of economics libraries. But they do serve the role of Lagrangian multipliers or shadow prices that, in the absence of competitive markets, might be employed by a central planning agency in computing ideal socialist pricing, as Pareto [77], Barone [6], Taylor [108], Lerner [58], Lange [53], Hayek [6], and other economists have argued. (A socialist might redistribute ownership in the V_i and their income-fruits.)

A question, for theoretical and empirical research and not ideological polemics, is whether real life markets—the Chicago Board of Trade with its grain futures, the London Cocoa market, the New York Stock Exchange, and the less-formally organized markets (as for staple cotton goods), to say nothing of the large Galbraithian corporations possessed of some measure of unilateral economic power—do or do not achieve some degree of dynamic approximation to the idealized "scarcity" or shadow prices. In a well-known passage, Keynes [49] has regarded speculative markets as mere casinos for transferring wealth between the lucky and unlucky, the quick and the slow. On the other hand, Holbrook Working [115]–[118] has produced evidence over a lifetime that futures prices do vibrate randomly around paths that a technocrat might prescribe as optimal. (Thus, years of good crop were followed by heavier carryover than were years of bad, and this before government intervened in agricultural pricing.)

3. Stochastic cob-web cycles. Let me describe a process famous in economics for more than forty years.[1] A crop, call it potatoes, is auctioned off for what it will fetch today according to a demand relation. But the amount supplied in the next period is a lagged function of today's price. The demand and supply relations are respectively

$$p_t = D[q_t], \qquad D' < 0,$$

(3.1)
$$q_t = S(p_{t-1}), \qquad S' > 0,$$

$$p_t = D[S(p_{t-1})] = P(p_{t-1}), \qquad P' < 0.$$

These nonlinear difference equations, subject to initial conditions q_0 or p_0, generate a determinate solution

$$q_t = Q(t; q_0), \qquad p_t = P(t; p_0), \qquad t > 0.$$

A stationary solution to the dynamic equations is defined by the intersection of the curves

(3.2)
$$p^* = P(p^*),$$

$$p^* = D[q^*], \qquad q^* = S(p^*).$$

---

[1] Discovered simultaneously around 1929 by Tinbergen, Ricci, and Henry Schultz, this has already reached the elementary textbooks as in Samuelson [82, p. 382].

This is locally unstable if

(3.3) $|P'(p^*)| = |D'[S(p^*)]S'(p^*)| > 1$

with every-other-period oscillations exploding away from (p^*, q^*).

If, as could be seen in a diagram, there exists a motion of period 2, we have repeating terms $(\cdots, f_0, f_1, f_0, f_1, \cdots; \cdots, g_0, g_1, g_0, g_1, \cdots)$

(3.4)
$$p_t = f_t \equiv f_{t \pm 2} \neq f_{t+1},$$

$$q_t = g_t \equiv g_{t \pm 2} \neq g_{t+1},$$

with

(3.5)
$$f_0 = P(f_1), \qquad f_1 = P(f_0),$$

$$f_1 = D[g_1], \qquad f_0 = D[g_0],$$

$$g_1 = S(f_0), \qquad g_0 = S(f_1).$$

As Leontief [56] showed, it will suffice for local stability of the periodic motion that $p_{t+2} = P(P(p_t)) = P_2(p_t)$ be a stable difference equation, with

(3.6) $P'(f_0)P'(f_1) = |D'[g_1]S'(f_0)D'[g_0]S'(f_1)| < 1$.

All this is intuitively obvious, but can be verified by a theory of difference equations with periodic coefficients that parallels the familiar Floquet theory of differential equations with periodic coefficients. (See Samuelson [97] for discussion parallel to Coddington and Levinson [15].)

The system (3.1) has a certain vogue in agricultural economics as being related to a supposed corn-hog cycle. It has the great merits that it solves with a stroke of the pen how to get, from one set of (p_t, q_t) data, *both* an identified demand function *and* an identified supply function. As readers of Haavelmo [35] and F. Fisher [33] know, the specified lag structure permitted older writers such as H. L. Moore and his pupil Henry Schultz to crack the identification puzzle.

But surely the cob-web cycle is an oversimplification of reality. If prices varied year after year in a predictable fashion, why shouldn't farmers and the agricultural information services recognize this, or at least why wouldn't commodity speculators or the board of trade do so? Such recognition would lead to an alteration of the postulated $q_t = S(p_{t-1})$ relation, perhaps replacing it by

(3.7)
$$q_t = S \text{ (price expected at period } t)$$

$$= S(\Pi_t).$$

Thus, in the absence of chance variations in harvests or in tastes, experience with (3.1) might lead after a time to the self-warranting inference

(3.8)
$$\Pi_t \equiv \Pi_{t+1} \equiv p^*,$$

$$q_t \equiv q^* = S(p^*).$$

Real life can hardly be so simple since there are, at the least, chance variations in supply harvested. To illustrate one might replace (3.8) by

$$(3.9) \qquad\qquad q_t = S(\Pi_t) + X_t,$$

where X_t is an independent random variable

$$\text{Prob}\,\{X_t \leq x\} = F(x) \quad \text{for all } t.$$

Intuitively, depending upon whether the chance draw of X_t has its outcome knowable late or early in the intention-to-plant stage, one would expect (3.8)'s stationary equilibrium to be replaced by kind of a Brownian-motion vibration around equilibrium: when adverse X_t is drawn, p_t tends to be high. Depending upon how much one can infer about the unknown probability distribution $F(x)$, farmers will form different decision rules on how to guess Π_t, and hence how to decide what amounts to plant of each crop.

The next sections will pursue this issue of stochastic variation.

4. Bachelier's absolute-Brownian motion. It is not easy to get rich in Las Vegas, at Churchill Downs, or at the local Merrill Lynch office. That price changes of common stocks and commodity futures fluctuate somewhat randomly, something like the digits in a table of random numbers or with algebraic sign-patterns like that of heads and tails in tosses of a coin, has commonly been recognized. Just as men try to develop systems and hunches to outguess random devices, so speculators purport to be able to infer from charts certain "technical" patterns that enable profitable prediction of future price changes.

As against the chartist-technicians, who are in as low repute as ESP investigators because they usually have holes in their shoes and no favorable records of reproducible worth, there are the "fundamentalists" and economists who think that the future algebraic rise in the price of wheat will have something to do with possibly discernible patterns of what is going to happen to the weather in the plains states, the price of nitrogen fertilizer, the plantings of corn, and the fad for reducing diets. It came as something of a surprise to these fundamentalists that Alfred Cowles [17]–[20] and M. G. Kendall [48], along with occasional earlier writers, found that their computers could hardly tell the difference between random number series and historical price differences. As Kendall put it, in discussing over 2,000 weekly price changes in Chicago spot wheat recorded for years between 1883 and 1914:

The series looks like a "wandering" one, almost as if once a week the Demon of Chance drew a random number from a symmetrical population of fixed dispersion and added it to the current price to determine next week's price [16, p. 87].

As measured by the absence of significant serial correlation, 18 English common-stock-price series were found also to look much like random walks.

The only cases of systematic serial correlation or dependence Kendall found were in such monthly series as New York spot cotton; but Working [119] and S. S. Alexander soon independently showed that these weak effects were precisely what one should expect from random-difference series averaged in the overlapping monthly fashion of Kendall's series.

In 1900 a French mathematician, Louis Bachelier, wrote a Sorbonne thesis [5] on the *Theory of Speculation*. This was largely lost in the literature, even though Bachelier does receive occasional citation in standard works on probability. Twenty years ago a circular letter by L. J. Savage (now, sadly, lost to us), asking whether economists had any knowledge or interest in a 1914 popular exposition by Bachelier, led to his being rediscovered. Since the 1900 work deserves an honored place in the physics of Brownian motion as well as in the pioneering of stochastic processes, let me say a few words about the Bachelier theory.[2]

After some incomplete observations about the difference between objectivist-frequency notions of probability and subjectivist-personal notions of probability as entertained by (a) the buyer of a stock, (b) its seller, (c) the necessarily-matched resultant of buyers' and sellers' pressures to form, so to speak, the probability in the "mass-mind of the market" (my phrase, not Bachelier's), he in effect posits

$$(4.1) \qquad \text{Prob} \{X_{t+T} \leqq x_T | X_0 = x_0\} = F(x_T - x_0 ; T).$$

Here x_0 is the known price of, say General Motors stock, now at $t = 0$. GM's price T periods from now is a random variable, X_T, following the indicated probability distribution. Although Bachelier does not linger sufficiently long over the fact, evidently t and T are not to be restricted to integral values corresponding to discrete time periods, but are to be real numbers. Today we would call this a Wiener Brownian-motion process involving infinitely-divisible independent *increments*.

Bachelier gives three or four proofs, or purported proofs, that the resulting distribution for F must have the normal de Moivre–Laplace–Gauss form. Since we can go from here to there in two intermediate jumps, he anticipates a form of

---

[2] Since illustrious French geometers almost never die, it is possible that Bachelier still survives in Paris supplementing his professorial retirement pension by judicious arbitrage in puts and calls. But my widespread lecturing on him over the last 20 years has not elicited any information on the subject. How much Poincaré, to whom he dedicates the thesis, contributed to it, I have no knowledge. Finally, as Bachelier's cited life works suggest, he seems to have had something of a one-track mind. But what a track! The rather supercilious references to him, as an unrigorous pioneer in stochastic processes and stimulator of work in that area by more rigorous mathematicians such as Kolmogorov, hardly does Bachelier justice. His methods can hold their own in rigor with the best scientific work of his time, and his fertility was outstanding. Einstein is properly revered for his basic, and independent, discovery of the theory of Brownian motion 5 years after Bachelier. But years ago when I compared the two texts, I formed the judgement (which I have not checked back on) that Bachelier's methods dominated Einstein's in every element of the vector. Thus the Einstein–Folker–Planck Fourier equation for diffusion of probabilities is already in Bachelier, along with subtle uses of the now-standard method of reflected images.

the Chapman–Kolmogorov relation and, in effect,[3] writes

$$(4.2) \qquad F(x; T_1 + T_2) = \int_{-\infty}^{\infty} F(x - u; T_1)F(du; T_2).$$

He purports to deduce that (4.2) implies

$$(4.3) \qquad F(x; t) \equiv F\left(\frac{x - \mu t}{\sigma\sqrt{t}}; 1\right) \equiv N\left[\frac{x - \mu t}{\sigma\sqrt{t}}\right],$$

where the well-known Gaussian integral is defined by

$$(4.4) \qquad N[y] = \frac{1}{\sqrt{2\pi}} \int_{-\infty}^{y} e^{-u^2/2} \, du.$$

Since any member of the Lévy–Pareto stable-additive class satisfies (4.2), and since all the members of this class that lack finite second moments are non-Gaussian, such a demonstration is invalid. The recent works of Mandelbrot [61]–[64] and Fama [25]–[31] suggest that the non-Gaussian Lévy distributions, with so-called kurtosis α between the 2 of the Gaussian distribution and the 1 of Cauchy distribution, must be taken seriously in evaluating empirical time series. Thus, when we supply Bachelier with the regularity conditions, such as finite second moment, to make his deduction valid, we must do so as a temporary loan and with some reservations.

Bachelier goes from (4.2) to (4.3) by varied arguments. He verifies (p. 30) the sufficiency of (4.3) for (4.2) by direct substitution, still leaving open the problem of necessity. Later (pp. 32–34) he uses the familiar demonstration, by Stirling's approximation, of the central limit law for the binomial process. Still later he gives two arguments, one (p. 39) involving random movements in discrete time on a discrete lattice of points, and the other (p. 40) reminiscent of Einstein's approximation involving zero probabilities outside an infinitesimal range in short-enough time intervals, to deduce the Bachelier–Einstein Fourier equation

$$(4.5) \qquad c^2 \frac{\partial F(x; t)}{\partial t} - \frac{\partial^2 F(x; t)}{\partial x^2} = 0$$

with well-posed boundary conditions at $t = 0$.

Bachelier applies this theory to observations in the Paris market of 1894–1898, with what he considers impressive corroboration and which we must regard as

---

[3] I say "in effect" because I write down cumulative probability distributions rather than his probability densities, which in my notation involve

$$F'(x; T_1 + T_2) = \int_{-\infty}^{\infty} F'(x - u; T_1)F'(u; T_2) \, du.$$

Bachelier also assumes that the expected value of $X_T - X_0$ is by hypothesis zero, as in an unbiased random walk, an assumption I do not yet make. Note: all my page references are to the English translation in Cootner [16]. The Stieltjes integral that I write as $\int_{-\infty}^{\infty} f(x)P(dx)$ can also be written as $\int_{-\infty}^{\infty} f(x) \, dP(x)$.

not uninteresting. To illustrate his typical researches, let me sketch his rational theory of warrant or call pricing.

Axiom. The expected value of a common stock's price change $X_{t+k} - X_t$, is always zero, as in a fair game or "martingale." An option enabling you to buy it at an exercise (or "striking") price of a dollars exactly T periods from now is to be given a market price today, W, such that it also faces you with a fair-game process.

I shall not spell out in detail the arguments. But notice that if X_T ends up below the exercise price a, you will not want to exercise and will lose what you paid for the warrant; and for every dollar X_T exceeds a, you make a dollar of gross profit by exercising. Hence, the value of the warrant that makes your net profit zero must be the following function of the time left for the warrant to run T, and the current price of the common stock, x:

$$(4.6) \qquad W(x; T, a) = \int_a^\infty (u - a) F[d(u - x); T].$$

Assuming that F does satisfy Bachelier's Gaussian form of (4.3), it is easy to derive

$$(4.7) \qquad W(a; T, a) = k\sigma\sqrt{T},$$

where k is a simple normalizing constant and σ is a parameter measuring the "volatility" of the stock's unbiased random walk per unit time period.

Thus, such a warrant or "call" with 2 years to run will be worth only about 40 percent more than one with 1 year to run (since $\sqrt{2} \simeq 1.4$). To be double the worth of a one-year warrant, we must pick a 4-year warrant. This morning I checked the newspaper ads for puts and calls and verified that this square-root-of-T law does hold approximately for call quotations over 30-day, 60-day and 180-day periods.

As another empirically good approximation when price changes can be represented by a probability density that is symmetrically distributed around zero—as Bachelier deduces and Kendall's observations loosely confirm over short time intervals—we can differentiate (4.6) to get, as I did some 20 years ago,

$$(4.8) \qquad \partial W(x; T, a)/\partial x = +\tfrac{1}{2} \quad \text{at } x = a.$$

This confirms the market rule of thumb: for each dollar rise or fall in market price above or below the exercise price, a warrant and call is marked up or down by approximately $\$\tfrac{1}{2}$. Perhaps this common rule was developed from the cruder argument that the chances are $1/2$ that the option will be worth exercising and that you will collect that dollar above the exercise price.

Note that the Bachelier model has only one parameter in it to be estimated, namely σ. When that is known, all kinds of random variables that depend on x —such as $W(x; T, a)$, such as the probability of making a positive profit on a warrant—take on a determinable probability distribution whose parameters can be compared with observed statistics of performance. Bachelier makes several such tests, with results he considers highly satisfactory.

Moreover, here art has improved on nature. Many modern researchers on warrant pricing, such as Shelton [105] and Kassouf [45], [46], have come out with regressions that sometimes deny the significance of a stock's volatility. This result I consider incredible—imagine paying as much for a warrant on sluggish AT&T as on jumpy Ling–Temco, price and durations being similar. Bachelier's formulas show that volatility is the name of the game. Indeed, if stock A has twice the σ volatility of stock B, then as much will happen to A in one year as to B in 4 years and A's 1-year warrant will have the same value as B's 4-year warrant. Specifically, for F Gaussian with zero mean, we can write

$$(4.9) \qquad W(x; T, a, \sigma) \equiv aW(x/a, \sigma^2 T, 1, 1),$$

where

$$(4.10) \qquad W(x; \tau, 1, 1) = \frac{1}{\sqrt{2\pi\tau}} \int_1^\infty (u - 1) \exp\left\{-\tfrac{1}{2}(u - x)^2/\tau\right\} du$$

a definite integral easy to tabulate.

5. Absurdity of unlimited liability.

Seminal as the Bachelier model is, it leads to ridiculous results. Thus, as the running period of a warrant increases, its value grows indefinitely, exceeding any bound (including all the money that there is in the universe)! A perpetual warrant, of which Tricontinental or Alleghany are only two out of numerous examples, should sell for an *infinite* price; but why would anyone in his right mind ever pay more than the value of the common stock itself for a perpetual call on it—since owning it is such a perpetual call, and at zero price?

I have skipped the details of how Bachelier allows for accruing interest (or dividends) since it is the discussion of these tedious details at the very beginning of his book that has served to lose him many readers. It suffices to say that the absurdities of the model do not trace to this feature of the problem.

Before I had become aware of Bachelier's work, my own experiments with random walks and those of Richard Kruizenga [51], [52], who was writing his put-and-call thesis[4] under my direction, had shown the untenability of an absolute random-walk model except as a short-run approximation. An ordinary random walk of price, even if it is unbiased, will result in price becoming negative with a probability that goes to 1/2 as $T \to \infty$. This contradicts the limited liability feature of modern stocks and bonds. The General Motors stock I buy for $100 today can at most drop in value to zero, at which point I tear up my certificate and never look back.

---

[4] Graduate students have a recurring nightmare that just as they are completing their Ph.D. theses with their stellar contributions, someone will turn up in the ancient literature many of their findings. This happened to Dr. Kruizenga when the Savage letter of inquiry arrived just as he was dotting the final i's on his own independent researches.

The absurdities to which the negative prices of the absolute random walk leads[5] are a result of its supposition that independent absolute increments

$$(X_{t+1} - X_t) + (X_{t+2} - X_{t+1}) + \cdots$$

can lead to $X_T - X_0$ losses indefinitely greater than the original X_0 principal. Since the warrant buyer avoids these alleged indefinite losses, if he is to experience a fair game he must pay an indefinitely high price for the warrant.

There is a hidden subtlety that must be unearthed here. Bachelier, a European, always has in mind what I have called in [90] a "European" rather than an "American" warrant. In America a warrant with T time to run can be exercised at any time in the interval from now to then, i.e., at any t' in the interval

$$t_0 \leqq t' \leqq t_0 + T.$$

Moreover, the American warrant holder has paid for it in advance and can throw the warrant away whenever he wishes to. By contrast, a European warrant is exercisable only at the end of the period, at $t_0 + T$, and final settlement involving the premium originally agreed upon for the warrant must be made then. The warrant holder cannot simply walk away from his obligation in the interim.

Now it is a theorem that the European warrant and the American warrant have the same value, and that an American warrant will *never* rationally be exercised prior to its termination date—*provided* the common stock and the warrant are postulated to earn the same mean percentage return per unit of time (in Bachelier's fair-game case, a common zero expected return) with all accruing dividends or interest being ignorable. See Samuelson and Merton [95] and Appendix footnote A4.

Let us now "Europeanize," so to speak, the holding of the common stock and suppose that at the end of some stipulated time period T, say at the time when it is known that I will die, I must settle my stock holding, receiving positive dollars if $X_T > 0$ and having to pay negative dollars if $X_T < 0$. I am not sure that I, as a prudent concave-utility maximizer, would ever dare hold a common stock that involves such *unlimited* European liability. Certainly I would not hold it in preference to cash at Bachelier's postulated zero mean return!

To summarize: The absolute-Brownian motion or absolute random-walk model must be abandoned as absurd. My own solution was to fasten upon Gertrude Stein's lemma: "A dollar is a dollar is a dollar." This leads naturally to the geometric Brownian motion of the next section.

---

[5] Bachelier in [16, p. 28] shows a guilty awareness of the defect in his model involving negative prices, as his translator, A. J. Boness, notes. Bachelier says, "We will assume that it [stock price, X_t] might vary between $-\infty$ and $+\infty$, the probability of a spread greater than X_0 [i.e., $|X_T - X_0| > X_0$, or $X_T < 0$] being considered completely negligible, *a priori*." For T large, this is a self-contradiction to his own absolute-Brownian-motion theory.

6. The economic geometric Brownian motion. The simplest hypothesis to circumvent difficulties is the postulate that every dollar's worth of a common stock's value is subject to the same probability distribution. That is,

(6.1) $$\text{Prob}\,\{X_{t+T} \le x_T | X_0 = x_0\} = P[x_T/x_0; T]$$

with $x_T \ge 0$. Since

$$x_{T_1+T_2}/x_0 = (x_{T_1+T_2}/x_{T_1})(x_{T_1}/x_0)$$

we can write

(6.2) $$P(x_{T_1+T_2}/x_0; T_1 + T_2) = \int_0^\infty P(x_{T_1+T_2}/x_{T_1}; T_2)P[d(x_{T_1}/x_0); T_1],$$

where x_0 is a given constant.

Warning: This explicitly assumes "independence" of the various ratios $(X_{T_1+T_2}/X_{T_1}, X_{T_1}/X_0)$. In terms of more general conditional probabilities, one would have to write

$$F(x_{T_1+T_2}|x_{T_1}, x_0) \not\equiv F(x_{T_1+T_2}|x_{T_1}).$$

When writers speak of the "random-walk theory of speculative prices," there are actually many ambiguous possibilities being implicitly contemplated. Sometimes price changes, or changes in such a function of prices as $\log X_t$, are assumed to be subject to probability distributions independent of all previous prices. But sometimes no more is meant than that the expected value of such a price change is uniformly zero (or some other prescribed drift parameter) regardless of past known prices. Almost every random-walk theorist assumes, at a minimum, the Markov property that conditional probabilities of future prices depend at most on present prices, in the sense that knowledge of X_{0-k} does not add anything about X_{0+T} once X_0 itself is specified. When this is denied, theoretical formulas of warrant prices $W(x; T)$ have to be written as $W(x, y; T)$, where y is some vector of past common-stock prices.

Equation (6.2) obviously is the multiplicative counterpart of (4.2)'s additive process. Were it not for the complication that there may be a positive probability of ruin, i.e. $P(0, T) > 0$, we could work with the logarithms

(6.3) $$y_t = \log x_t, \quad y_t - y_0 = \log (x_t/x_0)$$

and employ analogous integrals to those in the Bachelier absolute Brownian motion. At Bachelier's level of rigor, which ignores infinite-moments of Lévy–Pareto additive distributions and infinitely divisible distributions involving discrete probabilities of the Poisson type, we could state that the only solution to (6.2) for T_i nonnegative real numbers would be the log-normal distribution

(6.4) $$P(x; T) = L(x; \mu T, \sigma\sqrt{T}),$$

where

$$L(x; \mu T, \sigma\sqrt{T}) = N\!\left(\frac{\log x - \mu T}{\sigma\sqrt{T}}\right),$$

N being the normal distribution of (4.4), and where

$$\mu = E\left\{\log \frac{X_1}{X_0}\right\} = \int_0^\infty \log x L(dx;\mu,\sigma)$$

$$= \frac{1}{\sqrt{2\pi}\sigma} \int_{-\infty}^\infty y \exp\left[-\frac{1}{2}\frac{(y-\mu)^2}{\sigma^2}\right]dy,$$

$$\sigma^2 = \text{Var}\left\{\log \frac{X_1}{X_0}\right\} = \frac{1}{\sqrt{2\pi}\sigma}\int_0^\infty (y-\mu)^2 \exp\left[-\frac{1}{2}\frac{(y-\mu)^2}{\sigma^2}\right]dy,$$

(6.5)

$$e^\alpha = E\left\{\frac{X_1}{X_0}\right\} = \int_0^\infty x L(dx;\mu,\sigma)$$

$$= \frac{1}{\sqrt{2\pi}\sigma}\int_0^\infty e^y \exp\left[-\frac{1}{2}\frac{(y-\mu)^2}{\sigma^2}\right]dy$$

$$= e^{\mu + \frac{1}{2}\sigma^2}$$

Even if (6.2) holds only for integral values of T and T_i, the central limit theorem will ensure in a large variety of cases—e.g., where specified moments are finite and $P(0;1) = 0$—that $P(x;T)$ is "approximated" by $L(x;\mu T, \sigma\sqrt{T})$ as T becomes large. This means that certain normalized variates, such as

(6.6) $[\log(X_T/X_0) - T E\{\log(X_1/X_0)\}][T^2 \text{Var}\{\log(X_1/X_0)\}]^{-1/2}$

have a distribution that is well approximated by $N[\cdot]$. This fact does not mean that necessarily we get a tolerable approximation of the form

(6.7) $E\{X_T/X_0\} \exp[T(\mu + \frac{1}{2}\sigma^2)]^{-1} = 1 \quad \text{as } T \to \infty$

as uncritical combination of (6.5) and (6.6) might suggest.

Actually, if $P(x;1)$ is not itself log-normal, we shall have

(6.8) $E\{X_1/X_0\} = \exp(\mu + \frac{1}{2}\sigma^2 + b),$

where b is not zero save for singular coincidence. In that case the left-hand side of (6.7) becomes e^{bT} which departs ever farther from unity as $T \to \infty$! This will come as no real surprise to students of limits.

Having altered Bachelier's assumption of an absolute to a relative random walk, I might as well generalize his assumption that the random walk is an unbiased profitless-in-the-mean fair game.

Instead I assume that the mean or expected outcome grows like compound interest at the rate $\alpha \geq 0$. That is,

$$E\{X_T/X_0\} = \int_0^\infty x P(dx;T)$$

(6.9)

$$= e^{\alpha T} = \left\{\int_0^\infty x P(dx;1)\right\}^T.$$

Bachelier's special case is that where $\alpha = 0$.

The value of a warrant can be directly calculated by quadrature if we stipulate that holding it is also to produce a mean return per unit time, β, and with β to be exactly equal to α.

As shown in Samuelson [90], the rational price of a warrant, as a function of present stock price, x, time to run, T, and exercise price, a, becomes, with $\alpha = \beta$ and the log-normal distribution,

$$W(x, T; \sigma^2, a, \alpha) = e^{-\alpha T} \int_0^\infty \max(0, xZ - a)L(dZ; T\mu, T\sigma^2)$$

$$= e^{-\alpha T} \int_{-\infty}^\infty \max(0, xe^Y - a)\frac{1}{\sqrt{2\pi}\sigma\sqrt{T}}$$

$$\cdot \exp\left[-\frac{1}{2}\frac{(Y - T\mu)^2}{\sigma^2 T}\right] dY$$

(6.10)

$$= xN[v] - a e^{-\alpha T}N[v - \sigma\sqrt{t}],$$

$$v = [\log(x/a) + (\alpha + \tfrac{1}{2}\sigma^2)T]/(\sigma\sqrt{T}).$$

By substitution it is easy to show that this can be reduced to

(6.11) $$W(x, T; \sigma^2, a, \alpha) \equiv a e^{-\alpha T}W(x e^{\alpha T}, T\sigma^2; 1, 1, 0),$$

where

$$W(Z, t) = W(Z, t; 1, 1, 0)$$

$$= \frac{1}{\sqrt{2\pi t}} \int_{-\log Z}^\infty (Z e^Y - 1)\exp[-\tfrac{1}{2}(Y + \tfrac{1}{2}t)^2/t] dY$$

(6.12)

$$= ZN[(\log Z + \tfrac{1}{2}t)/\sqrt{t}] - N[(\log Z - \tfrac{1}{2}t)/\sqrt{t}]$$

can be tabulated once and for all for a convenient range of t values.

My version of the geometric Brownian motion based on the log-normal rather than normal distribution does remove Bachelier's objectionable feature of having the warrant price grow indefinitely with T, since for my case

(6.13) $$\lim_{T \to \infty} W(x, T; \sigma^2, a, \alpha) \equiv x.$$

But we still retain the advantage of Bachelier's behavior for short T, since

(6.14) $$W(a, T; \sigma^2, a, \alpha) \sim k\sigma\sqrt{T}$$

for T sufficiently small, just as in (4.7).

The notion of skewness of price ratios is an old one in economics. A century ago when Jevons computed his first index numbers, the geometric rather than arithmetic mean suggested itself. Wesley Mitchell's extensive report on World War I price changes confirmed this asymmetry for all but the shortest-run price variations. The log-normal distribution, dependent on a law of "proportional effect," was popularly referred to in the economics literature of 30 years ago as Gibrat's law, after the French engineer and econometrician Gibrat [34]. See Aitchison and Brown [1] for its properties.

Independently of my replacement of the absolute or arithmetic Brownian motion by the relative or geometric Brownian motion, the astronomer Osborne [76] noted the empirical tendency (i) for a cross-section of common stock prices to be approximately distributed by the log-normal distribution, and (ii) for an even better approximation by that distribution to an array of price changes of each stock. Other investigators have found similar approximations to the price ratios of single stocks. To rationalize these empirical facts, Osborne made frequent reference to the Weber–Fechner law in psychology. The validity of that law in the field of psychology itself has perhaps been overrated: in any case I would regard Weber–Fechner analogies more as scientific metaphors for the prosaic fact of proportional effects than as independent rationalization. Where the poetry may have gotten in the way of the prose is in connection with Osborne's hypothesis [76, p. 108] that $E\{\log(X_{t+1}/X_t)\} = 0$, a logical deduction that I cannot follow and which is at some variance with his assumption two pages earlier that men act to maximize the first moment of money itself rather than of a strongly-concave function of money. Moore [75] gives a modified paraphrase of Osborne's argument, which depends upon the doubtful postulate that men generally have Bernoulli logarithmic utility, $U(W) \equiv \log W$, in which case an either/or choice of all cash or one stock would become a matter of indifference on Osborne's postulate. Actually if $\log(X_{t+1}/X_t)$ has a zero first moment for each stock, a combination of two stocks can be expected to have a positive first moment. Why neglect the opportunity of people to trade in paired units? I am afraid that the Weber–Fechner arguments lack economic cogency.

As will be seen in § 9's discussion of possible martingale properties of prices, one cannot in economics insist upon necessary absence of price bias. (Osborne, in his taking note of inflation as a separate reason for price change, must ask himself whether in Germany's 1920–1923 hyperflation, when interest rates were millions of percent per month, $\log\{P_{t+1}/P_t\}$ was ex ante or ex post a martingale? Let me add that the array of prices in Wall Street today depends upon how corporations choose to split their stock and pay stock dividends: if price ratios, X_{t+1}/X_t, were otherwise log-normal and all firms split every stock 4-to-1 when it reached 100 in price, the resulting distribution would be skew but not log-normal.)

My own preoccupation with price ratios rather than price differences came from the fact that, in an ideally competitive market, each small investor can, except for brokerage charges, do the same with one dollar as with a million. The homogeneity-of-degree-one property of investment opportunity, plus the simplification of stationarity of opportunity whether a stock is quoted in units of $20 or of $40, suggested the identity

$$P(X_T, X_0; T) \equiv P(X_T/X_0; T)$$

from which log-normality emerges as an asymptotic or instantaneous result.

Let me say a word about Lévy–Pareto alternatives to Gaussian distributions for X_t or X_{t+1}/X_t. Mandelbrot [61]–[64] and Fama [25]–[31] have found some evidence for Lévy–Pareto distributions with fat-tail parameters $\alpha \simeq 1.9 < 2$ of the Gaussian cases. All investigators have noted that there tend to be many more outliers than in the log-normal or other Gaussian approximations. On the other hand, as later sections will suggest, I am inclined to believe in Merton's conjecture that a strict Lévy–Pareto distribution on $\log(X_{t+1}/X_t)$ would lead, with $1 < \alpha < 2$, to a 5-minute warrant or call being worth 100 percent of the common! Evidently the all-wise market does not act as if it believes literally in Lévy–Pareto distributions, even though it may sense that there is some validity to the alternative notions of "subordinated processes" discussed by Clark [14], Press [80], and Feller's classic text, and which also lead to fat tails with abnormally-many outliers.

7. The general case where warrant and stock expected yields differ. The above analysis, which agrees with results of Sprenkle [106] and other writers, assumed the special case of $\beta = \alpha$, for which one can easily prove that conversion will never take place prior to expiration of a warrant, so that there is no advantage over a European warrant (that must be exercised only at the end of the T period) for an American warrant with its privilege of exercise at any time at the option of the holder.

Since warrants may be more volatile in price than stocks, concave utility maximizers might require that they have $\beta > \alpha$. Certainly in real life perpetual warrants do not sell for as much as the common stock itself, as (6.13) of the $\beta = \alpha$ theory requires. In any case, if the common is paying out a dividend at an instantaneous percentage rate of its market value of $\delta > 0$, at the least we should expect

$$(7.1) \qquad \beta = \alpha + \delta > \alpha \geqq 0.$$

Hence, in my 1965 paper [90], I tackled the tougher mathematical problem of $\beta > \alpha$, for which conversion of a warrant with T periods to run becomes mandatory when

$$(7.2) \qquad X_t/a > c(t; \beta, \alpha, \sigma^2), \qquad \lim_{t \to \infty} c(t; \beta, \alpha, \sigma^2) = c(\beta, \alpha, \sigma^2) < \infty.$$

Some very hard boundary problems to the partial differential heat equations arise, as the reader can verify by referring to the mathematical appendix to [90] that H. P. McKean, Jr., generously provided in [68]. Exact solutions for the W function are known only for the perpetual log-normal and Poisson cases, and for warrants of all time periods in the rather special case where

$$(7.3) \qquad \begin{aligned} &\text{Prob}\{X_t/X_0 = e^{gT}\} = e^{-bT}, \\ &\text{Prob}\{X_T/X_0 = 0\} = 1 - e^{-bT}. \end{aligned}$$

However, Robert Merton and I have made good computer approximations to the general solution and hope some day to publish abbreviated tables.

Dividends aside, the need for the difficult $\beta > \alpha$ case has been lessened by the alternative theory of warrant pricing that Merton and I worked out in [95], based upon utility maximization.

More important, a fundamental paper by Black and Scholes [8] restores the $\beta = \alpha$ case's mathematics to primacy. My 1965 paper had noted that the possibility of hedging, by buying the warrant and selling the common stock short, should give you low variance and high mean return in the $\beta > \alpha$ case. Hence, for dividendless stocks, I argued that the $\beta - \alpha$ divergence is unlikely to be great. I should have explored this further! Black and Scholes show that, if the posited probabilities hold, transaction costs aside, in a world where all can borrow and lend at a riskless interest rate r, by instantaneously changing hedging proportions in an optimal way, one could make an infinite arbitrage profit over the period to expiration unless warrants get priced according to the (6.10) $\beta \equiv \alpha$ formula

$$W(x, T; \sigma^2, a, r) = xN\left(\frac{\log (x/a) + (r + \tfrac{1}{2}\sigma^2)T}{\sigma\sqrt{T}}\right) - a\,e^{-rt}N\left(\frac{\log (x/a) + (r - \tfrac{1}{2}\sigma^2)T}{\sigma\sqrt{T}}\right).$$

This is indeed a valuable breakthrough for science.[6]

Since my audience includes mathematicians, I have asked Robert Merton to sketch in the Appendix the continuous-time Brownian-motion aspects of the warrant problem. Merton deduces the Black–Scholes solution in elegant form.

8. Speculative price a "fair game"? Why should the spot price of wheat in Chicago have a zero mean change? At harvest time, price should be low; to motivate people to store it through the months after harvest and before the next harvest, its spot price ought to rise systematically—and it does! With price indexes showing inflation predominantly throughout this century, indeed throughout the history of capitalism and for that matter the preceding centuries of recorded history, is there any jury which believes or will act upon the belief that the observations of spot-wheat price changes to come over the eons of time ahead always have a first moment of zero?

If Kendall's serial correlations in [48] do not pick up any systematic movements in spot prices, so much the worse for the power of such short-run statistical methods. Had Kendall's observations been on "wheat futures" (i.e., the price changes of a contract to deliver spot wheat at some one specified future date)

---

[6] Under such pricing, the expected instantaneous percentage return on the warrant is no longer a constant β: instead β will grow when x/a is low and also when T is low, approaching down toward α as either of these gets large.

Warning: If the Black–Scholes pricing is violated, the universe will not explode as it would if (8.1)'s true-arbitrage situation were to hold. The market need not believe in the Black–Scholes formula in the way that it *must* believe in formulas that prevent (8.1) from being possible. Thus, how can a rational arbitrager "know with certainty" what the σ is that he needs to do the arbitrage? A more hypothetical arbitrage is involved in the Black–Scholes formalism, namely the following. Query: What pattern of pricing, *if* it were known to hold with certainty (if, if!), would prevent the possibility of arbitrage? What pricing pattern will yield no profits to locked-in arbitrage strategy that must be engaged in until expiration time? Answer: the Black–Scholes pattern of pricing and no other. See the Samuelson review [94] for a similar critique of the Thorp–Kassouf [109] allegedly sure-thing arbitrage in reverse-hedging of expiring warrants. That the Black–Scholes formalism cannot cover all cases is shown by the case where complete ruin is possible with finite probability. Thus, let $P(0; T) = 1 - e^{-bT}$ as in (7.3) and $P(0 + x; T) = (1 - e^{-bT}) + e^{-bT}L(x; T, \overline{T})$, so that only for $b = 0$ do we have (6.4). The possible discrepancy from Black–Scholes pricing, intuition suggests, must grow with b.

rather than on spot or actual physical wheat at *different* dates, that would have been quite a different matter, as I shall show. Then there are some new and different reasons to expect an approach to fair-game or martingale properties. Aside from experience with spot prices, think of their theoretical causation. Wheat price will depend on, inter alia, the weather and the business cycle. Causes of changes in the weather are numerous but they are surely not independent through time. Persistence patterns of positive autocorrelation are commonplace. Business cycle components, such as GNP or price levels, are not themselves serially-independent series—far from it—even if some of the exogenous shocks that the endogenous system cumulates may approximate to such patterns of independence.

Everything that I have said of a price like that of spot wheat can be equally said of the quantity of wheat produced, consumed, sold or stored. If these magnitudes are random variables, there is no reason why at every time scale they should follow probability distributions that lack dependence through time.

However, returning to price—particularly to the speculative price of a common stock or a commodity future, quoted in competitive markets in which there are many buyers and sellers, each free to buy and sell at posted prices without having to worry that his actions will greatly alter quoted prices—we find repeatedly in the literature a special reason why expected price change should be zero or small. The argument goes as follows.

Argument. Expected future price must be closely equal to present price, or else present price will be different from what it is. If there were a bargain, which all could recognize, that fact would be "discounted" in advance and acted upon, thereby raising or lowering present price until the expected discrepancy with the future price were sensibly zero. It is true that people in the marketplace differ in their guesses about the future: and that is a principal reason why there are transactions in which one man is buying and another is selling. But at all times there is said to be as many bulls as there are bears, and in some versions there is held to be a wisdom in the resultant of the mob that transcends any of its members and perhaps transcends that of any outside jury of scientific observers. The opinions of those who make up the whole market are not given equal weights: those who are richer, more confident, perhaps more volatile, command greater voting power; but since better-informed, more-perceptive speculators tend to be more successful, and since the unsuccessful tend both to lose their wealth and voting potential and also to lose their interest and participation, the verdict of the marketplace as recorded in the record of auction prices is alleged to be as accurate ex ante and ex post as one can hope for and may perhaps be regarded as more accurate and trustworthy than would be the opinions formed by governmental planning agencies.

The above long paragraph is purposely made to be vague, in faithful reproduction of similar ideas to be found repeatedly in the literature of economics and of practical finance. For sample passages dealing with the notion that competitive anticipations must, or often do, make price changes a fair game, the reader may dip into the Cootner symposium [16], where views of such diverse writers as H. Working, Taussig, Cootner, A. B. Moore are to be found. More recently,

Samuelson [90], Mandelbrot [62], [64], Fama [31], and many others have grappled with this same notion of "efficient markets." This Fama reference gives a valuable survey.

The discussion has come full circle. The economists who served as discussants for Kendall's 1953 paper [48] were outraged, as he expected them to be, at the notion that there is no economic law governing the wanderings of price, but rather only blind chance. Such nihilism seemed to strike at the very heart of economic science. But more recently there have been plenty of economists to aver that, when speculation is working out its ideal purpose, the result must be to confront any observer with a price-change pattern that represents "pure white noise."

Sometimes competitive-discounting-leading-to-fair-game-price-changes is deemed to be practically a tautology, based upon the definition of competition. Actually, I would argue, the purported assertion is empirically untrue. Yet what we have here is a suggestive, heuristic principle. Most passages dealing with this problem, you will find when you put magnifying glasses on them, are quite unclear as to what theorems are being stated and what modes of proof or validation are being proposed.

Recall that spot wheat price series. Better still, concentrate on nonstorable fish or sweet corn. Suppose everyone knew that next year fish will be more plentiful and its price lower. How could anyone arbitrage out that insight in order to bring fish price today, when the catch is small, into equality with next year's price? Or with the next decade's price? (My final section will discuss commodity models where spot prices are anything but martingales.) Similarly any economist who stops to think about the matter will realize that there is nothing anomalous about a low-coupon bond, say one now paying 3 percent a year, being confidently expected to rise in every period from now until its maturity date if during that period the market rates of interest are expected to stay far above the bond's coupon rate. Not only can such a discount bond have a positive first moment of price change, arbitrage equilibrium requires its price to rise. So it may be with common stocks. If inflation raises index numbers of goods' prices by 10 percent per year and can be expected to do so, no doubt the safe interest rate will have the expected 10 percent built into it; and anyone who expects a common stock to form an unbiased random walk, lest he be able to arbitrage out the expected price rise, would be crazy in view of the fact that the interest cost or "opportunity cost" of buying stocks now for resale later will no doubt involve interest rates and needed stock-price appreciation rates of at least 10 percent to make the venture worthwhile.

And which is zero, absolute price change, or logarithmic price change? Why not the change in $f(X_t)$, where $y = f(x)$ is a monotone two-way mapping of x and y? Most writers do not even think to ask these questions, being content with the primitive notion that if you can buy a thing at one price and know with certainty you can sell it at a higher price, then there is a patent contradiction. This kind of classical sure-thing arbitrage is portrayed by the following infinite-value linear programming problem:

You can exchange gold at the U.S. mint for silver in a 17–1 ratio; with the silver achieved, you can go to the Asian Mint and get gold at a 1–16 ratio; thus your terminal gold can become an infinite amount X_1, namely the solution to the trivial problem

$$(8.1) \qquad \max (17 - 16)X_1 \quad \text{subject to} \quad X_1 \geqq 0.$$

Commodity and stock markets offer no such easy arbitrage to the speculator, save in singular cases not germane to the present discussion.

Mandelbrot, one of the few authors who attempts a serious discussion of advanced discounting, in [64] couples with an arbitrary time series $P_0(t)$, a new arbitraged time series $P(t)$, where

$$(8.2) \qquad E\{P(t + T) - P(t)\} \equiv 0$$

and where $P(t)$ is "constrained *not* to drift from $P_0(t)$ without bound." Actually, he concentrates mostly on cases where $P_0(t) - P_0(t - 1) = \Delta P_0(t)$ is itself generated as a linear function of a series of past random variables ("innovations") which are of finite variance and serially uncorrelated:

$$(8.3) \qquad \Delta P_0(t) = \sum_{-\infty}^{t} L(s)N(t - s).$$

When the $L(s)$ coefficients are suitably convergent and the underlying probability distributions are subject to suitable restrictions, the new arbitraged $\{P(t)\}$ sequence can be defined so that $\Delta P(t)$ is proportional to $N(t)$, or what is the same thing, to a calculable linear sum of present and past $[P_0(t)]$ values, the coefficients to be selected so as to minimize the mean least-squares drift of $P(t) - P_0(t)$.

I have not done justice to Mandelbrot's discussion, nor to his extension to imperfect arbitraging, both because of space limitation and the imperfection of my understanding of how his mathematics relates to economic models. So let me in § 10 give an economist's version of what can be expected to be arbitrageable in an idealized commodity market. In concluding this section, I shall sketch briefly my own deductive derivation of the martingale property of competitively-anticipated prices. This is the only unambiguous statement known to me of what seems to be the root notion in the long passage labeled Argument.

Let a spot price, say of wheat, be designated as $P_0(t)$, and let it be subject to any known stochastic process, which need not even be a stationary one. Examples are the following:

$$(8.4) \quad P_0(t + 1) = .5P_0(t) + u_{t+1}, \qquad u_t \text{ an independent random variable,}$$

$$(8.5) \quad \text{Prob}\{P_0(t + 1) = j | P_0(t) = i\} = a_{ij},$$

where $[a_{ij}]$ is a Markov transitional probability matrix with nonnegative coefficients and row sums that add up to unity.

In the first of these cases

$$Y_T = E\{P_0(t + T)|P_0(t)\} = (.5)^T P_0(t) + E\left\{\sum_0^{T-1} (.5)^t u_t\right\}$$

(8.6)
$$= (.5)^T P_0(t)$$

if the expected values of the error terms are always zero. At the end of one period, we shall have

$$Y_{T-1} = E\{P_0(t + 1 + T - 1)|P_0(t + 1)\} = (.5)^{T-1} P_0(t + 1)$$

(8.7)
$$= (.5)^{T-1}(.5)P(t) + (.5)^{T-1} u_1,$$

$$E\{Y_{T-1} - Y_T\} = (.5)^{T-1} E u_1 = 0.$$

Similarly

(8.8) $$E\{Y_{t-1} - Y_t\} = 0,$$ $$t = T, \cdots, 1,$$

making the sequence $[Y_T, Y_{T-1}, \cdots, Y_0 = P_0(t + T)]$ a martingale. Note that the Y's are a new time series, $P(t)$, distinct from $P_0(t)$ but related to it.

In the second example

(8.9) $$Y_T = E\{P_0(t + T)|P_0(t) = i\} = \sum_1^n a_{ij}^T j,$$

where

$$a^T = a \cdot a^{T-1} = [a_{ij}^T],$$ $$T = 1, 2, \cdots.$$

Note that Y_T is a random variable taking on different values for each $i = 1, \cdots, n$.
Also

$$Y_{T-1} = E\{P_0(t + 1 + T - 1)|P_0(1) = i\} = \sum_1^n a_{ij}^{T-1} j,$$

$$E\{Y_{T-1} - Y_T|P_0(t) = i\} = \sum_{k=1}^n \dot{a}_{ik} \sum_{j=1}^n a_{ij}^{T-1} j - \sum_1^T a_{ij} j$$

(8.10)
$$= \sum_{j=1}^n (a_{ij}^T - a_{ij}^T) j$$

$$\equiv 0.$$

Again the market price quoted for the future contract payable at fixed time T from now will oscillate through the sequence $[Y_0, Y_1, \cdots, Y_T = P_0(t + T)]$ but as a martingale

(8.11) $$E\{Y_{t-k} - Y_t\} = 0.$$

This is evidently a general principal, as embodied in the following theorem.

THEOREM ON DRIFTLESS ANTICIPATIVE SPECULATIVE PRICE. Let

$$\text{Prob}\{P_0(t + T) \leqq x_T | P_0(t) = x_0, P_0(t - 1) = x_{-1}, \cdots\} = F_T[x_T; x_0, x_{-1}, \cdots],$$

(8.12)
$$Y_T \overset{\text{def}}{=} E\{P_0(t + T)|x_t, x_{t-1}, \cdots\},$$

$$Y_{T-k} \overset{\text{def}}{=} E\{P_0(\{t + k\} + \{T - k\})|x_{t+k}, x_{t+k-1}, \cdots\}.$$

Then

(8.13)
$$E\{Y_{T-1} - Y_T | x_t, x_{t-1}, \cdots\} \equiv 0.$$

By induction,

(8.14)
$$E\{Y_k - Y_j\} = 0, \qquad k, j = 0, 1, \cdots, T.$$

The proof is immediate from repeated use of the identity

(8.15) $\quad F_T[x_T; x_0, x_{-1}, \cdots] = \displaystyle\int_0^\infty F_{T-1}[x_T; x_1, x_0, \cdots]F_1[dx_1; x_0, x_{-1}, \cdots]$

as in Samuelson [89], where it is shown that $P_0(t)$ and x_t can be given a vector interpretation so that price changes of wheat may depend on price data for corn and on weather elements of the vector.

The strict martingale property is more than one can expect to occur economically when there is a cost (interest, psychic disutility of bearing risk, etc.) to maintaining a position. In that case, rather than equaling the $[Y_{T-i}]$ sequence, the futures price, $P(t)$, may instead be related to a transformed variable $[Z_{T-i}]$, where

(8.16)
$$Z_0 = Y_0,$$
$$Z_1 = \lambda_1^{-1}Y_1,$$
$$Z_2 = \lambda_1^{-1}\lambda_2^{-1}Y_2,$$
$$Z_T = \lambda_1^{-1} \cdots \lambda_T^{-1}Y_T.$$

These present-discounted-values have the quasi-martingale property, for Z_t known,

(8.17)
$$E\{Z_{t-1}|Z_t\} = \lambda_t E\{Y_{t-1}|Y_t\} = \lambda_t.$$

Here $\lambda_t = 1 + \rho_t$ is a kind of an interest premium that the risky futures price must yield to get it held. (Remark: Unless something useful can be said in advance about the $[\lambda_{T-i}]$—as for example $\lambda_t - 1$ small, or λ_t a diminishing sequence in function of the diminishing variance to be expected of a futures contract as its horizon shrinks, subject perhaps to a terminal jump in λ_1 as closing-date becomes crucial—the whole exercise becomes an empty tautology.)

I leave this subject of perfect discounting of price changes by "perfect speculation" with some needed remarks about the benefits and losses from speculation. Populist electorates often regard speculation as sharp-dealing at worst, as gambling at best. Apologists for bourses and for laissez-faire by contrast regard the speculator as a noble and nimble operator who takes on his shoulders the irreducible risks of society for zero or little risk-premium : successful speculation, and the apologists think this to be dominant in the long run, enriches the speculator only by virtue of the fact that it enriches society even more.

Briefly, let me state what correct analysis suggests.

1. To the degree that speculation brings about an equilibrium pattern of inter-temporal prices, society benefits in the Pareto-optimality sense : in the absence of equilibrium, there exists in principle a movement that could simultaneously make everybody better off. See, for example, a textbook discussion like that in Appendix Chapter 21 of Samuelson [82], or see Samuelson [87], [99].

2. There is some empirical evidence, as already mentioned in connection with Working and others, that some organized commodity markets approximate to equilibrium intertemporal price patterns.

3. The conclusion does not follow that the speculator necessarily "deserves" his gains. As demonstrated in Samuelson [87, p. 209], a man who is quicker in his response reflexes to new information by only epsilon microseconds might capture 100 percent of the transfer rents created by the new data. He would become rich as Croesus but, in this strong case will have conferred only an epsilon degree of benefit to society—say a nickel's worth.

4. Some speculators can be destabilizing; and, where imperfections of competition prevail or where self-fulfilling processes are possible (as in the case of exchange rate speculation that depreciates a currency and induces the increase in central-bank money supply that "justifies" the depreciation), these destabilizing speculations can be profitable. Also, existence of speculative markets can serve as an attractive nuisance to cause those who are over-optimistic to incur losses, to incur deadweight brokerage charges, and to hurt themselves and their families.

5. Finally, as in Samuelson [101] it can be proved that, under specifiable general conditions, the unsuccessful speculator, in hurting himself, does add benefit to the rest of the community—but in amount less than the hurt to himself. This sounds as if the utilities of incommensurable minds are being compared. But, actually all that is being asserted is that unsuccessful speculation destroys Pareto-optimality : if it could be reversed, everyone could be made potentially better off. (Indeed, in the commodity model of my last section, mistaken carryover of grain by half the identical population, under the mistaken belief that next year's crop will be definitely short, will do first-order harm to the speculators and confer infinitesimal benefit—i.e., benefit of a second order of smallness—on the rest of the community.)

A fair conclusion is that a priori dogmatism in this matter is unwarranted. Pragmatic evaluation of the costs and benefits of empirical speculative institutions and their alternatives is needed for eclectic decision and opinion making.

We have seen that much of the vague discussion about "random walks" of stock or commodity prices does not distinguish closely between processes involving independent increments of price changes or price ratios and unbiased martingales.

In the language of autocorrelation, an independent-increment process will involve zero serial correlation of lagged price ratios or differences. For this there is some evidence. Against this, some evidence has been marshaled. One attempt, which partially misfires, is that by Shelton [104]. He points out that the universe of entrants to the Value Line contest, in which each entrant selects a portfolio of 25 stocks out of a much longer list, ends up with a subsequent distribution of portfolio gains that has a mean greater than the mean of a portfolio made up of the larger universe of eligible stocks. The difference in means could not remotely arise by pure chance. I do not regard this as a cogent refutation of the hypothesis that each and every stock is subject to an independent increment random process. Shelton's findings are consistent with the alternative hypothesis: Volatile, high-variance stocks require a higher mean gain than the rest; people who enter contests correctly go for volatility in terms of that game's payoff function. This explains why Shelton's observations have such high variance, and could explain their superior mean performance.

In very short periods, there is weightier evidence in favor of some negative serial correlation. Thus, if by chance, more people want to sell GM today than buy it, the specialist in GM will oblige them but at lower and lower prices. Tomorrow, when by chance, more people want to buy than sell, the specialist will oblige them on an up scale, perhaps returning to his same normal inventory but having made an adequate profit by virtue of having bought cheaper than he sold.

Mathematically, this kind of negative serial correlation would occur in the first differences of prices (or, better, their logarithms) as a result of an assumption that the levels of prices are subject to a uniformly and independently distributed probability. Thus, replace

$$(8.18) \qquad \mathrm{Prob}\,\{X_{t+1} - X_t \leqq \Delta x_t | \Delta x_{t-1}\} = F(\Delta x_t)$$

by

$$(8.19) \qquad \mathrm{Prob}\,\{X_{t+1} \leqq x_t | x_{t-1}\} = G(x_t).$$

Then $\mathrm{Prob}\,\{X_{t+1} - X_t \leqq \Delta x_t | \Delta x_{t-1}\}$ will increase as Δx_{t-1} grows, in the same way that my electric bill tends to be lower in a month after it has been high when random errors in meter reading are involved.

This negative serial correlation is presumably weak and confined to short periods. It presumably gives the specialist, scalper or floor-trader his *raison d'être*. This simplest model of this process I can describe as follows.

Suppose that the net algebraic amount that people want to sell of a stock in any period, X, is a random variable with a systematic part that is a weakly increasing function of its price above some perceived normal level, e.g., is proportional to $P_t - P^* = p_t$, plus a purely random-noise component with zero mean, fixed variance, and zero serial autocorrelation. Suppose that the specialist lowers (or raises) his price in proportion to algebraic net sales X_t. Then our stochastic equation becomes

(8.20)
$$p_t - p_{t-1} = -aX_t = -abp_t - au_t, \qquad a > 0, \quad b > 0,$$
$$p_t = cp_{t-1} + v_t, \qquad 0 < c = (1 + ab)^{-1} < 1, \quad v_t = -a(1 + ab)^{-1}u_t.$$

Price will then perform a Brownian-like vibration around the normal level P^*, and there will be an ergodic probability

(8.21)
$$\text{Prob} \{P_{t+T} \leq y | P_t\} = Q_T(y; P_t),$$
$$\lim_{T \to \infty} Q_T(y; P_t) = Q(y) \quad \text{independently of } P_t.$$

The specialist stands to make a mean profit per unit time, subject to finite variance, and proportional to $a\sigma_X^2$. What determines a is not clear: perhaps the specialist stands to lose his monopoly position if he makes a too large.

The above presupposes that the specialist is not unpleasantly surprised by an unperceived permanent change in the P^* level. Thus, if P^* rises permanently for some fundamental reason and the specialist does not recognize that this is going on, he will be selling out his normal inventory at too-low prices and be able to replenish it only at a loss. There seems to be a basic conflict of interest: the specialist is a small and steady winner from purely random fluctuations, but stands to be a big loser if he bucks unforeseen fundamental trends. (In connection with the present heuristic remarks, I am indebted to an unpublished Bell Laboratory memorandum on related matters by Kreps, Lebowitz and Linhart [50].)

9. Portfolio optimization. The 1965 theory of economic Brownian motion sketched in the last section might explain how, if we had futures markets for stocks, the *futures* price quoted for General Motors common to be delivered on October 11, 1972, might fluctuate like a quasi-martingale for the 12 months between now and then. In the notation of the last section, we would be talking about a $P(t)$ or (Y_{T-k}) of GM futures price and not a $P_0(t)$ or X_t of GM common stock. None of the last section's content touches the question of the probability laws that the common stock might *itself* be expected to satisfy. In the present section I cannot hope to outline a complete general equilibrium theory of stock pricing, since that subject is still in its infancy. For a start on such a complete theory, see Lintner [59], [60], Sharpe [103], Fama [27], Hirshleifer [39], Merton [72], and Samuelson and Merton [95]. To salve my conscience, I do present in § 10 one complete general equilibrium model of stochastic speculative price, namely one for a commodity market.

In the present section I shall merely sketch some typical models of portfolio decision making. I do this with the thought that such models provide some of the indispensable building blocks out of which a complete theory will have to be built.

First, it is common to assume that a decision maker facing stochastic uncertainty acts to maximize the expected value of the concave utility of his wealth (as dependent on the outcomes he faces), namely

$$(9.1) \qquad \overline{U} = \int_0^\infty U(W)\, dP(W) = E\{U(W)\} < U(E\{W\}),$$

where $U(\cdot)$ is a concave von Neumann utility function. (After all, von Neumann's work does apply! The von Neumann and Morgenstern classic [113] revived interest in notions which have been endemic in economics since the eighteenth century days of Daniel Bernoulli [7], Laplace, and Bentham, and many others. I have a slight preference for the axiomatic approach of Ramsey [81], Marschak [66], [67] and Savage [102], as I have discussed in [85]. A good general reference is Arrow [4].)

It was long known that in choosing between safe cash and a zero-mean asset with positive variance, all of one's wealth would be put into cash if $\overline{U}$ is to be maximized. Pioneering work by Domar and Musgrave [23], Markowitz [65] and Tobin [111], [112], turned economists' attention to models involving two parameters: a mean of money gain and a measure of riskiness, or in the case of the last two, mean and variance

$$\mu = \int_0^\infty W\, dP(W),$$

$$(9.2) \qquad \sigma^2 = \int_0^\infty (W - \mu)^2\, dP(W),$$

$$\overline{U} \simeq f(\mu, \sigma^2) \quad \text{with } \partial f/\partial W > 0 > \partial f/\partial \sigma^2.$$

In Markowitz's valuable version, let a dollar invested in each of $i = 1, 2, \cdots, n$ securities give rise respectively to the random variables $Z_1, \cdots, Z_n$ with joint probability distribution

$$(9.3) \qquad \text{Prob}\{Z_1 \leqq z_1, \cdots, Z_n \leqq z_n\} = P(z_1, \cdots, z_n)$$

with probability density

$$(9.4) \qquad p(z_1, \cdots, z_n)\, dz_1 \cdots dz_n = (\partial^n P/\partial z_1 \cdots \partial z_n)\, dz_1 \cdots dz_n.$$

Then the terminal wealth W_1, will have the probability density

$$(9.5) \qquad \begin{aligned} &d(W_1 W_0^{-1}) f(W_1 W_0^{-1}; w_1, \cdots, w_n) \\ &= d(W_1 W_0^{-1}) \int_0^\infty \cdots \int_0^\infty w_1^{-1} p\Bigg(w_1^{-1} W_1 W_0^{-1} \\ &\qquad\qquad - w_1^{-1} \sum_2^n w_j z_j, z_2, \cdots, z_n\Bigg) dz_2 \cdots dz_n \end{aligned}$$

with mean and variance

$$(9.6) \qquad E\{W_1 W_0^{-1}\} = \mu(w_1, \cdots, w_n) = \sum_1^n w_j E\{Z_j\},$$

(9.7) $$V\{W_1 W_0^{-1}\} = \sigma^2(w_1, \cdots, w_n) = \sum_1^n \sum_1^n w_i \sigma_{ij} w_j,$$

where

(9.8) $$\sigma_{ij} = E\{(Z_i - E\{Z_i\})(Z_j - E\{Z_j\})\}.$$

If p were a joint normal distribution, the solution to the maximum expected utility problem would have to involve a (μ^*, σ^*) choice that represents a solution of the following quadratic programming problem:

(9.9) $$\min_{w_i} \sigma^2(w_1, \cdots, w_n) \quad \text{subject to} \quad \mu(w_1, \cdots, w_n) \geq \mu^*, \quad \sum_1^n w_j = 1.$$

This defines an "efficiency frontier" $\sigma^* = M(\mu^*)$, and depending upon one's degree of risk aversion one will pick the best of these frontier points, with its implied (w_i^*) strategy.[7]

It is absurd to expect p to be literally a joint normal distribution since that would violate the axiom of limited liability. An alternative defense of this Markowitz–Tobin procedure is possible in the case where $U(W)$ is quadratic. However, this assumption is known to lead to the odd result that, as I become wealthier, I become *more* rather than less risk averse. See Samuelson [91], [98], Borch [9], and Feldstein [32] for critiques of mean-variance analysis. The best defense of it, I think, is as a good approximation when the probability distributions are relatively "compact," as discussed in Samuelson [98]. For in such cases, the true solution (w_i^{**}) to the general problem

(9.10)
$$\max_{w_i} \overline{U}(w_1, \cdots, w_n) = \max_{w_i} \int_0^\infty \cdots \int_0^\infty U\left(W_0 \sum_1^n w_j z_j\right) p(z_1, \cdots, z_n) \, dz_1 \cdots dz_n$$
$$= \overline{U}(w_1^{**}, \cdots, w_n^{**})$$

will be close to a (w_i^*) solution on the Markowitz frontier.

Many of the results that the mean-variance analysis can establish can be also established by rigorous analysis for any strictly-concave $U(W)$ with convergent first moment. Here are a few representative theorems.

THEOREM 1. *As between* (i) *safe cash or holding a safe security with yield* $1 + r$ *and* (ii) *holding a risky security with positive variance, one will never hold the risky security if its mean return is not greater than* $1 + r$. *If its mean return,* μ_i, *is greater than* $1 + r$, *one must prefer to hold some of it, i.e.,* $w_i^{**} > 0$, *to holding cash alone.*

---

[7] For the independence case where $p(z_1, \cdots, z_n) = q_1[z_1] \cdots q_n[z_n]$, and each $q_i[z]$ has the Lévy–Pareto distributions with the same α kurtosis and β skewness coefficient, being of the form $q_i[z] = q[(z - \mu_i)/\varepsilon_i]$, Samuelson [92] has shown how the Markowitz efficiency-frontier analysis of quadratic programming can be generalized to a solvable concave programming problem,

$$\min_{w_i} \sum_1^n w_j^\alpha \varepsilon_j^\alpha \quad \text{subject to} \quad \sum_1^n w_j \mu_j \geq \mu^*, \quad \sum_1^n w_j = 1, \quad w_j \geq 0.$$

The resulting ε^* minimand forms with μ^* the efficiency frontier $[\mu^*, \varepsilon^*] = [\mu^*, f(\mu^*)]$, and the usual portfolio theorem follows. Because a joint Lévy distribution is not convenient, one goes beyond independence assumptions, in the Sharpe [103] and Fama [25] way, by considering returns with a common component added to the Z_i, namely $Z_i + c_i Y$ and where Y satisfies the $q[(Y - \mu_0)/\varepsilon_0]$ form.

THEOREM 2. *A risky security, with mean greater than that of a safe security and not less that that of any other security, and which is not perfectly correlated (in a nonlinear or linear sense) with any other security, must be held in positive amount.*

THEOREM 3. *If a group of securities are independently distributed each with a mean greater than that of the safe security being held, all must be held in positive amount.*

THEOREM 4. *If security i has a greater mean than any other security, and if it is independently distributed from all other securities, it must be held in positive amounts.*

THEOREM 5. *If all risky securities are subject to a probability distribution symmetric as between securities, i.e., with*

$$(9.11) \qquad P(z_1, z_2, z_3, \cdots) \equiv P(z_2, z_1, z_3, \cdots) \equiv P(z_3, z_2, z_1, \cdots) \equiv \cdots,$$

then they must be held in the same proportions, $w_i^* = 1/n$.

On the other hand, special $U(W)$ functions, which satisfy the condition

$$(9.12) \qquad U'/U'' = a + bW$$

are subject to some special decomposition theorems as discussed in Tobin [112] and Cass and Stiglitz [11]. Included are the important cases

$$(9.13) \qquad U = \log W, \qquad U = W^\gamma/\gamma, \quad 0 \neq \gamma < 1,$$
$$U = -e^{-\lambda W}, \qquad U = a^2 W - b^2 W^2.$$

Often analysis is wanted for maximization of terminal wealth, W_T, after $T > 1$ periods of time, during which the probabilities repeat themselves independently. Thus, we are sequentially to pick vectors $[w_i(1)], [w_i(2)], \cdots, [w_i(T)]$ to give the greatest $E\{U(W_T)\}$, where W_T is the random variable defined by

$$W_T = W_{T-1} \sum_1^n w_j(1) Z_j(T),$$

$$(9.14) \qquad W_{T-1} = W_{T-2} \sum_1^n w_j(2) Z_j(T-1),$$

$$\cdot \quad \cdot \quad \cdot$$

$$W_1 = W_0 \sum_1^n w_j(T) Z_j(1),$$

where the vectors $[Z_i(t)]$ are, for $t = 1, \cdots, T$, all independently distributed according to a common probability distribution, namely,

$$(9.15) \qquad P[z_1(1), \cdots, z_n(1)] P[z_1(2), \cdots, z_n(2)] \cdots P[z_1(T), \cdots, z_n(T)].$$

PAUL A. SAMUELSON

The exact solution is given by the Bellman-like dynamic programming sequence

$$\max_{w_i(1)} \int_0^\infty \cdots \int_0^\infty U\left(W_{T-1} \sum_1^n w_j(1)z_j\right) p(z_1, \cdots, z_n)\, dz_1 \cdots dz_n$$

$$= \int_0^\infty \cdots \int_0^\infty U\left(W_{T-1} \sum_1^n w_j^*(1)z_j\right) p(z_1, \cdots, z_n)\, dz_1 \cdots dz_n$$

$$= U_1(W_{T-1}), \quad \text{a concave function,}$$

$$\max_{w_i(2)} \int_0^\infty \cdots \int_0^\infty U_1\left(W_{T-2} \sum_1^n w_j(2)z_j\right) p(z_1, \cdots, z_n)\, dz_1 \cdots dz_n$$

(9.16)

$$= \int_0^\infty \cdots \int_0^\infty U_1\left(W_{T-2} \sum_1^n w_j^*(2)z_j\right) p(z_1, \cdots, z_n)\, dz_1 \cdots dz_n$$

$$= U_2(W_{T-2}), \quad \text{a concave function,}$$

$$\cdot \quad \cdot \quad \cdot$$

$$\max_{w_i(T)} \int_0^\infty \cdots \int_0^\infty U_{T-1}\left(W_0 \sum_1^n w_j(T)z_j\right) p(z_1, \cdots, z_n)\, dz_1 \cdots dz_n$$

$$= \int_0^\infty \cdots \int_0^\infty U_{T-1}\left(W_0 \sum_1^n w_j^*(T)z_j\right) p(z_1, \cdots, z_n)\, dz_1 \cdots dz_n$$

$$= U_T(W_0).$$

Note that this yields a best portfolio strategy at each instant of time as a function of that period's initial wealth.[8]

(9.17) $$w_i^*(T - t) = f_i(W_t; T - t), \qquad i = 1, \cdots, n.$$

May I call to your attention for future use the fact that, when all the probability distributions are symmetric in the various securities, the optimal portfolio shares will involve equal dollar investments in all securities.

---

[8] The problem in which one maximizes consumption over time, subject to stochastic return was solved by Phelps [78]. Combining this with sequential portfolio making leads to problems like

$$\max_{w_i(t),\, c(t)} \sum_1^T \lambda^{-t} u[c_t] + U(W_T),$$

where $\lambda \le 1$ and

$$c_t = W_{t-1} \sum_1^n w_j(t)z_j(t) - W_t.$$

This has also been solved by Hakansson [36], [37], Leland [57], Mossin [74], Samuelson [96] and by Merton [70], [71] for continuous t. The reader is alerted to some unsettled results when T is large. Hakansson [38] suggested attention then go to the mean and variance of average return per period; these can be surrogates for mean and variance of the logarithms of portfolio change, which Samuelson [100] misleadingly said were "asymptotically sufficient" for the decision process—a correct statement not as $T \to \infty$, but as $n/T \to \infty$, where n is the number of segments in which a fixed time T is divided, and Merton's infinitely-divisible log-normals become valid. H. E. Leland (and, later, S. Ross and Merton–Samuelson) proposed conditions under which $T \to \infty$ leads to a "turnpike theorem" in which $[w_j(t)] \to [w_j]$ appropriate to W^γ/γ, where $\gamma = \{[W U''(W)/U'(W)] + 1\}$ as $W \to \infty$.

THEOREM. *The optimal T-period solution to* (9.16), *when* $P(z_1, z_2, \cdots)$
$\equiv P(z_2, z_1, \cdots) \equiv \cdots$, *the symmetric case, involves*

$$(9.18) \qquad\qquad w_i^*(T - t) = 1/n.$$

The proof is immediate. Concavity of U guarantees that any local extremum is
a global maximum. By a legitimate use of the principle of sufficient reason, a
deductive symmetry argument, we know there is no reason to invest more in
one security than another. This completes the proof.

Finally, mention may be made of the special case where

$$(9.19a) \qquad\qquad U(W) = W^\gamma/\gamma, \qquad 0 \neq \lambda < 1,$$

or

$$(9.19b) \qquad\qquad U(W) = \log W.$$

This is the family of constant-relative-risk aversion, as discussed by Pratt [79]
and Arrow [3], a special case of (9.12) that leads to portfolio fractions and other
decisions that are proportional to the wealth level. That is, in (9.17)

$$(9.20) \qquad\qquad w_i^*(T - t) \equiv f_i(1; 1), \qquad\qquad t = 0, \cdots, T - 1.$$

Warning: $f_i(1; 1)$ will, generally, be different for each different γ. Only for
$\gamma \to 0$, will $f_i(1; 1)$ approach the solution given by the case where $E\{\log W\}$ is the
maximand. I must mention the Williams [114], Latané [54], Kelley [47], Brieman
[10], Markowitz [65], Hakansson [38] and Thorp [110] discussions which seem
almost to recommend that, for $T \to \infty$,

$$(9.21) \qquad\qquad f_i(W; T) \equiv f_i(1; 1)_{\log W},$$

which are the portfolio weights that maximize $E\{\log W_i\}$ at each single stage—
yet such proposals cannot be valid for rigorous $E\{U(W_T)\}$ maximizers. Such Latané
strategies do, for T sufficiently large, give a result that is with indefinitely great
probability, i.e., $P \to 1$, going to be better than the results of any other uniform
strategy. But that is another matter, quite different from expected utility maximizing, as Samuelson [88], [100] has argued. Note that, for general $U(W)$ and
$P(z_1, \cdots)$, no *uniform* w_i^* strategy is optimal at every time period.

Let me put this apparatus to work to discuss a problem relevant to a more
complete general equilibrium determination. Jen [42] reviews writings by those
such as Jensen [43], Cheng and Deets [12], Evans [24], Latané and Young [55],
devoted to the question: Suppose you begin by putting equal dollars in all
securities. At the end of one period, should you just continue to hold the now-
unequal dollar amounts? Or transaction costs aside, is it better to rebalance your
portfolio back to equal proportions? Which is better, buy-and-hold (BH) or continual rebalancing of portfolio to equal proportions (CRE)?

This question can be given a definite answer in that one case where equal
proportions are to be recommended in the beginning, namely when the joint

distribution of price rations is *symmetric* in the different stocks in each period and, for simplicity, independent of earlier period outcomes. As was shown earlier in (9.18), under these circumstances CRE is better than any other strategy for a concave utility maximizer. Thus, CRE does beat BH.

However, the asserted primacy of equal-proportions proves too much. How can everybody hold as much of dollars in General Motors as in Ford? One company is bigger than the other and there will not be enough to go around for equal-proportions holdings. The set up, looked at from a general equilibrium view in which everybody acts the same way, is self-contradictory. Even if Ford and GM start out with equal total values, under a symmetric $P(z_1, \cdots, z_n)$ distribution they must be expected to become unequal after one period, and increasingly unequal as T becomes large. Clearly the assumption of $P(z_1, \cdots, z_n)$ as a symmetric function has got to go in a good general equilibrium model.

Of course, in real life people differ: perhaps risk-averse widows will begin to buy the sluggish AT&T's and young[9] M.D.'s with sporting blood and fat prospects will buy the small and volatile stocks; and securities will get *repriced* so as to make them *all* be held.

However, if we seek a general equilibrium model of rock-bottom simplicity, it will involve all investors being alike. And then each will want, in effect, to pursue a buy-and-hold strategy, each of N people owning $1/N$ of all there is to be held. Is there any model which can rationalize such a buy-and-hold philosophy? (Note: I rule out the merits of buy-and-hold when you are *learning* inductively which stocks have the better expected value and are astutely letting your winners ride and become an increasing fraction of the total. I shall pretend that all similar men *know* the $P(z_1, \cdots)$ functions that each faces.)

Here then is a new idealized model which does seem to meet the challenge of making buy-and-hold motivated even in a world where people are alike in their information and probability expectations but possibly different in their wealths and degree of risk-aversions.

Axiom. Call all outstanding shares of each company one unit, so that the prices of such units $\{X_t\}$ are merely the total outstanding values of those stocks. (Splits are ignorable as dividends will be for the present terse exposition.)

I posit that each price, the high price for large GM or the low price for American Motors or some new firm, is proportional to the number of independent "profit-centers" or "molecules" in the firm. Each price changes as each molecule or profit-center in that firm proliferates into $0, 1, 2, \cdots$ succeeding molecules according to probability laws which are the *same* for every molecule in society *regardless of in which firm any one molecule may happen to belong.*

"What," you will ask, "could the size of an auto firm grow indefinitely, going beyond that fraction of the capitalized wealth of society that auto capacity could ever hope to attain under present tastes for autos and nonautos?"

Such a question holds no terror for the present model. If the age of conglomerates had not already dawned, the notion of companies which have profit centers that

---

[9] In Samuelson [96], it was shown that "businessman's risk" cannot be explained by a tendency to be more venturesome when you maximize terminal W_T with T large, in the sense that one with $U(W) = W^\gamma/\gamma$ or $\log W$ will have uniform (w_i^*) unless inabilities to borrow or other realistic factors are introduced into the idealized setup.

are not tied to any one industry but are free to go everywhere and to compete in search for a share of the consumer's dollar wherever spending tastes may direct such dollars—such a notion would have had to be invented to dramatize the present firm-as-collection-of-unrelated-molecules model. In the present model we are back to symmetry of results to be expected, but the symmetry is not with respect to equal dollars invested in each security but is rather nicely gauged so that, by the principle of sufficient reason, every concave utility maximizer will be motivated to make all of his portfolio proportions faithfully mirror all that there is to buy of total social wealth. If GM is three times the size of Ford, each of us will want to hold three times as much of GM as Ford, i.e., $w_i/w_j = 3$, and each w_i is directly proportional to the total values of outstanding stocks.

Call Z_j the number of new profit-centers or molecules that the jth present molecule will give rise to; then, independently of the firm in which any molecule may be, we face a symmetric probability distribution

$$P(\cdots, Z_i, \cdots; \cdots, Z_j, \cdots; \cdots; \cdots) \equiv P(\cdots, Z_j, \cdots; \cdots, Z_i, \cdots; \cdots; \cdots),$$

where the placing of the semi-colons indicates the boundaries of the firms, GM, Ford, GE, etc. A special case of this symmetry would be where each molecule is subject to an *independent* distribution similar to that of any other molecule, whether inside the same firm or outside of it; or, perhaps, the case where each such molecule is subject to independent variation except for a common business-cycle component of the Sharpe type. In the case of complete independence, consider two firms of unequal size, one containing say M_1 molecules and the other M_2 molecules. Let Y_1 and Y_2 represent, respectively, the random variables depicting the ratio of X_{t+1}/X_t for the respective firms. Then in terms of the following notational convention, we can prove the theorem that the portfolio proportions will indeed be proportional to outstanding market value:

$$P_1(y) = P(y), P_2(y) = P_1(y) * P_1(y) = \int_0^\infty P_1(y - u)\, dP_1(u),$$

$$\cdots$$

$$P_M(y) = P_1(y) * P_{M-1}(y) = \int_0^\infty P_1(y - u)\, dP_{M-1}(u).$$

In terms of this notation the probability distribution for $Y_1, Y_2, \cdots$ pertaining to firms of respective number of molecules and respective market values $M_1, M_2, \cdots$ will be of the form

$$P_{M_1}(y_1)P_{M_2}(y_2) \cdots .$$

And now it is easy to show that the resulting optimal proportions become proportional to firms' outstanding total market values or proportional to the M's.

This completes the description of the molecular model that can rationalize a buy-and-hold-all-there-is-to-hold philosophy. Rebalancing to equal proportions or adhering to any uniform proportions would definitely be suboptimal. (Remark: A Latané–Kelley expected-log maximizer would, in this environment, not adhere to uniform proportions but would rather do what every rational concave-utility maximizer would be doing even if his name were not Bernoulli or Weber or Fechner, namely, he would be buying his quota of outstanding total market value.)

Is there not a possible objection to this model—I mean beyond the usual intrusions of the reality of market imperfections, transaction charges, informational disagreements, and so forth? What will happen to the size distribution of firms over time? One would have to work out the answer for each different kind of symmetric function. But it is intuitively evident that the spread of firm size would widen through time. An ergodic state would not be achieved, unless we altered some of the assumptions of the model. The reader must decide whether the bulk of the evidence suggests that a model of dispersing firm size should be admired or rejected, and must be referred to works on the stochastic dynamics of industry size, such as that by Steindl [107].

10. Speculative stochastic price. A survey cannot be encyclopedic. Let me bring this bird's-eye view to an end by discussing, all too briefly, one self-contained model which does settle the economic issue of whether or not prices form a martingale or merely a stationary time series with a well-defined ergodic state as the resultant of Brownian vibrations around a level of equilibrium.

I consider an idealized model of a single spot commodity, like that analyzed in Samuelson [86], [87], [99]. The crop comes in intermittently, say every autumn; at first we may ignore all stochastic variations and let the crop be an arbitrary time sequence $(\cdots, H_t, H_{t+1}, \cdots)$. At first we may ignore all storage and suppose that consumption, C_t, does equal the harvest, H_t, in every period. Each C_t, so to speak, gets auctioned off for what price it will bring, along a conventional demand function

$$(10.1) \qquad\qquad P_t = P[C_t], \qquad P'[C] < 0.$$

Now let the crop be a stochastic variable, subject for simplicity to a time-independent uniform probability distribution

$$(10.2) \qquad \text{Prob}\,\{H_t \leq h\} = F(h), \qquad F(h_1, h_2, \cdots) = F(h_1)F(h_2)\cdots.$$

Obviously price will vibrate stochastically around the mean level $P[E\{H\}]$. Obviously, $P(t)$ will not be a martingale or, in any meaningful sense, a semi-martingale. Obviously, the conditional probabilities will be extremely simple, being of the form

$$(10.3) \qquad \text{Prob}\,\{P_t \leq p|P_{t-1}, P_{t-2}, \cdots\} \equiv \Pi(p), \qquad \Pi(P[h]) = F(h).$$

Now let us introduce into the problem the possibility of storage and arbitrage through time. Suppose that there are interest costs reckonable at r per period and that all physical storage costs can for simplicity be subsumed under the assumption that if I carry over Q_t in grain from the end of t for use or sale in the period $t + 1$, only a fraction a of that will become available in the next period, namely aQ_t, to be added to the new harvest H_{t+1}.

Samuelson [87] shows by standard methods that, in the absence of stochastic variations, the equilibrium pattern of prices is determined by the following nonlinear difference equations and inequalities:

$$(1 + r)^{-1}aP[H_{t+1} + aq_t - q_{t+1}] - P[H_t + aq_{t-1} - q_t] \leq 0,$$

$$(10.4) \quad q_t\{(1 + r)^{-1}aP[H_{t+1} + aq_t - q_{t+1}] - P[H_t + aq_{t-1} - q_t]\} = 0,$$

$$t = 0, 1, 2, \cdots, T, \quad q_{-1}, q_T \text{ specified},$$

with determinable solutions for the unknowns $q_0, q_1, \cdots, q_{T-1}; p_0, p_1, \cdots, p_T$. Actually, if $U'[C] \equiv P[C]$, these conditions can be given a Kuhn–Tucker dynamic programming interpretation

$$(10.5) \qquad \max_{q_0, \cdots, q_{T-1}} \sum_0^T (1 + r)^{-t} U[H_t + aq_{t-1} - q_t]$$

with $H_0, H_1, \cdots, H_T; q_{-1}, q_T$ prescribed.

It is further suggested how to handle the case of stochastic harvests. An obvious generalization of the nonstochastic programming problem of (11.5) is the following dynamic stochastic programming problem:

$$(10.6) \qquad J_T[H_0 + aq_{-1}] = \max_{q_0, \cdots, q_{T-1}} E\left\{\sum_0^T (1 + r)^t U[H_t + aq_{t-1} - q_t]\right\},$$

$$q_t \geq 0, \quad q_{-1}, q_T \text{ prescribed}.$$

The solution to this is given by the usual Bellman recursive technique and leads to the following general type of condition:

$$(10.7) \quad (1 + r)^{-1}aE\{P_{t+1}\} - P_t \leq 0, \qquad q_t\{(1 + r)^{-1}aE\{P_{t+1}\} - P_t\} = 0,$$

$$t = 0, 1, \cdots, T.$$

More specifically, solving the optimal control problems gives us a decision function for optimal carryover strategy of the form

$$(10.8) \quad \begin{aligned} q_{T-n}^* &= f_n(H_{t-n} + aq_{t-n-1}; q_T), & 0 &\leq \partial f(x; q_T)/\partial x \leq 1, \\ \lim_{t \to \infty} f_n(x; q_T) &\equiv f(x), & 0 &\leq f'(x) \leq 1. \end{aligned}$$

When we substitute these strategy functions f_n into the determining conditions of the problem, we emerge with a well-defined stochastic process. With $T \to \infty$, we can calculate the conditional probabilities

$$\text{Prob }\{P_{t+1} \leq p | P_t = p_0\} = \Pi_1(p; p_0), \cdots, \text{Prob }\{P_{t+k} \leq p | P_t = p_0\} = \Pi_k(p; p_0),$$

$$k = 1, 2, \cdots,$$

$$\text{Prob }\{P_{t+k} \leq p | P_t = p_0, P_{t-j} = p_{-j}\} = \Pi_k(p; p_0),$$

$$(10.9) \qquad \lim_{k \to \infty} \Pi_k(p; p_0) = \Pi(p), \quad \text{an ergodic-state probability},$$

$$E_{k \to \infty}\{P_{t+k} | p_0\} = \int_0^\infty p \, d\Pi(p).$$

This model portrays in a satisfying way many of the properties we should wish for a stochastic model of commodity prices. It fails to "explain" the Keynes–Houthakker "normal backwardation" of futures prices; it fails to explain "convenience yields" of inventory and "negative carrying charges" for carryover. The first failure can be removed, I believe, as soon as we introduce the realistic fact that some people have a comparative advantage in producing and holding this grain; the rest of the community has an interest in consuming it. The diversity of their interests ought to lead to normal backwardation. Interestingly, the magnificent Arrow finding, that there must be as many "securities" as there are possible states of nature if Pareto-optimality is to hold, suggests that organized markets do not go all the way in doing the job of optimally spreading risks among producers, consumers and well-informed speculators. See Arrow [2] and Debreu [21, Chap. 7].

I have discovered inductively that one can only scratch the surface of stochastic speculative price in any one lecture.

Acknowledgment. I owe thanks to Professor Robert C. Merton of MIT for the valuable Appendix on continuous-time analysis, and for other stimulus; also thanks to Jill Pappas and K. Iwai for editorial aids.

APPENDIX: CONTINUOUS-TIME SPECULATIVE PROCESSES

ROBERT C. MERTON

Let the dynamics of stock price x be described by the stochastic differential equation of the Itô-type[A1]

$$(A.1) \qquad dx = \alpha x \, dt + \sigma x \, dz,$$

where α is the instantaneous expected rate of return, σ is the instantaneous standard deviation of that return, and dz is a standard Gauss–Wiener process with mean zero and standard deviation one. It is assumed that α and σ are constants, and hence, the return on the stock over any finite time interval is log-normal.

Suppose we are in the world of the Samuelson 1965 theory [90] where investors require an instantaneous expected return β to hold the warrant and β is constant with $\beta \geq \alpha$. Let $W = F(x, \tau; \sigma^2, a, \alpha, \beta)$ be the price of a warrant with exercise price a and length of time until expiration τ. Using Itô's lemma,[A2] the dynamics of the warrant price can be described by the stochastic differential equation

$$(A.2) \qquad dW = F_1 \, dx + F_2 \, d\tau + \tfrac{1}{2} F_{11} (dx)^2,$$

where subscripts denote partial derivatives. Substituting for dx from (A.1) and

---

[A1] For a complete discussion of Itô processes, see the seminal paper of Itô [40], Itô and McKean [41] and McKean [69].

[A2] See McKean [69, pp. 32–35 and 44] for proofs of the lemma in 1 and n dimensions. For applications of Itô processes and Itô's lemma to a variety of portfolio and option pricing problems, see Merton [70], [71] and [73].

noting that $d\tau = -dt$ and $(dx)^2 = \sigma^2 x^2 \, dt$, we can rewrite (A.2) as

(A.3) $$dW = [\tfrac{1}{2}\sigma^2 x^2 F_{11} + \alpha x F_1 - F_2] \, dt + \sigma x F_1 \, dz,$$

where $[\tfrac{1}{2}\sigma^2 x^2 F_{11} + \alpha x F_1 - F_2]/F$ is the instantaneous expected rate of return on the warrant and $\sigma x F_1/F$ is the instantaneous standard deviation. Applying the condition that the required expected return on the warrant is β to (A.3), we derive a linear partial differential equation of the parabolic type for the warrant price, namely,

(A.4) $$0 = \tfrac{1}{2}\sigma^2 x^2 F_{11} + \alpha x F_1 - \beta F - F_2$$

subject to the boundary conditions for a "European" warrant:

(a) $F(0, \tau; \sigma^2, a, \alpha, \beta) = 0$,

(b) $F(x, 0; \sigma^2, a, \alpha, \beta) = \max[0, x - a]$.

Make the change of variables $T \equiv \sigma^2 \tau$, $S \equiv x\, e^{\alpha\tau}/a$, $f \equiv F\, e^{\beta\tau}/a$, and substitute into (A.4) to obtain the new equation for f,

(A.5) $$0 = \tfrac{1}{2}S^2 f_{11} - f_2$$

subject to

(a) $f(0, T) = 0$,

(b) $f(S, 0) = \max[0, S - 1]$.

By inspection, f is the value of a "European" warrant with unit exercise price and time to expiration T, on a common stock with zero expected return and unit instantaneous variance, when investors require a zero return on the warrant, i.e.,

(A.6) $$f(S, T) = F(S, T; 1, 1, 0, 0)$$

which verifies the homogeneity properties described in (6.11). To solve (A.5), we put it in standard form by the change in variables $y \equiv \log S + \tfrac{1}{2}T$ and $\phi(y, T) \equiv f(S, T)/S$ to arrive at

(A.7) $$0 = \tfrac{1}{2}\phi_{11} - \phi_2$$

subject to

(a) $|\phi| \leq 1$,

(b) $\phi(y, 0) = \max[0, 1 - e^{-y}]$.

Equation (A.7) is a standard free-boundary problem to be solved by separation of variables or Fourier transforms.[A3] Hence, the solution to (A.4) is

$$F = \frac{e^{-\beta\tau}}{\sqrt{2\pi\sigma^2\tau}} \int_{\log(a/x)}^{\infty} (xe^Z - a)\exp\left[-\frac{1}{2}\frac{(Z - (\alpha - \frac{1}{2}\sigma^2)\tau)^2}{\sigma^2\tau}\right]dZ$$

(A.8)
$$= e^{-(\beta-\alpha)\tau}xN\left[\frac{\log(x/a) + (\alpha + \frac{1}{2}\sigma^2)\tau}{\sigma\sqrt{\tau}}\right]$$

$$- ae^{-\beta\tau}N\left[\frac{\log(x/a) + (\alpha - \frac{1}{2}\sigma^2)\tau}{\sigma\sqrt{\tau}}\right]$$

which reduces to (6.11)–(6.12) when $\beta = \alpha$.

The analysis leading to solution (A.8) assumed that the warrant was of the "European" type. If the warrant is of the "American" type, we must append to (A.4) the arbitrage boundary condition that

(A.4.c) $F(x, \tau; \sigma^2, a, \alpha, \beta) \geq F(x, 0; \sigma^2, a, \alpha, \beta).$

It has been shown [A4] that for $\beta = \alpha$, (A.4.c) is never binding, and the European and American warrants have the same value with (A.8) or (6.11)–(6.12) the correct formula. It has also been shown that for $\beta > \alpha$, for every τ, there exists a level of stock price, $C[\tau]$, such that for all $x > C[\tau]$, the warrant would be worth more if exercised than if one continued to hold it (i.e., the equality form of (A.4.c) will hold at $x = C[\tau]$). In this case, the equation for the warrant price is (A.4) with the boundary condition

(A.4.c′) $F(C[\tau], \tau; \sigma^2, a, \alpha, \beta) = C[\tau] - a$ appended   and $0 \leq x \leq C[\tau].$

If $C[\tau]$ were a known function, then, after the appropriate change of variables, (A.4) with (A.4.c′) appended, would be a semi-infinite boundary value problem with a time-dependent boundary. However, $C[\tau]$ is not known, and must be determined as part of the solution. Therefore, an additional boundary condition is required for the problem to be well-posed.

Fortunately, the economics of the problem are sufficiently rich to provide this extra condition. Because the warrant holder is not contractually obliged to exercise his warrant prematurely, he chooses to do so only in his own best interest (i.e., when the warrant is worth more "dead" than "alive"). Hence, the only rational choice for $C[\tau]$ is that time-pattern which maximizes the value of the warrant. Further, the structure of the problem makes it clear that the optimal $C[\cdot]$ will be independent of the current level of the stock price.

[A3] For the separation of variables solution, see Churchill [13, pp. 154–156], and for the Fourier transform solution, see Dettman [22, p. 390].

[A4] Samuelson [90] gives a heuristic economic argument. Samuelson and Merton [95] prove it under more general conditions than those in the text. An alternative proof, based on mere arbitrage, is given in Merton [73].

In attacking the difficult $\beta > \alpha$ case, Samuelson [90] postulated that the extra condition was "high-contact" at the boundary, i.e.,

$$(A.9) \qquad F_1(C[\tau], \tau; \sigma^2, a, \alpha, \beta) = 1.$$

It can be shown that (A.9) is implied by the maximizing behavior described in the previous paragraph. In an appendix to the Samuelson paper, McKean [68, p. 38–39] solved (A.4) with conditions (A.4.c') and (A.9) appended, to the point of obtaining an infinite set of integral equations, but was unable to find a closed-form solution. The problem remains unsolved.

In their important paper, Black and Scholes [8] use a hedging argument to derive their warrant pricing formula. Unlike Samuelson [90], they do not postulate a required expected return on the warrant, β, but implicitly derive as part of the solution the warrant's expected return. However, the mathematical analysis and resulting needed tables are identical to Samuelson [90].

Assume that the stock price dynamics are described by (A.1).[A5] Further, assume that there are no transactions costs; short-sales are allowed; borrowing and lending are possible at the same riskless interest rate, r, which is constant through time.

Consider constructing a portfolio containing the common stock, the warrant and the riskless security with w_1 = number of dollars invested in the stock, w_2 = number of dollars invested in the warrant, and w_3 = number of dollars invested in the riskless asset. Suppose, by short sales, or borrowing, we constrain the portfolio to require net zero investment, i.e., $\sum_1^3 w_i = 0$. If trading takes place continuously, it can be shown [A6] that the instantaneous change in the portfolio value can be written as

$$(A.10) \qquad w_1\left(\frac{dx}{x} - r\,dt\right) + w_2\left(\frac{dW}{W} - r\,dt\right),$$

where the constraint has been eliminated from (A.10) by substituting $w_3 = -(w_1 + w_2)$, and so, any choice of w_1 and w_2 is allowed. We can substitute for dx/x and dW/W from (A.1) and (A.3), and rearrange terms, to rewrite (A.10) as

$$(A.11) \qquad \begin{aligned} & [w_1(\alpha - r) + w_2(\tfrac{1}{2}\sigma^2 x^2 F_{11} + \alpha x F_1 - F_2 - rF)/F]\,dt \\ & + [w_1\sigma + w_2\sigma x F_1/F]\,dz. \end{aligned}$$

Note that w_1 and w_2 can be chosen so as to eliminate all randomness from the return; i.e., we can choose $w_1 = w_1^*$ and $w_2 = w_2^*$, where

$$(A.12) \qquad w_1^*/w_2^* = -xF_1/F.$$

[A5] The assumptions and method of derivation presented here are not those of Black and Scholes [8]. However, the method is in the spirit of their analysis and it leads to the same formula. For a complete discussion of the Black and Scholes model and extensions to more general option pricing problems, see Merton [73].

[A6] See Merton [70, pp. 247–248] or Merton [73, § 3].

Then, for this particular portfolio, the expected return will be the realized return, and since no net investment was required, to avoid positive "arbitrage" profits, this return must be zero. Substituting for w_1^* and w_2^* in (A.11), combining terms, and setting the return equal to zero, we have that

$$(A.13) \qquad\qquad 0 = \tfrac{1}{2}\sigma^2 x^2 F_{11} + rxF_1 - F_2 - rF.$$

Equation (A.13) is the partial differential equation to be satisfied by the equilibrium warrant price. Formally, it is identical to (A.4) with "$\beta = \alpha = r$," and is subject to the same boundary conditions. It is important to note that this formal equivalence does not imply that the expected returns on the warrant and on the stock are equal to the interest rate. Even if the expected return on the stock is constant through time, the expected return on the warrant will not be,[A7] i.e.,

$$(A.14) \qquad\qquad \beta(x, \tau) = r + \frac{xF_1}{F}(\alpha - r).$$

Further, the Black–Scholes formula for the warrant price is completely independent of the expected return on the stock price. Hence, two investors with different assessments of the expected return on the common stock will still agree on the "correct" warrant price for a given stock price level. Similarly, we could have postulated a more general stochastic process for the stock price with α itself random, and the analysis still goes through.

The key to the Black–Scholes analysis is the continuous-trading assumption since only in the instantaneous limit are the warrant price and stock price perfectly correlated, which is what is required to form the "perfect" hedge in (A.11).

REFERENCES

[1] J. AITCHISON AND J. A. C. BROWN, *The Lognormal Distribution, with Special Reference to Its Uses in Economics*, Cambridge University Press, Cambridge, 1957.

[2] K. J. ARROW, *Le rôle des valeurs boursières pour la répartition la meilleure des risques*, Econometrie, Centre National de la Recherche Scientifique, Paris, 1953, pp. 41–48; English transl., *The role of securities in the optimal allocation of risk-bearing*, Rev. Economic Studies, 31 (1963–4), pp. 91–96; reprinted in [4, pp. 121–133].

[3] ———, *Aspects of the Theory of Risk-Bearing*, Academic Bookstore, Helsinki, 1965; reprinted in [4, pp. 44–120, 134–193].

[4] ———, *Essays in the Theory of Risk-Bearing*, Markham, Chicago and North-Holland, London, 1970.

[5] L. BACHELIER, *Théorie de la speculation*, Gauthier-Villars, Paris, 1900. Cf. English transl. in [16].

[6] E. BARONE, *The ministry of production in the collectivist state*, Collectivist Economic Planning, F. A. Hayek, ed., Routledge and Kegan Paul, London, 1935, pp. 245–290.

[7] D. BERNOULLI, *Specimen theoriae novae de mensura sortis*, Commentarii Academiae Scientiarum Imperiales Petropolitanae, 5 (1738), pp. 175–192; English transl., *Exposition of a new theory of the measurement of risk*, Econometrica, 12 (1954), pp. 23–36.

[8] F. BLACK AND M. SCHOLES, *The pricing of options and corporate liabilities*, J. Political Economy, (forthcoming).

[A7] In this respect, the Black–Scholes result is closer to the Samuelson and Merton [95] case, where $\beta = \beta(x, \tau) \geqq \alpha$ (and where no premature conversion takes place), than to the case of Samuelson [90].

[9] K. Borch, *A note on uncertainty and indifference curves*, Rev. Economic Studies, 36 (1969), pp. 1–4.

[10] L. Brieman, *Investment policies for expanding business optimal in a long run sense*, Naval Res. Logist. Quart., 7 (1960), pp. 647–651.

[11] D. Cass and J. E. Stiglitz, *The structure of investor preferences and asset returns, and separability in portfolio allocation: a contribution to the pure theory of mutual fund*, J. Economic Theory, 2 (1970), pp. 102–160.

[12] P. L. Cheng and H. K. Deets, *Portfolio returns and the randomwalk theory*, J. Finance, 26 (1971), pp. 11–30.

[13] R. V. Churchill, *Fourier Series and Boundary Value Problems*, McGraw-Hill, New York, 1963.

[14] P. K. Clark, *A subordinated stochastic process model with finite variance for speculative prices*, Econometrica (forthcoming).

[15] E. A. Coddington and N. Levinson, *Theory of Ordinary Differential Equations*, McGraw-Hill, New York, 1964.

[16] P. Cootner, ed., *The Random Character of Stock Market Prices*, revised ed., MIT Press, Cambridge, Mass., 1967.

[17] A. Cowles, *Can stock market forecasters forecast?* Econometrica, 1 (1933), pp. 309–324.

[18] A. Cowles and H. E. Jones, *Some a posteriori probabilities in stock market action*, Ibid., 5 (1937), pp. 280–294.

[19] A. Cowles, *Common Stock Indexes, 1871–1937*, Principia Press, Ind., 1938.

[20] ———, *A revision of previous conclusions regarding stock price behavior*, Econometrica, 28 (1960), pp. 909–915.

[21] G. Debreu, *Theory of Value*, John Wiley, New York, 1962.

[22] J. W. Dettman, *Mathematical Method in Physics and Engineering*, 2nd ed., McGraw-Hill, New York, 1969.

[23] E. Domar and R. A. Musgrave, *Proportional income taxation and risk-bearing*, Quart. J. Economics, 58 (1944), pp. 384–422.

[24] J. L. Evans, *An analysis of portfolio maintenance*, J. Finance, 25 (1970), pp. 561–572.

[25] E. F. Fama, *The behavior of stock market prices*, J. Business, 38 (1965), pp. 34–105.

[26] E. F. Fama and M. Blume, *Filter rules and stock market trading profits*, Ibid., 39 (1966), pp. 226–241.

[27] E. F. Fama, *Risk, return and equilibrium*, Rep. 5831, Center for Mathematical Studies in Business and Economics, Univ. of Chicago, Chicago, June 1968.

[28] E. F. Fama and R. Roll, *Some properties of symmetric stable distribution*, J. Amer. Statist. Assoc., 63 (1968), pp. 817–836.

[29] E. F. Fama, L. Fisher, M. Jensen and R. Roll, *The adjustment of stock prices to new information*, Internat. Economic Rev., 10 (1969), pp. 1–21.

[30] E. F. Fama, *Multiperiod consumption-investment decisions*, Amer. Economic Rev., 60 (1970), pp. 163–174.

[31] ———, *Efficient capital markets: a review*, Mimeograph, 1971.

[32] M. S. Feldstein, *Mean-variance analysis in the theory of liquidity preference and portfolio selection*, Rev. Economic Studies, 36 (1969), pp. 5–12.

[33] F. M. Fisher, *Identification Problem in Economics*, McGraw-Hill, New York, 1966.

[34] R. Gibrat, *Les Inegalités Economiques*, Paris, 1931.

[35] T. Haavelmo, *The structural implication of a system of simultaneous equations*, Econometrica, 11 (1943), pp. 1–12.

[36] N. H. Hakansson, *Optimal investment and consumption strategies for a class of utility functions*, Doctoral dissertation, University of California at Los Angeles, 1966.

[37] ———, *Optimal investment and consumption strategies under risk for a class of utility functions*, Econometrica, 38 (1970), pp. 587–607.

[38] ———, *Multi-period mean-variance analysis: toward a general theory of portfolio choice*, J. Finance, 26 (1971), pp. 857–884.

[39] J. Hirshleifer, *Investment decision under uncertainty: applications of the state-preference approach*, Quart. J. Economics, 80 (1966), pp. 611–672.

[40] K. Itô, *On stochastic differential equations*, Mem. Amer. Math. Soc., no. 4, New York, 1951.

[41] K. Itô and H. P. McKean, Jr., *Diffusion Process and Their Sample Paths*, Academic Press, New York, 1964.

[42] F. C. JEN, *Multi-period portfolio strategies*, Working paper 108, State University of New York at Buffalo, School of Management, May, 1971.

[43] M. C. JENSEN, *Risk, the pricing of capital assets, and the evaluation of investment portfolios*, J. Business, 42 (1969), pp. 167–247.

[44] ———, *The foundations and current state of capital market theory*, Bell. J. Economics and Management Sci, 3 (1972) (forthcoming).

[45] S. T. KASSOUF, *A theory and an economic model for common stock purchase warrants*, Doctoral dissertation, Columbia University, New York, 1965.

[46] ———, *Stock price random walks: some supporting evidence*, Rev. Economics and Statistics, 50 (1968), pp. 275–278.

[47] J. L. KELLEY, JR., *A new interpretation of information rate*, Bell System Tech. J., 35 (1956), pp. 917–926.

[48] M. G. KENDALL, *The analysis of economic time-series. Part I: Prices*, J. Royal Statist. Soc., 96 (1953), pp. 11–25; reprinted in [16, pp. 85–99].

[49] J. M. KEYNES, *General Theory of Employment, Interest and Money*, Macmillan, London, 1936, pp.154–164.

[50] D. KREPS, J. L. LEBOWITZ AND P. B. LINHART, *A stochastic model of a security market*, AT&T memorandom, December, 1971.

[51] R. KRUIZENGA, *Put and call options: A theoretical and market analysis*, Doctoral dissertation, M.I.T., Cambridge, Mass., 1956.

[52] ———, *Introduction to the option contract*, and *profit returns from purchasing puts and calls*, both in [16, pp. 377–391 and 392–411].

[53] O. LANGE, *On the economic theory of socialism, Part I and Part II*, Rev. Economic Studies, 4 (1936 and 1937), pp. 53–71 and 123–142.

[54] H. A. LATANÉ, *Criteria for choice among risky ventures*, J. Political Economy, 67 (1956), pp. 144–155.

[55] H. A. LATANÉ AND W. E. YOUNG, *Test of portfolio building rules*, J. Finance, 24 (1969), pp. 595–612.

[56] W. W. LEONTIEF, *Verzögerte Angebotsanpassung und partielles Gleichgewicht*. Z. National-ökonomie, 5 (1934), pp. 670–676.

[57] H. E. LELAND, *Dynamic portfolio theory*, Doctoral dissertation, Harvard Univ., Cambridge, Mass., 1968.

[58] A. P. LERNER, *Economic theory and socialist economy*, Rev. Economic Studies, 2 (1934), pp. 51–81.

[59] J. LINTER, *The valuation of risk assets and the solution of risky investments in stock portfolio and capital budgets*, Rev. Economics and Statistics, 47 (1965), pp. 13–37.

[60] ———, *Security prices, risk, and maximal gains from diversification*, J. Finance, 20 (1965), pp. 587–615.

[61] B. B. MANDELBROT, *The valuation of certain speculative prices*. J. Business, 36 (1963), pp. 394–419.

[62] ———, *Forecasts of future prices, unbiased markets and "martingale" models*, Ibid., 39, Special Supplement (1966), pp. 242–255.

[63] B. B. MANDELBROT AND H. M. TAYLOR, *On the distribution of stock price differences*, Operations Res., 15 (1967), pp. 1057–1067.

[64] B. B. MANDELBROT, *When can price be arbitraged efficiently? A limit to the validity of the random walk and martingale models*, Rev. Economics and Statistics, 53 (1971), pp. 225–236.

[65] H. MARKOWITZ, *Portfolio Selection: Efficient Diversification of Investments*, John Wiley, New York, 1959.

[66] J. MARSCHAK, *Probability in the social sciences*, Mathematical Thinking in the Social Sciences, P. Lazarsfeld, ed., Free Press, Glencoe, Ill., 1954, pp. 166–215.

[67] ———, *Rational behavior, uncertain prospects, and measurable utility*, Econometrica, 18 (1950), pp. 111–141.

[68] H. P. McKEAN, JR., *Appendix: a free boundary problem for the heat equation arising from a problem in mathematical economics*, Industrial Management Rev., 6 (1965), pp. 32–39.

[69] ———, *Stochastic Integrals*, Academic Press, New York, 1969.

[70] R. C. MERTON, *Lifetime portfolio selection under uncertainty: the continuous-time case*, Rev. Economics and Statistics, 51 (1969), pp. 247–257.

[71] ——, *Optimum consumption and portfolio rules in a continuous-time model*, J. Economic Theory, 3 (1971), pp. 373–413.

[72] ——, *An intertemporal capital asset pricing model*, Working paper 588-72, Sloan School of Management, M.I.T., Cambridge, Mass., February, 1972; forthcoming in Econometrica.

[73] ——, *Theory of rational option pricing*, Working paper 574-71, Sloan School of Management, M.I.T., Cambridge, Mass., October, 1971.

[74] J. MOSSIN, *Optimal multi-period portfolio policies*, J. Business, 41 (1968), pp. 215–229.

[75] A. B. MOORE, *Some characteristics of changes in common stock prices*, in [16, pp. 139–161].

[76] M. F. M. OSBORNE, *Periodic structure in the Brownian motion of stock prices*, Operations Res., 10 (1962), pp. 345–379; reprinted in [16, pp. 262–296].

[77] V. PARETO, *Cours d'Economie Politique*, 2 vols., Libraire de l'Université, Lausanne, Switzerland, 1897.

[78] E. S. PHELPS, *The accumulations of risky capital: a sequential utility analysis*, Econometrica, 30 (1962), pp. 729–743.

[79] J. W. PRATT, *Risk aversion in the small and in the large*, Ibid., 32 (1964), pp. 122–136.

[80] S. J. PRESS, *A compound events model for security prices*, J. Business, 40 (1968), pp. 317–335.

[81] F. P. RAMSEY, *Truth and probability*, The Foundations of Mathematics and Other Logical Essays, Kegan Paul, London, 1931, pp. 156–198.

[82] P. A. SAMUELSON, *Economics*, 8th ed., McGraw-Hill, New York, 1970.

[83] ——, *The Collected Scientific Papers of Paul A. Samuelson*, vols. I and II, J. E. Stiglitz, ed., M.I.T. Press, Cambridge, Mass., 1966; hereafter abbreviated as CSP I and CSP II.

[84] ——, *The Collected Scientific Papers of Paul A. Samuelson*, vol. III, R. C. Merton, ed., M.I.T. Press, Cambridge, Mass., 1972; hereafter abbreviated as CSP III.

[85] ——, *Probability, utility, and the independence axiom*, Econometrica, 20 (1952), pp. 670–678; reprinted in CSP I, Chap. 4, pp. 137–145.

[86] ——, *Spatial price equilibrium and linear programming*, Amer. Economic Rev., 43 (1953), pp. 283–303; reprinted in CSP II, Chap. 72, pp. 925–945.

[87] ——, *Intertemporal price equilibrium: a prologue to the theory of speculation*, Weltwirtschaftliches Archiv, 79 (1957), pp. 181–219; reprinted in CSP II, Chap. 73, pp. 946–984.

[88] ——, *Risk and uncertainty: a fallacy of large numbers*, Scientia, 57 (1963), pp. 1–6; reprinted in CSP I, Chap. 16, pp. 153–158.

[89] ——, *Proof that properly anticipated prices fluctuate randomly*, Industrial Management Rev., 6 (1965), pp. 41–50; reprinted in CSP III, Chap. 198, pp. 782–790.

[90] ——, *Rational theory of warrant pricing*, Ibid., 6 (1965), pp. 13–32; reprinted in CSP III, Chap. 199, pp. 791–810. Also contains [68, pp. 810–817].

[91] ——, *General proof that diversification pays*, J. Financial and Quantitative Anal., 2 (1967), pp. 1–13; reprinted in CSP III, Chap. 201, pp. 848–860.

[92] ——, *Efficient portfolio selection for Pareto–Lévy investments*, Ibid., 2 (1967), pp. 107–122; reprinted in CSP III, Chap. 202, pp. 861–876.

[93] ——, *Two generalizations of the elasticity of substitution*, Value, Capital and Growth: Papers in Honour of Sir John Hicks, J. N. Wolfe, ed., Edinburgh University Press, Edinburgh, 1968, pp. 469–480; reprinted in CSP III, Chap. 133, pp. 57–70.

[94] ——, *Book review of E. O. Thorp and S. T. Kassouf* [109], J. Amer. Statist. Assoc., 10 (1968), pp. 1049–1051.

[95] P. A. SAMUELSON AND R. C. MERTON, *A complete model of warrant pricing that maximizes utility*, Industrial Management Review, 10 (1969), 2, pp. 17–46; reprinted in CSP III, Chap. 200, pp. 818–847.

[96] P. A. SAMUELSON, *Lifetime portfolio selection by dynamic stochastic programming*, Rev. Economics and Statistics, 51 (1969), pp. 239–246; reprinted in CSP III, Chap. 204, pp. 883–890.

[97] ——, *Classical orbital stability deduced for discrete-time maximum systems*, Western Economic J., 8 (1970), pp. 110–119; reprinted in CSP III, Chap. 158, pp. 328–337.

[98] ——, *The fundamental approximation theorem of portfolio analysis in terms of means, variances and higher moments*, Rev. Economic Studies, 37 (1970), pp. 537–542; reprinted in CSP III, Chap. 203, pp. 877–882.

[99] ——, *Stochastic speculative price*. Proc. Nat. Acad. Sci., 68 (1971), pp. 335–337; reprinted in CSP III, Chap. 206, pp. 894–896.

[100] ———, *The "fallacy" of maximizing the geometric mean in long sequences of investing or gambling*, Ibid., 68 (1971), pp. 2493–2496; reprinted in CSP III, Chap. 207, pp. 897–900.

[101] ———, *Proof that unsuccessful speculators confer less benefit on the rest of society than their losses*, Ibid., 69 (1972), pp. 1230–1233.

[102] L. J. SAVAGE, *The Foundations of Statistics*, John Wiley, New York, 1954.

[103] W. F. SHARPE, *Portfolio Theory and Capital Market*, McGraw-Hill, New York, 1970.

[104] J. P. SHELTON, *The Value Line contest: a test of the predictability of stock-price changes*, J. Business, 40 (1967), pp. 251–269.

[105] ———, *Warrant stock-price relation, Parts I and II*, Financial Analysts J., May–June (1967), pp. 143–151, July–August (1967), pp. 88–99.

[106] C. SPRENKLE, *Warrant prices and indicators of expectations and preferences*, Yale Economic Essays, 1 (1961); reprinted in [16, pp. 412–474].

[107] J. STEINDL, *Random Processes and the Growth of Firms: A Study of the Pareto Law*, Hafner, New York, 1965.

[108] F. TAYLOR, *The guidance of production in a socialist state*, Amer. Economic Rev., 19 (1929), pp. 1–8.

[109] E. D. THORP AND S. T. KASSOUF, *Beat the Market: A Scientific Stock Market System*, Random House, New York, 1967.

[110] E. D. THORP, *Optimal gambling systems for favorable games*, Rev. Internat. Statist. Inst., 37 (1969), pp. 273–293.

[111] J. TOBIN, *Liquidity preference and behavior towards risk*, Rev. Economic Studies, 25 (1958), pp. 65–86.

[112] ———, *The theory of portfolio selection*, The Theory of Interest Rates, F. Hahn and F. Brechling, eds., Macmillan, London, 1965.

[113] J. VON NEUMANN AND O. MORGENSTERN, *Theory of Games and Economic Behavior*, 2nd ed., Princeton University Press, Princeton, N.J., 1947.

[114] J. B. WILLIAMS, *Speculation and the carry-over*, Quart. J. Economics, 50 (1936), pp. 436–455.

[115] H. WORKING, *Theory of inverse carrying charge in future markets*, J. Farm Economics, 30 (1948), pp. 1–28.

[116] ———, *Future trading and hedging*, Amer. Economic Rev., 43 (1953), pp. 314–343.

[117] ———, *New ideas and methods for price research*, J. Farm Economics, 38 (1958), pp. 1427–1436.

[118] ———, *A theory of anticipating prices*, Amer. Economic Rev., 48 (1958), pp. 189–199.

[119] ———, *Note on the correlation of first differences of average in a random chain*, Econometrica, 28 (1960), pp. 916–918; reprinted in [16, pp. 129–131].

241

Proof that properly discounted present values of assets vibrate randomly

Paul A. Samuelson

Institute Professor
Massachusetts Institute of Technology

Even the best investors seem to find it hard to do better than the comprehensive common-stock averages, or better on the average than random selection among stocks of comparable variability. Examination of historical samples of percentage changes in a stock's price show that, when these relative price changes are properly adjusted for expected dividends paid out, they are more or less indistinguishable from white noise; or, at the least, their expected percentage movements constitute a driftless random walk (or a random walk with mean drift specifiable in terms of an interest factor appropriate to the stock's variability or riskiness). The present contribution shows that such observable patterns can be deduced rigorously from a model which hypothesizes that a stock's present price is set at the expected discounted value of its future dividends, where the future dividends are supposed to be random variables generated according to any general (but known) stochastic process. This fundamental theorem follows by an easy superposition applied to the 1965 Samuelson theorem that properly anticipated futures prices fluctuate randomly—i.e., constitute a martingale sequence, or a generalized martingale with specifiable mean drift. Examples demonstrate that even when the economy is not free to wander randomly, intelligent speculation is able to whiten the spectrum of observed stock-price changes. A subset of investors might have better information or modes of analysis and get above average gains in the random-walk model; and the model's underlying probabilities could be shaped by fundamentalists' economic forces.

■ Consider a random vector sequence: $\ldots, X_t, X_{t+1}, \ldots, X_{t+T}, \ldots$. The dividend of a particular common stock, say General Motors, might be the ith component of that vector: $\ldots, x_{it}, \ldots, x_{i\,t+T}, \ldots$; and the jth component might, as in 1965 Samuelson,[1] denote the price of spot wheat at time t. Under some known stochastic process generating the random variables, there will be defined basic conditional probabilities

$$\text{Prob}\{X_{t+T} \leq x_{t+T} \mid X_t = x_t, X_{t-1} = x_{t-1}, \ldots\}$$
$$= P_T(x_{t+T}; x_t, x_{t-1}, \ldots; t) \quad (1)$$

Paul A. Samuelson received the B.A. from the University of Chicago in 1935 and the M.A. and the Ph.D. from Harvard University in 1936 and 1941, respectively. He is Institute Professor at the Massachusetts Institute of Technology, where his research embraces analytic micro and macro economics.

The author owes thanks to the National Science Foundation for financial aid, and to Kathryn Kaepplein for valuable assistance.

[1] See [3].

and conditional expected values

$$E\{X_{t+T} \mid X_t = x_t, X_{t-1} = x_{t-1}, \ldots\} = {}_{t+T}Y_t$$

$$= \int_{-\infty}^{\infty} x P_T(dx; x_t, x_{t-1}, \ldots; t)$$

$$= {}_{t+T}F_t(x_t, x_{t-1}, \ldots) \tag{2}$$

$$E\{{}_{t+T}Y_{t+1} \mid X_t = x_t, X_{t-1} = x_{t-1}, \ldots\}$$

$$= \int_{-\infty}^{\infty} {}_{t+T}F_{t+1}(x_{t+1}, x_t, \ldots) P_1(dx_{t+1}; x_t, x_{t-1}, \ldots; t)$$

$$= E\{{}_{t+T}Y_{t+1} \mid {}_{t+T}Y_t\} \quad \text{for short.} \tag{3}$$

Here a Stieltjes integral is written as $\int_{-\infty}^{\infty} f(x)g(dx)$; and when x is a vector, a *multiple* Stieltjes integral is written as $\int_{-\infty}^{\infty} f(x)g(dx)$.

The two basic 1965 theorems can now be recapitulated.

Theorem 1: For $\tau > t$, the sequence $({}_\tau Y_t, {}_\tau Y_{t+1}, \ldots)$ has the martingale property

$$E\{{}_\tau Y_{t+k} \mid {}_\tau Y_t\} \equiv {}_\tau Y_t, \quad (k = 1, 2, \ldots, \tau - 1). \tag{4}$$

Theorem 2: For the "discounted" sequence,

$${}_\tau Z_t \equiv {}_\tau Y_t / \prod_{j=1}^{\tau-t} \lambda_{t+j}$$

$$E\{{}_\tau Z_{t+1} \mid {}_\tau Z_t\} = \lambda_{t+1} {}_\tau Z_t \tag{5}$$

$$E\{Z_{t+k} \mid {}_\tau Z_t\} = \lambda_{t+1}\lambda_{t+2}\ldots\lambda_{t+k} {}_\tau Z_t.$$

2. Expected present discounted values

■ Suppose that the ith component of the vector X_t represents the dividend of a given stock that is to be paid out at time t. Then if $\lambda_{t+1} - 1$ is the interest rate paid at the end of period t on each dollar invested at time t, and if x_{it} were a nonrandom sequence, the classical Fisher present discounted-value rule of capitalization (slightly generalized) defines the value of a stock as

$$V_t = \sum_{T=1}^{\infty} (x_{i\ t+T} / \prod_{j=1}^{T} \lambda_{t+j}) \tag{6}$$

$$V_{t+1} = \lambda_{t+1} V_t - x_{i\ t+1}. \tag{7}$$

If $\lambda_t \equiv 1 + r$, the above denominator takes on the more familiar form $(1 + r)^T$.

But now revert to the supposition that $x_{i\ t+T}$, and hence V_t, are random variables; and assume that *the market capitalizes the stock at the expected value of V_t*, namely at v_t defined by

$$v_t = E\{V_t \mid X_t = x_t, X_{t-1} = x_{t-1}, \ldots\} = \sum_{T=1}^{\infty} {}_{t+T}Z_t \tag{8}$$

$$E\{v_{t+1} \mid v_t\} = \sum_{T=2}^{\infty} E\{{}_{t+T}Z_{t+1} \mid {}_{t+T}Z_t\}. \tag{9}$$

Now, by simple use of the principle of superposition, we can derive from (5) our needed generalization or corollary of Theorem 2, namely that stock prices themselves have a martingale or random-walk property.

Theorem 3. If stocks are capitalized at their expected present discounted values defined by (8) and (9), then

$$E\{v_{t+1} | v_t\} = \lambda_{t+1} v_t - E\{x_{i\ t+1} | X_t = x_t, X_{t-1} = x_{t-1}, \ldots\}. \quad (10)$$

Clearly (10) is the fundamental stochastic generalization of the fundamental nonstochastic relation (7). Note that it holds even for the Pareto-Lévy distributions that lack a finite variance but possess a defined first moment.

Proof of the theorem follows immediately from substituting Theorem 2's relation (5) into each term of (9) and then identifying what remains by use of (8).

■ Suppose that the ratio of dividend to earnings is a constant payout fraction. Let earnings at time t be proportional to a random variable satisfying an independent multiplicative relation. Then we can deduce that dividends will be generated by the stochastic process

3. Example of Brownian ramble

$$x_{i\ t+T} = x_{it} Z_1 \ldots Z_T, \quad (11)$$

where the Z's are positive random variables subject to uniform and independent probability distributions

$$\text{Prob}\{Z_i \leq z\} = P(z) \quad (12)$$

$$E\{Z_i\} = \theta, \ E\{x_{i\ t+T}\} = \theta^T x_{it}$$

$$E\{\log Z_i\} = \mu < \log \theta, \ \text{Var}\{\log Z_i\} = \sigma^2.$$

Finally, assume a constant interest rate, $\lambda_t \equiv 1 + r > \theta$, which is large enough to keep v_t a finite converging series

$$v_t = x_{it}\left[\frac{\theta}{1+r} + \frac{\theta^2}{(1+r)^2} + \cdots\right] = x_{it}\theta(1 + r - \theta)^{-1} \quad (13)$$

$$\text{Prob}\{v_{t+1}/v_t \leq z\} = P(z) \quad (14)$$

$$E\{v_{t+1} | v_t\} = \theta v_t \quad \text{from (12)}$$

$$= (1 + r)v_t - E\{x_{i\ t+1}\} \quad \text{from (10).}$$

Actually this model generates the economic or multiplicative Brownian motion of Osborne and Samuelson[2] with the asymptotic log-normal distribution

$$\lim_{T \to \infty} \text{Prob}\left\{a \leq \frac{\log(v_{t+T}/v_t) - \mu T}{T^{\frac{1}{2}}\sigma} \leq b\right\} = \frac{1}{\sqrt{2\pi}}\int_a^b e^{-\frac{1}{2}s^2} ds \quad (15)$$

and its price changes have the white-noise property

$$E\{\log v_{t+1} - \log v_t - \mu\} \equiv 0 \quad (16)$$

$$\text{covariance}\{\log v_{t+T}, \log v_t\} \equiv 0, \quad T > 0. \quad (17)$$

Granger[3] has arrived at similar results, including the interesting case where variables are generated as the (possibly infinite) sum of

[2] See [2] and [4], respectively.
[3] In [1].

white-noise random variables. Shiller[4] also offers valuable related contributions, particularly in connection with prediction algorithms and also the term structure of interest rates.

4. Probabilities that obey economic law

■ A second model provides an interesting contrast to the endless wandering of the above model. In it, earnings and dividends continue to have a probability distribution that stays within the same general central range; thus dividends have an ergodic distribution that is determined by economic law, by the fundamentals of the industry's resource scarcities and the capacity of its goods to meet peoples' needs and demands. But, and this is the beauty of the present martingale process, the movement of the stock price that capitalizes these determinate dividends is itself a white-noise generalized martingale!

Specifically, let dividends satisfy a damped autoregressive process

$$\log x_{i\,t+1} = a \log x_{it} + \eta_t, \quad |a| < 1, \tag{18}$$

where η_t is an independently and uniformly distributed random variable, with cov $(\eta_t, \eta_{t\pm k}) = 0$ for $k \neq 0$.

Then, for $|a| < 1$,

$$\lim_{T \to \infty} \text{Prob}\{x_{i\,t+T} \leq x \,|\, x_{it} = y\} = \lim_{T \to \infty} P_T(x, y) = P(x), \tag{19}$$

a limiting ergodic probability distribution that is independent of initial value for x_{it} and which is not log-normal.

Even though dividends and their changes have a nonwhite spectrum, with nonvanishing covariance $\{x_{it}, x_{i\,t\pm k}\}$, the martingale property of Theorem 3's (10) will still be valid. Thus, if the corporation had zero dividend payments over a time interval, and the λ_{t+j} discount factor were at or near unity, the spectrum of $v_{t+k} - v_t$ would be white, in the sense of zero first-order autocorrelation and zero expected values.

The present case of an ergodic probability distribution differs significantly from the log-normal models upon which so much of warrant and option valuations has been based. As applied to calls, which are typically warrants *protected* for dividend payouts, the difference is not so great. Indeed, as my colleague Robert Merton reminds me, even for the present model, once we ask what will be the cumulative value over time of a portfolio that invests back all dividends in this company's common stock, the relevant probability distribution derived from (19) will have properties much like that of (15). In fact, in the following special case, we shall have exactly the same form as (15).

Suppose the corporation selects its optimal algebraic dividend payout so as to leave within the company only that sum of wealth or money which can optimally earn more there than elsewhere. (If the indicated dividend is negative, think of the corporation as selling new shares; for that matter, transaction costs and tax complications aside, a corporation might choose always simply to buy shares *algebraically* in the open market, so that any positive dividend situation would work itself out in each of my shares' becoming more valuable.) Suppose further, for simplicity, that *ex ante* always the

⁴ In [5].

same total wealth is to be left in the company: all the random events of the period just past show up in the variable algebraic dividend. Finally, let the relevant interest rates be constant, $\lambda_t \equiv 1+r$. Then each dollar left invested and reinvested in this company will be subject to the multiplicative probability distribution of (11)'s form; and (15)'s log-normal limit will apply. Even if the amount the company is to reinvest is not completely independent in probability from period to period, the white martingale property assures zero auto-correlation and unbiased means; consequently a slight generalization of the central-limit theorem, to unautocorrelated rather than independent added variates, ought still to enable derivation of a log-normal limit.

■ One person, too small to affect market prices appreciably, could make systematic speculative gains in excess of those shown in (10), if he had more or better information or a better way of evaluating existing information. This would enable him to improve upon the probability distribution of (1). Thus, suppose at time t he could know x_{t+1} exactly, or have a more accurate way of estimating it than from $P_1(x_{t+1}; x_t, x_{t+1}, \ldots; t)$.

5. Qualifications

An example would be where this investor had private knowledge, or private recognition, of an additional datum m_t, in terms of which he has the probability distribution $Q_1(x_{t+1}; x_t, x_{t-1}, \ldots; m_t; t)$ with the property that $P_1(x_{t+1}; x_t, x_{t-1}, \ldots; t)$ is the "marginal distribution" of $Q_1(\ )$ with m_t integrated out. Suppose

$$P_1(x_{t+1}; x_t, x_{t-1}, \ldots; t) \equiv \int_{-\infty}^{\infty} Q_1(x_{t+1}; x_t, x_{t-1}, \ldots; dm_t; t), \quad (20)$$

and

$$Q_1(x_{t+1}; x_t, x_{t-1}, \ldots; m_t; t)P_1(x_{t+1}; x_t, x_{t-1}, \ldots; t)^{-1}$$
$$\neq \text{ a function of } m_t \text{ alone.}$$

Then knowledge of m_t gives extra predictive power of $x_{i\,t+T}$ and of V_{t+k}. Having such knowledge when others do not is highly profitable, since depending upon the level of m_t, the stock becomes an especially good or an especially bad buy. Of course, if this private knowledge becomes widespread, the relevant $P_1(\ )$ will become $Q_1(\ )$ itself, with Theorem 3 and (10) holding in terms of it, and with m_t being just one more element in the relevant x_t. In summary, the present study shows (a) there is no incompatibility in principle between the so-called random-walk model and the fundamentalists' model, and (b) there is no incompatibility in principle between behavior of stocks' prices that behave like random walk at the same time that there exist subsets of investors who can do systematically better than the average investors.

References

1. GRANGER, C. W. J. "Some Implications of the Fundamentalist's Valuation Model." May 25, 1973 paper for Berlin Workshop on International Capital Markets, September 1973.

2. OSBORNE, M. F. M. "Brownian Motion in the Stock Market." *Operations Research*, Vol. 7, No. 2 (March–April 1959), pp. 145–173. Also in P. H. Cootner, *The Random Character of Stock Market Prices*, Cambridge, M.I.T. Press, 1967, pp. 100–128.

3. SAMUELSON, P. A. "Proof That Properly Anticipated Prices Fluctuate Randomly." *Industrial Management Review*, Vol. 6, No. 2, pp. 41–49. This is reproduced as Chapter 198 in Samuelson, *Collected Scientific Papers, Volume III*, Cambridge, M.I.T. Press, 1972.

4. ———. "A Rational Theory of Warrant Pricing." *Industrial Management Review*, Vol. 6, No. 2, pp. 13–39. This is reproduced as Chapter 197 in *Collected Scientific Papers, Volume III*.

5. SHILLER, R. J. "Rational Expectations and the Structure of Interest Rates." Unpublished Ph.D. dissertation, M.I.T., 1972.

242

IS REAL-WORLD PRICE A TALE TOLD BY THE IDIOT OF CHANCE?

Paul A. Samuelson*

Professor Rutledge's investigation[1] on the variability of prices of a futures contract as it approaches its terminal date is a model of excellence. Because it touches on an issue that is at the heart of economics, I venture to add a few thoughts.

Law or Chance?

Is the price of wheat or bread a mere random walk? If we wait long enough, should we feel no surprise if a pound of bread sells for a penny or a billion dollars? For a trillion Cadillacs or 0.01 of a Cadillac?

If the sequence of prices is truly a Wiener or white-noise process, with logarithmic price changes independently and uniformly distributed through time, then economic price can truly wander anywhere in enough time. Just as west of the Pecos there is no law, in the Wiener long run we are not only all dead, but are dead in a universe not subject to any economic law, subject to no pull toward normal value or cost.

Few economists can cheerfully believe in the random, lawless world. That is why they at first bristled when statisticians like Maurice Kendall[2] began

Received for publication December 30, 1974. Accepted for publication January 21, 1975.

* I owe thanks to the National Science Foundation for financial aid and to Kate Crowley for editorial assistance.

[1] D. J. S. Rutledge, "A Note on the Variability of Futures Prices," this REVIEW, this issue (Feb. 1976).

[2] M. G. Kendall, "The Analysis of Economic-Time Series, Part I: Prices," *Journal of the Royal Statistical Society*, 96 (1953), pp. 11–25. See P. A. Samuelson, "Mathematics of Speculative Prices," 12th von Neumann Lecture (reproduced in *Mathematical Topics in Economic Theory and Computation*, SIAM, 1972), which among its more than

to mutter about white noise. Later, after more economists had been impressed by the quasi-random appearance of time series of speculative price, they reasoned, "If you can't beat 'em, join 'em and work the other side of the street." Economists embraced random walks of speculative prices *as a sign that economic law was alive and working in the marketplace of speculation.*

But still, but still . . . Even if one had to go to the stake for it, walking to the stake, an economist would have to whisper under his breath, "Dammit, the price of bread, the wage of an hour's unskilled labor, the rate of earnable interest or profit, the velocity of circulation of currency, aren't going to wander anywhere and everywhere at the *same* rate — even if the seismographs of the econometricians aren't sensitive enough to pick up the difference."

To the Rescue

At this point, my 1965 article on how anticipated speculative prices vibrate randomly[3] enabled the economist to mend his split personality: to reconcile his simultaneous belief in ultimate economic law and in efficient speculative markets (finally given a meaningful definition). What I was able to show there and in its cited 1973 sequel is this:

> A determinate trend in the long-run normal price of bread is quite compatible with the fact that speculators will discount in advance all discernible events and ensure that the violin string of speculative prices will fluctuate stochastically (and with only the profit-bias needed to coax out risk-taking) in response to the stochastic plucking of new random events and information.

---

one hundred references cites relevant publications by L. Bachelier, Holbrook Working, A. Cowles, E. F. Fama, B. Mandelbrot, R. C. Merton, and many others.

[3] P. A. Samuelson, "Proof that Properly Anticipated Prices Fluctuate Randomly," *Industrial Management Review* 6 (now *Sloan Management Review*) (Spring 1965), pp. 41–50, reprinted in P. A. Samuelson, *Collected Scientific Papers* III, chap. 198, pp. 782–790 (Cambridge, Mass: M.I.T. Press, 1972, ed., R. C. Merton); and "Proof That Properly Discounted Present Values of Assets Vibrate Randomly," *Bell Journal of Economics and Management Sciences,* 4 (Autumn 1973), pp. 369–374.

Similarly, GM stock price vibrates stochastically, but it is not the case that it could be anywhere with equal probability in a long time from now: if autos can command only some limited fraction of the GNP and GM some limited fraction of the auto market, the fact that GNP in real terms is limited by resources and technology implies that GM stock in the long run obeys an ergodic probability distribution which is not a Wiener process that spreads out indefinitely with the square root of elapsed time.

An Exact Ergodic Model

For readers not familiar with the concept of an ergodic distribution, I refer to my 1971 model[4] in which a competitive grain is subject to random harvest and stationary demand. Call $[\ldots, p_{t-1}, p_t, p_{t+1}, \ldots]$ the sequence of spot prices of physical grain or their logarithms. Let

$$\text{Probability } [p_{t+T} \leqq p \text{ given that } p_t = p_0] \quad (1)$$
$$= \Pi_T(p; p_0).$$

Then in the "damped" 1971 model,

$$\lim_{T \to \infty} \Pi_T(p; p_0) = \Pi(p), \quad (2)$$

independently of initial current price, p_0.

$\Pi(p)$ is the asymptotic ergodic probability distribution and constitutes the proper stochastic generalization of a normal equilibrium level, p^*. (As the variability of spot-price changes goes to zero, the ergodic distribution narrows to a determinate equilibrium value, around which actual price vibrates.)

But note this. Prices of futures contracts are given, not by $[\ldots, p_t, \ldots]$, but by the terminating sequence $[\ldots, y_{\theta,t}, y_{\theta,t+1}, \ldots, y_{\theta,\theta-1}, y_{\theta,\theta} = p_\theta]$, where $y_{\theta,t}$ is defined as the price quoted at time t for a grain futures contract calling for delivery of spot grain at time θ, which is $\theta - t$ time periods ahead. (Note: What I defined in 1965 as $Y(T,t)$ is the same thing as $y_{t+T,t}$ defined here.) Because the spot grain can be used to deliver against the futures contract, we have the final equivalence that links up the stochastic series of y's with that of p's.

[4] P. A. Samuelson, "Stochastic Speculative Price," *Proceedings of the National Academy of Sciences* 68 (Feb. 1971), pp. 335–337, reprinted in *Collected Scientific Papers* III, chap. 206, pp. 894–896.

If we adopt one of my 1965 hypotheses, that first one of zero risk premium which Rutledge tests, we posit:

$$y_{\theta,t} = \text{Expected Value at } t \text{ of } p_\theta$$
$$= E[p_\theta | p_t, p_{t-1}, \dots]. \tag{3}$$

In that case, it was easy to show that the finite time sequence of y's shows zero mean gain or loss, even though there exists a definite pull of normal value to bias the movements of spot prices themselves, or p's. Thus, the y's are shown to be what is technically called a "martingale," which is the proper way to interpret the loose phrase, "a random walk."

The variance of the y-changes is, however, another matter. There is no reason why it should be constant from period to period. Indeed, if we contemplate very long-lived futures contracts that will not mature for a very long time, we can deduce from the existence of (1)'s ergodic probability distribution and certain regularity conditions on (1) and certain regularity conditions on (1)'s rate of convergence, the strong result

$$\lim_{T \to \infty} \text{var} \left[y_{\theta, \theta - T + 1} - y_{\theta, \theta - T} \right] = 0. \tag{4}$$

This states unequivocally that near futures contracts show more variability than (sufficiently far) distant ones — *which seems in contrast to the fact that the variance of our guesses for distant spot prices is somewhat greater than the variance of our guesses for nearby spot prices.*[5]

There is no paradox or conflict between these opposite-sounding statements once one grasps the 1965 analysis.

Testing the Pudding

What light do the present Rutledge tests throw on the basic issues of economic law? If his basic data and tests had high power to help answer the

---

[5] See the Mathematical Appendix for the autorecursive stochastic-linear case. In P. A. Samuelson, "Optimality of Sluggish Predictors under Ergodic Probabilities," *International Economic Review* (Feb. 1976), I justify by means of the hog-cycle cobweb model the general fact alluded to at the end of the present appendix, that present predictions of the future should *rationally* be more sluggish than the actual future will turn out to be.

question we want answered, and if we take his findings literally, they would seem to suggest a fifty-fifty answer: Economic law may hold for silver and cocoa, but not necessarily for wheat and soybean oil.

Although my own guess would have been that 1970 wheat was *more* subject to economic law than 1970 silver (for reasons not worth mentioning here), Rutledge's lack of support for economic law, as I have phrased that concept, is I think typical of what most econometric exercises have hitherto suggested. From Holbrook Working's basic Stanford wheat studies of half a century ago to the present date, most commodity and stock relative price changes have displayed a vague Wienerish look of random and Gaussian independence.

Still, under my breath and without implying any criticism of the vast econometric literature, I have to affirm belief in economic law. Applying tests to *short-run* changes is *not*, I would think, a powerful way of discriminating between the basic antinomies I have been discussing.[6] To most children the world does appear flat: no playground experience denies that hypothesis. Yet the world is actually round. Accumulating the barely perceptible angle changes of the earth's surface does in the end add up to $360°$ and not $0°$!

I consign to a mathematical appendix elucidation of the general linear stochastic case, where the problem of law reduces not so much to monotonicity of variance as to the existence of damped roots and *ultimate* monotonicity.

MATHEMATICAL APPENDIX

My 1965 paper gave as an example the first-order linear autoregressive model for spot prices:

$$p_{t+1} = a\, p_t + u_t \tag{A1}$$

where $\{u_t\}$ stands for a sequence of independently and uniformly distributed variables, independent of the distribution of $(u_t, u_{t-1}, \ldots, p_t, p_{t-1}, \ldots)$.

[6] None of this implies any criticism of Rutledge's analysis, which was not directed towards cosmic questions of determinacy in economics, and which does well what it set out to do, namely to test whether variance per unit time of futures is systematically greater a few months before maturity date or several months before.

Rutledge adjoins for analysis the special second-order difference equation:

$$p_{t+2} - (1 + \beta)p_{t+1} + \beta p_t = u_t \qquad (A2)$$

where $\{u_t\}$ has the same properties of independence and time invariance, and where presumably $|\beta| < 1$ so that the system is not strongly anti-damped.

By examining the characteristic quadratic equation associated with (A2)'s difference equation, we see that this system is *not* damped, having a root equal to unity in virtue of Rutledge's formulation in terms of price *differences* only; and in consequence of this lack of dampening, even when $\beta \neq 0$, we do find that the absolute level of spot price will wander stochastically without being pulled back to any equilibrium zone. Thus,

$$\lambda^2 - (1 + \beta)\lambda + \beta = (\lambda - 1)(\lambda - \beta) = 0. \quad (A3)$$

I propose to dispose of the most general linear case involving a whole vector of variables, P_t, namely

$$P_{t+1} = P_t A + U_t \qquad (A4)$$

where P_t is a 1-by-n row vector, A is a square n-by-n matrix, and U_t a sequence of row vectors of n random variables with joint probability distributions that are as before independent and uniform through time, and have finite variances and covariances.

In order that this be a determinate, non-wandering system, it is necessary and sufficient that all of the characteristic roots of the matrix A be less than one in absolute value (including any complex roots, of course). In other words, "damped stability" requires that determinant $[A - \lambda I] = (\lambda_1 - \lambda) \ldots (\lambda_n - \lambda) = 0$,

$$|\lambda_n| \leqslant |\lambda_{n-1}| \leqslant \ldots \leqslant |\lambda_1| < 1, \qquad (A5)$$
$$\lim_{T \to \infty} A^T = 0.$$

In that case, there will exist an asymptotic ergodic probability distribution as defined in (A2), namely,

$$\text{Prob } [P_{t+T} \leqslant P | P_t = P_0] = \Pi_T(P; P_0)$$
$$\lim_{T \to \infty} \Pi_T(P; P_0) = \Pi(P).$$

$$(A6)$$

A special case of (A4) is given by

$$p_{t+n} = c_1 p_{t+n-1} + \ldots + c_n p_t + \{u_t\}. \qquad (A7)$$

This covers both the 1965 (A1) and Rutledge's (A2). For (A2) we find, after some straightforward calculations

$$V_T = \text{var } [y_{\theta, \theta - T - 1} - y_{\theta, \theta - T}], \, (T = 1, 2, \ldots)$$
$$= \dot{w}_T^2 \, \text{var } [u_t] = w_T^2 \sigma^2 \qquad (A8)$$

where w_T satisfies the same difference equation as

p_t, namely (A7), but with special canonical initial conditions:

$$w_{T+n} = c_1 w_{T+n-1} + \ldots + c_n w_T$$
$$(w_0, w_{-1}, \ldots, w_{-n+1}) = (1, 0, \ldots, 0). \tag{A9}$$

When the system is damped, we have

$$\lim_{T \to \infty} w_T = a_1 \lambda_1{}^T [(a_2/a_1)(\lambda_2/\lambda_1)^T + \ldots] = 0. \tag{A10}$$

This justifies the general statement:

Theorem: For every damped system,

$$P_{t+1} = P_t A + U_{t+1}$$

very distant futures have less per-period variance than nearby ones; indeed zero variance is the limit as $T \to \infty$. (But this does not deny that as T first grows, V_T can transiently rise.)

Here is a brief proof. By definitions

$$P_{t+T} = P_t A^T + U_{t+1} A^{T-1} + \cdots$$
$$+ U_{t+T-1} A + U_{t+T} \tag{A11}$$
$$Y_{t+T,t} = E[P_{t+T}|P_t] = P_t A^T + 0$$
$$+ \ldots + 0 \tag{A12}$$
$$\text{var}\,\{Y_{t+T,t+1} - Y_{t+T,t}\} = \text{var}\,\{P_{t+1} A^{T-1} - P_t A^T\}$$
$$= \text{var}\,\{P_t A^T + U_{t+1} A^{T-1} - P_t A^T\}$$
$$= \text{var}\,\{U_{t+1} A^{T-1}\} \to 0 \text{ as } T \to \infty \text{ and } A^{T-1} \to 0. \tag{A13}$$

For max $|\lambda_i| = |\lambda_1| < 1$, clearly A^{T-1} becomes small as T becomes large and the theorem is proved.

For $|\lambda_1| > 1$, we have the possible, albeit paradoxical, case where the distant futures contract imposes more current risk per period than a nearby future, and even indefinitely large risk as the time horizon grows indefinitely large. If $\lambda_1 = 1$ and $0 < |\lambda_2| < 1$, as with Rutledge, the riskiness grows, but grows more slowly, converging to a maximum variance per period.

To handle the nth order recursive system involving a single variable, as in (A7), let A be a companion matrix

$$A = \begin{bmatrix} 0 & 0 & \ldots & 0 & c_n \\ 1 & 0 & \ldots & 0 & c_{n-1} \\ 0 & 1 & \ldots & 0 & c_{n-2} \\ & \cdot & & & \\ & \cdot & & & \\ & \cdot & & & \\ 0 & 0 & \ldots & 1 & c_1 \end{bmatrix}, A^k = [a_{ij}{}^k], k \gtrless 0$$

Then by the Cayley-Hamilton theorem

$$A^{n+k} - \sum_1{}^n c_j A^{n-j+k} = 0, k \gtrless 0$$

and

$$w_k \equiv a_{nn}{}^k, (w_0, w_{-1}, \ldots, w_{-n+1})$$
$$= (1, 0, \ldots, 0).$$

Here is a numerical example of a damped system of the second order, where economic law does prevail, but yet a Rutledge test would correctly show that $V_2 > V_1$:

$$p_{t+2} = .1\, p_{t+1} + .2\, p_t + \{u_t\}$$
$$(\lambda^2 - .1\lambda - .2) = (\lambda - .5)(\lambda + .4) \qquad \text{(A14)}$$
$$9w_T = 4(.5)^T + 5(-.4)^T, \lim_{T \to \infty} w_T = 0$$
$$V_1 = (.1)^2\sigma^2 < (.21)^2\sigma^2 = V_2 > V_3$$
$$= (.041)^2\sigma^2 > V_{3+k}.$$

Note that for any root anti-damped, so that $|\lambda_1| > 1$, V_T eventually grows exponentially with T. In Rutledge's case where $\lambda_1 = 1$, V_T does grow with T but converges to a constant level, as one might intuitively expect of any system involving only first differences, namely,

$$\Delta p_{t+n} = \sum_{1}^{n-1} a_j \Delta p_{t+n-j} + \{u_t\}$$

where

$$\lambda^{n-1} - \sum_{1}^{n-1} a_j \lambda^{n-1-j} = (\lambda - \lambda_2)$$
$$\ldots (\lambda - \lambda_n)$$
$$|\lambda_n| \leqslant \ldots \leqslant |\lambda_2| < 1.$$

The moral is that for a certain number of periods near maturity, variability may "transiently" reverse its direction; but ultimately, in a damped system, the variability does decline steadily with distance from maturity.

This result is reasonable. Consider the price of cocoa in July 1999. Let 1 month pass, as December 1975 turns into January 1976. How different will be your evaluation and mine of that ultimate 1999 price? But, by contrast, consider the price of cocoa in March 1976. Surely we shall learn much about *it* as our 3-months horizon turns into a 2-months horizon.

Rutledge and I can't test this common sense relation because, even though in Arrow's treatises there is sense to a 1975 quotation for a 1999 futures, in the real world there are "indivisible" costs that render such markets non-viable.

Still, even if we can't measure something econometrically, we may still have strong grounds for believing in it—which is fortunate, since there is so little that can as yet be given decisive econometric testing.

478

243

Challenge to judgment

Perhaps there really are *managers who can outperform the market consistently – logic would suggest that they exist. But they are remarkably well-hidden.*

Paul A. Samuelson

Once upon a time there was one world of investment — the world of *practical* operators in the stock and bond markets. Now there are two worlds — the same old practical world, and the new world of the academics with their mathematical stochastic processes.

These worlds are still light-years apart: as far apart as the distance from New York to Cambridge; or, exaggerating a bit, as far apart as the vast width of the Charles River between the Harvard Business School and the Harvard Yard. Perhaps there has been in recent years some discernible rate of convergence between these disparate worlds. In any case, I would expect the future to show some further approach between them.

Indeed, to reveal my bias, the ball is in the court of the practical men: it is the turn of the Moun-

tain to take a first step toward the theoretical
Mohammed.

CAN ANYONE PERFORM?

Let me explain. If you oversimplify the debate,
it can be put in the form of the question,

Resolved, that the best of money managers
cannot be demonstrated to be able to deliver
the goods of superior portfolio-selection performance.

Any jury that reviews the evidence, and there
is a great deal of relevant evidence, must at least
come out with the Scottish verdict:

Superior investment performance is un-
proved.

Let me not be misunderstood. The Morgan
Bank people did do better in certain years than the
average mutual fund. That is not in doubt. Nor is it
denied that the T. Rowe Price organization achieved
greater increments of wealth in certain years than did
many other organizations. And both of these may
well turn out to perform better than the market as a
whole in the future. Yet, recall that there were years
when the Dreyfus Fund, or the Enterprise Fund, or
Fidelity Funds seemed greatly to outperform the
mob. And there were other years when they didn't.

What is at issue is not whether, as a matter of
logic or brute fact, *there could exist a subset of the decision makers in the market capable of doing better than the
averages on a repeatable, sustainable basis.* There is
nothing in the mathematics of random walks or
Brownian movements that (a) *proves* this to be impossible, or (b) *postulates* that it is in fact impossible.

The crucial point is that when investigators —
like Irwin Friend, William Sharpe, Jack Treynor,
James Lorie, Fischer Black, and Myron Scholes, or
any Foundation treasurer of fair-minded and serious
intent — look to identify those minority groups or
methods endowed with sustainable superior investment prowess, they are quite unable to find them.
The only honest conclusion is to agree that a loose
version of the "efficient market" or "random walk"

hypothesis accords with the facts of life. This truth, be it emphasized, is a truth about New York (and Chicago, and Omaha); and it is *as* true in New York as in Cambridge.

DEADWEIGHT TRANSACTION COSTS

This does not say that many people, or even most people, are not capable of frittering away the funds given them. To lose money, all you have to do is flip a coin, buying GM on heads and selling it on tails. That way you'll do worse than the averages, and worse even than holding GM or avoiding it. The money you lose — and the odds are overwhelmingly against you — will go to lower the losses of your hard-pressed broker. Similarly, the transaction volume generated by the non-random decisions of the vast majority of the big and small investors, who all *think* they have "flair" but do not demonstrably have it, serves only to suck economic resources out of useful GNP activities like osteopathy and rock singing into broker solicitations and bookkeeping.

This is not a condemnation of market activity: even if eight out of ten transactions are wasteful, who is to say which are the two that are not! It is, however, a useful hint to most pension and trust managers that their clients would in all likelihood be ahead if their turnover rates were halved and their portfolios were more broadly diversified. They also serve who only sit and hold; but I suppose the fees to be earned by such sensible and prosaic behavior are less than from essaying to give it that old post-college try.

EQUALITY OF AVERAGE AND ALL

What logic can demonstrate is that not everybody, nor even the average person, can do better than the comprehensive market averages. That would contradict the tautology that the whole is the sum of its parts.

What statistics can suggest is this: If you select at random a list of, say, 100 stocks and buy them *with weights proportional to their respective total outstanding market values*, although your sample's performance will not *exactly* duplicate that of a comprehensive market average, it will come close to doing so — closer than if you throw a dart at only one stock, but of course not quite as close as with a sample of 200, 300, or all the stocks available in the marketplace.

EUTHANASIA OF PERFORMERS

Do I really believe what I have been saying? I would like to believe otherwise. But a respect for evidence compels me to incline toward the hypothesis that most portfolio decision makers should go out of business — take up plumbing, teach Greek, or help produce the annual GNP by serving as corporate executives. Even if this advice to drop dead is good advice, it obviously is not counsel that will be eagerly followed. Few people will commit suicide without a push. And fewer still will pay good money to be told to do what it is against human nature and self-interest to do.

Emerson said that the world would beat a path to the door of the person who invented a better mousetrap. That showed what he knew about economics. Wells Fargo set out a trial balloon in the way of a sensible non-managed fund that embodied essentially the whole market. Batterymarch has done likewise. One of the American Express funds also experimented with such an outlet for pension fund money. The story is not yet over, but one is left with the impression that much underbrush has been growing up before the doors of these deviants into good sense.

At the least, some large foundation should set up an in-house portfolio that tracks the S & P 500 Index — if only for the purpose of setting up a naive model against which their in-house gunslingers can measure their prowess. Instead, most portfolio committees bolster their self-esteem by showing that they have done better than the Value Line 1500 Index. And no wonder: that being a geometric-mean index, I can outperform it merely by buying *its* stocks in its proportions; and can do so both in down markets and up markets — since money is only sophisticated enough to grow arithmetically, dollar on top of (algebraic!) dollar.

Perhaps CREF, which pioneered the variable annuity and the variable pension plan, can be induced to set up a pilot-plant operation of an unmanaged diversified fund, but I would not bet on it. I have suggested to my colleague, Franco Modigliani, who presumably will be President of the American Economic Association in 1976 (if there is a 1976), that economists might want to put their money where their darts are: the AEA might contemplate setting up for its members a no-load, no-management-fee, virtually no transaction-turnover fund along Sharpe-Mossin-Lintner lines. But there may be less supernumerary wealth to be found among 20,000 economists than among 20,000 chiropractors. For as Shaw should have said: "Those who have, don't know; those who know, don't have."

TEST OF PUDDINGS

How does one judge the validity of what I have been asserting? Certainly we don't want to replace old dogmas about "selectivity in search for quality" with new dogmas, however scientific their nomenclature. The sad truth is that it is precisely those who disagree most with the hypothesis of efficient market pricing of stocks, those who pooh-pooh beta analysis and all that, who *are least able to understand the analysis needed to test that hypothesis.*

First, they simply assert that it stands to common sense that greater effort to get facts and greater acumen in analyzing those facts will pay off in better performance somehow measured. (By this logic, the cure for cancer must have been found by 1955.)

Second, they always claim they know a man, a bank, or a fund that does do better. Alas, anecdotes are not science. And once Wharton School dissertations seek to quantify the performers, these have a tendency to evaporate into the air — or, at least, into statistically insignificant "t" statistics.

It is not ordained in heaven, or by the second law of thermodynamics, that a small group of intelligent and informed investors cannot systematically achieve higher mean portfolio gains with lower average variabilities. People differ in their heights, pulchritude, and acidity. Why not in their P.Q. or performance quotient? Any Sheik with a billion dollars has every incentive to track down organizations with such high P.Q.' (But, paradoxically, it takes P.Q. to identify P.Q., so it is not easy to get off the ground.)

Anyone with special abilities earns a differential return on that flair, which we economists call a rent. Those few with extraordinary P.Q. will not give away such rent to the Ford Foundation or to the local bank trust department. They have too high an I.Q. for that. Like any race track tout, they will share it for a price with those well-heeled people who can most benefit from it.

It is a mistake, though, to think that *so much money* will follow the advice of the best talents *inevitably, as a matter of the logic of competitive arbitrage alone,* to leave everyone else facing a "white noise" random-dart situation, in which every security of the same expected variability has the same expected mean return. From the nature of the case, there must always be a measure of uncertainty and of doubt concerning how much of one's money one can entrust to an adviser suspected of having exceptional P.Q. Many academic economists fall implicitly into confusion on this point. They think that the truth of the efficient market or random walk (or, more precisely, fair-martingale) hypothesis is established by logical tautology or by the same empirical certainty as the proposition that nickels sell for less than dimes.

The nearest thing to a deductive proof of a theorem suggestive of the fair-game hypothesis is that provided in my two articles on why properly anticipated speculative prices do vibrate randomly.* But of course, the weasel words "properly anticipated" provide the gasoline that drives the tautology to its conclusion. As I pointed out at the conclusion of the second cited article, any subset in the market which has a better ex ante knowledge of the stochastic process that stocks will follow in the future is in effect possessed of a "Maxwell's Demon" who tells him how to make capital gains from his effective peek into tomorrow's financial page reports. To be sure those possessed of such special competence must stay a subset of the market; if they become big enough to dominate the process of present stock price formation, that will falsify the presumption that they are still possessed of differential, undiscounted, ex ante valuable knowledge.

What is interesting is the empirical fact that it is virtually impossible for academic researchers with access to the published records to identify any member of the subset with flair. This fact, though not an inevitable law, is a brute fact. The ball, as I have already noted, is in the court of those who doubt the random walk hypothesis. They can dispose of the uncomfortable brute fact in the only way that any fact is disposed of — by producing brute evidence to the contrary.

* P. A. Samuelson, "Proof That Properly Anticipated Prices Fluctuate Randomly," *Industrial Management Review* (now *Sloan Management Review*), 1965, 6, 41-49; reproduced as Chapter 198 in Samuelson, *Collected Scientific Papers, Volume III*, Cambridge, M.I.T. Press, 1967. See also my "Proof That Properly Discounted Present Values of Assets Vibrate Randomly," *Bell Journal of Economics and Management Science*, Autumn 1973, 4, 369-374.

244

Foreword

"Those who can, do; those who can't, teach." According to this dictum of Shaw, the writings of professors of economics and finance should be of interest only to themselves. Practical men, interested in making a buck, should profitably ignore such academic writings and stick to their studies of corporate earnings, technical conditions of the market, and hot tips down at the midday eating club. Shaw, however, was a notorious joker, not one for the prudent man of investment to rely on. Writings of the last twenty years on the theory of speculative prices are not only of enormous interest for their own sake, but also should be of interest to the practical man who can understand them.

Let me give some illustrations. "Don't put all your eggs in one basket." The wisdom in this old saw gains new dimensions from the models of Harry Markowitz, William Sharpe, and others. Many portfolio men have not realized how strong is the positive correlation among the many securities they hold. They do not have nearly as many effectively different eggs in their baskets as they think.

Or take the question of good performance. The Ford Foundation, in a notable report directed toward non-profit institutions, urged them to be more rational in their investment policies. Who could object to that? Unfortunately, many who read that Report gleaned from it the message, "Be bold!", and this just at a time when the stock market went into its end-of-the-1960s tailspin. Readers who had been familiar with the kinds of analysis represented in this book would not have made this mistake. They would have realized that great performance in a bull market may be simply a reflection of great risk-taking: if two brothers, Cain and Abel, invest in identical securities, but Cain amplifies his leverage and risk by borrowed funds, then in a bull market Cain will spuriously appear to be the great investment genius. Even men innocent of analysis can see this, in the cold dawn of the morning after a bull-market binge. But it takes some analytical sophistication and knowledge of the Sharpe "beta" coefficient to see that certain institutional investors were accomplishing this same enhancement of mean return at the expense of greater risk, not by borrowing a cent, but rather by investing in highly volatile securities. I do not say you have to have read a book like this to sense these subtleties. The best practitioners I have known, many of them never having enjoyed formal schooling in mathematics beyond long division or high school algebra, realized things like this. But that is just the point that needs to be made. Investors who are successful over a long period of time, whether they are self-consciously aware of the fact or not, are essentially following precepts that can only be formulated and defended in terms of quite complicated mathematics.

Here is a final illustration of the need for statistical sophistication. Years ago mutual funds generally could not perform as well as the Dow-Jones or some other index of general stock prices. People in the industry resented this being pointed out, asserting the nonsense that you can't buy the averages. (Nonsense, because if it were true that a portfolio of those thirty stocks could really be expected to do better than the average of the best and most expensive money managers, it would be the duty of money managers simply to invest in the thirty Dow-Jones stocks, thereby bringing down the commission costs to small investors and bringing management fees down to a negligible amount.) In some years of the 1960s, however, mutual funds generally out-performed the Dow Jones or other index numbers of stock prices, and naturally the mutual fund industry called attention to this fact. There is, moreover, an understandable tendency for studies to be made to see which funds have been the most successful in recent years: those that seem to stand out get recommended, and certain of the go-go funds like those of Dreyfus or Fidelity have at times grown mightily at the expense of the rest. What is not sufficiently realized is that, by chance alone, if one picked different samples of fifty securities purely at random from the financial page, some samples would show more past growth than others; but that would not necessarily warrant the slightest credence in the expectation of their superior performance in the future. (It is like a famous study by Alfred Cowles III before World War II of seventeen different forecasting methods; the one that did the best was the "Dow theory," but it was not at all clear that this best performer did any better than the best of seventeen purely-random methods could be expected to do by chance alone.)

Ignoring the crucial question of whether good performance in the past can throw any light at all on good performance in the future. I note the further observation that in any year the fund that seems to show most rapid growth tends generally to be a small rather than a giant fund. People in the industry, who ought to know better, conclude from this fact alone that performance is likely to suffer with growth to giant size. No doubt there are some legitimate reasons to expect this; and to the degree that they are valid, they militate in the direction of starting new funds and stabilizing the size of giant funds. But there is also statistical reason to think that the size effect is spurious. Smaller funds tend to be less diversified; less diversified funds must be expected to show *both* higher and lower *extremes* of performance solely because of their smaller number of stocks held. For it to be legitimate to conclude that mere size hurts performance, we should have to have evidence that across *all* small funds the performance averages out worse than across *all* large funds, and with a deviation that is statistically significant according to the usual probability tests of hypotheses. Such evidence I have never seen marshalled; and casual inspection of what the performance has been of the aggregated portfolios of ten small companies chosen at random, and compared with one giant that is ten times as large, suggests to me that the adverse effects of size are exaggerated. (In any case, a large fund could, in principle, conduct itself like ten independent small funds.) In concluding these practical considerations deduced from the most elementary of sampling considerations, let me mention that contests like that conducted recently by the Chase

Bank among different analysts ought to be appraised for the import of their results by analysts experienced both in stochastic processes and game theory: contestants can rationally go for broke, knowing that the gains to them from purely lucky guesses may outweigh the loss to them of being a big rather than a small loser.

My pitch in this Foreword is not exclusively or even primarily aimed at practical men. Let them take care of themselves. The less of them who become sophisticated the better for us happy few! It is to the economist, the statistician, the philosopher, and to the general reader that I commend the analysis contained herein. Not all of science is beautiful. Only a zoologist could enjoy some parts of that subject; only a mathematician could enjoy vast areas of that terrain. But mathematics as applied to classical thermodynamics is beautiful: if you can't see that, you were born color-blind and are to be pitied. Similarly, in all the branches of pure and applied mathematics, the subject of probability is undoubtedly one of the most fascinating. As my colleague Professor Robert Solow once put it when he was a young man just appointed to the MIT staff: "Either you think that probability is the most exciting subject in the world, or you don't. And if you don't, I feel sorry for you."

Well, here in the mathematics of investment under uncertainty, some of the most interesting applications of probability occur. Elsewhere, in my 1971 Von Neumann Lecture before the Society for Industrial and Applied Mathematics, I have referred to the 1900 work on the economic Brownian motion by an unknown French professor, Louis Bachelier. Five years before the similar work by Albert Einstein, we see growing out of economic observations all that Einstein was able to deduce and more. Here, we see the birth of the theory of stochastic processes. Here we see, if you can picture it, radiation of probabilities according to Fourier's partial differential equations. And finally, as an anticlimax, here we see a way of making money from warrants and options or, better still, a way of understanding how they must be priced so that no easy pickings remain.

One of the troubles of being no longer young is that great experiences are behind you. If I had not already read all the detective works of Dashiell Hammett, I would now look forward to reading them. So I must envy any reader of these essays who reads them for the first time. He has an intellectual treat in store for him!

Paul A. Samuelson
Massachusetts Institute of Technology

245

FALLACY OF THE LOG-NORMAL APPROXIMATION TO OPTIMAL PORTFOLIO DECISION-MAKING OVER MANY PERIODS*

Robert C. MERTON and Paul A. SAMUELSON

*Sloan School of Management and Department of Economics,
M.I.T., Cambridge, Mass. 02139, U.S.A.*

Received August 1973, revised version received October 1973

The fallacy that a many-period expected-utility maximizer should maximize (a) the expected logarithm of portfolio outcomes or (b) the expected average compound return of his portfolio is now understood to rest upon a fallacious use of the *Law of Large Numbers*. This paper exposes a more subtle fallacy based upon a fallacious use of the *Central-Limit Theorem*. While the properly normalized product of independent random variables does asymptotically approach a log-normal distribution under proper assumptions, it involves a fallacious manipulation of double limits to infer from this that a maximizer of expected utility after many periods will get a useful approximation to his optimal policy by calculating an efficiency frontier based upon (a) the expected log of wealth outcomes and its variance or (b) the expected average compound return and its variance. Expected utilities calculated from the surrogate log-normal function differ systematically from the correct expected utilities calculated from the true probability distribution. A new concept of 'initial wealth equivalent' provides a transitive ordering of portfolios that illuminates commonly held confusions. A non-fallacious application of the log-normal limit and its associated mean-variance efficiency frontier is established for a limit where any *fixed* horizon period is subdivided into ever more independent sub-intervals. Strong mutual-fund Separation Theorems are then shown to be asymptotically valid.

1. Introduction

Thanks to the revival by von Neumann and Morgenstern, maximization of the expected value of a concave utility function of outcomes has for the last third of a century generally been accepted as the 'correct' criterion for optimal portfolio selection. Operational theorems for the general case were delayed in becoming recognized, and it was appropriate that the seminal break-throughs of the 1950's be largely preoccupied with the special case of mean-variance analysis.[1] Not only could the fruitful Sharpe–Lintner–Mossin capital

---

*We thank M.B. Goldman for scientific assistance. Aid from the National Science Foundation is gratefully acknowledged.

[1]Notable exceptions that deal with the general case can be found in the works of Arrow (1965), Rothschild and Stiglitz (1970), and Samuelson (1967a). Along with mean-variance analysis, the theory of portfolio selection when the distributions are Pareto–Lévy has been developed by Fama (1965) and Samuelson (1967b).

asset pricing model be based on it, but in addition, it gave rise to simple linear rules of portfolio optimizing. In the mean-variance model, the well-known Separation or Mutual-Fund Theorem holds; and with suitable additional assumptions, the model can be used to define a complete micro-economic framework for the capital market, and a number of empirically testable hypotheses can be derived. As a result, an overwhelming majority of the literature on portfolio theory have been based on this criterion. [2]

Unfortunately, as has been pointed out repeatedly, the mean-variance criterion is rigorously consistent with the general expected-utility approach only in the rather special cases of a quadratic utility function or of gaussian distributions on security prices – both involving dubious implications. Further, recent empirical work has shown that the simple form of the model does not seem to fit the data as well as had been previously believed, [3] and recent dynamic simulations [4] have shown that the behavior over time of some efficient mean-variance portfolios can be quite unreasonable.

Aside from its algebraic tractability, the mean-variance model has interest because of its separation property. Therefore, great interest inhered in the Cass–Stiglitz (1970) elucidation of the broader conditions under which a more limited form of a 'separation theorem' must hold regardless of the probability distribution of returns. The special families of utility functions with constant-relative-risk aversions or constant-absolute-risk aversions further gained in interest. [5] But it was realized that real-life utilities need not be of so simple a form.

The desire for simplicity of analysis led naturally to a search for approximation theorems, particularly of the asymptotic type. Thus, even if mean-variance analysis were not exact, would the error in using it become small? A defense of it was the demonstration that mean-variance is asymptotically correct if the risks are 'small' (i.e., for 'compact' probabilities); closely related was the demonstration of the same asymptotic equivalence when the trading interval becomes small (i.e., continuous trading). More recently, it has been shown that as the number of assets becomes large, under certain conditions, the mean-variance solution is asymptotically optimal. [6] And the present authors in another paper (1974) have developed a generalized mean-variance approximation procedure that is somewhat described by that paper's title. This enables

---

[2] The literature is so extensive that we refer the reader to the bibliography. Additional references can be found in the survey articles by Fama (1970) and Jensen (1972), and the book by Sharpe (1970).

[3] See Black, Jensen and Scholes (1972) and Friend and Blume (1970).

[4] See Hakansson (1971c).

[5] Cass and Stiglitz (1970) showed that these utility functions were among the few which satisfied the separation property with respect to initial wealth for arbitrary distributions. Other authors [Hakansson (1970), Leland (1968), Merton (1969, 1971) and Samuelson (1969)] have previously made extensive use of these functions.

[6] For the first, see Samuelson (1970); for the second, see Merton (1969, 1971); for the last, see Ross (1972a).

all those with utility functions that are near to a particular utility function to develop close approximations to optimal portfolios along a mean-variance trade-off frontier generated by a series expansion around that base function; this not only generalizes the standard Markowitz–Tobin mean-variance analysis of money outcomes, but can sometimes also validate the Hakansson efficiency frontier of expected average compound return and of its variance.

A particularly tempting hunting ground for asymptotic theories was thought to be provided by the case in which investors maximize the expected utility of terminal wealth when the terminal date (planning horizon) is very far in the future. Recourse to the Law of Large Numbers, as applied to repeated multiplicative variates (cumulative sums of logarithms of portfolio value relatives), has independently tempted various writers, holding out to them the hope that one can replace an arbitrary utility function of terminal wealth with all its intractability, by the function $U(W_T) = \log(W_T)$: maximizing the geometric mean or the expected log of outcomes, it was hoped, would provide an asymptotically exact criterion for rational action, implying as a bonus the efficiency of a diversification-of-portfolio strategy constant through time (i.e., a 'myopic' rule, the same for every period, even when probabilities of different periods were interdependent!). So powerful did the max-expected-log criterion appear to be, that it seemed even to supersede the general expected utility criterion in cases where the latter was shown to be inconsistent with the max-expected-log criterion. For some writers, it was a case of simple errors in reasoning: they mistakenly thought that the sure-thing principle sanctified the new criterion.[7] For others, an indefinitely large probability of doing better by Method A than by Method B was taken as conclusive evidence for the superiority of A.[8] Still other converts to the new faith never realized that it could conflict with the plausible postulates of von Neumann maximizing; or, still others, more sophisticatedly, have tried to save the approximation by appealing to bounded utility functions.[9]

Except to prepare the ground for a more subtle fallacy of the same asymptotic genus, the present paper need not more than review the simple max-expected-log fallacy. It can concentrate instead on the asymptotic fallacy that involves, not primarily the Law of Large Numbers, but rather the Central-Limit Theorem. It is well known that portfolio strategies that are uniformly the same in every period give rise to a cumulative sum of logarithms of returns that do approach, when normalized under specified conditions easily met a gaussian distribution – suggesting heuristically a Log-Normal Surrogate, whose two parameters : each period's expected log of return, and variance of log of return – will become 'asymptotically sufficient parameters' for efficient portfolio managing, truly an enormous simplification in that all optimal portfolios will lie on a new efficiency frontier in which the first parameter is maximized for each different value of

[7]See, for example, Aucamp (1971).
[8]See Breiman (1960) and Latane (1959).
[9]See Markowitz (1959, 1972).

the second. This frontier can be generated solely, by the family $U(W_T) = (W_T)^\gamma/\gamma$, and for $\gamma \neq 0$, this leads away from the simple max-expected-log portfolio. So this new method (if only it were valid!) would avoid the crude fallacy that men with little tolerance for risk are to have the same long-run portfolio as men with much risk tolerance. Furthermore, since the mean and variance of average-return-per-period are asymptotic surrogates for the log normal's first two moments (in a sense that will be described), Hakansson (1971b) average-expected-return – which to many [such as us in paper (1974)] has no interest as a criterion for its own sake – seems to be given a new legitimacy by the Central-Limit Theorem. Furthermore, suppose the Log-Normal Surrogate were valid, so that the true portfolio distribution could then be validly replaced by a log-normal with its $E\{\log W_T\}$ and var$\{\log W_T\}$. In that case, the criterion of expected average compound return (which has no interest for any thoughtful person whose utility function is far away from log W_T) could when supplemented by the variance of average compound return, be given for the first time a true legitimacy for all persons with $U = W^\gamma/\gamma$. Furthermore, this would hold whether $1 - \gamma$ is a small positive number or whether γ is a very large negative number. The reason for this is that mean and variance of average compound return can be shown to be 'asymptotic surrogates' for the Log-Normal Surrogate's two sufficient parameters, $TE\{\log W_1\}$ and Tvar$\{\log W_1\}$, W_1 being any single period's portfolio outcome. But, as we shall show, it is a fallacy of double limits to try to use the (unnormalized) Log-Normal Surrogate. And for people with $U = W^\gamma/\gamma$ and γ far from zero, the result can be disasterously bad.[10] What about the argument that expected average compound return deserves analysis because such analysis may be relevant to those decision makers who do not have a max $E\{U(\ )\}$ criterion and who just happen to be interested in average-compound-return? After some reflection, we think an appropriate reaction would go as follows: It is a free country. Anybody can set up whatever criterion he wishes. However, the analyst who understands the implications of various criteria has the useful duty to help people clarify the goals they will, on reflection, really want. If, after the analyst has done his duty of explaining the arbitrariness of the usual arguments in favor of average compound return, any decisionmaker still persists in being interested in average compound return, that is his privilege. In our experience, once understanding of the issues is realized, few decisionmakers retain their interest in average compound return.

One purpose of this paper is to show, by counter-examples and examination of illegitimate interchange of limits in double limits, the fallacies involved in the above-described asymptotic log-normal approximation. What holds for

[10]In a spin-off paper [Samuelson and Merton (1974)] to this one, we show that for $U = W^\varepsilon/\varepsilon$ and ε very small, a perturbation technique involving $E\{\log W_1\}$ and var $\{\log W_1\}$ can – quite independently of any log-normality – give a generalized mean-variance frontier for efficient local approximation. The two asymptotic moments of average compound return can, properly normalized, serve the same local-approximation purpose for $1/T$ small enough.

normalized variables is shown to be generally *not* applicable to *actual* terminal wealths. Then, constructively, we show that, as any fixed horizon planning interval is subdivided into a number of sub-interval periods that goes to infinity (causing the underlying probabilities to belong to a gaussian infinitely-divisible continuous-time probability distribution), the mean-log and variance-log parameters are indeed asymptotically sufficient parameters for the decision; so that one can prepare a (μ, σ) efficiency frontier that is quite distinct from the Markowitz mean-variance frontier of actual returns and not their logarithms; this logarithmic (μ, σ) frontier now provides many of the same two-dimensional simplifications (such as separation properties). The limit process involving breakdown of a finite T into ever-more subperiods is, of course, quite different from a limit process in which the number of fixed-length periods T itself goes to infinity.

There is still another kind of asymptotic approximation that attempts, as $T \rightarrow \infty$, to develop in Leland's (1972) happy phrase a 'turnpike theorem' in which the optimal portfolio proportions are well approximated by a uniform strategy that is appropriate to one of the special family of utility functions, $U(W_T) = (W_T)^\gamma/\gamma$, where $\gamma - 1$ is the limiting value of the elasticity of marginal utility with respect to wealth as $W_T \rightarrow \infty$. Letting γ then run the gamut from 1 to $-\infty$ generates a new kind of efficiency frontier, distinct from that of ordinary mean-variance or of $[E\{\log W\}, \text{var}\{\log W\}]$, but which obviously generalizes the single-point criterion of the would-be expected-log maximizers. It generalizes that criterion in that we now rationally trade-off mean return against risk, depending on our own subjective risk tolerance parameter γ. There is some question[11] as to the robustness of the Leland theorem for utility functions 'much different' from members of the iso-elastic family; but the main purpose of our paper is to uncover the booby traps involved in log-normal and other asymptotic approximations, and we do not examine this question in any depth.

2. Exact solution

In any period, investors face n securities, $1, \ldots, n$. One dollar invested in the jth security results at the end of one period in a value that is $Z_j(1)$, a positive random variable. The joint distribution of these variables is specified as

$$\text{Prob}\{Z_1(1) \leq z_1, \ldots, Z_n(1) \leq z_n\} = F[z_1, \ldots, z_n] = F[z], \quad (1)$$

where F has finite moments. Any portfolio decision in the first period is defined by the vector $[w_1(1), \ldots, w_n(1)]$, $\Sigma_1^n w_j(1) = 1$; if the investor begins with initial wealth of W_0, his wealth at the end of one period is given by the random variable

$$W_1 = W_0[w_1(1)Z_1(1) + \ldots + w_n(1)Z_n(1)]. \quad (2)$$

[11]Ross (1972b) provides a rather simple example where the Leland result does not obtain.

By the usual Stieltjes integration over $F[z_1, \ldots, z_n]$, the probability distribution of W_1 can be defined, namely

$$\text{Prob}\{\log(W_1/W_0) \leq x\} = P_1[x; w_1(1), \ldots, w_n(1)] \tag{3}$$
$$= P_1[x; w(1)].$$

An investment program re-invested for T periods has terminal wealth, W_T, defined by iterating (2) to get the random variable

$$W_T = W_0[\sum_1^n w_j(1)Z_j(1)][\sum_1^n w_j(2)Z_j(2)] \ldots [\sum_1^n w_j(T)Z_j(T)] \tag{4}$$
$$= W_T[w(1), \ldots, w(T)].$$

It is assumed that the vector of random variables $[Z(t)]$ is distributed independently of $Z(t \pm k)$, but subject to the same distribution as $Z(1)$ in eq. (1). Hence, the joint probability distribution of all securities over time is given by the product

$$\text{Prob}\{Z(1) \leq z(1), \ldots, Z(T) \leq z(T)\}$$
$$= F[z_1(1), \ldots, z_n(1)] \ldots F[z_1(T), \ldots, z_n(T)] \tag{5}$$
$$= F[z(1)] \ldots F[z(T)].$$

Since W_T/W_0 consists of a product of independent variates, $\log(W_T/W_0)$ will consist of a sum of independent variates. Therefore, its probability distribution is, for each T, definable recursively by the following convolutions,

$$\text{Prob}\{\log(W_T/W_0) \leq x\} = P_T[x; w(1), \ldots, w(T)] \tag{6}$$

$$P_2[x; w(1), w(2)] = \int_{-\infty}^{\infty} P_1[x-s; w(2)]P_1[ds; w(1)]$$

$$P_3[x; w(1), w(2), w(3)] = \int_{-\infty}^{\infty} P_1[x-s; w(3)]P_2[ds; w(1), w(2)]$$
$$\vdots \qquad\qquad\qquad\qquad \vdots$$
$$P_T[x; w(1), \ldots, w(T)]$$
$$= \int_{-\infty}^{\infty} P_1[x-s; w(T)]P_{T-1}[ds; w(1), \ldots, w(T-1)].$$

Here, as a matter of notation for Stieltjes integration, $\int_{-\infty}^{\infty} f(s)dg(s) = \int_{-\infty}^{\infty} f(s)g(ds)$.

The investor is postulated to act in order to maximize the expected value of (concave) terminal utility of wealth

$$\max_{\{w(t)\}} E\{U_T(W_T[w(1), \ldots, w(T)])\}$$
$$= \max_{\{w(t)\}} \int_{-\infty}^{\infty} U_T(W_0 e^x)P_T[dx; w(1), \ldots, w(T)] \tag{7}$$
$$\equiv \bar{U}_T[w^{**}(1), \ldots, w^{**}(T); W_0].$$

Here, $U_T(\ )$ is a concave function that can be arbitrarily specified, and $[w_j(t)]$, for each t, is understood to be constrained by $\sum_1^n w_j(t) = 1$.

For a general U_T, the optimal solution $[\ldots, w^{**}(t), \ldots]$ will not involve portfolio decisions constant through time, but rather optimally varying in accordance with the recursive relations of Bellman dynamic programming, as discussed by numerous authors, as for example in Samuelson (1969). But, here, we shall for the most part confine our attention to uniform strategies

$$[w_1(t), \ldots, w_n(t)] \underset{t}{\equiv} [w_1, \ldots, w_n]. \tag{8}$$

For each such uniform strategy, $\log(W_T/W_0)$ will consist of a sum of independent and identically distributed variates. We write the optimal uniform strategy as the vector $w(t) \equiv w_T^*$, and abbreviate

$$P_T[x; w] \equiv P_T[x; w, \ldots, w], \qquad T = 2, 3, \ldots, \tag{9}$$

$$W_T[w] \equiv W_T[w, \ldots, w],$$

$$\bar{U}_T[w^*; W_0] \equiv \bar{U}_T[w^*, \ldots, w^*; W_0].$$

Actually, for the special utility functions,

$$U_T(W) = W^\gamma/\gamma, \gamma < 1, \gamma \neq 0 \tag{10}$$

$$= \log W, \gamma = 0,$$

it is well known that $w^{**}(t) \equiv w^*$, independent of T, is a necessary result for full optimality.

3. Max-expected-log (geometric-mean) fallacy

Suppose Z_n represents a 'safe security' with certain return

$$Z_n = e^r \equiv R \geq 1. \tag{11}$$

If the other risky securities are optimally held in positive amounts, together their uncertain return must have an expected value that exceeds R. Consider now the parameters

$$E\{\log(W_1/W_0)\} = E\{\log(\sum_1^n w_j Z_j)\} = \mu(w_1, \ldots, w_n) = \mu(w), \tag{12}$$

$$\text{var}\{\log(W_1/W_0)\} = E\{[\log(\sum_1^n w_j Z_j) - \mu(w)]^2\} = \sigma^2(w_1, \ldots, w_n)$$

$$= \sigma^2(w).$$

For $w = (w_1, \ldots, w_n) = (0, 0, \ldots, 0, 1)$, $\mu(w) = r \geq 0$. As w_n declines and the sum of all other w_j become positive, $\mu(w)$ must be positive. However, $\mu(w)$ will reach a maximum; call it $\mu(w^{\dagger\dagger})$, and recognize that $w^{\dagger\dagger}$ is the max-expected-log strategy.

As mentioned in sect. 1, many authors fallaciously believe that $w^{\dagger\dagger}$ is a good approximation to w^* for T large, merely because

$$\lim_{T\to\infty} \text{Prob}\{W_T[w^{\dagger\dagger}] > W_T[w]\} = 1, \quad w \neq w^{\dagger\dagger}. \tag{13}$$

A by now familiar counter-example occurs for any member of the iso-elastic family, eq. (10), with $\gamma \neq 0$. For a given γ, $w^*(t) \equiv w^*$, the same strategy, independent of T; since each γ is easily seen to call for a different w^*, it must be that $w^* \neq w^{\dagger\dagger}$ for all T and $\gamma \neq 0$, in as much as $w^* = w^{\dagger\dagger}$ only when $\gamma = 0$ and $U_T(W) = \log W$. Hence, the vague and tacit conjecture that w^* converges to $w^{\dagger\dagger}$ asymptotically as $T \to \infty$, is false.

Others, e.g. Markowitz (1972, p. 3), who are aware of the simple fallacy have conjectured that the max-expected-log policy will be 'approximately' optimal for large T when $U_T(\ )$ is bounded (or bounded from above). I.e., if $U_T(\ )$ is bounded (or bounded from above), then the expected utility maximizer, it is argued, will be 'approximately indifferent' between the $\{w^*\}$ and $\{w^{\dagger\dagger}\}$ programs as T becomes large.

The exact meaning of 'approximate indifference' is open to interpretation. A trivial meaning would be

$$\lim_{T\to\infty} EU_T(W_0 Z_T[w^*]) = M = \lim_{T\to\infty} EU_T(W_0 Z_T[w^{\dagger\dagger}]), \tag{14}$$

where M is the upper bound of $U_T(\ )$. This definition merely reflects the fact, that even a sub-optimal strategy (unless it is too absurd) will lead as $T \to \infty$ to the upper bound of utility. For example, just holding the riskless asset with positive return per period $R = e^r > 1$, will, for large enough T, get one arbitrarily close to the bliss level of utility. Hence, even if eq. (14)'s definition of indifference were to make the conjecture true, its implications have practically no content.

A meaningful interpretation would be indifference in terms of an 'initial wealth equivalent'. That is, let $\Pi_{ij} W_0$ be the initial wealth equivalent of a program $\{w^i\}$ relative to program $\{w^j\}$ defined such that, for each T,

$$EU_T(\Pi_{ij} W_0 Z_T[w^i]) \equiv EU_T(W_0 Z_T[w^j]). \tag{15}$$

$(\Pi_{ij} - 1)W_0$ is the amount of additional initial wealth the investor would require to be indifferent to giving up the $\{w^j\}$ program for the $\{w^i\}$ program. Thus, we could use $\Pi_{12}(T; W_0)$ as a measure [12] of how 'close' in optimality terms the $\{w^1\} \equiv \{w^{\dagger\dagger}\}$ program is to the $\{w^2\} \equiv \{w^*\}$ program. The conjecture that max-expected-log is asymptotically optimal in this modified sense would be true only if it could be shown that $\Pi_{12}(T; W_0)$ is a decreasing function

---

[12] $\Pi_{ij}(\ ;\ )$ could be used to rank portfolios because it provides a complete and transitive ordering. Note: if $\Pi_{ij}(\ ;\ ) > 1$ then $\Pi_{ji}(\ ;\ ) < 1$. However $\Pi_{ij}(\ ;\ ) \neq 1/\Pi_{ji}(\ ;\ )$.

of T and

$$\lim_{T \to \infty} \Pi_{12}(T; W_0) = 1,$$

or even if $\Pi_{12}(T; W_0)$ were simply a bounded function of T.

Consider the case when $U_T(\ ) = (\ )^\gamma/\gamma, \gamma < 1$. Then,

$$EU_T(W_0 Z_T[w^*]) = W_0^\gamma E[(Z_T[w^*])^\gamma]/\gamma \tag{16}$$
$$= W_0^\gamma \{ E[(Z_1[w^*])^\gamma] \}^T/\gamma,$$

by the independence and identical distribution of the portfolio return in each period. Similarly, we have that

$$EU_T(\Pi_{12} W_0 Z_T[w^{\dagger\dagger}]) = (\Pi_{12} W_0)^\gamma \{ E[(Z_1[w^{\dagger\dagger}])^\gamma) \}^T/\gamma. \tag{17}$$

Now, $\{w^*\}$ maximizes the expected utility of wealth over one period (i.e., for the iso-elastic family $w^{**} = w^*$), and since $w^* \neq w^{\dagger\dagger}$ for $\gamma \neq 0$, we have that

$$E[(Z_1[w^*])^\gamma) \gtreqless E[(Z_1[w^{\dagger\dagger}])^\gamma] \text{ as } \gamma \gtreqless 0. \tag{18}$$

From eqs. (15), (16), and (17), we have that

$$\Pi_{12}(T; W_0) = [\lambda(\gamma)]^{T/\gamma}, \tag{19}$$

where

$$\lambda(\gamma) \equiv E[(Z_1[w^*])^\gamma]/E[(Z_1[w^{\dagger\dagger}])^\gamma].$$

From eq. (18), $\lambda(\gamma) > 1$ and $T/\gamma > 0$, for $\gamma > 0$; $\lambda(\gamma) < 1$ and $T/\gamma < 0$, for $\gamma < 0$; and, since λ is independent of T and W_0, we have from (19) that, for $\gamma \neq 0$ and every $W_0 > 0$,

$$\partial \Pi_{12}(T; W_0)/\partial T > 0, \tag{20}$$

$$\lim_{T \to \infty} \Pi_{12}(T; W_0) = \infty.$$

Hence, even for $U_T(\ )$ with an upper bound (as when $\gamma < 0$), an investor would require as $T \to \infty$, an ever-larger initial payment to give up his $\{w^*\}$ program. Similar results obtain for $U_T(\ )$ functions which are bounded from above and below.[13] Therefore, the $\{w^{\dagger\dagger}\}$ program is definitely not 'approximately' optimal for large T.

Further, the sub-optimal $\{w^{\dagger\dagger}\}$ policy will, for every finite T however large, be in a clear sense 'behind' the best strategy, $\{w^*\}$. Indeed, let us apply the test used in the Eisenhower Administration to compare U.S. and U.S.S.R. growth. How many years after the U.S. reached each real GNP level did it take the U.S.S.R. to reach that level? This defines a function $\Delta T = f(\text{GNP}_t)$, and some Kremlinologists of that day took satisfaction that ΔT was not declining in time. In a new calculation similar to the initial wealth equivalent analysis above, let us for each level of $E[U_T(W_T)]$ define $\Delta T = T^{\dagger\dagger} - T^*$ as the difference in time

[13]See Goldman (1972) for some examples.

periods needed to surpass that level of expected utility, calculated for the optimal strategy $\{w^*\}$ and for the max-expected-log strategy $\{w^{\dagger\dagger}\}$; then it is not hard to show that $\Delta T \to \infty$ as $T \to \infty$. Again the geometric-mean strategy proves to be fallacious.

Finally, we can use the initial wealth equivalent to demonstrate that for sufficiently risk-averse investors, the max-expected-log strategy is a 'bad' program: bad, in that the $\{w^{\dagger\dagger}\}$ program will not lead to 'approximate' optimality even in the trivial sense of (14) and hence, will be dominated by the program of holding nothing but the riskless asset.

Define $\{w^3\} \equiv [0, 0, 0, \ldots, 1]$ to be the program which holds nothing but the riskless asset with return per period, $R \geq 1$. Let $\{w^1\}$ be the max-expected-log program $\{w^{\dagger\dagger}\}$ as before. Then, for the iso-elastic family, the initial wealth equivalent for the $\{w^1\}$ program relative to the $\{w^3\}$ program, $\Pi_{13}W_0$, is defined by

$$\frac{W_0^\gamma}{\gamma} \Pi_{13}^\gamma E[(Z_T[w^{\dagger\dagger}])^\gamma] \equiv \frac{W_0^\gamma}{\gamma} R^{\gamma T}, \tag{21}$$

or

$$\Pi_{13} = [\phi(\gamma)]^{-T/\gamma}, \tag{22}$$

where $\phi(\gamma) \equiv E[(Z_1[w^{\dagger\dagger}])^\gamma]/R^\gamma$.

To examine the properties of the $\phi(\gamma)$ function, we note that since $\{w^{\dagger\dagger}\} \equiv [w^{\dagger\dagger}, w^{\dagger\dagger}, \ldots, w^{\dagger\dagger}]$ does maximize $E \log(Z[w; 1]) \equiv E \log(\Sigma_1^{n-1} w_j[Z_j(1) - R] + R)$, it must satisfy

$$E\{[Z_j(1) - R]/Z[w^{\dagger\dagger}; 1]\} = 0, \quad j = 1, 2, \ldots, n. \tag{23}$$

Multiplying (23) by $w_{j\dagger\dagger}$ and summing over $j = 1, 2, \ldots, n$, we have that

$$E\{(Z[w^{\dagger\dagger}; 1] - R)/Z[w^{\dagger\dagger}; 1]\} = 0 \tag{24}$$

or that

$$E\{(Z[w^{\dagger\dagger}; 1])^{-1}\} = R^{-1}. \tag{25}$$

From eqs. (22) and (25), we have that

$$\phi(\gamma) > 0; \quad \phi(0) = \phi(-1) = 1. \tag{26}$$

Further, by differentiation,

$$\phi''(\gamma) = E\{(Z[w^{\dagger\dagger}; 1])^\gamma \log^2(Z[w^{\dagger\dagger}; 1])\} > 0, \tag{27}$$

and so, ϕ is a strictly convex function with a unique interior minimum at γ_{min}. From (26), $-1 < \gamma_{min} < 0$, and therefore, $\phi'(\gamma) < 0$ for $\gamma < \gamma_{min}$. Hence, since $\phi(-1) = 1$, $\phi(\gamma) > 1$ for $\gamma < -1$.

But, from (22), $\phi(\gamma) > 1$ for $\gamma < -1$ implies that for any R, $W_0 > 0$, and $\gamma < -1$,

$$\lim_{T \to \infty} \Pi_{13}(T) = \infty, \tag{28}$$

and therefore, such risk-averse investors would require an indefinitely large initial payment to give up the riskless program for the max-expected-log one.

Further, in the case where $R = 1$ and the riskless asset is non-interest bearing cash, we have that for $\gamma < -1$, $E[(Z_1[w^{\dagger\dagger}; 1])^\gamma] > 1$ which implies that

$$\lim_{T \to \infty} EU_T(W_0 Z[w^{\dagger\dagger}; T]) = \lim_{T \to \infty} W_0\{E[(Z[w^{\dagger\dagger}; 1])^\gamma]\}^T/\gamma$$

$$= -\infty, \tag{29}$$

so that such a risk-averse person's being forced into the allegedly desirable max-expected-log strategy is just as bad for infinitely large T as having all his initial wealth taken away! Few people will opt to ruin themselves voluntarily once they understand what they are doing.[14]

4. A false log-normal approximation

A second more subtle, fallacy has grown out of the more recent literature on optimal portfolio selection for maximization of (distant time) expected terminal utility of wealth.

After giving arguments based on maximizing expected average-compound-return that imply myopic and uniform strategies, $w(t) \equiv w_T$, Hakansson (1971b, pp. 868–869) proceeds to use the Central-Limit Theorem to argue that for large T, the distribution of terminal wealth will be approximately log-normal. Then, he approximates the mean and variance of average-compound-return by the first two moments of the associated Log-Normal Surrogate. To obtain an approximation to the efficient set for the mean and variance of average-compound-return, he (p. 871) substitutes the Log-Normal Surrogate for the true random variable portfolio return in an iso-elastic utility function and computes its expected value *prior* to any maximization. This done, he is able to use the property that maximization of W^γ/γ under the log-normal distribution reduces to a simple linear trade-off relationship between expected log of return and the variance of log return with γ being a measure of the investor's risk-return trade off. More generally, if a portfolio is known to have a log-normal distribution with parameters $[\mu, \sigma^2] \equiv [E \log(W_1/W_0), \text{var} \log(W_1/W_0)]$, then for all utilities, it will be optimal to have a maximum of the first parameter for any fixed value of the second. While it is not true that for a fixed value of μ, all concave utility maximizers would necessarily prefer the minimum σ^2, it is true that for a fixed value of $\alpha \equiv \log[E(W_1/W_0)] = \mu + \frac{1}{2}\sigma^2$, all concave utility maximizers would optimally choose the minimum σ^2.[15] Hence, the Hakansson derivation can

---

[14]Goldman (1972) derives a similar result for a bounded utility function. Thus, Samuelson (1971, p. 2495) conceded too much in his criticism of the geometric-mean policy when he stated that such a policy would asymptotically outperform any other uniform policy for utility functions bounded from above and below.

[15]See Merton (1973, appendix 2) for a proof.

F

suggest that there exists an asymptotic 'efficient frontier' in either of the two related parameter spaces $[\mu, \sigma^2]$ or $[\alpha, \sigma^2]$. In the special case of the W^γ/γ family, the γ determines the point on that frontier where a given investor's optimal portfolio lies. One of us, independently, fell into this same trap.[16]

Unfortunately, substitution of the associated log-normal for the true distribution leads to incorrect results, as will be demonstrated by counter-example. The error in the analysis leading to this false conjecture results from an improper interchange of limits, as we now demonstrate.

For each uniform portfolio strategy $\{w\}$, define as in eq. (2), the one-period portfolio return in period t by

$$Z[t; w] \equiv \sum_1^n w_i Z_i(t) = W_t[w]/W_{t-1}. \tag{30}$$

Given the distributional assumption about asset returns in sect. 2, the $Z[t; w]$ will be independently and identically distributed through time with

$$\text{Prob}\{\log(Z[t; w]) \leq x\} \equiv P_1(x; w). \tag{31}$$

The T-period return on the portfolio is defined, for any $T \geq 1$, by

$$Z_T[w] \equiv \prod_{t=1}^T Z[t; w] = W_T[w]/W_0, \tag{32}$$

with

$$\text{Prob}\{\log(Z_T[w]) \leq x\} \equiv P_T(x; w) \tag{33}$$

as in eq. (6) with the w's independent of time.

Define $Z_T^\dagger[w]$ to be a log-normally distributed random variable with parameters μT and $\sigma^2 T$ chosen such that

$$\mu T \equiv E\{\log(Z_T^\dagger[w]\} = E\{\log(Z_T[w])\} = TE\{\log(Z_1[w])\} \tag{34}$$

$$\sigma^2 T \equiv \text{var}\{\log(Z_T^\dagger[w])\} = \text{var}\{\log(Z_T[w])\} = T \text{var}\{\log(Z_1[w])\}.$$

We call $Z_T^\dagger[w]$ the 'surrogate' log-normal to the random variable $Z_T[w]$; it is the log-normal approximation to $Z_T[w]$ fitted by equating the first two moments in the classical maximum-likelihood Pearsonian curve-fitting procedure. Note that by definition

$$\mu = \mu(w) = \int_{-\infty}^{\infty} x P_1(dx; w), \tag{35}$$

$$\sigma^2 = \sigma^2(w) = \int_{-\infty}^{\infty} (x-\mu)^2 P_1(dx; w).$$

[16]The neatness of the heuristic arguments and the attractiveness of the results has led a number of authors to assert and/or conjecture their truth. See Samuelson (1971, p. 2496) where $\mu(w)$ and $\sigma^2(w)$ are misleadingly said to be 'asymptotically sufficient parameters', an assertion not correct for $T \to \infty$, but rather for increasing subdivisions of time periods leading to diffusion-type stochastic processes.

Since each $\log(Z[t; w])$ in $\Sigma_1^T \log(Z[t; w])$ is an identically distributed, independent variate with finite variance, the Central-Limit Theorem applies to give us the valid asymptotic relation.[17]

Central-Limit Theorem. As T gets large, the normalized variable, $Y_T \equiv [\log(Z_T[w]) - \mu(w)T]/\sigma(w)\sqrt{T}$, approaches the normal distribution. I.e.,

$$\lim_{T \to \infty} \text{Prob}\{Y_T \leq y\} = \lim_{T \to \infty} P_T[\sigma(w)\sqrt{T}\,y + \mu(w)T; w] \tag{36}$$

$$= N(y) \equiv (2\pi)^{-1/2} \int_{-\infty}^{y} e^{-\frac{1}{2}t^2} dt,$$

where $N(\ )$ is the cumulative distribution function for a standard normal variate.

Since $\log(Z_T[w]) = \log(W_T[w]/W_0)$, this is the valid formulation of the log-normal asymptotic approximation for the properly standardized distribution of terminal wealth.

In a more trivial sense, both $P_T(x; w)$ for $Z_T[w]$ and also its surrogate, $\eta(x; \mu T, \sigma^2 T) \equiv N[(x - \mu(w)T)/\sigma(w)\sqrt{T}]$ for $Z_T^{\dagger}[w]$, approach the same common limit, namely

$$\lim_{T \to \infty} P_T(x; w) = L = \lim_{T \to \infty} \eta(x; \mu T, \sigma^2 T), \tag{37}$$

where

$$L = 1, \mu(w) < 0, \tag{38}$$
$$= 0, \mu(w) > 0,$$
$$= \tfrac{1}{2}, \mu(w) = 0.$$

But it is not the case that

$$\lim_{T \to \infty} \{[L - P_T(x; w)]/[L - \eta(x; \mu T, \sigma^2 T)]\} = 1. \tag{39}$$

From the *terra firma* of the valid Central-Limit theorem, a false corollary tempts the unwary.

False Corollary. If the returns on assets satisfy the distributional assumptions of sect. 2, then, as $T \to \infty$, the optimal solution to

$$\max_{\{w\}} E[U_T(W_T[w])] = \max_{\{w\}} \int_{-\infty}^{\infty} U_T[W_0\, e^x] P_T(\mathrm{d}x; w),$$

over all[18] *uniform* strategies $\{w\}$, will be the same as the optimal solution to

$$\max_{\{w\}} E[U_T(W_0 Z_T[w])[= \max_{\{w\}} \int_{-\infty}^{\infty} U_T[W_0\, e^x] \eta'(x; \mu T, \sigma^2 T)\, \mathrm{d}x,$$

[17]To apply the Central-Limit Theorem correctly, the choice for $\{w\}$ must be such that $Z[t; w]$ is a positive random variate with its logarithm well defined. Our later discussion of optimal policies is unaffected by this restriction since the class of utility functions considered will rule out $Z[t; w]$ with a positive probability of ruin. Cf. Hakansson (1971b, p. 868).

[18]With reference to footnote 17, the corollary is false even if we restrict the set of uniform strategies considered to those such that Prob $\{Z_T[w] = 0\} = 0$ for all finite T.

where $\eta'(x; \mu T, \sigma^2 T) = (2\pi\sigma^2 T)^{-1/2} \exp[-(x-\mu T)^2/2\sigma^2 T] = N'[(x-\mu(w)T)/\sigma(w)\sqrt{T}]/\sigma(w)\sqrt{T}$. I.e., one can allegedly find the optimal portfolio policy for large T, by 'replacing' $Z_T[w]$ by its surrogate log-normal variate, $Z_T^\dagger[w]$.

Let us sketch the usual heuristic arguments that purport to deduce the false corollary. From eqs. (36) and (37), one is tempted to reason heuristically, that since Y_T is approximately distributed standard normal, then $\log(Z_T[w]) = \sigma\sqrt{T}Y_T+\mu T \equiv X_T$ is approximately normally distributed[19] with mean μT and variance $\sigma^2 T$, for large T. Hence, if X_T has a density function $P_T'(x;w)$ then, for large T, one can write the approximation

$$P_T'(x; w) \approx \eta'(x; \mu T, \sigma^2 T), \tag{40}$$

and substitute the right-hand expression for the left-hand expression whenever T is large. As an example, from eq. (40), one is led to the strong (and false!) conclusion that, for large T,

$$\int_{-\infty}^{\infty} U(W_0 e^x)P_T'(x; w)\, dx \approx \int_{-\infty}^{\infty} U(W_0 e^x)\eta'(x; \mu T, \sigma^2 T)\, dx, \tag{41}$$

in the sense that

$$\lim_{T\to\infty} \left[\int_{-\infty}^{\infty} U(W_0 e^x)P_T'(x; w)\, dx - \int_{-\infty}^{\infty} U(W_0 e^x)\eta'(x; \mu T, \sigma^2 T)\, dx\right]$$

$$= \int_{-\infty}^{\infty} U(W_0 e^x) \lim_{T\to\infty} [P_T'(x; w) - \eta'(x; \mu T, \sigma^2 T)]\, dx = 0. \tag{42}$$

But, actually eq. (42) is quite false as careful analysis of the Central-Limit Theorem will show.

A correct analysis immediately shows that the heuristic argument leading to (41) – (42) involves an incorrect limit interchange. From eq. (36), for each T, the random variable Y_T will be seen to have a probability function $F_T(y; w) = P_T(\sigma(w)\sqrt{T}y+\mu(w)T; w)$. By definition, we have that

$$\bar{U}_T = \int_{-\infty}^{\infty} U(W_0 e^x)P_T(dx; w)$$

$$= \int_{-\infty}^{\infty} U[W_0 \exp(\sigma\sqrt{T}y+\mu T)]F_T(dy; w), \tag{43}$$

and, for the surrogate-function calculation,

$$\int_{-\infty}^{\infty} U(W_0 e^x)\eta'(x; \mu T, \sigma^2 T)\, dx \tag{44}$$

$$= \int_{-\infty}^{\infty} U[W_0 \exp(\sigma\sqrt{T}y+\mu T)]N'(y)\, dy.$$

Further, from the Central-Limit Theorem, we also have that, in the case where $P_T(\ ; w)$ and $F_T(\ ; w)$ have densities, $\partial P_T/\partial x = P_T'(x; w)$ and $\partial F_T/\partial y = F_T'(y; w)$,

$$\lim_{T\to\infty} F_T'(y; w) = N'(y). \tag{45}$$

---

[19]The argument is that a constant times a normal variate plus a constant, is a normal variate.

However, to derive eq. (42) from (43) – (45), the following limit interchange would have to be valid for each y,

$$\lim_{T \to \infty} \{U[W_0 \exp(\sigma\sqrt{T}y + \mu T)]F'_T(y; w)\} \tag{46}$$

$$= \{ \lim_{T \to \infty} U[W_0 \exp(\sigma\sqrt{T}y + \mu T)]\}\{ \lim_{T \to \infty} F'_T(y; w)\}.$$

In general, as is seen from easy counter-examples, such an interchange of limits will be illegitimate, and hence, the False Corollary is invalid. In those cases where the limit interchange in eq. (46) is valid (e.g., U is a bounded function), the False Corollary holds only in the trivial sense of (14) in sect. 3. I.e., as already noted, in the limit as $T \to \infty$, there will exist an infinite number of portfolio programs (including holding one hundred percent of the portfolio in the positive-yielding, riskless asset) which will give expected utility levels equal to the upperbound of U. As we now show by counter-example, it is not true that portfolio proportions, w^*, chosen to maximize expected utility over the $P_T(\ ; w)$ distribution will be equal to the proportions, $w^\dagger$, chosen to maximize expected utility over the surrogate $\eta(\ ; \mu T, \sigma^2 T)$, even in the limit.

To demonstrate our counter-example to the False Corollary, first, note that for the iso-elastic family, the expected utility level for the surrogate log-normal can be written as

$$E(W_0 Z^{\dagger}_T[w])^{\gamma}/\gamma = W_0^{\gamma} \exp[\gamma\mu(w)T + \tfrac{1}{2}\gamma^2\sigma^2(w)T]/\gamma. \tag{47}$$

As Hakansson (1971b) has shown, maximization of eq. (47) is equivalent to the maximization of

$$[\mu(w) + \tfrac{1}{2}\gamma\sigma^2(w)]. \tag{48}$$

Hence, from eq. (48), the maximizing $w^\dagger$ for eq. (47) depend only on the mean and variance of the logarithm of one-period returns.

Second, note that because the portfolio returns for each period are independently and identically distributed, we can write the expected utility level for the true distribution as

$$E(W_0 Z_T[w])^{\gamma}/\gamma = W_0^{\gamma}\{E(Z_1[w]^{\gamma})\}^{T}/\gamma. \tag{49}$$

Hence, maximization of eq. (49) is equivalent to the maximization of

$$E(Z_1[w]^{\gamma})/\gamma, \tag{50}$$

which also depends only on the one-period returns.[20]

Consider the simple two-asset case where $Z[t; w] \equiv w(y_t - R) + R$ and where the y_t are independent, Bernoulli-distributed random variables with

[20]This is an important point because it implies that if the conjecture that $\{w^\dagger\} = \{w^*\}$ could hold for the iso-elastic family for large T, then it would hold for T small or $T = 1$! I.e., $\mu(w)$ and $\sigma(w)$ would be sufficient parameters for the portfolio decision for any time horizon.

$\text{Prob}\{y_t = \lambda\} = \text{Prob}\{y_t = \delta\} = 1/2$ and $\lambda > R > \delta > 0$. Substituting into eq. (50), we have that the optimal portfolio rule, w^*, will solve

$$\max_{\{w\}} \{[w(\lambda - R) + R]^\gamma + [w(\delta - R) + R]^\gamma\}/2\gamma, \tag{51}$$

which by the usual calculus first-order condition implies that w^* will satisfy

$$0 = (\lambda - R)[w^*(\lambda - R) + R]^{\gamma - 1} + (\delta - R)[w^*(\delta - R) + R]^{\gamma - 1}. \tag{52}$$

Rearranging terms in eq. (52), we have that

$$[(R - \delta)/(\lambda - R)] = [(w^*(\lambda - R) + R)/(w^*(\delta - R) + R)]^{\gamma - 1} \tag{53}$$

or

$$w^* = w^*(\gamma) = (A - 1)R/[(\lambda - R) + A(R - \delta)], \tag{54}$$

where

$$A \equiv [(R - \delta)/(\lambda - R)]^{1/\gamma - 1}.$$

From eq. (35), the surrogate log-normal for $Z_T[w]$ will have parameters

$$\mu = \mu(w) \equiv 1/2\{\log[w(\lambda - R) + R] + \log[w(\delta - R) + R]\}, \tag{55}$$

and

$$\sigma^2 = \sigma^2(w) \equiv 1/2\{\log^2[w(\lambda - R) + R] + \log^2[w(\delta - R) + R]\} - \mu^2. \tag{56}$$

The optimal portfolio rule relative to eq. (48), $w^\dagger$, will be the solution to

$$0 = 1/2\left\{ \frac{\lambda - R}{w^\dagger(\lambda - R) + R} + \frac{\delta - R}{w^\dagger(\delta - R) + R} \right\}$$

$$\left(1 - \frac{\gamma}{2}\log[(w^\dagger(\lambda - R) + R)(w^\dagger(\delta - R) + R)] \right)$$

$$+ \frac{\gamma}{2}\left\{ \log[w^\dagger(\lambda - R) + R]\left(\frac{\lambda - R}{w^\dagger(\lambda - R) + R} \right) \right.$$

$$\left. + \log[w^\dagger(\delta - R) + R]\left(\frac{\delta - R}{w^\dagger(\delta - R) + R} \right) \right\}, \tag{57}$$

which can be rewritten as

$$0 = \left(\frac{\lambda - R}{R - \delta} \right)\left[1 + \frac{\gamma}{2}\log(B) \right] - B\left[1 - \frac{\gamma}{2}\log(B) \right], \tag{58}$$

where $B \equiv [w^\dagger(\lambda - R) + R]/[w^\dagger(\delta - R) + R]$. Note that since both w^* and $w^\dagger$ are independent of T, if the False Corollary had been valid, then $w^* = w^\dagger$. Suppose $w^* = w^\dagger$. From the definitions of A and B and from eq. (53), we have that $B = A$ and $(\lambda - R)/(R - \delta) = A^{1 - \gamma}$. Substitute A for B in eq. (58) to get

$$H(\gamma) \equiv A^{1 - \gamma}\left[1 + \frac{\gamma}{2}\log(A) \right] - A\left[1 - \frac{\gamma}{2}\log(A) \right]. \tag{59}$$

For arbitrary λ, δ, and R, $H(\gamma) = 0$ only if $\gamma = 0$ (i.e., if the original utility function is logarithmic). Hence, $w^* \neq w^\dagger$ for $\gamma \neq 0$, and the False Corollary is disproved. The reason that $w^* = w^\dagger$ for $\gamma = 0$ has nothing to do with the log-normal approximation or size of T since in that case, eqs. (48) and (50) are identities.

This effectively dispenses with the false conjecture that for large T, the log-normal approximation provides a suitable surrogate for the true distribution of terminal wealth probabilities; and with any hope that the mean and variance of expected-average-compound-return can serve as asymptotically sufficient decision parameters.

5. A chamber of horrors of improper limits

It is worth exposing at some length the fallacy involved in replacing the true probability distribution, $P_T(x; w)$, by its surrogate log-normal or normal approximation, $\eta(x; \mu T, \sigma^2 T) = N[(x - \mu T)/\sigma\sqrt{T}]$. First as a salutary warning against the illegitimate handling of limits, note that by the definition of a probability density of $P_T(x; w)$, $\partial P_T(x; w)/\partial x$, where such a density exists

$$\int_{-\infty}^{\infty} P'_T(x; w) \, dx \equiv 1. \tag{60}$$

Also, as is well known when summing independent, identically-distributed, non-normalized variates, the probabilities spread out and

$$\lim_{T \to \infty} P'_T(x; w) \, dx \equiv 0. \tag{61}$$

Combining eqs. (60) and (61), we see the illegitimacy of interchanging limits in the following fashion:

$$1 = \lim_{T \to \infty} \int_{-\infty}^{\infty} P'_T(x; w) \, dx = \int_{-\infty}^{\infty} \lim_{T \to \infty} P'_T(x; w) \, dx$$
$$= \int_{-\infty}^{\infty} 0 \cdot dx = 0. \tag{62}$$

Similarly, as was already indicated for a non-density discrete-probability example in the previous section, from the following true relation,

$$\lim_{T \to \infty} [P'_T(x; w) - \eta'(x; \mu T, \sigma^2 T)] = 0, \tag{63}$$

it is false to conclude that, for $0 < \gamma < 1$,

$$\lim_{T \to \infty} \int_{-\infty}^{\infty} e^{\gamma x} [P'_T(x; w) - \eta'(x; \mu T, \sigma^2 T)] \, dx$$
$$= \int_{-\infty}^{\infty} e^{\gamma x} \lim_{T \to \infty} [P'_T(x; w) - \eta'(x; \mu T, \sigma^2 T)] \, dx$$
$$= \int_{-\infty}^{\infty} e^{\gamma x} \cdot 0 \, dx = 0. \tag{64}$$

Hence, trying to calculate the correct $\bar{U}_T[w]$, in eq. (7) even for very large T, by relying on its surrogate

$$\int_{-\infty}^{\infty} e^{\gamma x} \eta'(x; \mu T, \sigma^2 T) \, dx = \exp\{[\gamma\mu(w) + 1/2\gamma^2\sigma^2(w)]T\} \tag{65}$$

leads to the wrong portfolio rules, namely to $w^\dagger \neq w^* \equiv w^{**}(t)$.

Thus, we hope that the fallacy of the surrogate log-normal approximation with respect to optimal portfolio selection has been laid to rest.

In concluding this debunking of improper log-normal approximations, we should mention that this same fallacy pops up with monotonous regularity in all branches of stochastic investment analysis. Thus, one of us, Samuelson (1965), had to warn of its incorrect use in rational warrant pricing.

Suppose a common stock's future price compared to its present price, $V(t+T)/V(t) \equiv Z[T]$, is distributed like the product of T independent, uniform probabilities $P[Z]$. For T large, there is a log-normal surrogate for

$$\text{Prob}\{\log(Z[T]) \leq x\} \equiv \Pi_T(x). \tag{66}$$

Let the 'rational price of the warrant' be given, as in the cited 1965 paper, by

$$F_T[V] = e^{-\alpha T}\int_{-\infty}^{\infty}\max[0, V e^x - C]\Pi'_T(x) \, dx, \tag{67}$$

where C is the warrant's exercise price and $e^\alpha \equiv E\{V(t+1)/V(t)\}$. Although the density of the normalized variate $y \equiv (\log(Z[T]) - \mu T)/\sigma\sqrt{T}$ approaches $N'(y)$, it is false to think that, even for large T,

$$e^{\alpha T} \doteq \int_{-\infty}^{\infty} e^x \eta'(x; \mu T, \sigma^2 T) \, dx = \exp\{[\mu + 1/2\sigma^2]T\}. \tag{68}$$

Nor, for finite T, will we in other than a trivial sense, observe the identity

$$F_T[V] \equiv F_T^\dagger[V] \tag{69}$$

$$= \exp\{[-\mu - 1/2\sigma^2]T\}\int_{-\infty}^{\infty}\max[0, V e^x - C]\eta'(x; \mu T, \sigma^2 T) \, dx.$$

It is trivially true that $\lim_{T\to\infty}\{F_T[V] - F_T^\dagger[V]\} = V - V = 0$, but untrue that $\lim_{T\to\infty}\{(V - F_T[V])/(V - F_T^\dagger[V])\} = 1$. Of course, if $\Pi_1(x)$ is gaussian to begin with, as in infinitely-divisible continuous-time probabilities, there is no need for an asymptotic approximation and no surrogate concept is involved to betray one into error.

Similar remarks could be made about treacherous log-normal surrogates misapplied to the alternative 1969 warrant pricing theory of Samuelson and Merton.[21]

To bring this chamber of horrors concerning false limits to an end, we must stress that limiting inequalities can be as treacherous as limiting equalities. Thus, consider two alternative strategies that produce alternative random

---

[21]Samuelson and Merton (1969). Since Black–Scholes (1973) warrant pricing is based squarely on exact log-normal definitions, it is inexact for non-log-normal surrogate reasoning. See Merton (1973) for further discussion.

variables of utility (or of money), written as U_I and U_{II} respectively and satisfying probability distributions $P_I(U; T)$ and $P_{II}(U; T)$. Too often the false inference is made that

$$\lim_{T \to \infty} \text{Prob}\{U_I > U_{II}\} = 1 \tag{70}$$

implies (or is implied by) the condition

$$\lim_{T \to \infty} \{E[U_I] - E[U_{II}]\} > 0 \tag{71}$$

Indeed, as was shown in our refuting the fallacy of max-expected-log, yielding U_I rather than the correct optimal U_{II} that comes from use of $w^* \neq w^{\dagger\dagger}$, it is the case that eq. (70) is satisfied and yet it is also true that

$$E[U_I - U_{II}] < 0 \text{ for all } T \text{ however large.} \tag{72}$$

Or consider another property of the $w^{\dagger\dagger}$ strategy: Namely,

$$\text{Prob}\{Z_T[w^{\dagger\dagger}] \leqq x\} \leqq \text{Prob}\{Z_T[w] \leqq x\} \text{ for all } x < M(T; w), \tag{73}$$

where $M(T; w)$ is an increasing function of T with $\lim_{T \to \infty} M(T; w) = \infty$. Yet eq. (73) does not imply eq. (71) nor does it imply asymptotic First Order Stochastic Dominance. I.e., it does not follow from eq. (73) that, as $T \to \infty$,

$$\text{Prob}\{Z_T[w^{\dagger\dagger}] \leqq x\} \leqq \text{Prob}\{Z_T[w] \leqq x\} \text{ for } all \text{ } x \text{ independently of } T. \tag{74}$$

The moral is this: Never confuse exact limits involving normalized variables with their naive formal extrapolations. Although $a = b$ and $b = c$ implies $a = c$; still $a \approx b$ and $b \approx c$ cannot reliably imply $a \approx c$ without careful restrictions put on the interpretation of ' $\approx$ '.

6. Continuous-time portfolio selection

The enormous interest in the optimal portfolio selection problem for investors with distant time horizons was generated by the hope that an intertemporal portfolio theory could be developed which, at least asymptotically, would have the simplicity and richness of the static mean-variance theory without the well known objections to that model. While the analysis of previous sections demonstrates that such a theory does not validly obtain, we now derive an asymptotic theory involving limits of a different type which will produce the conjectured results.

We denote by T the time horizon of the investor. Now, we denote by N the number of portfolio revisions over that horizon, so that $h \equiv T/N$ will be the length of time between portfolio revisions. In the previous sections, we examined the asymptotic portfolio behavior as T and N tended to infinity, for a fixed $h(= 1)$. In this section, we consider the asymptotic portfolio behavior for a *fixed T*, as *N* tends to infinity and *h* tends to zero. The limiting behavior is interpreted as that of an investor who can continuously revise his portfolio. We leave for later the discussion of how realistic is this assumption and other assumptions as a description of actual asset market conditions, and for the moment, proceed formally to see what results obtain.

While the assumptions of previous sections about the distributions of asset returns are kept, we make explicit their dependence on the trading interval length, *h*. I.e., the per-dollar return on the *j*th asset between times $t-\tau$ and t when the trading interval is of length *h*, is $Z_j(t, \tau; h)$, where τ is integral in *h*.

Suppose, as is natural once time is continuous, that the individual $Z_j(\ )$ are distributed log-normally with constant parameters. I.e.,

$$\text{Prob}\{\log[Z_j(t, \tau; h)] \leq x\} = N(x; \mu_j\tau, \sigma_j^2\tau), \tag{75}$$

where

$$E\{\log[Z_j(t, \tau; h)]\} = \mu_j\tau \tag{76}$$

and

$$\text{var}\{\log[Z_j(t, \tau; h)]\} = \sigma_j^2\tau,$$

with μ_j and σ_j^2 independent of *h*. Further, define

$$\alpha_j\tau \equiv (\mu_j + 1/2\sigma_j^2)\tau \tag{77}$$

$$= \log[E\{Z_j(t, \tau; h)\}],$$

and

$$\sigma_{ij}\tau \equiv \text{cov}\{\log[Z_i(t, \tau; h)], \log[Z_j(t, \tau; h)]\}. \tag{78}$$

As in eq. (11), the *n*th asset is riskless with $\alpha_n = r$ and $\sigma_n^2 = 0$.

We denote by $[w^*(t; h)]$ the vector of optimal portfolio proportions at time *t* when the trading interval is of length *h*, and its limit as $h \to 0$ by $w^*(t; 0)$. Then the following separation (or 'mutual fund') theorem obtains:

Theorem. Given *n* assets whose returns are log-normally distributed and given continuous-trading opportunities (i.e., $h = 0$), then the $\{w^*(t; 0)\}$ are such that: (1) There exists a unique (up to a non-singular transformation) pair of 'mutual funds' constructed from linear combinations of these assets such that independent of preferences, wealth distribution, or time horizon, investors will be indifferent between choosing from a linear combination of these two funds or a linear combination of the original *n* assets. (2) If Z_f is the return on either fund, then Z_f is log-normally distributed. (3) The fractional proportions of respective assets contained in either fund are solely a function of the α_i and σ_{ij}, $(i, j = 1, 2, \ldots, n)$ an 'efficiency' condition.

Proof of the theorem can be found in Merton (1971, pp. 384–386). It obtains whether one of the assets is riskless or not. From the theorem, we can always work here with just two assets: the riskless asset and a (composite) risky asset which is log-normally distributed with parameters (α, σ^2).[22] Hence, we can reduce the vector $[w^*(t; 0)]$ to a scalar $w^*(t)$ equal to the fraction invested in the risky asset. If we denote by $\alpha^*(\equiv w^*(t)(\alpha-r)+r)$ and $\sigma_*^2(\equiv w^{*2}\sigma^2)$, the (instantaneous) mean gain and variance of a given investor's optimal portfolio, an efficiency frontier in terms of (α^*, σ_*) or (μ^*, σ_*) can be traced out as shown in either fig. 1a or 1b. The (α^*, σ_*)-frontier is exactly akin to the classical Markowitz

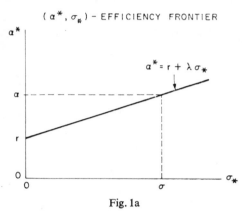

Fig. 1a

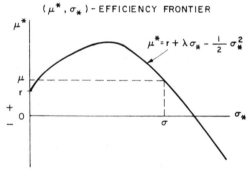

Fig. 1b

single-period frontier where a 'period' is an instant. Although the frontier is the same in every period, a given investor will in general choose a different point on the frontier each period depending on his current wealth and $T-t$.

In the special case of iso-elastic utility,[23] $U_T = W^\gamma/\gamma$, $\gamma < 1$, $w^*(t) = w^*$, a constant, and the entire portfolio selection problem can be presented graphi-

---

[22]See Merton (1971, p. 388) for an explicit expression for α and σ^2 as a function of the α and σ_{ij}, $i, j = 1, 2, \ldots, n$.

[23]See Merton (1969, p. 251 and 1971, pp. 388–394).

cally as in fig. 2. Further, for this special class of utility functions, the distribution of wealth under the optimal policy will be log-normal for all t.[24]

Hence, from the assumptions of log-normality and continuous trading, we have, even for T finite and not at all large, a complete asymptotic theory with all the simplicity of classical mean-variance, but without its objectionable assumptions. Further, these results still obtain even if one allows intermediate consumption evaluated at some concave utility function, $V(c)$.[25]

Having derived the theory, we now turn to the question of the reasonableness of the assumptions. Since trading continuously is not a reality, the answer will depend on 'how close' $w^*(t; 0)$ is to $w^*(t; h)$. I.e., for every $\delta > 0$, does there

PORTFOLIO SELECTION FOR ISO-ELASTIC
UTILITY FUNCTIONS

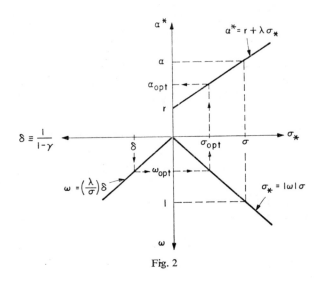

Fig. 2

exist an $h > 0$, such that $\|w^*(t; 0) - w^*(t; h)\| < \delta$ for some norm $\| \ \|$, and what is the nature of the $\delta = \delta(h)$ function? Further, since log-normality as the distribution for returns is not a 'known fact', what are the conditions such that one can validly use the log-normal as a surrogate?

Since the answer to both questions will turn on the distributional assumptions for the returns, we now drop the assumption of log-normality for the $Z_j(\ ; h)$, but retain the assumptions (maintained throughout the paper) that, for a

---

[24]See Merton (1971, p. 392).
[25]Further the log-normality assumption can be weakened and still some separation and efficiency conditions will obtain. See Merton (forthcoming).

given h,[26] the one-period returns, $Z_j(\ , h; h)$ have joint distributions identical through time, and the vector $[Z(t, h; h)] \equiv [Z_1(t, h; h), \ Z_2(t, h; h), \ldots, Z_n(t,h; h)]$ is distributed independently of $[Z(t+s, h; h)]$ for $s > h$.

By definition, the return on the jth security over a time period of length T will be

$$Z_j(t, T; h) \equiv \prod_{k=1}^{T} Z_j(kh, h; h). \tag{79}$$

Let $X_j(k, h) \equiv \log[Z_j(kh, h; h)]$. Then, for a given h, the $\{X_j(k, h)\}$ are independently and identically distributed with non-central moments

$$m_j(i; h) \equiv \underset{k}{E}\{[X_j(k, h)]^i\}, \quad i = 0, 1, 2, \ldots, \tag{80}$$

and moment-generating function

$$\psi_j(\lambda; h) \equiv \underset{k}{E}\{\exp[\lambda X_j(k, h)]\} \tag{81}$$

$$= E\{[Z_j(kh, h; h)]^\lambda\}.$$

Define the non-central moments of the *rate of return* per period, $Z_j(kh, h; h) - 1$, by

$$M_j(1; h) = \alpha_j(h)h \equiv \underset{k}{E}\{Z_j(kh, h; h) - 1\}, \tag{82}$$

$$M_j(2; h) = v_j^2(h)h + (\alpha_j(h)h)^2 \equiv \underset{k}{E}\{[Z_j(kh, h; h) - 1]^2\},$$

$$M_j(i; h) \equiv \underset{k}{E}\{[Z_j(kh, h; h) - 1]^i\}, \quad i = 3, 4, \ldots,$$

where $\alpha_j(h)$ is the expected rate of return per unit time and $v_j^2(h)$ is the variance of the rate of return per unit time.

Samuelson (1970) has demonstrated that if the moments $M_j(\ ; h)$ satisfy

$$M_j(1; h) = 0(h), \tag{83}$$

$$M_j(2; h) = 0(h),$$

$$M_j(k; h) = o(h), \quad k > 2,$$

then $\|w^*(t; 0) - w^*(t; h)\| = 0(h)$ where '0' and 'o' are defined by

$$g(h) = 0(h), \quad \text{if } (g/h) \text{ is bounded for all } h \geq 0 \tag{84}$$

---

[26]It is not required that the distribution of one-period returns with trading interval of length h_1 will be in the same family of distributions as the one-period returns with trading interval of length $h_2(\neq h_1)$. I.e., the distributions need not be infinitely divisible in time. However, we do require sufficient regularity that the distribution of $X_j(T; h)$ is in the domain of attraction of the normal distribution, and hence, the limit distribution as $h \to 0$ will be infinitely divisible in time.

and

$$g(h) = o(h), \quad \text{if} \quad \lim_{h \to 0}(g/h) = 0. \tag{85}$$

Thus, if the distributions of returns satisfy eq. (83), then, for every $\delta > 0$, there exists an $h > 0$ such that $\|w^*(t; 0) - w^*(t; h)\| < \delta$, and the continuous-time solution will be a valid asymptotic solution to the discrete-interval case. Note that if eq. (83) is satisfied, then $\alpha_j(h) = 0(1)$ and $v_j^2(h) = 0(1)$, and $\alpha_j \equiv \lim_{h \to 0} \alpha_j(h)$ will be finite as will $v^2 \equiv \lim_{h \to 0} v_j^2(h)$.

Given that $M_j(\ ; h)$ satisfies eq. (83), we can derive a similar relationship for $m_j(\ ; h)$. Namely, by Taylor series,[27]

$$m_j(1; h) = E\{\log(1 + [Z_j - 1])\} \tag{86}$$

$$= E\left\{ \sum_{i=1}^{\infty} (-1)^{i-1} [Z_j - 1]^i / i \right\}$$

$$= M_j(1; h) - 1/2 M_j(2; h) + o(h), \quad \text{from eq. (83)}$$

$$= 0(h),$$

and

$$m_j(2; h) = E\{\log^2(1 + [Z_j - 1])\} \tag{87}$$

$$= E\left\{ \sum_{p=1}^{\infty} \sum_{i=1}^{\infty} (-1)^{i+p} [Z_j - 1]^{i+p} / ip \right\}$$

$$= M_j(2; h) + o(h)$$

$$= 0(h),$$

and, in a similar fashion,

$$m_j(k; h) = o(h), \quad \text{for } k > 2. \tag{88}$$

Thus, the $m_j(\ ; h)$ satisfy eq. (83) as well. If we define $\mu_j(h) \equiv m_j(1; h)/h$ as the mean logarithmic return per unit time and $\sigma_j^2(h) \equiv [m_j(2; h) - \mu_j^2(h) h^2]/h$ as the variance of the log return per unit time, then from eqs. (82), (86) and (87), we have that

$$\alpha_j \equiv \lim_{h \to 0} \alpha_j(h) = \lim_{h \to 0} [\mu_j(h) + 1/2 \sigma_j^2(h)] = \mu_j + 1/2 \sigma_j^2$$

and $$\tag{89}$$

$$v_j^2 \equiv \lim_{h \to 0} v_j^2(h) = \lim_{h \to 0} \sigma_j^2(h) = \sigma_j^2. \tag{90}$$

Eq. (89) demonstrates that the true distribution will satisfy asymptotically the exact relationship satisfied for all h by the log-normal surrogate; from eq. (90), the variance of the arithmetic return will equal the variance of the

---

[27] The series expansion is only valid for $0 < Z \leqq 2$. Hence, a rigorous analysis would develop a second expansion for $Z > 2$. However, as is shown later in eq. (95), the probability that $Z > 2$ can be made arbitrarily small by picking h small enough. Thus, the contribution of the $Z > 2$ part to the moments $o(h)$.

logarithmic return in the limit. Hence, these important moment relationships match up exactly between the true distribution and its log-normal surrogate.

If we define $Y_j(T; h) \equiv \log[Z_j(T, T; h)]$, then from eq. (79), we have that

$$Y_j(T; h) \equiv \sum_{k=1}^{N} X_j(k, h), \quad \text{where } N \equiv T/h, \tag{91}$$

and from the independence and identical distribution of the $X_j(\ ; h)$, the moment-generating function of Y_j will satisfy

$$\phi_j(\lambda; h, T) \equiv E(\exp[\lambda Y_j(T; h)]\} \tag{92}$$

$$= [\psi_j(\lambda; h)]^{T/h}.$$

Taking logs of both sides of eq. (92) and using Taylor series, we have that

$$\log[\phi_j(\lambda; h, T)] = (T/h)\log[\psi_j(\lambda; h)] \tag{93}$$

$$= (T/h)\log[\sum_{k=0}^{\infty} \psi_j^{(k)}\ (0; h)\lambda^k/k!]$$

$$= (T/h)\log[\sum_{k=1}^{\infty} m_j(k; h)\lambda^k/k!]$$

$$= (T/h)\log[1 + m_j(1; h)\lambda + 1/2 m_j(2; h)\lambda^2 + o(h)]$$

$$= T[\lambda(m_j(1; h)/h) + (\lambda^2/2)(m_j(2; h)/h) + 0(h)].$$

Substituting $\mu_j(h)h$ for $m_j(1; h)$ and $\sigma_j^2(h)h + \mu_j^2(h)h^2$ for $m_j(2; h)$ and taking the limit as $h \to o$ in eq. (93), we have that

$$\log[\phi_j(\lambda; 0, T)] = \lim_{h \to 1} \log[\phi(\lambda; h, T)] \tag{94}$$

$$= \lambda \mu_j T + 1/2 \sigma_j^2 T\lambda^2,$$

and therefore, $\phi_j(\lambda; 0, T)$ is the moment-generating function for a normally-distributed random variable with mean $\mu_j T$ and variance $\sigma_j^2 T$.

Thus, in what is essentially a valid application of the Central-Limit Theorem, we have shown that the limit distribution for $Y_j(T, T; h)$ as h tends to zero, is under the posited assumptions gaussian, and hence, the limit distribution for $Z_j(T, T; h)$ will be log-normal for *all finite T*. Further from eqs. (89)–(90), the surrogate log-normal, fitted in the Pearsonian fashion of earlier sections, will, for smaller and smaller h, be in the limit, the true limit distribution for $Z_j(T, T; 0)$.

It is straightforward to show that if the distribution for each of the $Z_j(\ , h; h)$, $j = 1, 2, \ldots, n$, satisfy eq. (83), then for bounded $w_j(t; h)$, the 'single-period' *portfolio* returns, $Z[t; w(t), h]$, will for each t satisfy eq. (83). However, unless the portfolio weights are constant through time [i.e., $w_j(t) \equiv w_j$], the resulting limit distribution for the portfolio over finite time, will not be log-normal.

How reasonable is it to assume that eq. (83) will be satisfied? Essentially eq. (83) is a set of sufficient conditions for the limiting continuous-time sto-chastic process to have a continuous sample path (with probability one). It is closely related to the 'local Markov property' of discrete-time stochastic processes which allows only movements to neighboring states in one period (e.g., the simple random walk).

A somewhat weaker sufficient condition [implied by eq. (83); see also Feller (1966, p. 321)] is that for every $\delta > 0$,

$$\text{Prob}\{-\delta \leqq X_j(\quad ; h) \leqq \delta\} = 1 - o(h), \tag{95}$$

which clearly rules out 'jump-type' processes such as the Poisson. It is easy to show for the Poisson that eq. (83) is not satisfied because $M_j(k; h) = 0(h)$ for all k and similarly, eq. (95) is not satisfied since $\text{Prob}\{-\delta \leqq X_j(\quad ; h) \leqq \delta\}$ $= 1 - 0(h)$.

In the general case when eq. (95) is satisfied but the distribution of returns are not completely independent nor identically distributed, the limit distribution will not be log-normal, but will be generated by a diffusion process. Although certain quadratic simplifications still occur, the strong theorems of the earlier part of this section will no longer obtain.

The accuracy of the continuous solution will depend on whether, for reason-able trading intervals, compact distributions are an accurate representation for asset returns and whether, for these intervals, the distributions can be taken to be independent. Examination of time series for common stock returns shows that skewness and higher-order moments tend to be negligible relative to the first two moments for daily or weekly observations, which is consistent with eq. (83)'s assumptions. However, daily data tend also to show some negative serial correlation, significant for about two weeks. While this finding is inconsistent with independence, the size of the correlation coefficient is not large and the short-duration of the correlation suggests a 'high-speed of adjustment' in the auto-correlation function. Hence, while we could modify the continuous analysis to include an Ornstein–Uhlenbeck type process to capture these effects,[28] the results may not differ much from the standard model when empirical esti-mates of the correlation are plugged in.

[28]Cf. Merton (1971, p. 401).

References

Arrow, K.J., 1965, Aspects of the theory of risk-bearing (Yrjö Jahnssonin Säätiö, Helsinki).

Aucamp, D.C., 1971, A new theory of optimal investment, mimeo. (Southern Illinois Univer-sity, Carbondal, Ill.).

Black, F., M. Jensen and M. Scholes, 1972, The capital asset pricing model: Some empirical tests, in: M. Jensen, ed., Studies in the theory of capital markets (Praeger Publishers, New York).

Black, F. and M. Scholes, 1973, The pricing of options and corporate liabilities, Journal of Political Economy 81, 637–654.

Borch, K., 1969, A note on uncertainty and indifference curves, Review of Economic Studies 36, 1–4.

Breiman, L., 1960, Investment policies for expanding business optimal in a long-run sense, Naval Research Logistics Quarterly 674–651.

Cass, D. and J. Stiglitz, 1970, The structure of investor preferences and asset returns, and separability in portfolio allocation: A contribution to the pure theory of mutual funds, Journal of Economic Theory 2, 122–160.

Fama, E., 1965, Portfolio analysis in a stable Paretian market, Management Science 11, 404–419.

Fama, E., 1970, Efficient capital markets: A review of theory and empirical work, Journal of Finance 25, 383–417.

Feldstein, M., 1969, Mean-variance analysis in the theory of liquidity preference and portfolio selection, Review of Economic Studies 36, 5–12.

Feller, W., 1966, An introduction to probability theory and its applications, vol. II (John Wiley, New York).

Friend, I. and M. Blume, 1970, Measurement of portfolio performance under uncertainty, American Economic Review LX, 561–575.

Goldman, M.B., 1972, A negative report on the 'near-optimality' of the max-expected-log policy as applied to bounded utilities for long-lived programs, mimeo. (M.I.T., Cambridge, Mass.).

Hadar, J. and W. Russell, 1969, Rules for ordering uncertain prospects, American Economic Review 59, 25–34.

Hakansson, N., 1970, Optimal investment and consumption strategies under risk for a class of utility functions, Econometrica 38, 587–607.

Hakansson, N., 1971a, Capital growth and the mean-variance approach to portfolio selection, Journal of Financial and Quantitative Analysis 6, 517–558.

Hakansson, N., 1971b, Multi-period mean-variance analysis: Toward a general theory of portfolio choice, Journal of Finance 26.

Hakansson, N., 1971c, Mean-variance analysis of average compound returns, mimeo. (University of California, Berkeley).

Jen, F., 1971, Multi-period portfolio strategies, Working Paper no. 108 (State University of New York, Buffalo, N.Y.).

Jen, F., 1972, Criteria in multi-period portfolio decisions, Working Paper no. 131 (State University of New York, Buffalo, N.Y.).

Jensen, M., 1972, Capital markets: Theory and evidence, Bell Journal of Economics and Management Science 3, 357–398.

Latane, H., 1959, Criteria for choice among risky ventures, Journal of Political Economy 67, 144–155.

Leland, H., 1968, Dynamic portfolio theory, Ph.D. Thesis (Harvard University, Cambridge, Mass.).

Leland, H., 1972, On turnpike portfolios, in: G. Szegö and K. Shell, eds., Mathematical methods in investment and finance (North-Holland, Amsterdam).

Levy, H., 1973, Stochastic dominance among log-normal prospects, International Economic Review 14, 601–614.

Lintner, J., 1965, The valuation of risk assets and the selection of risky investments in stock portfolios and capital budgets, Review of Economics and Statistics XLVIII, 13–37.

Markowitz, H., 1959, Portfolio selection: Efficient diversification of investment (John Wiley, New York).

Markowitz, H., 1972, Investment for the long run, Rodney L. White Center for Financial Research Working Paper no. 20–72 (University of Pennsylvania, Philadelphia, Pa.).

Merton, R.C., 1969, Lifetime portfolio selection under uncertainty: The continuous-time case, Review of Economics and Statistics LI, 247–257.

Merton, R.C., 1971, Optimum consumption of portfolio rules in a continuous-time model, Journal of Economic Theory 3, 373–413.

Merton, R.C., 1972a, An analytical derivation of the efficient portfolio frontier, Journal of Financial and Quantitative Analysis 1851–1871.

Merton, R.C., ed., 1972b, The collected scientific papers of Paul A. Samuelson, vol. III (M.I.T. Press, Cambridge, 1972).

Merton, R.C., 1973, Theory of rational option pricing, Bell Journal of Economics and Management Science 4, 141–183.

Merton, R.C., forthcoming, An intertemporal capital asset pricing model, Econometrica.

Mossin, J., 1966, Equilibrium in a capital asset market, Econometrica 35, 768–783.

Ross, S., 1972a, Portfolio and capital market theory with arbitrary preferences and distributions – The general validity of the mean-variance approach in large markets, Wharton School of Finance Working Paper no. 12–72 (University of Pennsylvania, Philadelphia, Pa.).

Ross, S., 1972b, A counterexample taken from some portfolio turnpike theorems, mimeo. (University of Pennsylvania, Philadelphia, Pa.).

Rothschild, M. and J. Stiglitz, 1970, Increasing risk I, A definition, Journal of Economic Theory 2, 225–243.

Samuelson, P.A., 1965, Rational theory of warrant pricing, Industrial Management Review 6, 13–31; reprinted in Merton (1972b, ch. 199).

Samuelson, P.A., 1967a, General proof that diversification pays, Journal of Financial and Quantitative Analysis II, 1–13; reprinted in Merton (1972b, ch. 201).

Samuelson, P.A., 1967b, Efficient portfolio selection for Pareto Levy investments, Journal of Financial and Quantitative Analysis 107–122; reprinted in Merton (1972b, ch. 202).

Samuelson, P.A., 1969, Lifetime portfolio selection by dynamic stochastic programming, Review of Economics and Statistics LI, 239–246; reprinted in Merton (1972b, ch. 204).

Samuelson, P.A., 1970, The fundamental approximation theorem of portfolio analysis in terms of means, variances, and higher moments, Review of Economic Studies 37, 537–542; reprinted in Merton (1972b, ch. 203).

Samuelson, P.A., 1971, The 'fallacy' of maximizing the geometric mean in long sequences of investing or gambling, Proceedings of the National Academy of Sciences 68, 2493–2496; reprinted in Merton (1972b, ch. 200).

Samuelson, P.A. and R.C. Merton, 1969, A complete model of warrant pricing that maximizes utility, Industrial Management Review 10, 17–46; reprinted in Merton (1972b, ch. 200).

Samuelson, P.A. and R.C. Merton, 1974, Generalized mean-variance tradeoffs for best perturbation corrections to approximate portfolio decisions, Journal of Finance, forthcoming.

Sharpe, W., 1964, Capital asset prices: A theory of market equilibrium under conditions of risk, Journal of Finance XIX, 425–442.

Sharpe, W., 1970, Portfolio theory and capital markets (McGraw-Hill, New York).

Tobin, J., 1958, Liquidity preference as behavior towards risk, Review of Economic Studies 25, 68–85.

Tobin, J., 1965, The theory of portfolio selection, in: F. Hahn and F. Brechling, The theory of interest rates (MacMillan, New York).

246

GENERALIZED MEAN-VARIANCE TRADEOFFS FOR BEST PERTURBATION CORRECTIONS TO APPROXIMATE PORTFOLIO DECISIONS*

Paul A. Samuelson
Robert C. Merton

For investors with utilities "near" to logarithmic utility of terminal wealth, it is shown how use of the pair of parameters $E\{\log W\}$ and Variance$\{\log W\}$ can form an efficiency tradeoff frontier useful locally for people of different risk-return tolerances. Exact perturbation approximations are given in power series, and this two-parameter-tradeoff device is generalized to investors sharing the same general degree of risk tolerance, even if it is not near to $\log W$. Standard Markowitz mean-variance is seen to be one such special case. Another case is that of Hakansson's average-compound returns, whose expected value and variance—absurd and irrelevant as they are to those with utilities of terminal wealth *not* close to $\log W_T$—can be used as asymptotic surrogates for our locally-sufficient pair of parameters.

I. Solutions to Portfolio Decision Problem

A. *Local Perturbation Technique*

Exact solutions to the standard portfolio decision problem involves

$$\underset{\{w_i\}}{\text{Max}} \, E[U[W]] = \underset{\{w_i\}}{\text{Max}} \int_0^\infty U[W_o \Sigma_1^n w_j Z_j] P(dZ_1, \ldots, dZ_n) = U[w^*_2, \ldots, w^*_n] \tag{1}$$

where $U[\ ]$ is a strictly-concave function of terminal wealth, W, $P(Z_1, \ldots, Z_n)$ is the joint probability distribution of the non-negative random variables that depict each terminal outcome in dollars from one dollar invested in the jth security or program, $E\{\ \}$ is the operator for mathematical expectation, W_o is given initial wealth, $(w_2, \ldots, w_n)$ are fractions of wealth invested in each security, and $w_1 = 1 - \Sigma_2^n w_j$ is the amount invested in an available safe security.

Although general properties of the exact solution are known, its computation can be lengthy. Therefore, approximate solutions are legitimate objects of research.

Mistakenly, some have proposed replacing the general problem by $U[W] = \log W$, in the fallacious belief that such a maximizing strategy will give a good approximation to the true solution (or perhaps even "better" it) when there are many periods of independent reinvesting. See Williams [12], Latané

* This paper is a spin-off of a longer study [8] by the authors dealing with fallacious log-normal approximations in portfolio decision making. We owe thanks to the National Science Foundation for financial support.

[5], Kelly [4], Aucamp [1], Breiman [2], and their critique by Samuelson [10].

Some others have been attracted by the criterion of maximum expected average compound return discussed by Hakansson [3], in which the general U[W] can be replaced by $U[W] = W^{1/N}$ or by $W^{a/N}$, where N is an integer greater than or equal to two (and usually much greater) and $a \leqslant 1$, $a \neq 0$. (The case of $a = 0$ can be assimilated under the log W strategy already mentioned.)

However, it should be obvious that anyone whose true U[W] is far away from log W, as for example if it were $2W^{1/2} - W^{-1}$, $(1 + W)/(2 + W)$, or W^γ/γ for $|\gamma| >> 0$, will be badly served by the average compound return criterion—*no matter how numerous the periods of his independent reinvestings!* And supplementing its mean by its variance will not, in the general situation, remedy the failure of such a "maximum growth" policy.

Fallacies are fallacies. And they must be recognized as such. Nevertheless, we can ask the following question that will be of limited interest in some special cases.

Suppose there are two or more people, facing the same investment options, each with U functions near to W^ϵ/ϵ where $|\epsilon|$ is a small number. Thus, man B has $W^{1/9}/(1/9)$, man C has $-W^{-1/100}/(1/100)$, ... If by luck, some man A has solved the problem for log W, which is clearly "near" the other men's solutions, we should be able to develop a *perturbation technique* whereby supplementing A's E{logW} by Variance {logW} will give men B and C close approximations to their exact solutions.

How close is "close?" For any man we can write the optimal portfolio proportions as

$$w^*_i(\epsilon) = w^*_i(0) + \epsilon w^{*\prime}_i(0) + 0(\epsilon^2), \qquad (i = 2, \ldots, n). \tag{2}$$

Then $w^*_i(0)$ is the max E{logW} solution. And the best estimate for the correction-term coefficient $w^{*\prime}_i(0)$ is calculable from Var{logW}.

This means that we can validly generalize the classical absolute-mean-variance analysis of Markowitz [7], which works with arithmetic (rather than logarithmic) values E{W} and Var{W} and which must be viewed with caution when probabilities are not "compact" in the sense of Samuelson [9]. Now, we prepare once and for all a local efficiency tradeoff frontier between $\mu = E\{logW\}$ and $\sigma^2 = Var\{logW\}$, *which can be used* by all men like B and C to find their own best "risk-return" point to a high degree of approximation.

Warning: μ and σ^2 are "asymptotically sufficient" parameters for the problem only in the non-general case where ϵ in W^ϵ/ϵ is small enough so that the exact first correction in (2) is not swamped by the neglected remainder in the perturbation expansion.

If, however, ϵ's being small is a legitimate empirical hypothesis, then there are also other equivalent ways of arriving at the $w^{*\prime}_i(0)$ correction term. Thus, Hakansson's frontier of E{average compound return} and Var{average compound return} can equivalently be employed for this purpose—even by one who (like us) regards preoccupation with average compound return as gratuitous or fallacious.

B. *Sketch of Derivation*

In this preliminary report, we shall only heuristically present the argument. Replace W^ϵ/ϵ by its equivalent for maximization purposes

$$U[\epsilon;W] = (W^\epsilon - 1)/\epsilon \tag{4}$$

$$\lim_{\epsilon \to 0} U[\epsilon;W] = \log W$$

$$\lim_{\epsilon \to 0} \frac{\partial U[\epsilon;W]}{\partial \epsilon} = \tfrac{1}{2}\log^2 W.$$

Then, by Taylor's expansion,

$$U[\epsilon;W] = \log W + \tfrac{1}{2}\,\epsilon\log^2 W + 0(\epsilon^2) \tag{5}$$

and

$$E\{U[\epsilon;W]\} = \mu + \tfrac{1}{2}\epsilon(\sigma^2 + \mu^2) + 0(\epsilon^2) \tag{6}$$

$$= u[\epsilon;w_2(\epsilon),\ldots,w_n(\epsilon)]$$

$$= u[\epsilon;w] \text{ for short.}$$

Then,

$$\underset{\{w\}}{\text{Max}}\, u[\epsilon;w] = u[\epsilon;w^*(\epsilon)]\,|$$

is defined by the solution of the implicit equations satisfying the first-order maximum conditions.

$$0 = u_W[\epsilon;W^*] = u_W[0;W^*(0)] + \epsilon u_{WE}[0;W^*(0)]\epsilon u_{WW}[0;W^*(0)]W^{*\prime}(0) + 0(\epsilon^2), \tag{7}$$

where $u_w[\ ]$ stands for the row vector $[\partial u[\ ]/\partial w_2,\ldots,\partial u[\ ]/\partial w_n]$ and $u_{ww}[\ ]$ stands for the Hessian matrix of u's second partial derivatives, and similarly for the column vectors $u_{WE}[\ ], W^*(0),$ and $W^{*\prime}(0)$.

We calculate recursively new terms such as $w^{*\prime}(0)$ from relations of the type

$$u_w[0,w^*(0)] = 0. \tag{8a}$$

$$u_{WW}[0,W^*(0)]W^{*\prime}(0) = -\partial u_W[0,W^*(0)]/\partial\epsilon. \tag{8b}$$

For higher order terms, such as $w^{*\prime\prime}(0)$ or $w^{*(n+1)}(0)$, we have similar *linear* relations

$$u_{ww}[0,w^*(0)]w^{*\prime\prime}(0) = \text{a function of the partials of } u[0,w^*(0)]$$
$$\text{and of } w^*(0) \text{ and } w^{*\prime}(0). \tag{8c}$$

$$\overline{}$$

$$u_{ww}[0,w^*(0)]w^{*(n+1)}(0) = \text{a function of the partials of } u[0,w^*(0)]$$
$$\text{and of } w^*(0), w^{*\prime}(0),\ldots, \tag{8z}$$
$$w^{*(n-1)}(0), w^{*(n)}(0).$$

So long as ϵ is small, maximizing expected utility can be done neglecting terms in ϵ^2 and higher powers, i.e., the exact optimal solution $\{w^*(\epsilon)\}$ will satisfy (7) which can be rewritten as

$$0 = \partial\mu(w^*)/\partial w_i + \tfrac{1}{2}\epsilon(\partial\sigma^2/\partial w_i + 2\mu\partial\mu/\partial w_i) + 0(\epsilon^2), \tag{9}$$

$$(i = 2, \ldots, n)$$

when $U[\epsilon; W]$ is as defined in (4), while the (approximate) optimal solution $\{w^\dagger(\epsilon)\}$ obtained by maximizing $[\mu + \tfrac{1}{2}\epsilon(\sigma^2 + \mu^2)]$ will satisfy

$$0 = \partial\mu(w^\dagger)/\partial w_i + \tfrac{1}{2}\epsilon(\partial\sigma^2/\partial w_i + 2\mu\partial\mu/\partial w_i), \qquad (i = 2, \ldots, N). \tag{10}$$

However, maximization of $[\mu + \tfrac{1}{2}\epsilon(\sigma^2 + \mu^2)]$ is not the only way of obtaining a valid approximation to $\{w^*(\epsilon)\}$. Namely, if $w^{\dagger\dagger}(\epsilon)$ is the solution to

$$\underset{\{w\}}{\text{Max}}[\mu + \tfrac{1}{2}\epsilon\sigma^2], \tag{11}$$

then it will satisfy

$$0 = \partial\mu[w^{\dagger\dagger}(\epsilon)]/\partial w_i + \tfrac{1}{2}\epsilon\,\partial\sigma^2/\partial w_i, \qquad (i = 2, \ldots, n). \tag{12}$$

But, (10) can be rewritten as

$$0 = \partial\mu(w^\dagger)/\partial w_i + \frac{\epsilon}{2(1 + \mu\epsilon)}\,\partial\sigma^2/\partial w_i, \qquad (i = 2, \ldots, n) \tag{13}$$

$$= \partial\mu(w^\dagger)/\partial w_i + \tfrac{1}{2}\epsilon\,\partial\sigma^2/\partial w_i + 0(\epsilon^2).\text{[1]}$$

Therefore, $w^\dagger_i(\epsilon) - w^{\dagger\dagger}_i(\epsilon) = 0(\epsilon^2)$ and $w^*_i(\epsilon) - w^{\dagger\dagger}_i(\epsilon) = 0(\epsilon^2)$, $i = 2, \ldots, n$. Relation (11) as a criterion is of interest because it is a linear logarithmic mean-variance tradeoff and because all feasible solutions to (11) can be generated by an efficient frontier in logarithmic mean-variance space, i.e., man B and man C will each find their (approximate) optimal solutions on the frontier defined by

$$\text{Max } \mu(w_2, \ldots, w_n) \tag{14}$$

$$\text{s.t.} \qquad \sigma^2(w_2, \ldots, w_n) = \text{constant.}$$

Men with negative ϵ will wish to be slightly less risk-taking than man A with his maximum-growth (i.e., max μ alone) solution. Those with positive ϵ will want to be a bit less cautious—i.e., *both* branches of the frontier around A are definitely efficient.

C. *Graphical Depiction*

Figure 1 shows a rough heuristic sketch of the (μ, σ^2) efficiency tradeoff frontier. As noted, large σ^2 as well as small provide efficient points. Men like B will *want* to be on the declining branch. A*, B*, C* show the exact best strategies for the three men. B and C are our perturbation approximations, differing from true B* and C* by terms of $0(\epsilon^2)$. The tangency at A* of the exact curve to the tradeoff frontier constitutes the essence of our perturbation theorem.

Figure 2 shows the story in the strategy space. The equilateral triangle provides a barycentric diagram: the sum of the distances from any point in

---

1. $\underset{\{w\}}{\text{Max}}\mu = \underset{\{w\}}{\text{Max}} E\{\log W\}$ exists and is finite. Hence, $\mu\epsilon = 0(\epsilon)$.

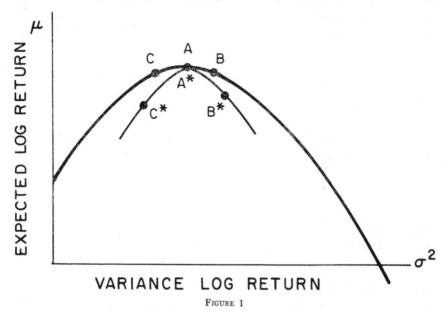

FIGURE 1

the triangle to the three sides is constant, taken to be unity. Then in a three-security case—say w_1 for fraction in cash, and w_2 and w_3 for fractions in two risky securities—the distance from the base (side 1) and the other two sides (sides 2 and 3) respectively depict $w_1 = 1 - w_2 - w_3$, w_2, w_3. The locus C A*B represents Figure 1's local approximations. Again tangency at A* epitomizes our power-series first approximations. (Note that the $w^*_i(0) +$

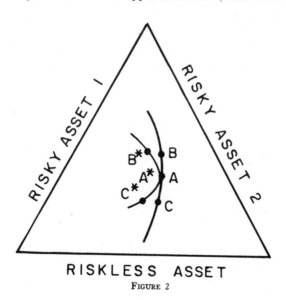

FIGURE 2

$\epsilon w^*_i{}'(0)$ approximation, which is very close to our C A*B locus, is not quite identical to it. But, of course, up to $O(\epsilon^2)$ there is no significant difference.)

D. *Higher-Order Conditions*

Remark: The same optimal solution, $w^*(\epsilon)$, is derived from any monotone stretching of $u[\epsilon;w]$ such as $g[\epsilon;w] \equiv G\{u[\epsilon;w],\epsilon\}$ with $\partial G/\partial u > 0$. Note that $g[\epsilon;w]$ will generally not have exactly the same coefficients in its power-series expansion in powers of ϵ (even though the solution to (7) and (8) for it must yield the same coefficients for $[w^*(0),w^*{}'(0), \ldots]$). This will explain why it happens that both $\text{Max}[\mu + \frac{1}{2}\epsilon(\sigma^2 + \mu^2)]$ and the different expression $\text{Max}[\mu + \frac{1}{2}\epsilon\sigma^2]$ in (11) can each yield the correct first-order approximating strategies—namely the same correct $[w^*(0),w^*{}'(0), \ldots]$ coefficients.[2]

Warning: Only in a near neighborhood of A's maximum will ϵ^2 terms be ignorable. To bring in a new second-order correction term $w^*{}''_i(0)$, we obviously need the third moment of skewness of $\log W$, μ_3, since (5) becomes

$$U[\epsilon;W] = \log W + \tfrac{1}{2}\epsilon\log^2 W + \tfrac{1}{6}\epsilon^2\log^3 W + O(\epsilon^3). \tag{15}$$

Now we need a tradeoff frontier in the three dimensions of logarithmic mean, variance, and skewness. And so it goes for fourth moment corrections to make the remainder $O(\epsilon^4)$. Every new power in the expansion involves a moment of one higher order, in analogy to Samuelson [9].

II. EXAMPLE

To illustrate that $w^*_i(\epsilon)$, $w^\dagger_i(\epsilon)$, and $w^{\dagger\dagger}_i(\epsilon)$ agree to $O(\epsilon^2)$, we consider the simple case of one risky and one riskless asset used in Merton and Samuelson [8]. The return per dollar on the riskless asset is R and the return per dollar on the risky asset is denoted by the Bernoulli-distributed random variable y where $\text{Prob}\{y = \lambda\} = \text{Prob}\{y = \delta\} = \frac{1}{2}$ and $\lambda > R > \delta > 0$. The optimal portfolio proportion in the risky asset was derived in [8] to be

$$w^*(\epsilon) = (A - 1)R/[(\lambda - R) + A(R - \delta)] \tag{16}$$

where

$$A \equiv [(R - \delta)/(\lambda - R)].^{\dfrac{1}{\epsilon - 1}}$$

Further, it was shown in [8] that the optimal solution to (11), $w^{\dagger\dagger}(\epsilon)$, satisfies

$$0 = \left(\frac{\lambda - R}{R - \delta}\right)[1 + \frac{\epsilon}{2}\log B] - B[1 - \frac{\epsilon}{2}\log B] \tag{17}$$

---

2. Actually, whenever $a(w) + \epsilon b(w) + O(\epsilon^2)$ is replaced by $a(w) + \epsilon f[a(w),b(w)] + O(\epsilon^2)$, we must get the same first-order conditions for $w^*(0)$, since $\{\partial f[\ ]/\partial a\} \{\partial a(w)/\partial w_i\}$ will vanish by virtue of the second factor's vanishing. So the presence or absence of a term like μ^2 in $\frac{1}{2}\epsilon(\sigma^2 + \mu^2)$ makes no formal difference. Of course, the proper $w^*{}''(0)$ cannot be found from $\mu + \frac{1}{2}\epsilon\sigma^2$ if the proper $O(\epsilon^2)$ terms are not taken into account.

where

$$B(\epsilon) \equiv [w^{\dagger\dagger}(\epsilon)(\lambda - R) + R]/[w^{\dagger\dagger}(\epsilon)(\delta - R) + R].$$

From (16), $w^*(0) = R(\lambda + \delta - 2R)/[2(R - \delta)(\lambda - R)]$, and $w^{\dagger\dagger}(0) = w^*(0)$. Since from (4), $E\{U[0,W]\} = E\{\log W\} = \mu$.
Differentiating (16), we have

$$w^{*\prime}(0) = \log\left[\frac{\lambda - R}{R - \delta}\right]\left[\frac{\lambda - \delta}{2(\lambda + \delta - 2R)}\right]w^*(0). \tag{18}$$

Applying the implicit function theorem, we have

$$\frac{w^{\dagger\dagger\prime}(0)}{w^{\dagger\dagger}(0)} = \frac{B'(0)}{B(0) - 1} - \frac{B'(0)(R - \delta)}{[(\lambda - R) + B(0)(R - \delta)]}$$

$$= B'(0)\left[\frac{1}{(\lambda + \delta - 2R)} - \frac{1}{2(\lambda - R)}\right](R - \delta), \tag{19}$$

and from (17),

$$B'(0) = \left(\frac{\lambda - R}{R - \delta}\right)\log\left(\frac{\lambda - R}{R - \delta}\right). \tag{20}$$

Combining (19) and (20), we have

$$w^{\dagger\dagger\prime}(0) = \frac{(\lambda - \delta)}{2(\lambda + \delta - 2R)}\log\left[\frac{\lambda - R}{R - \delta}\right]w^{\dagger\dagger}(0), \tag{21}$$

and using the result that $w^*(0) = w^{\dagger\dagger}(0)$ with (18) and (21), we have $w^{\dagger\dagger\prime}(0) = w^{*\prime}(0)$. Hence,

$$w^*(\epsilon) - w^{\dagger\dagger}(\epsilon) = w^*(0) + \epsilon w^{*\prime}(0) + 0(\epsilon^2)$$

$$- w^{\dagger\dagger}(0) - \epsilon w^{\dagger\dagger\prime}(0) - 0(\epsilon^2) = 0(\epsilon^2), \tag{22}$$

and $w^{\dagger\dagger}(\epsilon)$ is a valid approximation to $w^*(\epsilon)$ to $0(\epsilon^2)$.

To complete the illustration, we now show that $w^\dagger(\epsilon)$ is an equally good approximation. $w^\dagger(\epsilon)$ satisfies

$$\text{Max}\left[\mu + \frac{\epsilon}{2}(\sigma^2 + \mu^2)\right] = \text{Max}\left\{\frac{1}{2}\log[w(\lambda - R) + R]\right.$$

$$+ \frac{1}{2}\log[w(\delta - R) + R]$$

$$\left. + \frac{\epsilon}{4}(\log^2[w(\lambda - R) + R] + \log^2[w(\delta - R) + R])\right\}. \tag{23}$$

The first-order condition satisfied by $w^\dagger(\epsilon)$ is

$$0 = \frac{\lambda - R}{w^\dagger(\lambda - R) + R} + \frac{\delta - R}{w^\dagger(\delta - R) + R} + \epsilon\frac{(\lambda - R)\log[w^\dagger(\lambda - R) + R]}{w^\dagger(\lambda - R) + R}$$

$$+ \frac{(\delta - R)\log[w^\dagger(\delta - R) + R]}{w^\dagger(\delta - R) + R}. \tag{24}$$

Clearly, $w^{\dagger}(0) = w^{\dagger\dagger}(0) = w(0)$. Using this fact and the implicit function theorem, we have

$$\left(\frac{dw^{\dagger}}{d\epsilon}\right)_{\epsilon=0} = \frac{C(\lambda - R)[w^{\dagger}(\delta - R) + R]\log[C]}{(\lambda - R)^2 + C^2(\delta - R)^2} \tag{25}$$

where $C \equiv [w^{\dagger}(\lambda - R) + R]/[w^{\dagger}(\delta - R) + R]$. Using $w^{\dagger}(0) = w^*(0) = (\lambda + \delta - 2R)R/[2(R - \delta)(\lambda - R)]$ and hence that $C(0) = (\lambda - R)/(R - \delta)$, we simplify (25) to

$$\begin{aligned} w^{\dagger\prime}(0) &= \frac{R(\lambda - \delta)}{4(\lambda - R)(R - \delta)} \log\left(\frac{\lambda - R}{R - \delta}\right) \\ &= \frac{(\lambda - \delta)}{2(\lambda + \delta - 2R)} \log\left(\frac{\lambda - R}{R - \delta}\right) w^{\dagger\prime}(0). \end{aligned} \tag{26}$$

Comparing (26) with (21) and (18), we have $w^{\dagger\prime}(0) = w^{\dagger\dagger\prime}(0) = w^{*\prime}(0)$. Hence, $w^{\dagger}(\epsilon)$ and $w^{\dagger\dagger}(\epsilon)$ are equally good approximations to $w^*(\epsilon)$ with the error in either case of $0(\epsilon^2)$.

III. Generalization

Lest anyone think that there is something important about the neighborhood in which the γ in W^{γ}/γ is small, we could write down equivalent perturbations around any γ neighborhood, as, e.g., $\gamma = -3.14$.

Thus, in general

$$\frac{W^{\gamma+\epsilon}}{\gamma} = \frac{W^{\gamma}}{\gamma} [1 + \epsilon \log W + 0(\epsilon^2)], \tag{27}$$

and our asymptotically sufficient pair of parameters become $E\{W^{\gamma}/\gamma\}$ and $E\{W^{\gamma}\log W/\gamma\}$.

Even more generally, we need not consider constant-relative-risk averters with U functions in the class W^{γ}/γ. All we need is

$$U[\epsilon;W] = U[0;W] + \epsilon\partial U[0;W]/\partial\epsilon + 0(\epsilon^2) \tag{28}$$

and the pair of parameters, $E\{U[0;W]\}$ and $E\{\partial U[0;W]/\partial\epsilon\}$.

From this general viewpoint, we derive the original Markowitz (or for that matter Marschak [6] and Tobin [11]) mean-variance analysis by writing

$$U[\epsilon;W] = W - \epsilon bW^2 + 0(\epsilon^2). \tag{29}$$

However, for this approximation to be justified U must almost be linear while our earlier approximations required "near" log-linear. Hence, the earlier approximations are generally more relevant for concave utility maximizers. Warning: the approximation in (28) should not be confused with the justification of the use of mean-variance for "compact probabilities" which involves expansions like

$$U[\epsilon;W] = \epsilon(W - bW^2) + 0(\epsilon^2). \tag{30}$$

IV. DIGRESSION ON AVERAGE COMPOUND RETURN

We may briefly relate the Hakansson criterion of expected average compound return to our perturbation analysis. In the case of identical probability distributions in each period, serially independent of each other, the utility functions W^γ/γ will all give rise to "myopic" and uniform strategies. In that case, the Hakansson criterion (except for an additive constant) is defined as the $1/\epsilon$ power of $E\{1 + \epsilon U[\epsilon;W]\}$ where $\epsilon = 1/N$ and N is the number of periods.

Hence, it becomes

$$h[\epsilon;w] = \{1 + \epsilon u[\epsilon;w]\}^{1/\epsilon}$$

$$= \exp\left[\mu + \frac{1}{2}\epsilon\sigma^2 + 0(\epsilon^2)\right] \tag{31}$$

$$= e^\mu\left[1 + \frac{1}{2}\epsilon\sigma^2 + 0(\epsilon^2)\right].$$

Note that $h[\epsilon;w]$, $u[\epsilon;w]$, and $g[\epsilon;w] = \log h[\epsilon;w] = \mu + \frac{1}{2}\epsilon\sigma^2 + 0(\epsilon^2)$ have first-order coefficients different from one other.

Contemplating $g[\epsilon;w]$, we can give an affirmative answer to Hakansson's open question of whether, for N large and for ϵ small, his maximizing $\mu + \frac{1}{2}\epsilon\sigma^2$ yields a good approximation to his efficiency frontier. Note that no reference is made in our derivation to the treacherous assumption of a log-normal surrogate for the probability distribution of W/W_0 (i.e., of W_N/W_0).[3]

Up until now we have had no need to make explicit use of the variance of expected average compound return. Again with no recourse to log-normal surrogates, we calculate this as

$$V[\epsilon;w] = [E\{W^{2\epsilon}\}]^{1/\epsilon} - [E\{W^\epsilon\}]^{2/\epsilon} \tag{32}$$
$$= (1 + 2\epsilon u[2\epsilon;w])^{1/\epsilon} - (1 + \epsilon u[\epsilon;w])^{2/\epsilon}$$
$$= \exp[2\mu + \epsilon\sigma^2 + 0(\epsilon^2)](\exp[\sigma^2\epsilon + 0(\epsilon^2)] - 1)$$
$$= e^{2\mu}\sigma^2\epsilon + 0(\epsilon^2).$$

To keep this variance from vanishing (relative to the expected value) as $\epsilon \to 0$, we work with the normalized variance $\eta[\epsilon;w] \equiv V[\epsilon;w]/\epsilon$. It is apparent that $\eta[0;w]$ can provide the added information needed for the first-degree ϵ terms in $u[;]$, $h[;]$, and $w^*(\ )$. Hence, we can plot an efficiency frontier in the (h,η) pair, maximizing $h[0;w]$ for given values of $\eta[0;w]$.

Remark: Although $1/N < 0$ makes no immediate sense, there is no reason why we should not work in $h[\epsilon;w]$ with negative ϵ. What is useful about $h[\epsilon;w]$ is not its average-compound-return interpretation, but rather that it is a legitimate surrogate for $u[\epsilon;w]$.

Remark: In the usual indifference curve analysis of non-stochastic demand theory, when the utility indicator is stretched and renumbered, the utility

---

3. See Merton and Samuelson [8] for a discussion of the fallacies associated with such surrogates. Not even the Law of Large Numbers is involved in our derivations, since these are as valid for one-period as for many-period decision making.

contours themselves remain invariant. By contrast, in our diagram of first-order approximation, every stretching of the utility criterion—from $u[\ ]$ to $\{1 + \epsilon u[\ ]\}^{1/\epsilon}$ or $\log(1 + \epsilon u[\ ])/\epsilon$—definitely alters the shapes of the indifference contours in the diagram. But, and this is crucial, the proper tangency points of local optimality are *invariants* under the stretchings!

Figure 3 shows how the two parameters, expected-value-of average compound-return-minus-one and its variance, here called respectively $h_1[\epsilon; w_2,$

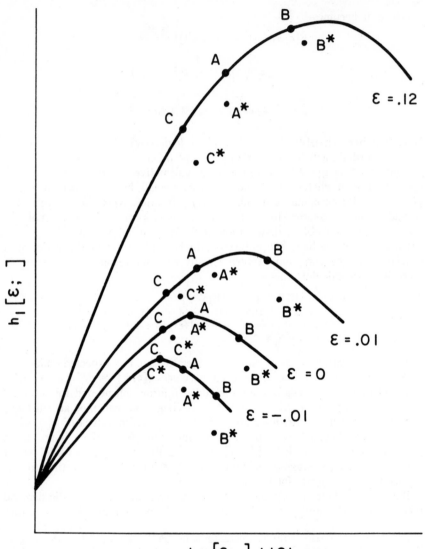

FIGURE 3

. . ., w_n] and $h_2[\epsilon; w_2, . . ., w_n]$ in honor of Hakansson, can be used as a surrogate for our local-approximation technique even by those who have no use for the average-compound-return criterion for its own sake. The horizontal axis plots the normalized variance $h_2[\epsilon; w]/\epsilon$ for reasons of convenience that will become apparent; the topology of the frontier is quite unchanged by this inessential monotone stretching. Actually, for $1/N$ small, the unnormalized variance shrinks to zero and would compress the diagram's scale to an unmanageable and inconvenient degree. (It also betrays people into thinking that there is something mandatory, or good, about pretending that men like B and C should forget that they have γ's a finite and irreducible distance away from A's $\gamma = 0$.) Further, as will be seen, with this normalization, the tradeoff frontiers approach a unique locus as $1/N \to 0$, one which depends only on the locally sufficient parameters $\mu(w) = E\{logW\}$ and $\sigma^2(w) = Var\{logW\}$. More exactly, $h_1[1/N; w] \to exp[\mu(w)]$, $Nh_2[1/N; w] \to exp[2\mu(w)]\sigma^2(w)$ as $1/N \to 0$.

Figure 3 shows several (h_1, h_2/ϵ) loci for various values of $1/N$. In every case, the points C*, A*, B* represent the exact $w^*(\epsilon)$ solutions corresponding to the same C*, A*, B* points of Figure 2 and Figure 1. In every case, the C, A, B points represent first-order approximations. Note that contrary to the mistaken notion that minimum variance of average compound returns (for a fixed mean) is a desirable thing, the declining branch of the frontier is efficient (for someone like B, for example).

Moreover, to debunk effectively the notion that expected average compound return is desirable for its own sake, Figure 3 plots an efficiency tradeoff locus for $1/N < 0$. Indeed, man C can get a much more accurate approximation— indeed an *exact* evaluation—if we set $1/N = \gamma_C = -.01$. Thus, C and C* coincide on the lowest curve shown, and both A and B are on the quite-admissible declining branch.

A. *Confused Defense of Average Return in Terms of Ranking Good Guessers About Future Probabilities*

The general criterion of average return has a certain plausibility about it. If in the last five years one mutual fund has had algebraic percentage gains, $+10, +20, -10, 0, +25$, and another has had $+12, +21, -10, 0, +5$, most people will prefer the first to the second since the first "dominates" the second in gains. Unconsciously, they will infer that those who run the first fund probably have better *inductions* about the probability distributions that we and Hakansson take as *exactly* (!) known. But probably, when ranking a third fund that scores close to $+9$ per cent in *each* of the five years, they will prefer this last to either of the other two funds, even though on a five-year basis it has no gain advantage over the first fund. Ask them, "Why do you prefer, out of two funds with the *same* average compound return for the time horizon *you* say is crucial to you, the fund with the lower intra-horizon *variance* of annual return?" A little thought will suggest the answer that an actual sample of decision-makers will give: "We naturally feel that the fund with the steady yield through thick and thin has an uncanny ability to come up with better guesses about the true [unknown] probabilities we are going to be running up against in the future. It will likely be better at avoiding losers."

The economist will understand this line of reasoning. But he will realize that it would be a *confusion* for him to regard it as a valid reason for being interested in the expected average compound return as a maximand in an analytical model where the decision maker is working with *prescribed* probabilities. We must warn in the strongest terms against confusing the conditions of real life with those of the scores of analytical articles in the financial journals, such as Hakansson's 1971 paper or the present one.[4]

B. *Comment on Hakansson*

Since those who have not thought the matter through are prone to find the criterion of average compound return appealing—and indeed are prone to read into it implications far beyond those that Hakansson has ever claimed on its behalf—it is worth digressing further to evaluate its merits, to respond to Hakansson's [3, p. 880] "Comment on Samuelson" to see whether he has cogently rebutted the critique made of the average return concept and to explain wherein post-Hakansson decision-makers are self-deceived.

1. We begin with Hakansson's three-quarter-page comment on the Samuelson [10] critique. This begins with his mention that the *median* capital, after a large number of periods, N, will be "approximately equal to" (in our notation, for the case of independent, identical probabilities in each period) $\exp[\mu N]$.

How should someone who adheres to the Ramsey-Savage-Neumann axioms of expected utility react to this heuristic enunciation of one facet of the Central Limit Theorem? If his utility function is far from $\log W_T$, he will receive this announcement with deservedly strong indifference. Let us hope that a new generation of thoughtless median maximizers does not arise on the scene!

2. Next Hakansson points out a facet of the Law of Large Numbers— namely, that average expected compound return converges in probability to $\exp[\mu N]$. Since $\exp\mu N$ increases with μ, the unwary will think that the sure-thing principle requires that he pick a higher μ in preference to a lower one. Yet, as our analysis has demonstrated, every rational maximizer of a $U(W_T)$ far from $\log W_T$ will greet this convergence in probability result with deserved indifference.

Indeed, the sophisticated probabilist will say "It is precisely because average expected return is *so badly normalized* as to converge in probability to $\exp[\mu N]$ that it is a confusing and undesirable variable for decision makers to pay attention to." To Hakansson's assertion that μ provides an "intuitively appealing measure[s] of growth," a sophisticated utility maximizer will reply,

---

4. The reader may ask: "How does one go about reaching the real life problem of inductive inference?" Briefly the answer is "If the statistician believes the array of 10,000 eligible stocks can be regarded as subject to a joint log-normal (or other distribution), he must use Bayesian, maximum likelihood, or other methods for guessing at the *future*(!) parameters of that distribution. There is, in any case, no warrant for anyone who has as his utility $U = -W_T^{-5}/5$ or $U = W_T^{7/8}/(7/8)$ to use $U = \log W_T$ or $W_T^{1/N}/(1/N)$ in his final calculations with *those separately estimated* probabilities."

"Informed intuition realizes that alleged 'measures of growth' are misleading to a rational expected utility maximizer." This agreed to, Hakansson's further observation, that σ^2 clearly is an indicator of the 'smoothness' of this growth," loses all interest and relevance to portfolio optimizing in the face of given probabilities.

3. Then Hakansson repeats and agrees with the literal correctness of Samuelson's statement that, although for large enough N the twin who maximizes μ will "almost certainly" end up with more terminal wealth than his brother who does anything else, that does not mean that the first twin will have as high expected terminal utility as will the twin who acts correctly to maximize the $E\{U(W_T)\}$ that they actually share as goals.

At this point Hakansson goes on to rule out risk tolerances greater than those of Bernoulli $\log W_T$ maximizers. When Einstein objected to the probability basis for quantum mechanics with the aphorism "God doesn't run a gambling casino," Bohr answered him with the reminder, "Who are we to tell Him how to run His business?" When Hakansson, more modest than Einstein, argues that long-run investors will not want to have certain concave utility functions hitherto deemed admissible, his chain of reasoning deserves careful examination.

Hakansson says: ". . . there is good reason to believe that few individuals with long-run goals and possessing all the facts about (the implications of) various utility functions would, upon reflection, emerge with preferences consistent with utility functions *other* than (in our present notation) $U(W_T) = -(W_T)^{-|\gamma|}$ or $U(W_T) = \log W_T$."

Note the sweep of this amazing dictum: $U(W_T) = W_T^{1/2}$, proposed by Cramer two centuries ago and deemed admissible by Bernoulli and Marshall, is now declared to be "on reflection" inadmissible. And what is the "good reason" offered to persuade one to renounce $W_T^{1/2}$ or $W_T^{.0001}$? It is Hakansson's belief that one should want, on reflection, to be on that branch of the Hakansson mean-variance frontier (recall our Figure 3) which *he* defines as the only efficient one.

What we have here is completely a case of *petitio principii*: assuming what needs to be proved—that it is natural to want to minimize the variance of average compound return for the same expected value of that (irrelevant!) animal.

Hakansson is correct that contemplation of the St. Petersburgh Paradox can alert most people to the fact that their utility is strictly concave rather than linear. But it would be a delusion to think that his defense of minimum variance of average returns has equal force for reflective people.

We two are people. We try to be reflective. Yet we reject his criterion. More important, not one of the dozen reflective people we have discussed that matter with were willing, *after* they understood the intricacies of the issue, to end up agreeing with the contention. And one who has read all of Hakansson's valuable work will not want to bet that the author himself will want to reaffirm: ". . . the preceding analysis suggests that all *risk-averse* utility functions other than those with constant relative risk aversion (at least as great as that of $\log W_T$) are implausible among (rational) long-run investors."

It is true that casual and systematic empiricism suggests that many people, perhaps most, have risk-aversion more like the utility functions $-W^{-1}$ or $-W^{-2}$ than like $W^{1/2}$ or $W^{7/8}$. But that same body of limited data suggests, we would guess, that more have risk aversions like $-W^{-1}$ or $-W^{-2}$ than like $\log W$ or $-W^{-.0001}$. And such an alleged fact, we have shown in this paper, would, if true, be fatal to would be maximum-growth-cum-smooth-growth strategies. For, as we have shown, someone with $U = -W^{-2}$ will find efficiency frontiers in our (μ, σ^2) or in Hakansson's (h_1, h_2) space grossly irrelevant for good approximating to his true optimal strategies. Many of Hakansson's casual readers, we have found, think that somehow $-W^{-2}$ gets *validly* converted into $-W^{-2/N}$ and hence for large N is brought near to $\log W$ for decision-making purposes. We emphasize that this is a false interpretation of what is valid and useful in Hakansson's work. We have other objections to average compound return arguments. But enough is enough.

V.　Conclusion

The powerful approximation methods developed here are seen to have nothing to do with multiplicity of periods of decision-making. In principle, these expansions are as valid for one-period as for one-thousand-period decision-making. And they do not depend upon the different periods' probability distributions being independent or even stationary.

REFERENCES

1. D. C. Aucamp. "A New Theory of Optimal Investment," (mimeo), Southern Illinois University (August 1971).
2. L. Breiman. "Investment Policies for Expanding Business Optimal in a Long-Run Sense," *Naval Research Logistics Quarterly* (December 1960).
3. N. Hakansson. "Multi-Period Mean-Variance Analysis: Toward a General Theory of Portfolio Choice," *Journal of Finance*, 26 (September 1971).
4. J. Kelly. "A New Interpretation of Information Rate," *Bell System Technical Journal* (August 1956).
5. H. A. Latané. "Criteria for Choice Among Risky Ventures," *Journal of Political Economy*, 67 (April 1959).
6. H. Marower and J. Marschak. "Assets, Prices, and Monetary Theory," *Economica*, V (1938).
7. H. Markowitz. *Portfolio Selection: Efficient Diversification of Investment* (New York: John Wiley and Sons, 1959).
8. R. C. Merton and P. A. Samuelson. "Fallacy of the Log-Normal Approximation to Optimal Portfolio Decision-Making over Many Periods," *Journal of Financial Economics* (March 1974).
9. P. A. Samuelson. "The Fundamental Approximation Theorem of Portfolio Analyses in Terms of Means, Variances, and Higher Moments," *Review of Economic Studies*, 37 (October 1970).
10. —————. "The 'Fallacy' of Maximizing the Geometric Mean in Long Sequences of Investing or Gambling, *Proceedings of the National Academy of Sciences*, 68 (October (1971).
11. J. Tobin. "Liquidity Preference as Behavior towards Risk," *Review of Economic Studies*, 25 (February 1958).
12. J. B. Williams. "Speculation and Carryover," *Quarterly Journal of Eonomics*, 50 (1936).

247

LIMITED LIABILITY, SHORT SELLING, BOUNDED UTILITY,

AND INFINITE-VARIANCE STABLE DISTRIBUTIONS

Paul A. Samuelson*

I. Introduction

I welcome the oppostunity to second the analysis of Davies and Ronning [4]. The considerations they raise crop up repeatedly in various contexts of uncertainty analysis and prompt the following remarks dealing with various topics described in my title.

II. Review

An investor with initial wealth W_0 (which by a dimensional convention can be set at unity and not explicitly written) faces a joint probability distribution of random-variable outcomes for a dollar invested respectively in securities $(1, 2, \ldots, n)$.

$$(2.1) \qquad \text{Prob} \{X_1 \leq x_1, \ldots, X_n \leq x_n\} = F(x_1, \ldots, x_n)$$

$$= F(\underset{\sim}{x}) \text{ for short.}$$

Being forced to invest all his initial wealth among these securities his final portfolio-wealth outcome, W, is a random variable defined as

$$(2.2) \qquad W = \sum_1^n w_j X_j , \quad \sum_1^n w_j = 1$$

where the portfolio weights may or may not be restricted to nonnegative values. For $u[W]$ his utility function of wealth, the expected value of his utility will, given the $F(\ )$ probabilities, be defined by the mutliple Stieltjes' integral

---

* M.I.T. The author owes thanks to the National Science Foundation for financial aid and to Vicki Elms for editorial assistance. Every economist working with stochastic processes has room to be grateful to Dr. Benoit Mandelbrot of IBM, for his pioneering work in extending finite-variance models to the infinite domain of Levy and beyond; and the author feels a particular debt to his works of the last 15 years.

(2.3) $$E\{u(W)\} = U(w_1,\ldots,w_n) = \int_\infty^\infty u[\sum_1^n w_j x_j] F(dx)$$

provided this integral converges. If it does not converge for some admissible choice of w's, the problem needs further defining.

Davies and Ronning [3] proved that if (a) $F(x_1,\ldots,x_n)$ is a symmetric function (i.e., the securities are "exchangeable"), if (b) it is nondegenerate (so that all securities are not perfectly riskless, a trivial case), if (c) $u[W]$ is a strictly concave function, if (d) it is bounded on the nonnegative interval for W, and (e) if the random variables in F, $(X_1,\ldots,X_n)$ are positive, then equal diversification, $w_j \equiv 1/n$, is the unique optimal solution.

Samuelson [20] had proved a similar result but without the restrictions (d) and (e), but with an additional different restriction [call it (d')], namely that every X_i have a finite variance. This (d') conditions is a sufficiency condition; but, as the 1974 result suggests, being overly strong, it is definitely not a necessary condition for the result. Condition (d') did serve to rule out the paradoxical Cauchy case, in which any (w_j) choice looks to be as good as any other; but, as remarked in Samuelson [20, p. 3], in any case the Cauchy distribution will not define a convergent expected value in (2.3) for *any* everywhere-strictly-concave u(W) function--as for example, $-e^{-W}$.

The present note illustrates, by means of stable distributions of Levy, how equal diversification may still be optimal even when various of the 1967 and 1974 restrictions are not imposed.

III. Metaeconomics

The 1974 invoking of nonpositive outcomes often makes good economic sense because it rules out unlimited liability in buying of common stocks. But, it would also rule out short-selling of any security with a right-hand tail of infinite range. And, as a related thing in a really perfect capital market, it will put restrictions on how much people might borrow for leverage purposes and on how much "margin money" must be put up on commodity and other contracts.

There is also some plausibility to the boundedness restriction (d)--in the presence of (e), of course (since if X_i and W can take on all real values, there can be no bounded u[W] function that is concave). For one thing, observing people and one's self may result in the empirical finding that people do have bounded utility (or that they *don't*, and seem to behave as if u[W] were log W or $W^{1/2}$, or $-W^{-1}$, or W^γ/γ for $1 > \gamma \neq 0$). Secondly, Arrow [1 and 2,

486

Chapter 2] and other authorities have given their authority to the view that, logically and aesthetically, the axioms of stochastic choice should include an axiom of boundedness of $u[W]$: (i) to avoid an otherwise constructable Super-Petersburg Paradox of the Menger [17] type; and (ii) so that *every* contemplated probability distribution, including the Cauchy distribution $F(x) = \pi^{-1} \tan^{-1} x$, $F'(x)dx = \pi^{-1}(1+x^2)^{-1} dx$, will have to define a convergent $E\{u[w]\}$ integral.

I must confess to some doubts about the force of the (i) argument. If you and I were alone in the universe, why could not the log W function actually guide our respective decisions? Under it, neither you, Peter, nor I, Paul, would agree to play the St. Petersburg game at any activity level other than zero; and the same will hold for the Menger supergames. What follows? We are thrown back on the empirical question of whether, on reflection, we do or do not possess bounded utility.

In connection with (ii), my views are more tentative. Do there exist in nature distributions that present nonconvergence properties? Or do they exist only in textbook exercises? I am not sure. But suppose that such prospects do exist. Won't we then genuinely want (α) to be "indifferent" between certain alternative choices? or (β) to break the ties in some definable fashion by constructing some "nonstandard" lexicographic ordering of the "infinities"? I leave these as open questions, and refer to Samuelson [23, pp. 354-5] for some similar discussion.

IV. Nonconcavity of Bankruptcy

Every market must face the fact that you can't get blood out of a turnip, or from a person what he doesn't have. Suppose someone makes a contract with me that results in a random-event outcome which leaves me owing him more than I have to pay. You may say, "The greater fool he to get himself in this pickle." But just try to devise a securities or commodities market, a bank, lending institution, or insurance company, that can perform its function and yet avoid such dire possibilities. Of course, one can try to set up safeguards: require collateral and margin money, arrange for stop-loss orders to sell out the cus-tomer while he still has positive margin equity, etc. But try as one may, it is not clear that orders can be executed in time and that some residual use of bankruptcy arrangements can be avoided.

How does this affect the decision maker who may face a W outcome that takes on algebraically negative values? He may or may not feel that such a loss involves him in a disutility of "dishonor" that obeys the concave-utility requirement. Instead he may feel *ex post*, and even *ex ante*, in terms of a utility function with $u[-|W|] \equiv u[0]$: i.e., "I might as well be hung for a

487

sheep as a lamb...." But this destroys the concavity of u[W] we need for various diversifications and risk-aversion theorems. (The same follows, as noted above, from adhering to Arrow's axiom of bounded utility over the $(-\infty,\infty)$ range for W.)

V. Mandelbrot-Lévy Stable Distributions[1]

To illustrate that my 1967 (d') restriction of finite variance is not necessary, one need only look at the companion paper to Samuelson [20], Samuelson [21], that had been submitted for publication at the same time, and which generalized the Markowitz [16] mean-variance efficiency frontier for the Gaussian case to a wider class of "stable" distributions of Lévy [16].

These form a four-parameter family of distributions, $L[(x-a)/b;\beta,\alpha]$, with the defining property that for X_1 and X_2 independent drawings from the same $L[x;\beta,\alpha]$ universe, their normalized sum follows the same distribution, namely

(5.1) $$\text{Prob } \{X_1 + X_2 \leq 2^{1/\alpha}\, x\} = L[x;\beta,\alpha] \ , \ 0 < \alpha \leq 2.$$

Also, the density to L, $L'[x;\beta,\alpha]$, has asymptotically the Pareto-slope property

(5.2) $$\lim_{x \to \infty} \{L'[x;\alpha,\beta]x^{-\alpha-1}\} = m < \infty \ , \ 0 < \alpha < 2.$$

Just as α is an inverse measure of how "fat" is the tail of outliers, so β is a measure of skewness (being 0 when $L'[\ ]$ is symmetric, +1 when its tail is skewed to the right, and -1 when to the left).

For $\alpha = 2$, $L[x;0,2]$ is the Gaussian distribution with finite moments of all order. For $\alpha < 2$, the variance is infinite in accordance with the absolute moment relation

(5.3) $$\int_{-\infty}^{\infty} |x|^h L'[x;\beta,\alpha]dx = \infty \ , \ h \geq \alpha < 2$$
$$< \infty \ , \ h < \alpha \ .$$

----

[1]Mandelbrot uses "Pareto-Lévy distributions" to describe the stable-additive functions with finite mean but infinite variance. However, as he points out, Pareto only knew their tail's asymptotic property; so my label is more fitting than that which Mandelbrot too modestly originally suggested; moreover, it can also be used for the stable case where the mean is not defined, an area to which Mandelbrot has also made great contributions.

The Mandelbrot-Lévy subset, which involves $1 < \alpha < 2$ and $\beta = 1$, has application to economics as in Pareto [1897], Mandelbrot [11, 1], 13, 14, 15], Fama [6, 7, 8], and Samuelson [19, 21, 24]. For it, we can adopt the convention that

$$(5.4) \qquad E\{X\} = \int_{-\infty}^{\infty} xL'[x;\beta,\alpha]dx = 0,$$

$$\int_{-\infty}^{\infty} xL'[x-a;\beta,\alpha]dx = a.$$

Unfortunately, $L[x;\beta,\alpha] > 0$ for every x including negative x. However, as shown in Mandelbrot, for the skewness parameter, which is at the ± 1 pole of its $[-1,1]$ range, $L[0;1,\alpha]$ can be very small indeed, actually of a smaller order of magnitude than in the symmetric stable case of Fama where $\beta = 0$. Still, no matter how sharply L[ ] goes to zero to the left, if u[W] were a function like log W, the least little probability of a negative X would have infinite disutility in all decision making.

Since such L[ ] deny the (e) restriction to positive variables, we must pick a u[W] defined on $(-\infty,\infty)$. The following concave example for u[W] shows that there do exist convergent $E\{u[W]\}$ for W, a Mandelbrot-Lévy variate:

$$(5.5) \qquad u[W] = 2W - e^{W} + 1 \ , \ W < 0$$

$$= 1 - e^{-W} \qquad , \ W > 0.$$

$$(5.6) \qquad \int_{-\infty}^{\infty} u[W]L'[W;1,\alpha]dW < \infty.$$

VI. Equal Diversification with Infinite Variance and Negative Outcomes

As in Samuelson [21], let $F(x_1,\ldots,x_n)$ be defined as a product of independent Mandelbrot-Lévy distributions:

$$(6.1) \qquad F(x_1,\ldots,x_n) = L[(x_1-a_1)/b_1;\beta,\alpha]\ldots L[(x_n-a_n)/b_n;\beta,\alpha] , \ 1<\alpha<2.$$

For the symmetric case of exchangeable variates $a_j \equiv a$, $b_j \equiv b$. Then

$$(6.2) \qquad \text{Prob } \{W = \sum_1^n w_j X_j \leq w\} = L[(w-a)/b^*,\beta,\alpha].$$

$$(6.3) \qquad b^* = b(\sum_1^n w_j^\alpha)^{1/\alpha}$$

$$\geq b(\sum_1^n n^{-\alpha})^{1/\alpha} = bn^{\frac{1-\alpha}{\alpha}}, \ \text{for } \sum_1^n w_j = 1, \ w_j \geq 0.$$

489

To maximize $E\{u[W]\}$ for a concave risk averter, we shall want the dispersion-scale parameter to be at its minimum. To see this consider any density, $f[(x-\mu)/b]$, where μ is its finite expected value $E\{X\}$ and where b^2 need not correspond to a finite variance. Then, for $u[W]$ concave and $E\{u[W]\}$ well defined, we have

$$(6.4) \qquad U(\mu,b) = \int_{-\infty}^{\infty} u[x]f[(x-\mu)/b]d[(x-\mu)/b]$$

$$= \int_{-\infty}^{\infty} u[\mu + by]f(y)dy.$$

$$(6.5) \qquad \partial u/\partial \mu = \int_{-\infty}^{\infty} u'[\mu + by]f(y)dy > 0 \quad \text{since } u'[\ ] > 0.$$

$$(6.6) \quad \partial u/\partial b = \int_{-\infty}^{\infty} y\, u''[\mu + by]f(y)dy$$

$$= u'[\mu] \int_{-\infty}^{\infty} yf(y)dy + \int_{-\infty}^{\infty} u''[\mu + b\theta(y)y]b(y)^2 f(y)dy, \; 0\leq\theta(y)\leq 1$$

$$= 0 + \text{negative number, since } u''[\ ] < 0.$$

This completes the proof that (d') is overly strong for the conclusion that $w_j = 1/n$ must be uniquely optimal for the case of exchangeable variables.

VII. The Case of Fractional α

For $0 < \alpha < 1$, and $\beta = 1$, we can have stable variates that obey the positivity restriction (e). Such cases arise in many stochastic processes. But being so fat-tailed and characterized by so many outliers that not even their mean, $E\{X\}$, is finite, they seem to have found no realistic role in economics and finance. Still they can nicely illustrate the equaldiversification conclusion of the 1974 theorem.

It will suffice to consider the one case, other than the $\alpha = 1$ Cauchy case and the $\alpha = 2$ Gaussian case, for which we know the explicit form for a stable density (and not merely its characteristic function). This is what Mandelbrot has called the Cournot density, in which $(\beta,\alpha) = (1,1/2)$, and which might also be called the inverse-chi-square distribution. (Samuelson [21, p. 3] erroneously called it the arc-sine distribution.) As shown in Feller [9, p. 173], we have

$$(7.1) \quad L'[(x-a)/b;1,.5] = (2\pi)^{-.5}[(x-a)/b]^{-1.5}\exp-[2(x-a)/b]^{-1}, \; x-a > 0$$

$$\equiv 0 \qquad\qquad\qquad\qquad\qquad , \; x-a < 0.$$

490

This is unimodal, with a peaked mode, a fat tail, and good behavior at a For it $E\{u[X]\}$ will be divergent for $u = X^{\frac{1}{2}}$ or $X^{\epsilon+\frac{1}{2}}$, $\epsilon > 0$.

As in (6.1) and (6.2), for the symmetric, exchangeable case, we deduce

$$(7.2) \qquad \text{Prob } \{\sum_1^n w_j X_j = W \leq w\} = L[(w-a)/b^*;1,.5].$$

where, now that α is less than one instead of being greater,

$$(7.3) \qquad b^* = b(\sum_1^n w_j^{.5})^{1/.5} \rightarrow b(\sum_1^n n^{-.5})^{1/.5} = bn.$$

Amusingly, now that there is no convergent mean (and the parameter a represents the minimum level that can occur for W), it only helps to have a *large* "dispersion-scale" parameter b^*![2] So, again we infer the truth of the equal-diversification portfolio choice, $w_j \equiv 1/n$.

To verify that we now wish *maximum* b^*, note the strong stochastic dominance over the range of positive $(x-a)/b$:

$$L[(x-a)/(b+\Delta b);1.,5] < L[(x-a)/b;1,.5], \quad \Delta b > 0$$

since $L[y;1,.5]$ is a strongly increasing function of positive y.

These Lévy distributions, in which various moments are undefined, warn us against the facile use of Taylor expansions like those in Samuelson [22].

VIII. Asymptotic Surrogates?

Even though Mandelbrot-Lévy distributions (and for that matter Gaussian distributions) must involve some negative outcomes, and even in situations where any negative outcomes are quite inadmissible, a defense of such distributions as "asymptotic approximating surrogates" needs investigation. As shown in Merton and Samuelson [18], log-normal surrogates can be tempting but treacherous for long-run decision purposes.

For simplicity, let $F(\ )$ consist of independent distributions and think of $n = 2m$ as "very large." Suppose it can be written as

$$(8.1) \qquad F(x_1,\ldots,x_m, x_{m+1},\ldots,x_{2m}) = [\prod_1^m P(x_j)][\prod_{m+1}^{2m} R(x_j)].$$

---

[2] While this paper was in the press, I learned from correspondence with Drs. Davies and Ronning that they have independently discovered this same phenomenon. See Davies and Ronning [5, Satz 1].

(8.2) $E\{X_j\} = \mu,$ $(j = 1,\ldots,2m).$

Because each of the two subsets of securities is exchangeable or symmetric, we can deduce at once that the optimal solution is

(8.3) $w_1 = \ldots = w_m = \omega/m,$ $w_{m+1} = \ldots = w_{2m} = (1-\omega)/m$

but where ω is an unknown positive fraction which depends upon the comparative properties of the $P(\ )$ and $R(\ )$ distribution. Thus, if $P(\ ) \equiv R(\ )$,

$\omega = \dfrac{1}{2} = 1-\omega$ by symmetry.

Alternatively, suppose that $2m = 4k$ and that means of any two of the first m securities have the same distribution as any one of the last m securities, so that

$$R(x) \equiv \int_0^\infty P(2x-x_1)P(dx_1).$$

Then the last m of the securities has the same means as does the first m, but has "smaller dispersions"; so, surely, $w_1 > w_{2m}$. Actually, for this special case

$$w_1 = \ldots = w_m = 1/(3m)$$

$$w_{m+1} = \ldots = w_{2m} = 2/(3m).$$

To see this, verify the symmetry properties

(8.4) $E\{u[a_1 \sum\limits_{j=1}^{k} (\frac{1}{2}X_j + \frac{1}{2}X_{m-j}) + a_2 \sum\limits_{j=1}^{k} X_{m+j} + a_3 \sum\limits_{j=1}^{k} X_{3_{k+j}}]\}$

$= U(a_1,a_2,a_3;m) \equiv U(a_2,a_1,a_3;m) \equiv U(a_3,a_2,a_1;m)$

$\leq U(a,a,a;m) = U(1/3k,\ 1/3k,\ 1/3k;\ 2k)$

$= U(\frac{1}{2}a,\ldots,\frac{1}{2}a,\frac{1}{2}a,\ldots,\frac{1}{2}a,a,\ldots,a,a,\ldots,a)$

$= U(\frac{1}{3}m,\ldots,\frac{1}{3}m,\frac{2}{3}m,\ldots,\frac{2}{3}m)$ Q.E.D.

Now let us revert back to our original case of (8.1) with two different $P(\ )$ and $R(\ )$ functions. As $n = 2m \to \infty$, the random variable

$\sum\limits_{1}^{m}[X_j - \mu)/m]$, when normalized by the factor $m/m^{1/\alpha}$, approaches $L[z/b_p;\beta,\alpha]$, where α is a computable value from the asymptotic right-hand tail of $P(x)$.

If $P(x)$ has a finite variance, we may set $\alpha = 2$ and identify $L[z;\beta,2] \equiv L[z;0,2] \equiv [L\ z;1,2]$ with the Gaussian distribution. If $P(x)$ never vanishes but $\rightarrow 0$ fast as x decreases, and has an infinite variance and finite mean, we are in the Mandelbrot-Lévy interval with $1 < \alpha < 2$ and $\beta = 1$. From now on $P(\ )$ and $R(\ )$ correspond to positive variates only, with equal means μ and, for simplicity, equal α's, which lie in the interval $1 < \alpha \leq 2$. (For brevity, I exclude the minor complications produced when $cP'(x)x^{-3} \rightarrow 1$ as $x \rightarrow \infty$.) As noted:

(8.5)
$$\text{Prob}\ \{\Sigma_{1}^{m}(X_j-\mu)m^{-1/\alpha} \leq z = Q_m(z).$$

(8.6)
$$\lim_{m\to\infty} Q_m(z) = L[z/b_p;1,\alpha]$$

where b_p is a scaling parameter that would be $[\text{Var}\{X_j\}]^{1/2}$ if $\alpha = 2$, and which is a determinate functional of $P(\ )$ for all admissible α.

By like reasoning

(8.7)
$$\text{Prob}\{\ \sum_{m+1}^{2m}(X_j-\mu)m^{-1/\alpha} \leq z\} = L[z/b_r;1,\alpha].$$

I define the "stable surrogate" to $P(\ )$ and $R(\ )$ respectively as

(8.8)
$$P(x)\ \llcorner\ L[(x-\mu)/b_p;1,\alpha]$$

$$R(x)\ \llcorner\ L[(x-\mu)/b_r;1,\alpha].$$

If these were *exact* approximations we could write the exact distribution of the random variable

$$W = \omega\Sigma_{1}^{m}(X_j/m) + (1-\omega)\sum_{m+1}^{2m}(X_j/m)$$

as

$$L[x-\mu)/b(\omega);1,\alpha],$$

(8.9)
$$b(\omega) = [b_p^{\alpha}\omega^{\alpha} + b_r^{\alpha}(1-\omega)^{\alpha}]^{1/\alpha}m^{1/\alpha} \leq [b_p^{\alpha}\overline{\omega}^{\alpha} + b_r^{\alpha}(1-\overline{\omega})^{\alpha}]^{1/\alpha}m^{1/\alpha}$$

where $\overline{\omega}$ is the unique (positive) root of $b'(\omega) = 0$: namely

(8.10)
$$\overline{\omega} = [b_r^{\alpha/(\alpha-1)}]/[b_p^{\alpha/(\alpha-1)} + b_r^{\alpha/(\alpha-1)}].$$

493

We know the approximations are not perfect. But suppose heuristically that "m is large," and that your u[W] function is such that its curvature, u"[W] is "not excessively large" for "extreme deviations" from the mean of W,μ, where the Levy-Gauss approximation "deteriorates." Then, subject to the ambiguities indicated by my copious use of quotation marks, one can hope that $(\bar{\omega},1-\bar{\omega})$ gives a "pretty good approximation" to the *true* optimizing portfolio fractions, (w_j).

If there is a justification for the use of Gaussian distributions in financial stochastic decision making, as in Fama [8], it would seem to me that it is included in the above heuristic generalization to Mandelbrot-Levy distributions. Note that the actual distributions never involve negative occurrences, and that when the number of securities is large enough for the above arguments to make sense, the surrogates will have *little* probability weight below zero.

This raises a question. Suppose m is "large" but fixed. Suppose that when m has that great size, so will the scaling parameters b_p and b_r be "large enough" so that the variation in the random variable W will be significant, no matter what the choice of the common ω and the common $1-\omega$. Will it then be simultaneously possible that $U(\omega/m,\ldots,[1-\omega]/m) = U(\omega)$ can still be very "sensitive" to the choice of ω (which is the case when optimization decision making is significant) at the same time that the Levy-Gauss approximations "remain useful"? I deal with this important question that has long needed an answer in a separate mathematical appendix.

Leaving my special and simple case where the securities divide into only two uniform classes, consider the more general case where all n probability distributions are different but do all happen to have right-hand tail behavior corresponding to the same β and α. (This could involve the finite variance case of $\alpha = 2$.) Now when n is in some sense large, but not so large as to reduce the problem to a triviality of "virtual certainty" for W, can one *usefully* approximate the distribution of

$\sum_1^n w_j X_n$ by a surrogate of the form $L[(w - \sum_1^n w_j\mu_j)/[\sum w_j^\alpha b_j^\alpha]^{1/\alpha};\beta,\alpha]$ so that the optimal (w_j^*) in

(8.11) $$\underset{a_j}{\text{Max}}\ U(w_1,\ldots,w_n) = U(w_1^*,\ldots,w_n^*)$$

occurs for a true best (w_j^*) in some sense "near to" the efficiency frontier defined, as in Samuelson [1967b[, by

494

$$\underset{w_j}{\text{Min}} \ \sum_1^n w_j^\alpha b_j^\alpha \quad \text{s.t.} \quad \sum_1^n w_j \mu_j \underset{=}{>} \text{ and } \sum_1^n w_j = 1$$

$$= \sum_1^n w_j (\mu)^\alpha b_j^\alpha ?$$

This remains an important question for investigation.

IX. Conclusion

Nothing in this paper serves to cast doubt on the various enunciated forms of the equal-fractional-share diversification theorem. On the contrary, it confirms them and shows how, in the domain of $(-\infty, \infty)$ outcomes, Mandelbrot-Lévy analysis can dispense with finite-variance assumptions; and how, in the $[0, \infty)$ domain, stable functions without a definable mean can provide similar demonstration even where the boundedness of utility need not hold--as with $L[x; 1, \frac{1}{2}]$ and with $u[W] = 2 - W$, $W \leq 1$, and with $u[W] = rW^{1/4} - 3$, $W \geq 1$, where a concave $u[W]$ is unbounded for low and high W.

My original beautifully simple argument by the Principle of Sufficient Reason holds without exception. If the securities obey symmetry and if the utility function is concave, then expected utility wherever it is defined must be a concave function of the portfolio parameters. Hence, by symmetry equal-fractional portfolio weights must provide a critical point which is maximal-- regardless of irrelevant moment convergence considerations.

495

As in Section VIII of my text, an excellent test of Gaussian approximation is provided by the example of two classes of independent, and respectively identical distributions of securities per \$ returns:

(A.1) $$\text{Prob}\{X_1 \leq x_1, \ldots X_m \leq x_m, \; X_{m+1} \leq x_{m+1}, \ldots, X_{2m} \leq x_{2m}\}$$

$$= [\prod_{j=1}^{m} P(x_j)][\prod_{j=m+1}^{2m} R(x_j)], \; P(x) \equiv 0 \equiv R(x), \; x < 0.$$

(A.2) $$E\{X_j\} = \mu, \; (j = 1, \ldots, 2m).$$

(A.3) $$\text{Var}\{X_j\} = \sigma_1^2 > 0, \; \sigma_1^2 < \infty, \; (j = 1, \ldots, m)$$

$$\text{Var}\{X_{m+i}\} = \sigma_2^2 > 0, \; \sigma_2^2 < \infty, \; (i = 1, \ldots, m).$$

With finite positive (but not necessarily equal) variances, we know that maximizer of expected concave utility will have optimal portfolio proportions

(A.4) $$w_1 = \ldots = w_m = \omega/m$$

$$w_{m+1} = \ldots = w_{2m} = (1-\omega)/m.$$

(A.5) $$E\{u[\omega\sum_1^m (X_j/m) + (1-\omega)\sum_1^m (X_{m+i}/m)]\}$$

$$= U(\omega;m) = U[\omega/m, \ldots, \omega/m; \; (1-\omega)/m, \ldots, (1-\omega)/m]$$

$$\leq U(\omega_m^*;m), \text{ where } \partial U(\omega_m^*;m)/\partial\omega = 0 \quad (m = 1,2,\ldots).$$

(A.6) $$U(\omega_1^*;1) < U(\omega_2^*;2) < \ldots < U(\omega^*;n) < U(\omega_{n+1}^*;n+1).$$

We can now define Gaussian "surrogates" for $P(x)$ and $R(x)$, namely as $N[(x-\mu)/\sigma_1]$ and $N[(x-\mu)/\sigma_2]$, those normal distributions computed by equating the first two moments to the respective means and variances of the $P(x)$ and $R(x)$ distributions. Although $P(x)$ and $R(x)$ are zero for negative x's, in accordance with "limited liability," this will definitely not hold for $N[(x-\mu)/\sigma_1]$, which will definitely have a positive value for $N[(0-\mu)/\sigma_1]$.

496

542

However, as m becomes large, the "surrogates" to the true distributions of

$$(A.7) \qquad Z_m = \sum_{j=1}^{m} (X_j/m), \quad V_m = \sum_{i=1}^{m} (X_{m+i}/m)$$

become respectively $N[(Z_m-\mu)/\sigma_1 m^{-1/2}]$ and $N[(V_m-\mu)/\sigma_2 m^{-1/2}]$,

with the property

$$(A.8) \qquad \lim_{m\to\infty} N[(0-\mu)/\sigma_i m^{-1/2}] = 0, \qquad (i=1,2).$$

Indeed, if we call the true distribution of Z_m and V_m, $P_m(z)$ and $R_m(v)$ respectively, we find

$$(A.9) \qquad \lim_{m\to\infty} P_m(x) = \lim_{m\to\infty} R(x)$$

$$= \lim_{m\to\infty} N[(x-\mu)/(\omega^2\sigma_1^2 + (1 - \omega)^2\sigma_2^2)^{1/2} m^{-1/2}] \qquad \begin{aligned} &\equiv 0, \ x < \mu \\ &\equiv 1, \ x > \mu. \end{aligned}$$

$$(A.9') \quad \begin{cases} \operatorname*{plim}_{m\to\infty} Z_m = \operatorname*{plim}_{m\to\infty} V_m = \operatorname*{plim}_{m\to\infty} \text{surrogate variates} = \mu. \end{cases}$$

This is merely the Law of Large Numbers applied to means of ever-larger samples; (A.9) is not itself a statement of the Central-Limit Theorem. For many $u[W]$ functions, as for example $\log W$, it makes no sense to calculate $E\{u[W]\}$ for the Gaussian surrogates. However, for $u[W]$ well-defined on $(-\infty<W<+\infty)$, as for example for $-e^{-W}$, the optimal value for ω when we use the normal surrogates is clearly given by

$$(A.10) \qquad \omega_m^{+} \equiv \omega^{+} \quad (n=1,2,\ldots)$$

$$= \sigma_2^2/(\sigma_1^2+\sigma_2^2)$$

since this is the ω that minimizes the variance of the portfolio at its common mean value of μ. By Jensen's inequality, $E\{\text{concave } u[W]\}$, when it is defined for the surrogate, is greater for a distribution that has the same mean as a second distribution and that has every outcome pushed toward the mean by the same fractional proportion.

Now, what is the relation between ω_1^{*} and ω^{+}, ω_2^{*} and ω^{+}, . . . , ω_m^{*} and ω^{+} for m "large," and ω_∞ and ω^{+}? The following theorem seems to provide for

497

surrogate Gaussian approximations some semblance of validity or usefulness:

Theorem. As $m \to \infty$, the true optimal ω_m^* does approach the surrogate

limit $\omega^\dagger$. I.e., $\lim_{m \to \infty} \omega_m^* = \omega^* = \omega^\dagger$

The proof is trivially simple and has nothing really to do with Gaussian surrogate approximations or with the Central-Limit Theorem. Rather it hinges on the basic fact that the Law of Large Numbers applies as shown in (A.9): with virtual certainty $U(\omega, m)$ becomes $u[\mu]$ for *all* ω as $m \to \infty$! Thus, what are called "compact" probability distributions in Samuelson [22] apply as m becomes large; and hence mean-variance analysis does asymptotically apply quite *without regard to any Gaussian approximations*. Q.E.D.

Figure I lists, for each of increasing m, the true expected utility in function of the portfolio proportions $(\omega, 1-\omega)$, namely $U(\omega; m)$. It will be noted that, as a corollary of the Law of Large Numbers:

(A.11) $$\lim_{m \to \infty} U(\omega; m) \equiv u[\mu].$$

(A.11') $$\lim_{m \to \infty} \partial U(\omega; m) / \partial \omega \equiv 0.$$

(A.11") $$\lim_{m \to \infty} \mathrm{Var}\{u[\omega Z_m + (1-\omega)V_m]\} \equiv 0.$$

Since $m = \infty$ is a meaningless polar case, any usefulness of these theorems must be their contents for "large m," as for example:

(A.11) $\left| \omega_m^* - \omega^\dagger \right|$ is "small" when m is "large."

But the usefulness of this is discounted when we realize that, for m large, *any* ω is very nearly as good as ω_m^*! I.e., from (A.10) we know that

(A.12) $U(\omega_m^*; m) - U(\omega; m)$ uniformly small when m large.

We may summarize as follows: Replication of sets of identical independently distributed securities does not require any reliance on surrogate normal Gaussian distributions to validate asymptotic mean-variance approximations; the "compactness" of probabilities that is implied by the applicable Law of Large Numbers suffices, without recourse to the Central-Limit Theorem, as is elaborated in Samuelson [25]. Moreover, the problem of optimization becomes

498

FIGURE I

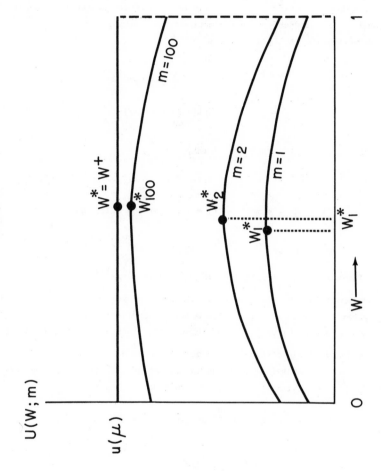

trivial when the portfolio outcomes become virtually certain: *any* weightings of a very large number of independently replicated securities will virtually wipe out risk (an observation worth noting in its own right).

In concluding, it is salutary to point out what happens when, as we increase the replications of securities m, we suppose that the variance of *each* is larger like m so that for all m we are left with the same final wealth variance. One can verify that the valid Central-Limit Theorem then has no relevance to the goodness-of-approximation of any Gaussian surrogates.

Now we rewrite (A.1)-(A.5)

(A.13)
$$\text{Prob}\{X_{1,m} \leq x_1, \ldots, X_{2m,m} \leq x_{2m}\}$$

$$= [\prod_{j=1}^{m} P(x_j;m)][\prod_{j=m+1}^{2m} R(x_j;m)]$$

$$P(x;m) \equiv 0 \equiv R(x;m), \quad x < 0.$$

(A.14)
$$E\{X_{j,m}\} = \mu \quad (j = 1,\ldots,2m; \; m = 1,2,\ldots).$$

(A.15)
$$\text{Var}\{X_{j,m}\} = m\sigma_1^2, \quad (j = 1,\ldots,m; \; m = 1,2,\ldots).$$

$$\text{Var}\{X_{m+i,m}\} = m\sigma_2^2, \quad (i = 1,\ldots,m; \; m = 1,2,\ldots).$$

At first I thought to require $P(x_j;m) \equiv Q[(x_j-\mu)/m^{1/2}\sigma_1]$, so that as m grows the spread around the mean is increased in proportion to $m^{1/2}$. But it became clear that with μ finite, this would impair limited liability for m large enough to make $Q[-\mu/m^{1/2}\sigma_1]$ positive rather than zero. So some other of the plentiful admissible sequence of functions must be used.

The surrogate Gaussian functions for $P(x;m)$ and $R(x;m)$ are respectively $N[(x-\mu)/\sigma_1 m^{1/2}]$ and $N[(x-\mu)/\sigma_2 m^{1/2}]$. Now consider

(A.16)
$$Z_{n,m} = \sum_{j=1}^{n} X_{j,m}/n, \quad n \gtrless m$$

$$V_{n,m} = \sum_{j=1}^{n} Y_{j,m}/n$$

where all $X_{j,m}$ are independently distributed by $P(\ )$, and all $Y_{j,m}$ are independently distributed by $R(\ )$. Write the distributions generated as

500

(A.17)
$$\text{Prob}\{Z_{n,m} \leq z_1\} = P_n[z_1;m]$$

$$\text{Prob}\{V_{n,m} \leq z_2\} = R_n[z_2;m].$$

It is not the case that, for m large, the following appeal to the Central-Limit Theorem is valid, namely

(A.18)
$$\lim_{m \to \infty} P_m[z_1;m] = N[(z_1-\mu)/m^{-1/2}\sigma_1 m^{1/2}]$$

$$\lim_{m \to \infty} R_m[z_2;m] = N[(z_2-\mu)/m^{-1/2}\sigma_2 m^{1/2}].$$

Indeed, these left-hand limits are not even necessarily defined.

What is undeniably true is the following correct version of the Central-Limit Theorem:

(A.19)
$$\lim_{(n/m) \to \infty} P_n[v_1\sigma_1(n/m)^{-1/2}+\mu] = N[v_1]$$

$$\lim_{(n/m) \to \infty} R_n[v_2\sigma_2(n/m)^{-1/2}+\mu] = N[v_2].$$

Since we have no useful way of contemplating a large n/m, this properly normalized Gaussian approximation is not the same thing as use of Gaussian surrogates, and (A.19) provides no useful way even for m large, of handling the probability distribution of the portfolio, $W_m = \omega Z_{m,m} + (1-\omega)V_{m,m}$ and of $E\{u[W_m]\}$.

This application of "compact probabilities" can be extended to handle cases where a common Sharpe factor, Z, is added as a random component to the random variables X_j and X_{m+i} of (A.1). For this, see a forthcoming 1976 paper entitled "Addenda on Compact Probabilities: Gaussian Surrogates in the Capital Asset Model and Convergence Pathologies." This also provides some warnings concerning possible lack of convergence of the formal series involved in the treatment of compact probabilities, and elaborates on the triviality implications for mean-variance analysis of (A.12).

[1]   Arrow, K. J. *Aspects of the Theory of Risk-Bearing.* Helsinki: Yrjö Jahnssonin Säätio, 1963.

[2]   _____. *Essays in the Theory of Risk-Bearing.* Chicago: Markham, 1967.

[3]   Davies, P. L., and G. Ronning. "Existence, Uniqueness and Continuity of Portfolio Choice." *Zeitschrift für Nationalökonomie,* vol. 34 (1974), pp. 137-143.

[4]   _____. "A Note on the Uniqueness of Portfolio Choice." *Journal of Financial and Quantitative Analysis,* vol. 10 (1975).

[5]   _____. "Einige exakte und asymptotische Ergennisse für das Standard modell der Portefeuille-Auswahl innerhalb einer Periode." Forthcoming in *Statistische Hefte* Band 16, 1975.

[6]   Fama, E. F. "Mandelbrot and the Stable Paretian Hypothesis." *Journal of Business,* vol. 36 (1963), pp. 420-429.

[7]   _____. "Portfolio Analysis in a Stable Paretian Market." *Management Science,* vol. 11 (1965), pp. 404-429.

[8]   _____. "Multiperiod Consumption-Investment Decisions." *American Economic Review,* vol. 60 (1970), pp. 163-174.

[9]   Feller, W. *An Introduction to Probability Theory and its Applications.* II. New York: Wiley, 1966.

[10] Lévy, Paul. *Théorie de l'Addition des Variables Aléatoires,* Paris: Gauthier-Villars, 1954.

[11] Mandelbrot, B. "The Pareto-Lévy Law and the Distribution of Income." *International Economic Review,* vol. 1 (1960), pp. 79-106.

[12] _____. "New Methods in Statistical Economics." *Journal of Political Economy,* vol. 61 (1963), pp. 421-440.

[13] _____. "The Variation of Certain Speculative Prices." *Journal of Business,* vol. 36 (1963), pp. 420-429.

[14] _____. "Forecasts of Future Prices, Unbiased Markets and 'Martingale' Models." *Journal of Business,* vol. 39 (1966), pp. 242-255.

[15] _____. "When Can Price Be Arbitraged Efficiently? A Limit to the Validity of the Random Walk and Margingale Models." *Review of Economics and Statistics,* vol. 53 (1971), pp. 225-236. (This contains references to other valuable Mandelbrot contributions.)

[16] Markowitz, H. M. *Portfolio Selection: Efficient Diversification of Investments.* New York: Wiley, 1959.

[17] Menger, K. "Das Unsicherheitsmoment in der Wertlehre." *Zeitschrift für Nationalökonomie,* vol. 4 (1934), pp. 459-485.

[18] Merton, R. M., and P. A. Samuelson. "Fallacy of the Log-normal Approximation to Optimal Portfolio Decision-making over Many Periods." *Journal of Financial Economics,* vol. 1 (1974), pp. 67-94.

[19]   Samuelson, P. A.   "A Fallacy in the Interpretation of Pareto's Law of
       Alleged Constancy of Income Distribution."   *Rivista Internazionale di
       Scienze Economiche e Commerciali,* vol. 12 (1965), pp. 246-253.

[20]   _____.   "General Proof that Diversification Pays."   *Journal of Finan-
       cial and Quantitative Analysis,* vol. 2 (1967), pp. 1-13.   (Reproduced as
       Chapter 201 in *Collected Scientific Papers of Paul A. Samuelson, III,*
       Cambridge: M.I.T. Press, 1972.)

[21]   _____.   "Efficient Portfolio Selection for Pareto-Levy Investments."
       Journal of Financial and Quantitative Analysis, vol. 2 (1967), pp. 107-
       122.   (Reproduced as Chapter 202 in *Collected Scientific Papers of Paul A.
       Samuelson, III,* Cambridge: M.I.T. Press, 1972.)

[22]   _____.   "The Fundamental Approximation Theorem of Portfolio Analysis
       in Terms of Means, Variances, and Higher Moments."   *Review of Economic
       Studies,* vol. 27 (1970), pp. 537-542.   (Reproduced as Chapter 203 in
       Collected Scientific Papers of Paul A. Samuelson, III, Cambridge: M.I.T.
       Press, 1972.)

[23]   _____.   "Comments on the Favorable-Bet Theorem."   *Economic Inquiry,*
       vol. 12 (1974), pp. 345-355.

[24]   _____.   "Refutation of Logically-Necessary Paretian Income Inequality."
       (February 1975 draft to be published in *PNAS.*)

[25]   _____.   "Addenda on Compact Probabilities: Gaussian Surrogates in
       the Capital Asset Model and Convergence Pathologies."   Forthcoming in
       Review of Economic Studies.

248

COMMENTS ON THE FAVORABLE-BET THEOREM

PAUL A. SAMUELSON*
Massachusetts Institute of Technology

Professors Taub and Bodenhorn[1] have demonstrated the useful theorem that, if your marginal utilities are well-defined at a point of no risk, you can judge among some small bets or investments by pretending that your marginal utilities are constant at the no-risk level. Although they cite a 1963 item from my *Collected Scientific Papers*, there are many items there that utilize various Taylor-expansion approximations to the expected utility function.[2] Thus, a closely related result is that an investor, who holds cash or a safe security and faces the option of an investment whose mean return per dollar exceeds that of the safe security, will necessarily benefit himself from investing some positive amount in that security.[3] Or to rescue mean-variance theory from its dubious dependence on quadratic utility, or on normal-Gaussian probability distributions, or on the confused view that any two-parameter family of distributions can have those parameters defined in terms of the first two moments alone (an irrelevancy when one realizes that a portfolio of two two-parameter distributions no longer is a 2-parameter family), recourse has been made[4] to the concept of "compact" probability distributions whose expected utility value can be asymptotically approximated by one-, two-, or any specified number of statistical moments.

I offer a few comments here that relate to corners in the utility function, to 2-way as distinct from 1-way unlimited-scale options, to problems of nonconvergence of the expected value of utility, to objective as against subjective definitions of "fair" and "favorable" investment or betting op-

*I owe thanks to the National Science Foundation for financial aid and to Kate Crowley for editorial assistance.

1. A.J. Taub and D. Bodenhorn, "Risk and the Scale of a Bet," *Economic Inquiry* (Sept. 1974), 12.

2. P A. Samuelson, "Risk and Uncertainty: A Fallacy of Large Numbers," *Scientia*, 6th Series, 57 (April-May, 1963), pp. 1-6, reproduced in my *Collected Scientific Papers*, II (MIT Press, Cambridge, Mass., 1965), Ch. 16, pp. 153-158. Similar considerations are utilized in Chs. 12, 15 and in *CSP*, III (1972), Chs. 200, 201, 202, 203, 204. In particular they lie at the heart of my works on portfolio decision making, since the betting or investing options discussed here can be easily modified to be relevant for alternative security investments of a given initial wealth.

3. P. A. Samuelson, "General Proof that Diversification Pays," *Journal of Financial and Quantitative Analysis*, 2 (March, 1967), pp. 1-13, reproduced as Chapter 201 in P. A. Samuelson *Collected Scientific Papers*, III (MIT Press, Cambridge, Mass., 1972), pp. 848-859. See particularly Corollary I, p. 6 or 853.

4. P. A. Samuelson, "The Fundamental Approximation Theorem of Portfolio Analysis in Terms of Means, Variances and Higher Moments," *Review of Economic Studies*, 37, (October, 1970), pp. 537-542, reproduced as Chapter 203 in *CSP*, III, pp. 877-890.

tions ("bets" for short), and finally to uncontrollable variations in the states of the world that go on whatever the investors decisions and which preclude him from having open to him a no-risk base and which have a bearing on the "subjectivity" of defining "fair?"

1. If a person has a corner in his utility function at the no-risk base point, then, as noted in 1963, the argument fails. To be sure, almost nowhere can a continuous-increasing function have corners. But suppose (as in the classic Domar-Musgrave analysis) the decision maker feels differently about gains than about losses. Then, so to speak, a corner follows such a "regretter" around to wherever he may land (just as a myopic Friedman-Savage bettor on long shots finds an inflection point waiting for him at some higher income than wherever he happens to land). When such corners occur, as Taub and Bodenhorn make clear, the usual conclusions have to be qualified. Example: at a corner a risk-averter will definitely shun favorable bets that are not "sufficiently" favorable.

2. It makes a difference whether a scale-free stochastic option is considered to be a 2-way rather than 1-way option. Thus, if eH and $-eK$ are the authors' vectors of gain and loss at probabilities p and $1-p$, we have a 2-way option only when the scale parameter that the investor is free to choose, e, can be negative as well as positive or zero.

If the bet is a two way option and is not originally a "fair" bet, one can always by picking the appropriate algebraic sign for e contrive a "favorable" bet. (Instead of "buying" an unfavorable option, one reverses its direction by "selling" it.)

The general theorem for 2-way options becomes this.

Theorem 1. If a 2-way option is not a "fair" bet, there must always exist an (algebraic) scale for it which is better than staying in the no-risk base situation. This is independent of whether the maximizer of *expected* (smooth) utility is a risk-averter (with strictly decreasing marginal utilities and concave utility), or is a risk-lover (with strictly convex utility), or is of mixed allegiance (as in the Friedman-Savage *curiosum*). But is is only in the first two of these cases that we can be assured that the final optimal decision, e^*, involves investing in the direction of the favorable bet. The risk-lover must plunge without limit into any favorable bet (a result incompatible with his remaining small enough to be realistically confronted by scale-free or unlimited scale investing options). The risk-averter can usually be expected to take only a finite optimal scale, e^*, for a given favorable bet, but examples can be easily found in which the bet will be so favorable compared to the rate at which his marginal utility decreases that he too will be an unlimited plunger (a result not possible however if his marginal utility of wealth satisfies "Inada" conditions of becoming infinite at zero wealth and zero at infinite wealth). For the mixed allegiance man, we cannot be sure that his final optimal e^* has the algebraic sign that it would have to have if he were confined to small-scale betting and thereby led in the direction of the favorable bet.

All "fair" bets will be rejected by risk-averters; be plunged into without limit by risk-lovers; but cannot have any fixed rule laid down for them in the case of mixed types.

The proof of this general theorem can be given for any case where you begin with a no-risk base situation, X, and face an option with random algebraic outcomes, Y, whose probability distribution is defined as

(1) $$Probability \; [Y \leqslant Z] = P(Z)$$

Then the expected value of any function of Y can be computed as an integral. In particular the expected value of utility of outcomes for any scale of bet e, which is the scalar quantity that is to be maximized with respect to e, is expressible as the following Stieltjes integral

(2) $$Expected \; u = v(e) = \int_{-\infty}^{\infty} u[X+eZ] \; P(dZ)$$

This provides convenient notation that can handle either discrete probabilities or continuous probability densities. Moreover, (2) may involve a multiple rather than single integral if we wish to let X, Y, and Z go beyond being merely the scalar magnitude of money wealth. Instead our notation handles for nothing, so to speak, the case where X is a row vector of goods and Y is a random vector of algebraic gains of those goods: $Y =$ (tea gained, . . . , salt gained), etc. In the case of scalar money wealth we denote by $u_X[X+A]$ the marginal utility of money wealth at the point $X+A$. But to handle the vector of goods case, we need merely interpret $u_X[X+A]$ to mean the column vector of marginal utilities of the respective goods or the gradient of $u[X+A]$.

Example: For the authors' case where the bet involves a gain of $(k_1, . . . , k_n)$ with probability p and a loss of $(h_1, . . . , h_n)$ with probability 1-p, our (2) would read, $pu[X+eK] + (1$-$p)u[X$-$eH]$.

To find the optimal e^* that maximizes $v(e)$, we differentiate (2) and look for an e root that makes the following first-derivative vanish

(3) $$v'(e) = \int_{-\infty}^{\infty} Zu_X[X+eZ] \; P(dZ) \; = \; 0$$

For risk-averters any e root will be sufficient to provide the maximizing e^*. For risk-lovers any possible e root would provide a minimum that is to be shunned; and hence we know that risk-lovers never have a proper finite-e^* optimum but instead must be plungers. For mixed types the necessary conditions of (3) are not enough to indicate where e^* will be and must be supplemented by secondary-condition investigations.

We are now in a position to give an exact definition of what constitutes a "fair," "favorable," or "unfavorable" bet to the person in question. Our criterion is to be the algebraic sign of $v'(e)$ at $e = 0$, or $v'(0)$: namely,

$$(4) \qquad v'(0) = \int_{-\infty}^{\infty} ZP(dZ)u_X[X] = Expected\ Yu_X[X]$$

These inner products are merely the expected values of the physical goods—tea, . . . , salt—summed and weighted by their respective marginal utilities in the no-risk situation. By definition a favorable bet involves $v'(0)$ positive; an unfavorable bet involves $v'(0)$ negative; and a fair bet involves $v'(0)$ zero. For Y a money scalar, this boils down to the original mathematicians' definition of fair and favorable. But in the vector case, unless every element of the vector involves a favorable bet in the physical commodity alone, we need to balance the favorable and unfavorable physical results by their respective marginal utility weights to arrive at an unambiguous definition.

Now suppose $v'(0)$ does not vanish. Then by picking a small e of its algebraic sign one will get a resulting $v(e)$ that must be better than $v(0)$. This is independent of the higher derivatives of $v(e)$ and hence establishes the first part of the theorem.

The second part of the theorem, that e^* must end up the same sign as $v'(0)$ for risk-averters follows immediately from the fact that if $u[X]$ is strictly concave so must be $v(e)$ for all non-trivial bets. If e^* were to be of opposite sign to $v'(0)$ for a strictly concave function, that would involve the contradiction that for such a function there would have to be a minimum e between e^* and 0, a patent absurdity for a concave function. When we examine the case of risk-lovers, we realize that the optimal e^* cannot be finite and that things do indeed get indefinitely better as one proceeds away from zero in the direction of a favorable bet. That e^* can be of opposite sign to $v'(0)$ in the mixed case is shown by the simple example of the Friedman-Savage guinea pig who faces an unfavorable long-shot bet. It would be better for him to reverse roles and take the function of a bookie in selling a small amount of such a bet as against standing pat; but so great is the marginal utility to him of being really wealthy that his optimal e^* is seen to be positive as he takes the bet in defiance of its negative $v'(0)$.

The final part of the theorem that I have added, which deals with fair bets, is proved as follows. For a risk-averter a fair bet provides a maximum at $e^* = 0$. A strictly concave function can have but one maximum. For a risk-lover $e^* = 0$ provides a minimum, from which he will certainly want to depart, gaining the more he does so. Finally, a mixed-allegiance person might or might not have distant reversals of his curvature that were strong enough to induce him into taking a given fair bet.

Note that where we have only a 1-way option, and e must be non negative, we can easily use Kuhn-Tucker programming to maximize $v(e)$, replacing the vanishing of $v'(e^*)$ by its being non-positive but being capable of being negative only if e^* vanishes. As the authors suggest, a risk-lover confronted by an unfavorable 1-way option will shun sufficiently small bets and (perhaps more surprisingly) may shun *all* unfavorable bets at any scale if they are not "sufficiently not too unfavorable." This last paradox can be shown to arise when the rising marginal utility is confined between upper and lower bounds.

3. The above discussion of large-scale bets alerts us to a warning that is needed anyway: the expected value of utility, $v(e)$, may not be well-defined for all e scales; and it may particularly not be defined for negative e. Thus, suppose that money Y has the log-normal distribution so beloved of finance theorists. Then the largest gain is infinite. But now suppose that Y is an unfavorable bet. As a 2-way option, selling Y short produces a favorable bet. But will one wish to choose a negative e, as indicated in Theorem 1? Certainly not if one's marginal utility goes to infinity at zero wealth, as seems reasonable and is implied by the Bernoulli utility function *log X* or by any member of the constant-relative-risk aversion family $u[X] = X^a/a$, $a < 1$. For such cases $v(e)$ is defined only for non-negative e and the 2-way option will never be relevant even if it is available. Risk averters will shun such a 1-way unfavorable or fair bet. Risk-lovers must plunge into fair 1-way bets but, as noted, may (if their strong convexity attenuates at high wealths) find it never pays to embrace at all highly unfavorable bets.

4. All that has been said so far hinges on the crucially important postulate that the decision maker has a no-risk base from which he can operate. Life need not be like that. Whatever we do there may be so many uncontrollable states of the world that could occur that we stand to face a variable outcome even if we stand pat. In that case the simple Theorem 1 has no fulcrum from which to operate.

Let me illustrate with a simple dollar-wealth case where X and Y are scalars. I begin at X of money wealth. I face the scale-free option eY. But no matter what my choice of e, I also am faced with uncontrollable dollar increments, S, that must be added to X—giving me in the end as final chance wealth outcomes $X + S + eY$, where I face a joint probability distribution for S and Y.

(5)
$$Prob \{ S \leqslant T \text{ and } Y \leqslant Z \} = P(T, Z)$$

Now I act to maximize

(6)
$$v(e) = \int_{-\infty}^{\infty} \int_{-\infty}^{\infty} u[X + T + eZ] P(dT, dZ)$$

and

(7)
$$v'(e) = \int_{-\infty}^{\infty} \int_{-\infty}^{\infty} Z u_X [X + T + eZ] P(dT, dZ)$$

And now the new fairness criterion would seem, as before, to hang on the algebraic sign of $v'(0)$ in

(8)
$$v'(0) = \int_{-\infty}^{\infty} \int_{-\infty}^{\infty} Z u_X [X + T] P(dT, dZ)$$

Note that this will by no means have to agree with the traditional dollar criterion of a fair gamble, since (8)'s new $v'(0)$ need *not* have the algebraic sign of

(9)
$$\text{Expected } Y = \int_{-\infty}^{\infty} \int_{-\infty}^{\infty} Z P(dT, dZ)$$

As shown in Samuelson-Merton,[5] we must replace the objective utility of $P(T, Z)$ by the "util prob" metric, $Q(T, Z)$, where by definition

(10)
$$Q(dT, dZ) \equiv u_X [X + T] P(dT, dZ)/c$$

$$c = \int_{-\infty}^{\infty} \int_{-\infty}^{\infty} u_X [X + T] P(dT, dZ)$$

There is, however, the special case where the betting options outcomes happen to be independently distributed from the S uncontrollable variations. The independence case involves

(11)
$$P(T, Z) \equiv R(T) P(Z)$$

With independence, our dollar fairness criterion does agree with the conventional definition, since now

(12)
$$v'(0) = \int_{-\infty}^{\infty} Z P(dZ) \; u_X [X + T] R(dT)$$

$$= (\text{Expected } Y) (\text{Expected } u_X)$$

With marginal utility always positive, the second factor in this last product

5. P. A. Samuelson and R. C. Merton, "A Complete Model of Warrant Pricing that Maximizes Utility," *Industrial Management Review*, 10 (Winter, 1969), pp. 17-46, reproduced as Chapter 200 in *CSP*, pp. 818-847. See particularly p. 19 or 820 and Appendix A's useful lemmas provided by Prof. David T. Scheffman, now of the University of Western Ontario. Robert Solow reminds me that (8) can be interpreted as "the expected value of 'Z' times 'the conditioned expected value of U_X, conditional on 'Z'" or *Expected* $[ZE\{U_X|Z\}]$ from which (12) follows intuitively in the independence case.

must be positive, giving $v'(0)$ the same algebraic sign as the first factor. Independence thus gives the same result with objective probability or with personal util-prob. These formulas hold also for X, S, and Y commodity vectors.

The independence case permits us to generalize Theorem 1. Now, both in the scalar dollar-wealth case and the vector many-commodity case, we can make the same inferences about "favorable" and fair scale-free 2-way options, provided only we carefully define "fair" bets so that, in the many-commodity case the expected values of the physical commodities are combined not with no-risk marginal utilities as weights, as in (4)'s $u_X[X]$, but rather with (12)'s expected marginal utilities as weights (the expectations being averaged over the $e = 0$ outcomes).

Theorem 2. Scale-free 2-way investing options whose outcomes are independently distributed from uncontrollable variations are subject to *all* the results of Theorem 1, provided our definition of fairness uses as weightings of physical-commodities' expected values (not the no-risk marginal utilities but rather the marginal utilities' expected values in the zero-bet situation). Thus, a bet that is not fair will at some small scale be better than an $e = 0$ decision . . . ; risk-averters will shun fair bets, just as risk-lovers will shun small unfavorable 1-way bets; . . . ; etc.

5. Actually, if we are willing to work with definitions of fairness that are completely subjective, *being different for each different person* (even in the scalar dollar-wealth case!), we can generalize both these theorems as follows.

Theorem 3. Applying as the criterion of fairness for a 2-way option $v'(0)$ in (8), we can validly state *all* the conclusions of the two earlier theorems on how risk-averters, risk-lovers and mixed-type persons will behave. In addition, new conclusions are valid such as the following: A risk-averter will definitely want to accept a bet that is "fair in *objective* money (or every-commodity) terms" provided it is distributed in probability in *negative dependence*[6] on the no-bet S outcomes, in the sense that

(13)   *Conditional probability* $[Y < Z$ when $S = T] = P(Z|T)$

with $P(Z|T_1) > P(Z|T_2)$ if $T_1 > T_2$.

6. For more on this see P. A. Samuelson, "General Proof that Diversification Pays," cited in footnote 3. Theorem III is particularly relevant. Note: a printer's error on p. 8 (or p. 855) prevents $\partial P(x_i|x_j)/\partial x_j > 0$ appearing as required here. See also the more difficult developments of this coal-and-ice company theorem in D. Scheffman, *Two Essays in Economic Theory*, MIT Doctoral Dissertation (1971), parts of which should be published in journal articles.

6. This lack of objectivity in the definition of a fair bet must at first seem distressing. Thus, Jones may rationally utilize Theorem 3 to make a dollar bet whose objective expected value he believes to be negative, even though Jones is a risk-averter. At the same time, risk-averter Smith may rationally bet in the opposite direction. (Recall Friedman-Savage's example.) Since economists often can only observe how people bet and not what their probability estimates are, doesn't Theorem 3 come close to saying, "The bets risk-averters make must be 'favorable' or they wouldn't have made them." "People do what they do" constitutes only an empty truism that rises to the level of a fatuity.

As the author's analysis makes clear, we were *already* in Theorem 1 in the morass of subjectivity when dealing with many-commodity vectors. Even if Smith and Jones agreed that tea's expected value in the bet was positive and salt's expected value was negative, they might rationally as risk-averters choose to be on opposite sides of the bet—provided that their relative marginal utilities for salt and tea differed in the no-risk situation.

However, one might have hoped—superficially as I shall show—to get rid of subjectivity as follows.

Suppose in the no risk situation, Pareto-optimality has somehow *already* been achieved. Then the $u_X[X]$ marginal-utilities vectors in (4) of two different persons will *already* have become proprotional to each other. Hence, speaking loosely, we can say that everybody "in the same market" will have the *same* "fair" bet criterion. (We speak loosely because Pareto-optimality need not come about from use of market pricing.)

Moreover, pushing along this same tempting logical path, we might try to bring Theorem 2 also into the *objective* camp by the following trick. Arrow-Debreu contingency-security markets, it is known,[7] can hope to bring about Pareto-optimality in stochastic situations. So let us hope that the random S that is added to each person's X—say $X^k + S^k$ for the k-th person—will already because of Arrow-Debreu contracts be arranged so that we have proportionality for all persons, k or otherwise, to the same weighting (column) vector *Expected* $u^k[X^k + S^k]$ in (8). If this hope can come true, Theorem 2 would seem to operate in terms of *objective* definitions of a "fair" or "favorable" bet.

7. However, before pushing our luck to trying to bring Theorem 3's general case on to the *terra firma* of objectivity, notice the fallacy of the hoped-for line of escape. Why should the *no-risk* situation's marginal utilities be made Pareto-optimal when in fact Theorem 1 says we shall all be

---

7. Cf. K. J. Arrow, *Essays in the Theory of Risk Bearing* (Markham Publishing Co., Chicago, 1971), especially Ch. 4, a 1963 English translation of Arrow's classic Paris paper of 1952; G. Debreu, *Theory of Value* (John Wiley and Sons, New York, 1959), final chapter.

departing from the no-risk bases? Arrow-Debreu Pareto-optimization ought to apply to the non-zero e^* states of the world, not to the $e = 0$ pre-bet states of the world.

Theorem 3 alerts us to the absolute need for subjective differences in "fairness," for it is just those differences that make it possible for Smith and Jones to both want to bet with each other. Some examples can illustrate.

Let Y be a fair bet in dollar terms. But let Y's gains tend to occur when risk-averter Smith's S shows losses and when risk-averter Jones' S shows gains. Then, as already noted, an arm's-length bet of Smith at positive e with Jones at negative e makes sense for *both* of them. They are mutually reinsuring in the Arrow-Debreu fashion! Mark Twain said that it is differences of opinion [about probabilities] that make horse races. We can add: Even with the same opinions about probabilities, it is differences in people's situations that make zero-sum bets possible.

8. I conclude by defining "a person's subjective marginal 'fair' bet, which is to be fair (not necessarily at the $e = 0$ level, but rather) at any specified scale level, e, and is to involve a zero $v'(e)$ there." The optimal scale for a 2-way bet is in the general case defined by e^*, at the root of e for which

$$(14) \qquad 0 = v'(e^*) = \int_{-\infty}^{\infty} \int_{-\infty}^{\infty} Z \, u_X [X + T + e^*Z] P(dT, dZ)$$

Hence, using the algebraic sign of $v'(e)$ as the criterion of "marginal favorability or fairness" at the scale e, we have the circular theorem.

Theorem 4. At the optimal scale for a bet, e^*, the bet must be *marginally* fair (with zero expected value under the util-prob there). All different securities one holds have the same "marginally fair" property with Samuelson-Merton util-prob expected values equal.

In a trivial sense, everyone in his e^* equilibrium experiences a marginal fair bet, but one man's $v'(e^*)$ vanishes at an e^* that is different from the e^* of the man he bets with.

9. I must not leave the impression that bets or investment gambles have to be zero-sum, with as much economic weight on one side as on the other. For each of us—and even Robinson Crusoe alone—can also make bets with Mother Nature, as for example when we plant seeds in the ground and reap a random harvest. Unlimited-scale bets, with other people or with Nature, are usually possible only when (a) each one of us is so small as to be a "bet *taker*" too unimportant to affect the odds; (b) and/or Nature's stochastic production function has *expected values* of outputs that are homogeneous-first degree functions of all inputs, (c) or, more strongly, has vector random outputs that are proportional to input

in the following sense—if H represents a vector of inputs and R a random vector of outputs, then

$$(15) \qquad Prob \quad R \leqslant Q|H = H \quad = \pi(Q|H°) \equiv \pi(mQ/mH°), \ m > 0$$

Does man have *limited liability* when it comes to bets with Nature? Often we have nothing to lose but our positive production inputs. But when we sow too much U-235, we may reap the whirlwind!

Axiom systems, like that of Arrow,[8] often assume utility to be bounded both above and below. And I do agree that many (perhaps most) people will, on introspection, feel that *their* utility is indeed bounded above; in the same way, even more people will feel that their utility is not linear in money. Sophisticated people in the latter group do not need to contemplate the famous St. Petersburg Paradox to learn that their marginal utility is decreasing; but some others may be made aware of this fact by such a dramatic example. Similarly, a super-St. Petersburg paradox of the Karl Menger type (as referred to by Arrow) may alert some subset of bounded-utility people to awareness of this fact. So much is not in dispute. But nothing said yet deprives a person from having linear utility, if on introspection he finds he really does. It's a free country! Two people in the universe with linear (or even convex) utility will gamble with each other inveterately even if an infinite-stakes game is feasible only in one-sided thought experiments. On the other hand, in a universe where everyone had a strictly-concave utility that is unbounded above, there would be no super-St. Petersburg game that can actually find a Peter to offer its option to the willing Pauls. So I fail to see the Menger theorem's compelling relevance. Nor do I think I should accept the bounded-utility axiom merely out of the fear that without it there may exist probability options that I am unable to rank by their first moments of utility—since their expected values may fail to exist. Am I ever likely to be confronted with choices among such option in the real world? I wonder.

As we saw with short-sales of IBM or other stocks, failure of convergence is most to be feared at low or zero levels of wealth. Bankruptcy or Death provides difficulties for any theory of finance or stochastic decision making. "One might as well be hung for a sheep as a lamb; or go bankrupt owing a million as a cent," are slogans that can cost one's fellowmen or co-passengers dearly—which is why every viable society tries to protect itself from *aprés-moi-le-deluge* rashness by placing crucial decision-making in staggered-age committees and family councils. These help defend the utility function from a relevant lower bound that destroys its strong con-

8. K. J. Arrow, *op. cit.*, Ch. 2, especially pp. 64-69.

cavity property on which the nice theorems about risk-averters must depend.[9]

Even if the utility function need only be defined for wealth outcomes that are non-negative, convergence difficulties can arise if marginal utility becomes infinite at zero wealth. This is because, in real life, no matter what one does, one may well face a finite probability of "ruin." (Like Socrates, all men are mortal.) In that case, no situation has a defined expected utility.

What to do? A case can be then made, I think, for the following lexicographic ordering that involves a minimax strategy.

1. Act always, between decision A and decision B, so as to select the option with lowest probability of literal ruin.

2. As between all options that share the same (lowest) probability of ruin, choose the one with the highest expected utility over *positive* outcomes.

Such a minimax (or maximin) strategy seems to be free of the usual minimaxer's paranoia which pretends that Nature is an omnipotent and malevolent adversary who will construe the worst.

---

9. The behavior of utility at lowest levels offers, I think, the more perplexing problems. I must confess I don't understand why anyone would permit me to make a short sale if (a) my wealth is finite, and (b) we both believe that the stocks' price is log-normally distributed with expected value not less than current price. But, as a thought experiment, I can still be permitted to shun any offered short sale on the ground that, if it results in a negative T outcome that makes my final outcome, $T+X$, negative, the dishonor of bankruptcy is deemed by me so infinitely bad as to make me prefer to the short sale any alternative that, with probability greater than $\epsilon > 0$, leaves me with no less than $0 + \eta > 0$, where ϵ and η are arbitrarily small. This does mean that my relevant $v(e)$ is not defined for negative e (or has to be defined as "minus infinity"). Whether $u[X+T]$ is termed concave for non-positive arguments is a semantic question of not much interest: certainly $u[-w^2]/u[w^2+a^2]$ is effectively zero for *all* w and for any positive a^2, however small.

249

OPTIMALITY OF SLUGGISH PREDICTORS
UNDER ERGODIC PROBABILITIES*

By Paul A. Samuelson[1]

FORECASTING MODELS rarely predict with complete precision. Often, they are observed to miss turning points in cyclical economic time series. The actual observations tend to be choppier than the predicted observations. Naturally, this gives rise to some dissatisfaction among forecasters and consumers of forecasts.

It is not clear what to do about this except to go back to the drawingboards for a better model and back to reality with more powerful telescopes and microscopes. One macro model builder was converted temporarily to monetarism, in the hope that introducing into his independent variables a choppy variate like the change in M_1, might serve to get what he regarded as excessive smoothness out of his model's predictions. (As a critic remarked, why didn't he add some random numbers to his forecasts if it was only extra variance he desired?) Other acts of desperation have been to replace least-squared-deviations by least-absolute-deviations, expecting that this will lead to less smooth (Gaussian?) estimates. Catering to their vanity of being able to claim to have been right at turning points, some forecasters have even suggested that in estimating coefficients of a model, extra weight be given in past sample data *to errors that take place at the turning points*, praying that such a method of fit will give coefficients that also produce reduced errors at *future* turning points.

A number of econometricians have pointed out that what is regarded as a defect actually represents optimal estimation procedures. Good forecasts *should* in many specifications be more stable than the reality they are forecasting. If the loss resulting from an error in forecasting is proportional to the square of that error—as with quadratic social welfare functions—what one gains in avoiding large errors between turning points is recompense for not doing better at the turning points themselves. After all, from the very definition of a trough or peak or turning point, the system is not there very long. Only if one had some special non-linear mechanism in mind, in which it is somehow a new ball game after each turn has been well established, would it make very much sense to be peculiarly concerned about errors at the turns themselves.

* Manuscript received September 5, 1975; revised October 27, 1975.
[1] I owe thanks to the National Science Foundation for financial aid, and to Kate Crowley for editorial assistance.

1

Hatanaka[2] has shown how "solely the logic of least squares" leads to optimal predicted forecasts that have "smaller variations than their counterparts in the actual series." One can only agree. What I should like to do here is to point out that, from the very nature of a "stable" stochastic process (one that in a genuine sense eventually forgets its past and therefore can be expected in the far future to approach an ergodic probability distribution), *it is both inevitable and proper that the best forecast made*—no matter what attribute of the dependent variable that is under consideration, as for example its expected value or arithmetic mean, its median, its geometric mean or any other parameter to be conditionally described, with or without use of least squares—*should become insensitive to the data now at hand*. It is therefore optimal that predictions of the future should be less variable than the actual data are then going to be revealed to be. Among other reasons, this is because the actual future data will have in them the strong effects of just-prior happenings, happenings which have as of this early time of prediction not yet happened.

To illustrate these truths about ergodic probabilities I shall analyze in detail the famous cob-web model[3] of price oscillation once it is made probabilistic.

1. THE DETERMINISTIC CASE

In its deterministic form, this assumes a well-behaved, Cournot-Marshall demand function relating current price, p_t, to current quantity supplied:

$$(1) \qquad p_t = D(q_t), \ D'(q) < 0, \ D(q) > 0 \qquad \text{when } q > 0$$

$$(1.1) \qquad p_t = \frac{1}{q_t}, \qquad \text{for example .}$$

On the supply side, it assumes that quantity in the next period, q_{t+1}, is a rising function of price now, p_t:

$$(2) \qquad q_{t+1} = s[p_t], \ s'[p] > 0, \ s[p] > 0 \qquad \text{when } p > 0$$

$$(2.1) \qquad q_{t+1} = 3p_t^{1/2} - 2, \ 0 \le p_t \le 1, \qquad \text{for example ,}$$
$$= 2.5 - 1.5 \exp(1 - p_t), \ 1 \le t .$$

Stationary equilibrium is unique at (q^*, p^*), the root of

$$(3) \qquad p^* = D(q^*), \ q^* = s[p^*]$$
$$p^* = D(s[p^*]) \overset{\text{def.}}{\equiv} f_1(p^*) .$$

[2] Cf. Hatanaka [3], who gives references to related work by Theil, Hart, Bossens and Modigliani, J. F. Muth, Mincer and Zarnowitz, and Granger and Newhold. My quotation is taken from [3, (151)].
[3] For references to the cob-web model, see [6]. Early work by Schultz, Tinbergen, and Ricci is cited in [2]. I parallel the analysis of Leontief [4]. Buchanan [1] cites Moore's important early work, as well as subsequent work by Kaldor and Lange, and questions whether farmers will continue to act on assumptions that are seen to be self-falsifying in the longer run.

It will be locally unstable when supply is more "elastic" than demand at the equilibrium, or when

$$(4) \qquad\qquad f_1'(p^*) = D'(q^*)s'[p^*] < -1.$$

Any divergence of equilibrium will asymptotically approach a periodic oscillation of determinate amplitude, defined as in Leontief [4] by the roots $(p^\dagger, q^\dagger; p^{\dagger\dagger}, q^{\dagger\dagger})$

$$(5) \qquad q^\dagger = s[p^\dagger], \ p^{\dagger\dagger} = D(q^\dagger), \ q^{\dagger\dagger} = s[p^{\dagger\dagger}], \ p^\dagger = D(q^{\dagger\dagger})$$

$$p^{\dagger\dagger} = f_1(p^\dagger), \ p^\dagger = f_1(p^{\dagger\dagger}) > p^{\dagger\dagger}$$

$$p^\dagger = f_1(f_1(p^\dagger)) \stackrel{\text{def.}}{=} f_2[p^\dagger], \ p^{\dagger\dagger} = f_2[p^{\dagger\dagger}]$$

$$f_2'[p] = f_1'(p)f_1'(f_1(p))$$
$$= s'[p]D(s[p])s'[D(s[p])]D'(s[D(s[p])]) .$$

To ensure that there is essentially only one cob-web box and periodic motion, it is assumed that

$$(6) \qquad\qquad 0 < f_2'[p] < 1, \ p \geq p^\dagger > p^* > p^{\dagger\dagger}.$$

In that case the solution to the system, when disturbed initially from equilibrium, will asymptotically approach a periodic motion of period 2. Write $p_t = p\{t; p_0\}$ as the solution to

$$(7) \qquad\qquad p_{t+1} = f_1(p_t), \ p_0 \text{ given}, \qquad\qquad (t = 0, 1, \cdots) .$$

Then

$$(8) \qquad p\{t; p^*\} \equiv p^* \qquad\qquad\qquad\qquad\qquad t > 0$$

$$[p\{2t; p^0\} - p^*][p^0 - p^*] \geq 0, \ [p\{2t + 1; p^0\} - p^*][p^0 - p^*] \leq 0$$

$$p\{t; p^\dagger\} \equiv \frac{1}{2}[(1)^t + (-1)^t]p^\dagger + \frac{1}{2}[(1)^t - (-1)^t]f_1(p^\dagger)$$

$$p\{t; f_1(p^\dagger)\} \equiv \frac{1}{2}[(1)^t + (-1)^t]f_1(p^\dagger) + \frac{1}{2}[(1)^t - (-1)^t]p^\dagger$$

$$\lim_{t\to\infty} p\{t; p^* + a^2\}p\{t; p^\dagger\}^{-1} = 1, \ a^2 > 0$$

$$\lim_{t\to\infty} p\{t; p^* - a^2\}p\{t; f_1(p^\dagger)\}^{-1} = 1 .$$

Figure 1 illustrates the deterministic case.

1(a) shows the familiar box motions, ABCD, surrounding the unstable intersection-equilibrium. 1(b) plots the $f_1(p_t)$ and $f_2[p_t]$ functions: the unstable e point is surrounded by the stable periodic-motion points a and c, corresponding to $p^\dagger$ aud $f_1(p^\dagger)$.

Prediction of data generated by the deterministic model is easy and exact. (It is too easy, since if farmers knew its dynamic laws—and they soon would infer them from experience—they would assuredly modify their $s[p]$ responses.

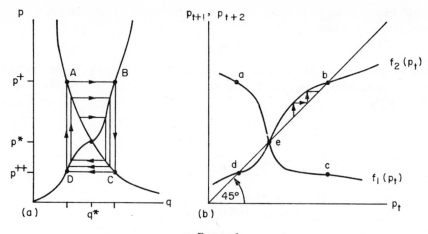

FIGURE 1

BECAUSE DB IN (a) HAS SMALLER ABSOLUTE SLOPE AT q^* THAN AC DOES, THE EQUI-
LIBRIUM IS LOCALLY UNSTABLE. PERTURBATIONS OF IT LEAD TO PERIODIC MO-
TIONS ALONG THE BOX ABCD, AS DO INITIAL POINTS OUTSIDE THE STABLE LIMIT
CYCLE. IN (b), THE POINT e IS LOCALLY UNSTABLE, BUT THE POINTS d AND b ARE
GLOBALLY STABLE, (EXCEPT FOR e): d AND b CORRESPOND TO THE LIMIT CYCLE
ABCD.

But never mind: the model is only used as an illustration.)

2. THE STOCHASTIC VERSION

Now let the harvest be a random variable, not the deterministic magnitude
$s[p_t]$. Specifically, assume a sequence of i.i.d. positive random variables, $\{U_t\}$,
is involved, namely

$$(9) \qquad Q_{t+1} = s[U_t P_t]$$

$$P_{t+1} = D(Q_{t+1})$$

$$(10) \qquad \text{Prob}\,\{U_t \geq u\} = F[u]$$

$$\text{Prob}\,\{U_t \geq u_0 \text{ and } U_{t\pm k} \geq u_1\} = F(u_0)F(u_1)$$

$$\text{Prob}\,\{U_t \geq u \,|\, P_t,\ P_{t-1},\ \cdots,\ P_{t-k},\ \cdots\} \equiv F(u)\,.$$

To show that prices and quantities are now random variables, I write them
as capital letters rather than with the lower case letters of the deterministic case.
Now as in Samuelson,[4] we can define conditional Markov probabilities:

$$(11) \qquad \text{Prob}\,\{P_{t+1} \leq p_1 \,|\, P_t = p_0\} = \Pi_1(p_1; p_0)$$

where the $\Pi_1(\ ;\ )$ function is related to the known $F[\ ]$ function by the relations

$$(12) \qquad \text{Prob}\,\{P_{t+1} \leq p_1 \,|\, P_t = p_0\} = \text{Prob}\,\{f_1(U_t p_0) \leq p_1\}$$

[4] See also [5, (chapters 198, 199, 200)].

$$= \text{Prob} \{U_t \geq f_1^{-1}(p_1)/p_0\} = F[f_1^{-1}(p_1)/p_0].$$

By the properties of Markov probabilities, we can recursively define for any positive integers T_1 and T_2

(13) $$\text{Prob} \{P_{t+T_1+T_2} \leq p_{T_1+T_2}| P_t = p_0\}$$

$$= \Pi_{T_1+T_2}(p_{T_1+T_2}; p_0)$$

$$\Pi_2(p; p_0) = \int_0^\infty \Pi_1(p; x)\Pi_1(dx; p_0)$$

$$\dotsb$$

$$\Pi_{T+1}(p; p_0) = \int_0^\infty \Pi_T(p; x)\Pi_1(dx; p_0)$$

$$\Pi_{T_1+T_2}(p; p_0) = \int_0^\infty \Pi_{T_1}(p; x)\Pi_{T_2}(dx; p_0)$$

$$= \int_0^\infty \Pi_{T_2}(p; x)\Pi_{T_1}(dx; p_0).$$

Given the strong dampening properties of the non-linear system, the conditional probabilities can be shown, under plausible regularity conditions, to approach an ergodic probability distribution that is independent of initial p_0, namely

(14) $$\lim_{T\to\infty} \Pi_T(p; p_0) = \Pi(p)$$

$$\lim_{T\to\infty} E\{g(P_T)|p_0\} = \lim_{T\to\infty} G_T(p_0) = G = \int_0^\infty g(p)\Pi(dp)$$

$$\lim_{T\to\infty} [G_{T+k}(p_0) - G_T(p_0)] = 0, \qquad \text{for any fixed } k.$$

Heuristically, any single disturbance dies out from the strong dampening; the system, so to speak, eventually forgets its distant past; when continually subjected to independent shocks, it reaches its ergodic Brownian vibration—the natural generalization of non-stochastic equilibrium—when there is a balancing of the shock energy imposed and the frictional energy dissipated by the dampening. These are, of course, loose words for a definable process.

This shows that predictions for the distant future become insensitive to present conditions. Even though the 1998–1999 prices will fluctuate, the most rational guess for them now is for them to be spread with determinable probabilities over the whole p terrain, above or below $p^\dagger$, $p^{\dagger\dagger}$, p^*.

If price is high in this odd year 1975, and if the variability of U_t is known to me to be small, I'll bet on high prices in odd years, 1977 and 1979. But I have little reason for confidence that 2077 will be appreciably higher than 2076. Indeed, I have less confidence about the rise in price from 1978 to 1979 than from 1976 to 1977. Blessedly, we in the present are spared the overwhelming burden of knowing every variation in the future: our present sins do gradually

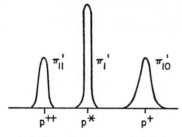

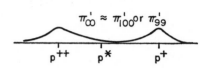

(a) Short-term probabilities

(b) Long-term probabilities where
Var $\{U_t\}$ is low

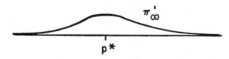

(c) Long-term probabilities where
Var $\{U_t\}$ >> 0

FIGURE 2

STARTING, SAY, AT $p^0 = p^*$ IN (a), ONE-PERIOD-AHEAD PROBABILITY DENSITY STILL CLUSTERS AROUND p^* TIGHTLY. 10 PERIODS AHEAD IT PERHAPS CLUSTERS SOMEWHAT AROUND $p^\dagger$; 11 PERIODS AHEAD SOMEWHAT AROUND $p^{\dagger\dagger} = f(p^\dagger)$. IN (b), STILL STARTING AT $p^0 = p^*$, FOR T VERY LARGE, THE SYSTEM CAN BE CONDITIONALLY EXPECTED TO BE SPREAD AROUND IN ITS ERGODIC DISTRIBUTION, π'_∞, PERHAPS BIMODALLY BUNCHED AROUND $p^\dagger$ AND $p^{\dagger\dagger}$. AS THE VARIANCE OF HARVEST INCREASES, THE DISTRIBUTION TENDS TO BECOME UNIMODAL AROUND THE p^* NEIGHBORHOOD, AS IN (c).

[NOTE: π'_T STANDS FOR $\partial \pi_T(p; p_0)/\partial p$ DENSITIES.]

wash out, and so do our good deeds!

What should spectral analysis reveal about this system? Old fashioned periodogram analysis, which attempts to decompose P_t into the following components

(15) $$P_t = a_0 + \sum_{k=1}^{N} [a_k \cos (2\pi kt/T) + b_k \sin (2\pi kt/T) + \text{error}$$

will fail miserably in a long time series for P_t on the interval $(0, T)$. As it should!

There is no fixed clock that stays synchronized in this universe, only one whose *phase* is constantly being perturbed. Still, as Var $\{U_t\}$ is made to diminish, the system should most of the time look like a linear periodic system, being "for long time periods near" $p^\dagger$ and $f_1(p^\dagger)$. I invite a reader to apply spectral analysis to Monte Carlo runs of this $\Pi_1(p; p_0)$ process that can be made to be almost log-normal for long time epochs by making Var $\{U_t\}$ small.

Figure 2 shows rough sketches of the $\Pi_T(p; p_0)$ probability distributions when Var $\{U_t\}$ is "small."

Massachusetts Institute of Technology, U.S.A.

REFERENCES

[1] BUCHANAN, N. S., "A Reconsideration of 'The Cob-Web Theorem,'" *Journal of Political Economy*, XLVII (February, 1939), 67-81.

[2] EZEKIEL, M., "The Cob-Web Theorem," *Quarterly Journal of Economics*, LII (February, 1938), 255-280. Reprinted in G. Haberler, ed., *Readings in Business Cycle Theory* (Nashville: American Economic Association, 1944).

[3] HATANAKA, M., "The Underestimation of Variations in the Forecasting Series: A Note," *International Economic Review*, XVI (February, 1975), 151-160.

[4] LEONTIEF, W. W., "Verzögerte Angebotsanpassung und Partielles Gleichgewicht," *Zeitschrift für Nationalökonomie*, Band V, Heft 5, 670-676. Reprinted in English translation in W. Leontief, *Essays in Economics: Theories and Theorizing*, Chapter 14 (New York: Oxford University Press, 1966).

[5] SAMUELSON, P. A., "Stochastic Speculative Price," *Proceedings of the National Academy of Sciences USA*, LXVIII (February, 1971), 335-337. Reprinted in Robert C. Merton, ed., *Collected Scientific Papers of Paul A. Samuelson*, Volume 3 (Cambridge, Mass.: MIT Press, 1972), 894-896.

[6] ———, "Mathematics of Speculative Price," 12th John von Neumann Lecture, *SIAM Review*, XV (January, 1973), 1-42. Reprinted in R. H. Day and S. M. Robinson, eds., *Mathematical Topics in Theory and Computation* (Philadelphia: Society for Industrial and Applied Mathematics, 1973), 1-42.

PART VI

International Economics

250

INTERNATIONAL TRADE FOR A RICH COUNTRY

by
Paul A. Samuelson

Lecture before the Swedish-American Chamber of
Commerce, New York City
May 10, 1972

Introduction

In these days of rapid change, when old traditions are being lost, it is necessary to forge new ones. I applaud the happy thought of the Federation of Swedish Industries to make it an annual custom for the Laureates of the Alfred Nobel Memorial Award in Economic Science, to give a lecture on some general subject in economics that will complement their official lectures on the intricacies of economic science. But though the spirit is willing, the flesh is weak: so overwhelming is the Swedish hospitality on the occasion of Nobel week that one more speech was just not possible for me. Worse than that, the awards one wins for scholarly research carry such public prestige these days that for the next year or so you live so to speak in the kind of whirl that must follow Miss America around in the year after her triumph—with the result that scientific scholarship itself must in some degree temporarily suffer.

All this is by way of apology for my own delay in taking part in this annual series. And it is by way of thanks to the Swedish-American Chamber of Commerce for making it possible for me to give this lecture in New York. If Mohammed cannot go to the mountain, so gracious is your hospitality that the mountain will come to Mohammed. One is all the more grateful for undeserved courtesies.

The Mark of Affluence

The topic I propose to think about today is the future of American international trade and finance. This happens to be of interest to the Swedish economy as well, by virtue of the fact that if we here in North America enjoy the highest per capita standard of living, then you in Sweden occupy the second place and have been closing the real wage gap between us.

The topic has an interest for all of western Europe and Australasia, since these are the continents in second place, also with a rapidly diminishing gap in comparison with the United States. The farseeing Japanese, who have the right to dream at night of that approaching date when their rapidly growing per capita real wages will equal and surpass our own, will have a natural interest in the same subject.

For, as I never tire of preaching in Scandinavia, the American pattern of things has a vital interest—not because there is anything special about being American, but because what one fool will choose to do at a high real income level so will another. The Americanization of Europe has little to do with forced infection imported from America: it is simply that everybody who gets to a real income of two or three thousand dollars a year per family member will want a car, a telephone, automatic heat, a winter vacation, and all the things that Americans by accident happened to have the opportunity to enjoy first. Our economy, so to speak,

6

is an analogue computer to show you the shadow of your own future. For better or for worse, I must add.

Our historians vie to formulate what it is that makes America distinctive. For that son of the middle border at the turn of the century, Frederick Jackson Turner, the fact of the *frontier* was the basic fact shaping America's history. If so, by now, the frontier of free land is ancient history. For long, America was the *newest* nation and the most modern democracy. Founded prior to the French Revolution, by now the United States is about the *oldest* of existing governments. David Potter, a distinguished historian of the last generation, asserted that what was the distinguishing feature in American history was the fact that we have always, even from our beginnings, been the *Land of Plenty.* Little wonder that Kenneth Galbraith's *Affluent Society* evoked a resonant response, equalling if not exceeding that of Thorstein Veblen's *Theory of the Leisure Class.* Potter would argue that this affluence, and our consciousness of it in comparison with the rest of the world, has been *the* central fact of the American experience.

Why is it harder for a rich man to enter into the kingdom of heaven than for a camel to pass through the eye of a needle? There must be a reason. And I suppose that reason is better known to Europeans who have had to put up with American tourists for a century than to American themselves. Affluence breeds self-confidence, even to the point of arrogance. As Samuel Butler said, there is always a certain lack of amiability about the go-getter. Admiration and fear aside, we tend to like a person in inverse relationship to his ability to survive in the struggle for success. If it is natural to expect a class struggle within a country based on differences in income and wealth, why is it not natural to expect international antagonisms based on the same economic disparities? If the class struggle had never existed, we should have had to invent it in order to explain the facts of modern life.

But what has all this to do with economics? In the

7

competitive equilibrium of Leon Walras, there is precious little room for the sociology of class warfare. Impersonal supply and demand dictate the final equilibrium. If in any sense there is personal rivalry of brother against brother, in a competitive market it is the substitutability of one identical worker against the other: the class struggle is an intra-class struggle, labor against labor in depressing the market wage, capitalist against capitalist in raising the real wage, depressing commodity prices and the rate of profit.

When Ricardo laid the foundations for the theory of international trade, in the form of the famous doctrine of comparative costs or comparative advantage, there was no particular role played by the *relative affluences* of the trading regions. What about the brute fact of *size,* that the United States aside from having highest per capita incomes has also been one of the economies of greatest land area and population? Herein we differ from Sweden or Switzerland in the same way that half a century ago the huge areas of Brazil and Argentina differed from the affluent "Switzerland of Latin America", Uruguay.

Mere size does not mean per capita affluence. Indeed, as the teeming millions of India and China illustrate, large absolute numbers when not matched by commensurate magnitudes of resources, makes for low productivity and poverty. As Adam Smith and Bertil Ohlin have emphasized, mere size may indeed be beneficial to the extent that it permits industries or society to realize the economies of mass production and scale that characterize many industrial processes. Increasing the extent of the market has always been a powerful argument in the arsenal of the free-trader. The Common Market is important to Western Europe in giving it the kinds of mass markets that the vast American continent has long enjoyed.

Nonetheless, once markets are large enough to afford competition among many efficient-scale producers, size ceases to be an important variable in the models of conventional international trade theorists. Thus, few of them would agree

8

with the contention of Oxford's Lord Balogh that small economies are at a disadvantage trading with the large United States—provided that the collusive power of concerted governmental action is not pursued by America. A cartel that monopolizes international markets is a bad thing, but a Dutch cartel would not smell more sweet just because it came from a small country; nor would the same cartel be more malevolent merely because of the giant size of its mother country.[1]

In summary, as far as competitive international trade analysis is concerned, there is no reason why mutually-profitable trade should not take place between affluent countries like America, Sweden, Australia, western Europe, among themselves, and between any of them and intermediate-income or underdeveloped nations—such as the countries of Latin America, Africa, Asia, and for that matter Eastern Europe (provided the latter's control authorities agree to balanced trade and follow the principle of importing those goods that can less cheaply be produced at home).

Needless to say, there is not unanimous agreement with these doctrines of classical and post-Keynesian establishment economics. My purpose here today is to subject them to searching reevaluation. Let me confess that my bias in the effort is to see whether I cannot find some merit in the suspicions and apprehensions of those who doubt and criticize the conventional wisdom.

To bring out the issues in the debate, let me state rather boldly and crudely an overly-complacent, optimistic view of the world taken by a naive student who has just learned the

---

[1] Actually, in the comparative advantage theory of Ricardo and Mill, small Portugal stands to gain a larger share of the advantage from international specialization than large England. Indeed, if English consumers are so numerous that their needs of Portugal's export goods have to be filled in part from domestic English production, Portugal gets 100 % of the gains from trade and England gets none. Under perfect competition smallness makes for rarity and advantage, largeness for abundance and selfish disadvantage.

9

classical doctrines of international trade. Then, as fairly as
I can, let me state what are some of the dire views and
apprehensions of that larger fraction of the world who have
not had a formal grounding in the theories of classical and
neoclassical economics.

10

Optimistic Conventional Views

For brevity, here is a dogmatic list

1. Until recently there was a weighty group of international finance experts who believed that the dollar was in some special sense a *key* international currency. Just as a sovereign government can issue money *ad lib* within a country and have it be acceptable (although, to be sure, at the cost of raising all prices), so the United States had in a sense the privilege of a counterfeiter. Therefore, by definition, we were hardly capable of running an international deficit since these deficits would *automatically* be financed by foreigners' accepting whatever dollars were thrust upon them. The dollar was, so to speak, not merely as good as gold: it was better than gold, particularly if the U.S. showed its determination to get rid of gold as an element in the international monetary systems by dumping our Fort Knox supply on the market for whatever price below the official price of $35 an ounce it would fetch from dentists, jewelers, and hoarders. (Few still hold to this comfortable view in its undiluted form. At best, it can be argued that the rest of the world has a desire to hold some *fraction* of its wealth in the form of dollars because of their convenience for exchange and as a store of liquidity, if only because the American GNP constitutes some thirty percent of world GNP and because ours has been a stable society that has protected private property rights in the past. It follows then

11

that to a limited degree the U.S. can finance a genuine deficit in its payments by issuing dollars that would be readily acceptable abroad in limited amounts).

2. Although in the historic past America was a high-tariff country—as in the Smoot-Hawley 1930 Act—under four decades of Reciprocal Trade programs, our duties have been cut in half, cut again and still again in half. As a result, though we are often regarded abroad as still being a protected market, this is only because of cultural lag: *America has become one of the freest markets in the world,* which is to the advantage both of our workers and of workers abroad. The substantial penetration of the American market by Japanese imports in the last two decades would be proof of this basic fact. (It may be added that, until recently, the endemic protectionist ideology of the American public had gradually been succeeded by a freer-trade ideology.)

3. Within the framework of the beneficial free-trade regime of the Bretton Woods system, even some optimists would admit that the *American dollar had prior to August 1971 become somewhat "overvalued."* To more this is merely a consequence of the post-1965 acceleration of the Vietnam war with its subsequent demand-pull and cost-push inflations. To others like me the overvaluation of the American dollar has been a longer-term phenomenon, related to the miraculous recovery of western Europe and Japan after the 1949 devaluation, to foreign investment desires of our corporations and to the expenditures and gifts of the United States in the Korean, Indochinese, and general cold-war efforts.

4. Even if the dollar is somewhat overvalued, this primarily *puts the onus on the surplus countries to unilaterally appreciate their currencies*—particularly the mark and the yen. Or else they should swallow our dollars of deficit without complaining. Running contrary to this comfortable policy of "benign neglect", enunciated both by conservatives and liberals among American economists, was the recogni-

12

tion by some of us that the regime of swallowing dollars could not be expected to last; and that, therefore, putting off the day of disequilibrium correction would only exacerbate the inevitable process of needed readjustment.

5. The true optimists held that *any overvaluation* of the dollar, even if it were fairly substantial, and more or less independently of its cause, *could be cured by the medicine of dollar depreciation or surplus-currency appreciation along the lines of the actual December 1971 Smithsonian Agreement in Washington.* Under the two-tier gold system, the free price of gold in the unofficial tier was of no importance; and within the official tier the only point in making a token upward revaluation of the dollar price of gold and SDR's was for the purpose of expediting agreement on new currency parities with lower dollar parities.

Since the dollar depreciation in December 1971 was substantial, averaging 12 per cent relative to other currencies, these "elasticity optimists" think that the therapy agreed upon in Washington should be ample to restore equilibrium in the reasonably near future. Indeed, some believe that even slight reductions in our export prices relative to prices of exports abroad will trigger off great improvements in our current credits and great improvements in our current debits; and these "elasticity super-optimists" have even been fearful that the dollar was depreciated too much in 1971 and will soon prove to be an undervalued currency. This will show itself, presumably, in the dollar soon rising to the top of the 2 1/4 per cent discretionary range agreed to in December 1971 when the official band of flexible exchange rates was more than doubled.

6. To such optimists as these, perhaps the whole August 15, 1971 crisis was unnecessary, being in the nature of an optical illusion, or being merely the self-fulfilling consequence of an irrational avalanche of speculation against the dollar. Likewise, the war of nerves that has been going on in the first half year following the Washington Agreement of last December, that is an irrational selfaggrevating move-

13

ment likely to come soon to an end. Or, if irrationality should carry the day, that will be an unfortunate and basically unnecessary outcome.

7. Almost all American economists now think it desirable that the fatal flaw of the Bretton Woods setup—its attempt to peg exchange rates—be removed in favor of (1) some kind of *gliding band,* in which parities can move up or down a few per cent in each year or (2) that we go outright onto some scheme of relatively-clean *floating* exchange rates, in which organized speculative markets will give exporters protection against fluctuating exchange risks and in which no deficits will ever again be possible.

8. Finally, with exchange rates flexible and with tariffs, import quotas, and other protective devices gradually removed, the American real wage will benefit in its rate of growth and the same will take place abroad, as everyone everywhere benefits from a more efficient international division of labor.

To be sure, in the ebb and flow of relative technological change and change in tastes, certain *specialized* workers within a country might find that their scarcity rents deteriorate when foreign competition takes away much of their advantage. And the same can happen to the rents enjoyed by capital and non-labor resources specialized to occupations no longer viable in the face of international competition. However, provided the country follows proper post-Keynesian fiscal and monetary policies, it should be able to ensure full-employment job opportunity for all. Displaced workers and machines will go into other lines of activity in which the country still has a comparative advantage, to the benefit of the real GNP and its broad factor-share claimants.

14

Economic Scares

I've now stated the optimists' case. Listen to it and you will not think of economics as the dismal science. Quite the contrary. One of the functions of economic analysis has been to rid people of their economic scares. In fact *Economic Scares* was the title of a little book, written by an economist of the World War I generation, old Edwin Cannan. For three decades he set the tone of teaching at the London School of Economics; and although the vulgar world used to associate that institution with the Fabian socialists, Bernard Shaw and the Webbs, and with the radical image of the late Harold J. Laski, those of us who know modern economics have always realized that it was more to be associated with Cannan, and with the laissez-faire-minded Lord Robbins and Friedrich Hayek.

One of the scares that Cannan claimed economics could rid you of is the perpetual mercantilistic scare that a country will chronically run an adverse balance of payments and be "drained" of its gold and precious reserves. I shall skip the details of his demonstration, based upon David Hume's assertion that after a country has lost enough money that will lower its prices and raise prices abroad, thereby causing its cheap exports to expand in value and causing the value of dear foreign exports to fall in value, until the equilibrium is restored with no further hemorrhaging of specie reserves.

All that I can say is that there are plenty of scares in

15

the present age, and economics has its work cut out for it if it is going to rid people of their fears. It was the Duke of Wellington who said: "I don't know whether my officers scare the enemy, but they sure as hell scare me." Well I am a sophisticated economist but I must confess to some apprehensions about the future of the American balance of payments and about the effects of future foreign trade developments on the average level of American real wages and living standards.

We live in the age of Freud. Now we know that often our anxieties are nameless dreads, and that if we can just get them out of our unconscious minds and viscera and lay them on the table for explicit and conscious examination in the light of economic principle, then we may be able to exorcize our fears and dreads. That is the purpose of this present investigation. And how much it is needed!

In every walk of American life, there is great uneasiness over foreign competition. The endogenous virus of protectionism which has infested all of American history from our earliest colonial days, and which still persisted in the years up to the 1929 crash, had indeed been laid to rest from, say 1933 when the Roosevelt-Hull Reciprocal Trade program began to lower American tariffs. By 1955, everyone in America—corporate managers, workers, union officials, editors, . . .—all seemed to have turned away from protectionism. I can testify that it was practically impossible in the 1950s to get anyone in Boston, the ancient citadel of Federalist conservatism, to debate in public with a professor on the issue of freer trade.

16

The New Protectionism

Those days are gone forever. In the last dozen years of the overvalued American dollar, one of the most baleful heritages of our ostrich-like policy of benign neglect of the international deficit has been the mushrooming up of protectionism. It is little exaggeration to say that everyone in America except a few academic economists has become a believer in protective tariffs, in mandatory or voluntary quotas. The few industrialists who still favor freer international trade, either have a commercial reason to do so because of their export positions, or I fear are right now hovering on the verge of a return to the protectionist fold. As an example, I offer you the automobile executives in Detroit. The workers there and their local unions have already turned protectionist, as you will verify if you go to any union meeting these days. Perhaps a few of the top executives, at least in their more public-spirited utterances, are still devotees of expanded international trade. But talk to the vice presidents in charge of domestic production and you will find a group of troubled men, who feel in their bones that by another decade North America may not turn out to be the place in which cars are to be viably built and sold in competitive markets. And, make no mistake about it, if it came to a choice between letting the auto business go abroad or protect it here at home by quotas, these executives will come down on the side of protectionism. To them it

17

is unthinkable that we should give up the auto industry. To do so would be criminally quixotic. And, in the view of all but the economics professors, the loss of basic industries like the auto industry would lower our real wage level and average standard of living.

To almost all Americans today it is an article of faith that using quotas on a wide scale—to save the textile, shoe, steel industries, and also the TV, electronics, auto, and tiddlywink industry—will be an important step in keeping real wages in America from deteriorating from their present all time peak levels.

Theoretical economists may quote comparative-cost examples until they are blue in the face. But the man in the street will not believe the assertion that high-paid American workers can compete with imported goods made by low-paid foreign workers. Throughout our history one of the most powerful weapons in the arsenal of protectionists has been the competitive threat from "pauper foreign labor". If it can be combined with the yellow peril, as in the threat from coolie labor, the argument is all the more powerful. And I am sorry to relate that this subconscious link with racism is not yet extinct: for some reason, Japanese Toyotas are more threatening than German Volkswagens or Swedish Volvos; the complaint against the Japanese today is, not that they are squat or bandy-legged sadists, but that they work too hard, save too much, are too well-educated, and are too darned smart. In short Max Weber's Protestant Ethic flourishes in the land of the rising sun. All the complaints that used to be made about Americans in the Europe of a generation ago are now made about the present-day Japanese.

Ironically, at the same time that high paid American workers have been frightened of the competition of low paid workers abroad, low-productivity countries have always been as frightened of the competition from the more affluent countries. *The American Challenge* by Servan-Schreiber illustrates in our own time how deep is the fear of the

18

American colossus. Nor is this a new phenomenon. Early in the nineteenth century it was England that represented the frontier of productivity. As Karl Marx pointed out, American economists of that day, such as the optimist Henry Carey, ended their advocacy of laissez faire at the country's boundaries. To quote from Marx's 1857 *Grundrisse,*

> "According to Carey, the harmony of economic conditions is based on the harmonious cooperation of town and country, industry and agriculture. This fundamental harmony . . . is ruined as a result of her (England's) competition in world markets and is the destructive element in general harmony. The only possible protection against it is constituted by tariff barriers—a forcible, national barricade against the destructive force of British heavy industry." (p. 50)

All through the last century, into our own times, the Marxian literature has generally held that mutually beneficial trade between the colonialized poorer nations and the affluent metropolitan center is impossible. Instead the relationship is intrinsically one of asymmetric exploitation, with the more affluent nation getting the lion's share of advantage from economic imperialism.

19

Needless to repeat at this stage, the classical theory of comparative advantage contended that, if even-handed competition prevailed between many suppliers and many demanders, then international specialization and trade, as well as capital movements, would work to the advantage of both countries—the poorer country as well as the richer, the exporter of capital who received his profit yield out of the enhanced real product of the capital-importing country, which now has its real wages increased by having each worker with more capital.

Let us bring American fears into the open. The textile industry is an easy case. How can our workers who must be paid more than two dollars an hour compete in standard textiles with the workers of Hong Kong, Singapore, India and Bengladesh? Textile manufacture is apparently one of the first activities that a developing country can do well in. With wages only small fractions of those in America, even if the foreign textile equipment is not quite as advanced as our own, costs of production abroad tend to fall lower than ours at home.

The theorist of comparative advantage agrees American resources should move out of cheap textiles, and for that matter shoes, and go to more efficient lines of production where our productivity is a larger multiple of foreigners' productivity. Yet when I said this over the New England

20

airwaves, I received a letter from a trade association official in the shoe industry that said: "Your words will go down in the infamy of history along with those of Marie Antoinette." More poignantly, what can my answer be to a letter from a 59-year-old woman textile worker, asking where at her age she can possible find another job. Shall I reply with the irrelevant contention that if immobile factors will let their wage fall flexibly far enough below the minimum wage, they may end up with a half a loaf of bread? At the least, the humane and politically savvy free-trader must urge support for governmental financial assistance to those workers and capital facilities whose competitive rents fall victim to the dynamics of changing international specialization.

The task of the proponent of freer trade is not over. It has just begun. A great many industries are believed to be in the predicament of textiles. Without quotas, shoe imports may grow. The steel industry has thrown in the sponge and now lobbies shamelessly for voluntary and mandatory quotas. Cameras, tape recorders, desk calculators, and an increasing variety of electronic products come from Japan and Europe.

The simple truth is this: American public opinion generally is of the firm conviction that America lacks comparative advantage in anything! Perhaps the man in the street will allow, as a purely temporary exception, that the United States may still have comparative advantage in the realm of aircraft and giant computers.

As mentioned, the situation in the automobile industry carries dramatic conviction to workers, executives, congressmen and newspaper editors, both in Michigan and everywhere throughout the land. Henry Ford and the auto are as much a part of the American saga as George Washington and the cherry tree. Yet more cars are being produced this year outside the United States than inside. Now that we no longer have the monopoly advantage to the economies of mass production, General Motors, Ford and Chrysler must

21

begin to wonder whether ten years from now North America will be at all the appropriate place to produce cars.

No doubt at night their international executives dream of getting bigger footholds in the production capacity of Japan and Europe. But down at the union halls there will be the greatest resentment at any attempt for the American industry to run away toward greener fields abroad. The Congressmen and Senators from the middle West will not sit by idly while comparative advantage works its remorseless change.

The academic economist must be aghast at this turn of public opinion. From the very definition of comparative advantage—repeat *comparative*—the economist maintains it is a logical impossibility for any country to lack comparative advantage in anything. To be sure, by the definition of what economists mean by an overvalued currency, if the dollar is overvalued, then fewer and fewer of our industries will be commercially viable in the comparative advantage sense. When that is the case the major premise of the free trader is denied: when workers are displaced from textiles, autos, you name it, it will not be because they've been sucked in to a more efficient line of production, but rather that they are pushed into unemployment and onto the dole.

I must correct myself: in the age after Keynes, we know how to expand fiscal deficits and monetary creation to keep purchasing power high even in the face of an overvalued currency. Displaced workers can be given jobs in public employment; or, as budget deficits lower overall thrift, they can find jobs in expanded output of those few lines in which we do still have comparative advantage. But such a post-Keynesian solution only magnifies and perpetuates the other side of the coin of currency overvaluation. It means chronic deficits in our balance of payments, which require that nations abroad swallow a torrent of unwanted dollars.

Try as I may to be heretical, *my reason will not let me agree with the man in the street that there is no depreciation of the dollar relative to surplus currencies that will*

22

permit America to have full employment under free trade.

The best econometric estimates that I have seen have been marshalled by Professor William Branson of Princeton University whom I am proud to count among MIT's former students. In the Brookings Papers on Economic Activity for mid-1972, Dr. Branson reviews the IMF, OECD, and Stephen Magee studies that generally suggest an improvement of $ 7—8 billion in America's current balance from the 12 per cent depreciation of the dollar at the December 1971 Washington Currency Agreement. I shall not quarrel with this as a best single estimate. But I must emphasize the large variance that any estimate is subject to. A famous earlier econometric estimate by Brookings economists, which expected equilibrium in America's balance of payments by 1968, went astray because of the unexpected Vietnam War. Who knows what may vitiate these new estimates?

23

A Summing Up

In closing, this much I must grant to the apprehensions of the man in the street. Were time not so short, my assertions could be less dogmatic.

1). No one knows the true size of the disequilibrium gap in the U.S. balance of payments just prior to August 15. *It may have been much larger than the experts think.* And the differential trends of productivity abroad relative to those here at home, which after all primarily created that gap, in my view, may still be working strongly against us in the years ahead following the Washington Agreement.

2). Therefore, the equilibrium parity of the dollar *may* have to be substantially downward in this coming decade. If such dollar depreciation is required, let us pray that gliding bands, crawling pegs, dirty floating, or clean floating will permit this to happen in an efficient way that preserves the fruitful international division of labor.

3). At home, traditional patterns of resource use may turn out to be *very far* from that equilibrium pattern necessitated by the vast changes in comparative advantage that have taken place over the last two decades and which may continue in the next. Even with post-Keynesian high employment, we know that the vested interests never give up their historic rents gracefully. The concentrated harm to themselves they see clearly and can make the public see; only the impractical eye of the academic economist sees clearly

24

the even greater benefit to the community at large from adaptation to dynamic comparative advantage.

4). Achieving equilibrium dollar parities and adapting to changing comparative advantage may only minimize America's loss of welfare from international trade. While the dollar was overvalued we enjoyed to a degree a higher standard of living from tangible goods imported in return for payment of mere dollar IOU's. Also our corporations acquired lucrative productive assets abroad partly in exchange for those American dollars that foreign central banks reluctantly had to swallow. Just as Germany or any country paying reparations suffers a primary burden from its unrequited payment, so will there be a *primary* burden upon America if we must replace our deficit by genuine export earnings. Beyond that, although a currency depreciation to restore equilibrium need not inevitably induce a deterioration of America's terms of trade, there is a real possibility that we shall be experiencing a *secondary* burden in the form of higher import prices relative to export prices. Indeed as western Europe and Japan close the gap between our overall productivity and theirs, quite aside from the financial aspects of currency parities, there could be a plausible trend against us in terms of lessened consumers' surplus from international trade.

In summarizing this point, I must guard against alarmist quantification. As long as America remains a continental economy whose imports stay in the neighborhood of not much more than 5 % of GNP, it is hard to see how even elasticity-pessimism can knock more than a few percentage points off the 50 % growth in our real GNP that the demography and productivity trends of the 1970's should bring in the coming decade.

5). Let me conclude with a possibility that has some ominous overtones for the share of labor, particularly the share in growing GNP or organized industries. Under modern trends of comparative advantage American management know-how (and for that matter management know-how anywhere) and American mobile capital may find that

25

their most efficient use is increasingly to employ foreign labor as a substitute for traditional American activities. Washington, New York City, Pittsburgh, and Denver are increasingly what Max Weber called *cathedral cities,* or in updated terminology, *headquarters cities. So under floating exchange rates and relatively free trade equilibrium, the United States might in time become a headquarters economy. Our emphasis in employment would shift to services and away from manufacturing.* It would become normal for us to enjoy an unfavorable balance of merchandise trade, reverting to the pre-1893 pattern in which the value of our merchandise imports exceeds the value of our exports. This trade deficit would be normally financed by our current *invisible* items of interest, dividends, repatriated or plowed-back profits, and royalties.

Though total American GNP would be the larger because of this free trade equilibrium, it is possible that *the competitive share of property would rise at the expense of labor's wage share.* This would present a problem for our welfare state—to expand tax and transfer programs to secure a more equitable distribution of income

6). Economics, alas, cannot be divorced from politics and from trends of ideologies hostile to absentee ownership. Suppose that economic equilibrium did dictate our becoming a service economy, living like any rentier on investment earnings from abrod. Let us grant that such an equilibrium, *if* permanent, could be optimal for the United States. But would it be safe for us to succumb to this natural pattern of specialization in a world of rising nationalism? Can one really believe that in the last three decades of the twentieth century the rest of the world can be confidently counted on to permit the continuing flow of dividends, repatriation of earnings, and royalties to large corporations owned here? I do not think I am paranoid to raise a doubt in this matter. There is certainly a danger that, *after* the United States has moved resources out of manufacturing and into the servicing-headquarter regime, it might then turn out that

26

nationalism impairs the successful collecting of the fruits of our foreign investments. We should then not only find ourselves poorer than we had expected but also facing the costly task of redeploying our resources *back* into the fields earlier abandoned. To be sure, private corporations may in some degree already take into account this danger of expropriation and thereby prevent an unwarranted redeployment of resources from taking place; but it is doubtful that they can be counted on to exercise the proper degree of prevision, particularly since they may well know that they can depend on our government to compensate them when such contingencies arise. Hence, there are rational grounds for some apprehensions concerning this aspect of spontaneous foreign-trade development.

I have tried to walk the mile with those who are fearful about international trends. Yet reason and experience have kept me from walking the whole mile with this overly pessimistic view. Let me conclude with a solemn warning.

Even if the most dire pessimists are correct in their belief that much of existing American industry can be preserved in its present form only by universal protective quotas of the Burke-Hartke type, it is a pitiful delusion to believe that such measures will enhance rather than lower the real standard of living of the American people.

27

251

TRADE PATTERN REVERSALS IN TIME-PHASED RICARDIAN SYSTEMS AND INTERTEMPORAL EFFICIENCY

Paul A. SAMUELSON*

M.I.T., Cambridge, MA 02139, U.S.A.

Received May 1975, revised version received July 1975

A timeless Ricardian system specializes geographically to minimize localized labor, just as a timeless neoclassical system specializes to minimize primary factor totals (in a vectoral sense). The steady states of a time-phased system, for *zero* interest or profit rate, similarly specialize to minimize primary factors. By contrast, when there is a positive interest rate, the observed steady states do *not* minimize primary totals. Thus, positive profit rates make a system superficially appear inefficient, much like systems with distorting taxes. However, from an intertemporal efficiency standpoint, which goes beyond steady states, it is shown that so long as the profit rates are geographically equal, the observed steady state is Pareto efficient, not Pareto inefficient. In contrast to the Emmanuel view that profit equalization leads to 'unequal exchange' and deadweight loss from trade, deadweight loss is shown to come from the *absence* of international lending markets. The present paper illustrates these truths, works out implications for factor-price equalization or nonequalization, gives conditions of trade equilibrium for time-phased systems, shows their multiplicity, and the possible Metcalfe–Steedman 'instability' from the standpoint of the global correspondence principle. A factor-price frontier is deduced, which gives the negative interest rate as a quasi-concave function of the real returns (in terms of any good) of the primary factors, and its well-behaved quantities *dual* is contrasted with the actual ill-behaved steady-state quantity relation.

1. Introduction

1.1. Review

I showed in the Halm *Festschrift*[1] that permanent positive-profit equilibrium in international trade, whether or not the different countries have equal profit rates, could (1) permanently *reverse* the geographical pattern of specialization

*I owe thanks to the National Science Foundation for financial aid, to Kate Crowley for editorial assistance, and to Professor Jagdish Bhagwati for stimulus to elaborate on these matters. I also owe thanks to a referee for alerting me to the valuable 1972 Metcalfe–Steedman paper, an important precursor of their paper that is to receive belated appearance in this journal, 'Reswitching, primary inputs, and the Heckscher–Ohlin–Samuelson theory of trade'; to Murray Kemp for valuable criticisms, and for the reference to the early gem of Acheson (1970); to Ian Steedman and J.S. Metcalfe for the Kemp and Khang (1974), Parrinello (1970, 1973), and Mainwaring references; and to Edwin Burmeister for critical stimulus.

[1]See Samuelson (1973). Of related interest is my (1975) contribution to the Bourneuf *Festschrift*.

compared to what is optimal in terms of Ricardian steady-state labor requirements, so that (2) *every person* could end up consuming less until the end of
time than he might consume in the zero-profit steady state; and this (3) even
if we work in the simplest model of fixed technical proportions, so that improved
steady-state outputs can never come from any increased 'roundaboutness' of
each industry's techniques.

The point of my paper was not to deduce that competitive equilibrium can
be Pareto-nonoptimal; but rather to point out (4) that even though a cum-
profit equilibrium involves *permanently* less of all goods than in a zero-profit
equilibrium, that does not necessarily imply that the cum-profit equilibrium
is non-Pareto-optimal (Pareto-inefficient), for the reason that (5) in going from
the cum-profit to the zero-profit steady-state equilibrium, we must traverse a
transient, non-steady-state path, which may *necessarily involve worsening the
consumptions of some periods in tradeoff for bettering the consumptions of some
later periods.*

This paradox, or seeming paradox, has elicited some interest, both in Marxian
and mainstream economics circles. So I welcome the invitation to expand upon
my terse exposition in the Halm volume (and to correct an arithmetic error in
my diagram, a slip which does not essentially affect the validity of my finding).
Also, I hope to go deeper into the equalized and unequalized profit cases,
qualifying my analysis for the latter case.

1.2. Assumptions

Like Ricardo, assume 2 countries (U.S. and U.K., designated by first subscripts, $i = 1, 2$) and 2 goods (say food and clothing, and designated respectively
by second subscripts, $j = 1, 2$); each industry in each country has specified
socially necessary labor requirements or 'costs', c_{ij}, the U.S. having comparative
advantage in food because $(c_{12}/c_{11}) > (c_{22}/c_{21})$. But unlike the usual textbook
exposition of Ricardian comparative advantage, I explicitly face up to the
realistic fact that the application of labor inputs must be time-phased (in the
Smith–Ricardo–Menger fashion of distinguishing between the direct labor
of each stage and the indirect labor of earlier stages, or in the Sraffa–Leontief
fashion of having commodities produced by labor inputs and also by the commodities themselves as needed inputs).[2] For simplicity, intrinsic joint production,
such as with mutton and wool, is at first assumed away, as is use of imports as
raw materials; hence, well-known nonsubstitution theorems, of zero-profit
or positive-profit steady-state equilibrium, do then hold, with the result that
we can deduce the price–wage ratios of those goods that are produced in a

---

[2] With time-phasing in the model, the socially necessary total labor, needed (directly and
indirectly) to produce 1 unit net of good j in the steady state, is of course more than its direct
labor requirement. Thus, if 2 labor produces a raw material and that plus 3 labor produces 1
finished product j, its Ricardian labor cost, or c_{ij}, will be $3 + 2$, not 3 alone.

country from its competitive unit costs *independently* of the composition of domestic and international demands. Finally, assume that trade must always balance, with zero capital movements; and postulate that profit or interest rates, r_1 and r_2, are given in each country, but not necessarily with $r_1 = r_2$.

1.3. Standard Ricardian analysis

Fig. 1(a) shows both countries' production-possibility (p-p) frontiers: the steep U.S. line, with comparative advantage in food, has absolute slope c_{12}/c_{11}, where c_{ij} depicts labor costs in country i of good j; the U.K. frontier has slope c_{22}/c_{21}, which has been assumed to be less than the U.S. ratio and slope, so that the U.K. has comparative advantage in clothing.

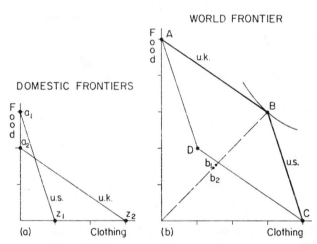

Fig. 1. From the domestic production frontiers on the left, a_1z_1 and a_2z_2, standard Ricardian comparative advantage deduces the concave world frontier, ABC, on which the $r_i = 0$ equilibrium will fall – as for example at B's 'tangency' with the homothetic contour. Only when one or both of r_1 and r_2 are positive, can equilibrium points on the interior ADC locus occur.

Fig. 1(b) shows the *world* production-possibility frontier derived from the 1(a) data. The concave locus ABC not only represents the maximal global amounts of one good producible for specified amounts of the other, but also represents the locus of production points that could be observed under zero-profit steady-state equilibrium. The AB facet comes from the U.K. line in 1(a); the BC facet from the U.S. line.

Where final equilibrium will fall on the locus, we have known since the time of Mill, must depend upon the patterns of domestic and international tastes and demand. Provided each good is wanted, so that its effective price will rise toward infinity as its supply becomes sufficiently small, we can be sure that something of each good will be produced somewhere in the world, and that the end points A and C can never be observed equilibria. At the B corner, the U.S. specializes in food alone, the U.K. in clothing alone.

One, and perhaps the simplest, way of handling Mill–Marshall conditions is to posit that *all* tastes are everywhere the same; no matter whether people are rich or poor, at one set of prices given them, they will spend each dollar or pound of income in the same proportions; consequently we can superimpose on fig. 1(b)'s world diagram the homothetic indifference contours, summarized by 1(b)'s curve. Provide the contour's slope at B is in between the slopes of AB and BC, the final equilibrium must be at B. (To determine each country's consumption share of the global production at B, examine the indicated b_1 and b_2 points. Why does the U.S. consume more than the U.K.? Because our p-p frontier, in comparison with their frontier, dictates that we end up with more than half the total when homothetic tastes are as shown.)

2. Paradox posed

2.1. Trade reversal

What my (1973) Halm article showed, in effect, was that we can construct interior sides parallel to the facets of the ABC world frontier, thereby forming the parallelogram ABCD. And I showed that, in cases where the 'time intensities or organic compositions' of the various goods are not equal, a move from zero to positive profit rates in one or both countries could cause *reversed* or 'perverse' patterns of geographical specialization, with the observed steady-state, cum-profit balanced-trade equilibria falling on the *inner* side of the parallelogram, on the interior ADC rather than the exterior ABC.

Thus, forevermore the whole world, and possibly each person in it, can consume less of both goods in a regime of positive profit than in the steady-state regime of zero profits.

Many, perhaps most, of my readers jumped to the conclusion that the points on the interior ADC are necessarily non-Pareto-optimal in comparison with those on the exterior ABC. Indeed some Marxian students in my seminars wondered whether I had not vindicated their critiques of capitalism and imperialism; whereas some of my orthodox friends wondered whether I had not made a mistake in my allegation that a point like D could be consistent with stable steady-state competition. I restored their faith, if not in my sanity, in the Smithian Invisible Hand of competition, when I proceeded to resolve the paradox by asserting the noncomparability of steady-states and the fact that, once we take into account the consumptions of all periods, including any involving *transient* paths from one steady state to another, it is *not* necessarily the case that the zero-profit observations truly 'dominate' (in the full Paretian sense) the cum-profit observations.

My earlier discussions can benefit from a more careful study of the alternative cases where the profit rates in the two countries are or are not equal. As some nice examples will show, a competitive equilibrium observed with *equal* profit rates has certain efficiency properties that may be lacking in the unequal profit case, a truth I failed to point out in my Halm paper. This is in a sense perhaps the reverse conclusion from that drawn by some readers of Emmanuel (1972), namely that the process of capitalistic *equilization* of profits is alleged to create some special deadweight loss in the world economy. If we require that trade be balanced without capital movements and the resulting *non*equilization of profit rates does result in some true permanent deadweight loss, then an analyst of competitive equilibrium, like Debreu or Arrow, may claim with some reason that it is the *absence* of natural competitive loan markets between nations that is responsible for the inefficiency, and *not the presence* of full 'capitalistic' competition.

2.2. Graphical depiction of reversals

To expose the possibility of reversed specialization on the ADC locus, let clothing be more 'time intensive' or 'roundabout' than food in the sole sense that increasing a country's profit rate r will raise the clothing–food cost ratio there. [*Example:* Food is produced in both places by labor invested for only one period, clothing being produced everywhere by labor invested for two periods. Hence raising any r_i above zero raises the new clothing–food ratio from (c_{i2}/c_{i1}) to $(c_{i2}/c_{i1})(1+r_i)$.]

What must happen when the U.K. has a very high profit rate and the U.S. has a low profit rate,[3] so that $r_2 \gg r_1$? Clearly, the U.K.'s original cost advantage in clothing is ultimately going to be lost; so eventually, production and exporting patterns will be completely reversed.

That is what is shown at D, which depicts world production of both goods from the same steady-state labor and technology, once geographical patterns of production are reversed from what they were at B. But could D actually be an observed competitive equilibrium? Yes.

To see this, stay with the simplifying assumption of homothetic tastes already encountered in fig. 1(b). Fig. 2 reproduces fig. 1(b), but now adds to the point D the two dashed lines that are steeper than AD, and which, respectively, depict the clothing–food cost ratios in the two countries after profit rates are

---

[3]The trade-reversal paradox could happen with equal profit rates. Thus, alter the numerical example above so that U.K. clothing requires labor to be invested for three periods rather than two periods. Then, at a high enough common profit rate, reversal of specialization must occur; but, as will be seen, the result is definitely not Pareto-non-optimal in a stronger sense than can be asserted for the unequal profit-rate case. Note also that which country can be presumed to be 'hurt' most is a question that admits of no simple answer. Indeed, one can contrive examples in which one country might be better off in the new positive-profit steady state, even though world productions are down.

high enough in the U.K. relative to the U.S. to make the latter's A_1D line less steep than the former's A_2D line.

Because the indifference slope through D happens to fall between the slopes of A_1D and A_2D, Mill's equation of reciprocal demand must intersect to put world production precisely at D, with the U.S. now the sole clothing producer and the U.K. the sole food producer. The allocation of the world production totals between the respective countries' consumptions is given at d_1 and d_2, which show, in comparison with fig. 1(b)'s b_1 and b_2, that *both* countries have suffered.[4]

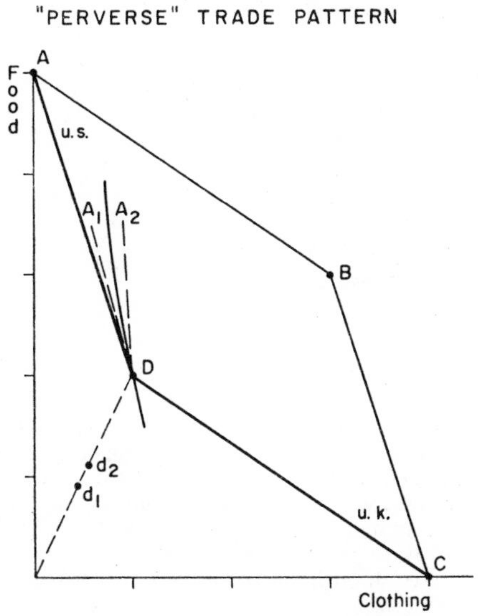

Fig. 2. When profit rates are high, clothing's costs are raised relative to food's. 'Perverse' specialization may occur at D, where U.K. specializes in food and U.S. in clothing despite the apparent 'lack' of (zero-profit!) Ricardian comparative advantage. The indifference slope at D is tangent to a P_2/P_1 line intermediate between A_1D and A_2D, permitting each place to specialize in 1 good.
[Note that this correction has been made in "Deadweight Loss in International Trade from the Profit Motive."]

The equilibrium shown at D in fig. 2 is one in which each country specializes in only one good. Fig. 3(a) shows the alternative 'limbo' equilibrium in which both goods are being produced in one of the countries. When clothing desire is much weaker than in fig. 2, we can be at E in 3(a), where the U.S. produces

[4]In my (1973) Halm diagrams, the contours and the AB and BC lines were made perfectly symmetric as between countries and commodities. The reader of the present exposition will realize that, in consequence, my E' point in the old fig. 9–2 should be on the AD limbo locus rather than at the D point as shown implicitly there. Moving E' west by 0.5″ and north by 1.0″ will (under the scaling shown there) rectify the error and give a proper reversed trade equilibrium. Asim Erdilek alerted me to the error in my 1973 fig. 9–2.

both goods because P_2/P_1 is at her new cost ratio: the homothetic contour through E is seen to be tangential to the U.S. A_1E line; the A_2E cost line of the U.K. is steeper than the ruling world price ratio, and hence she must specialize in food only.

Alternatively, if homothetic demand is very strong for clothing, equilibrium could have fallen at F in 3(a). There the U.K. is in limbo equilibrium producing both goods with a new cost ratio equal to the world price ratio: the indifference slope at F is tangential to the U.K.'s A_2F line; since the U.S.'s A_1F is less steep than world-price-ratio slope, U.S. specializes in clothing only. (Warning: in comparison with 1(b), 2   and 3(b), the horizontal scale of 3(a) has been expanded to bring out the correct detail.)

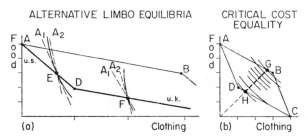

Fig. 3. At weak clothing demand, limbo equilibrium is at E on AD in 3(a), with U.S. producing both goods because the P_2/P_1 indifference slope there is tangent to U.S. cost line A_1E. Alternatively, with very strong clothing demand, limbo equilibrium could be at F on DC, with P_2/P_1 indifference slope tangential to U.K.'s A_2F line. In 3(b) is shown the singular case where r_2/r_1 is just such to make cost ratios equal in both countries: anywhere on ray segment *GH* can multiple equilibria fall, as shown by tangencies of homothetic contours along *GH* with P_2/P_1 ratio of that Engel ray or path; quantum jump from exterior ABC locus to interior ADC locus is seen really to go through this continuous, critical phase.

The reader may wonder how the equilibrium skips from being on the exterior ABC frontier to the interior ADC locus. Fig. 3(b) shows a case where the two profit rates are nicely adjusted so that both countries have the same cost ratios, which must be in excess of the AD slope. Now look at the ray segment *GH*, which represents the Engel's curve corresponding to the now-equalized cost ratios; final equilibrium can be anywhere inside the parallelogram along this Engel's path, depending upon taste conditions.[5] So, as we gradually increase the two profit rates from zero, there is no discontinuous jump from the outer to the inner locus, but rather a continuum of equilibria in between.

---

[5]Actually, depending on the steepness of the indifference contours relative to the slope at B and D, the *GH* ray could be clockwise or counterclockwise from the position shown in fig. 3(b). *Any* point in the parallelogram could be an equilibrium point provided the appropriate homothetic contours were specified.

3. The many-good case

Fig. 4 tells the story when there are 3 countries and 2 goods. It represents an obvious generalization of fig. 1(b)'s parallelogram; it now looks like the projection on the plane of a cube. The world production-possibility frontier, on which the zero-profit equilibrium must lie, is given by the concave, faceted frontier ABCD. With positive profit rates, equilibrium might come to lie on the convex interior locus AFED, in complete analogy with 1(b)'s 2-good case.

3-COUNTRY CASE

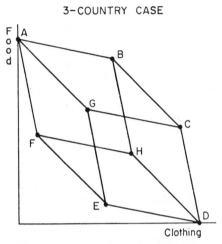

Fig. 4. With three countries, the world production-possibility frontier is given by the concave ABCD. With positive profit-rates, however, steady-state competitive equilibria with balanced trade could be observed at 'perverse specialization' points located at the interior corners F, E, G, or H. And various limbo equilibria could be observed along the various interior lines, such as AF, AG, GE, ED, BH, or HD. If, fortuitously, profit rates are such as to make cost ratios the same in all countries, we could end up anywhere inside the area bounded by ABCDEFA. If two countries have equal cost ratios and are each in limbo equilibrium producing both goods, we could end up in any parallelogram formed by their limbo lines as sides.

But now, instead of having only $2 = 2^2 - 2$ configurations in which every country specializes solely on 1 good, there are $2^3 - 2$, or 6, such configurations, corresponding to all the corners of the cube except A and D, the two axes points at which one of the goods fails to be produced at all. These specialization points are given by the intersection corners off the axes, namely B, C, E, F, G, H. Also, each country can have limbo equilibrium, wherein its cost ratio equals the world price ratio and in which it can produce both goods, in 4 different ways: thus, the country with steepest labor-requirements c_{i2}/c_{i1} ratio or slope is in limbo equilibrium along any of the 4 parallel lines AF, GE, BH, CD, differing according to whether the configuration of profit rates is such as to make the *other* countries be both producing food, both producing clothing, or respectively producing food and clothing or clothing and food. Thus, in all there are $12 = 3 \cdot 4$ distinct limbo possibilities. (For m countries capable of producing food and clothing, there are $m2^{m-1}$ distinct limbo regimes: namely, for $m = 2$, 3, 4, 5, . . ., no less than 2, 12, 32, 80, . . . limbo lines. And there are $2^m - 2$ different specialization configurations, or 1, 6, 14, 30, ...)

If the profit rates, (r_1, r_2, r_3), are singularly such that two countries have the same cost ratios, and if the pattern of world demand makes the world price ratio equal this common value, then equilibrium can occur *off* the lines: identify either of the two parallelograms that are generated by the parallel lines of those two countries, as for example AFGE and BHCD in the case where the two countries with the greatest labor-comparative advantage in food happen to have profit rates that give them the same world price ratio. Then *any* point within those two parallelograms could be the observed equilibrium. If *all* countries happen to be brought to common cost ratios by a particular configuration of profit rates, then *any* point in the ABCDEFA area could be an observed equilibrium.

To handle the case of 3 goods, the interested reader can draw a 3-dimensional diagram. For zero-profit equilibrium, we identify the concave, faceted world frontier much as in our previous 2-dimensional cases. Also, by identifying the most 'perverse' patterns of specialization, we can specify an interior, convex surface: the concave and convex surfaces enclose the admissible convex set of points that might be observed in equilibrium. And in this set various specialization and limbo sub-loci can be recognized and enumerated. Etc. Etc.

Turnover tax analogies. To begin to apprehend some of the subleties of intertemporal efficiency, the analogy of deadweight losses created by turnover taxes in each country will be illuminating. Instead of having profit rates r_1 and r_2, let us have percentage turnover tax rates v_1 and v_2. These differ from a value-added tax in that at each stage of production a levy is made on *all* cost inputs, labor as well as raw materials. Thus, the tax accumulates or compounds in exactly the same way that interest compounds: thus, we have the same $c_{ij}(v_i)$ functions as before. Even when all production can be regarded as instaneous rather than time-phased, it is obvious that trade equilibrium may be moved by turnover taxes from a zero-tax point like B to somewhere on the interior locus ADC. Provided that the receipts of the turnover tax collected in each country are either given back in a lump sum to all the citizens there, or that we introduce indifference contours for the government to generate the government's demands for food and clothing, we shall clearly have an equilibrium that is isomorphic in its steady-state phases with that of the cum-profit, steady-state balanced-trade equilibrium. Thus, all of the equations determinning equilibrium that I have written out in the mathematical appendix would be fully applicable to the turnover-tax equilibrium.

A trade reversal induced by such turnover taxes would correctly be interpreted to lead to deadweight loss. There is nothing controversial or surprising about this. Economists have always known that taxes which are not lump-sum will have distorting substitution effects and will create deadweight loss.[6]

If taxes can distort, why can't profit rates? This seems to be a legitimate question for critics of the present order to ask, whether they be Marxian or non-Marxian. And answering those reasonable questions seems to me to be a legitimate task for anyone who wishes to fair-mindedly appraise the workings of competition.

4. Paradox exposed: Intertemporal tradeoffs

The case of a time-phased system with geographical specialization patterns reversed can be quite different from the tax case. A simple example worked out in detail can illuminate the intertemporal tradeoff that lurks in the background of the steady-state formulation. The symmetric numbers of my Halm paper will do as well as any for the present purpose.

Let labor be invested for only one period in both U.S. and U.K. food production. Let labor be invested for two periods in U.S. clothing production and for three (!) periods in U.K. clothing production. In the U.S. 0.5 labor produces a unit of food; 2 labor produces a unit of clothing. In the U.K. these efficiencies are reversed: 0.5 labor produces a unit of clothing and 2 labor a unit of food.

Raising profit rates in each country will raise the cost ratio of clothing to food there. Under our present assumptions the domestic cost ratios are given, respectively, by

$$c_{12}(r_1)/c_{11}(r_1) = 2(1+r_1)^2/0.5(1+r_1) = 4(1+r_1),$$

$$c_{22}(r_2)/c_{21}(r_2) = 0.5(1+r_2)^3/2(1+r_2) = 0.25(1+r_2)^2.$$

It is evident that, even if both profit rates are equal, $r_i = r$ provided $r > 15$, the U.S. must perversely specialize in the steady state in clothing and the U.K. perversely in food. If labor supplies in both countries are 100, world production will be permanently (50,50) at D, instead of being permanently (200,200) at B. Under symmetric demand conditions consumptions in each country of food and clothing will be (25,25) instead of (100,100).

At first glance you might think that the world could be made four times better off by moving the equilibrium out to the frontier. But just try to do it. Table 1 shows the equilibrium phased in time as we move from the perverse D steady state to the more bountiful B steady state.[7] In periods -4, -3, -2, and -1

---

[6]How to minimize such deadweight loss under various feasibility constraints constitutes the theory of 'the second best' associated, for example, with Ramsey's brilliant 1927 work.

[7]See Samuelson (1966a), particularly table I on p. 581 for a similar worked-out transient path from one steady state to another. This paper is reproduced in Samuelson (1972); see p. 243 there.

the system is shown perversely stuck at D. To get the U.K. producing clothing and to phase out U.S. clothing production, we must in period 0 begin to shift labor to food in the U.S. and labor to the first-stage raw material for clothing in the U.K. Note that by period 3 the world is definitely better off, having quadrupled the productions and consumptions of all goods. But also note that in order to get from one steady stage to another, we had unavoidably to pass through period 2 in which, *temporarily*, there had to be a loss in clothing production and, with storage impossible, in clothing consumption. No matter how

Table 1[a]

Time (t)		...	-3	-2	-1	0	1	2	3	4	...
U.S.											
	$L_{11}(t)$		*0*	*0*	*0*	*100*	*100*	*100*	*100*	*100*	
	$q_{11}(t)$		**0**	**0**	**0**	**0**	**200**	**200**	**200**	**200**	
	$L_{12}(t)$		*100*	*100*	*100*	*0*	*0*	*0*	*0*	*0*	
	$q_{13}(t)*$		50	50	50	50	0	0	0	0	
	$q_{12}(t)$		**50**	**50**	**50**	**50**	**50**	**0**	**0**	**0**	
U.K.											
	$L_{21}(t)$		*100*	*100*	*100*	*0*	*0*	*0*	*0*	*0*	
	$q_{21}(t)$		**50**	**50**	**50**	**50**	**0**	**0**	**0**	**0**	
	$L_{22}(t)$		*0*	*0*	*0*	*100*	*100*	*100*	*100*	*100*	
	$q_{23}(t)^+$		**0**	**0**	**0**	**0**	**200**	**200**	**200**	**200**	
	$q_{24}(t)^{++}$		**0**	**0**	**0**	**0**	**0**	**200**	**200**	**200**	
	$q_{22}(t)$		**0**	**0**	**0**	**0**	**0**	**0**	**200**	**200**	
World											
	$q_1(t) = \Sigma_i q_{i1}(t)$		50	50	50	50	200	200	200	200	
	$q_2(t) = \Sigma_i q_{i2}(t)$		50	50	50	50	50	0	200	200	

[a]Italicized numerals represent labor allocations. Boldface numerals represent final outputs. Initial arrows show time-phased causal relations of production. Note in period 2, a shortfall of clothing output is inevitable. No matter how one goes from initial to terminal steady state, some period *must* have less than 50 clothing.

gradually one tries to contrive the dissaving in the U.S. clothing pipeline and the U.K. buildup in its clothing pipeline, there is no way to avoid some transient loss in clothing consumption. 'Waiting' in the old Senior and Marshall sense is seen to be more than propagandistic apologetics for capitalists: it is an ineluctible necessity under our simple time-phased technology.

Of course you may argue that chaps should not be so 'impatient' and that it would pay to sacrifice a little clothing now in order to get more of everything forever. But that is up to the participants of each generation to decide, and being permanently at the inferior reversal point D has been shown not to be a matter of deadweight loss and inefficiency, but perhaps no more than the reflection of the life-cycle wishes of each generation, or even the wishes of the planners in each system who don't feel that the present generation can 'afford' the extra sacrifices that would be needed to move from what is patently a 'non-golden-rule' state to the 'golden-rule state'. In the absence of international trade there is no paradox when people are observed with lower than golden-rule steady-state consumptions, quite possibly being there because they are unwilling to do the waiting and abstinence that bourgeois copybooks recommend to the young and the old.

So there is really no paradox. Even though techniques are fixed within each country, our possibility of balanced international trade in effect introduces the option for society to do some 'deepening' of capital – meaning by this, one hastens to say, only a move from a non-golden-rule configuration to a golden-rule configuration. Actually, as the beautiful work of Malinvaud[8] prepares us to understand, if a competitive equilibrium is viable at uniform profit rates – and this first special example involves equalized profit rates – then it is Pareto-optimal *in the full space of all intertemporal consumptions*. My mathematical appendix shows this by optimal-control methods in the section on equal profit rates.

5. Paradox revived

5.1. Nonequalized profit rates

A new depth of understanding can be attained if we modify our first numerical example in what will initially seem a trifling way. Now let clothing be producible in the U.K., as well as in the U.S., by labor invested for the *same* number of periods, namely two (rather than, as before, three for the U.K.). Sticking with our same symmetric numbers, 0.5 and 2, we can now contrive a perverse-specialization pattern only by having the profit rate in the U.K. considerably higher than in the U.S.: e.g., $r_2 = 16.0$ and $r_1 = 1.0$ will make clothing so expensive relative to food and relative to U.S. comparative costs that the U.K. could end up producing food and the U.S. producing clothing; the world is thus at an interior corner D rather than at a frontier corner B.

But now look at table 2. It is constructed on exactly the same lines as table 1. But lo and behold, notice that this time we can get from perverse D to efficient B by a transient path that does give the world *more* of *both* goods in *every* period. The critic of competitive profit regimes does now seem to have something of a case.

[8]See Malinvaud (1953); Mirrlees (1969); Samuelson (1966b, pp. 425–492) reproduces a 1949 Rand memorandum on envelope conditions for intertemporal efficiency; and Samuelson (1966b pp. 287–298) gives my 1959 Stanford Symposium paper, 'Efficient paths of capital accumulation in terms of the calculus of variations'. Its equations (5) do require strict relations among own rates of interest – or, in the present application to steady states, equality of profit rates everywhere in the world if intertemporal efficiency is to be realized.

However, to understand just what is the source of the alleged inefficiency, look again at the table. In period 1 the U.K. produces no final good at all: her labour is too busy producing the raw fiber for clothing at that time. Therefore, table 2 could never satisfy our basic assumption of *balanced* trade, since the U.K. has no final good to export. She could export IOUs if we would only relax our assumption. These IOUs could be backed up as collateral by the titles to the raw materials in her clothing pipeline; that way she is in effect exporting

Table 2[a]

Time (t)		-3	-2	-1	0	1	2	3	...
U.S.									
	$L_{11}(t)$	*0*	*0*	*0*	*100*	*100*	*100*	*100*	
	$q_{11}(t)$	**0**	**0**	**0**	**0**	**200**	**200**	**200**	
	$L_{12}(t)$	*100*	*100*	*100*	*0*	*0*	*0*	*0*	
	$q_{13}(t)$*	**50**	**50**	**50**	**50**	**0**	**0**	**0**	
	$q_{12}(t)$	**50**	**50**	**50**	**50**	**50**	**0**	**0**	
U.K.									
	$L_{21}(t)$	*100*	*100*	*100*	*0*	*0*	*0*	*0*	
	$q_{21}(t)$	**50**	**50**	**50**	**50**	**0**	**0**	**0**	
	$L_{22}(t)$	*0*	*0*	*0*	*100*	*100*	*100*	*100*	
	$q_{23}(t)$*	**0**	**0**	**0**	**0**	**200**	**200**	**200**	
	$q_{22}(t)$	**0**	**0**	**0**	**0**	**0**	**200**	**200**	
World									
	$q_1(t) = \Sigma_i q_{i1}(t)$	50	50	50	50	200	200	200	
	$q_2(t) = \Sigma_i q_{i2}(t)$	50	50	50	50	50	200	200	

[a]As before, italics represent country labor inputs and boldface numerals country final outputs. Note that the transition from 'inefficient' initial to efficient final state never involves loss of either world output. But note that in period 2, U.K. has no final outputs to use in balanced trade. Only if its buildup of intermediate clothing materials, $q_{23}(1+k)$, can be pawned for loans to finance imports, can an 'efficient' transient process be consummated. At no *uniform* profit rate could an inefficient initial state persist competively!

the q_{23} goods in process. Such capital movements in the form of IOUs or foreign investment would be fruitful if we will only allow it to happen. The world can increase fourfold its fruits, sharing them between labor in the two countries and capitalists in those countries, with part of the U.S. profits coming from U.S. owners of assets in the U.K.

5.2. International lending functionally understood

Note that widening our concept of the competitive market, from balance in every period of current merchandise exports and imports alone to balance of total payments inclusive of intertemporal loan transactions across national boundaries, does serve to destroy the 'inefficient' D state wherever it is inefficient. And in consequence of allowing capital movements, the steady state to which the system could settle down must now involve *equality* of steady-state profit rates (all riskiness being ignorable). And then, as we have seen already, any observed steady-state pattern with equal profit rates, $r_1 = r_2 = r$, even if it should look to be inside the zero-profit rate frontier, will in reality be Pareto-efficient in the full intertemporal space.

Suppose that loan contracts are not enforceable on other nations and on other nationals. Then trade may have to be balanced. Then optimizing capital-movement arbitrage may not be even transiently possible. And then permanent deadweight inefficiency may indeed prevail.

It is in this sense that there is truth in the dictum 'honesty is the best policy' – and so with enforceable contracts. These are seen to be more than self-serving copybook maxims. They have in them elements of truths relevant for utopias, socialist or otherwise. Even socialist states may benefit mutually from inter-temporal lending.

5.3. Digression on so-called 'unequal exchange'

One of the reasons for my papers in the Halm and Bourneuf *Festschrifts* was my wish to examine the merits of the views on unequal exchange by A. Emmanuel of the University of Paris, and on his reformulated Marxist theory of the imperialism of trade.[9] Unlike much of the Marxian literature that seems sterile as far as any application to the real world is concerned, Emmanuel purports to show by his analysis that there is substantial deadweight loss in a competitive trading world. He claims to demonstrate that Ricardian comparative advantage is logically erroneous in its claims for efficiency. And he hopes that his new analysis will throw light on the laws of motion of the deteriorating terms of trade of the poorer nations in their commercial relationships with the more affluent.

I have not found anywhere a clear exposition of Emmanuel's difficult argu-mentation. What seems to be basic to his thesis is a situation in which trade takes place between two regions with disparate real wage rates, but with profit rates that have been equalized. What the present analysis has established is that any analysis that attempts to trace deadweight loss to the equalization of profit rates, rather than to their nonequalization (as in my table 2) is 180° off the correct reason. This conclusion is a matter of logic, and could as well be applied to a community of socialist states or to trade within one multiregion socialist economy, as well as to an abstract model of competitive capitalism. None of my logical arguments here are intended to be applicable to a regime of monopoly:

---

[9]See Emmanuel (1972). This contains theoretical comments by Bettelheim and replies by the author.

thus, a cartel of oil producers, who hold up price by agreeing to curtail respective outputs to whatever can be sold at the pegged price, would of course bring in Chamberlinian and Robinsonian distortions of welfare.

6. Factor prices no longer equalized?

6.1. Labor-and-land technology

My colleague J. Bhagwati has asked me what the effect of profit in a time-phased system is on the well-known phenomenon of factor-price equalization. Space permits only a scratching of the surface here. The mathematical appendix goes more fully into the matter.

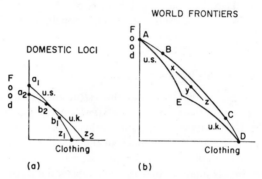

Fig. 5. Domestic production frontiers, a_1z_1 and a_2z_2, are shown on the left: the U.S. locus is steeper because we have relatively more land, the factor relatively most required for food in the steady state with zero profit rates. In 5(b) on the right, ABCD is the world frontier along which equilibrium must fall when $0 = r_1 = r_2$. The interior AED locus is observed only when profit rates are positive (as for example when $r_2 \gg r_1$). Between B and C on ABCD, both places produce both goods and $0 = r_1 = r_2$: AB corresponds to a_2b_2, the points with slopes lower than any of a_1z_1 slopes; CD corresponds to b_1z_1, points with slopes steeper than any of a_2z_2 slopes; on AB, the U.S. is producing only food, just as the U.K. is producing only clothing on CD. When regions differ only in land–labor endowments, so that $r_1 = r_2 > 0$ and tastes are similar, observed equilibrium could be along XYZ, as at Y, with factor prices equalized.

As before let the U.S. and U.K. produce food and clothing, but now by both labor and land as primary factors. Now also the time-phased technologies are to be the same in the two countries. For brevity, smoothly differentiable neo-classical functions are assumed prior to the mathematical appendix, and labor–land endowments are assumed to be initially not too far apart in the U.S. and U.K.

Figs. 5(a) and 5(b) are analogous to figs. 1(a) and 1(b). The zero-profit domestic frontiers are strongly concave rather than straight lines because the food industry involves greater land intensity than the clothing industry. Because the U.S.

land–labor endowment exceeds that of the U.K., our domestic frontier is steeper than theirs. The world production-possibility frontier, along which competitive zero-profit equilibria will fall in the zero-profit steady state, is shown as ABCD. Along the interval BC, where slopes have values common to both countries, both countries are producing both goods and factor prices are equalized: i.e., U.S. real wages and real rents are respectively equal to U.K. real wages and real rents. Along the AB interval the U.S. is producing no clothing; similarly, along CD, $q_{21} = 0$.

6.2. Unequal profit rates

Suppose profit rates can now be positive. If high r_i, ceteris paribus, raises the clothing–food cost ratio, for $r_2 \gg r_1$ we might be on the interior AE branch shown (which will be seen to come from the U.S. $a_1 z_1$ branch of 5(a) just as ED comes from the U.K. $a_2 z_2$ branch). Steady-state equilibrium along interior points of AED need involve no factor-price equalization, since both countries are *not* producing both goods there. But only with *unequal* profit rates can such interior perverse-specialization points be observed now that the laws of production are everywhere the same; and with such inequality of profit rates, as we've seen, intertemporal foreign loans would become optimal and would wipe out the intertemporal deadweight loss of AED points by making them inadmissible as steady states.

6.3. Equal profit rates

Now let us contrast zero profit rates to *equal* positive profit rates. Then, for certain possible patterns of demand, the equilibrium p_2/p_1 ratio will be in the range which is compatible with both countries producing both goods. And if that is the case and the common interest rate is still sufficiently near to zero, then labor and land factor returns will still be equalized, albeit at a lower level than when the profit rate was zero.

What about the domestic and world production patterns? The following example will show that positive profit might well shift the observed steady-state productions inside the old frontier, as indeed is the general expectation in any model that admits of rich substitution alternatives.

Suppose food is produced by labor and land invested for one period, and by a production function that is akin to the Cobb–Douglas or CES form. Suppose clothing is produced by first having a raw material or fiber produced by a neoclassical function of labor and land. And let clothing be produced by labor and by fiber, also involving a similar function. Then at high interest rates, it ought to pay to substitute labor in the late stage of clothing production for labor at the early stage; furthermore, the fact that the land in clothing is in effect invested for two periods rather than one means that high profit rates will raise the price of clothing relative to that of food. Since the zero-profit rate techniques used are the golden-rule techniques, and therefore maximal for steady-state production, it must be obvious that high and equal profit rates will cause the observed equilibrium with or without complete specialization to fall on domestic and world loci that lie *inside* $a_i z_i$ and ABCD.

As far as all pecuniary cost ratios are concerned, a rise to $1+r$ from $1+0$ can be thought of as a pseudo technological disimprovement, which, in every production function at every stage of production, raises each and every input requirement by the factor $1+r$![10] So we are left with the same new pseudo production relations in both countries when their r_i are equal. Then as we perturb a previously observed point on BC, in which zero-profit factor prices were equalized by small positive profit rates, we shall continue to have both countries producing both goods, and that does imply factor-price equalization.

Theorem. Provided steady-state equilibrium at equal profit rates causes both not-too-unequally-endowed countries to be producing both goods, we shall continue to have factor-price equalization – as along the XYZ interior locus in fig. 5(b). Any such observed equal-profit interior point will be intertemporally Pareto-efficient, even though it may spuriously appear to be 'dominated' by some point on the exterior frontier: thus, in going from y to a point on BC, the system will have to traverse a transient path that must require in some period 'abstinence' with respect to some good.

Inasmuch as the realizable ADC locus of fig. 2 was seen to be noncave, one realizes that the relevant *xyz* locus need not be concave. However, in view of the fact that the indifference contour will not be tangential to *xyz*, we are still able to assert that a shift of tastes everywhere in the world toward clothing will, with equalized world profit rates held constant, raise the relevant quantity

---

[10]Ever since my 1949 discussion of the nonsubstitution theorem, I have been using the valid trick of deriving all the *pecuniary* relations between prices of goods and factors in a time-phased system with a positive profit rate by simply introducing into any input, *wherever* it occurs in a technological relationship, the augmenting factor $(1+r)^{-1}$. The relationship between this and the so-called 'dynamic nonsubstitution theorem' is worth a word. Georgescu-Roegen and I independently arrived at the zero-profit nonsubstitution theorem in 1949. It was as much a 'dynamic' as a 'static' theorem: it applied to time-phased systems, hence 'dynamic', but it utilized the valid fact that steady-state relations for a time-phased system are *completely* time-free, hence 'static'. When later, as in the Akerman *Festschrift* (1961), I stated a positive-profit nonsubstitution theorem, that was just as 'static' as my 1949 theorem – since all pecuniary (P, r, W) relations were time free. And each theorem was just as 'dynamic' as the other. Once Mirrlees concedes the validity of the lemma that a positive-r system has precisely the pecuniary relations of a zero-r system with every input requirement blown up by the factor $1+r$, his (1969, fn. 8) gentle doubts about the rigor of my 1962 discourse should evaporate. The present mathematical appendix develops all this further. (Others probably have chanced on this same trick or lemma: thus see Metcalfe and Steedman (1972, p. 150, fn. 2), devoted to Champernowne. See also, Brock (1973), particularly section 2.3. See Samuelson (1966b, chs. 36, 37) for my 1949 and 1961 papers on the non-substitution theorem.

of clothing and lower that of food, and will, if anything, raise the equilibrium price ratio of clothing to food – but with the qualification introduced in the final appendix section that, as the Metcalfe–Steedman analysis suggests, time phasing may introduce multiple equilibria, some of which are 'unstable' and which by the 'correspondence principle' can be expected to have locally 'perverse' statical equilibrium relations.

6.4. Equalization of the interest rate by trade?

The question of Bhagwati's that I have attempted to answer above must not be confused with his 1960 question to me that was treated in my contribution to the 1965 Haberler *Festschrift*.[11] At that time the discussion did not presume interest rates to be given in the two countries (as, for example, by Ramseyan time preference), but rather assumed that something called capital endowments were given in the relevant short run. I was able to show some conditions under which free trade in goods would equalize interest rates and real wages, even in the absence of any possible capital movements. Thus, in a world of labor and one homogeneous capital good, in which food and clothing are produced by neoclassical production functions of different factor intensities, if the capital–labor endowments of the two countries are not too far apart, trade equilibrium will involve both countries producing both goods, and this suffices to equalize factor rents – and, with both places replacing capital, it equalizes the interest rate even under always-balanced rtade. I pushed my luck and went on to argue that a similar result could hold in a model involving many heterogeneous capital goods, provided that 'factor intensities' were such as to cause the ratio of costs of a pair of goods to move monotonically with respect to changes in the interest rate and if such a pair were simultaneously being produced in both countries. Bliss (1967), in the course of a long review of Samuelson (1966b),[12] criticized this formulation as being virtually empty. Among other things, he in effect pointed to what the reswitching literature had alerted us all to, namely that cost ratios of goods may wave up and down as the interest rate changes;

---

[11]See Samuelson (1965), reproduced in Samuelson (1966b, pp. 909–924). See also Bliss (1967, pp. 242–243). I owe thanks to a referee for calling to my attention two valuable papers: Metcalfe and Steedman (1972, 1973a), upon which I comment in later sections of my mathematical appendix.

[12]Once we are in a time-phased system, the relevant land–labor ratios are not those of *direct* labor to *direct* land. When two goods are equal in their direct labor–land intensities, if the first uses relatively much of a third raw material that is itself especially land-intensive, then we realize that the first good will be more land intensive than the second. See appendix section 15 for discussion to show that this formulation does not contradict the 1963 Vanek heorem cited by Metcalfe and Steedman in their 1972 paper. Also, as will be seen in the fuller appendix discussion, food could be more land intensive than clothing at a zero profit rate and yet at a sufficiently high profit rate, clothing might become the more land intensive. You might at first be tempted to think that the relative intensities could, even at a frozen profit rate, be changed and perhaps reversed merely by a change in the intensity of final food–clothing demand; but that happens not to be possible.

moreover, he showed that, if we used 'factor intensities' in the usual sense, we shall find that 'Wicksell effects' will enter into the relevant expressions to cloud the influence of mere factor intensities.

I must concede much merit to Bliss' critique: I should have been more explicitly guarded in my claims. However, the following consideration may still be of interest. My discussion of the heterogeneous-capital case did not precede, but rather followed, my discussion of what I called the 'local' factor-price-equalization theorem. The global theorem has unfortunately received virtually all the attention since my 1948 resurrection of the subject: this has to do with the question of whether, all over the world, factor prices get equalized by trade alone. The local theorem says in effect that even if factors could move between regions, almost always, before enough of them have moved to equalize geographical factor endowments, free trade in goods will step in to render the last migrations of factors unnecessary. Ruling out exact equality of factor intensities as constituting razor's edge cases of measure zero and infinitesimal probability, the real world will be divided into blocks of regions with equalized factor prices, and intermediate blocks in which complete 'specialization' permits factor-price divergences. Hence, my hypothesis about cost ratios can be easily reworded so as not to require global monotonicity but only to rule out the singularity of cost ratios invariant over an interval with respect to the profit rate. Moreover, examining Bliss' equations for the form of their Wicksell effects, we see that these have as a coefficient the interest rate itself. Therefore, a still more local factor-price-equalization theorem can be ventured, of the following type: for trading nations with sufficiently low profit rates and identical time-phased technology, equalization of commodity price ratios by trade can almost always bring about equalized real wages and interest rates. Admittedly this is straining for results and Bliss' caution must be commended.

7. Conclusion

This discussion has shown how positive profit rates can alter observed steady-state patterns of geographical specialization. It has shown that one must distinguish between unequal and equal profit rates: in the former case intertemporal inefficiency can emerge and can be attributed to absence of Pareto-optimal international lending operations; in the latter case of equalized own-rates of interest, the apparent steady-state deadweight loss is misleading, implying no intertemporal inefficiency. Thus, the Emmanual doctrine of unequal exchange, which if it were valid would be important, turns out to be the reverse of the truth to the degree that it believes profit equalization leads to inefficiency. Finally, factor-price equalization in time-phased systems is seen to be only moderately affected by time-phasing in regimes of equal profit rates; but, of course, prescribed unequal profit rates banish any expectation of equalized primary factor returns. In agreement with the analyses of Bliss and Metcalfe and Steedman, time-phasing is seen to introduce some special limitations on the degree to which the interest rate is equalized as a result of free trade in goods that are simultaneously being produced in two regions. However, there is seen to be some content in a 'local' version of the factor-price equalization theorem.

All these matters, and more, are explored at a deeper level in my lengthy mathematical appendix. The student of modern Sraffian analysis, even if he has no concern for international trade, will want to interest himself in the generalization to many primary factors of the nonsubstitution theorems, the factor-price frontiers, and other concepts of neo-neoclassical and neoclassical economics.[13]

Mathematical appendix

1. Universal supply conditions

With given time-phased technology and domestic profit rates, r_i, we take as known the resulting unit cost of each good relative to the wage rate, namely $c_{ij}(r_i)$ in each country. For $r_i = 0$, $c_{ij}(0)$ becomes the socially necessary labor required in country i to produce good j, namely c_{ij}. The supply of labor in each country is also given, namely (L_1, L_2).

The amounts of goods (q_{i1}, q_{i2}) producible in the steady state by L_i are known from c_{ij}, and are independent of the profit rates under fixed technological proportions. Also, the laws of arbitrage dictate that, at the given world price ratio for clothing–food, P_2/P_1 or p_2/p_1, a good cannot be produced in positive amount if it can be imported cheaper than the $c_{i2}(r_i)/c_{i1}(r_i)$ ratio says it can be produced at home. These considerations provide us with our needed supply conditions:

$$c_{i1}q_{i1} + c_{i2}q_{i2} = L_i \qquad (i = 1, 2),$$

$$q_{i1} = 0, \quad \text{if } c_{i2}(r_i)/c_{i1}(r_i) < (p_2/p_1),$$

$$q_{i2} = 0, \quad \text{if } c_{i2}(r_i)/c_{i1}(r_i) > (p_2/p_1). \tag{1.1}$$

2. The homothetic case

In the uniform homothetic case, all income is spent in the same way everywhere. The homothetic $u(q_1, q_2) =$ function might just as well be given the first-degree-homogeneous form $u(q_1, q_2) \equiv \lambda^{-1}u(\lambda q_1, \lambda q_2)$. Hence we can

---

[13]The following references have been called to my attention as being relevant to the present discussion: Acheson (1970), Metcalfe and Steedman (1973b), Kemp and Khang (1974), Parinello (1970, 1973) and Mainwaring (1974). Soon to be published writings by Kemp and Burmeister are also relevant.

aggregate world outputs, $q_{1j}+q_{2j}$, and determine in terms of them *as consumption levels* the marginal-rate-of-substitution or indifference slopes, namely $S(\text{world } q_2/\text{world } q_1)=(\partial u/\partial q_2)/(\partial u/\partial q_1)$, where $S'(\quad) < 0$ when the indifference contours are convex. This information gives us our needed demand and market-clearing conditions.

$$(p_2/p_1) = S([q_{12}+q_{22}]/[q_{11}+q_{21}]). \tag{2.1}$$

Under postulated regularity conditions, in which $S(x)$ goes monotonically from infinity to zero as x goes from zero to infinity, our equilibrium always exists, and is the *unique* solution of (1.1) and (2.1).

3. Demand conditions under intra-nation egalitarianism

Of course, there is no need to assume uniform homothetic tastes. But in denying that simplification, we must now identify the separate consumptions of the countries, namely (y_{ij}). Also we must replace the common $S(\quad)$ function by separate countries' nonhomothetic marginal-rate-of-substitution functions, $S_i(y_{i1}, y_{i2})$: for convex contours everywhere, we specify that everywhere $(\partial S_i/\partial y_{i2})-(\partial S_i/\partial y_{i1})S_i < 0$; for regularity, $S_i \to \infty$ as $y_{i2} \to 0$, and $S_i \to 0$ as $y_{i1} \to 0$. Also, we must now specify all countries' balance-of-trade or budget equations. Thus, we have our needed demand relations:

$$y_{i1}+(p_2/p_1)y_{i2} = q_{i1}+(p_2/p_1)q_{i2},$$

$$(p_2/p_1) = S_i(y_{i1}, y_{i2}), \qquad (i = 1, 2). \tag{3.1}$$

Equating of world supply and demand for good 2 (and then necessarily for good 1 too) would give our final (market clearing) relation for p_2/p_1:

$$y_{21}+y_{22} = q_{21}+q_{22}. \tag{3.2}$$

Eqs. (1.1), (3.1), and (3.2) complete the equilibrium, which exists but need not be unique once homotheticity is dropped.

4. Class structure equilibrium

Suppose workers receive only wage income and capitalists receive only their profit income. Then, in each country, we have to split up y_{ij} consumptions into separate laborer and capitalist components, namely Z_{ij} and z_{ij}, respectively. Now for each identical worker and identical capitalist, we need separate taste functions, $S_i(Z_{i1}, Z_{i2})$ and $s_i(z_{i1}, z_{i2})$. And we need a separate budget equation for each: workers spend the wages received from the industry where they work;

capitalists spend the rest of the national income, which will equal the total of competitive profits or interests. (*Warning:* The worker's real wage in any good is calculable from $c_{ij}(r_i)^{-1}$ only if the jth good is produced in i; otherwise, when j is an imported good, *its* real wage becomes $c_{ik}(r_i)^{-1}(p_k/p_j)$, where k is a home-produced good.) Our full demand relations are as follows:

$$Z_{i1} + (p_2/p_1)Z_{i2} = L_i \text{ Max } [c_{i1}(r_i)^{-1}, (p_2/p_1)c_{i2}(r_i)^{-1}],$$

$$z_{i1} + (p_2/p_1)z_{i2} = \{q_{i1} + (p_2/p_1)q_{i2}$$
$$- L_i \text{ Max } [c_{i1}(r_i)^{-1}, (p_2/p_1)c_{i2}(r_i)^{-1}]\},$$

$$(p_2/p_1) = S_i(Z_{i1}, Z_{i2}) = s_i(z_{i1}, z_{i2}), \qquad (i = 1, 2). \tag{4.1}$$

We close the system as before by adding market clearing of world supply and demand for each physical good, or in this case for good 2:

$$\{Z_{12} + z_{12}\} + \{Z_{22} + z_{22}\} = q_{12} + q_{22}. \tag{4.2}$$

Under our postulated technology and strong convexity conditions, an equilibrium solution to (1.1), (4.1), and (4.2) always exists. But in nonhomothetic cases, unique equilibrium is not assured. There could be a finite number of equilibria, some unstable; but for almost no choice of (L_1, L_2) will there be an infinity of different solutions.

A cheap generalization of the idealized case where capitalists receive no wages and workers receive no profit occurs when we posit for each of N population members a probability or frequency distribution of respective fractional shares of total labor and of total profit income, and specify common taste functions or taste functions for each income level or class status position.

My equilibrium equations are given for $n = 2$ goods. For $n \geq 2$, we merely make the summation in (1.1), (3.1) or (4.1) go over $(j = 1, 2, \ldots, n)$, rather than over 1 and 2 alone. For each jth nonnumeraire good, such as $(j = 2, 3, \ldots)$, we have relations in (1.1) just like those involving $c_{i2}(r_i)/c_{i1}(r_i)$, but now reading $c_{ij}(r_i)/c_{i1}(r_i)$. Similarly, (2.1) and (3.1) now, respectively, become

$$P_j/P_1 = \frac{\partial u\left(1, \sum_1^2 q_{i2} \middle/ \sum_1^2 q_{i1}, \ldots, \sum_1^2 q_{in} \middle/ \sum_1^2 q_{i1}\right) \middle/ \partial q_j}{\partial u\left(1, \sum_1^2 q_{i2} \middle/ \sum_1^2 q_{i1}, \ldots, \sum_1^2 q_{in} \middle/ \sum_1^2 q_{i1}\right) \middle/ \partial q_1}, \tag{2.1'}$$

$$\sum_1^n (P_j/P_1)y_{ij} = \sum_1^n (P_j/P_1)q_{ij}, \qquad (i = 1, 2),$$

$$P_j/P_1 = \frac{\partial u_i(y_{i1}, y_{i2}, \ldots, y_{in})/\partial q_{ij}}{\partial u_i(y_{i1}, y_{i2}, \ldots, y_{in})/\partial q_{ij}}, \qquad (j = 2, \ldots, n). \tag{3.1'}$$

5. Derivation of unit cost functions

Provided every final good is producible only by inputs of one country, we can easily apply the standard Leontief–Sraffa analysis to determine the $c_{ij}(r_i)$ functions as monotone increasing functions of the profit rate r_i. Thus, omit the country affix i, and let $(a_{0j}) = (a_{01}, a_{02}, \ldots, a_{0n})$ be the row vector of direct labour requirements per unit of the good. Let $a = (a_{kj})$ be the square matrix of input–output coefficients. Then our socially-necessary labor costs $[c_j] = [c_1, c_2, \ldots, c_n] = [c_j(0)] = c$ is known to be given by the row vector $a_0[I-a]^{-1} = c$ in a viable system. When a positive profit rate prevails, we find

$$[c_j(r)] = a_0(1+r)[I-a(1+r)]^{-1} \geq [c_j(0)], \qquad r \geq 0. \tag{5.1}$$

Our case has been one of only two final goods, food and clothing or 1 and 2. But that does not preclude that, in the background, there could be nonfinal goods $(3, 4, \ldots, n)$ such as coal, iron, corn, cotton, etc. We know that, always, $c_1'(r) > 0$, $c_2'(r) > 0, \ldots$. Unless $a_{0j}/c_j(0)$ is the same for all industries, increasing r must change some $c_k(r)/c_j(r)$; and we have supposed that $c_2(r)/c_1(r)$ rises with r. Any number of ups and downs in such a ratio can occur, if only n were large enough (and even for $n = 2$ if optimal techniques were feasible).

6. Intermediate goods traded

Realistically, if I can import a final good, I might well be able to import a raw material. *Example:* I produce clothing in the U.S. with U.S. labor and with fiber from the U.S. or U.K. If we allow this to happen, $c_{12}(r_1)$ can no longer be defined here independently of U.K.'s (a_{0j}) and (a_{kj}) matrices and U.K.'s r_2! We have lost the nonsubstitution theorem now that the trading world has *two* primary factors, L_1 *and* L_2. Or, as a Ricardian like Mill would put it, the labor theory of value breaks down once international trade enters the picture, whatever its merits otherwise.

All we need say in connection with 'perverse' specialization-pattern reversals is this: with $r_1 = 0 = r_2$, there will be a geographical pattern of productions and the world will be on its production-possibility frontier. With positive r's, the 'exterior' patterns may not be competitively feasible and the world will then permanently produce on a locus *inside* the concave frontier.

7. Durable inputs

These results could hold even if we allow durable capital goods as intermediate inputs for final goods. Thus, suppose that each kth input used to produce a unit of good j has only the fraction b_{kj} of itself used up in each period. Then we replace $(1+r)(a_{0j})[I-a_{kj}(1+r)]^{-1}$ by $(1+r)(a_{0j})[I-a_{kj}(b_{kj}+r)]^{-1}$ to take proper account of exponential depreciation in calculating our $[c_1(r),$ $c_2(r), \ldots]$.

8. Substitutional technology and growth rules

Finally, suppose with Sraffa, von Neumann, Wieser, and Walras that there is more than one column vector of the inputs that will produce a unit of one or more goods. Then, since $r_1 = 0 = r_2$ are the golden-rule profit rates for a world with fixed labor supplies (and, for that matter, land supplies), it is not surprising that positive profit rates lead to steady-state outputs that are less than those producible in the golden-rule state. However, in such cases econo-mists have rarely failed to realize that it would take 'waiting and sacrifice', on the part of someone to change the technology into that of the golden-rule state. There is no 'deadweight' loss, domestically, in starting with 'less time-intense' technology – i.e., with other-than-golden-rule technology. What is developed here is that specializing geographically involves a similar 'choice of alternative technologies' and that, for the world as a whole, it may take 'waiting' by someone, in the sense of trading off consumptions in the near future for permanently more in the further future, to be in Ricardo's global golden-rule state.

What follows for a Ricardian trading world with L's growing everywhere at the Harrod exponential rate $(1+g)^t$? Then, as von Weizsäcker[14] has stressed, it would be a wasteful tragedy if profit rates were zero, $r_1 < g > r_2$: in that case, per capita consumption would end up *inside* a specifiable concave world frontier; and, by the familiar Phelps–Koopmans theorem on permanent inefficiency, this does indeed involve a 'deadweight' loss. However, this is not so much a Marxian result as, in a sense, a non-Marxian result, since what it says is that *not charging a high enough profit rate is socially wasteful.*

9. Equalized profit rates and optimality

One way to see that an $r_1 = r_2 = r$ equilibrium at D (as in table 1) is not intertemporally inefficient is to show that such a steady-state pattern provides an optimal solution to maximize the following *world* optimal-control planning program for welfare. If the production pattern were truly inefficient, it would be thrown out of the optimal program; hence, if it survives, it cannot be in-efficient. Let $u[q_1, q_2]$ be a homogeneous-first-degree, concave function measur-ing world utility per period. Now maximize welfare over infinite time, utilizing table 1's technological assumptions:

$$\text{Max} \sum_0^\infty u[q_1(t), q_2(t)](1+r)^{-t},$$

[14]See von Weizsäcker (1971, pp. 20–31, 91–96; 1973); and von Weizsäcker and Samuelson (1971), reproduced in Samuelson (1972, pp. 312–314).

subject to

$$q_1(t) = q_{11}(t) + q_{12}(t) = 2L_{11}(t-1) + 0.5\,L_{21}(t-1),$$

$$q_2(t) = q_{21}(t) + q_{22}(t) = 0.5\,\{L_1 - L_{11}(t-2)\} + 2\{L_2 - L_{21}(t-3)\},$$

$$L_{11}(-t) \equiv 0,$$

$$L_{21}(-t) \equiv 100,$$

$$0 \leq L_{i1}(t) \leq L_i, \qquad (i = 1, 2). \tag{9.1}$$

We can convert (9.1) into the following Kuhn–Tucker saddle-point problem,

$$J = \mathop{\text{Min}}_{w_i(t)} \mathop{\text{Max}}_{L_{ij}(t)} \left\{ \sum_0^\infty (1+r)^{-t} u[c_{11}L_{11}(t-1) + c_{21}L_{21}(t-1), \right.$$

$$c_{12}L_{12}(t-2) + c_{22}L_{22}(t-3)]$$

$$\left. + \sum_0^\infty \sum_{i=1}^2 w_i(t)[L_i - L_{i1}(t) - L_{i2}(t)] \right\},$$

$$L_{ij}(t) \geq 0, \qquad w_i(t) \geq 0. \tag{9.2}$$

Necessary and sufficient conditions for the optimum are

$$\partial J/\partial L_{i1}(t-1) \leq 0, \qquad L_{i1}(t-1)[\partial J/\partial L_{i1}(t-1)] = 0, \qquad (i = 1, 2),$$

$$\partial J/\partial L_{12}(t-2) \leq 0, \qquad L_{12}(t-2)[\partial J/\partial L_{12}(t-2)] = 0,$$

$$\partial J/\partial L_{22}(t-3) \leq 0, \qquad L_{22}(t-3)[\partial J/\partial L_{22}(t-3)] = 0. \tag{9.3}$$

Let us now supply the initial conditions appropriate for a steady state, thereby finding stationary solutions to (9.3), with $L_{ij}(t) \equiv L_{ij}$, $w_i(t) \equiv w_i$, and with ratios of contemporaneous marginal utilities equal to p_2/p_1. We shall then find that (9.3) becomes equivalent to our (1.1) and (2.1).

Note: Suppose we alter the data given here as appropriate to table 1 to the data appropriate for table 2; to do this, we replace in (9.1) and (9.2) the term $c_{22}L_{22}(t-3)$ by $c_{22}L_{22}(t-2)$. We shall then find that when we solve (9.3), the point D can never be observed with $r_1 = r_2 = r$, for this last now implies that $[c_{22}(r)/c_{21}(r)] < [c_{12}(r)/c_{11}(r)]$ for *all* r, and equilibrium can never be interior to the ABC frontier. This warns us, even though it does not yet give a conclusive proof, that observed balanced-trade equilibrium at D, as a result of $r_2 \gg r_1$, may well be intertemporally Pareto-inefficient – a point that should have been emphasized in my Halm paper.

10. Optimality of equal (own) rates of interest

Before grappling with the intricacies of Pontryagin–Tucker inequalities, I have often found it heuristically convenient to use the old-fashioned calculus for qualitative understanding of the solution. Here therefore is such a heuristic demonstration, by the classical methods of the calculus of variations, that a stationary state (production pattern) which cannot be achieved with profit rates equalized between the two countries (i.e., with $r_1 = r_2 = r$) *cannot* be intertemporally efficient.

Let country 1, the U.S., have an instantaneous production-possibility transformation frontier, which relates its production of consumption goods, $q_{ij}(t)$ or q_{ij}, to its stocks of heterogeneous capital goods, $(K_1, \ldots, K_m)$, their rates of net investment growth, $(K'_1, \ldots, K'_m)$, and its unchanging stocks of primary factors, U.S. labor, U.S. land, . . ., or $(L_1, T_1, \ldots)$. I write it as

$$K'_1 = F[q_{11}, \ldots, q_{1n}; K_1, \ldots, K_m; K'_2, \ldots, K'_m; L_1, T_1, \ldots], \quad (10.1)$$

where F is a first-degree-homogeneous, concave function with smooth first and second partial derivatives.

The U.K. has its instantaneous frontier, which I write as

$$q_{21} = G(q_{22}, \ldots, q_{2n}; K_{m+1}, \ldots, K_{m+v}; K'_{m+1}, \ldots, K'_{m+v};$$
$$L_2, T_2, \ldots], \quad (10.2)$$

where G has properties similar to F.

World consumption totals satisfy

$$q_j(t) = q_{1j}(t) + q_{2j}(t),$$

or

$$q_j = q_{1j} + q_{2j}, \quad (j = 1, \ldots, n). \quad (10.3)$$

Substituting the relations (10.2) and (10.3) into (10.1), one can set up along my cited 1959 lines the variational condition for intertemporal efficiency, namely, for definable $\lambda(t)$ or λ,

$$0 = \delta \int_0^T \{(1-\lambda)K'_1 + \lambda F[q_1 - G(q_{22}, \ldots; K_{m+1}, \ldots;$$
$$K'_{m+1}, \ldots; \ldots), q_2 - q_{22}, \ldots, q_n - q_{2n}; K_1, \ldots;$$
$$K'_2, \ldots; \ldots]\} \, dt. \quad (10.4)$$

A word of explanation may be useful. Suppose the world starts with preassigned amounts of all capital goods; i.e., with preassigned $K(0) = [K_1(0)$

..., $K_m(0)$; $K_{m+1}(0)$, ..., $K_{m+v}(0)$]. Suppose it ends with preassigned capitals for all but $K_1(T)$, namely with $[K_2(T), \ldots; \ldots, K_{m+v}(T)]$. Suppose the totals for $[q_j(t)]$ have been prescribed over the whole $(0, T)$ interval. Then the path would be intertemporally inefficient if it did not maximize $K_1(T) - K_1(0) = \int_0^T K_1'(t) \, dt$. To maximize this integral, subject to the constraint of (10.1), we can set up the Lagrangian integrand $K_1' - \lambda(t)(K_1' - F[\ \ ])$; and it is the variation of such an integral that must vanish with respect to variations in arcs $K_j(t)$ and $q_{2j}(t)$, as expressed in (10.4).

The classic Euler–Lagrange necessary conditions for the extremals to this variational problem can easily be written down once we have prescribed time profiles of world total consumptions, $[q_j(t)]$. These differential-equation conditions will involve partial derivatives of F and G, and also $\lambda'(t)/\lambda(t)$. After simple manipulation, our optimality conditions for the arcs of $[K_1(t), \ldots, K_{m+v}(t)]$ and for geographical patterns of $[q_{21}(t), \ldots, q_{2n}(t)]$ take the following form:

$$-\lambda'(t)/\lambda(t) = \partial F/\partial K_1, \tag{10.5a}$$

$$d\{\partial F/\partial K_s'\}/dt = (\partial F/\partial K_s) + (\partial F/\partial K_1)(\partial F/\partial K_s'), \qquad (s = 2, \ldots, m), \tag{10.5b}$$

$$d\{\partial G/\partial K_s'\}/dt + (\partial G/\partial K_s')(\partial F/\partial q_{11})^{-1} d\{\partial F/\partial q_{11}\}/dt$$
$$= (\partial G/\partial K_s) + (\partial F/\partial K_1)(\partial G/\partial K_s'), \qquad (s = m+1, \ldots, m+v), \tag{10.5c}$$

$$\partial G/\partial q_{2j} = -\frac{\partial F/\partial q_{1j}}{\partial F/\partial q_{11}} = p_j/p_1, \qquad (j = 2, \ldots, n). \tag{10.5d}$$

If the terminal conditions are appropriate for steady-state solutions, all the terms of the form $d\{\ \}/dt$ must vanish, as must all K_s', and the p_j/p_1 ratios must be constants. We can then rearrange the (10.5b) and (10.5c) set to show equality of (own) interest rates in *both* countries:

$$\partial F/\partial K_1 = -\frac{\partial F/\partial K_s}{\partial F/\partial K_s'} = r_1, \qquad (s = 2, \ldots, m),$$

$$= -\frac{\partial G/\partial K_{m+v}}{\partial G/\partial K_{m+v}'} = r_2, \qquad (v = 1, \ldots, v). \tag{10.6}$$

This result, since it eschews all inequalities, presumes that 'interior' maximum solutions always prevail, so that complete specialization (with its patterns of zeros for some q_{ij}) does not take place. However, so long as $(L_1, T_1, \ldots)$ bear no simple relation to $(L_2, T_2, \ldots)$ and the technology embodied in G is not

identical with that in F, there is no reason why the trade that equalizes commodity prices, p_j/p_1, should equalize real factor returns to the $(L_i, T_i, \ldots)$
primary factors.

The most one might dare to assert is the weak local proposition on factor
price equalization:

> If the vectors $(1, T_1/L_1, \ldots)$ and $(1, T_2/L_2, \ldots)$ and the two countries'
> taste patterns are close enough together, if the technologies behind G and F
> are identical, if the autarky profit rates, r_1 and r_2, are 'not too large', and if
> we can rule out the 'improbable' and singular case where the common cost-
> ratio functions, $c_j(r; 1, P_T/P_L, \ldots)/c_1(r; 1, P_T/P_L, \ldots)$, are all constant over
> a whole interval near $r = 0$, then we can expect steady-state free trade in
> goods to be accompanied by complete equality of all factor returns in cases
> where the number of tradeable goods exceeds the number of primary factors,
> and where all phenomena of irreducible jointness in production are ruled
> out.

All the Bliss cautions, mentioned above, are in order in appraising the applicability of the above result.

What about the general case which lacks neoclassical smoothness and
differentiability? Fortunately, the classical 1953 article of Malinvaud, already
cited, states in its lemma 4 (p. 259) the general truth being asserted here: Only
those steady states that can be supported by equality of own interest rates can
be intertemporally efficient!

11. Time-phased multi-primary-factor equilibrium

We leave the simple world of nonsubstitution theorems behind when, along
with labor, we have land and other primary factors present and not reproducible at constant returns to scale within the system. Omitting the country
subscript, let us assume m different primary factors, whose totals are exogenously given as $[L_1(t), \ldots, L_m(t)]$. The amount of the kth primary input devoted
to the jth industry is written as L_{kj} (which is really short for $L_{i,kj}$ if the ith
country is involved), so that what was written in the previous section as L_i and
T_i could now be written as $L_{i,1}$ and $L_{i,2}$ or, for short, as L_1 and L_2.

Ruling out joint production, our time-phased production functions become

$$q_j(t+1) = Q_j[L_{1j}(t), \ldots, L_{mj}(t), q_{1j}(t), \ldots, q_{nj}(t)],$$

$$(j = 1, \ldots, n), \qquad (11.1)$$

where $Q_j[\ ]$ is concave, first-degree-homogeneous but not necessarily smoothly
differentiable in the neoclassical fashion. Thus, it could be of the Leontief
fixed-coefficient form,

$$Q_j[\ ] \equiv \text{Min} [L_{1j}/\lambda_{1j}, \ldots, L_{mj}/\lambda_{mj}, q_{1j}/a_{1j}, \ldots, q_{nj}/a_{nj}], \qquad (11.2)$$

where $[a_{ij}]$ is the familiar nonnegative n-by-n matrix of input–output conditions, and where $[\lambda_{ij}]$ is the m-by-n matrix of direct primary-input requirements. Thus, if L_1 is labor, the row vector $[\lambda_{1j}]$ is precisely what we previously called $[a_{0j}]$. Although some λ's and a's can be zero rather than positive, the system is interesting only if it is capable of steady-state finite consumption levels. Thus, we assume Hawkins–Simon conditions – as, for example, that all principal minors of $I-a$ be positive, so that $[I-a]^{-1}$ exists as a nonnegative matrix, A. If a were irreducible (as it need not be), A would be a positive matrix and we would only insist that at least one element of each row of $[\lambda_{ij}]$ be positive so that all designated primary factors are of interest.

The totals of all primary factors are allocated over all the industries; and the totals of goods produced are allocated as raw material inputs for the industries and as final-good consumptions, $(y_1, \ldots, y_n)$, namely

$$\sum_{j=1}^{n} L_{kj}(t) \leq L_k(t) > 0, \qquad (k = 1, \ldots, m),$$

$$\sum_{j=1}^{n} q_{ij}(t) + y_i(t) = q_i(t), \qquad (i = 1, \ldots, n),$$

$$L_{kj}(t) \geq 0, \qquad q_{ij}(t) \geq 0,$$

$$y_i(t) \geq 0, \qquad q_i(t) \geq 0. \tag{11.3}$$

When (11.1) takes the fixed-coefficient form of (11.2), (11.3) becomes equivalent to

$$\sum_{j=1}^{n} \lambda_{kj} q_j(t+1) \leq L_j(t), \qquad (k = 1, \ldots, m),$$

$$\sum_{j=1}^{n} a_{ij} q_j(t+1) \leq q_i(t) - y_i(t), \qquad (i = 1, \ldots, n), \tag{11.4}$$

or, in matrix notation,

$$\begin{bmatrix} \lambda \\ a \end{bmatrix} q(1+t) \leqq \begin{bmatrix} L(t) \\ q(t) - y_i(t) \end{bmatrix}.$$

For steady-state analysis, we set

$$L_{kj}(t) = L_{kj}, \qquad L_k(t) = L_k,$$

$$q_{ij}(t) = q_{ij}, \qquad q_j(t) = q_j,$$

$$y_i(t) = y_i, \qquad (k = 1, \ldots, m; i, j = 1, \ldots, n), \tag{11.5}$$

and (11.1) and (11.3) take the time-free form

$$q_j = Q_j[L_{1j}, \ldots, L_{mj}, q_{1j}, \ldots, q_{nj}],$$

$$\sum_1^n L_{kj} \leqq L_k,$$

$$\sum_1^n q_{ij} + y_i = q_i, \qquad (i, j = 1, \ldots, n; k = 1, \ldots, m). \tag{11.6}$$

The one-technique case of (11.2) and (11.4) reduces to the time-free linear inequalities

$$\begin{bmatrix} \lambda \\ a \end{bmatrix} q \leqq \begin{bmatrix} L \\ q-y \end{bmatrix}, y \geqq 0, \quad q \geqq 0. \tag{11.7}$$

So long as all n goods are valuable and are to be produced, we can rewrite (11.7) as

$$q = [I-a]^{-1}y = Ay,$$

$$\lambda Ay = Cy \leqq L, C = \lambda[I-a]^{-1}$$

$$= \begin{bmatrix} c_{11} \cdots c_{1n} \\ \vdots \quad \vdots \\ c_{m1} \cdots c_{mn} \end{bmatrix}. \tag{11.8}$$

Each $[c_{kj}]$ coefficient has the obvious interpretation as the minimum-socially-necessary kth-primary factor required (directly and indirectly) to produce a unit of the jth good (i.e., so much Marxian labor, so much Ricardian land, etc.).

In effect, we can short-circuit for steady-state production analysis the whole Leontief input–output whirlpool and write our net production relations when there are no optional techniques simply as

$$y_j = \text{Min} [\tilde{L}_{1j}/c_{1j}, \tilde{L}_{2j}/c_{2j}, \ldots, \tilde{L}_{mj}/c_{mj}],$$

$$\sum_{j=1}^n \tilde{L}_{kj} \leqq L_k, \qquad (k = 1, \ldots, m; j = 1, \ldots, n), \tag{11.9}$$

where $[\tilde{L}_{kj}]$ represents not direct labor, L_{kj}, but direct and indirect labor needed to produce net y_j.

As discussed in Samuelson (1966b, p. 51), even when there are alternative techniques that can be chosen either out of a finite or infinite set, short-circuited net production functions can be written for the $r = 0$ case as

$$y_j = Y_j[\tilde{L}_{1j}, \ldots, \tilde{L}_{mj}], \qquad (j = 1, \ldots, n), \tag{11.10}$$

where $Y_j[\ ]$ are concave, homogeneous-first-degree functions respectively definable by the following solution to a maximum problem. For brevity, I write out the procedure only for y_1, since for any other good the same logic applies.

By definition

$$y_1 = Y_1[\tilde{L}_{11}, \ldots, \tilde{L}_{m1}]$$

$$= \underset{L_{kj}, q_{ij}}{\text{Max}} \left\{ Q_1[L_{11}, \ldots, L_{m1}, q_{11}, \ldots, q_{n1}] - \sum_1^n q_{1j} \right\},$$

subject to

$$Q_i[L_{1i}, \ldots, q_{ni}] - \sum_{j=1}^n q_{ij} \geqq 0, \qquad (i = 2, \ldots, n),$$

$$\sum_{j=1}^n L_{kj} \leqq \tilde{L}_{k1}, \qquad (k = 1, \ldots, m),$$

$$L_{kj} \geqq 0, \qquad q_{ij} \geqq 0. \tag{11.11}$$

In every case, dual to $Y_j[\tilde{L}_{1j}, \ldots, \tilde{L}_{mj}]$ is the unit-cost-of-production function,

$$C_j[W_1, \ldots, W_m] = \underset{\tilde{L}_{jk}}{\text{Min}} \left\{ \sum_1^m W_k \tilde{L}_{kj} / Y_j[\tilde{L}_{1j}, \ldots, \tilde{L}_{mj}] \right\}, \tag{11.12}$$

where $C_j[\ ]$ is concave, homogeneous-first-degree just like $Y_j[\ ]$. For the zero-profit-rate steady state, a convex factor-price frontier relates the real wages in good j of the different primary factors, namely

$$1 \leqq C_j[W_1/P_j, \ldots, W_m/P_j]. \tag{11.13}$$

In the fixed-coefficient case, (11.13)'s equality has the special linear form

$$P_j = W_1 c_{1j} + W_2 c_{2j} + \ldots + W_m c_{mj}$$

$$= \sum_{k=1}^m W_k \lambda_{kj} + \sum_{i=1}^n P_i a_{ij}, \tag{11.14}$$

where the $[c_{kj}]$ are defined as in (11.7).

As a digression, dual-variable marginal productivities can be defined for the smooth neoclassical case in which all optimal choices are definable by interior maxima.

Then the maximum problem of (11.11) implies

$$P_j \partial Q_j / \partial L_{kj} = W_k, \qquad (k = 1, \ldots, m),$$

$$P_j \partial Q_j / \partial q_{ij} = P_i, \qquad (i, j = 1, \ldots, n). \tag{11.15}$$

where the $(P_1, \ldots, P_n, W_1, \ldots, W_m)$ are the commodity and factor prices expressed in terms of any convenient numeraire.

For this neoclassical case, zero-r, regard $[\lambda_{kj}]$ and $[a_{ij}]$ not as fixed constants but as unknown nonnegative real variables constrained by the Euler identities:

$$1 = Q_j[\lambda_{1j}, \ldots, \lambda_{mj}, a_{1j}, \ldots, a_{nj}], \quad (j = 1, \ldots, n), \quad (11.16)$$

$$[P_j] = \left[\sum_{k=1}^{m} W_k \lambda_{kj}^* + \sum_{i=1}^{n} P_i a_{ij}^* \right]$$

$$= \left[\sum_{k=1}^{m} W_k c_{kj}^* \right]$$

$$= W\lambda^*[I - a^*]^{-1} = WC^* \quad (11.17)$$

$$= \min_{\lambda_{kj}, a_{ij}} W\lambda[I - a]^{-1} \quad \text{subject to (11.16)},$$

where the optimal $(\lambda_{kj}^*, a_{ij}^*)$ are determinate functions of the factor-price ratios $(W_2/W_1, \ldots, W_m/W_1)$ in consequence of (11.15).

By the envelope-Jacobian theorem of Samuelson (1953, pp. 5, 15) the c_{kj}^* are definable as

$$\text{grad } C_j[W_1, \ldots, W_m] = (\partial C_j[W]/\partial W_k) = (c_{kj}^*[W/W_1]). \quad (11.18)$$

12. Positive-profit commodity and factor prices

When the common profit rate is given as $(1+r) > 1$, the steady-state pricing relations are just as in (11.14) or (11.17), but with $[\lambda_{kj}]$ and $[a_{ij}]$ replaced by $[\lambda_{kj}(1+r)]$ and $[a_{ij}(1+r)]$. Hence, we generalize the zero-profit-rate A and C matrices to:

$$[A_{ij}\{1+r\}] = A\{1+r\} = [I - a(1+r)]^{-1} \geqq A\{1+0\} = A,$$

$$[c_{kj}\{1+r\}] = C\{1+r\} = \lambda(1+r)[I - a(1+r)]^{-1} > C\{1+0\} = C,$$

$$(12.1)$$

where

$$\det [I - a(1+r)] > 0 \quad \text{for} \quad 1+r < 1+R \leqq \infty. \quad (12.2)$$

Warning: From now on, what was written as $c_j(r)$ is to be written as $c_{1j}\{r\}$ or $c_{1j}\{1+r\}$, or, once techniques are substitutable, as $c_{1j}\{1+r; W_1, \ldots, W_m\} = c_{1j}\{1+r; W\}$.

Our competitive prices for goods actually produced domestically are given by $P\{r; W\} = [P_j\{r; W_1, \ldots, W_m\}]$. In the fixed coefficient case, these satisfy

$$
\begin{aligned}
P\{r; W\} &= W\lambda(1+r) + P\{r; W\}a(1+r) \\
&= W\lambda(1+r)[I - a(1+r)]^{-1} = W\lambda(1+r)A\{r\} \\
&= WC\{r\} \\
&= [W_1 c_{1j}\{r\} + \ldots + W_m c_{mj}\{r\}].
\end{aligned}
\tag{12.3}
$$

One special, but interesting, case is where $n = m$, as when $n = 2 = m$. Then, provided the two goods ('food and clothing') differ in their factor intensities ('labor–land'), as measured by the inequality $c_{21}/c_{11} \neq c_{22}/c_{12}$, we know that, for endowment ratios L_2/L_f in an admissible positive interval, the equalities in the last relations of (11.9) can be satisfied. Some authors call this a condition of 'full employment', with perhaps the inkling of a suggestion that if some inequality holds, the primary factor in question should be thought of as experiencing some 'unemployment'. There is no real objection to such terminology. Sticking with it, one could go on to say that 'fully-employed' specified L_1 and L_2 determine uniquely (independently, so to speak) final outputs y_1 and y_2.

However, most writers in the programming field prefer to think of a factor as redundant and 'free' when the inequality $\sum_1^n L_{kj} < L_k$ holds, rather than as 'unemployed' in the Keynesian macroeconomic sense. Therefore, whether $W_k = 0$ or $W_k > 0$ is to be determined by factor supplies, L_1 and L_2, working with demand conditions. Thus, if the latter are given by the homothetic utility function $u = q_1^\alpha q_2^{1-\alpha}$, for L_2/L_1 between Min $(c_{21}/c_{11}, c_{22}/c_{12})$ and Max $(c_{21}/c_{11}, c_{22}/c_{12})$, it will depend upon α whether any factor is redundant. Thus, as α rises from 0 to 1, W_2 is at first zero and land is free; then at a critical fraction for α and up until a second critical α, both W_1 and W_2 are positive and neither factor is redundant; finally, for α in an interval sufficiently near to 1, land-intensive food is in such demand that labor is redundant with $W_1 = 0$.

When there are alternative choices possible for $[\lambda_{kj}]$ and $[a_{ij}]$, subject to (11.16), the best choices for them depend on r and $(W_1, \ldots, W_m)$, or $(W_1, \ldots, W_m)/W_1$ or $(W_1, \ldots, W_m)/(\text{any } W_k)$. In the strong neoclassical case, these will be unique functions, $[\lambda_{kj}^*\{r; W_1/W_1, W_2/W_1, \ldots, W_m/W_1\}]$, $[a_{ij}^*\{r; W_1/W_1, \ldots, W_m/W_1\}]$. When there are a finite number of alternative techniques, for almost all $(W_1, \ldots, W_m)$ the $[\lambda_{kj}^*, a_{ij}^*]$ choices will be uniquely determinate; but along critical rays in the $[W_1, \ldots, W_m]$ space there may be indifferent ties for $[\lambda_{kj}^*, a_{ij}^*]$, but all lead to determinate minimized $P_j\{r; W_1, \ldots, W_m\}$ functions.

An excellent heuristic way to define $P_j\{r; W_1, \ldots, W_m\}$ is to realize that they are given by the dual $C_j[W_1, \ldots, W_m]$ functions of (11.13), but generated from $Q_j[\quad]$ functions *that have the factor $(1+r)$ introduced as an amplification coefficient for every input requirement.* Here is a review of the general case.

Consider the row vector of functions $Q_j[L_{1j}/(1+r), \ldots, q_{nj}/(1+r)]$ as in (11.1), from which, by the (11.11) procedure, we define the 'fictitious' functions $Y_j[1+r; \tilde{L}_{1j}, \ldots, \tilde{L}_{mj}]$.[15] Then, exactly as in (11.17) and (11.18), we define from these fictitious functions concave dual minimum-cost functions, which serve as nonfictitious(!) costing relations,

$$(C_j\{1+r; W_1, \ldots, W_m\}) \equiv \alpha^{-1}(C_j\{1+r; \alpha W_1, \ldots, \alpha W_m\}), \qquad (12.4)$$

$$(\partial C_j\{1+r; W_1, \ldots, W_m\}/\partial W_k) = (c_{kj}^*\{1+r; W_1/W_1, \ldots, W_m/W_1\})$$

$$= C^*\{1+r; W/W_1\}$$

$$= \lambda^*\{1+r; W/W_1\}$$

$$\cdot (1+r)[I - a^*\{1+r; W/W_1\}1+r]^{-1}$$

$$= \lambda^*\{1+r; W/W_1\}$$

$$\cdot (1+r)A\{1+r; W/W_1\}, \qquad (12.5)$$

where the starred coefficients are almost everywhere determinate functions of $1+r$ and the relative W's.

The factor-price frontier giving, for each $1+r$, the convex contour relating all primary factors' domestic real returns in terms of a good, $(W_1/P_j, \ldots, W_m/P_j)$, is given by

$$1 = C_j\{1+r; W_1/P_j, \ldots, W_m/P_j\}, \qquad (12.6)$$

$$1+r = \psi_j[W_1/P_j, \ldots, W_m/P_j], \qquad (12.6')$$

where $\psi_j[\ ]$ is a decreasing function of its arguments with convex contours, so that $-\psi_j[x_1, \ldots, x_m]$ is a quasi-concave function. Holding the W's constant, or their ratios constant, as at $W_{k+1}/W_1 = \bar{w}_k$, the resulting ratio between any price and the composite-wage magnitude, $P_j/\bar{W}$ and $\bar{W}/P_j$, behave exactly as in the labor-only analysis of Sraffa. Thus, the $(\bar{W}/P_j; 1+r)$ frontier, $1+r = \psi_j[W_1/P_j, \ldots, \bar{w}_m W_1/P_j] = \Phi_j[\bar{W}/P_j]$ can have any number of inflection points on it, depending on the number of goods and of viable techniques, and a ratio P_j/P_1 or P_j/P_i can have any number of maxima and minima as r alone varies.

---

[15] *Warning:* The $Y_j[1+r; \tilde{L}_j]$ function does not give the *net output* of y_j producible out of $L_j = (L_{1j}, \ldots, L_{mj})$, but rather that smaller net output, call it Z_j as in (4.1) and (4.2), which is available to an owner of *all* the primary factors L but who receives no profit income at all, receiving only his $\Sigma_1^m W_k L_{kj}$ ('discounted'!) income. Moreover, when an equilibrium is observed, at a given positive r, with the following observed variables, $(L_{kj}, L_k, q_j, q_{ij}, q_j - \Sigma_1^n q_{ij} = y_j = Z_j + z_j, P_j, W_k)$, in general the $\tilde{L}_{kj}$ variables are not observable except as ratios of slopes of the $\psi_j[\ ]$ functions, or as computable from $[L_{kj}/q_j](1+r)[I-(q_{ij}/q_j)(1+r)]^{-1}$ and the y's, and as such will generally not be the same as the observable L_{kj}.

Fig. 6(a) shows the convex contours defined for descending profit rates in equal steps. The fact that the visual distances between the contours can both rise and fall is confirmed in 6(b), where for W_2/W_1 constant along any ray in 6(a), the real-wage and profit tradeoff frontiers can vary in their curvatures. We see in fig. 6(c) that the price ratios, as r changes and W_2/W_1 stays the same, can rise or fall any number of times, just as in Sraffa's one-primary-factor case. (As will be seen, when there is only one choice of technique, as in (12.3), the factor-price frontier of (12.6′) can be put in linear form provided we work with Sraffa's standard-reference commodity, whose price is $\sum_1^n P_j X_j^*$, where X^* is the von Neumann positive eigenvector that satisfies $aX^* = (1+R)X^*$, and where our real wages are $W_k/\sum_1^n P_j X_j^*.)$[16]

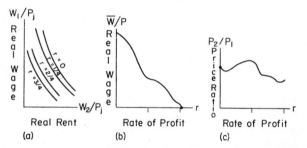

Fig. 6. Convex contours of real-wage and real-rent tradeoffs are shown in 6(a) for each profit rate. Although higher r implies lower contour, equal reductions in r need not produce equi-spaced contours. As a function of $(W_1/P_j, W_2/P_j, \ldots)$, $-(1+r)$ need only be 'quasi-concave', not concave. Holding W_2/W_1 constant, as along a ray in 6(a), the profit versus real wage tradeoff in 6(b) can be of variable curvatures, à la Sraffa. Also P_2/P_1 may reverse directions as r changes, as in 6(c).

Even if the profit rate is taken as given, one cannot usefully take relative W's to be given ratios that remain constant. Their values have to be endogenous unknowns of the problem, to be determined by the interplay of demand for final goods and the amounts that will be producible from given supplies of primary factors, $(L_1, \ldots, L_m)$ under competitive pricing conditions.

To sketch how general equilibrium defines a solution in a closed time-phased model with many primary factors, it will suffice to consider uniform homothetic tastes, expressible by the concave, first-degree-homogeneous utility function $u[y_1, \ldots, y_n] = u[Y]$. In this case we need not worry about the

---

[16]See the Steedman appendix to the Metcalfe and Steedman (1972) paper for this nice result. Its truth is apprehended intuitively once we realize that freezing relative $(W_1, \ldots, W_m)$ converts many primary factors into a single Hicksian composite factor with all the properties of a single factor: thus $\sum_1^m W_k \lambda_{kj}$ has all the properties of a_{0j} or Wa_{0j} in (5.1), and hence all the usual Sraffa results do apply. When alternative techniques are viable, the $\psi[\ ]$ frontiers of (12.6′) are still well defined, but no longer can we expect to preserve linearity – any more than one can expect linearity once Sraffa encounters more than a single viable technique.

breakdown of income and demand between workers, land-owners, and profit receivers. The rate of profit will be taken as given, $r \geq 0$; thus, it might be 6 percent because ours is an economy of a Ramsey planner, whose 6 percent rate of time preference leads to a zero-net-saving economy only at 6 percent; or, in a life-cycle saving model, 6 percent might be the rate at which total net asset holdings of all age groups just match the value of assets to be held; etc.

Consumer equilibrium is given by the usual budget relation and tangency conditions, and can be reduced to

$$P_j/P_1 = (\partial u[Y]/\partial y_j)/(\partial u[Y]/\partial y_1), \qquad (j = 2, \ldots, n). \tag{12.7}$$

The factor-and-goods price relationships can be summarized in various ways, perhaps most economically by using the relations established in (11.12), (11.10), (11.17), and (11.18) to establish valid dual functions:

$$(P_j) = (C_j\{1+r; W_1, \ldots, W_m\}) = (C_j\{1+r; W\}) \tag{12.8}$$

$$(C_j\{1+r; W\}) = \left(\sum_{k=1}^{m} W_k c_{kj}^*\{1+r; W\} \right)$$

$$= \left(\sum_{1}^{m} W_k \lambda_{kj}^*\{1+r; W\}(1+r) \right.$$

$$\left. + \sum_{i=1}^{n} C_i\{1+r; W\}a_{ij}^*\{1+r; W\}(1+r) \right)$$

$$= W\lambda^*\{1+r; W\}(1+r)[I-a^*\{1+r; W\}](1+r)]^{-1}$$

$$= \operatorname*{Min}_{\lambda, a} \{W\lambda(1+r)[I-a(1+r)]^{-1}\}, \tag{12.9}$$

subject to

$$1 = Q_j[\lambda_{1j}, \ldots, \lambda_{mj}, a_{1j}, \ldots, a_{nj}], \qquad (j = 1, \ldots, n).$$

Both in the neoclassical *and general case*, these relations define the admissible techniques $(\lambda_{kj}^*, a_{ij}^*)$ for each choice of $(1+r; W_1, \ldots, W_m)$. In the fixed-coefficient case, λ_{kj}^* and a_{ij}^* are given constants. In the regular neoclassical case, they are definable as unique roots of the marginal-productivity relations

$$(1+r)^{-1}P_j\partial Q_j[\lambda_{1j}^*, \ldots, a_{nj}^*]/\partial L_{kj} = W_k, \qquad (k = 1, \ldots, m),$$

$$(1+r)^{-1}P_j\partial Q_j[\lambda_{1j}^*, \ldots, a_{nj}^*]/\partial q_{ij} = P_i, \qquad (i, j = 1, \ldots, n). \tag{12.10}$$

Finally, we have the 'supply' conditions:

$$y_i = q_i - \sum_1^n a_{ij}^*\{1+r; W\}q_j, \qquad (i = 1, \ldots, n), \tag{12.11}$$

$$0 \leqq L_k - \sum_{j=1}^n c_{kj}^*\{1+r; W\}y_k = \alpha_k, \quad \alpha_k W_k = 0,$$

$$(k = 1, \ldots, m). \tag{12.12}$$

For given r, the set (12.7), (12.8), (12.9), (12.11) and (12.12) define a complete solution for $(y_j, q_j, q_{ij}, L_{kj}, P_j/P_1, W_k/P_1)$. Similarly, if we abandoned our simplification of homothetic demand, split y_j into $Z_j + z_j$ and distinguished tastes for the primary-factor-owning and the profit-receiving classes as both $U[Z_1, \ldots, Z_n]$ and $u[z_1, \ldots, z_n]$, we could define a complete equilibrium solution, although now the possibilities for multiple solutions are of course richer.

The comparative statics of how the equilibrium changes as r rises from zero and of the effects of a change in factor supply, become quite complicated once we leave the simplest parables behind us. Later, in connection with the analysis of Metcalfe and Steedman, some of these complications will be noted.

Kemp has suggested the desirability of summarizing the steady-state relations that hold for consumptions observable, $(y_1, \ldots, y_n)$, when primary factors are given as $(L_1, \ldots, L_m)$, under specified production functions, $Q_j[\ldots, L_{kj}, \ldots, q_{ij}, \ldots]$, specified profit rates r, and under *all possible* taste patterns (which might as well for this purpose be assumed to be homothetic and even of Cobb–Douglas form $\prod_1^n y_j^{k_j}$, where the fractional k_j sum to unity and independendently run the gamut from 0 to 1).

The case of one primary factor only, say labor or land, is straightforward enough. With joint production ruled out, the nonsubstitution theorems apply to it at each r. And the following hold when $m = 1$.

(a) For $r = 0$, observations will fall on a *concave outer frontier*, which will be strictly linear, a *hyperplane* in the n-space of goods.

(b) For r positive and above this golden-rule state, there will also be a hyperplane, which will if anything lie *inside* the golden-rule zero-r outer frontier.

(c) For r small enough positive numbers, the relationship between the hyperplane and r is monotone decreasing; but outside the neighborhood of zero, as simple reswitching dramatizes, the relationship between the hyperplane and r *need not be monotone*.

(d) For different r, the respective hyperplanes may have points in common; but if they do, they must coincide everywhere, since one plane can never cross the other.

However, when there are more than 1 primary factors, much less can be said.

(a′) For $r = 0$, the observations must lie along an outer concave frontier. But now, this need not be linear; and 'almost always' it will not be linear.

(b′) There is an invisible-hand theorem which guarantees that for each r away from the golden rule, the observations will also lie out on a frontier. (For if along any ray at fixed r an observed point were dominated by another observable point, the first point could not have been the solution to a Ramsey planner problem involving as time preference the stated positive r; and hence, it could not have been a competitively viable point.) But do we now have any reason to be sure that the locus is *concave*? Our regional trade examples warn us that we do not. Still, the locus for any r must lie inside (or along) the zero-r golden-rule locus.

(c′) For r near zero, the new locus must (if anything) be monotone decreasing in r. But, as in (c) above, for r outside the neighborhood of zero, the relationship with r need not be monotone.

(d′) Now if the same point is observable at two different r's, there seems no obvious reason why the respective loci may not cross. Given the leisure, I suspect I could fabricate an illustrative example.

13. Interest-rate and factor-price equalization?

We can now enunciate conditions for equalization of primary-factor prices and profit rates between two regions of similar geographical 'endowments and tastes'. Suppose $m+1$ goods are produced in common in two regions of identical technology: renumber them so that they are goods ($j = 1, 2, \ldots, m$, $m+1$). Then, suppose that in both countries (for whatever reason, such as similarity of endowments and tastes),

$$P_j/P_1 = \frac{c_j\{1+r; W_1/W_1, W_2/W_1, \ldots, W_m/W_1\}}{c_1\{1+r; W_1/W_1, W_2/W_1, \ldots, W_m/W_1\}},$$

$$(j = 2, \ldots, m+1). \qquad (13.1)$$

These are m implicit equations for the m unknowns on the right-hand side, $(1+r; W_2/W_1, \ldots, W_m/W_1)$. Then, except in the case that 'almost never' happens, when the following Jacobian matrix is singular,

$$J = \det [\partial(P_j/P_1)/\partial(1+r), (\partial P_j/P_1)/\partial(W_{1+k}/W_1)] = 0, \qquad (13.2)$$

we know from the [local!] implicit function theorem that (13.1) has a unique nearby solution for domestic profit rate and relative factor prices.

Theorem. Two regions enough alike in tastes and endowments will, if they have identical technologies, 'almost always' have their steady-state real factor returns and profit rates equalized by completely free trade if the number of distinct tradeable goods produced in common exceeds the number of primary factors and there is no joint production. (It is to be understood that any observed production relation, such as $q_j = Q_j[L_{kj}, \ldots, q_{ij}, \ldots]$ could, except for chance have been a 'little bit different' from what it is, so that only along razor's edges of zero measure will any two goods have identical factor intensities, etc.)

This local theorem does not assert that regions of vastly different endowments, tastes, and time preferences will be brought into the same factor-price equalization: they may specialize in a disjoint set of commodities; and there may well be disparate regions which inhabit points in the $(1 + r; W_{k+1}/W_1)$ space so far apart that there will always be between them a reversal of sign of the Jacobian, J, in (13.2). Also, if regional rates of time preference are constant and different and lending is feasible, there will be a tendency for borrowing to go on forever – until one is of derisory economic weight compared to the other.

Still the local theorem does have content: thus, it alerts us to the fact that before 'migration' of all factors leads to a world of uniform geography, free trade in goods would lead to a uniform production world; and it tells us that a finite globe will, under costless trade in many producible goods, divide into a finite number of geographical blocs, each with its own set of uniform returns but separated by a continuum of specialization regions with returns inbetween. It is to be noted that the equalization of long-run steady-state interest rates does not require that international borrowing be feasible in any short run.

14. Equal profit rates and factor-return equalization

So far in this appendix Bhagwati's 1960 query about trade itself (including always-balanced trade) as equalizing interest rates has exclusively been dealt with. If we consider his more recent query concerning the effect of *given* profit rates on equalization of factor returns, the answer is of course more clearcut.

(a) If profit rates are stipulated to be unequal, no equalization of real wages or land rents is to be expected. For one thing, unless the golden-rule technologies are optimal at *all* interest rates, the different regions can then be expected to use different techniques even if effective knowledge is the same everywhere. Even if the same technique is to be used, the different profit rates will produce different costing relations and different real factor prices (as for example, the necessity that the region with the higher profit rate will have to have at least one real factor price, W_k/P_j, lower no matter which P_j is used as numeraire).

(b) If profit rates are equalized by loans, and we've seen that this is in a sense mandatory for intertemporal efficiency, then we are back in the conventional non-time-phased discussion of factor-price-equalization – the only difference being that we work with $C_j[1+r; W_1, \ldots, W_m]$ functions rather than with the $C_j[1+0; W_1, \ldots, W_m]$ functions. Thus, if certain strong 'intensity' restrictions hold on the Jacobian matrix $(\partial C_j[1+r; W]/\partial W_k)$, such as that all its principal minors are positive in the nonnegative orthant for $(W_1, \ldots, W_m)$, and if m goods are produced in common in the two regions, then by the famous Gale–Nikaido Theorem, there exists only one solution in the large for $(W_1^*, \ldots, W_m^*)$ in terms of admissible $(P_1^*, \ldots, P_n^*)$ of

$$P_j^* = C_j[1+r; W_1, \ldots, W_m], \qquad (j = 1, \ldots, m). \tag{14.1}$$

15. Brief historical remarks on time-phased factor-price equalization

The previous paragraph has summarized the essence of the conclusions about time-free factor-price equalization, as discussed by Samuelson, McKenzie, Pearce, Chipman, Nikaido, and Gale.[17] With time-phasing, the interindustry aspects of the problem become important, as in discussion by Samuelson (1953, 1966b), by Vanek (1963), and by Metcalfe and Steedman (1972, 1973a, pp. 50–60).

The nice Vanek theorem applicable to the 2-good, 2-primary-factor case is worth mentioning. It demonstrates that if food is always '*directly* more land intensive' than clothing, it will also be '*totally* more land intensive' provided the only nonprimary inputs used for either good are food and clothing themselves.

In present terminology, it is asserted that

$$\Delta = \det [c_{kj}^*\{1+r; W\}] \gtreqless 0 \leftrightarrow \partial(P_2\{1+r; W\}/P_1\{1+r; W\})/$$
$$\partial(W_2/W_1) \gtreqless 0,$$

$$\Delta = \det [\lambda_{kj}^*\{1+r; W\}] \det A\{1+r; W\}$$

$$= \det [\lambda_{kj}^*\{1+r; W\}]/\det [I - a^*\{1+r; W\}(1+r)].$$

But this last denominator is positive by the well-known requirement of (12.2) that the profit rate be in the admissible interval below $R \leq \infty$.

There is a generalization of Vanek's theorem that I can assert for $m = n \geq 2$, provided the direct-labor Jacobian $[\lambda_{kj}^*\{1+r; W\}]$ satisfies certain strong

---

[17]See Samuelson (1966b, chs. 66–71) for my papers relevant to factor-price equalization of 1940, 1948, 1949, 1953, and 1965; also, Samuelson (1972, ch. 161). The latter appeared as Samuelson (1967) and gives references to the other participants in that symposium, namely McKenzie and Pearce, as well as to earlier 1950 work by Meade, 1951 work of Pearce and James, and McKenzie's classic 1955 paper. Also see Gale and Nikaido (1965).

sufficiency conditions related to McKenzie's diagonal dominance and the Gale–Nikaido conditions.[18]

The Vanek result can be misinterpreted. Realistically there need not be the same number of tradeable final goods as the number of total goods. Thus, as in the example mentioned in footnote 11, let food and clothing both require 1 of direct labor and 1 of direct land. But let food also require a_{31} of raw material, while that raw material requires 1 of land. Then *totally* food does require more of land even though *directly* it and clothing have the same land–labor intensity.

Our Jacobian relations, written for simplicity for $r = 0$, now become

$$
\begin{bmatrix} c_{11} & c_{12} & c_{13} \\ c_{21} & c_{22} & c_{33} \end{bmatrix} = \begin{bmatrix} \lambda_{11} & \lambda_{12} & \lambda_{13} \\ \lambda_{21} & \lambda_{22} & \lambda_{23} \end{bmatrix}
$$

$$
\cdot \begin{bmatrix} 1-a_{11} & -a_{12} & -a_{13} \\ -a_{21} & 1-a_{22} & -a_{23} \\ -a_{31} & -a_{32} & 1-a_{33} \end{bmatrix}^{-1}
$$

$$
= \begin{bmatrix} 1 & 1 & 0 \\ 1 & 1 & 1 \end{bmatrix} \begin{bmatrix} 1 & 0 & 0 \\ 0 & 1 & 0 \\ -a_{31} & 0 & 1 \end{bmatrix}^{-1}
$$

$$
= \begin{bmatrix} 1 & 1 & 0 \\ 1+a_{31} & 1 & 1 \end{bmatrix},
$$

$$
\det \begin{bmatrix} 1 & 1 \\ 1+a_{31} & 1 \end{bmatrix} < 0 = \det \begin{bmatrix} 1 & 1 \\ 1 & 1 \end{bmatrix}.
$$

Actually, factor-price equalization will take place in this case of $n = 3 > 2 = m$, whenever food and clothing are produced in both places and the profit rates have been equalized by loans, i.e.,

$$
P_1^* = W_1(1+r) + W_2[(1+r) + a_{31}(1+r)^2],
$$

$$
P_2^* = W_1(1+r) + W_2(1+r),
$$

[18]I owe thanks to Robert Solow for help in formulating and proving this conjecture. Let $[\lambda^*_{ij}\{1+r; W\}]$ for all admissible $1+r$ and $(W_1, \ldots, W_m)$ be 'nearly' positive-diagonal or, after a dimensional transformation, 'nearly' the identity matrix – so that $[\lambda_{ij}] = I + [e_{ij}] = [I - \alpha_{ij}]^{-1}$, where α_{ij} are small enough to satisfy Hawkins–Simon conditions. Then

$$
(1+r)^{-1}[c^*_{ij}\{1+r; W\}] = [I - \alpha^*]^{-1}[I - a^*(1+r)]^{-1}
$$
$$
= [I - a^*(1+r) - \alpha^* + a^*(1+r)\alpha^*]^{-1}.
$$

However, for off-diagonal λ^*_{ij} and α^*_{ij} sufficiently small, the right-hand matrix is the inverse of a matrix, call it $I - \beta^*\{1+r; W\}$ that also satisfies Hawkins–Simon conditions. Then $[I - \beta^*\{1+r; W\}]^{-1}$ is known to have all its principal minors positive, which is sufficient by the Gale–Nikaido conditions to generalize the Vanek theorem: namely, the very strong conditions on the direct-factor matrix λ^* which would guarantee factor-price equalization will also suffice to produce factor-price equalization when production of commodities by commodities is involved. See McKenzie (1955) and Gale and Nikaido (1965).

does have a *unique* (W_1^*, W_2^*) solution for admissible positive (P_1^*). But the point is that this cannot be deduced from the Vanek theorem, which is simply not applicable. It must be deduced from the intensity properties of the net $Y_j[1+r; \tilde{L}_{1j}, \ldots, \tilde{L}_{mj}]$ and $C_j[1+r; W]$ functions.

Knowledge of the existence of these functions, as discussed in my (1965) Haberler *Festschrift* paper, traces to Vanek's 1963 paper, and in its dual $C_j[1+ r; W_1, \ldots, W_m]$ form to the cited 1953 Samuelson paper, eq. (51). The Haberler *Festschrift* paper worked with an equilibrium in which, instead of the profit rate r being given, the stock of one physical capital good, K, or the stocks of a vector of such a physical good, was taken as given. Thus, within the framework of that assumption the capital goods are just like any other primary factor: labor and one capital good, (L, K), become just like labor and land, (L_1, L_2); or in the case of $m-1$ capital goods, $(L, K_1, \ldots, K_{m-1})$, we are dealing with $(L_1, \ldots, L_m)$. These 1965 cases differ from the discussions just above: thus, there we are facing $(L_1, L_2; 1+r)$, where the $1+r$ is independently variable, whereas in the 1965 model, the steady-state profit rate is deducible from the W_2/W_1 ratios, which in turn are deducible from the specified (L_1, L_2) factor supplies once the pattern of tastes (say, homothetic) is given. By contrast, the present exercise, once it has specified $1+r$ and demand compositions, will deduce what K/L or L_2/L_1 must be for a closed economy in a steady state. So to speak, as Metcalfe and Steedman (1973a) point out at the beginning of their paper (p. 52), the 1965 can be regarded as primarily 'short-run' equilibrium. Agreed. However, this is not to deny that within every long run there is also a short run; and if different geographical compositions of final-good production can coexist with implied different regional K/L ratios in the short run (and also in the long run) at equalized levels of *all* returns, that is knowledge which is intimately bound up with the nature and structure of the equations that lie at the heart of the traditional factor-price equalization literature of Heckscher, Ohlin, and their modern developers.

Bliss's (1967) comments on the 1965 paper have already been discussed in my text. One need only add, and this not by way of any disagreement with the letter or spirit of his critique, that there are *some* cases recognizable in advance where one can correctly assert that clothing is 'more time intensive' than food at every profit rate. Later I shall give some examples, and it suffices to point back to my illustrative Ricardian examples which did have the deducible property of $\partial(P_2/P_1)/\partial r > 0$, and which are admittedly very strongly special. Once one enters into the time-phased universe, such special conditions may validly be regarded as even more special and strong than in the non-time-phased models of traditional factor-price-equalization. Again agreed. But is there really a difference in kind or in logical method involved in my 1965 syllogisms? All conclusions are, to the perfect reasoning mind, 'already' latent in their premises. 'You begged your conclusions in your assumptions', is not from this angle a genuine reproach. After all, no informed person ever claimed after

1948 that Ohlin's complete factor-price-equalization had to take place in every case – but only that, under some specifiable conditions not completely fantastic or unrecognizable in advance, the conclusion would follow. What I am grateful to Bliss for stressing, and to Metcalfe and Steedman for even deeper analysis, is that once we are in the Sraffa world of explicit time-phasing, we should recognize how many nonmonotonic relations may be introduced and how treacherous becomes unsophisticated intuition in making guesses and surmises. Robinson and Sraffa are the sung heroes of this saga, and I sound my lyre in admiration for their Trojan deeds.

16. Metcalfe and Steedman analyses

Of the cited 1972 and 1973a papers, the latter one deals most specifically with the major topics of my text, namely where the number of primary factors, m, is one, namely labor. The case of a single capital good is not in doubt, and my 1965 conclusion stands that trade in 2 goods produced by it, with one involving greater labor intensity than the other, will in the absence of specialization equalize the interest rate even without borrowing. Actually, we can go a bit further without running into the Bliss cautions: if any two goods are producible by labor alone and themselves as inputs, then the one with uniformly lower direct labor costs will fall in relative price monotonically as r grows. Thus, let hammers, labor, and axes produce hammers and axes with no joint production but with time phasing: suppose that hammers and axes depreciate at the same percentage rate (this only for simplicity), and that the fraction of wage cost-outlay to hammer-plus-axe-cost outlay is always higher in the axe producing industry. Then with this 'intensity' assumption, $P_{\text{hammer}}/P_{\text{axe}}$ rises with r, and trade equilibrium with both places producing both goods is possible only with $r_1 = r_2$.

But adding lathes to hammers and axes makes n exceed 2 and, as all three authors point out, one cannot infer from the fact that relative wage cost in the axe industry is highest of all that its price will fall relative to the other two prices when r rises: actually, as r continues to grow, a P_2/P_1 ratio can reverse its direction of change, thereby vitiating equalization of profit rates. That being the case, Metcalfe and Steedman have to warn those who try to work with the money value of many heterogeneous capital goods *as if* it were a single versatile capital good, that they are on treacherous ground. A casual reading of the 'practical' literature, with its Leontief Paradoxes and aggregative analysis, reveals that such warnings are not academic, and I shall not here try to pronounce on the hard empirical question as to whether such practical work does or does not convey useful approximations and insights.

The 1973 paper does not purport to find my 1965 work *logically* assailable, since that never did work with an aggregative money magnitude of capital; the reader must not infer anything but formal similarity between my fig. 2 as cited by these 1973 authors and their own fig. 4.1, which involves a capital magnitude defined by them as follows (p. 52): 'In this paper we . . . assume that each country has a given endowment of 'capital value' measured, let us say, in terms of the first consumption commodity.' My figure involved K_1, whereas theirs involves $\sum(P_{k_j}/P_1)K_j$. Still I do concur with their warnings about the use of such aggregate capital magnitudes, which only work in certain Santa Claus cases (surrogate capital and worse).

After reflecting on Bliss's charge of emptiness, I have been able to think of some fairly complicated models in which one can specify, *in advance*, conditions that do guarantee global monotonocity of P_i/P_j ratios as r changes. Perhaps that is only testimony to my I.Q. and long familiarity with such models (or my stubborness). But here is one example, not so much congenial to a neoclassical apologist as to one who hopes to use a Marxian aggregated two-department model. Let

$$
\begin{bmatrix} a_0 \\ \hline a \end{bmatrix} = \begin{bmatrix} 0.4 & 0.8 & 1.6 & 0.1 & 0.2 \\ \hline 0.2 & 0.4 & 1.6 & 0.3 & 0.6 \\ 0.1 & 0.2 & 0.8 & 0.15 & 0.2 \\ 0.05 & 0.1 & 0.4 & 0.075 & 0.15 \\ 0.0 & 0.0 & 0.0 & 0.0 & 0.0 \\ 0.0 & 0.0 & 0.0 & 0.0 & 0.0 \end{bmatrix} + \begin{bmatrix} e_{0j} \\ \hline e_{ij} \end{bmatrix},
\tag{16.1}
$$

where the e_{ij} are 'small' plus-or-minus perturbations. Without the latter, the system 'aggregates nicely'[19] into a Marxian model with a capital goods department and a consumers good department, namely

$$
\begin{bmatrix} a_{0,\mathrm{I}} & a_{0,\mathrm{II}} \\ \hline a_{\mathrm{I},\mathrm{I}} & a_{\mathrm{I},\mathrm{II}} \\ a_{\mathrm{II},\mathrm{I}} & a_{\mathrm{II},\mathrm{II}} \end{bmatrix} = \begin{bmatrix} 0.4 & 0.1 \\ \hline 0.6 & 0.9 \\ 0.0 & 0.0 \end{bmatrix},
\tag{16.2}
$$

with P_{II}/P always rising with r. It follows that if good 1 and good 5, or any two goods representing both departments, are observed being produced in two regions, we can know the regions have equal profit rates.

The 1972 Metcalfe and Steedman paper gives an illuminating survey of the properties of the time-phased model in which land is a primary factor along with

[19]For all admissible r, $P_2/P_1 \equiv 2$, $P_3/P_1 \equiv 4$, $P_4/P_5 \equiv 2$, with P_{3+i}/P_{4-j} rising with r for every admissible positive value for i and j. This last remains true when $0 < |e_{ij}| < e$, and e is not too large. The example is chosen as a disguised dimensional transformation of a system in which goods 1, 2, 3 are 'alike' and goods 4 and 5 are 'alike'. A smell of surrogate lingers in the air, but it could easily be exorcized.

labor, and I must refer the reader to its many graphical and logical insights. Rather than relate their terminology to my $c_{kj}^*\{1+r; W\}$ notation, let me merely make a few selective commendatory comments.

If we hold proportions constant in $(W_1, W_2, \ldots, W_m)$, as noted earlier, we can treat the outlay on primary factors $\sum W_k \lambda_{kj}^*$ as a Hicksian composite, just like $W_1 a_{0j}$ in a labor-only Sraffa–Leontief system. The conclusion of Bliss and Sraffa follows at once that, when $n > 2$, $P_2\{1+r; W\}/P_1\{1+r; W\}$ can reverse its sign even when the relative direct *wage costs* are equal. By the same Hicksian trick we verify the elegant result of the 1972 Steedman appendix showing that for any number of primaɩy factors, Sraffa can define his standard reference commodity with a straight-line factor-price frontier.

A new and valuable finding of the 1972 paper deserves notice here. When $r = 0$, increasing the ratio of land rent to real wage must, if anything, induce less land-intensive techniques of production. And an increase in the supply of land alone can be expected to depress rent and the relative price of the good that is land intensive, in the same way that a shift away from the land intensive good can be expected to depress rent relative to wage, W_2/W_1. So all remains well-behaved in a time-phased system when the profit rate is zero, as the legend to fig. 7(a) will confirm and as fig. 8(a) will reconfirm. What Metcalfe and Steedman point out is that, once the profit rate becomes a large enough positive number, an increase in W_2/W_1 may cause the system to move to a permanent new position in which a *greater* L_2/L_1 intensity may prevail everywhere!

Once you are alerted to the possibility that high W_2/W_1 and (L_2/L_1)-intensive techniques can go together, reflection shows why this can happen. The system is no longer being urged by the invisible hand of competition to conserve on the actual use of the factor that has become dear; with positive r in the picture, the invisible hand is effectuating the economizing on 'dated L_2/dated L_1', where the r penalty is very great on those elements in the infinite progression $[\lambda_{kj}^*](1+r)[I + \{a^*(1+r)\} + \{a^*(1+r)\}^2 + \ldots + \{a^*(1+r)\}^t + \ldots]$, with large coefficients of high powers of t in the past.

One can sense how a 'turnover tax' in the form of the profit rate, $1+r$, pyramids throughout the stages of production as we go from $1+0$ to larger $1+r$, having complicated and different effects on the land and labor components, depending on the exact detail of the $[\lambda_{kj}]$ and $[a_{ij}]$ coefficients that are feasible. It is this which needs to be analyzed.

17. Case of multiple equilibrium

Here is a simple example. Let 1 of food be producible by 1 of land alone: $\lambda_{21} = 1$, $\lambda_{11} = 0$. Let 1 of clothing be producible by 3 labor and 1 of food-raw-material: $\lambda_{12}' = 3$, $a_{12}' = 1$. Or, alternatively, by 1 of labor, 1 of land, and 0.16 of food itself as raw material: $\lambda_{12}'' = 1$, $\lambda_{22}'' = 1$, $a_{22}'' = 0.16$. Note that clothing is always more labor intensive than food by either technique, since food requires land only. So at every uniform geographical r, production and trade of both goods in both places suffices to equalize factor returns.

Which of the alternative clothing techniques will be used when $r = 0$? That depends on whether food or clothing is much demanded. If food is much demanded, then land, its intensive factor, will be the major bottleneck and the first technique will be used. Why? Because in total by the first technique, clothing requires only 1 of land (via the 1 of food-raw-material produced by 1 of land); by contrast, the second technique requires 100/84 of land (to produce $q_1 = 100/84$, of which 16/84 goes for q_{22} and 84/84 for y_2).

If, however, clothing is much demanded, labor, its intensive resource, will be the main scarcity to be economized; so the second technique will then be viable, involving only 100/84 of labor rather than 3 of labor.

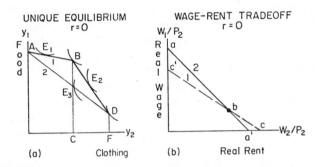

Fig. 7. At zero profit rate, a shift in tastes toward clothing and away from food will produce alternative equilibrium points in 7(a): E_1 on AB with labor redundant, $W_1/W_2 = 0$, and technique 1 alone viable; E_2 where both techniques coexist, and P_2/P_1 and W_1/W_2 are at the higher 'switch' levels; D where technique 2 is alone viable, and P_2/P_1 and W_1/W_2 are above their switch levels. At positive r, E_3 on the interior locus AD can prevail in the steady state, with the indifference slope at E_3 steeper than AD's absolute slope; such an interior point is not intertemporally inefficient.

In 7(b), the zero-profit factor-price frontier is shown as *cba*, the convex outer envelope of technique 2's solid aa' line and technique 1's dashed c'c line. Always, for $r = 0$, enhanced taste for clothing or diminished supply of labor will, if anything, raise W_1/W_2 and P_2/P_1.

Fig. 7(a) shows ABC as technique 1's steady-state frontier when $r = 0$. It shows ADF as technique 2's frontier. The final optimal frontier is, so to speak, their concavely-blended outer envelope, or ABD. If homothetic indifference contours are tangent on AB, as shown at E_1, labor will be redundant and $W_1 = 0$. If tastes shift toward clothing, equilibrium moves to tangency at B, with W_1/W_2 ever more positive the steeper the price-line tangency is at B. Finally, when clothing is wanted enough to raise its price enough to create tangency on BD, as at E_2, both techniques are viable and we are at a 'switch ratio' of wage to rent, namely at $W_1/W_2 = w^* = 2/19$, determined by

$$P_2 = 3W_1 + W_2 = (100/84)(W_1 + W_2),$$

$$(W_1/W_2) = w^* = 2/19,$$

$$[(W_1/P_2)^*, (W_2/P_2)^*] = [2/21, 19/21] \tag{17.1}$$

Finally, if tastes favor clothing enough, the tangent slope will come at D, steep enough to lift (W_1/W_2) above the w^* switch ratio, so that only the second technique is viable: the steeper the indifference slope at D, the greater equilibrium (W_1/W_2) will be. At $r = 0$, any increase in the relative wage, (W_1/W_2), can only serve to induce a more labor-saving technique – as from technique 1 to technique 2. [With $r = 0$, you can ignore E_3 in fig. 7(a).]

If both regions have the same L_1/L_2 ratio and there are uniform homothetic tastes, factor returns at $r = 0$ will be equal and autarky will prevail. Assuming that L_1 is not redundant, now increase L_1 in one region, say the U.K., freezing all other factor supplies elsewhere. Then the U.K. will begin to export clothing, and U.S. to export food; and world consumption of clothing, the labor intensive good, will relatively rise, as P_2/P_1 falls. Factor returns will stay equalized geographically, but W_1/W_2 will fall everywhere.

Suppose the U.K.'s L_1 increases indefinitely much. Then its old AB and AD lines will increase proportionally in length. Eventually the new D' will fall on the clothing axis itself, and ultimately U.K. labor will be so plentiful as to be redundant. Just as that happens, U.K. will specialize in clothing only and we are on the verge of losing factor-price equalization.

The reader can verify that if, instead of raising U.K.'s L_1, we had raised its L_2 from endowment equality of L_2/L_1 with the U.S., world P_2/P_1 will rise, raising W_1/W_2 equally in both places until only the technique 2 is used everywhere. Always, at $r = 0$, any change in technique induced by a factor's dearness is toward economizing on that factor.

Fig. 7(b) shows, for $r = 0$, each of the two straight-line wage-rent frontiers corresponding respectively to the two techniques: abc is the envelope of the solid aba' line for technique 2 and the dashed $c'bc$ line for technique 1. As one moves clockwise in 7(a) to ever higher P_2/P_1 and W_1/W_2, one moves in 7(b) from c to b to a. Production on AB means labor is redundant and we stay at c with $W_1 = 0$. When production is at B, the steeper the price slope there, the nearer on ab we will be to the switch ratio w^* and the point b itself. While production is on BD with both techniques blended, we stay at the switch point b. When production moves to D, the second technique prevails and we move higher upward on the solid ba the steeper is the price slope at D. (We never quite reach a if both goods stay scarce.)

Comparing all cases, we see that whatever has favored clothing has indeed also favored the wage of labor, clothing's intensive factor. Nothing is perverse here, with $r = 0$.

Now consider in detail the case where the profit rate is positive. By calculation one can verify that, if r is very large, over 525 percent, $1+r > 1+5.25 = 1/0.16$, technique 2 can never be viable. (Fig. 8(b) will later show how this comes about.) Indeed, for $1+r > 1+4$, technique 1 can be shown to dominate technique 2 for *all* patterns of demand. Calculation will also show that, for the profit rates between 25 percent and $316\frac{1}{2}$ percent, $0.25 < r < 3\frac{1}{6}$, technique 2 will dominate technique 1 for *all* patterns of demand.

Fig. 7(a) shows for r in this range an apparently 'perverse' equilibrium at E_3, southwest of some points on the ABD frontier. The price ratio at E_3 is equal to the indifference slope shown there, which exceeds the AD slope because of the profit markup that happens to be greatest on the 'more-time-intensive' clothing.

Actually, despite superficial appearance to the contrary, E_3 is not intertemporally inefficient. A planner with a rate of time preference in the above range, say 30 percent or 600 percent per period, might well aim to deliberately end up at E_3 in the steady state; and if you were to begin her or him in a steady state on ABD northeast of E_3, the rational decision would be made to consume some of the food raw material used in the technique 1 there, 'abstinence' being, so to speak, no longer rationally forthcoming.

The most interesting case, to which the 1972 Metcalfe and Steedman analysis alerts the reader, occurs for profit rates between $316\frac{1}{6}$ percent and 400 percent, $3\frac{1}{6} < r < 4$, as for example, $r = 3.5$. Fig. 8 illustrates what can and must happen in this case. If tastes for clothing are initially very weak, equilibrium might occur at E_4 in 8(a) with labor redundant, $W_1/W_2 = 0$, and technique 2 alone viable for $r = 3.5$. When tastes for clothing are stronger, equilibrium might alternatively come at E_5, or even at D itself. When clothing desire is very strong indeed, equilibrium might come only at B itself, *with P_2/P_1 and W_1/W_2* indefinitely high and technique 1 alone viable. Finally, we might have observed an equilibrium at E_5' on BD itself, with both techniques viable and W_1/W_2 at the new switch level for w^* appropriate to $r = 3.5$.

We shall see in a moment that, whereas E_4 is a *unique* equilibrium level, for intermediate degrees of clothing desire there will be *multiple* equilibria: 2 'stable' equilibria (like E_5 and B, or like D and B) with an 'unstable' equilibrium between them (like coexistence E_5').[20]

Before examining the phenomena of multiple equilibria and what that implies for the comparative-statical incidence of tastes change or factor-endowment change, let us use fig. 8(b) to understand the effects of higher r on the factor-price contours that give the tradeoff between real wage and real

---

[20]Rigorously, let food–clothing tastes be given by the first-degree-homogenous and concave utility function, $u[y_1, vy_2]$, where v is a parameter of clothing desire. Then when v is sufficiently small, we'll have unique E_4 equilibrium. For v sufficiently large, we'll have a steep-slope B equilibrium that is also unique. However, for v in some intermediate range, we must have 3 equilibria – two like E_s and B, stable involving each technique alone, and between them one like E_s', unstable involving both techniques on BD. Fig. 9(b)'s topological diagram will demonstrate why all this is so.

rent. For $r = 0$, 8(b)'s outermost convex frontier merely copies that of fig. 7(b) already seen.

Now increase r slowly. The old aa' and $c'c$ lines now move inward: aa' shifts in a parallel way and very slowly at first; $c'c$ shifts faster and steepens, so that the new b intersection moves southeastward. At $r = 2.5$, the new b just reaches the horizontal axis as shown by the two short lines radiating from b_1: for r just above 0.25, technique 2 clearly dominates technique 1 and is alone viable.

However, all the time that r has continued to increase toward 3, $c'c$ has been continuing to steepen, eventually becoming even steeper than aa'. Exactly at

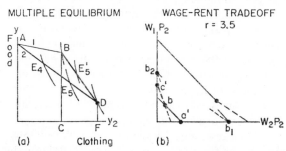

Fig. 8. At the intermediate profit rate, $r = 3.5$, a shift in tastes toward clothing produces alternative equilibrium points in 8(a), and can even produce multiple equilibria. With very weak tastes for clothing, the E_4 equilibrium is unique, with $W_1/W_2 = 0$ and technique 2 alone viable. With tastes very weak for food, unique equilibrium could occur at B, with technique 1 alone viable and both P_2/P_1 and W_1/W_2 indefinitely high. With tastes for clothing and food moderately strong, there must occur multiple equilibria: an 'unstable' one at E_5' on BD, with P_2/P_1 and W_1/W_2 at new switch levels where both techniques coexist; surrounding the E_5' equilibria, are the two 'stable' equilibria – at E_5 (or at D with E_5's price slope), with labor redundant, $W_1/W_2 = 0$, and technique 2 alone viable, or at B with high P_2/P_1 and W_1/W_2 and only technique 1 viable. In 8(b), the redrawn convex outer-envelope of 7(b) now has both its facets shifting inward as r rises. Since technique 1's dashed line shifts in faster and steeper, the point of intersection travels southeastward until, at $r = 0.25$, the lines intersect on the $W_1 = 0$ axis as shown at b_1. For $0 < r < 3\frac{1}{4}$, technique 2 dominates, as at E_3 in 7(a). For $r = 3$, the technique 1's dashed line, now steeper than the dashed line, intersects it on the $W_2 = 0$ axis at b_2. For $r = 3.5$, c'ba is the factor-price frontier: in the Metcalfe–Steedman fashion, a rise in W_1/W_2 induces a shift to the labor-using technique 1. For $r > 4\frac{1}{4}$, $c'c$ has disappeared into the origin.

$r = 3$, the curves again intersect, this time on the vertical axis, as shown at b_2; but now, for r just above 3, both techniques are again viable as shown by the new $r = 3.5$ locus $c'ba$. As r grows in this Metcalfe–Steedman interval, from 3 toward 4, the new b intersection travels towards the horizontal axis (albeit southwestward), reaching the horixontal axis where $r = 4$ at a point not shown (but near the origin). The $c'c$ line of technique 2 has shrunk into the origin itself!

What interests us is the new $(W_1/P_2, W_2/P_2)$ frontier for $r = 3.5$. Note how, as indicated in the 1972 paper, higher W_1/W_2 implies a shift to the *more*-labor-intensive technique 1, as the system now tries to economize on 'dated or marked-up labor', not on 'actual' labor!

To understand the implications of this case, we need a rigorous topological analysis of the full general equilibrium.

18. Topology of steady-state equilibrium

Fig. 9 nicely portrays the uniqueness of equilibrium when $r = 0$ in 9(a); and in 9(b) is shown the various possibilities of multiple or unique equilibrium when we are in the Metcalfe–Steedman regime, say with $r = 3.5$.

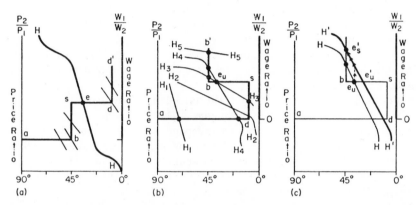

Fig. 9. The topology of 7(a) and 8(a) is shown here in 9(a) and 9(b): the angles of rays from the origin give declining P_2/P_1 on any HH demand locus. On supply loci, the of P_2/P_1 cost ratios corresponding to 7(a)'s AB fall on ab; those corresponding to B's ever steeper slope fall along bs; those corresponding to BD's coexisting techniques and the switch price and wage ratios fall along sd; finally, ever steeper price slopes at D in 7(a) occur here on dd'. Straight line segments of alternative H_iH_i show alternative unique equilibrium points on ABD locus. Always for $r = 0$, greater clothing demand or land supply raises P_2/P_1 and W_1/W_2. In 9(b) supply locus $adsbb'$ bends back on itself, thereby permitting intersections that are unique (as with H_1H_1 or H_2H_2 or H_5H_5); or triple equilibria (as with H_3H_3 or H_4H_4), with 'unstable' e_u surrounded by 2 stable equilibria. To see effect of enhanced clothing desire, 9(c) presents arrows that show the move from e_u, not to nearby e_u', but rather to stable e_s' near to old stable e_s and with the rise in P_2/P_1 and W_1/W_2 predicted by the global correspondence principle.

Since homothetic tastes give the price ratios that prevail from the demand side as determined by rays going from 90° to 0°, the HH locus in 9(a) gives the corresponding P_2/P_1 of the homothetic indifference slopes: this P_2/P_1 is a declining function, with no particular curvature, that goes from $+\infty$ on the left to 0 on the right. To complete the equilibrium, the supply locus d' gives the competitive cost–price ratio that has to prevail at each point where the varying rays intersect the ABD exterior frontier of 7(a). Thus, the horizontal branch ab

in 9(a) gives cost ratios for the points on AB in 7(a), where labor is redundant and P_2/P_1 is determined by technique 1's land costs alone. The vertical bs branch represents the B point in 7(a) with s representing the 'switch' price ratio corresponding to 7(b)'s switch-wage-ratio point. The points on sd correspond to blend points on DB, with $W_1/W_2 = w^*$ and P_2/P_1 such that both techniques can coexist. Finally, the d' correspond to the D point in 7(a), but with ever steeper slope there moving us higher on df.

The $r = 0$ final equilibrium must come at the unique intersection of demand's HH with supply's $absd'$. By considering all the alternative patterns of tastes that could prevail, we could make HH intersect at any of the points on $absdf$, as shown by the various short line-segments. Our topological diagram has confirmed the uniqueness of $r = 0$ equilibrium.

Now look at the $r = 3.5$ regime of 9(b). As before, demand's HH can take any of the alternative H_jH_j patterns shown. What is novel is the new supply locus $adsbb$, which in this regime must bend back on itself as shown in 9(b). It is this bent-back shape that creates the possibility of multiple intersections and of an unstable equilibrium.

Along ad, which corresponds to AD in 8(a), labor is redundant with $W_1/W_2 = 0$, and P_2/P_1 is determined by technique 2's land costs alone – as in the E_4 equilibrium of 8(a). The ds points correspond to various equilibria at D in 8(a), with the ever higher P_2/P_1 slope pulling W_1/W_2 ever higher toward the w^* switch ratio of 8(b) that must hold at the switch point s. The whole sb interval corresponds to the blending DB facet in 8(a) where both techniques coexist. Finally, along bb', equilibrium is at technique 1's B, with an ever steeper indifference slope there implying ever higher P_2/P_1 and W_1/W_2.

What is of interest is the triple equilibrium shown by the intersection of $adsbb'$ and either H_3H_3 or H_4H_4. Either case generates an 'unstable', 'co-existence' equilibrium on sb and DB, as shown at e_u; this is surrounded by two 'stable' equilibria respectively involving each of the *single* techniques. We can now appreciate and understand the Metcalfe–Steedman phenomenon, in which a relative rise in wage cost (i.e., in W_1/W_2) would induce a change to the *more* labor-intensive technique 1.

Several decades ago, I (1947, chs. 10, 11) stated the 'correspondence principle' that alerts the analyst to the heuristic fact that anomalous comparative-statics incidence and dynamic instability tend to go hand in hand. So all the more gratitude is due the 1972 authors for pointing out how positive profit in a time-phased system can create special new sources of multiplicity of equilibrium. Without detracting from their analysis, and in full agreement with it, one wants to explore exactly what that phenomenon implies. Just what does the unstable equilibrium mean?

Does it mean that if we start at e_u and then raise the supply of labor, the new equilibrium must involve a *higher* W_1/W_2 equilibrium?

Does it mean that if we start at e_u and then have a taste shift toward the labor-intensive clothing good, the new equilibrium will involve a *lower* rather than higher W_1/W_2 equilibrium?

A proper understanding of the global correspondence principle[21] suggests that the answers to these questions are in the negative, so that 'normal' directions of displacement of equilibrium will 'naturally' ensue, with new labor abundance ending up with lower wages and new extra derived demands for labor ending up with higher wages. However, to decide the validity of these suggested answers requires that we be able to specify the contemplated transient-dynamics of how the system moves from one steady state to another. This is not the place to go into the complex details of such a dynamic analysis, and therefore my discussion will be oversimplified.

First, consider a Ramsay planner who has long been in steady-state equilibrium at e_u. If he were *temporarily* perturbed from e_u, say by a fire that burns some food or clothing raw material, his optimal plan will *not* go back to e_u, which is a verifiable content to its being called an 'unstable' equilibrium. (Instead, depending on whether it was technique 1's or 2's raw material that was burned, the new transient program will approach asymptotically a new steady-state equilibrium in the near vicinity of one of the old stable equilibrium points.)

Armed with this reminder, now consider giving a Ramsay planner who is at e_u a new enhanced taste for clothing – as represented by a shift in 9(c) of HH to H'H'. His new optimal transient program will approach a new steady-state equilibrium. Will it involve 'perversely' *lower* W_1/W_2? No! Beginning at e_u, the planner is shown by the arrows to be shifted to e_s, the new stable equilibrium near to the old stable equilibrium of e_s (not to e_u', the new unstable equilibrium near e_u!). And now we verify that the increased demand for the labor-using good clothing does in fact result in a permanent increase in the wage rate. This is despite the fact that there is shown in 8(b) the Metcalfe–Steedman anomaly in which the witnessed rise in W_1/W_2 moves the system to the labor-using technique 1 rather than away from it; indeed, in the $r = 3.5$ regime, such an effect is the necessary way for the system to achieve its rendezvous with a raising of the wage rate.

What does all this mean for the status of e_u'? There is no initial state from which it will be reached (except from itself). A move from e_u to e_u', if it were possible as it is not, would in this example just escape being 'perverse' in its effect on W_1/W_2: W_1/W_2 just barely holds its own rather than perversely falling. But I believe I can fabricate a neoclassical example with Cobb–Douglas pro-

---

[21]See Samuelson (1971), particularly pp. 341–344 that discuss the global correspondence principle. This is reproduced in Samuelson (1972, ch. 163, pp. 374–398), see particularly pp. 388–391; it complements rather than contradicts the Metcalfe–Steedman discussion.

duction functions,[22] in which a move from e_u to e'_u would indeed be perverse in that an increased taste for clothing would seem to *reduce* clothing's price and the wage of the factor it uses relatively much of. But the point is that such a movement from unstable e_u to unstable e'_u simply will *not* happen, a subtlety I insufficiently appreciated when I originally enunciated the corrsepondence principle before World War II.

I leave to the reader the sizable task of going beyond the Ramsey–planner normative model, replacing it by what he regards as the realistic positivistic dynamics that governs a system after it has been perturbed out of steady-state equilibrium and while it is pursuing a transient dynamic path to a new steady state.

As scrutiny of fig. 9 of Metcalfe and Steedman (1972, p. 154) will suggest, new land abundance needs to be absorbed in the new equilibrium; however, since any induced drop in W_2/W_1 will result near e_u in a shift of technology toward technique 1's land-saving rather than land-using mode of production, there will have to be a considerable cheapening of the land-intensive good to encourage enough of its incremental production to absorb both the new increment of land and also land released by the shift to the land-saving technique. Thus, even for an infinitesimal increment of exogenous land near an observed unstable e_u, there must result a noninfinitesimal displacement of equilibrium.

---

[22]The enclosed heuristic diagram will now replace 9(c), I believe. Note that the shift from e_u to e'_u would lower P_2/P_1 and W_1/W_2 but, as the arrows indicate, the actual effect of the postulated enhanced taste for clothing will be to move equilibrium from e_u to e'_s.

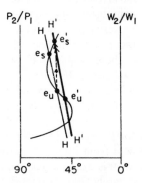

I have not checked out the rigorous calculations of this footnote's example; but the indicated drop in P_2/P_1 from e_u to e'_u will, I believe, be verified if one checks out the Cobb–Douglas model:

$$q_1(t+1) = L_2 - L_{22}(t) = y_1(t+1) + q_{12}(t+1),$$

$$q_2(t+1) = 4[L_1 q_{22}(t) q_{12}(t) L_{22}(t)]^{\frac{1}{4}} = y_2(t+1) + q_{22}(t+1),$$

for an intermediate value of r.

This is just what the global correspondence principle warns us is characteristic of unstable equilibria.

Fortunately, by the serendipity of logic and the essence of things, Nature abhors unstable equilibria, polarizing the glimpses of her petticoat that she grants us into bifurcated or bimodal concentrations around stable equilibria, with quantum skips in between.

References

Acheson, K., 1970, The aggregation of heterogeneous capital goods and various trade theorems, Journal of Political Economy 78.

Bliss, C., 1967, Review of collected scientific papers of Paul A. Samuelson, vols. I and II, Economic Journal 76.

Brock, W.A., 1973, Some results on the uniqueness of steady states in multisector models of optimum growth when future utilities are discounted, International Economic Review 14, 535–559.

Emmanuel, A., 1972, Unequal exchange: A study of the imperialism of trade (Monthly Review Press, New York); originally: 1969, L'exchange inégal (Librarie Francois Masparo, Paris).

Gale, D. and H. Nikaido, 1965, The Jacobian matrix and global univalence of mappings, Mathematische Annalen 159, no. 2, 81–93.

Kemp, M. and C. Khang, 1974, A note on steady-state price: Output relationships, Journal of International Economics 4, 187–198.

Mainwaring, L., 1974, A neo-Ricardian analysis of internal trade, Kyklos, 537–553.

Malinvaud, E., 1953, Capital accumulation and efficient allocation of resources, Econometrica 21, 233–268.

McKenzie, L.W., 1955, Equality of factor prices in international trade, Econometrica 23, 239–257.

Metcalfe, J.S. and I. Steedman, 1972, Reswitching and primary input use, Economic Journal 82, 140–157.

Metcalfe, J.S. and I. Steedman, 1973a, Heterogeneous capital and the Heckscher–Ohlin–Samuelson theory of trade, in: M. Parkin, ed., Essays in modern economics: The proceedings of the Association of University Teachers of Economics, Aberystwyth, 1972 (Longman, London).

Metcalfe, J.S. and I. Steedman, 1973b, On foreign trade, Economia Internazionale 26.

Mirrlees, J., 1969, The dynamic non-substitution theorem, Review of Economic Studies 36, 67–76.

Parinello, S., 1970, Introduzione ad una teoria neoricardiana del commercio internazionale, Studi Economici.

Parinello, S., 1973, Distribuzione, sviluppo e commercio internazionale, Economia Internazionale, May.

Ramsey, F.P., 1927, A contribution to the theory of taxation, Economic Journal 37, 47–61.

Samuelson, P.A., 1947, Foundations of economic analysis (Harvard University Press, Cambridge).

Samuelson, P.A., 1953, Prices of factors and goods in general equilibrium, Review of Economic Studies 21, 1–20.

Samuelson, P.A., 1965, Equalization by trade of the interest rate along with the real wage, in: Trade, growth, and the balance of payments: Essays in honor of Gottfried Haberler (Rand McNally, Chicago), 35–52.

Samuelson, P.A., 1966a, A summing up, Quarterly Journal of Economics 80, 568–583.

Samuelson, P.A., 1966b, Collected scientific papers of Paul A. Samuelson, vol. I and vol. II (MIT Press, Cambridge).

Samuelson, P.A., 1967, Summary on factor-price equalization, International Economic Review 8, 286–295.

Samuelson, P.A., 1971, On the trail of conventional beliefs on the transfer problem, in: J. Bhagwati et al., eds., Trade, balance of payments, and growth: Essays in honor of Charles P. Kindleberger (North-Holland, Amsterdam), 327–351.

Samuelson, P.A., 1972, Collected scientific papers of Paul A. Samuelson, vol. III (MIT Press, Cambridge).

Samuelson, P.A., 1973, Deadweight loss in international trade from the profit motive, in: C.F. Bergsten and W.G. Tyler, eds., Leading issues in international economic policy: Essays in honor of George N. Halm (D.C. Heath, Lexington, MA).

Samuelson, P.A., 1975, Illogic of neo-Marxism doctrine of unequal exchange, in: D. Belsley et al., eds., Inflation, trade and taxes: Essays in honor of Alice Bourneuf (Ohio State University Press, Columbus).

Vanek, J., 1963, Variable factor proportions and inter-industry flows in the theory of international trade, Quarterly Journal of Economics 77, 129–142.

Von Weizsäcker, C.C., 1971, Steady state capital theory (Springer–Verlag, Berlin).

Von Weizsäcker, C.C., 1973, Morishima on Marx, Economic Journal 83, 1245–1255.

Von Weizsäcker, C.C. and P.A. Samuelson, 1971, A new labor theory of value for rational planning through the use of the bourgeois profit rate, Proceedings of the National Academy of Sciences 68, 1192–1194.

252

Illogic of Neo-Marxian Doctrine of Unequal Exchange

Paul A. Samuelson

The theory of comparative advantage is one of the few bits of statical logic that economists of all schools understand and agree with. A. Emmanuel in *L'échange inégal* (1969)[1] devotes more than four hundred pages to refuting that theory, replacing it with the view that the poverty of a poor nation, trading with a rich nation and importing capital from it, is importantly related to this asymmetric pattern of trade.

The thesis, if correct, is important and novel. It is seriously presented by a serious scholar. It is one of the few attempts to put Marxian analytics to work on a genuine real-world problem. Two distinguished savants, Professors Charles Bettleheim and Henri Denis, have thought it valuable enough to have given the author the benefit of their criticisms. The argument deserves a fair-minded examination. Since, at the request of students in an MIT graduate seminar, I invested some hours in studying its arithmetical tables and syllogisms in order to form a judgment of the merits in the doctrine of unequal exchange, my provisional negative findings may be of some usefulness to others.[2]

I am grateful to the National Science Foundation for financial aid.

1. Translated as *Unequal Exchange: A Study of the Imperialism of Trade* (New York and London: Monthly Review Press, 1972).

2. My 1972 paper "Deadweight Loss in International Trade from the Profit Motive," in C. Fred Bergsten and William G. Tyler, eds., *Leading Issues in International*

I. RICARDO'S RED HERRING

Begin, as Emmanuel does, with Ricardo's traditional Portugal-England wine-cloth arithmetic. In backward England it takes 100 labor to produce [her needed 1 of] cloth; and 120 labor to produce [1 of] wine. In rich Portugal it takes only 80 labor for [that 1 of] wine; and only 90 labor for [that 1 of] cloth. Ricardo, and everybody (including Emmanuel), will agree that with labor immobile between countries and competitive balanced trade freely possible between countries, England will end up specializing in cloth, exporting it to Portugal in return for wine imports from Portugal, which specializes in wine production and imports cloth.

Moreover, the final post-trade ratio of cloth's price to wine's price, it is agreed, must end up somewhere between 100/120 and 90/80. We know that J. S. Mill first told Ricardo's readers where, on that closed interval, the equilibrium terms of trade would fall. Ricardo, presumably only by way of giving a hypothetical example, says, "Thus England would give the produce of the labour of 100 men, for the produce of the labour of 80" (*Principles*, ed. Sraffa, p. 135). This suggests

$$\frac{100}{120} \leq (P_c/P_w)^* = 1 \leq \frac{90}{80}$$

For this gratuitous case (or for any other arbitrarily selected terms-of-trade point in the open interval), the real wage in both countries rises: English workers get one of their needed subsistence goods for less work than before (the imported one); and so do Portuguese workers. Emmanuel does not disagree with this. He does not claim that poor country's labor is impoverished by the example's trade. He does not even go into the ill-posed question, "Which nation has the *higher* percentage improvement in real wage, the rich nation or the poor?" Those who know modern economic theory know that no one answer could possibly be given; before (and *after!*) trade, all we can validly know is this:

$$\frac{80}{120} = Min \left[\frac{80}{120}, \frac{90}{100} \right] \leq \frac{U.K. \; real \; wage}{Portugal \; real \; wage}$$

$$\leq Max \left[\frac{80}{120}, \frac{90}{100} \right] = \frac{90}{100}$$

Economic Policy: Essays in Honor of George N. Halm (Lexington, Mass.: Lexington Books, 1973), discusses some paradoxes of apparent (but illusory) steady-state inefficiencies under competition.

It is easy to supply examples in which trade brings either country to either pole of these limits, with the other country garnering *all* the gains from trade.

And even in Ricardo's gratuitous case, where we are made to end up at $P_c/P_w = 1$, it is not possible to say which of the countries has had real wages improved by the bigger percentage. The U.K. real wage always stays the same as before in cloth; only in wine does trade ever benefit it. The Portugal real wage rises only in imported cloth.[3] Equality-of-percentage rise in the respective imported-goods' real wages can take place only if the equilibrium price ratio P_c/P_w, ends up at the geometric mean of the two limits:$[(100/120)(90/80)]^{1/2} = \sqrt{15/16}$. But it would be wrong to think that Ricardo's choice of $1 = 16/16$ for the post-trade terms of trade of the United Kingdom implies, necessarily, that poor English labor gets the larger percentage gain in real wage, for imported wine might loom small in their total consumption budget. Even in the cases of uniform homothetic tastes, an exact index number of trade-induced relative real wages movements could take on any value. (By the way, Ricardo's example gratuitously suggests that England wants the *same* wine and cloth after trade as before trade—as if the benefits from trade are spent on leisure. Perhaps this is merely a figure of speech. By his own Malthusian theory of labor supply, Ricardo would presumably suppose that trade benefits are frittered away in mere creation of more human lives. As usual, Ricardo operates simultaneously at many levels of abstraction: although his arithmetic involves only labor costs, his explanation is that of any broker talking about shifts of "capital" between various projects, and so on.)

Emmanuel's unequal exchange, he is careful to warn us (p. 92, for example), is not at all concerned with the question: Granted that both countries gain from trade in real wages, does one get more than what might be considered the point

3. For convenient reference in connection with later appraising of Emmanuel's tables, let me pin down with admissible numbers Ricardo's pre-trade and post-trade equilibrium. Suppose before trade that each country consumes 1 (or 1 million) of wine (quarts) and cloth (yards). Portugal has the higher per capita income because 170 man-hours ($= 80 + 90$) of labor produce there what it takes 220 man-hours ($= 120 + 100$) to produce in England. Suppose that after trade, all of England's fixed labor goes to produce 2.2 m. cloth; and all of Portugal's goes to produce $2^1/_5$ wine. Humoring Ricardo with his 1-to-1 post-trade terms of trade, suppose millian reciprocal demand causes $1^1/_9$ m. wine to be exported by Portugal for $1^1/_9$ m. English cloth. Profit not having reared its ugly head, *all can agree that trade benefits both countries.* Poor England (but not so poor as before trade) now ends up consuming $1^1/_9$ m. wine and $1^1/_{72}$ m. cloth; rich Portugal ends up consuming $1^4/_{45}$ wine and $1^1/_9$ cloth. So runs the harmonious classical story. Will Emmanuel's Marxian version of the true situation, inclusive of profits equalized by international capital movements, successfully refute comparative cost? The last section will give a definite negative answer to the question.

of fair division[4] of trade blessings? For, as he says, from that viewpoint "unequal exchange does not represent a real loss but merely a failure to gain." Emmanuel's unequal exchange is designed to bare the *harm* from the trade, not its *benefit*.

II. HARM TO WORKERS WHEN POOR COUNTRY IMPORTS PROFIT-EQUALIZING CAPITAL?

To deduce trade's evil, we must abandon Ricardo's labor-only arithmetic. Now let there be profits as well as wages, surpluses, surplus values, indirect labor (in the form of Marxian constant capital) as well as direct labor (variable capital in Marxian terminology).

Now we still keep labor immobile as between countries. But let us suppose with Emmanuel that, in the absence of trade, the profit rate is lower in the nation with high real wages. We have at least two choices. We could merely introduce balanced merchandise trade in wine and cloth, not permitting any borrowing or lending. Always, current merchandise balance of payments must then balance.

However, it seems more realistic to recognize that capital is mobile between countries. Thus, Emmanuel says (p. 54), "Let us now suppose that free circulation of capital is introduced between countries, and, as a result, equalization of profit takes place."

Before looking at his Tableaux, we may ask ourselves: "What would the conventional international textbook models give as an answer to the positive-profit unbalanced-trade case?"

III. CONVENTIONAL TEXTBOOK PROOF OF TRADE-INDUCED RISE IN REAL WAGES OF CAPITAL-IMPORTING COUNTRY

In the oversimplified world of the texts, Heckscher-Ohlin two-factor production functions are made to replace labor-only Ricardian functions. Before trade, poor England has less homogeneous capital ("leets"), K, relative to its labor supply, L. Her profit rate, equalized between wine and cloth industries, is presumably higher than in rich Portugal, with its plentiful capital. Apparently, wine must be capital-intensive relative to cloth if we are to use Heckscher-Ohlin explanations for Portugal's comparative advantage in wine.

What are the effects of trade in the textbook models?

4. Emmanuel here takes Graham's simple case where A produces in 10 hrs. 40 wheat or 40 watches, while B's 10 hrs. produces 40 wheat and 30 watches. Naïvely, some writers have thought 40 and 35 (= 1/2 of 30 + 40) represents fair division—not Ricardo's gratuitous case, but one equally gratuitous.

1. Mere balanced trade in wine and cloth, with no IOUs or movement of physical capital goods allowed, will raise real wages of the abundant factor in the poor country England, as free trade in goods serves as a partial substitute for factor mobility. The high real wage of Portugal drops as relatively specializing there in non-labor-intensive wine economizes on its initially scarce labor. In England the high interest or profit rate drops as it relatively specializes on labor-intensive cloth.

2. If we supplement free trade in goods by free movement of physical capital, the differentials in real wages between rich Portugal and backward England are further reduced. Indeed, if the only reason for England's inferiority is scarcity of capital goods, real wages must be equalized by capital flows. (Indeed, we know from the classical factor-price equalization theorem that, even before enough capital has moved to equalize capital/labor endowments, real wages will already have become equal.)

To sum up: conventional 2-factor models lead to the opposite of the "unequal-exchange" thesis. Labor in the capital-poor countries gains the most from trade and from foreign investment and absentee-ownership.[5]

IV. NEOCLASSICISM REPLACED BY NEO-NEOCLASSICISM

Although the international-trade texts have not caught up with the frontier of debates about reswitching and complexities of heterogeneous-capital vectors, we must see how Joan Robinson or Sraffa or an MIT student handling dated-input models would evaluate the probabilities of immiserating unequal exchange.

Let us begin with a Leontief-Sraffa model where primary-factor labor produces all goods at constant returns to scale but with the help of produced goods themselves as inputs needed to work with primary labor.

Make the bizarre assumption of Ricardo that England is poor and Portugal rich. If we measure poverty by lowness of the real wage alone and assume the same Leontief-Sraffa technologies everywhere in the world, then Emmanuel is

5. Imagine a 3-factor world with production functions like $Q = F(L,K,T)$, where T is immobile land. Obviously, if K had some singular pattern of rivalry with L, rather than complementarity, as shown by negative $\partial^2 Q/\partial L \partial K$, free geographical movement of K could *hurt* real wages in the land-poor country. But, contrary to the unequal-exchange thesis, the combined income of the poor country, its return from the combined dose of immobile labor-cum-land, would have to go up rather than down. (None of this denies that import of *new* technology from a rich country might sometimes lower real wages in a poor country. Thus, the green revolution of hybrid wheat and rice strains could lower rural real wages while raising proprietors' property incomes.)

right in supposing that the poor country must have the higher profit rate, for a lower real wage can occur only with a higher profit rate, as students of the factor-price frontier know.

However, we need not assume the same technological options in terms of labor and non-primary inputs. In that case, it is possible but not mandatory for the high-profit region also to be what Emmanuel wishes it to be, the low-wage region.

Now we can ask the question: "Suppose by free movement of capital, trade in goods takes place between countries that have come to a common rate of profit. Will the real wage rise in the capital-importing country whose profit rate has been brought down in contradiction to Emmanuel's alleged fall in real wage?"

The only proper Sraffa answer is clear. "Yes. Mobile-goods trade and capital flows, which permanently lower the backward country's profit rate, must permanently *raise* (not lower) its real wage.

"Moreover, the real wage will presumably be induced to rise even more than the same drop in the profits rate would induce in a no-trade autarky. This is because, in addition to the rise in real wage obtainable without trade, the possibility that one can permanently exchange goods at price ratios different from those of autarky, will (if anything) lower some equilibrium prices relative to domestic wage rates at the postulated lower profit rate and give an extra boost to real wages in terms of imported goods."

So once again, the immiseration conclusions of unequal exchange are not validated—but rather their reverse.[6]

6. Here is a paradox discussed in my cited Hal m Festschrift paper. Suppose Ricardo's data (100, 120; 90, 80) hold for *total* labor requirements. If profit rates are both zero, Portugal exports wine and England exports cloth. But suppose (in this note only) that Portugal's wine requires its labor in two periods, half to produce grape juice and half to turn grape juice into wine; suppose U.K. wine is producible in one period. Cloth everywhere is produced in one period. Then, we discover that a high-enough profit rate, equal in both countries, will give England a cheaper cost ratio of wine to cloth. England will export wine in the steady state, and Portugal will specialize in cloth production! The world *seems* to be no longer efficiently on its global production-possibility frontier.

I have italicized the word *seems* because there is no true paradox. All this is quite as it should be. The world never has a choice of going at once from one steady state to another: to do that, it would have to build up stocks of heterogeneous capital goods in some places and reduce them in others. And there is nothing "inefficient" about the reversed geographical pattern. Actually, that pattern would be efficiently reached asymptotically if the two countries (1) permitted free balanced trade in goods, (2) permitted no interregional borrowings or absentee ownership, and (3) had Ramsey planners who engineered optimal growth patterns for their stationary populations with the same high time-preference rates in the two countries.

V. SOME MARX-LIKE TABLEAUX

We are now armed to examine Emmanuel's arguments. He envisages countries A and B, with unequal profit rates in autarky, e.g., 20% and $33^1/_3$%. After trade with mobile capital, they emerge with a common intermediate profit rate, e.g., 25%. (Each country has three industries, e.g., I wine, II cloth, . . .). Relevant tables from his chapter 2 are presented in table 1 below.

System A gives [Portugal's] low-profit before-trade situation. System B gives [England's] pre-trade high-profit situation. Systems A and B together give the alleged after-trade situation at a common intermediate profit rate.

A word of explanation may be helpful. The usual assumptions of Marxism Tableaux are made here. Thus the second column, Variable Capital, represents expenditures on direct labor, and the first column, Constant Capital, represents the cost of raw materials (or other capital goods) used. The column Surplus Value is based upon an assumed constancy of the rate of surplus value in all industries: in these first tables, more or less a happenstance, Emmanuel assumes that the rate of surplus value is the same in both countries before trade, mainly, 100%. Much less admissibly, he assumes that, although each country's

TABLE 1

SOME MARXIAN TABLEAUX

Branches	c Constant Capital	v Variable Capital	m Surplus Value (1.0)v	V Value $c + v + m$	T Rate of Profit $\frac{\Sigma m}{\Sigma c + \Sigma v}$	p Profit $T(c + v)$	L Price of Production $c + v + p$
				System A			
I	80	20	20	120		20	120
II	90	10	10	110	20%	20	120
III	70	30	30	130		20	120
	240	60	60	360		60	360
				System B			
I	40	20	20	80		20	80
II	50	10	10	70	$33^1/_3$%	20	80
III	30	30	30	90		20	80
	120	60	60	240		60	240
				Systems A and B Together			
IA	80	20	20	120		25	125
IIA	90	10	10	110		25	125
IIIA	70	30	30	130		25	125
IB	40	20	20	80	25%	15	75
IIB	50	10	10	70		15	75
IIIB	30	30	30	90		15	75
	360	120	120	600		120	600
A	240	60	60	360		75	375
B	120	60	60	240	25%	45	225
	360	120	120	600		120	600

Source: Adapted from Emmanuel, *L'échange inégal*, pp. 53–55.

rate of profit is equalized after trade, nevertheless each country continues to have the same rate of surplus value as it had before trade. Those who have had experience with Marxian categories will realize that there cannot in general be such extreme independence between the rates or profit and of surplus value. (E.g., when the organic compositions of capital are the same in different industries, or very nearly so, a large change in the profit rate must generate a sizable change in the rate of surplus value.)

In the final section of the table I have added two final rows that respectively consolidate the totals for the two countries. Emmanuel regards these totals as crucial because of his belief—wrong, as we shall see—that it is essentially the totals that are needed to describe the effects of international exchange.

How does the author use these tableaux?

Emmanuel seems to think that, if mobility of capital were not permitted to equalize profit rates, the goods would exchange between A and B at the price ratios from the final columns of A and B: 80 of B for 120 of A. Since capital mobility brings down the profit component of B's prices and raises that of A's prices, Emmanuel thinks that B's terms of trade are necessarily hurt by the process and that she must now trade 75 of B for 125 of A.

But this act is at its heart a nonsense calculation. Before trade, there was autarky: not 80 of B for 120 of A but 0 of B and 0 of A, with the terms of trade a meaningless and indeterminate form, $0/0$ = gibberish. And even if I change the comparison, and construct two post-trade situations—one where capital is immobile and the domestic profit rates are not equalized and the other where profit rates are equalized—still Emmanuel's comparison is a nonsense one. By his way of reckoning, an invention in the advanced country that lowered all costs of production there would impoverish it. Yet every college sophomore knows that a reduction in the terms of trade that is offset by productivity improvement may be highly beneficial to *both* countries.

By Emmanuel's kind of fallacious reasoning, one's heart would bleed for the capitalists in underdeveloped countries. Whenever capital imports bring down their profit rates, their whole nation suffers. Emmanuel even claims that hundreds of billions of dollars of extra real income—perhaps 30 or 40%!—could be secured for workers in the less-developed countries if his kind of unequal exchange were somehow ruled out.

The illogic of the whole procedure is much greater than has yet been indicated. GNPs (inclusive of double, triple, and multiple countings of gross raw materials at the different stages of production), of course, don't exchange against each other in international trade. Therefore, when Emmanuel uses such totals, as in 375 of A against 225 of B, we must reasonably infer that he regards these as differing only in scale (by a factor of 3 in a 3-branch model) from actual commodity prices, which is fair enough.

But it is profoundly wrong to leave after-trade industry totals what they were before trade. The whole effect of trade is to cause specialization and production shifts: Portugal contracts (even to zero) production in its cloth branch and expands it in its wine branch; in England the opposite takes place.

In Emmanuel's tables, both before trade and "after," there is no possibility of any wine-cloth trade. In every case his domestic price ratios, P_2/P_1 and P_3/P_1 are *identical* between countries both before and after trade! If Ricardo had postulated wine-cloth cost ratios as $80/100 = .8$ in Portugal and $96/20 = .8$ in England, he would have ended up with zero trade in everything.

Let us, however, extricate Emmanuel from his unfortunate choice of initial numerical examples. Let us give his argument all the rope it can use, to see fair-mindedly whether there is anything insightful—even imperfectly so—in his whole approach.

VI. THE ACID TEST: RICARDO'S EXAMPLE

What could provide a better test case of the root merit of the theory of unequal exchange than Ricardo's own simple case of comparative advantage? After all, Professor Bettelheim, in his sponsorship of the Emmanuel work, has important doubts about Emmanuel's analysis. The principal merit of Emmanuel's work in Bettelheim's eyes is that it refutes Ricardian comparative advantage. Thus, Bettelheim claims:

> Emmanuel's critique constitutes an extremely important contribution to the over-turning of what might be called the "dogma of the theory of comparative costs and of the benefits of the capitalist international division of labor. . . .
>   . . . One of the essentially interesting aspects of Emmanuel's book is, I think, that it brings out the profound inadequacy and illusory character of the classical and "neoclassical" theory of international trade.

Does the theory of unequal exchange succeed in any sense in undermining the theory of comparative advantage? Or in limiting its realism and relevance? Or in amplifying and improving it in any way?

I believe any analytically trained fair-minded reader who goes to the trouble of examining unequal exchange seriously will conclude as I have that the answers are No, No, and No. The following analysis, by the correct Marxian technique, of Ricardo's classical case should close the books on the matter.

Three tables are presented in table 2 dealing with the Ricardo example along proper Marxian lines: System A, System B, and System A and B, in the Emmanuel style. To be fair to his thesis, my example assumes differences in real wage rates in poor England and rich Portugal prior to trade. Also, to correspond with his emphasis upon equalization of profit rates by trade, I have amplified Ricardo's wine-cloth example to allow for profit. So that every Marxian can agree with the analysis, I have worked with an example in which there are no differences in organic composition of capital to put a wedge between analysis of Marx's Volume I "values" and Volume III "prices." Indeed, in the present simple Ricardo example, all constant capital is zero—permitting no one to explain away or to minimize the higher real wages of one country as the result of labor there working with more and better machinery. There is no room here for the apologetics of thrift.

To parallel Emmanuel's arbitrary profit rates, I use his pre-trade rates of 20% and 33⅓%. Like him, I use post-trade equalized rates of profit of 25%. But I do not follow Emmanuel's incorrect supposition that we can pool *after* trade his *unchanged* pre-trade surpluses. Of course, the specialization forced by trade will alter all such magnitudes, and the changed profit rates will affect the surpluses. Emmanuel fell in the same small trap here that Marxians (Sweezy, Dobb, et al.) and non-Marxians (Bortkiewicz, Seton, Samuelson,[7] et al.) agree Marx fell into when he gave his Volume III form of the transformation algorithm for going from "values" to "prices." In any case, Emmanuel is free to change my 25% to any other intermediate equalized profit rate he likes: my refutation will not thereby be affected at all. And he can use other than these admissible terms-of-trade outcomes, which I have made in table 2 to agree with an earlier footnote's version of the Ricardo case.

Let me give a word of explanation. I assume (see system B of table 2) that England consumes 1 (million or) m. qts. of wine before trade and 1 m. yds of cloth. She has a labor supply of 220 m. hrs., both before and after trade.

I assume (see system A) that rich Portugal consumes about an eighth more per head; the same 1 m. qts. of wine and 1 m. yds. cloth for her 170 m. hrs. labor, as against England's 220 m. hrs. labor.

Both before and after trade, labor is fixed in each country: at 170 m. hrs. for Portugal and 220 m. hrs. for England. I humor Ricardo in his choice of 1-cloth-to-1-wine post-trade terms of trade: to fix the numbers, I pick levels consistent with convex preference contours in each country—1⅑ m. yds. of English cloth exports to balance 1⅑ m. qts. of Portuguese wine exports. Finally, with Emmanuel, I assume free capital mobility creates equality of profit rates at 25%, bringing down the poor country's 33⅓% and bringing up the rich country's 20%. (It is not possible to humor Emmanuel and keep post-trade rates of surplus value at pre-trade levels because the case has such balanced organic composition. So I resist doing the impossible.)

The postulates of the example are now complete. It is just a question of working out all the numerical entries of the three tableaux, adhering to standard

7. I have reviewed this in the 1971 *Journal of Economic Literature*.

Marxian c + v + . . . calculations. Table 2 presents the corrected analysis, whose results are quite contrary to the unequal-exchange claims. To move beyond the fetishistic level of prices and aggregates, I have appended two columns to show actual physical commodity outputs—in quarts of wine and yards of cloth. Subtracting exports, or adding in starred imports, the final column shows national consumptions. With the profit rates known, the physical per capita consumptions or workers can be easily calculated by the reader.

VII. UNEQUAL EXCHANGE REFUTED

Emmanuel and Bettelheim will, I am sure, now agree with me that this careful and valid exercise, in which Ricardo's comparative-cost case has profit rates appended to it—and which do get equalized by trade—does benefit both countries in exactly the same manner that Ricardo claimed! See the last two columns of table 2, and note its identity with Ricardo's results (e.g., as spelled out carefully in an earlier footnote). Moreover, even if we improve on Ricardo's gratuitous way of selecting one of the possible range of final equilibria, we see that no single valid point has been scored by this Marxian model of unequal exchange against classical or neoclassical trade theory. Q.E.D.

Of course, wine is traded against cloth in the model. Anyone who wants to

TABLE 2

CORRECTED ANALYSIS OF RICARDIAN CASE

Branches	c Constant Capital	v Variable Capital	m Surplus Value	T Rate of Profit	p Profit $T(c + v)$	L&V Price and Value $c + v + p$	Q Physical Production	Consumption (Q-exports) or (Imports*)
			System A: Rich Portugal before Trade (170 m. hrs. total labor)					
I Wine	0	80 m.	16	20%	16	96 m.	1 m. qts.	1 m. qts.
II Cloth	0	90 m.	18		18	108 m.	1 m. yds.	1 m. yds.
	0	170 m.	34		34	204 m.		
			System B: Poor England before Trade (220 m. hrs. total labor)					
I Wine	0	120 m.	40	33⅓%	40	160 m.	1 m. qts.	1 m. qts.
II Cloth	0	100 m.	33⅓		33⅓	133⅓ m.	1 m. yds.	1 m. yds.
	0	220 m.	73⅓		73⅓	293⅓ m.		
			Systems A and B: After Trade and Profit Equalization (Unchanged Total Labor Hours)					
IA Wine	0	170 m.	42½	25%	42½	212½ m.	2⅛ m. qts.	1¹/₇₂ m. qts.
IIA Cloth	0	0	0		0	0	0	1¹/₉ m. yds.*
	0	170 m.	42½		42½	212½ m.		
IB Wine	0	0	0	25%	0	0	0	1¹/₉ m. qts.*
IIB Cloth	0	220 m.	55		55	275 m.	2¹/₅ m. qts.	1⁴/₄₅ m. yds.
	0	220 m.	55		55	275 m.		

say that a certain number of high-wage hours of A has been traded against a certain larger number of hours of low-wage B is free to do so. (David Ricardo did.) But that tautology does not mean that there is a meaningful par for such a ratio and that a deviation on one side from it represents "unequal" exchange. Unequal exchange in this sense is not the result of wage differentials; nor is it the cause of wage differentials; rather, it is tautologically a restatement of the fact of assumed wage differentials!

It is a cruel hoax on the laborers in poor countries to pretend that there is some way of increasing their real incomes[8] by 100% or 200% or even 2% by choking off trade, or by some other proposed way of eliminating unequal exchange. Indeed, romantic dilettantism has always been the enemy of social progress for the masses. Whether wrapped in Marxism symbolism or otherwise, logical nonsense is logical nonsense.

VIII. CONCLUSION

I have spared the reader further details of a thorough post-mortem on the Emmanuel model of unequal exchange, including a careful auditing of his dialogue with Professor Bettelheim. Because it is less mainstream economists than Marxians who are interested in the model, I have checked my negative autopsy report by *redoing his analysis completely in terms of Volume I "values," eschewing all prices.* The same negative finding emerges.

No new light has been thrown on the reason why poor countries are poor and rich countries are rich. What is a quite different and less important matter, no flaw in the theory of comparative advantage has been uncovered, and no improvement on that theory is provided by the doctrine of unequal exchange.

Let me also report that there is much else in *Unequal Exchange* to disagree with and to agree with. The analysis has the merit of being clear, if incorrect, a compliment that not all critiques and defenses of modern economics can warrant.

8. Actually, the trade-induced reduction in the poor country's profit rate adds an additional increase to the real wage there; i.e., along with the higher real wage in terms of the cheaper imported good, there is an increase in real wage in terms of its home product too. The trade-induced rise in the rich country's profit rate must depress its workers' real wage in terms of the exported good, and this same factor *could* even wipe out the higher real wage in terms of the imported good, leaving the rich-country employers with all the gains from trade.

253

Deadweight Loss in International Trade from the Profit Motive?

Paui A. Samuelson

The theoretical models of international trade, from Ricardo to the latest textbooks of mainstream economics, usually ignore profit rates—and their alleged tendency to be higher in the capital-poor underdeveloped world than in the advanced nations. Can the existence of profit differentials negate the verities of the theory of comparative advantage?

When I began to investigate this highly-relevant question, I had not enjoyed the opportunity of reading the interesting Marxian analysis by Dr. A. Emmanuel, entitled *Unequal Exchange.*[1] The present finding does not have a direct bearing on the Emmanuel thesis that equalization of the profit rate, by capital mobility from the low-interest advanced world to the capital-poor less developed nations, represents *unequal* exchange—and helps to explain both the lowness of real wages in the poor regions and how those wages can be raised by substantial percentages. So I leave to another occasion an audit of unequal exchange,[2] and tackle head on the vital question of whether the existence of profit vitiates efficient international trade.

Before Profit

Suppose Asia, with ten times the population of America, can produce only about the same amounts of food and clothing as America. But suppose the ratio of labor costs of food to clothing is 2-to-1 in Asia as against 1-to-2 in America. Suppose everyone everywhere spends half his income on food and half on clothing.

Then on the understanding that labor is the only factor of production and that profit rates are zero in both countries so that all time-phasings of labor inputs can be ignored, we can state the following properties of competitive equilibrium:

1. Asia will specialize on clothing in which she has Ricardian comparative advantage. America will specialize on food. Asian food imports will equal in value America's clothing imports; on our special demand assumptions, half of the GNP will be in the foreign trade sectors.

I owe thanks to the National Science Foundation for financial aid.

2. Despite the fact that America ends up ten times better off in per capita real incomes, people in both regions gain from this competitive trade: trade brings gains to the typical Asian and also to the typical American. (It is not very meaningful to ask, Which gains most in trade?)

Worldwide, more of both food and clothing is produced as a result of the geographical specialization and trade. Figure 9-1 shows world production possibilities in the steady state, FEC, with specialization. Compare the post-trade equilibrium at E with the autarky total of world production at A. Specialization permits, in this example, a 33 1/3 percent increase in every output and in average world productivity.[3]

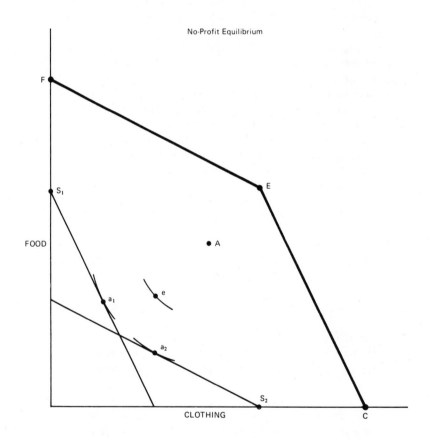

Figure 9-1. Deadweight Loss in International Trade from the Profit Motive

Effect of Positive Profit Differentials

All the above is elementary Ricardian comparative advantage. Being elementary, it ignores the time-phasing of labor inputs and the effects of that on relative unit costs of production when the competitive profit rate is positive, $r>0$. Now, as Marxian and non-Marxian economists recognize, steady-state autarky price ratios will differ from ratios of embodied-labor costs, the degree of the differences depending upon the height of the rate of profit.

Let us suppose that there will be balanced trade between continents, but no borrowing or lending. Let us concentrate on equilibria that will be observed under steady states, when productions, consumptions, wages, and prices never change. Suppose for whatever reason—it could be greater Ramsey-Böhm systematic time preference—the profit rate is higher in Asia than in America. And suppose that clothing production is more roundabout than that of food in both countries, in the unambiguous sense that the domestic cost ratios of clothing to food increase uniformly with respect to increases in the profit rate r.

Then, under autarky, America's clothing-food price ratio would be raised a bit above 2/1 by our low, positive r. Under autarky, Asia's clothing-food price ratio would be raised very much above 1/2 by the high r there. If the profit differential is large enough both before and after trade—remember that no lending is permitted that could serve to erode that differential or wipe it out—Asia may be *forced to specialize in food for which we have seen she was unfit in terms of socially necessary labor costs.* America will be *forced to specialize in clothing, for which she had a comparative disadvantage at zero profits.*

Figure 9-2 shows final equilibrium at E', with less of each product than at E, the zero-profit equilibrium. Consumption standards are shown for America and Asia, at e_1 and e_2, where both are worse off than at the e point in Figure 9-1's zero-profit equilibrium. Furthermore, the citizens of Asia are worse off in this positive-profit free-trade equilibrium than they would have been under autarky (either with or without positive profits). Apparently the existence of positive profit rates has not only wiped out all the gains from trade, it has even produced losses of production from a false and distorted geographical pattern of specilization. The reader must not think that any capitalists gain what the workers lose: actually, if production had been as at E, and allocated among the continents in any reasonable way, there would be enough extra to give capitalists more real profit income than they are getting at the actual competitive equilibrium of E' and still to leave enough left over to make every worker in the world better off. Indeed, prohibitive tariffs, while they cannot undo the loss of E's beneficial geographical specialization, can at least undo the harm of the "perverse specialization" created by the profit differentials and free trade.

One is tempted to conclude, therefore, the following:

Positive profit rates—more particularly positive profit differentials—create deadweight losses of production, consumption, and welfare even when there is no

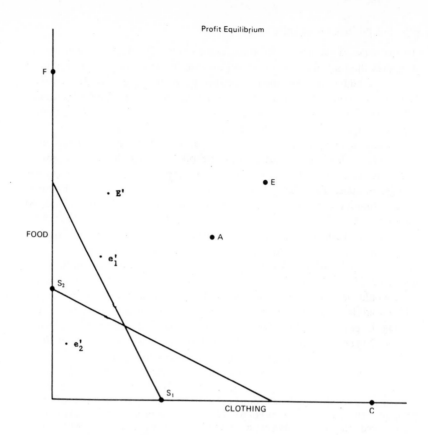

Figure 9-2. Deadweight Loss in International Trade from the Profit Motive

[Note: This figure was altered by Samuelson in 1977.]

monopoly, no externalities, no political or imperialistic exactions, and no using up of exhaustible resources, and so forth.

A formulation like the above, if it has not yet appeared in the writings of socialist critics, some day will.[4] Therefore, it is important to appraise it unflinchingly.

A Crushing Paradox?

Russell noted that the logical system of Frege was open to a contradiction in connection with the paradox involving the class of all classes. This was recognized, by Frege, Russell, and others, as a crushing objection, requiring major repair work.

Do we have here a similar paradox? Competitive equilibrium has been proved—by Bergson, Arrow, Debreu, and earlier writers—to be Pareto-optimal, involving zero deadweight loss. I.e., not everybody can be made better off by a feasible departure from the competitive equilibrium position. Here, we seem to confront a similar contradiction: the free-trade equilibrium cum competitive profit differentials is alleged to be non-Pareto-optimal and to involve deadweight loss.

My own conclusion is otherwise. *No, there is not deadweight loss in the strict sense of the term. The contradiction is only apparent.* The argument founders on a subtle pitfall involved in stead-state comparisons.

There are many ways to explain this subtle point. Perhaps the simplest is to begin at the competitive equilibrium shown at E' in Figure 9-2. Show, if you can, that there is a feasible path of going from E' to E, the better steady-state configuration, so as to make *every* American and *every* Asian better off in the transition. I say, *You cannot find such a path; it does not exist.* Comparing A and E is really comparing cheese and chalk, comparing life as it is with life as it might be if popsicles grew on trees; or, more accurately, comparing E' and E is comparing life now with what it *could* be after someone has abstained from current consumption goods in order that somewhere in the world there would be a greater accumulation of goods-in-process or equipment in the clothing industry.

To be sure, if we let America lend to Asia, building up there the capital goods in clothing needed to make the E steady state possible, there would be enough extra output brought into existence by that lending process to enable the debt to be repaid with interest and still leave enough left over to make every Asian (and every noncapitalist and capitalist in America) better off than in the pre-lending equilibrium at E'.

In brief, as Joan Robinson has been warning economists for the last twenty years, you must not look at a steady-state locus like FEC in Figure 9-1, and think that the world is free to choose indifferently among the points on it. Such a locus implies synchronization of time-phased inputs and presupposes in the background requisite stocks of heterogeneous capital goods that are different in quantities at each point. To go from points inside such a frontier to the frontier will involve sacrifices of some goods at one time in return for more goods at another later date.[5]

Conclusion

Competitive profit differentials as such cannot create wht is literally deadweight loss, whatever they may do to the inequity of the distribution of laissez-faire incomes.

Notes

1. Monthly Review Press, New York, 1972, a translation of L'ÉCHANGE INÉGAL, (Paris: Libraire Francois Maspero, 1969), including two Appendixes by the distinguished Marxist, Professor Charles Bettelheim of the École Pratique des Hautes Etudes of the Sorbonne. The full English title is UNEQUAL EXCHANGE¾ A STUDY OF THE IMPERIALISM OF TRADE.

2. I deal with this in a forthcoming paper entitled "Illogic of Neo-Marxian Doctrine of Unequal Exchange."

3. If instead of the numbers 2-to-1 I had used 4-to-1, or 1 1/2-to-1, the gains in per capita productions would have been 66 2/3, or 20, percent. The extreme symmetry assumptions make such definite statements possible.

4. Cf. the cited work on UNEQUAL EXCHANGE, which does not quite reach the present findings.

5. Reswitching phenomena do not affect this argument. But we should be aware of the possibility that a point like E', although it may be dominated in the steady state by some point northeast of it, say A, might have a superior potentiality for getting to some other third point! The present argument is not critically affected by the question of whether intermediate goods themselves can be traded internationally. Thus, semi-fabricated cloth if it can be traded, may get exported to Asia to be finished there.

254

OHLIN WAS RIGHT*

Paul A. Samuelson

Massachusetts Institute of Technology, Cambridge, Mass., USA

I was originally led to study the problem of complete factor-price equalisation by the need to explain to a class in international trade Bertil Ohlin's seminal proposition that, although free mobility of factor inputs in international trade will equalise factor returns all the way, free mobility of goods can serve only to move factor-prices *toward* (but not all the way to) factor-price equalisation. As has been discussed elsewhere,[1] I found I could not quite prove the last part of the Ohlin proposition, that factor-price equalisation by trade would have to be necessarily partial and incomplete. Indeed, in the case where there are zero transport costs, no complete specialization in either country, and where two goods are strongly relative factor-intensive in their respective inputs of the two inputs available to society, with the same laws of knowledge operative everywhere, I ended up proving that Ohlin was wrong in the Pickwickian sense of being less than right: namely I proved (as was later learned Abba Lerner had done more than a decade earlier in an unpublished paper at the London School of Economics) that there would have to be more than partial factor-price equalisation—there would have to be *full* factor-price equalisation.[2]

I. Vindication

Recently in another connection I presented a simple, but rigorous, model of general equilibrium in international trade that could be expressed in terms of the two-dimensional diagrams of Marshall's partial equilibrium supply and

* Thanks go to the National Science Foundation for financial aid and to Mary Tanner for editorial assistance.

My score of indebtedness, mounting over the years, to B. Ohlin, *Interregional and International Trade* (Harvard University Press, Cambridge, Mass., 1933) will be self-evident. Forty years have not aged this classic which sprang full-blown from the brow of its youthful author.

[1] P. A. Samuelson, "International Trade and the Equalisation of Factor Prices", *Economic Journal*, Vol. 58 (1948), pp. 163–184. The vast literature on this topic is surveyed in P. A. Samuelson, "Summary on Factor-Price Equalisation", *International Economic Review*, Vol. 58 (1967), pp. 286–295, where reference is made to the contributions of Lerner, Tinbergen, Meade, Pearce, McKenzie, Nikaido-Gale, and many others.

[2] To my knowledge only one support for the necessarily-incomplete equalisation thesis appeared in the literature. H. Uzawa, "Prices of the Factors of Production in International Trade", *Econometrica*, Vol. 27 (1959), pp. 448–468, sets forth in Section 6 a linear-demand model in which necessarily-incomplete-equalisation was deduced: unfortunately, the Uzawa functions were assumed to have single-valuedness properties which contradict the constant-returns-to-scale technologies presupposed in the discussions; hence the argument is not germane. Uzawa does quote Haberler's approval of the Ohlin thesis, but that approval may well have had reference to realistic transport costs for goods which, all are agreed, will present complete equalisation of either goods' prices or factors' prices.

demand.[1] The supply conditions of that model are of interest for their own sake since they portray what might be called the Ricardo–Viner case of pure rent.[2] They provide what this intricate subject can use to advantage, an alternative *simple* model that can free the discussion from the straight-jacket of the box-diagram analysis which Stolper and I imposed on the trade literature decades ago.[3]

My old classmate from Chicago days, Martin Bronfenbrenner, recently wrote to complain that I had not explained the implications of the new model for factor-price equalisation. Always game to try to fill any pointed-out vacuum, I proceeded to provide that analysis. The conclusion of the effort was this: After all, Bertil Ohlin's contention for partial but not total factor-price equalisation is essentially vindicated in this technological model.

It is the purpose of the present paper to describe these findings.

II. Graphical Resumé

Before turning to the new model, I show in Fig. 1 a self-contained summary of how free mobility in goods must compensate completely in the Lerner–Samuelson model for immobility of factors in equalising factor returns, provided two regions differ by not too much in geographical endowments. The correct post-trade situation, the heavy *SPEP'S'* locus, is contrasted with the no-trade light *NT* locus and with the Ohlin-thesis broken line *OH* locus.

The horizontal axis portrays the labour/land endowment in Region A in ratio to that in Region B. Equality is at 1, the intersection of the axes. The vertical axis portrays the wage/rent outcome in Region A relative to that in B. The reader might, for simplicity, think of Region B as vastly greater than Region A; then he can imagine the relative endowment of Region A differing by more and more from unity in either direction. (If the goods come to inter-

---

[1] P. A. Samuelson, "An Exact Hume–Ricardo–Marshall Model of International Trade", *Journal of International Economics*, Vol. 1 (1971), pp. 1–18. There is also my contribution to the Kindleberger *Festschrift* (ed. J. Bhagwadi et al.), *Trade, Balance of Payments and Growth* (North Holland Publishing Co, Amsterdam, 1971), Part 6, Chapter 15; "On the Trail of Conventional Beliefs About the Transfer Problem". Although the present paper adopts the industry-supply relations of these papers, it abandons their Marshallian partial-equilibrium demand relations.

[2] Viner's famous 1931 article, "Cost Curves and Supply Curves", in which the draftsman Wong will not draw the envelope of costs incorrectly despite Viner's insistence, develops the case. The original reference is to the 1931 *Zeitschrift für Nationalekonomie*, but the article has been reproduced in many anthologies and the reader is best advised to consult a version which includes a new appendix written a decade later. Cf. K. E. Boulding & G. J. Stigler, *Readings in Price Theory* (Richard D. Irwin, Inc., Chicago, 1952), Chapter 1, pp. 198–232.

[3] W. A. Stolper & P. A. Samuelson, "Protection and Real Wages", *Review of Economic Studies*, Vol. 9 (1941), pp. 58–73.

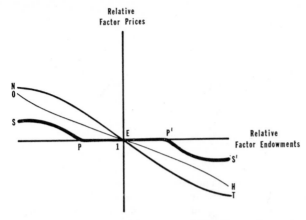

Fig. 1. As Region A's relative factor endowments diverge in ratio to Region B's from equality or unity, the No-Trade locus, *NT*, shows that inequality of relative factor prices can be expected under autarky. With trade serving to raise the demands for the cheap factor in each region, Ohlin claimed that the *OH* locus of partial but incomplete factor-price equalisation would result. However, the Lerner–Samuelson model is seen to have complete factor-price equalisation on the PEP' horizontal branch of SPEP'S'. Once complete regional specialization on a single commodity is induced, the *SP* branch shows that the wage-rent ratios are only partially equalised in the Ohlin manner, even for the Lerner–Samuelson model; and partial transport costs would produce a similar effect.

change factor intensities at distant factor prices, the *S'P'* branch could encounter another horizontal branch below the horizontal axis.)[1]

As Ohlin was the foremost to emphasize, difference in regional tastes can offset difference in regional factor endowments. Therefore, if both countries are of a comparable size, we can sidestep, or isolate, taste-difference complications by assuming the same tastes for all consumers all over the world no matter what their incomes ("uniform, homothetic preferences").[2]

III. The Ricardo–Viner case

This model assumes labour to be the only input transferable between industries. If labour worked alone at constant returns, this would give us the constant-cost case of classical comparative advantage. If, in addition, the laws

---

[1] Positive transport costs for the goods, of a constant percentage of price per unit, would cause the horizontal branches through *P* and *P'* to lie, respectively, above and below the horizontal axis, each terminating in the no-trade locus (which will, in the close neighborhood of *E*, be alone relevant).

[2] For derivation of the concept of social product in the simplifying case of homothetic, uniform tastes, see my contribution to the Hicks *Festschrift* (ed. J. N. Wolfe), *Value, Capital and Growth* (Edinburgh University Press, 1968), Ch. 19, "Two Generalizations of the Elasticity of Substitution", pp. 467–80, particularly Part II on homothetic general equilibrium and equation (20).

Swed. J. of Economics 1971

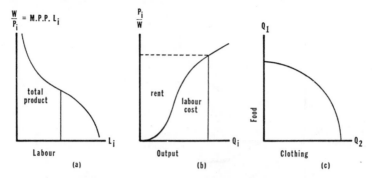

Fig. 2. For a typical industry i, the marginal-product and marginal-cost curves are shown in (*a*) and (*b*) respectively. If total L is successively divided into all for L_1 and none for L_2, half and half between L_1 and L_2, all for L_2 and none for L_1, ..., etc., we trace out the concave (from below) production-possibility frontier of (*c*). Diminishing returns to labour working in each industry with fixed specialized land makes concavity inevitable (save in the case where both lands are superabundant, with constant slope then set at relative labour costs only.)

of knowledge were everywhere the same, so that the simple labour production functions were everywhere the same, there would be no difference in production costs (no comparative advantages!) and no international trade would occur.

The kiss of Ohlin's analysis of increasing returns would bring to life the sleeping beauty of international trade even in a one factor world. However, in this paper we turn our backs on this aspect of Ohlin and Adam Smith and stay with the constant returns-to-scale assumption.

We go on to assume that there typically works with labour in each industry a non-transferable "land" specialized to that industry (food-land, clothing-land).[1]

Figs. 2*a* and 2*b* show the familiar marginal product and marginal cost curves. Fig. 2*c* shows the resulting regional bowed-out production-probability frontier. It looks like the similar frontiers of the Stolper–Samuelson model but now it could be a quarter circle with absolute slope running the gamut from 0 to infinity or 0° to 90°.

IV. One Region–Analysis

Within a single isolated region, the relative prices of goods (food and clothing) and relative factor prices (wages, food-land, clothing-land rents) will depend on the relative scarcity of the factors (labour, food-land, clothing-

---

[1] There could be more than one kind of specialized land, as we shall analyze.

Swed. J. of Economics 1971

land). The emerging general equilibrium will, of course, depend also on demand-tastes; but in the simplifying case where all tastes are uniform at all income levels, the system is in effect producing social product—i.e. food-clothing units whose constituent components depend only on the relative goods, prices once tastes are specified.

Labour abundance. Within a single region it is easy to see that an increasing abundance of any one factor—say, labour, first—will lower the real wage. Under our homothetic assumption, it must raise the output of both food and clothing, and hence by the law of diminishing returns to variable labour applied to fixed lands, the real wage will have to fall in terms of both goods and *a fortiori* in terms of social real product. By the same law, real rent of food-land must rise in terms of food; real rent of clothing-land must rise in terms of clothing.

But we have no way of knowing what increased labour abundance will do to the relative price of food and clothing. This could remain unchanged. Or, if food production happened to be more expandable by variable labour than is clothing production—as in the Cobb–Douglas case where labour's share in food costs exceeds its share in clothing costs—increased labour abundance must raise the ratio of clothing price to food price; hence the real food-land rent *in terms of clothing* need not necessarily be raised by labour abundance.

What about the effect of labour abundance on the real rent of clothing-land in terms of social product itself? No invariable result can be predicted. There is perhaps a presumption that labour abundance will be likely to raise any land's real rent—certainly all lands' rents together must be raised—but it is possible that the deterioration of food-land's real wage in terms of clothing could be so great as to make it drop in terms of social product.[1]

Summary. Labour abundance raises the real rents of each land in terms of its own products. Relative prices can move in either direction depending upon how strongly labour encounters diminishing returns in various industries. If a particular good's relative price is much raised, the other land may experience a drop in real rents relative to it (and even relative to social product).

A balanced increase in both lands is just like a reduction in labour alone. All rents together are lowered in terms of social product as the real wage in those terms rises (along a reversible two-variable "factor-price frontier").

Fig. 3*a* summarizes the effect of labour abundance in the production-possibility frontier. The new equilibrium must involve more of all goods, but otherwise there are no restrictions on the possibilities.[2]

---

[1] If labour and food-land are infinitely great substitutes and labour and clothing-land are infinitely-strong complements, the "perverse" result will follow at high labour supplies.

[2] To prove this, suppose the contrary that one good, say food, failed to increase. It's price would then rise relative to that of clothing. But how then could the extra supply of clothing have been coaxed out? Thus we are led to the proposition that both goods must increase.

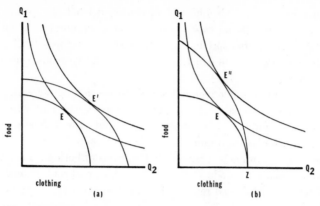

Fig. 3. (a) Labour abundance shifts us from E to E', lowering the real wage in terms of all goods and affecting food-clothing price ratio depending upon enhanced labour encounters diminishing returns in the respective industries. At least one real rent must rise in terms of social product; there is a weak presumption that both may rise. (b) Increased food-land pivots the production-possibility frontier vertically around unchanged maximum clothing intercept at Z. The quantity of food produced grows relative to that of clothing. The price of food will fall relative to that of clothing, and the real rent of food-land will fall in terms of all goods. If food-clothing demands are very low in elasticity of substitution, the real rent of the unchanged supply of clothing-land will rise and so will the real wage. If the food-clothing demand substitution is very elastic (as happens to be shown here), the real rent of clothing-land will fall in terms of clothing, social product, and even food.

Food-land-abundance. We may briefly describe the increase, in a closed economy with Ricardo–Viner technology and homothetic demand, of an increase in one land alone, say food-land. As Fig 2a shows, this tilts the production-possibility frontier vertically around the unchanged intercept of maximum clothing production. Hence food must be cheapened relative to clothing. The legend to Fig. 2a describes the reduction in food-land rent and probable[1] increase in the real wage and real clothing-land rents.

Summary. An increase in food-land lowers its real rent and the relative price of food. It will necessarily raise the real rent return of one other factor, labour- or clothing-land; it must raise their combined return. Elasticity-of-substitution of final demand tends to bring down clothing-land rent as food-land increases. Although food-land abundance always raises the real wage in terms of food, clothing might become so dear that the real wage in clothing could fall, and fall enough to reduce the real wage in terms of social product.

---

[1] Real social product is a concave homogenous-first-degree function of labour, food-land, clothing-land, $q = q(V_0, V_1, V_2)$, with real factor prices in terms of social product given by $[\partial q/\partial V_i] = [w_0, w_1, w_2]$ and $[\partial w_i/\partial V_j] = [\partial^2 q/\partial V_i \partial V_j] = [\partial w_j/\partial V_i]$. For any i, one $\partial w_i/\partial V_i$ must be positive. The symmetry of this Hessian matrix tells us that the case described two footnotes back, in which an increase in labour reduces real food-land rent, must here invoke a reduction in food land.

Factor shares. So far I have been discussing effects of a factor change on relative-factor and good prices. What about relative factor shares? Classical economists of Ricardo's day were perhaps susceptible to the confusion that an increase in a factor-price, as e.g. land rent, also means an increased share of rent in national income. We know that shares can move in any direction, depending upon elasticities of productivity and on elasticities of substitution. How relative shares are affected by factor-augmenting substitution, in which one of a factor now does the work of more than one, will depend on those same elasticities.

Cobb–Douglas case. Before leaving the closed economy, I should describe the double Cobb–Douglas case in which the proportions of the consumer dollar spent on the different goods are constant and the proportions of each industry's costs going to labour are also constant. In this case social output is itself a simple Cobb–Douglas function of the three factors

$$q = b V_0^{k_0} V_1^{k_1} V_2^{k_2}, \quad \sum_0^2 k_j = 1$$

Thus, suppose labour always gets three-fourths of national income with food-land getting 0.15 and clothing-land 0.10. Then $[k_0, k_1, k_2] = [0.75, 0.15, 0.10]$. This would result from a 0.70 labour share in food, a 0.80 labour share in clothing, and fifty-fifty expenditure on the two goods. If $[\lambda_1, \lambda_2]$ are labour's shares in the two industries and $[\alpha_1, \alpha_2]$ are the good's share of consumption dollar,

$$k_0 = \alpha_1 \lambda_1 + \alpha_2 \lambda_2, \quad k_1 = \alpha_1(1 - \lambda_1), \quad k_2 = \alpha_2(1 - \lambda_2)$$

$$k_i = \alpha_i(1 - \lambda_i)$$

In general, for any double Cobb–Douglas model, not necessarily Ricardo–Viner in technology, the factor shares in national income, $[k_i]$, are related to the factor shares in the jth industry, $[k_{ij}]$, and the shares of the j industry of the consumption dollar, $[\alpha_j]$, by the matrix identity,

$$[k_i] = [k_{ij}][\alpha_j]$$

The Cobb–Douglas case displays no perverse properties, as the following shows.

Summary. Increasing any factor lowers its real return, raises the real return of all other factors, and lowers the relative price of the good in which its factor-cost-share is relatively largest.

V. Various Geographical Endowments and Trade

Identical Endowments. If two regions have the same endowments of labour,

food-land, and clothing-land, uniformity of tastes will produce identical factor-prices, commodity prices and of course no international trade.

If the two regions differ in scale, but all factor proportions are the same,
the same absolute equalisation will result under our assumption of uniform
(homothetic) tastes. Not only will there be no international trade in goods;
even if factors could move between regions, there would be no incentive for
them to do so.

Disproportionate endowments. Suppose Region A has relatively more food-
land, Region B has relatively more clothing-land. Before trade, A will have
relatively cheap food and B will have relatively cheap clothing. Real wages
could be about equal in the two regions, the cheapness of one good just balancing the dearness of the other. Regional real outputs could also happen
to be equal; but of course food-land rents would still be relatively low in A,
and clothing-land rents relatively low in B.

If free trade is allowed, A will export food in exchange for B's exporting
clothing. Both regions will be better off at the equalised commodity prices.
With the international price ratio of clothing to food lower than Region A's
autarky prices, A will shift labour from clothing to food thereby somewhat
easing the redundancy and cheapness of its abundant factor, food-land. In
B, trade has the opposite effect causing it to produce for export the good for
which it has factor abundance: shifting labour from food to clothing tends to relieve the dearness of its scarce factor and relieve the cheapness of its plentiful
factor.

*All this leads, in the Ohlin manner, to partial but not complete factor-price
equalisation.*

To depict this Fig. 4 shows the autarky equilibrium for Region A at a, and
for Region B at b. Region B happens to have the higher national product by
virtue of its superabundance of, say, food-land. Perhaps its autarky real wage
is also higher.

Fig. 4 also shows the effects of the free interregional trade. A's final equilibrium is at E_a and and a'; B's final equilibrium is at E_b and b'; the common
international price ratio, which is intermediate between the two autarky prices,
is found on that common ray-from-the-origin, $0 E_a E_b$, at which the regions'
trade vectors $a' E_a$ and $E_b b'$ exactly match. Both regions get improved national
products, GNP's, from trade. But in each region there is a shift in production
toward greater specialization on the good which is relatively intensive in its
abundant factor; these trade-induced shifts in production raise the relative
factor prices of each region's relatively abundant factor from its autarky
cheapness, thereby *tending* to equalise factor prices internationally.

If Region A ends up with a real wage higher than in autarky but still lower
than that in Region B, the tendency toward equalisation will not have gone
all the way; it will have been only partial, in vindication of Ohlin's original
contention.

Swed. J. of Economics 1971

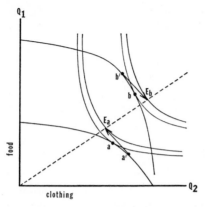

Fig. 4. Region B, above, has more food-land than Region A. In autarky, A at a has higher clothing-land price than B; at its autarky point b, Region B has relatively lower real rent of food-land. Free trade leads to equilibrium at E_a and E_b, where trade vectors $a'E_a$ and $E_b b'$ exactly match, and where the common international price ratio is between the autarky price ratios. Each region increases production of that good which has much of its relatively abundant factor: the move from b to b' involves shift of labour in B to food production, thereby relieving the cheapness of food-land and the dearness of clothing-land there; the move from a at a' has similar Ohlin influence, relieving the cheapness of A's relatively plentiful resource. Trade in goods partially equalises factor prices. [Alternate interpretation of diagram: suppose B has more labour than A, and food is more labour intensive than clothing. The production shifts due to trade then alleviate the dearness of A's labour and the cheapness of B's abundant labour.]

VI. Need for Factor Mobility

Mobility of goods has not been able to serve as a complete substitute for factor mobility in equalising all factor prices. With after-trade real wages lower in A than in B (in *all* goods!), labour has motivation to migrate from A to B if there are now no costs to such migration. As more and more labour migrates, A's real wage rises and B's falls. Finally, they must come into equality, at which point migration will cease. The present Viner–Ricardo technology has the remarkable property that none of the factors other than labour need migrate to achieve optimal world production and complete factor-price equalisation!

Theorem. In a general technology, when goods' prices are equalised by free trade, all the different factors may have unequal factor returns; factor-mobility *in all but one of the factors* will generally be needed to achieve full factor-price equalisation and maximal world production.

In a Viner–Ricardo technology, where labour is the only resource transferable between industries, it will always suffice for labour alone to be capable of migration to achieve full factor-price equalisation.

To prove this strong result, note that if the real wage at E_a is less (in every good) than at E_b, the fact that each region produces every good implies that

Swed. J. of Economics 1971

every real rent is greater in Region A than in B. A glance back at Fig. 2*a* confirms that, within each and every industry, there is a unique tradeoff between its real wage and real rent.[1] By the same token, as migration of labour from A to B proceeds far enough to achieve real-wage equality, it must lower all of A's real rents into exact equality with B's rising real rents, *Q.E.D.*

The point is that if the mountains will not come to Mohammed, Mohammed can go to the mountains. It does not matter that there are now many kinds of mountains—food-land, clothing-land, etc. For, these mountains do not have to interact with each other, but each need only interact with labour. The ability of labour migration to compensate by itself for immobility of all the other factors will hold in a Viner–Ricardo technology for any number of goods, $n \geqslant 2$, provided labour works with one specialized resource in each industry. It fails to hold wherever one or more industries involve more than one non-labour factor, which are distributed in unequal proportions among the regions: e.g., suppose the food-industry in Region A involves a different ratio of (food-land)' to (food-land)" than the ratio prevailing in Region B; then complete factor-price equalisation would involve, if you can imagine it, migration of one of these food-lands as well as labour.

VII. The Singular Case of Complete Equalisation By Trade

The case in the previous section, in which Region B begins with relatively more of food-land but in which labour migrates from A to B to equalise all factor prices, alerts us to an interesting possibility. Evidently there *can* be situations in which free trade in goods will alone suffice to equlaise factors returns all the way.

Consider the geographical configuration after labour has migrated enough to equalise the free-trade real wage. Region B still has more of food-land than does Region A. Suppose trade in goods is now prohibited, then autarky regimes will involve lower food-land rents in B, lower clothing-land rents in A, and lower food-clothing price ratio in B than A.[2]

---

[1] This suggests a slight paradox. Region A began with *relatively* much clothing-land, and hence at autarky *a* presumably began with lower real clothing-land rent than at B's autarky point *b*. But free trade ended A with higher real clothing-land rent, r_2, than in B. Hence, goods' mobility caused on overshoot in which this factor-price went from divergence in one direction over to divergence in the opposite direction. On reflection, we perceive no reason why this should not occur.

[2] The autarky real wage in terms of clothing will presumably be higher in A; in B the autarky real wage will presumably be higher in terms of food. Which region will have the higher autarky real wage in terms of social product—that is, which region will have workers "better off"—we cannot say. Suppose the real wage, $w = W/P_q$, happens to be the same in both regions. Then even if labour could migrate, it would not choose to do so. Why should it? Consequently, in the absence of goods' trade, the world will be stuck permanently in a geographical configuration which fails to maximize total world production of food and clothing. More precisely, we are not out on the world's maximal production-possibility frontier of $(Q_1 = Q_1^A + Q_1^B, \ Q_2 = Q_2^A + Q_2^B)$ production with world totals of $(L = L^A + L^B, \ V_1 = V_1^A + V_1^B, \ V_2 = V_2^A + V_2^B)$. But, if goods cannot be freely moved, what significance is there to a sum like $Q_i^A + Q_i^B$?

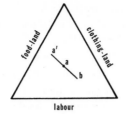

(a) Lerner–Samuelson Model   **(b) Ricardo–Viner Model**

Fig. 5. In the 5(a) model, all economies nearly like a given economy that is at *a* will have complete factor-price-equalisation—as shown by the two-dimensional shaded area. In the present 5(b) model, only those economies near the point *a* that are on a linear razor's edge will have equalised prices.

These geographical divergences of factor returns imply that if, and only if, two out of three factors of the factors are now free to migrate internationally, would world total products, as measured by global GNP measures or by p–p frontiers, be maximized in the absence of trade.

In short, only with free trade in goods does it suffice to have labour alone migrate in order to maximize world production efficiency. The previous theorem about Ricardo–Viner technology does not apply to autarky situations: for them, some mountains must move (along with labour) to another mountain.

But now revert to the situation in which labour mobility did give rise to the complete equalisation of factor returns under free trade. Freeze all factor movements from this point on. Nonetheless, by hypothesis, introducing free trade will equalise all factor returns. Since free trade succeeds in equalising all factor returns, and since they are not equalised in autarky, clearly we have produced a case in which—contrary to the strong Ohlin dictum—*free trade happens to lead to complete rather than partial factor-price equalisation.*

This singular case resembles the Lerner–Samuelson model in the sense that it contradicts the Uzawa–Ohlin dictum of *necessarily*-partial-rather-than-complete factor-price equalisation. However, I do think that the reader who re-examines Ohlin's argumentations and my 1948 exegesis of them could interpret him to believe that only-partial factor-price equalisation is most likely rather than that complete factor-price equalisation is logically impossible.[1] Ohlin, as a follower of Heckscher, could hardly have thought otherwise.

Ohlin's weaker dictum, that partial rather than complete equalisation is most likely, is confirmed, not refuted, by the present singular case. Thus, the

---

[1] It is Ellsworth's textbook, in its attempt to provide a proof for Ohlin, that does purport to demonstrate the logical impossibility of complete equalization. Cf. my 1948 discussion of P. T. Ellsworth, *International Economics* (MacMillan, London 1937). In a real sense, the present singular case does refute what might be called the Ellsworth–Uzawa contention.

present Ricardo–Viner example, precisely because it is singular, does differ from the Lerner–Samuelson model in which all-the-way equalisation is the rule rather than the exception. Fig. 5b shows how the present example differs from 5a's Lerner–Samuelson three-good three-factor model. In both cases, three factors, (V_0, V_1, V_2), are represented by points inside the equilateral triangles: the amount of V_i is proportional to the distance from any point to the ith side; and for all points the sum of the distances add up to the same normalization constant.

Consider the point a in 5a. All other regions, that have geographical endowments "near to" those of Region A, in the sense of falling into the two dimensional shaded are around a, will come into complete factor-price equalisation with Region A.

By contrast, look at 5b. Here, only on a singular razor's edge, the locus $a'ab$, will there be complete factor-price equalisation from trade alone. Elsewhere near a, and that means for "almost all" nearby points, the factor-price equalisation will be at best partial.

How do we recognize this singular locus along which free trade can achieve full factor-price equalisation. It is easy. Imagine both countries initially alike, at a. Now, take some fraction of the labour and food-land that work together in A's food industry and, without altering their proportion, send them both in a dose to Region B to work along with that same labour/food-land ratio in B's food industry. And, if you like, take some fraction of the labour and clothing-land in Region B and send them in a dose to A. Then the "new B" will be at b in Fig. 5b and the "new A" will be at a'. But with free trade in goods, it will be the case that the final equilibrium for a' and b will involve the same world productions (and consumptions) as at a's autarky; and exactly the same (equalised) factor returns; from a' clothing will be exported in return for an equal value of the food exported from b. It is no accident that the now-unbalanced productions of each region can be worked off by trade. By contrast, contemplate what happens at a' and b under autarky. At a' there would be too much clothing produced, if—as will actually happen under autarky—some labour were not shifted to the food-land there. Similarly, new Region B will, under autarky, shift some labour from food to clothing production. Hence, the pre-trade prices would, under uniform tastes, have been quite different at a' and b: the former has lower clothing and clothing-land prices, the latter, lower food and foodland prices. And it is free trade in goods that suceeds in restoring the complete equality of all relative prices that had prevailed at a. (The mathematical appendix explains why $a'ab$ is linear.)[1]

---

[1]Ricardo–Viner technology aside, such a singular case can always be found. Proof: start Regions A and B alike, with r factors and n goods. Send from A to B doses of factors in the proportions of one (or more) industry. Under autarky, this will hurt the over all well-being of both regions as domestic productions are distorted toward a "more balanced" configuration. But with free trade in goods, all regional productions can take place with the same factor-proportions of the original equal-endowment configuration. *Q.E.D.*

Swed. J. of Economics 1971

VIII. Conclusions

1. The simple Ricardo–Viner model, involving n goods, will involve $r = n + 1 > n$ factors, labour plus a specialised land for each good. We know from the standard analysis of factor-price equalisation that, when the number of factors exceeds the number of goods, no complete factor-price equalisation can be expected from trade alone. (E.g., with one good and two factors, corn produced by labour and land, no one expects regions of different labour/land endowments to end up with equal wages or rents in the absence of factor mobility.)

2. Nonetheless, taste differences aside, free trade in goods will benefit each region and *all* regions in the aggregate. Within this Ricardo–Viner model, the patterns of trade will, in the Ohlin fashion, involve each region's exporting the good whose input requirements it happens to have in special abundance. Production adaptations to trade will thus tend to raise the factor-prices of the most abundant inputs, which would otherwise be cheapest under autarky. The trade-induced movement of factor-prices toward equality, and away from geographically-induced diversity, will generally be only *partially* equalising. With labour's post-trade real wage ending up different in two regions, goods' trade falls short of permitting that maximal world production which migration of labour (of labour alone!) could effectuate.

3. If labour works with more than one immobile land, and if such lands do not occur in the same proportions geographically, we have $r > n + 1$, and there is no useful sense in which we can say labour produces within the "same" production functions internationally. Hence, no factor-price equalisation is to be expected.[1] Also, in real life, taste differences must be expected to complicate the analysis, particularly when they are not random.

Mathematical Appendix

1. Let the $(i = 1, 2, ..., n)$ outputs of the $(j = 1, 2, ..., J)$ countries be denoted by $[Q_i^j]$. Each is produced by the inputs (L_i^j, V_i^j), according to the concave homogeneous-first-degree production functions

$$Q_i^j = F_i(L_i^j, V_i^j) = V_i^j Q_i(L_i^j / V_i^j)$$

The total factor endowments of the jth country are given by

$$(L^j, V_1^j, ..., V_n^j) = (\sum_i L_i^j, V_1^j, ..., V_n^j).$$

2. Tastes and demand are summarized by a uniform homothetic set of indifference contours in terms of the n goods consumed, either in a region or in the world,

---

[1] When labour works with more than one specialized land, we need the Inada conditions to rule out the shutting down of production of some goods in some regions. Such specializations are actually realistic.

$$u = u[C_1, ..., C_n]$$

where u is a homogeneous-first-degree concave function.

For simplicity, regularity conditions are placed on the u and F_i functions so that they are smooth, with positive partial derivatives for positive arguments, and satisfying so-called Inada conditions whereby the partial derivative with respect to any variable goes from $+\infty$ to 0 as that variable goes from 0 to $+\infty$ for any positive levels of the other variables.[1]

3. Autarky equilibrium for any region with $(L, V_1, ..., V_n)$ endowment is defined by

$$P_i/W = Q_i'(L_i/V_i)^{-1} = S_i(Q_i) \quad (i = 1, ..., n)$$

$$L_1 + ... + L_n = L$$

$$\frac{P_i/W}{P_1/W} = \frac{\partial u[Q_1, ..., Q_n]/\partial Q_i}{\partial u[Q_1, ..., Q_n]/\partial Q_1} \quad (i = 2, ..., n) \tag{1}$$

Here W is the wage rate, $[P_i]$ the prices, $[W/P_i]$ the real wages in terms of the respective goods, and $S_i(Q_i)$ the rising marginal cost functions easily derivable from the production functions $Q_i(L_i/V_i)$, with $S_i(0) = 0$ and $S_i(\infty) = \infty$. The $3n$ variables, $[Q_i, L_i, P_i/W]$ are uniquely defined by the $2n + 1 + (n-1)$ equations of (1).

The comparative statics of the equilibrium, as we change any or all of $(L, V_1, ..., V_n)$, can be largely summarized in terms of the derivable function of social product

$$U = q(L, V_1, ..., V_n)$$

$$= \underset{L_i}{\text{Max}}\, u[V_1 Q_1(L_1/V_1), ..., V_n Q_n(L_n/V_n)]$$

subject to $\displaystyle\sum_{i=1}^{n} L_i = L \equiv V_0;$ $\tag{2}$

namely, by

$$w = r_0 = q_0(L, V_1, ..., V_n) = \partial q/\partial L = \partial q/\partial V_0$$

$$r_i = q_i(L, V_1, ..., V_n) = \partial q/\partial V_i$$

$$\partial r_i/\partial V_j = \partial^2 q/\partial V_i \partial V_j = q_{ij} = q_{ji} \quad (i, j = 0, 1, ..., n) \tag{3}$$

Here w is the real wage in terms of social product, r_i the similar real rents, and, by convention, L and V_0 are used interchangeably. By concavity and homogeneity (q_{ij}) is negative semi-definite.

---

[1] Inada conditions are more popular in the textbook than in the real world. If marginal productivities and marginal costs begin at positive intercepts, the equations below must be qualified by inequalities. When specialization causes some goods not to be produced at all in a particular region, that enhances Ohlin's case for partial rather than complete equalisation, just as in the Lerner–Samuelson model.

Continuing to use real social product, q, as numeraire, with $P_q \equiv 1$, the real prices $P_i/P_q = p_i$ are equal to

$$p_i = \partial u[Q_1, ..., Q_n]/\partial Q_i$$

$$= q_0(L, V_1, ..., V_n)/Q_i'(L_i/V_i) \quad (i = 1, ..., n) \tag{4}$$

Also

$$w = W/P_q = r_0$$

$$r_i = R_i/P_q = (R_i/P_i)p_i = [Q_i(L_i/V_i) - (W/P_i)(L_i/V_i)]p_i$$

For $n = 2$, it is not hard to show that

$$\partial(W/P_i)/\partial L < 0$$

$$\partial(W/P_i)/\partial V_i > 0. \quad (i = 1, 2)$$

For the limiting cases where the indifference contours are respectively of ∞ and 0 elasticities of substitution, the matrix

$$[\partial r_i/\partial V_j] = \begin{bmatrix} q_{00} & q_{01} & q_{02} \\ q_{10} & q_{11} & q_{12} \\ q_{20} & q_{21} & q_{22} \end{bmatrix}$$

has sign patterns $\begin{bmatrix} - & + & + \\ + & - & - \\ + & - & - \end{bmatrix}$ and $\begin{bmatrix} - & + & + \\ + & - & + \\ + & + & - \end{bmatrix}$,

but I do not see that, for intermediate cases, it is forbidden to have the pattern

$$\begin{bmatrix} - & - & + \\ - & - & + \\ + & + & - \end{bmatrix}$$

4. Free trade in goods leads to equilibrium defined by

$$P_i/W^j = Q_i'(L_i^j/V_i^j)^{-1} = S_i(Q_i^j), \quad (i = 1, ..., n; j = 1, ..., J) \tag{5 a}$$

$$L_1^j + ... + L_n^j = L^j \tag{5 b}$$

$$P_1(C_1^j - Q_1^j) + ... + P_n(C_n^j - Q_n^j) = 0 \tag{5 c}$$

$$P_i/P_1 = u_i[\textstyle\sum_j Q_1^j, ..., \sum_j Q_n^j]/u_1[\sum_j Q_1^j, ..., \sum_j Q_n^j], \quad (i = 2, ..., n) \tag{5 d}$$

$$\frac{P_i/W^j}{P_1/W^j} = u_i[C_1^j, ..., C_n^j]/u_1[C_1^j, ..., C_n^j] \tag{5 e}$$

Here $[C_i^j]$ is the amount consumed of the ith good in the jth country and

$u_i[\ ]$ stands for $\partial u[\ ]/\partial C_i$. The P's denote prices in *any* common international unit.

It is of interest to note that, if one is interested only in the equilibrium of international prices and real wages, and not in the pattern of trade and of regional consumption breakdown, all the relations of (5) involving C's, namely (5c) and (5e) can be ignored in this homothetic case: the equations (5a), (5b), (5d), which are $2nJ+J+(n-1)$ in number, suffice to determine uniquely the nJ $[Q_i^j]$, the nJ $[L_i^j]$, the J $[P_1/W^j]$ and the $(n-1)$ $[P_i/P_1]$.

If we then add the J balance-of-payments equations of (5c) and the $J(n-1)$ domestic consumption-demand equations of (5e), we further determine uniquely the remaining Jn consumption unknowns $[C_i]$.

Heuristically, and for that matter rigorously, we can determine all the post-trade real wages and rents from the following maximum problem:

$$U^*(L^1, V_1^1, ..., V_n^1; ...; L^J, V_1^J, ..., V_n^J)$$

$$= \underset{L_i^j}{\mathrm{Max}}\, u\left[\sum_{j=1}^{J} V_1^j\, Q_1(L_1^j, V_1^j), ..., \sum_{j=1}^{J} V_n^j\, Q_n(L_n^j, V_n^j)\right]$$

$$\text{subject to } \sum_{i=1}^{n} L_i^j = L^j \quad (j=1, ..., J) \tag{6}$$

If all prices, wages, and rent are expressed in a single currency unit, one can prove

$$W^j/W^1 = (\partial U^*/\partial L^j)/(\partial U^*/\partial L^1) \quad (j=2, ..., J)$$

$$R_i^j/W^j = (\partial U^*/\partial V_i^j)/(\partial U^*/\partial L^j) \quad (j=1, ..., J; i=1, ..., n) \tag{7}$$

Here R_i denotes the rent of the ith land in the jth country.

5. Equilibrium with factor mobility, which the text has shown need involve only labour mobility in the Ricardo–Viner model, is defined by the same equations as (5), but with the allocation of total L among regions now to be determined by the additional equations involving geographically-equalised real wages. In a free-trade world, if the real wage in terms of any good, say the first, is equalised regionally, *all* real wages are equalised. Hence, we can adjoin to (5)

$$P_1/W^1 = P_1/W^2 = ... = P_1/W^J \tag{5f}$$

These are the $J-1$ new equations needed to determine the new $J-1$ interregional allocations $[L^j]$ of the given world labor supply to achieve complete equalisation and efficiency.

6. Again, heuristically, we can determine the equilibrium real wages and real rents when both factors and goods are mobile, without using (5a)–(5f), but merely from (1) applied to world totals

$$w = q_0(\sum_j L^j, \sum_j V_1^j, ..., \sum_j V_n^j)$$

$$r_i = q_i(\sum_j L^j, \sum_j V_1^j, ..., \sum_j V_n^j) \quad (i = 1, ..., n) \tag{8}$$

7. A valuable heuristic way of analysing the differences between full and partial factor-price equalisation has been provided by Uzawa in the cited 1959 paper. Full equalisation achieves a higher-order of welfare realisation than partial; partial achieves a higher-order than autarky; autarky under perfect competition achieves a higher order than other feasible autarky allocations. All these welfare concepts can be unambiguously handled by the device of production-possibility frontiers; or even better, in our case of uniform homothetic demands, by reckonings of achieved real GNP's.

The following equations characterise the three stages: complete factor-price equalisation, partial, and autarky.

$$q(\sum_j L^j, \sum_j V_1^j, ..., \sum_j V_r^j)$$

$$= \max_{L^j} U^*(L^1, V_1^1, ..., V_n^1; ...; L^J, V_1^J, ..., V_n^J) \tag{9 a}$$

labour mobility and free trade

$$\geqslant U^*(L^1, V_1^1, ..., V_n^1; ...; L^J, V_1^J, ..., V_n^J)$$

$$= \max_{L_i^j} u[\sum_j F_1(L_1^j, V_1^j), ..., \sum_j F_n(L_n^j, V_n^j)] \tag{9 b}$$

free trade

$$\geqslant \sum_j q(L^j, V_1^j, ..., V_r^j)$$

$$= \sum_j \max_{L_i^j} u[F_1(L_1^j, V_1^j), ..., F_n(L_n^j, V_n^j)] \tag{9 c}$$

autarky

Fig. 6 shows, symbolically, these relations. The outer frontier shows the situation when all factors are mobile, migrating to equalise all factor returns and give the world maximal production possibilities. The middle frontier shows the results of free trade in goods. As each nation is improved by trade, total world GNP (reckoned at the homothetic tastes) is higher than it is at autarky; however, if labour cannot move to wipe out any post-trade geographical differences in the real wage, the aggregate GNP under goods trade falls short of that under factor mobility.

These two frontiers are the productions that would be observed as the homothetic tastes changed their food-clothing intensities, running the gamut from one extreme to the other. What then is the inner frontier? It represents the world sums of all autarky productions that would be engendered by the

Swed. J. of Economics 1971

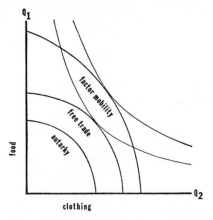

Fig. 6. The outer frontier shows world production possibilities when factors can move optimally—or, in the Ricardo–Viner case, when labour can move to equalise the post-trade real wage rate. The intermediate frontier shows world totals produced when goods can move freely in trade but factors are immobile. The inner curve shows what world production totals would be, as tastes changed uniformly in each county toward one good or the other, and when neither goods nor factors can move between regions. If resource endowments were the same in all regions, all three curves would coincide. In singular cases, the present Ricardo–Viner model could have the intermediate curve tangential to the outer frontier. This is in contrast to the Lerner–Samuelson model in which the two outer curves coincide for all regions that are near enough alike.

same change in tastes.[1] The fact that that this inner locus lies inside the middle one, represents the production inefficiency attributable to autarky. But, in a sense, there is a further consumption inefficiency as well: thus, suppose all countries under autarky have the same well-being. That "average level" will be less than the average level that would be read off the homothetic indifference contour going through the relevant point on the inner curve, even after proper allowance is made for the number of people: people are, so to speak, forced under autarky to consume "unbalanced" diets.

It is possible, as we have seen, for the singular case to occur in which free trade in goods is a full substitute for factor mobility. In such a case the middle frontier must touch the outer frontier in at least one place. However, save in the uninteresting case of identical geographical endowments—when all these curves are identical and no mobility will ever be used—the inner curve can never touch the intermediate frontier.

The mathematical condition for the singular case to occur can be written down briefly for the case of two regions, A and B. Suppose with balanced

---

[1] E.g., write a Cobb–Douglas $u = Q_1^k Q_2^{1-k}$ and let k go from zero to one. Or write a fixed-proportions $u = \mathrm{Min}\,[Q_1/k,\ Q_2/(1-k)]$ with $0 < k < 1$. These two alternatives will generate the same two outer frontiers, for the reason that those frontiers each represent solutions to maximal production problems under specified constraints. But the precise shape of the inner locus need not be the same.

endowments, equilibrium would take place with uniform world prices proportional to $(W, P_1, ..., P_n, R_1, ..., R_n)$ and with industry i everywhere using, per unit of output, a_{0i} of labour and a_{ii} of V_i. Let the migration of the ith factor from A to B be written as ΔV_i. Then, full factor-price equalisation will be preserved by free trade provided

$$\Delta V_0 = \sum_{i=1}^{n} (a_{0i}/a_{ii}) \Delta V_i \tag{10}$$

even though factor endowments have now become relatively different. After such migration, the same equilibrium prices will prevail under free trade, and the same total world productions and consumptions. However, were all tastes now to change, it would be virtually impossible for free trade in goods to continue to keep real wages geographically the same. Thus, if A now has relatively much food production and tastes turn toward food rather than clothing, how can that help but give B lower real wages? So the intermediate locus is touched only at the one singular point.

Examination of (9c) shows that (1) expresses the necessary condition for its maximum condition. Similarly, for (9b), the conditions (5a, b, d) are necessary. To achieve (9a), (5f) must be satisfied as well.

8. If labour works with more than one specialized resource in any industry, V_i must be interpreted as a vector, being short for $(V_{i1}, V_{i2}, ..., V_{ik_i})$, where k_i is the number of non-labour factors in the ith industry. Then (5a) must be replaced by

$$P_i/W^j = \partial F(L_i^j, V_i^j)/\partial L_i^j = S_i(Q_i^j), \quad (i = 1, ..., n) \tag{11}$$

$$P_i/R_{ik}^j = \partial F(L_i^j, V_i^j)/\partial V_{ik}^j, \quad (k = 1, ..., k_i)$$

and a similar rewriting of (1) is needed.

But now, migration of labour alone will not suffice to achieve complete factor price equalisation. The single condition of (5f) must be augmented, so that the numerous following all hold:

$$\frac{P_i}{R_{ik}^1} = \frac{P_i}{R_{ik}^2} = ... = \frac{P_i}{R_{ik}^J}, \quad (i = 1, ..., n; k = 1, ..., k_i) \tag{12}$$

Only if all (or all but one) of the $r = 1 + k_1 + ... + k_n$ factors can migrate freely, singular cases aside, will these conditions be guaranteed.

9. What if goods involve transport costs? The simplest case is the following: as any good goes from Region A to B, or vice versa, only the fraction f_i arrives there. Clearly, as every $f_i \to 1$, the Ohlin rule of partial factor-price equalisation will prevail. But now two regions that differ only by a trifle in factor endowments will not be able to trade; and their factor returns will necessarily differ by a trifle permanently. Free labour migration will almost, but not quite, equalise factor returns. It will equalise the real wage reckoned

in terms of the homothetic tastes; but in regions of food-land abundance, the real wage in food will be compensatingly high and in clothing will be compensatingly low, with the rents unequal in the opposite directions. In real life, tastes are not uniform, and sun lovers migrate toward the sun.

255

Equalisation of Factor Prices by Sufficiently Diversified Production Under Conditions of Balanced Demand

PAUL A. SAMUELSON*†

1.

If we have two factors ('labour and land') and one good, the slightest geographical difference in factor endowments will make factor prices unequal. If a second good is added that differs not at all in factor intensities from the first, the same conclusion holds.

If there are two goods that differ in their factor intensities and factor endowments are identical, factor prices will be equal. A slight perturbation in relative endowments will not suffice to upset this factor-price equalisation. But sufficiently large differentiation of geographical endowments must, even under strong differences in factor intensities of the two goods, ultimately destroy factor-price equalisation by leading to complete specialisation.

What happens as we increase indefinitely the number of goods[1] of 'intrinsically-differing factor intensities'? If demand is kept 'balanced', the present paper shows that such an increase in numbers must result eventually in factor-price equalisation

* Massachusetts Institute of Technology.

† I owe thanks to the National Science Foundation for financial aid and to Mrs Jillian Pappas for editorial assistance.

[1] J. Vanek and T. J. Bertrand have considered related problems in the Kindleberger *Festschrift*, Chapter 3, i.e. in J. Bhagwati *et al.*, *Trade, Balance of Payments and Growth*, (Amsterdam: North Holland Publishing Company, 1971). They provide references to earlier articles by Tinbergen (1949), Meade (1950), Samuelson (1953), Land (1959), Johnson (1967, 1969), Vanek (1968), Bertrand (1969) and others.

no matter how large is the original discrepancy of the relative positive land/labour endowments geographically. And the same can be said to hold when there are three or more factors of production. The reader is warned that the rabbit of necessary factor-price equalisation is plucked out of the hat only because some strong assumptions are put into the hat.

2.

Definitions: Demand among n goods is said to be 'balanced' when equal amounts are always spent on every good. (This strong assumption could be somewhat relaxed, but not in this paper.) Two goods are, by definition, 'of intrinsically-differing labour/land intensities' if the shares of the factors in their production are constant and systematically different between goods; a set of $n = 2m + 1$ goods, by definition, are 'of intrinsically-differing factor intensities' if their labour/land shares (b_i) satisfy the lattice equalities

$$(b_m, b_{m-1}, \ldots, b_1, b_0, b_{-1}, \ldots, b_{-m})$$
$$= (a^m, a^{m-1}, \ldots, a, 1, a^{-1}, \ldots, a^{-m}) \qquad a > 1 \quad (1)$$

For m large, this assures that all relative factor intensities are 'well represented', particularly the two extremes. (Example: for $a = 2$, $m = 1$, we have $n = 3$ Cobb–Douglas production functions proportional to

$$(V_1^{1/2} V_2^{1/2}, \; V_1^{1/3} V_2^{2/3}, \; V_1^{2/3} V_2^{1/3})$$

Theorem (two-factor case): As the number of goods of 'intrinsically differing factor-intensities' increases toward infinity, factor-price equalisation occurs between any two regions no matter how far apart are their geographical endowment ratios. More precisely, equalisation occurs for all endowments satisfying

$$1 > A^*(a, m) < \frac{(\text{Labour/Land})_{\text{Region 1}}}{(\text{Labour/Land})_{\text{Region 2}}} < A^{**}(a, m) > 1 \quad (2)$$

where
$$\lim_{m \to \infty} \begin{cases} A^*(a, m) = 0 \\ A^{**}(a, m)^{-1} = 0 \end{cases}$$

Hence for m large enough factor-price equalisation is assured.

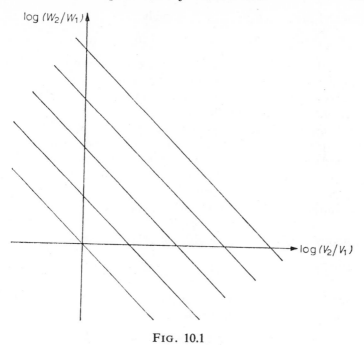

FIG. 10.1

Figure 10.1 can help explain the logic of what might otherwise seem like arbitrary assumptions. It portrays the well-known chart of factor/price ratio against factor proportions, but now on double-log scale so that the spread of the intensities can be identified with the statement that the parallel lines are distributed uniformly both on the right and the left of any intensity, *ad infinitum* in the limit.

3.

To generalise the result to any number of factors, retain the assumption of balanced demand. Now generalise the definition of a set of goods of 'essentially-differing factor intensities', in any one of a number of alternative ways, so as to ensure that the extreme poles – where each of r factors, taken by itself, suffices to produce a good – are increasingly well approximated as the number of goods is increased, i.e. the extreme points of relative shares of factors $(V_1, \ldots, V_1)$, namely

$$(1, 0, \ldots, 0) \cdots (0, 0, \ldots, \delta_{ij}, \ldots, 0), \ldots, (0, 0, \ldots, 0, 1),$$

$\delta_{ij} = 0$ if $i = j$ but $= 1$ otherwise, are each to be approximately approached in the limit by $1/r$ of the total expenditure. One such possible definition, suggested to me in talking with Professor Peter Diamond, is the following.

Definition: A set of goods are 'of essentially-differing r-factor intensities' if, for each of the r factors there is a sequence of goods which use it with its factor share being for a typical good of the sequence a^i times the shares of all the rest of the factors, all having equal shares, and where a^i becomes indefinitely great as the total number of goods increases.

Thus, for the first factor of $(V_1, \ldots, V_r)$, a typical sequence of goods would have the Cobb–Douglas functions

$$V_1^{c_i}(\prod_2^r V_k)^{(1-c_i)/(r-1)}, \quad c_i/(1 - c_i) = a^i \qquad (i = 0, 1, \ldots, m)$$

A similar sequence would occur for $V_2, \ldots,$ and finally for V_r, giving us $r(m + 1) = N$ goods in all.

> Theorem (for $r \geq 2$ factors): Under 'balanced demand', and for any number of factors, if there are enough goods N that are 'of effectively-differing factor intensities' equalisation of *all* factor prices is assured no matter how differentiated are geographical endowments of regions (provided only each region has positive amounts of all r factors.)

Specifically, factor prices are equalised between any two regions satisfying

$$1 > A^*(a, r, m) < \frac{[V_j \text{ endowment}/V_1 \text{ endowment}]_{\text{Region 1}}}{[V_j \text{ endowment}/V_1 \text{ endowment}]_{\text{Region 2}}} \qquad (3)$$

$$< A^{**}(a, r, m) > 1 \qquad (j = 2, \ldots, m)$$

with $\quad \lim_{m \to \infty} \begin{cases} A^*(a, r, m) = 0 \\ A^{**}(a, r, m)^{-1} \end{cases} \quad$ for $a > 1, r > 2$

Only a sketch of a proof will be given. Note that if an economy has two Cobb-Douglas functions, the factor share of any V_j would be the mean of the k_j coefficients of the two industries' production function, calculated by using as industry weights the industry's share of total demand. If there were n industries, the same weighted mean of the nk_j shares would give aggregate share of the jth factor. Now the definition of intrinsically-differing factor intensities is so contrived that, as $m \to \infty$ and the number of goods becomes larger and larger, the weight of expenditure becomes spent almost completely among the r polar cases where each of the r factors is in effect the *only* factor and is earning 100 per cent share in its industry's product. Thus, we end up indefinitely close to the case of a world characterised by r industries each using only one of the r factors peculiar to it. Obviously, a world with the production functions

$$Q_1 = V_1, Q_2 = V_2, \ldots, Q_r = V_r$$

will have the same real factor prices everywhere regardless of geographical partition of total factor endowments, provided only that all endowments are positive. With each factor working alone, regional specialisation is quite impossible. If any doubt about the proof remains, the reader can think of the above limiting case as being generated by the following kind of limit

$$Q_1 = V_1^{1-\varepsilon}\left(\prod_2^r V_j\right)^{\varepsilon/(r-1)}, \ldots, Q_r = (V_1 \cdots V_{r-1})^{\varepsilon/(r-1)} V_r^{1-\varepsilon} \quad (4)$$

with $\varepsilon \to 0$ as $m \to \infty$. Clearly, for any geographical dispersion of endowments, so long as every region has something of each factor, by making ε small enough we can ensure factor-price equalisation. The concept of 'diagonal dominance', first introduced by McKenzie, is used here with a vengeance.

Figure 10.2 illustrates, for $r = 3$ factors, the logic of the argument. Any industry point in Figure 2 represents, by its distance from the respective sides of the equilateral triangle, the relative shares of three factors in the indicated industry. As we move toward corner 1, say, the industry is more and more 'purely-labour (or V_1) intensive'. The definition of 'effectively-differing factor intensities' ensures that most industry points end up clustering indefinitely near one of each of the three corners being shown here, on the altitude lines,

$$[\tfrac{1}{2}, \tfrac{4}{5}, \ldots, 2^i/(1 + 2^i), \ldots]$$

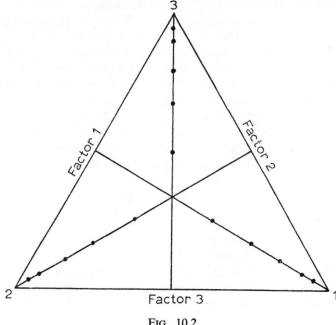

Fɪɢ. 10.2

fractions of the way toward the respective corners. That all the industry points fall on the angle-bisectors is a result of adopting the particular Diamond suggestion and is not an essential feature of a more general definition of 'differing factor intensities'.

4.

One singular, and surely objectionable, consequence of these strong assumptions of balanced demand and effectively-differentiated factor intensities is the fact that all r factors end up in the present model with equal shares. This is not at all an essential feature of the model: it would be easy to modify the assumption of balanced demand – as e.g. to assume that five times as much gets spent on land-intensive goods as on labour-intensive, with labour's final share of income being only one-sixth; but it is important for the present sufficiency conditions, that no significant expenditure must end up going for goods of mixed factor intensities, since otherwise one could not rule out completely specialised trade between diverse geographical regions.

It is of interest to note that the recent work of Professor Tinbergen has been with real-world models in which each nation should specialise in only a limited range of goods, which is in marked contrast with the non-specialisation results of the present artificial model. Empirical fact must decide among the competing theoretical models.

256

HERETICAL DOUBTS ABOUT THE
INTERNATIONAL MECHANISMS

P.A. SAMUELSON *

M.I.T. Cambridge, Mass.

1

An international system as illogical as the present one hardly has a long life expectancy. Its illogic was brought home to me when, in recent weeks, I tried to revise my elementary textbook to explain to the beginning student how the post-Smithsonian IMF system is supposed to operate. One realizes that the world is not made to suit the convenience of textbook writers; and no doubt an anthropologist describing the sex habits of Samoa or the unwritten constitution of British politics could not legitimately complain that his task had been made more difficult by the lack of logic of his subject matter. But surely in basic economics, if one is unable to discern an underlying efficacious mechanism contrived to restore equilibrium, that argues against the viability of the de facto arrangements.

Let me illustrate my meaning. The automatic gold standard with its Hume-specie-flow mechanism could be explained. And it could work. Or consider a clean-floating Chicago world. That can be explained and can presumably be made to work. The present system is, however, neither fish nor fowl. Currencies do not float freely; but when they are at their ceilings or floors in the widened 2¼ percent range, what is supposed to take place in the way of a disequilibrium-correcting mechanism in a world where the dollar is avowedly to remain inconvertible? I do not think that even Barnum could successfully resurrect the comfortable doctrine of benign neglect, in which the rest of the world is supposed to be content to swallow whatever dollars are thrust at it once the exchange rate has pushed the dollar to its allowed floor. And I doubt that there is any realism in an alternative mechanism which claims that (1) when other countries add dollars to their reserves, that automatically triggers off a new Hume mechanism in which their do-

* The author gratefully acknowledges aid from the National Science Foundation.

mestic money supply and cost levels rise proportionately, and that (2) when we lose dollars, this causes our M_1 (or M_2 or M_i) to fall proportionately, taking our flexible wages and prices down with it, and thereby (3) through differential cost-level movements finally raising the dollar's exchange rate into the middle of the widened band.

If you can believe that, you can believe anything. And I for one would not like to palm such an unconvincing doctrine off on innocent beginning students. Better to reserve it as the opiate of the international finance experts.

An alternative to this notion of the present system as a disguised Hume mechanism is the notion that, after the dollar has stayed for some not-very-long interval at its floor, that will be the excuse for another round of dollar depreciation relative to other currencies. If Mohammed will not adjust himself to the band, then we shall (without undue delay) move the band so that it manages to have Mohammed inside it. This second notion is equivalent to saying that the present scheme is a disguised form of free floating currencies à la Chicago.

This notion is not so absurd as the Hume one. But I wish I could believe that the present system could so simply turn itself into an effectively free-floating regime. After all, it took blood, sweat and tears to get the appreciations of 1971. Why should we expect this to become easier in the near future? (I mean the dollar adjustments, not the easier problem of floating for a small country like Canada or even, what is relevant as I write in late June, for the U.K.)

The most discouraging lines I have read in this symposium are those by Marcus Fleming in which he suggests that the gliding or crawling peg is an unlikely practical alternative in the near future. Discouraging because, in principle, such gradual currency parity adjustments could give us an equilibrating mechanism that is at least partway between the traditional Hume fixed-exchange and the free-floating regime of the utopian world ahead. If this halfway house is not feasible, we shall not, I fear, revert to one of the poles between which it is a non-golden mean. But rather, we are more likely, once the Smithsonian synthesis breaks down, to move into a regime of capital controls and of split exchange rates along the lines of the dual-franc.

With less but not negligible probability, once the Smithsonian agreement appears to have dissipated into anarchy and a mess, there is a danger that France will have gained adherents to the notion of bringing gold back as the basis of the international system. This will involve restoring a single-tier system, and doing so at the vastly higher dollar price of official gold that the South Africans, the French, the laissez-faire gold speculators, and the Milton Gilberts have so long been advocating. If this were to happen, it would be a shame – but not a tragedy. The best should never be made the ally of the bad. Seeking to demonetize gold is a worthy object. But if, for a variety of reasons, such an attempt breaks down and leads to a regime of widespread exchange controls, then make no mistake about it – such an outcome would be worse than a rewinding of the old gold-exchange standard at new generous valuations of gold. Such an outcome will mean a glorious opportunity lost – to replace gold by a more rational reserve asset. But it will not mean, despite the dreams of Zurich burghers or the hopes of Dr. Rueff, a new crucifixion of mankind on a cross of gold – or even a disciplining of the macroeconomic policies of modern mixed economies. If the price of gold were quadrupled, that would merely give Presidents and Chancellors a new ration of wild oats to sow. It would not mean price levels less inflated 10 or 20 years from now; but rather higher average prices then. Of all the gold bugs, only Sir Roy Harrod has seen this, and it is not his hopes that will be cheated in the event but the hopes of the gnomes and the Rueffs.

2

What is the major stumbling block to our fashioning a new and viable system? I don't think it is in the asymmetric position of the dollar, a factor much exaggerated by non-economists and somewhat exaggerated by international experts. To speak of a pre-1914 gold-pound standard and a pre-1971 gold-dollar standard is poetry not prose. And I don't think it's very good verse. Even the fact that exchange-rate interventions tend to be made in terms of dollars rather than official gold or SDR's does not, I believe, create a qualitative difference between an n-1 and an $n(n$-1$)/2$ system.[1]

---

[1] To be sure, there is a minor quantitative difference between how much (1) the *numeraire* currency, the dollar, can vary in ratio to any other currency, and (2) how much the ratio between two non-*numeraire* currencies can vary – when the IMF rule of a maximum 2¼% range is in effect.

$$\pi_i(1.0225)^{-1} \leq p_i/p_0 \leq \pi_i(1.0225)$$

Let me try to restate in a more prosaic and correct — albeit informal — manner the various factors upon which the special willingness to hold dollars (or any key currency) would depend. [2]

From 1933 to, say, 1955, the dollar was if anything undervalued. Attitudes grew up about the dollar that were based on that fact. Such attitudes were slow to change, but not impervious to change. In particular, Bretton Woods occurred when the American economy and the dollar were most dominant. And this explains many of the Bretton Woods arrangements, and also their inappropriateness and breakdown once America and the dollar lost their primacy.

The world has never been on a dollar standard, anymore than it was earlier on a pound standard. Under the automatic gold standard the dollar and gold were interchangeable: the dollar was as good as gold but no better; gold was as good as the dollar. The dollar could be better than gold only in the event that the automatic standard broke down in a downward revaluation of the dollar price of gold. As long as the dollar was undervalued, prudent men had to reckon the possibility of parity changes and revaluations; when prudent men did so, they had a right to think that the dollar might, after the next change, have its terms of trade improve vis à vis other stores of value. So, in 1948, you could still be deemed a prudent man if you thought the dollar was better than gold.

How long can you act like an idiot and still be deemed a prudent man? By the late 1950s, everybody but the bulk of the international experts could see that the next time there was to be a drastic change in currency parities and gold valuations it was going to be *against* the dollar, not in favor of it. Such an expectation does a lot to liquidity preference curves! (I mean genuine curves of what prudent men *want*, not those observed points which show where they are forced to be in a world where political power still can exert influence on America's allies.)

implies

$$(\pi_i/\pi_j)(1.0225)^{-2} \le p_i/p_j \le (\pi_i/\pi_j)(1.0225)^2.$$

So the mark/franc ratio can vary by at most about twice the 4½% that the mark/dollar ratio can vary.

[2] The next few paragraphs are literary renditions of $w = f(x_1, x_2, ...)$, where the x_i are factors such as the warranted belief that the key currency has been and is undervalued, the size of the key-currency country, the breadth of its money market relative to those abroad, its interest yields relative to yields elsewhere, stability of its political future, etc.

There would have been a more precipitous desire to rush away from dollar holdings but for the accidental fact that the New York market still, in the late 1950s, had little effective competition from other size-able money markets. By tradition, London offered an alternative; but of course the pound did not have the strength of the mark or the yen in those days. If only there had been a broad and resilient money market in Frankfurt or Tokyo, then you would have seen what a shift in liquidity preference means!

As Harry Johnson reminds us, the desire to hold dollars is not for the most part a desire to hold non-interest-bearing currency for its convenience in making transactions. Foreigners do not pay for their cigarettes in dollars. Nor would the fact that the dollar is the interven-tion currency create much of a demand to hold dollar currency, or even dollar treasury bills, if the world around 1960 had not already been de facto a regime in which people and countries were inhabitants of a system of non-free exchange rates. Specifically, if an act of imagination could convince you that in the decade of the 1970s exchange rates will generally find their equilibrium comfortably inside the post-Smiths-onian widened bands, and if central banks were free to please their fancies and perceived self-interest, you may be sure that they would hold sizeable stocks of dollar obligations or currencies only in those presumably rare periods when American interest rates were more fa-vorable than those abroad. They could sleep comfortably at night, knowing that at a price, they could always get hold of the dollars that are needed for intervention purposes.

The brute fact of America's size is of some importance. In 1945 when the IMF was launched, I would estimate that American real GNP was half that of the whole world. You can't laugh off such a fraction. By 1960 this had shrunk to below 40 percent. In 1972, American GNP is barely one-third that of the world. Any dolt can see the trend. By 1980 the Okita estimate that U.S. GNP will be down to one-quarter seems reasonable to me. (Remember by 1980, our per capita GNP of $8,000 per head will be matched by the per capita income of the Japanese. Don't ask about 1990.) Isn't it reasonable that the demand for American dollars as a medium of exchange and wealth-holding will decline in relative importance along with the declining economic do-minance of the United States? Moreover, our monopoly of a broad and resilient money market for short-term funds will be undermined in two ways: other markets will grow, and the so-called Euro-dollar market will convert itself into a Euro-mark and Euro-Euro market as well; also, hard going for the dollar is likely to result in proliferation of controls here, making our market a less desirable haven for foreigners and (in a degree) for Americans.

Even though we are a continental economy in which foreign trade does not bulk large in relative terms, the fact that we are so large has made it difficult for the American dollar to get itself depreciated relative to other currencies without their retaliating. This basic fact would still have existed even if the dollar had not become the intervention currency for the IMF system. Hopefully, as our relative size tapers off, there may be more scope in the future for the badly needed depreciations of the dollar relative to other currencies.

Herein lies the rub. Before Smithsonian, it was the American dollar's overvaluation that constituted the single greatest source of instability for the international system. Some experts think that out 12 percent average depreciation has cured all that. They may be right. I hope they are. But I am not confident in anybody's ability to be certain in making an estimate like this. I shall refer the reader to my Spring 1972 Nobel popular lecture, given on behalf of the Federation of Swedish Industries before the Swedish-American Chamber of Commerce in New York, for some of my misgivings and apprehensions concerning the further need for the American economy to adjust to an equilibrium state of international trade. I may well be wrong. I hope I am.

But certainly no prudent man can be sure that the major problem in the years immediately ahead may not be the requirement of further substantial changes in dollar parities. Doubling the size of our band, to put us even with the rest, would hardly meet this problem, a problem which could be much exacerbated if we ever agree to, or are forced into agreeing to, some form of convertibility of our liabilities abroad. The problem remains: the countries in surplus are, when the chips are down, loathe to make the adjustments that are implied by America's getting out of chronic deficit.

3

Next to this problem of getting the dollar parities into equilibrium and keeping them there − which is part of the basic problem of getting an efficacious equilibrating mechanism into the modern system − the problem of long-term liquidity of the system seems to me to be fairly trivial. Who could believe that, in the age after Keynes, depressions would ever again be caused by a failure of man to come up with sufficient double-entry bookkeeping items?

But I cannot agree with what I understand of Harry Johnson's remarks about the "now-indefensible theory of the 'deflationary bias' of the gold standard". [3] What makes that theory now-indefensible, one would presume, is the eagerness of nations to *depart* from the old rules of the gold standard with their unchanging gear ratios between monetary aggregates and gold-reserve bases. If the rules that Charles Rist and Jacques Rueff took for granted in 1929 were still to hold sway, their apprehensions would not be all that silly. This thesis that gold shortage was a primary cause of the great depression cannot correctly be attributed to a group labeled by Johnson as "radical Keynesians or Marxo-Keynesians": every other assistant professor in the Big-Ten of those days subscribed fervently to the thesis, and most of them thought that Rosa Luxemburg was the name of a Friml operetta. If one can invent the name for a unicorn, the animal must exist: so the set of Marxo-Keynesians can be defined, even if it is very nearly an empty set. Let me be specific.

Being a neo-mercantilist in the 1930s was anything but rare, or radical – or, one must add, foolish. Kalecki alone of the pre-war Keynesians had any genuine connection with Marx. (Lange's Keynesianism was in a different compartment of his thought from his interest in Marxism. People like Dobb played no creative role in the Keynesian revolution; and indeed most of the Left regarded the *General Theory* as an unwelcome palliative for saving capitalism by getting the real-wage down to expand employment. Mrs. Robinson and Kaldor seem to have discovered Marx only after 1939. When I wrote unkindly in a recent column that Galbraith was as innocent of Marx as Keynes, that dictum implied as a corollary: Keynes knew as little of Marx as Galbraith – a libelous statement albeit true! I could go on to discuss Kahn, Balogh, Harrod, or others whom Johnson may possibly have in mind, but Marxism would be – to coin a phrase – a red herring.)

Mrs. Schwartz and her collaborator may be correct in their surmises that the Fed could have created greater reserves for the banking system

---

[3] See his contribution to this symposium, particularly at the place where he first introduces "Marxo-Keynesians".

in the 1929—33 bank-failure debacle, but that would not make it wrong to realize that countries in the 1930s could beggar their neighbors of employment opportunities by being first and most vigorous in their devaluations.

Those who, at the end of World War II, feared a replay under Bretton Woods of an international scramble on the part of each nation to export its unemployment by beggar-my-neighbor policies were wrong. Dead wrong. But they were not wrong because of retrogressive Keynesianism that lacked understanding of the verities of monetarism. They were wrong because they did not correctly predict how Keynesian every mixed economy would be in creating domestic effective demand by non-orthodox budgetary and monetary policies. What I will grant to Professor Johnson is that a number of English Keynesians were insufficient appreciators of Hansenism — that doctrine which took seriously the comparative statics of the Keynesian models and led to shifts in the laissez faire schedules in the direction of full employment and over-full employment. (Anyone who, *after* 1940, worried about whether a capitalist system would suffer from "underconsumption" or would have to rely on imperialistic foreign investments and war expenditures for its creation of adequate purchasing power, was no Keynesian or post-Keynesian but still a Rip Van Winkle from the pre-Keynes era.)

If you teach a dunce the truths of monetary economics, which is not to be confused with the precepts of monetarism, you will not thereby (as Johnson seems to suggest) cure him of the errors of his ways in believing in "elasticity pessimism". There are correctly formulated systems in which elasticity pessimism is a correct doctrine rooted in irremovable real elements. [4] Our world may not be like such models. And no doubt many writers of the late 1940s were paranoid on this subject. That does not mean we can take as established, either by valid deductive reasoning or plausible inference from the experiences of the last two decades, that "elasticity optimism" is assuredly correct. The jury is still out on this empirical question, as well as on the sweeping Mundell dictum that devaluation of a currency (say the pound) is effective because it is a quick way of stripping a system of its *real M* (since its unchanged M must now face prices that will soon rise fully as much as the exchange rate has fallen).

---

[4] Bhagwati and Johnson specified an extreme instance in their well-known polemic with Sohmen.

If, as I think, the Marxo-Keynesians have been inappropriately characterized as critics of Bretton Woods by Johnson, the opposite error has been made in the overly-generous appraisal of the "key currency" critics of that system, such as John Williams. As one who lived in Cambridge, Massachusetts from 1935 to 1945, I can testify that there was always less than meets the eye to the "key currency" approach. Being sympathetic to it leads even so hard-boiled an analyst as Dr. Johnson to write such sentences as, "The 1971 crisis may in a sense be said to have been the result of a break-down of mutual understanding among the key currency countries." It would be as illuminating to give that as the reason for the Crimean War or the heroin traffic. It is true that Freud's reality principle made it unlikely that, once Bretton Woods was put into effect, the world would live happily ever afterwards. Maybe we needed a child to tell us that truth — or a professor over 50.

4

What was essentially wrong about Bretton Woods at its core, we had to re-learn from Dr. Friedman, a lone voice braying for so long in the wilderness that you can't peg exchange rates in a changing world where prices and wages are not two-ways flexible and in which people will not subject themselves to the discipline of the exchanges.

When Dr. Fleming tells us that gliding bands will not work, but rather we must depend on more frequent changes in for-a-period stable exchange rates, my heart sinks. It sinks because I hear that voice, in from the wilderness, pointing out that exchange depreciations which patently should be made *tomorrow* should have been made *yesterday* — if one-way speculation and panic breakdowns of parity are to be averted.

When I read Johnson's diagnosis that stability of the American price level a la Simons is a necessary condition for the viability of the non-flexible-exchange-rate 1945–65 system, my heart sinks. Such a diagnosis if correct represents the depths of pessimism, for there is not the slightest rational ground for betting with confidence that American prices will in the rest of this century average less than a 3 percent per annum rate of secular increase. My mock despair is lightened a bit by the consideration that the diagnosis is not too well-founded. And by my recollection that the system in the half dozen years before 1965 was not in any case a viable system. How can I shed tears over the announcement of the death of a pre-1965 system that I don't believe was then alive?

One must pinch oneself at the prospect of still another sophisticated expert who believes that *only after* the 1965 Vietnam inflation in America did the American dollar become overvalued. From 1959 to 1965, America tied its foreign aid, depreciated its military dollar de facto, introduced voluntary and mandatory capital controls on corporations and banks, initiated a temporary interest rate equalization tax that remained permanent, and dumped its farm products abroad. Yet it was losing gold and putting its allies in the position of taking on many more dollars than they really wanted during that period. The fact that our inflation during that period was more than matched by European inflations of those days did perhaps mean that there was a slow, but quite inadequate, improvement in the degree of dollar overvaluation in the first years of the 1960s; much of that, though, was merely a reflection of our intolerable level of unemployment inherited from General Eisenhower. All that one can justly say is that, after the Vietnam inflation, we ceased to make slow progress and went into reverse, until by 1970 the dollar's overvaluation finally became obvious even to the international experts.

Perhaps there is cold comfort in the reflection that all mixed economies seem to be subject to the same disease of creeping inflation. So long as the dollar holds its purchasing power as well as or better than other currencies, and so long as our interest rate structure has built into it an appropriate allowance for anticipatable inflation, a system truly based on dollars as reserves and nothing else [5] – that is what a dollar standard must mean if it is to mean anything significant – could survive. But I do not think that such a system would be feasible to create (since it never existed), even if we took the drunkard's pledge of temperance and succeeded in stabilizing our price level.

True, the postwar world has been one of inflation. But that has not, like drunkenness, been primarily the consequence of weakness of character of central bankers for no structural reasons. If as some monetar-

---

[5] Under the pristine gold standard, mercantilists had an exaggerated desire for gold, the stuff reserves consisted of. Under the pseudo-dollar world of 1959–1971, everyone longed to get rid of their plethora of dollars but could not succeed in doing so.

ists think, inflation is merely a matter of too much issue of exogenous *M*, then of course there can be no stability of exchange rates in a world of different rates of increase of average costs and prices. In nice models of neutral money, all real magnitudes and all "real prices" (of the form export price/import price or domestic price/domestic *M* supply) are invariant under nominal changes in prices and exchange rates. Price and exchange instability would then not really matter — particularly if price-level changes are anticipated and distortions of real money balances are deemed negligible in importance.

What should concern a student of world inflation are the chronic forces that act and react to prevent the creation of real prices that will clear markets. Just as a person can price himself out of the market by always demanding too high a real wage, any country can create permanent and substantive disequilibrium for itself by having cost-push inflation that keeps re-aiming at real wage and employment combinations that are just not feasible. Each exchange depreciation is soon frittered away in cost-level increases that recreate overvaluation. Indeed, most monetarists have only a superficial theory of the supply of money. *M* does not proliferate out of ignorance or a propensity of bureaucrats to run the printing-press crank. Often a profound theory of the reasons for "excessive *M* creation" will have to reckon with the structural factors that underly Phillips Curves, cost-push and sellers' inflation, and other realistic factors never dreamed of in the philosophies of neutral money and the conventional quantity theory.

5

To summarize, what do I worry about primarily in contemplating current international finance?

(1) The fact that the dollar has been out of equilibrium for stubborn and persistent reasons real and financial; and that it will be neither easy to get nations to agree to the corrective exchange rate parities needed nor painless to undergo those therapies.

(2) The fear that it is not feasible to have freely-floating exchange rates in the relevant intermediate-run future.

What is the best that I can hope for? That we move soon into a regime of *gliding bands*. Reading the other papers in this symposium has not added to my optimism concerning the years just ahead.

PART VII

Welfare Economics

257

Optimal Compacts for Redistribution

Paul A. Samuelson

A Theory of Justice by John Rawls (1971) has revived attention to concepts of "fairness" in welfare economics. It has also, by so to speak unnecessary co-incidence, brought back notions of minimaxing. I personally would consider it "unfair" if, under some banner of "fairness," people were forced into doing something none of them wants to do—such as acting in accordance with a mini-max principle. Sketched here are some strong, special cases in which minimaxing would appear to be definitely bad: this would seem to provide a counterexample to it as a *general* principle.

Within the realm of two-person, zero-sum von Neumann games, each of two ideally perfect players will find minimaxing not unattractive. But it was an act of desperation for statisticians of Wald's generation to try to base a system of decision making under uncertainty on minimaxing one's "possible loss." To be-lieve that Nature is an implacable enemy who will attempt to do you in is as good a definition of paranoia as any: Nature, I daresay, is too busy to concern herself so with little old you. Moreover, if the doctrine owes its appeal to your radical skepticism about your ability to form prior probability or plausibility judgments, following that radical skepticism to its logical conclusion will lead to morbid indifference: if no outcome can be ruled out as impossible, then there is no action you can take that will prevent the worst from happening. If, however, you do have some cogent way of separating events into those that can be speci-fied as "impossible" and those "possible," you have already taken the biggest qualitative leap, from which it is a small step to positing quantitative differ-ences in your personal beliefs about the "probabilities" of different events (their "betabilities" in the Ramsey sense.)

Notions of "fairness" can sometimes seem to point toward policies and atti-tudes that twentieth century intellectuals, a fairly well-defined object of anthropologists' studying, generally think of as "conservative" or even "reaction-ary." The minimax principle—whatever its true and intrinsic relation to those symmetry principles that, on sophisticated analysis, "justice" and "fairness" seem to boil down or degenerate to—may provide the opiate or placebo needed by the intellectual who wishes to avoid being reactionary. Thus, minimaxing can lead to egalitarian taxation, an obvious good thing. What is not always realized,

Financial aid from the National Science Foundation is gratefully acknowledged. I have benefited from discussions with Kenneth Arrow, but I fear he still regrets some of my rejec-tions of minimax regret.

minimaxing can lead to too much of what seemed like a good thing—even from the viewpoint of a non-conservative concerned with the good.

Regardless of its relationship to Rawlsian concerns, the following analysis has significance in its own right as an excursion into the theory of optimal redistributive taxation and of revealed preferences among social compacts.

Scenario for a Social Compact

Persons $1, 2, \ldots, n$ contemplate forming a compact to determine how their respective non-negative real incomes $(X_1, \ldots, X_n)$ are to be taxed.[a] Each ith person has a concave von Neumann utility function, $u_i[X_i]$, whose expected value he acts to maximize in any stochastic situation. These utility functions need not agree: thus $u_i[X_i]$ may show more or less risk aversion than $u_j[X_j]$, as in the cases $u_i = \log X_i$, $u_j = X_j^{\frac{1}{2}}$; but always $u_i''[X_i] < 0$.

No person knows what his actual pre-tax income will turn out to be. But each person has reason to believe (or, in alternative scenarios, is convinced that he has such reason) that there is a joint probability distribution that will govern the $(X_1, \ldots, X_n)$ outcomes:

$$\text{Prob}\left\{X_1 \leqslant x_1, \ldots, X_n \leqslant x_n | i\text{'s beliefs}\right\} = P_i(x_1, \ldots, x_n). \quad (11\text{-}1)$$

If there is a true, objective-frequency probability distribution that obtains, and each person's subjective (or personal, or Bayesian) probability agrees with it, then each $P_i(\ )$ and $P_j(\ )$ will be identical, say

$$P_i(x_1, \ldots, x_n) \equiv P(x_1, \ldots, x_n), (i = 1, \ldots, n) . \quad (11\text{-}2)$$

But we are free to reject (11-2)'s special case and to stick with the more general case of different subjective probabilities.

An important model is that in which each probability distribution is assumed to be *symmetric,* namely

$$P_i(x_1, x_2, \ldots) \equiv P_i(x_2, x_1, \ldots) \equiv \ldots$$

$$\equiv P_i(x_n, x_{n-1}, \ldots), (i = 1, \ldots, n). \quad (11\text{-}3)$$

This means that I think my chances of high or low incomes are no better or

---

[a] Any X_j may be a scalar, such as so many chocolates, or so many market baskets of goods of given composition, or so many dollars spendable at unchanged prices. But it could also be a vector of goods; $X_j = (\text{tea}_j, \text{coffee}_j, \ldots)$, etc.

worse than anyone else's; but it does not mean that the probabilities of low and high incomes are equal to those of middling incomes, as with Laplace's equal-probability axioms.

Egalitarianism Deduced

What will the optimal tax formula be that the ith person would opt for if given his choice? Clearly, consulting his own uncertain (symmetric!) prospects and aversion to risk, he will *solipsistically* vote for completely egalitarian taxa-tion *when incentive distortions can be ignored.*

Concretely, consider the family of tax formulas parameterized by α, the fractional degree to which each person is pushed toward the mean income:

Y_i = after-tax income of person i when all incomes are $(X_1, \ldots, X_n)$

$$= (1 - \alpha)X_i + \alpha\left(\sum_1^n X_j/n\right), 0 \leqslant \alpha \leqslant 1. \tag{11-4}$$

If $\alpha = 1$, we have completely progressive taxation; if $\alpha = 0$, we have laissez faire and no redistributive taxation.

EGALITARIAN THEOREM. A person with concave utility, wishing to maximize the expected value of his final after-tax income $u_i[Y_i]$*, or in terms of the self-defining notation of Stieltjes multiple integrals,*

$$\bar{u}_i(\alpha) = E\{u_i[Y_i]\}$$
$$= \int_0^\infty \cdots \int_0^\infty u_i\left[(1 - \alpha)x_i + \alpha\left(\sum_1^n x_j/n\right)\right] P(dx_1, \ldots, dx_n) \tag{11-5}$$

will choose for his *optimal* α, $\alpha_i^* = 1$. *I.e.,*

$$\underset{\alpha}{\text{Max }} \bar{u}_i(\alpha) = \bar{u}_i(1) = u_i\left[\sum_1^n x_j/n\right].$$

This is proved by verifying

$$\bar{u}_i'(1) = \int_0^\infty \cdots \int_0^\infty u_i' \left[\sum_1^n x_j/n \right] \left[x_i - \left(\sum_1^n x_j/n \right) \right] P(dx_1, \ldots, dx_n)$$

$$= 0 \text{ from symmetry of } P(\ ). \tag{11-6}$$

Even without differentiability, this proof by the principle of Sufficient and Reason applies.

> *UNANIMITY COROLLARY: By unanimous vote, a group of risk averters, each of whom conceives of himself as facing a symmetric prospect of pre-tax income, will opt for completely egalitarian taxation merely out of a selfish desire for mutual reinsurance.*

It should be remarked that if each person is a "minimaxer" (or maximizer of his minimum possible outcome), the same egalitarian unanimity follows. But this is a sufficient, not a necessary, condition. And formally it can be regarded as the special polar case of our theorem in which $\gamma \to -\infty$ in $u_i[X_i] = X_i^\gamma/\gamma$, $1 > \gamma \neq 0$. As γ goes to $-\infty$, maximizing (11-5) can be approximated arbitrarily closely by $\text{Max}\{\text{Min}[Y_i \text{ outcomes}]\}$, or so-called minimaxing.

The present theorems are pre-Rawls, going back at least to the analysis in Samuelson (1958, 1966) or Lerner (1944). The next section's advances are developments of what is hinted at in Samuelson (1974a) and earlier suggested as long as thirty years ago by Vickrey (1945).[b]

---

[b] I owe thanks to Kenneth Arrow for reminding me that what I though was original with me in 1964 is actually attributable to William Vickrey, who wrote

> ... If utility is defined as that quantity the mathematical expectation of which is maximized by an individual making choices involving risk, then to maximize the aggregate of such utility over the population is equivalent to choosing that distribution of income which such an individual would select were he asked which of various variants of the economy he would like to become a member of, assuming that once he selects a given economy with a given distribution of income he has an equal chance of landing in the shoes of each member of it ...
>
> Assuming that the marginal utility of money declines with increasing income, maximizing the total utility derived by a population from a given fixed aggregate income implies that this income be distributed equally, due allowance being made for varying needs. On such a basis, the exact shape of the utility function is irrelevant to a determination of the proper distribution.

Vickrey goes on to consider the effects on incentives of redistributive taxation and formulates in the following passage essentially the problem of my next section:

> ... It is generally considered that if individual incomes were made substantially independent of individual effort, production would suffer and there would be less

Deadweight Costs and Limited Redistribution

Suppose we recognize that it may cost something when we take taxes from one person and give transfers to another, that something of real output may be lost in redistributing because of administrative costs, grafts, inefficiencies, and frictions or because of incentive distortions stemming from any feasible taxes. This should temper the amount of egalitarianism that each person will want to have achieved in the social compact (although it may make each want *more* rather than less progression in the tax structure so that at least a little will filter down to a person when he is most destitute!).

Now we will want to replace (11-4) with its assumption that the total of after-tax incomes remains as high as that of pre-tax incomes. The simplest assumption about deadweight loss is that only a fraction, β, of all positive taxes collected ends up being successfully transferred to those who "receive negative taxes."[c]

Let the algebraic tax function that is to be adopted be written as $t(\ )$. If people are to be treated as similar except for differences in their X_j incomes, the tax must be *impersonal* with the special property

$$t_1(x_1, x_2, \ldots, x_{n-1}, x_n) \equiv t(x_1; x_2, \ldots, x_{n-1}, x_n)$$

$$\equiv t(x_1; x_n, \ldots, x_2, x_{n-1}) \equiv \ldots$$

$$t_i(x_1, x_2, \ldots, x_{n-1}, x_n) \equiv t(x_i; x_1, x_2, \ldots)$$

$$\equiv t(x_i; x_2, x_1, \ldots) \equiv \ldots$$

$$\equiv t(x_i; x^i) \text{ for short, } (i = 1, 2, \ldots, n) \tag{11-7}$$

---

to divide among the population. Accordingly, some degree of inequality is needed in order to provide the required incentives and stimuli to efficient cooperation of individuals in the production process. As soon as the need for such inequality is admitted, the shape of the utility curve becomes a factor in determining the optimum income distribution (1945, p. 329).

Then he sets up (pp. 330–331) a variational optimum problem that I would reformulate as follows: Each person's utility depends on his after-tax chocolate consumption and how much he labors; but his pre-tax chocolate output depends probabilistically on his quantity of labor. Any tax formula that depends only on his chocolate output will distort his labor-leisure decision; but subject to this recognized distortion, he selects that tax formula which would maximize his expected utility on the symmetric probability supposition that his productivity luck is the same as anyone else's.

I also owe to Arrow a reference to a similar investigation: J.A. Mirrlees (1971); also a reference to Vickrey (1960).

[c]Since these words were written, I learn that my model is similar to the famous "leaky-bucket experiment" of Arthur M. Okun (*Equality and Efficiency: The Big Tradeoff* [Washington, D.C.: The Brookings Institution, 1975], pp. 91–95).

where $x^i = (x_1, x_2, \ldots, x_{i-1}, x_{i+1}, \ldots, x_n)$ and $t(\ )$ is to be symmetric in the arguments of x^i.

"Positive taxes" are denotable by $\text{Max}[0, t(x_i; x^i)]$ and "transfers received" by the absolute value of negative taxes or by $\text{Max}[0, -t(x_i; x^i)]$. Assuming that only β of all positive taxes end up available as effective transfers, the choice of tax functions available for the social compact is limited by the non-analytic constraint:

$$\sum_{j=1}^{n} \text{Max}[0, -t(x_j; x^j)] - \beta \sum_{j=1}^{n} \text{Max}[0, t(x_j; x^j)] = 0. \tag{11-8}$$

This is non-analytic because $\text{Max}[0, z]$ is not an everywhere differentiable function.

OPTIMALITY EXISTENCE THEOREM: Each person, given his $u_i[X_i]$ *and* $P_i(x_1, \ldots, x_n)$ *functions can now determine in principle the optimum tax function,* $t(x_i; x^i)$, *that he would prefer to have apply to himself (and, of course, under impersonal taxation to each and every other person). The same holds even (a) if each* $u_i[X_i]$ *depends not solely on the* X_i *variable but altruistically or malevolently on all* $(X_1, \ldots, X_n)$ *variables; (b) if each* X_i *is not a scalar of "real income" but rather a vector of diverse goods and services of one date or different dates; (c) if* $\bar{u}_i(\ )$ *of one person's preference is replaced by some Bergson Social Welfare function provided by any ethical observer, the implications of which for optimal taxation we wish to explore.*

Formally, person i must solve a problem in the calculus of variations for *his* solipsistic unknown optimal tax function, which we can denote by $t_i^*(x_k; x^k)$, the affix k being used to emphasize that person i realizes the impersonal tax formula applies to *every* person, $i \gtrless k = 1, 2, \ldots, n$. Formally, he solves for

$$\underset{t(x_i; x^i)}{\text{Max}} \quad \int_0^\infty \cdots \int_0^\infty u_i[x_i - t(x_i; x^i)] \, P(dx_1, \ldots, dx_n) \tag{11-9}$$

where $t(x_i; x^i)$ is subject to (11-8). This is not a standard problem because in the Lagrangean-multiplier expression occasioned by the constraint (11-8), terms like $t(x_i; x_1, \ldots)$ and $t(x_1; x_i, \ldots)$ *both* appear. However, in principle the general optimal problem can be solved.

Numerical Example

A simplest case would be a two-person world with only two possible income outcomes characterized by

$$\text{prob}\{ X_1 = 1, X_2 = 3\} = \frac{1}{2} = \text{prob}\{X_1 = 3, X_2 = 1\}. \tag{11-10}$$

Then the sole degree of freedom to be voted on would be how much should be taxed away from the person who happens to get the highest real income for the benefit of the other person: i.e., person i solves (11-9) for his optimal tax function, which reduces to *his* optimal constant value for $t_i^*(3; 1)$. Call it t_i^* for short and derive it from

$$\underset{t_i}{\text{Max}} \left\{ \frac{1}{2} u_i[3 - t_i] + \frac{1}{2} u_i[1 + \beta t_i] \right\}$$

$$= \frac{1}{2} u_i[3 - t_i^*] + \frac{1}{2} u_i[1 + \beta t_i^*] = \bar{u}_i(t_i^*). \tag{11-11}$$

$$0 = -u_i'[3 - t_i^*] + \beta u_i'[1 + \beta t_i^*]. \tag{11-12}$$

Interestingly, for $\beta < u_i'$ (11-3) u_i' (11-1), (11-12) must be replaced by an inequality and *no* redistribution is worth its deadweight cost. We can deduce from (11-11) and (11-12) an expression for the optimal t_i^*, call it $\tau_i(\beta)$, and for the optimal post-tax income spread, call it $\sigma_i^* = \sigma_i(\beta)$:

$$t_i^* = \tau_i(\beta), \tau_i(1) = 1$$

$$\sigma_i^* = \sigma_i(\beta) = 3 - t^* - 1 - \beta t^* = 2 - (1 + \beta)\tau_i(\beta), \sigma_i(1) = 0$$

$$\tau_i(\beta) \equiv 0 \text{ and } \sigma_i(\beta) \equiv 2 \text{ for } \beta < u_i' (11\text{-}3)/u_i' (11\text{-}1).$$

$$\tau_i'(\beta) = \frac{u_i'[1 + \beta t^*] + \beta t^* u_i'' [1 + \beta t^*]}{-u_i''[3 - t^*] - \beta^2 u_i''[1 + \beta t^*]}$$

$$\tau_i'(1) > -\frac{1}{2}, \sigma_i'(1) < 0. \tag{11-13}$$

The last expression deduces the intuitive result that when we introduce a little deadweight loss in the system, we increase the optimal after-tax income spread from zero to a positive amount. The expression for $\tau_i'(\beta)$ shows that adding a little loss will increase the degree of tax progression so long as the Pratt-Arrow coefficient of relative risk tolerance, reckoned at the mean income as $-2u_i''[2]/u_i'[2]$, is less than 2: this occurs when people are more risk averse than any person who calculates the certainty equivalent of a lottery ticket as the harmonic mean of its prizes; such a person is definitely more risk averse than a Bernoulli with logarithmic utility, but is not so risk averse as a paranoid minimaxer.

All this general analysis can be confirmed in the special case where the person in question has constant relative risk aversion and has for his utility function $u_i[X_i] = X_i^\gamma/\gamma$, where $\gamma < 1$. Then (11-13) becomes

$$t_i^* = \tau_i(\beta; \gamma_i) = (3 - \beta^\theta)/(1 + \beta\beta^\theta), \, \theta = 1/(\gamma_i - 1) < 0$$

$$\sigma_i \equiv \sigma_i(\beta; \gamma_i) = 2 - (1 + \beta)(3 - \beta^\theta)(1 + \beta\beta^\theta)^{-1}. \qquad (11\text{-}14)$$

$$\tau_i(1; \gamma_i) \equiv 1 \text{ for all } \gamma_i, \, \sigma_i(\beta; -\infty) = 0 \text{ for all } \beta > 0. \qquad (11\text{-}15)$$

For $\beta = 1$ and no deadweight loss, (11-14) and (11-15) confirm our previous section's egalitarian solution no matter what γ_i is. For $\gamma_i = -\infty$, we confirm the minimaxer solution of egalitarianism no matter how small β becomes (and we note that an increase in taxation's *inefficiency* increases the optimal degree of redistributable taxation away from the rich for $\gamma < -1$). For any fixed fractional β, the more risk averse the person is, the larger $1 - \gamma_i$ is, the greater will be the degree of egalitarianism he will vote for. But, unless he is *completely* risk averse (and few such people seem ever to have been observed), he will wish to stop short of complete final income equalization: the last epsilon of mutual re-insurance has too great a deadweight loading cost.

> GENERAL THEOREM. *If all persons had the same degree of risk aversion and faced the same symmetric probability distribution of fates, they would selfishly agree on a unanimous vote on an optimal compromise between redistributive taxation and the deadweight loss involved therefrom. If no person has infinite risk aversion, they will unanimously suffer from an imposed minimaxer's regime of complete (and costly) egalitarianism, preferring to be spared that version of non-Pareto-optimal "fairness" or "justice."*
>
> *If the persons differ in their risk tolerances, and even if they agree on a symmetric probability distribution, it seems unclear whether their sense of "fairness" or "justice" would lead them (a) to be able to identify and calibrate the person who is "hurt most" under any given tax system, $t(x_k; x^k)$, and (b) to agree that the "best" system is to be that $t^{**}(\;)$ which leaves the "worst-off person" in the "best feasible position."*

Remark: If any person rejects the applicability of a *symmetric* probability distribution, to the degree that the asymmetry is "small," the qualitative conclusions of the present chapter will apply to some degree of approximation. But, of course, if some person knows that *he* will end up affluent, and if he behaves solipsistically and selfishly, then given the chance he would veto any agreement on egalitarian taxation. As Marx and Pareto observed, the last is not a fanciful possibility. To the degree that a person exaggerates his chances for a high (or low) income, he will opt for less egalitarian (or more egalitarian) tax structures: if all exaggerate in the same direction, they may even by unanimous vote agree on a tax structure that would be non-optimal for each were he in command of the true odds.

Negligibility of "Incipient" Deadweight Loss

The example used here to typify "deadweight loss" from redistribution, shrinking of a constant fraction of real incomes transferred with $\beta < 1$ and β a constant, probably exaggerates such costs. Thus, suppose the only important redistributive costs come from distorted "substitution effects" attributable to society's not finding feasible "ideal lump-sum taxes" but instead having to depend on some Ramsey pattern of (so-called "second best" or) optimal-feasible pattern of algebraic excises. And suppose that government has no other function than to provide redistribution (i.e., there is no army, judiciary, or village green concerts—or, if there are any, they are financed out of publicly owned land rents). Finally, continue our assumption that each person conceives of himself as being subject to a symmetric probability distribution as in (11-3).

Can it then be the case that laissez faire is better than *some* degree of egalitarian redistribution? We saw that, with β a small enough fraction, zero redistribution was called for. But once we recognize that β is generated by tax wedges between the prices sellers get and buyers pay(as in a unit or *ad valorem* tax on each bushel of wheat sold), we realize that β is not a constant: we realize that, at the "beginning" of redistribution, β is almost exactly unity, and the initial rate at which deadweight loss is incurred is negligible. This is a basic truth that rarely is explicitly enunciated: yet it follows from the fact that consumer-surplus triangles of deadweight loss, heuristically written as $\frac{1}{2}\Delta p \Delta q$, are of "a second order of smallness" compared to Δp or $q\Delta p$; as $\Delta p \to 0$ or $\alpha \to 0$ in (11-4), $\beta \to 1$—and hence α_i^* *must* be above zero.

The above analysis constitutes the basis for the long reiterated paradoxical theorem of Samuelson (1958, p. 333): a good "frontier" society with "small" public-good responsibilities has for its first responsibility some redistributing of incomes no matter how limited are its feasible tax systems. Actual history, however, which is not a drama playacted in Hegel's seminar room, chose to pursue its own logic.

A Digression of Minimaxing Regret[1]

A discussion that pays some attention to minimaxing should spare a word, a brief word, for the criterion of "minimaxing regret" (or loss in comparison with how one might have fared if a different and more lucky tax decision had been made). In the absence of deadweight distributive cost, $\beta = 1$, the previous numerical case calls for *taxation halfway toward egalitarianism* if maximum regret is to be minimized; i.e., if t_i^* has to be chosen from the real numbers on the interval $[0, 1]$ (and in a moment we shall weaken this requirement and *thereby* change the whole base of calculation of regret!) setting $t_i^* = 1/2$ will minimax regret. If this seems odd (as it does to me at first blush) reflect on the theorem that, if you apply a silly criterion, you must not be surprised at a silly answer (a tautology, since it is by such odd fruits that we learn how odd the tree is).

To see this, note that when you strike it rich, your regret (from not having voted for laissez faire and zero tax rate) is t_i^* itself; when you strike it poor, your regret (from not having voted for completely egalitarian taxation) is $1 - t_i^*$. Therefore, minimax regret requires $\text{Min}\left\{\text{Max}\,[t_i^*, 1 - t_i^*]\right\}$, which is attained at $1/2$, where $t_i^* = 1 - t_i^* = 1/2$.

Actually, minimaxing regret does not lead to transivity, since it can violate the principle of Independence of Irrelevant Alternatives and leave its practitioner at the mercy of the agenda he confronts. Thus, suppose you had considered it feasible to have taxed *either* outcome by 100 percent. Then your minimaxed regret would be $\text{Min}\left\{\text{Max}\,[4 - 3 + t_i^*, 4 - 1 - t_i^*]\right\}$, which requires egalitarian taxation, $t_i^* = 1$: that way you never cry over more than two of spilt potential income.

If there is deadweight cost of redistribution, $\beta < 1$, and again *any* degree of taxation is feasible, we achieve $\text{Min}\left\{\text{Max}\,[3 + \beta - 3 + t_i^*, 1 + 3\beta - 1 - \beta t_i^*]\right\}$ by taxation that falls short of egalitarianism, namely by

$$t_i^* = 2\beta/(1 + \beta) = 1/[1 - \tfrac{1}{2}(1 - \beta^{-1})] < 1 \text{ if } \beta < 1.$$

Actually, the egalitarian solution for the minimaxing of regret, deduced above for our numerical example when $\beta = 1$, holds valid for *any* case in which no two persons can ever have *exactly* the same income. To see this without complicated mathematics, concentrate on after-tax incomes $(Y_1, \ldots, Y_n)$. Compare any possible outcome with the utopia where you get all, $Y_i = \Sigma Y_j$; if ever the tax system could leave you with more than the mean income $\Sigma Y_j/n$, it must leave someone with different income (and that means *you* for a different roll of the die) with an income below the mean and therefore with the high regret greater than $\Sigma Y_j - (\Sigma Y_j/n)$; to keep the high regret at a minimum, you must opt for every after-tax income at the mean! Q.E.D.

However, this simplicity is lost if (a) you really accept the notion of impersonal taxation with $t(X_1; X_2, \ldots) \equiv t(X_2; X_1, \ldots)$ when X_1 and X_2 happen to be equal. In any outcome with two tied incomes, say $X_1 = 3 = X_2$, $X_3 = 1$, it is not feasible under impersonal taxation to compare for regretting purposes t_2 (3; 3, 1) with -(3 + 3 + 1 - 3). Your wishful thinking can only go so far as dreaming of a feasible $Y_2 = 7/2 = Y_1$ that comes from dividing total incomes evenly among all of you with the same income. Minimaxing regret then leads to solving for Min$\{$Max$[7/2 - 3 + t_2(3; 3, 1), 7 - 1 - 2t_2(3; 3, 1)]\}$, which yields the optimum tax $t_i^*(3; 3, 1) = 2\ 1/6$. Incredible as it may seem, picking the optimum tax structure that minimaxes regret when two men are rich and one poor leads to an after-tax income where the poor loner gets much more income than the rich, namely: (3; 3, 1) of pre-tax income leads to (5/6, 5/6, 5 1/3) of post-tax income, a case of progression with such vengeance as to lead to reverse inegalitarianism. (However, the effect depends on relative numbers, not on class position in the income scale: if two poor men and only one rich man occur, (1, 1, 3), the same reasoning leads to after-tax incomes of (5/6, 5/6, 3 1/3), which comes from taxing the (numerous) poor to subsidize the sparse rich!)

Does all this sound silly? That is because minimaxing regret is a criterion that has only to be understood to be laughed at.[d]

Conclusion

"There but for the grace of God go I." This consideration lies, I believe, at the basis of much of the modern welfare state. Mutual reinsurance is good business. That is why, to improve on Calvin Coolidge, The business of America is (also) government. The present theorems, which avoid all interpersonal comparisons of utility, indicate the sense in which this is true. I would hope that any Rawlsian can reformulate or interpret his syllogisms to agree with the results here deduced.

---

[d]Samuelson (1974b) shows that using it for portfolio decision making requires you, when faced with a choice of safe cash and an only-fair bet (such as the toss of a fair coin that returns you $2 for heads and $0 for tails for each dollar you ante up), to put exactly *half* your wealth into the gamble! Most people would have no such tolerance for profitless and pointless risk. Worse for minimaxing regret is that it makes you put almost half your money in a (slightly) unfavorable bet: thus, if on heads you got only $(2 - \epsilon)$ and on tails $0, you'd have to put $(1 - \epsilon)/(2 - 3)$ of your wealth in the unfavorable gamble; for $\epsilon = \frac{1}{2}$, corresponding to a gamble that gives you nought when a fair coin comes up tails and only 1½ when it comes up heads, you'd still put one-third of your wealth in the gamble and only two-thirds in cash with its safety and higher mean yield. *Remark*: Wald, Savage, and the original discussants of minimaxed regret never recommended it when adequate Bayesian probabilities were present, a reminder that present-day portfolio managers should take to heart.

Notes

1. Savage (1954) discusses minimaxing of regret in statistical decision making. Pye (1974) applies the concept to portfolio decision making (and gives further references); Samuelson (1974b) points out pathologies to which the concept leads.

References

Lerner, A.P. *Economics of Control.* London: Macmillan, 1944, particularly Ch. 3.

Mirlees, J.A. "An Exploration in the Theory of Optimum Income Taxation." *Review of Economic Studies* 38 (1971): 175–208.

Pye, Gordon. "A Note on Diversification." *Journal of Financial and Quantitative Analysis* 9 (January 1974): 131–136.

Rawls, John. *A Theory of Justice.* Cambridge, Massachusetts: Harvard University Press, 1971.

Samuelson, P.A. "Aspects of Public Expenditure Theories." *Review of Economics & Statistics* 40 (1958): 332–338, particularly pp. 332–333; reproduced as Ch. 94, P.A. Samuelson, *Collected Scientific Papers,* II. Cambridge, Massachusetts: MIT Press, 1966.

Samuelson, P.A. "A.P. Lerner at Sixty." *Review of Economic Studies* (1964), pp. 169–178, particularly pp. 173–176; reproduced as Ch. 183, in *CSP* III, (1972).

Samuelson, P.A. "Remembrances of Frisch." *European Economic Review* 5 (1974a): 13–15, particularly around footnote 4.

Samuelson, P.A. "Overdiversification from Minimizing Vain Regret." Paper presented at the Bell Laboratories on Economics of Uncertainty, July 29, 1974(b).

Savage, L.J. *Foundations of Statistics.* New York: John Wiley & Sons, 1954, particularly Ch. 9.

Vickrey, William. "Measuring Marginal Utility by Reactions to Risk." *Econometrica* 13 (1945): 319–333.

Vickrey, William. "Utility Strategy, and Social Decision Rules." *Quarterly Journal of Economics* 74 (1960): 507–535.

258

A CURIOUS CASE WHERE REALLOCATION CANNOT ACHIEVE OPTIMUM WELFARE

PAUL A. SAMUELSON

Richard Musgrave's classic *The Theory of Public Finance* presents a multiple theory of the public household. The first branch has to do with allocation of resources to public goods (defense, lighthouses, etc.) and to merit-want rectification of private demands (making the purchase of heroin illegal; provision of rehabilitation services for alcoholics instead of providing abstract purchasing power that will be dissipated in liquor).

The third branch has to do with macroeconomic stabilization (anti-cyclical public works, tax reductions to reduce unemployment). The remaining branch with which I am concerned in the present discussion has to do with the distribution of income.

If the distribution of income under laissez-faire creates greater inequalities between rich and poor than correspond to ethical notions of equity, or if its results fail to allocate income between those deemed deserving and those undeserving, thus failing to maximize a prescribed social welfare function, then the tax system may be used to rectify the situation. It is a fundamental theorem of modern welfare economics, glimpsed vaguely by Adam Smith in his doctrine of the Invisible Hand, but not really understood by economists until the middle third of the 20th century, that ideal lump-sum taxes and transfers can move a perfectly competitive system free of externalities along the utility-possibility frontier of Pareto-optimal points, until the absolute maximum of a prescribed social-benefit function is attained.

1. A Regular Case

Let us begin with a simplest possible example of pure exchange. A million

* Aid from the National Science Foundation is gratefully acknowledged.

145

PAUL A. SAMUELSON

identical women trade food and clothing with a million identical men in a perfectly competitive market. Because male and female tastes and endowments differ, women end up supplying clothing and demanding food.[1])

In the box diagram in fig. 1, men's indifference contours are related to the lower left-hand corner. Women's contours are related to the upper right-hand corner: a southwest movement in the box involves more clothing for women and less for men, and also more food and less clothing for women.

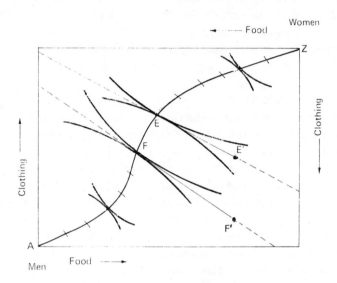

Fig. 1. Lump-sum redistribution from E' to F' will attain optimum welfare at F.

The contract curve AZ is the locus of possible competitive equilibria. Thus from the initial endowment point E', or from any alternative endowment point along the extended line through $E'E$, laissez-faire will result in market equilibrium at E. As the diagram is constructed, each initial endowment in the box results in *one* determinate competitive outcome along the AZ contract locus.

---

[1]) Instead of working with fixed endowments, one could allow production to be variable and still use the same Edgeworth box diagram provided Meade's trade-indifference contours are used.

Now suppose an ethical observer has a social welfare function that respects the tastes of the individuals but which attains its maximum at a point different from E, the laissez-faire point, say southwest of it at the point F. (If the reader pencils in closed contours of social welfare, the top of the mountain is seen to be at F and not at the laissez-faire point E.) Then, by a tax on men and a subsidy to women that moves us from E' to a new endowment point such as F', we can achieve the Bergson welfare maximum at F as the post-redistribution free-market equilibrium.

Should the tax and transfer be levied in terms of clothing alone? In terms of food? In terms of some composite market basket of food or clothing?

In the example in fig. 1 it does not matter. Indeed, if we use some kind of a *numeraire* or any measure of abstract purchasing power – perhaps dollars – then it is an important finding of modern welfare economics that one need usually only use algebraic lump-sum taxes and transfers designated in terms of abstract purchasing power. The people in the market place can be counted on to spend their money according to their own desires and best interests.

2. An Odd Case of Instability

What I should now like to point out is that cases can arise, and they are not necessarily far-fetched ones, in which society is unable to achieve a *stable* welfare optimum merely by having the distribution branch of the public finance authority levy its taxes in terms of one of the goods alone, or some simple combination of all goods, or even by the mere transfer of abstract purchasing power in the form of dollars.

Figure 2 illustrates such an oddity. The reader may pencil in on it the closed contours of social welfare, so that on the resulting topographical map F is seen to depict the true top of the welfare mountain, exactly as was the case in fig. 1. And now we note that, if we have begun at the endowment point E', we can achieve the rectified endowment point F' by lump-sum taxes of about one vertical inch on the men used to supply one vertical inch of clothing to the women. But now we will find that *any of three different* market equilibria are the outcome starting from F'.

The two offer curves generated by F', the so-called Marshall–Mill reciprocal demand curves, intersect three times: in F, but also in F_1 and F_2. The outer equilibria are seen to be stable, whereas F itself is seen to corre-

spond by bad luck to unstable equilibrium in both the Marshallian and
Walrasian senses. Thus, even if F were momentarily attained, the slightest
disturbance would send the system off either to F_1 or F_2. Like the case of
an egg standing on its end, the impact of a single molecule will destroy the
unstable optimality equilibrium and make it in practice not an equilibrium
at all.

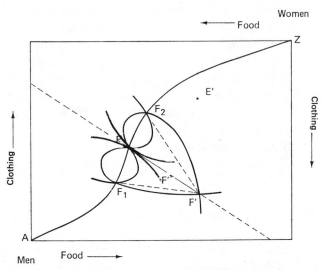

Fig. 2. A lump-sum transfer from E' to F'' will lead to optimum-welfare point F only as a
unstable market equilibrium. To achieve stability, we might need a reallocation such as
$E'F''$, which involves tax of one good and subsidy of another rather than a net transfer of
abstract purchasing power. Direct rationing might be almost as feasible and effective.

Note that both F_1 and F_2 are ethically inferior to F itself. Clearly there is
no way to achieve the optimum F permanently from F' by the freely competitive mechanism of the market.

3. Corrective Measures

Can nothing be done? Modern economic analysis enables us to diagnose
why F can be an unstable equilibrium: it is because of troublesome income
effects. Economic theory having come to the rescue, we can discover a lump-
sum tax transfer which will rectify the distribution of wealth and permit the

market to reach a stable intersection at F. What is needed is to tax the men heavily on food in combination with giving them (the men!) a transfer of clothing: the proceeds of these algebraic operations are given to the women who are taxed on clothing and subsidized on food. The Internal Revenue Service is now in the merchandizing business, contriving a northwest vector reallocation such as $E'F''$. (If initially we had been at F', the second branch of public finance would have to contrive an odd kind of redistribution, one such as that shown by the $F'F''$ vector in which the treasury *net* collects nothing in value terms.)

What has been accomplished? Now, as the reader can verify from fig. 2, a point like F'', which is *sufficiently near to the optimal state* of F, will generate offer curves which intersect only *once* and hence in a stable way. Modern theory assures us that all income effects are proportional to the amounts exchanged; hence if not too much has to be exchanged because F'' begins rather near to F, the well-behaved substitution effect will prevail and will ensure stability of market equilibrium.

In a sense, if it is comfort, it is cold comfort that there does exist some lump-sum vector of redistribution which can, *together with the market*, achieve an optimum. For after all, an omniscient socialist, who could contrive *from the beginning* vectoral reallocations from any initial point to the optimum itself, would have no need for the market at all! What is being said here is that the market can perform the last part of the journey; yet how can one be sure that this last part is an appreciable part of the task?

4. Conclusion

In concluding, let me emphasize that no perversities of increasing returns, of monopolistic market imperfections, or of externalities are involved in the present *curiosum*. And all the nice convexities of the indifference contours that a Debreu might desire are met with in our example. It may also be remarked that no inferior goods are involved.

Although my example gratuitously involves men and women, it is possible that given the inherited condition of our society, the problem of achieving equity between the sexes could involve lump-sum transfers that are considerable. And the same problem could arise in achieving equity as that between whites and blacks. When the inherited distortions of society have gradually evolved away, the resulting differences between men and women may well remain greater than between black and white. Full equality between the sexes need not mean merely that a woman has a right to be like a man but that each has the right to be different from the other. Now it is precisely when differences between market participants are great that the process of market exchange will involve long vectors of exchange and the definite possibility that income effects can perversely make for instability. Once-and-for-all redistributions of wealth endowments, rather than year-to-year redistribution by income taxation, may then be in order to achieve social optimality. Equity may require that women – or will it be men? – should be born with silver spoons in their mouths.

259

FROM GNP TO NEW

Thomas Carlyle complained that economics is the *dismal* science. That was last century. Today the complaint is that economics is the *complacent* science. Supposedly it tells us, if we were to listen, how to grow, grow, grow.

But who is to say that more is better? Certainly not an expert on the cells of malignant cancer. To many thoughtful people, the prospect of "healthy" growth in the gross national product (GNP) is not unlike the spectacle of an arrogant young racer, barreling along in his Ferrari down a dead-end country road. The smile on his healthy face is a measure of his ignorance that, at the end of the way, there lies an immovable brick object.

From this viewpoint, the post-World War II miracle of GNP growth in Western Europe and Japan is tragedy, not progress. The human race occupies a spaceship with limited room and exhaustible resources. Like fruit flies in Professor Pearl's glass bottles at Johns Hopkins, the passengers multiply. And suddenly, with the help of Merlin the New Economist, those in first class on the spaceship have learned how to pre-empt, on one last inglorious binge, the dwindling rations that will be needed by all.

No wonder critics say, "Gross national product is too . . . too gross. Economics is bankrupt if the only wares it can deal with are material wares, wares that despoil the habitat and defraud the future."

As an economist, I have to agree that the accusation, *if valid*, would indeed be a serious one. But those who take the time to investigate economics seriously—I mean modern economics, not that of your great-uncle Dudley—can satisfy themselves that the bill of indictment is a faulty one.

NET ECONOMIC WELFARE

Political economy is increasingly concerned, these days, with net economic welfare (or NEW). What is this?

NEW is the corrected version of GNP—corrected (1) to subtract from the conventional calculation those *non-material disamenities that have been accruing as costs to our economy* whether or not they have been recognized and charged against the industries and activities that cause them, and corrected (2) to add in items irrationally excluded from GNP (such as housewives' services in the home, value of expanded leisure and so forth).

Accruing costs and disamenities include, of course, effluents that pollute our rivers and lakes: the mercury from industry and the phosphates from home washers. Included are the hydrocarbons that darken our skies: carbon monoxide, sulfur, nitrogen compounds. No need to enumerate more.

Included too are the disamenities of modern urban life. Your tedious commuting trip to and from work is really a cost that must be subtracted from your cushy income that goes into the GNP.

We can be grateful that two Yale economists, William Nordhaus and James Tobin, have made a valiant effort to estimate the quantitative adjustments that have to be made in going from GNP to a measure of economic welfare. I refer interested readers to their 1972 monograph, written to help celebrate the 50th anniversary of the National Bureau of Economic Research, and entitled "Is Growth Obsolete?" Here are ome of their findings.

THE SCORE

NEW has been growing in America. But it has been growing at a considerably lower rate than per-capita real GNP—say, by 1.1 per cent per year rather than by 1.7 per cent.

Although my rough extrapolations of the Nordhaus-Tobin data suggest that NEW will fall behind GNP's growth increasingly in the future, all this is not inevitable. Modern economics teaches us that we can trade off some GNP growth for more healthy NEW growth.

It's up to us, the public. If we will it, we can give up half a per cent of conventional GNP yearly growth, in order to achieve perhaps an extra quarter of a per cent rate of NEW growth. And a good bargain many of us would judge such a trade-off.

But can we afford to let GNP languish? Won't that spell depression?

Modern economics, in the age after Keynes, *does* know how to limit GNP's material growth in the good cause of healthier welfare growth. Grass need not grow in the streets in the process (as indeed might well have been true in Calvin Coolidge's era of rugged individualism).

In short, modern political economy is the calculus of *quality* of life, and not merely that of material *quantity*.

260

Proof That Unsuccessful Speculators Confer Less Benefit to Society Than Their Losses

(mathematical analysis/unnecessary positive carryover model)

PAUL A. SAMUELSON

Department of Economics, Massachusetts Institute of Technology, Cambridge, Mass. 02139

Contributed by Paul A. Samuelson, March 10, 1972

ABSTRACT   It is well known that successful speculation can be a boon to society, whether or not the successful speculator is ruled to be the legitimate appropriator of his profits. It is also understood that unsuccessful speculation can naturally impose losses on the unsuccessful speculator himself. Little, however, is known about the effect of the unsuccessful speculator on the rest of society: one view is that the others gain what he loses, so that in a sense he is their benefactor and only his own enemy; a more plausible view is that his loss must in some sense exceed the gain splashed on others. Nothing seems to have been proved in a rigorous way in this matter.

Here, the problem is subjected to mathematical analysis. It is shown that others do definitely gain from an act of unsuccessful speculation, thus providing rigorous proof of what has long been surmised. But it is also shown that their gain is necessarily less, in an objective sense, than the loss to the speculator himself. Indeed, in the model of unnecessary positive carryover of grain into the future, the gain to the nonspeculators is proved to be actually of a second-order of smallness of infinitesimals compared to the speculator's loss.

ASSUMPTIONS

Assume two goods (say, soybeans and manufactures, or soybeans and "money," in the sense of abstract purchasing power over the composite goods and services that make up the nongrain totality of the standard of living).

Assume two periods (say, now and next year).

Assume $2N$ persons, who are identical in their tastes, incomes, and equal endowments in the two periods of both

goods. However, the first N people all make the identical
mistake of thinking wrongly that next year's soybean crop
will be small. Acting on this wrong view, they are the unsuccessful speculators who mistakenly carry over some of good 1
into the next year, mistakenly thinking that the price will
then have risen enough to compensate them for (i) the fraction of grain, $1 - a$, that will "evaporate" as the sole cost of
storage, and for (ii) the rate of interest, r, that prevails in the
economy because of standard time preference.

The remaining N people are not speculators at all. They
have no adverse view about the future. Since they were not
intending to carry any grain over into the future, they cannot
counterspeculate by reducing such carryover to offset the
aberration of the others. Nor do we permit them to arrive at
side-bets and bribes that might undo some of the action of the
speculators. They are passive people who, this time, happen to
be right.

The notation followed will be close to that of Samuelson
[1].

RESULTING EQUILIBRIUM

From now on, I call the first group of speculators Man A or A;
the rest, B. All in each group do exactly the same thing; however, with N large, they do not act at all collusively, but
rather each acts competitively and *independently* ends up with
the same actions because of the symmetry of the conditions.

Man A will carry over q of grain into the next period—mistakenly. But he will not in this period cut down on his grain
consumption by the full amount of q: Man B, confronting a
now-higher present price of grain, will be motivated to sell
some of his consumable grain to A, with the result that in an
extreme case everybody might cut down his present grain
consumption by $q/2 = y$. Man B consumes in the first period
more of the other good (which I shall call "money") and Man
A consumes that much less of it.

In the second period, all this is reversed. Together, they
consume aq extra of grain: A sells off some of this to B for
money, up to the extreme of half, so that each consumes ay
extra of grain. Now A consumes more money, by the amount
that B pays him for the grain. Had A been a successful rather
than unsuccessful speculator, his money receipts of the second
period would exceed his money outlay of the first by as much
or more than his interest and shrinkage-storage costs. But,
since his mistaken carry-over lowers price in the second period
when he sells and raises it in the first when he buys, he
definitely experiences a money loss, which is all the greater
when we take into account interest and storage charges.
Because of storage and interest costs, it might at first be
thought that the monetary loss to the speculator must be even

greater than the monetary gain to the rest. Actually, however, total money is conserved by hypothesis; so money gains and losses differ only in sign. But, we miss the important part of the story if we stay at the superficial level of monetary gains and losses. We must examine the welfare or utility involved for A and B from an optimal or suboptimal time phasing of the enjoyments from the steady flow of goods over time.

Since we know that all crops are in fact steady over time, soybeans not suffering a shortfall, it is easy to prove that the maximum welfare for A, B, and society is with zero carry-over, $y = 0$. We can now write down the utilities of A and B as respective determinate functions of y, $W_A[y]$, and $W_B[y]$, and examine their derivatives, $W_A'[y]$ and $W_B'[y]$, for positive y near zero. Because of time's arrow, the second law of thermodynamics, and the impossibility of simply reversing time and carrying grain back from future to the present, y is a nonnegative variable and the Kuhn-Tucker [2] programming techniques must be invoked to supplement the standard calculus of extrema.

The conclusions reached by mathematical analysis are that

$$W_A[0] > W_A[y] = W_A[0] - \alpha y + \dots, \qquad y > 0, \qquad \alpha > 0$$

$$\text{(1)}$$

$$W_B[0] < W_B[y] = W_A[0] + 0y - \beta y^2 + \dots, \qquad \beta > 0$$

where the remainders involve higher powers that can be ignored for sufficiently small positive y.

MATHEMATICAL PROOFS

To disprove the strong conjecture that others gain what the unsuccessful speculator loses, any one counterexample would suffice. To establish the presumption that the gain to others is, in a meaningful sense, less than the harm to them, we must examine a model that has some claim to representativeness. Here I use the 1970 canonical model already cited in which Marshallian partial-equilibrium is rigorously equivalent to Walrasian general equilibrium. In this model the second good, "money," has strictly constant marginal utility, so that there is the greatest possible significance to be attached to money as such. The first good, grain, is assumed to have standard diminishing marginal utility, a concept that can be given a purely ordinal, as opposed to cardinal, meaning in this strong model. Utilities in the second period have the same additive properties, but are discounted at the equilibrium rate of interest, $(1 + r)^{-1}$, which agrees in long-run stationary equilibrium with the psychological rate of subjective time preference. With proper choice of units, each man's utility can be written as

$$W = \{U[c_1(t)] + c_2(t)\}$$
$$+ (1 + r)^{-1}\{U[c_1(t + 1)] + c_2(t + 1)\}, \; U'' < 0 \quad (2)$$

Here utility has had its units chosen so that one unit of money has one of utility. And, with proper choice of units, the equal endowments per capita per period can be made to be unity.

Now suppose that half the people decide each to carry over q of grain to the next period. For these utility functions, a typical A will end up consuming exactly what a typical B consumes, since this is the only condition of short-term equality between the relative marginal utilities of the two goods to all persons. Each consumes $1 - y$, A having bought $y = q/2$ from B in return for money payment of $yU'[1 - y]$. In the second period the extra grain is aq, $a < 1$, and each man consumes $1 + ay$, with A now collecting $ayU'[1 + ay]$ from B: within each period total money is conserved, but A pays more money now than he collects later.

We can now express the final, reduced-form utilities of the respective people as a function of ay, the mistaken positive carry-over per head:

$$W_A[y] = \{U[1 - y] + 1 - yU'[1 - y]\}$$
$$+ (1 + r)^{-1}\{U[1 + ay] + 1 + ayU'[1 + ay]\} \quad (3)$$
$$W_B[y] = \{U[1 - y] + 1 + yU'[1 - y]\}$$
$$+ (1 + r)^{-1}\{U[1 + ay] + 1 - ayU'[1 + ay]\}$$

Differentiation of these functions with respect to y easily establishes that the first is at its maximum when $y = 0$—actually at a strong boundary maximum there with negative derivative; and that the second is at a local minimum there, but with vanishing derivative at the origin so that the benefit is of a second order of smallness in y.

For A we have

$$W_A'[y] = \{-U'[1 - y] - U'[1 - y] + yU''[1 - y]\}$$
$$+ (1 + r)^{-1}\{aU'[1 + ay] + aU'[1 + ay]$$
$$- a^2yU''[1 + ay]\} \quad (4)$$
$$W_A'[0] = -2U'[1][1 - (1 + r)^{-1}a] < 0$$

which is a sufficient Kuhn–Tucker condition for W_A to be at its maximum when $y = 0$. Note that, for the smallest y, the loss in utility is linear in y, in contrast to ordinary, smooth interior maxima. The erring speculator hurts himself much. [This is a somewhat special feature, stemming from the assumption that the speculators make so gross an error about the crop shortfall that they are motivated to overcome the storage and interest cost barrier. If it had been truly optimal for there to be positive carryover, because the future crop was definitely known to be sufficiently less than this year's, and if now the A group had overdone the carry-over by a small positive overshoot of $2y$, Eq. (4) would show a vanishing derivative at the origin for y, and going on to the second derivative would reveal that the harm to A was greater than the benefit to B, but of the same quadratic order of smallness.]

For the nonspeculator B, we have

$$W_B'[y] = \{-U'[1 - y] + U'[1 - y] - yU''[1 - y]\}$$
$$+ (1 + r)^{-1}\{aU'[1 + ay] - aU'[1 + ay] + a^2U''[1 + ay]\}$$
$$(5)$$

$$W_B'[0] = 0(-U''[0])[1 - (1 + r)^{-1}a^2] = 0$$
$$W_B''[0] = (-U''[0])[1 - (1 + r)^{-1}a^2] > 0$$

Again we have sufficient conditions, but now for a minimum of ordinary type.

There is no commensurability to utilities in different minds. But the fact that the gains to the nonspeculator are of a higher order of infinitesimals alerts us to the fact that when an elaborate calculation is made in terms of transfer or compensation payments, made either in terms of money or anything else, it can be shown that incorrect speculation disturbs Pareto-optimality. I.e., if we could reverse the mistake and set y equal to zero, *everyone* could definitely be made better off. The truth of this highly plausible result would be apparent even in the case where the two kinds of algebraic benefits were of the same quadratic order of smallness, since in this highly symmetric case we would find that the loss of the speculator (expressed in terms of *transferable* money) exceeds the gain of the nonspeculator.

Finally, the fact that monetary loss and gain on speculative transactions does not capture the full incidence of the problem can be demonstrated. Money loss, on a present-discounted-value basis, is defined as

$$L[y] = -yU'[1 - y^* - y]$$
$$+ (1 + r)^{-1}ayU'[x + ay^* + ay] \quad (6)$$

where up until now $x = 1$ and $y^* = 0$. If $x \ll 1$, the optimal carryover per head, y^*, is the positive root of

$$0 = U'[1 - y^*] + (1 + r)^{-1}aU'[x + ay^*] \quad (7)$$

By definition,

$$W_A[y] = U[1 - y^* - y] +$$
$$(1 + r)^{-1}U[x + ay^* + ay] + L[y] \quad (8)$$
$$= u[y] + L[y]$$
$$W_B[y] = u[y] - L[y]$$

where $u[y]$ is the total two-period utility from grain alone.

By differentiation, we find

$$L'[y] = -U'[1 - y^* - y] +$$
$$(1 + r)^{-1}aU'[x + ay^* + ay] + y\{U''[1 - y^* - y] +$$
$$(1 + r)^{-1} a^2 U''[x + ay^* + ay]\} \quad (9)$$
$$= u'[y] + yu''[y]$$
$$W_A'[y] = u'[y] + L'[y] = 2u'[y] + yu''[y]$$
$$W_B'[y] = u'[y] - L'[y]$$

It is evident that in all cases W_B is at a minimum when $y = 0$, and an ordinary minimum. For the other functions, we must distinguish the two cases: where optimal carry-over is positive before the unsuccessful speculative overshoot of carry-over and where it would take a larger future crop shortfall to justify any positive carry-over.

In the latter case, with $x = 1$ and $y^* = 0$

$$0 > L'[0] = u'[0] = \tfrac{1}{2}W_A'[0] \quad (10)$$

Here the speculator's welfare loss is twice that of his monetary loss, in contrast to the nonspeculator's gain, which was seen to be negligible in welfare terms compared to his nominal money gain.

In the case of optimal positive carry-over, with $x \ll 1$ and $y^* > 0$, Eq. (7) implies the vanishing of $u'[0]$, $L'[0]$, and $W_A'[0]$, along, of course, with $W_B'[0]$. To compare the limiting ratios $\Delta W_A/\Delta L$ and $\Delta W_B/\Delta L$, the ratios of welfare to monetary changes, we calculate for this case

$$0 > L''[0] = 2u''[0]$$
$$= \tfrac{2}{3}W_A''[0] = \tfrac{2}{3}(3u''[0]) \quad (11)$$
$$= -2W_B''[0] = -2(u''[0])$$

I know of no way of making intuitive the fact that these limiting ratios take on the Platonic rational fractions $(\tfrac{3}{2}, -\tfrac{1}{2})$ and $(2,0)$ in the respective cases. (Of course if $u[y]$ should have a stationary inflection point at 0, we would have to go on to higher even-order derivatives and new fractions would emerge; such singular cases, since they almost never occur, can be safely ignored.)

Concepts taken from the theory of revealed preference help to make intuitive the smallness of the nonspeculator's gain. Note that the nonspeculator will face, *after* the erroneous carryover, market prices that would still permit him to buy *exactly* the same batch of goods as he did before: thus, he is splashed by what is called in Samuelson [3] a bare "over-compensated" change. At the new prices, though, he can and will choose to buy a still better batch of goods—a proof that he is benefitted. But, as is well known from the classical works of

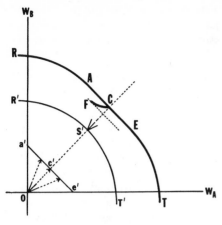

FIG. 1.

Slutsky, Henry Schultz, Hicks, and Wald, the difference between an over-compensated and a "just-compensated" change
is of a second order of smallness, vanishing like the squares of
price or quantity divergences and not their first powers.
(As discussed in Samuelson [4], the theorems of Waugh and
Oi that purport to show that price instability is in some sense
a good thing, find a valid application here.) Because the speculator cannot, after erroneous y has been carried over, buy his
"previous" pattern of consumptions at the new prices, or
even at the old prices, he is definitely worse off, but by an
amount whose order of smallness revealed preference cannot
predict.

Although the present analysis assumed N speculators and N
nonspeculators, this was only for expositional symmetry.
The number of speculators could be small relative to the rest,
provided it was still numerous enough to ensure perfect competition, and only obvious alterations would be needed in our
per capita formulas. Nor need tastes for grains be uniform
among people or independent between periods. Provided
ratios of the type $[\partial W/\partial c_i(t+1)]/[\partial W/\partial c_i(t)]$ are caused by
speculators to diverge from the true marginal rates of trans-
formation or storage of c_i between periods, everybody could
be made better-off by avoidance of the unsuccessful speculation.

The next section sums up the topology of this non-Pareto-
optimality (and, hence, of non-optimality in terms of any
social welfare function that purports to make interpersonal
ethical evaluations). In our special case of concave cardinal
W's, we need only solve the parametric concave programming
problem

$$\text{Max}\,\{wW_A + (1-w)W_B\}, \qquad 0 \le w \le 1 \qquad \textbf{(12)}$$

with respect to all feasible lump-sum transfers between A and

B of all grains and monies of all periods, and for all possible feasible w weightings. Straightforward Kuhn–Tucker conditions are both necessary and sufficient for the indicated solution.

GRAPHICAL DEMONSTRATION OF NON-OPTIMALITY

Because mathematical demonstration that positive y is non-Pareto-optimal is straightforward, it can be omitted here. Fig. 1 shows the full story in terms of society's utility–possibility frontier attainable in the absence of unsuccessful speculation, namely the frontier $RACET$. Erroneous y moves us from C to F, improving Man B slightly and hurting Man A much. The fact that CF moves inside the frontier is the objective meaning of "A's loss necessarily exceeding B's gain." As the dotted subfrontier through F indicates, with the wrong carry-over, society's best frontier is uniformly inside $RACET$; and, from such a suboptimal frontier, northeast movements are feasible that make everybody better off. The fact that CF begins with a horizontal slope is the objective meaning of the finding that B's gain is of a higher order of smallness than is A's loss. (If some positive carry-over, y^*, were optimal, CF would begin at C tangential to $RACET$.)

To explain why the frontier has the straight-line branch ACE, note that this corresponds to lump-sum money transfers between the two men. This will be evident from a terse description of how the frontier is generated. The inner straight line $a'c'e'$ shows each man's utility from money, the second good, alone: the fact that the line is given a slope of -1 does not mean that utilities are comparable across persons, but only that the symmetry of the problem helps in the exposition. The symmetric curve $R'S'T'$, which resembles a quarter circle only by coincidence, shows the grain utilities feasible for both men by reallocations of grain alone. To "add" the two curves "optimally," we add to the coordinates of S' the northeast vectors Oc', Oa', Oe', . . . , as indicated. Then, the branch AR is constructed by adding to the point a' the coordinates of the points on the upper-eight of the circle $S'R'$: in effect the shape of $S'R'$ is preserved just as if the diagram were made out of wire. Likewise ET is constructed identical in its shape to the lower branch $S'T'$, by adding the latter coordinates to the coordinates of the point e'. The subfrontier through F begins as a straight line there, as money is transferred among men: the subfrontier is inside the ACE frontier by the deadweight loss of grain $(1 - a)y$, amplified by the time-preference distortion of the time-phasing of consumptions.

In conclusion, when the analysis is freed from any one privileged cardinal measurement of utilities by monotone, nonlinear stretchings of the W_A and W_B axes, we lose concavity and other metric properties. But all topological properties, such as tangency, signs of slopes, northness, and eastness, are invariants.

I thank the National Science Foundation for financial assistance and Ms. J. Pappas for editorial aid.

1. Samuelson, P. A. (1971) "Stochastic Speculative Price," *Proc. Nat. Acad. Sci. USA* **68,** 335–337; also (1972) in *Collected Scientific Papers, III* (M.I.T. Press, Cambridge, Mass.).
2. Kuhn, H. W. & Tucker, A. W. (1950) in "Nonlinear Programming," *Proceedings of the Second Berkeley Symposium on Mathematical Statistics and Probability* (University of California Press, Berkeley), 481–92.
3. Samuelson, P. A. (1953) "Consumption Theorems in Terms of Overcompensation Rather Than Indifference Comparisons," *Economica* **20,** 1–9; also (1965) in *Collected Scientific Papers, II* (M.I.T. Press, Cambridge, Mass.)
4. Samuelson, P. A. (1972) "The Consumer Does Benefit From Feasible Price Stability," *Quart. J. Econ.* **86,** in press.

261

THE CONSUMER DOES BENEFIT FROM
FEASIBLE PRICE STABILITY *

Paul A. Samuelson

This paper could appropriately carry the subtitle, "Even Though The Consumer Would Benefit From (Waugh's) *Infeasible* Price Instability," in recognition of the deductive validity of the elegant Waugh theorem — that buying at variable prices is better than having to buy at the constant level of prices represented by their simple mean. My main title conveys the point that Waugh's result can *never* be applied so as to permit a society to lift its welfare by its own bootstraps through manufactured instability.

The General Overcompensated Theorem

First, I state a more general proposition, familiar from revealed-preference and standard demand theory. It will include the Waugh theorem as a special case in which the quasi-concave ordinal preference function is symmetric in the consumptions of different time periods. The truth of the theorem is not restricted to cases where utilities are independent or where consumer surplus areas are valid indicators of welfare.

THEOREM 1. *Suppose, at initial price vector* [1] $P^a = [P_j^a]$, *the consumer buys the quantity vector* $[Q_j^a]$, *paying* $P^aQ^a = \Sigma P_j^a Q_j^a$. *Then offering the consumer a new price vector* P^b, *with the same (or lower)*

* This answer, in reply to F. V. Waugh, "Does The Consumer Benefit From Price Instability?" this *Journal*, LVIII (1944), 602–14, was accepted for publication over a quarter of a century ago; but when the manuscript was lost in the editorial process, the exigencies of war did not seem to warrant preparing a new copy. The present reconstitution was prompted by a recent discussion with Professors Kenneth Arrow, Frank Hahn, Daniel McFadden, and Robert Bishop. My thanks go to the National Science Foundation for financial aid, and to Mrs. Jillian Pappas for editorial assistance.

1. Note: since absolute changes in money price levels and in money incomes have no significance, all the prices I speak of could be "real prices" of the form P_j/I, P_j^a/I^a, P_j^b/I^b, etc. where $I = \Sigma P_j Q_j = PQ$ is money income.

mean than that of P^a *(as measured by averaging the* P_j^b/P_j^a *ratios with the* initial *value weights* $P_j^a Q_j^a$), *will make the consumer with the same money income better off. I.e.,*

$$\frac{P^b Q^a}{P^b Q^b} < 1 = \frac{P^b Q^b}{P^a Q^a},$$

implies that Q^b *is better than the* Q^a *(limiting cases of cornered indifference contours being ignored).*

The truth of this theorem can be seen geometrically.[2] Its truth can be proved analytically by the consideration that the consumer could have, at P^b prices, bought Q^a; having chosen instead to buy Q^b, he thereby reveals that Q^b is better than Q^a. Q.E.D.

THE WAUGH TIME-SYMMETRIC CASE

How does Waugh's result fit in as a special case? Merely let the ordinal preference function be symmetric in the consumptions of the different n time periods, $Q = (Q_1, \ldots, Q_t, \ldots, Q_n)$. Let P^a represent a stable price vector $(p, \ldots, p)$, so that assuredly Q^a represents equal quantities consumed $(q, \ldots, q)$. Now consider a new unstable price vector P^b, such that its unweighted mean (which is its mean calculated with the weights of the initial P^a situation, which are here specified to be all equal) is the same as the common P^a price. Thus, $p = (P_1^b + P_2^b)/2$ is an example. Then clearly Theorem 1 tells us that the Q^b from unstable prices is definitely better than the constant q of the stable P^a situation.

INAPPLICABILITY OF THE WAUGH THEOREM

Unless the system has an outside Santa Claus, we can now demonstrate that *a closed system, when it goes from stable prices to unstable prices, must necessarily have those unstable prices average out to higher than the stable prices* — so that the Waugh theorem can never feasibly apply. Indeed the unstable prices will be shown in the next section to average out so high compared to the stable price that we can apply my generalized theorem *in reverse* and

2. In the later Figure I, Q^b, being on the "offer" or "overcompensated" locus generated by Q^a as a pivot, is seen to be better than Q^a. Provided $P^a Q^a = P^b Q^b$, the fact that the budget line through Q^b just passes through Q^a shows that the mean price of P^b does meet the condition of the theorem. See P. A. Samuelson, *Collected Scientific Papers* (M.I.T. Press, 1966), Ch. 9 for a 1953 *Economica* paper developing demand theory in terms of over- and under-compensation.

demonstrate by it the anti-Waugh conclusion — that stable prices are definitely better than any *feasible* unstable ones.

What are the set of feasible prices? I shall postulate the case most favorable to Waugh's claim, namely, a case where goods can be stored forward in time at zero cost. Indeed, to give his analysis all the rope it can use, I shall assume that carryback in time, borrowing from the future on a one corn for one corn basis, is somehow costlessly feasible.

I begin with the only case where any pre-Waugh writer would have considered stable prices a possible norm — namely, the case where all harvests are equal. With natural supply as well as consumer demand time-symmetric, under laissez faire equilibrium prices will necessarily be stable.

Normatively, this equal-consumption case is seen to be optimal in the sense of maximizing the feasible well-being of every representative man.[3] Only when equi-marginal utilities are realized in all periods can there be optimality, and with time symmetry this implies stable quantities and stable prices.

Assume now that the common p of Q^a were to be accompanied by a feasible variable P^b with mean as defined earlier equal to the common p. That would, by Theorem 1 (in its Waugh version), make Q^b better than Q^a even though the latter was shown to be *the best feasible* point. This would be a contradiction, and hence we can rule out applicability of the Waugh theorem to a closed system not aided by Santa Claus. (If there is a Santa Claus, it is his bounty, and not Waugh's instability, which makes us all better off!)

The Anti-Waugh Theorem

Actually, Figure I, which relates closely to Waugh's Figure 3, tells the whole story. With total harvests constant at level $nq = 2q = Q_1 + Q_2$ and with costless carryforward and carryback, feasible equilibrium must be on nature's 45° NN locus. The point Q^a on NN, being the symmetric point, must provide the *optimum optimorum* in this time-symmetric quasi-concave case. Any point that meets the condition of Waugh's theorem must be a point like Q^b that is seen to be infeasibly beyond the NN frontier.

Consider an actual unstable price point, like Q^c, that is truly

3. Even if people differ in tastes or endowments, Pareto optimality will require equal consumptions in all periods by any individual; through optimal lump sum interpersonal transfers the best of these Pareto optimal states can be assured.

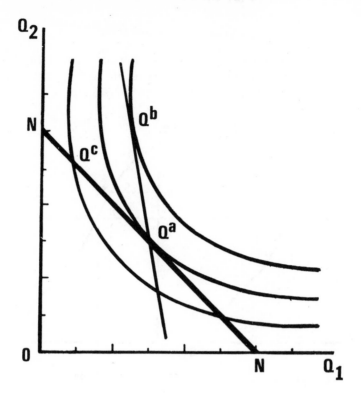

FIGURE I

Feasibility locus, with zero carryover costs, is NN of total available ΣQ_j. Although prices at Q^a are simple means of prices at Q^b, the superior Q^b situation is simply not feasible. A feasible unstable situation like Q^c is worse than stable Q^a, because the stable price level is below the unweighted mean, being instead equal to the mean of P^c prices using the Q^c weights that give greater weight to low prices.

feasible as shown by its lying on NN above or below Q^a. A close glance at Q^a in relation to Q^c will show that it is in the same over-compensated, revealed to be better status as Q^b was seen to be in relation to Q^a. Hence, the correct application of my theorem exactly reverses the roles of the unstable and stable prices, and leads to the conclusion that the stable price — in a comparison involving the unstable price's value weights — is always low enough in mean to reveal the stable consumptions to be preferable. I.e.,

$$\frac{P^aQ^c}{P^cQ^c} = \frac{\Sigma(P_j^cQ_j^c)(P_j^a/P_j^c)}{\Sigma P_j^cQ_j^c} < 1 = \frac{P^aQ^a}{P^cQ^c}.$$

Utility Areas Versus Consumer Surplus Areas

Figure II portrays the special case in which marginal utilities are assumed to be cardinally measurable, to be independent and constant through time, and where there is assumed to be in the

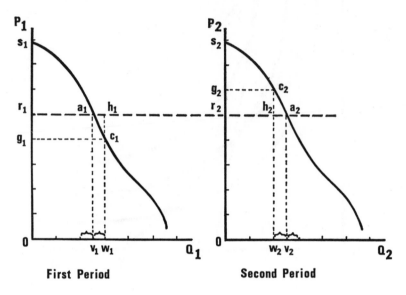

First Period   **Second Period**

FIGURE II

Total utility, $\Sigma s_j a_j v_j 0$, is maximal at price stability. Consumer-surplus triangles, $\Sigma s_j c_j g_j$, represent a false criterion. Correct consumer surplus criterion is $\Sigma s_j a_j v_j 0 - \Sigma r_j h_j w_j 0$, which is optimal at steady prices.

background a further good, call it Q_0, with strictly constant marginal utility at all times (as, e.g., leisure, or labor with constant marginal disutility). Now the prices on the vertical axes may be interpreted as price ratios, P_j/P_0, i.e., as prices relative to the background good as numéraire. If we measure utility in units of the good with constant marginal utility, demand curves and marginal utility curves become identical, with areas under the demand curves measuring rigorously the total utilities from the Q_j of each jth period. No one of these strong assumptions can be dispensed with, but two periods suffice for our graphical demonstrations.

Define $Q_1 + Q_2 = nq = 2q$, where q may be taken as given for all time; or where, in the longer run, each Q_i can be manufactured out of the background good at *constant* opportunity cost, r (which by proper choice of units could be made unity).[4] In the long-run case, q will be determined where the horizontal cost line r_1r_2 intersects the demand curves at the a_i points, where marginal costs and utilities are equated.

The total utility from this good for the two periods equals the sum of the areas under the demand curves, namely $\Sigma s_i a_i v_i 0$. But of course the cost rectangles $r_i a_i v_i 0$ measure foregone utility that could have been enjoyed from the background good; so only the triangular areas $s_i a_i r_i$, to the left of the demand curves and above the cost levels, measure consumer surpluses from Waugh's foreground good. This properly calculated consumers' surplus is maximized by steady prices, at (P^a, Q^a) corresponding to (a_i) and (q, q).

Total utility areas best prove this. With total output allocable over the two periods given at $2q$, a feasible unstable allocation is shown at (c_1, c_2), defined by the equal-spaced brackets on the Q_i axes (and definitely not on the P_i axes!) so as to conserve the means of the Q's (with means of P's doing whatever they then must do, depending on whether the demand curves are linear, convex, or concave).

Provided only that demand curves are negatively sloped, and regardless of their curvatures, we see that steady prices maximize total utility areas since $\Sigma s_i a_i v_i 0$ is bigger than any feasible $\Sigma s_i c_i w_i 0$. I.e., the closer c_i comes to a_i, and the less is feasible instability, the greater is total utility. This is demonstrated by the fact that the gained utility area in low-price time, $a_1 c_1 w_1 v_1$, is necessarily smaller (being shorter) than the lost utility area in high-price time, $a_2 c_2 w_2 v_2$.

Just as physicists contrast anti-matter to matter, I have used area analysis like Waugh's — but applied to total utility areas that go down to equal-bracketed horizontal Q axes, rather than to alleged consumer surplus areas that go leftward to equal-bracketed vertical P axes — to *reverse* Waugh's dictum that instability is optimal. The geometric reason for the reversal of conclusion comes from the fact that utility areas have limits of integration from $Q = 0$ to the Q in question, whereas Waugh's areas have limits of integration from the P in question through higher-than-market prices until infinitely high prices are reached.

Which is right for economic feasibility? There can be no doubt that my total utility areas are the right ones. (See my earlier gen-

4. Increasing cost cases can be handled, in which because of limited land, specific to each period's Q_i production, diminishing returns takes place. See P. A. Samuelson, "An Exact Hume-Ricardo-Marshall Model of International Trade," *Journal of International Economics*, I (1971), 1, pp. 1–18 for rigorous general equilibrium in terms of partial equilibrium Marshallian crosses.

eral analytic proofs, or Figure I's Q^c and Q^a comparisons.) Waugh's error, for feasibility application to the question of whether manufactured instability is a good or bad thing, was not in using consumer surplus areas — as I shall show in a minute, one can get the correct result by this indirect route *properly* traversed — but in calculating the wrong consumer surplus areas.

To expose this error, it would suffice to take the singular case of straight line demands where conserving the mean of Q_1+Q_2 just happens to conserve the mean of P_1+P_2. When Waugh charges a higher price, as at c_2, is the consumers' surplus enjoyed given by the area $g_2c_2s_2$, as his calculations implicitly aver? Surely not. Arguing that way is tantamount to thinking that, whenever we raise the price of wheat (by making it scarce), we thereby raise in equivalent proportion the *utility* of the background good(s) on which the money spent on wheat could otherwise be spent. This is money illusion with a vengeance (illusion be it noted on the part of the economist observer, not on the part of the consumer)!

What then is the correct consumer surplus at high-price c_2? It is the same in every case — namely, the signed total utility area $0w_2c_2s_2$ minus the foregone utility that could have come from spending the resources on this good on alternative goods: in this case, the foregone utility of the background good, as measured by the cost rectangle area $0w_2h_2r_2$. Thus, the proper consumer surplus area is not that above Waugh's P_2 but rather that above the true cost level r_2. Maximizing these correct consumer surplus areas $\Sigma r_i h_i c_i s_i$ is now seen to be the same as maximizing the total utility areas $\Sigma 0w_ic_is_i$, since these two sums differ by only a *constant* of total cost rectangular area provided we consider feasible alternatives that involve the same $\Sigma Q_i = nq$ means. Q.E.D. [5]

5. In going from stable P^a to unstable P^c, it is not feasible to assume that money income to be spent on the foreground goods in the two periods remains the same and that price means are conserved. Correctly, we can work with "real prices," regarding all components of P as $P_j/I = (P_j/P_0)/(I/P_0)$, where I is total expenditure on all periods, including the amount available to be spent on the background good (which will, for $Q_1+Q_2=2q$ frozen, be a frozen constant). Feasible means of such real prices will always be subject to my anti-Waugh theorem. On p. 611 of the cited Waugh article, the author shows recognition of the fact that fixity of the ΣQ_j total negates applicability of his theorem. But he argues that in other cases applicability remains: "If we were setting the toll for using a bridge for example, it would be perfectly possible to establish a toll of seventy-five cents one month and twenty-five cents the next month. . . ." It is true that, if marginal cost of a bridge ride is zero, this might be a better pattern than a stable price of fifty cents every month. But, I would add, stable prices at twenty-five cents, or for that matter at less than one cent, would under this hypothesis be better than the suggested unstable prices. And, as will be indicated explicitly in the final footnote, if for some reason the bridge must raise in tolls all or some fraction of its historic

Second-round Discussion and the Dual Waugh Theorem

If memory serves, the above lines more or less reconstruct the content of my original criticism of Waugh. In the meantime others were also busy, and contributions by L. D. Howell and Gertrud Lovasy evoked an interesting reply from Dr. Waugh.[6] As a result of the critiques, Waugh was led to adjoin to his original theorem about stable prices at the unweighted arithmetic mean as adding to consumer well-being, a dual theorem that *stabilization of prices at the weighted mean, using the weights of the unstable prices* (which would automatically give greater weight to the lower prices) *would reduce the common price enough to make the consumer better off.*

This is also a correct theorem, and it is the special case of my general formulation in which stable Q^a in Figure I was shown to be better than feasible unstable Q^c (that is, we reverse roles and make the initial P vector unstable, and the terminal one stable). Since the dual theorem, in a sense, sings the praises of price stability, one would have thought that its discovery by Waugh would have led him to correct his previous misapprehension about the virtues of boot-strap improvement through contrived instability. But, apparently by 1945 it still had the opposite effect, for he says that its effect is "to add to my statement" rather than, as I would have thought, to subtract from that part of his statement which has to do with policy applications.

Unfortunately, the new discussants uncritically accept Waugh's faulty calculation of relevant consumer surplus areas rather than the correct one. At the risk of overkill, therefore, let me present simple numerical counterexamples which show that neither the original thorem nor its dual (cf. pp. 301–02 of the 1945 reply) can be used by themselves to judge whether a particular pattern of unstable prices is better or worse than a comparison path of stable prices.

For all the different comparisons, I shall accept Waugh's own example of unstable prices. Here (with zeros omitted) we have $(P_1{}^d, Q_1{}^d; P_2{}^d, Q_2{}^d) = (2, 3; 3, 2)$. Now, repeating contentions of the earlier pages, I shall produce an example that has stable prices at the unweighted arithmetic mean but that makes every consumer worse off rather than better. It will suffice to take straight line de-

---

cost, stable prices will still be the best way for the discriminating monopolist to maximize his gross receipts (save in the singular case of rising marginal revenue curves).

6. Cf. L. D. Howell, "Does the Consumer Benefit from Price Instability?" this *Journal*, LIX (1945), 287–95; G. Lovasy, "Further Comment," *Ibid.*, 298–301; F. V. Waugh, "Reply," *Ibid.*, pp. 301–03.

mand curves between the above points, since this will get rid of the red herring that conserving the unweighted mean of prices is usually not the same thing as conserving the unweighted mean of quantities (the latter being appropriate for feasibility arguments). Our comparison point of stability thus conserves both means:

$$(P_1^e, Q_1^e; P_2^e, Q_2^e) = (2.5, 2.5; 2.5, 2.5).$$

Of course, this does not keep the consumers spending the same incomes on corn, the foreground good, but this is a problem that the discussants should have worried about in all cases of nonunitary demand. It is not a problem for one who measures consumer surplus properly. Since 2.5 is the unweighted average of 2 and 3, an uncritical application of Waugh's first theorem would lead to the conclusion that the consumer does benefit in going from stable P^e to unstable P^d. And apparently, this conclusion is valid without our being told anything about the level of the cost of corn! One pinches oneself that correct cost allocation of resources is of no significance in deciding the point of maximum consumer well-being. So let me add some assumption about the cost level. Let the marginal and average cost, in terms of foregone utility of the background good that provides us with the firm measuring rod of utils appropriate to any consumer surplus area calculations, be also 2.5. Now the issue is joined. Waugh says every consumer in the society is benefited by leaving the stable point P^e, where social marginal costs just equal social marginal utilities in every period. I say he is wrong. Can the jury be in doubt as to the verdict?

Now let me try to work the other side of the street and test Waugh's dual theorem — or rather, test its applicability to policy. I shall now consider, for comparison with unstable P^d, an alternative stable P^f, which came not from straight line demand but rather from a specially constructed step function that represents a possible form demand might take. The reader may take his pencil and draw the following curve between the points $(3, 2)$ and $(2, 3)$. "At the highest price let the demand curve be horizontal for all $Q_i < 2$; vertical at $Q_i = 2$ between prices 3 and 2.4; horizontal between Q's of 2 and 3 at the price level 2.4 (or if you prefer, between 2 and $3 - \epsilon$); and then, finally, vertical at $Q_i = 3$, from 2.4 down to say zero price." Needless to say, this example could have its corners rounded off and be made smooth. Now all three discussants, using the dual theorem of Waugh, would presumably agree that the stable point

$$(P_1^f, Q_1^f; P_2^f, Q_2^f) = (2.4, 3-\epsilon; 2.4, 3-\epsilon) \text{ is better than}$$

P^d — for the reason that the common

$$P^f = [Q_1^d P_1^d + P_2^d Q_2^d]/(Q_1^d + Q_2^d) = [2(3) + 3(2)]/(2+3) = 2.4.$$

(Here at least, by definition of the dual test criterion, the same total expenditures are taking place.) The discussants reach their conclusion before they are told anything about the costs of the good! Let us again assume that costs are 2.5 and test whether the unstable P^d is really worse than stable P^f as the dual theorem alleges. According to my calculation of total utility areas from corn in both periods corrected by the marginal utility of what could otherwise be done with the money (that is, what could otherwise be done with the *resources* not spent on corn but rather spent on the background good at its true social costs without any Santa Claus or Devil), the unstable point is the better. The reason it is better is not its instability: variety and change may be the spice of life, but Waugh's argument has nought to do with that kind of utility. The unstable point is better because it is a nearer approach to optimal allocation at the point where all marginal costs and marginal utilities are in balance. Neither stipulated situation is truly optimal, but the stable one involves so much *underpriced* goods as to be worse. In other words, because of considerations never touched on in Waugh's articles, *prices too low are just as bad for the consumer as prices too high.* Of course they would not be if his money income and consumption of background goods remained constant, but it is simply not feasible to give society such Santa Claus choices. Prices below marginal cost hurt every citizen (assumed for simplicity to be identical) since of course the government or whoever names prices and fills demand at those prices must, through whatever form of taxation and resource commandeering you may care to supply, be depriving the citizenry of more utility from alternative background goods than they are getting incrementally from those goods whose prices have been lowered. (If the government is selling out of past surplus storage, the principle is unchanged: stable prices allocate the same total more optimally.) In short, there is no substitute for general equilibrium analysis.

Lapsing for only a moment into symbols, I shall denote the demands as $P_i = p(Q_i)$ and $Q_i = q(P_i)$. The discussants seem to think attainable welfare is measured by consumer surplus triangles

$$F = \Sigma \left\{ \int_0^{Q_i} p_i(q)\,dq - Q_i p(Q_i) \right\} = \Sigma \int_{P_i}^{\infty} q_i(p)\,dp$$

whereas true welfare is measured by consumer surplus quadrilaterals

$$T = \Sigma \left\{ \int_0^{Q_i} p_i(q)\,dq - rQ_i \right\} = F + \Sigma Q_i[r - p(Q_i)]$$

where r is the cost level in terms of the background goods. The final discrepancy factor between T and F represents the ignored calculation of foregone background utility in comparison with foreground utility.

Needless to say, when we posit more realistic general equilibrium demand and utility functions than those appropriate to Marshall's simple geometrical areas, the purported demonstrations of the advantage contrived from price instability more patently fails.

Lest in correcting error I obscure truth, let me reaffirm that Waugh has proved two beautiful and significant theorems,[7] and none of my generalizations purport to go beyond them or discredit them. It is their possible applications to policy that I have warned against, and have done so in the spirit of replying to his modest statement that he was publishing his tentative results in order to call them to the critical attention of other scholars.

Of course, if the consumer's tastes value variety, as shown by indifference contours that are not quasi-concave, boundary maxima and jumps in demand will take place spontaneously. In that case, by the law of large numbers or some other device, it would be optimal to have half the consumers eat lobster on Monday, Wednesday, and Friday, eating none on Tuesday, Thursday, and Saturday, while the other half have the complementary pattern. It will still not be true that varying market prices can improve upon this statistically stable equilibrium. Indeed the slightest periodic deviation in prices will cause the variety-seeking speculator to adjust to the re-

---

7. They can be summed up in the statement that the consumer's maximized utility, as a function of prices and income or of real prices, will be *convex* in the case where there is being consumed a good with strictly constant marginal utility. By definition, $U^* = U^*(P_0/I, \ P_1/I, \ \ldots, \ P_n/I) = $ Max $cQ_0 + u(Q_1, \ \ldots, \ Q_n)$ subject to $P_0Q_0 + P_1Q_1 + \ \ldots \ + P_nQ_n = I$. So long as all goods are being consumed it is easy to see that U^* takes the special form $U^* = cI/P_0 + u^*(P_1/P_0, \ \ldots, \ P_n/P_0)$, where $-u^*$ is a concave function completely dual to $u(Q)$. With u^* and U^* convex, Waugh's first theorem boils down to the statement that a chord between any two points on a convex function lies *above* the surface. The Howell-Lovasy-Waugh dual theorem boils down to the fact that any tangent line to a convex surface will lie *below* the surface. Armed with this, we may state what Waugh has clearly understood: as applied to a many-good, say corn-oats complex, spending the same money income on unstable prices whose weighted index number of prices (using the value weights of the different goods in the steady price situation) is the same as a similar index number of steady prices, will make the consumer better off. The reader may similarly generalize the dual theorem. But in all cases no feasibility arguments for instability will emerge. For references to the maximized utility function U^*, a concept associated with the names of Hotelling, Roy, Court, Houthakker, and others, see P. A. Samuelson, "Using Full Duality to Show that Simultaneously Additive Direct and Indirect Utilities Implies Elasticity of Demand," *Econometrica*, XXXIII, No. 4 (Oct. 1965), pp. 781–96; and to appear in the forthcoming Volume III of my *Collected Scientific Papers*.

gime that gives him the lower price, and market totals will begin to deviate from true marginal cost positions. A genuine case for variety rather than stability would occur if, as at Woodstock, there are consumption externalities across people so that we all want to have our lobster binges together: in that case laissez faire would lead to "instability," but extra instability contrivable by Waugh would not improve matters.[8]

THIRD-ROUND DISCUSSIONS:
PRODUCER BENEFIT FROM PRICE INSTABILITY?

When I sent recently a copy of the above to Dr. Waugh, he kindly referred me to a 1966 paper of his [9] which put the emphasis not on "manufactured price instability," but upon price stabilizing. This is a welcome emphasis but does not render my above analysis otiose. Moreover, Waugh's 1966 bibliography alerted me to a similar confusion in the literature attributable to a 1961 article by Walter Y. Oi.[1] Since this too has been accepted by an array of commentators, I had better kill two false birds with the same analytical stone.

Professor Oi, apparently unaware of Waugh's 1944 analysis, develops essentially the same theorem for the supply rather than the demand side of the market. If the same thing is independently discovered, surely that vouches for its truth and relevance? Not at all. The history of science is replete with independent discovery of error and of misleading applicability. All this shows is that certain slips are tempting!

In response to the Oi article, I would reverse his title, "The Desirability of Price Instability Under Perfect Competition," by adding one word and the prefix "un": then it would more correctly

8. Whether price instability can increase overall welfare is a problem not to be confused with the more trivial question: does price instability increase the gross receipts of producers? If demands are inelastic, of course raising prices will raise more revenue to the producers or the government operating as their agent. If demands are elastic and marginal revenues downward sloping, unequal prices cannot raise more gross revenue from the same ΣQ_i; if marginal revenues are rising, even though positive, instability of prices will raise more revenue for the producers, but of course their gain is less than the loss of welfare to the consumers — in the sense that unequal prices violate Pareto optimality and produce deadweight loss.

9. Frederick V. Waugh, "Consumer Aspects of Price Instability," *Econometrica*, XXXIV, No. 2 (1966) pp. 504–08.

1. *Ibid.*, p. 508. Walter Y. Oi, "The Desirability of Price Instability under Perfect Competition," *Econometrica*, XXIX, No. 1 (1961), pp. 58–64; Clem Tisdell, "Uncertainty, Instability, Expected Profit," *Econometrica*, XXXI, No. 1–2 (1963), pp. 243–47; Albert Zucker, "On the Desirability of Price Instability," *Econometrica*, XXXIII, No. 2 (1965), pp. 437–41.

read, "The Undesirability of Feasible Price Instability Under Perfect Competition."

Just as Waugh showed that the consumer would benefit from buying at varying prices rather than at prices stabilized at their simple mean, Oi shows that producers will get more profit from selling at varying prices than from selling at prices stabilized at their simple mean. This follows at once from the well-known fact that maximized profit, regarded as a function of the competitive prices at which the producer can sell, is a convex function (from below) of those prices. Obviously a straight line joining any two points on a strictly convex surface lies above the surface: hence, the average of profits from high and low prices is greater than the profit from the average price. Exactly the area analysis that Waugh applied to consumers surplus, Oi applies to producers surplus. The resulting theorem is correct, and it can be generalized to the wider correct theorems that Howell-Lovasy-Waugh provided for the consumer case. But the price instability needed to make the theorem applicable to Oi's title is simply not feasible. In other words, no bootstrap operation of manufactured price instability can accomplish the wonderful promises of the Waugh and Oi prospectuses, namely to make *both* producers and consumers simultaneously better off.

Indeed I can add some erroneous, but tautological, theorems of my own. "A country is better off if its exchange rate is destabilized so as to have the same mean level as its equilibrium rate." But do not get caught in the following fallacy: If instability helps both countries A and B, a world of two countries must be best off under instability.

No Perpetual Motion Machine Of the Third Kind In Economics

Classical physics takes it as axiomatic that no perpetual motion machine of the first kind is possible, since that would violate the first law of thermodynamics, that total energy cannot be created. Classical physics takes it as axiomatic that no perpetual motion machine of the second kind is possible, since that would violate the second law of thermodynamics, that total entropy cannot decrease. By knocking the heads together of Oi and Waugh, I can prove that no economic perpetual motion machine of the third kind is possible — that is, unless you have a Santa Claus; but then if you do have a Santa Claus available, who needs the Waugh-Oi theorems?

Figure III consolidates on one diagram Waugh's demands curves

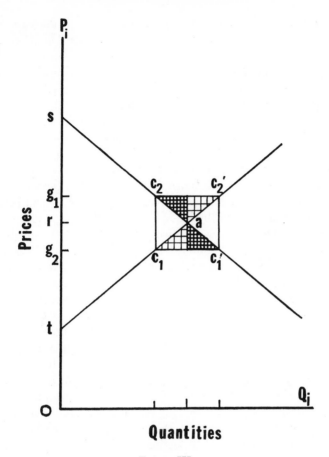

Figure III

The dark- and light-shaded triangles represent respectively the Waugh and Oi alleged gains for consumers and producers from price instability, . .g_1g_2. . , in comparison with price stability at the mean level, . .aa. . . Actually, from a utility standpoint, the shaded areas equal the net social *loss* from instability: geometrically, the unshaded triangles adjacent to the shaded triangles are of the same area and they do represent the loss of consumer-cum-producer surplus. The speculator's loss to the government or outside Santa Claus is shown by the rectangle, $c_2c_2'c_1'c_1$, to be twice as large as the shaded areas.

of Figure II, along with Oi's supply curve, ta. With prices stable in both periods, equilibrium will be at the a intersection point: it is easy to prove that this is optimal since it maximizes the total utility of society from both the utility for corn and the total utility in the background from labor and leisure. A way of seeing this is by confirming that the algebraically signed area between the curves, the sum of consumer and producer surplus, is greater that it would be from any other pricing pattern.

On forsaking this known optimum, what is the result of "manufacturing" a little price instability by having the price be first at the low g_1 level and then second at high g_2 level, with their average being the same as the stable r price? The reader can verify that the alleged Waugh gain is the area of the two shaded triangles above and below a, also that the Oi gain and profit is given by the adjacent lightly shaded triangles. How wonderful it all is! The harm of producers in the first period is more than compensated by their gain in the second period; the harm done consumers in the second period is more than compensated by their gain in the first period. Oi and Waugh together are allegedly two times as good: the shaded triangles represent their combined alleged advantages. So good are they that we ought to destabilize prices further, without limit!

Alas, there is always a catch. When we lapse into feasibility and common sense, we recognize that the shaded triangles represent the actual net utility *loss* to society from price instability — i.e., the correctly calculated loss in consumer and producer surplus. To go through the combined Waugh-Oi scenario requires in the high-price second period more labor demanded by the producers than the consumers will supply, and it requires in the low-price first period less employment by producers than consumers will supply. Just as running over a pedestrian cannot be canceled out by running the truck back over him in reverse, these plus and minus labor discrepancies cannot be canceled against each other. Unfortunately superficial examination of areas involved in partial equilibrium Marshallian crosses cannot reveal what is being presupposed in the background. The reader can be referred to my cited 1971 international trade article on Hume-Ricardo-Marshall to remedy the deficiency. This shows that producers are not different beings from consumers in a closed system and how, when one correctly handles the rent to land, the alleged areas of gain are incorrect representations of welfare.

Without some outside intervention — by Santa Claus, by the government, by some country abroad — the unstable price pattern . .g_1g_2. . is just not feasible. Let us make it feasible by fiat or some kind of intervention. Because I have used straight line curves, the argument is given all the rope it needs: let us suppose the government buys up the excess output of the high-price period and uses it to supply the excess demand of the low-price period. What does it buy these corn outputs with? With money. But in any rigorous model in which the partial equilibrium curves of Marshall are to be compatible with true general equilibrium, the money must stand for the numeraire good in the background in terms of which the marginal utility is constant, namely for labor-leisure in our example.

What we are having the government do is to *buy goods when they are dear and sell them when they are cheap,* which is not quite the recipe for success. Obviously what the producers and consumers are gaining is being done at the expense of the government losses.

But what is government? It is we the people. It begins with nothing and ends with nothing. It must tax whenever it spends. The case most favorable for the argument will be where the taxes and expenditures are all in lump sum form, say in terms of labor: then in the high-price year the government will tax us for the amount of labor needed to enable producers to produce at the stipulated c_2' point; in the low-price year the government gives us a lump sum positive transfer of labor so that we will choose the greater leisure compatible with the low production that is going on at c_1.

But here comes the rub: more labor is involved in the tax to manufacture instability than is involved in the transfer; the difference represents the government's loss from uneconomic "counterspeculation" and is measured by the rectangle $c_2 c_2' c_1' c_1$. In Figure III, this is seen to be twice the deadweight loss of the community's utility. Part of this deadweight loss is precisely the magnitude of the excess profit that Oi is glad to see producers get, namely, the light-shaded triangle. This shows how badly titled his paper is. In common sense terms we are being whipsawed by the law of diminishing returns: instead of producing the two-periods' total of grain by allocating labor until its marginal product is equal in each period, we are deliberately nonequalizing them, gaining less in leisure than we lose in unnecessary work.

Of course the net loss in welfare to the community is greater than Oi's production inefficiency loss. We must not forget the Waugh consumption inefficiency loss — the heavily shaded/ triangles — a point already sufficiently belabored.[2]

2. The discussion has dealt with the case of straight line demand and supply, the case in which stable prices give the same totals of production over a full cycle as do unstable prices. For the straight line case, algebraic analysis shows deadweight social loss to be proportional to $\sigma_p^2[E_s + |E_d|]$, where E_s is the elasticity of the positively sloped supply, $|E_d|$ is the absolute elasticity of the negatively sloped demand, and σ_p is the standard deviation of prices around the mean. This exactly equals the indicated sum of Oi and Waugh alleged "gains." The "speculator loss" to the "government" from buying dear and selling cheap will be twice as great, but half is cancelable rather than

The whole matter can be summed up in a theorem I have long expounded in lectures:

When a speculator unsuccessfully distorts the pattern of equilibrium to his own loss, all the others in the market gain. But they generally gain less than he loses.[3]

Enough has been said to show that, just as every perpetual motion scheme can be shown to draw on a hidden source of energy or entropy and to involve in that sense a Santa Claus, so every demonstration that purports to show a gain from manufactured price instability must rely upon a loser in the background.

I should stress that price stability is not optimal when underlying conditions of supply and demand are variable. Then what is required is optimal adaptive price flexibility. Thus, we do not properly judge whether an organized futures market in onions should have been abolished by looking to see whether prices were more stable when there was a market than when there was not such an organized market. A proper demonstration requires us to show that the organized market served to give a better approximation to the called-for amount of price instability.

Finally, it should be said that the 1966 Waugh and the 1944–45 Waugh are not identical. In 1966, Waugh concluded:

Price stability, in itself, appears to be neither a virtue nor a vice. . . . It all depends on the level at which the price is stabilized and whether one is concerned with the welfare of the consumer or the producer. [p. 508]

Although this is a welcome step away from possible misunder-

---

deadweight loss. Even for nonlinear relations, these will be good approximations for σ_p small. (In Figure III, the two elasticities are shown equal so that Oi and Waugh losses are equal; in the more general case of unequal elasticities, it is more tedious to verify the equality of the area of loss of consumer-cum-producer surplus to the shaded triangles' areas.)

3. Cf. P. A. Samuelson, "Intertemporal Price Equilibrium: A Prologue To The Theory of Speculation," *Weltwirtschaftliches Archiv*, LXXIX (1957), 181–219, for a warning against the facile assumption that a successful speculator "deserves" his profits. "Suppose my reactions are not better than those of other speculators but rather just one second quicker. . . . I make a fortune . . . every day. . . . Would anyone be foolish enough to argue that in my absence the equilibrium pattern would fail to be reestablished? By hypothesis, my sole contribution is to have it established one second sooner than otherwise. . . . The worth of this one-second's lead time to society is perhaps $5. Actually, however, I get a fortune. . . ." This article is reproduced as Ch. 73 in *The Collected Scientific Papers of Paul A. Samuelson* (Cambridge: MIT Press, 1965), ed. Joseph E. Stiglitz. See also, P. A. Samuelson, "Stochastic Speculative Price," *Proceedings Of The National Academy Of Sciences*, LXVIII (1971), 335–37, and P. A. Samuelson, "Proof that Unsuccessful Speculators Confer Less Benefit to Society than their Losses," *Proceedings of the National Academy of Sciences*, LXIX (1972), 1230–33.

standing, I should prefer to state the matter more like the following:

Price stability is, other things equal, in itself a definite virtue. This is so whether one takes the view of producers or consumers or both, in the following sense: Under stable conditions of supply and demand, or more basically of technology and tastes, departures from price stability usually violate Pareto optimality; to the extent that producers or consumers gain, the loss to the other parties is "greater" than their gain (i.e., the losers could bribe the winners not to destabilize and all could end up better off under stability than under manufactured instability). It is definitely a Santa Claus illusion to think that both parties can simultaneously gain, an illusion avoidable if one correctly measures underlying utility areas rather than misleading consumer and producer surplus areas.

Conclusion

Where competitive laissez faire leads to stability, deliberate interference by the government or anyone else to create instability as such is shown to be harmful. Common sense is, in the end (if somewhat belatedly), vindicated.

Massachusetts Institute of Technology

262

REJOINDER

Paul A. Samuelson

I welcome Dr. Waugh's statement of his views and Professor Oi's affirmation that he had never envisaged "contrived" instability in connection with his deductive argument, but rather had in mind the irreducible stochastic variability of real life — shipwrecks, weather fluctuations, and the like.

This raises the question, to which neither Oi nor I have assayed a comprehensive analysis: "Will reducing stochastic variability as such — for example, by introducing better lighthouses and radar warnings against shoals, or by inventing hybrid seeds more impervious to weather variations — be expected to hurt producers' profits, absolutely or in relationship to total GNP?" An affirmative answer to this question would be of considerable interest for its own sake, aside from any enhancement it might have for the Waugh-Oi deductive theorems. A few brief remarks may thus be in order.

Although it is possible to produce models in which profits and variability are positively correlated (I shall do so in a moment), I do not believe that any invariable relationship or even general presumption can be asserted. It is certainly possible to produce models of considerable plausibility in which the reverse relationship prevails, namely, in which an increase in exogenous instability reduces both profits and total output.

Let me illustrate with a bare-bones general equilibrium model. Let labor be the only factor transferable between the food and clothing industries: in food, it works with fixed food–land alone; in clothing, with fixed clothing–land alone. For simplicity, let Cobb-Douglas functions give labor 50 percent factor shares in each industry. And suppose *all* consumers, laborers or landowners, always spend half their incomes on food and half on clothing. Total labor and leisure are assumed strictly constant.

Now let us concentrate on the "profits" of the hiring factors, most particularly on the "rents" of the food-land owners, who are to be the "producers" in the industry that shall be assumed to be subject to *external* stochastic variation. Exogenous risk will be introduced into the clothing production function in the form of a productivity parameter that is a random positive variable with mean of unity. We can now uniformly increase or decrease the spread of this probability distribution by varying a parameter that I shall call s.

Query: As the measure of external variability, s, grows, is there a presumption that the long-run profits of food producers will also grow?

To give a definitive answer we must postulate how people react to risk. The simplest hypothesis is that every man has a Bernoulli utility function whose expected value he seeks to maximize: i.e., $U(X) = \log X$, with marginal utility halving every time income doubles. Finally, it is crucial whether society must allocate its labor between industries *before* or *after* the draw of the random variable is made. Thus, we must analyze two different cases.

The first case, which seems to me to be the more realistic one, is that where ex ante decisions have to be made before the outcome of uncertain variables can be known. In this case our model gives [1] a simple and unequivocal answer. Increasing the exogenous risk parameter, s, reduces total mean GNP. It reduces the well-being of every man in the sense that the mean utility enjoyed goes down even more than mean real income goes down. In particular, the "profits" of food-land owners, which constitute their incomes, are reduced on the average — and since they are risk averters by hypothesis their ex ante and ex post welfare is reduced still further.

I shall not attempt a rigorous proof of these assertions here. But the reader will notice that relative shares are always the same, one half to labor and one quarter to each kind of land. So we need only calculate mean or expected real GNP, which can be shown to decline by virtue of the law of diminishing returns and marginal rates of substitution. Thus, increasing s has no effect on the 50–50 split of labor between the industries, but it does have the effect of increasing the dispersion of clothing around the same mean. Since an increment of unbalanced goods, clothing, will have less of an augmentation on real social product than an equal loss of that

---

1. As Professor Nissan Liviatan pointed out after reading these lines, this unequivocal answer can be given not just for simple models like this one, but for *any* concave economy (i.e., one with convex technology not capable of increasing returns to scale), provided it is confined to ex ante adjustments in the face of any kind of stochastic variation of inputs and intermediate processes around unchanged means. And, I would add, it is not always unrealistic to speak of anticipatable variation that is benevolent: e.g., in evolution, where only the best can be selected, variability is a benefit, not a loss; or in connection with mineral resources, uneven distribution of copper or coal is better than even, if man can recognize and exploit the rich veins, eschewing the others. If the entropy of the world had already reached its maximum, the heat death would no doubt be bad for GNP and General Motors.

good — which is merely to say that GNP is concave in clothing alone — clearly instability is bad for expected income and profits. Q.E.D.

In the second case, nature so to speak tosses a coin and the weather for the crop year is determined. After farmers know what the weather will be like, the transferable pool of labor gets allocated optimally by competition between the food-land and clothing-land. Now what will be the expected or mean GNP and the expected level of food producers' profits as a function of the instability parameter, s?

If we adhere strictly to our constant-share-of-everything straightjackets, the answer is again that high s is bad for mean GNP and mean incomes of everybody, including profit receivers from food-land. But this case, in which ex ante knowledge will happen to lead to no change in decisions in comparison with ex ante ignorance, is clearly too special. Waiting upon a more complete analysis, I can report that when we replace the assumption of proportions spent on the goods that are independent of relative prices by more general assumptions and when we replace logarithmic utility by more general concave utility, we shall find that expected utility will be higher when ex ante adjustments are made than when they are not made. But even these higher levels of expected real GNP *will be lower, the greater is s.* With expected GNP hurt by instability, there is perhaps a vague presumption that so will be any one factor's share, such as food-land profits. However, I am sure that one can produce models in which the consumption elasticity of substitutions are such as to give higher rather than lower food profits. So no firm rule is possible.

We can also modify the character of the exogenous random variable to produce models in which mean GNP is raised by an increase in riskiness. At first this may seem paradoxical and perverse. But when one realizes that this happens usually in cases where society is given an ex post peek before it must make its adjustments, we begin to understand. Suppose you offer me a heads-tails bet of a dollar gained against a dollar lost. I shall refuse if I have concave utility. But if you let me first peek at the outcome, I shall gladly accept when I am a sure-thing winner and decline otherwise. My mean utility cannot help but be raised! Just as I expect to meet few such opportunities in real life, I can wonder whether there is relevance to a social comparison in which variables are constant or in which, after they are determined, one can select the more favorable outcome; in a sense, the mean "productivity" is not being held constant while the variability alone is being altered, and no one ever doubted that an improvement in *mean* productivity, other things equal, would probably imply an improvement in welfare.

MASSACHUSETTS INSTITUTE OF TECHNOLOGY

263

Is the Rent-Collector
Worthy of His Full Hire?*

PAUL A. SAMUELSON†

The answer is No.

I. Statement of the Theorem

Allyn Young and Frank H. Knight have set straight the Marshall-Pigou fallacy that all increasing cost industries ought to be socially penalized: Young and Knight point out that the bidding up of rents to factors scarce to an industry are "transfer" costs to society; and, further, that such rents have to be charged if social efficiency is to be achieved. Otherwise land will get non-optimally utilized; fishing seas and roads may become overcrowded.

I take this all to be standard doctrine. Charging rents serves an efficiency purpose for a *laissez faire* or communistic society, even if we do not want any class called landlords to receive an income from rents.

The problem I pose here is this:

Suppose that "landlords" are not made to give up any of their rents to laborers.

* This paper was written in February 1962 but not published. In the meantime, Professor Martin Weitzman (then at Yale, now at M.I.T.) has independently originated a similar theorem and applied it brilliantly to the enclosure movement. Cf. Martin Weitzman and Jon S. Cohen, "A Marxian Model of Enclosures," July 31, 1972, unpublished. I owe thanks to the National Science Foundation for financial aid, and to Kate Crowley for editorial assistance.
† Institute Professor of Economics, M.I.T., Cambridge, Mass.

Can it be true that the service these landlords create in improving the allocation of labor will be more than enough to pay their rent charges and still leave labor better off than before?

Were the answer to this Yes, labor would find it advantageous to vote unanimously for the institution of landlordism if the only alternative was that no rent would be charged by anyone. The present theorem states that Yes would be the wrong answer.

Under the conditions postulated,[1] *the rent collected by landlords always represents more than the extra output society thereby achieves*; so in a certain sense, rent collection subject to no tax represents a subtraction (if not "exploitation") of labor.

I present this theorem not primarily for its interest as political economy. But it may have some implications for welfare analysis and it is a beautiful example where intermediate reasoning can establish what first appears to be a formidable problem viewed merely as cold mathematics.

[1] General diminishing returns and statical conditions—the latter because it is obvious that *laissez-faire* crowding of fishing waters could wipe out the last fish couple and *permanently* impoverish fishing labor.

II. A Test Example

Following in Robert L. Bishop's tradition at M.I.T. I set in January 1962 the following examination question for first-year graduate students.

> A village owns given amounts of grade A and grade B land. The average physical product schedules for corn of identical labor on the two types of land are given by
>
> $$APP_L^A = 8 - \frac{1}{2}L_A \text{ and } APP_L^B = 6 - \frac{1}{2}L_B.$$
>
> The total number of available identical labor is $L = 6$. The village uses the land as communal property dividing the lots to give each man an equal produce. Then at Ricardo's advice they charge rent (giving it back in an equal social bonus). Explain the reasons for this advice; derive the numerical value of the proposed rent; show in what way and by what amounts each villager will end up better off?

The good student, lending Ricardo Knight's insight, answers as follows. Prior to the collection of rents, labor overcrowded the good land, with equilibrium being at the point where average corn product was equalized on all lands used. (Five L_A and one L_B gave a wage rate of 5½ corn per worker and a total output for society of that much times the labor supply, or 33 corn in all.)

After the collecting of rent, the *marginal* rather than average labor productivities were equated: this relieved good land of the people who were there only because they could gain a slice of the high intra-marginal productivity such land would yield without them; the shift of labor to the poor land, where its marginal product was higher, does add to society's total output. (Arithmetically, with 4 and 2 for L_A and L_B, the wage is now at the equated marginal product

level of 4 each per worker: the "residual rents" on the A and B land are 8 and 4 corn respectively. The total wage plus rent bill now adds up to 34, the increase over 33 being attributable to the efficiency aspects of rent collection on allocation. Note: though the total social pie has gone up, the amount that wage labor now ends up getting *as wages* has gone considerably *down*. This straight-line case therefore is one instance confirming my theorem that the total of rent always subtracts more from product than efficiency adds.)[2]

III. Literary Proof

We can begin with the case of but two plots of land, because that is simpler and because, fortunately, the case of any number of plots yields to essentially the same reasoning.

Before rent is charged, labor divides itself on the two plots so as to equalize their real wage rates at a common *average labor product* level. When the marginal products are unequal, it is evident we can add to total product by switching labor from the low to the high marginal-product areas. After land is appropriated by rent collectors, they will charge rent and ensure that the new configuration ends up with a common wage level at the now-equalized *marginal* products. Thus, in the new situation total output will have been increased by the new efficient allocation of labor. At the initial

---

[2] One student, regarding the initial situation as a problem of "fair division," supposed that initially each worker was allocated exactly one-sixth of A *and* one-sixth of B. Then if we can disregard waste-motion involved in working two plots, each will on his own small scale solve society's labor allocation problem. If he equalizes *marginal* productivities, technocratically or by charging *himself* rents, the optimum is achieved. This perhaps illustrates the efficiency merit of "private property" in the sense of providing *exclusive* use, without regard to rental pricing.

allocation of labor the respective *marginal labor products* will because of universal diminishing returns, each be less than their respective average products and hence less than the equalized wage level.

To compare the new and old wage rates, it is crucial to realize that the plot which has gained labor will, by the law of diminishing returns, end up with a lowered marginal product. But its initial marginal product was already shown to be less than the initial average-product wage rate. Hence, we have proved that the terminal marginal-product wage rate is definitely inferior to the initial average-product wage rate. This completes the proof that rent-collecting has definitely lowered pure wage income.[3]

The generalization to any number of land plots is fairly simple. First, we have the configuration yielded by the wage at equated average products; second, that yielded by the wage at equated marginal products. Except in the singular case so easily disposed of, there will be at least one plot of land that has had positive labor added to it. Hence, the proof from the two-plot case directly applies: On such a plot, the terminal marginal product wage is less than (or equal to) its initial marginal product, which is less than the initial average-product wage. *Q.E.D.*

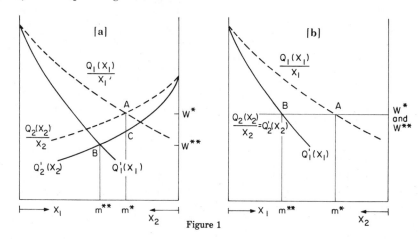

Figure 1

In Figure 1a, $w°°$ at B is less than C which is less than A's $w°$—as can be seen at a glance. [Figure 1b shows a borderline case in which the strong diminishing returns assumption has been relaxed on Land B, and where the rent triangle above B just matches the increment-of-total-social product triangle below BA.]

[3] The singular case, in which the equating of average products happens to coincide with the equating of marginal products, can be easily disposed of. In this case rent-collecting does not add to output at all; so, of course, collecting positive rents must lower wage incomes. (Alternative proof: Initial APP > Initial MPP = terminal MPP.) In the limiting case of everywhere-uniform-horizontal marginal productivity curves, there will of course be no rent under private property and no change in anything.

That the ultimate loss in wages can be indefinitely large and the property return be grossly in excess of any function performed by the rent collector is shown by an example where the two plots have Cobb-Douglas functions with the same negligible exponent on labor, but with proportionality constants differing negligibly. In that case landlords get 99.9% of the product for achieving little or no improvement of the total product.

IV. Graphical Formulation and Proof

The good student presents the following graphical solution to the problem: First, he adds the average product curves horizontally; then he intersects the resulting curve with an inelastic labor supply schedule. The intersection gives him the common wage level and from the original individual curves he deduces the initial labor allocations and products. To get the terminal allocations, he adds the individual marginal product curves horizontally; again he finds the intersection of the vertical labor supply curve with this new aggregate curve, thereby getting the new common wage and so forth. (All this is rather like the Yntema-Robinson graphs for discriminating monopoly.)

For the two-good case, the Jevons-Wicksell diagram of Fig. 1 is even more convenient, and of course straight lines are not necessary.

V. Mathematical Formulation

To illustrate the power of economic intuition, one might present the following equivalent problem to an expert mathematician to see how rapidly he can solve it.

Theorem: We are given n non-negative strongly-concave monotone and smooth functions $Q_i(x)$ each with the property

that $Q_i''(x) < 0$, $x > 0$. Then $w^{\circ\circ} < w^{\circ}$, where

$$w^{\circ} = \frac{Q_1(x_1^{\circ})}{x_1^{\circ}} = \frac{Q_2(x_2^{\circ})}{x_2^{\circ}} = \ldots \frac{Q_n(x_n^{\circ})}{x_n^{\circ}},$$

$$x_i^{\circ} > 0$$

$$0 < x_1^{\circ} + \ldots + x_n^{\circ} = x = x_1^{\circ\circ} + \ldots + x_n^{\circ\circ},$$

and

$$w^{\circ\circ} = Q_1'(x_1^{\circ\circ}) = Q_2'(x_2^{\circ\circ}) = \ldots = Q_n'(x_n^{\circ\circ}), \quad x_i^{\circ\circ} > 0.$$

The mathematical problem would look even more formidable if we replaced the above equalities by the following type of inequalities of modern programming type $w^{\circ\circ} \geqslant Q_i'(x_i^{\circ\circ})$, $x_i^{\circ\circ}\{w^{\circ\circ} - Q_i'(x_i^{\circ\circ})\} = 0$, and so forth. Yet the theorem and proof would still be valid.

VI. Final Word

I draw no deeper welfare implications in this paper. Some may wish to note that here is one of the innumerable examples that can show the arbitrariness of those old new-welfare arguments which used to say: "If situation II could be better than situation III for everyone with proper compensating redistributions being made, then whether or not [!] such redistributions (or bribes) are made, society should overtly select II over I." Pareto-optimality is never enough.

PART VIII

Theory of Money and Inflation

264

Reflections on the Merits and Demerits of Monetarism[1]

PAUL A. SAMUELSON

"Monetarism" is a doctrine which holds two basic tenets. First, it holds that change in the money supply is the only *systematic* factor influencing the overall level of money spending. Not tax rate changes, loan financed public spending, nor even bursts of private investment and consumption spending have any predictable influence. Its second tenet is a consequence of the first, and goes as follows: the only macroeconomic policy needed to run a prosperous economy is for the central bank to stabilize, at all times, the rate of growth of the money supply at some agreed upon and announced annual rate — say 4 or 5 per cent.

In sharp contrast to monetarism is the main stream of modern economics today which (for want of a better name) I shall call "Post-Keynesian Economics." Modern economics, as represented by men like James Tobin, Franco Modigliani and myself, basically believes that changes in the money supply engineered by Federal Reserve policy have important effects upon the level of money, Gross National Product and, depending upon the state of slackness in the employment market, upon real output and the price level.

The significant distinction between this position and crude monetarism can be clarified by the following three post-Keynesian propositions which are all quite incompatible with the monetarist hypothesis:

(1) Even when the money supply is held constant any significant changes in thriftiness and the propensity to consume can be expected to have systematic independent effects on the money value of current output, affecting average prices or aggregate production or both.

(2) Even when the money supply is held constant an exogenous burst of investment opportunities or animal spirits on the part of business can be expected to have systematic effects on total GNP.

(3) Even when the money supply is held constant, increases in public expenditure or reductions in tax rates — and even increases in public expenditure balanced by increases in taxation — can be expected to have systematic effects upon aggregate GNP.

1. Financial aid from the National Science Foundation is gratefully acknowledged. My thanks, and the reader's, go to Felicity Skidmore, who translated my spoken words into prose, but who is exonerated from any recriminations.

It can be said by one man: "Monetarism, that's me." That man, of course, is Milton Friedman.[2] Fortunately Professor Friedman good humoredly gives it out that he loves combat. We have been friends for 37 years. We have disagreed, and that has not yet jeopardized our friendly relations. So I feel free to throw some punches today in his direction, and when he returns them, I shall receive the blows with whatever grace I can muster.

I have dwelt in detail upon the controversy between monetarists and post-Keynesians, and examined the evidence and research on both sides of that argument, in another place.[3] The purpose of the present paper is merely to summarize the historical record, and to discuss some recent work from both sides.

THE POST-KEYNESIAN POSITION ON MONEY

One of the principal preoccupations of the post-Keynesian economists has been to trace out the *causal* mechanisms whereby monetary and fiscal variables produce their effects upon the total of spending and its composition.

Thus, an open-market purchase of Treasury bills by the Fed first bids up bond prices and lowers their yield; this spreads to a *reduction in yields* on competing securities, such as longer-term government bonds or corporate bonds or home mortgages. The lowering of interest costs will typically be accompanied by *a relaxation in the degree of credit rationing,* and this can be expected *to stimulate investment spending* that would otherwise not have taken place. The lowering of interest rates generally also brings about an *upward capitalization of the value of existing assets,* and this increase in the money value of wealth can be expected to have a certain *expansionary influence on consumer spending,* and in a degree on business spending for investment. As a limit upon the stimulus stemming from money creation by orthodox open-market operations, must be reckoned the fact that as the central bank pumps new money into the system, it is in return taking from the system *an almost equal quantum of money substitutes* in the form of government securities. In a sense, the Federal Reserve or the Bank of England is merely a dealer in second-hand assets, contriving transfer exchanges of one type of

---

2. The description given above is, of course, my summary of Friedman-type monetarism. No doubt he would word things somewhat differently. And I should like to emphasize that there are many qualifications in his scientific writing which do not logically entail the *simpliste* version of monetarism outlined above. Indeed, one of my purposes below is to emphasize the point that the weight of the evidence on money, theoretical and empirical, does not imply the correctness of crude monetarism. Speaking for myself, I can say the excessive claims for money as an exclusive determinant of aggregate demand have, if anything, slowed down and delayed my appreciation of money's true quantitative and qualitative role.

3. In "Monetarism Objectively Evaluated," originally prepared for a still-born South African financial publication, and abridged in Paul A. Samuelson, *Readings in Economics,* 6th edition (McGraw-Hill, New York, 1970), pp. 145-154. Small sections of this paper are used below.

8

asset for another, and in the process affecting the interest rate structure that constitutes the terms of trade among them.[4]

What needs to be stressed is the fact that one cannot expect money created by this process *alone* (with, say, the fiscal budget held always in balance) to have at all the same functional relationship to the level of the GNP and of the price index as could be the case for money created by gold mining or money created by the printing press of national governments or the Fed and used to finance public expenditures in excess of tax receipts. Not only would the creation of these last kinds of money involve a flow of production and spendable income in their very *act of being born,* but in addition the community would be left *permanently richer* in its ownership of monetary wealth. In money terms the community *feels* richer, in money terms the community *is* richer. And this can be expected to reflect itself in a higher price level or a lower rate of unemployment or both.

Money created through conventional central-bank operations, quite divorced from the financing of fiscal deficits or the production of mining output, does not entail an equivalent permanent increase in net wealth as viewed by people in the community. Post-Keynesians emphasize that extinguishing the outstanding interest-bearing public debt, whether by a capital levy or by open-market purchase of it, does rationally make the community *feel poorer* than would be the case if the same amount of money existed and the public debt had been unreduced.

All men are mortal. Most men do not concern themselves with the well-being of their remote posterity. Hence, government bonds as an asset are not completely offset in their minds by the recognition of the liability of paying taxes in perpetuity to carry the interest on those bonds. Only if people live forever, foreseeing correctly the tax payment they (or the posterity as dear to them in the most remote future as is their own lifetime well-being) must make on account of the perpetual future interest payments on government bonds — only then would it be true to say that retirement of public debt would have no substantive effects upon the reckoning of wealth, the levels of spending, and the level of prices generally. Rejecting such a perpetual-life model as extreme and unrealistic, we must debit against an increase in money through open-market operations a partial offset in the form of retirement of some of the outstanding public debt.

My purpose here is to stress that wherever monetarism overlaps the post-Keynesian synthesis, it has validity. And in view of the importance of the matter, every economist should welcome the reinforcement monetarism gives to desirable macroeconomic policies. But where monetarism diverges from the main stream of economics, it cannot, in my opinion, stand up to the test of plausible economic analysis and the full range of empirical experience. There is a further

---

4. See P. A. Samuelson, "American Bankers Association Symposium" in the 1963 "Fiscal and Financial Policies for Growth." Reprinted in *Collected Scientific Papers of Paul A. Samuelson,* Vol. 2, ed. Joseph E. Stiglitz (MIT Press, 1966), pp. 1387-1404.

9

grave indictment that must be charged against monetarism. It not only hurts the cause of appreciating the proper role of money by its exaggeration, quite unnecessary assertions and denials. In addition, its reliance upon a naive form of empiricism — to call it "positivism" would be to libel a doctrine that is already vulnerable to legitimate criticism — obscures economic understanding of the mechanisms and linkages of monetary policy.

Monetarism says in effect, "Believe in me, not because I have prepared a reasoned explanation of the processes by which money works out to be the sole and invariant determinant of aggregate activity, but because my correlations are high and my historical regularities many. Mine is a 'black box' model in which money enters at one end as an input and, for reasons unexplained and not necessary to explain, invariably induces at the other end of the box an output response in GNP." All experience in economics and all theoretical principles make it impossible to believe in such naive causal relationships — so that, when we withhold our belief, we are left with nothing, only a "black box."

Monetarism can be expressed in exactly the same terms as the crude Quantity Theory of Money. The post-Keynesian eclectic position is incompatible with this. (It is not, however, incompatible with a sophisticated version of the Quantity Theory of Money.) The logic of neoclassical analysis leads to the view that less of any kind of inventory will be held if, other things equal, the cost of holding it has gone up. Thus, we can postulate that the *velocity of circulation of money is a rising function of the interest rate*. With this assumption the post-Keynesian (or even the simple Keynesian) model becomes compatible with a sophisticated Quantity Theory. And we find that an instructive way of looking at Keynesian liquidity preference is *as* a theory of the velocity of circulation.

It is natural that a Keynesian should resent monetarism as not doing justice to the richness of reality. A good neoclassical post-Keynesian should feel equally resentful. For, in its vulgar reversion to a simple equation of exchange, $MV=PQ$, monetarism takes (V) and sometimes even (Q) as *exogenous* parameters. To demonstrate this I may make reference to my recent attempt toward formulating a proper neoclassical model[5] in which a doubling of the money supply will (if accompanied by a doubling of the deadweight public debt) lead to an exact doubling of all prices, wages, and value magnitudes in the longest run.

All we need to stress here is that the neoclassical model in its proper form has absolutely no need for an $MV=PQ$ fatuity. If one chooses gratuitously to adjoin such a relation to it, one must face up to the fact that equilibrium V is a homogeneous function of degree zero in all price variables and will depend substantively on real variables, including most notably having a positive dependence on the

---

5. P. A. Samuelson, "What Neoclassical Monetary Theory Really Was," *Canadian Journal of Economics*, Vol. I (1968) pp. 1-15.

10

rate of interest. As soon as this last dependence is admitted, one abdicates from monetarism and lapses into good sense.

HISTORY

"Main stream" good sense was not, however, always thus. And I am the first to agree that this modern position attaches to credit and money policy a greater importance than economists generally recognized at the end of the 1930's. How is it that some Keynesians should ever have become identified with the doctrine that money doesn't matter? After all, for a quarter century before 1936, Keynes was the principal exponent on monetary theory. The *General Theory* represented a continuation of culmination of many of his monetary doctrines, and his public and private writings until his death in 1946 affirmed his faith that, if the long-term interest rate could be brought low enough, monetary policy could play an effective role in curing depression and stagnation.[6]

Most converts to Keynesianism became so during the slump years of the late 1930's. Then the deep-depression polar case did seem to be the realistic case. In 1938, the interest rate on Treasury Bills was often a fraction of a fraction of a fraction of a per cent, and even a monetarist might despair of the potency of central bank monetary policy.

As one who lived through those times, I can testify how money got lost by economists. First, multiple correlation studies by people like Jan Tinbergen, of the Netherlands, who pioneered for the League of Nations macrodynamic models of the business cycle, invariably found that such variables as interest rates turned up with *zero or perversely-signed weights in their estimating equations*. Second, case studies at the Harvard Business School and elsewhere invariably registered the result that *the cost and availability of credit was not a significant determinant of business behavior and investment*. Third, large-scale questionnaire surveys, like those associated with the names of Sir Robert Hall, Sir Hubert Henderson, Sir Roy Harrod, Charles Hitch, and Phillip Andrews, uniformly recorded answers denying the importance of interest rates and monetary conditions.

Fourth, as Professor Alvin Hansen and other contemporary writers noted, the inflow to the States of billions of dollars of gold resulting from distrust of Hitler's Europe, produced almost a controlled ex-

---

6. When an author writes as much as did Keynes, it is inevitable that certain of his passages might seem to contradict others. There are *some* of his paragraphs written in the 1930's that do seem to play down the quantitative potency of monetary policy in times of deep depression. And those many writers, such as Sir John Hicks, Sir Roy Harrod, Professor James Meade, and the late Oskar Lange, who have codified the *General Theory* in the form of simple equations and graphs, are able to formulate a "deep-depression" polar case in which money does not matter (either because the liquidity-preference schedule displays infinite elasticity at a "liquidity-trap," or the marginal efficiency schedule of investment displays complete inelasticity to interest rate changes). But note that this is not the general case of the *General Theory*, but only a special polar case, just as the classical quantity theory of money is the special case at the opposite pole.

11

periment in which the reserves of the banking system were vastly expanded and yet no commensurate expansion in business activity or even in the total money supply was achieved. Finally, it was fashionable in those days for theorists to argue that interest was a negligible cost where short-term investment projects were involved; and where long-term projects were involved the irreducible uncertainties of expectations served to dwarf the importance of the interest rate as a controlling variable.

Then the real world changed and economics changed with it. Already in the war years, Professor Modigliani showed the logical need for placing greater emphasis upon stocks as against flows than had been done by the *General Theory's* first commentators. Professor Pigou, in a handsome recantation of his first rejection of the *General Theory*, supplied in the 1940's an important influence of the real money stock as it acts directly on the propensity to consume even in the absence of the interest rate effects that had been recognized in the *General Theory*. Recognition of this "Pigou effect" served to reconcile the deep cleavage between neoclassical theory and the Keynesian revolution. And by the 1950's and 1960's an accumulating body of analysis and data had led to a strong belief that open-market and discount operations by the central bank could have *pronounced macroeconomic effects upon investment and consumption spending in the succeeding several months and quarters.*

This is the place to clear up some doublethink and distortion of the historical record. Is it the case that in the years from 1930 to 1950 there was prevalent in the Chicago oral tradition a sophisticated analysis of the demand for money? A reader of Professor Friedman might be forgiven for believing that such was the case, at least up until the time that he read the definitive article by Don Patinkin[7] which shows this to be a complete figment of the imagination. Dr. Patinkin was a graduate student at the University of Chicago during the crucial years of the 1940's and happens to possess notes from all the principal courses given on money. His dissertation was in this area; and his lecture notes prove that no sophisticated demand-for-money analysis developed independently of Keynes as part of Chicago's "oral tradition."

I can complete the story. For, in the middle 1930's, before Patinkin appeared on the scene, I was a student at the University of Chicago who learned money from Professor Lloyd Mintz and who took courses from Professors Henry Simons, Aaron Director, Paul Douglas, and who upon numerous occasions heard Professor Frank Knight (in public and in private conversations) discuss the problems of effective demand. Let me make clear that these were the years in which my contemporaries were George Stigler, Milton Friedman, Albert Gaylord Hart, Martin Bronfenbrenner, Russ Nichols, and at one remove Homer Jones. I can certify that no sophisticated anticipations of

---

7. Don Patinkin, "The Chicago Tradition, the Quantity Theory, and Friedman," Journal of Money, Credit and Banking, Vol. I, No. I, (February, 1969) pp. 46-70.

12

Keynesian demand for money were involved in any of the reading assignments, in any of the formal courses, in any of the bull sessions of undergraduates and graduate students that I was privy to. In other words, there was no such oral tradition.

After this historical digression, let me now go back to monetarism, and discuss in detail a new model developed by Mr. Arthur B. Laffer.

THE LAFFER MODEL[8]

Before I discuss the model itself, some preamble is in order. At the beginning of 1971, most forecasters, whether monetarist or otherwise, Washington or from business and universities, projected a money GNP for 1971 in the general vicinity of $1,050 billion, which would represent about a 7 per cent increase over 1970's $977 billion. To the surprise of everyone, Nixon's Economic Report raised the ante to the neighborhood of $1,065 billion for 1971; by the 1972's midyear, according to the same official forecast, unemployment would be down from its current 6 per cent level to a 4½ per cent, with prices as measured by the GNP deflator rising at only about 3 per cent per annum.

This created something of a mystery. Within the Economic Report itself, there was no breakdown of the projected GNP; and the very words used suggested that the Council of Economic Advisers, while they believed the best guess for mean GNP would probably somewhat exceed the $1,045-$1,050 range, did not really claim that $1,065 was more than a possibility: i.e., a jury of statistical semanticists might interpret the CEA as claiming that a third-quartile estimate for GNP would be $1,065, not a median estimate. Moreover, the CEA was known to have given private briefings only some months before which were much more pessimistic, not only more pessimistic than the official version that eventually appeared but even more pessimistic than the so-called consensus forecast that gave rise to the $1,045-50 range.

All this gave rise to speculation in the press (as for example in dispatches by Leonard Silk of the *New York Times*) that Nixon and his White House Adviser George Shultz had reversed the professionals on the Council and made them accept at the last moment a significantly higher forecast. Whatever the origin of such speculations, they were quickly denied by the CEA and indeed some earlier speeches by Herbert Stein had discussed feasible paths toward early full employment consistent with the official forecast.

When George Shultz testified before the Joint Economic Committee, he claimed that the high forecast was shown to be a reasonable estimate by a money model developed by his assistant, Arthur B. Laffer, trained at Stanford and on leave from the University of Chi-

---

8. This section has been added subsequent to my 1970 lecture. For description of this model, see the February, 1971 manuscript, A. B. Laffer and R. D. Ranson, *A Formal Model of the Economy for the Office of Management and Budget.*

13

cago. Mr. Laffer, when interviewed by the press, admitted that he had a model which would out-perform the models used by conventional forecasters and which had the virtue of simplicity so that George Shultz could understand and have confidence in it. When the turn came for the CEA to testify, they claimed that their high forecast had not been based on the Laffer model. Their reasons to defend the $1,065 number were that it was consistent with the strength of rise in earlier postwar recoveries during their first year, that forecasters generally tended to be overconservative in their estimate of numerical changes, and most importantly that since this was a target forecast by government, the fact that government had the power and presumably the will to make it come true meant that it was to be believed. In particular, they were counting heavily on Dr. Arthur Burns and the Federal Reserve to engineer a strong growth rate in the money supply to help Administration deficit fiscal programs achieve this goal. A reading of the Economic Report suggested that perhaps a 5 or 6 or even 7 per cent rate of growth of M_1 (currency plus demand deposits) might do the trick; but later in Washington gossip one heard numbers ranging as high as 9 per cent per annum for M_1 growth. When Burns himself testified before the JEC, he expressed the view that the government forecast was overly high and that in any case the Federal Reserve was not going to engineer a dangerously high rate of growth of money at the cost of a reigniting of inflationary pressures just to keep such a forecast from going wrong.

Critics of the Administration, like me, cast considerable scorn on the $1,065 forecast and the case put up for it; most friends of the Administration also criticized $1,065 as being higher than the evidence warranted, but many thought it a good thing that actual GNP would fall below that estimate since otherwise the cost would be renewed inflation. Everyone agreed that $1,065 *might* be exceeded but that the evidence did not bear it out as the optimal estimate of central tendency. What is to be stressed is that monetarists, like Dr. Allan Meltzer of Carnegie-Mellon or the Federal Reserve Bank of St. Louis economists, had forecasts much like that of the modal group (which included the Wharton School model and many others).

The Laffer model is a three equation model. Its most important equation estimates by least squares procedure the percentage change in money GNP (not seasonally corrected) as dependent variable. The independent variables are dummy seasonals (which are in all equations), the current percentage change in M_1, the algebraic increase in the index of stock prices of the previous quarter, a current strike variable to allow for GM and similar work stoppages, and finally current government expenditures on goods and services as well as three previous periods' government expenditure treated as lagged variables. The effect of M_1 is instantaneous and marginally strong; stock prices also have a positive effect; but the immediate positive effect of government expenditures (which are after all actually *in* the GNP itself) is washed out very soon by negative coefficients on

14

the lagged government expenditure variables. The R^2 fit is good (.96 for the period 1948-69) and shows no systematic undervaluations at cyclical turning points.

I shall not say much here about the other equations of the Laffer model. The rate of price inflation is made to depend upon its own values at two earlier quarters and on the previous quarter's Treasury bill rate, the latter being a proxy in a model based upon the notion of "efficient markets" for people's best judgment about inflationary trends. The rate of change of money is also an independent variable with a direct effect on price levels. Of course, as a residual from the first two equations one can get an estimate of how real GNP changes with these same variables. The equation for unemployment is made to depend upon current and lagged real outputs and for some reason on stock-price change two quarters back and various other variables. What is interesting is that unemployment does not in the final Laffer equation have any direct effect upon price or wage changes except through indirect channels of causation. This is in contrast to much Phillips-curve reasoning.

What are we to think? The view that this is a laughable model on which to base an official forecast of a nation must be distinguished from the view that this is a laughable model from the standpoint of macroeconomic analysis and econometric methodology. Both views have adherents, sometimes overlapping. I see no reason why this effort should not get its fair day in court and be subject to sober evaluation. Here is evidently not the place for a full-scale review that does justice to the subject. Only some cursory remarks will be made.

First, in a sense this might be interpreted as a *reductio ad absurdum* attack on monetarism. After all it uses the methodology of crypto-positivism: how big are your R^2s compared to mine? To dismiss it at that is to prejudge the issue, but the point must be stressed that those most grievously wounded by the Laffer model, if it should be judged to be true, are monetarists such as Milton Friedman. All his years of showing that money has its effects distributed in a lagged way over a period of time are thrown to the wayside by the new findings. It denies the basic Friedman notion that, although money is all-important in comparison with any other systematic macro-variables to one who wishes to predict the future of price levels and nominal GNP, still there is so much "noise" in its effects that the authorities will do more harm than good if they try to pursue a discretionary monetary policy to stabilize the business cycle and achieve inflationless full employment. Were the Laffer model true, discretionary monetary activism on the part of the Fed would be both easy, efficacious, and mandatory. To anyone who points out that the good R^2s of the St. Louis model tend to confirm traditional monetarism, one can point to the even better R^2 of the Laffer model.

Second, as identified structural relations that enable the government or anyone else to predict the effects of various packages of policies and events, the Laffer model will appear to most economists, as it appears to me, to be of dubious validity. Of course, if year after

15

year, under a great variety of alternative policy packages, the model continues to generate high R^2s and lower errors of estimate than all rival models, then we shall presumably have to reform our Bayesian prior probabilities about the linkages of economic causation.[9]

Third, there are particular biases of identification that the model seems prone to. Much, perhaps too much, has been made of its use of seasonally unadjusted data and dummy seasonals. (Arthur Okun dismissed it as the "twelve months of Christmas" model.) After all the use of dummy variables is *one* method of handling seasonal variations, and one which is optimal under certain conditions. Still, by leaving seasonal variations in the dependent variables an uninteresting improvement in R^2 is attained.[10] And, if the degree of seasonality is not exactly constant from year to year, and if (as everyone tends to agree) the Christmas concomitant rise in M_1 and in sales is a reflection of the fact that the Fed adapts to the religious and other seasonal patterns, then some upward bias in the estimate of $\delta GNP/\delta M$ is imparted. For purposes of crude annual predictions, if the Fed continues to act in the future much as it has in the past — which most people, monetarists bitterly and post-Keynesians gratefully, think involves some tendency for the Fed to increase M in consequence of prior and contemporaneous changes in GNP — a Laffer or St. Louis reduced-form model may give fairly good estimates. But if the Fed begins in the future to do more of what monetarists urge upon them, namely stabilize the growth of M, or if they do more of what full employment zealots like me urge upon them, namely use activist M policy to offset inflationary and deflationary trends originating elsewhere, then the mididentified monetarist models of the Laffer type can be expected to do badly or less well. (Thus, imagine the thought experiment in which for only a single quarter money is raised: we could then discover whether Friedman and all of the eclectic Keynesians were right, that the effects are spread over a considerable period of time, or whether Laffer is right that the direct effects are exhausted in the single quarter — save possibly for some indirect effects via changes in bill rates as these reflect the efficient-market expectation of individuals.)

Fourth, the grain of truth in the "efficient markets" hypothesis must be handled gingerly in connection with macroeconometric model

---

9. Since writing these lines I have just learned that the Federal Reserve Board staff, in response to a request from the Joint Economic Committee, has done an analysis of the Laffer model which casts considerable doubt on its validity. Thus, if some Korean War years are omitted from the sample period as distorted, the model predicts $1,048 billion instead of the familiar $1,065 billion, suggesting an imprecision of identification perhaps due to multi-collinearity.

10. I am informed that Professor David Fand has been able to explain 91 per cent of the variance in GNP changes from dummy seasonals alone! To go from $R^2 = .91$ to $R^2 = .96$ begins to seem less impressive. One test to apply to a model based upon first differences is to subject it to simulation experiments during part or all of its own sample period. I understand that simulations of the Laffer model starting with the year 1960 show considerable drifting away from the actual course of developments. Of course no model can be perfect in this respect but the drift shown seems to be greater than that of, say, the St. Louis Federal Reserve Bank model commented on (below).

16

building. Use of efficient market variables, while they improve retro-active R^2s, may mask underlying identifications. Example: I wish to forecast the spot price of next December's corn. If I put into my regression both weather data and today's quoted December futures price, the latter is likely to eliminate the former (or to be collinear with it in certain cases). "So what?" might retort a crude empiricist, "I am interested in accurate forecasts and so much the worse for underlying fundamental variables of weather if they do not help me in my task." However, even the crude empiricist is likely to find himself let down by the use of such proxy variables. Suppose we try to guess the December spot price 18 months from now. We have no futures price for it yet. Later we will get one. So, to use the regres-sion based on such a variable, we must *ex ante* estimate the value of this "independent variable."

And now all that has been done is to put off an analysis in terms of the fundamentals of supply and demand of spot prices in order to perform such an analysis on futures prices. That this is not an idle point can be illustrated by a question arising as I write: during this spring, Treasury bill rates have firmed. Is this a valid sign of re-newed expectations of inflation, or are the straws in the wind of price increase abatements in the consumers price index a more valid indi-cation of reduction of inflationary expectations? How can Laffer (or we) know what it is that the speculators in government bills are efficiently forecasting? We encounter a problem of "efficient" interpretation of efficient market happenings.

I do not wish to give the impression that there is no possible evidence that would convert me to monetarism. Its tenets are clear cut and are operationally refutable in principle. Thus, a study by the St. Louis Federal Reserve Bank, using what is technically called a reduced-form 4-quarter lagged regression model, finds that money had a significant positive effect on GNP in the 1952-70 sample period. Tax-rate changes had no significant effect. Public expenditure changes had weak positive effects for two quarters, followed by weak negative effects two quarters later that wiped out any net steady-state effect.

Now I do not believe that such a reduced form analysis correctly specifies the macroeconomic model that needs to be estimated. But I would say that evidence like this does have a bearing on whether the monetarists or the post-Keynesians are more correct. It is at first blush impressive that by money alone one can at least retroactively "explain" in the usual multiple-correlation sense about half the total variance in the change in GNP. But when one examines the whole sample, inclusive of the fifties and the sixties, one sees that all the good fit is in the sixties. The multiple-correlation coefficient (R^2 to be technical) is not at all large in the fifties. We thus are confronted essentially with only one epoch, one experiment upon which to base our new monistic faith in monetarism.

Those of us who know the 1960's, who were part of the decisions made and who have a much more intimate feel for the causations than can be given in one crude statistical time series, cannot in ac-

17

cordance with the best modern theories of Bayesian inference believe that the 1960's are best understood in terms of a "money only matters" model. (Specifically, our cross-sectional judgmental data suggest that if Kennedy had frozen the budget at a low balanced level and then made the M supply grow as it did, the vector of economic development would have been very different — in contrast to a crude use of the St. Louis reduced-form equations.) [11]

I have said enough about crude monetarism. In rejecting it or watering down its claims, however, we must not make the opposite error of embracing a crude anti-monetarist position.

THE KALDOR CRITIQUE OF MONETARISM

One such example of anti-monetarism is that of Professor Nicholas Kaldor, who has recently presented a vigorous criticism of monetarism.[12] Much that Dr. Kaldor says one can readily agree with. His insistence that δM will not have an invariant value regardless of how the M came into existence and the regime of rules and policies being pursued. His point that, to the extent that the central bank is stabilizing interest rates or trying to attenuate its responses to changes in the strength of aggregate demand, M changes will be induced by prior and simultaneous changes in income however those were brought about. His cogent example of Canada, in which the M supply had decreased only a fraction of what was the case in the United States during the great depression but in which the Canadian drop in output was nonetheless comparable to that in the United States. His trenchant criticism of Friedman for claiming that the Fed was guilty in the great depression of cutting the total of high-powered M when, on Friedman's own figures, the M base grew more in the years 1929-32 than it had in the previous years of prosperity. And many other well-put points.

But, after demolishing Professor Friedman, Dr. Kaldor proceeds to put in the place of his one-sided doctrines the new one-sided doctrine that the monetary authorities have essentially no *exogenous* control over the money supply, saying:

> "What then governs, at least in the U.K., the changes in the 'money supply?' In my view, it is largely a reflection of the rate of change in money incomes . . . . This basic relationship between the money supply and GNP is modified, however, in the short period I

11. Since these lines were written, the Federal Reserve Board-MIT-Penn model of the economy, under the general supervision of Franco Modigliani, has undertaken some interesting simulations. The model, which definitely is not a monetarist model, was made to run off data to which reduced form equations of the Federal Reserve Bank of St. Louis type were fit. The results were dramatic. The St. Louis regression equations falsely reported that money was the sole causal agent! Evidently such methodology is of low power to resolve the true identification problem, and no one should be misled by high R^2 coefficients.

12. N. Kaldor, "The New Monetarism," *Lloyd's Magazine* (1970), Summer, pp. 1-17.

18

am convinced that the very short run variations in the 'money supply' — in other words the variation relative to trend — are very largely explained by variation in the public sector's borrowing requirement." [p. 16]

I cannot agree with Kaldor's belief that velocity of M will adjust to offset any induced changes in M (a remnant of the Radcliffe Committee heresy), nor with his odd belief that the interest elasticity of the demand for money and of V does not matter, since in any case the central bank will never be able to pursue an independent monetary policy because that would result in changes in interest rates and security prices which would be catastrophic and intolerable.

I am prepared to admit that there are important institutional differences between the money market in the U.K. and the United States, so that the Bank of England cannot under present practices exercise monetary policy in exactly the way that the Federal Reserve can. Yet experience shows that Kaldor is simply wrong in thinking that the Fed can never follow the monetary policy that would be desired by post-Keynesians or even that which would be desired by monetarists; and I suspect that he is even wrong when it comes to the London market which he knows best. Both under its present institutional arrangements and after various desired reforms in practice have been introduced, the Bank of England has broad leeway in determining what the money supply shall be in the face of concomitant fiscal policy, and it is indeed an important matter what is the elasticity of the demand for money with respect to interest rate changes and what is the elasticity of the stream of investment and consumption spending to such changes.

All will agree that central banks have often in the past chosen to moderate somewhat the fluctuations in interest rates and credit conditions that would have been induced by cyclical ups and downs of spending propensities. This moderating of interest rate oscillations was possible only by their permitting some components of the money supply to react passively to prior and contemporaneous changes in GNP.

Even the monetarists agree to this, nay even insist on it in their heated indictments of the central bankers. Long before Professor Kaldor, critics of monetarism — such as Professors Tobin, Modigliani, and myself — have demonstrated that this indictment for reacting passively, if true, ought to weaken any inference that a high multiple correlation between M and GNP "identifies" the potency of the former to control the latter.

And all will agree that central banks have often accommodated fiscal deficits and surpluses by contriving faster or slower rates of growth of the money supply. Thus, the monetarists have a valid point when they insist that the separate potency of fiscal policy is often hard to identify historically because of concomitant monetary changes. So one can welcome Dr. Kaldor's debunking of the evidence for money's exclusive potency by stressing the fact that, *in the past*

19

to a significant degree, the money supply did have an endogenous component respondent to GNP and fiscal policy.

Does it follow from that, as Professor Kaldor argues in his characteristic confident and persuasive manner, that the central bank is only a constitutional monarch, which can reign only so long as it does not rule? Is it true that in the U.K. — or in the United States or Timbuctoo — exogenous changes in the money supply are quite impossible without bringing on such violent instabilities in the capital markets as to cause those independent monetary policies to be soon reversed? Can it be true that the potency of monetary policy is unaffected by the question of whether the marginal-efficiency-of-investment schedule is interest-inelastic and the liquidity-preference schedule is infinitely elastic — as even the Neanderthal Keynesians are able to recognize?

I am not an expert on the London market. But none of the meagre evidences offered by Professor Kaldor, either in *Lloyd's Bank Review* or at the World Econometric Congress last September in Cambridge, is at all convincing on the point that exogenous monetary policy is simply impossible.

This is worse than a reversion to Neanderthal Keynesianism, for even that doctrine admits that money can be changed if you are willing to countenance the completely-offsetting changes in its velocity that will allegedly thereby be induced.

As far as I can make out, we have here simply Humpty-Dumptyism — assertions based upon neither facts nor plausible reasonings.

During the German hyper-inflation of 1920-23, the head of the Reichsbank kept insisting that he was powerless to pursue an exogenous monetary policy. He was no more to be believed than would be a Governor of the Bank of England or the Federal Reserve who, in the face of the fact that Daltons and Victory Loans have fluctuated from 100 to down below 50, claimed impotence to act except endogenously.

CONCLUSION

Science is public knowledge. It should never be subject to the whims and idiosyncracies of one man. There is no way to explain why monetarists, i.e., those who believe in the impotence of fiscal policy and of investment fluctuations to affect overall inflation and money spending, should also believe that the money supply should follow this or that simple rule, should believe that wages and prices are downward flexible and the Phillips curve is a mirage, should believe in a natural rate of unemployment, should peculiarly believe that inflation has an effect upon the money interest rates, should believe that employment is always full in the long run — there is no reason why monetarists should believe this except that all of these notions happen to be believed by the one man, Professor Friedman.

In leaving the subject of a sophisticated demand for money, I

20

have to stress that once you believe in it, with full recognition that such demand depends negatively on interest rates and significantly on the amounts of other assets (public debt, private bonds, claims to wealth, and various money substitutes), you cease to be a monetarist and have rejoined the human race. As Professor Tobin recently remarked in deflating the claims of Professor Harry Johnson that the monetarists had been doing sophisticated work in measuring the demand for money, the truth is that every econometric study of the demand for money concludes that there is a strong negative dependence upon the interest rate — that is everyone with the notable exception of Professor Milton Friedman, the sole scholar unable or unwilling to detect such an effect.

Finally, in none of the modern sciences would it be respectable to believe in the pseudo-positivism which prevails among the monetarists. It makes one ashamed for one's science, and provides us with still another reason why the peculiar tenets of monetarism have to be rejected.

21

265

SAMUELSON ON THE NEOCLASSICAL DICHOTOMY: A REPLY*

PAUL A. SAMUELSON   *Massachusetts Institute of Technology*

Don Patinkin's comment[1] on what neoclassical theory really was is most welcome, for he is rightfully hailed as both the culmination of that tradition and a progenitor of the theories that go beyond it.

Let me register agreement with basic points he makes, and then take this occasion to add some further reflections.

Agreements

1. Some writers, before and after Patinkin's seminal 1949 article,[2] believed in what he and I call the invalid (A', B') dichotomy: namely, they write down a set of pure "barter-type" relations, which after we have eliminated unknown quantities of goods can be usually written in the form of homogeneous-of-degree-zero relations

$$A': \qquad 0 = f_i(P_1, P_2, ..., P_n) \equiv f_i(1, P_2/P_1, ..., P_n/P_1) \qquad (i = 1, 2, ..., n)$$

*I owe thanks to the National Science Foundation for financial assistance.
[1] D. Patinkin, "Samuelson on the Neoclassical Dichotomy: A Comment," this JOURNAL, V, no. 1 (Feb. 72), 279–83. I hope on another occasion to clarify some other matters that have proved puzzling in my earlier papers, "What Classical and Neoclassical Monetary Theory Really Was," this JOURNAL, I (1968), 1–15, and "Nonoptimality of Money Holding under *Laissez Faire*," *ibid.*, II (1969), 303–8.
[2] D. Patinkin, "The Indeterminacy of Absolute Prices in Classical Economic Theory," *Econometrica*, 17 (1949), 1–27. See also his "The Invalidity of Classical Monetary Theory," *ibid.*, 19 (1951), 134–51, and his *Money, Interest, and Prices* (Evanston, Ill., 1st ed., 1956; 2nd ed. 1965).

and in which any one of the functions is functionally dependent on all the rest and can be ignored as redundant.

A useful example for later comment would be exchange of apples and nuts between two classes, each with an equal number of identical people and with members of each class endowed respectively with $(q_1{}^\dagger, q_2{}^\dagger)$ and $(Q_1{}^\dagger, Q_2{}^\dagger)$, and where for simplicity all men spend equal amounts on each of the two goods. Then my A' can be reduced down simply to

$$(1) \qquad P_2/P_1 = (q_1{}^\dagger + Q_1{}^\dagger)(q_2{}^\dagger + Q_2{}^\dagger)^{-1}.$$

Writers may then append to the A' relations a B' relation of either of the following two types:

B_1': $P_1 = 1$, good 1 being set as "numeraire."

Alternatively, with some money stuff constant at $M = M^\dagger$, an equation-of-exchange type relation is assumed

B_2': $P_1Q_1{}^* + P_2Q_2{}^* + \ldots + P_nQ_n{}^* = \bar{V}M^\dagger$

where the $Q_i{}^*$ are the real solutions to A' and $\bar{V}$ is an alleged constant or quasi-constant.

In terms of our example, B_2' would become

$$(2) \qquad P_1(q_1{}^\dagger + Q_1{}^\dagger) + P_2(q_2{}^\dagger + Q_2{}^\dagger) = \bar{V}M^\dagger.$$

Combining the examples A' and B_2', we get the familiar quantity-theory proportionality of every price to the exogenously given money supply, namely

$$(3) \qquad P_i = \{\bar{V}(2q_i{}^\dagger + 2Q_i{}^\dagger)^{-1}\}M^\dagger \qquad (i = 1, 2).$$

2. We can further agree that B_2' is a pretty unsatisfactory theory of money holding and money spending. If barter really works so nicely in the A' apple-nut sector, why should wampum or greenbacks be held at all in the B' sector? Why shouldn't the wampum become *free* pebbles on the beach? And the greenbacks become worthless bits of waste paper? In other words, to repeat what Frank Knight observed many years ago,[3] if there were no stochastic uncertainties about the timing of transactions, no lack of synchronization between receipts and expenditures, no indivisibilities and frictions giving rise to brokerage and other transaction costs – then any velocity parameter, $\bar{V}$, would become infinite. Or what is the same thing, the $k = 1/\bar{V}$ parameter of the Cambridge school's propensity to hold money in relation to income would go to zero, taking the "value of money" down to zero with it. Once we let $\bar{V} \to \infty$, all absolute prices go to infinity, $P_i \to \infty$, and become meaningless; but we are still left with well-determined price ratios or "real terms of trade," P_i/P_j, as allegedly determined in A' alone.

Anyone who really faces up to this natural disappearance of all money as

---

[3]F. H. Knight, *Risk Uncertainty and Profit*, a Cornell thesis (1916), first published in 1921, and reprinted in 1933, 1948, and 1957. For the following quotation, taken from the preface to the 1933 reissue, see the Augustus M. Kelley reprint of economics classics, p. xxii: "If the exchange-medium of a society has no intrinsic service value, the velocity of circulation must approach infinity, as the amount of uncertainty affecting the individual's need for money is reduced toward zero."

an economic good, will probably retreat back from B_2' to B_1' with its trivial *numeraire* solution to absolute prices.

At the least, to defend B_2' as a supplement to A', one would have to stipulate that some "implicit theorizing" has been going on in the background, postulating that the A' allegedly-barter transactions did involve lack of synchronization of receipts and payments and those stochastic uncertainties and frictions that one appeals to when explaining why anyone holds inventories of anything – as, for example, why a wholesaler holds a stock of mousetraps, and why he doesn't hold a larger one.

3. So we can agree that any economist, such as the young Patinkin of 1949, could make a real contribution to the subject in formally putting M – i.e. real honest-to-goodness money, whether in the form of shells, coin, or greenbacks – into the heart of the economic market system, thereby abandoning the unsatisfactory (A', B') dichotomy in favour of a more satisfactory (A, B) dichotomy – to which I now turn.

Now one stipulates that the unknowns $(M, P_1, ..., P_n)$ can be related by homogeneous-of-degree-one-or-zero type, as e.g.

$$A: \qquad 0 = F_i(M, P_1, ..., P_n) \equiv MF_i(1, P_1/M, ..., P_n/M),$$
$$(i = 1, 2, ..., n; \text{ or } i = 0, 1, ..., n).$$

Note that if we choose to write down $n + 1$ rather than n relations in A, one of them will be functionally dependent on the rest and be ignorable as redundant.

With luck A can be solved for all n equilibrium ratios $(P_i/M)^*$. Then we can append to A the stipulated quantity of (what today we would call "outside") money

$$B: \qquad M = M^\dagger.$$

Thus, the absolute prices are determined, and they do have the quantity-theory property of being proportional to the stock of exogenous money:

$$P_i = (P_i/M)^* M^\dagger, \qquad (i = 1, ..., n).$$

To illustrate this valid (A, B) dichotomy with the apple-and-nut example, let us suppose that there is a convenience of having an average cash balance – in order to avoid irregularities and minimize variance of apple-nut consumptions around their mean annual magnitudes, to bridge transactions and offset lack of synchronization of in-payments and out-payments, and perhaps in order to avoid irksome effort and leisure sacrificed in making more frequent trips to the bank when cash balances dip low.[4] For simplicity, suppose everyone

---

[4] Another time I hope to illustrate how one can deduce an individual's preference function of the form $U(q_1, ..., q_n; M, P_1, ..., P_n) \equiv U(q_1, ..., q_n; \lambda M, \lambda P_1, ..., \lambda P_n)$ with $\partial U/\partial q_i > 0$, $\partial U/\partial M > 0$, $\partial U/\partial P_i < 0$. Thus, interpret q_i as "expected" or mean q_i per unit time, $q_i \equiv \bar{q}_i = \exp\{q_i(t)\}$. Let σ_{ij} = the covariance matrix $\exp\{(q_i(t) - \bar{q}_i)(q_j(t) - \bar{q}_j)\}$ and suppose that, for each set of prices $(P_1, ..., P_n)$, larger M permits you to have reduced covariances and higher well-being. Thus, we deduce a function $U(\bar{q}_1, ..., \bar{q}_n; M, P_1, ..., P_n)$ of the postulated neoclassical type. Another time I hope to describe dynamic paths as against steady-state paths, in which each man can hope to spend out of his cash and non-cash wealth, by making his $dM^\dagger(t)/dt$ negative, etc.

will pay half of what he spends on apples or what he spends on nuts in order to get the convenience utility from the average cash balance he holds: this cost of having an average cash balance is incurred in the form of explicit interest on his borrowed cash; or, if he is endowed with titles to cash, the cost is in the form of implicit or opportunity-cost interest incurred for that part of his cash endowment that he forebears from lending out at the market rate of interest, r, per unit time.

Then A can be written

(4) $\qquad P_1(q_1{}^\dagger + Q_1{}^\dagger) = P_2(q_2{}^\dagger + Q_2{}^\dagger) = 2rM,$

where M is the aggregate of cash balances demanded and where, for simplicity, we can let the interest rate be set by the long-run time-preference parameter, $r = \rho$.

This is equivalent to either of the following A formulations

(5) $\qquad (P_i/M)^* = 2\rho(q_i{}^\dagger + Q_i{}^\dagger)^{-1} \qquad (i = 1, 2),$ or

(6) $\qquad P_2/P_1 = (q_1{}^\dagger + Q_1{}^\dagger)(q_2{}^\dagger + Q_2{}^\dagger)^{-1},\ P_1/M = 2\rho(q_1{}^\dagger + Q_1{}^\dagger)^{-1}.$

Adjoining B gives

$\qquad M = M^\dagger,$

and the resulting (A, B) system displays the quantity-theory proportionalities

(7) $\qquad P_i = \{2\rho(q_i{}^\dagger + Q_i{}^\dagger)^{-1}\} M^\dagger, \qquad (i = 1, 2).$

In concluding this list of agreements, let me make clear that I did not, prior to 1949, write out such a complete (A, B) system. Nor do I claim to be able to recall that someone else did. And I do not mean to deny that some writers, even after 1949, still continued to insist upon the validity of (A', B') – as such, or as against that of (A, B).

Caveats: literary-mathematical dichotomies

Having agreed on so much, let me make some observations.

Quite aside from the dichotomy between A' and B' or between A and B, there has been a different kind of dichotomy in the neoclassical literature – a dichotomy between *accepted literary* views on the role of money and prices and the *mathematization* of the subject.

For every writer Patinkin (or I) can name who, prior to 1932 or between 1940 and 1971, embraced the invalid (A', B') dichotomy, we can name dozens of neoclassical writers whose literary versions (and I do mean their *behaviour* relations) were incompatible with that invalid (A', B') dichotomy. When Lloyd Mints at Chicago assigned me an undergraduate book to read in 1932, it was Dennis Robertson's Cambridge handbook, *Money*. In it you will find no (A', B') dichotomy. And I could multiply this example fifty-fold. To save time, let any reader thumb through Howard Ellis' valuable survey, *German Monetary Theory* (Cambridge, Mass., 1934). It contains every kind of monetary theory – commodity theories, state theories, quantity theories – but no remote approximation to the (A', B') equation set.

I had the best undergraduate training in economics that the 1930s could provide. Except for reading a section of Cassel's classic *Theory of Social Economy* on the "arithmetic of prices" – and that was not in the money course – I do not think I ever encountered an (A', B') formulation. At Harvard, in Schumpeter's unsystematic lectures on Walras, I probably did meet it. But if I ever got from him the (A', B_2') quantity-equation-of-exchange version, I am sure that I got the (A, B_1') *numeraire* version much, much more often. And note: the (A', B_1') dichotomy involving a *numeraire* convention of some $P_1 = 1$, so that relative prices and absolute prices are trivially identical, is in no sense illogical or self-contradictory; it does not pretend to be a theory of "money" – it is a way of *avoiding* such a theory of money and absolute prices – and it does not provide such a theory.

What classical and neoclassical monetary theory was really about is, I would argue, Marshall, Fisher,[5] Pigou, Robertson, Cannan, Ellis, *et al.* and not the rare and esoteric mathematizations attempted by Divisia, Cassel, or Schneider – or, in later times, the re-creations of Archibalds and Lipseys. The difference between science and anecdotes (or the case method) is some authentication of relative empirical *frequencies*. By this test the (A', B') analysis is of primary interest as a rare (and therefore valuable), but not-quite-successful, attempt to capture in mathematics what neoclassical writers were saying over and over again in words: "Money is useful"; "Money is *indirectly* useful, useful for the work it does in buying commodities, and when prices are high, it takes more money to provide the same useful service"; etc., etc.

When I chaired that 1949 Christmas session that Patinkin refers to (which, incidentally, may have been the last one that Schumpeter attended), I felt that Leontief and Hickman spoke for themselves and a limited subset of

---

[5]Fisher is an interesting case, worth commenting on because of his pre-eminence as a monetary theorist and because Patinkin has commented on him on pp. 600–2 of his 1965 book. Fisher never clearly stated a proper A set of equations, we can agree on that; and Patinkin may be right in suggesting that Fisher is in some confusion between a B_2' formulation of his 1911 $MV = PQ$ type and a B_1' formulation of his 1892 type – or, as I might prefer to put it – Fisher thought that a B_2' equation could play the same role in completing his A' set as a B_1' equation could. Fisher's A' set is pretty clearly of the type that can be approximated by n independent equations in the n ratios $[P_i/\bar{P}(p_1, ..., p_n)]$, where $\bar{P}$ stands for "the price level" and is a first-degree homogeneous function in the Ps. Such an A' does determine *all* equilibrium relative price ratios, $(P_i/P_j)^*$, that are "independent of" M or $M^\dagger$. This property of A' is no crime, since a proper A also has this property, a conclusion of my version of neoclassical theory that Patinkin has also independently arrived at. However, a proper A set, save in the special case of "separability" (as in my nut-apple example, where utility functions take the additive form $U[q_1, ...] + u[M, P_1, ..., P_n])$, has final reduced-form solutions independent of M; but, the relations determining the solutions are not "independent of" M/P_i magnitudes. So Fisher's A' is too special. (Note: it can be defended against a charge of being self-contradictory by reference to the separability possibility.) Since Patinkin himself uses an index number construction, $\bar{P}(P_1, ...)$, he has not criticized Fisher as being too special in this direction. But I – gently – must criticize them both for yielding to this unnecessary (and generally inadmissible) specialization. I concur in regarding Fisher's $MV = PQ$ supplement B' to his A' as being unnecessarily special, although two sections on I *deduce* that precise form for the special apple-nut-money case involving additive logs. Finally, to do Fisher justice, the real-balance effects and stability analysis that Patinkin hankers for can validly be contained in Fisher's B_2' relation in those special cases where his A' happens to be a legitimate form of A.

neoclassical writers; I felt indignant that this should represent the neoclassical tradition.

In insisting on this dichotomy between the literary substance of neoclassical monetary theory and the (A', B') or other mathematizations, I am only insisting on what Don Patinkin himself has claimed – namely, that his 1949 and, even more so, his later writings do capture the spirit of what is implicit in the earlier quantity-theory writers and are closer to what the original propounders had in mind. All the more credit is due to Patinkin for his contributions.

The reader who has read this far will see that there is no essential disagreement between Patinkin and me. However, let me record in the next section a few minor comments that do represent some unimportant (to me at least) differences in emphasis between some of our formulations.

Identities, excess demands, and stability

Notice that my A' and also my A equations are not necessarily in the form of "excess-demand" functions. The nuts-apples example brings this out. Although these relations could often be recast in the form of excess-demand relations, it is a more faithful rendering of the pre-1932 discussions *not* to use this particular device, which was brought into prominence only *after*[6] John Hicks' 1939 *Value and Capital*. Oskar Lange, in his subsequent writings on Say's Law,[7] emphasized this Hicksian formulation, as did my own work on the dynamic-stability of markets. But all this came *after* the age of neoclassicism, which died a violent death the month Keynes' *General Theory* appeared in 1936. Oskar Lange, who was Patinkin's teacher and my friend, had a glorious decade in economics from 1935 to 1945. His work on Marxian economics, socialist pricing, capital models, Keynesian macroeconomics, stability analysis, and welfare-economics methodology, are enough to assure him permanent fame in economics. But, at the time of the early 1940s, I thought his work on Say's Law represented something of a detour. Since I was accustomed in those days to put my fingers into every pie, I recall feeling somewhat guilty that I could not become more interested in the then-popular game of reconciling "loanable-funds" and "liquidity-preference" theories of interest determination by reference to the Hicks-Walras formulations that, if all but one market is in equilibrium, then the Budget Identity (Say's Law, in some versions) would ensure that that last market would necessarily be in equilibrium. I never felt that indifference-curve analysis of the triad, money, goods, and bonds, had the fruitfulness of such analysis of tea, salt, and apples. I regarded listing of abstract equations with specified homogeneity properties as a somewhat

[6]Some of Walras is almost in this form, as e.g., when we equate $S_i(...)$ and $D_i(...)$ functions. Fisher's 1907 interest models are precisely of this form, as are Viner's 1931 lecture on international trade and subsequent trade articles by Lerner and Leontief. But it is to Hicks that we must give the major credit for the widespread emphasis on excess-demand functions.
[7]O. Lange, *Price Flexibility and Employment* (Bloomington, Indiana, 1944); this makes reference to his earlier articles on similar subjects. See P. A. Samuelson, *Foundations of Economic Analysis* (Cambridge, Mass., 1947), chaps. 9 and 10, which give references to my earlier articles on related subjects.

bloodless and arid procedure that lacked concrete substance and as not doing justice to the history of Say's Law or to doctrines of full employment via flexible wage rates and prices, as in contemporaneous discussion by Pigou and others of so-called Pigou effects. As mentioned elsewhere, I no longer feel guilt for having sat out that Lange dance. Inevitably that part of Patinkin's first work that took off from the Lange formulations interested me less than its heartland, in which the moneyness of money, for facilitating transactions and for holding, is given its long overdue formulation in explicit equational form.

Thus, consider what Patinkin tells us:[8] "In technical terms, my criticism of the $[(A', B_2')]$ dichotomy was that, because of Walras' Law, the excess-demand function for money – say $\phi(...)$ – has the form

$$\phi(...) \equiv - \sum_{i=1}^{n} p_i X_i(p_2/p_1, ..., p_n p_1),$$

which – by virtue of its being homogeneous of degree 1 in the p_i – is inconsistent with the form of the function as presented in B' [i.e., in B_2']."

This reason for rejecting (A', B') was stressed by Patinkin in his 1949 writings. But in his later writings, he more nearly approached the view that I expressed in 1968 and that follows here. Valuable as was the 1949 breakthrough, it was the later more general, less technical, objections that I think come closer to making sense out of the Robertsons and earlier neoclassicals.

In any formulations, whether at dates 1932, 1949, or 1968, I never found it particularly useful or interesting to think of "money" as a Hicks-Lange $(n + 1)$th commodity. The holding of money – i.e. the "renting" of money balances for transactional purposes (present or future) – has for its "price" the interest rate r (the rent per unit time of money expressed as a ratio to principal, and hence with dimensionality of a pure number per T, or ($MT^{-1}M^{-1}$ $= T^{-1}$) and *not* a P_{n+1} or a P_{n+1}/P_1. Certainly one does not speak for Robertson, Marshall, Pigou, Fisher, Ricardo, Hume, or Locke when one uses these Hicks-Lange formulations.

What do neoclassical and later writers find wrong with the (A', B_2') formulation? Consider A' in my apple-nuts model, which is due to pre-Walras writers such as Jevons of 1870 or J. S. Mill of 1848. There is in it no "technical" contradiction of A' with the quantity-equation-of-exchange formula of B_2' of the kind that Patinkin in the quoted passage says offended him. No Walras' identity is being raped, or even being referred to. The Walras identity of "apples traded for nuts of *equal value*" is already well in the background of my example's reduced-form relation, $P_2/P_1 = (q_1^\dagger + Q_1^\dagger)(q_2^\dagger + Q_2^\dagger)^{-1}$.

What is wrong with B_2' and the (A', B_2') formulation is this: (i) either it leaves the determination of $\bar{V} = 1/k$ at a finite level as a ridiculous absurdity, for reasons already mentioned; or (ii) it leaves the cogent reasonings for the finiteness of V, and for V being a constant rather than a complicated function of $(P_1, ..., P_n, M)$ – and of $r!$ – in the background as implicit theorizing; or (iii) it gratuitously denies the possibility that nuts-apples decisions could be influenced by the transactions aspects of a money-using system, thereby postulat-

---

[8]This quotation, except for my bracketed insertions, is taken from Patinkin, "Comment." 280.

ing a special and vulnerable kind of "neutrality" of money in comparison with "barter" – a "separability" neutrality which is quite different from the quantity-theory version of neutral money.

This difference with Patinkin in viewpoint or emphasis is, I insist, minor. But it may explain to the reader why there has been some apparent talking at cross purposes, and also what the last part of my 1968 paper is all about; it should set clear why Patinkin's new footnote 5 does not represent a correction that I can agree is needed. My objection to the inadequacy of the usual (A', B') formulation is not, I think, closely related to Patinkin's point that B' is a "mirror reflection" of A' and hence it is illogical to think that A' could be free of M while B', its twin so to speak, is made dependent on M'. Even where B' is *in no sense* such a mirror, it is wrong in principle to think that relative prices are unaffectable by changes in those behaviour patterns and institutions that are peculiarly tied up with M's velocity and liquidity properties; it would take more than "separability" to make such a strong version of "neutrality" generally valid.

The elaboration of my differences with Lange, and with some of Patinkin, may also explain why I have not been more concerned with something that Patinkin apparently regards as important – namely his footnote 11 complaint of neglect of real balance effects and of stability analysis. Patinkin speaks of his "... basic criticism of neoclassical monetary theory – which is that it did not fully integrate the real-balance into its analysis ... in support of this criticism ... the first and main bit of evidence presented in chap. VIII:1 of my book is the absence of stability analysis (with reference to the absolute price level) in the monetary theory of Walras and the Cambridge economists."

One hardly expects in pre-1932 writers much of post-1939 Hicks-Samuelson-Lang-Metzler-Arrow-Hurwicz stability discussion. And I find it less significant than Patinkin does that Walras pays less attention to *tâtonnement* in one part of his book than in others. At the heuristic level neoclassical writers are replete with discussions of how Spanish gold caused people to spend more and bid up prices. The same holds for the printing press in the German hyper-inflation of 1921–3. I was brainwashed into believing a monetary version of the business cycle, of the Hawtrey and Robertson's *Banking Policy and the Price Level* type, in which the price level in floating down to restore full employment would overshoot past equilibrium but then, inevitably after a time, recovery would take place. One could better accuse the modern writing of the arch quantity theorist, Milton Friedman, of neglecting channels of causation and stability than the primers I was brought up on. Just as peasants speak prose all their lives, those who fail to write anywhere a differential equation, relating d(price level)/dt to some discrepancy between the cash balance wanted at the given level of prices and what there is to be held by people, are not thereby convicted of neglect of an equilibrating process. Patinkin himself quotes examples of this kind of recognition from Wicksell and other great masters.

In any case, formalization of statical systems usually precedes formalization of dynamical systems, both in physics and economics. The fact that my 1968 paper scrupulously deals only with the statical conditions of equilibrium does not mean that I have in any way overlooked or left unintegrated any real balance effects. The early writers would not agree with any censuring of me on that account: the least I can do is desist from throwing stones at them on that same account.

In concluding this discussion of minor lack of agreements and prior to a technical digression on the distinguishability of (A, B) from (A', B'), let me emphasize anew that the best neoclassical theory (like post-Keynesian theory) had no need for (i) $MV = PQ$ formulations; (ii) the dubious assertion that velocity, V, is independent of interest rates, r, or very nearly so – since all that can be said of V is that it is homogeneous-of-degree-zero in the full set of variables $(P_1, ..., P_n, M, ...)$; (iii) use of aggregate price level concepts, $\bar{P}$, as against the whole vector $(P_1, P_2, ..., P_n, W, ...)$, or postulating of "separability" conditions; (iv) explicit use of a "real balance" variable of the form $M/\bar{P}$ as against homogeneous functions of degree zero in the vector $(M, P_1, ..., P_n)$; (v) the odd notion that M affects PQ *only* through its effects on P – in a real world where Q is *fluctuating* in different degrees below its full-employment level. Only when $Q = Q^*$ is assured, does M affect P proportionally in accordance with neoclassical standard theory.

A technical digression

There is no canonical form for the correct A. Many alternative formulations are admissible, both for unreduced and reduced forms. Sometimes it is natural for the relations of an impeccable A to contain a subset that looks like the questionable A'. Our apples-nuts example provides a case in point. Instead of

$$A \qquad P_i/M = 2\rho(q_i^\dagger + Q_i^\dagger)^{-1}, \qquad (i = 1, 2)$$

$$B \qquad M = M^\dagger,$$

we can write its *exact* equivalent

$$A' \qquad P_2/P_1 = (q_1^\dagger + Q_1^\dagger)(q_2^\dagger + Q_2^\dagger)^{-1},$$

$$B_2' \qquad \sum_1^2 P_j(q_j^\dagger + Q_j^\dagger) = (4\rho)M^\dagger.$$

Here in my version of B_2' the non-constant velocity of circulation, $V = 4\rho$, is a deduced behaviour equation, and not an exogenously given parameter.

These equivalent (A, B) and (A', B_2') relations involve no implicit theorizing, being deducible from my 1968 utility function for each person

$$(9) \qquad U(q_1, q_2; M, P_1, P_2) \equiv U(q_1, q_2; \lambda M, \lambda P_1, \lambda P_2) =$$
$$\exp\{0.4 \log(q_1 q_2) + 0.1 \log(M^2/P_1 P_2)\}.$$

Of course, the fact that M drops out of all M/P_i terms in A' is due to the accident that U here has the "separability" or "tree" property

$$(10) \qquad U = F[f(q_1, q_2); M, P_1, P_2].$$

In a general case, as for instance,

$$U = f(q_1; M/P_1) + g(q_2; M/P_2),$$

P_2/P_1 would not be independent of the (M, P_1, P_2) variables.

However, even in the general case, one could usually choose to express the A set as

(11) $0 = F_i(1, [P_1/M], [P_1/M][P_2/P_1], ..., [P_1/M][P_n/P_1])$ $(i = 1, ..., n)$.

Any one of these functions might have already been solved to express P_1/M in terms of the $(P_2/P_1, ..., P_n/P_1)$ remainder. This would then be of a B_2' form and the rest with P_1/M eliminated would be of the A' form. Hence, a mathematician or logician who was no economist, could not go all the way with my earlier rejection of the (A', B_2') dichotomy as illegit'mate. Nor would I quarrel with him: provided the moneyness of money is in the warp and woof of the analysis, who cares how the relations are *presented?*

Conclusion

Summary of so varied an argument must be brief. After agreeing with Patinkin's major contention that pre-1949 neoclassical theory was in need of the reformulation he has provided, I elucidate some minor differences with his formulation of the (A', B') and (A, B) equations in necessarily excess-demand form, and I suggest how alien from 1932 "classical neoclassicism" was the post-*Value and Capital* Lange treatment of M as just another q_{n+1} good, and of Say's Law as having an intrinsic relation to Walras' budget identities or to post-1939 stability analyses of dynamic excess-demand processes. If I am right, there is no belittlement of the Patinkin contribution involved.

My review of the literature for this occasion leaves me in no doubt that Patinkin is correct in his major contention: we pre-Keynes neoclassicals were not clear in our own mind on *exactly how* to tie up monetary theory of absolute prices with our analysis of the equilibrium relative prices that were known to be unaffected by the quantity of outside money. 1932 is not 1950 or 1968 or 1972. This granted, one is still left after reading Patinkin with a feeling that quality will out: how well Walras, Wicksell, Fisher, Marshall, and the great masters score even though none gets it quite right from the standpoint of Patinkin's 1949 preoccupation with excess-demand and stability formulations[9] or, I may add, from the 1972 common ground that Patinkin and I share with modern analysts. Indeed, we still lack in 1972 a really adequate theoretical structure that encompasses the foundations of a money economy. On to the drawing boards!

[9]Some of the masters' failings are merely that they do not use Patinkin's terminology, surely venial rather than mortal sins. Thus, the rectangular hyperbola relating the "value of money" or $1/\bar{P}(P_1, ...)$ to the stock of money M†, although it may not be a demand curve in Patinkin's sense, is one in Gregory King's original sense or in the reduced-form sense of the locus of observed points traced out by changes in the supply of M†.

266

FOREWORD:
THE GEOGRAPHY OF
ECONOMIC INFLATION

by
Paul A. Samuelson
Professor of Economics
Massachusetts Institute of
Technology

ARCHIMEDES' lever is useless without a fulcrum to rest it on, and even angels need the point of a needle to dance upon. So too must prices be located in *space* as well as in time. Unlike released cannonballs, competitive prices follow a reverse law of gravity and *climb* the gradient of transport costs.

Corn downstream cannot sell for more than the extra costs to get it there. It can sell for less, but then it won't move from here to there. Along the geodesic where corn is flowing, competitive price rises predictably as the integral of the transport costs incurrable at each point along the way.

To the one-track mind of a corn addict, the globe is covered with isobars of equal corn price, consisting of closed contours surrounding maximum points in cities. Cities are not only sinks of iniquity, they are also sinks of consumption and hence mountaintops of price. Between nearby cities, markets are separated by border frontiers or great divides, on one side of which goods go east and on the other side west. Losch's ideal pattern for similar cities forms a grid of regular (spherical) hexagons. Where three borders meet, that is, where three altitudes of the equilateral triangle formed by the cities meet, occur valleys of price minima: their surrounding closed contours ascend in price until finally tangency is reached with the descending closed contours of the cities; such tangencies occur at passes or saddlepoints halfway between two cities. Along the line joining the two nearest cities (fore and aft on the horse) price is at a minimum on the saddlepoint; on the line perpendicular to this (starboard to port of the horse), price is at its maximum on the saddlepoint. All this is in accord with the mathematical topology of Clerk Maxwell and Marston Morse. (Of course, if the cities are far enough apart, the borders will cease to be lines and will become thick no-man's-lands where the price surface is so flat as to enforce self-sufficiency in corn. These autarky zones are like the dough left over in the cookie sheet when your mother stamps out circular cookies, and on them price can vary gently according to local variations in soil fertility and demands.)

As von Thunen established in his classic 1826 *The Isolated State*, the contours of price go along with congruent isopleths of land rent and population density: rent and density rise and fall with price on a homogeneous plain. The geodesic rays of goods movement pierce perpendicularly (really pierce "transversally") the isobar wave fronts, in the style of Huyghens, Hamilton, and Caratheodory.

GEOGRAPHICAL ASPECTS
OF
INFLATIONARY PROCESSES

What has all this to do with the geography of price inflation? *Everything. From knowledge of how prices are connected in space, we understand how spatial price patterns change over time.*

Consider the mythology of a Kondratieff cycle based on a California, Australia, or Klondike gold discovery. Near the mines goods are scarce and gold is abundant. An unfresh egg can sell for $5 so long as the cost to transport an egg to California in a short period of time is astronomical. Given more time, transport costs are less; but they are still large enough to keep prices and wages in the gold fields higher than those in the East. With transport of goods, prices become lower in California than they were, and higher in the East than they were, even though staying higher in California than in the East. California is exporting some of its gold-occasioned inflation.

But this *supply effect* is not all. As gold accumulates in the East and provides export surpluses there, unemployment and excess-plant capacity are less there. Cost-push pressures begin to operate. Furthermore, as the stock of gold grows, the money supplies in the world are growing. By the Quantity Theory of Prices and Money, in the longer run this will increase price and wage levels. Such a theory is adequate to explain how Spanish specie (mainly silver, not gold) raised European price levels in the centuries after Columbus.

Can the modern Federal Reserve similarly raise prices in Europe by creating more U.S. money supply? As demand here raises prices here, under a pre-1971 regime of pegged exchange rates this has to raise prices abroad since our import surplus reduces supplies of goods abroad (as with the Eastern eggs that went to the gold fields). Reinforcing this supply effect is the fact that the exchange rate of the dollar and, say, the mark can be maintained in the face of a U.S. payments deficit only by the German government and central banks taking in our dollars (our I.O.U.'s) and giving German exporters in return newly printed German currency. So the increase in our money supply increases Europe's money supply: more money in the world in the end will make for higher world-wide prices.

Is there no defense from importing New World inflation (along, say, with New World vulgarity and syphilis)? Under floating exchange rates, of the post-1971 variety, there is such a defense. A fully employed Germany can let the mark appreciate relative to the dollar so that higher U.S. dollar prices and wages are in equilibrium with unchanged German prices and wages. There is then no transitional U.S. import surplus, and no stimulus to the German export industries.

My impressionistic comments serve as only an overture to the arias that follow in this fruitful interdisciplinary concert of economists and geographers.

267

Economic Policy –
Where Is It Leading?

Paul A. Samuelson

ONCE UPON A TIME there was a general who was so stupid that eventually the other generals noticed it. Now, alas, in 1974 the recession has so intensified that even the President of the United States has finally noticed that the American economy is in a recession. For many months I have been saying that we are in a recession by every definition except one, namely the definition of the National Bureau for Economic Research, and that many of us go whole hours without thinking about the National Bureau.

President Ford and his Administration did not hastily accord diplomatic recognition to the recession. Thus at the September Summit meetings, twenty-three of the twenty-eight economic experts drawn from a broad spectrum of American life told the President that the Federal Reserve's monetary policy had been too tight and that he, the President, could not formulate his optimal policies as if inflation alone were the enemy. If twenty-three economic experts are going to go to heaven, my good friend Kenneth Galbraith would just as soon pass up the opportunity rather than be found dead in that company. He is not by temperament one who grabs for the middle position, and I verify from the Summit transcripts that John Kenneth Galbraith and Milton Friedman walked hip-to-head along the path of the minority.

Dr. Geoffrey Moore, who was Nixon's Commissioner of Labor Statistics, and who is the man at the National Bureau who years from now will decide whether this is a kosher economic recession, has as recently as December eighth reiterated his doubts on the matter. In the December first Sunday *New York Times'* financial section, Mr. Julius Shishkin, who is Ford's Commissioner of Labor Statistics, and who used to be the Custodian of the Leading Indicators of the National Bureau for Economic Research, also stated doubts, basing his reservations on the fact that prices have not been falling as with earlier recessions, and on the more rational fact that employment of labor has been unaccountably growing in the current period of stagnation. The Administration's Assistant Secretary of Commerce, Sidney Jones, characterized our current situation of economic unpleasantness as merely "a business spasm." Chairman Alan Greenspan of the Council of Economic Advisors, and Emeritus

---

These views on present economic problems were presented at a panel discussion at Boston University on December 4, 1974. Even though some of the statistics and governmental policies have changed since then, the basic arguments have not.

Professor William Fellner, his associate on the CEA, have, like Bre'er Rabbit, said "nuf'in' " on the subject. But, if you have a baby in the dormitory and simply stuff it in a drawer, that won't really dispose permanently of the matter. During and since the Summit the business situation has so patently deteriorated that canny Arthur Burns, now Chairman of the Federal Reserve, but earlier the guru at the National Bureau of Moore and Shishkin, has long since declared us to be in a recession; Professor Paul McCracken of the University of Michigan, Ford's informal advisor, admitted that we are in a recession. But he added the reassuring news that it will have a V-shaped bottom in 1975, and will be followed by a vigorous recovery. When my wife asked me how McCracken knew that, I was not able to give her a satisfactory answer.

Las Vegas paid off recession bets right after the Fourth of July when it became clear that U.S. Real GNP growth was negative in the first two quarters of the year. Since then the third-quarter data have become available, and we've had three quarters of decline, so to speak, back-to-back. No expert doubts that the current final quarter of 1974 will show further and intensifying real output decline. I have just been examining a baker's dozen of next year's forecasts and I find that, with the exception of one Harvard Assistant Professor, they all expect a down quarter early in 1975. You only begin to get a serious division among the experts when it comes to the second and third quarters of 1975.

Some experts, perhaps a plurality, think that sometime after Easter the trough of the 1973–1975 recession will occur. Others put the date after the Fourth of July, and you are called a pessimist in the fraternity of forecasters if you don't expect recovery by Thanksgiving Day, 1975. Yet I should warn

you that the fraternity of experts have been generally overly optimistic about the weakness in the economy; they've atoned for their overestimation of job opportunities by their equally optimistic underestimation of the virulence of our two-digit price and wage inflation.

And so, to repeat my opening lines, finally even President Ford has had to admit that we are in a recession. Like the Victorian housemaid who when charged with the heinous crime of being with child argued in self defense by way of extenuation that it was only a little fetus, so President Ford asserted at this week's press conference that it was really only a little recession, nothing to worry about seriously, so to speak, no worse than a bad cold.

Policy Past

My assigned topic is economic policy. To begin to understand the problems that this conjures up, let me repeat what I have been saying for a long, long time. If you turn this recession upside down and look at its bottom, it says, plainly written, "Made in Washington."

Do I claim this because I am a Democrat and it is Republicans who have been doing whatever they do in the White House? No. I am a Democrat, but my experience in serving on expert committees to advise the opposition party has been that the Democrats have no constructive policy programs to put forth. I have heard Leon Keyserling make proposals. I have heard Paul Samuelson make proposals. I have heard James Tobin, Arthur Okun, and Otto Eckstein make proposals. I have even heard John Kenneth Galbraith make proposals. But, if required to testify under oath, I would have to admit that the Washington policies which have been followed in the score of months prior to our present uncomfortable situation have been the joint work of both political parties.

Did Washington produce the present rate of unemployment of six going on seven percent because of errors in forecasting by the economic experts? Not at all. The turn from an overstrong to an overweak economy came after the first quarter of 1973, in other words after the re-election of Richard Nixon was safely over. For once the forecast crowd was very quick in realizing that the turn had come. This weakness in production has been by design, not by accident, and not primarily as a result of acts of God and of the King's enemies. Herbert Stein, the last chairman of the Council of Economic Advisors, and George Schultz, the last Secretary of the Treasury, and Arthur Burns, the perpetual chairman of the Federal Reserve, *all desired* that the economy be cooled off. This is not because they are sadists. As far as I know they were each Boy Scouts who helped little old ladies across the street and who exude the milk of human kindness. They hope to contrive a slowdown in the good and necessary cause of fighting the accelerating inflation.

In a measure most of us Democratic advisors went along. We conceded that the old Kennedy-Johnson goal of a four percent unemployment rate had to be at least temporarily given up. But few of us Democrats were prepared to favor six and seven percent unemployment as the necessary cost of fighting inflation. James Tobin of Yale broke away when unemployment became five percent; Okun and Samuelson turned ornery at five-and-a-half percent; Otto Eckstein and the rest draw their line at six percent.

Policy Future

What makes policy prescription so hard is the following objective finding of modern economic researchers. Once upon a time when Queen Victoria and President McKinley reigned, relatively small increments of unemployment bought you large increments of price stability. Today the tradeoff is worse, damnably worse for anyone who will take out his pencil and do a cost-benefit analysis on the net advantages of pursuing the Greenspan-Friedman-Ford policy of slowing down the economy in order to cool off the inflation.

What should have dominated the Summit discussions was the nature of this tradeoff. Yet when many of us so-called experts were asked to present memoranda at the Second Summit, I was aghast to learn in a telephone conversation that no one had thought about this problem of how much or little you buy in inflation abatement for each degree of investment in the sadism of unemployment. After I called this omission to the attention of the White House, they asked Eckstein (of Harvard and DRI) and David Grove (the economist for IBM) to take a hard look at this issue. For once academic gown and executive-suite gray flannel were in complete agreement: Eckstein and Grove confirmed the finding that Tobin had earlier stated at the Federal Reserve and at Brookings — namely, that in going from six percent unemployment to six-and-a-half percent unemployment, you only succeeded in reducing the next eighteen months' rate of inflation from, say, nine-and-three-quarters percent to nine-and-a-half percent.

What did the sage of Cook County, Professor Milton Friedman, say when confronted with this dire prospect? He said: "I don't believe in mathematical models." Well, it is possible that going by the bullet in your knee is a better method than going by econometric models. But how can we account for the fact that bullets in Republicans' knees always seem to tell a different story from those in Democrats' knees?

It is the death of rationality to disregard evidence and experience. If a person has better evidence, let him produce it. If he has a more plausible way of analyzing existing evidence, let him set it forth so the jury can ponder over its cogency. Let me quote from Lewis Carroll's *Through the Looking Glass:*

> "When *I* use a word," Humpty Dumpty said in rather a scornful tone, "it means just what I choose it to mean — neither more nor less."
> "The question is," said Alice, "whether you *can* make words mean different things."
> "The question is," said Humpty Dumpty, "which is to be master — that's all."

I am against Humpty Dumptyism when it comes to economic policy or for that matter military policy.

Just because Mr. Friedman says that it probably won't take a lot of unemployment in order to ease the inflation, that's not good enough for me if reasoned analysis of relevant patterns of experience do not confirm his intuition.

This is not a criticism that I make simply against those on the right. When I hear my good friend of long standing, Ken Galbraith, speak about the merits of permanent price-wage controls, administered this time by people who really believe in them and who apply them mainly to the few hundred largest corporations and a few dozen unions they bargain with, I stubbornly think of the post-World War II experience with price-wage controls, on several occasions, of Sweden. And of Norway. And of Holland. And of the U.K. And of Japan and Germany. And I examine in my mind's eye a dozen different books which have tried to describe, analyze, and appraise these twenty or more experiments by modern mixed economies. And I cannot help but wonder whether to follow the bullet in Galbraith's knee or to take note of the disappointments and skepticisms in the data of actual experience.

Samuelson's Rx

Let me conclude with my own policy recommendations.

1. Ford faces stagflation, not simple old-fashioned demand-pull inflation. He has two enemies, not one: recession and inflation, inflation and recession.

2. The Federal Reserve must loosen its tight money tourniquet. The housing industry is dying on the vine. Autos and consumers' durables are hard hit. Lower interest rates and faster growth can help make certain that the recession of 1973–1975 does not become the recession or depression of 1973–1976.

3. Ford should withdraw his proposal for a five percent tax surcharge on personal and corporate incomes. He should deny that he ever urged the Nixon proposal that American families save an extra one-and-one-half percent of their incomes. He might melt down those WIN buttons.*

4. He should welcome the fact that his budget is going to go deeply into deficit. The President knows the $300 billion spending limit can't possibly be achieved. He should stop applying the meat ax of budget cutting to human well-being programs. Yes, wasteful defense programs should be cut. Yes, welfare programs that have proved ineffective should be phased out in favor of more efficient programs. But no, it is not the case that since 1969 Washington spending has been out of control and that it is this factor which allegedly explains our inflation.

I admit it is easier to fight recession than inflation. But with the unemployment rate threatening to move to seven percent, I believe that the four prescriptions I have just given are not incompatible with our present rate of inflation moving down by next Labor Day to say eight percent. Eight percent inflation is bad. But the alternative to it threatens to be worse.

My final advice to President Ford is: scale down your targets and your claims. When

---

*In his State of the Union address in January, President Ford proposed a tax rebate.

we come to July 4, 1976 and are celebrating our bicentennial, President Ford can't possibly hope to have achieved stable prices without inflation. If we are lucky, we can go from low two-digit price inflation to high one-digit price inflation in one or two years. And with still more luck, we might get to five percent annual price inflation. But I see nothing in the evidence that will support on a reasonable basis the conclusion that we can do much better than that.

Margaret Fuller, our nineteenth-century Concord transcendentalist said, "I accept the universe." When told of this, Thomas Carlysle replied, "By gad, she'd better."

I suggest that President Ford and the American Congress accept the universe. It is the only one we have.

PART IX

Lectures and Essays on Current Economic Problems

268

Worldwide Stagflation

The following article was written by Professor Paul A. Samuelson of the Massachusetts Institute of Technology. The article is adapted from a memorandum prepared last autumn by Dr. Samuelson for the West German Council of Economic Advisers. Copyright © 1974 by Paul A. Samuelson.

THE international economy has seen in recent years a reacceleration of inflation in virtually every region. Creeping inflation that had earlier displayed a 3% or 4% or 5% average yearly trend has generally more than doubled that rate. Although the sharpest upswing has been in the prices of those staples that move heavily in international trade—food, fiber, fuels, and metals—there also has generally been a decided quickening in the pace of wage inflation and of price increases for domestic services and goods.

The current inflation, to be sure, has not represented hyperinflation or galloping inflation of the 1920-23 German experience or the Hungarian and Chinese experiences after World War II; nor is it akin to the 300% rate of inflation reached in Chile at the end of the Allende regime, or (as yet) akin to the chronic Latin American inflation that has averaged out to more than 20% per year for decades and even generations. However, the magnitude of the inflation makes it a matter of acute concern and public debate, particularly because of widespread uneasiness that it may well accelerate further. Inflation is indeed a prime election issue in many countries.

Compounding the economic problem of inflation is the fact that, often and in many countries, there persists a simultaneous problem of unemployment and stagnant growth. "Stagflation" is a new name for a new disease: stagflation involves inflationary rises in prices and wages at the same time that people are unable to find jobs and firms are unable to find customers for what their plants can produce.

Fallacious single-cause explanations

A variety of monistic explanations have been offered for the current inflation. The monetarists, of course, identify excessive growth of the money supply as the sole or prime cause. Other economists trace the global speedup of inflation principally to the long string of balance-of-payments deficits experienced by the U.S. in the 1960s. And for still others, wage-push is the villain, with the wage explosion that has occurred so widely in recent years attributed to various structural changes in the labor market that are said to have worsened the so-called Phillips-Curve trade-off between movements in unemployment and wages.* Other monistic explanations of current inflation relate to forces disturbing individual commodity or labor markets: to droughts, floods, strikes, cartel behavior, and so on. And a great number of people are convinced, of course, that our inflationary troubles trace to the rise in both the official and unofficial prices of gold—that is, to the general devaluation of currencies vis-à-vis gold that has occurred in the last several years. A related explanation runs in terms of the additional depreciation of particular currencies—such as the dollar—against other major currencies, a phenomenon that links domestic

---

* The Phillips Curve takes its name from A. W. Phillips, a New Zealand economist who concluded from study of data covering almost a century of British experience that percentage changes in money wage rates can be explained largely by the level of unemployment and the rate of change of unemployment. Oversimplified, Phillips' thesis is: The softer the job market, the weaker are wage pressures.

cost and price increases to exogenous forces abroad.

One could expand the list of monistic explanations. They make for dramatic reading. But, alas, the claims of one cause to be the sole cause invalidate such claims for the rest. As we apply the best tools of modern economic analysis to the pattern of available evidence, I believe that no monistic theory can be validly maintained. One is forced by the facts of experience into an eclectic position. It is not a case where intellectual indecision or uncertainty leads to a hedged position of eclecticism. It is rather that explanation of the varied pattern of ongoing experience calls for bold combination of causations.

I certainly have no doubt that the Asian and African droughts and Soviet crop shortfalls have been one critical element in the international run-up of food prices. Sudden supply shifts combined with sudden demand shifts obviously tend to produce dramatic price fluctuations, particularly in an area such as agriculture where changes in prices do not quickly induce either enlarged supply or reduced demand. Microeconomic commodity inflation — whether in food, in fuels, or indeed in any important sector of the domestic or international economy — refuses to remain microeconomic. It is true that a family which spends more on beef or electricity than it has been spending previously may spend less for other things, tending thereby to depress their prices. And one could conceive of money wage rates falling when bad harvests or dear Near-East oil induces a lower real wage rate. But this sort of offsetting occurrence seems to happen only in history books. In the world in which we actually live, strong upside price pressures originating in a particular sector tend to disturb the whole price structure and raise its average level. This is partly because fiscal and monetary policies — for reasons I explore in the paragraphs that follow — generally work in a way that prevents compensatory price declines from occurring. It is also because existing institutional arrangements (such as escalator clauses in collective-bargaining contracts) tend to set in motion a phase of price-wage leapfrogging whenever a major instance of microeconomic inflation erupts. If one focuses narrowly on some especially visible part of the complicated transmission process — on explosive wage behavior or rapid monetary growth—it may well seem that the critical causal element has been identified. But that is illusory. Monetary expansion, for instance, is typically more the result than the cause of sustained general inflation, simply because in the end central bankers—like governments—must be responsive to public opinion of populist electorates. They must be accommodative and avoid policies that would acutely worsen short-run unemployment and stagnation problems. The whole explanation of the inflation we are experiencing is something more than the sum of its separate parts. But it is not something other than the combination of those analytically distinguishable separate strands of causation.

Overview of global inflation

I believe that the present inflation is rooted deep in the nature of the mixed economy. And it is the mixed economy—which is not laissez-faire capitalism any more than it is centrally-controlled state socialism—that characterizes most of the world today: North America, Western Europe and Australasia, Japan, and much of the developing world outside of Eastern Europe and mainland Asia.

For one thing, we live in the Age After Keynes. Electorates all over the world have eaten of the fruit of the tree of modern economic knowledge and there is no going back to an earlier age. High

4

employment or full employment is everywhere a goal insisted upon by the electorate of all political persuasions. A half century ago there was no comparable political sentiment effective against incurring prolonged depression or even stagnation; rather there was often a preoccupation with the perils of inflation, of budget and foreign-trade deficits. This shift in populist attitudes of governments necessarily shifts the odds against stable prices (and of course against falling prices). No longer can one expect half the peacetime years to experience falling prices. If general price levels rarely stand still and often rise, then the secular trend of prices must be upward on the average.

What needs emphasis is the universal character of this common *Zeitgeist*. It used to be said, of course, that Germany was an exception. Because of traumatic memories of the inflation of the early 1920s, the German voter, it used to be claimed, would put effective political pressures on the side of price stability—even at the cost of considerable transitional unemployment. Whatever plausibility that hypothesis once had, its credibility surely has gradually weakened as the years have passed? Only a fraction of the population now alive could actually have experienced the hyperinflation. The vividness of any memory must be attenuated through time. This is not to deny that the German Phillips Curve of earlier years represented, in some respects, the envy of most other industrialized nations. However, although I cannot profess to be anything of an expert on local German conditions, the available statistical evidence strongly suggests to me that *since 1969 there also has been a deterioration in the trade-off relation between German labor market conditions and wage inflation.* Thus, even in Germany, we seem to have a new bias toward chronic inflation.

The present diagnosis is in some ways *not* a pessimistic one. The microeconomic laws of supply and demand that have pulled the prices of major staples to high levels can be expected at least in some instances to pull those same prices downward. Indeed, the prices of many key farm products are now well below earlier peaks, and outside the U.S. a number of metal prices have recently come down appreciably. Microeconomic commodity inflation—except perhaps for OPEC oil—does not have the irreversible character that we properly associate with cost-push inflation in the mixed economy. Moreover, the pre-World War II pattern of a common synchronous business cycle has to a considerable extent reappeared. The coincidence of business cycle exuberance widely throughout the world in 1972-73 was a prime reason for the intensity of inflationary pressure. Now, we seem to be witnessing a widespread relaxation of demand in many countries at the same time. The old-fashioned business cycle has been tamed in the Age After Keynes, but it is by no means yet dead.

A pessimistic diagnosis?

But in a deeper sense, for anyone who is nostalgic for an era in which prices are reasonably stable and in which the purchasing power of money might even rise under the impact of cost-reducing technical change and innovation, the present general diagnosis may be profoundly pessimistic. The modern mixed economy simply will not tolerate that large numbers of people starve or suffer. The old dictum, "He who will not take any kind of work that is offered him, however disagreeable and low-paid it may be, must be starved into doing so," just does not hold any more. And its degree of relevance fades with each passing decade. So be it. Few of us, in the affluent West at least, would want to turn back the clock to an earlier epoch. But it is a corollary of this deep-seated structural change in both attitudes and institutions that prices and wages are increasingly rigid against downward movement. In 1921 general wage rates in urban Britain or America might drop by 10% or even 20%. Today, even relatively large numbers of unemployed put little effective downward pressure on general wage and cost levels. Thus, during the U.S. recession of 1969-70, the rate of unemployment went from 3⅓% of the labor force up to 6% without doing very much even to slow down the positive rate of increase of money wage rates; and it never did slow the rate of wage increase down to the level of average labor-productivity improvement in the American economy. Looking beyond 1974, one must expect that union wage settlements will lose their "moderate" character and move from the 5%-to-7% annual range up toward the 10%-to-12% range.

Specific factors in recent inflation

Besides the broad deep-rooted structural changes here and abroad that have created a new bias toward inflation, the acceleration of price increases in recent years traces to a number of special disturbances — most of which I have enumerated. The food and fuel problems are uppermost in the minds of people at the moment perhaps, but a great deal of attention—deservedly so—also has been paid to balance-of-payments disequilibrium, particularly to the U.S. payments deficits of the 1960s. From 1959 to 1971, the U.S. dollar was overvalued in my view. Even if this opinion is not accepted for the first five years of this period, after the Viet Nam War few could doubt that the overvaluation of the dollar was worsening. This must, in some degree, have contributed to inflation in Western Europe and Japan.

The mechanisms through which the overvaluation of the dollar contributed to global inflation are multivarious but are not in doubt. The swelling of U.S. imports of goods and services provided strong export markets for the surplus countries such as Germany and Japan. Export orders, microeconomically, raised the prices German firms could charge; they also reduced the excess capacity in the export sectors, raising real marginal costs there and hence the mark prices charged to either Germans or non-Germans. The enhanced incomes enjoyed in the export sectors were, in turn, respent on local goods and services, putting upward price and wage pressures in those sectors. Thus, whether we use the language of microeconomics or the Keynesian multiplier language of macroeconomics, one understands how the international U.S. payments deficit contributed to inflation in other countries. (In the U.S., the ability to get goods from abroad did—but in an inadequate degree—do something to lessen upward pressure on the U.S. wage and price level.)

The tendency for the rest of the world to import some inflation from the United States was reinforced, moreover, by the workings of the Bretton Woods system. Prior to 1971, the surplus countries generally supported the official parity of the U.S. dollar. This meant that firms and persons in Western Europe were, in the end, given local currencies by their own central banks. This added to their local supplies of money. And one does not have to be an over-simple monetarist to recognize that the effect of such an increase in money is to strengthen the direct stimulative multiplier effect that flows from an export surplus. Inevitably, of course, the policy of "benign neglect" in the U.S. with regard to the payments deficit was bound to create apprehension and to induce a speculative flight out of the dollar and into the undervalued currencies of the surplus countries. When that hap-

6

pened, a further bulge occurred in local money supplies outside the U.S., thereby intensifying the multiplier process.

Could not the nations with undervalued currencies have insulated themselves from importing some inflation from the American deficit? Of course they could have. But it would not have been technically all that easy. And it would have involved many politically unpopular measures.

A surplus country, for instance, could have refused to support the dollar at its official parity. Instead it could have let its currency appreciate against the dollar without limit. This would have stopped the stimulative multiplier process. No dollars would have come into the surplus country, and hence there would have been no enlargement of the local money supply via central banking absorption of dollars. In time, the appreciation of the surplus country's currency could have been expected to have stimulated imports and weakened exports. And with the risks from speculation becoming two-sided under a regime of freely fluctuating exchange rates, there presumably would have ceased to be one-way speculative movements. These possibilities are not, of course, entirely academic. The German government on several occasions most particularly did follow a deliberate policy of currency appreciation beginning in the early 1960s. The results, it is true, were not wholly in keeping with textbook doctrine, especially as regards Germany's trade surplus. *But appreciation of the mark undoubtedly did keep the price level in Germany from being as high as it would have been otherwise.* The German man in the street understandably complains about the inflation he has experienced: he would have more to complain about under a Bretton Woods regime of pegged exchange rates at the 1960 dollar-mark parity.

Alternatively, while still supporting an overvalued dollar's official parity, the monetary and

fiscal authorities of any country in payments surplus, could, in principle, have *offset* the inflationary pressures imported from abroad. Higher taxes and lower government expenditures could have been employed to produce a negative fiscal-policy multiplier effect just large enough to offset the stimulative export multiplicand. And as the central bank of the surplus country absorbed dollars (or SDRs or, before 1967, official gold), it could have arranged *offsetting sterilization operations* to keep its domestic supply of money from expanding. The central bank, that is, could have engaged in whatever open-market sale of government securities was needed to keep the supply of currency plus demand deposits at a target set by some perfectionist monetarist. None of this would have been easy; and it would have run into great political resistances. But, in principle, it would not have been unfeasible.

Trade and payments considerations

For the future, there is reason to think that the American dollar is no longer overvalued from a long-run point of view. This has to be a tentative judgment, especially because of the difficulties involved in assessing the outlook for food exports and oil imports over a several year span. But with the dollar now showing a cumulative trade-weighted average depreciation of about 18% from June 1970 parities vis-à-vis 14 other major currencies, it is not unreasonable to think that the period of chronic balance-of-payments disequilibrium for the U.S. is over, at least in relation to other oil-consuming industrialized countries. (Germany may still be an exception to this: she still runs a surprisingly strong payments surplus in mid-1974.) If this is so, the stimulative multiplier process described above that prodded global inflation rates higher may have run its course. Countries no longer with chronic surpluses thus could get some relief from "imported" inflationary pressures. This would be decidedly the case if the overhang of dollars accumulated prior to the Spring of 1973 was gradually to be reduced by U.S. payments strength. However, it's a bit premature as yet to count on such a relative surplus trend.

There is another facet of international economic relations that must be analyzed if we are to understand the recent worldwide speeding up of the rate of inflation. Ten years ago the need to compete for world export business served effectively to hold down many prices in the European and Japanese economies. Professor Erik Lindahl of Sweden and others have described the dual-price system that emerged: a domestic price index of commodities sheltered from international competition rose steadily in the early 1960s at 4% per annum or more; at the same time a price index of standardized goods moving in international trade was held down to virtual stability by the need to compete with exporters abroad. What was true for Sweden was also true for other countries: Italy and Japan provide good examples of the dual-price system at work; a striking contrast exists between them and the United States, which because of its continental size and tradition of domestic orientation lacked such a dual-price system.

What needs emphasis is the fact that for many years this element of international competition did serve to restrain price increases for industrial goods and to moderate the over-all rate of inflation. It is a nice analytical question as to how equilibrium could be maintained for long in a common labor market between two such disparate sectors—one with selling prices rising several percent more per year than the other. Undoubtedly, a squeezing of profit margins in the competitive international sector provides part of the explanation. The influence of keen competition in that sector also may have done much to induce more rapid technical productivity advances and rationalizations than occurred in the domestic sector. Gradually, however, it clearly became more and more difficult to insulate the two sectors from one another. *And some part of the explanation for the recent worldwide quickening of inflation of industrial prices must be found in the fact that, at long last, stability in the price levels of internationally traded goods did come to an end.*

On the brighter side

Precise forecasting of global price trends during the next several years is beyond my ability. For the relatively near-term, I am encouraged chiefly by two considerations: first, by the incipient evidence that high prices recently for food and fibers may well be inducing a significantly enlarged flow of goods onto markets; second, by the indications that simultaneity in business-cycle situations in different countries—characteristic of the century before World War II—is reconstituting itself. In 1974, this second consideration carries disinflationary implications because we seem to be witnessing a rather general easing of demand pressures. Indeed, some concern is being voiced (e.g., an article in *The Economist* of June 1 titled, "The Approaching Depression") that we have entered into an oil-affected period of sluggishness internationally that will cumulate into very serious unemployment. While the extreme view strikes me as unjustifiably alarmist, I do believe that the fact that the present circumstance of economies tending to be in step together heightens prospects that price increases will moderate for a while. Parenthetically, I would note that I see no compelling reason why in the Age After Keynes this coming of business cycles into goose step should have to

8

prevail in the future. As in the 1950s and 1960s, America can still have its minirecessions when other countries are having their booms — and vice versa.

The longer-run outlook

Apart from the relatively near-term, however, I do not think anyone ought to count strongly on persistent improvement in price performance. Certainly, it seems only realistic to perceive the outlook for the mixed economies not as an outlook for stable prices but rather for a series of compromises which will make for creeping or trotting inflation. The problem is how to keep the creep or trot from accelerating. This includes the challenge of finding new macroeconomic policies beyond conventional fiscal and monetary policies that will enable a happier compromise between the evils of unemployment and of price inflation. The rhetoric of John Kenneth Galbraith notwithstanding, direct wage and price controls are not an incomes policy that, in my assessment of experience, modern mixed economies know how to use effectively in other than the short run. Periodically, for short periods, price-wage freezes and phases of price-wage regulation for large-scale economic units can be used to advantage. Presidential or Ministerial wage-price guidelines and guideposts also have a limited function; but experience does not make one optimistic that these can be relied on much in the longer run.

Manpower and labor market programs to reduce the structural elements of unemployment certainly need to be explored further; but it is not clear from experience in the United States or in Europe that they have anywhere been able to solve the problem of giving a much-improved Phillips Curve to any economy.

Since I have been stressing that, even with creeping inflation, we are left with stagflation imperfections and trade-offs as people increasingly come to anticipate any maintained rate of inflation and to become habituated to that unchanging rate—then why do I not recommend a Draconian policy of insisting upon absolutely stable prices at whatever cost to current unemployment and short-run growth, always in the hope that after this original costly investment in fighting inflation has been made the economy can live happily ever afterwards with stable prices and nothing worse than moderate amounts of unemployment? I think making any such recommendation is academic, since in any modern mixed economy — featured politically by very limited tolerance of policies of constraint — it will assuredly never be followed. But more than that: I am not persuaded by the force of theoretical argument, or by the statistical and historical data so far available for different mixed economies, that even in the longest run the benefits to be derived from militant anti-inflationary policies don't carry excessive costs as far as average levels of unemployment and growth are concerned. And even if the benefits did decisively outweigh the costs in the longest run, history is a onetime thing and mankind at this stage of the game can ill afford to make irreversible academic experiments whose outcomes are necessarily doubtful and whose execution could put strains on the already-strained political consensus of modern nations.

What is not academic is the more relevant debate going on behind the scenes of official life: Would it not be desirable, in the interests of keeping inflation from accelerating, to countenance and even contrive slow U.S. growth for two or three years, so that unemployment will remain above the 5½% level? Even if desirable, is such austerity feasible in the present American political environment?

269

STATEMENT OF PAUL A. SAMUELSON, PROFESSOR OF ECONOMICS, MASSACHUSETTS INSTITUTE OF TECHNOLOGY

Mr. SAMUELSON. I am going to concentrate in my prepared remarks on the problems that I do know best, the economics of a modern mixed economy, its distribution of income, and how these are affected by present practices and procedures with respect to male and female employment. Others who specialize in the fields of social psychology, biology, political science, and education will speak, and also those who specialize on human power like Barbara Bergmann here, and have spoken to other issues.

Now, by reason of custom, law, discrimination, and motivations, women who are capable of holding jobs across the full spectrum of American economic life are in fact confined to a limited group of industries and occupations and positions and status within those industries. Even if a woman is not excluded from an industry, it may still be that she finds herself at the bottom of the heap in those industries. This is very well documented by all students of the subject. And it is very well known that these ghettos into which women tend to be restricted are not the executive suites at the top of the corporate enterprise, they are not the prestigious professions and the highest paid jobs generally. The typical woman worker is lucky if she earns 50 or 60 percent of the typical man worker, even though tests show that her IQ, diligence, and dexterity cannot account for the difference in pay status. And the differential remains around 20 percent even when we correct for the fact, as we should—that there is a difference in the length of time that a typical woman has been continuously in the labor force. This continuity is more of a relevant variable than it ought to be in the long run—that is, we should so readjust our society that, if women out of choice wish to go in and out of the labor market more than men do, for perfectly good reasons that we can all understand, then their previous expertise should not be wasted.

A man can transfer from one company to another without penalty, where there really is no transferability, whereas the woman who shows on her résumé that she has been out of the labor market awhile raising young children for a few years is very heavily penalized.

That is in the nature of the present pattern; it is part of the attitudes which have been built up and which perpetuate this situation.

In the absence of extensive census research, I offer you something which struck me a few years ago. The class at Radcliffe of 1937, which happens to be my wife's class, was more highly selected and gifted by every objective test than the class of 1937 at Harvard. You can check this by looking at IQ's, the number of honor awards, and grades. And yet I was appalled 25 years later when I came to study the income statistics of the reunion classes. These gifted and motivated women, even those who had never left the labor market by reason of marriage and motherhood or anything else, generally topped out at incomes just where the lucky males began their incomes.

A man is considered to be low paid often if he teaches in a primary or secondary school or is a librarian. If you look at the facts of the census, these are high-paid jobs for women. And yet all this was nobody's fault; it was just the way the system worked.

One of the greatest frontiers to improve U.S. productivity, U.S. GNP—and what is more important these days, our net economic welfare, the GNP corrected for the things which are not in it, disamenities of urban life, leisure and other things—is the present unused potential of women in our economy. If because of the dead hand of custom and discrimination half of our population have a quarter of their productive potential unrealized—and that may be an understatement—then by simple arithmetic a gain of between 10 and 15 percent in living standards is obtainable, by ending these limitations and discriminations. Maybe my arithmetic is oversimplified. And maybe it hasn't made sufficient allowance for their actual cost in the home. So subtract something from that number if you like. But also add something, because what we impute to women in the home and the status that they have in the home will be improved if their opportunity cost in industry is the higher figure that it ought to be.

So this may be a conservative, minimum estimate. And note that it is a permanent increment to our standard of life and well-being, not just a temporary dividend.

Well, a big question is: Will these economic gains to women come largely at the expense of male workers?

Will it structurally change the income differential between different occupations and skills? What are the repercussions on the family and the birth rate, quantitatively and qualitatively?

These aren't easy questions for anyone to answer. I certainly don't have firm answers to them. But there are so many unfounded assertions that go the rounds on these vital topics, implicitly and explicitly, that it is worth making an attempt to give approximate guesses on what research will some day give us as the justified answers.

First, it has to be said that by and large these gains that come to living standards and national income by additional productivity of a new group are not at the expense of the previous groups in society. No man's masculinity is really going to be threatened, and his paycheck is not going to be threatened. This kind of an effect that I am speaking of has been demonstrated again and again by the history of U.S. immigration, by the long overdue upgrading of black Americans' economic opportunities, by the increasing education of all classes of American society. Each group produces more, it consumes more, it saves more. In other words, it carries its own weight.

Now, I haven't forgotten about the law of diminishing returns. And that law as it would apply to a largely agricultural economy of the Malthus type would say that there would be effects of subtraction on the wage and marginal productivity of the existing workers if you add a new group. But that is of a secondary and tertiary magnitude in an advanced economy like that of the United States or of Western Europe, in my judgment.

Second, it is only reasonable to suppose that just as the broadening of education lowers the differential returns of those who previously had a monopoly position at the top of the income pyramid, so will the gradual self-emancipation of society from sexual discrimination slightly reduce the degree of inequality of earnings.

For example, if as many women in the United States go into dentistry as in Finland, the quite high professional earnings of dentists might cease to be quite so high. I am not saying that nobody gets hurt. But I am taking broad categories and weighing the advantages and the disadvantages.

Certainly certain particular monopoly groups are benefited by the exclusion of women now. But that is the exception.

Third, an economic upgrading of women's status should in our materialistic society also rub off on general human status. Women will not be spiritually degraded by their economic advance, but on the contrary, will come into their long overdue social desserts. We have such a materialistic society where it is money that talks. Your status is automatically upgraded if your pay is upgraded.

Fourth, high-earning women, the statistics suggest, do tend to marry high-earning men. So the improvement in degree of inequality that comes from better opportunities for female heads of household bread-winners will be offset. There will still be need for concern about the disparity in the distribution of income. This is not a panacea.

Let me say, by the way, as a digression, that by and large our rules should involve symmetry. A person is a person. This would call for fair shares, equal treatment for women. But consider the fact, which somehow sadly is a fact, that women are given a special residual role with respect to children—they are the ones to whom the buck is passed in the last analysis. Then there is a strong case to be made for pushing toward more than fair shares. Now, there is no danger that we are going to hit equality and overshoot the mark. But when further progress is made, there will be room for still more.

Fifth, I think that better economic opportunity for women can be expected to accelerate the already strong trend toward smaller families and leveling off of population. That class of 1937 at Radcliffe— and I only use that as typical of its vintage—would have had many fewer children had job opoprtunities been more challenging and had social attitudes adjusted to this fact. Unless we are able to devise better programs for good care of infants and children of working women, the more affluent and more educated will be providing a smaller fraction of the generations to come.

61

I'm stating that not as a problem but as a probability.

Now, I am ready to expand on any of these themes, or try to answer any questions, and perhaps put something in the record.

But I realize that I have not said enough about what to do about this matter. And in my closing paragraph let me say that I don't think that the improvement will come about of itself. It must come about through pressure. It must come about through pressure of the citizenry on the Congress, it must come about through the pressure of Congress and the Executive on business and on unions and on all of us.

It must come about through coercion.

There are great similarities between the problem of discrimination against women and the problem of discrimination against other groups. And there is beginning at last to be in the data on the earnings opportunities of black Americans, as against white Americans, something seems to be in the data since 1965 for the first time that shows a ray of hope which is more than just an upswing in a war economy or an upswing in a boom economy, something that seems to require a dummy variable. And I suggest that that dummy variable that is in those regression equations has to be the continuous pressure of Government. You cannot change attitude by laws alone. But it is amazing how ephemeral attitudes are when laws make you change them.

Try not discriminating, and you may find you will like it.

I was at Clintonville, Va., visiting a Dupont plant on the day that by force of the fact that Government contracts would be refused to Dupont, the word went out and was implemented that black workers no longer had to just sweep the floor. Personnel officers called in these small town southern workers, and these personnel officers in their southern dialects said, "Now, look here, we don't like this any better than you do. But these are your jobs, we just won't have work for you unless you change your attitudes. And we want you to know that head management in Wilmington is behind this."

You have got to put the fear of God not just down the line, but up the line, too.

[The following paper was attached to Mr. Samuelson's statement:]

ECONOMICS OF SEX: A DISCUSSION [1]

(By Paul A. Samuelson, professor of economics, Massachusetts Institute of Technology)

Women with jobs receive much lower pay than do men with the same education, general mental aptitudes (I.Q. etc.), and years of work experience. This common sense observation is documented by the papers of Professors F. Weisskoff and H. Zellner, who each show that women tend to be segregated in lower-paying occupations. Indeed, my colleague Robert Hall has shown in the Brookings Papers on Economic Activity (1970, 369–410), that the only group in our economy who continue to get higher earnings beyond the middle-twenties ages are white men: i.e., black men and all women have essentially no gains in pay or status to look forward to with age.

One cannot help agreeing with Professor Zellner and Weisskoff that the pattern of female segregation does not represent a rational equilibrium based on intrinsic inferiority of females as factors of production. Instead it must for a large part represent a process of discrimination against women, unconscious and conscious. Like discrimination against blacks, Jews, homosexuals, immigrants, and radicals, sex discrimination often has in it a self-fulfilling vicious circle: women become less self-assured, less possessed of crucial experience under the self-

[1] Paper presented at the American Economic Association meeting, New Orleans, La., Dec. 28, 1971.

perpetuating regime; those males (and females) who begin without sex prejudice become contaminated by it; and those who themselves think they do not have it feel they must in their self-interest engage in discrimination "to please" their customers, or employees, or boss, or banker, or . . .

If segregation stems even in part from discrimination based on prejudice and on misinformation—and note we do not have to wait upon future research to isolate these from some possible genetic and permanent-cultural superiorities of either sex over the other—then society has much to gain from reducing sex discriminations. Women themselves, and their families, have no doubt the most to gain from such a change; and men, as a group, no doubt have something to lose from removal of their privileged status; but, on the whole, in a specifiable sense, the totality of society stands to gain—in the sense that there will be enough increase in total product to make everybody potentially (i.e. through feasible Pareto-optimal side payments) better off.

Since the papers have just come to me, and since the subject is so interesting and important as to require no sprightly badinage, I propose to use my few minutes of scarce time to explore the simplest model of sex discrimination that I could think of. Here it is.

1. We have an equal number of women and men workers, really alike in all productive traits, and with zero algebraic emotional problems in working with each other in any indifferent combinations.

2. We have three, identical, independent occupations, each having declining marginal-productivity demand curves for labor (expressed in money of constant purchasing power, and with "consumer-surplus triangular areas above their rectangular-area wage bills" that represent competitive rents to the fixed hiring factors).

3. Women are arbitrarily segregated to work only in occupation 1; men can work in 1, 2, or 3.

Warning.—There are genuine asymmetries in real life between men and women that escape the model. Thus, if women desire to take maternity and post-maternity leaves in a degree that men will not, we face the old problem: How can one treat unequals equally? Recall Shaw's ammendment to the golden-rule dictum of treating your neighbor as you would have her treat you. Shaw asserted: "Don't treat your neighbor as you would be treated. He—I mean she—may be different."

Query.—

A. What are the costs to women of discrimination?

B. What are the gains to men of discrimination?

C. What are the effects on total wages of discrimination?

D. What are the effects on total competitive profits?

E. What are the effects on total welfare or total real incomes of discrimination?

I give definite answers to all these questions, under the special assumption of linear demands. I have not yet investigated [2] how much my conclusions depend on strict linearity (but it is obvious from classical investigations of "small taxes" that, as discrimination becomes incipiently small, some of this linear analysis becomes increasingly exact.)

Three of my answers are obvious, corroborating common-sense expectations that sex discrimination hurts women workers, helps men workers, and hurts total real product. What is not so obvious—at least, to me, it came as a surprise—it turns out in this model that sex discrimination (in either direction) helps the residual profits or competitive rents of the hiring factors (which presumably, because of past sex discriminations, are predominantly owned by men).

Figure 1 tells the story. The line ABC represents the demand for Industry 1. The line ZYX represents the horizontally-aggregated demands of Industries 2 and 3; because the workers are allocating themselves half to each industry, this line falls more gently than ABC, having half its slope; and since the employment in these industries grows as people are shifted away from Industry 1, ZYX falls

---

[2] Since giving this orally, I have ascertained that, for non-linear demands, it is not assured that non-discrimination minimizes total profits and maxmizes total wages. Thus, let the demand curve follow AB as in the figure, but below B break almost horizontally: then the discrimination will lower the profit total; and it will raise the wage total but, since total welfare still must fall, the wage rise will be less than the profit drop. Even without a corner at B, as when the demand curve through B is very convex (from below), this same phenomenon will be observable. The fact that total wages can have a local minimum and profits a local maximum at zero discrimination shows that linear analysis is not always applicable even for incipiently-small discrimination—despite my oral optimism.

from right to left. The horizontal line FOM represents total labor, female plus male; moving right from F to O, female labor increases; and, moving left from M to O, male labor increases.

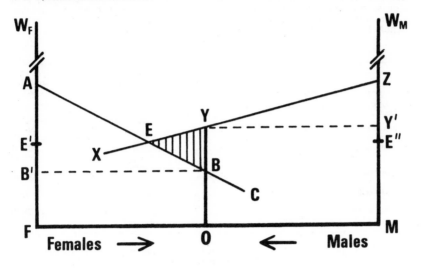

FIGURE 1

Under complete segregation of women out of Industries 2 and 3, all women go to Industry 1 and end at the low wage shown at B. No man can afford to go to Industry 1 at so low a wage; hence, all men go to Industries 2 and 3, necessarily equally if they pursue most advantageous wage, and all men end up at the high wage at Y. The wage differential, BY, results from discrimination.

The reader may verify the respective wage bills: FOBB' for women and OMY'Y for men; the profit triangles B'BA in Industry 1 and only YY'Z in both other industries! The total of social welfare, measured in real output (or dollars of constant purchasing power or, if consumers of both sexes owned land equally and were hedonistically commensurate, in some kind of cardinal utility units) is given by AFOB+YOMZ.

Now we remove all segregation, which by hypothesis is completely irrational in our model. The new wage equilibrium for everybody is at E as either (1) one-third of the females "invade" Industries 2 and 3 in equal proportions, bringing down the wage rates there and raising it in Industry 1 to equality, or (2) at random, we indifferently allocate the work force, FM, to get equal totals in all industries at the common wage. The triangle formed by EBY measures the gain in "social utility" from abolishing discrimination, non-inclusive of psychic and ethical advantages of enjoying equity. Notice: E stands for "equilibrium," "equality," "efficiency" and "equity"—they are equivalent in this model. Note too that, with linearity, E is one-third way eastward in longitude from F to M, and it lies north of B by two-thirds of the latitude toward Y. Therefore, if the reader will draw the horizontal E'EE", he will find that the total wage bill under discrimination is less than under freedom. But if he compares the sum of this discrimination-regime profit triangles

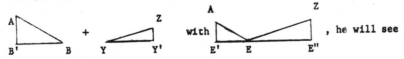

that employers get more competitive profits under discrimination than they do under equality of treatment. [*Query.*—Does unconscious realization of this influence and reinforce prejudice, particularly on the part of those employers who deign to reap the extra profits of hiring low-cost women? Such canny types can gain from fanning prejudice in other employers.]

Table 1 shows the quantitative magnitudes in the linear case.

TABLE 1

	With no discrimination	With discrimination
Female labor	1	1
Male labor	1	1
Female wages	100	$100-\dfrac{2\Pi}{4}$
Male wages	100	$100+\dfrac{\Pi}{4}$
Total wages	200	$200-\dfrac{\Pi}{4}$
Total profit	Π	$W+\dfrac{\Pi}{8}$
Total welfare	$200+\Pi$	$(200+\Pi)-\dfrac{\Pi}{8}$

As a final postscript, let me point out that imperfections of competition—in the sense of conditions of Chamberlin-Robinson-Knight monopolistic competition, for reasons of increasing returns and other factors unrelated to sex discriminations—are almost a necessary condition for the observed patterns of segregation. By this I mean the following:

If constant returns to scale prevailed perfectly without artificial barriers to entry, if knowledge were complete, if women are actually or potentially the equivalent of men as factors, both productively and in terms of affect, then the condition shown in E would tend to be approximated in the real world. Proof: in the Wicksell fashion, women could hire land and plant and men and women to produce this ideal regardless of sex-bigotry on the part of much of the population. (Also, with competitive profits higher in the ghetto area, fixed factors would be attracted there, resulting, as in the famous factor-price equalization theorem, in a tendency toward equalization of wage rates: if Martha is forbidden to go to the mountain, the market can come to her.)

Alas, I conclude from this not that sex segregation and discrimination will soon improve. But rather that the real world departs significantly from the posited perfect-competition model.

The Convergence of the Law School and the University

PAUL A. SAMUELSON

L AW IS AN OCCUPATION. Although the number of economists in the United States, I am told, only equals the number of chiropractors, there must be ten times as many lawyers. God did not decree this number. Ten years ago, when Dean Griswold gave the Hamlyn Lectures in London, he rather apologized for this abundance of riches. It is not because we are naturally more litigious, he suggested, that we have two and one-half times as many lawyers per capita as the British Isles, but rather because, in addition to the federal legal system, we have some fifty-five other legal systems.

Not only must almost half a million lawyers be fed, they must also be trained. For despite the urgings of Milton Friedman that anyone be allowed to hang up his shingle as a lawyer—or, for that matter, as a brain surgeon—we have retreated from the golden age of a century ago. Then, in my native state of Indiana, the doctrine used to be: "Every person of good moral character, being a voter, shall be entitled to admission to practise law in all courts of justice." As we are beginning to realize, however, women are also persons; but, alas, they were not then voters in Indiana. Hence, with that flexibility for which the Anglo-Saxon common law is so justly famous, the 1893 supreme court of Indiana held that a woman, even though she could not vote, was entitled to practice law in the state, provided she be of good character. Thus,

⊘ PAUL A. SAMUELSON is professor of economics at M.I.T. and author of the widely used textbook, *Economics*. In 1970 he was the recipient of the Alfred Nobel Memorial Prize in economic science. This article is adapted from the first Sulzbacher Distinguished Lecture given at the School of Law at Columbia University under the title "Economists and Lawyers."

along with the Prudent Man doctrine, was born the Good Woman doctrine.

Where are lawyers to be trained? In university law schools, where else? But that was not ordained in heaven. One does not learn plumbing in the university. Universities long were havens of culture and wild oats—not, theology excepted, vocational schools for the establishment. Before and after colonial times, America tended to imitate the eighteenth-century English pattern, which would never dream of regarding Oxford or Cambridge as the proper place to learn to be a barrister or a solicitor. Only if one wanted to be a philosopher about the law or, failing to make the grade in the actual practice of law, determined to teach about it, would one benefit from academic law. Two centuries later, things are not all that different in Britain. It is only recently that one who aspires to be a chartered accountant, or a physician, or a lawyer, or an actuary, would be well advised to waste the most creative years of his life attending a university. Special schools, isolated from the mainstream of college life, dealt with these professional matters.

On the Continent, it was otherwise. In the medieval curriculum of the proper university, law, medicine, and theology do appear, all vocational subjects *par excellence*. This does not seem an odd arrangement only because it has been hallowed by tradition. But just try to introduce into a German university the study of industrial relations, and one may be told that such a vocational study is not proper for a proper university, an argument that collapses once one points to the parallel example of clinical work there in the removal of appendixes.

For better or worse, the American law school has wormed its way into a corner of the university campus. Today one does not apprentice oneself to a practicing lawyer and thereby qualify for the bar. It was only yesterday that night school was an important avenue for legal training; in Boston one could be a legislator during the day, kill the hours of dusk in a handy saloon, later working one's way down Beacon Hill for lectures on contracts and torts. The lights are going out all over the world where night schools

257

are concerned. Affluence is killing them off. Economists who study the importance of investing in human capital know how important vocational training—and that includes part-time and on-the-job training—can be. So there may be something lost as well as gained from the changing trends.

We must not be misled by the fact that in this country one goes to a university law school rather than taking a certain number of meals and instruction at Lincoln's or Gray's Inn. Yes, the law school does have the same zip code as the rest of the university; but an anthropologist who has spent forty years, as I have, observing the strange practices of American universities can testify that, until recently, the same zip code often used to be about all the law school and the university had in common.

Thus, though for many years I resided in Leverett House at Harvard, I can hardly remember ever meeting a professor of law at the tutors' table or in the Senior Common Room. The few exceptions tended to be professors of constitutional law, often a euphemism for an overpaid historian. Paul Freund, who *is* a proper law professor, has in recent years been one of the most popular lecturers in Harvard College; just as hard cases are said to make poor law—a doubtful dictum if I ever heard one—so rare exceptions are noticed in the social sciences precisely because they are a deviation from the common run of things and because they may be swallows of a glorious spring to come.

To clinch that law schools were long an alien and unassimilated element in the body politic of the university, I submit the fact that law schools are, with rare exceptions, the only places known to me that put strong emphasis on being a good teacher. Tenure depends on classroom performance. Law professors even make a point of grading their own exams! The enormity of this can only be appreciated if one knows the rest of the university. Until the recent student uprisings—and such special liberal colleges as Amherst and Swarthmore aside—one would never advise a son seeking success in an academic career: "Son, spend your time getting to know your students. Brood about the Socratic method, and the relative merits of true-false or essay tests." Instead, a decent respect for the unvarnished truth would compel you to say: "Research performance is what makes the dean move. Einstein couldn't have received tenure on his teaching ability. One can best understand the decisions of appointment committees at the top score of universities in terms of the following criteria: 'Next time the Rosenwald Foundation determines the comparative ratings of biochemistry departments, will this appointment help move us up from rank 7 to rank 57?' "

I don't say this is as it should be. Don't shoot the anthropologist who only reports to you the facts. But let me add, as an aside, that the hardest appointments a college ever has to make are those to be based on teaching performance alone. To be sure, in the realm of research science, there is also many a slip between hope and performance; but nowhere is the standard deviation of appointments greater than in the pure teaching realm, where so often the charmer of age thirty is the bore of age fifty-five.

Apparently one of the reasons why the law schools set so much store on teaching is that teaching is what most good law professors do. This was brought home to me a few years ago when I served on the Commission for the Social Sciences, set up to advise the government and the National Science Foundation on the funding of the social sciences. After a number of solemn consultations, we decided that there was no need to set up a new foundation that would parallel the existing National Science Foundation. We also decreed that, just because a person was in the law school, he should not be deprived of all access to research funds. We consulted a distinguished law scholar—he was, at least, a dean—who pointed out that until recently law professors were not considered eligible to do genuine research; and that, in the short time since such a right had been recognized, the quality of the applications had revealed some uncertainty as to what constituted an appropriate research topic and program.

What, then, do teachers of law do? Until recently, at least, they tended to the law. A Williston or Corbin or Prosser or Wigmore achieves fame for codifying a branch of the subject and for writing a successful textbook. When I became a successful textbook writer, I had to live down that fact by producing more and better scientific research. The law reviews tell the same novel story. Shortly after the last World War, I heard a friend order milk in a three-star Paris restaurant. The aggrieved waiter replied, "Madame, in this country we reserve the milk for children." In the law, the best reviews are reserved for the young, apparently being written by, and run by, students. This is so incredible that I had better quote authority, Dean Griswold being as good as anyone else for this purpose. He remarked in those same Hamlyn Lectures, ". . . the achievement is a remarkable one, that in a learned profession the basic periodical commentaries are written and edited by students." And apparently it is good for the students' training that they should edit the *Harvard Law Review* or any of the hundred other law reviews.

The academic mind boggles at the thought of graduate students writing or even soliciting papers for the *Physical Review,* the *Annals of Mathematics,* or *Comptes Rendus.* Even in my comparatively soft subject of economics, not only could graduate students not remotely edit *Econometrica,* they couldn't begin to edit the *American Economic Review,* which is supposed to be the common denominator publication of the official association. Likewise at the other end of the age scale, there is the phenomenon that an excellent law school in California can be staffed exclusively by emeritus professors, some carrying on into their mid-seventies. Can one imagine a distinguished department of physics, microbiology, or economics similarly staffed? C. P. Snow spoke some years ago of the two cultures; apparently it is really a case of the seventeen and one-half different cultures.

A key element of teaching in law schools, at least in the first year or so, is classes that would be deemed large in the faculty of arts and sciences. I refer to classes of, say, something more than a hundred students. Perhaps it was the triumph of the case method, as pioneered at the Harvard Law School, that permitted this to be a useful process. Such a group is large enough to build up tension and affect; yet it is small enough to permit interchange, and not all of that voluntary, between student and professor. Contrast this with the few large lectures in Economics I or Sociology A involving as many as a thousand students and, at some universities, even overflow rooms with closed circuit television. Most state and less-than-most-affluent schools have to settle for these monstrosities in the basic courses. These, however, work well only if there is a magnificent lecturer, one who is both showman and sage. Where, these days, does one get that person? And how does one keep him or her in the elementary lecture room? The answer is that generally one does not get a Taussig, or a Keynes, or a Joan Robinson to perform this function. Moreover, the current generation of students has low tolerance levels for the kind of showman who kept their fathers and grandfathers entertained at old Siwash.

As a result, departments, to play safe, do what they try to do in any case at the upperclass levels—proliferate small classes or sections. The best law schools are not immune to this trend either. Such proliferation of courses reaches its polar limit in the concept of education as consisting of Mark Hopkins at one end of a log and the student at the other end. Mark Hopkinses do not come cheap. Professors' wives must eat too, and ours, the teaching profession, is one of those laggard industries in which technological progress is almost nonexistent—teaching machines and TV notwithstanding. That is why the cost of tuition is one of the most steeply rising items in the price index.

Without having made a study of the matter, it is my impression that law schools differ from other parts of the university in the sense that the student's tuition can essentially pay for his own training—at least if that is the standard old-fashioned training. Think how different this is from the medical schools, where the student's tuition goes only a small fraction of the way toward defraying the expenses of his education. As an economist, I must expect these differences in technology to have profound repercussions on the competitive conditions in the two industries: the industry in which physicians work and that in which lawyers work.

261

One's predictions are confirmed by the historical facts. When I prepared the first edition of my textbook *Economics,* just after World War II, lawyers and doctors had about the same median earnings, with the lawyers being a bit ahead in the mean. When I come to prepare the tenth edition next summer, I shall find that the doctors have forged well ahead of the lawyers both in the median and in the mean. Not fair, you say? Well, that's the way the supply-and-demand cookie crumbles.

Averages and means, of course, tell only part of the story. The dispersion of lawyers' incomes tends to be greater than that of physicians'. The range between the top lawyers in the large urban firms and those at the bottom, who are really living only in disguised unemployment, is greater than the range between top surgeons and family practitioners. No doctors ever run out of work. Indeed, Parkinson's law does characterize the medical profession: in counties that have a single doctor, he works harder and concentrates on the most important cases. In posh urban areas, when the density of physicians doubles and redoubles, doctors simply work less hard and move down the curve of diminishing returns—but not diminishing incomes—from pneumonia to hay fever and from phlebitis to hangnail, with discretionary hysterectomies and appendectomies being the great budget balancers.

As Adam Smith pointed out years ago, and as the latest Irish sweepstakes will bear out, people are unduly attracted by a few large prizes. Therefore, even when many lawyers are unemployed, people will flock to law schools in the hope of becoming a Charles Evans Hughes. Each overestimates his own chances. As an example, a law student told me recently that of her entering freshman class, only 35 out of 550 would make the law review, but that in a secret poll 75 percent confided their expectation that they would make it.

What are the implications of this? It seems to me that in these postactivist times on the campus, students are flocking to the medical schools and law schools like lemmings swarming toward the cold waters of the Norwegian fjords. The high costs of medical education, the limited number of places in the medical schools, and the restrictive guild-practices of the AMA ensure that physi-

262

cians will not be coming out of our ears. I am not so sure that the same safety valves will operate in the field of law. Most of those lemmings will find a friendly law school ready to embrace them and their tuition dollars: it won't be a Columbia, or Stanford, or Yale, but any industry in which the consumer is self-financing of the product he buys is likely to see supply expand to meet enlarged demand.

The Clayton Act says that people are not to be treated as commodities. But I fear that the marketplace answers to a different drummer than the pieties of Congress. Just as there is a corn-hog cycle, in which high price eliciting too much corn at one time eventually leads to too much bacon and farm bankruptcy at another, so should one expect that, after the period of gestation needed to produce a member of the bar, there should be some softening for that commodity. As they say on Wall Street, when the paddy wagon comes, it takes the good girls along with the bad; in time of surfeit, the bell tolls even for graduates of the Ivy League, albeit not so dolefully.

Let us make a deposition that through thick and thin able lawyers will do well. It has been my experience that they will also endeavor to do good. We are used to the academic economists who go back and forth, from university to Washington and back to the university. Their number is as nothing compared to the lawyers: for every Heller and Burns I can cite for you five McCloys, Pattersons, Deans, and Balls. When I had to recruit talent for the Kennedy administration, I found the economists very hard to ensnare. By contrast, the lawyers vied to get back near the seats of power. Galbraiths, Tobins, and Ackleys took prudent leave from their universities; Coxes and Surreys cheerfully gave up tenure at their nation's call. I used to ask myself, why this difference? Can life with Sullivan & Cromwell be all that boring? In desperation I was even driven to a Marxist hypothesis: just as it used to be said that only the very rich and the very poor can afford good medical care in America—little more than a half truth at best—so it may well be that only the rich and the poor can afford to work for the government. Most academics come in between.

263

An economist does not better himself much, in the internal revenue sense, from serving a tour of duty in Washington. Lawyers seem to arrange things better; the path from the Department of Justice to IBM or Goldman-Sachs is a short one; every good tax lawyer has done his apprenticeship on the other side of the counter.

I say this not by way of criticism. Thus, the tax bar has been outstanding in serving the public interest. Once the client's private interest has been given its one bite, men like Randolph Paul and Laird Bell have told the Treasury how to close that unintended loophole. I wish I could report the same thing about other branches of the law. I well remember when one leading attorney told me that he had refused to serve on a blue-ribbon commission concerning the antitrust laws so as not to dilute his fervor on behalf of clients. Self-admissions or boasts like that, I understand, have special weight as testimony. Or take the practice of labor law and negotiation. Just as investment banking houses used to divide off into those that were Jewish and those that were not, in this arena a firm too often must choose one side and stick to it, referring a stray would-be client to the fellow down the street.

Just as some cultures are hag-ridden, ours has been counsel-ridden. Our congressional cup runneth over with lawyers. And that has always been the case. Lawyers were strongly represented among the signers of the Declaration of Independence. They formed a large bloc at the Constitutional Convention. The predominance of lawyers in American political life is nowhere better summarized than in the oft-quoted words of de Tocqueville:

In America there are no nobles or literary men, and the people are apt to mistrust the wealthy; lawyers consequently form the highest political class and the most cultivated circle of society. . . . If I were asked where I placed the American aristocracy, I should reply without hesitation, that it is not composed of the rich, who are united by no common tie, but that it occupies the judical bench and the bar.

This dominance of lawyers in politics continues into our own day, though with somewhat reduced virulence. If challenged to

264

provide an explanation for this peculiar fact, I should have eclectically to weigh many diverse causal factors. For one thing, lawyers tend to be intelligent. They are even more articulate, displaying a swollen verbalization-to-IQ ratio. I should also have to invoke a Marxist-functionalist argument. Lawyers cannot advertise; that would be bad form. But in an electoral contest it is often better for a lawyer to have run and lost than never to have run at all. And perhaps it is more exciting to be the governor in the State House than the senior partner in Ropes Grey. Leisure time misspent in studying the autobiographies of twenty-fifth-reunion classes gives me the casual impression that doctors and academics generally show greater self-complacency over their choice of vocation than do lawyers and businessmen. I once even heard a former president of Du Pont seriously muse out loud: "Maybe I should have stayed in chemistry and won a Nobel prize."

I am not the one, and this is certainly not the place, to investigate the question of whether lawyers have a disproportionate role in the establishment. I know that economists in the upper ranks of the civil service claim that they do. But we do not require a Marxist cannon to crush so small a peanut. Lawyers have a way of making themselves indispensable. One has to take off one's hat to an industry that coined and forced into circulation the maxim, "He who is his own lawyer has a fool for a client." Charles Darwin would have given higher marks to that one than to Bernard Shaw's gift to the academic world: "Those who can, do; those who can't, teach."

Much of the foregoing is ancient history. The training for the law used to be a narrow training, and the mind boggles at the prospect of putting the country in the charge of men who had only the legal training typical of the generation before last. In those days one could justly say with Kipling, "What do they know of the law who only the law know?" One had to hope that a Henry Stimson or a Robert Taft or a Dean Acheson received at Yale that general education which he was certainly not going to have deepened at the Harvard Law School. So perhaps it was

265

just as well that, being an affluent nation, we early imposed an undergraduate education as a prerequisite for professional training at the bar.

In the last couple of generations, and particularly in the years since World War II, the moat between the law school and the rest of the university has been narrowing. Perhaps it all started with the Yale Law School and its interdisciplinary approach. But now the trend is universal. I seem to remember that while the size of the student body at the Harvard Law School changed but little in the 1950s, the size of the faculty doubled.

The cancer of research is beginning to invade the law schools. And by this I do not mean research *inside* the law itself, the compilation and organization of court decisions and precedents. Just as colleges have poets and painters in residence, gracing the campus to replace the stately trees felled by the Dutch elm disease, so law schools are beginning to have house economists and even sociologists. It all starts innocently—a visiting professorship here, a joint appointment there, even a distinguished lecture series with an interdisciplinary cast. But that is the innocent way cancer so often begins, with nothing worse than a bad pimple.

Like Will Rogers's friend who knew how to spell *banana* but just didn't know when to stop, research never knows when to stop. To deepen understanding of the law of capital gains, one countenances research projects in the law school on the economics of uncertainty. The next thing you know, a Lasswell at the Yale Law School may be investigating the frequency of masturbation among judges over sixty.

Like most amateur futurists, I used to think that the older countries of Europe set the pattern for us in America. What Bismarck and Lloyd George did there for state pensions before World War I, Franklin Roosevelt did here in 1937. So I was amused to be told by the former Danish prime minister, Jens Krag, an economist fallen from grace, that he too had thought America would become like Europe—until actual experience showed him that Europe was increasingly becoming like America.

266

If I am right in discerning some convergence between the law schools and the university, who is coming toward whom? Discounting the fact that I live on the university mountain, I must be candid and record the impression that the mountain of the university is not moving closer to the Mohammed of the law school.

Only at the Harvard Business School, where something called the case method is in vogue, can I discern a movement in the universities toward standard law school techniques. And in view of the width of the Charles River that separates it from Harvard Yard, one would scarcely consider the "B School" to be a typical part of the university. Nor am I sure that the famous case method at the Harvard Business School is any more than a pun on the case method used in the law school. After all, legal litigation does come naturally packaged in actual cases: *Marbury v. Madison* is a legitimate atom for taxonomy and study. The case of the crying waitress is another genus altogether, as are, one will also perceive on reflection, Freud's cases of the boy who was bitten by a horse and of the regiment of girls who attested to having been raped by their respective fathers.

Yet the Harvard Business School, and its case method, does enable me to verify by triangulation the distinction between a faculty that superlatively trains its students for a vocation and a faculty that adds to scholarly and scientific knowledge. The B School is tops: its graduates make the most money and run the biggest businesses. Its rivals and critics do not dispute this fact, even though some of them may argue over whether this is attributable to the education acquired there or to the self-fulfilling myth that enables it to attract and select out those who already have the advantages needed to get ahead through energy, ability, and inherited status.

I am prepared to concede that the training given at the Harvard Business School is an important factor in the success of its graduates, and that the case method—which constitutes a kind of role-playing and a simulation of the mixed-upness that in real life characterizes actual managerial decision-making—in all probability provides good training for the command post in the execu-

267

tive suite. Still, what toughens the hands of the karate expert may spoil the fingers of the violinist or surgeon. The mixed-upness that characterizes life is the enemy of scientific induction. That is why the natural scientist tries to control his experiments so that he can infer the effects of one thing at a time; and that is why the social scientist (or the meteorologist or astronomer) has to atone by elaborate statistical analysis for his inability to make controlled experiments. The case method by itself is like folk wisdom. There is no wisdom in folk wisdom, for folk wisdom recognizes all the things that can happen—including their opposites. "Absence makes the heart grow fonder." How true. "Out of sight, out of mind." How unfalse. Only when case instances, or when the modern elaboration of cases that we term simulations, are accorded some measure of relevant frequency, have we made more than the first step toward scholarly knowledge.

I am overstating my case about the Harvard Business School. But that, after all, is really what the case method was invented for. Those cases don't fall from heaven; they are fabricated in every sense of the word. I admit that Robert Schlaifer and Howard Raiffa and John Pratt and John Lintner have added greatly to the body of economic and statistical knowledge, and yet they have done their work at the Harvard Business School. And I could enumerate still other names. But I also know that when you ask the stars at the other graduate schools of business to rate themselves and their peers as contributors to the corpus of knowledge about managerial economics, finance, industrial organization, and accounting principles, the greatest business school of them all does not come near the top of their lists. Faithful to the case method, I sum up with a story that is not the worse for being true. A student recently went to one of the Harvard Business School deans and said: "Here is the syllabus of the finance taught at Brand X University. See how much better it is than what we are getting." The dean looked over the material—noting, I suppose, how it bristled with the multiple integrals of stochastic processes— and replied judiciously: "Yes, and if you want to be director of research for some New York money management concern, perhaps you should go there. But if you want to be president of the company, I think you should stay here."

Out of the mouths of deans comes wisdom. There is a conflict of interest, let us face it, between training people for a career and the creation of scholarly knowledge. The Institute for Advanced Studies at Princeton and Rockefeller University are expensive places; one cram school for the bar turns out more product in a year than they do in a century. Although America is an affluent nation, we cannot afford to produce an Oxford in every county. We can't even afford to produce a Berkeley in every state, and in recent years it has become an open question whether we can afford to produce a Berkeley in Berkeley.

If I am right in thinking that the standard law school has been changing in the last generation, rejoining the university or in a sense joining it for the first time, that trend will itself have to be subjected to the economists' cost-benefit analysis. As Walter Heller said in connection with the need for a similar cost-benefit calculus applied to ecological and environmental concern, the Hudson River ought certainly to be made cleaner than it now is; but, given that it flows between two populations as dense as those of Manhattan and Jersey City, it is doubtful that a free and affluent people will opt to spend enough in the way of resources so that Columbia undergraduates may once again swim in the Hudson River.

The law schools have the task not simply of training those who will become president of the company or senior partner in the firm. They have the task of training those who will become presidents of the United States and creators of the law. Throughout most of American history, scholarship has been at a discount among our pragmatic and materialistic citizenry. When I was a boy reading H. L. Mencken in the 1920s, the professor was an object of good-natured derision. Then came the Great Depression and Roosevelt's Brain Trust; then came the Manhattan Project and the atomic bomb. There followed a bull market in science, which filtered down even to sociology and classical studies. That

269

movement peaked out some years ago. Physicists feel guilty about what they have wrought; molecular biologists are fearful of what they may conjure out of their black boxes. Economists berate themselves that their juries are hung up on the solution to stagflation.

All the more important if our professional schools are going to rise in relative importance while the universities are shedding some of their bull-market gains—all the more important that the professional schools embody some of those virtues associated with the higher learning. The convergence of the law school and the university that I have hinted at seems to parallel an overdue convergence of the medical school and the university. When chronic student unrest in Mexico City closed down all economic study there for several years, I suddenly had the vision that civilization as we have known it might have to live on in the business schools of the world.

All change—I hesitate to call it progress—is bought at a price. I have already indicated that the case method is likely to be at least a partial casualty in the brave new world of the future. Another casualty, and I am not here thinking about the first few semesters of study, may well be the Socratic method. It is a good method to sharpen up the students' wits in an adversary procedure. But it is a terrible method if Mark Hopkins has a great deal of knowledge and understanding that must be imparted to the new generation of students. Just imagine teaching topological dynamics by the Socratic method: you would scarcely get past Newton's second law before the Thanksgiving vacation intervened, much less impart the intricacies of the Einstein-Lorenz transformations.

The adversary method, I understand, is one method nominated for arriving at truth. Apparently it is a good enough method for all those fifty-odd legal systems that the lawyer has to grapple with. Yet is it not curious that science, which is supposed to be the search for truth pure and simple, does not rely on the adversary method as it is known in a court of law? Or to put it differently:

270

All scientists sit in judgment on the work of *any* scientist. Indeed, as Sir Karl Popper has so nicely put the matter, each scientist tries to be his own most devastating critic, committing an abortion here, an infanticide there, and of course an incestuous assassination of the works of his fathers and grandfathers. A lawyer might properly be disbarred for interrupting his eloquent discourse to say, "Oh, I've discovered the *nonsequitur* in my syllogism and would like to alter my client's plea from innocent to guilty." Yet a Galileo achieves immortal fame when he discovers that what he believed thirty years earlier, and what Descartes may have gone to his grave believing, is false—namely, that how far a cannonball has fallen after being released is not proportional to its velocity attained or the time elapsed but rather to the square of those magnitudes, a self-rectification that leads eventually through Newton, Leibnitz, Lagrange, and Helmholtz to the magnificent law of the conservation of energy.

The far-reaching implications of the changes I have discussed go beyond mere methodology. The very economics of producing and reproducing lawyers and judges stands to be significantly altered in ways I do not dare to guess. And as Wittgenstein almost said, of that which we cannot speak it is better to be silent.

271

Lessons from the Current Economic Expansion

By Paul A. Samuelson*

I shall take literally my assignment on this panel and discuss what lessons we have learned from recent macroeconomic experience. This means noting some surprising departures from previous patterns of experience. But it also means pinching ourselves and asking, What went right?

Here, then, in ten minutes are ten lessons learned or to be learned, which is at the rate of one lesson a minute.

Lesson 1. *Economists cannot forecast the future with precision.*

Lesson 2. *Neither can anyone else,* and the forecasts made by professional economists are systematically better than any made by brokers, bankers or businessmen. (Together, these lessons might constitute the "random dart" theory of getting a forecast: throw a coin at any one of the couple of dozen leading practitioners of the forecasting art, and you'll do about as well as if you try to pick out the very best one. In fact, it won't matter much where your coin lands, you'll get almost the same forecast anyway—which leads to the next lesson.)

Lesson 3. *Economists can succeed in forecasting like each other.* Roy Blough's dogma still holds. Economists are like eight Esquimaux in one bed—the only thing you can be sure about is that they are all going to turn over together. I may add as a corollary to Blough's Law: most economists are going to be all correct together, or all wrong together. The dispersion between forecasts by a score of university, bank, government, and corporation ana-

lysts is much less than the dispersion of their best guesses around where the future reality will lie.

Lesson 4. *Some economists manage to forecast worse than others.* But a Darwinian process of selection—often self-selection when one deals with rational men with alternative uses for their leisure time—does serve to eliminate those whose comparative advantage lies in cosmology or in futurism. After a man has said a dozen times, "If this forecast doesn't turn out correct, I'll hang up my gloves," he finally does. However, there are exceptions to this rule: some masochists make a nice living out of being wrong in an interesting way, predicting every other year that the Dow-Jones average will go down to 200, where it will meet the dollar price of gold. Businessmen, who like to have their adrenalin run listening to a ghost story, will pay as much to listen to these ever-losers as to informed analysts. But my Darwinian proposition becomes irrefutable when I base it on the tautology that the born losers who stay in the forecasting game cease to be regarded as economists by members of our guild.

Lesson 5. *An automatic computer can forecast better than an official government agency.* But an analyst with judgment can do better than an automatic computer. This is borne out, not only by the rather sad performance of the reduced-form monetarist model of the Federal Reserve Bank of St. Louis, but also by Ray Fair's audit of his own Princeton model, which does without any inputs of "judgment" and which thereby runs up a larger mean

* Massachusetts Institute of Technology.

square error than the leading judgmental-computer models of the Wharton, Michigan, *DRI*, Chase, or other type.

Lesson 6. *Judgmental analysts cannot do without the computer.* So much of the information that comes to any man of judgment these days has been massaged by a computer that the era is past when one could have a fair contest between a non-analytical observer such as Sumner Slichter and a giant post-Keynesian macro computer model. Were Slichter alive today, he would make his forward strides of shrewdness while riding on the escalator of the computer.

Lesson 7. *Economists can forecast (well, almost forecast) everything but prices.* In this sense they are the reverse of Oscar Wilde's cynics, who know the price of everything and the value of nothing. When it comes to next March's price of wheat, why should any Ph.D. be able to forecast that better than people who know a lot about the crops and milling industry and who have a lot of money riding on the outcome of their best guesses? All the things that are easy to forecast—that is, easy enough for a mere professor to foresee—can be expected to have already been taken into account by the speculative market. Indeed, if there were in Las Vegas or New York a continuous casino on the money *GNP* of 1974's fourth quarter, it would be absurd to think that the best economic forecasters could improve upon the guess posted there. Whatever knowledge and analytical skill they possess would already have been fed into the bidding. It is a manifest contradiction to think that most economists can be expected to do better than their own best performance. But I am saying something more devastating than that. I am saying that the best forecasters have been poor in predicting the general price level's movements and level even a year ahead. By Valentine's Day 1973 the best forecasters

were beginning to talk of the growth recession that we now know did set in at the end of the first quarter. Aside from their end-of-1972 forecasts, the fashionable crowd has little to blame itself for when it comes to their 1973 real *GNP* projections. But, of course, they did not foresee the upward surge of food and decontrolled industrial prices. This has been a recurring pattern: surprise during the event at the virulence of the inflation, wisdom after the event in demonstrating that it did, after all, fit in with past patterns of experience. I know of no exception to this generalization. Monetarists have generally done no better in this regard, although some have thought that there is somehow a closer link between M and P than between M and money $GNP = P \times Q$. To be sure, some have been less unlucky in their guesses than others, but we all know what the corollary of that is. What seems to have thrown economists off is the fact that the Phillips Curve seems to have worsened, both in the eyes of those who believe in the Phillips Curve and in the eyes of those who don't (and use a different language to describe the same disappointing effect upon wages and costs generally of each degree of stagnation). Improvement in the rate of inflation is a mirage that economists see eighteen months ahead; but just as the railroad tracks never seem to meet as they appeared to do ten miles back, so that return to "normalcy" never seems to occur—not even after we have euphemistically redefined normalcy to permit of 2.5 percent annual inflation or more. Paradoxically, as soon as the analysts stopped underestimating wage increases, they began to underestimate general price increases. One suspects that two things are involved: wishful thinking and perhaps a change in the structural difficulty of the economy in having steady or slowly growing price levels. When their predictions go wrong, people usually find alibis in contrafactual predictions incapable of being falsified or corroborated. Thus, some say, "It is price controls that cause the error in my forecasts (in either direction!); but, of course, we shall never know what the world would have been like without those price controls." Or they say, "If the Fed would do something (which the odds are against its doing), then the reality would agree with my forecast." Much of the disagreement for policy, but not all, comes from differences between advisers on how much sacrifice of short-term welfare they are willing to invest in now and in the near future for some hypothetical better behavior of the economy in the more distant future. Those with a low rate of time discount, who will cheerfully recommend a flyer in sadomasochistic austerity, are likely by the Darwinian process of politics to find themselves not in power for the period of time they say their therapy requires.

Lesson 8. *In recent years the U.S. economy has been remarkably unprone to swings of inventory accumulation such as characterized our past history.* Those who prior to the energy crisis predicted a genuine recession for 1974 were counting on such an inventory slingshot effect to give them their downturn. But they may have to look elsewhere for their recession.

Lesson 9. *A microeconomic event such as an Arab oil boycott can loom large as a macroeconomic depressant.* Most experts now think that if the boycott is more than a charade and a passing thing, real output will decline in the first half of 1974. But we now realize that our Fisher-Keynes macro models do not tell us how to handle such a microeconomic restriction on supply and productivity. It is not even clear that we should call such a downturn a recession, since it may not involve much wastage between our actual *GNP* and our producible *GNP*. However, to the extent that gasoline scares hurt the auto business and the suburban building market, some of the same secondary effects of conventional recession will become operative, calling for some of the conventional lean-against-the-wind policy measures.

Lesson 10. *The conventional wisdom that currency depreciation will improve the balance of payments seems in 1973, at long last, to receive some support from the factual evidence.* There have been more important things to worry about in recent years than which way the dollar would move in a regime of somewhat-flexible exchange rates.

I've still not drawn all the lessons taught by our recent times. Perhaps I may be permitted to give one final lesson, to grow wise on, so to speak.

Lesson 11. *Events of the last half dozen years have shown us how much economics remains an art rather than a science.* Economics is exciting because what we study is hard, not easy. Once again, I think, experience has taught us the hard way that eclecticism in economics is, to paraphrase Justice Holmes, not so much a desirability as a necessity.

272

Foreword

by Paul A. Samuelson

What is the single most frequent question I encounter when I lecture to students, businessmen, Congressional committees? There is no better way to learn what is bothering people than to chart the changes in the cry that emerges from the heart of a concerned audience.

Ten years ago, with monotonous regularity, I encountered this query: "How are we going to handle the soaring public debt?" Those burdens that were supposed to bow down the backs of Eisenhower's grandchildren were certainly bothering many of his contemporaries. Five years ago, particularly abroad, the question had changed. "Professor Samuelson, isn't it true that America's prosperity depends on Cold War expenditures and imperialistic ventures abroad?"

Today, things have changed once again. Without doubt, the burning question of the day, especially among young people, has to do with our national growth. "To William James, the bitch goddess of America was success. Isn't worship of a zooming GNP a reversion to idolatry of the golden calf?" As one earnest student put it, "To me, GNP is gross national pollution. I wish it could halve, not double."

As one who lived through the horrible days of the Great Depression, when GNP did indeed drop by half, I can testify that this is the hard way to purify the atmosphere and restore the serenity of a simple life. And yet I can sympathize with the concern now being shown about unwanted babies, unbridled population growth, the tasteless piling up of baubles. And those who ask these questions today are among the finest human beings one meets, whereas those who used to ask about the public debt were decent enough citizens, honest people who honored their contracts and kept their fences mended, but not human beings with whom you would want to share a lifeboat.

Biology, however, is too important to leave to the biologists. We need scholars like Peter Passell and Leonard Ross —young men whose hearts are on the side of the angels—to separate from the incredible nonsense that is now being written about overpopulation and doomsday the unavoidable kernel of truth. Pascal said, "The heart has its reasons which reason knows nothing of." Indeed it does. And so do astrologers and charlatans, zealots and computers. The research scientist who wins fame for himself, too often begins to sound like a race-track tout when he leaves the laboratory.

What can I be thinking about, when I recommend this present, careful audit of the costs and benefits accruing from different kinds of growth? Don't I know that a computer at MIT has revalidated for our time the curse of Malthus— that population grows in a remorseless geometric progression, while subsistence and resources grow arithmetically at best? How could I not know this?

Yes—but let me tell a story about the machine, a true

story. Long ago, there was a marvelous machine that could meet and best any man in chess. It traveled all through Europe, taking on each village champion and adding to its list of victories. Finally, it met a skeptical man of the enlightenment who looked deep into its structure. And there, curled up inside the machine, he found a little man—dwarfed, but still a man, with two eyes and one brain.

I reveal no secret when I say that curled up inside every modern computer, if only you can see him, there is a man—its programmer. Water does not rise above its own source. The theorems of a model can be no better than its axioms.

Peter Passell and Leonard Ross seek to appraise the axioms of growth and antigrowth. We can all learn from their effort.

273

CHRISTMAS ECONOMICS

BY PAUL A. SAMUELSON

'There is no free lunch." How often we hear that tired substitute for thought, that fractional truth which is a fractional untruth.

My whole life has been one long free lunch—and not just in the first year of life. I have always been over-paid to do that which I would pay to do. But I am simply one of the lucky ones, you say? That's precise-ly my point.

Our virtues, like our faults, are in the stars we never made. We see it in every family: one child has dyslexia, another total recall; one is born, as William James put it, with a bottle of champagne to his credit, another chronically owing a night's sleep. What, after all, did the sister of Helen of Troy look like? All such gifts are the gifts of the gods.

So it is with nations. A 5-foot-10 American citizen with a certified IQ of 101 is paid eight times what his fellow man in Central America gets. He is paid one and a half times as much as his fellowperson in the United States even if she has one-third more IQ. He is paid three times the real income of that great-grandfather who boasted of the same 101 IQ and had to work much harder.

Notice that I speak of what one gets "paid," not of what one "earns." Econ-omists, from Madame Pompadour's medical counselor to last June's newly minted Ph.D., have always realized that there is only the most tenuous connection between rewards and de-servingness. When Queen Victoria offered Lord Melbourne the Order of the Garter, he said, "What I like about the Order of the Garter is that there is no damned merit about it." A sheik's son on his way to Monte Carlo could say as much.

COMMUNITY

I have quoted in many editions of my economics textbook wise words of Britain's greatest sociologist (and I mean L.T. Hobhouse and not Her-bert Spencer!) to summarize all this:

"The organizer of industry who thinks he has 'made' himself and his business has found a whole social sys-tem ready to his hand in skilled work-ers, machinery, a market, peace and order—a vast apparatus and a perva-sive atmosphere, the joint creation of millions of men and scores of genera-tions. Take away the whole social fac-tor and we have not Robinson Crusoe, with his salvage from the wreck and his acquired knowledge, but the na-tive savage living on roots, berries and vermin."

Or, as a native sage has put it:

"Carry the notion of the individual to its limit and you get a monstrosity . . . not Nietzsche's superman, but Wolf Boy."

What has this to do with econom-ics? Just this. Altruism, like vintage burgundy, you might think, is a lux-ury that can be afforded only by the affluent. And when we reflect on the evolutionary process of natural selec-tion, we can understand why the preference a mother gives to her own infant might have survival value and therefore have survived. But by the same logic we realize that altruistic mother love, like concern to be a good neighbor, also has survival value and is part of nature's grand design.

WE, INC.

Modern industrial societies typical-ly devote a larger fraction of their total resources to government than do subsistence economies. Democracy is the greatest system of mutual rein-surance ever invented. When we see a friend in the line for unemployment compensation, we each say, "There but for the grace of supply and demand go I."

Justice Oliver Wendell Holmes laid down the doctrine, "Taxes are what we pay for civilized society." Although he was the one who also said, "Life is painting a picture, not doing a sum," I believe his political arithmetic cannot be faulted. In the case of Justice Holmes this was more than high-sounding rhetoric. For, like the Athenians of old, he left his not inconsiderable estate to the United States people.

When the husband in O. Henry's story pawned his gold watch to buy the tortoise-shell set to comb the beautiful tresses the wife had sacrificed to buy him a watch chain, that was indeed a splendid Christmas Day. But 364 additional such days each year would be too much. Just because government expenditures stem from the highest human motive is no reason for them to be undertaken inadvisedly—or inefficiently. Governments, like Casanova, too often never know when to stop.

Still, we are told, of faith, hope and charity, the greatest of these is charity. And the wisest translate the word as love.

PART X

Essays on the Evolution of Economics

274

The balanced-budget multiplier: a case study in the sociology and psychology of scientific discovery

Paul A. Samuelson, October 1974

Introduction

This is an instance that would delight Columbia's Robert K. Merton, whose studies in the sociology of science have demonstrated that single-tons in the discovery of new scientific results can be expected to be the exception rather than the rule. Of course at the moment of discovering the theorem, I was pretty sure that it had not already appeared in the literature and that it was new. But shortly thereafter, in a conversation with Bill Salant, I discovered that he too had discovered essentially the same theorem. And it was not long afterwards, I seem to recall, that Alvin Hansen, in his book with Harvey Perloff came upon some if not all of its essential content. Also, I knew that Harold Somers, in a *Canadian Journal* paper, had arrived at a parallel (but not isomorphic) result. But not until later did I learn that Nicholas Kaldor's arithmetical exercisᵉ ⅃ for Beveridge had also recognized how full employment could be acnieved by a budget balanced at a high enough level. I am not able to recall even the approximate date—during the war, I believe—when Bill Salant told me that Keynes had also implicitly used the theorem in a wartime budget he had written for the Chancellor of the Exchequer (Kingsley Wood), which made the point that if you added £1,000 m. of new war expenditure to a full-employment economy, you would have to raise taxes by *more* than £1,000 m. (from which part of the b-b-m theorem follows). Some of the reasons for the delay in publication of Salant and Samuelson results, will, I presume, be apparent from Walter Salant's posthumous presentation of his brother's contributions.

What I propose here is to undertake a psychological experiment that may be of some interest for its own sake—namely, to let the filter of memory give my offhand recollections of the sequence of events. Only after this Monte Carlo run will I do a little cursory research to warn against the more glaring distortions that memory and unconscious self-interest are bound to create. The errors in my account may be of more interest to a psychologist concerned with how scholars actually behave than will be the banal details that happened a third of a century ago.

The dog that didn't bark

To me the remarkable thing was not that I discovered the unitary balanced budget mutliplier around 1942 (plus or minus one year), but that I did not discover it earlier—or, more exactly, that such a truth remained to be discovered much after 1936. And as a matter of fact, it was there in a 1938 article that I gave at the Detroit Annual Meetings of the American Economic Association on the invitation of Alvin Hansen, already then my fatherly friend and teacher. But of course I didn't recognize that it was there in my equations. (This is like the experience at the time of the famous Lee-Yang-Wu parity experiment in physics. A physicist friend of mine told me that he already had that result in his notebook of experiments, as he realized in retrospect; but either he had not appreciated its significance, or he dismissed such a discrepancy from parity as presumed experimental error. A second instance is given by Glenn Seaborg in his foreword to the American edition of Otto Hahn's autobiography. Seaborg had devoured every word Hahn had written in the years before he learned in 1939 about the Hahn-Strassmann-Meitner-Frisch splitting of the uranium atom with a release of energy. When he heard of that experiment and its interpretation, he walked the streets of Berkeley for much of the night wondering how he had missed this obvious resolution of the experimental data he knew so well.)

There was a first special reason why a dozen members of the Hansen School had not discovered the theorem in the late 1930's. This reason will seem incredible to the modern generation of economists, and I doubt that a future-generation historian of doctrines would pick it up in his researches. I am referring to the fact that Simon Kuznets, our pioneering source on the definition and the data of GNP and national income, in the years just before World War II included in his definition of GNP, not government expenditure on goods and services, but *only that fraction of such expenditures which was financed by taxes rather than deficits.* By the war years, this peculiar Kuznets definition (which one must realize was not without some reasonable rationalization) had become quite untenable, since at the wartime peak as much as a quarter of all GNP would have been excluded if one had stubbornly adhered to the definition.

If one defines national income or GNP by the relations $Y_K = C + I + T = c[C + I + G - T] + I + T$ rather than by the present-day (and more correct-seeming) relations $Y = c[Y - T] + I + G$, then one will not be led to the unitary-balanced-budget multiplier of $dY/dG \equiv 1$ whenever $dT/dG \equiv 1$—or, rather it will appear to be an uninteresting fatuity. Here T stands for total tax collections, I for net investment, G for government expenditure on goods and services (not to be confused with government expenditures on transfers, which I'll write as Tr), C for total consumption expenditures, and $c[y]$ is the functional relation between consumption and "disposable income after taxes," y or $Y - T$, with c' the derivative of $c[y]$ being the marginal propensity to consume, assumed in conventional Keynesian theory to be a fraction less than 1, and where Y_K is my symbol for the odd-seeming Kuznets income definition of those pioneering days.

There was a second chain of events that were relevant in the genesis of the theorem. Economists then, as now, sought to measure how stimulative or restrictive fiscal policy really was. Thus, Lauchlin Currie and the too-soon-departed Martin Krost computed at the Federal Reserve Board a time series that purported to measure this multiplicand. Such a measure, it was hoped, would reveal that the recession of 1937 was triggered off by federal fiscal tightness at the beginning of the year when Secretary of the Treasury Morgenthau tried to balance the budget and when the new Social Security taxes began to bite in before expenditure transfers amounted to much. Later Henry Villard privately attempted similar estimating of the government's net-income-creating contribution. By and large it was the government deficit, $G - T$ (or, in those early days, $G + Tr - T$), that was thought to constitute the government stimulus. Hence, a high balanced budget would still represent a zero stimulus! (I am skipping over the attempt to elaborate the concept by giving larger weights to expenditures directed toward poor and presumably ready spenders with high marginal propensities to consume.)

A third channel of influence relative to the budget theorem came from Bill Salant's and my preoccupation (and that of Machlup, Colin Clark, D. H. Robertson, Harrod, Haberler, and above all Metzler) with *international trade* multipliers. It was obvious that two-country analysis had much the same analytics as the private-and-public sectors. In particular the debate about whether the "multiplicand" should be exports, X, or the balance of exports over imports, $X - M$, was relevant, as was the fact that tax revenues (T), like imports (M), are usually best regarded as an "endogenous" or "induced" variable rather than as an "exogenous" or "autonomous shift" parameter.

The thing itself

My own perception of the balanced-budget theorem came in a form that I still regard as the best of many ways[1] of looking at the matter (and which I put in my 1948 Hansen festschrift exposition).

The change in private disposable income, y or $Y - T$, and not in $Y = C + I + G$, is indeed validly determined in the simplest Keynesian models by the $1/(1 - c')$ multiplier as applied to the budget-deficit multiplicand. I.e., equilibrium y^* is the root of

$$y = c[y] + I + (G - T),\ 0 \leqslant c'[y] < 1, \tag{1a}$$
$$y^* = m[I + (G - T)], \tag{1b}$$
$$dy^*/d(G - T) = m'[\quad] = 1/(1 - c') > 1. \tag{1c}$$

But if that is so, presto—the unitary balanced-budget-multiplier theorem is perceived:

> Increasing G and T together so that $G - T$ and y^* never change makes $Y^* = y^* + G$ grow exactly one for one with growth in G.

This is a remarkable result. It is one of those quantitative econometric magnitudes that is independent of our empirical measurements of the strength of the marginal propensity to consume c'. It is almost suspect for being such an invariant, one that holds uniformly provided only that c' is any non-negative magnitude less than 1.

Given such a recognizably important result, one's natural inclination is the Mertonian one of publishing it rapidly to make it available to the world for policy use and to gain the commendation of one's scholarly peers for good work and good luck.

Two minds with a single thought

But the years 1939–1945 were busy wartime years. And in any case, in an encounter with William Salant whose exact date and place eludes me, I learned that he had come upon essentially the same result. It is my recollection that he wrote down for me the geometric series multiplier for a dollar of G expenditure and its negative counterpart for a dollar of T tax collection: namely,

$$= \dfrac{\begin{array}{l} 1 + c' + (c')^2 + \cdots \\ - c' - (c')^2 - \cdots \end{array}}{1} \qquad \text{Eureka!}$$

1. I can recall not caring for other explanations of the theorem that tried to rely on shorter lags in government than in private spending and/or allegedly faster velocity of public rather than private dollars.

We agreed to prepare a joint publication. But William Salant got tied up in war service and I never thought it fair to carry the matter any further.

Priority sans disclosure

In the meantime I had of course communicated my result to Alvin Hansen, whom I saw often both in Cambridge and in Washington, and I learned that he had arrived at the notion of government adding to GNP even in the absence of a deficit by thinking of government as having a unitary propensity to consume, and therefore no leakage: so the private GNP could ride piggyback on the solid baseload governmental GNP; if you lift the base an elephant stands on by one cubit, then the height of his head will rise by one cubit. Q.E.D.

Back in the fifteenth century, when a Renaissance mathematician discovered the formula for a cubic or quadric, he often announced a Latin anagram that gave his rivals no useful clue to his algorithm. But should they subsequently discover his magic formula on their own, he could produce his anagram to demonstrate in retrospect that he had indeed had legitimate claims to priority. I suspect it was before my conversation with Salant that I prepared my contribution to one of Seymour Harris's many symposium volumes, his *Postwar Economic Problems*. In my paper, a paper that to this day reads very well to its author's eyes (as for example in its anticipation of the elements which are valid in the permanent-income hypothesis, of the counterclockwise hysteresis ratchet effects of consumption in declines, and the secular increase in consumption-living requirements), I announced the balanced-budget theorem but reserved it for a future discussion.

Thus, when Henry Wallich came to write his *Quarterly Journal of Economics* version of that theorem, he sent me a draft of his paper and asked whether he had in effect earned the guinea for correctly deducing the content of my announced result. (My imperfect recollection is that essentially he had indeed done so.)

The everafter

As Alfred Marshall should have known when he delayed publishing some of his findings for as long as thirty years, you cannot expect the rest of the world to stand still just because you've gone fishing or are a perfectionist author. So naturally the balanced-budget theorem became a standard feature of the postwar macroeconomic literature, particularly after much of a whole issue of *Econometrica* (April 1946) was devoted to it, containing such important names as Trygve Haavelmo, Everett Hagen, Gottfried Haberler, and Richard Goodwin. (It was only much later, after Rasmussen's 1958 *Economic Journal* article, that I became aware that my admired friend, Jørgen Gelting,[2] had published a 1941 Danish article on the essential theorem.)

To improve upon Voltaire and Napoleon, history is a set of myths *temporarily* agreed upon. When you read the standard saga of how in the middle of the seventeenth century Pascal and Fermat originated probability theory in answering the gaming queries of the profligate Chevalier de Méré, you know that the story falsifies itself on its face. The questions posed were sophisticated ones and prepare one to believe that probability theory dates back to an earlier century (as in the writings of Cardano). If memory is correct, Haavelmo was not so much concerned to prove the simple truth of the balanced-budget relation as to *refute* the facile explanation given for it—namely, that its validity stems allegedly[3] from the fact that some of new taxes will come out of income that would otherwise be saved, whereas all of (exhaustive) government expenditures enters into national product. Thus I seem to remember his specifying the $c' = 1$ borderline case where this facile explanation would run into some difficulty. (On the other hand, when $c' = 1$ we could avoid an unstable system provided that T were not taken to be an autonomous constant but instead satisfied an induced relation like $T = \tau Y$, with my 1938 implication that any increment in G would then automatically eventually induce an equivalent increment in T, with the unitary-balanced-budget theorem thereby holding.)

One subsequent expository development of the u-b-b-m theorem worth remembering is Arthur Smithies' demonstration that if induced investment depends on total Y and not on $y = Y - T$, one could even

2. My debts to Jørgen Gelting are great, and not only for friendship with him and his wife in the late 1940's in postwar Cambridge and Copenhagen. In 1948, when I was lecturing on modern welfare economics at the University of Copenhagen, his questions rearoused my interest in two public-finance topics that soon preoccupied me: Ramsey's 1927 theory of optimal (feasible) taxation, and the theory of public goods in the Lindahl and general-equilibrium versions. But these are two other stories, each worth retelling if the present one is.

3. Actually, in my elementary textbook's many editions' expositions of why a dollar increment of G and of T will expand equilibrium Y^*, I have repeatedly (and correctly) stressed that with $c'[Y - T]$ fractional, a unit rightward shift of the CC consumption schedule will shift it down by less than a unit (by only the fraction c' of a unit). This explanation does require that $c' < 1$, as does William Salant's cancellation-of-infinite-series explanations (which for $c' = 1$ would become $[1 + 1 + \cdots] - [0 + 1 + 1 + 1 + \cdots]$, an undefined magnitude). Thus, in the influential survey of fiscal impact in the 1930's of E. C. Brown (1956), a *valid* first pass at the government "multiplicand" was provided by $G - (T - Tr)c'[\ ]$. In the most general formulation, we can let $c'[\ ]$ exceed unity provided it falls short of $1/(1 - T) > 1$: the system will still be dynamically stable, but when $1 - c' > 0$, $G - T$ declines as G increases—even though Y^* and y^* still rise determinately with G.

succeed in overbalancing the budget by spending more, a comforting doctrine that liberals of those days liked to use in selling expansionary fiscal policy to the electorate. Noteworthy too was Thomas Schelling's use of like analysis to show that paying out more in wages could *raise* profits; and also Schelling's neat graphical exposition of the unitary-balanced-budget theorem in the *Review of Economics and Statistics.*

You know that a theorem has really arrived and even gone by its full bloom when the literature begins to add rebuttals and qualifications to it. I remember putting in this genus the paper by William Baumol, questioning the realism of expecting $dY/dG \equiv dY/dT$ to be identically unity. I thought then that any expositor of the theorem would cheerfully agree; and if pressed for a best estimate of the realistic departure from unity he might, monetary limitations not assumed to be pressing in the background, expect the multiplier to be greater rather than less than unity.

And a modern theorem is finally classical when people come to feel (as Gelting apparently did in 1941) that it was already in Ricardo (something I am inclined to doubt since Ricardo never departed from Say's Law in the modern Keynesian manner).

Conclusion

Professor Merton has pointed out that scholars do have concern for priorities, and provides argumentation as to why this is so. He also points out, with Newton and Darwin serving as good instances, that scholars also are uncomfortable in their concerns over matters of priority. All this Mertonian wisdom is borne out by various abortive efforts by William Salant and me to publish some of the details of the present account, and also by the hesitations involved in these attempts. It is also the case that one good friend, for reasons that I never quite grasped, advised strongly against any postwar publishing on this subject. He may well have been right.

POSTSCRIPT FROM THE LIBRARY STAIRS

1. I have now read the galley proofs of the William and Walter Salant items, and of the Gelting and Bent Hansen items. And I have paged through the bound library backfiles of some of the relevant economic journals. In the light of this, how does my previous remembered account stand up? It seems to me that it stands up fairly well; if it stood up too well, that would itself be a suspicious circumstance. Most of the actual errors and ambiguities are of no particular importance.

There are, however, some systematic failures of memory that Robert Merton or a historian of science and of the reward system in science will find extremely interesting. And so would Sigmund Freud. The filter of memory is not an unbiased filter: it tends to decide ambiguities in the direction of personal wish fulfillment. So what else is new?

2. Here I shall briefly indicate what seem to be the important defects in my earlier account, and shall also provide some references for the reader interested in most easily looking up the subject. Thus, for the many writings of Robert K. Merton, I cite his book of collected essays on science, Merton, 1973. Parts 4 and 5, written for the most part over the last sixth of a century, are most relevant, in particular his 1957, 1961, and 1963 items dealing with singletons and multiples in scientific discovery; but really many more of the essays could be beautifully corroborated by this one test case.

3. For the reader of published print the whole matter might be summed up as follows. A trained economist who knew the literature in all languages would say that the first statement in print of the balanced-budget-multiplier theorem was that of Gelting 1941 in Danish. Somers 1942 came close to *some* of its content. And so did Keynes in his treasury memorandum for Chancellor Sir Kingsley Wood's Budget Address of April 1941, which made the point which Gelting attributes to Ricardo[4] in 1821 and which Milton Friedman 1942 was also to make in connection with the size of taxes needed to close an inflationary gap. Hansen and Perloff 1944 also came close. In the English literature, Wallich 1944 has received too little notice: it makes the essential point in a nonmathematical, nongraphical way and cites Samuelson 1943 for its bare announcement of the theorem and mentions that William Salant had an unpublished paper of 1942 on the subject.

The theorem enters the conscious public literature in a dramatic way in Haavelmo 1945 and the discussion it spawned in the April 1946 *Econometrica*—Haberler-Hagen-Goodwin-Haavelmo 1946. An omniscient reader might have noted the theorem's spoor in Musgrave 1945. And important aspects of the matter came to the larger public's attention in Kaldor 1944. Samuelson 1948 provides exposition of it. Smithies 1948 and Schelling 1946 and 1948 provide supplementary aspects of it.

---

4. As I suspected in my earlier account, Ricardo's point, as quoted by Rasmussen (1958, p. 156) from Ricardo (1821, paragraph that overlaps pp. 393–94 of Sraffa 1953 ed. of Ricardo's *Principles*) in connection with Gelting's contention, really refers to a microeconomic point about an aggregative Say's Law system: all that Ricardo intends to say is that a shift in final demand toward a *more* "labor-intensive" good (Napoleonic-war soldiers rather than clothing) will increase the long-run equilibrium level of employment (and population!). One must live with Ricardo to realize how far he was from Keynes and Hansen, to say nothing of the pre-Keynes Malthus.

The beginnings of systematic discussion of the history of the theorem do not come until after the mid-1950's, a dozen years after its genesis, as for example in Rasmussen 1958, with its calling attention to the Gelting article in Danish; and, of course, we have in this issue of *HOPE* the Salant-Salant-Hansen-Gelting-Samuelson symposium (1975).

4. To a member of the "invisible college" who knows all that there is to know about the matter, including that which is *not* in print (Walter Salant or Alvin Hansen come close, as I might), we can sum up thus. Not knowing of Gelting's work, William Salant and Paul Samuelson independently discovered the theorem, probably in the first half of 1942, and this fact was indirectly communicated to a number of interested American economists, only a few of whom were provided with the 1942 Salant memorandum or the details of the Samuelson formulation. Also aspects of the theorem were independently discovered by Keynes, Hansen-Perloff, and Kaldor.

With respect to "independence" of discovery, Gelting, Samuelson, Salant each made the discovery not knowing that anyone else had done so. Wallich and Haavelmo independently rediscovered the theorem, knowing only that some other persons had earlier established it in *some* form or other but not knowing anything about their modes of argument. (Thus, although Haavelmo comments on Wallich's published discussion, it is clear that he did not know that paper existed when he submitted his own first version to *Econometrica*.)

Cary Brown, who has kindly read this postscript, emphasizes that the invisible college still did not appreciate the balanced-budget phenomenon until a late date: he vividly recalls a Treasury meeting "(probably in late 1944 or 1945) of a distinguished panel of economists— Haberler, Viner, J. M. Clark, Henry Simons, . . .—who specifically disagreed with Hansen's contention that a dollar of tax reduction is not the same thing as a dollar of expenditure increase." Brown thinks that somewhere in the Treasury minutes this demonstration of the novelty of the b-b-m theorem at that date could be corroborated.

To appreciate Walter Salant's subtle remarks differentiating between the Salant-Samuelson result and related results like those of Kaldor, Keynes, and perhaps Somers, one must add to his exposition the following consideration: (i) there is the unitary balanced-budget-multiplier theorem proper, with its emphasis on 1.0; (ii) there is also the more general theorem, not at all obvious to prewar consumers of Currie-Krost deficit-multiplicand and related analysis, that equal increments in government expenditure on goods and in tax receipts will have *some positive* effect on income and employment. To establish only the latter important result, one need *not* have apprehended the former, and evidently Keynes, Friedman, and perhaps Kaldor did not.

Also, and what is a different point, if $dY/dG = dY/dT$ is not unity, à la Baumol-Peston, that invalidates (i) but not the important (ii).

5. Now I turn to the biases in my memory's filter, which will be of interest to those concerned with the psychology of scholars and with antiquarian history, and which those interested only in substance can skip.

The following "errors" were all essentially in my favor, and hence of possible Freudian origin.

(a) There are no equations in Samuelson 1938 as I had thought. Those equations are in Samuelson 1942: in particular, contrary to Walter Salant's failure to find in this latter article relevant b-b-m material, the third from the last equation in Samuelson 1942, p. 584, n. 1, is, except for notation and the linearity assumption (a limitation shared with Gelting and William Salant), precisely equivalent to the crucial Equation (1a). That does not mean that in the months before Christmas 1938 the earlier paper did not have similar equations: it may well have had them, because its text states theorems that encapsulate some of them, including the final 1942 footnote equation.

Two more Freudian points about the 1938 paper. Why did I forget that it did not appear until 1940? Unconscious predating in my own favor? Certainly it gives signs of possible contamination by my own post-1938 thinking. Second, on p. 504 in paragraph 2, *almost* a direct denial of the balanced-budget's expansionary effects is explicitly stated!

(b) My memory seems to have conveniently forgotten Haavelmo's first, 1945 article, the one that come closest to my own mathematical formulation. I remembered only the 1946 symposium that gave the Haberler, Hagen, and Goodwin reactions to Haavelmo's original article. Also, I forgot Musgrave 1945, which I must have known even though I was still at the Radiation Laboratory doing wartime mathematics of a noneconomic nature early that year.

(c) My memory remembered only the $(1 + c' + \cdots) - (c' + \cdots)$ contribution of William Salant, although there was much more there. I now rather think that my original lunch conversation with Bill Salant predates this memo in its July 1942 form. I seem to recall his telling me *after* that lunch something like, "Our mutual discovery is not so unanticipated after all; I've discovered that Keynes wrote a speech for the Chancellor's Budget Address that had an inkling of it."

6. A few final thoughts for the Mertonian buff. Why did Wallich get so little notice from economists and Haavelmo so much? In part, a Matthew Effect[5] (to him that hath shall be given): Haavelmo, and

5. The joint article by Baumol and Peston provides another example of the Matthew Effect: I forgot the junior author's name! This is quite another thing

certainly Haberler-Hagen-Goodwin were collectively "better known" than Wallich was then. Also, Wallich had no equations, tables, or graphs. An advantage, you say? Well, if you do, you don't know twentieth-century economics. A theorem is lost among mere words; Hansen-Perloff suffered somewhat from the same factor; Kaldor's tables fared better. Then too, publication just *after* a war can be better than during the war when scholars are otherwise preoccupied: thus Slutsky's classic 1915 paper on consumer demand theory, appearing in a wartime Italian journal, had to be rediscovered almost a score of years later.

7.   Having now done some retrospective research, I could improve upon my earlier account and could amplify it in several worthwhile directions. But enough is enough.[6]

REFERENCES

Baumol, W. J., and M. H. Peston. "More on the Multiplier Effects of a Balanced Budget." *American Economic Review* 45 (March 1955):140–48; "Reply," ibid., 46 (March 1956):160–62.

Brown, E. C. "Fiscal Policies in the 'Thirties: A Reappraisal." *American Economic Review* 46 (Dec. 1956):857–79.

Currie, L., and M. Krost. *Explanation of Methods of Computing Net Contribution.* Board of Governors of the Federal Reserve System, Washington, D.C., February 10, 1939, mimeographed.

---

from talking often about Hansen, and only rarely about Hansen-Perloff; one presumes (what one cannot always validly presume) that the collaborator who is a specialist in one of the many fields written on is the one primarily involved in the part of the book dealing with that specialty. Does Merton have a name for the following effect? Russell and Whitehead jointly authored *Principia Mathematica;* because Whitehead soon thereafter stopped publishing on mathematics and logic, many (like Keynes) tended to refer to it as Russell's. The fact that Keynes had resentments against Whitehead, his thesis reader and family's friend, may also be germane. Another point that Merton should give a name to if he hasn't already is the following: If you tell me that you have built a successful hydrogen bomb, I am put at an immense advantage. Example: From 1937 to 1946, I off and on tried to prove that "If what is now (properly) called Houthakker's strong axiom of revealed preference is not to be violated, then non-integrability of the more-than-2-good indifference-slope field is ruled out." No success. When I learned in 1950 that Hendrik Houthakker, then a young Dutch graduate student at Cambridge, England, had quite independently formulated the theorem and proved it conclusively, I sat down and at once hacked out my own proof. My friends Kenneth Arrow and Nicholas Georgescu-Roegen had independently notified me earlier that Jean Ville (1946) had provided such a proof; but as best I could make out with my graduate student's knowledge of French, Ville had not done all that needed doing and what Houthakker first did. Now that Ville's beautiful and important paper has been translated, I still think the task awaited its Houthakker; but even a hasty 1947 glance at Ville's line integrals probably hastened my duplication of the Houthakker syllogism.

6. I owe thanks to the National Science Foundation for financial aid, and to Kate Crowley for editorial assistance.

Friedman, Milton. "Discussion of the Inflationary Gap." *American Economic Review* 32 (June 1942):314–20.

Gelting, J. "Nogle Bemaerkninger om Finansieringen af offentlig Virksomhed." *Nationalökonomisk Tidsskrift* 79 (1941):293–99; translated in this issue under the title "Some Observations on the Financing of Public Activity."

Goodwin, Richard M. "Multiplier Effects of a Balanced Budget: The Implications of a Lag for Mr. Haavelmo's Analysis." *Econometrica* 14 April 1946):150–51.

Haavelmo, Trygve. "Multiplier Effects of a Balanced Budget." *Econometrica* 13 (Oct. 1945):311–18; "Reply," ibid., 14 (April 1946):156–58.

Haberler, Gottfried. "Multiplier Effects of a Balanced Budget: Some Monetary Implications of Mr. Haavelmo's Paper." *Econometrica* 14 (April 1946):148–55.

Hagen, E. E. "Multiplier Effects . . . ," *Econometrica* 14 (April 1946): 152–55.

Hahn, Otto. *My Life: Autobiography of a Scientist.* New York, 1970.

Hansen, Alvin H., and Harvey S. Perloff. *State and Local Finance in the National Economy.* New York, 1944. Esp. pp. 244–46.

Hansen, Bent. "Introduction to Jørgen Gelting's 'Some Observations on the Financing of Governmental Activities.'" In this issue.

Houthakker, Hendrik S. "Revealed Preference and the Utility Function." *Economica* 17 (May 1950):159–74.

Kaldor, Nicholas. "The Quantitative Aspects of the Full Employment Problem in Great Britain." Appendix C of W. H. Beveridge, *Full Employment in a Free Society* (London, 1944; American ed. New York, 1945).

Keynes, J. M. "Treasury Memorandum for April Budget Message of Chancellor of the Exchequer Sir Kingsley Wood," as reproduced in R. S. Sayers, *Financial Policy, 1939–1945* (London, 1956).

Merton, Robert K. *The Sociology of Science: Theoretical and Empirical Investigations.* Chicago, 1973. A collection of earlier papers and lectures edited by N. W. Storer.

Metzler, Lloyd A. *Collected Papers,* Cambridge, Mass., 1973. Esp. articles bearing on many-region multipliers and transfer problems.

Musgrave, Richard A. "Alternative Budget Policies for Full Employment." *American Economic Review* 35 (1945):387–400.

Rasmussen, P. N. "A Note on the History of the Balanced-Budget Multiplier." *Economic Journal* 68 (March 1958):154–56.

Ricardo, David. *The Works and Correspondence of David Ricardo:* vol. 1. *Principles,* ed. Piero Sraffa. Cambridge, 1953.

Salant, Walter S. "Introduction to William A. Salant's 'Taxes, the Multiplier, and the Inflationary Gap.'" In this issue.

Salant, William A. "Taxes, the Multiplier, and the Inflationary Gap." 30 July 1942. In this issue.

Samuelson, Paul A. "Theory of Pump Priming Reexamined." *American Economic Review* 30 (Sept. 1940):492–506. Reproduced as chap. 85 of *The Collected Scientific Papers of Paul A. Samuelson,* II, ed. J. E. Stiglitz (Cambridge, Mass., 1966), pp. 1125–39.

Samuelson, Paul A. "Fiscal Policy and Income Determination." *Quarterly Journal of Economics* 54 (Aug. 1942):575–605. Reproduced as chap.

86 in *The Collected Scientific Papers of Paul A. Samuelson,* II, ed. J. E. Stiglitz (Cambridge, Mass., 1966), pp. 1140–70.

Samuelson, Paul A. "Full Employment After the War." In *Postwar Economic Problems,* ed. S. E. Harris (New York, 1943), pp. 27–53. Reproduced as chap. 108 in *The Collected Scientific Papers of Paul A. Samuelson,* II, ed. J. E. Stiglitz (Cambridge, Mass., 1966), pp. 1429–55.

Samuelson, Paul A. "The Simple Mathematics of Income Determination." In *Income, Employment and Public Policy: Essays in Honor of Alvin Hansen,* by L. A. Metzler et al. 1948. Reproduced as chap. 91 in *The Collected Scientific Papers of Paul A. Samuelson,* II, ed. J. E. Stiglitz (Cambridge, Mass., 1966), pp. 1197–1219.

Samuelson, Paul A. "The Problem of Integrability in Utility Theory." *Economica,* Nov. 1950, pp. 355–85. Reproduced as chap. 10 in *The Collected Scientific Papers of Paul A. Samuelson,* I, ed. J. E. Stiglitz (Cambridge, Mass., 1966), pp. 75–105.

Samuelson, Paul A. *Economics.* 9th ed. New York, 1973.

Schelling, Thomas C. "Raise Profits by Raising Wages." *Econometrica* 14 (July 1946): 227–34.

Schelling, Thomas C. "Income Determination: A Graphic Solution." *Review of Economics and Statistics* 30 (Aug. 1948):227–29.

Smithies, Arthur. "The Impact of the Federal Budget." *Review of Economics and Statistics* 29 (Feb. 1947):28–31.

Smithies, Arthur. "The Multiplier." *American Economic Review* 38 (May 1948):299–305.

Somers, Harold M. "The Impact of Fiscal Policy on National Income." *Canadian Journal of Economics and Political Science* 8 (Aug. 1942): 364–85.

Villard, H. H. *Deficit Spending and the National Income.* New York, 1941.

Ville, J. "The Existence of a Total Utility Function and of an Index of Price." *Review of Economic Studies* 19 (1951) 128–32. A translation of a 1946 paper from the *Annales de l'Université de Lyon.*

Wallich, Henry C. "Income-Generating Effects of a Balanced Budget." *Quarterly Journal of Economics* 59 (Nov. 1944):78–91.

275

THE ART AND SCIENCE OF MACROMODELS OVER 50 YEARS

PAUL A. SAMUELSON

Massachusetts Institute of Technology, Cambridge, Massachusetts

1.1. Prologue

We are gathered together for a birthday celebration to celebrate 50 years of effort and research on econometric models of the overall economy. A birthday party is a time for fun, for looking backward and reminiscing, for looking forward and dreaming.

A birthday party is not a time for criticizing. Only the good fairies are invited. Cold champagne, not cold water, is the order of the day. As the first speaker, my role ought to be peculiarly honorific. Unlike the overture, which outlines and samples the goodies that are to come, the keynote speech is supposed merely to fill in that awkward pause while the late arrivers are getting seated and the symposium is getting itself organized.

I shall attempt to play my part: to serve as the aperitif to whet your appetites and prepare your stomachs for the good roast beef that is to come. As I review the troops, I shall drop names – names of the illustrious dead and of those on active duty. But no matter how polite I try to be, the fact that this is a scientific gathering keeps breaking in. Science is an austere club with stiff rules. Perhaps that is why, like so many ancient clubs these days, it is losing its appeal to new members. The one thing science cannot do is to prove scientifically that the rules of the scientific game are to be followed. Of course, like any enclave of gentlemen, science can eject the cad who breaks the code, stripping him of his badge of membership; but, by definition, cads don't mind not being gentlemen.

Scientific accuracy therefore impels me at the beginning to point out that there is a 20% error in the assignment title '50 years of macrodynamic model building.' Try as I can, I am unable to trace back the beginnings of our subject more than 40 years. Jan Tinbergen's 1935 econometric model of the Dutch economy is our fountainhead and source. I do not think I am stretching things if I include Ragnar Frisch's famous propagation-and-impulse macrodynamic model of the 1933 Gustave Cassel *festschrift*; if you argue that this is a purely theoretical system, Frisch's 1932 circulation-planning model can be pointed to as an ambitious attempt to chart an economy and–what has never been far from our subject–an attempt to improve on economic policies and performance.

It would take us back more than half a century to the 1919 attempt by Warren Persons at Harvard to divide economic time series into those that lead and those that lag. This is a case of the god that failed, that failed twice–once with a bang, once with a whimper: first when the A-B-C barometers of the Harvard Economic Society failed completely to warn of the 1929 stock market crash; second, when Arthur Burns, Geoffrey Moore, and Julius Shishkin revived the methodology in the form of the leading indicators and diffusion indexes, perfecting the techniques just when the ups and downs of the old-fashioned business cycle became secondary to the problems of chronic inflation and excessive gap between actual and potential output. The leading indicator approach I regard as supplementary to macromodel building, not competitive with it. There is no reason why the method should have been particularly useful in preventing speculative stock market losses; after all, lead relationships as historically used, even when accurate, gave no indication of quantitative magnitude of the contraction to follow, and could at best have been helpful in the 1930 and later period when optimists persuaded themselves that the storm was over; in any case general business had turned down in mid-1929, *before* the Crash, an uncharacteristic case where the follower went ahead of the leader and plunged the method into lower repute than was warranted.

Henry L. Moore's *Generating Economic Cycles* of 1923 would take us back almost to our 50 years. But this seminal work more primarily inspired the partial-equilibrium econometrics of Henry Schultz, Bowley Allen, Jacob Marschak, Herman Wold, Richard Stone, and other measurers of demand elasticities. Its connection with macromodeling is more tenuous. To be sure, the estimating of demand curves alerted economists to the problem of 'identification.' The work of Moore, Elmer Working, Wassily Leontief, Ragnar Frisch, Jacob Marschak, Hans

Staehle, Lloyd Metzler, and others culminated finally in the pathbreaking synthesis of Tryggve Haavelmo, which in turn stimulated contributions by Herman Wold, Tjalling Koopmans, Franklin Fisher, Hans Theil, Robert Basmann, and a host of others. But fortunately good old least squares was good enough for Tinbergen; else our subject might have been stillborn. For I can remember the time, just about 25 years ago, when two, three, or *n*-stage least squares had not yet been invented, and when computing facilities for complete, or limited-information estimating were not available, with the result that empirical measurement was grinding to a standstill in the fear of identification bias.

Having just mentioned the name of Moore, I am reminded of a certain kind of macromodel that goes back twice 50 years. Moore didn't believe in sunspots and business cycles: he believed in the transit of Venus–whatever that is!–and business cycles. But before him, Stanley Jevons did believe in sunspots: over the last century, the method of the periodogram or other harmonic analyzers have been applied in the attempt to isolate periodicities in business aggregates. Today, using the more sophisticated Fourier techniques of Norbert Wiener and Andrei Kolmogorov, statisticians have revived spectral analysis. This is not so much a case of a god that failed as one of a god that has not yet succeeded. However, periodicity theory did lead 50 years ago to attempts by Sir Gilbert Walker and G. Udney Yule to work with autoregressive stochastic relations. Eugen Slutsky, the hero who successfully in 1915 executed Vilfredo Pareto's search for the comparative-statics properties of utility maximization, had already shown that random shocks can be cumulated by moving averages and other linear processes into coherent waves that mimic business cycles. This naturally raised the question of whether business cycles are merely mimicking exogenous random shocks that are accumulated by the endogenous properties of the system. And then we are brought full circle back to the early macromodels of Frisch and Tinbergen and to the fertile 1938 thesis of Herman Wold.

Besides, there is a more direct connection between partial-equilibrium elasticity estimation and macrodynamic models. It is via the famous cobweb theorem, in which delayed supply couples with contemporaneous demand to produce a self-exciting corn-hog cycle. One cannot exaggerate the importance to science of parables, of strong images of the cobweb or accelerator–multiplier type. Being simple enough to comprehend and complex enough to excite, they point the way to more sophisticated analysis. Around 1929, Rici, Henry Schultz, P. N. Rosenstein-Rodan, and Tinbergen all glimpsed the dynamics of the cobweb, which indeed had already been implicit in Moore's measuring of potato elasticities. In his maiden voyages, Tinbergen had been led to investigate echo and other cycles in ship-building, phenomena akin to the cobweb but with greater macroeconomic potential.

Now I must change my pace. Like Tristram Shandy, who took years to write up weeks of his birth, I am using up most of my time in just getting our birthday child born. At this rate I shall never finish!

Let me therefore briefly enumerate some stepping-stones.

(1) In World War II, various econometric models were developed to describe and prescribe for wartime economic development and postwar planning. The famous consensus forecast by government economists of great postwar unemployment did not advance the prestige of the method. But in the hands of the Committee for Economic Development, Charles Roos, W. S. Woytinsky, and other econometricians, similar methods had produced more accurate visions of the postwar world. (There were also literary economists on both sides of this debate.)

(2) We next move into what can be called the age of Klein. But he would be the first to insist that it is also the age of many other econometricians and model builders. More important, science is public knowledge, not personal knowledge, i.e. science is committee knowledge, jury knowledge, man-in-the-street knowledge for anyone who cares to put out the effort to learn what there is to know and teach. Therefore we are now in the age of the Norwegian and Dutch governments' macromodels, of the Wharton School, Ann Arbor, Federal Reserve Bank of St. Louis, Social Science Research Council–Brookings, FRB–MIT–Penn, OBE, Data Resources, Inc., Chase Econometrics, Fair–you name your favorite system of national income estimation.

1.2. Models and forecasting

How are we doing in economic forecasting? What progress is there to report in the technique of macromodel forecasting and policy diagnosis? I am serving up the aperitif, not the meat or dessert. And this is a birthday party, not a wake. You couldn't expect me to take inventory of the birthday girl and say: 'True, she is fair and her eyes are blue. But if you look closely at her forehead, unmistakable signs of acne peer out through the cosmetic powder.'

No, I shall not abuse my access to this captive audience to air my half-baked impressions about the art and science of macromodeling. Although I am getting there, I am not yet old enough to become a common scold over the newer trends. In 1939, when our subject was still new, John Maynard Keynes subjected Tinbergen's League of Nations Study to a famous critique and scolding. Barely a month before Joseph Schumpeter died, he spoke at the November 1949 National Bureau Conference on Business Cycles. Although he had all his life been an admirer and patron of mathematical economists, in his next-to-the-last public utterance, Schumpeter felt compelled to stick up for the *historical* approach to business cycles as against its neglect in favor of econometric techniques. Corrado Gini, also a founder of the Econometric Society and a prolific writer on inequality and much else, warned late in life against the 'delusions' of econometrics, a warning seconded by Nicholas Georgescu-Roegen. Ragnar Frisch, the moving spirit among the founders, spoke out, I am told, at the Rome World Econometric Congress against modern excesses in econometrics. Perhaps it is in maturity, as well as in one's wine cups, that one's tongue speaks the truth. Certainly it was not here a case of La Rochefoucauld's aphorism: 'The old give us good advice when they can no longer set us a bad example.' For all of these men were producing scholars at the time they spoke.

Let me speak otherwise. I once said that we scholars work for our own applause, i.e. we seek to work so well that a jury of the best-informed professionals will agree that our results are correct, relevant, and stimulating. It is a corollary to this proposition that the most useful criticism of a subject must often bore from within. That is part of what Thomas Kuhn implies when he says it takes a new paradigm to kill off an old one.

A decade back, Tjalling Koopmans took a year off to write some essays on the foundations of economics. He came to my office in Cambridge to ask my opinion on, among other things, how well our scientific forecasts would be improved in the years to come. I think I disappointed him a little with my cautious answer. I said, 'I think their accuracy will improve, particularly as we get better data and bigger computers to store, find, and analyze these data. But I feel almost as if there is a Heisenberg indeterminacy principle dogging us, which will limit the asymptotic accuracy of forecasting we shall be able to attain.' In a stochastic world, such a conclusion should perhaps not be surprising. But my caution went beyond that. I felt that, so to speak, providence itself does not know, has not committed itself yet, to what will be the exact outcome of entrepreneurial animal spirits determining next year's investment.

In the years that have elapsed since our conversation, Koopmans has written a great book. And the art of macromodeling has, I think, made steady progress. But I suspect it is yet the case that the best judgmental forecasts are still about as good or as bad as the best computer forecasts. Indeed, something like this must be at the heart of the fact that, with the exception of a few, almost all model builders adjust their constants by various quasi-judgmental procedures and believe that this does improve their batting averages. There used to be a marvelous chess machine that could beat all comers. But alas it turned out that curled inside the machine was an actual man. It would be ironic if, inside the Wharton model, we found in the end, Lawrence Klein.

For, I repeat, science is public knowledge, reproducible knowledge. When Robert Adams wrote an MIT thesis on the accuracy of different forecasting methods, he found that 'being Sumner Slichter' was apparently one of the best methods known at that time. This was a scientific fact, but a *sad* scientific fact. For Slichter could not and did not pass on his art to an assistant or to a new generation of economists. It died with him, if indeed it did not slightly predecease him. What we hope to get by scientific breakthrough is a way of substituting for men of genius men of talent and even just run-of-the-mill men. That is the sense in which science is public, reproducible knowledge.

1.3. Conclusion

Therefore let me conclude with an anecdote in which I sold off the truth for a wisecrack. One day I was looking over a wad of computer printout. My colleague Edwin Kuh, who knows how rare it is that I get contaminated by data, asked what it was. I replied: 'This is an OBE picture of what's going to happen to *GNP* and all its components for eight quarters ahead. This is the way we live now.'

Ed Kuh inquired: 'How long, Paul, will it be until the computer makes you obsolete?'

Since the question was asked in a malicious way, I gave a malicious answer: 'Not in a thousand years, Ed.' When I used to lecture out on the story, I would add the qualifier, 'Of course, I could be wrong by a factor of 10.'

The incident may serve as a story, but of course it is wrong in two important ways. First, however good is the qualitative judgment of myself or some person who follows events more closely than I, our judgment has been formed and is kept tuned up by looking at computer forecasts. I would no more dream of tackling the back of an envelope before I had looked at the Wharton, and Michigan, and St. Louis models than I would dream of doing so on the basis of tea-leaves or rereading Alfred Marshall's *Principles*. In other words, we dwarfs of judgment see as far as we do because we stand on the shoulders of computer giants.

But equally important: suppose it were the case that my judgment were much more accurate than it is and were more accurate than that of computer models and other practitioners. Suppose, in short, that I were not Napoleon but Sumner Slichter. An anointed king is a king forever. But a top tennis player is king only for a day. Judgment is something you have until you don't have it any more. And you are the last to be able to judge your own judgment. For if you knew enough to recognize its slipping away from you, maybe it wouldn't be escaping. When Antoine Lavoisier fell victim to the guillotine, his friend and admirer Joseph Lagrange said bitterly: 'It took the revolution but a minute to take that head, and Europe will not be able to grow another like it for a century.' But all was not lost, we realize, since, as Lagrange had already noted, Lavoisier had made elementary chemistry 'as easy as algebra.' Those scientific contributions represented Lavoisier's immortality.

All men are mortal. Scientists are men. Ergo scientists are mortal. But science is immortal. Just as poetry is that which escapes in translation, scientific knowledge is that Cheshire residue which remains after you have boiled off the scientist cats.

One of the advantages of living a long time is to see how the children of your friends turn out. I wish I could be here 50 years hence when we gather for the centennial celebration. Until then, I venture the prophecy that our bonny birthday girl will develop into a beautiful goddess.

1.4. Epilogue

As the ink was drying on the above argument, I noted a possible flaw in my reasoning. Suppose that the best forecasting remains an individual art rather than a reproducible science. That is, suppose it were the case that macromodels repeatedly fail to do as well as certain specifiable Slichters. If true, that is a scientific fact which it is within the province of science to note and which it is the duty of science to report. What follows? That we should try to improve the performance of computer models? Of course: that goes without saying. But suppose the hoped-for improvement is not forthcoming or is long delayed; what then? I think it would be the duty of science to try to understand how the Slichters do it, wherein lies the source of their intuitive judgments. There is no evidence that transcendental mysticism is involved. Slichters are rare but not unique. They can be sought and perhaps identified. It is possible that workshops of judgmental forecasters would then be deemed to be in order, in which masters help apprentices become masters, so that the death or decay of one man does not fatally perturb the continuing good prediction performance of the group. Like the Lord's house, science has many mansions, and Ph.D.s do not live by computers alone.

276

Adam the Immortal

By Paul A. Samuelson

A few words in behalf of the 18th-century giant of economics by the 20th-century laureate

IN the field of political economy, Adam Smith stands first. He is our Christopher Columbus. But better than Christopher Columbus, it was Adam Smith who first created the continent that he came to discover and explore—I mean the continent of political economy itself. As some sage has observed in *Newsweek* magazine, Smith was well-named Adam.

T. S. Eliot's *The Wasteland* has not eclipsed the *Iliad* or the *Odyssey*. Keynes's 1936 *General Theory* represents a culmination of Smith's 1776 *Wealth of Nations,* not its *coup de grace.* Even Karl Marx could derive from Adam Smith's analysis of the division of labor elements of his own notions of alienation; and in any week when inspiration lagged in the Reading Room of the British Museum, Karl could keep his knife sharp by whittling away at what he conceived to be Adam Smith's inadequacies.

On Adam Smith himself, I can be brief. Of Homer we know only his literary remains. I say "his," but we cannot be sure that "hers" or "theirs" might not be the preferred pronoun. I can add two further bits of information: Homer was blind, and at least once Homer nodded. But now I have shot my bolt.

With Adam Smith it is much the same. We know that romance only once touched his life. At the age of six he was kidnapped by gypsies. I have always wondered whether they returned the right child and whether, as with William Shakespeare, we are dealing with an imposter. Beyond this, the gossip columnists would find Adam Smith a dull subject. As he said in connection with his splendid library, "I am a beau only to my books." And yet when we sniff around where it is no business of ours to sniff, we find few traces of maladjustment or repressed neuroses. At least, I hope that Smith's absent-mindedness and unworldly manner is not a symptom of some pathological condition. If so, every faculty club in this land would be decimated in a fortnight by the jailing psychiatrist. The worst a psychologist could say about Adam Smith is that he loved his Mother.

Reaching for piquant detail, I can record that Adam Smith was once called a son of a bitch by the renowned Dr. Samuel Johnson. You must not think it was in a barroom quarrel, . . . but I shall spare you the details.

I must not linger over the few bare facts we know about Adam Smith's life. At a tender age, namely 14, he went up as a student at the University of Glasgow. His later sojourn at Oxford University convinced him that the professors there

were a lazy and not very erudite bunch.
(What else is new?) He even taught
literature for a while, until, at the age of
28, he was elected professor of logic at
Glasgow—and a year later to a professorship of moral philosophy. Then, in his
early forties he became tutor to the son of
a duke, deriving thereby the advantage of
a couple of years residence in France,
where he was able to hobnob with various
of the *Philosophes* and proceeded to
retire at a very young age. And, in retirement, wrote his masterpiece, the *Wealth
of Nations*.

Nature arranges that when a flower
has blossomed and achieved its purpose in
life, it proceeds to die. Adam Smith
adhered to this timetable in a more lei-
surely manner. He lived on for another 14
years after 1776, long enough to add a
few commas and some new insertions and
emendations to four more editions of his
masterpiece. Appropriately, his grave-
stone simply marks the burial place of
Adam Smith, the author of the *Wealth of
Nations*.

This great economist, the exemplar of
the virtue of self-interest, was found to
have left little of an estate behind him—
a blemish his surprised biographer
explains away by the pious supposition
that "he often gave large sums in secret
to charity."

What shall I say about Adam Smith's
economics itself? Already this year I have
given several speeches on that subject,
two on March 9, the very day of publication of the *Wealth of Nations*. Such papers
bristle with mathematical equations, using
modern duality theory to vindicate Smith
from patronizing comparisons with
Ricardo, and cogently defending Smith
from Karl Marx's thousands of words of
criticism in Volume 2 of *Das Kapital*—
the best volume in that treatise of two
million words, but the one nobody reads.

Since the clichés written about Adam
Smith turn out to be broadly true, it is
mandatory that I say a few words about
Adam Smith's famous doctrine of the
Invisible Hand. His words have been
much quoted, and they deserve to be.
They sum up his importance in the history
of ideas. And they sum up much of his
current importance to our own generation
of economists. Here are Smith's words:

Every individual endeavors to employ his
capital so that its produce may be of
greatest value. He generally neither
intends to promote the public interest, nor
knows how much he is promoting it. He
intends only his own security, only his own
gain. And he is in this led by an INVISIBLE
HAND to promote an end which was no
part of his intention. By pursuing his own
interest he frequently promotes that of
society more effectually than when he
really intends to promote it.

I think you'll grant that those are
eloquent words, elegantly written. But
what do they really mean? Adam Smith
could not have answered the catechism of
what they mean—not in 1776, nor on
July 17, 1790, when he died. David
Ricardo and John Stuart Mill, his illustrious followers as classical economists,
also could not have received a passing
grade on an examination question dealing
with the doctrine of the Invisible Hand.
At least not a passing grade at the M.I.T.
graduate school of economics.

And yet, and yet . . . One feels that
more than rhetoric is involved in Smith's
message. After the 1890s, Vilfredo
Pareto began to sense its valid core. As
every child reveals, you don't have to
know *exactly* what you mean in order to
carry on a meaningful discussion. Exact
understanding comes later, if at all.

When I began graduate study in economics, I could not learn from some of
the world's greatest authorities the answer
to this simple question: "I know that price
ought to equal marginal cost, but *why*
should it?" I made myself something of a
bore in the Chicago Quadrangle and the
Harvard Yard, buttonholing Frank
Knight, Jacob Viner, and Joseph
Schumpeter with this query. Indeed, not
until a few years later, when my fellow
graduate student at Harvard, Abram
Bergson, cleared the matter up in a justly
famous 1938 article on welfare economics, could I put down my lantern of
Diogenes. In Valhalla, the shade of Adam
Smith must have then found peace.

There *is* content in Smith's doctrine of
the Invisible Hand. It tells us an important half-truth. A half-truth is a half-
falsehood. The blunder of Dr. Jekyll was
his failure to realize that you must never
administer a powerful potion without
also being able to supply its antidote.

Competitive equilibrium does not represent the best state of the world. It says in Chapter 3 of an elementary economics textbook that functionally the auction markets may be doing what they are designed to do, and yet John D. Rockefeller's dog may get the milk that could keep a slum urchin from being crippled for life in limb and intellect. Properly formulated, the correct version of the Invisible Hand doctrine does not allege that dollar votes are distributed by the competitive regime of laissez faire so as to have equal ethical value. Its correct versions say, and it is important to know this, that once the initial distribution of wealth and economic voting power has been ethically rectified by non-laissez-faire forces, the algorithm of perfect market competition, if you could attain it, could *efficiently* achieve production and allocation of economic goods and services —efficient in the sense of avoiding deadweight loss, so that it will never be possible to better the condition of some without sacrificing the well-being of others.

As the economists in the socialist countries of Eastern Europe are painfully aware, the market mechanism still does have a pragmatic function to perform. The debate going on today concerning deregulation shows that even from a twentieth-century perspective, the notions of Adam Smith do, for better or worse, live on. That is Darwinian immortality few scientists can hope to achieve.

Let me propose therefore that we declare Adam Smith to be a winner of the Nobel Prize in Economics, entitled to all the emoluments and rights pertaining thereto. To use an expression borrowed from economics itself: never was an honor more *richly* deserved.

277

LIBERALISM AT BAY*

BY PAUL A. SAMUELSON

In America a liberal is someone who in his time flirted with Teddy Roosevelt's progressive movement. He was swept up by hope in Woodrow Wilson's New Reconstruction. Par excellence, a liberal was moved by the New Deal Revolution of Franklin Roosevelt and its heritage in the form of the Fair Deal, The New Frontier, and the Great Society. He does not expect society a decade from now to be the same as now: the changes he looks to are generally in the direction of an increase in welfare expenditure by the state, probably an increased fraction of the GNP going through the government's hands, possibly an erosion of the individual's freedoms to act as he would himself choose to act (particularly in the realm of business freedoms—as for example his right to exploit the patents he has won or to set the rents charged on the property that he owns).

From many viewpoints he is a dull fellow. The drum beat he marches to is muffled. By and large he is a small-picture man: when he reads Spengler and Toynbee and Sorokin and Frazer and Schumpeter and Marx—and he is the only one who reads them *all*—it is in the spirit of reading a detective story or science fiction. Justice Holmes put it well in one of his innumerable letters to Pollock—or was it Laski? I quote from imperfect memory, and any corruption of text well be all the more interesting from a Freudian point of view: "Have just been reading Spengler. He is a rascal of course—but the rascal does give you a run for your money."

Now I am not here today to give you a ramble through the

* Delivered as the Second Gerhard Colm Memorial Lecture, New School for Social Research, on March 5, 1971.

history of intellectual thought. I am here as an economist, honoring Gerhard Colm, a great economist who was himself the kind of liberal my branch of the social sciences has produced. Liberalism in economics can, roughly speaking, be equated with the so-called "new economics." It is the economics which fought its way against the orthodoxies that prevailed for some sixty years before 1935—in America, in Britain, in Scandinavia, in the Netherlands, and to a degree in Germany. Of course its most dramatic novelties were in the field of Keynesian macroeconomics. It is quite impossible for those who did not live in the *ancien regime* to realize how great were the impacts of Keynes' *General Theory*. Although this 1936 book is not one that the lay public could ever read with profit, its general message—that full employment was not the normal state of the world, but rather fluctuations in the aggregate level of spending, production, and employment—was a message that came through loud and clear to the world outside of economics. More importantly, after Keynes no one could fail to realize that *it is within the capability of a modern mixed economy to contrive fiscal and monetary policies designed to iron out the cruel business cycle and achieve a more tolerable approximation to full employment and vigorous growth.*

That economics did face something new under the sun can be indicated by a few illustrations. Although Franklin Roosevelt's New Deal administration came into power in 1933 with a Brain Trust, it was a brain without intelligence: it had no idea of how to grapple with the Great Depression. A horse doctor from the Cornell School of Agricultural Economics thought that devaluation would reinflate the price level: okay, let's give it a whirl. A retired general thought that raising prices and cartelizing industries would restore prosperity: and so the NERA was born. It was not until Roosevelt's second term that the key to restoration of prosperity by means of activist fiscal policy was clearly understood—in consequence of Alvin Hansen's application of the new Keynesian theories.

Or, to take another example, I used earlier the familiar word of "macroeconomics." The word itself is of postwar coinage. Recently Dr. Edwin Nourse, the first chairman of the Council of Economic Advisers under the Employment Act of 1946 and Gerhard Colm's employer, wrote to me saying: "I inquired from Professor Alvin Hansen who first used the term macroeconomics and he replied, 'I think it was Samuelson.'" I have a lot to answer for in heaven, but that one was news to me. So I looked up the first 1948 edition of my textbook and, as I thought, the word was not yet there. Subsequently I was able to trace it in *both* of its present meanings to the period of this past quarter century.

Here is a last example of the irreversible changes that Keynes has wrought. When Roosevelt was just swinging into his stride, the cream of the Harvard faculty got together on a book entitled, *The Economics of the Recovery Program.* I stress the fact that these were not the old fogies of the department: *their* reactions were generally unprintable. As a reviewer put it, Harvard's second team found the New Deal wanting. As history will put it, Harvard's second team stepped up to bat and struck out. I invite any of you to go back and read Schumpeter's opening chapter. Schumpeter was then in his veritable prime, at the pinnacle of his international fame. What then is his diagnosis of and solution to the Great Depression? As to diagnosis, the Depression was as bad as it was because fate ordained that the forty-month inventory cycle of Kitchen-Crum just happened to be in phase with the eight-year major cycle of Juglar and with the long waves of Kondratieff making troublesome noises in the background. Lucky it was that the intermediate-length fifteen-year construction cycle of Kuznets had not yet been invented or Schumpeter would have administered Extreme Unction to the capitalistic system. And what was his recommended therapy for an epoch that involved all the banks being closed down and grass growing on both Main Street and Wall Street? It was in effect: sweat it out. Depressions are the cleansing and cathartic phases of a business cycle that is inexorably rooted in the very nature of the capitalist society. This from a man who always believed that capitalism was *economically* sound but politically unstable!

Although the Keynesian Revolution in macroeconomics—and its subsequent reconciliation with neo-Classical economics by Pigou in Cambridge and many others, including at the New School the young and brilliant Franco Modigliani—is best known to the lay public, there were two other advances that mark off the new economics from the old. Whereas the older economics had regarded most of the world that could be manageably analyzed as perfectly competitive, with only an occasional reference to the pure case of perfect monopoly, there came to pass in the early 1930s what has been called the monopolistic or imperfect competition revolution. Applied economists had always studied imperfections of competition, particularly after the trust movement at the turn of the century; but not until the 1933 books of Edward Chamberlin and Joan Robinson did this become a really respectable subject for the theoretical seminar room. Those of you who are acquainted with Thomas Kuhn's seminal work, *The Structure of Scientific Revolutions,* will recognize that in economics, as in the more exact branches of the natural sciences, it makes a tremendous difference whether a new paradigm has been found that gives the scientists a coherent way of thinking about previously known facts. This new paradigm was provided, belatedly some might argue, by the monopolistic competition revolution.

A final trend that has characterized the new economics in the decades since 1930 has been the increasing mathematization of economics. That is one of the mortal sins for which I shall have to do some explaining when I arrive at heaven's pearly gates. Along with the fruits of econometric measurement of the relationships of economic reality, and along with the techniques of operational research and actual decision-making under uncertainty by business and government, the modern symbolic methods have imparted a more powerful logical understanding of the big issues of the subject. In particular, the whole subject of *welfare economics*—its scope and its limitations—has been understood for the first time. I make reference here to the writings of economists like Abram Bergson, the late Oskar Lange of Poland, the young Kenneth Arrow—to say nothing of writers like Abba Lerner (some of which took place here at the New School), Sir John Hicks, and Nicholas Kaldor.

It is good advice to always study the preconceptions of a science or a school of thought. The utilitarianism of Bentham and Mill and Sidgwick and Edgeworth represented just such preconceptions of the neo-Classical economist. But by the early 1930s the simple addition of cardinal utilities of different minds in order to maximize the greatest good for the greatest number was no longer something to be accepted by such young economists as Gunnar Myrdal and Lionel Robbins. Would economics then have to cease to pretend to be a political economy and revert simply to a positivistic description of the behavior of different industries or the average level of prices and productivities? To be concrete, what meaning could be given to the ancient statement by Adam Smith that a competitive market system, concerned with atoms pursuing only their own narrow self-interests, would be led "as if by an invisible hand" to achieve the good of all? Was this right? Was it wrong? Demonstrably wrong? Or was it a meaningless statement such as purity weighs more than *amo-amas-amat* and less than zigzag? Not until Bergson's 1938 article in the *Quarterly Journal of Economics* did I have an adequate idea of how to go about answering such questions.

It is not my purpose here today to argue whether this making economics more mathematical is a good or bad thing or whether it has been carried into the realms of decadence. Nor do I wish on this occasion to discuss the communication problems all this raises and the psychological anguish among those who happen to be born with a burning interest in political economy but not with a zest for symbolic manipulation. In reserving such matters for another occasion, I perforce have something of a bad conscience since one of the key objections to the new economics has precisely to do with this issue of its formalistic structure.

I wish instead to concentrate on the status of the new economics, within the scholarly profession itself and with various sectors of the public at large. How did it come to receive wider acceptance after a stormy initial reception? What competing paradigms did its acceptance tend to displace? Has its vogue reached a peak, permanent or temporary? What counterforces does the new economics face today? And, most important of all, what can one say intelligently about its future?

All success stories are dull, including those for scholarly doctrines. So I can be brief in saying that the successive editions of my own textbook reflect well the gradual acceptance of the new doctrines. My first edition in 1948 brought, a decade late, into the classroom and teaching process what was already widely accepted at the frontier of the profession itself. So to speak, I embalmed Keynesianism and the general equilibrium approach, packaged and sold it. I was well rewarded for my efforts from the beginning, but the coin for which any ambitious scholar works is not that of money itself, for otherwise he would have become a plumber or a brewer in the first place. The coin for which he works is influencing the mind of a generation.

I will not bore you with the ancient history of the denunciations that my book, and all the similar books that emerged, were subjected to. One of your local department-store owners went around the country lecturing to Rotary audiences on my dangerous doctrines; William Buckley received his first baptism of success in his book, *God and Man at Yale,* under the first heading of which the New Haven chaplain came in for a lot of criticism and under the second heading of which I received my due. It all sounds funny in retrospect; and as far as I personally was concerned no real trauma or anguish was involved. But if you were a teacher at many a school around the country and the Board of Regents of your university was on your neck for using subversive textbooks, it was no laughing matter.   Man-months were involved in preparing mimeographed documentation of mis-quotations on the part of critics and so forth.   Make no mistake about it, intimidation often did work in the short run.

Let me record here that these bitter critiques did have an effect upon my formulations.   Recall that the coin I sought was wider dissemination of what I regarded as a more accurate eco-nomic understanding.   My last wish was to have an intransigent formulation that would be read by no one.   But at the same time there was no point in keeping an audience by giving up the sub-stance of the economic understanding I was trying to impart. Let me hasten to say that no esoteric heresies were involved, but merely correct thinking about what would be the consequences of achieving a balance in the federal budget in each and every year, and similar matters not today considered much in doubt. As a result I followed an Aesopian policy of paying careful atten-tion to every criticism of every line and word of my text.   When I felt I was wrong, I uncheerfully made the change; but being a bumptious fellow, I fear that not very often did I find that I was wrong.   The kind of errors my pen tended to make were errors that only my learned colleagues could spot, not the likes of William Buckley who, when all is said and done, has an under-standing of conservative economics that cannot remotely be com-pared with that of Milton Friedman or Frank Knight.   More often when I felt that my point was not wrong, I carefully rephrased the argument so that its logic and empirical cogency would stand out.   And I also, almost lawyerlike, arranged my prose so that an unfriendly critic could not conveniently leave out a word like "not" and distort my meaning.   In a sense this care-ful wording achieved its purpose: at least some of my critics were reduced to complaining that I played peek-a-boo with the reader and didn't come out and declare my true meaning.

Nevertheless, such defensive writing weakens the élan of a book.   And I reread today, say the fifth edition of the book, with certain irritation for the care with which many matters are formulated. I do not dwell on these matters of history for their own sake, but because they have a relevance to the present-day debates about the status of economics. Let me illustrate. One business-man who was a severe critic of my textbook and of all the post-war texts, whether written by Heilbroner or Bach or whomever, challenged me to sit down with him and go over his page-by-page criticisms. I learned something at that session I have never for-gotten, something which is completely of relevance today when I sit down with someone, like my daughter, who is impatient with the pace of economic progress. My businessman critic would say: "Turn to page 115. You say there, 'The fraction of GNP going to government has increased in this century.'" At first I could not make out what was eating him. On page 115 sure enough my pen had written that the government sector has risen in relative importance in recent decades, and various rather pretty charts and tables chronicle this fact. Puzzled, I asked naïvely, "Isn't that true? Have I distorted the facts or used some corrupt histori-cal source? Do you have some facts that show this to be false?" My critic squirmed and squirmed and finally uttered the words that I have never forgotten and which gave me an insight for which I am eternally grateful. My critic haltingly said, "Yes, it may be true. But *you must never state a fact like that without deploring it!*"

Today the shoe is on the other foot. It is not businessmen and boards of trustees who subject the teachers of elementary economics to critical pressure. Often it is students, and not merely students militantly involved in the New Left, but the gen-eral run of students. Suppose a textbook writer states a fact like the following: "The inequality of the distribution in the United States has remained roughly constant since 1945." Although this is correct according to most authorities, such as Herman Miller of the U. S. Census or Simon Kuznets or the late Selma Goldsmith, the simple statement of this fact has not infrequently been criticized as an expression of apologetics for the present established order. Some years ago such a reaction would have puzzled me. But thanks to the conversation with my business critic that I have reported on, I was quite prepared for this reaction. For according to one who fundamentally is opposed to the existing order, you must never state a fact like this one without deploring it.

Actually, I personally do deplore it. But just as we climb mountains because they are there, we must first establish the facts that are there to deplore. Moreover, what inference is one to draw from the fact of a rather persistent inequality of the distribution of income, as measured, say, by a Lorenz curve or perhaps a Pareto coefficient? One wish is that it ought to be changed. Frankly that is my reaction to cancer and cardiac insufficiency. But I am also impressed that the elimination of something like cancer will not be an easy or immediate task. And the very persistence of inequality suggests to the canny critic of the present order that there may be some rather stubborn and persistent forces that will not easily be exorcized.

As I see it the new economics is now under attack from four fronts. First, there is simply the rejection of it by the conservative interests. Although in terms of *realpolitik* this may be the most potent and long lasting of the oppositions, this historic rejection lacks intellectual interest. Either you feel it or you don't, and there is not much intellectual arguing about it that can be done.

Second (and I am, roughly speaking, working my way from right to left), we have the assault from within the profession of economics against the new economics by Libertarians. Names like Frank Knight, Friedrich Hayek, and Milton Friedman are associated with this general school. If you have to have but one name, Milton Friedman will do. Among the lay public, under the banner of Ayn Rand and avowed self-interest, there is a new radical right [1] that is allied with the academic movement of the

[1] It is curious, and upon reflection perhaps not surprising, that there is a tendency for the radical left and the radical right to join in their attack on the conventional economics. This is not merely a matter of tactics, like that involved in the Weimar Republic just before Hitler's successful rise to power. Rather it

Chicago School. With these fellow travelers I have no interest here. Within the profession the Friedman camp is still only a minority. But it is a growing minority. It has established beachheads outside of Cook County—at UCLA, Virginia, and for all I know, there is a secret cell with a mimeograph machine operating here. This movement supplies analytical and empirical arguments that no scientist can refuse to face, but the present occasion is not the appropriate time to go into these technical arguments. Let me simply say that Professor Friedman's function in reminding us of what it is that market pricing accomplishes, and what are some of the penalties to society of disregarding these lessons, is an important one. I would be lynched to assert before a New York audience like the present one that there are certain deficiencies in the present system of rent control; but like Galileo who kept insisting that the world is after all a globe that does move, I must mutter under my breath that Friedman is right in this insistence and in his insistence that the fixed exchange-rate system set up at Bretton Woods is fatally flawed in a world where countries will not deflate and inflate according to the old rules of the international gold standard. To the public though, Professor Friedman is known as a monetarist, as an alleged challenger to the mantle of Keynes. Here I shall simply record the opinion that his notion that only rates of change in the money supply can be expected to have predictable effects on the aggregate of money GNP have not been found convincing by most economists. I believe the jury of posterity will agree with this verdict. When *Newsweek* asked me last year, "Is Keynes dead?" I replied, "Yes. And so are Newton and Einstein."

A third challenge to the new economics comes from John Kenneth Galbraith. By now even high-school students are familiar with his work, *The Affluent Society,* and his *New Industrial State.* Followers of Dr. Friedman think he is the new

is a fact that radical libertarianism is a form of anarchism not all that different from the antibureaucratic anarchism of the New Left.

Keynes. Galbraith, I suspect, thinks that it is *he* who is the real
Napoleon.   Ten years ago in a Presidential Address to the
brethren within the economists guild, I said that the non-
economists take Galbraith too seriously but that we in the profession do not take him seriously enough.   In this brief time it is
not possible for me to evaluate what it is about Galbraith that
differs from the new economics and is also likely to be deemed
valid in the future.   His emphasis upon the importance of programs in the public sector in comparison with expansions of
private spending is not really unique to him nor even originating
with him, as the earlier espousal of this cause by Alvin Hansen
makes clear.   In any case, without basing the case so strongly
on the artificiality of private wants as shaped by advertising and
social emulation, I would agree with this thesis of Galbraith's,
and to him I say, "Right on."

Galbraith's notion that large corporations are important represents a healthy reemphasis of the Berle-Means thesis about the
separation of ownership and control in the modern corporation.
It is not at all clear that much follows from this distinction, either
for positive description or for social policy.   And indeed many
of Galbraith's own inferences, such as his pooh-poohing of antitrust controls on the large corporations, seems to me to be in the
reactionary and conservative direction.   Like Schumpeter he
often becomes enamored with the power he describes.   It is really
a rope trick that Galbraith often appears to be on the side of
radical economics: the optical illusion is enhanced by the fact
that both groups know that they don't like the new economics.
I find Galbraith's notion that there is a technostructure which
really runs our corporations and government, and which represents
a convergence of form and function with the technostructure
which runs Russia and China, to be a naïve notion bred in part
out of exaggerated self-esteem.   I'd like to think that our MIT
students will inherit the earth—what am I saying?—but reality
keeps breaking in.   They, like the large corporation itself, are
constitutional monarchs who reign only as long as they don't

rule. Just let some computer tell Henry Ford, or for that matter
the General Motors Board, that they've got to do something he
wants but which they don't think is in accordance with their
long-run interest, and see how fast he draws his severance pay.
On serious matters, such as whether we should have permanent
wage-price controls, the Galbraith position consists of little more
than elegant reiteration. He has simply not yet done his home-
work on how such measures work out in Scandinavia, Britain,
and elsewhere. Anyone who has a notion that a few men in a
Washington office can keep tabs on the prices and wages charged
by the few hundred largest corporations and the unions they
deal with should better occupy himself writing a best seller about
Utopia.[2]

I must move on to the critique of modern economics that
comes from the left.[3] This, I think, represents a movement that

[2] In his fascinating essays, *Between Capitalism and Socialism*, Robert Heilbroner quotes a passage written by Lenin just before taking office, in which the
activities of running a socialist state are described as having been *"simplified
by capitalism to the utmost, till they have become the extraordinarily simple
operations of watching, recording, and issuing receipts, within the reach of anyone who can read and write and know the first four rules of arithmetic."* I trust
the reader of Heilbroner's essay will realize that in the famous contest between
von Mises and Lange about the merits and demerits of socialist planning, it was
Hayek, with his point about how a market system brings information to bear upon
the outcome, who really won the debate.

[3] In discussion with students after the lecture, I was asked why I had not included in the list of schools critical of modern economics the rejection of neo-Classicism
by the so-called Anglo-Italian school of Joan Robinson, Nicholas Kaldor, Piero
Straffa, Luigi Pasinetti, and others. I, myself, had debated whether to do so, but
had decided against it on the ground that this involved a rather esoteric dispute
within the domain of economic theory itself. On reflection I am inclined to
regret this decision, and in a longer discourse such discussion would certainly
be in order. Let me, therefore, offer some too-brief words on the subject. First,
relatively few policy implications seem to follow from this critique. Advisers to
the President or Finance Minister from the two divergent schools would be likely
to provide the same spectrum of advice about central bank or fiscal policy—
although on price-wage controls and collective bargaining there might emerge
significant differences. Secondly, there is nothing intrinsically radical about
these critics: true, their agnosticism about, and rejection of, the apologetics of
marginal productivity models of income distribution creates a vacuum of ideology
which makes way for various "isms" from the left; on the other hand, the Kaldorian
macroeconomic distribution theory offered as an alternative is reactionary in its
reversion to a belief in spontaneous full employment, and despite the many sweet

is here to stay for a long, long time.   To illustrate the changed times we live in, let me recount the fact that I was a so-called Hoyt Visiting Fellow at Yale in the spring of 1964.   I lived for a week in Calhoun College and got to talk to many students and junior faculty.   Everywhere I looked there were banners then for Barry Goldwater, and this long before he received the Republican nomination.   All the debate came from conservative students.   I was told that it was not the village Marxist who was the "troublemaker" in the elementary economics classroom as had been the case in the 1930s, but rather the conservative critic. How things have changed.   Last year, if my memory is correct, there were only eighteen active members at Yale in the Marching and Chowder Society of Conservatives for Freedom. No doubt that was below par for the course.   After all, at a place like Yale we have to expect conservative strength to average out much stronger than that, just as from sociological considerations alone one would guess that in the long run conservative opinion at a cosmopolitan place like the New School ought to be relatively weak.

I know professors are saying, as they touch wood, that the campuses are cooling off.   And so they are in comparison with the height of the Cambodian crisis.   In my judgment not too much should be made of this short-run wiggle.   The generation gap is a real thing, in America and elsewhere.   The children of affluence, even after the Vietnam war is blissfully behind us, will, according to the timetable forecast by Schumpeter thirty years ago, turn increasingly critical of the established system. To be sure, many, perhaps most, will outgrow this phase.   But the frequency with which disaffection will remain, and the base level of acquiescence from which it starts, will I think be secularly changing.

I shall leave to the social psychologist the study of the dynamics

words that Joan Robinson often devotes to the name of Karl Marx, her scalpel of criticism has undoubtedly been the most damaging of all, being the more so because she so patently does not write from a procapitalist point of view.

of this social phenomenon. Here I have barely time to mention
the economic thrust of radical economics. In politics they say
you can't beat somebody with nobody. What model of analysis
will the New Left be able to develop to displace the current paradigms of thought? Thomas Huxley once said, "To Herbert
Spencer, the saddest thing in the world is a beautiful theory killed
off by an ugly little fact." Thomas Kuhn would not agree that in
the scientific world it is such brutal facts that are the giant killers.
It takes a new theory to displace an old theory. And properly
so. In science it is always a case of, "The king is dead. Long
live the new king." Scientific theories are made in order to be
superseded.

In most of the world, ruling as a substitute for modern economics as we have known it for the past century and a half, there
prevails the model of what I called Marxian economics. It is
natural for the New Left to begin with this structure of the old
left. Unfortunately, Marxian economics has for forty years been
in a decadent state. Such an evaluation might well be expected
of me as a lackey who lives off surplus value; but it is as well
the verdict of Marxians themselves, and I remind you that we
are here talking of the economics of Marx as embodied in the
three volumes of *Das Kapital,* in the *Theories of Surplus Value,*
in the *Grundrisse,* and other writings.[4]

The fact that Marxians can never—never? well almost never—
agree among themselves on even such basic notions as the proper
method of transforming from *Capital*'s Volume I labor-theory-
of-value tableau to Volume III's equal-profit-rate tableaux is
indicative of the failure of that engine of analysis to lay bare the
laws of motion and development of competitive capitalism. The
hour is too late to go into these niceties. It suffices to say that
the timetable of a falling rate of profit along with an immiseration
of real wages was realized to be in grave jeopardy by Marxists as

[4] For a complete list of references together with discussion, see P. A. Samuelson,
"Understanding the Marxian Notion of Exploitation: A Summary of the So-called
Transformation Problem between Marxian Values and Competitive Prices," *Journal
of Economic Literature,* 1971, Vol. IX, No. 2, June 1971, pp. 399–431.

early as the turn of the century.[5] (Let me add that those trends were never validly deduced from the logical structure of the cost-of-production-of-labor foundations of Marx's own exploitation theory, but that is a matter for the seminar room and not the real world.)

As far as I know there is only one Marxist left who believes that real wages have actually steadily declined in the century since the 1867 publication of *Capital*. I refer to Professor Jurgen Kuczynski of the East Berlin University whose statistics struggle valiantly to maintain this thesis, but who is ridiculed even by Marxist colleagues. It is more common to explain the failure of the real wage to stagnate with the kind of argument which Cambridge's Maurice Dobb has put forth, namely: were it not for the growth of the trade union movement and pro-labor legislation, wages would have fallen. For the U. S. of 1867 to, say, 1929, the rise in the real wage was strong and could not possibly have been so explained. But suppose it could? Does Dobb really want to be counted in with Edward Bernstein and the other Fabian revisionists who were so castigated by Kautsky and Lenin for precisely such abandonments of the scientific content of Marxian economics?

In our own time a more interesting reconciliation is attempted. Often, it is claimed, Marx was speaking ambiguously when he predicted immiseration of workers. All he meant by low wages

[5] In the Edwardian era Marxism experienced an Indian summer. The writings of Hilferding, Luxemburg, and Lenin come to mind. Aside from a fruitful emphasizing of monopoly elements, interesting theories of imperialism emerged. Whatever merits such critiques may have had for the days of Queen Victoria or of William Howard Taft, in the post-Keynesian, post-Kaleckian epoch it is an atavism to believe that third markets and Cold War offshore expenditures are needed to keep the system from developing realization crises and underconsumptionist stagnation. Budget deficits and money creation by the central bank are efficacious vaccines against such diseases, and populist democracy in all the mixed economies of the post-World War II world have been only too prolific in creating purchasing power. The resulting tendency toward cost-push creeping inflation is a malady not dreamed of in the Luxemburg-Lenin system, and its leading to stop-go operation is indeed a blemish—some would say the principal blemish—of the modern mixed economy; but not one related to Imperialism.

was wages low relative to the growth of the total social pie. Or
even in cases where the wage share was maintained, and that is
what most statisticians think to have been the case for most advanced economies, the worker is in modern times more "alienated"
in some sense of that word. Charlie Chaplin's *Modern Times,*
in which a possibly well-paid worker merely turns one screw in an
automatic factory, is the paradigm for this viewpoint. It comes
as no surprise that the young Marx is increasingly popular with
the young. What used to be considered his juvenilia, the laundry
lists of a great mind on its way to greatness, are now taken to be
the real thing. This infatuation with "Marx before he became
a Marxist" represents, I think, no passing phase; it performs a
sociological and ideological function.

It is not in developments of the old Marxism that one would
expect progress to come from the New Left. When it comes to
understanding the actual laws of motion of our system in the
next decades and in the past century, some sage has said, Marxism
is the opiate of the Marxists. By concentrating on what is thought
of as the big picture, reality itself is lost.

Let me conclude on an optimistic note. I believe that the
future is longer than the present. It is even longer than the past.
Man did not evolve from the slime and the waters, climb down
from the trees, only to become New Dealers and virtuosos of
functional finance. Fruit and light have not yet emerged from
the workshops of the radical economists. But the movement is
young and that will—no, I must in all honesty reword this to—and
that *may* change. Every scientist must say to this and to every
other movement: By your fruit and light will you be known.

278

PAUL A. SAMUELSON

Economics in a Golden Age: A Personal Memoir

ON ALFRED NOBEL's last birthday, in Europe's most beautiful building of this century, Professor Arne Tiselius spoke of a visit he once made to a Scottish chemistry laboratory. Through some failure of communications he did not realize until ushered into a large auditorium that a lecture was expected from him. When he asked what they would like to hear him discuss, someone called out, "How does one go about getting a Nobel Prize?" Professor Tiselius confessed he could not be responsive to the question.

When my turn came for the usual Stockholm remarks of gratitude and humility, I departed from my polished text to say, "I can tell you how to get a Nobel Prize. One condition is to have great teachers." And I enumerated the many great economists whom I had been able to study under both at Chicago and Harvard.

Although necessary, this condition is not by itself sufficient. "One must also have great collaborators." And, again, from Robert Solow down, I was able to count my own blessings. "Of course, one must have great students," following which went a recital of famous names.

Finally, in a crescendo of humility, I said, "And more important than all of these, one must have LUCK."

I stand by all these impromptu remarks. But with the shade of Samuel Johnson hovering over me and warning against all cant, I must add some afterthoughts. In the dark of the late October night, when a reporter phoned my home to ask my reaction to having received the Alfred Nobel Memorial Prize in Economic Science for 1970—and I spell out the title to emphasize that economics is a latecomer at the festive table with an award that is not quite a proper Nobel Prize—my first response was, "It's nice to have hard work rewarded." My children told me later it was a conceited remark.[1] Nonetheless one must tell the truth and shame the devil. It has been one of the sad empirical findings of my life: other things equal—with initial endowments and abilities held constant—the man who works the hardest tends to get the most done, and the one who saves the most does, alas, end up richest. To find these copybook maxims valid is as vexing as to learn that the horror stories told in my youth against cigarette smoking are after all true.

One must also tell the truth and shame the angels. So I must add what I might not have felt it necessary to add twenty years ago, namely that one must have been blessed with analytical ability. Great intellects— Newton, Lagrange, Gauss, and Mill will do as examples—have often been accused of false modesty. Newton said that however he may have appeared to others, to himself he appeared like a child playing with pretty pebbles on the beach. Lagrange explained his success in solving difficult problems by "always thinking about them." In similar words, Gauss discounted his superiority over other great mathematicians, saying in effect that, if you had thought as hard as he had about these matters, you too would be a Gauss. Finally, John Stuart Mill, who seems to have had the highest IQ ever observed, tells us in his autobiography, in words that are as charming as they are naïve, "Aw, shucks, anyone could have learned Greek at three and written a history of Rome at five"—and, I may add, have a nervous breakdown by nineteen—"if only he had the advantage of a teacher like James Mill."

What are we to make of these absurd disclaimers? Certainly Newton, who anonymously led the battle against Leibniz' claims to the calculus and who declared he would go to his grave without writing up the universal law of gravitation if he were required to make acknowledgment that Hooke had also some notions about attraction according to the inverse square of the distance, was anything but a truly modest man. And the record for Gauss is not that of a generous person. (When an old friend wrote to tell that his son had discovered non-Euclidean geometry, Gauss could not forebear from saying that he himself had already done that in unpublished work decades earlier. Worse than to kiss and tell is to not publish and claim.) A truly generous scholar, Euler—who made sense of Maupertuis' mystical principle of least action but refused to take the credit for it, and who delayed his own publications in the calculus of variations so that the youthful Lagrange could publish his novelties first —did not go around belittling himself or his work. Only in the case of Mill was pathological modesty a characteristic feature. (Actually when we read his remarks about (1) his father, (2) that paragon of all intellectual and other virtues, Harriet Taylor, and finally (3) his stepdaughter, with whom he lived after Harriet's death, we do not have to be a Freud to recognize that we are in the presence of neurotic pathology. Besides, Mill's notions of radical philosophy—utilitarianism, feminism, and much else—required him to have a belief in the environment as the prime determiner of all abilities.)

Properly understood, there is much truth and not merely cant in the disclaimers of these men. A fish has no reason to be aware of the water he has never left. As we live inside our own skulls, our findings become transparently clear. We not only see our discoveries; but, particularly among profound minds, we also see through them. The excitement is in the chase. Once we have conquered the theorem, there is, as Mach has stated, an inevitable feeling of letdown, almost I would say a postorgasmic relaxation. When Newton was asked how he knew that gravitational attraction would lead to Keplerian ellipses for planetary motion, he could say simply, "I calculated it." When one heard the late John von Neumann lecture spontaneously at breakneck speed, one's transcendental wonder was reduced to mere admiration upon realizing that his mind was grinding out the conclusions at rates only twice as fast as what could be done by his average listener. Is it so remarkable that a few leading scholars will again and again lead the pack in the conquering of new territory? If you think of a marathon race in which, for whatever reason, one clique gets ahead, then you will realize that they need subsequently run no faster than the pack in order to cross each milestone first.

But let us make no mistake about it. Although there is much truth in the quoted disclaimers, there is also much nonsense. Mere work will not make a bookkeeper into a Gauss: it will not even make a Jacobi into a Gauss. And John D. Rockefeller did not get that rich by saving more dimes than other people. Talent, natural talent, is a necessary even if not sufficient condition for success in these realms. My old colleague in the Society of Fellows, Stanislaus Ulam, used to tell the story of a mathematician friend who had worked out a wonderful formula for success. Success in life turned out to be a many variable function, which depended *inter alia* on how handsome you were, how wellborn, and a great variety of other matters. "Ability," said Ulam, "did enter into the formula, but after much manipulation it was found to enter both in the numerator and the denominator and could be neatly cancelled out of the final answer." That is a good story to tell at a cocktail party. But, outside the fields of college administration, it is utter poppycock. Ulam himself provides an excellent counterexample: it was not his brown eyes that explain the invention of the hydrogen bomb, the development of the Monte Carlo method, and numerous advances in the area of topology.

As mentioned, twenty years ago I would not have insisted on these trite assertions. However, by pure chance, I was for a time given some medication that excellently treated the symptoms for which it was prescribed. But during that period, I felt that it took the fine edge off my mind. Suddenly I realized how the other half lives! It was not that my performance suffered so visibly to the outer world. During that very period I wrote one of my best articles, but to myself it was clear that I was living on capital. (Paderewski used to say that if he quit practicing for one day, *he* noticed it; if he quit for two days, the critics noticed it;

if he quit for three days, the whole world noticed. Luckily I was able to change my diet before the third day.) It was not merely that my ability to discover new truth was lowered; in addition the zest to discover new truth was diminished by a more passive participation in the struggle against ignorance. In sum, there is a chemical element in intellectual achievement and one is a fool to take great pride in the chance circumstance that one's chemistry happens to be a favorable one. I may add as a corollary that it would be nice to give Newton and Gauss a potion to show *them* what they were really like.[2]

The Time and the Place: The Midway

The year 1932 was a good time to come to the study of economics. "May you live in interesting times" may be a curse against happiness, but it is surely a benison for any scientist. Louis Pasteur in Eden would have become merely a brewer of beer.

The University of Chicago was a great place to study economics then. Frank Knight and Jacob Viner were at the top of their form. Henry Schultz, with energy and passion, was introducing the new mysteries of econometrics. Paul Douglas and Henry Simons catered to the needs of the young for relevance and commitment. Outside of the Economics Department, the rest of the university was in its finest hour. The new broom of Hutchins swept in exciting innovations of undergraduate curriculum and had not yet become the wand that paralyzes and destroys.

When I appeared on January 2, 1932, at 8:00 A.M. to hear Louis Wirth lecture on Malthus' theories of population, my mind was literally the tabula rasa of John Locke's psychology. Not yet graduated officially from high school, I had never heard of Adam Smith. (I later discovered that *The Wealth of Nations* had always been in our family library, disguised as a few inches of the five-foot Harvard Classics. But having sampled to my displeasure *Two Years Before the Mast* and being conditioned against the volume on the *Aeneid* which I had used as a trot—or, as we called it in those days, a "pony"—I forewent the pleasures of a liberal education in favor of research on sex in the eleventh edition of the *Encyclopaedia Britannica* and of browsing through the debates on Christianity and socialism that my father had picked up in the second-hand bookstores. For my money, Clarence Darrow and Robert Ingersoll always won the arguments: at fourteen turning the other cheek seemed merely stupid.)

I was prepared to find college difficult. True, I had always been a bright student. Although it was fashionable then to say you hated school, I always secretly liked it as a child and looked forward to the coming of September. Before the sociologists at the university showed me that all differences in performance rest on environmental opportunities, I was a naïve Francis Galton.[3] To ourselves, my brothers and I seemed perceptibly "smarter" than our cousins, who in turn were definitely smarter than the general run. It was with incredulity that I discovered in the second grade a boy who could add faster than I, but I could rationalize this by the fact that I was always being "skipped" a term, something that was particularly easy to do under the unconventional semester plan which characterized the innovative Gary school system. However, I reached my finest hour just before my hormones changed and turned me into an underachiever. Coming into college a term behind my class, I therefore thought that hard work would be necessary to survive, an agreeable error that launched me into scholarly orbit. As Wirth, himself a distinguished sociologist and excellent lecturer, expounded the 1-2-4- . . . and 1-2-3- . . . arithmetic of Malthus, it was all so simple that I was sure I must be missing the essential point. Since then I have come to realize that Malthus was just as simple as it seemed to me at sixteen, and hence I have never been surprised by the popularity of Malthusian doctrines with the man in the street and Ph.D.'s in biology.

Although there was a minute in my sophomore year when I toyed with the notion of becoming a sociologist, my real stimulus came from an old-fashioned course in elementary economics that remained in the curriculum as a fossil from the pre-Hutchins "old plan" days, and which I was put in by virtue of my late arrival. Having missed the cosmic aspects of economics, as expounded by Harry Gideonse and the really excellent staff in Social Science Survey I, I was expected to be able to catch up by learning about marginal cost and elasticity of demand. By luck, my teacher was Aaron Director, a strong libertarian of the Knight-Hayek school. (A local joke was that, later, he used to refer to Milton Friedman as "my radical brother-in-law.") Director was also an analyst and an iconoclast, whose cold stare terrorized the coeds in the class but captivated me. In any case, even if I had had Mr. Squeers for a teacher, the first drink from the economic textbooks of Slichter and Ely would have been like the Prince's kiss to Sleeping Beauty. It was as if I were made for economics.[4] I could not believe that the rest of the class were making heavy weather of such problems as to what would be the effect upon the price of kidneys of Minot's discovery that liver cured anemia, or the effect of mutton price if orlon were invented.

Chicago was a good place to learn economics at that time precisely because it was a stronghold of classical economics, a subject which had reached its culmination thirty years earlier in the work of Cambridge's Alfred Marshall. Economics itself was a sleeping princess waiting for the invigorating kiss of Maynard Keynes, and if one had to spend one's undergraduate days marking time before that event, Chicago was a better place to do so than would have been Harvard, Columbia, or the

London School. Cambridge University was never within my ken, but since economics was also waiting for the invigorating kiss of mathematical methods, it would have been a personal tragedy if I had become merely a clever First in the Economics Tripos there. (I like to think I might have risen above the tragedy, but as Wellington said of Waterloo, it would have been a "damned close-run thing.")

I have written elsewhere that, for an economic theorist, the last half of the nineteenth century was a bad time to be born. The really great work in neoclassical economics was all done in the years 1865 to 1910. Jevons, Menger, Walras, Böhm-Bawerk, Marshall, Wicksteed, Wicksell, and Pareto had gone beyond the classical synthesis of Smith, Ricardo, and Mill. Even the Marxian branch of the classical tree, save for one brief period of Indian Summer, shows clear sign of degeneracy after the turn of the century and the demise of Marx and Engels.

I do not say that 1915 was the perfect year to be born. Much as every family thinks that it would be happier with 20 per cent more income, every scientist thinks that if he had turned up just a bit earlier many of the delays in his subject might have been avoided and many more of the victories would have been his alone. Right before my time came the wonder generation of Frisch, Hotelling, Harrod, Myrdal, Tinbergen, Ohlin, Haberler, Hicks, Joan Robinson, Lerner, Leontief, Kaldor, and others too numerous to mention. Still to a person of analytical ability, perceptive enough to realize that mathematical equipment was a powerful sword in economics, the world of economics was his oyster in 1935. The terrain was strewn with beautiful theorems begging to be picked up and arranged in unified order. Only the other day I read about the accidental importation into South America of the African honey bee, with a resulting decimation of the local varieties. Precisely this happened in the field of theoretical economics: the people with analytical equipment came to dominate in every dimension of the vector the practitioners of literary economics.[6]

Elsewhere in this volume, Talcott Parsons tells how he moved out of economics and into sociology more or less by chance and the necessity to make a career. It seems to me that this was a great stroke of luck for him. Although his genius might have turned economics in the direction of methodological system building, it would have been the Lord's own work and definitely against the tides of change. What were the major tides of economics in the decades after my 1935 graduation?

Back around 1950, at a Princeton Inn meeting of the American Economic Association's executive committee, Frank Knight once announced in his cracker-barrel Socratic manner: "If there is anything I can't stand it's a Keynesian and a believer in monopolistic competition." Being not much more than half his age at the time, but definitely old enough to behave myself better, I asked, "What about believers in the use of mathematics in economic analysis, Frank?" When told he couldn't stand them either, I realized that the indictment fitted me to a "T." And I thanked my lucky stars once again that by chance and necessity, I, like Parsons, had been forced to leave the womb. Having been the usual A student and local bright boy at Chicago, I naturally thought it to be Mecca. Why leave Mecca?

Aside from its genuine excellences as a leading center for economics, Chicago had an additional attraction for me.[6] Although still an undergraduate, I had the opportunity to take Jacob Viner's celebrated course in graduate economic theory—celebrated both for its profundity in analysis and history of thought, but also celebrated for Viner's ferocious manhandling of students, in which he not only reduced women to tears but on his good days drove returned paratroopers into hysteria and paralysis. I, nineteen-year-old innocent, walked unscathed through the inferno and naïvely pointed out errors in his blackboard diagramming. These acts of Christian kindness endeared me to the boys in the backroom of the graduate school: George Stigler, Allan Wallis, Albert Gaylord Hart, Milton Friedman, and the rest of the Knight Swiss guards. As I performed various make-work tasks for the department—dusting off the pictures of Böhm-Bawerk, Menger, and Mill in the departmental storage room which Stigler and Wallis had squatted in—we would gossip for hours over the inadequacies of our betters and the follies of princes who try to set right the evils of the marketplace.

Karl Marx, though, was right in his insistence on the economic determinism of history, including the history of economists. For a few pieces of silver I left Olympus. The Social Science Research Council tried the experiment of picking the eight most promising economic graduates by competitive exam and, in effect, subsidizing their whole graduate training. My comfortable fellowship carried only one stipulation: leave home. As a scholar, I sighed; as an opportunist, I obeyed.

But where to go? Foreign study was frowned on. The choice, and it tells us as much about the state of economic institutions as would a Carnegie or Rosenwald Report, was either Columbia or Harvard. Most of my teachers and friends advised Columbia. Harry Gideonse, whose influence along with that of Eugene Staley on my choice of economics as a major was insufficiently stressed in my earlier remarks, said: "How could anyone give up Morningside Heights in preference for New England?" (How times change!) Wallis, Friedman, and many of the Chicago students of that day and since tended to have Columbia ties as well. They advised me, only too correctly, that I would not learn any modern statistics at Harvard if I passed up the chance to attend Hotelling's Columbia lectures.

The decision was made, as so many important ones are, by nonrational processes and miscalculation. I picked Harvard. Why? It was not because of the great Schumpeter. Actually I was warned that he was kind of a brilliant nut who believed that the rate of interest was zero in a stationary state, an impossibility that had been demonstrated at length by our local sage. I had never heard of Leontief or the mathematical physicist Edwin Bidwell Wilson (not to be confused with my Society of Fellows contemporary, E. Bright Wilson, Jr., the physical chemist also at Harvard), two great reasons for studying economics at Harvard. My teacher in money, Lloyd Mints, told me that John Williams was a good man but to watch out for the inflationist Seymour Harris. (Since Harris was still an orthodox protégé of Harold Hitchings Burbank, this judgment says much for Mints's prophetic powers to smell out evil.) I must confess that glances into Edward Chamberlin's recent and great book on *Monopolistic Competition* carried some small weight in the balance in favor of Harvard.

But in the end my decision was made on quite nonscholarly grounds. Gideonse did not know his man. I went to Harvard in search of green ivy. Never having been east (I don't count Florida as east) before the age of twenty, I picked Cambridge over New York in the expectation that the Harvard Yard would look like Dartmouth's Hanover common. Expecting white churches and spacious groves, I almost returned home after my first view of Harvard Square, approached by bad chance from the direction of Central Square. No wonder I annoyed Chairman Burbank at first encounter: I told him that I (1) would not take E. F. Gay's famous (and sterile and dull) course in economic history, but instead would take Chamberlin's course given to second-year graduate students, (2) intended to "skim the cream" of Harvard since it was by no means certain that I would choose to stay more than a year, and (3) had not made advanced application to do graduate study at Harvard for the simple reason that in those days any paying customer, to say nothing of an anointed Social Science Research Council Predoctoral-Training Fellow, could get in anywhere. It was not love at first sight. But it really would not have mattered since Burbank stood for everything in scholarly life for which I had utter contempt and abhorrence.[7]

The Golden Days of the Harvard Yard

"In 1935 a brash young student from the University of Chicago appeared at Harvard."[8] Luck was with me. Harvard was precisely the right place to be in the next half dozen years. When I once told Edward Mason that I proposed to write a memoir on the golden days for economics in the Harvard Yard, he suggested I wait "until we are up again." Well, there will never be a better time than now to sing of the Age of Hansen—and of Schumpeter, and of Leontief, and (for me) of E. B. Wilson. And I can sing for all my comrades at arms—Alan and Paul Sweezy, Kenneth Galbraith, Aaron [R. A.] Gordon, Abram Bergson, Shigeto Tsuru, Richard Musgrave, Wolfgang Stolper, and others who were already established when I arrived in the graduate school, September 1935; and for many yet to come—Lloyd Metzler, Robert Triffin, Joe Bain, James Tobin, Robert Bishop, John Lintner, Richard Goodwin, Henry Wallich, Cary [E. C.] Brown, Emile Despres, Walter and William Salant, Sidney Alexander, Benjamin Higgins, to say nothing of postwar diamonds such as James Duesenberry, Robert Solow, Carl Kaysen....

Harvard made us. Yes, but we made Harvard. By the time of World War II the dominance in economics of Harvard had become almost a scandal. The old-school tie counted for much, too much no doubt—but it does save time to have familiar faces around. (When I came to do mathematical work at the Radiation Lab during the war, I found that the old Princeton tie had a similar role in moving you up the mathematics queue.) When the American Economic Association commissioned an official survey volume on the state of modern economics, George Stigler, in a scholarly review, drew up a statistical matrix of index references and mutual citing of the Harvard constellation in order to document the dominance I speak of. I do not suppose he would have gone to the trouble if he had not thought it a distorted reflection of the intrinsic worth of the barbarians outside the walls: Stigler has always insisted on the old-fashioned distinction between value and market price!

And yet, that this involved more than mutual backscratching was brought home to me by a later event. In 1948 when Alvin Hansen turned sixty, some of his fond students banded together to present him with a *Festschrift*.° Since he had at that time spent no more years teaching at Harvard than he had teaching earlier at Minnesota, our committee naturally thought to invite students from his Minnesota days to contribute. From the Harvard vintages, there was almost an embarrassment of riches to choose from. Yet despite an extra effort the final disproportion was striking. Years later I happened to ask Alvin why that should have been so. He said that he had indeed had some very good students at Minnesota but that, by and large, the very best students had tended to bubble off (with his blessing) to the few largest centers. This confirmed the advice that I used to give young students: If you have any reason to think you are good, beg, borrow, or steal the money to come to the top place. If you go to Rome, it is your classmates who will be the next cardinals and who will be picking popes. I presume that these casual observations from experience confirm the views about "the institutionalization of a discipline" that Edward Shils discusses elsewhere in this book.

° Published as *Income, Employment, and Public Policy* (Norton, 1958).

Readers who are noneconomists will not wish me to elucidate the many features of graduate study at Harvard in those days. Let me summarize it all by saying that my transfer from Chicago to Harvard put me right in the forefront of the three great waves of modern economics: the Keynesian revolution, of which I shall give an account presently, the monopolistic or imperfect-competition revolution, and finally, the fruitful clarification of the analysis of economic reality resulting from the mathematical and econometric handling of the subject—including an elucidation for the first time of the welfare economics issues that had concerned economists from the days of Adam Smith and Karl Marx to the present.

Much of Harvard analysis was crude and unrigorous, as I discovered to my intense surprise. But it had life and it lacked closure. The mistakes one's teachers made and the gaps they left in their reasonings were there for you to rectify. You were part of the advancing army of science. There was an extra advantage: in that pluralistic environment there was plenty of opposition to every one of the new doctrines. You were not an Uncle Tom if you enlisted in the wave of the future. Schumpeter repudiated Keynes. Williams and Hansen conducted a famous dialogue, the courtesy of which in the face of fundamental disagreement does both men credit. (The greatest capital for undercutting a colleague in asides with students would have accrued to Hansen, and all honor must go to him that never once did he indulge in such personal criticisms. I was one of his favorites and intimates and the farthest I could push him to go was to say, when I praised a colleague long dead, that the man had in effect been a closet-Keynesian who, to curry favor with businessmen, had camouflaged his wisdoms and insights.)

All autobiography loses interest when success arrives. So let me simply say that the years 1935-1940 were good to me. As a junior fellow I was completely happy, turning out paper after paper. I once had a student who told me that he could have spent his whole life hitting fungoes to his brother on the farm back in Illinois but he had a suspicion it couldn't last. I could have remained a junior fellow all my life. Indeed it was fortunate that no one offered me a permanent fellowship at Harvard—lecturer was the name given for those with second-class membership in the club— because I would certainly have happily accepted it.

In 1940 I was offered the princely post of instructor in the Department of Economics and tutor in the Division of History, Government and Economics. I gladly took it and continued in my same Leverett House office. When a month later a better offer came from MIT and when I learned that my departure would not cause irreparable grief, I took the offer.[9] My last qualm in doing so was overcome as a result of a long handwritten letter from my revered teacher of mathematical economics and statistics, E. B. Wilson, about his Hegira from Yale to MIT early in the century. Wilson was the last of the universal mathematicians. He was

Willard Gibbs's favorite student, and one of the first to do work in a variety of fields: vector calculus, functionals, mathematical physics, aeronautical engineering, vital statistics, psychometrics, and most important for me, mathematical economics. He was the only intelligent man I have ever known who loved committee meetings. He also loved to talk and we had hours of conversations following his lectures. What a teacher's pet I have always been! I was also a favorite protégé of his. In the letter he told how his agonizing decision to leave Yale for MIT which friends had warned him against as a barbarian outpost, had been the beginning of a fruitful and happy epoch. Until you leave home, he said in effect, you are a boy and not the master of your own house. (In Virginia Woolf's diary there is a striking entry, which I quote from imperfect memory: "Father [Leslie Stephen, the biographer, historian, and mountain climber] would have been ninety today. Thank God he died. I could never have realized myself otherwise.")

Since gossip always likes a good story, and since McGeorge Bundy and the cited Breit-Ransom book have commented in print on the fact of my leaving Harvard, a few words on the event may not be out of order. I left Harvard in 1940 for the same reason that James Tobin left it in 1950: I got a better offer. Just as Lord Melbourne said he liked getting the Order of the Garter because there was "no damned merit to it," my parting was eased by the fact that no one, least of all me, thought that it was lack of merit that kept me from a chair in economic theory. Those were the depression days, the days of the Walsh-Sweezy hearings, in which President Conant was rationalizing Harvard's budget and tenure procedures after the benevolent despotism of President Lowell. Even my beloved mentor, Wassily Leontief, did not yet quite have tenure in my time. It was not for another decade that, under the so-called Graustein formula for spacing departmental appointments, a theorist was appointed at Harvard. It is frustrated expectations that make for disappointment and bitterness: from the first day I appeared in Boylston Hall in 1935, I never received any letter, oral promise, or clairvoyant message even hinting that a permanent appointment awaited me. When last year a Harvard Crimson reporter asked why I had not responded favorably to a couple of calls from Harvard in the later days of Bundy and Pusey, I heard myself stating the simple, prosaic truth: "After a cost-benefit analysis, I decided to stay put."

In any case, on a fine October day in 1940 an *enfant terrible emeritus*[10] packed up his pencil and moved three miles down the Charles River, where he lived happily ever after.[11]

What Economics Is About

It is easy for the artist to write about himself as a young man, but hard for him to write about his art. Has there ever been even one good

novel about a scholar or artist that conveyed any notion of his work? It
was Hans Zinsser who said that when any genuine biologist reads Arrow-
smith's prayer in the Sinclair Lewis novel, he wants to throw up. (Yet
I have seen elsewhere the biography of at least one distinguished scientist who was led into the field by reading that same book.) When my
wife was a girl, she thought of her father, a small-town banker, as doing
nothing down at work except sitting with his feet upon the desk. That
I suspect is every child's view of what his parent does during that hiatus
between morning and dusk. If James Joyce were to write the account of
a single day in the life of a scientist, that would be unutterably dull except to another scientist.

G. H. Hardy claimed that the one romance of his life as a Cambridge mathematician was his collaboration with Ramanujan, the self-
taught Indian genius. The great romance in the life of any economist
of my generation must necessarily have been the Keynesian revolution.
Perhaps the best impression I can convey of its impact is given by the
following quoted passage, taken from a eulogy I was invited to write on
the occasion of Keynes's death in 1946, less than a decade after the
period I have been writing about:

I have always considered it a priceless advantage to have been born as an
economist prior to 1936 and to have received a thorough grounding in classical
economics. It is quite impossible for modern students to realize the full effect of
what has been advisably called "The Keynesian Revolution" upon those of us
brought up in the orthodox tradition. What beginners today often regard as
trite and obvious was to us puzzling, novel, and heretical.

To have been born as an economist before 1936 was a boon—yes. But not
to have been born too long before!

"Bliss was it in that dawn to be alive,
But to be young was very heaven!"

The *General Theory* caught most economists under the age of 35 with the
unexpected virulence of a disease first attacking and decimating an isolated
tribe of South Sea islanders. Economists beyond 50 turned out to be quite immune to the ailment. With time, most economists in-between began to run the
fever, often without knowing or admitting their condition.

I must confess that my own first reaction to the *General Theory* was not at
all like that of Keats on first looking into Chapman's Homer. No silent watcher,
I, upon a peak in Darien. My rebellion against its pretensions would have been
complete except for an uneasy realization that I did not at all understand
what it was about. And I think I am giving away no secrets when I solemnly
aver—upon the basis of vivid personal recollection—that no one else in Cambridge, Massachusetts, really knew what it was about for some 12 to 18 months
after its publication. Indeed, until the appearance of the mathematical models
of [it] there is reason to believe that Keynes himself did not truly understand
his own analysis.

Fashion always plays an important role in economic science; new concepts
become the *mode* and then are *passé*. A cynic might even be tempted to

speculate as to whether academic discussion is itself equilibrating: whether assertion, reply, and rejoinder do not represent an oscillating divergent series, in which—to quote Frank Knight's characterization of sociology—"bad talk drives out good."

In this case, gradually and against heavy resistance, the realization grew that the new analysis of *effective demand* associated with the *General Theory* was not to prove such a passing fad, that here indeed was part of "the wave of the future." This impression was confirmed by the rapidity with which English economists, other than those at Cambridge, took up the new Gospel; . . . and still more surprisingly, the young blades at the *London School* . . . who threw off their Hayekian garments and joined in the swim.

In this country it was pretty much the same story. Obviously, exactly the same words cannot be used to describe the analysis of income determination of, say, Lange, Hart, Harris, Ellis, Hansen, Bissell, Haberler, Slichter, J. M. Clark, or myself. And yet the Keynesian taint is unmistakably there upon every one of us . . .

Instead of burning out like a fad, today ten years after its birth the *General Theory* is still gaining adherents and appears to be in business to stay. Many economists who are most vehement in criticism of the specific Keynesian policies—which must always be carefully distinguished from the scientific analysis associated with his name—will never again be the same after passing through his hands.

It has been wisely said that only in terms of a modern theory of effective demand can one understand and defend the so-called "classical" theory of unemployment . . .

Thus far, I have been discussing the new doctrines without regard to their content or merits, as if they were a religion and nothing else . . .

The modern saving-investment theory of income determination did not directly displace the old latent belief in Say's Law of Markets (according to which only "frictions" could give rise to unemployment and overproduction). Events of the years following 1929 destroyed the previous economic synthesis. The economists' belief in the orthodox synthesis was not overthrown, but had simply atrophied . . .

Of course, the Great Depression of the Thirties was not the first to reveal the untenability of the classical synthesis. The classical philosophy always had its ups and downs along with the great swings of business activity. Each time it had come back. But now for the first time, it was confronted by a competing system—a well-reasoned body of thought containing among other things as many equations as unknowns. In short, like itself, a synthesis; and one which could swallow the classical system as a special case.

A new *system*, that is what requires emphasis. Classical economics could withstand isolated criticism. Theorists can always resist facts; for facts are hard to establish and are always changing anyway, and *ceteris paribus* can be made to absorb a good deal of punishment. Inevitably, at the earliest opportunity, the mind slips back into the old grooves of thought since analysis is utterly impossible without a frame of reference, a way of thinking about things, or in short a theory.[12]

The final lines of this quoted passage contain certain notions that have brought fame to Thomas Kuhn, who argues in *The Structure of Scientific Revolutions* (University of Chicago Press, 1962) the importance of scientific paradigms in conditioning the thought of each school of science. This is a seminal idea, but, as expressed in the first edition of that work, one which fails to do justice to the degree to which "better" theories, and I mean intrinsically better theories, come to dominate and replace earlier theories. Now if Dr. Kuhn had been talking about the softer science of economics, I could provide him with much grist for his mill. And yet I must confess to the belief that truth is not merely in the eye of the beholder, and that certain regularities of economic life are as valid for a Marxist as for a classicist, for a post-Keynesian as for a monetarist.

In short, economics is neither astrology nor theology.

REFERENCES

1. They were apparently not alone. In a recent biographical work, W. Breit and R. L. Ransom, *The Academic Scribblers: American Economists in Collision* (New York: Holt, Rinehart and Winston, 1971), the authors quote the remark, with the prefacing words: "He was characteristically brash about his own achievements and prize." Despite some acknowledgments of help from me in personal correspondence on some fine points of doctrine, the authors' account does not jibe with my views on a number of matters.

2. Reminiscing one night at the Society of Fellows, I. A. Richards told me that the great Cambridge philosopher, Frank Ramsey, whose death at twenty-six was such a tragedy to economics as well as philosophy, found it hard to believe that others could not solve complicated syllogisms of mathematical logic in their heads. "Can't you *see* it?" he would ask. No they couldn't. (A good joke about von Neumann is in order. According to legend, when asked the old problem of how much distance a fly traverses in running back and forth between two approaching locomotives, von Neumann is supposed to have given the right answer—by *summing* the series. The other night, instead of counting sheep, I tried to do the same in my head. Although I dislike puzzles, it turned out to be fairly easy—given *all* the time one needs.)

3. A few years ago on a plane from Chicago to Washington, conversation with a fellow passenger enabled me to infer that he must be a Chicago professor of sociology. Without identifying myself, I chanced to remark: "At the University of Chicago I was taught to believe that differences in abilities and achievements are almost solely a function of differences in the environment. But now that I have become the father of six children, three of them triplets, I have had to modify my views." This drew down upon my head the following reproof: "Actually, you were right the first time. It *is* environment which is all important. Just to illustrate, take my own case: you may not realize it, but I am a distinguished professor and scholar. Yet I had two uncles who I can assure you were of the caliber to hold a chair in any great university in the world; but being poor immigrant boys, they were deprived of environmental opportunity." I could not resist replying: "Isn't it remarkable that a man who doesn't believe in the importance of heredity could report that no less than three of his immediate family were capable of being great scholars." Fortunately, he never turned his head.

4. Years ago I heard Boris Goldovsy interviewed on radio. He was asked whether his son had talent, and replied: "Of course both his mother and father are musical, but still it is uncanny. Even at the age of five, when he goes to the piano it is as if his fingers have a wisdom that the little boy himself does not know." Or to vary the analogy, no cat ever took to catnip the way our first-born, Jane, reacted at the age of several months to her first taste of ice cream: her eyes rolled to know that such delights existed, and if she could have climbed a tree or rassled a bear she would have. So with me, on looking into economic books. Possibly, I would have done well in any field of applied science or as a writer, but certainly the blend in economics of analytical hardness and humane relevance was tailor made for me or I for it.

5. That the apparatus of marginal revenue and imperfect competition should have had to be painfully rediscovered at the beginning of the 1930's, almost a century after Cournot's definitive 1838 work, testifies to the decadence of economics at that date. Or to illustrate with a harder problem that my economist readers will understand: in 1936, after I had already taken graduate courses in economic theory from Jacob Viner at Chicago and Joseph Schumpeter at Harvard, I still had to go around the Harvard Yard like Diogenes asking, "Why is it necessary for optimality that price should have to equal marginal cost?" And I was to receive no definitive understanding on the matter until my classmate Abram Bergson gave his 1938 definitive reformulation of modern welfare economics.

6. It is fashionable to recall how much one hated school days at Eton, and it is subtly self-flattering to state how badly one was educated at college. (Henry Adams even complained that he was never assigned *Das Kapital* in Harvard College, which demonstrates that the faculty there was already up to its tricks of not assigning books not yet written.) I had a great education at the University of Chicago from 1932 to 1935, and one of my resentments against Robert Hutchins is that, by the time of his retirement, he had reduced a thriving college of 5,000 undergraduates into a few hundred under-age neurotics. To be sure the withdrawal of Rockefeller's princely patronage also contributed to the decline. Among the great noneconomist lecturers I heard, and got to know outside of class, were the mathematician Gilbert Bliss, the biologist Anton Carlson, the anthropologists Fay-Cooper Cole and Robert Redfield, the paleontologist Alfred Romer, and nearer to my own field, Frederick Schuman and Harold Lasswell in political science, Louis Wirth in sociology, and W. T. Hutchinson in American history (the single best course lecturer I have heard anywhere). My education was more in width than depth, not a bad way to spend the years sixteen to nineteen prior to specialized research. In a 1972 obituary article of Jacob Viner, to appear in the March-April *Journal of Political Economy,* I include some further recollection of the Chicago scene.

7. It tells much about the Harvard of President Lowell's days that such men received office space and held power. But to admit the rich texture of life, I repeat a conversation between the late Alfred Conrad, Richard M. Goodwin (Hoosier, Rhodes Scholar, former Harvard don, and now a fellow in Peterhouse College at Cambridge) and me, as we were driving back to Boston from Joseph Schumpeter's funeral in Connecticut. Conrad: "Say what you will about Burbie, knowing that I had tuberculosis at Saranac, never a week went by that he did not ask me about my health. No one else in the huge Harvard environment seemed to know whether I was dead or alive. You were in a human relation with Burbank." Goodwin: "Indeed you were. He once said to me, 'Dick, I'd like to do with you

what my father once did to me. Tie you to the wheel of a wagon and apply a long black whip to your back.'" One should add that he was genuinely fond of Goodwin. During the war years a dear friend of ours was Burbank's secretary, but we avoided all strain by not talking about the man she worshipped and I despised.

8. Breit and Random, *Academic Scribblers*, p. 111.

9. A couple of months later, Ed Chamberlin, serving as an interregnum Harvard chairman, phoned to ask whether MIT was paying me a full-year's salary despite my late-October recruitment. When I said yes, he asked me whether I would not in that case return my September Harvard check, saying "you wouldn't want to deprive a young scholar of a full-year's income." I meekly returned the check, although it occurred to my wife that perhaps there might have been found a different solution for that poor man's problem.

10. A phrase of Provost Peter Kenen of Columbia, not mine.

11. A distinguished foreign economist who read this memoir commented to me: "You know, the popular explanation for your leaving Harvard is that you were a victim of antisemitism." I replied, "I suppose that would be the *simplest* explanation." "As a scientist," he asked, "aren't you required to accept the simplest explanation?" I do use Occam's Razor to slice away the reasons when they are otiose; but if a simple hypothesis cannot explain all the facts, I don't think it mandatory to embrace it. Lest I be misunderstood, let me state that before World War II American university life was antisemitic in a way that would hardly seem possible to the present generation. And Harvard, along with Yale and Princeton, was a flagrant case of this. So if anyone wants to understand why Jews, in relation to their scholarly abilities, were underrepresented on the Harvard faculty in those days, he can legitimately invoke the factor of antisemitism. (In many of the humanities faculties, bigots genuinely believed that Jews were no good; in science and mathematics, the belief was that they were too good; one could, so to speak, have one's cake and eat it too by believing—as did the eminent mathematician George D. Brikhoff and, to a degree, the eminent economist Joseph Schumpeter —that Jews were "early bloomers" who would unfairly receive more rewards than they deserved in free competition. Again, lest I be misunderstood, let me hasten to add the usual qualification that these two men were among my best friends and, I believe, both had a genuine high regard for my abilities and promise.) To illustrate, though, the failure of any one factor to account for the richness of reality, the following questions can be asked of those who know economists of that period well. (1) Why was Lloyd Metzler not given a tenure post at Harvard, since he suffered only from the disability of being from Kansas? (2) If you contemplate the academic careers in America of three men—Oskar Lange, Jacob Marshak, and Abba Lerner, not all Jewish—how can you cover the facts with the simple theory of antisemitism?

12. Quoted, with grateful acknowledgment to the original journal, from "Lord Keynes and the General Theory," *Econometrica*, 14 (1946), 187-199, and reprinted in P. A. Samuelson, *Collected Scientific Papers*, II (Cambridge, Mass.: MIT Press, 1966), pp. 1517-1533.

279

Reminiscences of Shigeto Tsuru

Paul A. Samuelson

I frst met Shigeto Tsuru in Ec 11, the Harvard economic-theory seminar, which Frank Taussig had made famous by his masterful use of the Socratic method, and which Joseph Schumpeter was then teaching for the first time. In 1935 Harvard economics was just entering its golden decade, though no one knew it then. Leontief was not yet 30; Schumpeter was in his prime, unbelievable as it must now seem to me, still much younger then than I am now; Haberler and Hansen were about to join the team; and the worlds of Keynesian econo-mics, Bergsonian welfare economics, Chamberlin-Robinson monopolistic competition, and mathematical economics were still in their erupting stages.

There were 20 to 30 of us beginning graduate study in that depression year: Robert Triffin from Belgium; I from Chicago and the middle west; David Lusher from McGill in Canada (later to be, until his death, the single best GNP fore-caster in the U.S. government); Russ Nixon, fresh from campus politics at the same University of Southern California from which, decades later, Nixon's Watergate crew were recruited; and many others. Already on the scene, as I have recorded elsewhere, were Alan and Paul Sweezy, Richard Musgrave, Alice Bourneuf, R. A. Gordon, Wolfgang Stolper, Abram Bergson, and a long list of now-famous names. Soon

52

to come were Sidney Alexander, Lloyd Metzler, Joe Bain, John Lintner, Henry Wallich, James Tobin, Benjamin Higgins, Robert Solow, and the many stars who made the Harvard sky shine so brightly in the age of Hansen.

Tsuru, you must understand, was a proper Harvard man —a graduate of Harvard *College*, and not, like such outlanders as me, merely a member of Harvard *University*: in those days the social niceties still counted, and a gentleman's C was the best grade a chap could desire. Because I soon distinguished myself in Schumpeter's seminar by talking so much—too much about Frank Knight, the Chicago sage I had just left behind, I was told!—I caught Shigeto's ear and he invited me to dinner with him at Adams House, his Harvard house in undergraduate years. As a graduate student I lived across the Charles River at the Harvard Business School (not because I ever betrayed any interest in business-school education, but because there were luxurious vacancies there in those years of depression when people could not afford a Harvard education). Shigeto lived in Claverly Hall, essentially a "gold coast" overflow house for Adams House, and where, according to legend, the aristocratic Franklin Roosevelt had once lived (or was it William Randolph Hearst?).

How shall I describe that Shigeto Tsuru? As a young boy, already involved in the ideological generation gap, Shigeto had come to, of all places, Lawrence College in Appleton, Wisconsin, deep in what might be called the American "middle-border." In that small community for farm boys and local bourgeoisie, he learned our language and customs in a way that would not have been easy in a cosmopolitan center like Harvard or Berkeley. After two years he correctly sensed that he had exhausted the benefits of that environment,

53

and cannily decided to transfer to Harvard for his final undergraduate years. That was a good thing for Tsuru. But it was an even better thing for me. It made possible my marriage to Marion Crawford. In Japan in those days marriages were arranged. In America they were made in heaven. But even heaven needs a helping hand, and without that of Shigeto I would never have met Marion. Returning to Wisconsin in the summers of 1934 and 1935, it was Shigeto who told Marion Crawford that after two years at Lawrence College she should follow his example for her final two years of undergraduate study, and move on to the big-time at Radcliffe College. Not only did Shigeto arrange for my bride to arrive in Cambridge just when I was to arrive; he also, at a student's restaurant on Church Street off Harvard Square, introduced us to each other. After that assist, Heaven took over, and I have been ever since the grateful beneficiary.

Shigeto's outstanding characteristic even then in his early 20's was his being "deep." There is a stereotype, not completely fanciful, of the uneasily smiling oriental. Nothing could be farther from Tsuru's demeanor, then or since. What would fit better would be the stereotype of the inscrutable oriental; or, indeed, the omniscient dignity of an American Indian chieftain. With calm assurance, Shigeto would tell you at a track meet that the runner in third position would win the mile event; sometimes he was right, but never in doubt. Tsuru was, for a Japanese, tall. Except that he is not now so slim, and that some gray has infiltrated his hair, I cannot see much in the way of change in him over the years. (But he used to always warn me that Americans are not very good in judging the ages of Japanese.)

Let me tell a story to illustrate his uncanny control. Going

54

back to Japan during a summer vacation then involved a boat trip of three weeks or more. On one of those voyages, Shigeto ate some fish which caused him to break out in hives. The itching was unbearable. But the ship's doctor had instructed him not to scratch. "What did you do?" I asked. "How did you manage this impossible situation?" He replied, and we believed him, "I exercised my will power." Even in sleep, he was always perfectly in control.

We played squash together. We argued about economics. We went to the Boston Symphony, to the Old Howard burlesque show in what used to be Scollay Square. He lent me his old rumble seat roadster, and on one occasion when I grazed a fender while he was in Japan, an honest woman later identified Shigeto, a Japanese, as me, the American driver of the car. I have never had much confidence in eyewitnesses since.

On my first visit to Japan in 1959, I lectured in Tokyo, Nagoya, Osaka, and Fukuoka to large crowds. In those days before simultaneous translation, I was lucky to have Shigeto as my superlative translator. At the beginning of each lecture I would express some words of thanks for my good fortune in having for translator "my old companion-at-arms from Harvard days." The thought of us staid professors as bold young blades invariably tickled the fancy of the audiences, and a titter of laughter would surface twice—once during my English rendition, and then again in greater volume during Tsuru's deadpan translation. So let me record for posterity that, although there used to be a libel that Japanese do not have strong heads for alcohol, Shigeto could hold his own with anyone. At our wedding party in 1938, his was the last toast when all others had given up. Still no mortal is a god, and in the spring of 1940, when the Nixons gave a party to celebrate

55

the completion of Ph. D dissertations by Tsuru, Nixon, Slitor, Bergson, and others of that vintage year, the stress of last-minute compositions took its toll—and without exception the new entrants into the company of learned scholars succumbed to the kiss of martini cocktails.

Harvard did much for us. But, as I have had occasion to say in the past, we did much for Harvard too. And Tsuru in particular brought to that rather complacent citadel of mainstream economics, a knowledge of and an interest in Marxian economics. His undergraduate thesis had been, I seem to recall, on Marx's commodity fetishism—anything but a conventional topic. Abe Bergson and I used to puzzle over Tsuru's contention that "It is not that Marx has a 'labor theory of value,' so much as that he has a 'value theory of labor.'" I hope someday to understand this. Paul Sweezy's *The Theory of Capitalist Development*, which still serves as one of the best expositions of Marxian economics for economists trained on mainstream lines, was written at Harvard in this period. Tsuru's appendix to the book, relating the steady and expanded reproduction tableaux of Marx to Quesnay's *tableau economique* and to Leontief-Keynes' circular flows, occupies a permanent place in the history of economic docrines.

In the course of time the young scholar grew up into the world authority. Shigeto and Masako Tsuru's return to Japan was a loss for American economics. But this came at a time when, as never before, a go-between was needed for Japanese and American economists. No one has ever fulfilled this role better than Tsuru and both countries have been blessed by the role he plays. And the much needed dialogue between mainstream and Marxian economists owes as much to the work of Shigeto Tsuru as to any other single scholar.

56

All this belongs to public scene. The publication of the many volumes of collected papers of Shigeto Tsuru will help to mark his scholarly achievements, but only his loving friends of 40 years standing can know fully the other Tsuru, the one whose fading snapshots fill our photo albums, and whose unfaded memories fill our hearts.

280

Foreword

"All successful scholarly careers are alike." What rot. Only this element of truth lies in this Tolstoyan paraphrase: scratch a professor and you find, usually in his vita, plenty of A's and honors. It is only after the rat race we call graduate study is over that the *summas* separate themselves into the creative and the competent.

So it was with Joe Bain. He took his A.B. (Phi Beta Kappa, with highest honors) from UCLA when it was just emerging from its cocoon as a normal school: as I can say about my hometown of Gary, Indiana, that UCLA Department of Economics was a good place for a Bain or a Domar to come from. Having an interest in the economics of accounting, Bain wisely chose to spend 1935–36 in graduate study at Stanford, where John B. Canning was taking an enlightened approach to that rather prosaic subject. The West Coast, with Canning at Stanford, and Hatfield, Staehling, and Mooritz at Berkeley, was then several time zones ahead of the East in the economic analysis of accounting–i.e., in accounting: they are really the same thing!

So when Bain arrived at Harvard in 1936, he was one up on us Eastern yokels–which included Schumpeter, Chamberlin, and Mason on the faculty, and in the student body such stalwarts as the two Sweezys, Musgrave, Bergson, Bourneuf, Stolper, Samuelson, Bishop, and Tsuru, as well as those soon to arrive such as Metzler, Lintner, Wallich, and other immortals. By taking surprisingly few courses, Bain completed his Ph.D. dissertation within three years: in those happy days, there was so little to learn in graduate school and so much time to think. (It was in Usher's economic history course that the Bains met: women then had to sit in the front rows and B came so high in the alphabet as to give Bain a chance to make contact, a privilege denied to us S's.) By the summer of his first year he had already published his first *Quarterly Journal* article, which must seem surprising in the modern age when an unusual student may submit his first article by his third or fourth year, and see it in print some two to three years after its formal acceptance.

The only pretense toward a Harvard meritocracy in those days was the statistics and accounting teaching staff for the pathologically shy Professor Frickey: along with R.A. Gordon, A. Bergson, W. Hance, L. Metzler, and G. Hauge, Bain prepared each October the June quizzes. Dr. Frickey ran a tight ship.

Berkeley, under the entrepreneurship of Robert Calkins, soon called. Bain replied and never looked back. For more than a third of a century—almost a dozen college generations—Bain pursued at Berkeley a research and teaching program in industrial organization. The learned journals and the library bookshelves testify to his fecundity in an area where it was not easy to be fecund. As a theorist, like Picasso, there is no afternoon when I cannot contrive a new gemlet. But in the study of real world markets, one must collect and analyze data for years in order to make relevant contributions.

Thoreau said that if, by forty, fame has not knocked at your door, forget it. Joe Bain could stop holding his breath early on, even before his classic analysis of barriers to entry and his independent discovery, along with Sylos-Labini, of the Bain-Sylos-Modigliani theory of oligopoly price as limited by potential entry.

This volume testifies that Joe Bain, although he is not your run-of-the-mill rotarian, has had profound influence on students and colleagues in the field of price theory. A pearl in his own right, he is also the clam shell around which pearls have formed. The students of his students will form a multiplier chain whose convergence to a finite sum is in doubt. No scholar can wish for more. And more his friends cannot wish for him.

281

Preface

This volume is a testimony to Alice Bourneuf. That cannot be said in the same sense of every Festschrift, for often the continental mode prevails in which a scholar who has a stranglehold on an important university and area of study has tribute exacted from his students: paying such *Danegeld* is like paying taxes, a necessary cost of doing business. Bourneuf commands only our respect.

I count more than nine lives for Alice Bourneuf as a scholar. She was both of the age of Taussig and the age of Schumpeter at Harvard in the 1930s. And for that matter of the age of Hansen. Once when I wrote of how Schumpeter gave only A's to women where Taussig gave them only C's, a friend gently reminded me that Bourneuf's A was a person's A.

To the current generation, idle gossip of that bygone time has the unreality of the Trojan Wars or the medieval era. Was it really the case within the present half-century that Radcliffe females could not discuss Shakespeare in the same room with Harvard males for fear that a six-letter word might occur? (President Emeritus Lowell once asked me indignantly, "Would you want *your* sister to discuss Macbeth with men?" I have no sister, but still. . . .) Economics, at the graduate level, was emancipated already by the 1930s; only at the under-graduate level did the charade persist of having a Mason give his hour class to 60 Harvard men, and then repeat it later to 9.7 Radcliffe women. Also, female dissertations had to be shorter because, although Radcliffe graduate students had stack privileges in Widener Library, they had to leave at 6 P.M.; any midnight oil was to be burned in their own garrets.

All of us in the 1930s were children of the depression. The fact that there were no jobs was liberating: if one had a little, one could pursue the unhurried life on that little. But all good things, and depressions, come to an end.

Bourneuf went to study at Louvain in Belgium just in time to be caught by World War II's outbreak. After a term in Seymour Harris's research galleys, she proceeded to the Office of Price Administration. The late Stephen Enke, in his algebraically sweet manner, once asserted: There are three kinds of economists—competent economists, incompetent economists, and OPA economists. He was more right than he realized. Kenneth Galbraith, Dick

Gilbert, Walter Salant, Victor Perlo, Jacob Mosak, David Lusher, Murray Geissler—the list is long—were alumni of that remarkable wartime group whose names came to be heard of. I can remember a visit in the early 1940s to one of the hot temporaries on the Mall, where every economist I knew was frantically tearing up completed contributions to a treatise on the subject and reversing their contents: Leon Henderson and J. K. Galbraith shifted gears from "no freeze" to a "general freeze." Everyone but Bourneuf, who had time to chat. Why this exception? I asked. I'm alright, Jack, she replied in effect, my chapter is on the *history* of price controls and not even Ken Galbraith can change that.

Again, all good things come to an end, and Alice Bourneuf moved over to the Federal Reserve. Those were great days at the Fed because of the carpetbaggers from the universities: Dick Musgrave, Robert Triffin, Lloyd Metzler, Evsey Domar, Gottfried Haberler, Alex Gerschenkron, Howard Ellis, Agnete (Laursen) Kalckar. A regret of my life is that I never heard Keynes at his two wartime Federal Reserve seminars. Like Moses, it was not given me to enter into the promised land of the 1944 Bretton Woods meetings, where Ajax and Hector—I mean, White and Vinson and Keynes—did mighty battle. But, like Joshua, Bourneuf was there. A muckraker might say she was there to set up the International Monetary Fund, where she proceeded to get a job. It is not documented that she contrived to create the Marshall Plan so that she could go to Norway. But bliss was it in that dawn to be alive and be Dick Bissell's plenipotentiary in the Norway that Brofuss was propelling into the twenty-first century.

Good Americans go to Paris when they die. Lucky Americans go there on a U.S. payroll while they live. Alice Bourneuf moved "down" from Oslo to Paris just when the Marshall Plan was at its zenith. How can you get them back on the Washington farm after that? Moreover, Joseph McCarthy's Washington was no great place to be, even for those who had never signed a petition for the release of Mooney or sold cookies for Spanish Refugee relief. Our victories yet to come, in Indochina and elsewhere, had to be won in the seminars of Mt. Holyoke. The Eisenhower years provided a rich spectacle for the scholar and teacher in macroeconomics. The long academic vacations provided the leisure to write up the Norwegian experience, and investigate the undulations of inventories. From a distance of 100 miles, I can guess that Bourneuf's voice was heard in the Holyoke senior common room. I recall once hearing her indignation when one of her honors students, who had written an original analysis of an accelerator-multiplier model, was asked in her oral examination by an interdisciplinary colleague: "But what is the *sociology* of your model?"

Two years as a visiting professor at the exciting and turbulent Berkeley of the 1950s may have made Bourneuf a loose ion. In any case, when Boston College called, she jumped. Never one to tolerate sexual discrimination, her indignation was unsparing when someone proposed that another woman be appointed to share an office with Bourneuf. And never underestimate the powers of an activist: many a dean at B.C. must have divided time into "Before and After Bourneuf." At AEA conventions, when Father McEwen and Alice Bourneuf appeared, department heads quaked for the ivory they were hoarding. The results are now history.

It is not meet to register in a public place the bonds of affection this remarkable economist has inspired. She is living disproof of the Durocher Theorem that good guys end up last. A female scholar in a Neanderthal age of men, a Catholic in the American university of the first half of the twentieth century when there was a shameful trace of truth in the phrase "Anti-Catholicism is the antisemitism of the intellectual," such a person could be forgiven for becoming abrasive. Not so Bourneuf. The militance I wrote of had no self-pity or resentments in it. She sought excellence, and learned some of the Jesuit arts of persuasion and feasibility in its pursuit. Sharp elbows are not shapely, and people are loved, some sage has said, in inverse relationship to their ability to take care of themselves in the Darwinian struggle for existence. Alice Bourneuf has been much loved. Her friends and colleagues—but I repeat myself—feel honored in presenting these birthday gifts.

282

Jacob Viner, 1892–1970

Paul A. Samuelson

Massachusetts Institute of Technology

When I attended the University of Chicago in the early 1930s, it had the best Department of Economics in the country. Every locality knows that its department is the best, but ours really was the best because it had Frank Knight, Jacob Viner, and Henry Schultz—not to mention Paul Douglas and Henry Simons, Simeon Leland and Harry Millis, Aaron Director and Lloyd Mints. Schultz represented the new econometric wave of the future, but Knight and Viner represented the giants of the present. Frank Taussig at Harvard was in his twilight years; Allyn Young had died recently in London; Schumpeter and Leontief were but newly arrived in Harvard Square. Columbia fielded a mighty team with Wesley Mitchell, John Maurice Clark, and Harold Hotelling. But we had Viner and Knight.

Viner was my teacher. I heard many lectures by Knight and had chances to talk to him. However, it was chance of the draw that the famous 301 graduate course in economic theory, which oscillated between Frank Knight and Jacob Viner, happened to be given by Viner in the winter quarter of 1935, my senior year and just after I had learned Marshallian economics from Paul Douglas. It was no easy matter for anyone to get into Viner's course (and, as we shall see, still harder to stay in it). For an undergraduate it was still harder, but Paul Douglas said he would write a letter on my behalf.

Fortunately for me, Viner had just returned from his tour of duty in Morgenthau's treasury and must have been in an indulgent mood. With about thirty-five other aspirants, who I recall included Martin Bronfenbrenner and Warren Scoville, we lined up around a huge seminar table in the basement of the then new Social Sciences Research building. Viner appeared, holding our names on index cards; and after a speedy inquisition, five of us were found wanting in previous preparation or motivation. But that was only the beginning.

My impression of Viner never changed from that first glimpse. He was short and intense, like a bantam cock. His upper lip, usually bedewed by a bead of moisture, curled in what seemed half a smile. In my imperfect memory his hair was then red, and his complexion matched. His suit coats were on the short side and his posture was not that of a West Point cadet. How I remember anything about his person I do not know, since every eye in the room was fastened upon the diabolical deck of index cards in his hands through which he shuffled nervelessly. To be scrupulously honest, subsequent legend has contaminated my account. I was too innocent to be nervous. In contrast to the graduate students present, I had nothing at stake. But for them, their whole careers and professional futures were in jeopardy each time he riffled through the cards.

Viner was a student, *the* prize student of Frank Taussig, that master of the Socratic method. Taussig played on his classes as Pablo Casals plays on his 'cello. He knew which idiot would botch up Ricardo's trade-off between profit and the real wage; he knew which cantankerous student had to be kept out of the classroom verbal interaction lest he short-circuit the dialogue. Viner added one new ingredient: terror. Members of the seminar sat tensely around the table, and when the name of the victim was read off the cards, you could almost hear the sighs of relief and the slumping back into chairs of those who had won temporary respite. Indeed, the stakes were high. Three strikes and you were out, with no appeal possible to any higher court. And this was no joke. I remember an able graduate student who, having failed to give an acceptable answer on two previous occasions, was told by Viner: "Mr. ——, I am afraid you are not equal to yourself or this class." This man barely managed to retrieve his position at the final moment. If a graduate student was refused admittance to 301, the basic course in theory, he had no choice but to drop out or to transfer to the slums of political science or sociology. (Years later when I discussed with Jack Viner the legend of his ferocity, he said that the department had given him the function of screening the candidates for higher degrees. It was not work for which he was ill-equipped.)

What shall I say about the course? By reputation it was considered the best course in economic theory being given in the America of those days. On reflection, I think it probably deserved that accolade. I shall comment more on Wesley Mitchell's famous course on schools of thought later, and need only mention that the magnificient J. M. Clark was never noted as an outstanding classroom lecturer. The year 1934–35 was the last year in which Taussig taught in his famous Ec. 11; actually Schumpeter took over in the second semester, as can be detected from the grade book which records a quantum jump in the grades of women. The fact that the Taussigian method was overpraised to Harvard men of my generation tends to make me unfairly critical of it; and as I have written elsewhere, Taussig told me before he died that Ec. 11 was vastly over-rated in the after-1919 years.[1]

To my regret, the notes that I took for Viner's course, if they still exist, are not in any location known to me. But that is perhaps just as well, for Viner was vehement in his belief that it was a sacrilege to take skimpy notes from a course and present it to the world as a fair sample of the course's quality. To his indignation, a student had done just that around 1930, and a mimeographed copy of the notes was on deposit in Harper Library. In 1935 the course that I took was noticeably different in scope and coverage from the 1930 version. To buttress his sensitivity on this point, Viner made reference to Wesley Mitchell's famous course at Columbia. Without authorization, a student circulated rather elaborate mimeographed notes (which, subsequent to my conversation with Viner, were published by Augustus Kelley). Viner had read these notes and reported that their content was extremely disappointing, a fact he blamed on the unauthorized paraphraser, not on the quality of Mitchell's thought. (If I am honest, I must report that my own reading at that time of Mitchell's lectures on a subject like, say, Jevons's utilitarian model of exchange raised doubts in my mind that the classroom discussion was more penetrating than the notes had recorded. If I had raised my eyes from the dirt floor to observe the beautiful blue Mediterranean, perhaps my youthful judgment would have been less harsh.)

I do remember being fascinated by Viner's first lecture. In it he eluci-dated the nature of continuing equilibrium by means of the analogy of a well-balanced aquarium. Before and since I have heard much of the circular flow of Quesnay and Schumpeter and Walras, but I cannot recollect a similar treatment of this issue. As might have been expected, Viner put considerable store on the historical development of the subject. Since this was my first graduate course, I did not know there was any other way to do it. Viner made clear at the beginning that he would not be covering the latest wrinkles in the theory of imperfect or monopolistic competition. However, since Viner himself, along with his student Theodore Yntema, had independently discovered the marginal cost–marginal revenue conditions for maximization of an imperfect competitor's profits, much of what was contained in the Chamberlin and Robinson treatises was adequately covered. Although I had the best undergraduate education in economics that opportunity could provide at that date, only once, and then in Viner's graduate course, was I exposed to the mysteries

[1] His exact words were something like this: "After the interruption resulting from my serving as price administrator in Washington under President Wilson, I never really felt I could catch up in economic theory. That's why I went back into a new career in international trade theory." I may add that Taussig's 1927 *International Trade,* written when he was in his late sixties, is truly a classic, both in its originality and its peerless exposition; the theses of his gradute students, including Viner's own classic, are a priceless addition to the literature.

of indifference curves and the production possibility frontier (this latter under the heading of Pareto's "production indifference" curve). In the first minute of the course Viner made clear that a proper prerequisite for it would be knowledge of the calculus. But that since the instructor lacked that qualification, he would waive it for the rest of us.

As economists of this generation know well, Jacob Viner was a respecter of mathematics, but also both critical and defensive about it. Let me make clear that Viner possessed in superlative degree what might be called native mathematical ability. I used to think it a pity that his generation had been deprived of proper training in that subject—the more so in that he could properly complain that the Harvard Graduate School of 1914–16 had consisted largely of mediocre fellow students and, the magnificent Taussig aside, of overrated professors of economics who did not tax his energies as a student. But I now realize in retrospect that the subject of economics gained from having Viner concentrate upon those areas of wisdom and erudition for which he had a unique comparative advantage, and that more mathematical facility might merely have diverted him from his appointed task.

In writing these reminiscences of Viner as a teacher at Chicago I have consulted with a number of eminent scholars who took his graduate courses both before and after the 1935 term I have spoken of. Suffice it to report that there is a legend about how fierce he seemed at first contact. Legends grow on legends, and an experienced psychologist will be amused to learn that the 1946 Viner at Princeton was "mellow," and the 1946 Viner of Chicago was "unmellow." The truth is that he used a teaching technique which to the best students was inordinately stimulating. I could quote testimony after testimony to this effect. I myself found his course enormously stimulating. Evsey Domar, who took it in 1940, tells me it was the best course he has ever taken, and in part because of Viner's challenging manner. Martin Bronfenbrenner, who took many of Viner's Chicago courses, recalls that it was a custom to sit in on the same course year after year because of the new insights to be gleaned.

After I left Chicago I learned that I was something of a legend myself in Viner's course of that year. Legends grow on legends. So let me set the record straight. The prosaic fact is that Viner had a custom of coming to class with complicated diagrams to be copied on the blackboard. Such transcriptions are notoriously subject to minor errors in which curves intersect on the wrong side of axes, and so forth. Fools rush in where angels fear to tread, and so it was left to the only undergraduate in the course to point out such occasional petty aberrations which detracted nothing from his evident erudition and keenness.

Few of us like to be wrong. Jacob Viner, consummate scholar that he was, and meticulous in his knowledge of the literature, was no exception in this respect. Yet I would argue that it is the occasional errors of geniuses like Viner which make the reputations of mere mortals, and which also seminally advance the body of science. Who in economics would remember Dr. Wong if his memory had not been perpetuated by his correcting of Viner's long-run cost-curve envelope? Precisely because Viner was so Jovianly impervious to error, the economics profession got a modicum of *Schadenfreude* at his expense over the envelope incident. Certainly he had no need to be sensitive about it. The controversy with the draftsman occurred in Viner's truly masterful article of 1931 on "Cost Curves and Supply Curves." This has appeared in all the anthologies, and its reprints have circulated all over the world. Within the last year I have found myself writing two or three different articles based upon the beautifully simple Ricardo-Viner technology discussed in one part of that article. By 1935 Viner reported to the class that Wong had been right in 1931 and he, Viner, had been wrong, mathematically and economically. "But" he said to me privately just as the class bell had rung, "although there seems to be some esoteric mathematical reason why the envelope cannot be drawn so that it passes smoothly through the declining bottoms of the $\cup$-shaped cost curves, nevertheless I can do it!" "Yes," I replied impishly, "with a good *thick* pencil, you can do it."

I found later at Harvard that the great Joseph Schumpeter remained confused in this matter. He always insisted that somewhere in the third dimension of the parametrized surface of $\cup$-shaped cost curves, the envelope did go through Viner's bottom points. Yet in the same 1931 volume of the *Zeitschrift für Nationalökonomie* there appears, bound with Viner's, a paper by Erich Schneider; here, in the guise of total- rather than average-cost curves, appears a clear depiction of the proper envelope relations. And of course Roy Harrod later set the matter straight in terms of $\cup$-shaped curves.[2]

There has never been a greater neoclassical economist than Jacob Viner. This is high praise indeed. Over the years he engaged in a running battle with Lionel Robbins, Frank Knight, and Gottfried Haberler on the doctrinal question of whether the Austrian notion of opportunity-cost in some genuine theoretical and empirical manner superseded a contributing role of classical, real, or disutility costs. No matter how much his opponents appealed to terminology involving labor as displaced leisure or supply as algebraically reversed reserve-demand, Viner took his position with Marshall that both blades of the scissors had to form the equilibrium

---

[2] To linger for a moment on the pregnant errors of a master scholar, I should point out that half a dozen years before Joan Robinson published her geometrical analysis of discriminating monopoly, it had all been worked out by Theodore Yntema in this *Journal*. Yntema was led to this 1928 investigation to *correct* a conjecture in the theory of dumping which Viner had arrived at in his classic on the subject by the sometimes treacherous method of investigating different numerical examples.

intersection; and that, empirically, both blades have to be considered as cutting save in singular polar cases. By stubbornly standing his ground, Viner in the end was victorious, explicitly or implicitly.

I have been asked by the editors of the *Journal of International Economics* to discuss in detail Jacob Viner's colossal contributions to the modern theory of international trade. Together with his work on partial equilibrium, this constitutes the unforgettable core of his analytical contributions to economics. Let me then merely say here that his 1937 *Studies in the Theory of International Trade* is without peer in its magisterial review and evaluation of the literature. Moreover, it contains in it material from the 1931 lecture, which he gave at the London School of Economics, that anticipates completely the later models of Lerner and Leontief in international trade and of Hicks in the statical production-exchange model of general equilibrium. It should go into the record that these contributions to international trade were part of Viner's value-added during the Chicago years.

When President Harper launched with Rockefeller money a new great university, aside from plundering the faculties of existing universities, he made the great innovation of supporting learned journals. It would take an essay to enumerate the advantages to a research center and the general community of a learned journal. It is enough to mention here that the *Journal of Political Economy* was a great Chicago contribution to the development of economics. For many years Frank Knight and Jacob Viner were coeditors, a magnificent team. Viner's own contributions as an editor have never been adequately recorded. But scores of writers for the *JPE*, now of international eminence but then often neophyte scholars, will know how valuable were his editorial improvements and suggestions. Many have reason to thank him for his rejections. As befits the editor of a house journal, Viner was particularly sensitive to the need for objective justice where controversies involving Chicago faculty and graduates were concerned. The *JPE* may even have leaned over backwards in refusing to review books by Chicago economists.

Jacob Viner must always have been a prodigious worker. I am saying nothing here of his contributions as a policy adviser during his great-depression and World War II days at the U.S. Treasury. The obituaries in the public press naturally stressed these aspects, and I recognize that Viner himself enjoyed a certain satisfaction from knowing that he had served his times. But those of us in the field of economics were understandably irritated that the world should not realize it had lost a scholar as well as a statesman.

I have to shudder at the thought of how a great treatise like the *Studies* could have been written in the same years that frequent trips to Washington were being undertaken. And I now realize why, when I used to go to his office for help and discussion, he would open the door a crack and stand there puffing on his pipe, conversing through the few degrees of angle of that door. It powerfully shortens idle conversation to conduct tutorials on the hoof.

Jacob Viner was a great eclectic. For this I now value him. When I learned in my teens that most members of the Chicago economics department had signed a petition in favor of One Hundred Percent money, I found it almost incredible that Viner was unwilling to put his name to the document. Today I would sympathize fully with his reservations.

Being sensible does not mean lacking courage. Viner was justly proud that he and the whole Chicago economics department had issued in 1931 a famous memorandum explicitly recommending unbalanced budgets to fight the great depression. He was a great exponent of the neoclassical theory of money, but that did not lead him to overlook the effects on the velocity of circulation of money that budget deficits and surpluses can have. Henry Simons used to remind me that when many of the Keynes converts had still been Say's-Law deflationists, the Chicago economists had baited fiscal orthodoxy. On the other hand it is a perversion of history to believe that there was an oral tradition at the University of Chicago which had already anticipated the valid nucleus of Keynesian analysis.

It was a tragedy of Moses that he was never to be permitted to enter into the Promised Land. I have always thought it was the good fortune of Jacob Viner that, after a creative and sometimes stormy passage at Chicago, he was able while at the very prime of his powers to move into the serene harbor of Princeton.

Where he and his wife Frances did live happily ever after.

283

FRANK KNIGHT, 1885-1972

One of America's most influential intellectuals died recently. But few people would recognize his name.

Frank Knight was professor of economics at the University of Chicago for half a century. He never retired; when he died in his 80s his fountain pen was still full. Knight was the founder of the Chicago School in economics: if he was Abraham, Henry Simons was Isaac and Milton Friedman is Jacob.

Although, as far as I know, Knight was never invited to the White House, you can see his influence on Washington in the decisions that Secretary George Shultz will be making on foreign-exchange rates and in the mordant wit of Herbert Stein, chairman of the Council of Economic Advisers. But this is only the visible peak of the iceberg. Even radical economists, as I shall argue, bear the stamp of Frank Knight's thought.

CRACKER-BARREL SOCRATES

How did The New Yorker miss doing a profile on so singular a personality? A profound philosopher and superb economic technician, he was also the village atheist and a sage of the Will Rogers vintage. These days professors tend to come from Exeter Academy or the Bronx High School of Science. Knight was of that turn-of-the-century generation who—like Karl and Arthur Compton and Wesley Mitchell—came off the farm.

He used to say in his squeaky voice that he became an economist because his feet hurt him following the plow. Perhaps nearer the truth was the fact that when he was a graduate student in philosophy at Cornell, he was given an ultimatum: "Stop talking so much, or leave the philosophy department." This gave Knight no choice but to gravitate down into economics. (It also made him an authority on the laws of talk, as in his dictum: "Sociology is the science of talk, and there is only one law in sociology. Bad talk drives out good.")

Frank Knight was a skeptic who doubted the ability of man through government to better his condition. Capitalism—alas!—is the best we can settle for. Thus, if Doctor Friedman is one of those optimists who thinks that capitalism is the best of all possible worlds, Dr. Knight was one of those pessimists who is afraid that this is indeed the case.

I shall not argue here the issue of determinism vs. free will. But if you believe that man can hurry forward the clock of evolution—that a Marx or Lenin can advance the date of the inevitable revolution—then you must concede man can retard that clock. From 1932-1945, faith in the market-pricing mechanism as the organizer of the economy sold at a discount.

THE COUNTER-REVOLUTION

It was the priceless contribution of Frank Knight and the Chicago School to remind us of the market's merits. This is a message that falls on deaf ears in the common rooms of Britain's ancient universities. But it is one whose relevance a Russian, Yugoslav or Czech can understand.

And make no mistake about it. Rumors of the death of the market, like those of Twain's death, are greatly exaggerated. In Britain and Scandinavia, Socialist governments have in the last quarter of a century often been displaced from office. In America, too, the pendulum swings. The role of Frank Knight in this counter-revolution is pivotal.

A central feature of Knight's thought is his antipathy toward the mixed economy. As he put it, a planned economy is simply a well-managed penitentiary. It was this simplistic element that came to disillusion me with my boyhood idol. And I fear it made Knight a poor prophet of events that were to come after 1932, as when in a moment of despair, he declared that the only choice was between Communism and Fascism and he for one preferred Communism.

Knight's antipathy toward the prevalent post-New Deal world is not unlike that of a Herbert Marcuse. Many of the New Left are Knight without the market.

As a sage has said: "The ideas of economists and political philosophers, both when they are right and when they are wrong, are more powerful than is commonly understood. Indeed, the world is ruled by little else. Practical men, who believe themselves to be quite exempt from any intellectual influences, are usually the slave of some defunct economist ... I am sure that the power of vested interests is vastly exaggerated, compared with the gradual encroachment of ideas."

Although, as J.M. Keynes also said, "in the long run we are all dead," Frank Knight lives on.

284

SEYMOUR HARRIS AS POLITICAL ECONOMIST

Paul A. Samuelson (M.I.T.)

Seymour Harris was legendary for being so productive a scholar. As the number of his books came to be reckoned in the scores, he became the subject of a good deal of badinage within the profession of economics. But instead of becoming sensitive on the issue, Harris took pride in the product of his vineyard. His opening words before Congressional committees would proclaim, "I am Seymour Harris, Professor of Economics at Harvard University and author of 33 [or 45] books. . . ."

When Friedrich Lutz was still at Princeton, he summed up the phenomenon aptly: "That man Harris can't hold his ink." I once asked Seymour whether G. D. H. Cole had not caused fully as many trees of the forest to be ground up into paper pulp as he had. After giving the remark the deliberation it deserved, Harris replied: "First, Cole is not really an economist. And besides it's an unfair comparison: Cole suffered from insomnia."

An Oxford partisan of Cole might have offered in rebuttal that Seymour Harris himself was more than a mere economist in his many writings, and also that many of Harris's books were edited symposia rather than solo accomplishments. Although Harris did write dozens of books as sole author, it is also true that he was the most interesting editor of his times. It was this aspect of Harris's productivity that prompted Gottfried Haberler to provide the most memorable introduction of a lecturer in the annals of our guild. Before that famous World War II Federal Reserve seminar, which Keynes twice addressed (even though he never gave a lecture at Harvard) and which served to keep alive the scholarly interests of academics drafted to the war effort, Haberler said:

> There is no need for me to introduce to you Dr. Seymour Harris, since those of you who are not busily engaged in reading his works are busily engaged in writing them.

The reader will notice that my pen has fallen back into the same affectionate badinage that for forty years Seymour Harris evoked from a wide circle of colleagues. But I must not leave the picture so distorted.

The future historian of thought is apt to miss out on the important influence that a scholar like Seymour Harris has had on the course of American economics. So let me, while memories are still green, comment on Harris (1) as a scholar, (2) as an activist ideologist who promoted Keynesianism and the New Economics, and (3) as a human being.

Scholar

Harris was a prodigious worker even in the contemporary Harvard stable of prodigious workers. Some people — Bertrand Russell comes to mind as an excellent example — are prolific because they write easily and do not shame to let their dictated words pass directly into print. Not Harris. He knew himself to be a clumsy writer. For him it was a matter of much input for each bit of output. He used to tell a story about the great Barry Wood, Harvard football star as well as brilliant scholar:

> After seeing Barry's fantastic football victory over Yale, imagine my surprise to find him an hour later industriously studying in the Dunster House library.

Seymour never seemed to realize that it was also a story on him!

Harris made important contributions to conventional areas of economic investigation. Two typical ones come to mind.

1. When Britain left the gold standard in 1931, and the United States followed in 1933, the economics of currency depreciation became an obvious target for a Harris book. The result of his researches was, for the attentive reader, to correct the understanding of his contemporaries. Generally speaking, economists thought that what was important about an exchange rate depreciation was its "beggar-my-neighbor" effect to expand the exports of the depreciating country, thereby improving its depression level of employment at the expense of its neighbors. Aside from this, the pre-Harris economists

questions as, whether Roosevelt's dollar depreciation would restore the 1926 price level generally concerned themselves with such price (shades of Dr. Warren, the Cornell farm economist who caught FDR's ear for a brief time in 1933), or whether the terms of trade of the depreciating countries would deteriorate much.

Harris's findings properly turned attention to the most crucial point, namely that the *depreciation of the currency by the sterling bloc was primarily important in that it permitted them to pursue expansionary fiscal and monetary policies at home without having to fear for the induced balance-of-payments consequences; and the domestic expansion that the depreciation permitted served in turn to expand the imports of the depreciating countries, thereby resulting in negligible harm perpetrated by the depreciating country on the countries that willfully stayed pat.*

Much of this had been foreseen by the genius of Keynes in his Macmillan Committee and subsequent years; but it was Harris who tenaciously put the matter to historical testing. Only those who are unaware of the fashionable myths that beclouded the thinking of the time, and who do not appreciate how important is the role of fashionable myth in science, will fail to sense the importance of the Harris investigations.

2. When Harris set out to write his book on social security, the economics of the subject was in a woeful state. The 1935 Act had envisaged tax collections large enough in relation to disbursements to build up a sizeable so-called Social Security Reserve Fund. Indeed, the recession of 1937 was attributable in part to the fact that the system began operations by collecting more than it was disbursing. However, both conservative and liberal critics of the system soon began to develop the notion that the reserve fund was a myth: the future elderly will have to be supported out of the then current product of the working classes; so why did the financing matter? Although Harris as a new adherent of the *General Theory* was all too aware of the potentially deflationary aspects of tax collections in excess of disbursements in a time when the short-term interest rate was a fraction of a fraction of one per cent, he punc-

tured the defective logic of Senator Vandenberg and other important critics of the time by pointing out that (1) what mattered was not what you chose to *call* the accumulated surplus of taxes, e.g., a "reserve fund" or whether or not you put actual government bond certificates "in it," but rather (2) whether your excess tax collections were to result in unemployment or in easier money and more capital formation now than would otherwise have taken place, and out of whose incremental fruits some fraction of the future retirement burden could be borne. All this was long before James Buchanan's revival of pre-Keynesian debt analysis. And even though Harris was not able to reach the depths of profundity of the current Modigliani-Diamond analysis of life-cycle savings and public debt-social security incidence, as Schumpeter would say, Harris's was a stellar performance for its time and not one which was fully appreciated then perhaps because of the difficulty of his prose.

Since space does not permit further samplings of Harris's contributions, let me merely point out that Harris was the spearhead in the movement to have economists tackle the varied important problems of the day: social security, economics of education, regional economics, economics of Harvard, wartime economics, price-wage controls — no area was off-limits for his probing research. When most of the profession was fiddling with the niceties of the Kahn-Keynes multiplier, the definitions of saving and investment, and the intricacies of Böhn-Bawerk's average period of production, Seymour Harris was digging into the real problems of the present and the future.

It is worth pointing out that all this was before the days of the National Science and Ford Foundations. At Harvard in the late 1930's, a Schumpeter lined up with a dozen other professors to compete for the secretarial services of the half-time not occupied by the *Quarterly Journal of Economics* duties of the department's second secretary. Harris carried on his many researches on a shoestring, maneuvering to afford a research assistant (such as Crawford, Bourneuf, Wolfert, and others) and a secretary (such as Thorp and Buller). No one was overpaid in that shop, history will record.

Activist

When a fabulous Social Science Research Council fellowship for graduate study forced me to leave the Chicago Midway against my will, Columbia and Harvard were my logical second choices. Most of my Chicago faculty friends favored going to Columbia. But, an ungrateful child, I opted for the green ivy of Cambridge. I remember being warned against Seymour Harris as an "inflationist" (John Williams, however, was a "sound" man). This was indeed prescient, since in mid-1935 Harris was still a protégé of the conservative Harold Hitchings Burbank: it was like the remarkable prescience of de Tocqueville in recognizing the weakness of the American presidency — especially remarkable, since before de Tocqueville's time there had been such strong Presidents as Washington, Jefferson, Quincy Adams, and Jackson.

Early in 1936 Keynes's *General Theory* appeared. Also, after hanging on at Harvard for more than fifteen years without tenure, an existence not to be recommended to the weak or proud, Harris became an Associate Professor. In any case, soon he was riding the front seat of the Keynesian bandwagon. Except for Alvin Hansen, who was appointed to the new Littauer School after 1938, Harris had little company as a Keynesian on the Harvard faculty of those days. Williams was skeptical; Schumpeter was opposed; Chamberlin and most of the other faculty never to their dying day read the *General Theory*. How wrong the reactionary *Veritas* Foundation was in its view of fair Harvard as then in the clutches of radical Keynes-Marxists.

Human Being

Harris was tireless and fearless. He was the most partisan of men, with a lower-case *p*. Having no children of his own, he made Harvard, the Democratic Party, Stevenson and Kennedy, New England, and his students part of his extended family. Having adopted me as a "brilliant" person (his word, and the word he genuinely applied to Schumpeter, Tobin, Arthur Schlesinger, Galbraith, Solow, and many others), I could do no wrong. After my

hair was flecked with gray, he was still introducing me as a brilliant *wunderkind*. I used to tell him that if I submitted my laundry list (or Milton Friedman's latest confection in disguise) to the *Review of Economics and Statistics*, he would publish, muttering only to himself that it was not quite up to my usual standard. Whenever we met he expressed regret that the MIT department could not be merged back into the Harvard Department of Economics.

His sense of loyalty was so great that, if he lived a fortnight in a boarding house, he undoubtedly would have begun to defend its cooking. When President Kennedy named Harris to Douglas Dillon's Treasury, it was no time at all before he was mediating between it and Tobin and his other protégés at the Heller Council of Economic Advisors.

It is proper that I confine myself to Seymour Harris as an economist. But he was much more than that at Harvard. He ordered the economics books for Widener for decades, with few realizing how that collection kept growing. It was Harris who was directly responsible for Harvard's part in pulling out of TIAA, an event which together with Vannevar Bush's threatened rebellion at the Carnegie Institution led to the creation of CREF as an implementation of William Greenough's Harvard Ph.D. thesis on variable annuities. Harris was senior tutor for years at Dunster House. He was chairman of the Economics Department after Burbank was deposed, and he made an active chairman. Today people will hardly believe that Schumpeter was opposed as President of the American Economic Association on the bigoted grounds that he was not trained in this country; against great odds, Seymour Harris led the successful fight to make Schumpeter president. Since that time, I would suppose that the average scholarly quality of the numerous foreign-born AEA presidents has been, if anything, higher than our native lot.

Seymour disagreed with the Harvard alumnus who said that Good Americans go to Paris when they die. His notion of Valhalla was the Harvard Yard. It was characteristic that he left his not inconsiderable savings of a lifetime to fund a Harvard chair in economics. One of the last letters I received from him, after he was already a very sick man, was an uncharacteristic request for financial advice. It was not for himself, he explained, but only because of his anguish that the money he was leaving to Harvard was shrinking under Republican misrule. The future of the Dow-Jones Industrials not having been vouchsafed to me, I wrote back by way of comfort that, undoubtedly the Harvard portfolio was shrinking just as rapidly as his own nest egg, so that the incremental importance of his gift to Harvard could not be affected by anything that man in the White House did.

Vale!

I see that I introduced my contribution to Harris' last Harvard symposium with the following words:

> "One of the great pleasures in my life has been preparing chapters for various Seymour Harris symposia, and I should like nothing better than to spend the next hundred years doing the same at five-year intervals."

Now that he is gone and I am ten years older, I'd like to up the ante to "the next thousand years."

285

ALVIN HANSEN AS A CREATIVE ECONOMIC THEORIST

Paul A. Samuelson

Early syntheses, 27. — The scholar reborn, 29. — Conclusion, 31.

Much has been written about Alvin Hansen, the teacher and scholar — by others in this symposium and by me elsewhere.[1] My purpose here is to describe his contributions to the corpus of economic analysis: when all personal influences decay exponentially through time as they must, there remains imperishably locked in the developed corpus of a subject the value-added contributions of a scholar. Men are mortal. Their theorems and inductive inferences are permanent.

From the early 1930's on, Alvin Hansen had an international reputation among economists. He was also of renown to the general public, to governmental officials, and to international agencies. His oral and written testimony was widely sought; his tireless pen wrote not only for his academic colleagues and for students, but also for the wider public at large. At Harvard, in the policy areas of macroeconomics, despite his nonaggressive manner, he came to overshadow his colleagues in an almost embarrassing manner; considering the strategic importance of Harvard at that juncture in history, Hansen through his hold on students wielded a tremendous influence on the course of modern economic stabilization policy. (His colleagues included, to name but two scholars important in their own right, Joseph Schumpeter and Sumner Slichter: for different reasons, neither of these developed a coterie of followers to amplify his own influence. And the important influence of John Williams, both in his own person and through that minority of able students who did march primarily to his beat, was often by way of contrast and qualification to the bolder theses of Hansen and his circle. Gottfried Haberler provided a critical audit that was both creative and valuable.)

This public extra-academic stature of Hansen I particularly stress. Its bright light tends to obscure his analytical importance as an economist. Anyone who has studied the parallel career of Gustav Cassel will realize that, precisely because Cassel came to be overpraised by the public toward whom so much of his writing was ad-

1. P. A. Samuelson, "Alvin H. Hansen, 1887–1975," *Newsweek*, June 16, 1975, p. 72; "In Search of the Elusive Elite," Op.Ed., *New York Times*, June 26, 1975, p. 31; "Alvin H. Hansen, 1887–1975," to appear in the *American Economic Review* (sometime in 1976).

dressed, he came to be underpraised by contemporary academics. The parallel ends here, in that Cassel was among the most egotistical of scholars and never underplayed his own worth. Hansen, on the other hand, though stubbornly insistent on the value of his own conclusions, was not by temperament one to blow his own horn. Schumpeter, Galbraith, and any historian of science could join with me in pointing out that the world makes the great mistake of taking you at your own claims: if Alfred Marshall insisted that he had done independently what Jevons and Walras had done earlier, the jury of history would fail to write this off to his discredit but rather would chalk him up as an original thinker.

There is still another minor reason why Hansen's originality may tend to be overlooked as the passing years obliterate personal memories. By 1935 economics entered into a mathematical epoch. It became easier for a camel to pass through the eye of a needle than for a nonmathematical genius to enter into the pantheon of original theorists. A kind of Gresham's Law operated, as those of us who benefited from it know only too well.

But by all odds the major reason why Hansen is in danger of getting less than his full share of recognition as an important analyst is the fact that he came to be known as "the American Keynes." There is much that is just about such a title. No one in America did as much as Hansen in shaping and applying the analysis of Keynes's *General Theory* to the American scene. To say this is to accord Hansen great praise. And that praise is augmented when one adds that, after 1936, it was Hansen and his circle that did the major work in spelling out the implications of the Keynes macroeconomic model for fiscal policy. (Turning the pages of the *General Theory*, we remind ourselves that in this work Keynes chose to say less about its various implications for expenditure and budget policy than he had said earlier in *Can Lloyd George Do It?* (1929) and in *The Means to Prosperity* (1933). Richard Kahn came to the nucleus of Keynes's theory of income determination, Kahn's famous 1931 article on the multiplier, by way of antidepression public works spending; but by 1936, the emphasis is on which schedules intersect to determine what, and not on which contrived shifts in the schedules might be used to realize prescribed full employment targets.)

Though Hansen was most generous in his acknowledgements of Keynes's influence, an influence he had resisted at first, Hansen was much more than the American Keynes, being an important creator in his own right.

To bring out this evaluation of the man, let me quote from a letter that I wrote a dozen years ago when asked to make nominations for a Nobel-like prize in economics. This was long before a proper Nobel Prize for economics was set up by the gift of the Bank of Sweden on its 300th anniversary. The effort to establish the prize in question, the Balzan Prize, was ended in a legal tangle before an award in economics came to be made; but the fact that Komolgorov in mathematics and Admiral Morison in history received Balzan awards made it a coveted honor.

My 1963 words included:

> Of all living men, and here I measure my words, Professor Hansen has made the widest and most original contributions to the theory of income determination and macroeconomics generally. If Lord Keynes were alive, I should have to alter this judgment. . . . Hansen himself has always made acknowledgments to the macroeconomic contributions of Keynes. [Still] connoisseurs of income policy and modern fiscal economics realize that from shortly after 1936 there grew up in America a fruitful development of the subject; not only are most of the contributions originally due to Hansen himself, but in addition many done by others have been the direct or indirect result of his inspiration.

I ought to add here that one reason to explain Hansen's importance in carrying the post-1936 ball is that America, rather than Britain, was the natural place where the Keynesian model applied: the United States was largely a closed, continental economy with an undervalued dollar that gave ample scope for autonomous macroeconomic policies; Hansen's first Harvard years of the late 1930's, when gold was flowing into this country and, as Hansen said at the time, was providing a massive controlled experiment to show the weak elasticity responses to normal easing of credit, that was the era par excellence when an approximation to Keynes's liquidity trap prevailed. On those same Monday and Friday afternoons when Hansen and Williams were holding their famous Fiscal Policy Seminars, the banks down the road were earning only 3/8 of 1 percent on their marginal assets. A student like me, even armed with a letter from his pastor, could not get a Cambridge bank to take his deposit: in the end I had to settle for a Postal Account, which could not refuse to take my money. (Incidentally, the fruitful differences of opinion between Williams and Hansen in the seminar did not at that time revolve around any differences in view between the scholars on the potency of monetary policy: John Williams was even more skeptical about the stiffness of the string on which monetary policy was to push; he used to say, "even if I believed completely in your credit worthiness and you offered me 10 percent interest, I wouldn't make you a loan." A rhetorical exaggeration, no doubt, but indicative of how badly burned bankers had been in the earlier years of the great depression.)

EARLY SYNTHESES

Keynes had Marshall and Pigou to teach him monetary theory. I had Viner, Schumpeter, Leontief, Haberler, and Hansen to teach me modern analysis. Hansen was not so lucky. The leap from a frontier homestead to the University of Wisconsin was for him the strategic quantum jump. Wisconsin was still in its most fruitful institutionalist phase under John R. Commons, Richard T. Ely, and their disciples. In terms of preparing himself for what was later to become his primary field of interest, Hansen was lucky in happening to pick business cycles as a thesis topic. This was perhaps the primary area of economic *analysis* in which the institutionalists were able to make much of a contribution.

Wesley Clair Mitchell, who called himself an institutionalist and who was indeed hostile toward economic theory (the only sure badge identifying an institutionalist), wrote his great *Business Cycles* in 1913, just as Hansen was getting enough money together to go to graduate school. The subject of cycles was so new that Mitchell's naive Baconian empiricism could play a useful role. Hansen's Ph.D. thesis seems to have been a Mitchell-like survey of monthly statistical movements here and in principal countries abroad. Fortunately, Hansen did not follow Mitchell's example to move down curves of diminishing returns in trying to let the facts tell their own story about what sometimes happens in business cycles and what sometimes does not happen.

Perhaps because of interest in his own Scandinavian background, Hansen moved away from the views fashionable in the Anglo-Saxon literature of the trade cycle. He was attracted to the Continental view that the great swings in economic activity have been of *quasi-exogenous* origin, being associated with intermittent waves of innovational activity, of population, and of over- and undershots in the process of capital formation. He had seen with his own eyes ordinary men on the frontier carried into prosperity just by virtue of being in the right place at the right time; and their brothers, no less worthy, by the luck of the draw plunged into bankruptcy and ruin.

His mentors were writers like Arthur Spiethoff (a permanent

influence) and Wicksell (who too often is remembered only for his monetary analysis of secular price disequilibrium, and not for his view that the business cycle is like a rocking horse that is set into motion by the exogenous blows of innovation and growth and that responds endogenously to those cumulative shocks according to its own *endogenous* structure and resonance); Schumpeter, Tougan-Baranowsky, Marx, Cassel, and neo-Wicksellians generally influenced Hansen in the 1920's; Dennis Robertson was perhaps the sole important writer in English who, like Hansen, looked beyond the veil of money to explain the historic rhythms of capitalism.

The Hansen of this period took on some of the faults as well as the virtues of these writers. Thus, like them, he sometimes wrote of the depression as being due to overinvestment — absolutely, or in relation to undersaving. Usually the authors were unclear on their time-period analysis, and one seemed to confront the paradox of too much investment as *weakening* contemporaneous aggregate demand! Readers had to struggle to arrive at the understandable commonplace that, if there is too much investment at one time, it may overdo things in terms of profitability and, in a regime of sticky wages, prices, and interest rates, usher in a period of low investment; it is this *subsequent* low investment that constitutes the contemporaneous depression.

His 1927 *Business Cycle Theory* is worth rereading today. It has verve and wisdom. But few readers realize that it is a redrafting of an essay submitted to win the prize offered by the Pollak Foundation for the best critique of the underconsumptionist writings of Foster and Catchings. An idiosyncratic work, inferior to Hansen's, won the first prize, but this origin of Hansen's 1927 book explains its lopsided character and overemphasis on Foster's views. Amusingly, the 1927 Hansen signs himself as a believer in Say's Law, stating that anyone who looks carefully into the debates between Malthus and Ricardo on the subject cannot fail to realize that Ricardo is the logical victor in his demonstration that unemployment due to too little purchasing power is an impossibility.[2]

---

2. A. H. Hansen, *Business Cycle Theory* (Boston: Ginn & Co., 1927), p. 101 says: "Say, Ricardo, and Mill were quite right in their insistence that overproduction is inconceivable." At the end of the work (p. 206) appears one of those famous-last-word proclamations, written just before the Great Depression set in:

> . . . the character of the business cycle is changing. The violence of the oscillations of the business cycle during the last hundred and fifty years is the result of a rapidly growing capitalism. In the end it may well be that the cycle phenomenon itself, at least in its extreme manifestations, will be seen to have been a disease which came and passed in the few swift centuries during which the world was made over from a rural, local economy to a highly industrialized world economy.

By the time of his 1932 *Economic Stabilization in an Unbalanced World,* the realities of the great depression had taught Hansen to soften his view that overproduction is impossible.

He recognizes there, in Chapter X, that wage and price rigidities may enable structural unemployment to persist. Still, on the basis of his pre-1936 writings, Hansen would have to be graded as an important but not outstanding analyst. Lest this be judged a harsh verdict, let me add that what Keynes wrote up to and through his 1930 *Treatise on Money* was enough to make him the greatest economist of a nonvintage epoch in economics; but only on the basis of his subsequent, largely unpredictable, breakthroughs in analysis can the jury of historians declare Keynes to have been the greatest economist since Adam Smith and Leon Walras.

THE SCHOLAR REBORN

I have always hazarded the guess that Hansen received his call to Harvard by miscalculation. They did not know what they were getting. And neither did he. His 1936 review of the *General Theory* must have struck a Harvard committee as an unfavorable review; only Hansen remembered it as being among the most favorable reviews that Keynes received. (Viner, Taussig, Haberler, Pigou, and even Hicks wrote reviews and commentaries that are more amusing to read in retrospect than they seemed at the time.)

On the train from Minnesota, so to speak, Hansen must have seen the light. There followed a dozen golden years of important achievements. To illustrate the wave-like character of fertility in a scholar's own life, let me mention the case of the 1948 Festschrift for Hansen's sixtieth birthday. The other editors and I tried to enlist his Minnesota as well as his Harvard students. In the end, even though he had been as long there then as at Harvard, the few that we got had all followed him to Harvard. Later when I asked him to explain the discrepancy, he hypothesized that the best students tended to bubble off to the few leading places. With respect, this is only part of the story. It was because of the great depression and *General Theory* stimulus that Hansen, wherever he might have subsequently been, attained his full stride and stature as an important scholar.

Along with discovering the incidence of tax and expenditures and other fiscal parameters upon a Keynesian system built around the multiplier, the marginal efficiency of capital, and the schedule of liquidity preference, Hansen was the first to develop the interactions between the multiplier and the accelerator. (The Minnesota visit

of Frisch in 1931 was important for Hansen's quick integration of
the acceleration principle into the Keynesian system; his review of
Harrod's 1936 *Trade Cycle* shows the prepared mind at work.) I
have recorded elsewhere how my own early reputation received
much too much credit for merely analyzing mathematically what
was essentially Hansen's own system. Hansen was able to resist
even my harmful influence. I kept insisting, rightly but misleadingly, that there was no net stimulus from the accelerator in a
multiplier model that oscillates around a horizontal trend. Hansen,
like Keynes in his famous *Eugenics Review* article,[3] realized what
Harrod and Domar were later to formalize, that in an economy of
growth the accelerator was an important factor in the genesis of
net spending stimulus or multiplicand.

Hansen's famous doctrine of impending long-term maturity or
stagnation, in consequence of declining growth rates in population,
of the exhausted frontier of abundant land and other natural resources, of possible decline in vast new capital-using innovations,
and of possible enhanced internal corporate saving — this was an
important doctrine that I never felt it necessary to make up my
mind about. When the birth rate began to rise beyond any rational
basis for prediction, Hansen early recognized the fact of it. And
it is interesting to note that such famous "refutations" of Hansen,
as that by the able George Terborgh, accepted his logic of the incidence of growth trends but denied his implicit projections of how
those trends were likely to continue to work out.

Those who have not read Hansen carefully have often misinterpreted him. He was never pessimistic about the growth potential of the system. Hansen believed productivity trends were as good
as ever, and perhaps even better. Hansen never believed we had to
stagnate: he believed that any tendency toward ineffective demand
could be offset by macroeconomic policy. Paul MacCracken,
Richard Bissell, S. Morris Livingston, and others in the wartime Department of Commerce who used Hansen's analysis without accepting his conclusions, helped provide the intellectual basis for the new
Committee for Economic Development. That Hansen's view of the
post-World War II world was the correct one — even though he
did not win the $25,000 Pabst competition — can be seen by com-
paring what happened in the postwar period to what a typical
National Bureau publication thought was going to happen.

Already in 1945 Hansen, like Beveridge, saw the need for an
incomes policy and the likelihood that full employment would bring

3. J. M. Keynes, "Some Economic Consequences of a Declining Population," *Eugenics Review* (April 1937).

with it creeping price inflation. He was uncannily accurate in his back-of-the-envelope estimates of our potential GNP in the 1945–1970 epoch. Hansen correctly predicted no end-of-the-war stagnation, correctly foreseeing that inventory restocking and inherited backlogs of demand and liquidity would ease the conversion period. (Some of his disciples were not so prescient!)

But on this occasion, my emphasis is on his analytic contributions, not on his superlative judgments in political economy. When any schoolperson today uses the familiar CC and $C+I+G$ schedules of income determination, he is merely employing a watered-down version of what Hansen was creating in the late 1930's and what some of us in his circle formalized and packaged for educational use. A good indicator of Hansen's importance to the theory of income determination is a review of the many persons who contributed to the balanced budget-multiplier theorem. Of the dozen odd persons recently shown to have played a key role, some two thirds were directly connected with Alvin Hansen. And if none of them had ever written, Hansen would in any case have been sufficient to alert the world to the crucial point involved.

Conclusion

Time must call a halt. But I should not like to end without paying a tribute to two fine men. The times were such that Alvin Hansen and John Williams could understandably have engaged in ideological and personal battle over the important issues of the time. It is much to their credit that courtesy, civility, and friendship persisted throughout. In a sense, Hansen's capacity and opportunity for undercutting the less popular doctrines of his colleague might have been the greater; students of that day could have been turned against any more conservative analyst. Neither in face-to-face confrontation nor in separate lectures did either snipe at the other.

I saw a lot of Alvin Hansen outside the classroom, but I never heard him utter a critical word about a colleague. Only years later when he was in retirement did Hansen respond to a commendatory remark I made about still another colleague, but even then the most this gentle scholar could say was that he had always regarded the person in question as in effect a "closet" Keynesian.

Hansen did not regard economics as an ego trip. To him it was the fascinating study of how to improve the lot of humanity.

Massachusetts Institute of Technology

286

In Search of the Elusive Elite

By Paul A. Samuelson

CAMBRIDGE, Mass.—Is the country run by an Eastern establishment, a coterie of academics, journalists, and businessmen somewhat removed from the mainstream of American life?

This question was brought home to me at the first meeting of economists last September in the White House. When my turn came, President Ford turned to me and said,

"Let's have an Eastern opinion on the state of the economy."

Cognizant of my education in the Big Ten, I set the record straight by beginning, "Mr. President, my Middle Western credentials are impeccable. . . ."

Still I have lived these many decades in Cambridge, Mass. And I did receive my graduate school finishing at Harvard. Perhaps Lysenko and Lamarck are right, and environment is indeed more important than heredity.

But who were my teachers at Harvard and my fellow students? Were they William Jameses and Henry Adamses? Bowditches and Gibbses? No. They were from Kansas, Iowa, Wales, Ontario, Wisconsin. . . .

I do not mean to deny that there is reality to the belief of an alien and alienated Eastern élite. Any good anthropologist will confirm that such a belief is widespread.

Not long ago I appeared on an economic outlook panel in Chicago. An esteemed colleague, who spent what Sigmund Freud and Erik Erikson would agree were his formative years in an industrial city of northern New Jersey, told a cheering business audience that it was the nervous hysteria of Wall Street and Eastern intellectuals that constituted our real problems.

It was recently brought home to me how treacherous must be any analysis of its putative validity.

Alvin Hansen, who died earlier this month, was certainly the founder and leader of an important school of economic thought and ideology. He was more than the "American Keynes," but not less. Singlehandedly, he converted a generation of Harvard (and American!) economists away from an ancient orthodoxy in macroeconomic policy.

It is no exaggeration to say that his disciples dominated the World War II Washington ideology in economics. We live in the world Hansen helped to shape.

Yet Hansen was fifty when called from Minnesota to Harvard (called there, his students used to say, by miscalculation). The son of Danish immigrants, he had to talk his father into letting him finish high school; had to teach school to finance graduations from Yankton College, South Dakota, and the University of Wisconsin.

A generation ago when I was a Guggenheim fellow, pins to mark the birthplace of all fellows were distributed pretty much uniformly over the map. By contrast, pins to mark the current location of fellows at the time they earned appointments tended to be bunched on the two coasts. As our meritocracy grinds on, a generation from now the birthplaces of Guggenheim fellows no doubt will become more bunched, a banal truth that is independent of whether you believe in the primacy of genetic nature or environmental nurture.

And yet it will continue to be the case that if a William James were to visit the college towns that serve as oases of culture and of uncomfortable ideas far from the the Atlantic Ocean—in Ames or Iowa City, Ann Arbor or East Lansing, Madison or Ripon—he would feel he had never left home.

The Internal Revenue Service gives as a rough and ready definition of legal residence the test: Domicile is where you intend to return. Alvin Hansen, who also had never left home, returned for burial last week to Viborg, S. D., to the farm his parents had homesteaded and which he still owned.

287

Alvin H. Hansen, 1887-1975

As far as political economy is concerned, the golden age of the Harvard Yard might more appropriately be called the Age of Hansen. Alvin Hansen, who died last week full of years and honors, was often called the American Keynes. But the title does not do him justice.

It is true that Hansen was the leading interpreter in America of the path-breaking and novel methods of economic analysis of John Maynard Keynes. And this is all the more remarkable since Hansen was already middle-aged when the 1936 Keynesian classic, "The General Theory of Employment, Interest and Money," was written. As the great Max Planck, himself the originator of the quantum theory in physics, has said, science makes progress funeral by funeral: the old are never converted by the new doctrines, they simply are replaced by a new generation. Hansen was an exception. He read Keynes, and disagreed. He read again, and agreed.

More important, he worked out the implications for economic policy—primarily fiscal policy, but monetary policy too—of the new Keynesian paradigms. The U.S., being an affluent and vast continental economy, turned out to be actually a more appropriate object for Keynes's new theories than his native England.

DEPRESSION THERAPY

Franklin Roosevelt was, in the beginning, not at all a Keynesian. He stumped against Hoover on a promise to balance the budget. His early braintrusters were, at their most radical, Veblenian planners as innocent of the intricacies of modern macroeconomics and econometrics as the elderly bankers they inveighed against.

By Roosevelt's second term, the facts of life had sunk in: the NRA and fireside chats would not themselves restore prosperity; planning rhetoric could not provide the monetary demand industry needed to provide jobs for the quarter of our population who were involuntarily unemployed. Budget deficits, far from being an unfortunate concomitant of the Depression, were something deliberately to be contrived if the country was to get moving again. It was Hansen, and his Harvard-trained economists, who gradually converted the President and the Congress to an understanding of these facts of economic life.

To the public at large, Alvin Hansen's fame stemmed from his theory that an affluent country like ours was likely to face a long-term problem of stagnation. The frontier with its free land was gone. (Hansen, brought up on the farm in South Dakota that his Danish parents had homesteaded, understood the significance of this.)

Along with growth of land, Hansen's dynamic version of the Keynesian system required, for its vigorous balance of saving and investment, buoyant growth in population. Yet to informed demographers, the pre-World War II evidence pointed toward a continued decline in birth rates and rates of population growth. Finally, Hansen and his Harvard colleague Joseph Schumpeter stressed the role of innovation and invention in providing the motives for private investment spending. Scanning the record on corporate saving to provide internal sources of finance, on capital-saving as against labor-saving techno-logical change, Hansen formulated his doctrine of possible long-run stag-nation under undiluted capitalism.

FISCAL Rx FOR MATURITY

This message made Hansen unpop-ular in conservative circles. Few love the prophets of doom. But even more unpopular is a prophet who proposes that the government do something about the problems he warns against. Hansen was the militant apostle of positive fiscal policy, both to stabilize the ups and downs of the business cycle and to maintain long-run bal-ance of full-employment saving and investment.

World War II banished all these concerns for a time. Alvin Hansen was one of the honorable few who correct-ly foresaw that the end of the war would not bring mass unemployment, but instead a restocking boom. And Hansen was one of the first to dis-cern—no less than 30 years ago!—that no mixed economy can simultaneous-ly have full employment, steady price levels and free-market wage and price determination.

Hansen lived to see his vision ful-filled. The Employment Act of 1946, which put the government on record as responsible for job opportunity, is his permanent legacy.

288

The 1972 Nobel Prize for Economic Science

In the fourth awarding of this new honor, the committee of the Swedish Royal Academy of Science continues to emphasize scholarly achievement within the discipline of political economy rather than more popular and direct influence on policy. Two distinguished theorists share the award: Sir John Hicks (born in 1904), emeritus Oxford professor [and earlier holder of academic posts at the London School of Economics (LSE) and at the Universities of Cambridge and of Manchester]; and Kenneth J. Arrow (born in 1921), now at Harvard but long the sparkplug of a brilliant group of economists at Stanford University.

Although the citation groups the two "for their contributions to general equilibrium," each has done quite different work in this common field. And, although the citation properly points out the difference in their ages, informed scholars are aware that Hicks continues to make contributions of the first rank, just as he has been doing for 40 years.

Arrow is one of the new breed who come to economics with good training in economics and statistics. Hicks, who read PPE (Politics, Philosophy, and Economics) at Oxford, is self-taught and necessarily more intuitive and heuristic (1).

Both men made their first breakthroughs just before the age of 30: In the case of Hicks (2), *The Theory of Wages* (1932) and (with R. G. D. Allen in 1934) research in demand theory that culminated in *Value and Capital* (1939); in the case of Arrow (3), his Impossibility Theorem for Ideal Democratic Resolution of Divergent Preferences (1949–1951), and in 1952 his revolutionary reformulation of the theory of risk by means of the concept of contingent securities. In this age when patronage of pure science by government and foundations is much discussed, it is worth noting that Arrow's social welfare theories first saw the light of day as Rand Corporation memos; the finished form *Social Values and Individual Choices* (1951) appeared as a Cowles Foundation monograph at the University of Chicago; his 1952 risk breakthrough was aided by an Office of Naval Research grant.

I can only sample typical researches by such prolific authors. I begin with Hicks.

Dynamics of the Distribution of Income

In the *Theory of Wages*, Hicks supposes real gross national product (GNP), Q, to be subject to neoclassical models of distribution:

$$Q = Q(V)$$
$$= Q(V_1, V_2, \ldots),$$
$$= \lambda^{-1} Q(\lambda V), \qquad \text{a concave function}$$

first-degree homogeneity

$$= \sum_1^n V_j \partial Q(V) / \partial V_j,$$

Euler's theorem

$$w_i = \partial Q(V) / \partial V_i,$$

marginal-product factor pricing

$$\alpha_i = \{V_i \partial Q(V)/\partial V_i\}/Q(V),$$

relative factor shares in GNP

Here, (w_j) are the real prices of the respective (V_j) factors; w_1 is the real wage of labor, V_1; w_2 is the rent of land, or (as Hicks tells us he now regrets as oversimplified) w_2 is the interest rate of some homogeneous aggregate of capital V_2.

For the most part Hicks worked with labor and capital only. He correctly perceived that capitalism has shown greater growth of capital than of labor. Without technical change, he verifies that the interest or profit rate would fall, and the real wage rise—this by virtue of

$$\partial^2 Q/\partial V_i^2 < 0 < \partial^2 Q/\partial V_i \partial V_j$$

What happens to property's relative share in GNP, $\alpha_2 = (V_2 \partial Q/\partial V_2)/Q$ as V_2/V_1 grows? Hicks shows that α_2 will fall, rise, or stay the same, depending upon whether his newly defined "elasticity of substitution,"

$$\sigma = (\partial Q/\partial V_1)(\partial Q/\partial V_2)/Q\partial^2 Q/\partial V_1 \partial V_2)$$

is less than, greater than, or equal to unity. (Implicitly, Hicks seemed to believe $\sigma < 1$.)

Even more important is his analysis of how technical invention affects distribution. Put a technical change parameter, t, in $Q(V_1, V_2; t)$ with $\partial Q/\partial t > 0$. Then its effect on relative shares depends, Hicks shows, on whether invention is labor-saving or capital-saving; that is on whether

$$\partial/\partial t\{(\partial Q/\partial V_2)/(\partial Q/\partial V_1)\}$$

is greater than or less than zero.

Hicks develops the notion of Marx that, every time capital accumulation tends to raise labor's share, this induces labor-saving technological research and development—with the result that the relative share in GNP of

wages has been remarkably constant (the so-called Bowley's Law).

Pure Theory of Demand

The analytical core of *Value and Capital* defies brief synopsis. Without having known of E. Slutsky's 1915 work in Italian, Hicks built consumer-demand theory on the behavioristic basis of "The Batch of goods A preferred to Batch of goods B," with no attempt to say "There exists numerical utility, $U(X^A) = U(x_1^A, x_2^A, \ldots)$, which is greater than $U(X^B)$."

But now what happens to our commonsense notions: "Coffee and tea are *substitute* goods. Tea and lemon are *complementary* goods." The old test fails: "If the sum of increments of utility that I get from experiments that increase but one good at a time exceeds the increment of utility I get from increasing both goods *together*—then (like tea and coffee) they are *substitute* goods."

Hicks ingeniously proposed an alternative behavioristic test: "Raise the price of coffee and raise the consumer's income just enough to leave him as well off as before. If the amount bought of tea now goes up, tea and coffee are *substitutes*; if the amount of cream goes down, cream and coffee are *complements*." Then, just as Clerk Maxwell had proved reciprocity relations in thermodynamics (dependent on $\partial^2 E/\partial V \partial S \equiv \partial^2 E/\partial S \partial V$), Hicks proves that

$$(\partial x_i/\partial P_j)_v \equiv (\partial x_j/\partial P_i)_v$$

that is, if tea is a substitute for coffee, coffee must be a substitute for tea.

All this he applies to bonds and stocks as well as consumption goods, contributing to the revolutionary advances in business cycle control that we associate with Keynes's *General Theory of Money, Interest and Employment*.

Existence of General Equilibrium and Its Dynamic Stability

Before describing what I regard as Arrow's two greatest analytical contributions, let me connect some of his work with that of Hicks. Hicks reduced the general equilibrium of production and exchange of n goods to the following homogeneous-of-degree-zero net demand functions involving prices, $P = (p_1, \ldots, p_n)$

$$0 = - F(P) = - f_j[p_1, \ldots, p_n] \equiv - F[\lambda P]$$

He demonstrated that a unique solution to price ratios, P^*/p_1^*, would be assured if everyone always spent each extra dollar of income in the same way.

In that case, I and others proved that the system would be dynamically stable, in the sense that the following algorithm of price formation would converge to P^*/p^*

$$\dot{P} = (\dot{p}_j) = (- k_j f_j[P] = - KF[P]$$
$$\lim_{t \to \infty} P(t)/ P(t) = P^*/p_1^*, \quad \text{for any } P(0) > 0$$

Here K is a diagonal matrix with positive, but arbitrary, k_j elements.

Arrow, in collaboration with Leonid Hurwicz of the University of Minnesota, explored global stability when the Jacobian matrix $[\partial f_i/\partial p_j] = F'[P]$ is not symmetric but does have positive off-diagonal elements.

Arrow, in accordance with the new tradition stemming from topological work by A. Wald and J. von Neumann, went beyond the mere counting of equations and unknowns in $F[P] = 0$. The question of the existence of at least one equilibrium solution, P^*, had to be explored in terms of the use of inequalities, usually involving delicate fixed-point theorems of the type developed by Brouwer and Kakutani. Collaborating with G. Debreu, Arrow not only established such existence and uniqueness theorems for positivistic sys-

tems, but also for normative formulations of how a system should optimally function.

I shall briefly refer to Arrow's work in the area of risk and decision theory, as summarized in his collected papers on the subject. In 1952, he stated for the first time the necessity for optimal allocation of risk-bearing of so-called Arrow-Debreu contingent-securities (which pay different returns depending on which one of all possible contingent states of the world materialize).

I conclude with an indication of what is involved in his celebrated Impossibility Theorem, which is to mathematical politics something like what Gödel's 1931 impossibility theorem is to mathematical logic.

Imagine 3 (or more) states: for example, Taft is elected President in 1912, Wilson is elected, Roosevelt is elected. Imagine 3 (or more) individuals, each of whom has a preference ordering of these states. Thus, $(WRT)_1$ means man 1 prefers Wilson to Roosevelt or Taft, and Roosevelt to Taft.

Arrow asks: Given *any* 3 of the $(3!)^3$ choices for $(\quad)_1, (\quad)_2, (\quad)_3$, how can we define a social preference ordering, call it $(\quad)_0$, that obeys a few appealing axioms? (Thus, each man's vote is sometime to count. If Roosevelt dies or lives, *that* should not affect choice between Taft and Wilson. And so forth.)

He then proves by elegant reasoning that it would involve a self-contradiction for there to be a solution satisfying all of these appealing axioms.

Aristotle must be turning over in his grave. The theory of democracy can never be the same (actually, it never was!) since Arrow.

The Scientists' Way

Scholars make their primary contribution through their writings. We judge them as men by their influence on students and co-workers. Both Hicks and Arrow have been blessed in this regard, and have shed blessing.

For sociologists of science, like R. K. Merton, Hicks and Arrow each demonstrate that one need not be at the outstanding university of the moment to make one's scientific mark. Hicks, at LSE and Manchester, helped elevate those places to distinction in economics. Stanford gave Arrow his chance before he was famous. He rewarded it by creating the Stanford school of economic theorists. It says something for academic life that both men were recognized as being deserving of the most prestigious academic posts, and were able to exercise choice among numerous opportunities.

PAUL A. SAMUELSON
Massachusetts Institute of Technology, Cambridge 02139

Notes

1. Sir Roy Allen is said to have told the story of how, when Hicks asked him about determinants—no doubt matrices were still too esoteric—he lent Hicks Netto's little book on the subject, and in three weeks Hicks had worked out the essence of *Value and Capital*, his magnum opus. Even if the anecdote is not literally exact, it is well told.

2. A Hicks bibliography, complete through 1968, appears in J. N. Wolfe, Ed., *Papers in Honor of Sir John Hicks, Value, Capital and Growth* (Edinburgh University Press, Edinburgh, 1968), pp. 531–537. Important items are *Theory of Wages* (1932, 1963), *Value and Capital* (1939, 1946), *The Social Framework: An Introduction to Economics* (1942, 1952, 1960), *A Contribution to the Theory of the Trade Cycle* (1950), *A Revision of Demand Theory* (1956), *Capital and Growth* (1965), *A Theory of Economic History* (1969), and various collections of articles, such as *Essays in World Economics* (1959), and *Critical Essays in Monetary Theory* (1967).

3. A selected bibliography for Arrow would include *Social Choice and Individual Values* (1951, 1963), *Essays in the Theory of Risk Bearing* (1971), *Studies in Linear and Non-Linear Programming* (1958, with co-authors L. Hurwicz and H. Uzawa), *Studies in Mathematical Theory of Inventory and Production* (1958, with co-authors S. Karlin and H. Scarf), *Public Investment, The Rate of Return, and Optimal Fiscal Policy* (1970, with co-author M. Kurz), and *General Competitive Analysis* (1971, with co-author F. H. Hahn).

289

Pioneers of Economic Theory

Future Legislation May Grow Out of Their Writings

By PAUL A. SAMUELSON

Sir John Hicks of Oxford and Kenneth Arrow of Harvard are essentially "economists' economists." Neither writes for the popular press or runs for political office. But their esoteric-appearing writings provide the new theoretical systems out of which legislation of the future will be shaped. Hicks's magnum opus, "Value and Capital," was published back in 1939 when Arrow was still an earnest student at C.C.N.Y. The book bristles with mathematical equations. The equations are misleadingly penned into an appendix ghetto, but their spirit permeates the innocent-looking pages of text.

An Appraisal

Hicks's chapter heads may quote from Milton and Congreve and Hardy, but that will not serve to wash out one row of his determinants or resolve the definiteness of his quadratic forms.

"Value and Capital" established for the first time the general properties of the economic market system. Every tyro knows that a plentiful apple crop will probably send down the price of apples. But once we are faced with hundreds and thousands of commodities, who is to say that all things are not possible—includ-ing even the possibility that the price of apples will rise in a plentiful crop!

What Could Be Predicted

Sir John (then, austerely J.R.) showed what could and could not be predicted for a general equilibrium system.

In science, a culmination is a beginning. When the young Arrow came to economics in the late nineteen-forties—at Columbia, Chicago, and ultimately at Stanford where he made his great contributions — he faced problems opened up by the Hicksian breakthroughs: How can the economic system handle risk? Granted that there exists a system of prices that will clear the interconnected market for goods and securities, can we be sure that real live people, starting from scratch, will be ablet to find their way dynamically to that equilibrium?

It was as if Hicks was the Archimedes who established the stationary equilibrium of a pendulum's bob. What was needed was a Newton who could rationalize the oscillations of the pendulum around its way to equilibrium.

Different Backgrounds

C. P. Snow has written of the two cultures—the humanities and the sciences. At first glance, Hicks represents the older culture of the humanities, the urbane, purposely stuttering Oxford don. Arrow is the mathematicially trained wave of the future — at home in Russell's logic and von Neumann's game theory, rather than steeped in the poetry of Eliot and Pound.

But this is to do an injustice to both men. Hicks is better regarded as the last of the intuitionists — the self-trained generation of mathematical economists. (When he asked his friend R. G. D. Allen, what these new-fangled determinants were that apparently his new theories required, Allen lent him a slim German book by Netto on determinants and matrices—and in a few weeks, Hicks had worked out "Value and Capital"!)

Kenneth Arrow came to economics with a good grounding in mathematics and statistics. His two greatest contributions, I think, were those written when he was just about 30 years of age—his revolutionary formulation of welfare economics, and his path-breaking theory of risk. The first is not only a stellar contribution to economics, it is as well a breakthrough for political science and, I would dare assert, for philosophy itself.

Paradox of Voting

Men have always sought ideal democracy—the perfect voting system.

Aristotle, Hobbes, Calhoun, and Jim Farley have grappled with the question of how big a majority must be for its decisions to be decisive. But profound minds have known for centuries the paradox of voting. Just as Harvard may beat Yale at football, and Yale beat Princeton, but Princeton beat Harvard, the same may happen in a three-man election.

As in 1912 between Woodrow Wilson, William Howard Taft and Theodore Roosevelt, suppose each third of the population has the preference orderings: W T R, R W T, T R W.

Who wins the election? Run Wilson against Taft, and Wilson wins. Run Wilson against Roosevelt, and Roosevelt wins. But run Roosevelt against Taft, and Taft wins! What is needed, you will think, is a new genius to invent a voting system that will banish forever such ties and eliminate the possibility of manipulating the outcome by rearranging the order of choice.

What Kenneth Arrow proved once and for all is that there cannot possibly be found such an ideal voting scheme: The search of the great minds of recorded history for the perfect democracy, it turns out, is the search for a chimera, for a logical self-contradiction.

Arrow's argument is beautiful, but difficult. (It used to be said that only 10 men understood Einstein's theory of Relativity. That was an exaggeration. But it is no exaggeration to say that only a score of scholars were able to follow Arrow's early researchers in these esoteric fields.)

Now scholars all over the world—in mathematics, politics, philosopsy, and economics —are engaged in trying to salvage what can be salvaged from Arrow's devastating discovery that is to mathematical politics what Godel's 1931 impossibility-of-proving-consistency theorem is to mathemat-

In the field of risk, people knew before Arrow that General Mills can benefit from hedging the wheat it holds in inventory by selling futures on the Chicago Board of Trade. What Arrow discovered was that, to get a perfect hedge, you must be able to set up a different market for every outcome of the chancey world—a separate market and security or contract, in case it rains in the eastern Midwest and McGovern wins, etc.

The economics of insurance, medical care, prescription drug testing—to say nothing of bingo and the stock market—will never be the same after Arrow.

290

NOBEL LAUREATE LEONTIEF

It used to be said that only twelve men in the world understood Einstein's theory of relativity, and all but one were Germans. Actually, that was an overstatement. But it did illustrate how rarely the general public can grasp the intricacies of a great scientist's work.

Wassily Leontief of Harvard has just been awarded the Nobel Prize in Economics for 1973. This is richly deserved for his pioneering work on the input-output structure of an economy's industries. Input-output is a fairly complicated statistical technique for analyzing both the anatomy and the physiology of the economy. Beyond its value as a tool of description, it is valuable as a device for prediction and for planning. On the theory that what one fool can learn so can another, let me try to explain the simple logic of input-output.

It takes labor and iron to produce coal. But to produce iron, along with labor, it takes coal. Don't we have a vicious logical circle here? Coal depends upon iron; but iron depends on coal.

No. There is circular interdependence. But the circle is a virtuous one. It can be resolved by solving the simultaneous equations of your high-school algebra class. (Recall Jack and Jill. Jill is half Jack's age. Jack is five years older than Jill. No vicious circle here. Since Jill will double her age in five years, she must now be 5; knowing that, we calculate Jack to be 10. We've just solved two simultaneous equations by eliminating one of the unknowns—Jack's age—through a clever substitution, ending up with one easy equation for the one remaining unknown—Jill's age.)

They give $120,000 in Nobel Prizes for this? Wait. Note the immensity of Leontief's statistical estimations.

THE GRAND TABLEAU

What Leontief did was to break down the aggregate gross national product into manageable industry sub-aggregates. At first he worked with but ten industries: agriculture, manufacturing, transportation, government, etc. From actual data, he measured how much each needs of the other per dollar of flow. To make the problem statistically manageable, he made the heroically simplifying assumption: when we shift from war to peace, from isolation to free trade, the ratio of inputs that any industry needs from other industries will remain either constant or will change according to trends that can be recognized and estimated.

Ten by ten coefficients is bad enough. But by the time he had data on 100 by 100 industries and 400 by 400, the number of his coefficients began to run in the hundreds of thousands; and the number of operations needed to solve them simultaneously to run in the millions. The giant calculator was invented just in time. And Leontief has been its leading customer.

Moreover, so far I have been describing only the Model T statistical version of Leontief's input-output. In recent years, he and his team—aided by grants from foundations, the Bureau of Labor Statistics, the National Science Foundation—have built a dynamic version that calculates the investment needs of an economy growing at various projected rates.

FRUITS OF SCIENCE

A prophet is with even greater honor outside his own country. The United Nations, the World Bank, government agencies in Scandinavia and Western Europe, the five-year plans of the developing countries—all have taken up input-output budgeting.

The supreme compliment came when the U.S.S.R. decided that input-output is OK (in Auden's verse, what is not forbidden is required) and, like wireless, is really a Russian invention after all. Since Leontief was part of the earlier wave of emigrant scientists who have enriched American scholarship, this nationalistic predating of the record is harmless enough.

I list some uses of input-output:
■ After the Indochina war, what will be the effects on total employment and on skill requirements of a shift of $1 billion of GNP from war to peace purposes? (Leontief's result, an *expansion* of employment, must have specially delighted him, since he is one of the exceptions to the rule that as a scholar grows older he becomes more reactionary.)
■ Leontief was the first to discover that U.S. exports are relatively more *labor intensive* than our imports—a paradox since reconfirmed.
■ Congress used his tableau to detect the great weight of steel-price hikes on the 1950s cost-push inflation.

I could go on for pages. A great scholar's work is never done.

291

Nobel Choice:
Economists in Contrast

The following article was written by Paul A. Samuelson, professor of economics at the Massachusetts Institute of Technology, who was awarded the Nobel Memorial Prize in Economic Science in 1970.

Economists all over the world will think it a happy choice of the Swedish Royal Academy of Science to have selected Gunnar Myrdal and Friedrich A. von Hayek for this year's Nobel Memorial Prize in Economic Sci-

An Appraisal

ence. Although both men were said to have been selected primarily for their stellar contributions to monetary analysis—macroeconomics as it came later to be called—each has made outstanding contributions in the wider realms of policy and the social sciences.

In no sense has their work been joint. Indeed, their policy conclusions, if followed literally would be at loggerheads and self-cancelling.

Dr. von Hayek's 1931 work on business cycles, "Prices and Production," concluded that excess civic expansion and deficit spending by Government plus central bank money creation were the roots of all evil.

Non-Intervention Sought

The best cure for the Depression was to sweat it out.

The worst thing, Dr. von Hayek and his Austrian School counterparts believed, was for the government to provide unemployment compensation and other supplements to consumers' incomes, for that would merely put off the bitter day of reckoning and only worsen the "under saving" that the economist thought was the villanous cause of every depression.

By contrast, Dr. Myrdal's "Monetary Equilbrium," written at about the same time, was an important anticipation by the Stockholm School of John Maynard Keynes' "General Theory," published in 1936. Dr. Myrdal has been anything but a believer in laissez-faire, having been an important architect of the Swedish Labor Party's welfare state.

Just as Dr. von Hayek has had to pine for a return to the 19th century Whig era of limited government, Dr. Myrdal has seen his heart's desire realized.

Even his important work alerting Sweden to the imminence of population decline, done jointly with his wife, Alva Myrdal, herself a leading scholar, ambassador, and cabinet officer, has turned out after a wartime booming of population to be prescient of present day trends.

Fear of Favoritism

The Swedish academy´ is

apparently very zealous to keep its Nobel awards "scientific." Although Dr. Myrdal might have received one of the first few awards, they no doubt felt that such a decision might smack of provincial favoritism.

Moreover, it is often charged that such award-granting committees are influenced by political beliefs, so that a "liberal" like Jan Timbergen of the Netherlands stands a better chance than a free-market "conservative" like Milton Friedman.

This may explain the coupling together of the interventionist do-gooder Dr. Myrdal with the unreconstructed Dr. von Hayek, who argued in his best-selling book "The Road to Serfdom," that mild piecemeal reforms lead inevitably to the totalitarian hell of Hitler and Stalin.

The citation that goes with the awards seems to have gone out of its way not to stress the roles of these two great scholars as ideologists. But one remembers that when Einstein was finally given his Nobel Prize in the early nineteen-twenties, the citation went out of its way to exclude relativity, a fact hat did not escape his proud notice when he chose to give his official Nobel lecture on that topic.

Personal Contrasts

Both of this year's winners are great and prolific scholars, whose activities continue at an intense rate although both are in their seventies, but they are of quite different temperaments.

Dr. Myrdal is anything but the taciturn, emotionless Swede: his volubility would do credit to any Viennese coffee house.

Dr. von Hayek, by contrast, is reserved, possessed of an Old World courtliness, displaying emotion oniy in the skillful editing of the love letters of John Stuart Mill and Harriet Taylor. Although Dr. von Hayek held a chair for many years at the London School of Economics and answered to Chancellor Robert Hutchins's call to pursue philosophy and economics at the Uuniversity of Chicago, when he began to approach the retirement age he preferred to go back to a lifetime chair in a European university.

Dr. Myrdal seems a continental by accident; Dr. von Hayek, who is a kinsman of the great philosopher Ludwig Wittgenstein, always seemed more of a visitor in the Anglo-Saxon world, even when being honored by the British Academy.

Bridge to Socialists

At the time of the Marshall Plan, when the cold war seemed to be opening the divide between Western and Eastern Europe ever further, Dr. Myrdal, as head of the United Nations for Europe, provided an important bridge with the Eastern Socialist countries. He gathered to his headquarters in Geneva such brilliant economists as Lord Nicholas Kaldor of England and Walt Whitman Rostow of the United States.

Throughout his life, Gunnar Myrdal has been carrying on a lover's quarrel with the United States; even in his majesterial 1944 study of our racial problem, an "American Dilemma" he has held up to us the American credo in which we profess belief but too often honor in rhetoric only.

Perhaps a bit bored with the perfections of the affluent Swedish welfare state, Dr. Myrdal has turned his attention in recent years to criticism of mainstream economics and to the problems of economic development in southeast Asia.

India, Bangladesh. and Pakistan present problems intrinsicly more difficult than those of the advanced world. Time and again the believer in the use of social intelligence had to point out the emptiness of much of what goes by the name of governmental planning.

Debate on Allocation

Before World War II there was a great debate as to whether there could be rational allocation of economic resources under Socialism.

The late Ludwig von Mises said no. The late Oskar Lange of Poland, and Abba P. Lerner, transplanted to our shores from Britain, seemed to win the debate by pointing out that the planners might hope to use the market-pricing tools of the capitalistic order, but purged of its monopolistic and profit-seeking imperfections.

Friedrich von Hayek provided the important rebuttal that we live in a world of uncertainty; decentralized enterprise, he suggested, is an efficent way of having each individual bring his little quantum of information into useful play.

Anyone who overhears the current discussion in the law schools of America on the relationship of information to contracts, torts, and public regulation will appreciate that the Hayekian contribution lives on.

The 1974 joint Nobel award underscores the need in political economy for tolerance and eclecticism.

Milton Friedman

The economics profession has long expected that Milton Friedman would win the Nobel Prize in Economics. His 1976 award is fitting recognition of his scientific contributions and his scholarly leadership.

There is no need for me to describe in these columns his important views as a conservative economist. His own words speak eloquently for themselves.

What I have to emphasize is that Friedman is the *architect* of much that is best in our conservative tradition and not merely the *expositor* of that viewpoint. Furthermore, the adjective "conservative" does not do proper justice to a thinker who would refuse the steel industry its import quotas, strip Texas of its oil subsidies and deprive the railroads and the trucking interests of their protective regulations.

Why is Milton Friedman "an economist's economist"? Let me point out the ways.

CURRICULUM VITAE

He started as an undergraduate student of Arthur Burns at Rutgers. No bad beginning. He went on to become a graduate-student star at Columbia and Chicago.

The "Chicago School," with its emphasis on human freedoms and the efficiency of market pricing, can be said to have been founded by Frank Knight, his revered teacher. Under Friedman it has been led to new heights of influence and profundity.

MIT, Harvard, Oxford and every topnotch economics department would today feel deprived and one-sided if the fruitful Chicago viewpoint were not represented on its faculty. This new fact is a tribute to one great leader.

Scholars are known by their original scientific discoveries. Friedman early made his mark in statistics and mathematical economics. Without being a Keynesian, he pioneered early budgetary measurements of income-consumption patterns and taught our wartime Treasury how to reduce the inflationary gap. Abraham Wald's great breakthrough in the statistical technique called "sequential analysis" stemmed in part from Friedman's realization that it is not necessary to finish testing every egg to infer that a batch is bad. Does this seem simple? So now does Newton's falling apple.

If it pays to reduce risk by insuring, how at the same time can it pay to increase risk by backing long shots? Friedman (with L.J. Savage) provided an answer. Also, Friedman (with Simon Kuznets, Nobel laureate 1971) first analyzed and measured "human capital," the investment we make in our medical and other education and the interest return on this investment.

Do not the rich save more from each dollar than the poor? If so, redistributing income from rich to poor will raise consumption spending and stimulate business. Friedman's investigation of "the *permanent income* hypothesis" revealed that, once we get used to being permanently at a higher income, we in fact save *much the same fraction* of income! That this finding stood up so well to adversary attack demonstrated his Nobel caliber.

Of course it is monetarism that marks Friedman's lifework of the last twenty years. His monumental "A Monetary History of the United States 1867-1960," written with Anna Schwartz, clinched his international reputation.

MISSIONS ACCOMPLISHED

The story the facts tell Friedman is that the price level is determined in the long run by the quantity of money. Contrary to the view of 1939 Keynesians and the stubborn 1959 view of many English economists, the short-run changes in the money supply provide the one factor reliably related to half the variance in nominal GNP changes. The rest being primarily noise, M growth is the only such significant factor. From this follows his basic prescription: *Keep aggregate M growth constant.*

What I have failed to convey is Milton Friedman's bounce and gaiety, his rapier intelligence, his unfailing courtesy in debate. The world admires him for his achievements. His intimates love him for himself.

The fact that he and I, despite our policy disagreements and scientific differences, have remained good friends over 40 years says something perhaps about us, but even more I dare to think about political economy as a science.

CONTENTS

Volume I

Contents

Contents of Volume II

Acknowledgments

CONTENTS

Volume II

Book Three
Trade, Welfare, and Fiscal Policy

Contents

CONTENTS

Volume III

Contents

Part IV. On Ricardo and Marx

Book Four

Economics and Public Policy

Part XII.   Pure Theory of Public Expenditure

Part XIII.   Principles of Fiscal and Monetary Policy

Part XIV.   The Individual and the State

Book Five

Economics—Past and Present

Contents

Contents of Volumes I and II

Acknowledgments

Index

ACKNOWLEDGMENTS

The author, editors, and The MIT Press wish to thank the publishers of the following essays for permission to reprint them here. The selections are arranged chronologically, with cross references in brackets to the chapter numbers used in this collection.

Foreword to *The Retreat From Riches: Affluence and Its Enemies*, ed. by Peter Passell and Leonard Ross (New York: Viking Press, Inc., 1971). Copyright 1971, 1972, 1973 by Leonard Ross and Peter Passell. Reprinted by permission of The Viking Press. [Chapter 272]

"Reflections on the Merits and Demerits of Monetarism," in J. J. Diamond, ed., *Issues in Fiscal and Monetary Policy: The Eclectic Economist Views the Controversy* (Chicago: DePaul University, 1971), pp. 7–21. Copyright © 1971 by DePaul University. [Chapter 264]

"Paradoxes of Schumpeter's Zero Interest Rate," *The Review of Economics and Statistics*, Vol. LIII, No. 4 (November 1971), pp. 391–392. Copyright 1971 by the President and Fellows of Harvard College. [Chapter 217]

"Ohlin Was Right," *The Swedish Journal of Economics*, Vol. 73, No. 4 (December 1971), pp. 365–384. [Chapter 254]

"Jacob Viner, 1892–1970," *The Journal of Political Economy*, Vol. 80, No. 1 (January/February 1972), pp. 5–11. Copyright 1972 by the University of Chicago. [Chapter 282]

"Liberalism At Bay," *Social Research*, Vol. 39, No. 1 (Spring 1972), pp. 16–31. Copyright 1972 by New School for Social Research. [Chapter 277]

"The Economics of Marx: An Ecumenical Reply," *Journal of Economic Literature*, Vol. X, No. 1 (March 1972), pp. 51–57. Copyright © 1972 by The American Economic Association. [Chapter 227]

"Proof That Unsuccessful Speculators Confer Less Benefit to Society Than Their Losses," *Proceedings of the National Academy of Sciences, U.S.A.*, Vol. 69, No. 5 (May 1972), pp. 1230–1233. [Chapter 260]

"Samuelson on the Neoclassical Dichotomy: A Reply," *The Canadian Journal of Economics*, Vol. V, No. 2 (May 1972), pp. 284–292. © Canadian Economics Association/Association canadienne d'Economique 1972. [Chapter 265]

"Frank Knight, 1885–1972," *Newsweek* (July 31, 1972), p. 55. Copyright 1972, by Newsweek, Inc. All rights reserved. Reprinted by permission. [Chapter 283]

"The General Saddlepoint Property of Optimal-Control Motions," *Journal of Economic Theory*, Vol. 5, No. 1 (August 1972), pp. 102–120. Copyright © 1972 by Academic Press, Inc. [Chapter 223]

"International Trade for a Rich Country," (Stockholm: Federation of Swedish Industries, August 1972). Copyright 1972 by Paul A. Samuelson. [Chapter 250]

"The Consumer Does Benefit From Feasible Price Stability," *The Quarterly Journal of Economics*, Vol. LXXXVI, No. 3 (August 1972), pp. 476–493. Copyright 1972 by the President and Fellows of Harvard College. [Chapter 261]

"Rejoinder," *The Quarterly Journal of Economics*, Vol. LXXXVI, No. 3 (August 1972), pp. 500–503. Copyright 1972 by the President and Fellows of Harvard College. [Chapter 262]

"Mathematics of Speculative Price," in R. H. Day and S. M. Robinson, eds., *Mathematical Topics in Economic Theory and Computation* (Philadelphia: Society for Industrial and Applied Mathematics, 1972), pp. 1–42. [Chapter 240]

"Economics in a Golden Age: A Personal Memoir," in G. Holton, ed., *The Twentieth-Century Sciences: Studies in the Biography of Ideas* (New York: W. W. Norton and Co., Inc., 1972). [Chapter 278]

"Heretical Doubts About the International Mechanisms," *Journal of International Economics*, Vol. 2, No. 4 (September 1972), pp. 443–454. © North-Holland Publishing Company, 1971. [Chapter 256]

"Unification Theorem for the Two Basic Dualities of Homothetic Demand Theory," *Proceedings of the National Academy of Sciences, U.S.A.*, Vol. 69, No. 9 (September 1972), pp. 2673–2674. [Chapter 212]

"Pioneers in Economic Thought," *The New York Times* (October 26, 1972), p. 71. © 1972 by The New York Times Company. Reprinted by permission. [Chapter 289]

"The 1972 Nobel Prize for Economic Science," *Science*, Vol. 178 (November 3, 1972), pp. 487–489. Copyright 1972 by the American Association for the Advancement of Science. [Chapter 288]

"Samuelson's 'Reply on Marxian Matters,' " *Journal of Economic Literature*, Vol. XI, No. 1 (March 1973), pp. 64–68. Copyright © 1973 by The American Economic Association. [Chapter 228]

"From GNP to NEW," *Newsweek* (April 9, 1973), p. 102. Copyright 1973, by Newsweek, Inc. All rights reserved. Reprinted by permission. [Chapter 259]

"A Quantum Theory Model of Economics: Is the Coordinating Entrepreneur Just Worth His Profit?," Chapter 18 in J. Bhagwati and R. S. Eckaus, eds., *Development and Planning, Essays in Honour of Paul Rosenstein-Rodan* (London: John Allen and Unwin, Ltd., 1973), pp. 329–335. [Chapter 214]

"Deadweight Loss in International Trade from the Profit Motive?," in C. F. Bergsten and W. G. Tyler, eds., *Leading Issues in International Economic Policy, Essays in Honor of George N. Halm* (Lexington, Mass.: Lexington Books, D. C. Heath and Co., 1973), pp. 149–154. [Chapter 253]

"Optimality of Profit-Including Prices Under Ideal Planning: Marx's Model," *Proceedings of the National Academy of Sciences, U.S.A.*, Vol. 70, No. 7 (July 1973), pp. 2109–2111. [Chapter 226]

"Economics of Sex: A Discussion," Joint Economic Committee, 93rd Congress, 1st Session, *Economic Problems of Women*, July 10, 1973. (Washington: U.S. Government Printing Office, 1973), pp. 58–64. [Chapter 269]

"Relative Shares and Elasticities Simplified: Comment," *The American Economic Review*, Vol. 63, No. 4 (September 1973), pp. 770–771. Copyright © 1973 by The American Economic Association. [Chapter 213]

"Proof That Properly Discounted Present Values of Assets Vibrate Randomly," *The Bell Journal of Economics*, Vol. 4, No. 2 (Autumn 1973), pp. 369–374. Copyright © 1973, American Telephone and Telegraph Company. [Chapter 241]

"Nobel Laureate Leontief," *Newsweek* (November 5, 1973), p. 94. Copyright 1973, by Newsweek, Inc. All rights reserved. Reprinted by permission. [Chapter 290]

"Is the Rent-Collector Worthy of His Full Hire?," *Eastern Economic Journal*, Vol. I, No. 1 (January 1974), pp. 7–10. © Eastern Economic Association 1974. [Chapter 263]

"Insight and Detour in the Theory of Exploitation: A Reply to Baumol," *Journal of Economic Literature*, Vol. XII, No. 1 (March 1974), pp. 62–70. Copyright © 1974 by The American Economic Association. [Chapter 229]

"Rejoinder: 'Merlin Unclothed, A Final Word,'" *Journal of Economic Literature*, Vol. XII, No. 1 (March 1974), pp. 75–77. Copyright © 1974 by The American Economic Association. [Chapter 230]

"Generalized Mean-Variance Tradeoffs For Best Perturbation Corrections to Approximate Portfolio Decisions," *The Journal of Finance*, Vol. XXIX, No. 1 (March 1974), pp. 27–30. Copyright 1974 by the American Finance Association. [Chapter 246]

"Scale Economies and Non-Labor Returns at the Optimum Population," *Eastern Economic Journal*, Vol. I, Nos. 1 and 2 (April/June 1974), pp. 125–127. © Eastern Economic Association 1974. [Chapter 238]

With R. C. Merton, "Fallacy of the Log-Normal Approximation to Optimal Portfolio Decision-Making Over Many Periods," *Journal of Financial Economics*, Vol. 1, No. 1 (May 1974), pp. 67–94. © North-Holland Publishing Company, 1974. [Chapter 245]

"Lessons From the Current Economic Expansion," *The American Economic Review*, Vol. 64, No. 2 (May 1974), pp. 75–77. Copyright © 1974 by The American Economic Association. [Chapter 271]

"Remembrances of Frisch," *European Economic Review*, Vol. 5, No. 1 (June 1974), pp. 7–23. © North-Holland Publishing Company, 1974. [Chapter 211]

"Worldwide Stagflation," *The Morgan Guaranty Survey* (June 1974), pp. 3–9. Copyright 1974 by Paul A. Samuelson. [Chapter 268]

"Marx as Mathematical Economist: Steady-State and Exponential Growth Equilibrium," in G. Horwich and P. Samuelson, eds., *Trade, Stability, and Macroeconomics, Essays in Honor of Lloyd A. Metzler* (New York: Academic Press, 1974), pp. 269–307. Copyright © 1974, by Academic Press, Inc. [Chapter 225]

Foreword to *Investment Portfolio Decision-Making*, ed. by J. L. Bicksler and P. A. Samuelson (Lexington, Mass.: Lexington Books, D. C. Heath and Co., 1974). [Chapter 244]

"Equalisation of Factor Prices by Sufficiently Diversified Production Under Conditions of Balanced Demand," in W. Sellekaerts, ed., *International Trade and Finance, Essays in Honour of Jan Tinbergen* (London: Macmillan, 1974), pp. 213–219. Copyright 1973 by Paul A. Samuelson. [Chapter 255]

"A Curious Case Where Reallocation Cannot Achieve Optimum Welfare," in W. L. Smith and J. C. Culbertson, eds., *Public Finance and Stabilization Policy, Essays in Honor of Richard A. Musgrave* (New York: North-Holland/American Alsevier Co., 1974), pp. 145–150. © North-Holland Publishing Company, 1974. [Chapter 258]

With J. Yellin, "A Dynamical Model For Human Population," *Proceedings of the National Academy of Science, U.S.A.*, Vol. 71, No. 7 (July 1974), pp. 2813–2817. [Chapter 234]

"A Biological Least-Action Principle for the Ecological Model of Volterra-Lotka," *Proceedings of the National Academy of Sciences, U.S.A.*, Vol. 71, No. 8 (August 1974), pp. 3041–3044. [Chapter 232]

"Capital Shortage, or Glut?," *Newsweek* (August 26, 1974), p. 73. Copyright 1974, by Newsweek, Inc. All rights reserved. Reprinted by permission. [Chapter 219]

"Analytical Notes on International Real-Income Measures," *The Economic Journal*, Vol. 84, No. 335 (September 1974), pp. 595–608. Reprinted from *The Economic Journal* by permission of Cambridge University Press. © Copyright 1974 by the Royal Economic Society. [Chapter 210]

With S. Swamy, "Invariant Economic Index Numbers and Canonical Duality: Survey and Synthesis," *The American Economic Review*, Vol. 64, No. 4 (September 1974), pp. 566–593. Copyright © 1974 by The American Economic Association. [Chapter 209]

"Comments on the Favorable-Bet Theorem," *Economic Inquiry*, Vol. XII, No. 3 (September 1974), pp. 345–355. Copyright 1974 by the Western Economic Association. [Chapter 248]

"Challenge to Judgment," *The Journal of Portfolio Management*, Vol. 1, No. 1 (Fall 1974), pp. 17–19. Copyright © 1974 Institutional Investor Systems, Inc. [Chapter 243]

"Nobel Choice: Economists in Contrast," *The New York Times* (October 10, 1974), OpEd page. © 1974 by The New York Times Company. Reprinted by permission. [Chapter 291]

"Complementarity: An Essay on the 40th Anniversary of the Hicks-Allen Revolution in Demand Theory," *Journal of Economic Literature*, Vol. XII, No. 4 (December 1974), pp. 1255–1289. Copyright © 1974 by The American Economic Association. [Chapter 208]

"Steady-State and Transient Relations: A Reply on Reswitching," *The Quarterly Journal of Economics*, Vol. LXXXIX, No. 1 (February 1975), pp. 40–47. Copyright 1975 by the President and Fellows of Harvard College. [Chapter 216]

"Seymour Harris As Political Economist," *The Review of Economics and Statistics*, Vol. LVII, No. 1 (February 1975), pp. i–v. Copyright 1975 by the President and Fellows of Harvard College. [Chapter 284]

"Economic Policy—Where Is It Leading?," *Boston University Journal*, No. 1 (April 23, 1975), pp. 30–36. Copyright 1975 by Paul A. Samuelson. [Chapter 267]

"The Balanced Budget Multiplier: A Case Study in the Sociology and Psychology of Scientific Discovery," *History of Political Economy*, Vol. 7, No. 1 (Spring 1975), pp. 43–49. Reprinted by permission of Duke University Press. [Chapter 274]

"The Convergence of the Law School and the University," *The American Scholar*, Vol. 44, No. 2 (Spring 1975), pp. 256–271. Copyright 1975 by Paul A. Samuelson. [Chapter 270]

"Alvin Hansen, 1887–1975," *Newsweek* (June 16, 1975), p. 72. Copyright 1975, by Newsweek, Inc. All rights reserved. Reprinted by permission. [Chapter 287]

Review of V. K. Dmitriev, *Economic Essays on Value, Competition, and Utility* in *Journal of Economic Literature*, Vol. XIII, No. 2 (June 1975), pp. 491–495. Copyright © 1975 by The American Economic Association. [Chapter 231]

"In Search of the Elusive Elite," *The New York Times* (June 26, 1975), OpEd page. © 1975 by The New York Times Company. Reprinted by permission. [Chapter 286]

"The Art and Science of Macromodels Over 50 Years," in G. Fromm and L. R. Klein, eds., *The Brookings Model: Perspective and Recent Developments* (New York: North-Holland/American Elsevier, 1975), pp. 2–10. © North-Holland Publishing Company, 1975. [Chapter 275]

"Social Darwinism," *Newsweek* (July 7, 1975), p. 55. Copyright 1975, by Newsweek, Inc. All rights reserved. Reprinted by permission. [Chapter 239]

"The Optimum Growth Rate for Population," *International Economic Review*, Vol. 16, No. 3 (October 1975), pp. 531–538. Copyright © 1975 by the Wharton School of Finance and Commerce, University of Pennsylvania, and the Osaka University Institute of Social and Economic Research Association. [Chapter 221]

"Optimum Social Security in a Life-Cycle Growth Model," *International Economic Review*, Vol. 16, No. 3 (October 1975), pp. 539–544. Copyright © 1975 by the Wharton School of Finance and Commerce, University of Pennsylvania, and the Osaka University Institute of Social and Economic Research Association. [Chapter 220]

"Trade Pattern Reversals in Time-Phased Ricardian Systems and Intertemporal Efficiency," *Journal of International Economics*, Vol. 5, No. 4 (November 1975), pp. 309–363. © North-Holland Publishing Company, 1975. [Chapter 251]

"Alvin Hansen as a Creative Economic Theorist," *The Quarterly Journal of Economics*, Vol. XC, No. 1 (February 1976), pp. 24–31. Copyright 1975 by the President and Fellows of Harvard College. [Chapter 285]

"Optimality of Sluggish Predictors Under Ergodic Probabilities," *International Economic Review*, Vol. 17, No. 1 (February 1976), pp. 1–7. Copyright © 1976 by the Wharton School of Finance and Commerce, University of Pennsylvania, and the Osaka University Institute of Social and Economic Research Association. [Chapter 249]

"Is Real-World Price a Tale Told by the Idiot of Chance?," *The Review of Economics and Statistics*, Vol. LVIII, No. 1 (February 1976), pp. 120–123. Copyright 1976 by the President and Fellows of Harvard College. [Chapter 242]

"Time Symmetry and Asymmetry in Population and Deterministic Dynamic Systems," *Theoretical Population Biology*, Vol. 9, No. 1 (February 1976), pp. 82–122. Copyright © 1976 by Academic Press, Inc. [Chapter 235]

"The Optimum Growth Rate for Population: Agreement and Evaluations," *International Economic Review*, Vol. 17, No. 2 (June 1976), pp. 516–525. Copyright © 1976 by the Wharton School of Finance and Commerce, University of Pennsylvania, and the Osaka University Institute of Social and Economic Research Association. [Chapter 222]

"An Economist's Non-Linear Model of Self-Generated Fertility Waves," *Population Studies*, Vol. XXX, No. 2 (July 1976), pp. 243–247. [Chapter 237]

"Interest Rate Determinations and Oversimplifying Parables: A Summing Up," in M. Brown, K. Sato and P. Zarembka, eds., *Essays in Modern Capital Theory* (Amsterdam: North-Holland, 1976), pp. 3–23. © North-Holland Publishing Company, 1976. [Chapter 215]

"Speeding Up of Time With Age in Recognition of Life as Fleeting," Chapter 7 in A. M. Tang, F. M. Westfield, and J. S. Worley, eds., *Evolution, Welfare, and Time in Economics, Essays in Honor of Nicholas Georgescu-Roegen* (Lexington, Mass.: Lexington Books, D. C. Heath and Co., 1976), pp. 153–168. [Chapter 233]

"Illogic of Neo-Marxian Doctrine of Unequal Exchange," in D. A. Belsley, E. J. Kane, P. A. Samuelson, and R. M. Solow, eds., *Inflation, Trade, and Taxes* (Columbus: Ohio State University Press, 1976), pp. 96–107. Copyright © 1976 by the Ohio State University Press. All rights reserved. [Chapter 252]

Preface to *Inflation, Trade and Taxes, Essays in Honor of Alice Bourneuf*, ed. by D. A. Belsley, E. J. Kane, P. A. Samuelson, and R. M. Solow (Columbus: Ohio State University Press, 1976). Copyright © 1976 by the Ohio State University Press. All rights reserved. [Chapter 281]

"Optimal Compacts for Redistribution," in R. E. Grieson, ed., *Public and Urban Economics* (Lexington, Mass.: Lexington Books, D. C. Heath and Co., 1976), pp. 179–190. [Chapter 257]

Foreword to *The Geographical Aspects of Inflationary Processes*, ed. by P. B. Corbin and M. Sabin (Pleasantville, New York: Redgrave Publishing Co., 1976). Copyright © 1976 by Docent Corporation, Pleasantville, New York. [Chapter 266]

"Reminiscences of Shigeto Tsuru," in Shigeto Tsuru, ed., *Ad Multos Annos! Looking Back and Ahead on Shigeto Tsuru* (Tokyo: Dai Nippon Printing Co., Ltd., 1976). [Chapter 279]

Foreword to *Essays on Industrial Organization, Essays in Honor of Joe S. Bain*, ed. by R. Mason and P. D. Qualls (Cambridge, Mass.: Ballinger, 1976), pp. xvii–xviii. [Chapter 280]

"Limited Liability, Short Selling, Bounded Utility, and Infinite-Variance Stable Distributions," *Journal of Financial and Quantitative Analysis*, Vol. 11, No. 3 (September 1976), pp. 485–503. Copyright 1976 by the Graduate School of Business Administration, University of Washington. [Chapter 247]

"Resolving a Historical Confusion in Population Analysis," *Human Biology*, Vol. 48, No. 3 (September 1976), pp. 559–580. © Wayne State University Press, 1976. [Chapter 236]

"The Periodic Turnpike Theorem," *Nonlinear Analysis, Theory, Methods and Applications*, Vol. 1, No. 1 (September 20, 1976), pp. 3–13. Reprinted with permission from author, title C, Copyright 1976, Pergamon Press Ltd. [Chapter 224]

"Milton Friedman," *Newsweek* (October 25, 1976), p. 89. Copyright 1976, by Newsweek, Inc. All rights reserved. Reprinted by permission. [Chapter 292]

"Adam the Immortal," *The Pennsylvania Gazette* (November 1976), pp. 26–27. Reprinted with permission from The Pennsylvania Gazette, alumni magazine of the University of Pennsylvania. Copyright © 1976 by The Pennsylvania Gazette. [Chapter 276]

"Christmas Economics," *Newsweek* (December 25, 1976), p. 54. Copyright 1976, by Newsweek, Inc. All rights reserved. Reprinted by permission. [Chapter 273]

"Economics of Forestry in An Evolving Society," *Economic Inquiry*, Vol. XIV, No. 4 (December 1976), pp. 466–492. Copyright 1976 by the Western Economic Association. [Chapter 218]

INDEX